BUSINESS STUDIES

Reference Copy Sept '97

DAVE HALL

ROB JONES

CARLO RAFFO

Edited by
IAN CHAMBERS

Causeway Press

Dedication

To Elaine, Amanda Jane, Kath, Sandra, Georgina and Rebecca for all their love and support in the writing of this book.

Cover design by Susan and Andrew Allen

Cover illustration provided by The Telegraph Colour Library

Graphics by Caroline Waring-Collins and Elaine Marie-Anne Cox

Photography by Andrew Allen and Dave Gray

Typing by Ingrid Hamer and Pauline Groome

Editor – Dave Gray

Acknowledgements

The publishers wish to thank the following for permission to reproduce photographs and copyright material.
Andrea Marks public relations/Dillons Bookstore p.370; Bemrose Corporation p.69; Castings Ltd p.274, p.289, p.292, p.312; EGA Ltd p.358; Employment Gazette p.394; Executive 2000 p.270; Ford Motor Company p.10, p.308; HMSO, Inland Revenue p.268; Ian McAnulty p.34, p.232, p.237; Innovations p.252; Latimer International p.372; Manchester Evening News p.376; Metropolitan Borough of Wigan p.217; Mike Gibbons p.24, p.138; Morgan Motor Company p.248; Sally and Richard Greenhill p.2, p.37 (bottom), p.70, p.284, p.370; Sefton Photo Library p.23, p.74, p.199 (top), p.208 (top), p.250 (bottom), p.255 (top right), p.341; Skandia Life p.506; SMCL p.407; The Midland Bank p.179; The Observer p.175; Topham Picture Source p.30, p.37 (top), p.199 (bottom), p.208 (bottom), p.213 (middle), p.214 (top and bottom), p.254; Travel Photo International p.170.

All HMSO sources are Crown copyright - reproduced with the permission of the Controller of Her Majesty's Stationery Office.

Every effort has been made to locate the copyright owners of material used in this book. Any omissions brought to the notice of the publisher are regretted and will be credited in subsequent printings.

British Library Cataloguing in Publication Data
A catalogue record for this book is available from the British Library.

ISBN 1-873929-09-9

Causeway Press Limited
PO Box 13, Ormskirk, Lancs, L39 5HP
© Dave Hall, Rob Jones, Carlo Raffo, Ian Chambers
1st impression, 1993
Reprinted 1994 (twice), 1995, 1996 (twice), 1997

Typesetting by John A. Collins and Elaine Marie-Anne Cox (Waring-Collins Partnership)
Printed and bound by Cambus Litho Ltd, Nerston, East Kilbride.

Contents

Contents

Preface

Business studies does not provide a step-by-step guide to how to be 'good at business'. There is no simple set of rules that can be applied at **all** times which will **always** be successful. However, by being analytical, rigorous and critical it may be possible to develop skills and approaches which can be useful, at certain times and in certain situations, when making business decisions. It is possible that different approaches will be used by different people in business and there may be disagreement as to which approach to take.

Business studies is integrated and different areas of business are interdependent. There are links, for example, between:

■ what is being produced and the funds available to pay for it (production and finance);
■ the selling of the product and ethical considerations (marketing and ethics);
■ the type of business and many aspects of its operation.

Being aware of these aspects of business will help us to understand how and why business decisions are made, and how they affect a variety of people, both within and outside the business. The aim of this book is to help those studying business to understand business decisions and to be analytical, rigorous and critical in their business thinking. A number of features are included which we believe will help this task.

Comprehensive The book contains material which should meet the demands of a wide range of business studies courses including GCE A level and AS level, the content range of Advanced GNVQ in Business, professional courses and introductory higher education courses.

Flexible unit structure The unit structure allows the lecturer or teacher greater freedom to devise the course. Business studies teachers and lecturers often teach different aspects of the course in different orders. So, whilst there is a logical order to the book, it has been written on the assumption that teachers or lecturers and students will piece the units together to suit their own teaching and learning needs.

Cross referencing has been used in many of the units. This helps the teacher, lecturer or student to follow the course as they want. It will also be useful for modular courses and courses where business studies is only one part of the total course. The units in the book which relate to specific aspects of business, such as marketing or accounting, can be used in specialist courses or provide a short course in that area. Cross referencing also helps to stress the integrated nature of business studies and the interdependence and possible conflict that may exist in many areas.

Accessibility The book has been written in a clear and logical style which should make it accessible to all readers. Each unit is divided into short, easily manageable sections.

A workbook The text is interspersed with a large number of questions. The questions which appear as part of the units mostly refer to preceding information. Answers in most cases are expected to be fairly short and simple. Questions are based on a variety of case studies, data, articles, photographs, etc. They should allow the student and

teacher/lecturer to assess whether the information has been understood. One longer question appears at the end of each unit. This is a data or case study question. It draws on information contained in the whole unit and answers are expected to reflect this.

All questions are designed to develop understanding and knowledge of concepts, problem solving and decision making skills, ability to use data and analytical, evaluation and comparison skills. A summary in the form of short answer questions is also included at the end of each unit.

Use of business examples, case studies and data Modern technology has allowed much of the book to proceed from manuscript to book form in a very short period. This has meant that we have been able to use statistics and business examples which were available up to September 1993. Materials used have been chosen to demonstrate appropriate arguments and theories. They should, therefore, allow students to answer questions which require knowledge of what has happened 'in recent years' or 'over the past decade', as well as questions which deal with current debates.

Examination practice At the end of a number of units are case studies, data questions, investigations and essays. These are designed to be longer, more detailed, pieces of work, often reflecting the level of answer required for an examination or a piece of coursework.

Key terms Many units contain a key terms section. Each section defines new concepts, which appear in capitals in the text of the unit. Taken together, they provide a comprehensive dictionary of business terms.

Presentation Great care has been taken with how the book has been presented. It is hoped that the layout of the book, the use of colour and the use of diagrams will help learning.

We would like to thank the following for their efforts in the preparation of this book: Richard Dunill, for keeping the debate sharp and yet accessible; Mike Kidson and Lisa Fabry for the unenviable task of proof reading; Ingrid Hamer for her long hours of typing; Nigel Lewis; Michael J. Forshaw of David J Quine Chartered Accountants for bringing a 'real' accountant's view to the book; all staff and students at South Bolton College, King George V College and Loreto College; Diane Wallace, Steve Robertson and Ian Chambers for working on the early development of the book; Alain Anderton for sharing his style ideas.

Finally, the authors would like to make a special acknowledgement to Dave Gray at Causeway Press and Ian Chambers. Without their commitment, skillful co-ordination, drive and encouragement this book could not have been produced. Thank you.

David Hall
Rob Jones
Carlo Raffo

What is business activity?

In 1986, Bob and Ann Jones bought 'The Rowehouse', a small guest house in Horton-in-Ribblesdale, for £80,000 cash. They had searched for such a property for many months. They both liked the countryside and wanted to run a small Bed & Breakfast business before they retired in 10 years time. The previous owner had let the business slip. Bob and Ann decided to make some changes. They:

■ completely decorated and refurbished the dining room and lounge;

■ fitted 'ensuite' facilities into 5 of the bedrooms;

■ offered guests a 4 course evening meal emphasising traditional country fayre;

■ advertised 'The Rowehouse' in national newspapers;

■ printed some new 'glossy' leaflets to send out.

In running the business Bob concentrated on the catering side. For two years he attended Skipton Technical College where he developed his cooking skills and obtained some City and Guilds catering qualifications. Ann's main role was to deal personally with the guests and prepare the rooms each day. She also managed the financial side and dealt with the administration.

Over a 4 year period the business gradually expanded. Many of the guests returned several times having enjoyed their stay so much. Guests were particularly complimentary about the personal service provided by the owners and the 'homely' atmosphere in 'The

Rowehouse'. However, in 1991 the number of guests staying fell quite sharply. Bob and Ann felt that this was almost certainly due to the recession. There was little they could do about this, but since they did not have to borrow any money to buy the guest house, they felt that they could survive for a couple of years. Fortunately, in 1993, there was an upturn in business.

The above case illustrates many features of business activity.

■ Business activity produces an **output** - a good or service. An accommodation service is provided by Bob and Ann.

■ Goods and services are **consumed**. Paying guests consumed the service provided by Bob and Ann.

■ **Resources** are used up. Money, food, furniture and fuel are just a few examples of resources used by Bob and Ann.

■ A number of **functions** are carried out. Administration, decisions about finance and decisions about production are some examples.

■ Businesses can be affected by **external factors**. The recession caused a decline in guests in 1991.

Figure 1.1 shows a diagram which illustrates the nature of business activity. All types of business may be represented by this diagram - a building society, a window cleaner, a multinational chemical company or a shoe manufacturer.

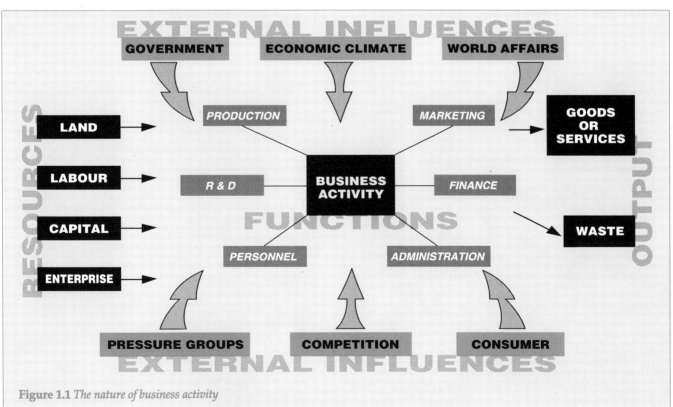

Figure 1.1 *The nature of business activity*

Business resources

Businesses use resources or FACTORS OF PRODUCTION in business activity. These are usually divided into four groups.

Land Land is not just a 'plot of land' where business premises might be located. It also includes natural resources, such as coal, diamonds, forests, rivers and fertile soil. The owners of land receive **rent** from those who use it.

Business activity uses both **renewable** and **non-renewable** resources. Renewable resources are those like fish, forests and water which nature replaces. Examples of non-renewable land resources are mineral deposits like coal and diamonds, which once used are never replaced. There has been concern in recent years about the rate at which renewable resources are being used. It is argued that seas are being so 'overfished' that some species of fish may die out.

Labour Labour is the workforce of business. Manual workers, skilled workers and management are all members of the workforce. They are paid **wages** or **salaries** for their services. The quality of individual workers will vary considerably. Each worker is unique, possessing a different set of characteristics, skills, knowledge, intelligence and emotions.

It is possible to improve the quality of **human resources** through training and education. Human resources become more productive if money is invested by business or government in training and education.

Capital Capital is sometimes described as the **artificial** resource because it is made by labour. Capital refers to the tools, machinery and equipment which businesses use. For example, JCB make mechanical diggers which are used by the construction industry. Capital also refers to the money which the owners use to set up a business (☞ unit 39). Owners of capital receive **interest** if others borrow it.

Enterprise Enterprise has a special role in business activity. The **entrepreneur** or businessperson develops a business idea and then hires and organises the other three factors of production to carry out the activity. Entrepreneurs also take risks because they will often use some personal money to help set up the business. If the business does not succeed the entrepreneur may lose some or all of that money. If the business is successful, any money left over will belong to the entrepreneur. This is called **profit**.

Business functions

Figure 1.1 showed that businesses have a number of functions. A business is a SYSTEM - it has parts that work together to achieve an objective. The functions are all parts of the system. A business is also part of other systems such as the economic and political systems (☞ unit 6). What functions does a business carry out?

■ **Production** involves changing natural resources into a product or the supply of a service (☞ unit 28). Most business resources are used up in the production process. Examples of production can be seen on a building site where houses are constructed, in a dental surgery where dental treatment is given and in a coal mine where coal is extracted.

■ **Marketing** has become very important in recent years due to an increase in competition in business. It is concerned with identifying consumer needs and satisfying them. Examples of marketing activities are market research, advertising, packaging, promotion, distribution and pricing.

■ The **finance** department is responsible for the control of money in a business. It has a number of important duties. This includes recording transactions, producing documents to illustrate the performance of the business and its financial position and controlling the flow of money in the business.

■ Dealing with enquiries, communicating messages and producing documents for the workforce are all examples of **administrative** tasks.

■ The **personnel** function involves the management of people. The personnel department looks after the welfare of the workforce, and is responsible for such things as recruitment, selection, training, appraisal, health and safety, equal opportunities, payment systems and worker disputes.

■ **Research and development (R&D)** involves technical research, for example, research into a new medicine or a new production technique. R&D can be very expensive. Consequently, many businesses do not have a R&D department but rely on adapting new products and new technology developed by other companies.

QUESTION 1

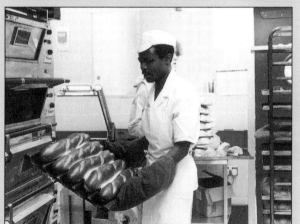

Look at the photograph.

(a) Draw up a list of resources which the above business activity is using and state whether they are land, labour or capital.

(b) Assuming that the entrepreneur is not in the picture, what might he or she be doing? Explain your answer.

In a large business these functions should be easy to spot. However, a self-employed window cleaner will also carry out these functions.

- Production - cleaning windows.
- Marketing - distributing business cards to potential customers.
- Administration - dealing with enquiries from potential customers and recording their personal details in preparation for a first visit.
- Personnel - recruiting and supervising part time helpers during busy periods.
- Finance - keeping records of all financial transactions.

Business activity is highly integrated. For example, production is heavily influenced by marketing activities. If marketing is effective and more of the product is sold, then more will have to be produced. Also, the finance department, for example, will carefully watch the amount of money used by other departments.

What does business activity produce?

All business activity results in the production of a good or a service. CONSUMER GOODS are those which are sold to the general public. They fall into two categories.

- **Durable goods** such as cookers, televisions, books, cars and furniture can be used repeatedly for a long period of time.
- **Non-durable goods** such as food, confectionery, cigarettes and shoe polish are used very soon after they are purchased. Some of these goods are called

fast moving consumer goods, such as soap, crisps and cornflakes.

CAPITAL GOODS are those goods purchased by businesses and used to produce other goods. Tools, equipment and machinery are examples of capital goods.

The supply of **services** has grown in recent years. Banking, insurance, hairdressing, car valeting and gardening are examples of this type of business activity.

Business activity also results in the production of waste materials. Most waste is useless and some waste, like radioactive nuclear waste, is very dangerous and expensive to dispose of. Some production techniques result in **by-products** which can be sold. For example, the brewing process generates yeast which is sold to the producers of Bovril and Marmite. Most waste, more than 70 per cent, is generated by farming, mining and quarrying.

External factors

Business activity is affected by a number of external forces, some of which are shown in the diagram in Figure 1.1. These are beyond the control of the individual business. In some cases they constrain a firm's decisions (☞ unit 7) and may prevent its growth and development.

- **The government** has a great deal of influence over business activity. In most countries the government will be in favour of business development. A **legal framework**, where all individuals abide by the law and offenders are punished, will help this. A country also needs an **infrastructure** including roads, railways, telecommunications, schools and hospitals. These items are often provided by the state (☞ unit 4). Government policy can also influence business. For example, profits and many goods and services which businesses produce are taxed.
- The economic climate can have a tremendous impact on business activity. For example, in the early 1990s the UK suffered from a recession and a falling demand for goods and services. This resulted in considerable hardship for many firms - around 62,000 firms were forced to close in 1992.
- World affairs such as the Gulf War in 1990 can affect business activity. Firms in the defence industry benefited from increased orders from the government. The development of the European single market in 1992 (☞ unit 70) has meant that UK firms have easier access to European markets and there are fewer restrictions on goods sold to member countries.
- Some individuals form **pressure groups** (☞ unit 71) in order to influence firms. For example, the Animal Liberation Front (ALF) have protested about the testing of products on animals for a number of years. Due to this pressure some firms have reduced such activities.
- Most businesses face **competition** from other firms. Competitors' behaviour can influence a firm's activities. For example, when Virgin Airways began to offer cheap flights to America in the early 1980s, other airline companies were forced to do the same.

QUESTION 2

Look at the photographs.

(a) State which of the above shops sell: (i) non-durable goods; (ii) durable goods; (iii) services.
(b) What capital goods might these shops require in order to operate?

■ **Consumers'** tastes often change. Companies are forced to update, modify and change their products in order to satisfy consumers' demands. It is unlikely that the clothes bought five years ago would be popular today, although they might be in 20 years time!

> **QUESTION 3** Farmers frequently complain about the uncertainty which exists in agriculture. They are unable to plan effectively for the future. This is because it is so difficult for them to predict what their revenue will be from the sale of crops. In addition, some farmers have been forced to cut back what they produce by the EC.
>
> (a) Explain two external factors which might affect farmers.
> (b) Would farmers be hit severely by a recession? Explain your answer.

Satisfying needs and wants

The success of a business activity depends on many factors. The most important is to supply a product that consumers want to buy. Businesses must satisfy consumers' NEEDS and WANTS to be successful. People's needs are limited. They include things which are needed to survive, such as food, warmth, shelter and security. Humans also have psychological and emotional needs such as recognition and love. Wants, however are infinite. People constantly aim for a better quality of life, which might include better housing, better health care, better education, longer holidays, and more friends. Unit 6 deals with the way in which an economy attempts to satisfy people's needs.

Markets

The **goods** and **services** produced by businesses are sold in MARKETS. A market exists when buyers and sellers communicate in order to exchange goods and services. In some cases buyers and sellers might meet at an agreed place to carry out the exchange. For example, many villages and towns have regular open air markets where buyers and sellers exchange goods and services. Also, buying and selling can be carried out over the telephone. For example, the First Direct banking facility allows customers to conduct nearly all of their banking business over the telephone. Buying and selling can also take place in high street shopping centres, in newspapers and magazines, through mail order, and more recently, through television.

The goods and services of most businesses are bought by market CONSUMERS to satisfy their wants and needs. A business may be interested in some of the following markets.

■ Consumer goods markets - where products like food, cosmetics and magazines are sold in large quantities.
■ Markets for services - these are varied and could include financial services for individuals or industrial cleaning.
■ Capital goods markets - where items used by other businesses are bought and sold, such as machinery.
■ Labour markets - where people are hired for their services.
■ The housing market - where people buy and sell properties.
■ Money markets - where people and institutions borrow and lend money, such as commercial banks.
■ Commodity markets - where raw materials, such as copper and coffee are bought, mainly by business.

> ## QUESTION 4
>
> Table 1.1 *Information on national newspaper circulation*
>
> **NATIONAL NEWSPAPER CIRCULATION TRENDS 1986 - 1991**
>
> | | 1986 '000 | 1987 '000 | 1988 '000 | 1989 '000 | 1990 '000 | 1991 '000 |
> |---|---|---|---|---|---|---|
> | **National Dailies** | | | | | | |
> | Daily Express | 1,729 | 1,690 | 1,637 | 1,575 | 1,585 | 1,519 |
> | Daily Mail | 1,732 | 1,810 | 1,759 | 1,723 | 1,708 | 1,684 |
> | Daily Mirror | 3,139 | 3,128 | 3,157 | 3,092 | 3,083 | 2,881 |
> | Daily Record | 765 | 764 | 773 | 771 | 778 | 760 |
> | The Star | 1,278 | 1,137 | 967 | 891 | 912 | 838 |
> | The Sun | 4,050 | 4,045 | 4,219 | 4,017 | 3,855 | 3,665 |
> | Today | 307 | 340 | 548 | 589 | 540 | 460 |
> | Popular dailies | **13,000** | **12,914** | **13,060** | **12,658** | **12,461** | **11,806** |
> | The Daily Telegraph | 1,132 | 1,169 | 1,127 | 1,103 | 1,076 | 1,058 |
> | Financial Times | 254 | 307 | 278 | 288 | 289 | 287 |
> | The Guardian | 507 | 460 | 438 | 431 | 424 | 410 |
> | The Independent | 303 | 361 | 387 | 412 | 411 | 372 |
> | The Times | 467 | 447 | 436 | 428 | 420 | 387 |
> | Quality dailies | **2,662** | **2,744** | **2,666** | **2,662** | **2,620** | **2,514** |
>
> Source: adapted from *A.B.C data*.
>
> (a) Describe the market which the data in Table 1.1 represents.
> (b) State three changes that have taken place in this market over the time period.

Specialisation

One feature of modern businesses is SPECIALISATION. This is the production of a limited range of goods by an individual, firm, region or country. Specialisation can take place between firms. For example, McDonalds supply a limited range of fast foods, Ford manufacture cars, ICL produce computers, Heinz process food products and MFI supply furniture products. Examples of regional specialisation might be Kidderminster, which specialises in carpet production, Stoke-on-Trent, which produces pottery and Kent, which is one of the country's main hop growers. Different countries also specialise. For example, Scotland specialises in the distilling of whisky, Saudi Arabia in oil extraction and South Africa in the supply of gold.

Specialisation within a firm is an important part of production. Departments specialise in different activities, such as marketing, purchasing, personnel and finance.

People specialise in different tasks and skills. This is called the DIVISION OF LABOUR and allows people to concentrate on the task or skill which they are best at. In business, production is divided amongst workers, who each concentrate on a limited range of tasks. For example, the building of a house involves an architect to draw up the plans, a bricklayer to build the structure, a joiner to undertake woodwork, a roofer to lay the tiles etc. It is argued that the division of labour raises the productivity and efficiency of business and the economy. There are a number of reasons for this.

■ Workers can concentrate on the tasks that they do best, leaving other tasks to more specialist workers.

■ People's skills are improved by carrying out tasks over a long period of time. It is also possible to develop a brand new skill.

■ Time is saved because workers are not constantly changing tasks, moving from one area to another or collecting new tools.

■ The organisation of production becomes easier and more effective.

Specialisation, however, does have disadvantages.

■ Work can become tedious and boring. This can result in poor worker motivation with the likelihood of a higher rate of absenteeism and increased staff turnover.

■ Problems can also occur when one stage of production depends on another stage. If one stage breaks down, production might be halted.

■ Over-specialisation can pose problems when there is a change in demand. If people are only competent in one skill they may have to retrain, causing delays in production. Some are not able to retrain and become unemployed.

QUESTION 5 In June 1993, Peter Wyper decided to make a radical change in his business. For ten years he had supplied a household appliance repair service in the Swindon area. His advert in the *Yellow Pages* offered a service with a guarantee that he would repair any household appliance within twenty-four hours. However, in the last three years he had experienced a number of problems with the growing range of electrical appliances now on the market. His four staff, who were originally refrigeration engineers, could not cope with the electronics in some of the new appliances. This had resulted in some complaints from customers when guarantees could not be met. In fact, Peter had lost money on many calls because some of the work had to be contracted out. He finally decided to change his advert and specialise in kitchen appliances.

(a) What might be the: (i) advantages; (ii) disadvantages; of Peter's decision to specialise in the repair of kitchen appliances?

(b) What might have been an alternative strategy for Peter?

The importance of money

MONEY is anything which is generally accepted as a means of exchange. It is essential for the smooth exchange of goods and services in markets and helps specialisation.

Without money goods have to be exchanged using a BARTER SYSTEM. This involves swapping goods directly, which is inefficient. It is necessary for the wants of individuals to be perfectly matched. Searching for the perfect match in a barter deal can be very time consuming. It is also difficult to value different goods without money. In addition, giving change can be a problem when the values of the goods being exchanged do not match exactly. Money also has a number of other functions. It:

■ allows individuals to save some of their income and buy goods and services at a later date;

■ enables all goods and services to be valued in common units, for example, a house which costs £60,000 is worth exactly 10 times more than a car which is valued at £6,000;

■ allows payments to be deferred, ie goods can be bought and payment made at a later date.

In the UK, money includes bank notes and coins, bank accounts (both current and deposit) and building society deposit accounts. Cheques and credit cards are not examples of money. They are means of transferring money rather than money itself.

The government often measures the amount of money in the economy. M0 is a narrow measure of money and includes all notes and coins in circulation plus any deposits which commercial banks hold at the Bank of England. M4 is a broad measure and includes M0 plus money held in a range of bank and building society accounts.

Levels of business activity

Business activity is often classed by the type of production that takes place.

PRIMARY production includes activity which takes the natural resources from the earth, ie the extraction of raw materials and the growing of food. Mining, fishing, farming and forestry are examples of primary business activity. SECONDARY production involves manufacturing, processing and construction which transform raw materials into goods. Car production, distilling, baking, shipbuilding and office construction are examples of secondary sector activity. TERTIARY production includes the provision of services. Hairdressing, distribution, security, banking, theatre and tourism are all examples of business activity in this area. Other methods of classifying business include by:

■ size (☞ unit 31);

■ geographical area (☞ unit 30);

■ sector (☞ units 3 and 4);

■ ownership (☞ unit 3).

Changes in business activity

Over time the UK has experienced some radical changes in the structure of the economy. Before the Industrial Revolution most resources in the UK were employed in primary production. This included producing food and household needs such as coal for heating. During the nineteenth century secondary production expanded rapidly. The Industrial Revolution resulted in a rapid growth in manufacturing.

Since around 1960 tertiary production has grown continually at the expense of the secondary sector. Today about 70 per cent of all business activity is the provision of services, such as recreation, retailing and cleaning.

The decline in manufacturing is often called DE-INDUSTRIALISATION. Changes in consumer demand in favour of services, a lack of competitiveness amongst UK manufacturers, a lack of investment, unhelpful government economic policy and restrictive trade unions are some of the arguments put forward to explain the decline. De-industrialisation has had an effect on businesses. For example, many have been forced to change their product range, adopt new working practices, re-locate, find new markets and reorganise. Also, many firms have failed to survive the changes.

QUESTION 6

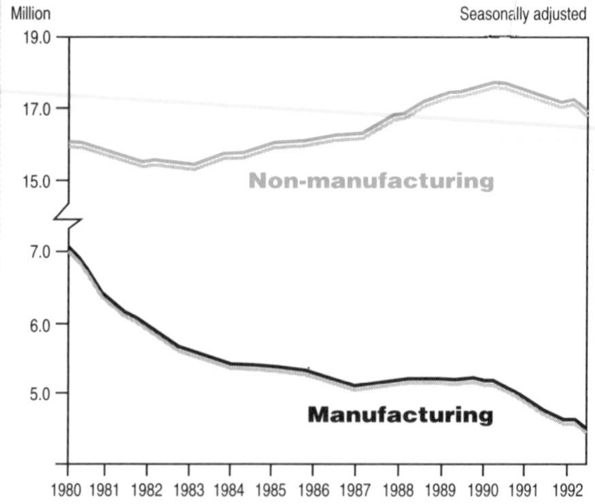

Figure 1.2 *Employment in manufacturing and non-manufacturing industry, UK 1980 - 1992*

Source : adapted from *Employment Gazette*, 1993

(a) Explain the terms:
   (i)   manufacturing
   (ii) non-manufacturing;
   in Figure 1.2.
(b) What effects might the trends in employment have on:
   (i)   an engineering business;
   (ii) a skilled engineer;
   (iii) a tertiary company?

Key terms

Barter - a system of exchange which involves the swapping of goods between individuals.

Capital goods - goods used to produce other goods, such as tools, equipment and machinery.

Consumers - individuals who buy goods and services to satisfy their needs and wants.

Consumer goods - goods produced for general use by the public; they can be durable and non-durable.

De-industrialisation - the decline in manufacturing.

Division of labour - specialisation in specific tasks or skills by individuals.

Factors of production - resources used by business to produce goods and services.

Market - anywhere that buyers and sellers communicate to exchange goods and services.

Money - any substance which is generally accepted as a means of exchange.

Needs - human requirements which must be satisfied for survival.

Primary production - activities which involve the extraction of raw materials from the earth and the growing of food.

Secondary production - activities such as manufacturing which transform raw materials into finished goods.

Specialisation - in business, the production of a limited range of goods.

System - parts that work together to achieve an objective; a system can be a communications system, a business, an economic or a political system.

Tertiary production - activities which involve the provision of services.

Wants - human desires which are unlimited.

Question

Sanjay's Balti House

Sanjay had been employed as a cook in a family restaurant business in Birmingham for ten years. The restaurant, Azim's Balti House, was one of the first of its kind in Britain. It specialised in Pakistani cuisine offering a unique 'Balti' dish - a special rich curry, flavoured with freshly chopped coriander and served sizzling in a wok at the table. Its clientele were a mixture of local residents, students from Aston University and curry enthusiasts. Azim's also benefited from passing trade due to its location on the very busy Lozells Road. Over a ten year period the owners of the business became very wealthy indeed.

Sanjay had business ambitions of his own. During his employment at Azim's he saved £20,000. In 1992 he enjoyed a weekend golfing holiday in Southport. For twelve months Sanjay had been looking for a suitable place to locate a Balti House of his own and decided that Southport would be ideal for the following reasons.

■ Southport had no restaurant which offered this unique type of cuisine.

■ It enjoyed busy holiday trade at weekends and in the summer.

■ Unemployment was relatively low in the town.

■ Supplies of ethnic foodstuffs could be obtained from nearby Preston.

■ He thought that Southport would be a pleasant place for his family to live. The local schools had a good reputation, he liked the architecture and the town centre was pretty and lively.

Finding suitable premises was easy. Sanjay leased a shop on Eastbank Street, the main road into Southport.

Whilst viewing the premises he noticed how busy the traffic was in the street. This would be another advantage, he thought. He took out a five year lease for £10,000, spent a further £3,000 converting the premises into a restaurant, and bought £4,000 worth of furniture and other equipment. Two weeks before he opened Sanjay placed some adverts in the local newspaper. He also installed a large green and white flashing neon sign in the window, 'Sanjay's Balti House'.

After four months of trading Sanjay was deeply concerned. The income generated by the business was not even sufficient to cover his running costs, ie rates, heating, lighting, advertising and staff. He posted leaflets to about half the houses in Southport as a last attempt to increase demand. After seven months he had to close; there was virtually no interest in the restaurant. He and his family moved back to Birmingham; the failed business venture had cost £28,000. Sanjay was fortunate to get his old job back at Azim's where business continued to boom.

(a) **What classification of production would Sanjay's business have fallen into? Explain your answer.**

(b) **State two examples of land, labour and capital that Sanjay may have used in his business venture.**

(c) **Explain why Sanjay could be said to have been an entrepreneur when setting up his new business.**

(d) **Using examples from the case study, explain the external factors that:**
   (i) influenced Sanjay to set up;
   (ii) may have influenced the lack of success of the business.

Summary

1. What are the four factors of production?
2. What is the financial reward paid to each production factor?
3. Why is capital said to be an artificial resource?
4. Describe 6 functions involved in business activity.
5. Why is business activity highly integrated?
6. Explain the difference between needs and wants.
7. What is the difference between capital and consumer goods?
8. What is meant by specialisation in business?
9. State 3:
   (a) advantages;
   (b) disadvantages; of specialisation.
10. Briefly describe the role of money in business.
11. List 10 business activities in your local town. State which of these are examples of:
    (a) primary production;
    (b) secondary production;
    (c) tertiary production.
12. What are the possible causes of de-industrialisation in recent years?

People in business

Business activity exists because of people. People set up in business. They employ others to manage the business and work for them. Business activity results in goods or services which are bought by people. The people who buy these goods and services may work for businesses to earn income. There are arguably four groups of people that can be identified in business activity:

- owners or shareholders;
- managers;
- employees;
- consumers.

  These are shown in Figure 2.1. Notice that there is an overlap between the groups. The owner of a large company may be a shareholder and may also be a manager. An employee might also be a shareholder and may be a consumer of the goods or services the company produces. Most managers will also be employees of the company. The first three groups mentioned above are all part of a business. Consumers are not part of a company itself, but they are vital to business activity.

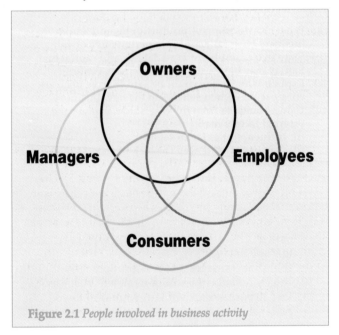

Figure 2.1 *People involved in business activity*

Owners

A business is the property of its owner or owners. The owner of a van can use it to earn income by hiring it out. The owner of jewellery can wait for its value to increase and then sell it. It is possible for the owners of a business to do these things as well.

  Not all owners are the same. The owner of a small business, such as a small retail outlet selling watches, may be the only person in the business. The owner would make all of the decisions, possibly use personal finance to start the firm and carry out all tasks, such as selling, ordering stock and recording transactions. In very large companies there can be thousands of joint owners. They all own **shares** (☞ units 3 and 40) in the company. This entitles them to a share in the profit, known as a DIVIDEND and a vote each year to elect the DIRECTORS of the company. Examples of shareholders might be the Moores family owning shares in Littlewoods, or the people all over the UK who own shares in British Telecom or ICI. The involvement of shareholders in the business will depend, perhaps, on their position in the business and the amount of money invested in it. Figure 2.2 shows a summary of the different types of business owner.

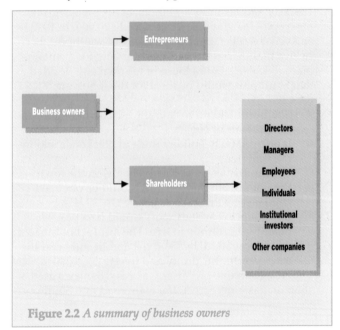

Figure 2.2 *A summary of business owners*

The entrepreneur

Unit 1 showed that **enterprise** was a **factor of production**. Arguably, it is the most important. Without an **entrepreneur** to organise the land, labour and capital, business activity would not take place. What is an entrepreneur? People who have this role usually perform three functions in business.

Innovation Business activity usually begins with the entrepreneur having a business idea. The entrepreneur could be said to be innovative. He or she is forming a new business where one did not exist before. When Anita Roddick opened the first Body Shop in March 1976 in Brighton, she created a new business idea of her own. This was to sell toiletries and cosmetics with conservation, the environment and animal rights in mind. Even when ideas are copied, it could be argued that the entrepreneur is being innovative. For example, Aldi, the German based supermarket chain, could be said to be innovative. They compete with existing UK supermarket chains, but sell less well known brands at low prices.

Organisation Land, labour and capital are hired by the entrepreneur and organised to produce goods or services. Decisions about the location of the premises, the method of production, product design, prices and wages are often made by the entrepreneur. Also, if the firm grows, it is likely that some of these tasks may be passed down to others.

Risk taking Setting up a business is risky. Money has to be paid out in advance to buy materials, business premises, equipment and pay wages. The entrepreneur may use some personal money to meet these costs. There is no guarantee that the final product or service will be sold. If goods are unsold then the entrepreneur will have to suffer this loss. It is not possible to insure against **unquantifiable** risks, such as these, so the entrepreneur bears all the costs of failure.

The type of people who become entrepreneurs is extremely varied. Some, like Richard Branson, the former owner of Virgin Records, start businesses when they are young and help them to grow. Some people extend their hobbies to a business situation, some leave their jobs voluntarily to start a business, some use redundancy money to set up and some inherit businesses.

Entrepreneurs often tend to be associated with small firms. This is because the entrepreneur will face risk and will control all aspects of the business activity. Many small businesses do become large businesses and thus the role of the entrepreneur may well change. In large business organisations many people bear the risk, are innovative and are responsible for control. People such as Rupert Murdoch, the owner of *The Sun* and *The Times* newspapers, are arguably examples of entrepreneurs in large companies.

> **QUESTION 1** In January 1993, Rahila Ahmed decided to leave her job as a systems analyst at a computer manufacturer. She had built up a fund of £25,000 to set up in business as a computer programmer. Rahila bought £20,000 worth of computer equipment. She designed computer software for children with learning difficulties. She selected this specialism because a friend's daughter had quite serious learning difficulties and Rahila had designed a number of programs to help her read, count and spell. Because there was a desperate lack of software in this area Rahila very quickly sold her programs. Within six months she had generated £55,000 worth of sales and had employed a salesperson and a secretary.
>
> (a) In what way is Rahila an entrepreneur?
> (b) What risks did Rahila face when deciding to become an entrepreneur?
> (c) If the business continues to grow, how might Rahila's role as an entrepreneur change?

Type of shareholder

Certain types of business do not have shareholders, such as sole traders and partnerships. Limited companies can raise money by issuing shares (☞ unit 3). Shareholders become the 'joint owners' of the business. The shareholder or group of shareholders with the majority of shares, ie 51 per cent, will be the majority shareholder in the business. Examples of these shareholders are shown in Figure 2.2.

Directors Directors are elected by the shareholders each year and are responsible for running the business. They do not have to hold shares in the companies they run, but generally they do. Some directors have quite large shareholdings, sometimes large enough to exert control, such as in a family business.

Managers Managers are usually appointed by directors and are actively involved in running the business. Some managers own shares in their companies, but they do not have to. Sometimes they are allowed to buy shares or are given shares as a bonus. It is argued that if managers own shares in the company it might motivate them to perform well in their jobs. This is because if they perform well, profits may be higher and higher dividends can then be paid to shareholders like themselves.

Employees Most employees in large business organisations are not shareholders. However, in the last decade the government has encouraged people to own shares in their companies. Companies have also offered shares to employees as bonuses. Sainsbury's is an example of one company which does this. It is unlikely that employees will own enough shares to have any control in the running of the business.

Individuals It is possible for individuals to own shares in companies. Any member of the public is allowed to buy shares in any **public limited company** (☞ unit 3). One common way of buying them is through a **stockbroker**. Individuals generally buy shares because they want to earn dividends. Buying shares is an alternative to other methods of saving, for example putting money in a building society account. Such people play no role in running the business. Also, they rarely have any control since they own only a small fraction of the total number of shares. If individuals are not happy with the performance of the company they may sell their shares.

Institutional investors These are financial institutions (☞ unit 40) such as insurance companies, pension funds and unit trusts who buy shares to earn income. They buy and sell very large numbers of shares, but rarely participate in the running of the companies. Their aim is to hold those shares which pay the most attractive dividends. In some cases they may exert control, since they own such large blocks of shares.

Other companies Some firms hold shares to earn income, some to control other companies and some to build up stakes in other companies with a view to taking them over in the future (☞ unit 32).

Managers

Firms of all sizes employ managers. A MANAGER may be defined as an individual who is accountable for more work than he could undertake alone. In a small firm the owner is likely to be responsible for all managerial tasks. When a business grows the responsibility for some decision making is often **delegated** to others since it is not possible for one person to carry the whole burden.

There are a number of common functions of managers in business.

Organising and decision making Businesses are often divided into departments. A smaller business may have production, marketing, finance and administration departments. The owners may appoint one manager to control each department. The manager will have responsibility for all activities and employees in the department. For example, he may have helped to recruit employees, must make decisions about how the department should be run and ensure that department objectives are met. Employees in the department will look to the manager for leadership, to solve problems, to communicate information to them, settle disputes, motivate them and represent the department at meetings.

Planning and control Managers are also likely to contribute to the overall planning of company activities along with the owner and other managers. They also have a controlling role in the business. This may involve control of finance, equipment, time and people, for example. In larger business organisations managers become more specialist and concentrate on a narrower aspect of management.

Accountability Managers are accountable to the owners. If the production department does not achieve a satisfactory level of output, the manager may have to 'shoulder the blame'. This might mean a loss of a bonus payment.

Entrepreneurial role Although managers may not risk their own money, they might risk their job. A manager might make a decision to install some revolutionary new machinery. This could be successful and the manager might be promoted. However, if the machinery is unsuccessful, leading to heavy losses, the manager may be sacked. The manager is, arguably, in carrying out this task, innovating and risk taking.

Employees

The role of employees in business is to follow the instructions of employers. Employees are hired by firms to help business activity. A business needs people with a range of skills and knowledge. Many provide a training programme for new employees to familiarise them with the firm's policies and working practices. Employees will be more productive if they are taught good working practices from the time they start at a new company. Note that managers of the business are usually employees.

Employees normally sign **contracts of employment** (☞ unit 53) agreeing to follow all reasonable instructions related to their job. In return for their time and effort they receive a payment, ie a **wage**. The amount workers are paid depends on a wide range of factors such as age, experience, qualifications, the type of industry and the level of skill required.

The role of employees in business has begun to change in recent years.
- They have had to cope with the introduction of new technology.
- They have been encouraged by some companies to participate more in problem solving and decision making.

- They have become more flexible and have adapted to the introduction of new working practices. For example, many employees are trained in a number of tasks and are expected to be able to change from one job to another.
- Increased emphasis has been placed on training and learning new skills. For example, departmental managers have been encouraged to develop personnel skills.

Consumers

Consumers are not members of a business, but they are vital to business activity. Consumers are the customers for the goods and services that a business produces and their spending generates income for the firm. Consumers are usually individual people, although firms produce capital goods so their customers can be other businesses.

It is important for a business to understand the needs of consumers buying its products. It is often said that consumers are **sovereign**. This means that consumers dictate the pattern of business activity, ie firms will only supply goods and services which consumers want to buy. Firms that produce goods which are not wanted by consumers will fail. For example, the *Sunday Correspondent* is an example of a newspaper that failed as a result of a lack of demand.

Consumers and business have many different relationships.

- Contact between businesses and consumers takes place when goods or services are bought. This can vary. When services are bought there is usually a personal contact between the two groups, as there would be when a client makes an appointment to see a solicitor. In the case of water supply, the contact for many customers is limited, ie through the post when the quarterly bill arrives.
- Businesses need to communicate with consumers to find out what they want. **Market research** (unit 9) helps a business to collect information about their potential customers.
- As well as collecting information from consumers, businesses also pass on information about the nature of products, the price charged, how products work and where they might be bought. **Advertising** (unit 24) is often used to do this.
- Consumers are more aware today about products that are available, prices, channels of complaint and product performance. Consumers have more income than ever before, and much greater expectations of products. Businesses must take these expectations into account when designing, manufacturing and marketing products. For example, 20 years ago, a radio in a new car would have been an 'extra'. Today, a complete 'sound system' in a car is virtually a necessity.
- Businesses operate in a world where consumers have increasing rights and protection. This is dealt with in unit 73.

Because of increased consumer expectations and awareness, improved consumer rights and fiercer competition in business, the vast majority of companies work hard at promoting good customer relations. Indeed, more and more firms are happy to give consumers a lot more than their strict legal rights. Most high street stores will accept returned goods and reimburse customers. without too much investigation. Free after sales service is common and sales staff receive a lot more in the way of 'customer care' training.

QUESTION 4

(a) In what ways might the consumers in the above photographs be different?
(b) In what ways might the businesses communicate with their potential customers.
(c) How might the two groups of consumers exercise their rights if they were not satisfied?

Interdependence

There is a significant degree of interdependence within business. In large firms the owners are dependent upon the skill and ability of the management team. If managers perform well then the business is likely to make more profit which will benefit the owner. Managers rely on business owners for their jobs and to support their decisions.

Managers and other employees are also dependent upon each other. Employees rely on the guidance of management in order to do their jobs. Management depend on workers to produce output according to their instructions. Management will be accountable to the owners of the business if workers are inefficient.

Businesses are dependent on consumers. Business activity would not take place if consumers did not buy goods or services. However, consumers can only purchase these goods and services if they have income. They may earn this income from employment in business. Thus, business owners are dependent upon consumers for their income, and consumers, in their role as employees and managers, are dependent upon business owners for their income.

Conflict

Conflict can exist between many of the groups working in business.

Employees and owners What might lead to conflict between the employees and the owners of a business?

- Levels of pay. In most businesses, rates of pay are negotiated every year. Bargaining (☞ unit 59) takes place between employees and owners or managers. It is common for the two sides to disagree on new wage levels. This is because workers generally want more than the owners or managers are prepared to pay.
- Working conditions. Conflict may arise if, for example, the working environment is too cold for employees to do their jobs.
- Changing practices. In recent years a number of new working practices have been introduced in business. Disputes have occurred when employees have been asked to perform new tasks or change the way they undertake existing tasks. Employees often feel that they are being asked to do more work.
- Redundancy. When employees are faced with the threat of losing their jobs, quite naturally they react. In the early 1980s and early 1990s there were a very large number of redundancies. Workers are often angry when their jobs are replaced by machines.

Owners and managers In some businesses the management team may become powerful and influential. When this happens they may pursue their own interests rather than those of the owners. This might involve paying themselves high salaries or organising their time to suit their own needs, whilst achieving satisfactory levels of profit, which would not be in the owners' interests since profits would be lower. Such conflict may result in some owners selling their shares. This is often referred to as a divorce of ownership and control (☞ unit 5).

It is in everyone's interests to settle conflict as quickly as possible. Conflict can lead to lower levels of output and loss of profits for the owners. Managers and other employees may suffer from poor motivation, a lack of job security and loss of wages.

Consumers and business What might lead to conflict between consumers and business?

- Price. Owners may wish to maximise their profit which might involve charging the highest possible price. However, consumers want to buy goods as cheaply as possible. If competition exists in the market (☞ unit 22) consumers will generally benefit. If there is a lack of competition, as there is in the gas distribution industry, for example, consumers do not have a choice, except to go without.
- Quality. Consumers may be dissatisfied with the quality of the products they have bought. If consumers return goods then businesses lose income, so disagreements often occur as to whether a firm should accept returned goods.
- Delivery time. Customers are often keen to receive the goods which they have ordered as quickly as possible. A dispute would occur if, for example, a business cannot deliver a wedding dress promised for the day of a wedding.
- After sales service. Consumers may be upset by poor after sales service. For example, if a person buys a hi-fi system, and finds that it does not work, a dispute might emerge if the business refused to investigate the problem.

QUESTION 5 Henley Garden Centre is owned by Sandra Thompson who is retired and lives in Venice. She employs a manager who has an assistant to help run the business. The manager concentrates on finance and administration while his assistant is responsible for production, selling and staff. Thirty staff are employed in the large garden centre and they have just been offered a 4 per cent wage increase. They had requested a 13 per cent pay rise on the grounds that in the previous two years they had agreed to a pay freeze. The staff are very angry with this final offer and they have all agreed not to work at weekends. The management have always been unpopular with the employees because they feel that they are being exploited. For example, the manager and the assistant manager both drive company BMWs and take it in turns to take time off to play golf three times a week. However, since the owner lives abroad, is reasonably satisfied with the profit made by the company and is not entirely aware of the circumstances, the situation is unlikely to change.

(a) Identify possible sources of conflict between the management and the employees.
(b) How might the conflict between the management and employees affect the business?
(c) Explain whether there might be a conflict in this case between the owner and management.

Management buy-outs

A MANAGEMENT BUY-OUT has traditionally been where the management team in a business becomes the owner, usually by buying the shares from the existing owners. It would raise the finance itself from banks and other institutions. The 1980s saw an increasing number of buy-outs taking place. Some of these were when financial institutions took control of a company (known as a LEVERAGED BUY-OUT), often paying large amounts of money. In 1989 there were 500 recorded deals in the UK alone. The early 1990s saw a drop off in the number of buy-outs and their valuations. Only 354 deals took place in the whole of Europe in 1991, the largest being the £140 million paid to Allied Lyons for Gaymer Group Europe, owners of Babycham and Olde English Cider. Over the period 1982-1992 more than 4,200 deals took place.

Evidence shows that the majority of buy-outs are still small scale, less than £10 million, and that the high spending of the 1980s has fallen. Why have buy-outs by the management of a company taken place in the UK?

- It is an alternative to full or partial closure of a family business or its subsidiary. For example, in 1992 Miller & Bryce, the 100 year old Scottish research company, was bought by the management.
- Sometimes large companies sell off parts of their business which do not fit into their future plans. For example, Forte, the hotel group, sold Gardner Merchant, Europe's biggest caterer, for £342 million to a management buy-out team in 1992.
- To resurrect a company that had already gone into receivership (☞ unit 67). For example, in 1989, Kosset Carpets was bought from the failed Coloroll empire.
- As part of the privatisation programme (☞ unit 4) of the UK government. The government allowed some managers to buy subsidiaries of state owned industries, such as British Steel and Austin Rover. In the case of the National Freight Corporation they permitted an entire management buy-out.

What might be the advantages of a management buy-out? From the sellers' point of view it lets them to raise finance for a possibly ailing firm or subsidiary, which might otherwise have closed down. From the managers' and employees' point of view it would enable them to keep their jobs in the same occupation and area as they had before. It is also argued that the efficiency of the business would be improved by a buy-out. This is perhaps because there is an increased incentive for managers to perform well. Following a buy-out the management team will benefit financially from any profit made by the company, so there is an incentive to keep costs down and motivate the workforce, for example. In addition, the potential for conflict between the owners and the managers is reduced because after a buy-out the owners are the managers.

Generally, it seems that buy-outs are successful as they keep the business going. A study by the Warwick Business School reported that management buy-outs outperformed their industry average for the first three years. However, after that, they tended to underperform. Other, longer term, studies have suggested that performance after the first three years continued to be better than the industry average.

Management buy-ins

Interest in MANAGEMENT BUY-INS, where an outside management team takes over a business, began in the mid-1980s. In 1985 there were less than 30 buy-ins, rising to 111 in 1991. Most of the deals arose out of family owned businesses with no clear line of succession when the head of the family retires. Many small business owners prefer their companies to remain independent, albeit outside family control, rather than be swallowed up by conglomerates. One example was F & AE Lodge, a Huddersfield based supermarket chain. Edward Lodge the chairman, sold the business to a group of outside managers when the Lodge family decided to retire.

QUESTION 6 In September 1992, Whitbread, the brewing and retail group, sold 233 public houses to a management buy-in team. The sale was forced by the government. This followed an investigation which ruled that some of the big firms in the industry should sell their 'tied houses' to increase competition. The buy-in team was led by Paul Smith, the former group manager of Devenish, a West Country brewery. The aim of the new company, Discovery Inns, was to enhance the traditional values that once made Britain's public houses renowned throughout the world for their good ale and for the hospitality of their landlords. The deal was arranged and led by Kleinwort Benson Development Capital and backed by other City institutions. Bank finance was supplied by NM Rothschild.

Source: adapted from *The Times*, 15.9.1992.

(a) What is the difference between a management buy-out and a management buy-in?
(b) Why might Whitbread want an outside management team to take over the running of their public houses?

Key terms

Directors - people elected by shareholders to run companies.
Dividend - a proportion of a company's profits paid to owners of shares in that company.
Leveraged buy-out - a situation where a group of financial institutions takes control of a company.

Manager - an individual who is accountable for more work than he or she could undertake alone.
Management buy-in - the sale of a business to an outside management team.
Management buy-out - the sale of a business to the existing management team.

Summary

1. Briefly explain why people are important to business activity.
2. List 3 functions of an entrepreneur.
3. Why are entrepreneurs often associated with small businesses?
4. State 5 possible groups of shareholders.
5. Briefly explain 4 roles of management.
6. 'The role of employees in business is changing.' Explain this statement using an example.
7. What is meant by 'consumer sovereignty'?
8. Briefly explain 3 ways in which businesses and consumers are related.
9. Why are owners, managers and employees interdependent?
10. Explain one source of conflict between: (a) owners and managers; (b) managers and employees; (c) businesses and consumers.
11. Explain how management buy-outs might benefit the buy-out team.

Question

Fosters

Fosters are a high street retail chainstore which sell mainly menswear. They have around 350 shops and operate in a very competitive market. Their main strength is considered to be casual wear. During the 1980s Fosters experienced mixed fortunes. They made money in good times and lost money during the recession. In 1992 the chain made heavy losses and the owners, Sears, sold it to a management buy-out group. Sears felt that the cost of turning the company around was not justified. They believed that the business faced certain problems.

- It covered only 40 per cent of the market.
- The shops were in the wrong place.
- It needed £10 million to £15 million to put things right.

Sears wanted to concentrate on its more promising operations which included the department store Selfridges, its shoe empire, speciality retailing such as Adams childrenswear, Olympus sportswear, womenswear chains such as Miss Selfridge, Wallis and Warehouse and Freemans the mail order business.

The buy-out deal appeared quite attractive. Fosters were sold to the buy-out group for just £1. Sears retained ownership of the properties but handed over all of the fixtures and fittings, stock and cash valued at £29 million. The transaction cost Sears £18 million in total cash outlay. However, Sears said that Fosters would have cost them £16 million if they had not sold out. They added, that Fosters had drained £30 million from group resources in the last two years. This is the second time that Sears have given away a business. In 1991 they sold the Hornes menswear chain to a management group for £1.

David Carter-Johnson, the leader of the buy-out group, was optimistic about the future of Fosters. He believed that the recession of the early 1990s was not the cause of Fosters' problems. His view was that Fosters were a 'jack-of-all-trades and master of none'. They were trying to sell everything in a space half the size of Burtons, so they did everything half as well. His solution was to concentrate on the casual wear

strength and drop suits and sportswear. They aimed to raise sales per square foot from £200 to £300 and embark on a cost cutting strategy. The buy-out was funded largely by Hambros European Ventures, the development capital business. In exchange for their financial backing they took a 40 per cent share in the business.

Source : adapted from *The Guardian*, 22.9.1992.

(a) In what way is the buy-out of Fosters a traditional management buy-out?
(b) In what way might the management group be described as entrepreneurial?
(c) How might the role of the managers change after the management buy-out?
(d) Write a report explaining the advantages of the buy-out to:
 (i) the owners, Sears;
 (ii) consumers;
 (iii) managers;
 (iv) employees.
(e) Why might the interdependence between the managers and the employees be more important after the buy-out?
(f) Suggest 3 possible sources of conflict that may result between the management and the employees after the buy-out.

What is a business organisation?

Businesses are often referred to as organisations. An ORGANISATION is a body that is set up to meet needs. For example, the St. John's Ambulance organisation was originally set up by volunteers to train the public in life saving measures.

Business organisations satisfy needs by providing people with goods and services. All organisations will:
- try to achieve objectives (☞ unit 5);
- use resources;
- need to be directed;
- have to be accountable;
- have to meet legal requirements;
- have a formal structure (☞ unit 63).

Private sector business organisations

Unit 1 showed the different methods of classifying business. One of these methods was by sector. The PRIVATE SECTOR includes all those businesses which are set up by individuals or groups of individuals. Most business activity is undertaken in the private sector. The types of business in the private sector can vary considerably. Some are small retailers with a single owner. Others are large multinational companies (☞ unit 70), such as ICI and Trafalgar House. Businesses will vary according to the legal form they take and their ownership.
- Unincorporated businesses. These are businesses where there is no legal difference between the owners and the business. Everything is carried out in the name of the owner or owners. These firms tend to be small, owned either by one person or a few partners.
- Incorporated businesses. An incorporated body is one which has a separate legal identity from its owners. In other words, the business can be sued, can be taken over and can be liquidated.

Figure 3.1 shows the different types of business organisation in the private sector, their legal status and their ownership. These are examined in the rest of this unit.

The sole trader

The simplest and most common form of private sector business is a SOLE TRADER or SOLE PROPRIETOR. This type of business is owned by just one person. The owner runs the business and may employ any number of people to help. Sole traders can be found in different types of production. In the primary sector many farmers and fishermen operate like this. In the secondary sector there are small scale manufacturers, builders and construction firms. The tertiary sector probably contains the largest number of sole traders. They supply a wide range of services, such as hairdressing, retailing, restaurants, gardening and other household services. Many sole

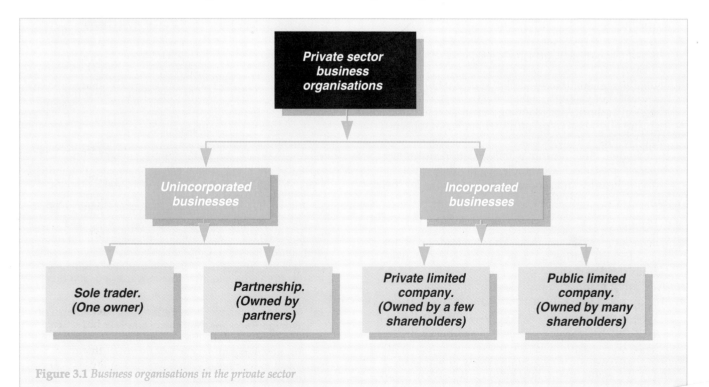

Figure 3.1 *Business organisations in the private sector*

traders exist in retailing and construction where a very large number of shops and small construction companies are each owned by one person. This can be seen in Figure 3.2. Although there are many more sole traders than any other type of business, the amount they contribute to total output in the UK is relatively small.

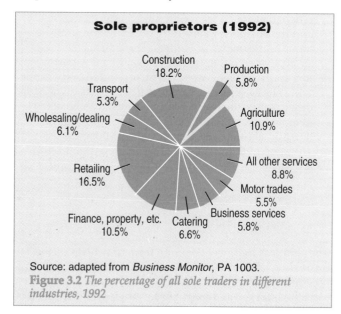

Sole proprietors (1992)

Construction 18.2%
Production 5.8%
Transport 5.3%
Agriculture 10.9%
Wholesaling/dealing 6.1%
All other services 8.8%
Retailing 16.5%
Motor trades 5.5%
Finance, property, etc. 10.5%
Catering 6.6%
Business services 5.8%

Source: adapted from *Business Monitor*, PA 1003.

Figure 3.2 *The percentage of all sole traders in different industries, 1992*

Setting up as a sole trader is straightforward. There are no legal formalities needed. However, sole traders or self-employed dealers do have some legal responsibilities once they become established. In addition, some types of business need to obtain special permission before trading.

- Once turnover reaches a certain level sole traders must register for VAT.
- They must pay income tax and National Insurance contributions.
- Some types of business activity need a licence, such as the sale of alcohol or supplying a taxi-service or public transport.
- Sometimes planning permission is needed in certain locations. For example, a person may have to apply to the local authority for planning permission to run a fish and chip shop in premises which had not been used for this activity before.
- Sole traders must comply with legislation aimed at business practice. For example, legally they must provide healthy and safe working conditions for their employees (☞ unit 56).

Advantages of sole traders

- The lack of legal restrictions. The sole trader will not face a lengthy setting up period or incur expensive administration costs.
- Any profit made after tax is kept by the owner.
- The owner is in complete control and is free to make decisions without interference. For many sole traders independence is one of the main reasons why they choose to set up in business.
- The owner has flexibility to choose the hours of work he or she wants and to take holidays. Customers may also benefit. Sole traders can take special needs into

account, stocking a particular brand of a good or making changes to a standard design, for example.
- Because of their small size, sole traders can offer a personal service to their customers. Some people prefer to deal directly with the owner and are prepared to pay a higher price for doing so.
- Such businesses may be entitled to government support (☞ unit 8).

Disadvantages of sole traders

- Sole traders have UNLIMITED LIABILITY. This means that if the business has debts, the owner is personally liable. A sole trader may be forced to sell personal possessions or use personal savings to meet these debts.
- The money used to set up the business is often the owner's savings. It may also come from a bank loan. Sole traders may find it difficult to raise money. They tend to be small and lack sufficient **collateral**, such as property or land, on which to raise finance. This

QUESTION 1 George Saunders was employed by a national newspaper but was made redundant in January 1992. He spent seven months searching for another reporting job, but eventually gave up and decided to set up his own business. He had always enjoyed books and opened up a second-hand book shop in Cardiff. In a room above the bookshop he opened up a small cafe. He used £4,000 of his own savings and a £1,000 bank loan to meet the set up costs. He also qualified for £40 per week from the government's Enterprise Allowance Scheme. George employed two part time students to help out in the cafe during weekends and school holidays. After a slow start business picked up and his cafe gained popularity with students from three local colleges. He spotted an opportunity and lowered prices slightly to encourage even more students to visit.

After one year he extended his bank loan to £2,000 and bought some more kitchen equipment to provide substantial lunch time meals. Again he kept prices low and targeted the student market. The business expanded and George was beginning to enjoy good profits. The book shop only made a small contribution to turnover, but George felt that it helped the image of the cafe which attracted his customers.

One morning when he was opening, a local authority representative arrived unannounced to inspect the business premises. After a two hour investigation the inspector left saying that George would hear from the authority the next day. A letter from them informed George that his kitchen must conform to a long list of health regulations. George estimated that the cost would be £3,000. He arranged a meeting with the bank that same afternoon. Unfortunately they could only lend him half the amount. George was eventually forced to borrow from a private loan company, paying high rates of interest.

(a) What features of a sole trader does the example of George Saunders' business show?
(b) In what ways does the above case highlight the:
 (i) advantages;
 (ii) disadvantages;
 of being a sole trader?

means money for expansion must come from profits or savings.

- Although independence is an advantage, it can also be a disadvantage. A sole trader might prefer to share decision making, for example. Many sole traders work very long hours, without holidays, and may have to learn new skills.
- In cases where the owner is the only person in the business, illness can stop business activity taking place. For example, if a sole trader is a mobile hairdresser, illness will lead to a loss of income in the short term, and even a loss of customers in the long term.
- Because sole traders are unincorporated businesses, the owner can be sued by customers in the event of a dispute.
- This type of business lacks continuity. When the owner dies it is necessary to 'wind up' the firm. The business may be sold, but begin trading again under another name.

Partnerships

A PARTNERSHIP is defined in **The Partnership Act, 1890** as the 'relation which subsists between persons carrying on business with common view to profit'. Put simply, a partnership has more than one owner. The 'joint' owners will share responsibility for running the business and also share the profits. Partnerships are often found in professional services, such as accountants, doctors, estate agents, solicitors and veterinary surgeons. After sole traders, partnerships are the most common type of business organisation. It is usual for partners to specialise. A firm of chartered accountants with five partners might find that each partner specialises in one aspect of finance, such as tax law, investments or VAT returns.

There are no legal formalities to complete when a partnership is formed. However, partners may draw up a DEED OF PARTNERSHIP. This is a legal document which states partners' rights in the event of a dispute. It covers issues such as:

- how much capital each partner will contribute;
- how profits (and losses) will be shared amongst the partners;
- the procedure for ending the partnership;
- how much control each partner has;
- rules for taking on new partners.

If no deed of partnership is drawn up the arrangements between partners will be subject to the Partnership Act. For example, if there was a dispute regarding the share of profits, the Act states that profits are shared equally amongst the partners.

Advantages of partnerships

- There are no legal formalities to complete when setting up the business.
- Each partner can specialise. This may improve the running of the business, as partners can carry out the tasks they do best.
- Since there is more than one owner, more finance can be raised than if the firm was a sole trader.

- Partners can share the workload. They will be able to cover each other for holidays and illness. They can also exchange ideas and opinions when making key decisions. Also, the success of the business will not depend upon the ability of one person, as is the case with a sole trader.
- Since this type of business tends to be larger than the sole trader, it is in a stronger position to raise more money if necessary.

Disadvantages of partnerships

- The individual partners have unlimited liability. Under the Partnership Act, each partner is equally liable for debts.
- Profits have to be shared amongst more owners.
- Partners may disagree. For example, they might differ in their views on whether to hire a new employee or about the amount of profit to retain for investment.
- The size of a partnership is limited to a maximum of 20 partners. This limits the amount of money that can be introduced from owners.
- The partnership ends when one of the partners dies.

QUESTION 2 Dribble, Crisp, Macon and Crudgington are a firm of solicitors based in Cleethorpes. They set up their partnership in 1986 in a town centre office. Because they were all such good friends from university days they did not think it necessary to draw up a deed of partnership. They traded for six years and enjoyed modest profits. However, their scope for increasing profit was limited. They tended to attract a less wealthy clientele, they thought due to drab offices.

In 1992 Crisp suggested that they move to some new offices on the outskirts of Grimsby. Dribble agreed, but Macon and Crudgington were actually content with the current situation. After a very lengthy and heated discussion, Crisp convinced them that taking out a five year lease and relocating would be a good business move. The next week Crisp signed a ten year lease with a property company for the offices. This annoyed Macon and Crudgington since Crisp had led them to believe that the lease would be for five years. The initial outlay on the ten year lease was more than they could all afford, but Crisp argued that a friend of his, Drinkwell, would like to become a sleeping partner. After more discussion and disagreement, they were left with little option but to follow Crisp's suggestions.

After 9 months the financial position of the business was poor and the company faced trading problems. The monthly payments on the offices were crippling, the partnership had lost more than half of its old clients, Macon had been absent for six months with a stress related illness, and they had been unable to attract many new clients in their new location. In August 1993 they decided to cease trading, owing a total of £26,000.

(a) Describe the ways in which the case illustrates the disadvantages of partnerships.
(b) How would the loss be divided between Dribble, Crisp, Macon, Crudgington and Drinkwell? Explain your answer.
(c) Why do you think Drinkwell was content to become a sleeping partner?

The partnership must be wound up so that the partner's family can retrieve money invested in the business. It is normal for the remaining partners to form a new partnership quickly afterwards.

- Any decision made by one partner on behalf of the company is legally binding on all other partners. For example, if one partner agreed to buy four new company cars for the business, all partners must honour this.
- Partnerships have unincorporated status, so partners can be sued by customers.

Limited partnerships The **Limited Partnerships Act 1907** allows a business to become a LIMITED PARTNERSHIP, although this is rare. This is where some partners provide capital but take no part in the management of the business. Such a partner will have LIMITED LIABILITY - the partner can only lose the original amount of money invested. She can not be made to sell personal possessions to meet any other business debts. This type of partner is called a **sleeping partner**. Even with a limited partnership there must always be at least one partner with **unlimited liability.** The Act also allows this type of partnership to have more than 20 partners.

Companies

There are many examples of LIMITED COMPANIES in the UK. They range from Garrick Engineering, a small family business, to British Airways which has many thousands of shareholders. One feature is that they all have a separate legal identity from their owners. This means that they can own assets, form contracts, employ people, sue and be sued in their own right. Another feature is that they all have **limited liability**. If a limited company has debts, the owners can only lose the money they have invested in the firm. They cannot be forced to use their own money like sole traders and partners to pay business debts.

The **capital** of a limited company is divided into **shares**. Each member or **shareholder** (☞ unit 2) owns a number of these shares. They are the joint owners of the company and can vote and take a share of the profit. Those with more shares will have more control and can take more profit.

Limited companies are run by **directors** who are appointed by the shareholders. The board of directors, headed by a **chairperson**, is accountable to shareholders and should run the company as the shareholders wish. If the company's performance does not to live up to shareholders' expectations, directors can be 'voted out' at an **Annual General Meeting (AGM).**

Whereas sole traders and partnerships pay income tax on profits, companies pay corporation tax.

Forming a limited company

How do shareholders set up a limited company? Limited companies must produce two documents - the **Memorandum of Association** and **Articles of**

Association. The Memorandum sets out the constitution and gives details about the company. The **Companies Act 1985** states that the following details must be included.

- The name of the company.
- The name and address of the company's registered office.
- The objectives of the company, and the scope of its activities.
- The liability of its members.
- The amount of capital to be raised and the number of shares to be issued.

A limited company must have a minimum of two members, but there is no upper limit.

The Articles of Association deal with the internal running of the company. They include details such as:

- the rights of shareholders depending on the type of share they hold;
- the procedures for appointing directors and the scope of their powers;
- the length of time directors should serve before re-election;
- the timing and frequency of company meetings;
- the arrangements for auditing company accounts.

These two documents, along with a statement indicating the names of the directors, will be sent to the Registrar of Companies. If they are acceptable, the company's application will be successful. It will be awarded a **Certificate of Incorporation** which allows it to trade. The registrar keeps these documents on file and they can be inspected at any time by the general public for a fee. A limited company must also submit a copy of its annual accounts to the Registrar each year. Finally, the shareholders have a legal right to attend the AGM and should be told of the date and venue in writing well in advance.

Private limited companies

Private limited companies are one type of limited company. They tend to be the smaller type and their business name ends in Limited or Ltd. Shares can only be transferred 'privately' and all shareholders must agree on the transfer. They cannot be advertised for general sale. Private limited companies are often family businesses owned by members of the family or close friends. The directors of these firms tend to be shareholders and are involved in the running of the business. Many manufacturing firms are private limited companies rather than sole traders or partnerships.

Advantages
- Shareholders have limited liability. As a result more people are prepared to risk their money than in, say, a partnership.
- More capital can be raised as there is no limit on the number of shareholders.
- Control of the company cannot be lost to outsiders. Shares can only be sold to new members if all shareholders agree.
- The business will continue even if one of the owners dies. In this case shares will be transferred to another owner.

Disadvantages

- Profits have to be shared out amongst a much larger number of members.
- There is a legal procedure to set up the business. This takes time and also costs money.
- Firms are not allowed to sell shares to the public. This restricts the amount of capital that can be raised.
- Financial information filed with the Registrar can be inspected by any member of the public. Competitors could use this to their advantage.
- If one shareholder decides to sell shares it may take time to find a buyer.

QUESTION 3 Katrina Lau owns a small manufacturing company in Kidderminster producing carpet making equipment for local carpet manufacturers. She employs six people in a small factory located in Broad Street. Although the local carpet industry had declined in recent years, Katrina had established herself as a leading and respected supplier in the area. She was now in a position to expand. Katrina had plans to build an extension to her factory and install some new machinery which would enable her to treble output in the future. The expansion would cost £120,000 and although Katrina had enjoyed many profitable years as a sole trader, she had not retained very much of that profit in the business. Her bank manager suggested that she should form a limited company as a means of raising the money.

(a) Imagine that you are Katrina's bank manager. Write to her explaining:
    (i) why she might set up as a limited company;
    (ii) how to form the company.
(b) How might Katrina find suitable shareholders for her company?
(c) What might be the disadvantages for Katrina in forming this company?

Public limited companies

The second type of limited company tends to be larger and is called a **public limited company**. This company name ends in PLC. There are around 500,000 limited companies in the UK but only 3 per cent of them are public limited companies. However, they contribute far more to national output and employ far more people than private limited companies. The shares of these companies can be bought and sold by the public on the stock exchange. To become a public limited company, a Memorandum of Association, Articles of Association and a **Statutory Declaration** must be provided. This is a document which states that the requirements of all the Company Acts have been met. When the company has been issued with a **Certificate of Incorporation**, it is common to publish a **Prospectus**. This is a document which advertises the company to potential investors and invites them to buy shares before a FLOTATION. Some examples of companies which have 'gone public' recently are Manchester United in 1991 and Carpetright in 1993. It was also announced in July 1993 that the House of Fraser

was to go public (with the exception of Harrods). 'Going public' is expensive. This is because:

- the company needs lawyers to ensure that the prospectus is 'legally' correct;
- a large number of 'glossy' publications have to be made available;
- the company may use a financial institution to process share applications;
- the share issue has to be **underwritten** (which means that the company must insure against the possibility of some shares remaining unsold) and a fee is paid to an underwriter who must buy any unsold shares;
- the company will have advertising and administrative expenses;
- it must have a minimum of £50,000 share capital.

A public limited company cannot begin trading until it has completed these tasks and has received at least a 25 per cent payment for the value of shares. It will then receive a Trading Certificate and can begin operating, and the shares will be quoted on the Stock Exchange (☞ unit 40).

Advantages

Some of the advantages are the same as those of private limited companies. For example, all members have limited liability, the firm continues to trade if one of the owners dies and more power is enjoyed due to their larger size. Others are as follows.

- Huge amounts of money can be raised from the sale of shares to the public.
- Production costs may be lower as firms may gain economies of scale (☞ unit 31).
- Because of their size, PLCs can often dominate the market.

Disadvantages

- The setting up costs can be very expensive - running into millions of pounds in some cases.
- Since anyone can buy their shares, it is possible for an outside interest to take control of the company.
- All of the company's accounts can be inspected by members of the public. Competitors may be able to use some of this information to their advantage. They have to publish more information than private limited companies.
- Because of their size they are not able to deal with their customers at a personal level.
- The way they operate is controlled by various Company Acts which aim to protect shareholders.
- There may be a divorce of ownership and control (☞ unit 5) which might lead to the interests of the owners being ignored to some extent.
- It is argued that many of these companies are inflexible due to their size. For example, they find change difficult to cope with.

Some public limited companies are very large indeed. They have millions of shareholders and a wide variety of business interests situated all over the world. They are known as **multinationals**, which means that they have production plants in a number of different countries. For example, Kellogg's is an American based multinational company with a production plant and head office situated in Battle Creek, USA. Kellogg's also has factories in

Manchester, Wrexham, Bremen, Barcelona and Brescia near Milan.

QUESTION 4 Amstrad, the computer company, were subject to a shareholder battle in 1992-93. Alan Sugar, the chairman, built up the company and enjoyed a great deal of success in the 1980s. In 1988 the company's annual profit peaked at £160 million. However, since then the company's fortunes reversed. In 1991-92 they made a pre-tax loss of £70.9 million. Alan Sugar held 205 million shares which was a 35 per cent stake in the company. He wanted to change the status of the business back to a private limited company. He offered the 31,000 shareholders 30p per share compared with the stock market price of 28p (at its peak in 1988 it was over 200p). If they had accepted the offer, it would have cost him £113 million. The shareholders questioned the motive for the buy-out. Sugar argued that he had the shareholders' interests at heart and that 30p was the best offer they were likely to get in view of the company's recent poor performance. However, many shareholders were suspicious. They believed that once Sugar had taken the company back completely, he would turn it around and enjoy all future profits for himself. The final vote was close. The shareholders decided to reject the offer by a 58.7 per cent majority.

Source : adapted from *The Observer*, 6.12.92 and updated.

(a) Explain why Alan Sugar lost complete control of the company when it originally went public.
(b) Calculate how many shares the company has issued.
(c) Why might Alan Sugar want to take back the ownership of Amstrad from a public to a private limited company?

Holding companies

Some public limited companies operate as HOLDING COMPANIES. This means that they are not only a company in their own right, but also have enough shares in numerous other public limited companies to exert control. This type of company tends to have a very diversified range of business activities. For example, the Kingfisher group owns a number of companies including Woolworth, B & Q, Superdrug, Comet and a property arm Chartwell.

The main advantage of this type of company is that it tends to have a diverse range of business activities. This helps protect it when one of its markets fails. Also, because it is so large, it can often gain economies of scale.

Co-operatives

A CO-OPERATIVE is a business organisation where:
- all members have equal voting rights - one vote for each member;
- all members participate in the running of the business and share the work load, responsibility and decision making;

- the profits are shared equally amongst the members;
- sometimes decision making is delegated to a manager, leading to specialisation and improved efficiency.

During the 1980s the number of businesses setting up as co-operatives grew, possibly as a result of the desire to share risks. One important type of co-operative is a producers' or workers' co-operative. This is where a group of individuals organise themselves collectively to produce goods or services, such as in a farming co-operative.

Another type is a retail co-operative. 'Co-op' shops or supermarkets can be found in high streets all over the country. The first 'Co-op' was set up in Rochdale in 1844. A group of workers called the Rochdale Pioneers pooled their resources and purchased food from wholesalers, which they sold to their colleagues. Their colleagues became members of the group by paying £1 for a share. This entitled them to a vote at meetings where a president of the local co-operative society would be elected. They also enjoyed goods at lower prices and a share of the society's profits, which were distributed according to the amount members spent.

The principles of the modern Co-op are very much the same. Customers are issued with stamps according to how much they spend in the shops. These can be saved and exchanged for goods. Co-ops are involved in a variety of retailing activities, such as groceries, dairy products, banking, travel, funeral direction and bakeries. The largest single retailing co-operative is the Co-operative Retail Society which is based in Manchester.

The overall structure of a business organisation

A business will be organised so that it can run efficiently. There are a variety of different structures that a business organisation can have. The structure could be based on one or a combination of the following:
- Organisation by function. Many businesses are organised into departments, which undertake different activities. Departments common to most firms include marketing, production, personnel, finance etc.
- Organisation by process. When production is based on a number of operations, the business may be organised into areas that specialise in these different tasks. For example, a printing company may be organised into typesetting, paper buying, printing and binding of books or magazines.
- Organisation by geographical area. A business may be divided into regional or national sections, which concentrate on certain areas of the country or parts of the world. An example might be a multinational company which has different divisions worldwide.
- Organisation by product. This is where each different part of a business concentrates on the production of a product or the provision of a service. The demerger of ICI resulted in two companies (☞ unit 32). ICI concentrated on chemicals, explosives and paint while Zeneca would produce pharmaceuticals. Figure 3.3

shows the division of a French holding company, Suez. The company is organised so that each part concentrates on a particular service.

■ Organisation by customer. A business may be organised so that certain sections deal with the needs of different groups of consumers. Accountants or solicitors, for example, may be organised to deal with the different needs of particular clients.

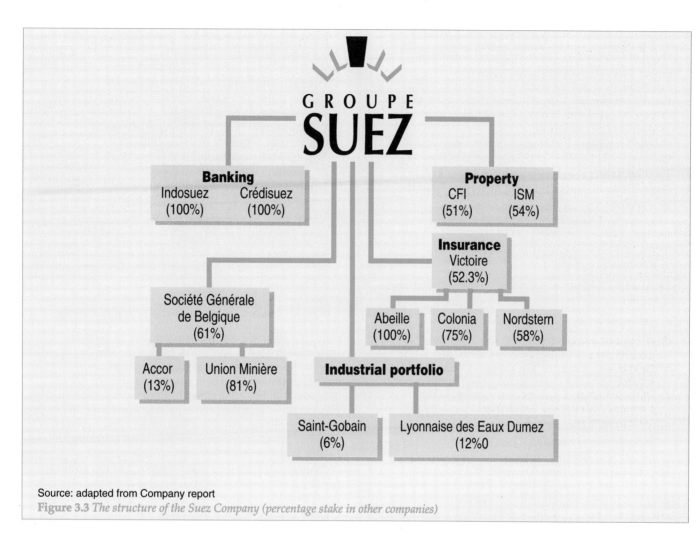

Source: adapted from Company report

Figure 3.3 *The structure of the Suez Company (percentage stake in other companies)*

Summary

1. What is the difference between a corporate body and an incorporated body?
2. State 3 advantages and 3 disadvantages of being a sole trader.
3. What is the advantage of members drawing up a deed of partnership when forming a partnership?
4. State 3 advantages and 3 disadvantages of partnerships.
5. What is meant by a sleeping partner?
6. What is the role of directors in limited companies?
7. What is the difference between the Memorandum of Association and the Articles of Association?
8. What is a Certificate of Incorporation?
9. Describe the advantages and disadvantages of private limited companies.
10. What are the main legal differences between private and public limited companies?
11. Describe the advantages and disadvantages of public limited companies.
12. How is a company prospectus used?
13. State 2 advantages of a holding company.

Key terms

Co-operative - a business organisation which is run and owned jointly by the members who have equal voting rights.
Deed of Partnership - a binding legal document which states the formal rights of partners.
Flotation - the process of a company 'going public'.
Holding company - a public limited company which owns enough shares in a number of other companies to exert control over them.
Limited company - a business organisation which has a separate legal entity from those of its owners.
Limited liability - where a business owner is only liable for the original amount of money invested in the business.

Limited partnership - a partnership where some members contribute capital and enjoy a share of profit, but do not participate in the running of the business. At least one partner must have unlimited liability.
Organisation - a body set up to meet a need.
Partnership - a business organisation which is usually owned by between 2-20 people.
Private sector - businesses that are owned by individuals or groups of individuals.
Sole trader or sole proprietor - a business organisation which has a single owner.
Unlimited liability - where the owner of a business is personally liable for all business debts.

Question

Stagecoach Holdings

Brian Souter, a chartered accountant, formed Stagecoach in 1980 along with his sister, Mrs Ann Gloag, who was a nurse. He acquired a handful of buses and operated a service between Dundee and London. He employed his father as a driver and undercut the established Scottish bus company to break into the market.

The company expanded when the National Bus Company was broken up and privatised in 1985. Stagecoach bought bus companies in Hampshire, Cumbria and the East Midlands. Further acquisitions were made from failed management buy-outs and a few Scottish bus companies. Following each purchase tiers of management were eliminated, routes were re-examined, different sized buses were introduced, heavy investment in new fleets was made, productivity deals with the workforce were agreed and middle management were allowed to flourish. In addition, from time to time the company profited from property deals. For example, as a result of privatisation the company acquired the Keswick bus station for £55,000 which it sold for £705,000. In another deal it sold the bus station in Whitehaven for £1.1 million having bought it for £165,000.

Stagecoach at the time employed 11,000 people and operated 3,300 buses. They also had business interests in Kenya, Malawi, New Zealand and China. In 1992 Stagecoach's pre-tax profits were £8.2 million compared with £2.5 million in 1991. This improvement was achieved on a turnover growth from £103.3 million to £140.7 million.

In 1993 Brian Souter announced that Stagecoach would be floated on the Stock Exchange. The flotation, Mr. Souter said, would give the company the resources it needed to continue its expansion. About 35 municipal bus companies in England were due for privatisation over the following two years and the government was also going to sell the London Buses. Another possible opportunity was the franchising of British Rail services.

Stagecoach Holdings was being sold to the public for about £100 million. At the time, of the company's 21 million issued shares Mr. Souter the chief executive owned 9.1 million and Mrs. Gloag the managing director owned 8.7 million. In addition, some Scottish financial institutions had an important financial interest in the business and were expected to take between 16 and 25 per cent of the shares.

Source: adapted from the *Financial Times*, 26.1.1993.

(a) **How would the official name of the company have changed if Stagecoach had 'gone public'?**
(b) **What evidence is there in the case to suggest that Stagecoach holdings was originally a private limited company?**
(c) **Explain why Mr. Souter decided to 'go public'.**
(d) **What problems may Mr. Souter have faced in going public?**
(e) **Based on the information in the case, explain the benefits to investors that may have been used in a prospectus advertising the sale of the company.**

Public sector organisations

The PUBLIC SECTOR is made up of organisations which are accountable to central or local government. They are funded by the government and tend to supply public services rather than produce products. There are a number of different organisations which are part of the public sector.

Public corporations Like incorporated bodies in the private sector (☞ unit 3), these have a separate legal identity to their owners, the government. They are also organised in a similar way. A government minister will appoint a chairperson and a board to run the organisation. The board will have overall responsibility for policy and will be accountable to that minister. Public corporations can take a number of forms.
- NATIONALISED INDUSTRIES are previously private businesses which were taken into state ownership, such as British Coal.
- Public utilities are organisations which supply important services like water, gas and electricity. Most of them have been transferred to the private sector in recent years. One example of remaining organisations is the Scottish Water Authorities.
- The BBC is a unique organisation. The chairperson is accountable to the Home Office and it raises most of its revenue from TV licence money. It is a non-trading service.
- The Bank of England, which has a special role in the monetary system, is headed by a governor who is accountable to the Chancellor of the Exchequer.
- Nuclear Electric was formed when electricity generation was split into three separate businesses. Powergen and National Power were transferred to the private sector whilst Nuclear Electric was retained as a public corporation, arguably because the private sector would not want the business.

Local and central government departments Local government departments supply a variety of services which are stated in Parliamentary Acts, such as education and housing. Central government departments administer the policy of the government. There are around 20 of these, such as the Treasury, the Department of Health and the Foreign Office.

QUANGOs These supply specialist services which are politically non-controversial. They are accountable to different government departments depending on their area of specialism. Some examples are research councils, advisory bodies, tribunals and marketing boards like the Milk Marketing Board. In recent years the role of bodies such as TECs (☞ unit 8) has increased.

The amount of business activity in the public sector has fallen since 1979. This is as a result of government policy. Services which had previously been provided by the state were reduced in favour of private sector schemes, such as private dental practices. Also, many nationalised industries were privatised. This is discussed later in this unit.

Which goods and services does the public sector provide?

It has been argued that certain PUBLIC GOODS and MERIT GOODS need to be provided by public sector organisations.

Public goods have two features.
- **Non-rivalry** - consumption of the good by one individual does not reduce the amount available for others.
- **Non-excludability** - it is impossible to exclude others from benefiting from their use.

Take the example of street lighting. If one person uses the light to see her way across the street, this does not 'use up' light for someone who wants to look at his watch. Also, it is impossible to stop using the light shining across the street. This means that it would be unlikely that people would pay directly for street lighting. If you paid £1 for light to cross the street, someone else could use it for free! If people will not pay, then businesses cannot make a profit and would not provide the service. Other examples of public goods may include the judiciary, policing and defence, although in some countries private policing does exist. These public goods are provided free at the point of use. They are paid for from taxation and government borrowing.

It is argued that some merit goods should be provided by the public sector. Examples include education, health and libraries. These are services which people think should be provided in greater quantities. It is argued that

QUESTION 1

(a) Is the example in the photograph above a public or a merit good? Explain your answer.
(b) Explain why a business in the private sector may be unlikely to produce this 'product'.

if the individual is left to decide whether or not to pay for these goods, some would choose not to or may not be able to. For example, people may choose not to take out insurance policies to cover for unexpected illness. If they became ill they would not be able to pay for treatment. As a result it is argued that the state should provide this service and pay for it from taxation. The provision of merit goods is said to raise society's standard of living (☞ unit 67).

Nationalised industries

Between 1945 and 1979 nationalised industries played an important role in the UK economy. They included British Telecom, British Gas, British Steel and Rolls Royce. Some of them like British Gas and British Telecom were huge organisations which dominated the industry. Others like British Airways competed with firms in the private sector. After 1979 the government sold many of these to the private sector.

Nationalisation was common government practice after the Second World War, especially between 1945 and 1951. It involved taking control of firms which had previously been privately owned. Numerous reasons have been put forward for nationalisation.

■ To supply services which are unprofitable. In the private sector, services are only provided if a profit can be made. Rail, bus, and postal services are examples of services which the private sector may not provide in isolated regions where costs exceed revenue.

■ To avoid wasteful duplication. The supply of services in the private sector might result in competing firms offering the same service. For example, there may be several rail links between the same destinations. This is clearly a waste of resources. One rail link run by an organisation in the public sector would prevent this. Such organisations are called NATURAL MONOPOLIES. This is because even if there was just one firm in the industry, it is impossible to gain all **economies of scale** (☞ unit 31). It is always possible to lower costs by producing more.

■ To protect employment. Some firms have been nationalised to maintain their existence and save jobs. In 1975 British Leyland was rescued by the government. It took the company into the public sector and allowed it to continue operating even though it made losses.

■ To control strategic industries. It is argued that certain industries should remain under government control because they are vital for the country. Stability in key industries such as energy, water supplies and transport is best guaranteed under direct government control. Also, the government has used nationalised industries to help it achieve economic objectives (☞ unit 65). For example, in the 1970s and perhaps the 1990s the government has restricted wage increases in the public sector as a means of setting the standard for wage increases in the private sector.

■ To prevent exploitation. Many of the nationalised industries were monopolies (☞ unit 22) which dominated the market. It was argued that consumers

can be more easily protected from exploitative business practice if they are under government control.

■ Political ideology. One political view is that the rewards from business activity should be controlled by the state rather than individuals. If a nationalised industry makes a profit it is passed on to the government. The government can then use this to spend on behalf of the people. In view of this it is not surprising that most nationalisation has taken place when a Labour government has been in power.

The few nationalised industries which remain today are run under strict guidelines. They are expected to return a profit if this is possible and are set performance targets in each trading year. It is likely that some of them will be privatised in the future, such as British Rail.

QUESTION 2

(a) What might be the motives for the public sector supplying the service in the photograph?
(b) What problems might arise if this service was provided by the private sector?

Local authority services

Some services in the UK are supplied by local authorities. Their structure, composition, and responsibilities are laid down mainly in the **Local Government Act 1972**. Local authorities include district councils, county councils, metropolitan boroughs, and London boroughs. They provide many services which are essential to local businesses and the local community.

■ Education and recreation. Local authorities are responsible for controlling most of the money allocated by government to education. Sports halls, libraries, swimming pools, community centres and parks are all examples of services provided by local government. Increasingly in the early 1990s schools and colleges chose to 'opt out' of local government control. This meant that an individual school was accountable to the board of governors rather than the local authority. The governors are accountable directly to the Department for Education.

- Housing. This includes the provision of council housing, amenities for the homeless, house renovation grants and rent allowances.
- Environment and conservation. Refuse collection, litter clearance, pest control, street cleaning and beach maintenance are examples of these services.
- Communications. Local bus services have been the responsibility of local authorities up until recently. However, the Transport Act of 1985 allowed competition from the private sector. The maintenance of roads and traffic control are other examples of such services.
- Protection. This involves the provision of a fire, police and ambulance service and local justice, and also consumer protection. Local authorities employ trading standards officers and environmental health officers to investigate business practice and premises.
- Social services. Local government is also responsible for providing services such as community care, social workers etc.

These services are paid for from a variety of sources. Central government pays the largest proportion, through a direct grant to local authorities. In addition, local corporations can raise local taxes, such as the council tax. In some cases they make a charge for certain services, such as sports halls and swimming pools.

There are reasons why such services are provided by local rather than central government. Firstly, it is argued that the local community is best served by those who are most sympathetic to its needs. Thus, local authorities should have the knowledge to evaluate those needs and supply the appropriate services. Secondly, central government is made up of large departments which often have communication problems. The decentralisation of many services should help to improve communication between the operators of services and the public. Finally, local councillors are accountable to the local electorate and if their policies are unpopular in the local community it is unlikely that they will be re-elected.

Central government departments

Central government departments supply some important services. These departments are also used by the government to implement policy.
- **The Treasury** is responsible for the government's economic strategy. This involves controlling the level of government expenditure, collecting government revenue, monitoring economic indicators and making economic forecasts.
- **The Department of Social Security** is a relatively new department formed out of the old Department of Health and Social Security (DHSS). Its main aim is to provide benefits for those individuals who qualify for them. The department assesses the needs of people who cannot work. It then makes sure that regular and correct payments are made.
- **The Department of Defence** is responsible for the provision and maintenance of the armed forces, both

in the UK, and in bases located in other parts of the world.
- **The Department of Trade and Industry's** role is to ensure that company law is enforced. It also aims to protect the community against business and financial fraud. One example of its activities is the work carried out by the **Monopolies and Mergers Commission** (☞ unit 73) investigating the market power which a company might have following a takeover.
- **The Department of Transport** carries out the planning of the overall transport strategy. It is also responsible for all aspects of roads, motorways and rail links.

Departments may change depending on the needs of the country and the priorities which political parties emphasise. One new department formed in 1992 was the **Department of National Heritage.**

Much of the work carried out by local and central government benefits private sector business. For example, some local authorities employ builders to carry out maintenance and repair work to buildings like hospitals and schools. Also, the Department of Transport gives contracts to large construction companies, such as Wimpey and Costain, to build roads and motorways.

QUANGOs

Some activities carried out by government are politically non-controversial. These are controlled by QUANGOs. They tend to be specialised bodies providing services that central government does not have the resources or the expertise to carry out. The Sports Council and the Arts Council are well known QUANGOs. They give funds to different sports and arts projects. They also promote and represent their members' interests. In 1992 the Higher Education Funding Council (HEFC) was formed to allocate government funds to higher education institutions and monitor their performance.

Executive agencies

In 1988, the 'Next Step' report put forward recommendations for the supply of services by government departments. The report argued that the supply of services, such as benefit payments, prisons and the passport office, should be separated from the policy making body and carried out by **executive agencies**. A chief executive was to be appointed, accountable to a government minister, in charge of the delivery and efficiency of a particular government service. Many of these chief executives have been appointed from outside the Civil Service. For example, Derek Lewis, head of the prison service, was formerly a chief executive with the Granada Group. The general policy of the government departments remains the responsibility of the permanent secretaries and senior civil servants. The idea is to run the supply of services in a more 'business like' way and eventually privatise the activities.

QUESTION 3 The effects of the new executive agencies are beginning to be observed. One of the features of these organisations is that they are set efficiency targets. The agency and its employees are judged by their results and rewarded according to their performance. For example, chief executive salaries have a performance related bonus of up to 35 per cent extra. Managers have been given more flexibility to implement pay-and-reward systems for their staff. Some improvements in government services have been reported. For example:
■ social security payments are now cheaper and quicker to administer;
■ the Northern Ireland Driver and Vehicle Testing Agency has been able to bring down charges, making them 30 per cent cheaper than on the mainland;
■ it now takes 7 days to process a passport application compared with the previous average of 3¹/₂ weeks.

However, questions have been raised as to whether some agencies have the ability to meet their performance targets, or whether the correct targets have been set in the first place.

Source: adapted from *The Independent*, 27.5.1993.

(a) Why do you think the government has introduced executive agencies?
(b) What evidence does the case provide to suggest that the supply of such services will be delivered in a more 'business like' way by executive agencies?

Privatisation

PRIVATISATION is the transfer of public sector resources to the private sector. It has been an important part of Conservative government policy since 1979. Table 4.1 shows those industries which have been privatised since 1979. The most publicised were the sales of the nationalised industries, such as British Telecom, British Gas, British Airways and the regional water boards. However, privatisation involves several other activities.

The sale of parts of nationalised industries The government chose to break up some nationalised industries by selling parts of them. One example was the sale of the Jaguar car company for £297 million, which was part of British Leyland. Also, in 1984 British Rail's Sealink was sold for £40 million.

Deregulation This involves lifting restrictions that prevent private sector competition. For example, in 1984 when British Telecom was privatised Mercury was allowed to supply telecommunication services. Deregulation also allowed bus services to be run by the private sector.

Contracting out Many government and local authority services have been 'contracted out' to private sector businesses. This is where private contractors are given the chance to bid for services which used to be supplied by the public sector. Examples include the provision of school meals and the cleaning of schools and hospitals. In 1992 a French company, Onyx (UK), won the contract to collect refuse in Liverpool.

Table 4.1 *Sale of state owned companies to the private sector since 1979*

Date begun			
1979	* British Petroleum	1986	British Gas
	* ICL	1987	British Airways
	* Ferranti		Rolls Royce
	Fairey		Leyland Bus
1981	British Aerospace		Leyland Truck
	* British Sugar		Royal Ordnance
	Cable and Wireless		British Airport Authority
	Amersham International	1988	British Steel
1982	National Freight Corporation		British Leyland
	Britoil	1989	British Water Authorities
1983	* Associated British Ports	1990	Electricity Area Boards
	British Rail Hotels	1991	Electricity Generation
1984	British Gas Onshore Oil		
	Enterprise Oil		To be privatised
	Sealink Ferries		British Coal
	Jaguar Cars		British Rail
	British Telecom		Post Office
	British Technology Group		

* Partly owned by the government at the time of sale.

The sale of land and property Under the 1980 Housing Act, tenants of local authorities and New Town Development Corporations were given the right to buy their own homes. Tenants were given generous discounts, up to 60 per cent of the market value of the house, if they agreed to buy. During the 1980s about 1.5 million houses were sold. Few realise that the sale of land and properties has raised almost as much money as the sale of nationalised industries.

The reasons for privatisation

When the Conservative party was elected in 1979 they made it clear that business activity in the public sector would be reduced. They believed that businesses should be owned and run by individuals or groups of individuals. What reasons were put forward for such a policy?
■ The sale of state assets generates a great deal of income for the government. For example, British Gas was sold for £6,533 million, British Petroleum for £6,090 million and the water companies for £5,240 million.
■ Nationalised industries were inefficient. They lacked the incentive to make a profit, since their main aim was arguably to provide a public service (☞ unit 5). As a result their costs tended to be high and they often made losses. Also, many believed that they were overstaffed. Supporters of privatisation argued that if they were in the private sector, they would be forced to cut costs, improve their service and return a profit

for the shareholders.

- As a result of deregulation, some organisations would be forced to improve their service and charge competitive prices. For example, in many areas, private firms began to compete for passengers on bus routes. In some cases prices were reduced. Consumers would benefit from this and should also have greater choice. In addition, it is argued that there would be more incentive to innovate in the private sector.

- Once these organisations had been sold to the private sector there would be little political interference. They would be free to determine their own investment levels, prices and growth rates. In the past government interference has affected the performance of nationalised industries. For example, during the 1970s, in an attempt to control inflation, the government stopped many nationalised industries from raising their prices.

- Privatisation would increase share ownership. It was argued that this would lead to a 'property owning democracy' in which more people would have a 'stake' in the success of the economy. For example, if you bought shares in British Telecom, you would be a part

owner of the company and get a dividend each year. Workers were encouraged to buy shares in their companies so that they would be rewarded for their own hard work and success.

- Privatisation should improve accountability. The losses made by many of these nationalised industries were put down to the fact that they were operating a public service. In the private sector these industries would be accountable to shareholders and consumers. Shareholders would expect a return on their investment and consumers would expect a quality service at a fair price. For example, if shareholders were not happy with the dividends paid, they could sell their shares.

Impact of privatisation on business

How have businesses changed after transferring to the private sector?

- Profit has become a more important objective. For example, the profits of British Telecom have increased from around £1,000 million in 1984, when the company was first privatised, to over £3,000 million in 1991.

- In some cases prices have changed. For example, water prices rose by 15 per cent in the year after privatisation. This was above the inflation rate. In addition, buyers of new homes have been charged up to £1,900 to be connected to the mains water supply, compared with a standard charge of £30 before privatisation. In contrast, some of BT's telephone charges have fallen in recent years. The formula for setting price in the early 1990s was the rate of inflation minus 6.25 per cent. This was enforced by the industry regulator (☞ unit 73), and since inflation was around 3 per cent for much of this time, prices had to be cut.

- Some of the companies have reorganised their internal structure. During the early 1990s, British Telecom cut their staff and reorganised their workforce. During 1990 alone 18,000 jobs were shed, including 6,000 management posts. Since then there have been further cuts.

- Many of the newly privatised businesses have attempted to improve their image and have become more consumer orientated. For example, BT spent a great deal of money on TV adverts trying to portray a new 'improved' image, introduced a new logo and changed the colour of their vans. In 1984, public confidence in BT was at an all time low and 25 per cent of all call boxes were out of order. By 1991, 95 per cent were in working order and 90 per cent of faults were repaired within one day.

- Many companies have increased investment since privatisation. For example, capital expenditure by Manweb has increased from £34.7 million in 1987 to £67.8 million in 1991. The water companies have also spent a lot of money to meet EC water standards. New sewerage systems and water purification plants have been built, for example. They have increased investment from around £2 billion to £3 billion since 1989.

QUESTION 4

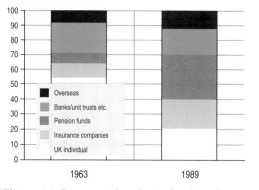

Figure 4.1 *UK shareholders as a percentage of the adult population*

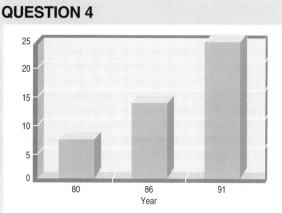

Figure 4.2 *Component bar charts showing who owned shares in the UK in 1963 and 1989*

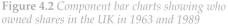

(a) In what way do the data support the view that one of the objectives of privatisation was to widen share ownership?

(b) In what way might wider share ownership improve the accountability of these organisations?

Some of the companies have begun to offer new services and to diversify. For example, Manweb now offer large customers who wish to buy electricity at a wholesale price the right to do so. North West Water bought two new businesses in 1991-92, Wallace and Tiernan, chemical feed and disinfection equipment producers, and Edwards and Jones which makes and sells high performance sludge dewatering equipment.

Some of these changes may not have been a direct result of privatisation. Some may have taken place even if they had remained a public sector business.

QUESTION 5 In January 1993, BT cut telephone charges following an announcement by Mercury regarding price changes. BT said it might cut prices by more than was required by Oftel, the industry watchdog, to encourage more calls. BT's change in pricing policy was prompted by:
■ increased competition;
■ tighter regulation;
■ the arrival of executives who have experience of market driven industries.

Some of the price reductions included cuts of between 3 per cent and 10 per cent for USA and Canadian calls, and cuts between 0.6 per cent and 4.1 per cent for business calls. However, the average residential telephone bill was expected to rise by 2.4 per cent.

Source : adapted from the *Financial Times*, 1993.

(a) What evidence is there in the above case to suggest that BT has become more aware of consumers' desires?
(b) Why is it important for Oftel, the industry watchdog, to monitor BT's price changes?

Arguments against privatisation

Arguments against privatisation have been put forward on both political and economic grounds. Most of the criticisms below are from the consumer's point of view.

■ Privatisation has been expensive. In particular, the government was criticised for the amount of money spent advertising each sale. The money spent on expensive TV advertising was at the taxpayer's expense.

■ It has been argued that privatisation has not led to greater competition. In some cases public monopolies with no competition have become private monopolies. These companies have been able to exploit their position.

■ Nationalised industries were sold off too cheaply. In nearly all cases the share issue has been over-subscribed. This shows that more people want to buy shares than there are shares available. When dealing begins on the stock market share prices have often risen sharply. This suggests that the government could have set the share prices much higher and raised more revenue. For example, in 1984 BT shares were selling for 90 per cent more than the original issue price.

■ Natural monopolies have been sold off. Some argue

that they should remain under government control to prevent a duplication of resources.

■ Once part of the private sector, any parts of the business which make a loss will be closed down.This appears to have happened in public transport. Bus services on non-profitable routes have been cut or stopped completely since deregulation.

■ Share ownership arguably has not increased. Many who bought shares sold them very quickly after. In addition, a significant number of new shareowners only own very small shareholdings in just one company.

■ Many of the nationalised industries are important for the development of the nation. To put them in private hands might jeopardise their existence. For example, one of the reasons why British Steel was nationalised was to save it from possible closure. If business conditions change for the worse a private company may not guarantee supply. Also, since the shares are widely available, it is possible for overseas buyers to take control of strategic UK firms.

Regulation of privatised industries

One criticism of privatisation was that dominant industries, which were previously state owned, now operate as private sector businesses. They may be able to exploit their position by increasing their prices or reducing services. Because of this they must be controlled. Control of private sector firms is nothing new. The Monopolies and Mergers Commission was set up to monitor firms which might act against the public's interest. They investigate cases where large dominant firms or firms merging might act to exploit their position. Because privatisation created some private monopolies, the government set up specialist 'watchdog' agencies to protect the public. Examples of these bodies include Oftel (the telecommunications industry), Ofgas (the gas industry) and Ofwat (the water companies). These are discussed in more detail in unit 73.

QUESTION 6 Since privatisation, water charges have increased in three years by 60 per cent. This has prompted consumers to question whether privatisation has been successful, and whether there is enough protection from Ofwat. The problem is that the water companies have to set prices which generate enough profit to keep shareholders happy, and at the same time, fund huge capital investment programmes to meet EC water quality standards. Critics of water privatisation maintain that customers carry too much of the cost of investment. Ofwat has warned that household bills could double in real terms by the year 2005 because the true cost of meeting EC and national environmental rules was underestimated in the run up to privatisation. Critics also argue that shareholders should bear a bigger burden of the costs. Share prices have more than doubled since privatisation and dividends have risen from between 6 per cent and 10 per cent a year. In addition, it is almost impossible to introduce competition in the supply of water to households and the treatment of sewage. Environmentalists argue that the water industry should make more of an effort to pass on some of these costs to the 'culprits'. By this they mean the polluters of water. However, the water industry argues that it is difficult to identify them. One area of conflict in the water industry concerns 'the reasonable rate of

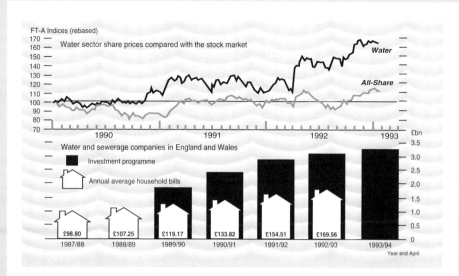

Figure 4.3 *Information about share prices, investment levels and household bills in the water industry*

return' which water companies are allowed to earn from their capital. The dispute is about how to define that 'reasonable rate of return'. The water companies would naturally argue for higher 'reasonable rates'.

Source : adapted from the *Financial Times*, 20.1.1993.

(a) What evidence is there in the case to suggest that privatisation has not been in consumers' interests?
(b) Why is Ofwat's task in setting prices for the water companies a difficult one?
(c) Why do you think that the share price for water companies has risen faster than an average of all other shares?

Key terms

Merit goods - goods which are underprovided by private sector businesses.
Nationalised industries - public corporations previously part of the private sector which were taken into state ownership.
Natural monopoly - a situation where production costs will be lower if one firm is allowed to exist on its own in the industry, due to the existence of huge economies of scale.
Privatisation - the transfer of public sector resources to the private sector.
Public goods - goods where consumption by one person does not reduce the amount available to others and, once provided, all individuals will benefit.
Public sector - business organisations which are accountable to central or local government.
QUANGOs - Quasi Autonomous Non Government Organisations.

Summary

1. What is meant by a public corporation?
2. What is meant by non-rivalry and non-excludability when describing public goods?
3. Why are merit goods provided by the public sector?
4. List 5 reasons for nationalisation.
5. Why do local authorities provide some public sector services?
6. How are local authority services funded?
7. Describe the responsibilities of 3 government departments.
8. Explain the difference between deregulation and contracting out as methods of privatisation.
9. What are the disadvantages of privatisation?
10. What is the function of Ofgas, Ofwat and Oftel?

Question

Wolds Remand Centre

Wolds Remand Centre was Britain's first privately run prison service. The Home Office granted the Group 4 security company a £5 million a year contract to run the Humberside low security remand centre. It is believed that about eight companies bid for the contact. It was opened in April 1992 at a cost of £135.6 million and is being run on an experimental basis. The government made 'the Wolds' a showpiece prison for further privatisation. The prison was built to house a maximum of 320 remand prisoners serving courts in South Yorkshire. The chief executive of Group 4 said that it wanted to produce a 'secure but humane' environment for prisoners. Stephen Twinn, the director of Wolds (prison governor), emphasised that the prisoners in the centre were theoretically innocent, and thus would be subject to the minimum of restrictions. They hoped to break a 200 year prison regime tradition of broken promises, frustration and ill feeling. Of the 160 staff employed at the centre, Mr. Twinn is one of only five recruited from the existing state prison service. The Wolds contains a number of unique characteristics which are aimed at improving the prison environment.

- All cells are single, each one with a lavatory.
- Each prisoner has a cell key to provide privacy; prison staff can over-ride the locks if necessary.
- Staff are called security supervisors rather than prison officers.
- Staff will wear uniforms consisting of blazers, light grey trousers, clip on tie and the Group Four logo.
- Inmates can spend all their waking hours outside their cells.
- Two hours per day can be spent outdoors.
- Each block of cells has three televisions and a video for recording late schedules, a pool table, soft seating and a dining area.
- Meals are brought on heated trays from a central kitchen 'airline style'.
- The staff supervisor sits and eats the same meal with the prisoners.

Since the opening of the prison in April 1992 the centre has experienced some problems. Three separate incidents have questioned whether Group 4's approach of treating prisoners like 'consumers' has been successful. One incident involved 42 prisoners refusing to return to their cells at the end of the day after a protest over food. The prisoners did not like the way in which the food was distributed in plastic trays. They preferred the old system of being served from a hatch on plates. The prison management conformed with their wishes. A second incident involved complaints about medical care and the third occurred when £5,000 worth of damage was caused in a disturbance. This was in June 1992 and again resulted from prisoners refusing to return to individual cells. In addition, critics of prison privatisation have described it as a 'step backwards in prison policy'. Eight

A prison custody officer at Wolds Remand Centre.

prison unions have threatened to isolate the Wolds. Mr. Paul Sullivan, spokesman for the Prison Officers Association, said that turning to the private sector failed to address the central needs of the prison service. It was 'ethically wrong, irresponsible and impracticable'. Between 9,000 and 10,000 remand prisoners would be detained in sub-standard conditions. Inmates at the Wolds would be 'feather -bedded' in 'paradigms of excellence'. In 1993, a Prison Reform Trust report argued that public accountability was hindered. This was because financial details of Group 4's contract with the Home Office were confidential. 'The company is not required to produce an annual report to the Home Office and, if it was, presumably this too would have been secret. This would prevent proper 'value for money' comparisons being made.

Source: adapted from *The Independent*, 7.11.1991, 6.7.1992, 7.7. 1992, *The Times*, 30.6.1992 and updated.

(a) **What branch of privatisation does this case fall into? Explain your answer.**
(b) **Describe the possible motives for the government choosing to privatise the prison service.**
(c) **Why should a private sector business like Group 4 want to involve themselves in this type of activity?**
(d) **Explain the views of Mr Paul Sullivan in his objection to the privatisation of the prison service.**
(e) **How might a private sector business' approach to running prisons be different from a public sector organisation's?**

What are objectives?

All businesses have objectives. These are the **goals** which are set out by the people who lead or control the organisation. The performance of a business could be judged on how effectively it achieves its objectives. For example, if a self-employed carpenter aimed to make a satisfactory profit and actually made £10,000 he might consider that he had achieved his objective.

The objectives of businesses in the private sector used to be different from those in the public sector. However, since 1979, many of these differences have been eliminated. Most of this unit focuses on objectives in the private sector.

Survival

From time to time all businesses, regardless of their size and status, will consider survival important.

Early stages of trading Most firms begin on a small scale, establish themselves and then grow. The owners of a new firm will probably be happy to see the firm survive in its first few months (or even years) of trading. Firms may encounter a number of problems when they first begin trading including:
- a lack of experience;
- a lack of resources;
- competition from established firms;
- unforeseen problems such as unexpected costs;
- limited recognition by customers.

Also, in the early stages decision makers might make

QUESTION 1 Candor Hotels is a Brighton based hotelier with a chain of twenty five hotels based in different cities worldwide, seven of which are in the Middle East. Throughout the 1980s it enjoyed rising profits. However, in the 1990s the company began to struggle and profit fell sharply. In 1993 Candor Hotels reported its first ever loss, £1.8 million. Eric Swensson, the managing director was interviewed by the local press just after the loss was announced. He said: '...I have been in the hotel business for thirty years and I cannot remember trading conditions ever being as bad as this. Our company has been hit by the Gulf War, the world recession, falling property values and rising business costs...a loss of £1.8 million may not seem too bad given our overall strength, but quite frankly I am not optimistic about the future....we do not anticipate an improvement in trading conditions until the middle of 1994...we expect to make a loss again next year and possibly the year after...in order to survive we will have to close down some of our Middle East operations and cut costs...'

Write a brief report explaining to the workforce why the short term objective of Candor Hotels should be survival.

---

mistakes. As a result of this uncertainty the most important business objective might be to survive in the initial stages of trading.

When trading becomes difficult During a recession (☞ unit 67), for example, a business could face falling demand, bad debts and low confidence. During the early 1990s Polly Peck, Coloroll, Lowndes Queensway and the Canary Wharf development project all suffered as a result of the slump in the economy and had to cease trading. In 1992 alone, business failures totalled 62,000.

Threat of takeover Firms sometimes become targets for other firms to take over (☞ unit 32). When this happens the survival of the firm in its existing form may be the main objective. One way to achieve this is to persuade the owners (the shareholders) not to sell shares to the person or company bidding for them.

In the long term it is unlikely that survival would remain the only objective. Business owners tend to be ambitious and so pursue other objectives.

Profit maximisation

It is often argued that the main aim of private sector businesses (☞ unit 3) is to MAXIMISE their profits. This is achieved where the difference between the total revenue earned by the business from selling its products and the total costs of those products is the greatest. The manufacturer in Table 5.1 would produce 3,000 units as this is the output where its profit is highest. There are many definitions of **profit**. This is the accountant's definition (where total revenue − total cost is the greatest) and not the reward for risk to entrepreneurs, as explained in unit 1.

Table 5.1 *Profit maximising position*

£000

Output	Total costs	Total revenue	Profit
2,000	10	20	10
3,000	15	30	15
4,000	30	35	5

It may be reasonable to assume that firms aim for as much profit as possible. In practice a business is more likely to have a satisfactory level of profit as an objective. This is known as SATISFICING. Why is this likely to be a more reasonable objective?

Objectives of small firms Owners of small firms may not want to expand their output to a point where their profits are maximised. This may be because:
- it involves employing more workers, making more decisions and working longer hours;
- they may want to keep their turnover below the VAT

threshold, avoiding the need to charge their customers VAT and filling in VAT returns;
- they are happy with a satisfactory profit level and their current lifestyle.

Information In practice it may be difficult to identify precisely the level of output that will maximise profits. For a business to do this it must be able to measure all of its costs at every possible level of production. It must also be able to estimate accurately the prices it can charge for these levels of output.

Other aims A business might sacrifice short term profit maximisation for long term profits. This might explain why a firm lowers its price initially to build a market share and then increases price when competitors have left the market. It might also account for firms operating in the short term at a loss. In this case, the owners may be optimistic that in the future sales will pick up.

Growth

Many businesses pursue growth as their main objective. Business people argue that firms must grow in order to survive. Failure to grow might result in a loss of competitiveness, a decline in demand and eventual closure. If a firm is able to grow and dominate the market, in the future it may be able to enjoy some monopoly power and raise its price. By growing, a firm can diversify and reduce the risk of business enterprise. It can sell to alternative markets and introduce new products. If one market or product fails it will have a range of others to fall back on. Firms can exploit economies of scale if they grow large enough. This will enable them to be more efficient and enjoy lower costs. Motives for growth are dealt with in unit 31.

QUESTION 2 Webster's Ltd manufacture horse saddles. They are a small company which employ 3 skilled craft workers in a factory in Devon. The owner of the business is Wendy Webster. She enjoys running the business but the profit at the current level of output is only £15,000 p.a. Wendy is a talented horsewoman and spends 3 days a week eventing. Although this is a hobby, Wendy is able to generate some business through contacts which she makes during these events. Wendy knows that she could make a lot more profit by producing and selling more saddles, but she prefers not to expand output. The diagram in Figure 5.1 shows the total costs and the total revenue for Webster's Ltd. The current level of output which generates £15,000 profit is 200 saddles.

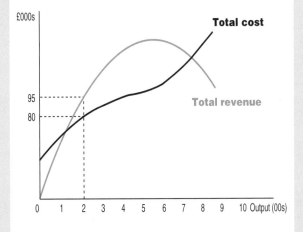

Figure 5.1 *The total costs and total revenue of Webster's Ltd*

(a) Estimate (to the nearest hundred) the level of output that would maximise profit for Webster's from Figure 5.1?
(b) Explain why Wendy might not wish to maximise profits.

QUESTION 3 In 1988, Sir James Ball, the chairman of JB PLC which manufactures domestic radiators, retired after 17 years of service. Moira Urquhart was appointed as a replacement and addressed a press conference to talk about the future of the company. She said: '...my main aim is to see this company establish itself as a market leader...I hope to treble turnover and raise employment...this company needs to grow to survive overseas competition...there will be a period of high investment, both in capital and in human resources....'

Table 5.2 *JB PLC profit reinvested, 1986 - 1992*

Year	Profit reinvested (£m)
1986	7
1987	11
1988	9
1989	20
1990	42
1991	50
1992	61

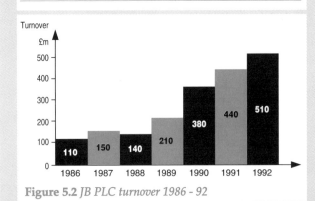

Figure 5.2 *JB PLC turnover 1986 - 92*

(a) What evidence does the data provide to support the view that JB PLC pursued a policy of growth from 1988?
(b) Why might Moira Urquhart be keen for the company to pursue a policy of growth?
(c) Why might the owners of the company object to this policy?

A number of people involved in business activity might benefit from growth.

- Employees may find their jobs will be more secure (although this might not always be the case if growth involves purchasing more machinery).
- Managers and directors will tend to have more power and status. For example, a director of British Gas is likely to enjoy more power and recognition than the director of a small manufacturer.
- The salaries of directors and the chairperson are often linked to the size of the firm.
- The owners of companies might have mixed feelings about growth. On the one hand, growth often means that current profits have to be invested to fund the expansion. However, growth might generate much higher profits in the future which will benefit the owners.

Managerial objectives

Sometimes the managers of a firm are able to pursue their own objectives. For this to happen there must be some divorce of ownership and control. In other words the owners of the company do not necessarily control the day to day running of it. This may be possible when there is a very large number of joint owners as in a public limited company. Each owner has such a small part of the firm that he or she is able to exert little control over its running. As a result management take control and run the company according to their own aims. These aims vary depending on individual managers. Some common examples might be to:

- allocate themselves luxury company cars;
- maximise personal salary;
- maximise their departmental budgets;
- improve their status and recognition;
- maximise the number of employees in their charge;
- maximise their leisure time;
- delegate as much as work as possible;
- maximise fringe benefits, such as expense accounts for entertaining.

If managers are seen by owners to be abusing their power they are likely to be fired. To protect their positions managers often pacify owners by ensuring that the business generates enough profit to keep them satisfied. Profit may also be important to managers if their salaries are linked to profit levels.

Sales revenue maximisation

SALES REVENUE MAXIMISATION was put forward by William Baumol in the 1950s. He argued that an objective of firms may be to gain the highest possible sales revenue. This objective will be favoured by those employees whose salaries are linked to sales. Managers and sales staff are examples of staff paid according to the sales revenue which they generate. Sales revenue maximisation is not the same as profit maximisation. In Table 5.1, the business maximised profits at an output of 3,000 units. Producing 4,000 units would have maximised sales revenue (£35,000).

QUESTION 4 Tim Reilly is the sales manager for the Bromwich Insurance Company. He earns a basic salary of £5,000 p.a. plus 5 per cent of the value of each insurance policy he sells. It has been the policy of the company in recent years to maximise sales. Tim's sales figures for the last five years are shown in Table 5.3.

Table 5.3 *Insurance policy sales data for Tim Reilly*

	1989	1990	1991	1992	1993
No.of policies sold	400	470	580	700	800
Average value of each policy	£500	£500	£500	£470	£450
Total value of policies (000s)	£200	£235	£290	£329	£360

(a) Calculate Tim's annual salary for each year.
(b) Why will Tim benefit from the company's policy to maximise sales?
(c) Explain why the owners of the company might be unhappy with the policy of maximising sales.

Image and social responsibility

In recent years firms have started to appreciate how important their image is. Many have also seen the benefit of showing responsibility to the people involved in business activity, such as customers, employees and suppliers. Why has this happened?

- Legislation has been passed which favours consumers.
- There have been changes in social attitudes.
- Competitive pressure has forced businesses to take into account the needs of others.

Customers Companies with household names such as Heinz, Kellogg's, Ford, Cadbury's and Sainsbury's would not wish the general public to think badly of them. Some companies have made serious efforts in recent years to improve their image. British Telecom is one very good example. They have replaced nearly all of the old red public telephone kiosks which were often criticised for being dirty and vandalised. They changed their logo and also launched a series of television advertising campaigns designed to develop a more friendly image.

Faced with competition, firms are likely to lose sales if they don't take into account the needs of customers. Increasingly, firms are giving free after sales service, replacing unwanted goods without question and training their staff to deal with the public.

Employees Government legislation and arguably trade unions have influenced how workers treat employees. A number of laws have been passed to protect workers (☞ unit 56). A recent example is legislation which affects workers who use visual display units (VDUs). Firms have to provide suitable work stations and give a minimum number of breaks in a given time period to avoid strain on the worker. One effect of legislation is that it protects companies with high standards of responsibility from those competitors who have little regard for health and safety at work. Unscrupulous firms will not be able to lower costs by neglecting health and safety because they will have to keep within the law.

Trade unions have argued for the rights of the workforce for many years. They have aimed to improve social facilities, wages and working conditions. In recent years the power of trade unions has been reduced (☞ unit 59) and some groups of workers may have suffered as a result.

Suppliers Some firms have benefited from good relations with suppliers of raw materials and components. One example is in manufacturing, where companies are adopting **Just-in-time** manufacturing (☞ unit 33). This means that firms only produce when they have an order and stocks of raw materials and components are delivered to the factory only when they are needed. Reliable and efficient suppliers are needed by firms if they order stocks 'at the last minute'. Maintaining good relations with suppliers is likely to help this process. Examples of good relations might be prompt payment to suppliers or regular meetings to discuss each other's needs.

QUESTION 5

(a) What image might the products in the photograph convey about the businesses that manufacture them?
(b) Why might the businesses wish to portray this image?

Behavioural theories

BEHAVIOURAL THEORIES assume that business objectives are not determined by owners and managers alone. They suggest that other interested parties, such as the government, consumers and pressure groups may affect the firm's objectives. The objective a company has will depend on the power of these groups to influence decisions. It is argued that groups inside and outside the business have certain minimum goals.
- The owners will require a certain level of profit to retain their interest in the business.
- Workers will demand a minimum level of pay and acceptable working conditions if they are to be

retained in employment.
- Managers will insist on enough resources to carry out their tasks (this might include an appropriate expense allowance, for example).
- The government will require the company to obey laws and pay taxes.
- Consumers will demand quality products at reasonable prices.
- Environmentalists will insist that pollution is avoided.

In practice, the group with the most influence will achieve its aims. The dominant group may change over time. For example, in the 1960s and the 1970s trade unions were powerful in many industries. They gained large pay rises, in some cases resulting in lower profits for the owners. Since then the power of trade unions has been reduced. A wide range of anti-trade union legislation (☞ unit 59) has been passed and unemployment has risen. This has contributed to a fall in trade union membership. As a result the position of the employer has strengthened.

Sometimes groups will compromise. The diagram in Figure 5.3 illustrates the total costs, total revenue and profit of a business. If it is dominated by the directors, they might have growth as an objective. This would be achieved at output level Q_1, where output is pushed to the limit before the firm makes a loss. However, the owners may prefer the business to produce a level of output Q_2 where profits are greatest. A compromise might be at Q_3, where a minimum level of profit is made for the owners, but output is high enough for some growth.

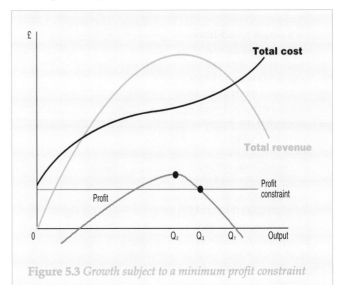

Figure 5.3 *Growth subject to a minimum profit constraint*

What determines business objectives?

Behavioural theories suggest that the group which dominates the business will determine the objectives. If the owners are in control they are likely to aim for profit. However, there are other factors that influence the choice of objective.
- The size and status of the firm. For example, many small businesses may be content with profit satisficing

or survival. Larger companies may aim for growth and market domination.

■ The age of the business. Businesses starting off may be content with survival. Later, when they are established, they may pursue other objectives.

■ The state of the economy may affect business objectives. During a recession many firms, both large and small, concentrate on survival. During normal trading conditions other objectives will be important.

■ Whether a business is in the public or private sector. Up until recently, organisations in the public sector were set up to provide a service whereas firms in the private sector pursued other objectives such as making a profit. This issue is dealt with in the next section.

Objectives in the public sector

Between 1950 and 1979, **nationalised industries**, such as coal, gas, electricity, water, rail and steel, played an important role in the economy. However, since 1979 it has been government policy to transfer most of these from the **public** to the private sector (☞ unit 3). Arguably nationalised industries had two objectives before 1979.

■ To provide a service to the nation.

■ To break-even, taking one year with another.

They aimed to provide services like rail links, bus routes, postal delivery, and other utilities to areas in the country which would be unprofitable. Privately owned firms would not supply to these regions as they would not make a profit. In addition, nationalised industries were expected to take into account externalities (☞ unit 72) in their activities. For example, the coal industry was expected to take the health and safety of their workforce into account even if it meant high costs. Many nationalised industries did not break even. In fact, many of them made a loss - a major criticism of their operation.

In the 1960s and 1970s the government changed its attitude towards nationalised industries. They encouraged a more commercial approach. For example, the government set targets for rates of return on investment projects. At the same time, though, governments prevented many of these organisations from raising prices, particularly during the 1970s when inflation was high. This had an adverse effect on the financial performance of these industries and most of them continued to make losses.

From 1979 onwards the Conservative government aimed to transfer a large number of these organisations to the private sector. Before this could take place the government had to make them attractive to potential buyers. This was achieved by setting profit as an objective. In some cases a new chairperson was appointed to bring about the necessary changes. Costs were cut by reducing the labour force and the firms were allowed to set their own prices. Once profitable they could then be sold. For example, before British Steel was privatised in 1988 they cut their workforce from 190,000 in 1979 to 50,000 in 1988, whilst maintaining output at around 12 million tonnes. In addition, they transformed their financial performance. In 1987-88 they made a profit of

£419 million compared with a £5 billion loss over the previous decade.

The few nationalised industries which are left are expected to aim for profit. Their performance is monitored closely and once they are consistently profitable they are likely to be privatised (☞ unit 4).

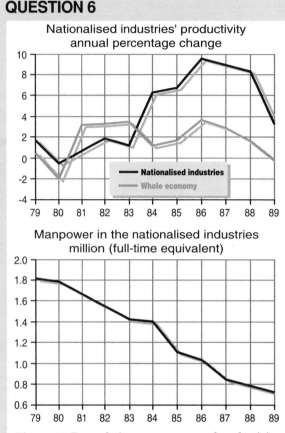

QUESTION 6

Nationalised industries' productivity annual percentage change

Manpower in the nationalised industries million (full-time equivalent)

Figure 5.4 *Data relating to manpower and productivity in nationalised industries*

(a) Explain how the data supports the view that nationalised industries pursued profit after 1979.

(b) What other objectives might nationalised industries like British Coal pursue?

Key terms

Behavioural theories - theories that state business objectives are determined jointly by groups of interested parties.

Profit maximisation - producing a level of output which generates the most profit for a business.

Sales revenue maximisation - producing a level of output where sales revenue is greatest.

Satisficing - generating sufficient profit to satisfy the owners, not necessarily at an output which gives greatest profit.

Question

Unsung heroes of the moral majority

Corporate responsibility is of as much concern to the small firm as the large, though their approaches and the issues involved can differ considerably. Larger firms talk about corporate codes, the responsibility of managers to owners, the activities of multinationals and employee management. But, as Ian Smedley, of the Institute of Directors, recently told a small firms conference in Southampton, some of these aspects have a lesser importance in the smaller firm.

'Individual moral responsibility can be clearly seen in the small firm. The owner-director sets goals for the business and acts in order to achieve them', he said. 'In small firms, the entrepreneur's personal moral decisions will be fundamental to the attitudes and activities of the business.'

The small firm owner confronts issues of ethics or corporate responsibility very directly in day-to-day operations, and the current emphasis on corporate responsibility is nothing new to the entrepreneur. 'Small firms and particularly entrepreneurs have been at the heart of corporate responsibility since the notion of corporate responsibility emerged', says Tom Cannon, visiting professor in that subject at Manchester Business School.

'The classic thing is the entrepreneurs of the past who preferred to spend their money on their factories and their employees instead of racing stables and Monte Carlo . . . the entrepreneurial philanthropist, reinvesting in the community. You wouldn't even have had the field of corporate responsibility if it hadn't been for owner-managers committing themselves to their community. Even today when you look around, for example, enterprise agencies, community groups, basically you see local small businessmen and women who are making things happen. For every seconded manager there are three or four local small business owners serving on an enterprise agency, the council of a university, on an NHS trust, or involved in environmental movements - right across the board of local corporate responsibility, small-firm owners playing their part in their local community.'

He points to projects like Cariocca Enterprises - a managed workspace for black entrepreneurs in inner-city Manchester which arose as part of an effort to regenerate the area following the riots of a few years ago.

'You find the same tradition, they're giving their time as well as their money because they get committed. If you look at local economic development, local school boards, school governors, at a whole range of community enterprise activities, it's the entrepreneur you keep coming across', says Prof. Cannon, whose recent book on corporate responsibility focuses mainly on large firm aspects.

At Cariocca Enterprises, a quarter of the board comprises small firm owners, none of them employing more than five staff, and their activities ranging from market trading to soft furnishing manufacture.

'Big firms are very skillful at capitalising on the public relations benefits, but what you've got in a lot of small business people is that they do it to some degree out of a sense of duty, to some degree out of a sense of personal commitment to that community. What they're not very good at is blowing their own trumpet, so we tend to assume that it's the IBMs, the ICIs who are involved everywhere', says Prof. Cannon.

He also believes that small firms are bigger providers of, say, computers for local schools than are larger enterprises. 'The bedrock of all corporate responsibility activity at present is in fact the small-business owner.' But there is also an argument that small firms could learn from the ethical experience of large corporations. Derek Archer, a consultant, says that large firms will often have procedures and practices for handling such matters, or resources such as specialised staff or departments.

He believes that there is vast experience available to small and medium sized enterprises, though there is at present no mechanism by which they can tap into it.

Some large firms had spent substantial amounts of money and manpower on research into the actuality and benefits of good business practice. 'Much of the work could be' comparatively easily translated into useful, low-cost tools of the trade for small businesses interested in and realising the value of an ethical approach to their endeavours.'

Source: *The Guardian*, 15.2.1993.

(a) Write a brief report explaining the benefits of corporate responsibility to business owners.
(b) Using examples from the article, describe the benefits which people will enjoy as a result of firms showing social responsibility.
(c) How might a recession affect the degree to which firms can be socially responsible? Explain your answer.
(d) Why might small firms show more social responsibility than large ones?
(e) How might an objective, such as showing greater responsibility, conflict with other objectives a firm might have?

Summary

1. Under what circumstances might survival be an important objective?
2. Why might a successful business still not survive in its existing form?
3. What is the difference between short term and long term profit maximisation?
4. Why might a business pursue growth as an objective?
5. Which group involved in the business is likely to pursue growth? Explain why.
6. List 5 examples of managerial objectives.
7. Who would favour sales revenue maximisation in an organisation?
8. Why has the importance of image and social responsibility as a business objective grown?
9. What factors determine business objectives?
10. In what ways might public sector business organisations have changed their objectives in the last decade?

The basic economic problem

Unit 1 showed that business activity involved satisfying consumers' **needs** and **wants**. Businesses aim to satisfy these wants and needs by producing goods and services. When food is produced or a bus service is provided **resources** (land, labour, capital and enterprise) are used up. These resources are scarce relative to needs and wants. In other words, there are not enough resources to satisfy all consumers' needs and wants. This is known as the BASIC ECONOMIC PROBLEM. This means businesses, individuals and the government must make **choices** when allocating scarce resources between different uses. For example, a printer may have to choose whether to buy a new printing press to improve quality or some new computer software to improve administrative efficiency.

Economics is the study of how resources are allocated in situations where they have different uses. The choices faced by decision makers can be placed in order of preference. For example, a business may be considering three investment options but can only afford one. The decision makers might decide that the order is:
1. a new computer system;
2. a fleet of cars for the sales force;
3. a warehouse extension.

The business will allocate resources to the purchase of the new computer system. The other two options are **foregone** or given up. The benefit lost from the next best alternative is called the OPPORTUNITY COST of the choice. In this example it would be the benefit lost by not having a fleet of new cars.

QUESTION 1 Lakes and Dales Ltd own sixty properties in the Lake District and Yorkshire Dales which they rent out to holidaymakers. They are considering the sale of ten cottages for £700,000 to a property speculator. The cottages under consideration - earned £100,000 rental income in the previous trading year. With the money raised they intend to convert some 'run down' farm buildings into a luxury hotel.

(a) Explain how the above example illustrates the concept of opportunity cost.
(b) What would be the opportunity cost if the sale went ahead?

The function of an economy

What is an economy? An ECONOMY is a **system** which attempts to solve the basic economic problem. In the national economy the resources in a country are changed by business activity into goods and services which are bought by individuals. In a household economy the family budget is spent on a range of goods and services.

Local and international economies also act in the same way, but at different levels. The function of an economy is to allocate scarce resources amongst unlimited wants. The basic economic problem is often broken down into three questions.

■ **What should be produced?** In developed economies the number of goods and services produced from resources is immense. The economic system must decide which resources will be used to produce which products. For example, what proportion of resources should be used to produce food, housing, cars, cigarettes, cosmetics or computers? Should resources be used for military purposes? Should resources be used to generate wealth for the future? In less developed countries the decision about what to produce may be simpler. This is because the choices available are limited. For example, a very poor African village might be faced with the decision whether to produce wheat or maize. However, this is still a question about resource allocation and what to produce.

QUESTION 2

Consider the photographs above. In each case decide:
(a) what goods or services are being produced;
(b) how production is being organised (where, what resources are used, how production is taking place);
(c) who it is being produced for.

- **How should it be produced?** The way in which goods and services are produced can vary. Decisions have to be made about such things as where production will take place, the method of production and the materials and labour that will be used.
- **For whom should it be produced?** An economy has to determine how the final goods and services will be allocated amongst competing groups. For example, how much should go to students, should the unemployed receive a share of output, should Ethiopia receive a proportion of total UK output, should managers get more than workers?

How the above questions are answered will depend on the type of **economic system**. It is usual to explain how resources are allocated in three types of economy - the free market economy, the planned economy and the mixed economy. The way business activity is organised will be different in each of these systems.

The organisation of production in different economic systems is also influenced by the **political system**. For example, in countries where there are free democracies, a significant proportion of goods and services are produced by independent businesses. On the other hand, in those countries which are dominated by the state, usually **communist** systems, the government plays a very important role in the production of goods and services.

Market economies

In MARKET ECONOMIES (also known as CAPITALIST ECONOMIES or FREE ENTERPRISE ECONOMIES) resources are allocated through markets (☞ unit 1).

The role of government in a free market system is limited. Its main functions are:
- to pass laws which protect the rights of businesses and consumers and punish offenders;
- to issue money and make sure that the monetary system (☞ unit 1) operates so that markets work efficiently;
- to provide certain essential products and services that would not be provided by firms, such as policing, national defence and the judiciary;
- to prevent firms from dominating the market and to restrict the power of trade unions. These activities will restrict competition and affect the workings of the market.

What to produce This decision is often made by consumers. Businesses will only produce goods if consumers will buy them and so firms must identify consumers' needs and respond to them. Firms which produce unwanted products are likely to fail.

Resources will be used to produce those goods and services which are profitable for businesses. If consumers buy more of a particular product prices will tend to rise (☞ unit 22). Rising prices will attract firms into that industry as they see the chance of profit. For example, in recent years, new firms have set up supplying accommodation for the elderly, to exploit rising demand as the population ages in the UK.

As demand for out of date and unwanted products falls their prices will also fall. Firms will leave these industries due to a fall in profit. They will sell unwanted resources like land, buildings and equipment and make labour redundant. These resources will be used by other businesses. For example, many cinemas have closed down due to a lack of demand. Some of the buildings used as cinemas have been bought by other businesses and used as bingo halls, night clubs or supermarkets.

How to produce In market economies businesses decide this. Businesses aim to make a profit. They will choose production methods (☞ unit 29) which reduce their costs. Competition in business forces firms to keep costs and prices low. Consumers will prefer to buy their goods from firms which offer lower prices, although other things such as quality will also influence them.

How are goods and services allocated? Firms produce goods and services which consumers purchase with money. The amount of money consumers have to spend depends on their income and wealth. In market economies individuals own the factors of production. For example, workers earn wages from selling their labour. Owners of capital receive interest, owners of businesses receive profits and the owners of land receive rent. All of these can be spent on goods and services. Those individuals with the most money can buy the most products.

In practice there are no pure market economies in the world. However, some countries such as the USA, Japan and Hong Kong have economies which possess many of the characteristics of market economies.

Implications of market economies

The working of a free market economy can affect business and consumers in many ways.
- Resources are allocated automatically by the forces of demand and supply (☞ unit 22). For example, if more people decide to buy a product, the business will expand output, hire more factors of production and earn more revenue.
- Resources are not wasted in the production of unwanted goods.
- There should be a wider choice of goods and services.
- Individuals are free to set up in business and to choose how to spend their income.
- Competition should lead to lower costs and improve quality as firms try to impress consumers. Innovation might also be more widespread as firms try to develop new products to offer more choice and new production techniques to lower costs.
- There is often an unequal DISTRIBUTION OF INCOME. Groups that cannot be involved in business activity, such as the old or the ill, may have little or no income.
- MARKET IMPERFECTIONS often occur. For example, large firms may dominate an industry by driving out competition. The company can then force up prices

and exploit consumers.

- Some goods are not provided by private firms. These include defence, but also services where they may not make a profit (☞ unit 4).
- A lot of time and money is wasted when businesses collapse. In 1992 around 62,000 firms ceased trading.
- Resources are often very slow to move from one use to another. For example, some workers may refuse to move from one area to another if a firm closes down resulting in underused resources.
- Consumers may lack the information to make choices when buying products. The range of products, their quality and their prices change so frequently that consumers find it difficult to keep up to date. Also, some firms use techniques to influence consumer choice.

QUESTION 3 The Japanese market had long been one that seemed to work according to its own rules. The difficulty of producing software which used the Japanese language allowed a handful of domestic manufacturers, led by NEC, to carve up the personal computer (PC) market amongst them.

Price wars began in October when Compaq, a US firm, introduced a machine at half the price of Japanese machines. IBM, also a US company, followed suit. 'We brought out low-priced models because it was the main way in which to differentiate between IBM's and NEC's machines', says Mr Tsutomu Maruyama, director of Personal Systems Operations at IBM's Japan General Business Company. IBM and Compaq both reported strong sales. In 1993, Dell, the US firm, announced a low price desktop computer for sale in the Japanese computer market. Shortly afterwards Toshiba announced its first low cost notebook PC.

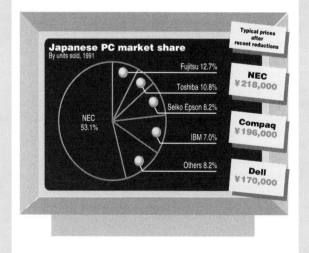

Figure 6.1 *Japanese PC market share, by units sold, 1991*

Source : adapted from the *Financial Times*, 2.3.1993.

(a) What possible problems of a market system are mentioned in the article above?
(b) Explain the effect of the changes in prices on the allocation of resources in the computer market.
(c) What might be the results of these changes for:
   (i) Japanese businesses;
   (ii) US businesses?

- In order to keep costs low, firms may choose pollute the environment. For example, they might discharge poisonous substances into rivers.

Planned economies

Until the late 1980s and early 1990s many Eastern European countries such as Romania, Poland and Russia could be described as PLANNED or COMMAND ECONOMIES. Today, examples might include Cuba and North Korea. Government has a vital role in a planned economy. It plans, organises and co-ordinates the whole production process. This is unlike a market economy, where planning and organising is carried out by firms. Another difference is that resources in planned economies belong to the state. Individuals are not permitted to own property, land and other non-labour means of production.

What to produce This decision is made by government planners. They decide the type and mix of goods and services to be produced. Planners make assumptions about consumers' needs. For example, they decide how many cars, how much milk, how many shirts and how much meat should be produced. Planners then tell producers, such as farms and factories, exactly what to produce.

How to produce Government also tells producers how to produce. **Input-output analysis** is often used to make plans. For example, with a given level of technology, the state may know the land, labour, tractors and fertiliser (inputs) needed to make 1 million tonnes of wheat (the output). If an area needs 20 million tonnes, it is possible to work out the inputs needed. A complex table is drawn up which helps planners calculate the resources needed to meet the various output targets. Plans are often for 5, 10 or 15 years.

How are goods and services allocated? Goods and services are distributed to consumers through state outlets. People purchase goods and services with money they earn. Prices are set by the planners and cannot change without state instruction. Sometimes there are restrictions on the amount of particular goods and services which can be bought by any one individual, cars for example. Some goods and services, like education and health care, are provided free by the state.

Implications of planned economies

How does a planned economy affect the businesses and consumers that operate in it?

- There tends to be a more equal distribution of wealth and income. The state provides a minimum level of payment to all individuals. In addition, people are not allowed to own property, so wealth cannot be accumulated through private ownership.

■ Resources are not duplicated. There is no competition in the supply of a service like public transport, where several buses might drive along the same road competing for the same passengers.

■ Production is for need rather than profit. Planners decide what is needed and what is produced. Resources are not wasted through businesses producing unwanted goods.

■ Long term plans can be made taking into account a range of future needs, such as population changes and the environment.

■ Many resources are used up in the planning process. Vast bureaucracies, employing large numbers of people, are needed to supervise, co-ordinate and carry out plans.

■ People tend to be poorly motivated. As there is no profit, there is no incentive to motivate entrepreneurs.

■ Planners encourage the production of standardised goods with little variety and choice for consumers.

■ Planners often get things wrong! This can lead to shortages of some goods and services and surpluses of others. Also, planner's choices are not necessarily those of individuals. For example, many command

economies produce large quantities of military goods.

■ Shortages of goods often result in long queues outside state shops. This often leads to black markets. Goods and services are sold unofficially by individuals well above the state imposed prices. It is argued that this leads to bribery and corruption.

■ The standard of living is often poor compared with countries which use other types of economic system.

Mixed economies

In reality, no country has an economy which is entirely planned or free market. Most economic systems in the world have elements of each system.

They are known as MIXED ECONOMIES. In mixed economies some resources are allocated by the government and the rest by the market system. All Western European countries have mixed economies. The public sector (☞ unit 4) in mixed economies is responsible for the supply of public goods and merit goods. Decisions regarding resource allocation in the public sector are made by central or local government. In the private sector production decisions are made by firms in response to the demands of consumers.

In the public sector, public goods and merit goods are provided free when used and are paid for by taxes. Examples might be roads, health care and street lighting. In mixed economies the state usually provides a minimum standard of living for those unable to work. In the UK the Welfare State provides benefits, such as unemployment benefit and sickness benefit. In the public sector the state will own a significant proportion of production factors.

In the private sector individuals are also allowed to own the means of production. Businesses are set up by individuals to supply a wide variety of goods and services. Competition exists between these firms. As a result, there will tend to be choice and variety. One of the roles of the government is to ensure that there is fair competition in the private sector. All private sector goods and services are allocated as in the market system described earlier.

What should be the 'degree of mixing' in this type of economy? The government will decide how much business activity there will be in the private sector and how much in the public sector. Some countries, like Sweden, allow the government to play a major role in the supply of goods and services than others, like the UK. For example, in Sweden the government spends around 60 per cent of national income, whilst in the UK the government spends around 40 per cent. In countries where the government plays an important economic role, social provision will tend to be greater, taxes higher and the distribution of wealth and income more equal. In countries where the private sector plays the most important economic role, social provision will tend to be lower with fewer free goods and services at the point of sale. Also, taxes will be lower and the distribution of wealth and income less equal. For example, in the last decade, income tax rates have fallen in the UK and fewer

---

QUESTION 4 Agriculture is Ukraine's most efficient and potentially profitable export industry. Last year, Ukraine's farms produced 39 million tonnes of grain, despite a mild drought. But the Ukrainian government, once responsible for 25 per cent of grain production in the entire Soviet Union, was forced to import 3 million tonnes of grain last year to make up the short-fall in its 17 million tonne state order.

Ukraine's new reform-minded government hopes that the agricultural sector will be the first to reap the fruits of reform and shake up Ukraine's 8,000 collective farms, many of which are inefficient and inert. It has abolished subsidies for almost all agricultural products, raised the food prices in state stores by 300-500 per cent and is preparing a package of agricultural reforms which aim to free farmers to sell their produce at market prices and dismantle the system whereby the state provided farms with all of their inputs.

The plan, intended to erode the power of Ukraine's vast agricultural bureaucracy and bankrupt the most inefficient farms, is politically risky. But Mr Viktor Pynzenyk, minister for the economy and architect of the government's overall reform programme, is confident that the government can succeed in implementing its agricultural package.

A decision to continue the old practice of setting a target for government grain purchases, with the official state order for 1993 pegged at 13 million tonnes, illustrates the reformers' technique for evading criticism by conservatives.

Source: the *Financial Times*, 27.1.1993.

(a) Using examples from the article, explain how resources were allocated to agriculture in the Ukraine under a planned system.
(b) Identify the potential: (i) benefits; (ii) problems; that the state systems had for farms in the Ukraine.

services have been supplied by the state. The distribution of income has changed in favour of the 'wealthy' during this time.

Problems of changing systems

In the late 1980s and the early 1990s major changes took place in a number of Eastern European countries. The former communist regimes were overthrown and replaced by some form of democracy. In most cases, the new governments wished to introduce market economies to replace the older planned systems which were thought to be inefficient. Although each country has had different experiences, there are some common features which all countries changing to a market system have faced. Many problems have arisen as a result of these changes. Businesses in these countries have had to change how they operate to cope with new demands.

Inflation Most countries have experienced inflation - a rise in the general price level. Under a planned system prices were set by the state and, in theory, inflation did not exist. In 1991-92 inflation in Poland was 80 per cent per annum. Inflation erodes the functions of money (☞ unit 1). In some countries businesses have reverted to bartering for resources, exchanging their products for other goods or services. Alternatively, they have exchanged their goods for currencies with stable values, such as the dollar.

Establishing the system A change to a market economy will not take place overnight. The institutions in Western economies which help the market system to work will take time to develop and operate in the former planned economies. Businesses may have problems raising finance due to a lack of banks etc. able to loan money. In many countries there is no stock market where shares in a company can be sold to raise finance. Other problems may result from the previous inefficiencies of planned systems. Transport, communications and markets for buying and selling goods are not yet ready for the level of business activity that will take place under a market

system. This can result in late deliveries, a lack of information and a restriction in selling opportunities.

Competition Businesses in former planned economies now face competition from both within the country and from abroad. Poland in particular has suffered from cheap foreign goods being sold in their economy. Prices of home produced goods and services are likely to be higher than before. Previously the state had kept the prices of resources low so that the prices of final goods were also low. Removal of these controls would mean having to increase prices to make a profit.

Unemployment In a planned system unemployment should not exist. The state provides work for all individuals and makes sure that they have minimum living standards. In March 1991, unemployment, after the introduction of market economies, was almost 3 per cent in Romania, 11.5 per cent in Poland and 7.5 per cent in Hungary.

Running the business The new entrepreneurs in former planned economies will be the managers and employees of ex-state run firms. In Hungary there were over 28,000 companies and 300,000 partnerships by the end of 1991 after a market system was introduced. These businesses have no experience of how to operate in a market system. They face the prospect of making a profit or going out of business, unheard of under a planned system. Also, businesses are not used to operating under a system where profit and earnings motivate people to work. Many would still suffer from the lack of initiative associated with the planned system. Finally, the ability to organise, run and motivate business activity in these countries may not exist, and many people require training, often from Western firms or training agencies.

Transfer of ownership One major problem facing all economies changing from a planned to a market system is the transfer of ownership. Previously all resources and businesses were state owned. Farms, factories and shops now have to be passed on to employees and managers. In East Germany all state firms were placed in the hands of an agency (the Treuhand) which sold them off. In the former USSR and Czechoslovakia, people were given vouchers which entitled them to a share of a company.

Key terms

Basic economic problem - how scarce resources with different uses are allocated to satisfy wants.
Distribution of income - the amount of income and wealth different groups have in a particular country.
Economy - a system which attempts to solve the basic economic problem.
Market economy or capitalist economy or free enterprise economy - an economic system which allows the market mechanism to allocate resources.
Market imperfection - any factor which hinders the free operation of markets, such as where one firm dominates resulting in exploitation.

Mixed economy - an economic system which allows both the state and the market mechanism to allocate resources.
Opportunity cost - the benefit of the next best option foregone when making a choice between a number of alternatives.
Planned economy or command economy - an economic system in which the state is responsible for resource allocation.

Summary

1. Why do businesses, individuals and government need to make choices about the resources they use?
2. Give 2 examples of opportunity cost.
3. What is the function of an economy?
4. What are the 3 questions an economy aims to answer?
5. Describe the benefits of market economies for: (a) firms; (b) consumers.
6. Describe the problems of planned economies for: (a) firms; (b) consumers.
7. What determines the degree of 'mix' in a mixed economy?
8. 'A free market system in former planned economies will take time to work.' Give 3 examples which support this statement.

Question

The power of sausages

The success of the Kyryshko brothers, a trio of bearded giants, each 6ft 6 inches tall and weighing in at more than 250lb, is one of the most hopeful signs that 70 years of Soviet rule has not snuffed out the entrepreneurial instinct of the Ukrainian people.

From their home base in Bila Tserkva, a provincial city 100km south of Kiev, the three brothers have built up a food processing empire which achieved a turnover of $1 million and 1.5 billion roubles in 1992.

The biggest obstacles the Kyryshkos face are the endless changes to Ukrainian law and the breakdown in trade with the former Soviet republics. The collapse of the inter-republican banking system, and the difficulties of trying to pay for raw materials with Ukraine's new currency, have persuaded the Kyryshkos to revert to barter in almost all of their trade outside Ukraine.

'We produce sausage', explains one of the brothers, Mr Ivan Kyryshko, 'and in the uncertain economic conditions of our country, sausage is better than money.'

To obtain glass jars for his vegetable canning factory last year, Mr Kyryshko was forced to journey to the distant forests of Siberia in order to buy lumber in exchange for sausage and a cash payment. The lumber was sent to Kazakhstan, so that steel could be made and shipped to Tiumen so that caustic soda could be sent to Kiev where Mr Kyryshko's glass jars were produced.

Building on the power of sausages, the Kyryshkos have created a business which has a staff of 175 and an additional 150 part time workers. The brothers have a contract with farmers in the southern Ukrainian region of Mykolaiv - chosen because the land there has not been seriously affected by Chernobyl - to produce vegetables for their canning factories and feed for their 2,000 cattle and 600 pigs.

Altogether Mr Ihor Kyryshko, another brother, says that the business produces as much meat and vegetables as the entire Bila Tserkva region.

The Kyryshkos also operate a textile factory, have shares in a leading Ukrainian bank and commodities exchange, and own three Ukrainian newspapers, a local TV station and a volleyball team.

The Kyryshkos bring a religious zeal to business. 'I only found real personal fulfilment after perestroika, when I could become a businessman', says Mr Ihor Kyryshko.

This attitude seems to be shared by the Kyryshkos' employees. Mr Serhii Kasianov, manager of the Kyryshko canning factory where 36 workers produce 8 million cans a year, explained that he has developed a new work ethic since he left his job at a state canning factory, not surprisingly as his salary is now triple the average Ukrainian wage.

Despite the many frustrations that Ukraine's fledgling entrepreneurs face every day, the Kyryshkos are cautiously optimistic about Ukraine's reform-minded government. They describe Mr Leonid Kuchma, prime minister and himself a former factory director, as a man who can get things done.

Businessmen are the people who should be running Ukraine, in the view of Mr Ihor Kyryshko, who does not rule out a political career for himself. 'If not us then who?' asks the man whom Ukrainian newspapers have dubbed 'The Capitalist of Bila Tserkva'.

Source: the *Financial Times*, 7.1.1993.

(a) Explain how the Kyryshko brothers made use of the barter system when running their business.
(b) In what way are the problems faced by the Kyryshko brothers typical of those faced in countries where the economic system is changing?
(c) What sort of 'work ethic' do you think the factory manager has developed in the canning factory?
(d) Why do you think that Mr Ihor Kyryshko has found 'real personal fulfilment' since becoming a businessman?
(e) How do you think:
(i) consumers;
(ii) workers;
have benefited in the Ukraine since the introduction of the market system?
(f) Write a letter to the Ukraine government explaining how they might help the development of business in the country.

Why businesses make decisions

Businesses are DECISION MAKING units. The decisions that they make might include:
- what to produce;
- where to locate the premises;
- what method of production to use;
- what price should be charged;
- what wages should be paid;

and many others.

Why do businesses make decisions? In each case above there are a number of choices a firm may make. For example, the choice might be to locate a new warehouse in Exeter, Plymouth or Torquay. This is an example of a **strategic decision** because it can affect the profitability and survival of the business. Many of the day-to-day decisions taken by business are called tactical decisions. An example might be when and how much stock to order or the setting of sales targets. These **short term control decisions** are often repeated on a regular basis. A business may also make **longer term control decisions**, such as planning to employ extra workers in future to take changes in the economy into account.

Decisions made by firms often involve some risk. Strategic decisions are likely to involve the most risk. For example, the decision to sell a new product in a foreign country involves great risk as there are many factors that can affect its success.

QUESTION 1 On March 30th 1993 Esso, the petroleum company, announced that it was cutting the maximum price of petrol at the pumps of its stations by 4.5p a gallon (1p a litre). The cut came after British Petroleum's (BP) announcement on the 26th March that it would be cutting its price by 6p a gallon. Figure 7.1 shows the new prices per gallon from 30th March onwards.

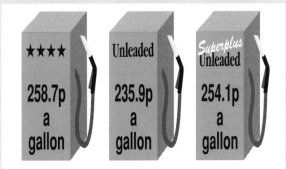

Figure 7.1 *Prices for petrol charged by Esso*

Source: adapted from the *Financial Times*, 30.3.1993.

(a) Suggest other alternative courses of action that Esso could have taken in response to BP's decision to cut its price by 6p a gallon.
(b) Why might there be a risk in Esso's decision to cut its price by 4.5p a gallon?

Who makes decisions?

Unit 2 showed that owners, managers and employees are involved in business activity. They will all make some decisions, although not of equal importance. Major decisions, such as the location of a new plant, will be made by the owners. Less important decisions, such as the amount of time spent waiting for a delivery before making an enquiry, are likely to be made by employees.

The size of the business can affect who makes decisions. In a small firm the owner will make most of the decisions because he or she is the person in control. Some decisions might be **delegated** if the owner trusts the employees. As a small firm expands, the owner might employ a manager to help run the business and take some responsibility for decision making. In very large businesses decisions are made at many different levels, by different people.

Decisions are often classified into three types.

Policy decisions These are decisions about the general direction and overall policy of the business. They might be the decision to buy another company, the closure of a plant making a loss, or whether or not to launch a new product. These decisions are the responsibility of the board of directors, who control the business on behalf of the shareholders. In small firms policy decisions are made by the owner, although such decisions are likely to be smaller, such as the opening hours of a local DIY store.

Management decisions Management decisions or **executive** decisions determine how policy decisions are carried out. An example of such a decision might be deciding the best way to close a loss making branch. For example, should it be closed immediately, gradually, over a period of time? Should the closure be negotiated or

---

QUESTION 2 Plasmo PLC are a very large business that manufactures plastic components for electrical appliances. They employ 7,000 people and have production operations in the UK, USA and Italy. The company has 150 different product lines. During the course of a week some of the decisions made in the business were as follows:
- Should a customer enquiry be dealt with by a letter or a telephone call?
- Should a new customer be allowed to buy £5,000 worth of goods on credit?
- Should the company discontinue a product which has rapidly falling sales?
- Should the company change its logo?
- Should the marketing department employ an artist or continue to pay an agency for artwork?
- Should red or blue litter bins replace the existing grey ones in the offices?

(a) Classify each decision in terms of: (i) policy; (ii) management; (iii) administrative.
(b) How might employees be affected if all decision making was made by management and directors?

enforced? Could a management buy-out (☞ unit 2) be considered? Management decisions should ensure that the policy decisions are carried out as efficiently as possible according to the general objectives of the company. Some management decisions might be taken by directors since some directors are also managers in the business.

Administrative decisions Administrators are often office staff or supervisors, they act according to general company policy and under the direction of management. They will have responsibility for a number of tasks. These may require lower level decisions to be made, such as the amount of time allocated to specific tasks or the choice of equipment. It is sometimes argued that the performance of employees can be improved by letting them become involved in decision making. This is said to improve motivation (☞ unit 48).

The decision making process

A business makes decisions in order to achieve objectives (☞ unit 5). For example, it might decide to launch a new product in order to diversify. Decisions are made at all levels in a business and it is useful to have a flexible process which can be followed by all involved. Figure 7.2 shows the stages in the decision making process.

Identifying objectives The objective of a business might be to halt a rapid decline in sales. This decision is quite complex and may be taken by the board of directors. Quite often the objective is to solve a problem. This might be planning for the future or deciding on a growth direction for the company. Lower level decisions, made by junior managers perhaps, often involve choosing between different courses of action, such as the selection of 5 new skilled workers from a possible 125 applicants.

Gathering information and ideas People need information and ideas to make decisions. The amount and nature of the information needed will depend on the decision. For example, the decision whether or not to launch a new product might require some information about possible sales levels and consumer reactions, costs of production and reactions of competitors. It could take several months to collect all this information. Other decisions could perhaps be made from information which the business already has. A decision whether or not to dismiss an employee might be made on the basis of information from the personnel department.

Where does the business gets its ideas? It might set up a working party to collect information and ideas from within the firm. The working party would then produce a report or make a presentation to the decision makers. Alternatively, individuals or departments might submit ideas and information. Another way of obtaining information and ideas is to hold discussions amongst staff in the firm.

Evaluation of ideas The next stage is to analyse these ideas on alternative courses of action. Analysis can range from a guess on the basis of the information to the use of complex decision making techniques (☞ units 16 and 17).

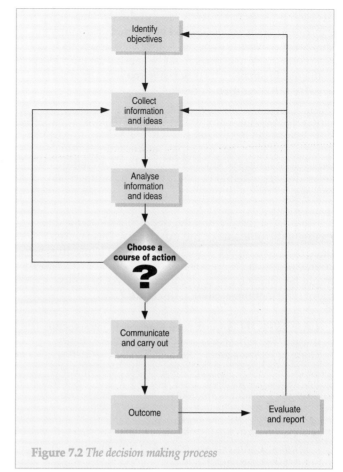

Figure 7.2 *The decision making process*

For example, there are a number of techniques which can be used to assess which investment project a firm should choose.

One popular method of analysis is SWOT analysis (☞ unit 21). For example, a firm could use this analysis if it was deciding between two possible locations for a plant. Decision makers could list the strengths, weaknesses, opportunities and threats of each location and then make a comparison.

Making a decision Next the decision has to be made. This is the most important stage in the process. Decision makers have to commit themselves to one course of action. It is difficult to change the decision, so getting it right is vital! For example, once production begins following the decision to launch a new product, it is difficult for the firm to change its mind. If the product does not sell, this can lead to a loss of money. Some decisions can be reversed. For example, if the owner of a shop decides to close on Tuesday afternoons, but then finds that the loss of sales is intolerable, the owner can easily reopen again.

Sometimes the decision makers feel that they cannot reach a decision. They may have to obtain more information and complete the previous two stages in the process again.

Communication Once a decision has been made, personnel are informed and the decision is carried out. Quite often the people making the decisions are not those that carry them out. Instructions may be passed by the decision makers to someone else, probably a manager, explaining what action should be taken. For example, if the directors decide to begin selling their products in a new country, instructions must be sent to the marketing manager. In smaller firms decision makers are more likely to carry out their own decisions.

Outcome Once a decision has been carried out it will take time before the results are known. Sometimes this can be quite a long time. For example, the companies which decided to build the Channel Tunnel will not know for several years whether or not it will be a commercial success.

Evaluate the results Finally, decision makers need to evaluate the outcome of their decisions. This is often presented as a report. It may be necessary to modify the course of action on the basis of the report. For example, it might be necessary to revise the objectives or collect some more information, as shown in Figure 7.2.

QUESTION 3 North East Electronics manufacture mobile telephones and employ 840 people in their Durham based factory. During the early 1990s they suffered a big drop in sales due to the recession and increased competition. They had to cut their costs and save £3.1 million in the coming financial year. Two courses of action have been suggested.
- Make 300 factory workers redundant.
- Close down their distribution operation. Sell off vans, lorries and warehouses and make only 80 workers redundant.

(a) What information might the firm need in order to make its choice?
(b) Suggest 3 ways in which the firm could have gathered ideas and information suggesting the possible courses of action.
(c) If the firm chose the option of selling the distribution centre, is this decision reversible? Explain your answer.

Constraints on decision making

Businesses cannot make decisions with complete freedom. In many situations there are factors which hinder, limit or restrict particular courses of action. These CONSTRAINTS may make the decision easier because they eliminate some courses of action. For example, what if a business is deciding to buy a new computer, has £900 available, and is faced with a choice of;
- Amstrad £600,
- Nimbus £1,000,
- Texas £900,
- IBM £1,200?

The firm can only buy the Amstrad or the Texas given the money it has available. It is left with a simpler choice and fewer options to choose from. However, although the money constraint has made the decision easier, it may also have prevented the business from buying the most suitable computer (perhaps the IBM) for its needs.

Internal constraints These may result from the policy of the business itself.
- Availability of finance. Decision makers are often prevented from choosing certain courses of action because the business cannot afford them.
- Existing company policy. For example, to control the wage bill, a firm's policy may be to restrict overtime to a maximum of 10 hours per week. The production manager may want to offer workers more overtime to reach a production target. However, she is not able to do so because of the firm's overtime policy.
- People's behaviour. Decisions may be limited by people's ability. For example, a manual worker is unlikely to be able to run a department if the manager is absent. People are also limited by their attitudes. For example, a company may wish to move three people into one office who work in separate offices at the moment, but this could meet with resistance.

External constraints These are limits from outside and are usually beyond the control of the business.
- Government and EC legislation. Businesses must operate within the law. For example, a manager may require a driver to deliver some goods urgently to a customer 600 miles away, which would require a 17 hour drive. The law restricts the amount of time a person can drive a commercial vehicle to about 10 hours per day.
- Competitors' behaviour. Say a firm is deciding to introduce a new product. If Mars are enjoying some success with a new product Cadbury's might copy Mars and decide to launch their own version of the product. Because competition has become greater in recent years, this constraint has affected more firms.
- Lack of technology. There are many examples of operations in business that in the past were slow or

---

QUESTION 4 West Barton Brick Company are considering an expansion of their operations. Their current factory is too small and the company is finding it increasingly difficult to meet demand. The management want to build a new factory near Lincoln. They are currently waiting for a decision from the planning department of the local council.

If the new factory is built, the firm's employees will have to travel 26 miles to work. The workforce have expressed their dissatisfaction at this possibility. They have requested a special travel allowance of £100 per month if they have to travel. However, it has been company policy for 20 years not to make special payments of any sort to employees.

The decision makers are also considering a price increase. This would raise revenue and profitability and also reduce demand, and thus the new factory would not be needed. The result of this decision, however, might be to attract new firms into the market. The outcome is not certain.

(a) Identify the constraints which the decision makers face and state whether they are internal or external.
(b) Under what circumstances will a business change its existing policies?

physically demanding. Today tasks as varied as loading cargo onto ships to computer aided design can be carried on effectively with the use of modern technology.

- The economic environment. It is argued that business activity moves through booms, where demand rises, and slumps (☞ unit 67). This can affect investment decisions. For example, if a company is deciding whether to build a larger plant, the decision makers may postpone the plan if the economy is in a slump and demand is low. During the recession of the early 1990s a large number of businesses cancelled investment projects.

The quality of decisions

If the right decisions are made the business will benefit. The quality of decisions depends on a number of factors.

Training If people are trained their performance is likely to be better. The people making important decisions in a business should receive training (☞ unit 54). Courses are offered by business schools and other educational institutions which concentrate on decision making.

Quantity and quality of information Decision making will be improved if there is access to information. For example, if a firm is thinking of a price increase, the more information it has on the reactions of customers, the more likely it is to decide whether this is the right course of action. Information technology in business (☞ unit 36) has helped decision makers a great deal. They are able to store more information, retrieve it instantly and change it into a form which is more useful to them.

Inadequate and inaccurate information can lead to the wrong decision being made and may cause serious problems. For example, when an insurance company is setting premiums for motor insurance, if the estimate of the cost of repairing cars is too low then premiums will be set too low.

Ability to use decision making techniques The ability to use decision making techniques will help accurate decisions to be made. For example, one technique used to evaluate the likely returns from choosing a particular course of action is the use of decision trees (☞ unit 16).

Risk Some decisions involve considerable risk, such as the launching of a new product. It is argued that UK managers are too cautious in their approach to decision making. This is because they prefer to choose courses of action which carry the lowest risk, and avoid taking riskier courses of action which might result in higher profits.

Human element Most decisions are made by people. Different people are likely to make different decisions. How do people differ?

- The level of experience might be different. More experienced decision makers will often, but not always, make more accurate decisions.
- The attitude to risk may differ. Cautious decision

makers will choose different courses of action to 'risk takers'.

- People have different capabilities. Those who are skilled at decision making will enjoy better results than those whose judgements are poor.
- Self-interest may affect the course of action chosen. For example, management and trade unions are likely to reach different conclusions when setting wage levels for the workforce.
- People often have different perceptions. This may influence the decisions they make. For example, two people on an interview panel for a new recruit may have different views of an interviewee's performance.

QUESTION 5 A soap manufacturer is thinking of diversifying. However, they are not sure which new product to manufacture although they have decided to stay with toiletries. The marketing manager believes that shampoo might be a good idea because the product is used by both males and females regularly. However, the production manager believes that there is too much competition in this market and the setting up costs for shampoo production would be too high. Information about the use of toiletries is shown in Table 7.1.

Table 7.1 *Penetration of toiletries*

PENETRATION OF TOILETRIES
Users per fortnight*

Product category	Total %	Men %	Women %
Talc	42.5	36.0	49.1
Anti perspirants/deodorants	80.0	74.9	85.0
Body spray	16.7	6.5	26.9
Soap	92.2	93.8	90.7
Bath additives	33.2	23.1	43.2
Shower products	24.2	25.2	23.3
Toothpaste/gel	94.5	94.0	94.9
Shampoo	95.8	96.0	95.7
anti-dandruff/medicated	26.7	33.1	20.5
other	75.3	68.2	82.4
Conditioner	25.3	11.2	39.3
Hair spray	27.9	11.1	44.6
Mousse	17.3	5.1	29.4
Gel	8.0	11.5	4.6
Fragrance (excl. body spray)	57.1	61.1	53.0
Skincare - Total			88.1
Creams			60.1
Lotions/Milks			60.8
Oil			7.1
Astringent/toner			22.1
Lipcare products			21.8
Medicated	11.8	10.8	12.8
Make-up			80.8
Mouthwash	13.4	12.4	14.3

*Men/women aged 11 - 64.

Source: adapted from Taylor Nelson Personal Care Panel, October, 1991 - March, 1992.

(a) Discuss 3 factors which might affect the quality of the decision about what to produce in the above case.
(b) How might the business make use of the information in Table 7.1 in its decision making about shampoo production?

Interdependence

Businesses are highly interdependent. Many businesses depend on others for supplies of materials and components. Other businesses supply ancillary services, such as cleaning, waste disposal, financial services and maintenance. When making decisions firms should consider how they affect these support services. In recent years some large businesses have put financial pressure on support businesses by delaying payments. This may lead to support services closing down.

Decision makers need to be aware of the interdependence between their own company and their competitors. In highly competitive industries one firm's decisions can affect the behaviour of other firms. For example, in the grocery trade if one supermarket decides to lower the prices of several hundred lines, other supermarkets may have to do the same or risk losing customers. This type of interdependence is particularly important in decisions concerning:
- price;
- launching new products;
- packaging;
- non-price competition,
- introducing new technology;
- exploiting new markets.

Key terms

Constraints - factors which restrict decision making.
Decision making - choosing between alternative courses of action.

Summary

1. Why do most business decisions involve some risk?
2. Who makes decisions in business?
3. Why might the size of the business affect who makes decisions in the business?
4. Explain the difference between a policy decision and an administrative decision.
5. Briefly describe the 7 stages in the decision making process.
6. List 3 internal and 3 external constraints on business decisions.
7. State 5 factors affecting the quality of business decisions.
8. 'Businesses cannot make decisions without considering the effects on their suppliers.' Briefly explain this statement.

Question

Camellias

Camellias are an up-market ladies fashion chainstore. They are an established and large business with around 200 high street stores. They have enjoyed a steady growth in sales and profit for the last fifteen years. Camellias' success has resulted largely from the quality of after sales service which the stores offer to their customers. They offer:
- low price fitting and adjustment services;
- an exchange facility for mistaken purchases;
- high class dry cleaning.

Many of their customers are regulars and have shopped there for many years. They also face very little competition in the areas where they operate. Another chainstore, Frock Shop, does offer a very similar service but operates in different regions to Camellias. As yet there is no high street in which both stores compete.

The board of directors are considering the purchase of 40 high street shops for £4 million from a regional shoe shop which has just ceased trading. Camellias are poorly represented in this region, but Frock Shop are very well represented. So far the directors of Camellias have deliberately avoided opening shops in streets where Frock Shop has stores. In addition, Frock Shop have never directly competed in high streets where Camellias have operated.

One of the directors involved in the decision is new to the company. She has an excellent record as a marketing director and was recruited with the overwhelming support of the company owners. They were impressed with her ideas on merchandising and also her commitment to rapid growth. The bank has told the directors to reach a decision on the purchase by the end of the month otherwise finance will no longer be available.

(a) Explain why the decision of Camellias might be regarded as a strategic decision.
(b) What might be the objectives of Camellias when making their decision?
(c) Identify the constraints that there might be on the decision of Camellias.
(d) What information might be helpful to Camellias in making its decision?
(e) What decision do you think Camellias might come to? Explain your reasons.
(f) How might the business evaluate the possible outcome of its decision?

Why set up?

What do ICI, the Virgin Group, Ratners the jewellers, your nearest newsagent and the local window cleaner all have in common? At some time in the past, these businesses have been **set up** by their owners. Many, though not all, began as small operations. They are often started by entrepreneurs (☞ unit 2) working in a small shop or factory, or from home. Alan Sugar, the businessman behind Amstrad, started by convincing customers they really were buying the last television he had left in his flat! The Body Shop began as one retail outlet opened in 1976 in Brighton by Anita Roddick, having previously sold her own cosmetics in the 1960s. According to the NatWest Small Business Start-up Index, more than 400,000 small businesses were formed in 1992. It is estimated in the UK that there are nearly 3 million businesses, of which over 95 per cent employ less than 20 people.

Why do people set up in business?

- Independence. Some people prefer to make their own decisions and take responsibility rather than being told what to do.
- To increase rewards. People setting up their own business often believe that they will earn more than if they were working for an employer.
- As a result of redundancy. Some businesses start when an employee is made redundant and decides to use her skills in her own venture. **Redundancy payments** can be used to fund the business.
- Commitment to a product. A business may be set up to sell a new invention or because of commitment to a product no-one else wants to produce. For example, Sophie Mirman worked for Tie Rack before setting up the Sock Shop. Banks would not lend her money, so she and her husband financed the business themselves. Initially in the UK, the Sock Shop was a success.
- Sometimes people extend their hobbies into a business. A stamp collector may set up a small stall at local markets, for example.

QUESTION 1 Gary Clarke worked for an industrial painting company for several years. He worked his way up to a position of pricing and writing bids for new work. He felt, however, that by setting up his own business he would gain a higher salary and have more flexibility in his work than at present. Gary had a good relationship with customers and believed his small business would be more efficient than the large company he worked for. He also felt that he would be more motivated working for himself. He had seen several self-employed painters used by the company and was impressed by their commitment.

(a) What factors were important in Gary's decision to set up on his own?
(b) What risks might Gary face in doing this?

- To satisfy creative needs. A worker on a production line packing biscuits may be artistic. Setting up a business to paint portraits may allow the individual to satisfy these needs.
- A person may want to work in a particular job, but can't find employment. Someone who has trained as a hairdresser or joiner may find that setting up their own business is the only alternative to being unemployed.
- An employee may be dissatisfied with their job. Setting up in business is one alternative to looking for a job with another firm.

Implications

What faces a person setting up their own business? He or she will come up against many problems and challenges. The way in which the entrepreneur works will probably be different to that of an employee. Take an example of a chef who has decided to 'go it alone' and open a cafe specialising in crepes and pancakes. At first, the chef would be uncertain about whether there is demand for this type of meal. Arguably this risk never goes away, but it is likely to be far greater at first until regular customers visit the cafe. The earnings of the chef are also likely to vary, depending on sales. Working for an employer, he would have earned a regular wage or salary.

The responsibility for the business would fall onto the owner. This means problems, from the non-delivery of ingredients to the placing of local adverts, will fall onto the chef. Even if employees are hired, the responsibility falls onto the owner. Many business people find that great personal commitment is needed. They must also be able to come up with new ideas and 'keep going' even if things get tough. This means the person must be single minded and self-sufficient.

Organisation of time is very important. He must decide what is to be done and place tasks in order of priority. He must also decide if the task can be done by someone else, ie what to **delegate**. Many people who set up in business talk about the lack of time to get things done. Working from 6am until midnight every night of the week is likely in the early stages. This places great stress on their personal and social life and their family and friends.

The entrepreneur must also consider the skills they have and whether they are enough. Working for an employer may demand skill as a chef. This technical skill will be important to the cafe. However, the chef will also need management skills. These include making sure that correct materials and equipment are available to having an effective stock control. As workers are hired, the entrepreneur must develop personnel skills to control, motivate and organise the workforce. The owner will also need to sell himself and the company, a skill that is unlikely to be part of his role as an employee. Most people find that their technical skills are much greater than their managerial skills. It is often this lack of managerial skills which leads to problems. If a skill is needed which the entrepreneur does not have, he can:

■ retrain, although there may be little time to attend a course and available courses are not always designed for specific needs;
■ hire full time employees with the necessary skills;
■ employ a specialist, such as an accountant, designer or market research agency, ideally for 'one off' tasks so that they do not become a full time cost;
■ find a partner or take over another business. This is dealt with later.

QUESTION 2 The questionnaire in Figure 8.1, is part of a publication designed by the National Westminster Bank. It aims to make business people aware of the demands on them if they start up in business.

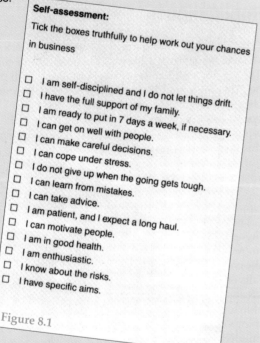

Figure 8.1

Source: *The Business Start-up Guide*, National Westminster Bank.

(a) Think of a business you might like to start. Carry out the questionnaire and ask one friend to do the same. Compare your results.
(b) If you didn't tick all the boxes, what would this imply if you decided to start a business?

Setting up

Whatever the reasons people want to set up in business, they must have a **business idea** before they can begin. It might be a specialist shop selling items for dolls houses, a door to door hairdressing service or a company producing computers. The idea can come from many places. It might be based on the skills or experience of the entrepreneur. It might be an idea from a colleague or advice from an independent. Often the idea is simply the same as other businesses, and the entrepreneur feels she can do it better.

It might just be inspiration!

The next stage is to **consider** whether the business is likely to be a success. This can depend on many factors, some of which are dealt with in the next section of this unit. If the entrepreneur is sure that the business will be a success and is prepared to take the risk, then she is likely to go ahead. Setting up the business without careful **planning** can lead to problems. It is advisable to plan the business and take advice before finally setting up, to avoid these problems.

One final decision that the entrepreneur must make is **how** to set up the company. She may set up on her own, with a partner, or by buying an existing business.

The process involved in setting up the business is shown in Figure 8.2.

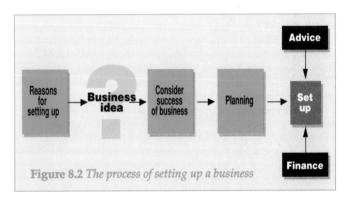

Figure 8.2 *The process of setting up a business*

The chances of success

Many businesses that are set up fail within a few years. Between 1989 and 1992, only 40 per cent of businesses were still trading three years after start up. If a business is going to be a success, the entrepreneur must consider a number of factors. Any one of these factors may be important. The Showering family made fine cider at a good profit in Somerset. When they produced a high quality drink from pears, in a champagne-like bottle and called it Babycham, they became millionaires.

Take an example of someone aiming to produce and sell training shoes. There are a number of questions that may help to make this idea into a success.

The basic business idea What business is the person entering and what will be sold? It may be better to sell 'high quality and performance sports shoes' rather than just 'trainers'. Who are the customers? It may be possible to target an audience, such as 25-35 year olds in a certain income bracket. How is the product used? The shoes could be designed to be hard wearing for sports, or with fashion in mind.

The market How many products exist already? Customers may prefer other types of shoes for fashion wear or a different type of design. What are the strengths and weaknesses of the competition? It may be possible to find a gap in the market, such as trainers that can be used for hiking, water sports or with a special design feature, such as a cut away back with flexible material.

Marketing What price can be charged? It may be possible to undercut competitors' prices or sell initially at less than unit cost (☞ unit 23) until the product begins to sell well. Can the business compete in some other way, such as advertising? American advertisers argue that every product has a UNIQUE SELLING POINT (USP). The business could identify this and promote it. For example, the trainers may be 'comfortable, but robust'. How will the product be sold? The producer may sell through a retailer, representative or direct to the public, for example.

People What are the main skills needed to run the business? What skills are needed to manufacture the product? The sports shoe manufacturer may need the skills of a designer or perhaps a sports scientist before production can begin. How workers can be attracted and retained in the business must also be considered. How much do you know about legislation regarding employment? The entrepreneur will have to take into account the health and safety of employees, for example.

Finance How much money is needed to start up? The business person will need to work out the costs of setting up, eg rent and rates, wages, machinery, sales and distribution costs and professional fees. How much is available to invest? The business person may have savings or insurance policies which can be used. According to the Midland Bank only 50 per cent of businesses borrow from a bank. Many people use redundancy cheques or sell their house to raise finance. Over and above the initial investment, how much more will be required before cash flows into the business? The sports shoe manufacturer may have orders but no cash flowing in until goods are sold. In the meantime, bills must still be paid. Often an overdraft is negotiated with the bank to see the business through this period. What other sources of finance can be used? If the entrepreneur approaches a third party to fund start up costs, control may be lost.

The product or service offered Is the product or service ready for sale? If not, how far has it been developed? It is unlikely that the sports shoe manufacturer will find a backer for the business if the idea has not yet been developed. Is the product idea safe? It may be possible to protect the idea by patent (☞ unit 28) or copyright before production takes place.

Is production cost effective? The manufacturer may want to consider the way the shoe is produced, the location of production, how production is organised and the materials used. Each of these will affect the cost and speed of production.

Risk, timescale and cost What are the main risks involved in the venture? How can they be reduced? The producer may try the product on a small scale basis before trading or work part time while still employed to reduce risk. Who can help and how? This is dealt with later in this unit.

QUESTION 3 Two years ago, Mary Balfour set up an agency for introducing people to one another. There are more than a thousand of these in existence and many fail after a short period. What made Ms Balfour enter such a high risk business?

According to Mary, 'I have always been fascinated by human relationships ... even before I set up in business. I had about 15 marriages to my credit as a result of people I had introduced on a non-professional basis. But I realised to be a success I would have to identify a gap in the market.'

Before taking the plunge, Mary spent 12 months researching the competition and what it had to offer. She decided that the best chance of success was to provide an up-market service for well off, well-educated, middle aged professional people. She felt that this would be a good market segment to target as such people were unlikely to form relationships in the usual way due to the nature of their work. Mary found almost immediately that the business was a success.

Identify the factors that may have influenced the success of Mary Balfour's business.

Planning

Although there are examples of businesses that just 'set up and prosper', these are limited. Most firms must plan carefully what they aim to achieve and how to do it. Answering the questions in the last section will help the business to produce a BUSINESS PLAN. This is a statement that outlines the way that the business will

QUESTION 4 Look at Figure 8.3 which shows part of a business plan of a small business selling signed and numbered limited edition artists' etchings, greetings cards and picture frames.

> **c Major competitors - their prices, strengths and weaknesses:**
> Major competition is from 'Anystore' which has a well-known prints department, but this helps more often than not, as customers are drawn to the area and the small print gallery is cheaper.
> Other competition is from all of the other shops selling gift items, but again they draw custom into the area.
> Strengths of the small print gallery are:
> Something for everyone at any price level. Once it is bought people cannot tell how much it costs.
> Numbered handmade prints are exclusive and special, and possibly an investment for the future.
> Weaknesses of the competition are that they are more expensive and less flexible. Jewellers, for instance have nothing under £18.00.
>
> Figure 8.3

Source: *The Business Start-up Guide*, National Westminster Bank.

(a) Discuss how competition can:
  (i) help;
  (ii) harm;
  the business.
(b) If the business was applying for a loan, why might a bank manager be interested in this information?

achieve its objectives (☞ unit 5).

An established business may produce a business plan to show how it will obtain the funds to pay back a loan for a new piece of machinery. For a business starting up, a business plan is vital. It can be used to:

- give a clear idea of its direction and operation;
- show a bank or other institution its likely position and its ability to pay back a loan;
- identify problems that may occur to allow the business to deal with them before they can become a problem;
- highlight its strengths and weaknesses.

What is included in a business plan? Table 8.1 shows the details that might appear in the plan of a business aiming to produce and sell specialist cycle equipment.

Table 8.1

Features	What is included	Examples
The business	Name and address of the business What the business aims to achieve Type of organisation	Cross-Harchard Partnership
The product or service	What is being produced What quantities will be produced The proposed price	Specialist cycles Average price £300
The market	Results of research or testing The size of the market If the market is growing or not Who will buy the product Competition and their strengths and weaknesses Methods of promotion and advertising	Growing demand for mountain cycles, racing cycles etc. Advertising in trade journals.
Personnel	Who is involved in the business What experience and skills people have	Former Raleigh workers
Buying and production	Likely costs of production Who the main suppliers are What benefits suppliers have	Production costs £30,000
Premises and equipment	The type of premises Location of premises and cost Age, style and value of machinery Replacement cost of machinery How to cope with expansion	Produced on industrial estate site

Profit	Likely profit based on:
	  * turnover (price x sales)
	  * costs
	  Break even point. This is the quantity sold where turnover is equal to costs
		Total costs = £55,000
		At £300 need to sell 183 to break even

Cash flow	When cash will come in When cash will go out If payments will be cash or credit Difference between cash in and cash out each month	Payment by cash and credit
Finance	How much cash owners will put in How much will have to be borrowed What money is needed for How much spending will cost What assets can be used as security How long borrowing will be for and when it will be paid back.	£5,000 put in by each of the partners

Who can help and in what way?

There is a variety of organisations that provide help and advice for new businesses. They range from those set up by government or private organisations to individuals with certain skills. Advice may be in the form of:

- a telephone number of a specialist who can help;
- a detailed discussion on the best way to run a business;
- telephone numbers of organisations providing funds;
- training videos or seminars;
- specialist information on markets and types of business.

Where can an entrepreneur obtain help?

Individuals It may be possible to get advice from people who have started their own business and have been through the process of setting up. They may be able to point out what they did right or wrong and how they might do things differently. Advice about specific skills needed for running a business might come from:

- an accountant - who can give advice on accounts, book-keeping, taxation;
- a solicitor - who can give advice on the legal requirements of the business;
- an insurance adviser - who can give advice on how to protect and cover such things as equipment and employees.

Banks All of the main commercial banks provide advice for potential business people. This ranges from information about sources of finance to helping to draw up a business plan. For example, the NatWest Start-up Service allows people to talk to a small business adviser at a local branch. The adviser can help to find out whether the business is entitled to a government or EC grant. The NatWest also produce a publication titled *The Business Start-up Guide,* as do other banks.

Training and Enterprise Councils (TECs) These are government agencies with offices all over the UK. TECs run a special Enterprise Allowance Scheme aimed at those unemployed who want to set up in business. Schemes are different, but most involve weekly payments for the first year until the business is up and running. The 1993 budget offered help to those starting a business, with training, counselling and a 15 month allowance as part of the Business Start-up Scheme.

Enterprise agencies These were created specially by the government to help small businesses. Most offer free advice on how to start up and run a business, training courses, contacts and information on potential investors. Local authorities often help in their setting up.

Other organisations Other organisations can offer help and advice.

- The Department of Trade and Industry runs, amongst other things, roadshows to areas of the country where consultants are available to help with business problems and a small firms service offering advice on marketing, exporting etc.
- Trade associations, such as The Wool Marketing board, The Association of British Travel agents or the Booksellers Association, can provide advice about certain types of business or industry.
- The Federation for Small Business produce a 'Be Your Own Boss' starter pack.
- The Prince's Youth Trust gives training, advice and sometimes funds to the under 25s.
- Livewire - is a scheme started by Shell to encourage

entrepreneurs between the ages of 16 and 25.

Business clubs These are regional organisations found all over the UK. They are made up of businesses in the area and are particularly useful for new firms. Often speakers from the Inland Revenue or insurance companies are invited to speak on tax, VAT, grants etc. A list of members is available and businesses provide information and advice to each other. A certain amount of inter-trading also takes place. This helps new firms to make contacts and removes some of the risk when first trading.

Getting finance

Where do new businesses find the finance that is needed to buy materials, pay wages etc? Funds can come from a number of sources.
- Personal savings or past earnings. A person aiming to set up a business in the future may have saved for some years or a redundant employee can use payments made when they became unemployed.
- Funds from partners or investors. Unit 3 showed the different types of partnership and limited companies that exist. A partnership can obtain finance from all partners, even if some are not actively involved in the business. Limited companies can raise large amounts of finance. Investors buy a 'share' of the company by purchasing shares. This is then used to finance business activity and the shareholders are paid with a dividend as a reward.
- It is possible to buy machinery and equipment and pay for it at a later date or over a period of time. Businesses may allow components or materials to be bought on CREDIT SALE or HIRE PURCHASE, where the goods are used and the cost is paid over time, plus interest. Businesses often sell goods and are paid at a later date (30, 60 or 90 days). This is known as **trade credit**.
- A business may decide to lease or hire equipment from a hire company. A small construction firm, for example, may hire scaffolding for a large building rather than buy their own which they might not use all the time.
- Banks or other financial institutions. Banks offer loan and overdraft facilities and charge interest. Services such as business accounts, insurance and salary payments are also available. They may be free for a time if the firm remains in credit. Banks often ask for security against a loan. This can be any assets owned by the business or perhaps the house of the owner. Banks also need convincing that the loan is secure. They will ask for a business plan, references or proof of trading in the past. Loans can be in many forms. Some allow only the interest to be paid off in the first one or two years. It may also be possible to use a mortgage to buy premises.
- Government funds. There are a variety of grants available from government and local authorities. One example would be the Enterprise Allowance Scheme in the last section. The government also run a Small Firms Loan Guarantee Scheme. This allows firms that do not have security or a track record to borrow. The government guarantees part of a loan (for 1993, this was 85 per cent), up to £250,000 over 2-7 years. The firm makes a payment to the government each quarter based on the amount of the loan still owing. A **Business Expansion Scheme** allows funds to be raised by shares. Buying shares is encouraged by tax relief of up to £40,000.
- EC Grants (such as the Regional Development Grant) are available from both the EC and the UK government for businesses in certain area of the UK. These assisted areas are dealt with in unit 30.
- The Department of Trade and Industry. The Enterprise Initiative offers help towards consultancy in areas such as design, marketing and planning.
- Certain industries can sometimes offer funds for businesses. Examples have included British Coal Enterprise giving low-interest loans to firms thinking of locating in coal mining areas and similar offers from the British Steel Industry.

QUESTION 5 Embroidery may not seem the most promising route to a successful business, yet Debra O'Mahony, whose clients include the Royal Opera House and the Bucks Fizz pop group, turned over £32,000 in her first nine months of trading. Ms O'Mahony, aged 24, created a bespoke design service through her innovative designs, time-saving technology and the experience she gained in holiday jobs with Next in Britain and in Paris and New York.

She graduated in textiles and fashion at Birmingham Polytechnic in 1989, with embroidery as her speciality. In that same year she won £500 in a student competition. She was advised to start her own business, and in February last year gave up her full-time job as a fabric designer and colourist with a London fashion consultancy. The next seven months were spent laying the foundations of the business.

Debra spent six weeks on the London Enterprise Agency's design business enterprise course, which included lectures, developing a business plan and researching the market. She also spent time finding a computer that could handle her accounts, publicity material, correspondence and, most crucially, her designs. Having taught herself computing, she chose a £7,000 IBM machine. She obtained £3,000 in grants from Wandsworth Economic Development Office, a £4,000 low- interest loan from the Prince's Youth Business Trust, and a further £2,000 loan from Greater London Business Incentive Scheme. Her family also contributed, but she did not approach the banks.

Etoile Design Associates were launched at the Fabrics Show in London in September 1991. In spring 1992, she won the London regional finals of Livewire, the scheme Shell UK started to encourage entrepreneurs between 16 and 25.

Source: adapted from *The Times*, September 1992.

(a) Identify the possible:
 (i) areas of advice;
 (ii) sources of finance;
 that were used by Debra O'Mahony.
(b) Why did Ms O'Mahony choose not to use banks as a source of finance?
(c) Under what circumstances might the business need to raise more finance in future?

How to set up

A business person must decide what form the new business will take. What alternatives are available?

Setting up a new business alone Perhaps the simplest way of starting a business is to set up alone. Unit 3 showed the possible advantages and problems of being a sole trader. There are few legal requirements and trading can begin straight away. However, the owner will have to take all the responsibility and bear all costs.

Setting up with others One way of avoiding the problems of a sole trader is to set up with others. A partnership would allow the business person to share the load of running the business and to raise more finance, without the demands of becoming a limited company. It is, of course, possible to start business as a limited company. This may be likely if a business is to be run as a family concern (a private limited company), or if a great deal of finances were needed because of the scale of the operation (a public limited company). Limited companies are dealt with in unit 3.

Buying a business A potential business person may be able to buy an existing business. There are many examples of this. An electrician made redundant from a large public limited company may 'buy out' a local retailer selling electrical goods who wants to retire. Managers, shareholders or directors may wish to leave one company and buy out the interests of another. In some cases the managers of a company may try to buy the business from the shareholders because they feel the company can be run better. This is an example of a **management buy-out** (☞ unit 2). It is also possible for a worker buy out to take place, where workers buy out the shareholders of a business.

Buying a franchise If a person wants independence, but is better at carrying out or improving someone else's ideas than their own, franchising might be the ideal solution. FRANCHISING has grown steadily. A survey by the National Westminster Bank and the British Franchise Association in 1992 showed 10 per cent annual growth in franchised units, with sales of £5.24 billion during the year. This was expected to grow to £12.5 billion by 1995.

There are many examples of franchises in the UK. They include names such as Wimpy, Dyno-rod, Body Shop, Holiday Inn and the British School of Motoring. What types of franchise exist?

- Dealer franchises. These are used by petrol companies, breweries and vehicle and computer producers. The companies (the **franchisors**) agree that other businesses (the **franchisees**) can sell their products. A written agreement between the two will cover areas such as the back up service of the franchisor, maintaining the image of the franchisor, sales targets, stock levels and the 'territory' of the franchisee. For example, Ford Motor Company do not allow dealers more than 5 dealerships or advertising outside the allocated 'area'. Ford does not charge a fee. It earns revenue by a mark up on sales to the dealer.
- Brand franchising. This is designed to allow an inexperienced franchisee to set up from scratch. It is used by firms such as Wimpy and McDonalds. The franchisor will already have a reputation for a product or service. It 'sells' the rights of these branded products to the franchisee. The intention is that a consumer will know they are buying the same product whether in London or Edinburgh. It is important that franchisees are monitored to make sure that the standard is maintained. To buy the franchise a business will pay between £15,000-£20,000 and a percentage of turnover (a royalty of usually 10 per cent). Often publicity, marketing and support services are carried out by the franchisor.

The benefits to the franchisor might be:
- using the specialist skills of a franchisee (as in the case of Ford dealers' retailing skills);
- the market is increased without expanding the firm;
- a fairly reliable amount of revenue (because royalties are based on turnover not profits, money is guaranteed even if a loss is made by the franchisee);
- risks and uncertainty are shared;

The advantages to franchisees might be:
- the franchisor might advertise and promote the product nationally;
- they are selling a recognised product so the chance of failure is reduced;
- services such as training and administration may be carried out by the franchisor.

Franchising is not without its problems. The royalty must be paid even if a loss is made. Also franchisees may be simply 'branch managers', rather than running their

---

QUESTION 6 In 1990 business was booming for Fastframe, a North-East company with 90 franchised outlets in the UK. Fastframe offered a quick framing service in high street premises. The end of the consumer spending boom meant some franchisees were unable to make royalty payments and some went out of business. Fastframe was left with falling income and expensive leasehold property. By 1993 receivers were called in by Ian Johnson, the founder.

Many of the franchisees, however, refused to be sold off as part of the liquidation. They argued that they were no longer bound by the agreement they had signed because the parent had failed to deliver support services for some time. Many had paid between £26,000 and £55,000 for their franchises, and believed they could be profitable as independent businesses. Paul Bell, a former franchisee of the year, believed the parent's marketing fell short, but he argues franchisees should not forget the parent's role in setting up. 'A lot of people want the proprietor's profit, but with the manager's responsibility.'

Source: adapted from the *Financial Times*, 1993.

(a) What type of franchise would Fastframe be described as? Explain your answer.
(b) How does the experience of Fastframe show:
  (i) the benefits of franchising to the franchisee;
  (ii) the problems for the franchisor?

own businesses, because of restrictions in the agreement. The franchisor has the power to withdraw the agreement and in some cases, prevent the franchisee from using the premises in future.

Running a business

When a business is set up, there are legal and operational tasks that must be carried out.

Keeping records All transactions which take place must be recorded. This includes all sales of goods or services, the purchase of all materials, equipment and the payment of all bills for heating, lighting, wages, transport etc. This information can be used to show how well the business is performing. There are also certain records that some businesses must keep by law. For example, a business must produce a profit and loss account. The accounts of a business are dealt with in units 38-46.

The use of documents When goods and services are bought and sold, a number of documents are used. They provide evidence and records of the transactions that have taken place. Some documents that might be used include:
- an invoice - a document sent with goods sold on trade credit, informing the purchaser that payment is due on a certain date;
- a cash receipt - a proof of purchase given when something is paid for in cash;
- a credit note - a document issued to a purchaser when they have overpaid, allowing 'credit' on future payments;
- proof of delivery - proof that items have been delivered and received at a certain destination.

If a business person employs workers, they will be given a contract of employment (☞ unit 53). This shows the terms under which the employee is hired and with which they must conform. Employees also need to be provided with wages or salary slips, showing their total earnings and any deductions.

The larger the business becomes, the more documents it is likely to use. Examples of documents that may be used internally include **memos** from, say, the production manager to the marketing manager, or **agendas** for meetings to discuss a new promotional campaign.

Tax and insurance Part of any revenue earned by a business must be paid to the government.
- Taxation. Profits made by a business are liable for tax. Government policy (☞ unit 65) has tried to reduce the corporation tax and income tax paid by businesses in the last decade to encourage growth and development. Businesses can claim allowances, which will reduce the amount of tax paid.
- Value Added Tax (VAT). Businesses must pay VAT on any goods they sell. Usually, they add this on to the price of a good or service. Some products in the UK are exempt from VAT. In the early 1990s, these included children's clothing, food and books. A business will have VAT placed onto the cost of materials, components and other items they buy.

- National Insurance contributions. Employers must make NATIONAL INSURANCE contributions to the government and must also remove employees' contributions from their wages. Employers' payments were based on a scale of 0-10.45 per cent in 1993. Employees paid 9 per cent of earnings if they were between £56 and £420 a week in 1993.

Key terms

Business plan - a statement made by a business, outlining the way it will attempt to achieve its objectives.

Franchise - an agreement where a business (the franchisor) sells rights to other businesses (the franchisees) allowing them to sell products or use the company name.

Hire purchase/credit sale - methods used to buy goods now and pay off the balance over a period of time. In the case of the former, the goods only belong to the buyer when the final payment is made.

National Insurance contributions - payments made by employees and employers to the government as a form of insurance premium

Unique selling point - a feature of the product or service that differentiates it from others and persuades people to buy it.

Summary

1. Give 6 reasons why people set up in business.
2. Briefly explain the likely changes an employee may find in their work if they become a business owner.
3. Where might a business idea come from?
4. What questions about:
   (a) the market;
   (b) finance;
   might a business person ask when starting a business?
5. How might a small business use a business plan?
6. List 6 aspects of a business plan.
7. What help and finance might:
   (a) a Training and Enterprise Council;
   (b) The Department of Trade and Industry;
   (c) a commercial bank;
   provide for a small business?
8. Why might a business club be particularly useful for a small new business?
9. What is the Business Start-up Scheme?
10. 'A franchise allows the franchisee and franchiser to do what they do best.' Explain this statement.
11. What problems might a small business setting up as a franchisee face?
12. Why might a business need to use documents?

■ Businesses will pay Business Rates to the local authority. This is a tax on the percentage value on any building owned by the business.

■ Insurance. It is sensible for an entrepreneur to insure against damages and theft. If production ceases for any reason, this could be a major problem for a new business. Revenue will not be earned and there may be cash flow problems (☞ unit 44) or the business may not be able to afford the immediate cost of repairing or replacing a piece of machinery. Some insurance is required by law. All businesses must have public liability, in case a customer or visitor to the premises is injured and makes a claim.

Question

Kidstuff

Kim and Judith Yip didn't think they had many problems. They had regular employment - Kim worked as a mechanic in a local garage and Judith for a large retailer in Liverpool. They were buying their own house on the Wirral, Merseyside and ran two cars.

Without warning both were made redundant within 3 months of each other. Faced with the possibility of a sharp drop in income, the need to support two young children and a mortgage, they thought long and hard about what to do next. Judith's mother persuaded them to set up in business. Judith had in the past made 'up-market' children's clothing for family and friends, such as party dresses. Their business was to be based around providing specialised, originally designed or unusual children's clothes. They could buy fabrics in bulk from wholesalers, make up clothes and sell them at local markets in the area. They would also offer a service where they would make up clothing at people's request.

Although Judith had the skills to make the clothes, she and Kim felt that they knew little or nothing about business. To solve this problem they both enrolled in a business course at a local college, where they were encouraged to write business plans which would help them in future. They also applied to be part of the Enterprise Allowance Scheme at a local TEC. This money, they hoped, would provide a safeguard in the early stages of the business.

Kim and Judith had to make some important decisions. The business, Kidstuff, was set up as a partnership between the two. They decided from the start to use their combined redundancy money of £11,000 to fund the business and not apply for a bank loan. Judith's mother also had savings of £5,000 which could be used in a crisis. Spending at first was to be kept to a minimum. The cars would be used to transport clothes to markets. It would, however, be necessary to employ part time machine operators to help make the clothes and pay them a wage.

Getting a 'feel' for the market was also thought to be important. Although Judith's clothes had been successful on a small scale, she did not know how large the market was in the region. Kim and Judith visited local markets and shops in the North West. They checked the prices of competitors, the products that seemed to sell best and the markets that most people visited. They also found that the average price of a stall per day was £15. The relative prices of wholesalers were also compared, so that the cheapest fabrics could be bought. Kim felt that it was important to reduce travel cost and time and so they concentrated on markets in the Merseyside and Lancashire area, rather than travel as far as Salford. For the business to be successful, they would have to sell for 5 out of 7 days a week, and perhaps attend craft fairs on a Sunday. There was actually no shortage of customers for the products given the number of stalls and shops in the area. Kim and Judith, however, felt that the service they were offering was different enough so that demand would be steady and they could charge a slightly higher price without losing sales.

The price of the clothes was to vary between £7 and £18, although the average price was found to be about £12. Kim also worked out that it would cost around £26,000 to run the business in the first year.

After a year of trading, an accountant was hired to produce the accounts. The business had done quite well, as shown in Table 8.2.

Table 8.2

	£
Sales	38,000
Costs	26,000
Net profit	12,000

The figure for costs included materials, the wages of operators, the hiring of stalls and some leaflets to advertise the business. Kim and Judith divided the profit of £12,000 equally between them.

(a) How does the case study of Kim and Judith illustrate the difficulties of setting up in business?

(b) Write a business plan for the business under the following headings:
  (i) the business;
  (ii) the product;
  (iii) the market;
  (iv) personnel;
  (v) production;
  (vi) premises and equipment;
  (vii) profit and break-even quantity;
  (viii) finance.

(c) If the business needed to raise finance in future, advise them on the benefits and problems of different methods.

Ski-weekends

In 1991, Danny Rodgers bought a second hand Fletcher powerboat and a variety of water-skiing equipment, including wet suits, life jackets and waterskis, for £5,000. Danny and his friend, Chris Hamilton, had always wanted to take up water-skiing since trying it on holiday in Corfu. They both lived in Manchester and planned to transport the boat to Lake Windermere every fortnight at weekends. Although Danny had been able to afford the cost of the boat and the equipment, he needed financial support from his friends to fund the weekends in Windermere. Chris travelled every fortnight and Danny found it easy to persuade two other friends to travel with them and help share the cost.

After a terrific summer in 1991, Danny began to wonder whether there was any money to be made in this hobby. All of his friends had taken to water-skiing. By the end of the season he was having to turn some of them down because the car was always full. He spent the winter discussing the possibility of forming a business partnership with Chris. Chris was a very useful ally because he was a qualified mechanic and could handle the maintenance and repairs on the boat. In the Spring of 1992, Danny and Chris decided to sell Ski-weekends in Windermere.

They had left the decision rather late and there was a lot to be done. They felt that a bigger, more powerful, boat would be required so they sold the Fletcher for £2,900. A more powerful boat would cost £6,000; they also thought that they would need about another £500 for advertising. Danny had already used his savings to buy the original boat. Chris could only contribute £1,000 so they needed a further £3,600 to set up. They would obviously need to borrow.

Danny suggested that they should try to calculate how much revenue they would earn in a season and what their costs would be, before visiting the local bank. They began by identifying some specific details:
- The boat could accommodate a maximum of five people per weekend.
- They decided to set a price of £89 per person for the weekend. This would include Bed & Breakfast, all skiing tuition and transfers from the guest house to the Lake. It would not include an evening meal and transport to Windermere.
- They would operate from May to September inclusive.
- They had agreed Bed & Breakfast rates with a local guesthouse of £11 per person for Saturday night.
- Petrol for the whole weekend would be about £90.
- They agreed that an important part of the weekend would be socialising on Saturday evening.
- They would continue to bring two friends each weekend from Manchester. They would be expected to pay their own accommodation bill and contribute £10 each for petrol.
- They would market the Ski-weekends by advertising in North West local newspapers.
- Some posters would also be produced which they planned to place in sports halls, leisure centres, F.E. colleges and night clubs.
- Simple informative pamphlets would be sent to respondents to advertisements and posters.

Each pamphlet would contain details of costs, a booking form and an itinerary of the weekend's activities which is shown in Table 1.

The itinerary in Table 1 allows Danny, Chris and friends to enjoy water-skiing themselves on Saturday morning, Saturday evening and Sunday afternoon before returning to Manchester on Sunday evening.

Table 1 *Itinerary for the weekend's activities*

Saturday	
12.30	Meet instructors at Guest House
13.00	Skiing on Lake Windermere
15.00	Break for refreshment
15.30	Skiing on Lake Windermere
17.30	Free time
21.00	Socialising in Bowness

Sunday	
9.00	Breakfast
10.00	Skiing on Lake Windermere
11.30	Break for refreshment
12.00	Skiing on Lake Windermere
14.30	Free time
17.00	Departure from Guest House

Danny and Chris drew up Table 2 to show the expected revenue for the venture. They did not assume that they would be fully booked every weekend during the season. They calculated their expected revenue on the basis of a four week month (enabling them to take the occasional weekend off) and three people per weekend except for July and August when they assumed that four people might book with them.

Table 2 *Expected revenue for their first season*

		(£)		
May	Jun	Jul	Aug	Sep
1,068	1,068	1,424	1,424	1,068

With this information, Danny and Chris went to the bank to ask for a £3,600 bank loan. They expected it to be a formality because both were in full-time employment. Unfortunately the bank manager was not in a position to make a decision. She said that they had over-looked some important costs and that a proper business plan must be drawn up.

(a) What motivated Danny and Chris to set up the business?
(b) State **three** possible costs which Danny and Chris may have overlooked.
(c) Draw up a business plan using the following headings:
   (i) the business idea;
   (ii) a full description of the services;
   (iii) the market;
   (iv) attracting customers;
   (v) equipment;
   (vi) an analysis of income;
   (vii) an analysis of costs;
   (viii) finance;
   (ix) likely profit in the first year.
(d) Explain **2** external factors which might affect their business in the future.
(e) What legal and financial advice might you give to Danny and Chris if they went ahead with the business and formed a partnership?

C & J Clark is a family business which was founded in 1825. Two quakers, James and Cyrus Clark, made sheepskin slippers as a sideline to the family farm. But by 1863 the business was virtually insolvent and William Stephens Clark took charge and built the company from a cottage industry into a mass market shoe maker. It is believed to be the country's fifth largest private company. The family own about 70 per cent of the shares, with the rest distributed equally between employees, trusts and institutions, including the Prudential and Legal & General.

In March 1993, a tense board meeting took place to discuss the terms of a £160 million bid for the company from Berisford International, the property and commodities group. The board was split; one side wanted to accept the bid and the other wanted the company to pursue an alternative strategy.

Both sides were desperate for a change in the company's fortunes. Pre-tax losses of £3.5 million were reported for the half year to July 1992, compared with a £2.5 million profit the year before. Dividends had dwindled from 3.5p at the interim stage to 1.75p.

One of the few things which unites the two sides of the family is the dislike of publicity. This intensely private Quaker company is trying to suppress news of the row. However, the identities of the two sides have emerged. The fight to keep Clarks an independent company is led by 56 year old Lance Clark who is supported by Caroline Gould, a non-executive director. On the other side is Walter Dickson, the first non-Clark chairman. He is backed by John Clothier, the millionaire managing director, Dan Clark, and three outsiders.

The current crisis stems from C & J Clark's rapid expansion and the cost of buying back £40 million of family shares 3 years ago. The company, with sales of £590 million, also owns the K-Shoes and Ravel brands. Cheap imports have also affected the UK shoe industry - about 7 out of 10 pairs bought in the UK are from abroad. Many shareholders are pessimistic, and want to sell their shares. Bids have come from Electra, an investment trust and Fii, a rival shoe company. Berisford's bid though, is the one most favoured by the board.

Lance wants to keep the company a family business, but introduce new personnel. He seeks the removal of Dickson and another non-executive director, outsider Jim Power. They would be replaced by Lance's nephew, Hugh Pym, an ITN journalist, and Michael Markham, a non-family businessman. Lance's cousin Richard Clark also backs this move and Roger Pedder, Richard's brother-in-law, makes up the four who between them have 13 per cent of the shares. The 30 per cent non-family shareholders also back the move to retain the company in private hands. Details of their strategy have not been made public but they may include:
- slimming down the board;
- raising finance to buy out disgruntled shareholders;
- possibly floating the company on the stock market in a couple of years.

The four argue that the Berisford bid seriously undervalues the company. Berisford would make C & J Clark one of four divisions within the group and push hard for sales abroad. Clark's workforce believe that a Berisford takeover would mean job losses. Critics also add that some UK factories would be closed, destroying the Quaker company's reputation for benevolence. A City analyst who feels that the Berisford bid

makes sense stated 'Maybe its time for Clark to bite the bullet and join the real world. If times are tough, the shareholders will seek sanctuary with the highest bidder'.

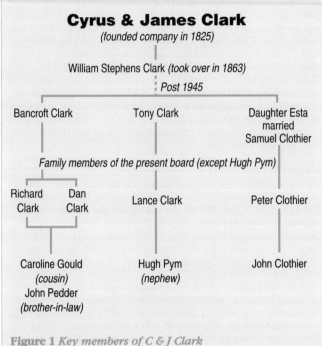

Cyrus & James Clark
(founded company in 1825)

William Stephens Clark (took over in 1863)

Post 1945

Bancroft Clark | Tony Clark | Daughter Esta married Samuel Clothier

Family members of the present board (except Hugh Pym)

Richard Clark | Dan Clark | Lance Clark | Peter Clothier

Caroline Gould (cousin) John Pedder (brother-in-law) | Hugh Pym (nephew) | John Clothier

Figure 1 *Key members of C & J Clark*

Source: adapted from *The Independent on Sunday*, 28.3.1993.

(a) Explain what the diagram in Figure 1 shows about the ownership of Clarks.
(b) Why do you think that C & J Clark have remained a private limited company for so long?
(c) What evidence is there in the case to suggest that one of Clark's objectives is to show social responsibility?
(d) Explain 2 reasons why Clarke's employees might want to own shares in the company.
(e) Why might institutions such as the Prudential have owned shares in C & J Clark?
(f) What internal and external factors might have contributed to Clark's poor trading position?
(g) Explain why you think a conflict has arisen amongst the directors.
(h) What choice would you make between the Berisford bid and the 'alternative strategy'? Explain your answer.

Battle of the radio waves

Broadcasting law reforms have made setting up a radio station much easier. It is also relatively cheap. Unlike television, there are no franchise fees to pay. Putting in a bid for one of the eight available London listening franchises cost only £2,500 in June 1993. Broadcasting equipment no longer has to be approved, and, in theory, you could start up with a tape recorder in your front room. Transmission costs (£50,000 to £200,000 depending on waveband and frequency) and music copyright fees (a flat rate of £60,000 for a music station) are only payable after your advertising income starts to come in.

The prospect of running one of these eight radio stations attracted 48 bids from a variety of people and organisations. Angus Deayton (the comic), Sebastian Coe (the athlete-turned-MP), London Transport, Cardinal Basil Hume, Joan Bakewell, Anne Diamond, Robert Smith (the lead singer of The Cure) and many others are behind companies and consortia who bid for the eight London franchises in June. Other bidders included some experienced 'players' in the media field - Reuters Holdings, Associated Newspapers, the publisher of the Daily Mail, London County Radio and Radio Africa.

So why all the interest?

- It is cheap to set up.
- For the generation that listened to Radio Luxembourg there is undeniable 'romance'.
- There is the lure of power and influence.
- According to Avtar Lit, the Chairman and chief executive of the ethnic station, Sunrise Radio, it is easy to make money.

Avtar Lit learnt his trade running a pirate Asian station in the UK and then two more in Los Angeles. He formed Sunrise Radio two years ago, broadcasting a mix of music, current affairs and chat in Hindustani and English to Indians and Pakistanis. £187,000 was invested by Mr. Lit and some Asian business colleagues. By the nineteenth day of broadcasting they had enough advertising business to pay for their studios in Hounslow. The business now makes profits of £250,000. In 1991 it bought the loss-making Bradford City Radio, renamed it Sunrise Yorkshire and it now makes a profit. A third station is operating in the East Midlands and the company plan to offer a satellite service to households with Astra receivers.

John Parcell, UK managing director of Reuters, is also confident of making a profit from radio. Reuters is planning to set up a service for the business community if its bid is successful. They predict an audience of around 80,000 for their mix of business news, personal finance advice and interviews. They also plan to broadcast news of economic indicators at 11.30 am, with immediate follow-up analysis by specialists. Reuters plan to spend £2 million setting up and expect to break-even in year two, with a profit of £1 million by year five. They are aiming to charge high rates for advertising space in anticipation of a wealthy business audience.

Reuters has already sampled the radio business. In the 1970s, they ran a service supplying recorded stories which were sold to radio stations around the world, including Mutual Broadcasting in the US. Reuters Radio lost money and closed down in 1980.

The only sources of income in radio broadcasting are advertising and sponsorship. Competition is fierce as newspapers, TV, posters and radio fight for a share of business advertising budgets. Of the total amount spent by business on advertising, only 2 per cent goes to radio. It is argued that it could rise to around 8 per cent, as it is in America, if wealthier listeners are attracted. One radio station, Classic FM, has already begun to attract some big advertisers; British Gas, Schroder Wagg and Time-Life have advertised on radio for the first time.

The consensus is that radio can attract more advertising revenue. Zenith Media, the media buying arm of Saatchi & Saatchi, forecast that revenue from radio advertising will grow by between 6-8 per cent this year - faster than television. Last year £144 million was spent by advertisers across 120 radio channels.

The launch of Richard Branson's Virgin AM 1215 in April, amid unprecedented hype, will probably help the cause of radio. It managed to attract advertising from Nestlé, McDonalds, Abbey National, Hewlett-Packard and other 'big' companies even before the launch.

Source: adapted from *The Independent on Sunday*, 13.6.1993.

(a) Explain 2:
   (i)   financial;
   (ii) non-financial;
   motives for setting up a business running a radio station.
(b) Explain 3 advantages which businesses currently supplying media services might have when setting up a radio station.
(c) What might be the benefits of buying a loss-making business?
(d) Explain 3 factors which Reuters might have considered when planning to set up a radio station.
(e) In what way is the service supplied by Avtar Lit, and the service planned by Reuters, specialised?
(f) How might TV and other advertisers react to the growth in radio advertising?
(g) What is meant by the phrases:
   (i)   'there are no franchise fees to pay';
   (ii) 'Putting in a bid for one of the eight available London franchises...';
   (iii) 'Reuters plan to....break-even in year two'?

investigations

Aims

• To investigate the process of setting up a business, identifying the various stages the owner or owners go through.
• To identify any problems which are encountered when setting up a new business.

Research

You should ideally conduct this investigation in pairs or small groups. Find a business in your locality which has set up in the last twelve months or so. Small businesses might be the best choice. The retail sector might be a good starting point. You might identify a new business by:

• asking local estate agents if some business premises have been let recently;
• walking around industrial or commercial areas looking for evidence of new business activity, such as 'under new management' signs or building or refurbishment on premises;
• asking parents, friends, business people, teachers etc.

Make an official appointment with the owner by telephoning or writing (use official school or college letter headings if possible). Always be flexible when arranging appointments to fit in with the business owner.

Once you have found a new business and made an appointment, you need to plan your visit. You may only have half an hour to interview the owner so you need to be thoroughly prepared. You can prepare by writing a questionnaire. Base your questions on the following issues.

• What was the owner's motive for setting up?
• Where did the business idea come from?
• What research was done into the validity of the idea?
• Who is involved in the business and what are their roles?
• How was the 'set up' financed and how much was needed?
• What legal requirements had to be satisfied?
• How was the location chosen?
• What important decisions had to be made?
• What help and advice did the owner get?
• Did the owner write a business plan? Can you see it?
• What problems did the owner encounter?
• How well is the business doing now?
• What plans do you have for the future?

If you are working in pairs or small groups you could specialise in particular areas.

During the interview you need to get as much information as possible. The following points might help you do this.

• Your questionnaire should only be used as a starting point.
• Try to get the owner to talk freely.
• Ask 'on the spot' questions when your curiosity is aroused.
• Ask permission to record or video the interview.
• Ask for copies of any business documents and details of any financial information. Remember that this information may be confidential. Do not show any disrespect to the owner if they choose not to let you see certain information.

(Your conduct is very important. You are representing your school or college and are in the process of building a link with the business community, and a link which you yourself might wish to use in the future.)

Presentation

Details of your interview should be presented formally to the rest of your class. Each member of your group must make a contribution. This will allow some specialisation and give each member an opportunity to practice presentation skills. To make your presentation interesting and effective the following points might be useful.

• Careful planning and preparation is the key to a good presentation.
• No more than 7 minutes per student should be used.
• Do not read directly from a script.
• Use headings on an OHP as the basis for your discussion.
• Use the OHP to show diagrams, charts and copies of documents etc.
• Use extracts from any tape or video recordings.
• Invite questions from the audience.

It might be a good idea to invite the business owner to your presentation. You could evaluate each other's presentations and offer suggestions as to how improvements might be made in the future.

Aims

- To identify the main reasons why businesses fail.
- To produce a personal file of real business case studies.

Research

You need to collect reports on 15-20 businesses which have collapsed in the last couple of years. In 1992 about 62,000 businesses failed, so there are plenty of examples. There are two main sources of information which you might use - CD ROM of a newspaper or past editions of newspapers themselves. If your school or college does not have CD ROM, try a town or city or university library. You may actually remember the names of some companies that have recently collapsed. You could enter these names in the CD ROM. Other useful entries to make could be under the following headings.

- Business failure.
- Liquidation.
- Receivership.
- 'Gone bust'.
- Closure.
- Takeover.
- Management buyout.
- Management buying.
- Ceased trading.
- Folded.
- Redundant.

   Either obtain printouts of the reports or make brief notes from the computer screen.

   The second source is equally valuable, but takes longer to obtain information. Your library is likely to have back copies of appropriate newspapers (*Financial Times, The Independent, The Guardian* etc.). Search through these back copies looking for reports on businesses that have collapsed. There will often be several reports on a particular business. To save time you could share the searching process with another class member. Once you have identified the names of companies which have failed you could contact them and ask for a copy of their published accounts. They often contain a great deal of information which could be used in your file. If the company has ceased trading this may not be possible, however.

Presentation

Your file could be organised under the following headings.

- Name of company.
- Location of its operations.
- Type of company, eg PLC, sole trader etc.
- Scope of activities, ie the type or types of business activity explaining what products or services the company supplies.
- Number of employees.
- Recent history of financial performance, eg losses, turnover, debts.
- Reason for collapse - write a report explaining the events that lead up to the failure of the business. Give details of any rescue attempts.

   You could produce graphs and charts which allow you to make comparisons between the companies you have identified. Some ideas are:

- a graph showing the sizes (in terms of turnover, capital employed or the number of employees) of the businesses which have failed;
- a pie chart showing the reasons for business failure;
- a graph showing the size of losses made by each company;
- a map showing where the failed businesses are located.

1. 'Profit maximisation is the most important business objective.' Critically evaluate this statement.

2. What motivates individuals to set up in business? In what way, if any, have these motives changed in the last decade?

3. Discuss the ways in which different business organisations are interdependent. Compare the degree of interdependence in the petrol industry and the restaurant industry.

4. Compare the roles of shareholders, managers and employees in businesses. Discuss the extent to which shareholders 'control' a business.

5. Explain the importance of producing a business plan when starting a business. Discuss three 'external factors' which might affect the outcome of a business plan.

6. Explain why the public sector provides most of the public and merit goods in the UK. Discuss why the government has allowed firms in the private sector to supply some of these services in recent years.

7. Outline the advantages to consumers of the deregulation of local and national bus services. What problems might a new bus operator have when entering the market?

8. One of the problems in running a small business is trying to raise finance to expand. Discuss the advantages and disadvantages of forming a partnership with a relative to help raise finance.

9. Describe the process of becoming a public limited company. Using examples, explain why some public limited companies have reverted to private limited status in recent years.

10. Describe the economic changes which have taken place in Eastern Europe in recent years. What opportunities might become available for Western businesses in the future?

What is market research?

Unit 1 explained that business activity will only be successful if the output produced can satisfy people's wants and needs. Information about the things people want will help firms to decide what to produce. This information is often found by MARKET RESEARCH.

Market research can be defined as the collection, collation and analysis of data relating to the marketing and consumption of goods and services. For example, firms might gather information about the likely consumers of a new product and use the data to help in their decision making process. The data gathered by this research might include:

- whether or not consumers would want such a product;
- the functions or facilities it should have;
- what style, shape, colour or form it should take;
- the price people would be prepared to pay for it;
- where people would wish to purchase it;
- information about consumers themselves - their age, their likes, attitudes, interests and life styles;
- what consumers buy at present.

Without market research, a firm might spend large sums developing and launching a product which may be unsuccessful. A sensible firm would find out the chances of success before a product is launched and carry out research to monitor how well the product is doing when sales begin.

The need for market research

A market is anywhere that buyers and sellers come together to exchange goods and services (☞ unit 1). Markets are in a constant state of change. As a result a business is likely to use market research on a regular basis for a number of reasons.

- Descriptive reasons. A business may wish to identify what is happening in its market. For example, a brewery may want to find trends in its sales of various types of beer over a certain period, or to find out the types of customers who are buying a particular beer.
- Predictive reasons. A business may wish to predict what is likely to happen in the future. For example, a travel company will want to discover possible changes in the types of holiday that people might want to take over the next 2-5 years. This will place them in a better position to design new holiday packages that will sell.
- Explanatory reasons. A business may want to explain a variety of matters related to its marketing. This may include sales in a particular part of the country. A bus company, for example, might wish to research why there has been a fall in the number of passengers on a specific route.
- Exploratory reasons. This is concerned with a business investigating new possibilities in a market. For example, a soft drinks manufacturer could trial a new canned drink in a small geographical area to test customer reaction before committing itself to marketing the product nationally.

Once a business has decided why it needs market research, the next stage is to identify the **aspects** or **areas** it wants to concentrate on. Table 9.1 shows the different areas that could be researched and some possible elements that might be considered in each.

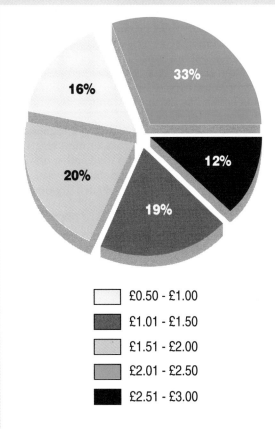

QUESTION 1 Dibble Designs are producers of artistic calendars, posters and greetings cards. They are considering extending the product line by making hand-made greetings cards. The average price of competitors' cards is £1.80. Figure 9.1 shows market research results of the prices people would be prepared to pay.

33%
16%
12%
20%
19%

☐ £0.50 - £1.00
☐ £1.01 - £1.50
☐ £1.51 - £2.00
☐ £2.01 - £2.50
☐ £2.51 - £3.00

Figure 9.1

(a) What does the market research tell the business and how might it use this information?
(b) Discuss the possible problems for Dibble Designs if it had not carried out this research.

Table 9.1 *The scope of market research*

Area of research	Elements to be considered
The market	Identifying market trends Discovering the potential size of the market Identifying market segments Building up a profile of potential/actual consumers Forecasting sales levels
Competition	Analysing the strengths and weaknesses of competitors Identifying relative market shares Identifying trends in competitors' sales Finding information on competitors' prices

Promotion	Analysing the effectiveness of promotional
	   materials
	Deciding upon choice of media for
	   promotions

The product	Testing different product alternatives Identifying consumer wants Developing new product ideas Assessing consumer reaction to a newly launched product
Distributing the product	Identifying suitable retail outlets Exploring attitudes of distributors towards products

Pricing the product	Discovering the value consumers place on
	   the product
	Identifying the sensitivity of the demand for
	   the product to changes in its price

QUESTION 2 Jiva Mountainwear are manufacturers of a range of leisure clothing for use in the outdoors. They are concerned about two aspects of their business. Firstly, they must maintain their present share of the market for waterproof jackets in the face of growing competition. Secondly, they want to extend the range of products into the area of footwear for use by mountaineers and walkers. Table 9.2 shows the sales of waterproof jackets over the last 5 years.

Table 9.2

	1989	1990	1991	1992	1993
Total sales	80,000	85,000	87,000	85,000	81,000
Percentage share of market	15	15	16	13	10

(a) What possible:
  (i) descriptive;
  (ii) predictive;
  (iii) exploratory;
  reasons might Jiva Mountainwear have for using market research?
(b) Given Jiva's objectives, identify any areas of the market for waterproof jackets they might want to research.

Desk research

Desk research involves the use of SECONDARY DATA. This is information which **already exists** in some form. It may be existing business documents or other publications. Business documents that a firm may use for market research include the following.

- Existing market research reports.
- Sales figures. The more sophisticated these are the better. For example, sales figures which have been broken down according to **market segments** (☞ unit 19) can be particularly useful.
- Reports from members of the sales force resulting from direct contact with customers.
- Stock movements. These can often provide the most up-to-date information on patterns of demand in the market. This is because they are often recorded instantly, as opposed to sales figures, which tend to be collected at a later date.

Secondary data will also be available from sources outside the business. Individuals or other organisations will have collected data for their own reasons. A firm might be able to use this for its own market research.

- Information from competitors. This may be, for example, in the form of promotional materials, product specifications or price lists.
- Government publications. There are many government publications which firms can use. These range from general statistical publications such as *Social Trends*, the *Census of Population* and the *Annual Abstract of Statistics* through to specialist publications, such as country profiles produced by the Department of Trade and Industry.
- International publications. There is a huge amount of information about overseas marketing published each year by organisations, such as the World Bank and clearing banks, the European Community, and the International Monetary Fund.
- Commercial publications. A number of organisations exist to gather data about particular markets. This information is often highly detailed and specialised. Mintel, Dun and Bradstreet and the *Economist* Intelligence Unit are examples of such organisations in the UK.
- Retail audits. The widespread use of EPOS (electronic point of sale) has meant that it is now much easier to collect detailed and up to the minute data on sales in retail outlets, such as supermarkets and other retail chains. Retail audits provide manageable data by monitoring and recording sales in a sample of retail outlets. Firms find these audits especially helpful because of the way in which they provide a continuous monitoring of their performance in the market. A well known example is data on the best selling records or CDs which make up weekly music charts. This information is collected from retail outlets in the UK.
- General publications. A business may use a range of publications widely available to members of the public for their market research. These include newspaper and magazine articles and the use of publications such as the *Yellow Pages*.

The main advantage of secondary information collected externally is that it has already been collected and is often available at little or no cost. However, it is not always in a form the firm would want. This is because it has been collected for another purpose. Consequently, secondary information needs to be adapted before it can be used in particular market research projects.

> **QUESTION 3** Stephanie and Tahira are considering setting up a bridal shop selling gowns and other wedding accessories in their home town of Bolton (population 260,000). Before doing so they have decided to research the market. The latest edition of *Social Trends* tells them that each year there are 252,000 first marriages. They calculate, with the UK's present population of 57 million, that this means one first marriage for every 226 people.
>
> (a) Why is the information which Stephanie and Tahira are using known as secondary data?
> (b) Explain how Stephanie and Tahira might use the information to predict likely sales. Suggest possible problems with using the data to predict demand.
> (c) What other sources of secondary data would you suggest that they use when examining the potential market?

Field research

Field research involves collecting PRIMARY DATA. This is information which does not already exist. In other words, it has to be collected by the researcher. Field research can either be carried out by a firm itself or by a market research agency.

The main advantage of primary data is that the firm which initially collects it will be the only organisation with access to it. Primary information can therefore be used to gain marketing advantages over rival firms. For example, a package holiday firm might discover through its field research that the use of a particular airline is a major attraction for its customers. This information can then be used to win a share of the market from rival firms by using it as a feature in promotional materials. The main disadvantage of primary information is that it can be very expensive to collect. This is because field research, if it is to generate accurate and useful findings, requires specialist researchers and is time consuming.

Most primary information is gathered by asking consumers questions or by observing their behaviour. The most accurate way to do this would be to ask or observe all consumers of a particular product (known as the **population**). However, in all but a few instances this would be either impractical to carry out or expensive. It is usual to carry out a survey of a **sample** of people who are thought to be representative of the total market. Methods of choosing samples are dealt with later in this unit.

Methods of field research

There are a number of different field research methods a business can use.

Field research using a questionnaire.

Questionnaires Personal interviews, telephone interviews and postal surveys (see below) all involve the use of questionnaires.

There are certain features that a business must consider when designing a questionnaire. If it is poorly designed it may not obtain the results the firm is looking for.

■ The balance between closed and open questions. **Closed** questions, such as 'How many products have you bought in the last month', only allow the interviewee a limited range of responses. **Open** questions, however, allow interviewees considerable scope in the responses which they are able to offer. Open questions allow certain issues to be investigated in great detail, but they do require a high degree of expertise in the interviewer. For example, an open question might be 'Suggest how the product could be improved'.

■ The clarity of questions. The questions used must be clear and unambiguous so that they do not confuse or mislead the interviewee. 'Technical' language should be avoided if possible.

■ The use of leading questions. Leading questions are those which encourage a particular answer. For example, a market research agency investigating the crisps market should avoid the question, 'Do you think that Smiths crisps are better than Walkers?' A better question would be, 'Which brand of crisps do you prefer - Smiths or Walkers?'

Personal interviews This involves an interviewer obtaining information from one person face-to-face. The interviewer rather than the interviewee fills out the responses to questions on a questionnaire, which contains mainly 'open' questions.

The main advantage of interviews is that they allow the chance for interviewees to give detailed responses to questions which concern them. Long or difficult questions can also be explained by the interviewer and the percentage of responses that can be used is likely to be high. If needed, there is time and scope for answers to be followed up in more detail. Interviews, however, can be time consuming and rely on the skill of the interviewer. For example, a poorly trained interviewer asking questions on a product she did not like may influence the responses of the interviewees by appearing to lack interest.

Telephone interviews This method allows the interview to be held over the telephone. It has the advantage of being cheaper than personal interviewing and allows a wide geographical area to be covered. However, it is often distrusted by the public and it is only possible to ask short questions.

Postal surveys This involves the use of questionnaires sent to consumers through the post. It is a relatively cheap method of conducting field research. It also has the advantage that there is no interviewer bias and a wide geographical area can easily be covered. Unfortunately, the response rate to postal questionnaires is poor, often falling to 10 per cent and below. In addition, questions must be short, so detailed questioning may not be possible. Questionnaires must also be well designed and easy to understand if they are to work.

Observation Observation is often used by retail firms 'watching' consumers in their stores. Observers look out for the amount of time consumers spend making decisions and how readily they notice a particular display. Its advantage is that a tremendous number of consumers can be surveyed in a relatively short space of time. However, observation alone can leave many questions unanswered. For example, it may reveal that a particular display at a supermarket is unpopular, but provide no clues as to why this is the case.

Consumer panels This involves a group of consumers being consulted on their reactions to a product over a period of time. Consumer panels are widely used by TV companies to judge the reaction of viewers to new and existing programmes. Their main advantage is that they can be used to consider how consumer reaction changes over time. Firms can then build up a picture of consumer trends. Their disadvantage is that it is both difficult and expensive to choose and keep a panel available for research over a long period.

Test marketing This involves selling a product in a restricted section of the market in order to assess consumer reaction to it. Test marketing usually takes place by making a product available within a particular geographical area. For example, before the Wispa chocolate bar was marketed nationally, it was test marketed in the North East of England.

QUESTION 4 Vegran is a company that has developed a healthy lunch bar made from carob and oats. Initially, it has decided to sell the bar in the South West for a trial period, before launching the product throughout the country. Before this, however, it wants to collect views of consumers on the taste and appearance of the bar. It is particularly interested to find out whether consumers would notice a difference in taste between chocolate and carob and their views on the bar's size and packaging.

Vegran is only a small company with a limited budget for its marketing projects.

(a) Comment on the usefulness of:
  (i)   postal surveys;
  (ii) consumer panels;
  (iii) personal interviews;
  for this company in gathering information.
(b) What potential advantages might test marketing have for Vegran?

Sampling

Carrying out a survey of every single potential consumer (known as the POPULATION) of a firm's product would be impractical, time-consuming and costly. Businesses still, however, need to collect enough primary data to have a clear idea of the views of consumers. This can be done by taking a SAMPLE of the population. This sample group should be made up of consumers that are representative of all potential buyers of the product.

There are a number of ways in which a sample can be chosen.

Random sampling This method gives each member of a group an equal chance of being chosen. In other words, the sample is selected at random, rather like picking numbers out of a hat. Today computers can be used to produce a random list of numbers which are then used as the basis for selecting a sample. Its main advantage is that bias cannot be introduced when choosing the sample. However, it assumes that all members of the group are the same (homogeneous), which is not always the case. A small sample chosen in this way may not have the characteristics of the population, so a very large sample would have to be taken to make sure it was representative. It would be very costly and time consuming for firms to draw up a list of the whole population and then contact and interview them.

One method sometimes used to reduce the time taken to locate a random sample is to choose every tenth or twentieth name on a list. This is known as systematic sampling. It is, however, less random.

Stratified random sampling This method of random sampling is often preferred by researchers as it makes the sample more representative of the whole group. The sample is divided into **segments** or **strata** based on previous knowledge about how the population is divided up. So, if the business was interested in how 'class' affected consumers' demand for a food product, it might divide the population up into different class groups, such as working class males, middle class females etc. A random sample could then be chosen from each of these groups making sure that there were the same proportions of the sample in each category as in the population as a whole. So if the population had 10 per cent upper class males, so would the sample.

Quota sampling This sampling method involves the population being segmented into a number of groups which share specific characteristics. These may be based on the age and sex of the population. Interviewers are then given targets for the number of people out of each segment who they must interview. For example, an interviewer may be asked to interview 10 males between the ages of 18 and 25, or 15 females between the ages of 45 and 60. Once the target is reached, no more people are interviewed from that group. The advantage of this sampling method is that it can be cheaper to operate than many of the others. It is also useful where the proportions of different groups within the population are known. However, results from quota sampling are not statistically representative of the population and are not randomly chosen. They must therefore be treated with caution.

Cluster sampling This involves separating the population into 'clusters', usually in different geographical areas. A random sample is then taken from the clusters, which are assumed to be representative of the population. This method is often used when survey results need to be found quickly, such as opinion polls.

Multi-stage sampling This involves selecting one sample from another sample. So, for example, a market researcher might choose a county at random and then a district of that county may be selected. Similarly, a street within a city may be chosen and then a particular household within a street.

Snowballing This is a highly specialised method of sampling. It involves starting the process of sampling with one individual or group and then using these contacts to develop more, hence the 'snowball' effect. This is only used when other sampling methods are not possible, due to the fact that samples built up by snowballing cannot be representative. Firms operating in highly secretive businesses such as the arms trade may use this method of sampling. Similarly, firms engaged in producing highly specialised and expensive one off products for a very limited range of customers may need to rely upon snowballing when engaged in market research. Examples might include firms engaged in the nuclear and power generating industries.

QUESTION 5 Late one Friday afternoon, the Senior Management Team of Northminster College, a large Tertiary college, had gathered to have a brief discussion on undertaking market research into the provision of a number of new courses in the next academic year. Due to financial constraints, it had already been agreed that the college would need to undertake its own research.

Sheila Whittle, the Principal, opened the discussion. 'This would have been a lot easier 20 years ago when I first started in this game. All of our students lived within five miles of the college and were aged between 16 and 19. Nowadays, we get a range of students and office workers some of whom live forty miles away. We also get adults returning for retraining and retired people wanting to study out of interest.'

Roy Erkule, the marketing manager, offered the first suggestion: 'Why don't we just draw up a list of our potential students and then take a random sample from the list? That way, everyone will have an equal chance of being selected and our results will be totally reliable.'

Kerry Chan, the finance officer, disagreed. 'I think that'll be far too complicated. We need to identify the different groups of students who might attend the college and then interview a specified number from each of these groups.'

Ian Jackson, the curriculum manager, was already tiring of the discussion: 'Look, I've got better things than this to do on a Friday afternoon. Can't we just select a group of students, give each one a set of ten questions and get them to pass them around their friends?'

(a) Is it necessary for Northminster College to use sampling when carrying out this research? Explain your answer.
(b) What might be the problems of using random sampling in this case?
(c) Identify the sampling methods mentioned by Kerry Chan and Ian Jackson.
(d) Which sampling method would you recommend to the college? Explain your answer.

The problems of market research

If market research was totally dependable, it would mean that firms could use market research into the design of products and then be completely confident as to how consumers would respond to them. This would mean that all new products launched onto the market, which had been researched in advance, would be a success. Similarly, no products would flop because firms would receive advance warning from their research and take any necessary measures.

In reality, things may be very different. It has been estimated that 90 per cent of all products fail after they have been initially launched. Some of this, no doubt, can be put down to a lack of, or inadequate, market research. However, a number of firms who have conducted extensive research amongst consumers before committing a product to the market place have launched products which have failed. Given estimates which suggest that the minimum cost of launching a new product nationally is

£1 million, this is a risky business.

Famous examples of thoroughly researched products which have turned out to be flops include the Sinclair C5, a cheap vehicle with more stability than a moped and lower costs than a car. In research, consumers enthused over this vehicle. In reality, it was almost impossible to sell. Similarly, when Coca-Cola launched 'New Coke' with a new formula flavour onto the market, research suggested it would be a huge success. In practice, 'New Coke' was quickly withdrawn from the shops.

The problem is often the **reliability** of primary data collected from field research. There are three main reasons why market research does not always provide reliable information to firms.

■ Human behaviour. Much market research depends upon the responses of consumers who participate in the collection of primary data. Whilst the responses of consumers may be honest and truthful at the time, it does not mean that they will necessarily respond in the same manner in future. This is because all human behaviour, including the act of consuming and purchasing goods, is to some extent unpredictable.

■ Sampling and bias. As noted earlier in this unit, when undertaking research amongst a given population, it is usual to base the research upon a sample of the total population. This is because it would be impossible and/or very costly to include every person when dealing with a large population. Results from a sample, however, may be different from those which would have been obtained if the whole population had been questioned. This is known as **statistical bias**. Clearly, the greater the statistical bias that occurs when sampling, the less will be the reliability of the data obtained. Some methods of sampling are likely to introduce a higher degree of statistical bias than others. At one end of the spectrum, random sampling introduces little or no bias into the sample because each member of the population has an equal chance of being selected. At the other end of the spectrum, there is likely to be a very high degree of statistical bias with snowballing as the sample selected is highly unlikely to be representative of the population as a whole.

■ Other forms of bias. It is not only the process of sampling which can introduce bias into market research. As mentioned earlier in the unit, questionnaires need to be carefully constructed to avoid the problem of encouraging particular responses from consumers through the use of leading questions. Similarly, the behaviour of interviewers can affect the outcome of interviews.

Key terms

Market research - the collection, collation and analysis of data relating to the marketing and consumption of goods and services.
Population - total number of consumers in a given group.
Primary data - information which does not already exist and is collected through the use of field research.
Sample - a group of consumers selected from the population.
Secondary data - data which is already in existence. It is normally used for a purpose other than that for which it was collected.

Summary

1. Why is market research important to firms?
2. Explain the difference between:
   (a) descriptive research;
   (b) predictive research:
   (c) explanatory research.
3. State 5 areas that market research could concentrate on.
4. What is meant by desk research?
5. What is meant by field research?
6. Why might field research be of benefit to a business?
7. In what circumstances might:
   (a) postal surveys;
   (b) questionnaires;
   (c) observation;
   be useful?
8. What is meant by sampling?
9. Why might a stratified random sample be preferred to a random sample?
10. Briefly explain how a firm would obtain a quota sample.
11. Why might sampling result in statistical bias?

Question

Bemrose Corporation PLC

In 1993 Bemrose Corporation PLC, a firm of printers, was in the process of making a decision about buying a new item of machinery. They wanted to be certain about the most suitable machinery to purchase and did not want to waste money buying technology which was unsuitable for their needs. They were also keen to keep pace with developments and did not want to lose vital orders from customers because of an inability to carry out work that was required. All concerned at the company agreed that information was needed before a decision could be taken.

Mr Roger Norton, the Southern area sales manager, was given the task of designing research into actual and potential customers. Customers were mainly businesses wanting books, magazines and manuals printed. Mr Norton drew up a questionnaire designed to discover information about the printing requirements of publishing companies. Part of the questionnaire concentrated on the colours required in each publication, the number of copies required, the types of publications they produced etc., as shown in Figure 9.2.

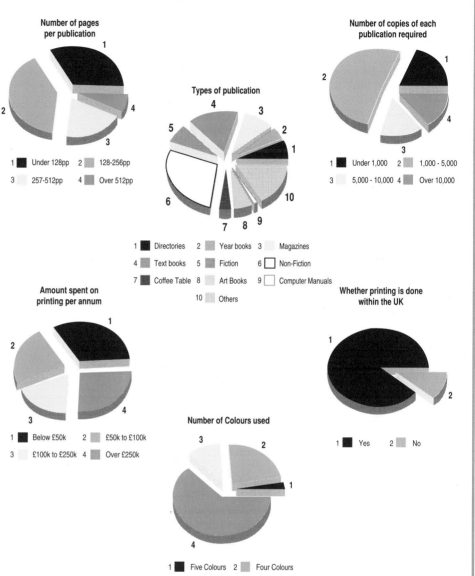

Figure 9.2

The questionnaire was sent by post to 1,653 book publishers based in the UK. Names of publishers were found from a list produced by J. Whitaker & Sons Ltd, which includes nearly all book publishers in the UK. Some small publishers, magazine publishers and large publishers (such as *Yellow Pages*) were excluded from the research, although these accounted for a very small proportion of the total number of publishers. A free pen was offered to all firms responding to the postal survey. 336 responses were received representing a rate of response of 20 per cent.

Source: Mr Roger Norton, *Bemrose Publishing Survey*, 1993.

(a) Would you describe the data gathered by Bemrose as primary or secondary data? Explain your answer.

(b) What reasons might Bemrose have had for carrying out the research?

(c) Comment on the choice by Bemrose to use a questionnaire to gather data, using the results of the survey to illustrate your answer.

(d) To what extent did Bemrose use sampling techniques? Explain your answer.

(e) What advice would you give Bemrose on the type of machinery they may require from the figures?

(f) Why might Bemrose need to be cautious about the results of the survey?

The costs of production

Unit 9 showed that a business needs information about its potential market. It also needs accurate and reliable cost information to make decisions. A firm that is aiming to expand production to meet rising demand must know how much that extra production will cost. Without this information it will have no way of knowing whether or not it will make a profit. You will be familiar with your own costs. These are the expenses you have, such as travel costs to school or college. Similarly, businesses have expenses. These might include wages, raw materials, insurance and rent.

Economists usually think of costs as **opportunity costs** (☞ unit 6). The opportunity cost is the value that could have been earned if a resource was employed in its next best use. For example, if a business spends £40,000 on an advertising campaign, the opportunity cost might be the interest earned from depositing the money in a bank account. A business is concerned, however, with ACCOUNTING COSTS. An accounting cost is the value of a resource used up in production. This is shown in the business accounts as an asset or an expense. For example, if a firm buys some fuel costing £5,500, this is shown as an expense in the accounts.

It is also important to understand how a firm's costs change in the SHORT RUN and the LONG RUN.

- The short run is the period of time when at least one factor of production (☞ unit 1) is **fixed**. For example, in the short run, a firm might want to expand production in its factory. It can acquire more labour and buy more raw materials, but it has a fixed amount of space in the factory and a limited number of machines.
- In the long run, all factors can vary. The firm can buy another factory and add to the number of machines. This will increase **capacity** (the maximum amount that can be produced) and begin another short run period.

Fixed costs

Costs which stay the same at all levels of output in the short run are called FIXED COSTS. Examples might be rent, insurance, heating bills, depreciation (☞ unit 43) and business rates, as well as **capital costs** such as factories and machinery. These costs remain the same whether a business produces nothing or is working at full capacity. For example, rent must still be paid even if a factory is shut for a two week holiday period when nothing is produced. It is worth noting that 'fixed' here means costs do not change as a result of a change in **output** in the short run. But they may increase due to, say, inflation. Figure 10.1 shows what happens to fixed costs as a firm increases production. The line on the graph is horizontal which shows that fixed costs are £400,000 no matter how much is produced.

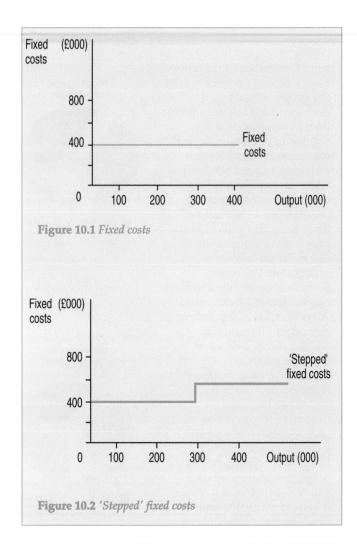

Figure 10.1 *Fixed costs*

Figure 10.2 *'Stepped' fixed costs*

QUESTION 1

(a) Using the photograph above, identify any fixed costs.
(b) Which of the costs in the photograph might rise in the short run?

What happens over a longer period? Figure 10.2 illustrates 'stepped' fixed costs. If a firm is at full capacity, but needs to raise production, it might decide to invest in more equipment. The new machines raise overall fixed costs as well as capacity. The rise in fixed costs is shown by a 'step' in the graph. This illustrates how fixed costs can change in the long run.

Variable and semi variable costs

Costs of production which increase directly as output rises are called VARIABLE COSTS. For example, a baker will require more flour if more loaves are to be produced. Raw materials are just one example of variable costs. Others might include fuel, packaging and wages. If the firm does not produce anything then variable costs will be zero.

Figure 10.3 shows a firm's variable costs. Assume that the firm buying new machinery in Figure 10.1 produces dolls and that variable costs are £2 per doll. If the firm produces 100,000 dolls it will have variable costs of £200,000 (£2 x 100,000). Producing 500,000 dolls it will incur variable costs of £1,000,000 (£2 x 500,000). Joining these points together shows the firm's variable costs at any level of output. As output increases, so do variable costs. Notice that the graph is **linear**. This means that it is a straight line.

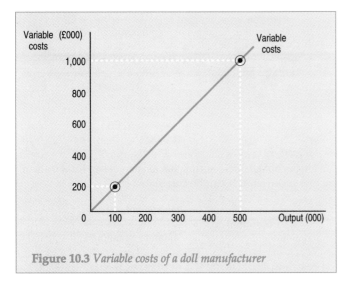

Figure 10.3 *Variable costs of a doll manufacturer*

Some production costs do not fit neatly into our definitions of fixed and variable costs. This is because they are not entirely fixed or variable costs. Labour is a good example. If a firm employs a member of staff on a permanent basis, no matter what level of output, then this is a fixed cost. If this member of staff is asked to work overtime at nights and weekends to cope with extra production levels, then the extra cost is variable. Such labour costs are said to be SEMI-VARIABLE COSTS. Another example could be the cost of telephone charges. This often consists of a fixed or 'standing charge' plus an extra rate which varies according to the number of calls made.

QUESTION 2 Josina Gerrard runs a small computer maintenance operation in Liverpool. She keeps very accurate business records and is anxious to monitor all business costs. An extract from her records is given below.

Table 10.1 *A summary of business motoring costs, 1993*

	£
Petrol	300
Oil	30
Service	50
Repairs	120
Insurance	200
Road licence	100
Depreciation	400
Total	1,200

(a) Which of the costs listed above might be regarded as fixed, variable and semi-variable? Give reasons for your answers.
(b) If Josina travelled 12,000 miles during the financial year, calculate the motoring cost per mile.
(c) Which of the above costs would increase if Josina had travelled 14,000 miles instead?

Total costs

If fixed and variable costs are added together they show the TOTAL COST of a business. The total cost of production is the cost of producing any given level of output. As output increases total costs will rise. This is shown in Figure 10.4, which again shows the production of dolls. We can say:

Total cost (TC) = fixed cost (FC) + variable cost (VC)

The business has fixed costs of £400,000 and variable costs of £2 per doll. When output is 0 total costs are £400,000. When output has risen to 300,000 dolls, total costs are £1,000,000, made up of fixed costs of £400,000 and variable costs of £600,000 (£2 x 300,000). This information is summarised in Table 10.2. In Figure 10.4, notice that as output increases fixed costs become a smaller proportion of total costs.

Table 10.2 *Summary of cost information for the doll manufacturer*

£000

Output (units)	Fixed cost	Variable cost	Total cost
0	400	0	400
300	400	600	1,000

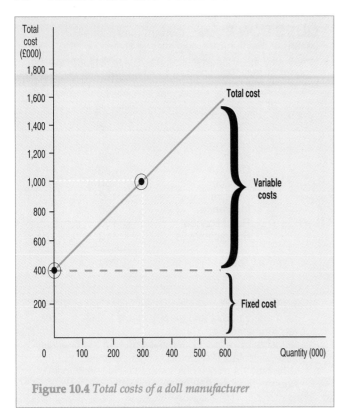

Figure 10.4 *Total costs of a doll manufacturer*

Direct and indirect costs

Costs can also be divided into direct and indirect costs. DIRECT COSTS or PRIME COSTS are costs which can be identified with a particular product or process. Examples of direct costs are raw materials, packaging, and direct labour. INDIRECT COSTS or OVERHEADS result from the whole business. It is not possible to identify these costs directly with particular products or processes. Examples are rent, insurance, the salaries of office staff and audit fees. Indirect costs are usually fixed costs and direct costs variable costs, although in theory both direct and indirect costs can be fixed or variable. The methods used to apportion indirect costs to individual products are discussed in unit 12.

Average and marginal costs

The AVERAGE COST is the cost per unit of production, also known as the UNIT COST. To calculate average cost the total cost of production should be divided by the number of units produced.

$$\text{Average cost} = \frac{\text{Total cost}}{\text{output}} \quad \text{or} \quad \frac{\text{Fixed cost} + \text{variable cost}}{\text{output}}$$

It is also possible to calculate **average fixed costs**:

$$\text{Average fixed cost} = \frac{\text{Total fixed cost}}{\text{output}}$$

and **average variable costs**:

$$\text{Average variable cost} = \frac{\text{Total variable cost}}{\text{output}}$$

Take the earlier example of the doll manufacturer with fixed costs of £400,000 and variable costs of £2 per unit. If output was 100,000 units:

$$\text{Average fixed cost} = \frac{£400,000}{100,000} = £4$$

$$\text{Average variable cost} = \frac{£2 \times 100,000}{100,000} = £2$$

$$\text{Average total cost} = \frac{£400,000 + (£2 \times 100,000)}{100,000}$$

$$= \frac{£600,000}{100,000} = £6$$

MARGINAL COST is the cost of increasing total output by one more unit. It can be calculated by:

$$\text{Marginal cost} = \frac{\text{change in total cost}}{\text{change in output}}$$

For example, if the total cost of manufacturing 100,000 dolls is £600,000 and the total cost of producing 100,001 dolls is £600,002, then the marginal cost of producing the last unit is:

$$\text{Marginal cost} = \frac{£600,002 - £600,000}{100,001 - 100,000} = \frac{£2}{1} = £2$$

The relationship between average and marginal cost and their uses for the business are discussed in unit 12.

Long run costs

Most of the costs discussed so far in this unit have been short run costs, ie the time period where at least one factor of production is fixed. In the long run, all production factors are variable, and the behaviour of costs are subject to new economic 'laws'. This is dealt with in detail in unit 11.

Total revenue

The amount of money which a firm receives from selling its product can be referred to as TOTAL REVENUE. Total revenue is calculated by multiplying the number of units sold by the price of each unit:

Total revenue = quantity sold x price

For example, if the doll producer mentioned earlier sells 300,000 dolls at a price of £5 each:

Total revenue = 300,000 x £5 = £1,500,000

Figure 10.5 shows what happens to total revenue as output rises. Notice that the graph is **linear**.

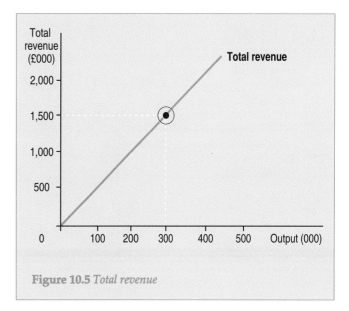

Figure 10.5 *Total revenue*

Profit and loss

One of the main reasons why firms calculate their costs and revenue is to enable them to work out their profit or loss (☞ unit 11). **Profit** is the difference between revenue and costs.

Profit = total revenue - total costs

For example, if the doll manufacturer in the earlier example produces and sells 300,000 dolls, they sell for £5, fixed costs are £400,000 and variable costs are £2 per unit, then:

Profit	=	£5 x 300,000 - (£400,000 + [£2 x 300,000])
	=	£1,500,000 - (£400,000 + [£600,000])
	=	£1,500,000 - £1,000,000
	=	£500,000

It is possible to calculate the profit for a business at any level of output using this method.

Key terms

Accounting cost - the value of an economic resource used up in production.

Average cost or unit cost - the cost of producing one unit, calculated by dividing the total cost by output.

Direct cost or prime cost - a cost which can be clearly identified with a particular unit of output.

Fixed cost - a cost which does not change as a result of a change in output in the short run.

Indirect cost or overhead - a cost which cannot be identified with a particular unit of output. They are incurred by the whole organisation or department.

Long run - the time period where all factors of production are variable.

Marginal cost - the cost of increasing output by one more unit.

Semi-variable cost - a cost which consists of both fixed and variable elements.

Short run - the time period where at least one factor of production is fixed.

Total cost - the entire cost of producing a given level of output.

Total revenue - the amount of money the business receives from selling output.

Variable cost - a cost which rises as output rises.

Summary

1. What is the difference between opportunity costs and accounting costs?
2. How do you account for a 'stepped' fixed cost function?
3. Why are some costs said to be semi-variable?
4. What happens to variable costs as a proportion of total costs when output rises?
5. Explain the difference between direct and indirect costs.
6. How is:
   (a) average fixed cost;
   (b) average variable cost;
   calculated?
7. How is total revenue calculated?
8. What information is required to calculate a firm's profit?

Question

Banbury Paper Supplies Ltd

Banbury Paper Supplies Ltd are a small paper manufacturer which produces rolls of newspaper for the *Oxford Chronicle*, a local newspaper. At the end of the year their current contract with the newspaper expires. It is rumoured that the *Oxford Chronicle*, which has always been supplied by the Banbury producer, is looking for a cheaper source of material in an effort to cut its costs. Gillian Cowbridge, the managing director and controlling shareholder of Banbury Paper Supplies Ltd, is obviously concerned. She is aware that the costs of her own company's operations have been escalating recently and profit margins have been squeezed. One of the problems is the location of the factory. Although it is small, it is located in the most expensive part of Banbury. The premises are owned by a property company who refuse to sell the freehold. Gillian has tried to get planning permission for alternative sites but applications have been repeatedly turned down by the local council.

Table 10.3

	£
Rent p.a.	30,000
Business rates p.a.	10,000
Raw materials (per batch)	200
Fuel (per batch)	100
Directors' salary p.a.	20,000
Labour (per batch)	1,700
Equipment leasing charge p.a.	16,000
General overheads p.a.	4,000

Banbury Paper Supplies Ltd do not have any debt, but lease all of their equipment. Rolls of newspaper are produced in batches of 100. Raw materials are very cheap since recycled paper is used. Details of all business costs are shown in Table 10.3.

(a) Determine which of the above costs are fixed or variable (assume that there are no semi-variable costs).
(b) Draw up a table of costs over a range of output from 0 to 20 batches. (Use only even numbers of output.) Include fixed cost, variable cost, and total cost.
(c) Plot the fixed, variable and total cost on a graph.
(d) Examine the cost breakdown of Banbury Paper Supplies Ltd. What is their main problem? What might Gillian do to overcome the problem?
(e) The *Oxford Chronicle* currently purchases 20 batches of newspaper per annum at an agreed price of £7,000 per batch. What is the level of profit made?
(f) After a meeting with the purchasing officer for the *Oxford Chronicle*, Gillian is told that the *Oxford Chronicle* is now only prepared to buy 20 batches at £6,500 or 10 batches at £8,500. On purely financial grounds which is the best deal for Banbury Paper Supplies?

Break-even analysis

Businesses often like to know how much they need to produce or sell to **break-even** (☞ unit 8). If a business has information about fixed costs and variable costs and knows what price it is going to charge, it can calculate how many units it needs to sell to cover all of its costs. The level of sales or output where total costs are exactly the same as total revenue is called the BREAK-EVEN POINT. For example, if a business produces 100 units at a total cost of £5,000, and then sells them for £50 each, total revenue will also be £5,000 (£50 x 100). The business will break-even at this level of output. It makes neither a profit nor a loss. Firms may use break-even analysis to:

- calculate in advance the level of sales needed to break-even;
- see how changes in output affect profit;
- see how changes in price affect the break-even point and profit;
- see how changes in costs affect the break-even point and profit;
- calculate the level of output needed to reach a target rate of profit.

Calculating the break-even point

It is possible to calculate the break-even point if the firm knows the value of its costs and the price it can charge. Take an example of a small producer, Joseph Cadwallader, who makes wrought iron park benches in his foundry. His fixed costs (FC) are £60,000 and variable costs £40 per bench. He sells the benches to local authorities across the country for £100. The break-even output can be calculated from the following total cost and total revenue formulae:

$$\text{Total cost} = \text{fixed cost} + \text{variable cost}$$
$$\text{or} \quad TC = £60,000 + £40Q$$
$$\text{and Total revenue} = \text{price} \times \text{quantity sold}$$
$$\text{or} \quad TR = £100Q$$

where Q is the quantity produced and sold. As the break-even point is where total cost is equal to total revenue, we can write:

$$TC = TR$$
$$£60,000 + £40Q = £100Q$$

To find Q we can calculate

$$60,000 = 100Q - 40Q$$
$$60,000 = 60Q$$
$$\frac{60,000}{60} = Q$$
$$1,000 = Q$$

At a level of output of 1,000 benches the firm will

break-even. The total cost and total revenue equations can also be used to calculate the amount of profit or loss the firm will make at particular levels of output. At any level of output below the break-even position the firm will make a loss. Output produced above the break-even level will yield a profit. Thus, if the bench manufacturer were to produce 1,200 benches, profit would be:

$$\begin{aligned}
\text{Profit} &= TR - TC \\
&= (£100 \times 1,200) - (£60,000 + [£40 \times 1,200]) \\
&= £120,000 - (£60,000 + £48,000) \\
&= £120,000 - £108,000 \\
\text{Profit} &= £12,000
\end{aligned}$$

An alternative way to calculate the break-even point is to identify the **contribution** and divide it into the total fixed cost. The contribution is the amount of money left over when we subtract the variable cost from the selling price. Contribution is discussed in more detail in unit 12. Using the example of Joseph Cadwallader, to determine the break-even level of output it is first necessary to calculate the contribution.

$$\text{Contribution} = \text{Selling price} - \text{variable cost}$$
$$\text{Contribution} = £100 - £40$$
$$\text{Contribution} = £60$$

The break-even point is now given by:

$$\text{Break-even point} = \frac{\text{Fixed costs}}{\text{Contribution}}$$
$$= \frac{£60,000}{£60}$$
$$= 1,000$$

This confirms our earlier answer that Joseph Cadwallader needs to produce 1,000 park benches to break-even. The value of his total revenue at this level of output will be £100 x 1,000 = £100,000 and the value of his total cost will be £60,000 + (1,000 x £40) = £100,000, ie total revenue and total costs are the same.

QUESTION 1 Steve Westwood, a young entrepreneur from Wantage, leased a Hotdog van for £3,000 p.a. He planned to sell hotdogs at Oxfordshire sporting venues during the weekends. He estimated that his variable costs would be 30p per hotdog and decided to sell them for 90p each.

(a) Show the formulae for: (i) total cost; (ii) total revenue; for the business.
(b) How many hotdogs would have to be sold to break-even?
(c) Calculate the profit or loss if 4,000 hotdogs are sold.

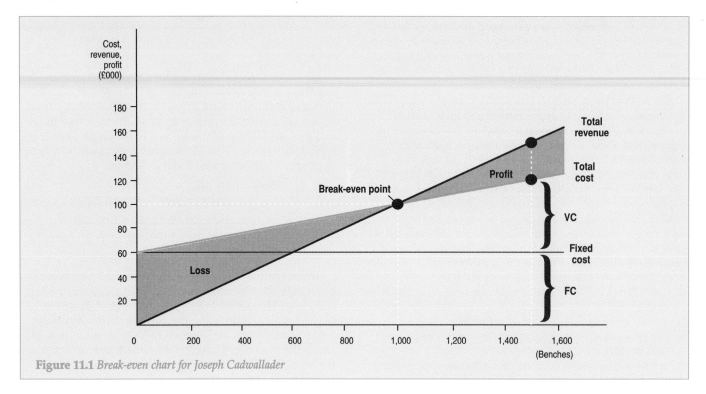

Figure 11.1 *Break-even chart for Joseph Cadwallader*

Break-even charts

The use of graphs is often helpful in break-even analysis. It is possible to identify the break-even point by plotting values of total cost and total revenue on a graph. This graph is called a BREAK-EVEN CHART. Figure 11.1 shows the break-even chart for Joseph Cadwallader's business. Output is measured on the horizontal axis and revenue, costs and profit are measured on the vertical axis. The first step when preparing this chart is to plot the total cost and total revenue functions. It was stated in unit 10 that the total cost and total revenue functions are linear. The lines can therefore be drawn by joining two points which lie on each function, for example at an output of zero and 1,500. The results are shown in Table 11.1.

Table 11.1

£

Q	TR	TC
0	0	60,000
1,500	150,000	120,000
	(1,500 x 100)	(60,000 + [1,500 x 40])

The selection of the two random production levels like this can cause problems. To help it would be useful to:
- always choose zero as one of the levels;
- calculate the break-even point mathematically;
- choose a second level of output which is higher (but no more than double) than this break-even level.

When the functions are plotted on the graph the break-even point is the level of output where the functions cross, ie where total revenue and total cost are the same, 1,000

benches in this example. The break-even chart in Figure 11.1 also shows that all output levels to the left of the break-even point will generate a loss. In addition, all output levels to the right of the break-even point will result in a profit.

What if the business is not producing and selling 1,000 benches, but 1,200 benches? It would be useful to know by how much sales can fall before a loss is made. The break-even chart in Figure 11.2 shows the MARGIN OF SAFETY when output is 1,200. This is the range of output over which a profit can be sustained. It is equivalent to the distance between the break-even level of output and the current level of output. Joseph Cadwallader's margin

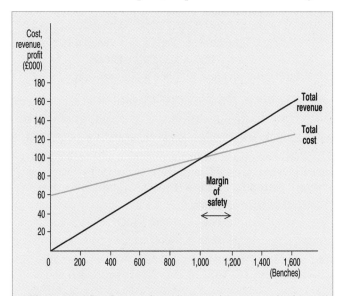

Figure 11.2 *Break-even chart showing the margin of safety for Joseph Cadwallader's business*

of safety if 1,200 benches are produced and sold is 200, ie output can fall by 200 benches before a loss is made. At an output of 1,200 the business has total revenue of £120,000 and total costs of £108,000 and so a £12,000 profit is made.

QUESTION 2 Nancy Lightfoot and Jennifer Price have been made redundant. The local hospital where they were both employed was closed due to government spending cuts. They decide to form a business partnership and rent a nearby petrol station. Nancy, who worked in the finance department at the hospital, draws Jennifer's attention to a list of costs which she has compiled. They are listed in Table 11.2.

Table 11.2

	£
Garage rent p.a.	20,000
Business rates p.a.	4,000
General overheads p.a.	6,000
Petrol per gallon	1.80

(a) Derive a total cost function and a total revenue function (assume that petrol is sold for £2.20 per gallon).
(b) Plot the functions on a graph and determine the amount of petrol (in gallons) which must be sold per annum to break-even.
(c) If Nancy and Jennifer managed to sell 100,000 gallons in a year, calculate: (i) their profit; (ii) their margin of safety.

Advantages of break-even analysis

The break-even chart is an easy visual means of analysing the firm's financial position at different levels of output. Business decision makers can see at a glance the amount of profit or loss that will be generated at different levels of production. The chart can also be used to see the effect on the break-even point, the level of profit and the margin of safety of changes in costs or price.

Changes in price Figure 11.3 shows the effect of a 10 per cent increase in price for Joseph Cadwallader. This causes the total revenue function to shift from TR_1 to TR_2 indicating that total sales revenue has increased at all levels of production. The higher price means that the firm will break-even at a lower level of output, ie 857 benches. It will also mean higher levels of profit (or lower losses) at every level of output. The margin of safety will also increase assuming an output of 1,200 benches is produced (this is not shown in Figure 11.3).

Increases in fixed costs Figure 11.4 shows the effect of an increase in fixed costs of £20,000 for Joseph Cadwallader. The total cost function makes a parallel shift upwards from TC_1 to TC_2. This occurs because a rise in fixed costs causes total cost to increase at every level of output by the same amount. As a result the break-even level of output rises to 1,333 benches. At all levels of production profit falls (or losses rise). There is no longer a

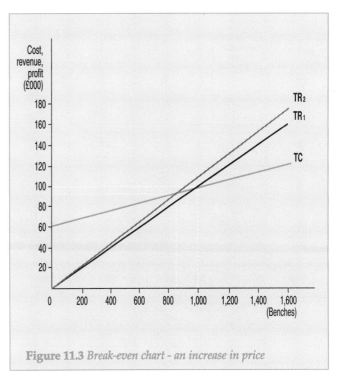

Figure 11.3 *Break-even chart - an increase in price*

margin of safety if 1,200 benches are produced. The firm will make a loss at this output.

Increases in variable costs An increase in variable costs will increase the gradient of the total cost function. This is illustrated in Figure 11.5 by a shift from TC_1 to TC_2. The break-even level of output for Joseph Cadwallader rises to 1,200 benches when variable costs increase by £10. At an output of 1,200 there is no margin of safety as the firm breaks even.

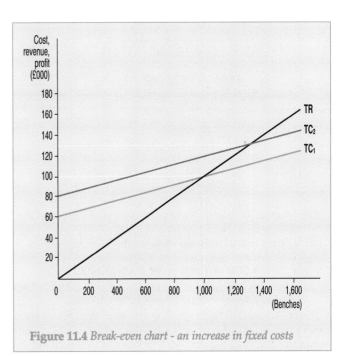

Figure 11.4 *Break-even chart - an increase in fixed costs*

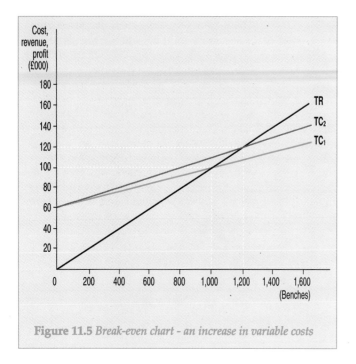

Figure 11.5 *Break-even chart - an increase in variable costs*

The break-even chart also shows clearly the relationship between fixed costs and variable costs. As output is increased it can be seen that fixed costs become a smaller and smaller proportion of total costs. This was illustrated in Figure 11.1.

Target rate of profit

Break-even analysis can also be used to calculate the amount of output needed to generate a certain level of profit. For example, if Joseph Cadwallader wanted to make a profit of £30,000, the level of output required to do this is:

$$\frac{\text{Fixed cost} + \text{profit target}}{\text{Contribution}}$$

$$= \frac{£60,000 + £30,000}{£60}$$

$$= \frac{90,000}{60}$$

$$= 1,500 \text{ benches}$$

Thus, when 1,500 benches are produced profit is given by:

Profit = total revenue - total cost

$= £100 \times 1,500 - (£60,000 + [£40 \times 1,500])$

$= £150,000 - (£60,000 + £60,000)$

$= £150,000 - £120,000$

$= £30,000$

Limitations to break-even analysis

Break-even analysis as an aid to business decision making does have some limitations. It is often regarded as too simplistic, and many of its assumptions are unrealistic.

■ The model assumes that all output is sold and no stocks are held. Most businesses hold stocks of finished goods to cope with changes in demand. There are also times when firms cannot sell what they produce and choose to stockpile their output to avoid laying off staff.

■ Break-even analysis is based on a static model. In the world of business, conditions constantly change. The break-even chart is drawn for a given set of conditions and cannot cope with sudden increases in wages and prices or changes in technology. Simple, dynamic models have proved difficult to develop.

■ The effectiveness of break-even analysis is dependent upon the quality and accuracy of the data used to construct the cost and revenue functions. If the data is poor and inaccurate, then conclusions drawn on the basis of the data are flawed. For example, if fixed costs are underestimated, the level of output required to break-even will be higher than that suggested by the break-even chart.

■ Throughout the analysis it has been assumed that the total cost and total revenue functions are linear. This may not always be the case. The shapes of the total cost and total revenue functions in practice are discussed in the next section of this unit.

QUESTION 3 Cornish Products Ltd are ice cream manufacturers based in Truro. They produce Cornish ice cream for the retail trade. Their fixed costs are £50,000 and variable costs 50p per kilo. The ice cream is distributed nationally and sold for 75p per kilo.

(a) How many kilos would the company need to produce in order to generate a profit of £125,000?
(b) How many extra kilos would the company need to produce to reach this profit target if fixed costs increased to £70,000?
(c) How might the usefulness of the above answers be undermined if the weather was particularly cool during the summer?

Total cost and revenue functions - an alternative

One criticism of break-even analysis, as we have seen, is that total cost and total revenue are drawn as straight lines. This indicates that as output increases, total cost and total revenue rise by the same proportion. What actually happens to total costs and total revenue as output increases?

Total cost Assume a factory is built for 1,000 workers. As more workers are employed they can specialise in different tasks (☞ unit 1). 500 workers are likely to be more productive than one, for example. At some point, however, the opportunity to take advantage of specialisation may be used up and although total output will continue to rise, each extra worker will be less productive. For example, if 2,000 workers were employed in the above factory, there would not be enough machinery available for all workers to be usefully employed.

This is called the law of DIMINISHING RETURNS. It states that as more of a variable factor (labour here) is added to a fixed factor (say capital) the output of the extra workers will rise and then fall. In other words output will rise but at a diminishing rate. In extreme cases output may even fall. This is called negative returns.

How does this affect the costs of a business? Table 11.3 shows the effect on output and total cost of hiring labour at £200 per week with fixed capital costs of £100 per machine. The output per worker always rises, but eventually at a diminishing rate. For example, when the fourth worker is employed output rises by 47 units, but the fifth worker adds only 28 units. Total costs rise as the firm employs more labour. The effect of diminishing returns on the firm's total cost function is shown in Figure 11.6. Notice that it is non-linear.

Table 11.3 *The effect on output and total cost as a firm employs more workers given a fixed amount of capital*

Capital (machines) costing £100 each	Labour (workers) costing £200 per week	£ Fixed costs (machinery)	£ Variable costs (Labour)	Total cost (£)	Output (units)
10	0	1,000	0	1,000	0
10	1	1,000	200	1,200	20
10	2	1,000	400	1,400	54
10	3	1,000	600	1,600	105
10	4	1,000	800	1,800	152
10	5	1,000	1,000	2,000	180
10	6	1,000	1,200	2,200	192

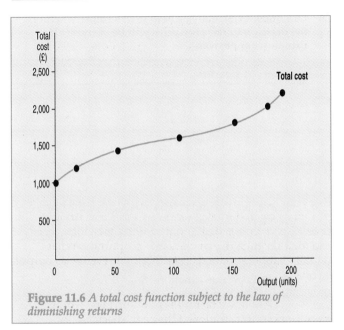

Figure 11.6 *A total cost function subject to the law of diminishing returns*

Total revenue The total revenue function drawn in unit 10 assumed that each unit would be sold for the same price. In reality, it is unlikely that a firm can continually sell its output for the same price. There reaches a point where additional sales can only be made if the price is lowered, for example a business may offer lower prices to customers who buy larger quantities. Figure 11.7 shows that as the price is lowered to encourage more sales the total revenue earned by the business falls.

The graph also shows a total cost function subject to diminishing returns. Notice that there are now two break-even points, Q_1 and Q_2. When linear functions are used on a break-even chart, as output is increased beyond the break-even level of output, profit continues to increase indefinitely. When non-linear functions are used profit can only be made over a particular range of output, ie between Q_1 and Q_2. If production is pushed beyond Q_2 losses are made.

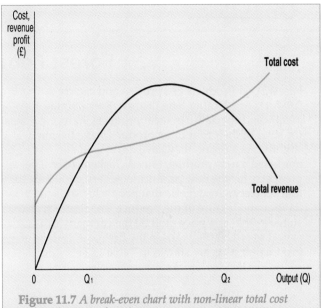

Figure 11.7 *A break-even chart with non-linear total cost and total revenue functions*

QUESTION 4 JT Edinburgh & Son manufacture standard housebricks. Their total revenue and total costs for a range of output between 1-100,000 tonnes are shown in Table 11.4.

Table 11.4 *Cost and revenue data for JT Edinburgh & Son*

Tonnes (000s)	0	10	20	30	40	50	60	70	80	90	100
Total costs (£000)	10	22	25	27	28	29	31	35	40	48	56
Total revenue (£000)	0	14	25	33	38	41	42	42	40	34	24

(a) Plot the total cost and total revenue functions for JT Edinburgh. Show the two break-even levels of output.

(b) Reading from your graph, what will be the profit or loss when 90,000 tonnes of bricks are produced?

(c) If the total revenue function was linear, how might the answer in (b) be different?

Key terms

Break-even point - the level of output where total cost and total revenue are the same.
Break-even chart - a graph containing the total cost and total revenue functions, illustrating the break-even point.
Diminishing returns - the eventual decline in output each extra worker adds to total output when the opportunity to specialise is used up.

Margin of safety - the range of output between the break-even level and the current level over which a profit is made.

Question

Forest Food Products Ltd

Forest Food Products Ltd process and can food products in a Nottingham factory. They employ 100 people and specialise in meat products. In recent years the sales of their four main products have declined slightly. As a result, they have developed and test marketed a new product, tinned chicken curry. The prospects for the new product look very good indeed. Market research suggests that people have taken to the flavour and texture of the product. The research also suggests that at a price of £1.50 the company can expect to sell 800,000 cans in the first year. Details of production costs are shown in Table 11.5.

Table 11.5 *Production costs for tinned chicken curry*

Overheads	£300,000
Raw materials (per can)	30p
Labour (per can)	40p
Packaging (per can)	20p
Distribution (per can)	10p

(a) Show the formulae for the total cost and total revenue functions given the data in the case.
(b) Calculate the break-even level of output.
(c) Construct a break-even chart and show the margin of safety if the firm produces and sells 800,000 cans.
(d) Reading from your graph, what level of profit will be made?

At the end of the trading year the directors meet to discuss the success of the new product. They are only moderately satisfied. The sales director suggests an increase in price. The company accountant agrees and suggests that a price increase to £2 might improve financial performance.

(e) Show the effect of the price increase on your break-even chart. Identify the new break-even level of output.
(f) Can break-even analysis help to determine whether the decision to raise the price will be successful? Explain your answer.

Summary

1. Why might break-even analysis be helpful?
2. How can the contribution be used to calculate the break-even level of output?
3. What is the advantage of a break-even chart?
4. What effect will a price increase have on the margin of safety?
5. What effect will a fall in fixed costs have on the margin of safety?
6. How will a rise in variable costs effect the break-even level of output?
7. What are the limitations to break-even analysis?
8. In reality, why is the:
   (a) total cost function;
   (b) total revenue function;
   likely to be non-linear?

Unit 12 Using Cost Data

Collecting cost data

A business incurs costs at all stages of production. It will have to pay for resources bought from outside the business, such as raw materials. There are also costs when a service is bought from another department within the business. Business managers must record all these costs as they occur. One method used to do this is to find a point where the costs occur and can easily be recorded (a cost collection point). These are known as COST CENTRES. A cost centre may be:

■ a geographical location, eg a factory, sales region or department;

■ a person, eg, a director, salesperson or maintenance worker;

■ an item of equipment, eg a photocopier, telephone line or vehicle.

Charging **direct costs** to a cost centre is simple. For example, a vehicle will be charged with the expenses it incurs, eg petrol, oil, repairs, servicing and road tax. Charging indirect costs is more involved, and is dealt with later in this unit.

Cost centres have two benefits for managers. Firstly, they provide a very sound foundation for a costing system. Secondly, they enable managers to make comparisons between the cost of operating a cost centre and the benefit it provides. For example, if a salesperson costs a company £30,000 per year and only generates £25,000 worth of sales, it may be more profitable to find

another method of selling.

Costing methods

The process of measuring the likely consequences of a business activity is called COSTING. Costing systems benefit a business in a number of ways. They provide managers with financial information on which to base decisions. They help to identify the profitable activities, avoid waste and provide information for cost cutting strategies. Costing can also assist the marketing department in setting the price of products. Examples of costing exercises include:

■ measuring the cost of manufacturing individual products;

■ calculating whether or not it would be more economical to contract out a particular business operation, eg security;

■ determining the cost of moving to a new business location;

■ estimating the cost of decorating the office.

There are usually three costing methods used by firms - full, absorption and marginal costing.

Full costing

When a business produces several products in the same factory and is trying to calculate the cost of producing one individual product, it faces a problem. How should it allocate indirect costs? In other words how can it decide how much each product is contributing to total indirect costs? FULL COSTING solves the problem by allocating indirect costs in an arbitrary way, such as, a percentage of direct costs. For example, a manufacturer which makes two metal components code named ZX 1 and ZX 2 may have the direct costs of producing 100,000 of each component shown in Table 12.2.

Table 12.2 *Direct costs for two components*

			£000
Component	ZX 1	ZX 2	Total
Direct cost	200	300	500

Assume that total indirect costs are £300,000. We need to calculate the percentage each component contributes to total direct cost.

$$\text{For ZX 1} = \frac{200}{500} \times 100 = 40\%$$

$$\text{For ZX 2} = \frac{300}{500} \times 100 = 60\%$$

QUESTION 1 Maria and Patricia Evans own a small chain of shoe shops in the South East. They have six shops in Croydon, Brighton, Dover, Bexley, Redhill and Crawley, all with similar turnover. Maria and Patricia employ managers in each shop. Maria is responsible for the day to day coordination of the business, whilst Patricia is responsible for buying and marketing. One reason for their success has been due to their effective cost control. Each shop is a cost centre. Annual total cost information for each centre, over a three year period, is shown in Table 12.1.

Table 12.1 *Total costs for Maria's and Patricia's shoe shop business*

£000

Year	Bexley	Brighton	Crawley	Croydon	Dover	Redhill
1991	49	53	32	45	50	43
1992	51	54	34	44	53	46
1993	52	56	37	43	57	48

(a) Explain the advantages to Maria and Patricia of recording costs using the cost centres described above.

(b) Given that all the shops have roughly the same annual turnover, what conclusions might you draw from the above information?

The £300,000 indirect costs can now be allocated to each component.

For ZX 1 indirect costs = 40% x £300,000 = £120,000
For ZX 2 indirect costs = 60% x £300,000 = £180,000

The total cost or **full cost** of producing 100,000 of each component can now be calculated. This is done by adding the allocated indirect costs to the direct costs.

For ZX 1 full cost = £120,000 + £200,000 = £320,000
For ZX 2 full cost = £180,000 + £300,000 = £480,000

Full costing is often criticised for the arbitrary way it allocates indirect costs. It could result in misleading costings because the allocation of indirect costs is not based on any actual indirect costs incurred.

QUESTION 2 Ponteland Beach Buggies Ltd manufacture two beach vehicles - the Sandmaster and the Dunedriver. Details of of the direct production costs are shown in Table 12.3. The company also incurs annual indirect costs of £60,000. It plans to produce 100 of each vehicle in the next year.

Table 12.3 *Cost information for Ponteland Beach Buggies Ltd*

	(Per vehicle)	
	Sandmaster	Dunedriver
	£	£
Direct labour	60	90
Raw materials	50	80
Components	65	80
Fuel	25	50

(a) Calculate the direct costs of producing 100 of each vehicle.
(b) Allocate the indirect costs of production to each product as a percentage of direct costs.
(c) Calculate the full cost of producing 100 of each vehicle.

Absorption costing

ABSORPTION COSTING is a traditional method of cost determination. It involves charging or 'absorbing' all the costs associated with business operations individually to a particular cost centre. This includes all direct and indirect costs. Absorption costing differs from full costing in the way indirect costs are allocated. Full costing uses a 'blanket' method, whereas absorption costing apportions indirect costs more accurately. How costs are **apportioned** can vary according to the nature of the indirect cost. For example:
- costs like rent, rates, heating and lighting can be apportioned according to the area or volume in a building that a particular operation occupies;
- personnel expenses could be apportioned according to the number of people employed in a particular operation;

- depreciation and insurance costs could be apportioned according to the book value (☞ unit 43) of the assets used.

To illustrate absorption costing take the example of Dudley Car Exhausts which manufacture three types of exhaust systems E1, E2, and E3. Factory time and direct cost details (per system) are shown in Table 12.4. Annual indirect costs include rent, selling costs, overheads and administration. These are £12,000, £18,000, £24,000 and £4,000 respectively. Rent is apportioned according to the factory time used by each system. Selling costs and overheads are apportioned equally between all systems. Administration is apportioned according to the labour input of each system (most administration costs in this case are labour related, eg wages). Dudley Car Exhausts produces 1,000 of each system every year.

Table 12.4 *Factory time and direct costs for Dudley Car Exhausts*

System	Labour (£)	Materials (£)	Fuel (£)	Factory time(hrs)
E1	2	3	1	1
E2	2	4	2	3
E3	4	4	2	2
Total	8	11	5	6

Using the absorption costing method it is necessary to allocate every single business cost to the production of the three systems. For E1 the total direct cost is calculated by adding labour, materials and fuel, ie $(2 + 3 + 1 = £6)$. To apportion rent to the production of one E1 system it is necessary to take into account the amount of factory time one E1 system uses, ie $1/6$ of the total time and also the number of E1 systems produced, ie 1,000 during the year. The following calculation must now be performed:

$$\text{Rent apportioned to one E1 system} = £12,000 \times \frac{1}{6} \times \frac{1}{1,000}$$

$$= \frac{£12,000}{6,000}$$

$$= £2$$

Selling costs and overheads are split equally between each system, so that selling costs are £6 and overheads £8 for each system. Administration costs are apportioned according to the amount of labour used to make each system. For the E1 system the allocation can be calculated as follows.

$$\text{Administration costs apportioned to one E1 system} = £4,000 \times \frac{£2}{£8} \times \frac{1}{1,000}$$

$$= £4,000 \times \frac{1}{4} \times \frac{1}{1,000}$$

$$= \frac{£4,000}{4,000}$$

$$= £1$$

The complete cost schedule for all three systems is shown in Table 12.5.

Table 12.5 *The cost of producing the three exhaust systems using the absorption method of costing*

(£)

System	Direct	Rent	Selling	Overheads	Admin.	Total
E1	6	2	6	8	1	23
E2	8	6	6	8	1	29
E3	10	4	6	8	2	30
Total	24	12	18	24	4	82

Some businesses use the absorption method to set the price of their products. Once the cost of each unit has been calculated a profit percentage is added to determine the selling price (☞ unit 23).

The absorption costing method is popular in practice, although there are some criticisms of its use. It is difficult to apportion indirect costs accurately to each unit when a firm produces a very wide range of products. Although less so than full costing, any method of apportionment will still be arbitrary to some extent. It is, therefore, important for a business to be consistent in the way it apportions indirect costs to different cost centres.

QUESTION 3 Using the information in the above text about Dudley Car Exhausts, answer the following questions.
(a) Show why the rent, per exhaust, is £6 for the E2 system.
(b) Calculate the selling price of each system if a 25 per cent mark-up is used.
(c) Using the absorption method, calculate the cost of producing each system if rent and selling costs double.

Marginal costing

Marginal cost is the cost of increasing output by one more unit. The MARGINAL COSTING approach used in business is based on this idea. It allocates direct costs (likely to be variable costs), but not indirect costs (likely to be fixed). In marginal costing, decisions are based upon the value of the CONTRIBUTION that a product or process makes to the indirect costs (fixed costs) and profit. The contribution is the amount of money left over after a sale when all the direct costs have been met.

Contribution = selling price - marginal costs (direct costs)

Take the example of the Lancaster Wellington Boot Company which manufactures wellington boots and walking shoes. Table 12.6 shows the revenue, direct costs and contribution.

Table 12.6 *Sales revenue, marginal costs and contribution for the Lancaster Wellington Boot Company*

£

	Wellington boots		Walking shoes	
Sales revenue		30,000		25,000
Direct materials	5,000		3,500	
Direct labour	10,000		4,500	
Other direct costs that can be apportioned	5,000		3,000	
Marginal cost		20,000		11,000
Contribution		10,000		14,000

Table 12.6 shows that wellington boots contribute £10,000 to fixed costs and walking boots contribute £14,000. If the total indirect (fixed) costs for the company were actually £12,000, then the profit would be:

Total contribution	£24,000
less Indirect (fixed) costs	£12,000
Profit	£12,000

In business, if a product makes a positive contribution then it is worth producing. However, even when a product or contract makes a negative contribution there may be reasons for continuing production. For example, a company may be promoting a loss leader (☞ unit 25).

QUESTION 4 Villa Road Office Supplies manufacture filing cabinets. They have just received an order for 20 cabinets from a company which is offering to pay £200 each for them. The production manager advises the sales department that there are two methods of production for the style of cabinet required by the customer. Method 1 incurs direct (variable) costs of £150 per cabinet and method 2 incurs direct (variable) costs of £170.

(a) Calculate the contribution to factory overheads each method would make if the order is met and decide which method should be chosen.
(b) If the direct (variable) costs rose to £210 for method 1 and £230 for method 2, calculate the new contributions.
(c) Given your answers in (b) state whether you would go ahead with the order. Explain your answer.

The relationship between marginal and average cost

Average total cost and marginal cost were defined in unit 10. These two curves are shown in Figure 12.1. Notice that the marginal cost curve cuts the average cost curve at its lowest point. Why? Consider a business building houses with an average cost of £50,000.
■ If another house is built (the marginal house) with a

higher than average cost, the average cost will rise;
■ if the marginal house cost less than the average cost, the average cost would fall;
■ if the marginal house cost £50,000 (the same as average cost) then the average cost would remain the same.

So the marginal and average costs are equal when average costs are constant. On a U-shaped average cost curve this is only at the one point, the lowest point. At all other points the average cost curve in Figure 12.1 is either rising or falling.

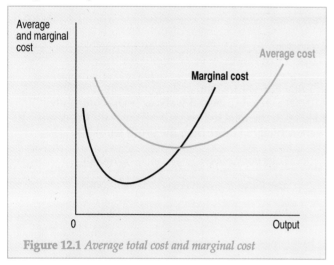

Figure 12.1 *Average total cost and marginal cost*

The closing-down point

In the short run it may be worth continuing production of a product even when a loss is being made. This can be shown for a whole company as well. Consider the case of a shop whose present cost and revenue conditions are shown in Table 12.7. If the shop remains open it incurs total costs of £1,500 and generates £700 in sales revenue. This results in a loss of £800. However, if the shop closes this loss is increased to £1,000. Although total costs fall to £1,000 because there are no variable costs to pay, total revenue falls to zero because there are no sales. Thus, in the short run it pays the shop to remain open because losses are lower. However, when revenue is incapable of covering variable costs the firm should close down.

Table 12.7 *Cost and revenue information for a shop*

		£
	Open	Closed
Fixed cost	1,000	1,000
Variable cost	500	-
Total cost	1,500	1,000
Total revenue	700	-
Loss	800	1,000

Diagrammatically, the CLOSING-DOWN POINT can be shown by combining the average total cost, average variable cost and marginal cost curves (☞ unit 10), as in Figure 12.2. The closing-down point is where marginal cost is equal to average variable cost. When the price falls below P_1 on the diagram, the firm can no longer cover its variable costs. At this point the firm may decide to close down.

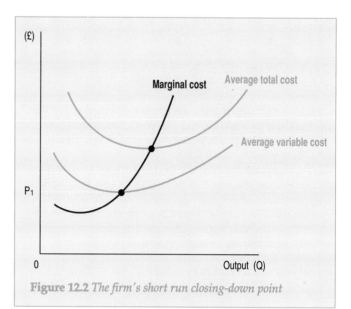

Figure 12.2 *The firm's short run closing-down point*

QUESTION 5 Cost data for an aircraft manufacturer is shown in Table 12.8

Table 12.8 *Cost data for an aircraft manufacturer*

£m

Output	FC	VC	TC	AVC	ATC	MC
1	10	25				
2	10	32				
3	10	36				
4	10	39				
5	10	40				
6	10	44				
7	10	50				
8	10	58				
9	10	70				
10	10	81				

(a) Complete the table by calculating TC, AVC, ATC and MC.
(b) Plot the AVC, ATC and MC functions on a graph.
(c) Show the price below which the business will close down.

Summary

1. Describe the benefits of costing.
2. What are the advantages of using cost centres?.
3. How might the following indirect costs be apportioned:
   (i) office wages;
   (ii) corporate advertising;
   (iii) factory insurance?
4. What is the difference between absorption and full costing?
5. What is the main advantage of the absorption costing method?
6. In what way is the absorption method limited?
7. How is the contribution calculated?
8. How are fixed costs treated in marginal costing?
9. In what circumstances might a loss making contract be accepted?
10. Explain when a firm should close down in the short run.

Key terms

Absorption costing - a method of costing which involves charging all the costs of a particular operation to a unit of output.

Closing-down point - the level of output in the short run where a firm should cease its operations, ie where marginal cost is equal to average variable cost.

Contribution - the amount of money left over after a sale when all direct (variable) costs have been covered, ie selling price minus direct costs.

Costing - the process of measuring the likely economic consequences of a particular business activity or operation.

Cost centre - a point where costs occur and can be easily recorded.

Full costing - a method of costing which apportions indirect costs as a blanket percentage of cost centres.

Marginal costing - the process of costing the production of one more unit of output.

Question

Bradford Engineering PLC

Bradford Engineering PLC produce a range of components for Diesel engines. One such component, the SPC 50, is made up of three other smaller components in a ratio of 4:2:1. The code names for the three smaller components are the SPC 4, the SPC 2 and the SPC 1. Planned output of the SPC 50 for the coming financial year is 5,000 units. The expected production costs for this level of planned output are tabulated below.

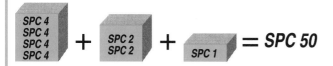

Table 12.9

	SPC 4	SPC 2	SPC 1
			£
Direct labour	80,000	37,000	44,000
Direct materials	20,000	13,000	22,000
Other direct costs	50,000	13,000	20,000
Fixed overheads (apportioned)	6,000	5,000	7,000

Bradford Engineering have been approached by a small engineering company in Newcastle, offering to supply the SPC 4s, SPC 2s and SPC 1s for £6.50, £4.60 and £14 per unit component respectively. However, the

Newcastle based company could not assemble the components and Bradford Engineering would incur a further £20,000 in assembly and transport costs. The two companies have a successful business relationship and their respective managing directors are very good friends.

The workforce at Bradford Engineering are highly skilled and thoroughly reliable. They are generously remunerated and there has not been any industrial unrest for 27 years. A large multi-national company has just located an engineering plant in nearby Leeds and are currently recruiting. Their terms of employment are extremely attractive and several Bradford workers have expressed an interest in the jobs to their colleagues.

(a) Calculate the cost of manufacturing 5,000 SPC 50s using the absorption method.
(b) On a purely financial basis, state whether or not it would be preferable to buy in the components from the Newcastle company.
(c) What non-financial factors should be taken into consideration in the decision to buy in?
(d) Assuming that Bradford Engineering rejected the supply offer, how many SPC 50s would have to be produced in order to break-even if they are sold for £70 each?
(e) Most of the apportioned overheads are administrative costs. How might they have been apportioned?

Why do businesses present data?

Information is a valuable resource. Knowing whether a profit is likely to be made, how well a product is selling, whether stocks are running low and how much cash is available are all vital for running a business. Firms will need access to a variety of information or DATA, including;

■ weekly or monthly sales figures;
■ financial information at the end of the year;
■ productivity rates of workers and capital;
■ market research findings (☞ unit 9);
■ the costs of production.

The data must be stored, retrieved and then presented in the most accessible and straightforward way. In some cases data is required immediately. A business can then analyse the data and use it to make decisions. Information technology (☞ unit 36) means that large amounts of data can now be stored on computer disk. The data can be easily 'called up' on a computer screen and presented in a form businesses can use.

Take an example of a firm collecting data on the groups of people likely to purchase a new soft drink. The data could be collected using market research techniques and stored in a database. It will then be possible to present the data as a graph or table on the computer screen showing which group of people is most likely to purchase the product. It is also possible to print out the information and distribute it to departments. There are many different ways in which the data can be presented. The method the firm chooses will depend on the type of data collected, who and what it is required for and how it is likely to be used.

Bar charts

A BAR CHART is one of the simplest and most common means of presenting data. Numerical information is represented by 'bars' or 'blocks' which can be drawn horizontally or vertically. The length of the bars shows the relative importance of the data. Table 13.1 shows data on the profit made by Ragwear PLC, a manufacturer, over the last six years. This is presented as a bar graph in Figure 13.1.

Table 13.1 *Profit for Ragwear PLC over a six year period*

	Yr1	Yr2	Yr3	Yr4	Yr5	Yr6 £m
Profit	2.1	2.9	3.8	4.1	3.2	4.9

The main advantage of using a bar chart is that it shows results very clearly. At a glance the reader can get a general feel of the information and identify any trends or

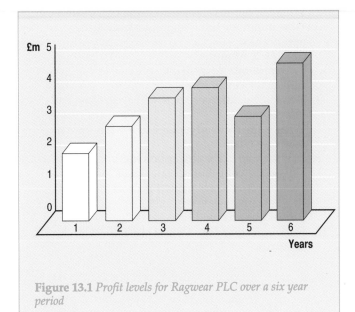

Figure 13.1 *Profit levels for Ragwear PLC over a six year period*

changes over the time period. Figure 13.1 shows that profit has continued to increase over the period apart from a 'dip' in year 5. This might indicate to the firm that trading conditions in year 5 were unfavourable or that the firm's performance was relatively poor. Bar charts are more attractive than tables and allow the reader to analyse the data more quickly.

The bars in Figure 13.1 are drawn vertically. They could also, however, be drawn horizontally. They are also 3 dimensional, but they could have been 2 dimensional.

It is possible to produce a bar chart from collected data, such as from market research. This data may be collected in a **tally chart** as in Table 13.2, which shows the results of research into the brands of toothpaste bought by a sample of supermarket customers. The total number of times each item occurs is known as the **frequency** (f). So, for example, the most popular from the survey is Colgate and the least popular is Kingfisher, a natural toothpaste. Figure 13.2 shows the data from Table 13.2 as a bar chart.

Table 13.2 *Survey results into the popularity of toothpaste*

Brand	Tally marks	Frequency
Colgate	.....	260
Macleans	.....	190
Sensodyne	.....	100
Mentadent	.....	50
Supermarket own brand	.....	230
Kingfisher	.....	20
Gibbs SR	.....	150
Total		1,000

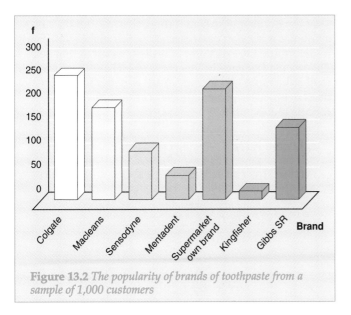

Figure 13.2 *The popularity of brands of toothpaste from a sample of 1,000 customers*

Component bar charts

A COMPONENT BAR CHART allows more information to be presented to the reader. Each bar is divided into a number of components. For example, the data in Table 13.3 shows the cost structures of five furniture manufacturers in 1993. The total cost is broken down into labour, materials and overheads.

Table 13.3 *Cost structures of five furniture manufacturers and overheads*

£000

	Oakwell	Stretton	Bradford	Jones	Campsfield
Labour	50	36	70	45	90
Materials	18	25	48	23	50
Overheads	10	10	19	13	25

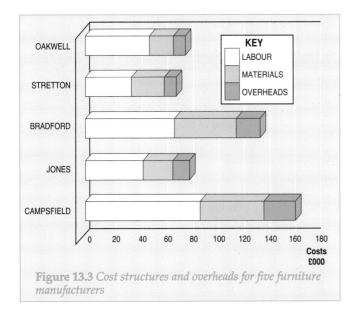

Figure 13.3 *Cost structures and overheads for five furniture manufacturers*

The data in the table are presented as a component bar chart in Figure 13.3. One advantage this chart has compared to the simple bar chart is that total costs can be seen easily. There is no need to add up the individual costs. It is also easier to make instant comparisons. For example, labour costs are the greatest proportion of total cost at Oakwell. This might suggest to a firm that Oakwell uses a more labour intensive production technique than the others. Also, labour costs at Oakwell are higher than at Stretton, but not as high as at Campsfield. This might indicate that Oakwell is less efficient than Stretton and a much smaller business than Campsfield.

Figure 13.4 shows three other styles of bar chart, illustrating data for AVC Holdings. This is a company that produces three types of machine tool, code named BAT 4, BAT 3 and BAT 2.

■ The first chart is a **parallel** bar chart. It shows the turnover contributed by each of the company's three products. Over the time period the turnover for BAT 4 has increased from £10 million to £40 million. Sales of BAT 3 have remained fairly steady at around £15 million each year. The turnover from BAT 2 has declined from £20 million to £7 million. This type of graph is similar to a component bar chart. The advantage is that it is easier to compare changes between the components, although it is more difficult to compare totals.

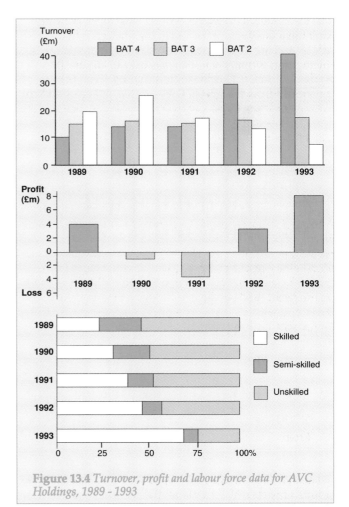

Figure 13.4 *Turnover, profit and labour force data for AVC Holdings, 1989 - 1993*

- The second chart is a **gain and loss** bar chart. It shows the profitability of the company over the time period. The performance of AVC Holdings worsened in the first three years and then improved. The profit in 1993 was £8 million. This type of chart distinguishes very clearly between positive and negative values.
- The third chart is a **percentage component** bar chart. It shows the breakdown of the workforce in terms of their skill with each section represented as a percentage of the workforce. In 1989 nearly 25 per cent of the workforce were skilled. In 1993 this had risen to around 70 per cent. The chart also shows that the numbers of semi-skilled workers have fallen as a percentage of the total.This might indicate that the firm has introduced new technology, leading to unskilled staff being replaced with skilled staff. One disadvantage of this presentation is that changes in the total size of the workforce are not shown.

A pictograph or pictogram

A PICTOGRAPH or PICTOGRAM is another form of chart. It presents data in a similar way to bar charts. The difference is that data are represented by pictorial symbols rather than bars. Figure 13.5 shows an example of the orders which GPA Group have received for their aircraft over a nine year time period. The pictograph shows a general decline in orders. This might indicate that there is a general decline in the market or that customers are delaying future orders. One problem with a pictograph is that it is not always easy to 'divide' the symbols exactly. This makes it difficult to read precise quantities from the graph. For example, in Figure 13.5, in

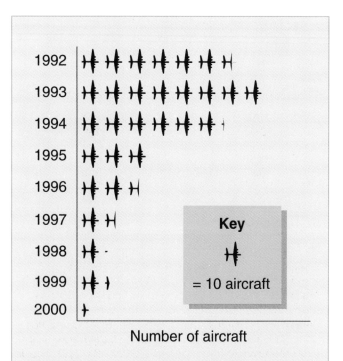

Figure 13.5 *A pictograph for GPA Group showing orders for aircraft in March 1992 for each year to 2000*

1994 the number of orders is more than 60, but the last symbol is a fraction of an aircraft which makes it difficult to determine the exact size of orders placed in that year. The main advantage of this method is that the graphs tend to be more eyecatching. Such a method might be used in business presentations to attract clients or in reports to the public.

QUESTION 1 Petfood Ltd manufacture three brands of canned catfood - Purrliver, Purrlamb and Purrfish. Their sales figures for a six month period are shown in Table 13.4. The managing director has requested this information from the sales department to be used in a board meeting.

Table 13.4 *Petfood Ltd sales figures from June to November*

						(000s)
	JUN	JUL	AUG	SEP	OCT	NOV
Purrliver	20	20	19	18	18	17
Purrlamb	20	30	40	45	50	59
Purrfish	30	28	28	25	21	18

(a) Present the data in Table 13.4 in an appropriate chart.
(b) Explain: (i) what the chart shows and what it might indicate for the business; (ii) why the sales department may have chosen this method of presentation.

Pie charts

In a PIE CHART, the total amount of data collected is represented by a circle. This is divided into a number of segments. Each segment represents the size of a particular part relative to the total. To draw a pie chart it is necessary to perform some simple calculations. Table 13.5 shows the details of monthly output at five European plants for a multinational brick producer. The 360 degrees in a circle have to be divided between the various parts which make up the total output of 50,000 tonnes. To calculate the number of degrees each segment will contain, a business would use the following formula:

$$\frac{\text{Value of the part}}{\text{Total}} \times 360°$$

Table 13.5 *Monthly brick output at five European plants*

	Bedford	Brescia	Lyon	Bonn	Gijon	Total
Output (tonnes)	10,000	8,000	5,000	15,000	12,000	50,000

Thus, the size of the segment which represents the monthly brick output in Bedford is:

$$= \frac{10,000}{50,000} \times 360°$$

$$= 0.2 \times 360°$$

$$= 72°$$

Using the same method it can be shown that the size of the other segments representing output at the other plants will be: Brescia 58°; Lyon 36°; Bonn 108°; Gijon 86°. The number of degrees in each segment added together make 360°. A pie chart can now be drawn using a protractor or a DTP package on a computer. The pie chart is shown in Figure 13.6. Bonn makes the largest contribution to monthly output with Gijon second. The company might use this information to compare with monthly production targets.

Pie charts are useful because readers get an immediate impression of the relative importance of the various parts. They can also be used to make comparisons over different time periods. There are however, drawbacks with pie charts.

- They do not always allow precise comparisons to be made between the segments.
- If a total consists of a very large number of components, it may be difficult to identify the relative importance of each segment.
- It is difficult to show changes in the size of the total pie. For example, if the total rises over time it is possible to make the 'pie' bigger. However, the exact size of the increase is often difficult to determine because it involves comparing the areas of circles.

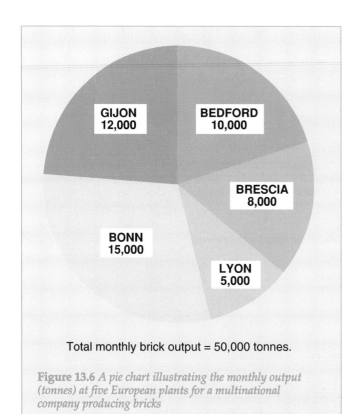

Total monthly brick output = 50,000 tonnes.

Figure 13.6 *A pie chart illustrating the monthly output (tonnes) at five European plants for a multinational company producing bricks*

QUESTION 2 Crosby Metal Springs (CMS) sell products nationally and organise their selling operation on a regional basis. The sales turnover figures in 1992 and 1993 are shown for each region in Table 13.6.

Table 13.6 *Regional sales turnover for Crosby Metal Springs*

	North West	North East	Scotland & Wales	Midlands	South West	South East	Total %
1992	12.7	14	5.3	21.3	19.3	27.4	100
1993	19.5	17.7	8.9	24.8	10.6	18.5	100

(a) Construct two pie charts illustrating the information in Table 13.6.
(b) What do the charts show?
(c) What might be a disadvantage of presenting the data in this way?

Histograms

Table 13.7 illustrates some data collected by market researchers on behalf of a football club. It concerns the age profile of a spectator sample at a Saturday afternoon Premier League fixture. The chart shows the number of spectators in the sample that falls into various age ranges (known as **classes**). The total number of times each item occurs in each class is known as the frequency (f). So the total number of spectators in the 10 - 19 age range is 290. This type of data is usually shown as a HISTOGRAM as in Figure 13.7. A histogram looks similar to a bar chart, but there are some differences.

Table 13.7 *The age profile of a spectator sample taken at a football club for a Saturday afternoon Premier League fixture*

Age range	Frequency
0-9	180
10-19	290
20-29	500
30-39	400
40-49	350
50-59	280
60-79	200
Total	2,200

- In a histogram it is the **area** of the bars which represents the frequency. In a bar chart it is the length or height of the bars. For example, in Figure 13.7, all the columns have the same width except for the last one where the age range covers two decades and not one. This means that the frequency in the figure is not 200 as shown in the table, but 100 (200÷2 = 100). This is because in the table 200 spectators fall into the age range 60 - 79, whereas the histogram shows 100 spectators in the age range 60 - 69 and 100 in the range

70 - 79. However, the area of the last bar coincides with the data in the table, ie it is equal to 200. The total area represented by all columns is equal to the sample size of 2,200.

■ Bar charts and histograms can be used for **discrete data** - data which only occur as whole numbers, such as the number of people employed in a store. Histograms are most useful when recording **continuous data** - data which occur over a range of values, such as weight or age.

■ Histograms tend to be used for grouped data (☞ unit 14), for example the number of people between the ages of 0 and 9.

The histogram in Figure 13.7 shows that the most frequently occurring age range for spectators is 20 - 29. The information might be used by the football club to help plan a marketing strategy. It is possible to show the information in Table 13.7 by plotting a curve called a **frequency polygon**. It is drawn using the histogram and involves joining all the mid-points at the top of the 'bars' with straight lines. The frequency polygon for the data in Table 13.7 is shown in Figure 13.7. Arguably, the visual pattern of the data is shown more clearly by the frequency polygon.

Tables

Tables are used to present many forms of data. They may be used:

■ if data are qualitative rather than quantitative;
■ where a wide range of variables needs to be expressed at the same time;
■ where the numbers themselves are at the centre of attention;
■ when it is necessary to perform calculations on the basis of the information.

Some would argue that the use of tables should be avoided if possible. However, a poorly or inaccurately drawn graph would be less effective than a neatly presented table. Table 13.9 shows information about the number of outlets various DIY businesses have. The parent company of each business is also listed. This data could not be shown effectively using a graph or chart. The data are largely qualitative and there is quite a large number of entries. The table shows that Magnet have the largest number of outlets with 306. Homebase, owned by J. Sainsbury/GB-Inno BM, have the smallest number with just 50 outlets.

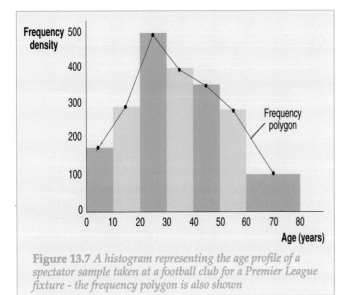

Figure 13.7 *A histogram representing the age profile of a spectator sample taken at a football club for a Premier League fixture - the frequency polygon is also shown*

QUESTION 3 Orrel Boxes Ltd produce cartons for cereal producers. The marketing manager was asked by the chairperson to supply information regarding the size of customer orders for the last month. After looking through the sales records she was able to draw up Table 13.8.

Table 13.8 *Information regarding the size of orders for Orrel Boxes Ltd*

Order size	Frequency
1,000 - 1,999	34
2,000 - 2,999	52
3,000 - 3,999	86
4,000 - 4,999	100
5,000 - 5,999	189
6,000 - 6,999	60
7,000 - 7,999	48
8,000 - 11,999	40

(a) Why would the marketing manager produce a histogram rather than a bar chart to present the data?
(b) Construct a histogram from the above information.
(c) How might a business make use of data presented in this way?

Table 13.9 *Leading DIY retailers, early 1990s*

Trading name	Company/parent	Number of Outlets
B&Q	Kingfisher	243
Homebase	J.Sainsbury/GB-Inno BM	50
Texas Homecare	)	
Sandfords	) Ladbroke Group	215
Texas Bulk DIY	)	
Manders Paint & Wallpaper	Manders (Holdings)	64
Great Mills	RMC	88
Do-it-All	WH Smith Group	114
Fads, Decor 8, Home Charm & Homestyle	) Boots (formerly Ward	106
Payless DIY	) White)	
Wickes, Builders Mate	Wickes	150
Magnet	Magnet	306
Jewson	Jewson	220
Wilko, Wilkinson Hardware	Wilkinson	85

Line graphs

LINE GRAPHS are probably the most common type of graph used by a business. A line graph shows the relationship between two variables. The values of one

QUESTION 4

Table 13.10 *Sources of management buyouts: number (per cent)*

Source	Pre-1982	1982	1983	1984	1985	1986	1987	1988	1989	1990	Total
Receivership	12.6	14.3	7.0	10.0	2.2	1.7	0.7	2.0	0.4	9.1	5.0
UK parent	59.2	62.8	66.0	63.0	61.4	59.5	51.1	52.0	55.8	46.2	57.0
Foreign parent	14.1	10.2	11.5	12.5	12.0	13.8	10.7	9.7	6.5	9.6	10.8
Family ownership	11.0	8.7	11.0	12.5	21.0	19.4	25.8	28.6	30.6	26.4	21.0
Privatisation	3.1	4.1	4.5	2.0	3.0	4.8	10.4	5.7	4.2	5.8	5.1
Going private	0.0	0.0	0.0	0.0	0.4	0.7	1.3	1.7	2.5	2.9	1.1
Total	100	100	100	100	100	100	100	100	100	100	100
Number	191	196	200	200	233	289	309	350	354	208	2,359

Source: adapted from CMBOR, an independent Research Centre founded by Touche Ross and Barclays Development Capital at the University of Nottingham.

(a) List three types of information that could be found in Table 13.10.
(b) Why might a table such as this be the best way of expressing the information?

variable are shown on the vertical axis and the values of the other variable are placed on the horizontal axis. The two variables must be related in some way. The values of the variables can be joined by straight lines or a smooth curve. If **time** is one of the variables being analysed it should always be plotted on the horizontal axis. Output is usually plotted on the horizontal axis. The main advantage of this type of graph is the way in which a reader can get an immediate picture of the relationship between the two variables. Also, it is possible to take measurements from a line graph when analysing data. It is much more difficult to do this when reading figures from a table. Quite often more than one line is shown on a line graph so that comparisons can be made.

QUESTION 5

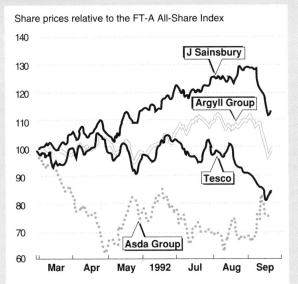

Share prices relative to the FT-A All-Share Index

Figure 13.8 *A line graph illustrating supermarket share performance*

(a) What relationships does the line graph in Figure 13.8 show?
(b) What are the advantages of illustrating the data in this way?

Cumulative frequency curves

When collecting data and recording it in a table, it is possible to show CUMULATIVE FREQUENCY. This is the total frequency up to a particular item or class boundary. It is calculated by adding the number of entries in a class to the total in the next class - a 'running total'. Table 13.11 shows the weights of cereal packages coming off a production line in a particular time period.

Table 13.11 *Cumulative frequency of package weights*

Weights falling within these ranges (grams)	Frequency	Cumulative frequency
198-199	30	30
199-200	50	80 (30 + 50)
200-201	150	230 (30 + 50 + 150)
201-202	70	300 (30 + 50 + 150 + 70)
202-203	40	340 (30 + 50 + 150 + 70 + 40)
203-204	5	345 (30 + 50 + 150 + 70 + 40 + 5)

The cumulative frequencies in the table can be plotted on a graph. The graph is called an **ogive** and is shown in Figure 13.9. It can be seen, for example, that 270 packages weigh below 201.5 grams.

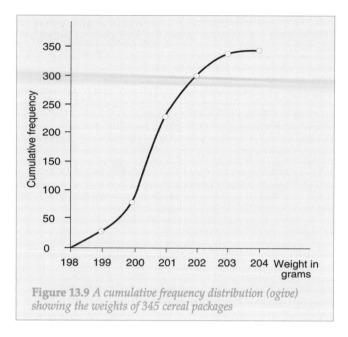

Figure 13.9 *A cumulative frequency distribution (ogive) showing the weights of 345 cereal packages*

A Lorenz curve

A LORENZ CURVE is a special type of line graph. It is a cumulative frequency curve which can be used to show the difference between actual distribution and an equal distribution. Figure 13.10 is a Lorenz curve which illustrates the way in which business is distributed between different hotels in a town. What does the curve show? If business was shared equally between all hotels then the line would be a straight 45° line. So, for example, 30 per cent of the town's hotels would get 30 per cent of all business, measured here as the number of rooms occupied. The Lorenz curve shows the actual distribution of business amongst the town's hotels. For example, 50 per cent of the town's hotels have only 10 per cent of the total hotel business. This obviously indicates a very

unequal distribution of business amongst the town's hotels. The further the Lorenz curve is drawn away from the 45° line the more unequal the actual distribution will be. A business might use this to analyse market share. The Lorenz curve is often used to show the distribution of wealth in a particular country.

Spreadsheets

Some types of numerical data can be presented effectively using a SPREADSHEET. A spreadsheet allows the user to enter, store and present data in a grid on a computer screen. Just as a word processor is able to manipulate text, spreadsheets can do the same with numerical data. The grid is made up of a number of cells. Each blank cell is able to carry information which will fall into one of three categories.
- Numeric data - these are the numbers entered by the user which will be manipulated by the program.
- Text - this refers to the words used in the spreadsheet, often headings.
- Formulae - these are the instructions given by the user which tell the computer to manipulate the numerical data, for example, add a column of entries to give a total.

An example of a spreadsheet is illustrated in Table 13.12. It contains data relating to a firm's production costs. Each column (from B to G) shows the costs of various items each month. Each row shows particular costs over the entire period. For example, row 1 shows the labour costs each month. Row 5 shows the total cost each month. The total cost is automatically calculated by the program.

Table 13.12 *An example of a spreadsheet which contains cost data*

	A	B	C	D	E	F	G
		JAN	FEB	MAR	APR	MAY	JUN
1	Labour	200	210	230	210	200	230
2	Materials	100	100	110	130	100	110
3	Fuel	35	35	35	30	30	20
4	O'heads	25	25	30	30	35	35
5	Total	360	370	405	400	365	395

In this case the formula for cell B5 would be B1 + B2 + B3 + B4. If the business changed any of the entries, the totals in row 5 would change automatically.

Some spreadsheets are much larger than the screen itself with up to 250 columns and 8,000 rows. The screen can only show part of the spreadsheet. Scrolling is used to solve this problem. This enables the user to scan over the entire spreadsheet until the section they need is shown on the screen. The advantages of spreadsheets are listed below.
- Numerical data is recorded and shown in a clear and ordered way.
- Editing allows figures, text and formulae to be changed easily to correct mistakes or make changes in the data.

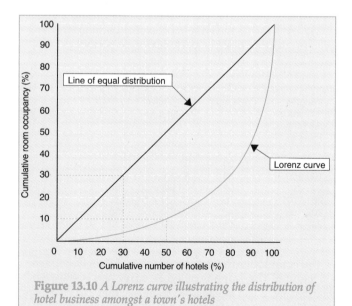

Figure 13.10 *A Lorenz curve illustrating the distribution of hotel business amongst a town's hotels*

- It is easy to copy an entry or series of entries from one part of the spreadsheet to another. This is particularly useful when one figure has to be entered at the same point in every column.
- The user can add, subtract, multiply and divide the figures entered on the spreadsheet.
- A spreadsheet can calculate the effect of entry changes easily. This is sometimes referred to as the 'what if' facility, eg what would happen to cell X (total costs) if the entry in cell A (labour costs) increased by 10 per cent? The answer can be found very quickly.
- Some spreadsheet programs allow graphs and diagrams to be drawn from figures in the spreadsheet.

One problem with spreadsheets is in printing the results. Some simple spreadsheets will tend to print everything being used. This can be time consuming and wasteful. Other programs allow the user to print specific rows, columns or cells. Some spreadsheets permit the sheet to be printed sideways to allow for a wide sheet to be printed. A further complication is what should be printed out for some of the cells, eg for a particular cell-should it be the result of a formula or the formula itself?

Databases

A DATABASE is really an electronic filing system. It allows a great deal of data to be stored. Every business which uses computers will compile and use databases. The information is set up so that it can be updated and recalled when needed. Table 13.13 shows part of a database of a finance company which gives details about their clients. The collection of common data is called a file. A file consists of a set of related records. In the database pictured in Table 13.13 all the information on Jane Brown, for example, is a record. The information on each record is listed under headings known as fields, eg name, address, age, occupation, income each year. A good database will have the the following facilities.

Table 13.13 *An extract from a simple database*

Name		Address			Age	Occupation	Income p.a
Adams	John	14	Stanley St,	Bristol	39	Bricklayer	£15,000
Appaswamy	Krishen	2	Virginia St,	Cardiff	23	Welder	£25,000
Atkins	Robert	25	Liverpool Rd,	Cardiff	42	Teacher	£21,000
Biddle	Ron	34	Bedford Rd,	Bath	58	Civil servant	£40,000
Brown	Jane	111	Bold St,	Newport	25	Solicitor	£22,000

- 'User-definable' record format, allowing the user to enter any chosen field on the record.
- File searching facility for finding specified information from a file, eg identifying all clients with an income over £24,000 in the above file. It is usually possible to search on more than one criterion, eg all females with an income over £24,000.
- File sorting facility for rearranging data in another order, eg arranging the file in Table 13.13 in ascending order of income.
- Calculations on fields within records for inclusion in reports.

In the world of business and commerce there is actually a market for information held on databases. It is possible to buy banks of information from market researchers who have compiled databases over the years. Names and addresses of potential customers would be information well worth purchasing if it were legally available. The storage of personal data on computer is subject to the Data Protection Act (☞ unit 36). Any company or institution wishing to store personal data on a computer system must register with the Data Protection Office. Individuals have a right under the Act to request details of information held on them.

Bias in presentation

Just as bias can affect the collection of data (☞ unit 9) it can also affect its presentation. When presenting profit figures to shareholders or sales figures to customers, managers will want to show the business in the best light. There is a danger that figures may be distorted in the way they are presented, in order to make performance look better than it was.

There are two main ways in which bias can occur.

- The method of presentation could exaggerate the actual rate of change shown by the data. This can be done by cutting and expanding one axis of a graph. Darrel Huff, an American statistician, called this a 'Gee-Whiz' graph. Figure 13.11 shows the same data presented in two different ways. In graph (b) the profit axis has been cut and extended. This gives a far better impression of the growth in profit than in graph (a). Similar bias can be introduced into bar charts, pie

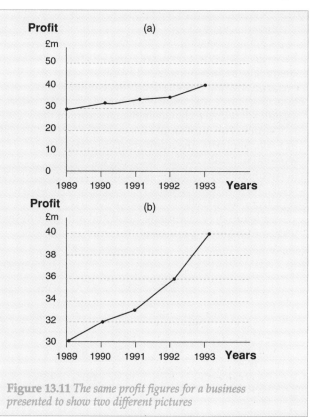

Figure 13.11 *The same profit figures for a business presented to show two different pictures*

charts and pictographs.

- A business could leave out figures that do not fit into the 'picture' it wants to portray. For example, in a presentation to customers a firm may show its sales figures have been rising over the past five years, but omit to show that the total market has been increasing at a faster rate. This, in fact, means that the market share of the business has been falling.

Summary

1. Why is it important for a business to present data clearly, accurately and attractively?
2. What are the main advantages of using bar charts?
3. What is the main disadvantage of using pictographs?
4. State 3 types of data that component bar charts can be used to illustrate.
5. What is the difference between a histogram and a bar chart?
6. Why are pie charts a popular method of data presentation?
7. What is the main disadvantage of using tables to present data?
8. State the three types of information which a cell in a spreadsheet can carry.
9. What are the main advantages of spreadsheets?
10. What are the advantages of databases for firms?

Key terms

Bar chart - a chart where numerical information is represented by blocks or bars.
Component bar chart - a chart where each bar is divided into a number of sections to illustrate the components of a total.
Cumulative frequency - the total frequency up to a particular item or class boundary.
Data - a collection of information.
Database - an organised collection of data stored electronically with instant access, searching and sorting facilities.
Histogram - a chart which measures continuous data on the horizontal axis and class frequencies on the vertical axis.
Line graph - a line which shows the relationship between two variables.
Lorenz curve - a type of cumulative frequency curve which shows the disparity between equal distribution and actual distribution.
Pictograph or pictogram - a chart where numerical data is represented by pictorial symbols.
Pie chart - a chart which consists of a circle where the data components are represented by the segments.
Spreadsheet - a method of storing data in cells in such a way that a change in one of the entries will automatically change any appropriate totals.

Question

Swift PLC

Between September 1992 and August 1993 Swift PLC, a chemicals manufacturer, underwent a radical re-organisation and automation programme. The size of the total workforce was reduced from 4,500 to 3,000. More significant was the change in the structure of the workforce. The number of factory workers fell from 3,000 to 1,000. Similarly, the numbers of administration workers fell from 700 to 500. In the marketing department employment was doubled from 500 to 1,000 whilst the finance department also enjoyed an increase in staff from 300 to 500.

As a result of this reorganisation and automation there were a number of changes in the company's fortunes.

Some of the key changes recorded on a monthly basis are illustrated in Table 13.14.

(a) **Choose appropriate charts or graphs and illustrate the changes in each of the categories of data.**
(b) **State the reasons for your choice of presentation method in each case.**
(c) **Using the methods you have chosen, explain the changes taking place and the implications for the company in the future.**
(d) **What possible problems might there be in accurately reflecting the changes taking place in methods of presentation?**

Table 13.14 *A monthly record of financial information for Swift PLC during their re-organisation and automation period*

	SEP	OCT	NOV	DEC	JAN	FEB	MAR	APR	MAY	JUN	JUL	AUG
Share price (p)	50	51	55	58	68	67	67	79	98	105	109	112
Cash bal. (£m)	-1.8	-1.9	-1.8	-1.0	-0.3	0.9	1.2	1.9	3.1	3.9	5.0	6.7
Sales (£m)	9.1	11.3	12.9	14.1	16.0	15.8	16.3	18.9	23.1	25.9	28.3	30.1
Labour costs (£m)	8.1	7.9	8.0	6.4	6.1	6.3	4.1	3.9	3.9	2.8	2.9	3.0
Labour costs (% of total)	67%	65%	66%	43%	45%	45%	28%	27%	29%	22%	24%	23%

Why analyse data?

A business can make great use of the data which it has collected about such things as costs, sales, markets and profits. Unit 13 showed that presenting the data will allow a firm to find out important information, such as the proportion of total costs accounted for by employees' wages. However, when looking at more complex problems, the data may need to be analysed in more detail. This can involve:
- finding out the most likely outcome, such as the most likely purchaser of a new product;
- forecasting what may happen in future, such as the need for extra employees;
- finding out variations, such as by how much output changes at different times of the week, day or year;
- finding out whether the quality of a product is being maintained.

Sometimes businesses can use data which has been analysed for them. Government departments produce information on factors which might influence businesses, such as the rate of inflation. Industry bodies may provide data, for example, ABTA give information on the market for tourism.

There are a variety of techniques which can be used to analyse data. This unit looks at measures of central tendency and dispersion, and the next looks at forecasting and predicting from data. While these methods can help a business to make better decisions, they must also take into account the nature of the data they are using. A certain amount of data is unreliable. It may be out of date, collected in less than a thorough way, or incomplete. Analysing this data, and making decisions based on incorrect figures, may cause problems. A firm that decides to increase its stocks because data show they are running low each week may have large quantities of unwanted goods if the data prove to be incorrect.

Central tendency

Much of the information that a business collects will be too detailed to be useful. It is necessary for this raw data to be organised into a form that decision makers can use more effectively. One method allows the business to discover the most **likely** or **common** outcome from the data. This involves calculating the CENTRAL TENDENCY from the data - usually known as the **average**.

Knowing the most likely outcome will be useful in a number of situations. A firm may be interested in:
- the level of stock ordered most often;
- the production level a department achieves most often;
- the average sales each month;
- the average number of days lost through injury.

Table 14.1 shows the amount of stock ordered by a small business over a period of time. How can the business find the average quantity of stock ordered each week? There are three ways of doing this - finding the **mean, median** or **mode.**

Table 14.1 *Amount of stock ordered by a business over a 40 week period*

6	8	10	12	8	10	8	10	14	10
10	8	10	12	10	12	12	14	12	12
8	14	10	12	12	12	10	10	12	12
6	10	14	12	8	12	8	12	10	8

Arithmetic mean The arithmetic MEAN is the figure that most think of as an average. Simply, it can be calculated by adding the value of all items and dividing by the number of items. The formula for calculating the arithmetic mean ($\overline{x}$) is:

$$\overline{x} = \frac{\text{sum of items}}{\text{number of items}}$$

The mean for the first four orders in Table 14.1 would be:

$$\overline{x} = \frac{6 + 8 + 10 + 12}{4} = \frac{36}{4} = 9$$

Working out the mean in this way for all figures is time consuming. Imagine a multinational adding up the stock needed by every department for a year!

One method used to save time and improve accuracy is to work out the frequency (f) from the figures. The frequency is the number of times an item occurs. The **frequency distribution** (☞ unit 13) for the figures in Table 14.1 is shown in Table 14.2.

Table 14.2 *Frequency distribution for stock ordered by a business over a 40 week period*

Quantity of stock ordered (x)	Frequency (f)	Quantity (x) x frequency (f)
6	2	12
8	8	64
10	12	120
12	14	168
14	4	56
	Σ f = 40	Σ f(x) = 420

where Σ = the sum of (adding up all the values).

The mean can be calculated by:
- multiplying the quantity of stocks ordered (x) by the frequency (f);
- adding up all these values and dividing by the total frequency.

The formula for calculating the mean of a frequency

distribution is:

$$\bar{x} = \frac{\Sigma fx}{\Sigma f} = \frac{420}{40} = 10.5$$

Therefore, when the business orders stock, on average it orders 10.5 units. The company might use 10.5 as its average order quantity for stock control (☞ unit 33).

The advantage of using the mean as a measure of average value is that it takes into account all data. It is also a figure which is generally accepted as representing the average. However, it can be distorted by extreme values, resulting in a figure which is untypical and which may be misleading. For example, if the stock ordered had been 6 + 8 + 10 + 12 + 69 in Table 14.2, the $\Sigma f(x)$ would have been 640 and the mean would have been 640 ÷ 40 = 16.

The median The MEDIAN is the **middle** number in a set of data. When figures are placed in order, the median would be half way. For example, the median of the figures 3, 6, 8, 10 and 12 would be 8. The median for 1, 2, 3, 4, 5, 6 would be 3.5, the half way point. If a firm had production figures of 200, 220, 240 and 260 units, the median would be half way between 220 and 240. In this case the median is found by an average of 220 and 240:

$$\frac{240 + 220}{2} = \frac{460}{2} = 230$$

Again, these are simple figures. Businesses, however, have large amounts of data and finding the median may require the use of the formula:

$$\frac{n + 1}{2} \text{ (for odd numbers) or } \frac{n}{2} \text{ (for even numbers)}$$

where n is the number of values or total frequency. In practice, with large numbers of figures, the latter formula is used.

In Table 14.2 there are 40 values. The median value would be 40 ÷ 2 = the 20th item if they were placed in order from smallest to largest, ie 6, 6, 8, 8 etc. This is orders of 10 units. You can see this from the cumulative frequency in Table 14.3. The 20th item in the cumulative frequency column must have been for an order of 10 units.

Table 14.3 *Cumulative frequency of stock ordered by a business over a 40 week period*

Quantity of stock ordered (x)	Frequency (f)	Cumulative frequency
6	2	2
8	8	10
10	12	22
12	14	36
14	4	40

The median is a useful measure of the average because, unlike the mean, it is not distorted by extreme values.

However, the problem with the median is that it ignores all data other than the middle value.

The mode This is the value that occurs most frequently. From the figures in Table 14.1, the MODE would be 12 units, as this is the order quantity which occurs most often (14 times). As with the median, the mode is unaffected by extreme values and has the added attraction of being easy to calculate. The main problem with the mode value is that it does not take account of all values and might, therefore, prove misleading when taken as a measure of the average. There might also be several modes within a set of data, which will make the measure less useful.

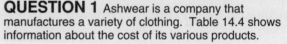

QUESTION 1 Ashwear is a company that manufactures a variety of clothing. Table 14.4 shows information about the cost of its various products.

Table 14.4

Cost of production	Number of products
£1	4
£2	12
£3	22
£4	15
£5	7
	60

(a) Calculate:
   (i)   the arithmetic mean;
   (ii) the median;
   (iii) the modal;
   cost of production.
(b) The firm is considering launching 2 new products and has estimated that they will both have a production cost of £8. Calculate the likely effect that this will have on your answers to question (a).

Grouped data

Data is often put into convenient groups, called **classes** (☞ unit 13). Table 14.5 shows the results of market research into the ages of people buying a particular firm's products. The quantity purchased by each age group (the frequency) is shown in the second column.

How does a business find the average? It is not possible to find the mode, but it is possible to find the **modal group**. This is the group with the highest frequency, in this case consumers between the ages of 30-39 (25).

To find the mean, take points at the centre of each age group, such as 24.5, which is the central point between the ages of 20 and 29. This is shown in column 3. Multiplying the frequency (f) by the central point (x) allows column 4 to be calculated. The **mean** can be found using the formula:

$$\bar{x} = \frac{\Sigma fx}{\Sigma f} = \frac{3,600}{100} = 36$$

where Σ is the sum of all values.

Table 14.5 *Market research results showing the ages of people buying a firm's products*

Ages of consumers	Quantity purchased (f)	Centre of of interval (x)	f x
0 - 9	3	4.5	13.5
10 - 19	10	14.5	145.0
20 - 29	21	24.5	514.5
30 - 39	25	34.5	862.5
40 - 49	22	44.5	979.0
50 - 59	14	54.5	763.0
60 - 69	5	64.5	322.5
	$\Sigma f = 100$		$\Sigma fx = 3,600.0$

The figure of 36 is an estimate because it has been assumed that the average age of the 10 people in the age group 10 - 19 is 14.5. In fact, it could have been more or less. This is true of all groups.

The **median** can also only be estimated. To find the median a business would need to calculate a cumulative frequency table. The information in Table 14.5 has been used to do this in Table 14.6 Part (a) shows the original table. Part (b) shows how a cumulative frequency table can be calculated. 3 goods were bought by consumers under the age of 9. 10 goods were bought by consumers aged 10-19, so 13 goods in all were bought by consumers under the age of 19. The last point is 100, showing the 100 goods bought altogether by all consumers. It is possible to draw this as a cumulative frequency polygon or **ogive** (☞ unit 13) as in Figure 14.1.

What is the median age of consumers buying the products? If there are 100 goods, the median value can be found by drawing a line at 50 to the cumulative frequency curve. This gives a median of 35.

Table 14.6 *Frequency and cumulative frequency tables*

(a)

Ages of consumers	Quantity purchased
0 - 9	3
10 - 19	10
20 - 29	21
30 - 39	25
40 - 49	22
50 - 59	14
60 - 69	5
	= 100

(b)

Ages of consumers	Cumulative frequency
10 or less	3
20 or less	13
30 or less	34
40 or less	59
50 or less	81
60 or less	95
70 or less	100

QUESTION 2 Table 14.7 shows the salary ranges of employees in a business.

Table 14.7

Salary range (£)	Number of employees
8,001 - 9,000	6
9,001 - 10,000	15
10,001 - 11,000	40
11,001 - 12,000	25
12,001 - 13,000	10
13,001 - 14,000	4
	100

(a) What is the modal salary group?
(b) Estimate the mean salary. Use approximate mid class values of 8,500, 9,500 etc.
(c) Estimate the median by drawing a cumulative frequency graph on graph paper.
(d) Why would it be important for the employee representatives at this company to calculate such average figures?

Dispersion

The previous section explained how a firm can calculate an average. The firm may also be interested in how wide the data are spread - the DISPERSION. It may be that information is widely spread or there is a narrow dispersion. If the data are widely spread, the average is likely to be distant from the rest of the data. If, however, there is a narrow spread, the average will be close to the rest of the data and more typical.

Table 14.8 *Monthly production figures*

Units

Month	Jan	Feb	Mar	Apr	May	Jun	Jul	Aug	Sep	Oct	Nov	Dec
Sales	40	46	52	54	54	52	58	56	54	56	42	36

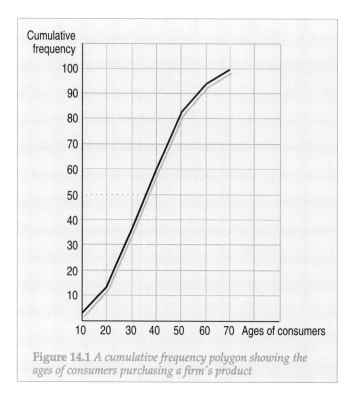

Figure 14.1 *A cumulative frequency polygon showing the ages of consumers purchasing a firm's product*

Table 14.8 shows the monthly output figures for a production plant. In order, the figures will be:

36   40   42   46   52   52   54   54   54   56   56   58

It is possible to calculate the spread in a number of ways.

Range The RANGE is the most simple method. It is the difference between the highest and the lowest value. In Table 14.8 this would be 58 - 36 = 22. The main problem with the range is that it can be distorted by extreme values. Just one rogue figure can vastly increase the value of the range out of all proportion to its size.

Interquartile range The INTERQUARTILE RANGE considers the range within the central 50 per cent of a set of data. It therefore ignores the bottom and top 25 per cent (quarter). This gives it the advantage of being far less prone to distortion by extreme values than the range.

In order to calculate the interquartile range it is necessary to arrange data with the lowest item first and the highest item last. The first quartile, which is a quarter of the way along, must then be found, followed by the third quartile, which is three-quarters of the way along. The difference between the first and the third quartiles provides the interquartile range.

Using the data in Table 14.8 it is possible to calculate the first quartile using the formula:

$$\text{First quartile (Q1)} = \frac{n}{4}$$

where n equals the number of values. The first quartile shows the value below which 25 per cent of all figures fall. So:

$$Q1 = \frac{12}{4} = 3$$

The third quartile can be calculated using the formula:

$$\text{Third quartile (Q3)} = \frac{3(n)}{4} = \frac{3 \times 12}{4} = \frac{36}{4} = 9$$

In the data the third item is 42 and the ninth is 54. So the interquartile range is 54 - 42=12. The interquartile range for these production figures is therefore narrower than the range. When dealing with large amounts of data **deciles** or **percentiles** may have to be used as they give more exact figures. Deciles are the 10, 20 etc. per cent values, whereas percentiles are the 1, 2, 3 etc. per cent values. In the production figures, the 50th per cent of the values will be 50 per cent of 12 (6), or the sixth value of 52 units of production.

Mean deviation The range and interquartile range only take into account the spread between two figures in a set of data. However, there are many figures and each will **deviate** from the mean. In business this could be for reasons such as:

- the results from market surveys varying between regions;
- sales varying on a monthly or weekly basis;
- the output from a machine varying in quality as parts begin to wear out;
- the quality of products received from different suppliers varying according to the specifications they have used.

In Table 14.8 the arithmetic mean of the production figures is:

$$\frac{600}{12} = \frac{\text{(total production over the period)}}{\text{(the number of months)}} = 50 \text{ units}$$

The deviation of each production total from the mean is shown in Table 14.9.

Table 14.9

Month	Production (x)	units Deviation $(x-\bar{x})$
Jan	40	-10
Feb	46	- 4
Mar	52	+ 2
Apr	54	+ 4
May	54	+ 4
Jun	52	+ 2
Jul	58	+ 8
Aug	56	+ 6
Sep	54	+ 4
Oct	56	+ 6
Nov	42	- 8
Dec	36	-14

$\Sigma (x) = 600$ $\Sigma (x-\bar{x}) = 72$ (ignoring signs)

The MEAN DEVIATION provides one figure, by averaging the differences of all values from the mean. It is usual to ignore the plus and minus signs and use the formula:

$$\text{Mean deviation} = \frac{\Sigma (x-\bar{x})}{n}$$

where Σ = the total of all values
$(x-\bar{x})$ = the difference between the mean and the value ignoring the sign
n = the number of values.

The mean deviation for the monthly production figures in Table 14.9 would be:

$$\frac{72}{12} = 6$$

This is the average deviation of all values from the mean. The larger the mean deviation, the wider the spread or dispersion. As a method of calculating dispersion, mean deviation has problems, notably the removal of the plus and minus signs. The next section shows two other measures of dispersion the **variance** and the **standard deviation**, which attempt to deal with this.

QUESTION 3 Table 14.10 shows the petrol consumption per annum for area sales representatives working for Quantex PLC, a producer of office equipment.

Table 14.10

Gallons per annum

Region	North West	North East	South West	South East	West Midlands	East Midlands	Wales	Scotland
Number of gallons used	1,200	1,360	1,140	1,000	1,150	1,300	1,250	2,000

(a) Calculate the mean deviation from the figures.
(b) Calculate the:
  (i) range;
  (ii) interquartile range;
  from the figures.
(c) Which of your answers to (b) do you think is of more use to the business?

The variance and the standard deviation

Both the range and the interquartile range are basic measures of dispersion. They only take into account the spread between two figures in a set of data. The mean deviation is also of limited use because of the cancelling out of positive and negative deviations. A more sophisticated measure of dispersion is needed if businesses are going to be able to gain accurate and useful conclusions from a set of raw data.

By using the VARIANCE a business can look at the average of the spread of all data from the mean. Table 14.11 shows the figures for production from Table 14.9. To remove the plus and minus figures the deviations have to be squared, rather than ignoring the signs as in the mean deviation calculation. This is shown in the fourth column of Table 14.11.

Table 14.11

Month	Production figures	Deviations from mean, $(x-\bar{x})$	Deviations squared, $(x-\bar{x})^2$
Jan	40	-10	100
Feb	46	- 4	16
Mar	52	+ 2	4
Apr	54	+ 4	16
May	54	+ 4	16
Jun	52	+ 2	4
Jul	58	+ 8	64
Aug	56	+ 6	36
Sep	54	+ 4	16
Oct	56	+ 6	36
Nov	42	- 8	64
Dec	36	-14	196
		$\Sigma(x-\bar{x})^2 =$	568

The variance can be calculated by:

$$\frac{\Sigma (x-\bar{x})^2}{n} = \frac{568}{12} = 47.333$$

The original figures were expressed in units of production, but the variance figures are expressed in units 'squared'. To return to the original units it is necessary to find the **square root** of the variance. This is known as the STANDARD DEVIATION, ie:

$$\sqrt{\frac{\Sigma (x-\bar{x})^2}{n}} = \sqrt{47.333} = 6.88$$

Using the variance and the standard deviation

It is possible to use the variance and standard deviation with far more detailed data. Say that a local council is interested in the age profile of its employees because it is considering the introduction of an early retirement policy, and it wants to calculate the likely costs of such a policy over the next few years. Table 14.12 shows how it might use the mean and the standard deviation.

■ As group data is shown in the table, the total frequency is found by multiplying the mid-point of each age class (column 2) by the frequency (column 4) and then adding these values (bottom of column 4). The mean age is then found by:

$$\frac{\Sigma f(x)}{\Sigma f} = \frac{8,365}{230} = 36.4 \text{ years}$$

■ The variance is found first by calculating how much each mid-point deviates from the mean (column 5). Next each of these values must be squared to cancel out the plus and minus signs (column 6). Finally, the frequency of these squared values can be found by multiplying column 6 by column 3 to give column 7.
■ The variance is the sum of column 7 divided by the total frequency so:

$$\frac{\Sigma f(x-\bar{x})^2}{\Sigma f} = \frac{37,673}{230} = 164$$

■ The standard deviation is:

$$\sqrt{\frac{\Sigma f(x-\bar{x})^2}{\Sigma f}} = \sqrt{164} = 12.8$$

The standard deviation is a measure of the average deviation from the arithmetic mean of a set of values. It is calculated by using the formula:

1 standard deviation equals $\sqrt{\dfrac{\Sigma f(x-\bar{x})^2}{\Sigma f}}$

Table 14.12

1 Age class	2 Age class mid-point (x)	3 Frequency (f)	4 Mid-point x frequency (fx)	5 Deviation from mean $(x-\bar{x})^2$ mean = 36.4	6 Deviations squared $(x-\bar{x})^2$	7 Frequency of deviations squared $f(x-\bar{x})^2$
16-20	18	25	450	-18.4	338.6	8,465
21-25	23	29	667	-13.4	179.6	5,208
26-30	28	32	896	- 8.4	70.6	2,259
31-35	33	36	1,188	- 3.4	11.6	418
36-40	38	27	1,026	1.6	2.6	70
41-45	43	23	989	6.6	43.6	1,003
46-50	48	18	864	11.6	134.6	2,423
51-55	53	17	901	16.6	275.6	4,685
56-60	58	13	754	21.6	466.6	6,066
61-65	63	10	630	26.6	707.6	7,076
		$\Sigma f = 230$	$\Sigma fx = 8,365$			$\Sigma f(x-\bar{x})^2 = 37,673$

Unlike the interquartile range it takes into account all items in a set of data. It is thus much less likely to be distorted by a 'rogue' piece of data within a range. In the example above of the local council, the data had a mean of 36.4 years with a standard deviation of 12.8 years. This would tell the organisation information about both the average age of its employees and the spread of ages.

The standard deviation can be used in a number of ways by a business.

- To establish whether the results of a market research survey are significant and show a difference to what was expected.
- To find out the quality of batches of products being bought (eg grain being bought by a flour mill) where it would be impossible to check all the batches.
- To check on the standards of output of a production line.
- To identify the likely range of productivity in a workforce where it would be impossible to carry out a work study of all those employed.

It is likely that a business, when carrying out these tasks, will rely on sampling information (☞ unit 9) as a basis for judging the performance of a whole population. This population might be customers, products, supplies or employees. The use of the standard deviation measure will help a business to decide if the data that they collect within a sample is a useful representation of the whole population, and if the results from the sampling data can be used as a basis for decision making. This is dealt with in the next two sections.

Probability and sampling

The reason that businesses carry out surveys and take samples is to try to reduce the risk and uncertainty that exists in every business decision. PROBABILITY is a technique that helps a business to quantify risk and it forms a basis for the analysis of sampling data.

A probability is a simple ratio between the event the business is interested in and the total number of events that could occur, ie:

$$\text{Probability (P)} = \frac{\text{Required event}}{\text{Total events}}$$

Take an example of a card drawn from a pack of 52 playing cards. The probability of drawing a 'Heart' would be:

$$P(\text{a Heart}) = \frac{13}{52} = \frac{1}{4} = 0.25$$

Similarly, for drawing a card that is from one of the other suits:

$$P(\text{a Club}) = \frac{13}{52} = \frac{1}{4} = 0.25$$

$$P(\text{a Diamond}) = \frac{13}{52} = \frac{1}{4} = 0.25$$

$$P(\text{a Spade}) = \frac{13}{52} = \frac{1}{4} = 0.25$$

There are three important laws of probability:
- The sum of the probabilities of all the possible events will equal 1. Thus the probability of drawing a Heart, a Club, a Diamond or a Spade will equal 1 (0.25 + 0.25 + 0.25 + 0.25 = 1).
- To obtain the probability of one event or another event occurring, **add** the probabilities (the addition

---

QUESTION 4 In a market research survey carried out amongst 1,000 consumers across the Midlands, Enigma Research was able to collect the information in Table 14.13 about the amount of milk that households are likely to buy in one week.

Table 14.13

Quantity of milk purchased (pints)	Frequency of response
0 - 2	5
3 - 5	18
6 - 8	55
9 - 11	137
12 - 14	269
15 - 17	271
18 - 20	149
21 - 24	62
25 - 27	22
28 - 30	12
	1,000

(a) From the figures calculate:
   (i) the mean rate of consumption per household;
   (ii) the variance in this sample;
   (iii) the standard deviation.
(b) What use might the Milk Marketing Board make of these figures?

rule). Thus the probability of drawing a Diamond or a Spade = 0.25 + 0.25 = 0.5.

■ To obtain the probability of one event and another occurring, **multiply** the probabilities (the multiplication rule). Thus the probability of drawing a Diamond and a Spade on two successive draws = 0.25 x 0.25 = 0.0625.

Two examples can be used to illustrate how probability might affect a business.

To quantify the risk associated with making a decision Say that a business has the following information about the launch of a new product.

■ Probability of gaining a high demand = 0.6, expected return £6 million.
■ Probability of gaining a medium demand = 0.2, expected return £3m
■ Probability of gaining a low demand = 0.2, expected return £1 million.

This information about the likelihood of high, medium or low demand would have been derived from market research. The likely outcome from the decision to launch the new product will be:

■ 0.6 probability of a return of £6m = 0.6 x £6m = £3.6m;
■ 0.2 probability of a return of £3m = 0.2 x £3m = £0.6m;
■ 0.2 probability of a return of £1m = 0.2 x £1m = £0.2m.

Given that these are the only three outcomes possible (the sum of the three probabilities = 1), then the average return the company can expect from the launch of such a product = £3.6m + £0.6m + £0.2m = £4.4m. If, for example, the cost to the business of launching such a product is £3m, then by the laws of probability, such a launch would be worth the risk. This use of probability is found in decision trees (☞ unit 16).

To establish the possible range of events that might occur in business situations Say an estate agency has three photocopiers in operation. The photocopiers are known to break down one day in every ten. What is the chance that all three are out of operation at once? There are a number of alternative combinations to consider.

■ All 3 copiers are working.
■ 2 copiers are working and 1 is faulty.
■ 1 copier is working and 2 are faulty.
■ All 3 copiers are faulty.

If a working copier is (w) and a faulty copier is (f), the possible combinations amongst the three machines are:

Machine	1	2	3	
	w	w	w	All 3 machines are working
	w	w	f	
	w	f	w	2 are working and 1 is faulty
	f	w	w	
	w	f	f	
	f	w	f	1 is working and 2 are faulty
	f	f	w	
	f	f	f	All 3 machines are faulty

If the probability of a working machine (p) is 0.9 then the probability of a faulty machine (q) is 0.1. It is possible to work out the probability of all these combinations.

■ All 3 machines working = 1 x 0.9 x 0.9 x 0.9 = 0.73 (or 73%).
■ 2 machines working and 1 faulty = 3 x 0.9 x 0.9 x 0.1 = 0.24 (or 24%).
■ 1 machine working and 2 faulty = 3 x 0.9 x 0.1 x 0.1 = 0.027 (or 2.7%).
■ All 3 machines are faulty = 1 x 0.1 x 0.1 x 0.1 = 0.001 (or 0.1%).

In algebraic terms the probabilities are worked out using the binomial expansion:

$$p^3 + 3p^2q + 3pq^2 + q^3 = 1$$

Thus for this business there is only a 0.001 chance (0.1 per cent) of all three machines being out of action at once. But there is a 0.24 (24 per cent) chance of at least one machine being out of action, which might be a problem for the company. Although 3 machines have been used in this example, a business might need to look at combinations involving 2, 4 or more machines. Probabilities would then be worked out using, for example:

$$p^2 + 2pq + q^2 = 1 \text{ (for 2 machines)}$$

$$p^4 + 4p^3q + 6p^2q^2 + 4pq^3 + q^4 = 1 \text{ (for 4 machines)}$$

QUESTION 5 Saunders PLC produces computer keyboards. In any batch of production they expect to produce 5 per cent which are rejected by their quality control department. The quality control department tests 4 keyboards out of each batch produced by operators in a day.

(a) What are the possible combinations of good and faulty keyboards that might occur during the testing?
(b) What is the probability that the quality control department will find:
  (i) no faulty keyboards;
  (ii) 1 faulty keyboard;
  in the batch of 4?

The normal distribution

The NORMAL DISTRIBUTION is a statistical model that will tell a business what the expected range of outcomes from a particular population will be. It is used where businesses have been carrying out large scale sampling (☞ unit 9), for example in market research or in quality control, where they want to find out what range of results to expect.

The normal distribution occurs in many different contexts. For example, if a large group of sixth form students, representing the full A level ability range, took a Business Studies examination, then the frequency distribution of their marks may resemble a normal distribution, as shown in Figure 14.2. Some students will do very well, some students will do very badly, but the majority of students will fall close to and either side of the average (mean) score.

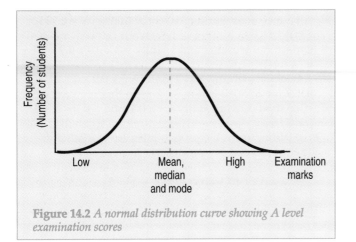

Figure 14.2 *A normal distribution curve showing A level examination scores*

The resulting curve shows all the possible outcomes (range of marks) and the frequency at which they occurred (number of students at each mark). It is 'bell-shaped' and symmetrical about the mean value.

Normal distributions will differ in their shallowness or steepness. The weights of people in a population are likely to be quite evenly spread as in Figure 14.3(a), whilst IQ scores in a population are likely to be more closely bunched around the average, with few high or low scores as in Figure 14.3(b). It is the spread of the data that

determines the curves' steepness or shallowness. This spread, as shown earlier in the unit, can be measured by the use of **standard deviations**.

Whatever the spread of the normal distribution curves, they have particular features in common.

- The curve is symmetrical about the mean.
- The mean, mode and median of the distribution is equal.
- 50 per cent of all values lie either side of the mean value.
- The curve can be divided into 3 standard deviations (SDs) either side of the mean.
  68 per cent of the population will lie between + or - 1 SD.
  96 per cent of the population will lie between + or - 2 SDs.
  99.8 per cent of the population will lie between + or - 3 SDs.

Thus nearly all results will lie within + or - 3 SDs of the mean. A small proportion (0.2 per cent) will lie outside this range, but this is so small businesses are not concerned about it in practice. The exact distribution of the range of results possible is shown in Figure 14.4. The normal distribution has a certain predictability. Therefore any results that lie outside the expected range become significant and unexpected.

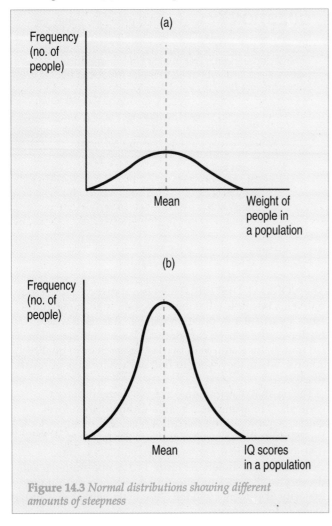

Figure 14.3 *Normal distributions showing different amounts of steepness*

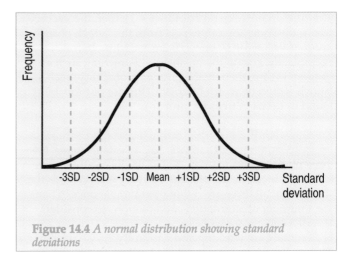

Figure 14.4 *A normal distribution showing standard deviations*

Using the normal distribution

One business context where the normal distribution can be used is in the analysis of market research data. A business might ask, 'was the result of a survey possible purely by chance or was there a significant difference between the actual result and the expected one?'

Say that a company which manufactures potato crisps has used a market research company to discover whether their new 'Sweet and Sour' flavour, which has been heavily promoted since its launch, is well known by the public. On average, the company would expect 50 per cent of those asked to recognise a flavour, but following the promotion they would expect a higher recognition. If the market research company asks 900 consumers, what results might the company expect to get to measure whether the promotion was successful?

The first stage in the use of normal distribution to answer this question involves the calculation of the expected range of results from such surveys. To do this it is necessary to calculate the mean and the standard deviation for this particular distribution.

The mean for a normal distribution can be calculated using the formula:

$$mean = n \times p$$

where n = the sample size
and   p = the probability of an event occurring.

The standard deviation for a normal distribution can be calculated using the
formula:

$$1 \text{ standard deviation (1SD)} = \sqrt{npq}$$

where n = the sample size;
        p = the probability of an event occurring;
and   q = the probability of an event not occurring.

For the market research on the 'Sweet and Sour' crisps:
    n = 900
    p = 0.5
    q = 0.5

Therefore, for such surveys as this:

$$mean = 900 \times 0.5 = 450$$

$$1SD = \sqrt{900 \times 0.5 \times 0.5} = \sqrt{225} = 15$$

The full range of results can be + or - 3SD from the mean where:

    2SD = 30
    3SD = 45

Therefore, the range for this normal curve will be:

    450 + or - 45 = 405 to 495.

The normal curve can now be drawn based on this information as in Figure 14.5.

For the company, this normal curve provides a tool to help it analyse any market research results.

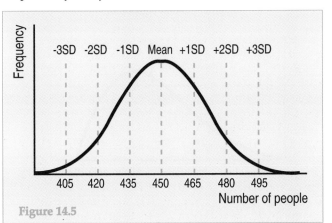

Figure 14.5

- 68 per cent of all results will show that between 435 and 465 people recognise the flavour (given a mean of 450).
- 96 per cent of all results will show that between 420 and 480 people recognise the flavour.
- 99.8 per cent of all results will show that between 405 and 495 people recognise the flavour.

Only if the market research results show more than 495 people recognising the flavour can the company be totally confident that its promotion has been effective in increasing recognition above the 50 per cent level. Suppose the actual result was 486 people recognising the product? How significant would this be? We can find this in terms of standard deviations (z) by using the formula:

$$z = \frac{x - m}{s}$$

where x = the value
m = the mean
s = the standard deviation

so:

$$z = \frac{486 - 450}{15} = \frac{36}{15} = 2.4 \text{ SDs from the mean}$$

To find out what percentage of the population lies between the mean and +2.4SDs, a normal distribution table, as in Table 14.14, can be used. This shows the areas under the standard normal distribution from the mean. Because this is a frequency distribution, the area represents the number in the population between each value.

Reading from the left hand column of the table, 49.18 per cent (or 0.4918) of the population will lie between the mean and +2.4SDs. To include all values up to and including 486 it is necessary to add this to the 0.5 or 50 per cent on the other side of the mean. This gives a total of:

$$0.5 + 0.4918 = 0.9918 \text{ or } 99 \text{ per cent}$$

This is shown as a shaded area on Figure 14.6.

The company can therefore be 99 per cent certain that a result of 486 represents an improvement over the 50 per cent average. If it wanted to be even more certain, it would need to take 3 standard deviations (rather than 2.4) into account.

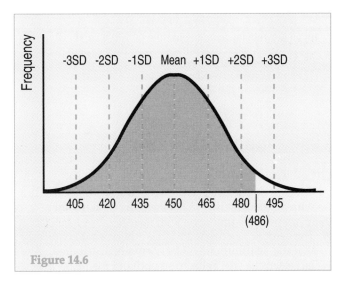

Figure 14.6

Table 14.14 *Table of standard normal curve areas*

(z)	.00	.01	.02	.03	.04	.05	.06	.07	.08	.09
0.0	.0000	.0040	.0080	.0120	.0160	.0199	.0239	.0279	.0319	.0359
0.1	.0398	.0438	.0478	.0517	.0557	.0596	.0636	.0675	.0714	.0753
0.2	.0793	.0832	.0871	.0910	.0948	.0987	.1026	.1064	.1103	.1141
0.3	.1179	.1217	.1255	.1293	.1331	.1368	.1406	.1443	.1480	.1517
0.4	.1554	.1591	.1628	.1664	.1700	.1736	.1772	.1808	.1844	.1879
0.5	.1915	.1950	.1985	.2019	.2054	.2088	.2123	.2157	.2190	.2224
0.6	.2257	.2291	.2324	.2357	.2389	.2422	.2454	.2486	.2517	.2549
0.7	.2580	.2611	.2642	.2673	.2704	.2734	.2764	.2794	.2823	.2852
0.8	.2881	.2910	.2939	.2967	.2995	.3023	.3051	.3078	.3106	.3133
0.9	.3159	.3186	.3212	.3238	.3264	.3289	.3315	.3340	.3365	.3389
1.0	.3413	.3438	.3461	.3485	.3508	.3531	.3554	.3577	.3599	.3621
1.1	.3643	.3665	.3686	.3708	.3729	.3749	.3770	.3790	.3810	.3830
1.2	.3849	.3869	.3888	.3907	.3925	.3944	.3962	.3980	.3997	.4015
1.3	.4032	.4049	.4066	.4082	.4099	.4115	.4131	.4147	.4162	.4177
1.4	.4192	.4207	.4222	.4236	.4251	.4265	.4279	.4292	.4306	.4319
1.5	.4332	.4345	.4357	.4370	.4382	.4394	.4406	.4418	.4429	.4441
1.6	.4452	.4463	.4474	.4484	.4495	.4505	.4515	.4525	.4535	.4545
1.7	.4554	.4564	.4573	.4582	.4591	.4599	.4608	.4616	.4625	.4633
1.8	.4641	.4649	.4656	.4664	.4671	.4678	.4686	.4693	.4699	.4706
1.9	.4713	.4719	.4726	.4732	.4738	.4744	.4750	.4756	.4761	.4767
2.0	.4772	.4778	.4783	.4788	.4793	.4798	.4803	.4808	.4812	.4817
2.1	.4821	.4826	.4830	.4834	.4838	.4842	.4846	.4850	.4854	.4857
2.2	.4861	.4864	.4868	.4871	.4875	.4878	.4881	.4884	.4887	.4890
2.3	.4893	.4896	.4898	.4901	.4904	.4906	.4909	.4911	.4913	.4916
2.4	.4918	.4920	.4922	.4925	.4927	.4929	.4931	.4932	.4934	.4936
2.5	.4938	.4940	.4941	.4943	.4945	.4946	.4948	.4949	.4951	.4952
2.6	.4953	.4955	.4956	.4957	.4959	.4960	.4961	.4962	.4963	.4964
2.7	.4965	.4966	.4967	.4968	.4969	.4970	.4971	.4972	.4973	.4974
2.8	.4974	.4975	.4976	.4977	.4977	.4978	.4979	.4979	.4980	.4981
2.9	.4981	.4982	.4982	.4983	.4984	.4984	.4985	.4985	.4986	.4986
3.0	.4987	.4987	.4987	.4988	.4988	.4989	.4989	.4989	.4990	.4990

QUESTION 6 Towey Ltd manufacture dresses for a large retail store, which imposes strict quality standards on their production. One example is in the sizes of the finished garments. The retail store expects the size 10-12 dresses to be of average length 160cm with a standard deviation of 0.25cm.

(a) Assuming that the production of dresses is normally distributed, what range of lengths of these dresses would be acceptable to the retailer? Show your answer on a sketch of a normal curve.

(b) If the retailer tested a sample of 100 size 10-12 dresses, what percentage would they expect to be:
   (i)   above 160.75cm;
   (ii)   between 160 and 160.4cm;
   (iii) below 159.6cm?

Limitations of the normal distribution

As with all models used in business decision making, there are possible problems with its use.

■ The sample size has to be large otherwise it is unlikely that the distribution will be normally distributed. A large sample size helps to smooth out the peaks and troughs in smaller frequency distributions.

■ The calculation of the mean and the standard deviation are based on probability figures that themselves might be based upon estimates rather than exact figures. In the example of market research, the 0.5 probability used to calculate the likely response to the market research on crisps was an estimate based upon previous experience.

■ Especially in the area of quality control, a 'one-off' reading which is a long way from the expected mean may not be sufficient to reject a batch or shut down a machine. Further sampling would be important to confirm the evidence of the first sample before costs are incurred by the business.

■ Not all large distributions will resemble the normal distribution. The distribution might be skewed and therefore not symmetrical about the mean. Figure 14.7(a) shows a positively skewed frequency distribution, which might represent the distribution of teachers' salaries in a school or college. In a positively skewed distribution, the mode will have a lower value than the median, which will have a lower value than the mean. Figure 14.7(b) shows a negatively skewed frequency distribution, which might represent the number of people per day attending a successful cinema over a period of time. In a negatively skewed distribution, the mode will have a higher value than the median, which will have a higher value than the mean. Normal distribution analysis could not be used with such skewed distributions.

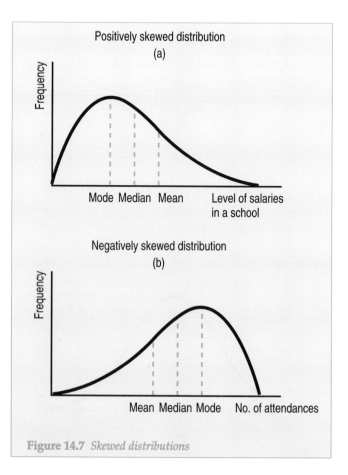

Figure 14.7 *Skewed distributions*

Summary

1. Why might businesses need to analyse data?
2. What are the differences between the mean, median and mode as measures of central tendency?
3. How is the mean of grouped data calculated?
4. List 5 measures of dispersion that might be used in analysing data.
5. Explain 2 possible uses in business of the standard deviation.
6. What does probability measure?
7. Why is the normal distribution a useful tool for businesses to use in analysing data?
8. What are the distinguishing features of a normal curve?
9. What is the difference between a normal distribution and a skewed distribution?

Key terms

Central tendency - a measure of the most likely or common result from a set of data (the average).
Dispersion - a measure of the spread of data.
Interquartile range - the range between the central 50 per cent of a set of data.
Mean - the value in a set of data around which all other values cluster; commonly used in business as the average of a set of data.
Mean deviation - the average deviation of all figures from the mean, which ignores plus and minus signs in its calculation.
Median - the value which occurs in the middle of a set of data when the data is placed in rank order.
Mode - the most commonly occurring item in a set of data.
Normal curve - a graphical representation of the normal distribution.
Normal distribution - a naturally occurring frequency distribution where many of the values cluster around the mean, but where there are a few high and low values away from the mean.
Probability - a quantification of the likelihood of an event occurring.
Range - the difference between the highest and lowest values in a set of data.
Standard deviation - the average deviation from the arithmetic mean of a set of data (accounting for plus and minus signs in the calculation) found by the square root of the variance.
Variance - the average deviation of all figures from the mean, which removes plus and minus signs by 'squaring' the deviation figures.

Question

Sarne Co.

The management of Sarne Co, a manufacturer of machinery for the textile industry, has set an objective of improving productivity on the assembly line.
A group of work study consultants were employed to analyse existing work methods on the production line and devise new ways of organising the production line. As well as carrying out discussions with the workforce and the production controllers, the consultants also studied the output of a random sample of 100 workers in order to establish their productivity before any changes. The results were as shown in Table 14.15(column a).

Two months later, following a substantial reorganisation both of the layout of machinery and the way the workforce carried out their jobs, the consultants returned to measure the output of another random sample of 100 workers. The results after the reorganisation were as shown in Table 14.15(column b).

(a) **Explain how the work study consultants might have chosen their random sample of workers.**
(b) **Calculate the mean and the standard deviation of output for this sample of workers before and after the reorganisation.**
(c) **Based upon this evidence, was the reorganisation a success? Explain your answer.**
(d) **What other factors would the management of Sarne Co need to take into account before deciding if the reorganisation is a success?**

Table 14.15

Products produced per hour	Number of workers producing these products	
	(a)	(b)
21 - 30	3	0
31 - 40	18	12
41 - 50	36	30
51 - 60	25	30
61 - 70	10	12
71 - 80	8	10
81 - 90	0	6

Forecasting

Unit 14 explained the methods a business might use to find the most **likely** or **average** result. This is based on past information that has been recorded. Businesses are also keen to know about what might happen in the future. Anything they can predict accurately will reduce their uncertainty and will allow them to plan. Predictions, of course, are based on current information, so the accuracy of these predictions will depend on the reliability of current data.

What would a firm like to predict with accuracy? Some examples might include:
- future sales of products;
- cash flow in the next year;
- changes in the cost of labour or machinery;
- economic or demographic changes.

A variety of techniques can be used to predict future results. One of the most popular is **time series analysis**, which is discussed in the next section.

Time series analysis

TIMES SERIES ANALYSIS involves predicting future levels from past data. The data used is known as **time series data** - a set of figures arranged in order, based on the time they occurred. So, for example, a firm may predict future sales by analysing sales data over the last 10 years. The firm, of course, is assuming that past figures are a useful indicator of what will happen in the future. This is likely to be the case if trading conditions are **stable** or if the firm needs to forecast trends in the short term. Time series analysis does not try to explain data, only to describe what is happening to it or predict what will happen to it.

There are likely to be four components that a business wants to identify in time series data.
- **The trend**. 'Raw' data can have many different figures. It may not be easy to see exactly what is happening from these figures and so a business often tries to identify a trend. For example, there may be a trend for a business to hold more and more stocks of goods to take into account fluctuations in the market.
- **Cyclical fluctuations**. For many businesses there may be a cycle of 'highs and lows' in their figures, particularly in sales figures, which rise over a number of years and then fall again. It is argued that these are a result of the recession-boom-recession of the trade cycle in the economy (☞ unit 67). In a recession, for example, people have less money to spend and so the turnover of a firm may fall in that period.
- **Seasonal fluctuations**. Over a year a firm is unlikely to have a constant level of sales, stock, costs etc. The seasonal variations are very important to a business such as a travel agent or a 'card' producer, where there

may be large sales at some times but not at others. A farmer may also have a seasonal demand for labour and so wage costs will vary at different times of the year.
- **Random fluctuations**. At times there will be 'freak' figures which stand out from any trend that is taking place. An example may be the sudden boost in sales of umbrellas in unusually wet summer months or increased costs due to the failure of an important machine.

Identifying the trend

An analysis of figures will tell a firm whether there is an upward, downward or constant trend. Identifying the trend allows the business to predict what is likely to happen in future. The first step is to smooth out the raw data. Take an example of a toy manufacturer, whose yearly sales over the past 10 years are shown in Table 15.1.

Table 15.1 *Yearly sales of a toy manufacturer (£000)*

1983	1984	1985	1986	1987	1988	1989	1990	1991	1992
300	500	600	550	600	750	850	900	1,000	1,100

It is possible to calculate a trend by using a MOVING AVERAGE. The average can be taken for any **period** the business wants, such as a year, a month or a quarter. For now we will assume the toy manufacturer uses a 3 year average. The average of sales in the first 3 years was:

$$\frac{300 + 500 + 600}{3} = \frac{1,400}{3} = 466.7$$

The first year's sales 'drop out' and the next year's sales are added to give a moving average. The average for the next three years was:

$$\frac{500 + 600 + 550}{3} = \frac{1,650}{3} = 550$$

If the business continues to do this, the results will be as shown in Table 15.2. Notice that the moving average is placed at the centre of the 3 years (ie the average for 1983-1985 is plotted next to 1984).

Table 15.2 *3 year moving average for sales of a toy manufacturer (£000)*

1983	1984	1985	1986	1987	1988	1989	1990	1991	1992
300	500	600	550	600	750	850	900	1,000	1,100
		466.7	550	583.3	633.3	733.3	833.3	916.7	1,000

What if the firm had used a 4 year period instead of 3 years? No one year is the centre point and simply placing the figure in between two years may result in misleading predictions in future. The solution is to use CENTRING. This uses a 4 and 8 year moving **total** to find a mid point. So, for example, in Table 15.1:

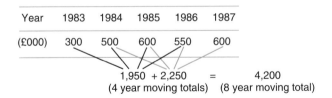

Year	1983	1984	1985	1986	1987
(£000)	300	500	600	550	600

1,950 + 2,250 = 4,200
(4 year moving totals) (8 year moving total)

This can then be used to find the mid-point, which is 1985. The trend or moving average can be found by dividing the 8 year moving total by 8, the number of years, as shown in Table 15.3.

Table 15.3 *Calculating a 4 year moving average for a toy manufacturer*

£000

Year	Sales	4 year moving total	8 year moving total	Trend (4 year moving average = 8 year moving total ÷ 8)
1983	300			
1984	500	1,950		
1985	600		4,200	525
1986	550	2,250	4,750	593.75
1987	600	2,500	5,250	656.25
1988	750	2,750	6,050	756.25
1989	850	3,300	6,800	850
1990	1,100	3,500	7,350	918.75
1991	800	3,850		
1992	1,100			

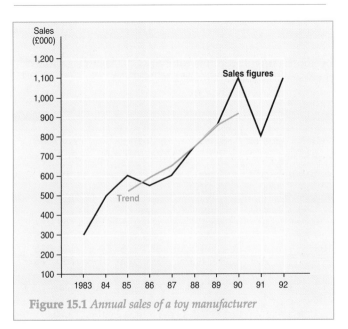

Figure 15.1 *Annual sales of a toy manufacturer*

Plotting the moving average figures onto a graph (as shown in Figure 15.1) shows the trends in the figures. It is clear to see that sales appear to be generally rising over the period. The trend line is 'smoother' than the line showing the actual sales figures. It eliminates any fluctuations in sales each year and gives a more obvious picture of the trend that has been taking place.

QUESTION 1 A business has recently gathered data on its sales revenue as shown in Table 15.4, and wants to calculate a 3 and 4 period moving average.

Table 15.4 *Sales revenue*

(£000)

Period	1	2	3	4	5	6	7	8	9	10
Sales revenue	100	130	160	175	180	190	190	180	220	250
3 period moving average			130	155						
4 period moving average			151.3							

(a) Calculate the 3 and 4 period moving averages for as many years as you can to complete the table.
(b) Plot the sales figures and both trend lines onto a graph on graph paper.
(c) Comment on the relationship between the trend and the actual sales revenue figures.

Predicting from the trend

Having identified a trend that is taking place the business can now predict what may happen in future. Figure 15.2 shows the trend data from Figure 15.1, but with a line drawn to predict the likely sales in 1993. The graph shows that sales of the toy manufacturer's goods may reach about £1,160,000.

The business has made certain assumptions when predicting this figure.

■ The broken line showing the prediction is extended from a line drawn through the trend figures. This is the LINE OF BEST FIT. It is the best line that can be drawn which matches the general slope of all points in the trend. The line is an average, where points in the trend on one side of the line are balanced with those on the other. In other words, it is a line which best fits **all** points in the trend.

■ No other factors are likely to change and affect the trend in 1993.

However, this is not likely to be an accurate prediction because it is taken from the trend, and the trend 'smoothed out' variations in sales figures. To make an accurate prediction, the business will have to find the average variation over the period and take this into account.

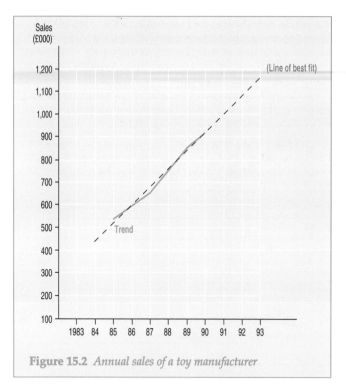

Figure 15.2 *Annual sales of a toy manufacturer*

We can find how much **variation** there is from the trend by calculating:

Actual sales - trend.

So, for example, the **cyclical** variation in Table 15.3 would be as shown in Table 15.5

Table 15.5

(£000)

Year	Sales	Trend (4 year moving average)	Variation in each year
1983	300		
1984	500		
1985	600	525	+75
1986	550	593.75	-43.75
1987	600	656.25	-56.25
1988	750	756.25	- 6.25
1989	850	850	-
1990	1,100	918.75	+181.25
1991	800		
1992	1,100		

The average of the variations over the period 1985-1990 is (in £000):

$$\frac{+75 - 43.75 - 56.25 - 6.25 +/-0 +181.25}{6} = \frac{+150}{6} = +25 \text{ (or + £25,000)}$$

If the predicted value based on the trend was £1,160,000, then adding £25,000 may give a more accurate predicted figure of £1,185,000.

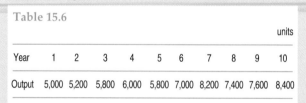

QUESTION 2 Table 15.6 shows the yearly production figures of a furniture manufacturer over a period of 10 years.

Table 15.6

units

Year	1	2	3	4	5	6	7	8	9	10
Output	5,000	5,200	5,800	6,000	5,800	7,000	8,200	7,400	7,600	8,400

(a) Calculate a four yearly moving average from the figures to show the trend taking place.
(b) Plot the trend onto a graph on graph paper and predict the likely output in year 11, stating your assumptions.
(c) Calculate:
   (i) the cyclical variation for each year;
   (ii) the average cyclical variation over the period.
(d) Explain how the average variation will give a more accurate figure, using your answers to (a)-(c).

Seasonal variations

Earlier it was stated that a business may be interested in variations in any one year. It is possible to predict from a trend and use **seasonal** variations to make a more accurate prediction. Table 15.7 shows sales of a business over a 3 year period, including sales in each quarter. A 4 quarter moving average has been calculated and also the variation in each quarter.

Carrying on the trend to predict the sales for the fourth quarter of 1992 might give a figure of £470,000. (It would be possible to find this by drawing and extending a line of best fit through the trend.) As we know, this is a 'smoothed out' figure. A more accurate prediction might be to calculate the **average seasonal variation** in the fourth quarter, for example (in £000):

$$\frac{-97.125 - 117.5}{2} = \frac{-214.625}{2} = -107.313$$

by subtracting it from the total of £470,000, this gives a more accurate prediction of £362,687.

Table 15.7

(£000)

Year	Quarter	Sales	4 quarter moving average	Variation
1989	3	460		
	4	218		
1990	1	205	328.5	-123.5
	2	388	346	+42
	3	546	358.25	+187.75
	4	272	369.125	- 97.125
1991	1	249	383.625	-134.625
	2	431	396.625	+34.375
	3	619	404	+215
	4	303	420.5	-117.5
1992	1	277		
	2	535		

Other methods of forecasting

There are two other methods of forecasting that are sometimes used.

Causal modelling Time series analysis only describes what is happening to information. Causal modelling tries to explain data, usually by finding a link between one set of data and another. A business, for example, may want to find a link between the rewards paid to workers and their productivity. Figure 15.3 shows various results that could have been found in a business. Once the results are plotted, the line of best fit can be found, which is the line that best represents the data. In Figure 15.3 the line shows that, generally, as bonuses increase the productivity of workers rises. This could help the firm to predict the effects on output of any increase in rewards in the future.

A business must be careful when making predictions from such data. The increase in production may have been the result of factors other than increased bonus payments, such as more efficient machinery.

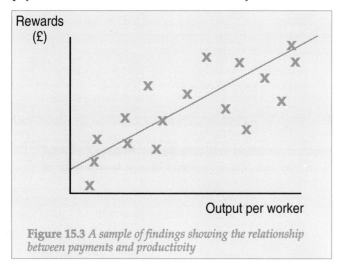

Figure 15.3 *A sample of findings showing the relationship between payments and productivity*

Qualitative forecasting Qualitative forecasting uses people's opinions or judgements rather than numerical data. A business could base its predictions on the views of so-called experts, or on the opinions of experienced managers in the marketing or production department. Such methods are usually used by firms:
■ where there is insufficient numerical data;
■ where figures date quickly because the market is changing rapidly.

Index numbers

When faced with large amounts of data, it may be difficult for firms to see exactly what is happening. Also figures are often for very large amounts and are measured in different values. This makes interpretation and comparison a problem.

One method to help a business analyse and interpret data is the use of INDEX NUMBERS. Table 15.8 shows the production figures and unit costs for a company manufacturing small components. It is not easy to immediately see the changes in production or costs from the data. Changing these figures into index numbers will make them easier to interpret.

The first stage in working out an index is to decide on a BASE YEAR. This is given a value of 100 and acts as the base from which all other figures in the index can be compared. In the example, 1988 is taken as the base year and has a value of 100 in the index. Next, all other figures must be changed into index figures based upon the base year.

Table 15.8 *Production levels and unit costs of a small component manufacturer*

Year	1988	1989	1990	1991	1992	1993
Production levels (units)	25,000	24,350	25,500	26,300	26,950	25,950
Unit costs (£)	1.23	1.25	1.24	1.27	1.30	1.31

For production levels in 1989, this is:

$$\frac{\text{Number produced in 1989}}{\text{Number produced in 1988}} \times 100 = \frac{24{,}350}{25{,}000} \times 100 = 97.4$$

In 1990, it would be:

$$\frac{\text{Number produced in 1990}}{\text{Number produced in 1988}} \times 100 = \frac{25{,}500}{25{,}000} \times 100 = 102$$

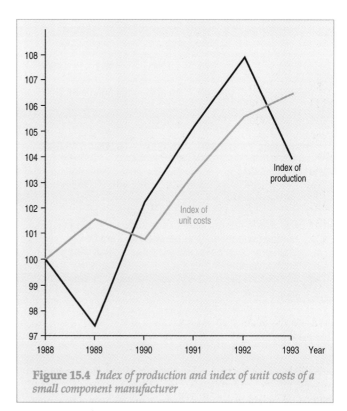

Figure 15.4 *Index of production and index of unit costs of a small component manufacturer*

A similar process would be carried out for the material costs. The results are shown in Table 15.9 and Figure 15.4.

Table 15.9 *Index numbers for production levels and unit costs of a small component manufacturer*

Year	1988	1989	1990	1991	1992	1993
Production levels	100	97.4	102	105.2	107.8	103.8
Unit costs	100	101.6	100.8	103.3	105.7	106.5

It is now easier for the firm to analyse this data. The firm could use the results in a number of ways.
■ To identify trends and forecasts.
■ The percentage increase in production or costs can be calculated. For example, between 1988 and 1993, the index of unit costs rose from 100 to 106.5 or 6.5 per cent.
■ To compare figures that are measured in different values. The production levels of the business are measured in units and costs are expressed in money values. It is possible to compare the trends in both on the same graph. This is particularly useful for the business. Between 1992-93, for example, production had started to fall whereas material costs were continuing to rise, although not at as great a rate.
■ Presenting the data in a clear and easy way for shareholders or managers.

QUESTION 3 A manufacturing company in the South East employs 100 workers. It has become concerned at the levels of pay settlement over recent years. Table 15.10 shows the average level of wages for some groups in the business.

Table 15.10

				£
	1990	1991	1992	1993
Managers	25,000	30,000	32,000	35,000
Administration	10,000	10,500	11,000	12,000
Production	12,000	15,000	16,800	18,000

(a) Using 1990 as a base year, calculate the index for each category.
(b) If 15 per cent of workers are employed as managers, 25 per cent in administration, 55 per cent in production (the other 5 per cent being cleaners etc.), calculate the total cost in 1993 of each category.
(c) How could the business use the index in future pay bargaining?

Problems of index numbers

A business will need to take care when producing its index.
■ Updating the base year. From time to time a business will need to change its base year which will affect index figures in the years that follow. After a number of years the firm will no longer be interested in comparing this year's figures with those of, say, 10 years ago (the base year). It will want to compare this year's figures with a more recent base year. So for example, in Table 15.8 if the base year was 1991 instead of 1988, the index of production in 1992 and 1993 would be:

1992 $\dfrac{26{,}950}{26{,}300} \times 100 = 102.5$

and 1993 $\dfrac{25{,}950}{26{,}300} \times 100 = 98.7$

■ Choice of base year. A firm must be careful to choose a base year which is representative. If a year is chosen where costs, prices or output are high, then index figures in later years will be lower than if a more appropriate year was picked. A base year where figures were low will inflate index numbers in following years.
■ Nothing has been said so far about the importance of different items that make up an index. A firm's unit costs would be made up of many different items. This is dealt with in the next section.

A weighted index

A more accurate index would take into account that changes in some items are more important than others. The costs of a firm may be made up of labour, capital, electricity, etc. The firm might be able to construct an index showing how costs change over a period. However, if it spends more on, say, machinery than labour, then the figures for spending on capital must be WEIGHTED.

Table 15.11 shows a firm which spends different amounts on various costs of production over a period. Using year X as the base year, the index of **total** costs is calculated by:

$$\frac{\text{Year Y index}}{n \ \text{items}} = \frac{424}{4} = 106 \text{ or 6 per cent}$$

where n = total amount.

Table 15.11

				£ per annum
	Year X	Year Y	Year X index	Year Y index ([Costs in Year X÷ costs in Year Y] x100)
Wage costs	100,000	103,000	100	103
Rent/rates	50,000	55,000	100	110
Materials	250,000	260,000	100	104
Production costs	100,000	107,000	100	107
Total costs	500,000	525,000	400 ÷ 4 = 100	424 ÷ 4 =106

This says nothing, however, about the weightings of the different costs. Looking at Table 15.11, it is possible to work out the proportion of spending on each item in year X.

Total wage cost = 20 per cent (100,000 ÷ 500,000) x 100
Rent/rates   = 10 per cent
Materials   = 50 per cent
Production costs = 20 per cent

A firm can now calculate a weighted index using these figures. This is shown in Table 15.12. The index in year Y is multiplied by the weighting, so the weighted index of, say, total wage costs is 103 x 20 per cent = 20.6.

Table 15.12

	Weighting	Year Y index	Weighted Year Y index (weighting x Year Y index)
Total wage costs	20%	103	20.6
Rates/rent	10%	110	11.0
Materials	50%	104	52.0
Production costs	20%	107	21.4
			105.0

The weighted index is now 105. When the percentage spent on each item is taken into account the increase in prices is 5 per cent rather than 6 per cent, as shown in Table 15.11.

A weighted index over time

The example so far has only dealt with an index over two years. Table 15.13 shows calculations for another 2 years based on changes in the index numbers. The proportion spent on each item is assumed to remain the same. This is known as the **base year** or **Laspeyre** method of calculation.

Table 15.13

	Year X Index	Year Y Index	Year Z Index	Year A Index
Total wage costs	100	103 x 20% = 20.6	105 x 20% = 21	106 x 20% = 21.2
Rent/rates	100	110 x 10% = 11	110 x 10% = 11	108 x 10% = 10.8
Materials	100	104 x 50% = 52	106 x 50% = 53	110 x 50% = 55
Production costs	100	107 x 20% = 21.4	110 x 20% = 22	115 x 20% = 23
Weighted index	100	105.0	107	110.0

It is also possible to recalculate the index each year based on the weightings in the current year. This is known as the **Paasche** method and can be useful if weightings change frequently. In Table 15.13 the weighting in year A (the most recent year) may have been:

Total wage costs   = 15 per cent
Rent/rates   = 10 per cent
Materials   = 45 per cent
Production costs   = 30 per cent

The index numbers for each year would have been multiplied by the current percentages and not the weightings for the base year. So in year A the weighted index using the Paasche method would be:

Total wage costs   106 x 15% = 15.9
Rent/rates   108 x 10% = 10.8
Materials   110 x 45% = 49.5
Production costs   115 x 30% = 34.5
                                 _____
                                 110.7

Firms can use weighted indexes in a number of ways, especially where there are a number of items which they wish to include in an index. For example, a firm which sells five products and wishes to construct a single index to show its changes in sales over the last ten years may consider using one. Products with high sales levels could be given a higher weighting than those with low sales levels. In this way, a weighted index would more accurately reflect overall changes in sales.

Probably the best known index in the UK is the Retail Price Index (RPI). This measures the rate of inflation by finding out how the average household spends its money and monitoring any falls or rises in the prices of those goods and services. The RPI is an example of a **weighted index** as it gives greater importance to some items than to others. For example, a rise in the price of petrol is given a higher weighting than a rise in the price of soap. A change in the price of a product with a high weighting will consequently have a relatively greater impact upon the index than a similar change in the price of a product with a low weighting.

QUESTION 4 Table 15.14 shows the expenditure by a bicycle manufacturer over a 3 year period.

Table 15.14

	£000		
	Year 1	Year 2	Year 3
Wages	150	180	195
Rent	90	90	99
Materials	90	91.8	93.6
Admin	50	60	70
Production costs	120	120	126
	500		

(a) Calculate the weightings for each cost item based upon the Year 1 expenditure figures.
(b) Using the base year method, calculate a weighted index for each of the following years.
(c) What are the advantages of presenting the data to the business as a weighted index?

Key terms

Base year - a period, such as a year, a month or a quarter, which other figures are compared to. It is given a value of 100 in the index.
Centring - a method used in the calculation of a moving average where the average is plotted or calculated in relation to the central figure.
Index number - an indicator of a change in a series of figures where one figure is given a value of 100 and others are adjusted in proportion to it. It is often used as an average of a number of figures.
Line of best fit - a line plotted through a series of prints which balances those on one side with those on the other, and best represents the slope of the points.
Moving average - a method used to find trends in data by smoothing out fluctuations. It involves calculating an average for a number of periods, then dropping the first figure and adding the next to calculate the average that follows.
Time series analysis - a method which allows a business to predict future levels from past figures.
Weighting - a process which adjusts an index number to take into account the relative importance of a variable.

Summary

1. Why might a business want to predict the future?
2. What are the four components of time series data that a business might be interested in?
3. What does a trend show?
4. How might a business use the calculation of a trend?
5. What is meant by causal modelling?
6. Why might a business use index numbers rather than actual figures?
7. State three uses that a business might have for index numbers.
8. Why might weighted index numbers be more useful than a simple index?
9. Explain the difference between the Laspeyre and Paasche methods of calculating a weighted index.
10. What does the Retail Price Index show?

Question

Shell Wrap Ltd

Shell Wrap Ltd is a UK based company that manufactures cling film wrapping. In the late 1980s the company experienced a rapid increase in sales and turnover as more companies found a use for the materials. In particular, orders came from food producers and confectioners. The company expanded as a result, taking on more workers and investing in equipment. Table 15.15 shows the index of costs over the period.

(a) Using a 4 quarter moving average, calculate the trend from the figures in Table 15.15 that the business might have found.
(b) Explain why centring might be used by the business when calculating the trend in (a).
(c) Calculate:
   (i) the seasonal variation for as many quarters as you can;
   (ii) the average seasonal variation for the fourth quarter.
(d) Plot the trend onto a graph and, using your answer to (c ii), predict the likely index of costs in the fourth quarter of 1990, stating any assumptions you have made.
(e) Why might Shell Wrap Ltd have used index numbers instead of actual cost figures to represent the cost data?

Table 15.15 *Index of costs for Shell Wrap Ltd*

Year	Quarter	Index
1987	3	115
	4	101
1988	1	112
	2	80
	3	105
	4	130
1989	1	115
	2	90
	3	105
	4	140
1990	1	125
	2	105

(f) Assume that the index for Shell Wrap is a weighted index. Choose any quarter and briefly explain how the business might have calculated the index figure.

Operational research

Businesses constantly make decisions. The production department may have to find the cheapest way to carry out a task. The marketing department may have to choose between two advertising campaigns. Unit 7 explained the steps involved in decision making. Businesses can use a number of **quantitative techniques** to help them make decisions and to solve problems that arise. These OPERATIONAL RESEARCH (OR) methods were developed by American scientists in the 1960s. They were based on problem solving methods used in Second World War operations, such as the most effective way to destroy submarines. OR methods use models (or simplified real world situations) to investigate solutions to the problems businesses may face. However, such models are only aids to decision making - the decision itself will still need to be taken and might involve other quantitative and qualitative data which is not included in the model. The types of decision where such models might be used include the following.

■ Where should a new plant be sited?
■ In what order should a new product be assembled?
■ Which method of distribution has the cheapest transport costs?
■ How should resources be allocated in production?
■ How should the launch of a new product be organised?
■ How can customer waiting time be reduced in busy retail outlets?
■ How can a building project be timetabled?

This unit deals with linear programming and decision trees while the next looks at network and cost-benefit analysis, and simulation.

Blending

BLENDING is a technique which shows a firm how 'best' to allocate its resources, given a number of constraints. Firms usually aim to allocate resources in a profitable and cost effective way. Blending is one example of LINEAR PROGRAMMING. This method sets out a business problem as a series of linear or mathematical expressions. A linear expression is an equation which links two variables such that their behaviour, if plotted on a graph, would be represented by a straight line. These expressions are then used to find the **optimal** or best solution. How can firms use blending? It may be used when they are making decisions about production. Take, for example, a firm producing two products, denim jeans and denim jackets with a number of constraints:

■ the same resources are used for each product;
■ the three main operations in their manufacture are cutting, sewing and studding;
■ the time taken for each operation is shown in Table 16.1;

Table 16.1

	Cutting	Sewing	Studding
			Minutes
Jeans (jn)	3	2	1
Jackets (jk)	1	2	2

■ in a working day there are 900 minutes of cutting time, 800 minutes of sewing time and 700 minutes of studding time;
■ the denim used in jeans costs £5 and in jackets £8;
■ jeans sell at £7 per pair and jackets at £11 each.

The firm has to decide what combination of jackets and jeans should be produced to maximise profits, given these constraints.

The cutting constraint The first step when using this technique is to show the information on constraints as a set of **inequalities** where ≤ means less than or equal to and ≥ means greater than or equal to. The firm knows that the amount of cutting time needed for jeans is three minutes and for jackets one minute. So the total cutting time is:

$$3jn + 1jk$$

There is also a constraint. The amount of cutting time must be no more than 900 minutes. So:

$$3jn + 1jk \leq 900$$

We can show this on a graph. If the firm used **all** its time for cutting to make jeans (and no jackets were made), it could make:

$$\frac{900 \text{ minutes}}{3 \text{ minutes}} = 300 \text{ jeans}$$

If all the time was used to make jackets (and no jeans were made), it could produce:

$$\frac{900 \text{ minutes}}{1 \text{ minute}} = 900 \text{ jackets}$$

The cutting constraint is shown in Figure 16.1. The line shows combinations of jeans and jackets that could be cut if all available cutting time is used. So, for example, the firm could make 300 jackets and 200 pairs of jeans. The area inside the line is called the **feasible region**. It shows all combinations of jackets and jeans that could be cut in the time available, ie when 3jn + 1jk ≤ 900.

Sewing and studding constraints The time available for sewing is 800 minutes. Sewing jeans and jackets takes

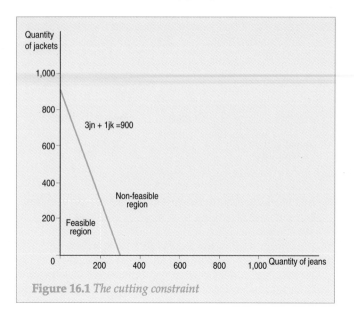

Figure 16.1 *The cutting constraint*

2 minutes each. So:

$$2jn + 2jk \leq 800$$

Similarly, the constraint for studding is 700 minutes. Studding jeans takes 1 minute and jackets 2 minutes. So:

$$1jn + 2jk \leq 700$$

Again we can illustrate these lines on a graph. If all sewing time available was used on jeans or on jackets, the firm could make 400 jeans **or** 400 jackets. If all the time available for studding was used on jeans **or** jackets the firm could make 700 jeans **or** 350 jackets. These two lines are added to the other constraint and are shown in Figure 16.2. All constraints are now illustrated on the graph. The shaded area represents the feasible region taking all these constraints into account. This shows all the combinations of jeans and jackets that **could** be made.

Deciding on a solution How will a firm allocate its resources to maximise profits? This depends on the profit level a firm chooses. The firm knows that the profit made from the sale of a pair of jeans is £7 - £5 = £2. From the sale of a jacket it is £11 - £8 = £3. So the total profit from both is:

$$2jn + 3jk$$

This line can be plotted on the graph. Say that the firm wants to make a profit of £300. This could be gained if the firm produced 150 pairs of jeans and no jackets:

$$£300 = (150 \times 2) + (0 \times 3)$$

or no jeans and 100 jackets:

$$£300 = (0 \times 2) + (100 \times 3)$$

This profit line is shown in Figure 16.3 (which shows the feasible region PQRS of Figure 16.2). A higher level of profit can be shown by moving the line parallel and to the right, eg £600. The optimal or best solution for the firm is at Q. If the profit line is moved away from the origin, this is the last point in the feasible region that the profit line would touch. The firm would produce 300 jackets and 100 pairs of jeans. The profit would be £1,100 (300 x £3 + 100 x £2). There is no other combination of jackets and jeans in the feasible region that will earn more profit. Profit will always be maximised on the edge of the feasible region.

Blending can be very useful when firms are deciding how to make best use of their resources. Businesses might use this method to allocate factors of production between different products so that profits are maximised or costs minimised. However, it does have problems. It is a production technique which does not take the demand for products into account. The example used here only uses two products. In practice, firms produce many different products. The **Simplex Method** is used to cope with this, but requires detailed calculations and the use of computers by business.

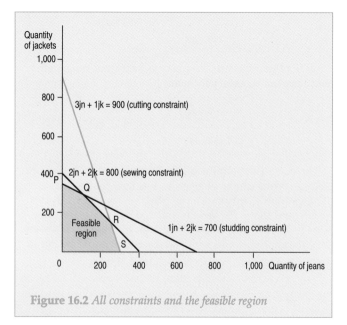

Figure 16.2 *All constraints and the feasible region*

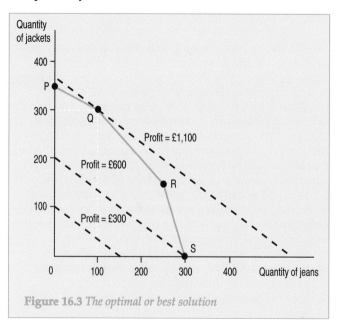

Figure 16.3 *The optimal or best solution*

QUESTION 1 Stonewold Brewery produce two types of ale, best bitter (BB) and strong ale (SA). Three brewing processes are required; malting, mashing and fermenting. The amount of time each process takes and the capacity available is summarised in Table 16.2. The profit made on a barrel of best bitter and strong ale is £24 and £30 respectively.

Table 16.2 *Time constraints for the three brewing processes*

	Malting	Mashing	Fermenting
Hours needed to (BB)	4	8	2
produce 1,000 barrels (SA)	6	4	3
Capacity, total hours available	240	240	150

(a) Write out the problem as three equations showing the constraints.
(b) Draw the constraints on a graph.
(c) On the graph, plot a **point** that shows the allocation of resources that will maximise profit.
(d) Calculate the profit that will be earned at this point.

Transportation

TRANSPORTATION is another linear programming method. It is useful when firms have the problem of transporting items from a number of different origins to various destinations. For example, distribution companies have to decide the most cost effective way to distribute goods from their warehouses to a number of customers. Take an example, where two factories, F1 and F2, supply three warehouses, W1, W2, and W3.

■ The output of each factory is constant at 14 and 23 loads per day respectively.
■ The warehouses need 16, 18 and 3 loads every day respectively.
■ The transport costs per load are shown in Table 16.3.

Table 16.3 *Transport costs from factories to warehouses*

£00s per load

	Warehouses		
Factory	W1	W2	W3
F1	3	4	2
F2	1	1	5

The firm must now decide on the most cost effective way of transporting the loads. The first step is to build a model which can be used to help decision making. The information is organised into a matrix as shown in Table 16.4. This shows that any factory can deliver to any warehouse. The small numbers at the top of each box show the transport cost per load in hundreds of pounds. Notice that the total output of both factories, 37 loads (14 + 23), is the same as the warehouses' demand (16 + 18 + 3).

Table 16.4 *A matrix showing transport costs, factory output and warehousing capacities*

	W1	W2	W3	Output
F1	3	4	2	14
F2	1	1	5	23
Demand	16	18	3	37

The firm must now decide which factories will supply which warehouses. One way of doing this is to start in the top left hand corner. Say that 14 loads are transported from F1 to W1. This is shown in the top left hand corner in Table 16.5. This represents the whole of F1's output. If W1, W2 and W3 need supplying, they must be supplied from F2.

Table 16.5 *The start of the solution*

	W1	W2	W3	Output
F1	3 14	4	2	14
F2	1	1	5	23
Demand	16	18	3	37

Now assume that F2 sends 2 loads to W1, 18 loads to W2 and 3 loads to W3. All output has been delivered to the warehouses. Also, the warehouses' demand for goods has been satisfied. This is known as a **feasible solution** and is shown in Table 16.6.

Table 16.6 *A feasible solution*

	W1	W2	W3	Output
F1	3 14	4	2	14
F2	1 2	1 18	5 3	23
Demand	16	18	3	37

It is now possible to work out the cost of this solution. The total cost will be:

(14 x £300) + (2 x £100) + (18 x £100) + (3 x £500) = £7,700

It is unlikely that this arbitrary method of deciding on deliveries will give the **least cost solution**. The solution for the firm is shown in Table 16.7.

Table 16.7 *The least cost solution*

	W1	W2	W3	Output
F1	3 11	4	2 3	14
F2	1 5	1 18	5	23
Demand	16	18	3	37

The cost of this solution would be:

(11 x £300) + (3 x £200) + (5 x £100) + (18 x £100) = £6,200

An alternative method used to find this optimal solution involves the use of **shadow costs** and **opportunity costs**. However, if the figures are simple it may be easier to use trial and error - keep manipulating the data until any further attempt to move the loads around would either increase the total cost or leave it unchanged. In business, a computer would be used to look at all possible combinations and choose the least cost solution.

QUESTION 2 Two warehouses W1 and W2 supply three retailers R1, R2 and R3. The supply capacity of the warehouses is 20 and 40 loads per week respectively. The demands of the retailers are 14, 20 and 26 loads per week respectively. The transport costs between the warehouses and retailers are summarised below.

Table 16.8

(£00s)

| Warehouse | Retailers | | |
	R1	R2	R3
W1	1	3	6
W2	4	10	3

(a) Set up a transportation model by constructing a suitable matrix showing, costs, demands, and supply capacities.
(b) Determine the least cost solution for the distribution of loads from warehouses to retailers using your answer to (a) and calculate the cost. (Use trial and error.)

Decision trees

Sometimes the decisions firms need to make are extremely risky. This may be because they have little information or because the outcome is uncertain. For example, the launch of a new product in a foreign market may carry a very high risk. Most, if not all, decisions involve some risk. When the outcome is uncertain, DECISION TREES can be used to help reach a decision. A decision tree is a method of tracing alternative outcomes of any decision, and comparing the likely results of those alternatives. They help a firm to minimise the risk involved.

Decision trees have a number of features. These can be seen in Figure 16.4 which shows the decision tree for a business that has to decide whether to launch a new advertising campaign or retain an old one.

■ Decision points. Points where decisions have to be made in a decision tree are represented by squares and are called decision nodes. The decision maker has to choose between two courses of action. In this example, the decision is whether to launch a new campaign or retain the old one.

■ Outcomes. Points where there are different possible outcomes in a decision tree are represented by circles and are called **chance nodes**. At these chance nodes it can be shown that a particular course of action might result in a number of outcomes. In this example, at 'B' there is a chance of failure or success of the new campaign.

■ The use of **probability** or **chance**. The likelihood of possible outcomes happening is represented by **probabilities** in decision trees. The chance of a particular outcome occurring is given a value. As was shown in unit 14, if the outcome is certain then the probability is 1. Alternatively, if there is no chance at all of a particular outcome occurring, the probability will be 0. In practice the value will lie between 0 and 1. In Figure 16.4, at 'B' the chance of success for the new campaign is 0.2 and of failure is 0.8.

■ Expected values. This is the financial outcome of a decision. It is based on the predicted profit or loss of an outcome and the probability of that outcome occurring. The profit or loss of any decision is shown on the right hand side of Figure 16.4. For example, if the launch of a new campaign is a success, a £15 million profit is expected. If it fails a loss of £2 million is expected.

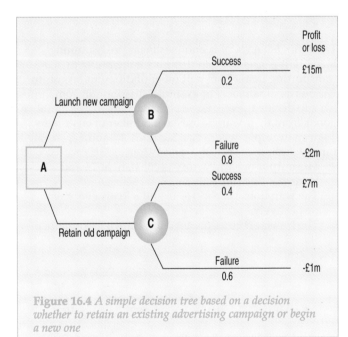

Figure 16.4 *A simple decision tree based on a decision whether to retain an existing advertising campaign or begin a new one*

What should the firm decide? It has to work out the **expected values** of each decision, taking into account the expected profit or loss and the probabilities. So, for example, the expected value of a new campaign is:

	Success		Failure
Expected value =	0.2 x £15m	+	0.8 x (-£2m)
	(probability) (expected profit)		(probability) (expected loss)
=	£3m - £1.6m		
=	£1.4m		

The expected value of retaining the current campaign is:

	Success	Failure

Expected value = 0.4 × £7m + 0.6 × (-£1m)

= £2.8m - £0.6m

= £2.2m

From these figures the firm should continue with the existing campaign because the expected value is higher.

A more detailed decision tree

In practice businesses face many alternative decisions and possible outcomes. Take a farmer who has inherited some land, but does not wish to use it with his existing farming business. There are three possible decisions that the farmer could make.

■ Sell the land. The market is depressed and this will earn £0.6 million.
■ Wait for one year and hope that the market price improves. A land agent has told the farmer that the chance of an upturn in the market is 0.3, while the probabilities of it staying the same or worsening are 0.5 and 0.2 respectively. The likely proceeds from a sale in each of the circumstances are £1 million, £0.6 million and £0.5 million.
■ Seek planning permission to develop the land. The

legal and administration fees would be £0.5 million and the probability of being refused permission would be 0.8, which means the likelihood of obtaining permission is 0.2. If refused, the farmer would be left with the same set of circumstances described in the second option.

If planning permission is granted the farmer has to make a decision (at node E). If the farmer decides to sell, the probability of getting a good price, ie £10 million, is estimated to be 0.4, while the probability of getting a low price, ie £6 million, is 0.6. The farmer could also develop the land himself at a cost of £5 million. The probability of selling the developed land at a good price, ie £25 million, is estimated to be 0.3 while the likelihood of getting a low price, ie £10 million, is 0.7.

The information about probability and earnings is shown in Figure 16.5. What decision should the farmer make? The sale of the land will earn £0.6 million.

The expected value of the second option is:

Expected value = 0.3 × £1m + 0.5 × £0.6m + 0.2 × £0.5m

= £0.3m + £0.3m + £0.1m

= £0.7m

Since this earns more than the first option, it would be a better choice. We can show this in Figure 16.5 by crossing the 'selling immediately' path with a / /, indicating that the first option will not be taken up. The expected value of the second option (£0.7m) is shown in the diagram at node B.

A **rollback** technique can then be used to work out the

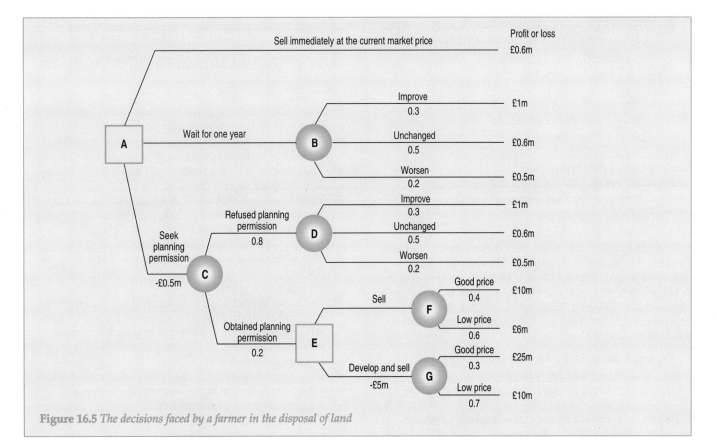

Figure 16.5 *The decisions faced by a farmer in the disposal of land*

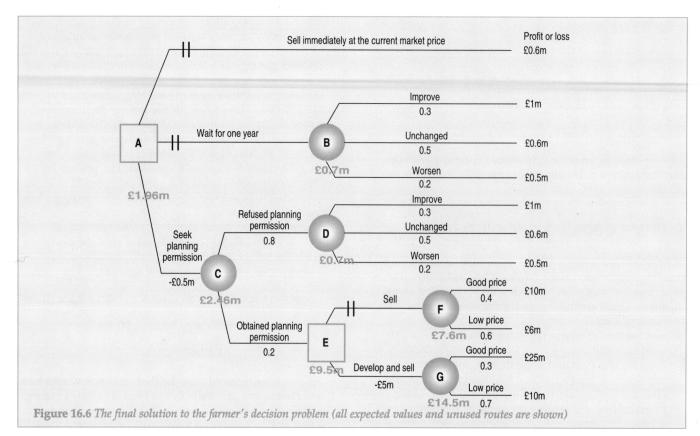

Figure 16.6 *The final solution to the farmer's decision problem (all expected values and unused routes are shown)*

expected value of the third option. This means working from right to left, calculating the expected values at each node in the diagram. The expected value at node D is:

Expected value = 0.3 x £1m + 0.5 x £0.6m + 0.2 x £0.5m

= £0.7m

The expected value at node F is:

Expected value = 0.4 x £10m + 0.6 x £6m

= £4m + £3.6m

= £7.6m

The expected value at node G is:

Expected value = 0.3 x £25m + 0.7 x £10m

= £7.5m + £7m

= £14.5m

At node E, a decision node, the farmer would choose to develop the land before selling it. This would yield an expected return of £9.5 million (£14.5 - £5 million) which is higher than £7.6m, ie the expected return from selling the land undeveloped. Thus, in Figure 16.6 the path representing this option can be crossed. The expected value at node C is now:

Expected value = 0.2 x £9.5m + 0.8 x £0.7m

= £1.9m + £0.56m

= £2.46m

Finally, by subtracting the cost of seeking planning permission (£0.5 million), the expected value of the final

option can be found. It is £1.96 million. Since this is the highest value, this would be the best option for the farmer. This means a // can be placed on the line to node B as £0.7 million is lower than £1.96 million. All of the expected values are shown in Figure 16.6.

Advantages and disadvantages of decision trees

Decision trees can be applied to much more complicated problems. They have some major advantages.
- Constructing the tree diagram may show possible courses of action not previously considered.
- They involve placing numerical values on decisions. This tends to improve results.
- They force management to take account of the risks involved in decisions and help to separate important from unimportant risks.

The technique also has some limitations.
- The information which the technique 'throws out' is not exact. Much of it is based on probabilities which are often estimated.
- Decisions are not always concerned with quantities and probabilities. They often involve people and are influenced by legal constraints or people's opinions, for example. These factors cannot always be shown by numerical values.
- Time lags often occur in decision making. By the time a decision is finally made, some of the numerical information may be out of date.
- The process can be quite time consuming, using up valuable business resources.

QUESTION 3 The owner of a popular Torquay restaurant, The Sea Gull's Table, has been advised by a doctor to take a month's holiday for health reasons. As a result the owner is faced with a dilemma regarding the running of his business in his absence. There are three possible courses of action open to him.

- Shut the restaurant for one month and suffer the financial loss which is estimated to be £1,000.
- Place the business in the hands of an inexperienced relative who would receive a payment of £1,000. The probability of the relative securing a good profit, ie £4,000, in the owner's absence is 0.2. The probability of modest profit, ie £2,000, is 0.8.
- Hire a professional manager experienced in the restaurant trade at a cost of £4,000. The probability of the manager making a good profit, ie £5,000, is 0.9, while the probability of a more modest profit, ie £3,000, is 0.1.

This information is shown in a decision tree in Figure 16.7.

(a) Calculate the expected values of the three courses of action.
(b) Which course of action is the most desirable on financial grounds?
(c) What non-financial information might need to be considered in making this decision?

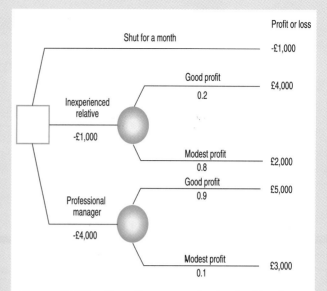

Figure 16.7 *The alternative courses of action faced by the owner of The Sea Gull's Table*

Summary

1. State 5 problems that operational research methods could be used to investigate.
2. Why are blending and transportation examples of linear programming?
3. Explain briefly two problems that businesses might have when using blending.
4. What does the use of blending show a firm?
5. What types of problem does the transportation technique help to solve?
6. What does the use of transportation show a firm?
7. When can decision trees be used to solve business problems?
8. What is the difference between decision nodes and chance nodes?
9. What information is needed to calculate the expected value of an outcome?
10. Describe the advantages and disadvantages of decision trees.

Key terms

Blending - a graphical approach to linear programming which deals with resource allocation subject to constraints.

Decision trees - a technique which shows all possible outcomes of a decision. The name comes from the similarity of the diagrams to the branches of trees.

Linear programming - a technique which shows practical problems as a series of mathematical equations which can then be manipulated to find the optimum or best solution.

Operational research - a logical and scientific approach to decision making which uses calculations.

Transportation - a method designed to solve problems where there are a number of different points of supply and demand, such as a number of manufacturers distributing their products to a number of different wholesalers.

Question

Stoke Precision Components Ltd

Stoke Precision Components Ltd manufacture high quality components for the defence industry. They are about to begin production on a new design and have to decide which method of production to use. The customer has insisted on a very high standard of quality. The 'quality factor' will be important when deciding on the method of production.

■ One alternative is to contract out some of the work. If the sub-contractors meet the quality standard, the potential profit from contracting out is estimated to be £10m. If they fail to meet the standard the firm will incur a £1m loss. The probability of the quality standard being met is 0.5.

■ If the company decides to manufacture the component itself, it has to make a further decision. There are two possible production methods. Method 1 involves using an existing technique which has a 0.7 probability of meeting the quality standard. The profit potential if the standard is met is £20m. However, if the standard is not met the firm stands to lose £10m. Method 2 is new. However, before production can begin there has to be an inspection of the

plant. This is to ensure that it meets EC Health and Safety standards. The probability of the plant passing the inspection first time is 0.4. A delay will reduce the profit potential of the contract. Once the plant has been passed as safe, the probability of the quality standard being met is 0.9. If production can begin immediately the profit potential is £40m. However, if the quality standards are not met a loss of £20m will be made. If there is a delay in production the potential profit is £30m. Also, a loss of £30m will be made if the quality standard is not met.

Figure 16.8 shows a decision tree with all of this information.

(a)   Explain the significance of nodes B and C.
(b)   Calculate the expected values of the three production methods.
(c)   On the basis of your answers in (b) which method would you choose?
(d)   What might be the limitations of the decision made in this way?
(e)   Why is the quality standard less likely to be met by a sub-contractor?

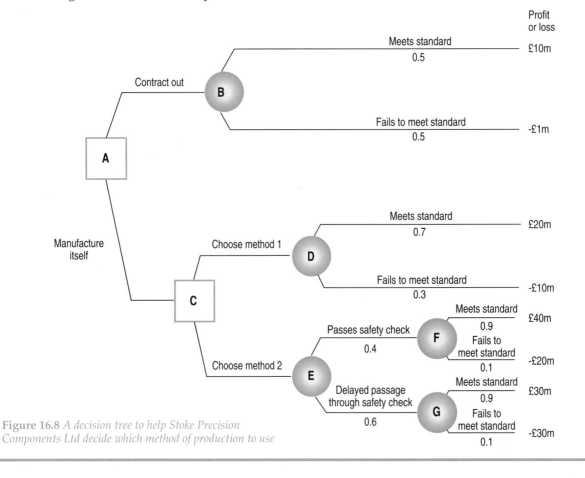

Figure 16.8 *A decision tree to help Stoke Precision Components Ltd decide which method of production to use*

Network analysis

Unit 16 showed that a variety of techniques can be used in a business to make more effective decisions. Some operations in business are carried out by large numbers of people, using a large amount of resources. Others are more straightforward.

NETWORK or CRITICAL PATH ANALYSIS is a technique which allows a business to:

- estimate the minimum time that could be taken to complete a possibly complex operation;
- identify whether resources are being used efficiently;
- anticipate any tasks that may or may not cause delays in the operation.

Network analysis is used in many industries, particularly manufacturing and construction. For example, a builder may consider the use of network analysis when planning the sequence of tasks to build a new house. In such industries the time and resources used are vital to the project.

Take a simple operation, such as painting a window frame, that a builder might carry out. This could involve many different tasks, for example:

- preparing the woodwork;
- applying the undercoat;
- waiting for the undercoat to dry;
- applying the gloss.

This is shown in Figure 17.1 as a **network diagram**.

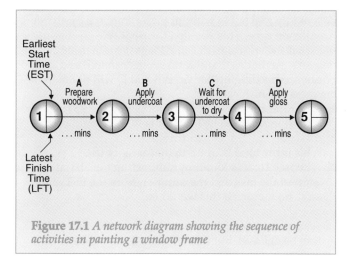

Figure 17.1 *A network diagram showing the sequence of activities in painting a window frame*

There are certain features in Figure 17.1 that are important when constructing any network.

- The circles are called **nodes** showing the start or finish of a task. The arrows show the tasks involved in painting the window. They use up resources as they are carried out. For example, even waiting for paint to dry uses up resources, such as time. The activities are **dependent** on each other. So the undercoat cannot be applied until the woodwork has been prepared.
- Nodes contain information. Figure 17.1 shows that

nodes are divided into three sections. In the left hand semi-circle the **node number** is written. This makes it possible to follow tasks more easily through the network. The number in the top right is the **earliest starting time** (EST). This shows the earliest time that the next task can begin. The number in the bottom right is the **latest finishing time** (LFT). This shows the latest time that the previous task can finish without delaying the next task.

- Arrows show the **order** in which the tasks take place. They often have letters next to them to show what the order is. The length of time each task takes is placed below the arrow.

Constructing a network

Figure 17.1 is a rather simple example of a network. In practice operations in business may be more complex with many different tasks, some of which can be carried out at the same time as others. For example, the tasks involved in producing an advertising campaign for a company could be:

- A - plan the advertising campaign;
- B - make a TV video;
- C - make a poster;
- D - test market the TV video;
- E - test suitability of poster;
- F - present campaign to the board of directors;
- G - communicate the campaign to all company personnel.

The estimated length of time for each task and the order, ie the tasks that **depend** upon others being completed, are shown in Table 17.1. The total estimated time is 49 hours, but this is not important because activities B and C, and D and E can be done at the same time by different employees.

Figure 17.2 shows the network for the marketing campaign summarised in Table 17.1. The tasks, node numbers and time durations are all included.

Table 17.1 *The order and times of tasks when producing an advertising campaign*

Tasks	Order/dependency	Estimated time (hours)
A	Must be done first	4
B	Can only start when A is complete	6
C	Can only start when A is complete	7
D	Can only start when B is complete	8
E	Can only start when C is complete	10
F	Can only start when D and E is complete	9
G	Must wait for D, E and F to be completed	5

Once the network has been constructed it is possible to 'fill-in' the earliest start times and latest finishing times, and then show the critical path. This will tell the business how long it will take to launch the advertising campaign, and indicate where delays could take place.

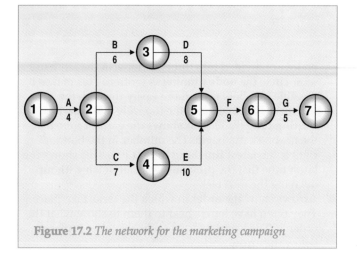

Figure 17.2 *The network for the marketing campaign*

Earliest start time Assuming that the **earliest time** task A can be started is hour 0 then tasks B and C cannot start for 4 hours (0 + 4), ie until task A has been completed. These are shown in the top right of nodes 1 and 2.

Task D cannot start until A and B have been completed, this takes 10 hours (0+4+6) which is shown in node 3. Task E cannot start for 11 hours (0+4+7) and is shown in node 4. Task F cannot start until E and D are complete. The EST for task F is 21 (0 + 4 + 7 + 10). It is important to choose the longest route when calculating the ESTs. The route A,B,D is only 18 (0 + 4 + 6 + 8). The EST of the longer route (21) is shown in node 5. The EST in the final node also shows the time it takes to complete the whole marketing campaign. It is 35 hours (0 + 4 + 7 + 10 + 9 + 5) and is shown in node 7. All this information is shown in Figure 17.3.

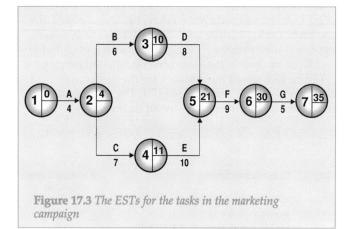

Figure 17.3 *The ESTs for the tasks in the marketing campaign*

Latest finish time The next step is to identify the **latest finish time** (LFT) of each task without extending the project duration. We must start at node 7 and work back. Task G must be completed by the 35th hour. This LFT is shown in the bottom right of node 7. To calculate the LFT for task F, we subtract the time it takes to perform task F from the previous LFT, ie 30 (35 - 5). This LFT is shown in node 6. The LFTs for tasks D and E are 21 (30 - 9), as shown in node 5. For task B the LFT is 13 (21 - 8) and for task C 11 (21 - 10). The LFT for task A is 4, following the

route that will give the earliest time, ie C (11-7=4) rather than B which would give (13-6=7) The LFTs for all tasks are shown in Figure 17.4.

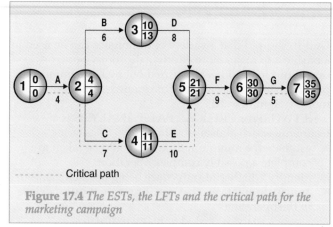

- - - - - - - Critical path

Figure 17.4 *The ESTs, the LFTs and the critical path for the marketing campaign*

The critical path Once all the LFTs have been identified it is possible to outline the CRITICAL PATH. This can be drawn through the nodes where the ESTs and the LFTs are the **same**. This means that there can be no delays between completing the preceding tasks and starting the next ones on this path without prolonging the total time of the marketing campaign. The critical path for the campaign, A, C, E, F, G, is shown by a dotted line in Figure 17.4. It is critical because any task on this path which is delayed will delay the whole campaign beyond the 35 hours identified earlier as the minimum time.

The float What about tasks which do not lie on the critical path, ie B and D? B and D together, could be delayed up to 3 hours without prolonging the campaign's completion time. This is called the **float**. We have already seen that the critical path is the longest route through the network. Activities C and E take longer than B and D by 3 hours, so speeding up activities B and D will not help the business to finish earlier.

- The **total float** is found by subtracting the EST and the duration from the LFT. So for task B it would be:
  13-6-4=3.
  This is the total float up to that activity (B).
- The **free float** is found by subtracting the EST at the start of the task and the duration from the EST at the end. So for task B this would be:
  10-6-4=0.
  This is the free float for that task. It shows that task B can be delayed, but this will interfere with other tasks, ie D.

Table 17.2 shows the total float after each task in the marketing campaign. The tasks without a float (shown by a *) are 'critical' - any delay in these and the whole campaign will be prolonged. Only non-critical tasks have a float.

It is important for a business to know how much float there is. If tasks in the operations could be delayed without delaying the whole job, then resources in these tasks, (such as labour, machinery etc.), could be used more productively elsewhere or shared between tasks. It is also important when tasks may take days or weeks. If an operation is delayed, a business will not be too worried if there is some float, only if the float disappears.

Table 17.2 *The duration, EST, LFT and floats for each task in the marketing campaign*

Task	Duration	EST	LFT	Total Float	Free Float
					(Hours)
A	4	0	4	0*	0
B	6	4	13	3	0
C	7	4	11	0*	0
D	8	10	21	3	3
E	10	11	21	0*	0
F	9	21	30	0*	0
G	5	30	35	0*	0

QUESTION 1 Figure 17.5 shows a network for the installation of a new piece of machinery. The times shown are for number of days taken.

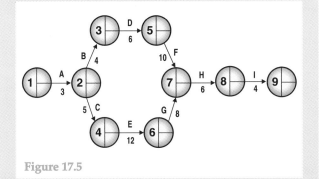

Figure 17.5

(a) Calculate the earliest start time for each task.
(b) Calculate the latest finish time for each task and the minimum time for the whole project.
(c) Determine the critical path.
(d) Identify the amount of total float and free float in a table.

A more complex network

Sometimes it is necessary to include a **dummy** activity or task in a network diagram. Take an example made up of

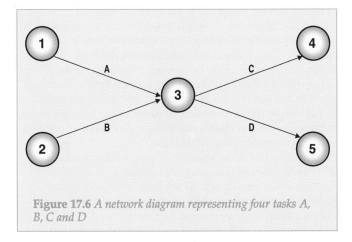

Figure 17.6 *A network diagram representing four tasks A, B, C and D*

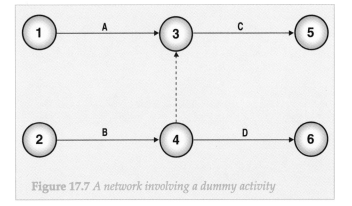

Figure 17.7 *A network involving a dummy activity*

four tasks A, B, C and D. Assume that task C cannot start until tasks A and B have been completed. Task D can only start when B has been completed. The network in Figure 17.6 appears to represent this sequence of tasks. However, the diagram also shows that task D cannot start until A and B have been completed, yet this is not a requirement in our example. In order to show a **dependency** the network can be redrawn using a dummy activity as shown in Figure 17.7. The dummy task is shown by a dotted line and now the diagram shows that task D is only dependent upon the completion of task B. Dummy activities do not use up any time - they always have a time duration of zero.

Let's look at a network which involves a variety of tasks and a dummy activity. Table 17.3 and Figure 17.8 show tasks involved in the assembly of a vehicle engine. The earliest start times and latest finish times have been calculated using the method in Figures 17.3 and 17.4 earlier. There are certain features about this network.

■ A dummy activity or task links J and K to the completion of C. This is because whilst J and K are dependent upon C finishing, they are is also dependent upon H finishing. It would be impossible to illustrate these dependencies in the network without the use of a dummy line, which shows a logical connection, but does not show any time passing.

■ The critical path through the network is shown by a broken (blue) line, linking activities A,C,J and L. Notice that these are the nodes where the ESTs and LFTs are equal. It is also the route with the longest

Table 17.3 *Tasks and their estimated time involved in assembling a vehicle engine*

Task	Order/dependency	Estimated time (hours)
A	Can start at the same time as B	2
B	Can start at the same time as A	2
C	Must follow A	6
D	Must follow A	3
E	Must follow B	1
F	Must follow B	8
G	Must follow C	2
H	Must follow D,E	1
J	Cannot start until C,H have finished	3
K	Cannot start until C,H have finished	3
L	Must follow G,J	4

The operation is complete when F, K and L have finished.

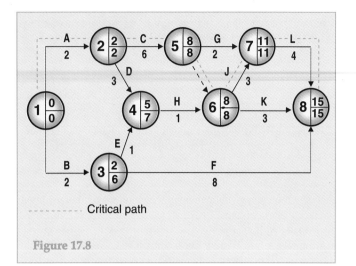

Figure 17.8

ESTs, as explained earlier in this unit.
- The minimum time to complete the assembly of the engine would be 15 hours.
- The float in the network is shown in Table 17.4.

Table 17.4

Task	Duration	EST	LFT	Total Float	Free Float
A	2	0	2	0*	0
B	2	0	6	4	0
C	6	2	8	0*	0
D	3	2	7	2	0
E	1	2	7	4	2
F	8	2	15	5	5
G	2	8	11	1	1
H	1	5	8	2	2
J	3	8	11	0*	0
K	3	8	15	4	4
L	4	11	15	0*	0

Advantages of network analysis

The major advantage of network analysis is that it provides decision makers with a picture of a problem which may be easier to interpret. It can be used to suit a range of circumstances and help solve a variety of business problems.
- Reduce the time lost between tasks, ensuring that projects run smoothly.
- Encourage forward planning. The process ensures that all the tasks in a particular operation have been identified and timed from start to finish. The construction of the network forces decision makers to consider all aspects of a project.
- Improve efficiency in production. The level of working capital can be minimised by ordering and receiving materials and components 'just-in-time'. By identifying float and critical activities, resources such as labour and capital can be used more effectively.

- Control cash flow. This is achieved by not ordering supplies too early and only making purchases when they are required.

QUESTION 2 A toy manufacturer has designed a new wooden toy. The construction of the toy involves 9 activities A to J. The order and the duration of tasks are shown in the network diagram illustrated in Figure 17.9. The time durations shown are in minutes.

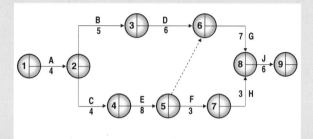

Figure 17.9 *Network diagram for the construction of a new wooden toy*

(a) What is the minimum construction time for the new toy?
(b) What is the critical path?
(c) If task D and task H were each delayed by one minute what would be the effect on:
  (i) the minimum construction time;
  (ii) the critical path?

Queueing and simulation

SIMULATIONS are models which try to reproduce in a dynamic way what is going on in reality. Business simulations, such as business games, have become common tools in management training and Business Studies teaching. But simulations can also be used to look at a very specific problem, such as queueing. People who are kept waiting in queues may look for a different place to buy goods and services. Queues also waste resources, such as time spent dealing with customer complaints.

Such problems often result when customers arrive at random. Examples may be people using a cashpoint or a public telephone, patients arriving at casualty or cars arriving at a toll booth. It is the random element which causes the problem. If people used these items regularly it would be easy to decide on the number of staff required to deal with customers without causing delay. This assumes, however, that the service time is constant. This is not always the case. Where the service time is variable, such as at a supermarket checkout, a problem will exist.

Take an example of how a simulation can be used to reduce queuing at checkouts in a supermarket. A number of variables need to be considered:
- The number of customers arriving at the checkouts.
- The number of checkouts in operation.
- The frequency of arrival at checkouts.
- The length of time each customer takes at the checkout.

A simulation will allow a business to work out the

number of checkouts it must operate at different times of the day to keep queues at a minimum.

The first stage is to collect information about how the system operates at present. The supermarket collected information about 100 customers who 'checked out' between 5.00pm and 5.30pm. Table 17.5 shows this information.

Table 17.5 *Information relating to customers arriving at a supermarket checkout*

Time between arrivals at checkout (mins)	Frequency (per cent)	Cumulative frequency	Time at check out (mins)	Frequency (per cent)	Cumulative frequency
0	8	8	1	7	7
1	20	28	2	25	32
2	32	60	3	32	64
3	21	81	4	16	80
4	9	90	5	12	92
5	10	100	6	8	100

Table 17.5 also shows the **cumulative frequency** (☞ unit 13) of people at the checkout. The information forms the basis of a model which will try to simulate the arrival of customers at checkouts. Random numbers are used to indicate the time between arrivals and the length of time spent at the checkout. Random numbers are obtained from computers and have no pattern provided they are used in a random way. For example a random series of 50 numbers may be:

```
20 84 27 38 66 19 60 10 51 20
35 16 74 58 72 79 98 09 47 07
98 82 69 63 23 70 80 88 86 23
94 67 94 34 03 77 89 30 49 51
04 54 32 55 94 82 08 19 20 73
```

Table 17.6 *Cumulative frequencies and allocated random numbers*

Time between arrivals (mins)	Cumulative frequency	Random numbers	Time at check out (mins)	Cumulative frequency	Random numbers
0	8	01 - 08	1	7	01 - 07
1	28	09 - 28	2	32	08 - 32
2	60	29 - 60	3	64	35 - 64
3	81	61 - 81	4	80	65 - 80
4	90	82 - 90	5	92	81 - 92
5	100	91 -100	6	100	93 -100

The random numbers are allocated to the 'Time between arrivals' and the 'Time spent at the checkout', according to the cumulative frequencies as shown in Table 17.6. The simulation can now begin, using the random numbers in the order they are shown above:

Random number 20 - customer 1 arrives after 1 minute
Random number 84 - customer 1 takes 5 minutes to be served

Random number 27 - customer 2 arrives 1 minute after customer 1
Random number 38 - customer 2 takes 3 minutes to be served

Random number 66 - customer 3 arrives 3 minutes after customer 2
Random number 19 - customer 3 takes 2 minutes to be served

The simulation can be recorded as shown in Table 17.7. It is assumed that there is just one checkout in operation to start with.

Table 17.7 *The results of the simulation showing the arrival times, waiting times, service times, and the leaving times of customers*

Customer	Random number Arrival	Random number Service time	Simulated times Between arrival (mins)	Simulated times Service time (mins)	Arrived at	Served at	Leaves at	Cust wait (mins)	Checkout wait (mins)
1	20	84	1	5	5.01	5.01	5.06	0	1
2	27	38	1	3	5.02	5.06	5.09	4	0
3	66	19	3	2	5.05	5.09	5.11	4	0
4	60	10	2	2	5.07	5.11	5.13	4	0
5	51	20	2	2	5.09	5.13	5.15	4	0
6	35	16	2	2	5.11	5.15	5.17	4	0
7	74	58	3	3	5.14	5.17	5.20	3	0
8	72	79	3	4	5.17	5.20	5.24	3	0
9	98	09	5	2	5.22	5.24	5.26	2	0
10	47	07	2	1	5.24	5.26	5.27	2	0

With just one checkout in operation, the average customer waiting time is about three minutes - this might be considered acceptable. Also, the checkout has been working constantly. Let us now run the simulation with two checkouts in operation. The results are shown in Table 17.8.

Table 17.8 *Results from simulation with two checkouts employed (the random numbers are excluded)*

Customer	Simulated times Between arrival (mins)	Simulated times Service time (mins)	Arrived at	Checkout number	Served at	Leaves at	Cust. wait (mins)	Checkout wait (mins)
1	1	5	5.01	1	5.01	5.06	0	1
2	1	3	5.02	2	5.02	5.05	0	2
3	3	2	5.05	2	5.05	5.07	0	0
4	2	2	5.07	1	5.07	5.09	0	1
5	2	2	5.09	1	5.09	5.11	0	0
6	2	2	5.11	2	5.11	5.13	0	4
7	3	3	5.14	1	5.14	5.17	0	3
8	3	4	5.17	2	5.17	5.21	0	4
9	5	2	5.22	1	5.22	5.24	0	5
10	2	1	5.24	2	5.24	5.25	0	3

With two checkouts in operation, customers are never kept waiting. However, both checkouts are waiting for customers on many occasions. The results from this simulation can help the supermarket decide whether it wants to operate one or two checkouts. The final decision will also depend on its policy towards customer queueing and staff productivity. For example, if its policy is to keep staff fully employed then it will use just one checkout. Simulations like this may appear cumbersome, but the use of a computer will help speed up the process. They are used quite commonly in business. Other OR techniques are too complex to deal with problems like queueing and congestion. However, simulations are only as good as the data upon which they are based. Inaccurate data could lead to incorrect conclusions being drawn. Also, the data may be expensive to collect in the first place.

QUESTION 3 A warehouse receives lorry loads of corn from local farmers. It currently operates one tipping facility. Table 17.9 shows the arrival intervals of successive lorries and the times taken to tip their loads.

Table 17.9 *Information regarding the arrival of lorries at a warehouse and the time it takes to tip their loads*

Time between arrivals (mins)	Frequency (per cent)	Cumulative frequency	Tipping time (mins)	Frequency (per cent)	Cumulative Frequency
3	5	5	10	12	12
4	10	15	11	20	32
7	45	60	12	30	62
10	30	90	13	28	90
13	10	100	14	10	100

(a) Use a simulation to show the: (i) arrival time; (ii) waiting time; of 10 lorries which begin arriving at 9.00am. Use the random numbers in the text on the previous page.
(b) Using another simulation, show the effect of operating two tipping facilities.
(c) Do you think a second tipping facility would be a worthwhile investment? Explain your answer.

Cost-benefit analysis

Many decisions in business are 'financial' decisions. When considering different courses of action decision makers often weigh up the financial costs against the financial benefits. Normally, a business will choose the course of action which generates the greatest net financial benefit. Recently, some firms have begun to consider the costs and benefits of their decisions to the rest of society. Take an example of a chemical company. It is likely to face the 'private' costs of machinery etc., but may also generate pollution into the atmosphere. Pollution is one example of **negative externalities** (☞ unit 72) or external costs. Similarly, the business will aim to sell its product to earn revenue (a private benefit), but may build a factory and a new road which eases traffic congestion in the area (an external benefit). We can say:

Social costs = private/financial costs + external costs.
Social benefit = private/financial benefit + external benefit.

COST-BENEFIT ANALYSIS is a method used to take into account social costs and benefits when making decisions. A business must place a monetary value on any social costs and benefits which a particular course of action might lead to. For example, consider a business calculating the cost of locating a new factory in a rural area. Part of the external cost might be the potential loss of wildlife. The business must find a way of evaluating this cost in monetary terms. Quite obviously this would be difficult and this is one of the

problems with cost-benefit analysis.

Cost-benefit analysis is more commonly used in the public sector. Government investment projects have often been the subject of cost-benefit analysis. For example, the decision whether or not to build a bypass would look at external costs, such as the loss of custom to local businesses when the traffic is diverted. These would be compared with the possible external benefits, such as less congestion and fewer accidents on the local roads. The overall decision would depend on both the external costs and benefits, and the financial costs of constructing the bypass. The abandoning of a Thames crossing at Oxleas Wood because of the impact it would have had on the environment is an example of a project that took social costs and benefits into account.

QUESTION 4 Daryl Cullen and Simon Duckworth ran a small chemical processing plant which is located next to the Wolverhampton Canal in the West Midlands. In the last 12 months, due to rising demand, the plant had proved to be too small. A number of breakdowns had occurred resulting in the discharge of waste into the canal. The company was fined £1,000 for polluting the canal and warned that any future discharges would be dealt with more severely. Daryl and Simon decided to relocate their plant on Teeside. Most of their customers were now from the North East and by locating on Teeside they qualified for some local government aid. The new site was a large area of land which had been derelict for 17 years. Local residents had complained about its 'ugliness' for many years. Daryl and Simon hoped to create 135 jobs when the new plant was built. However, there was opposition to the location from a Middlesbrough Horticulture Society. They argued that a rare species of orchid had become established on the site and would disappear if the plant was built. Despite their protests the relocation has taken place with the blessing of the local community and the local government.

(a) State two possible:
    (i) social benefits; (ii) social costs;
    of relocating the plant on Teeside.
(b) To what extent do you think Daryl and Simon would have considered the above costs and benefits when making their decision?

Key terms

Cost-benefit analysis - a technique which involves taking into account all social costs and benefits when deciding on a course of action.
Critical path - in an operation which consists of a sequence of activities, this is the one sequence which cannot afford any delays without prolonging the operation.
Network analysis or Critical path analysis - a technique used to find the cheapest or fastest way to complete an operation.
Simulation - a technique which imitates what might happen in reality by using random numbers.

Summary

1. What is meant by a network?
2. What does the critical path show a firm?
3. What is meant by a float in a network and what does it tell a business?
4. Briefly explain 3 uses of network analysis to a firm.
5. State 3 situations where a simulation might be used by a business.
6. Explain what is meant by:
   (a) private costs;
   (b) private benefits;
   (c) external costs;
   (d) external benefits.
7. 'The private costs of building a new motorway through a rural area are not the only costs that must be taken into consideration.' Briefly explain this statement.

Question

Precision Electronics PLC

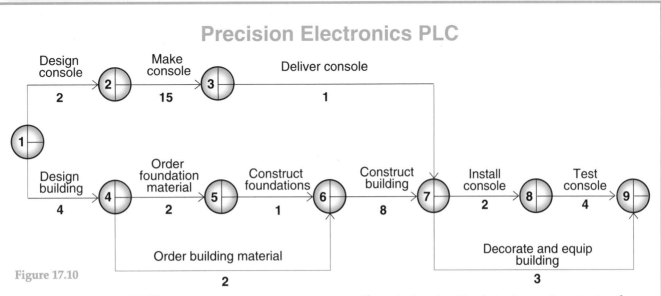

Figure 17.10

Precision Electronics PLC have won a contract to design and install a new traffic control system for a large city in the North of England which is introducing trams as part of the transport network. The contract covers both the design and manufacture of the electronic control system (the console) and the construction of a control building attached to the existing central bus station. For the construction work Precision would need to use outside contractors.

Table 17.10

Task	Weeks
Design console	2
Make console	15
Deliver console	1
Install console	2
Test console	4
Design control building	4
Order and deliver foundation material	2
Construct foundations	1
Order and deliver control building material	2
Construct central building	8
Decorate and equip building	3

The tasks involved in designing and equipping the new control units are shown in Table 17.10. In their planning for the construction, Precision had to draw up the network in Figure 17.10 in order to establish the time the contract would take and the likely bid it would put in.

(a) For these activities, calculate the:
   (i) earliest start time;
   (ii) latest finishing time;
   (iii) total float;
   (iv) free float.
(b) What would be the minimum time between Precision receiving this contract and the control building being fully operational?
(c) Which tasks lie on the critical path for the operation? Explain why.
(d) What would be the effect of a delay in making the console of 2 weeks?
(e) The outside contractors would be employed at the stage when the foundations of the building needed constructing. What would be the latest time at which they could start doing this without delaying the whole project?
(f) What are the limitations for Precision in using such an analysis in deciding their likely bid for the contract?

Lossie Ltd

Lossie Ltd are a family business based in Falkirk, Scotland. They produce tartan products for the tourist industry. The company is controlled by Lorraine and Angus Lossie who between them own 70 per cent of the shares. Their three children Maggie, Kit and Morag hold 10 per cent each. Maggie is a qualified accountant and is the company's financial controller. Kit is responsible for marketing and Morag looks after the administration and personnel side of the business. Angus spends a lot of his time in the factory overlooking production.

Lossie produce kilts, rugs and scarves. They employ 38 people and distribute most of their output to retailers in Scotland. The success of the business has been rather erratic in the last 6 years. Table 1 shows turnover, costs and profit for the period 1988-93. Maggie introduced the use of cost centres 6 years ago, making each product a cost centre.

Table 1 *Turnover, costs and profit for Lossie's 3 products 1988-93*

£000

	1988	1989	1990	1991	1992	1993
Kilts						
Turnover	400	600	470	500	300	400
Costs	250	360	300	300	200	350
Profit	150	240	170	200	100	50
Rugs						
Turnover	600	800	580	710	540	610
Costs	400	500	400	500	390	420
Profit	200	300	180	210	150	190
Scarves						
Turnover	200	230	220	260	180	100
Costs	170	180	180	220	200	150
Profit	30	50	40	40	-20	-50

Lorraine and Angus have arranged a board meeting to discuss the company's trading position. They are particularly concerned about the loss made by scarves in the last two years. Maggie has drawn up a break-even chart to show the current position of scarf sales. This is shown in Figure 1. Maggie is also in the process of converting the data in Table 1 into a more informative format, ready for the board meeting.

(a) Draw 3 component bar charts to illustrate the data shown in Table 1.

(b) State 3 advantages of illustrating the information in this way.

(c) Describe briefly what the graphs show.

(d) Using the break-even chart in Figure 1, determine:
  (i) the price of scarves;
  (ii) their fixed costs;
  (iii) their variable costs;
  (iv) the number of scarves needed to break-even.

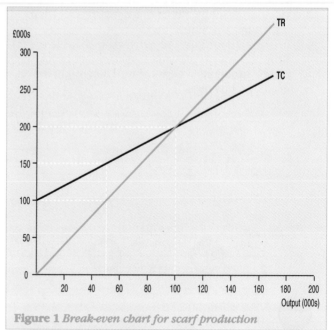

Figure 1 *Break-even chart for scarf production*

During the board meeting the discussion focused on the scarf business. Sales in 1993 were 50,000 which generated a loss of £50,000. Angus looked at the break-even chart, explained that factory space was short and that it would be impossible to produce enough scarves to break even. He also added that an investment of £25,000 would be necessary to expand capacity. By converting some unused storage space, capacity could be increased to 120,000 scarves. However, Morag wondered whether they could sell this many scarves.

Kit had some interesting ideas on this matter. He did not believe that increasing capacity was the answer. He had spent the last three months collecting some data regarding prices and demand for scarves from the retailers. The results are shown in Table 2. On the basis of the data in the table Kit suggested that the price should be increased. After further discussion two courses of action were identified.
• Raise price to £4.00.
• Raise price to £3.00 and invest £25,000 to increase capacity.

Table 2 *The predicted sales of scarves at different prices*

Price	Predicted sales
£1.00	150,000
£2.00	120,000
£3.00	70,000
£4.00	30,000
£5.00	15,000

(e) Calculate which of the above courses of action generates the most profit (state any assumptions that you make).

(f) Construct a new break-even chart and show the margin of safety for your answer in (e).

(g) Discuss 3 non-financial considerations in the above decision.

investigations

Aims

- To establish what is the existing level of service for customers based on the present number of pumps.
- To simulate the existence of an additional pump to see if the queueing time for customers is reduced.
- To investigate whether there are any benefits to the garage or to customers from having an extra pump.
- To consider other factors which might affect the garage's decision.

Research

You can carry out an investigation into a business problem using simulation as a decision making technique. The example here is to find out whether an extra petrol pump at a garage will reduce queueing, but other business situations where queueing exists, such as at a supermarket, in a doctor's surgery, or at a motorway toll booth, can also be examined.

From the garage's own records you can find out the level of sales per day and the pattern of sales during the day.

From this information identify a busy hour and a quiet hour and carry out a survey (by observation) of customer arrival time and customer service time, and thus any queueing time during those two hours. For each customer the time between their arrival, the time they are waiting, and the time for them to be served needs to be recorded. From this research, frequency distributions can be drawn up for the busy hour and the quiet hour, showing customer arrival time, customer service time, and customer queueing time. Averages can then be calculated to compare the results from the two hours.

Presentation

A simulation can now be attempted based on these frequency distributions.

Assuming that the garage has at present 2 pumps in operation, the simulation can be carried out for 3 pumps. Random numbers, allocated according to the observed frequency distributions for arrival time and service time during the busy hour, can be used to represent real customers. The simulation should take place for an hour of simulated time. A second simulation can be carried out using the frequency distributions from the quiet hour.

As a result of the simulation, has the customer waiting time been reduced? Has the number of customers being served increased? Would the costs of installing the third pump be outweighed by the benefits? Is there a substantial difference between the busy hour and the quiet hour? What would be the effect on business over a whole day or whole week?

You also need to take into account the limitations in using this technique as a basis for decision making? Some factors to consider include:

- were the research data, both primary and secondary, reliable?
- were the periods chosen for the research typical of the whole day?
- is the pattern of demand likely to stay the same in the near future?
- what other external factors are there to consider?
- are there alternative uses for the garage's resources?

investigations

Aims

- To establish the past and existing levels of sales for a particular product.
- To identify if there is any pattern in these figures.
- To forecast future sales using a numerate technique.
- To establish what other factors might affect the forecasted figures.

Research

Forecasting techniques can be used to predict future trends. You can use company information to predict what will happen in future periods. Make sure you choose a business where information is available. This may be a small business, where staff are willing to give you information, or a business where lots of data are published in secondary sources.

From the company records, draw up the quarterly sales figures over a period of time, eg 3 years. Using company reports and discussions with staff, try to establish the reasons behind any major changes in the pattern of sales over the three years.

Presentation

Using the sales data, calculate the trend figures for the quarters covered using a 4 period moving average (remember that you will need to centre the trend figure carefully). Plot the original sales figures on a graph and also plot the trend figures. Attempt to extend the trend into the future by drawing a line of best fit, and therefore forecast possible sales figures over the next 4 quarters.

As the figures are quarterly, you should also attempt to calculate the seasonal variation for each quarter from the existing data. Once this is done, you can adjust your original forecasts in line with the seasonal variation. This will then give you seasonally adjusted predictions for the sales of the product.

You may be able to use the predicted sales to make suggestions about how a business should react. For example, the business might be considering expanding production of a product. Your forecast will be able to tell the business whether this is a good idea.

There are, however, some limitations with forecasting which you should take into account in your suggestions.

- Is the past sales data a good indicator of future trends? Were there factors in the past which had a strong influence on sales which will not be repeated?
- Has the company the necessary resources for expansion, eg machinery, labour, factory space, finance?
- What changes in the external environment might influence the decision, eg the state of the economy, the actions of competitors?
- What alternative uses might the company make of the resources devoted to this product? How will its other products be affected?

Marketing - a possible definition

A market is any set of arrangements that allows buyers and sellers to exchange goods and services (☞ unit 1). It can be anything from a street market in a small town to a large market involving internationally traded goods. But what is meant by the term MARKETING? Some definitions which suggest that marketing is the same as advertising or selling are incorrect. One definition, from the Institute of Marketing, which has gained wide acceptance is that:

'Marketing is the management process involved in identifying, anticipating and satisfying consumer requirements profitably.'

There are some features of business marketing behaviour that may have led to this definition.

■ Consumers are of vital importance. A product has a far greater chance of being a success if it satisfies consumers' needs. Marketing must be aimed at finding out what these needs are and making sure that products meet them. Market research (☞ unit 9) is often used by businesses for this purpose. Managers, however, also place stress on having a 'feel' for the market. This could be very important in a market with changing trends, such as fashion clothing or home decoration products.

■ Marketing is a process. It does not have a start and an end, but is ongoing all the time. Businesses must be prepared to respond to changes that take place. This is shown in Figure 18.1. For example, a firm marketing its own range of office furniture would be unwise to decide on a strategy and then not take into account consumers' reactions. If the firm sold modern designs, but sales were poor, a better strategy might be to target offices wanting a traditional look.

■ Marketing is a business philosophy. It is not just a series of activities, such as advertising or selling, but more a 'way of thinking' about how to satisfy consumers' needs. A business selling good quality products, cheaply, may be unsuccessful in its marketing if it has dirty, badly organised or poorly lit facilities. Retailers such as IKEA, ASDA and Carpetworld have large 'superstores' with restaurants and play areas for children. They could be said to cater for all their consumers' shopping needs.

■ Marketing affects all aspects of a business. A production department would not continue making a product that does not satisfy the needs of the consumers at whom it is aimed. In the same way, pricing decisions cannot be made without knowing how much consumers are prepared to pay.

■ Marketing is not just about selling. Selling is only one part of the marketing process. Before selling their products, businesses carry out a range of activities which take into account consumer preferences. These include market research, the testing of products on consumers and the design of products.

■ Marketing and advertising are not the same. Advertising is just one of a number of tactics used by marketing departments. Other marketing methods include promotions, such as free gifts and competitions.

■ Many businesses regard profit making as their main objective (☞ unit 7). Firms in competitive markets must make a profit in the long run to survive. Marketing must therefore satisfy consumers' wants **profitably**. Even when profit is not the main objective, marketing has a vital role to play. Charities, such as Oxfam and public sector organisations such as colleges and hospitals, adapt and change the marketing of their services to satisfy their consumers' needs.

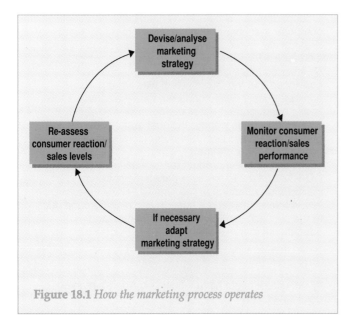

Figure 18.1 *How the marketing process operates*

Devise/analyse marketing strategy

Monitor consumer reaction/sales performance

If necessary adapt marketing strategy

Re-assess consumer reaction/ sales levels

QUESTION 1 In 1990 Timotei was the biggest selling shampoo in the world outside the US according to Unilever, its producers. It had annual sales of £175 million a year and estimated profits of about £19 million. Initially, however, it was a flop. Starting life as a deodorant in Finland (where its name means grass) it failed to catch on. In 1975 Unilever relaunched it in Sweden as a mild, natural shampoo, achieving 12 per cent of the market. A year later it was taken back to Finland and by 1983 it had been launched on the UK market, achieving 8 per cent of the market within three years.

By 1985 in Sweden, and 1988 in the UK, sales had slipped. The decline was arrested to some extent by advertising and also through the launch of Timotei skin care products and face wash in 1988. The company is hoping that Timotei anti-dandruff shampoo, first tested in California in 1990, will also be a success.

Source: adapted from *The Independent*, 1.3.1990.

To what extent would you say that Unilever 'identified, anticipated and satisfied consumer requirements profitably' from the information in the article?

The rise in the importance of marketing

It is only in the last forty years in the UK that marketing has begun to assume such an important role in business. What factors may have led to this?

Economic growth Economic growth (☞ unit 67) in the UK since the Second World War has led to an increase in the REAL DISPOSABLE INCOME of many consumers. This has resulted in a growth in demand for products and services and for a far wider range of choice. In response, businesses have developed an array of products and services which are available to the consumer. We need only think of goods that were not available twenty years ago, such as compact discs and personal computers. Services, such as credit cards and mail order, have also been developed in response to consumers' needs.

Fashion There have been considerable changes in fashion and in the tastes and lifestyles of many consumers. For example, large numbers of people today buy products for sports which were new or were mostly ignored just a few years ago. These include mountain biking, American football and hang gliding.

Technology Rapid technological change has taken place in recent years and continues to do so. Firms constantly invent, design and launch new and advanced products onto the market. One example is the electronics industry. During the 1980s and early 1990s, Sony were able to launch a range of products that were not previously feasible in technical terms. These included the compact disc player, the camcorder and digital audio tape players.

Competition The number of products competing for the consumer's attention is constantly increasing. There has been increased competition from foreign products in UK markets and a greater availability of foreign services. Competition is nothing new, but the scale of it is. Japanese and US firms, with efficient production methods and sophisticated marketing, have been successful in UK markets. More open trade in European Community countries (☞ unit 70) is also likely to create more competition for UK firms.

Effects on business

How have the factors in the last section affected the marketing of UK businesses?

Economic growth Businesses are now aware of the growth in demand and the wide variety of tastes of consumers. Successful marketing is essential if firms are going to gain their share of a growing market and increase their turnover and profit. Larger markets can pose a problem. The investment needed to launch a product onto a large market is enormous. Marketing must make sure that such products will succeed or the business can face large losses.

Fashion Tastes and fashions in today's markets are changing faster than ever before. Marketing must anticipate and respond to these changes. Toy manufacturers, for example, try to be aware of the next 'craze'.

Marketing has become more important as firms have realised that consumers' tastes may be influenced. There are a variety of techniques that can be used to achieve this (☞ units 23 and 25).

Technology Businesses must respond to changes in technology. A firm's products can become obsolete very quickly unless it is able to respond to such changes. Marketing and production departments now work closely together to anticipate new opportunities that arise. Marketing must also provide consumers with technical details about products. It is unlikely that consumers will know all the uses of new products which have previously been unavailable.

Technology has influenced the marketing methods that businesses use. Examples of technical marketing media now used by firms include electronic billboards and satellite TV.

Competition Competition, both at home and from abroad, has meant that successful marketing is vital to maintain a firm's market share. UK businesses have also had to respond to the sophisticated marketing techniques of US and Japanese companies. This has meant that the expenditure on marketing by many UK firms has risen as a share of total spending in the last few decades.

The British motorcycle industry serves as a warning to those firms which fail to respond. British companies such as Triumph and BSA had dominated the market for motor cycles in the UK ever since the 1930s. When the Japanese company Honda launched its 50 cc moped in the UK, British companies did not see this as a threat. Their lack of response allowed Honda and other firms, such as

---

QUESTION 2 In 1993, Apple, the world's largest manufacturer of personal computers, launched two new product ranges. The first was a portable 'notebook' computer that changed in seconds into a fully functional desktop computer. Called the Macintosh Duo System, it comprised a powerful portable computer which could be inserted into a desktop base unit. Apple were convinced that the Duo System was what portable computer users were crying out for. 'It addresses the user's need for the best of the portable and desktop computing worlds without the cost and inconvenience of maintaining two separate computers', Apple's product manager claimed.

The second new product range was the supply of CD-ROM drives to medium-priced mainstream computers. Although at the time CD-ROM sales were low, Apple anticipated a huge increase in demand due to the simplicity and availability of games and educational material on them.

Source: adapted from *The Independent*, 1992.

What factors might have influenced Apple's marketing decisions?

Yamaha and Kawasaki, to almost completely take over the market for motorcycles in the UK. By the 1980s, the British motorcycle industry had effectively collapsed.

Product and market orientation

A distinction is often made between two different approaches to running a business - a product orientated approach and a market orientated approach.

Product orientation Many businesses in the past, and some today, could be described as PRODUCT ORIENTATED. This means that the business focuses on the production process and the product itself. For example, it may try to develop efficient production methods or produce goods which are technically superior.

In the past, many firms producing consumer goods were product orientated. When radios and televisions were first produced in the UK, it was their novelty and the technical 'wonder' of the product that sold them. There were few companies to compete against each other, and there was a growing domestic market. There were also few overseas competitors. The product sold itself.

Some industries today are still said to be product orientated. The machine-tool industry has to produce a final product which exactly matches a technical specification. However, because of increased competition, such firms are being forced to take consumers' needs into account. The technical specification to which a machine-tool business produces might be influenced by what customers want, for example.

The Concorde aircraft project has often been described as being product orientated. The main question was whether the aircraft was technically possible. Whether or not it could be produced at a price which would attract companies was less important. The developers assumed that a supersonic aircraft would 'sell itself'. In fact the only airlines which did buy it were British Airways and Air France, largely because of the involvement of the British and French governments in its development. For other airlines the price was too high and the number of passengers Concorde could carry was too low. Several airports, most especially New York, had indicated that they might ban supersonic aircraft because of noise. Although the project was thought to be a technological success, its failure to take into account the needs of the market meant that it was not a commercial success.

Product orientated businesses thus place their emphasis on developing a technically sound product, producing that product and then selling it. Contact with the consumer comes largely at this final stage.

There will always be a place for product orientation. A great deal of pure research, with no regard to consumers' needs, still takes place in industry. However, success is more likely today if a business can match a product with consumers' wants.

Market orientation A MARKET ORIENTATED business is one which continually identifies, reviews and analyses consumers' needs.

Henry Ford was one of the first industrialists to adopt a market orientated approach. When producing the Model T, he did not just design a car, produce it as cheaply as possible, and then try to sell it to the public. Instead, in advance of production, he identified the price at which he believed he could sell large numbers of Model T's. His starting point was the market and the Model T became one of the first 'mass-market' products. This illustrates the market orientated approach - consumers are central to a firm's decision making.

Sony are one of many modern firms who have taken a market orientated approach. The Sony Walkman is an example of a product developed in response to the wishes of consumers.

A market orientated business will have several advantages over one which is product orientated.
- It can respond more quickly to changes in the market because of its use of market information.
- It will be in a stronger position to meet the challenge of new competition entering the market.
- It will be more able to anticipate market changes.
- It will be more confident that the launch of a new product will be a success.

QUESTION 3 What's yellow, tacky and very successful? The answer can be found easily in stationery shops throughout the country. The 'Post-it-note' has become as indispensable as paper clips in many offices and is a best seller for the company 3M in 50 countries around the world.

The 'Post-it-note' was the brainchild of Art Fry, a chemical engineer who was a researcher in product development at 3M. Initially he wanted to find something which stopped his notes falling out of a hymn book - a sort of 'book mark that stuck'. He remembered that a colleague had previously developed a rather strange low tack adhesive and wondered if he could use it. At the time the company had no idea what to do with it. Fry found it perfect for his ideas - not too sticky to rip the paper, but sticky enough to keep things in place. That was in 1975.

'The processing equipment and the marketing of the product then had to be invented', he said. In 1979, after an initial failure with 'press and feel' pads, Post-it-notes were given away free with detailed brochures on how they could be used. The company found 90 per cent of people receiving free copies wanted to buy more.

Source: adapted from *The Observer*, 16.8.1992.

(a) Would you describe 3M as product orientated or market orientated in their development of the Post-it-note?
(b) Identify reasons why the Post-it-note was ultimately a success.

Influences on product and market orientation

Whether a business places emphasis on the product or on the market will depend on a number of factors.

The nature of the product Where a firm operates in an industry at the edge of new innovation, such as bio-technology, pharmaceuticals or electronics, it must innovate to survive. Although a firm may try to anticipate consumer demand, research is often 'pure' research, ie the researcher does not have a specific end product in mind.

Policy decisions A business will have certain **objectives**. Where these are set in terms of technical quality or safety, the emphasis is likely to be on production. Where objectives are in terms of market share or turnover, the emphasis is likely to be on marketing.

The views of those in control An accountant as a managing director may place emphasis on cash flow, profit forecasts etc., a production engineer may give technical quality control and research a high priority and a marketing person may be particularly concerned with market research and consumer relations.

The nature and size of the market If production costs are very high, then a company is likely to be market orientated. Only by being so can a company ensure it meets consumers' needs and avoids unsold goods and possible losses.

The degree of competition A company faced with a lack of competition may devote resources to research, with little concern about a loss of market share. Businesses in competitive markets are likely to spend more on marketing for fear of losing their share of the market.

Implications of a market orientated approach

What effect will taking a market orientated approach have on a business? It must:
- consult the consumer continuously (market research);
- design the product according to the wishes of the consumer;
- produce the product in the quantities that consumers want to buy;
- distribute the product according to the buying habits and delivery requirements of the consumer;
- set the price of the product at a level that the consumer is prepared to pay.

The business must produce the right product at the right price and in the right place, and it must let the consumer know that it is available. This is known as the **marketing mix** (unit 21). We will consider each aspect of the mix in more detail in subsequent units. Here it is enough to say that it involves the product, price, promotion and place.

It would be wrong to assume that the adoption of a market orientated approach will always be successful.

Many well-researched products have been failures.

Coloroll, for example, a well known business which started in the wallpaper market, expanded into home textiles and soft furnishings. Their attempt to enter the DIY burglar alarm market, however, was a failure. The company's reputation and design skills had little value in that section of the DIY market compared with other companies, whose reputations were based on home security or electronics.

QUESTION 4 Texas Instruments are one of a number of firms in the competitive market for supplying micro-chips to computer manufacturers. They have found that placing greater emphasis upon winning customer approval has become an important means of competing effectively in this market. Indeed, in this hi-tech industry, many believe that customer satisfaction is becoming as crucial to success as technological skills or manufacturing capabilities.

One example of the changes which Texas Instruments have made has been in their dealings with ICL, the UK based (and Japanese owned) computer manufacturer. In the past, ICL staff receiving goods from Texas Instruments had to open each package, often with as many as 10,000 components, confirm the contents listed on the packing note and computerise the data. Now, the data provided in bar-code form by Texas Instruments is read by ICL's bar-code system and goes automatically into its computer system.

In the past, Texas Instruments would only see customers when they were trying to sell a product or when something went wrong. This has changed with teams of managers, design engineers and accountants talking to personnel of all ranks within companies that purchase Texas products.

Source: adapted from the *Financial Times*, 1992.

(a) What evidence is there that Texas Instruments have become more market orientated?
(b) Why do you think Texas Instruments have become more market orientated?
(c) Advise Texas Instruments on the implications of a move to a more market orientated approach.

Key terms

Marketing - the management process involved in identifying, anticipating and satisfying consumer requirements profitably.
Market orientation - an approach to business which places the requirements of consumers at the centre of the decision making process.
Product orientation - an approach to business which places the main focus of attention upon the production process and the product itself.
Real disposable income - the income with which consumers are left after taxes (other than VAT) have been deducted and any state benefits added on. Any changes in the rate of inflation are also taken into account.

Summary

1. What is meant by the term marketing?
2. Distinguish between marketing and advertising.
3. Why is marketing described as a process?
4. How can marketing techniques be employed by non-profit making organisations?
5. What factors have made marketing so important in today's business environment?
6. Why might product orientation still be important today?
7. What are the main advantages of a market orientated approach?
8. Why might a market orientated approach be unsuccessful?

Question

The Mini Disc v DCC

Sony, the Japanese based multinational company are one of the leading suppliers of electronic products to the worldwide marketplace. They have a reputation for innovation and have led the rest of the world with products, such as the Walkman. On 30 May 1991, they announced their latest product - the Mini Disc player. The mini disc was an audio disc which could be played on a machine the size of a cigarette packet.

At the time Sony believed the likely buyers would be young people wanting a product so small it could be pinned to a T-shirt. Unlike the compact disc (CD) machines, which had been mass-marketed in play only form, the Mini Disc machines would be able to record as well as play. Launching the Mini Disc player in Tokyo, Mr Norio Ohga, Sony's President, said, 'The young generation needs technology that offers quality sound and random access which can be easily operated'. The Mini Disc was to be more expensive than the Walkman although the blank discs would be the same price as blank metal audio cassettes and pre-recorded discs would be the same price as CDs. Sony were not prepared to forecast likely sales, although they were confident about the success of the product.

Sony said that they would continue to produce digital audio tapes (DAT), though they accepted that it was unlikely to become a mass-market product. It was estimated that fewer than 150,000 DAT players were sold worldwide in 1990, compared with 31.2m CD players and 146.5m old-fashioned audio-cassette machines.

The new product was launched in late 1992. Phillips, with their digital compact cassette player (DCC) already on the market by this time, provided Sony with their main competition. The DCC player plays music stored 'digitally' on cassette. This gives a more accurate quality. An important feature of Phillips' strategy was that they had the backing of the world's big music companies. Mr Gerry Wirtz, a senior product manager at Phillips, said that by asking the music companies to help with the development of DCC the Dutch company hoped to escape the problems experienced by DAT in gaining widespread acceptability.

Mr Charles Kopleman, chairman of the US based SBK record company, believed that the battle would be won by the machine that was the cheapest and easiest to use. 'At the end of the day, it's the consumers who will make their minds up', he said. However, others believed that the record companies would be influential because if they didn't provide the music, consumers could not safely invest in the machines. One possibility is a worldwide fit of indecision on the part of consumers with everybody taking the 'wait and see' option. This could result in both formats flopping, leaving Sony and Phillips to find another way of replacing the cassette.

By mid-1993, DCCs appeared to have a head start on mini-discs. There were two reasons for this. Firstly, DCCs had better software support in the form of 1,500 titles available on major labels such as Polygram, Virgin, EMI, Chrysalis and Decca. It could well be the software that determines their ultimate fate. Secondly, DCC machines at this time were already in the shops. It could be the record retailers who make or break one of these two. They won't be able to stock full ranges of DCCs and Mini Discs alongside CDs and cassettes, so they're likely to be forced to dump one or the other pretty quickly.

Source: adapted from the *Financial Times*, 31.5.1991; *Q Magazine*, May 1993.

(a) What evidence is there to suggest that Sony is market rather than product orientated?
(b) Examine the factors that might have influenced Sony's decision to become market orientated.
(c) Outline the possible advantages to Sony of becoming market rather than product orientated.
(d) What factors might determine whether the Mini Disc or compact cassettes will win the battle for market dominance?
(e) Why might a 'market orientated' product, like the Mini Disc, possibly fail?

The objectives of marketing

MARKETING OBJECTIVES are the **goals** that a business is trying to achieve through its marketing. A company's marketing objectives will be influenced by its corporate objectives (☞ unit 5). For example, if the objective of the business is to maximise profit, marketing will be geared at achieving this. Firms' marketing objectives are likely to include some of the following.

- To target a new market or market segment. A business must decide which markets it will aim to sell its products into. It might decide that a product will sell better in a market abroad than one at home. It may also decide to target a section or **segment** of the market. So, for example, the product could be sold to a certain 'class' of customer or a certain age group.
- To achieve or maintain market share. A business may attempt to gain a certain MARKET SHARE or percentage of a market. It may set goals, such as 'gaining 10 per cent of all market sales within three years of launching a new product'. Once a business has achieved a particular market share, it must decide how to maintain it or increase it in the face of competition.
- To develop a range of products. A firm might aim to develop products which market research has indicated would be successful. Goals may also be set on how existing products could be improved or how products can be differentiated from rivals' products.
- To increase profitability and revenue. A business might set profit or revenue targets. It may also set goals for making products more profitable and assessing which products give the greatest profit.
- To improve the image of products. Businesses must consider the image they convey about their products. The image that consumers have about a firm's products will often be determined by promotion (☞ units 24 and 25).

There is a relationship between these objectives. An attempt to 'market' to a particular segment by producers of, say, environmentally friendly products, such as Ecover or Ark, will affect the type of image they portray. Similarly, a business aiming to develop a new product is likely to be trying to increase its revenue and profit.

The marketing objectives chosen must also take account of the constraints under which the firm operates. For example, products such as Lada cars have traditionally been sold to lower income groups. Huge sales increases are unlikely amongst higher income groups in a short period of time. Also, a firm cannot expect to launch a major new product onto the market unless it has the finance. Other constraints may include legal requirements, competition that a firm faces and economic changes that may take place.

QUESTION 1

Table 19.1 *Chocolate: European market share (per cent)*

	Nestlé Switz	Mars US	Suchard Switz/US	Cadbury Schweppes UK	FERRERO ROCHER Italy	All others
UK	28	26	2	30	2	12
Germany	13	17	19	-	16	37
France	27	11	14	8	6	33
Italy	22	10	3	-	28	37
Spain	36	1	14	1	-	46
Netherlands	15	23	9	-	-	53
TOTAL EUROPE	20	16	12	10	9	33

Source: adapted from BZW estimates.

(a) Compare the relative market shares of Suchard and Cadbury/Schweppes in the UK and Spain from Table 19.1.
(b) What marketing objectives might:
   (i) Mars set in the UK;
   (ii) Ferrero Rocher set in the UK;
   (iii) Cadbury/Schweppes set in Italy?
   Explain your answers.

Market research

Businesses use information from market research (☞ unit 9) to help them decide how to achieve their objectives. Market research is used to gather, collate and analyse information relating to all aspects of the marketing and consumption of goods and services. It provides firms with data upon which to make marketing decisions. 'To manage a business well is to manage its future, and to manage the future is to manage information', is a phrase which is often repeated in many successful companies. Market research can provide information in the following areas.

■ The market. It may be possible to identify market segments, gauge the size of the market or find the most likely consumers of the product and their spending patterns.

■ The product. Consumers' preferences for packaging, colour, design etc. can be found. It is also possible to find opportunities for new products or to change existing ones. Sometimes a new product is tested on a small representative section of the total market. This is known as TEST MARKETING. The test market area should have similar characteristics to those found nationally. Although test marketing provides reliable marketing information, it is expensive. It also allows competitors to see the new product and the chance to take counter action before a national launch.

■ Advertising and promotions. How effective promotions will be, what advertising media should be used and any ideas for advertising campaigns can all be found from market research.

■ Competition. The unique selling points of competitors' products (☞ unit 8), their market share and the sales trends of their products can be analysed.

■ Distribution. Research can be carried out to investigate the most suitable, outlets for a firm's products.

■ Price. Consumer reaction to differing price levels can be gauged through market research.

Marketing objectives will only be achieved if a firm can gather and use the information it collects. It is important, therefore, that marketing managers receive information from sources other than market research. Whilst it may generate valuable **primary** data (☞ unit 9), it can miss other sources of market information, such as is found in magazines, government departments and trade journals. There are also less formal means of researching the market, such as talking to sales representatives, personal visits, and keeping an 'ear to the ground' to remain in tune with any market changes.

QUESTION 2 Mail Boxes Etc is a business operation which began in the United States of America in 1980. It consists of 2,200 stores in 13 countries throughout the world which specialise in offering fax, stationery and post services to small and medium sized businesses. The first British based store was opened in Marylebone High Street, London in early 1993 with plans for three more to be opened in the same year.

The idea for these stores began when the company spotted a gap in the US market for private mail box facilities. Although it soon had competitors, Mail Boxes tried to distinguish itself by offering extra business services, such as office supplies ranging from envelopes and stamps to paper and sticking tape.

Mail Box customers can use the centre's address for mail, which they believe looks more respectable than a PO Box number, and they have access to a fax machine and all the benefits this offers without incurring the set up and running costs of purchasing one.

Serena Long, UK marketing manager, said the company decided that the 'old fashioned, friendly approach' would be particularly attractive in Britain at a time when traditional Post Offices were showing signs of moving in the opposite direction. A Mail Box store is something many towns are crying out for. There is nowhere else which offers the same 'one stop' convenience and service.

Source: adapted from *The Independent on Sunday*, 16.5.1993.

(a) What were Mail Box Etc's likely marketing objectives when they entered the UK market?
(b) How might market research have helped the business to arrive at the decision to open stores in the UK?

Targeting the market

Sometimes businesses attempt to market products to all consumers. At other times they may **target** particular groups to concentrate on. What strategies might a business use in each case?

Undifferentiated marketing This is aimed at most sections of the market, or possibly the whole market. It is likely to be expensive because of the need to sell to the whole market. A business will probably face competition from those firms aiming at certain segments within the market. This strategy is likely to suit those products which cannot easily be differentiated to suit the needs of particular groups of people. Milk is an example, although it has been differentiated to some extent with the sale of skimmed and semi-skimmed milk.

Differentiated marketing This can involve marketing different products or services to different groups of people or promoting the same product by different means. An example of the former is the way in which banks have different types of bank accounts. There are now bank accounts specifically designed for teenagers and others geared up to the needs of retired couples.

Concentrated marketing This occurs when a firm concentrates its marketing upon a specific section of the market. An example might be a product that is only available to certain people, such as the under-26s European rail pass, or because the firm only expects a certain **market segment** to buy the product. This strategy is often used by small firms as well as those in specialist markets, as it is not as expensive as other methods.

QUESTION 3

Discuss whether a business would use undifferentiated, differentiated, or concentrated marketing for the above products.

A - Higher managerial, administrative or professional
B - Middle managerial, administrative or professional
C1 - Supervisory or clerical, junior managerial
C2 - Skilled manual workers
D - Semi and unskilled manual workers
E - Casual or lowest paid workers, unemployed.

It is usual for four categories to be used - AB, C1, C2, DE. (Sometimes AB and C1 are joined to give ABC1.) Figure 19.1 shows the number of holidays taken by different 'classes' of UK residents. A company selling family holidays in the UK may, for example, target social classes C1 and C2, aiming at those who don't take a holiday in these groups. Because of the regular changes in the pay and status of occupations, these categories are revised from time to time.

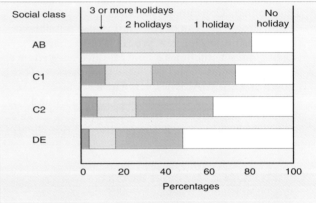

Source: adapted from British National Travel Authority; British Tourist Authority

Figure 19.1 *Number of holidays per year by social class (holidays of 4 nights or more by adult residents of GB in GB or abroad)*

Market segmentation

Producers may attempt to identify and target groups of people with similar needs and develop products or services for each of them. Breaking a market down into sub-groups with similar characteristics is known as MARKET SEGMENTATION.

Threshers, the off-licence chain, have made use of this technique. Each branch stocks goods which are suitable to the population of the area they are serving. Branches in towns such as Eastbourne or Cheltenham, for example, are more likely to promote whisky and sherry, rather than lager and vodka, to cater for 'older' customers.

There are a number of different ways in which firms can segment their market.

■ By age. Many firms are beginning to pay closer attention to the segment that includes the over 60s, as they are growing as a proportion of the total population. The marketing of financial services for older people has become popular in recent years.

■ By sex. Manufacturers may target females when marketing their products. A number of the major car manufacturers, for example, have targeted women in their promotional campaigns for smaller hatchbacks.

■ By level of education. This is usually whether or not consumers have studied at higher education. An example might be a magazine aimed at those with certain qualifications.

■ Social class. Social classes are often placed into six socio-economic categories.

■ Income. Income groups may differ from 'social classes'. For example, a self-employed skilled manual worker, such as an electrician, might receive the same income as a middle manager. However, because of their occupations, they will be in different socio-economic groups.

■ Religion. Food producers may specialise in Kosher food for Jewish people, for example.

■ Ethnic grouping. Some products, such as hair gels, are aimed at Afro-Caribbean groups.

■ Family characteristics. Examples of these segments include Young Singles, Married with no children (if both partners have jobs, such units might be referred to as 'DINKIES' - Double Income No Kids) and Older Singles.

■ Political voting preference. Newspapers are often targeted at consumers according to how they vote.

■ Geography. This might include considering the region of a country the consumer lives in (urban, rural, semi-rural or suburban). It may also consider the type of house or road people live in. This method can be especially useful in large or highly culturally diverse markets where buying patterns are influenced by region. For example, firms that regard the European Community as their market are likely to segment this market into more manageable chunks.

QUESTION 4

Table 19.2 *Participation in sports and exercise by sex and age*

Percentage in each group participating in each activity in the 4 weeks before the survey	Males				Females			
	16-19	20-29	30-59	60+	16-19	20-29	30-59	60+
Jogging, cross country/ road running	18	17	7	-	10	5	2	-
Swimming	24	20	14	3	24	20	14	3
Snooker, pool and billiards	65	49	23	6	23	11	3	-
Weight training	22	17	5	-	9	5	2	-
Keep fit/yoga, aerobics, dance exercise	5	6	5	3	24	20	12	5
Cycling	28	12	10	5	14	8	8	2
Sample size = (100%) Numbers in sample	706	1,725	4,476	2,179	678	1,923	4,826	3,016

Source: adapted from *Social Trends*, CSO.

Your company, Sportswear Ltd, is developing new ranges of leisure wear. Using the information above, write a report to the marketing director identifying the market segments the company should aim at and the type of clothing it might produce. You will need to justify your decisions.

■ Personality and attitude to life. Consumers are classified in this way according to their psychological characteristics.

The main aim of market segmentation is to increase profits by raising sales. More specific aims may be to assess the strengths and weaknesses of a product or service with a group of consumers or to identify segments to which sales might be targeted.

It is usual for firms to employ a variety of the segmentation methods above. So, for example, a manufacturer of luxury apartments may target a segment including single women or men, with no children, in the 30-40 age range, with very high incomes and in social class A.

Research into why firms are successful has shown why market segmentation is so important. One survey, for example, revealed that Japanese firms paid far more attention to market segmentation than British firms. A number of the UK firms surveyed did not see their market as being made up of segments. They felt that anyone in the market could be a customer and that there was little purpose in breaking down the market. As a result, such firms have been pushed into low quality, low price market segments. Japanese firms, however, have been able to successfully target more up-market segments.

Niche marketing

NICHE MARKETING involves a business aiming a product at a particular, often tiny, segment of a market. It is the opposite of mass marketing, which involves products being aimed at whole markets rather than particular parts of them. Tie Rack, Knickerbox and Classic FM are all examples of attempts to exploit niche markets.

Why do firms attempt this type of marketing?

■ Small firms are often able to sell to niche markets which have been either overlooked or ignored by other firms. In this way, they are able to avoid competition in the short run at least.

■ By targeting specific market segments, firms can focus on the needs of consumers in these segments. This can allow them to gain an advantage over firms targeting a wider market.

There are, however, a number of problems with niche marketing. These might include some of the following.

■ Firms which manage successfully to exploit a niche market often attract competition. Niche markets, by their very nature, are small and are often unable to sustain two or more competing firms. Large businesses joining the market may benefit from economies of scale which small firms are unable to achieve.

■ Many small firms involved in niche marketing have just one product aimed at one small market. This does not allow a business to spread its risks as a firm producing many products might.

■ Because niche markets contain small numbers of consumers, they tend to be faced by bigger and more frequent swings in consumer spending than larger markets. This may mean a rapid decline in sales following an equally rapid growth in sales.

QUESTION 5 Having worked for Marks and Spencers and Tie Rack for a number of years, Sophie Mirman believed that she had spotted a gap in a market traditionally dominated by large clothes retailers and department stores. One day she had been out shopping and discovered she couldn't find a pair of tights to match the new dress she had just bought. This discovery, combined with an earlier observation of women fighting their way through crowded department stores just to buy a pair of tights, convinced her that there was an opening in the hosiery market.

After eventually raising sufficient finance, Sophie, together with her husband Richard, opened the first branch of Sock Shop in Knightsbridge Underground station. It was an instant success and led to the opening of a number of other shops. By 1987, 47 shops had been opened and the company was valued at over £50 million. However, the success was short lived. An attempt to expand into the USA flopped with the loss of millions of pounds. In addition, an especially long and hot summer in the UK in 1989 led to a huge fall in the sales of both tights and socks. By 1990, the company had collapsed.

(a) Explain why Sock Shop was an example of niche marketing.
(b) Why do you think Sock Shop was so successful in their first few years of operation?

Key terms

Market niche - a small segment of a market.
Market segmentation - breaking a market down into sub-groups which share similar characteristics.
Market share - the proportion of total sales in a particular market for which one or more firms are responsible. It is usually expressed as a percentage.
Marketing objectives - marketing goals that businesses try to achieve.
Test marketing - testing a product out on a small section of a market prior to its full launch.

Summary

1. Identify 5 marketing objectives.
2. What constraints might be placed on a firm's choice of marketing objective?
3. What is the role of a market research department?
4. Explain the difference between differentiated and undifferentiated marketing.
5. What is meant by a market segment?
6. In what ways might a firm segment its market?
7. Give 2 examples of a niche market.
8. Why might a firm concentrate on niche marketing?

Question

Patak

In 1993 there were some 7,500 Indian restaurants in the UK. By 1996 there should be over 10,000. Most dishes are not original. They are made by chefs from spice bases. Almost 90 per cent of all dishes are made from spice bases produced by Patak.

Patak is run by Kirit Patak. The business was started by his father, Laxmishanker, after he arrived in the UK in 1957. It specialises in spice pastes for Indian dishes made from a special recipe. The secret of what is included is closely guarded - as close as the blend for Coca-Cola. The recipe is made by Kirit's wife Meena, based on traditional recipes.

In 1993 Patak employed over 160 people and sold well over £10 million of spices and pickles a year. How did the firm become so successful? The 1980s saw a boom in Indian restaurants and Indian meals. The business quickly decided that the 'Indian market in the UK was mature and switched its marketing to large supermarkets. Every effort was made to get products on the shelves of mainstream supermarkets and retail chains. This, and the growth of Indian restaurants, led to rapid expansion. Between 1975 and 1990 sales overseas also expanded, particularly in America and Australia. Patak have the ambition to be the world's number one supplier of Indian food ingredients.

In 1990 the company appointed David Page, former MD of Campbells UK, to make Patak a leading brand. Page was particularly keen to widen the marketing emphasis. Arguably the main sales had been to 'young AB and C1s'. The stress was now to be placed on 'anyone with a stomach'.

Kirit is looking to expand in future. One requirement is likely to be a new factory. He has also hinted that he is looking out for businesses to acquire.

Source : adapted from *Business Age*, May 1993.

(a) What evidence is there to suggest that Patak may have targeted part of the market in the past?
(b) How might this have affected the business?
(c) Explain the statements 'the main sales had been to young ABC1s' and 'stress would now be placed on anyone with a stomach'.
(d) What marketing strategy is suggested by your answer to question (c)?
(e) Discuss the possible marketing objectives of Patak in the future, using evidence from the passage.

Stages in the product life cycle

A business aiming to achieve its marketing objectives (☞ unit 19) must be aware of the PRODUCT LIFE CYCLE. The product life cycle shows the different stages that a product passes through and the sales that can be expected at each stage. Most products pass through six stages - development, introduction, growth, maturity, saturation and decline. These are illustrated in Figure 20.1.

Development During the development stage the product is being designed. Suitable ideas must be investigated, developed and tested. If an idea is considered worth pursuing then a **prototype** or model of the product might be produced. A decision will then be made whether or not to launch the product. A large number of new products never progress beyond this stage. This is because management are often reluctant to take risks associated with new products.

During the development stage it is likely that the business will spend to develop the product. As there will be no sales at this stage the business will initially be making a 'loss' on the product.

Introduction This stage is when the product is new on the market and sales are often slow. Costs are incurred when the product is launched. It may be necessary to build a new production line or plant, and the firm will have to meet promotion and distribution costs. Therefore, it is likely that the product will still not be profitable.

The length of this stage will vary according to the product. With brand new technical products, eg washing machines, compact disc players and personal computers, the introduction stage can be quite long. It takes time for consumers to become confident that such products 'work'. At first the price of such products may be quite high. On the other hand, a product can be an instant hit resulting in a very rapid sales growth. Fashion products and some FAST MOVING CONSUMER GOODS may enjoy this type of start to their life.

Growth Once the product is established and consumers are aware of it, sales begin to grow rapidly. The product then becomes profitable. If it is a new product and there is a rapid growth in sales, competitors may launch their own version. This can lead to a slow-down of the rise in sales.

Maturity At some stage the growth in sales will level off. The product has become established with a stable market share at this point. Sales will have peaked and competitors will have entered the market to take advantage of profits.

Saturation As more firms enter the market it will become saturated. Some businesses will be forced out of the market, as there are too many firms competing for consumers.

Decline Eventually sales of products will decline. This is usually due to changing consumer tastes, new technology or the introduction of new products.

Most products have a limited life, although some firms are still enjoying the profits from products which were launched many years ago. The familiar Oxo cube was launched in 1910, Kellogg's Cornflakes were launched in 1906 and Theakstons Old Peculiar, a strong ale, was launched in the eighteenth century. These products still sell well today. Once consumers lose interest in a product and sales fall, the firm may withdraw it from the market. It may be replaced by a new product. Sometimes products are withdrawn in case they damage the image of the company.

Because of the high cost of investment, car producers such as Rover in the UK, and Ford and Vauxhall in Europe, set product life cycles of 10 years for their models. It appears, for many products, that life cycles are getting shorter and shorter, especially in areas like electronics. In the computer industry, some models have become obsolete within months, as new versions appear which are more technically advanced.

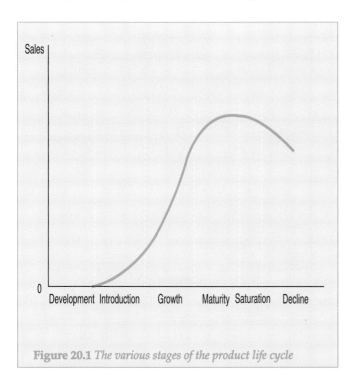

Figure 20.1 *The various stages of the product life cycle*

QUESTION 1

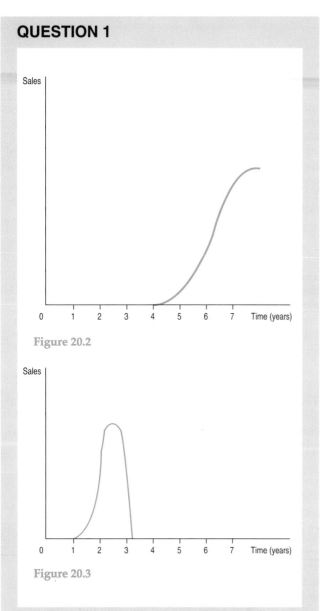

Figure 20.2

Figure 20.3

(a) Examine Figures 20.2 and 20.3. For each of these, list a product which you think might have a similar product life cycle.
(b) Why do some products have a very long life cycle (greater than 50 years)?
(c) Sketch the current product life cycle of three of the following products:
   (i)   ra-ra skirts;
   (ii)   ice cream Mars bars;
   (iii) skateboards;
   (iv)   Coca-cola;
   (v)   Hovis bread;
   (vi)   *Today* newspaper;
   (vii) compact discs;
   (viii) smoke alarms;
   (ix)   the Volkswagen Beetle;
   (x)   a football strip of a Premier League team.

Extension strategies

It is clear from the product life cycle that the sales of products decline, although at different rates. Firms can attempt to extend the life of a product by using EXTENSION STRATEGIES. They may decide to use one or more of the following techniques.

■ Finding new uses for the product. Video tape which had previously been used for video recorders attached to televisions was adapted to be used with portable camcorders.

■ Finding new markets for existing products. The late 1980s saw a boom in sports equipment and clothes being sold in retail outlets as fashion clothing and accessories.

■ Developing a wider product range. Supermarkets now sell freshly squeezed orange juice in 'one drink' bottles as well as in larger bottles. These are suitable for lunchtime drinks.

■ Changing the appearance or packaging. Deodorants have been repackaged into 'roll ons' rather than aerosol can sprays to make them more environmentally friendly.

■ Encouraging people to use the product more frequently. Wholemeal bread and fibre breakfast cereals have been promoted as products able to make up for the deficiency in our fibre intake.

The effect that an extension strategy can have on the product life cycle is shown in Figure 20.4. As the market becomes saturated and sales begin to fall, the decline in sales is delayed by the use of an extension strategy.

It would be sensible for a business to try to extend the life of a mature product **before** sales start to decline. Firms that can predict falling sales from **market forecasts** (☞ unit 15) may attempt to use extension strategies before the decline takes place.

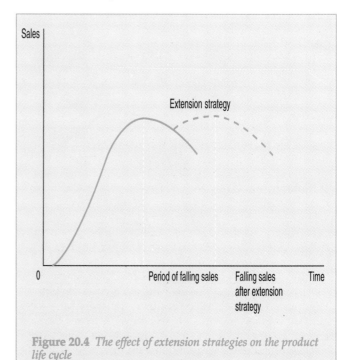

Figure 20.4 *The effect of extension strategies on the product life cycle*

QUESTION 2 1992 saw even the Mars bar suffer from the recession. Mars announced that in a bid to counter declining sales, a 3.2 per cent drop since 1990, they were changing the Mars bar from November onwards. The new bar would have the same ingredients, but a new blend and a new 'smoother and creamier' taste. Customers would also get a 6 per cent bigger chocolate bar for the same price. Ever watchful of current trends, Mars kept the same 452 calories in every 10 grams.

Bob Eagle, the Mars spokesperson, said 'Our research shows a clear consumer preference for a bigger size.' The company expected to sell more than a billion bars in 1992.

Along with the change in size came a change in slogan. The famous 'A Mars a day helps you work, rest and play' was replaced by 'Now there's more to Mars'.

Source: adapted from the *Daily Mirror*, 10 September, 1992.

(a) In what sense was Mars using an extension strategy in 1992?
(b) Identify and explain the extension strategy Mars used to extend the product life cycle of the Mars bar.
(c) Advise Mars on another extension strategy it could use in future.

The product mix

Product life cycle analysis shows businesses that sales of products eventually decline. It is possible to delay this decline using extension strategies.

A well organised business will attempt to phase out old products and introduce new ones. This is known as managing the PRODUCT MIX (or PRODUCT PORTFOLIO). With a constant launch of new products, a business can make sure a 'vacuum' is not created as products reach the end of their life.

Figure 20.5 shows how a business can manage its product mix. Say that a business over a particular time period aims to launch three products. By organising their launch at regular intervals, there is never a gap in the market. As one product is declining, another is growing and further launches are planned. At point (i), as sales of product X are growing, product Y has just been launched.

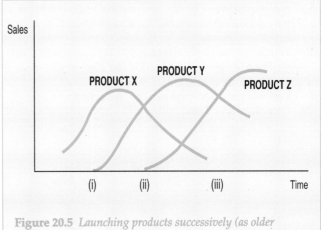

Figure 20.5 *Launching products successively (as older products decline, new products are launched onto the market).*

This means that at point (ii), when sales of product X have started to decline, sales of product Y are growing and product Z has just been launched.

This simple example shows a 'snapshot' of three products only. In practice, a business may have many products. It would hope that existing products remain in 'maturity' for a long period. The profit from these mature products would be used to 'subsidise' the launch of new products. New products would be costly at first, and would make no profit for the business.

Examples of businesses that have successfully managed their product mix are sweet manufacturers. Companies such as Nestle produce a wide range of products, including KitKat, Milky Bar and Yorkie, and constantly look to launch new products.

The product mix includes **product lines**. These are groups of products which are closely related to each other. One example is the launch of a range of products associated with a new film. Product lines in this area include anything from T-shirts and mugs to plastic dolls and comics for films such as Batman. One of the most successful product lines of all time has been the Mickey Mouse merchandise of the Walt Disney Company.

Managing the product mix

One problem for firms in planning their product mix is that it is very difficult in practice to tell what stage of the life cycle a product is at. Also, there is no standard lifetime for products. For example, young people's fashion clothing has life cycles which can be predicted with some certainty. Others are less reliable. Who, for example, could have predicted the lengthy life cycles of products such as Heinz baked beans and the VW Beetle, or the short life of products such as the Sinclair C5?

A useful technique for allowing firms to analyse their product mix is the **Product Portfolio Matrix** developed by the Boston Consulting Group. It is sometimes called the **Boston Matrix**. This matrix places products into four categories.

■ 'Star' products are those with a large share of a high growth market.

- 'Problem children' might have future potential as they are in growth markets, but their sales are not particularly good.
- 'Cash cows' are those which are able to generate funds, possibly to support other products. They are mature products with a stable market share.
- 'Dogs' are products that may be in decline.

These are shown in Table 20.1.

Table 20.1 *The Product Portfolio Mix (Boston Matrix)*

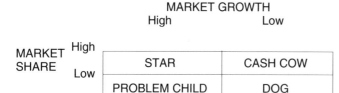

		MARKET GROWTH	
		High	Low
MARKET SHARE	High	STAR	CASH COW
	Low	PROBLEM CHILD	DOG

Firms must ensure that their product mix does not contain too many items within each category. Naturally, firms do not want lots of 'Dogs', but they should also avoid having too many 'Stars' and 'Problem children'. Products on the left hand side of the table are in the early stages of the product life cycle and are in growing markets, but the cost of developing and promoting them will not yet have been recovered. This will drain the firm's resources. Balancing these with 'Cash cows' will mean the revenue from the 'Cash cows' can be used to support products in a growing market. The development cost of 'Cash cows' is likely to have already been recovered and promotional costs should be low relative to sales.

This does not mean though that firms would want lots of 'Cash cows' and few 'Problem children' and 'Stars'. This is because many of the 'Stars' and perhaps some 'Problem children' might become the 'Cash cows' of the future.

New product development

Planning the product mix requires the continual development and launch of new products. New products are needed to replace products coming to the end of their life cycle and to keep up with changes in the market. This is called **new product development**.

In some industries the need to plan ahead is very important. In the chemical industry, development work is done on products which might not reach the market for over ten years. In the motor industry many cars take over five years to develop.

New products normally pass through five stages when they are being developed.

Generating ideas The first stage is when firms generate ideas. Ideas for new products come from a variety of sources.

- Identifying gaps in the market, perhaps through market research. An example of this has been the development of vegetarian microwave dishes by food producers.
- Scientific research. Firms such as ICI devote huge amounts to research and development expenditure. As a result they have developed products ranging from 'non-drip paint' to bio-degradable plastics.
- Creative ideas or 'brainstorming'. Products such as the jet engine have come about as a result of this.

Analysis The second stage is the analysis of those ideas generated in the first stage. There are a number of questions a firm might ask. Most importantly, it must find out if the product is marketable - if enough consumers wish to buy it to allow the firm to make a profit. Businesses must also decide if the product fits in with the company's objectives, if it is legal and if the technology is available to produce it.

Development The third stage is the actual development of the product. This may involve technical development in the laboratory or the production of a prototype. Such work will be carried out by the **research and development** department. An important part of this process is the actual design of the product (☞ unit 28). Some preliminary testing may be carried out to find out whether or not the product actually meets consumers' needs.

Test marketing Stage four involves the test marketing (☞ unit 19) of the product. This is done because of the high cost of launching on the national market. It is less expensive to make mistakes on a smaller scale.

QUESTION 3 Lokotronics are a company producing a range of electrical goods. Table 20.2 shows the sales from just four of their products over the period 1984-1992.

Table 20.2

Sales (000)

Year	Product A	Product B	Product C	Product D	All products
1984	2	8	-	-	
1985	4	10	-	-	
1986	8	6	9	-	
1987	12	3	15	-	
1988	18	1	18	2	
1989	20	-	16	6	
1990	22	-	11	15	
1991	22	-	10	20	
1992	21	-	8	25	

(a) From the sales figures, describe the product life cycles of:
    (i) Product A;
    (ii) Product B.
(b) Calculate the total sales of all products in each year.
(c) Comment on the management of the product mix over the period.

Launch and commercialisation The final stage is the launch and commercialisation. Here any problems found during test marketing must be solved. The firm will then decide on the 'marketing package' it will use to give the product launch the greatest chance of success.

At each of the five stages, many ideas are rejected. This means that very few ideas generated in the first stage will actually end up as a product launched onto the market. In Figure 20.6 and Table 20.3, an example is shown where 40 ideas were put forward for a new product. In this company the majority of ideas do not get beyond the first stage. The pass rate at this stage is only 1 in 5, with 4 out of 5 ideas being rejected. After that, the number of ideas which survive from one stage to the next increases as the pass rate falls from 1 in 5 ideas to 1 in 2. At the end of the process, only 1 out of a total of 40 ideas has survived to be launched onto the market.

Table 20.3

Stage	Number of ideas	Pass rate
Generation of ideas	40	1 in 5
Business analysis	8	1 in 2
Development	4	1 in 2
Test marketing	2	1 in 2
Commercialisation and launch	1	1 in 1

Constraints on new product development

There is a wide range of **constraints** on firms. These will restrict the number of new products developed.

Availability of finance and resources In highly competitive markets firms find that their profit margins are squeezed. This means that financial and human resources are often not available to develop new products. An example of this is in the market for budget fashion clothing. Firms in this market tend to copy products developed by others.

Cost Even when firms have resources, the cost of developing new products may be prohibitive. The development of products in the electronics market can cost millions of pounds. As technological boundaries have been pushed forward, the cost of even modest new product development has risen sharply. Also, in many markets products have increasingly shorter life spans. This means that less time is available to recover development costs.

Market constraints There is little point in a firm developing a new product unless consumers are prepared to purchase it at a price which can cover development and production costs. Many so-called 'tremendous ideas' for new products have been abandoned. This is because firms believe they cannot find a profitable market for the product.

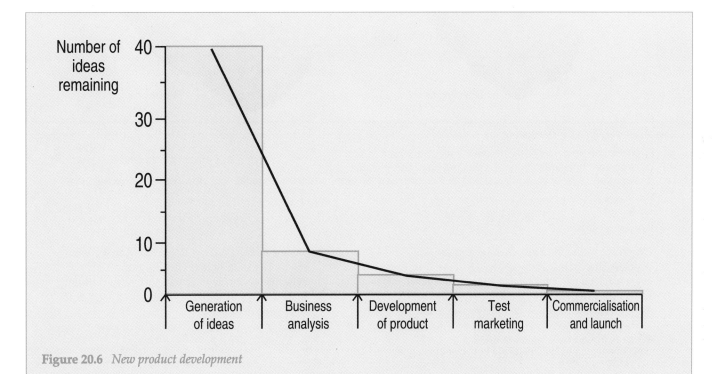

Figure 20.6 *New product development*

Legal constraints Firms cannot develop whatever new products they wish. Legislation must be taken into account. For example, a pharmaceutical company wishing to develop a new product must be sure that it adheres to health legislation.

QUESTION 4 In 1992, an international consortium including AT and T, the US telecommunications group, and Matsushita of Japan, the world's leading consumer electronics company, were poised to win the race to launch the world's first 'personal communicator'. This was to be a combined pocket telephone and personal computer. It was an example of a new class of portable devices, combining the power of personal computers with the communications abilities of a cellular telephone. The developers of this new product hoped that it would have as much impact on person-to-person communication as the telephone had in the early 1900s. It was estimated that $38 million had been spent to bring this product to the market.

The personal communicator

Aerial for cellular radio

Voice telephony

Screen

Screen for electronic mail, facsimile and personal computing

Keyboard for computing

Voice telephony

NotePhone

FlipPhone

Source: adapted from the *Financial Times*, 1.10. 1992.

(a) What are the advantages to the consumer of this new product?
(b) Where might the ideas for such a product have come from?
(c) Unlike many, this product has passed all the stages of development through to launch. How would you explain this?

Summary

1. Briefly describe the various stages in the product life cycle.
2. Why might a product have a 'steep' life cycle?
3. How can a firm extend the life of its products?
4. Explain how a business can prevent a 'vacuum' in its product mix.
5. What is meant by a product line?
6. What is meant by the Product Portfolio Matrix?
7. How can the Product Portfolio Matrix help a business to manage its product mix?
8. What is meant by new product development?
9. State 2 ways in which a business can generate new product ideas.
10. What is meant by the 'pass rate' of new products?

Question

Murphy Drinks Ltd

Murphy Drinks Ltd had been producing powdered chocolate drinks for just over thirty years. The company was set up as the market for vending machines producing hot drinks had just begun to mushroom in the early 1960s. Their first product, 'Murphy's Vending Chocolate', came onto the market in 1963.

Its success in gaining a 35 per cent share of the market for vended chocolate drinks in under five years acted as the foundation stone for the future actions of the company. Ever since 1968, the percentage market share held by Murphy's vending chocolate had never fallen below this 35 per cent mark and, at times, had risen as high as 42 per cent. Sales generated by this product were in excess of £160,000 in the financial year ending in 1992.

The success of the vending chocolate gave Murphys the confidence to develop a new product in 1969 called 'Catering Chocolate'. This was aimed at the hotel, canteen and restaurant market. Although 'Catering Chocolate' was successful in gaining a 20 per cent share of its market, the cost of developing it made Murphys cautious about attempting to launch any further products. In total, almost £15,000 was spent over a two year period in the process leading up to the product being marketed to hotels, restaurants and canteens throughout the country.

It wasn't for another eighteen years that Murphys attempted to launch a new product. This time, in response to changing tastes in the hot drinks market, they developed a low calorie chocolate drink called 'Lifestyle'. This low calorie drink was sold in sachets and distributed mainly through the larger supermarket chains. Despite their past successes, Murphys initially found it difficult to establish a firm footing for this product. However, the last two years, 1991 and 1992, had witnessed a substantial growth in the sales of 'Lifestyle' as consumer and retailer resistance to it was broken down by a series of promotional campaigns. Sales revenue in 1992 amounted to over £100,000.

Encouraged by the success of 'Lifestyle' in the retail sector, Murphys had made the decision in 1992 to launch a product line which they had been developing for a number of years. This was a range of flavoured chocolate drinks called 'Hi-lifes'. There was a high degree of initial interest from consumers in this product range, but it was too early - only six months after the launch - to evaluate its likely success.

Murphys also wanted to develop a new chocolate drink (called Bliss) and had a number of ideas which needed to be considered. However, members of the board of directors were split on this issue. Some were keen to go ahead with the new product development programme for two main reasons: firstly, out of concern about the falling sales of 'Catering Chocolate' and secondly, because they felt that now was the time to capitalise upon their recent success with 'Lifestyle'. Other members of the Board were much more cautious. Not only were they concerned about upsetting their present product mix, but there were worries about the cost of developing this product.

Table 20.4 shows the different stages involved in the development of this new product and the cost at each stage.

Table 20.4 *Cost of developing a new chocolate drink (Bliss)*

	Cost per idea	No. of ideas	Pass rate
Generation of ideas	£50	40	1 in 5
Analysis of ideas	£500	8	1 in 2
Development	£8,000	4	1 in 2
Test marketing	£13,000	2	1 in 2
Launch and commercialisation	£35,000	1	1 in 1

(a) At what stage of the life cycle were each of Murphy's products in 1992?
(b) Describe Murphy's existing product mix. Do you think it is well managed?
(c) What extension strategies would you recommend for Catering Chocolate?
(d) From the figures given in the table, calculate the total cost to Murphys of developing the new chocolate drink, Bliss.
(e) Other than cost, what might prevent Murphys from developing a new product?

The marketing mix

In order to achieve its marketing objectives (☞ unit 19), as well as the overall objectives of the company, a business must consider its MARKETING MIX. The marketing mix refers to those elements of a firm's marketing strategy which are designed to meet the needs of its customers. There are four parts to the marketing mix - product, price, promotion and place. These are often known as the four 'Ps', as illustrated in Figure 21.1. To meet consumers' needs, firms must produce the right product, at the right price, make it available at the right place, and let consumers know about it through promotion.

Product Unit 20 showed the importance of the product life cycle and the product mix to a firm's marketing. Businesses must make sure their product is meeting the needs of their customers. This means paying close attention to a number of the features of the product.

- How consumers will use the product. A furniture manufacturer would market different products for home use than it would for office use. Products created for the office would need to be sturdy, able to withstand regular use and long lasting. Products created for the home would need to stress features such as the quality of the fabric, design and the level of comfort.
- The appearance of the product. This is likely to involve a consideration of such things as colour. Food manufacturers, for example, go to great lengths to ensure that their products have an appealing colour. In some cases this means adding artificial colourings to

alter the appearance. There are many other factors to be taken into account during the product's design (☞ unit 28). These include shape, taste and size. Deodorant manufacturers and toilet cleaning fluid producers might also consider aroma.
- Financial factors. There is little point in a firm producing a product which meets the needs of consumers if it cannot be produced at the right cost. All things being equal, a good produced at high cost is likely to be sold for a high price. Unless consumers are convinced that a product is **value for money**, they are unlikely to purchase it.

Price The pricing policy that a business chooses is often a reflection of the market at which it is aiming. Prices will not always be set at the level which will maximise sales or short run profits. For example, a firm may charge a high price because it is aiming to sell to consumers who regard the product as exclusive rather than because production costs are high. The way in which the market influences the pricing policy of a firm is dealt with in unit 22. However, factors such as production costs do also influence pricing to some extent (☞ unit 23).

Promotion There are a number of promotional methods a business can use including above the line promotions, such as TV advertising, and below the line promotions such as personal selling (☞ units 24 and 25). A firm will choose a promotion method it feels is likely to be most effective in the market in which it operates. For example, methods such as '10 per cent off your next purchase' are used with 'fast moving' consumer goods, such as canned food and packets of biscuits. National television

Figure 21.1 *Elements of the marketing mix*

advertising will only be used for products with a high sales turnover and a wide appeal.

Place This refers to the means by which the product will be distributed to the consumer (☞ unit 26). The product must get to the right place, at the right time. This means making decisions about the way in which the product will be physically distributed, ie by air, sea, rail or road. It also means taking into account how the product is sold. This may be by direct mail from the manufacturer or through retail outlets such as supermarkets.

QUESTION 1 First Direct, a part of Midland Bank PLC, was launched in 1989 as a completely new concept in banking. It is a bank that has no branches, but can be contacted by telephone 24 hours a day, 365 days a year. Through the savings it makes on not having High Street branches, it is able to offer higher interest rates on current accounts in credit and lower rates of interest on customer loans than most of its competitors.

The new bank was launched with a £3.5 million advertising campaign. Much of this was spent on a bizarre series of television advertisements in which a frozen image of a fish and a bucket appeared together with the First Direct logo. The principal aim of this was to put the new bank on the map by attracting customer attention.

By the end of 1990 the bank had attracted 100,000 customers. It has been estimated that there are three to five million potential customers in the UK for First Direct and that this figure may grow substantially as the concept of direct banking becomes accepted.

Source: adapted from *The Observer*, 26.5.1991.

(a) Identify the elements of the marketing mix that First Direct is emphasising.
(b) Why might First Direct be able to gain a competitive edge in the banking market?

Choice of marketing mix

Each firm must decide upon its own marketing mix. It is important that the right **balance** between price, product, promotion and place is achieved. It could be argued that as firms become more market orientated all elements are important. However, at times firms may stress one or more elements of the mix. The mix a firm chooses will depend upon certain factors.

■ The type of product they are selling. For example, a firm marketing highly technical products is likely to emphasise its products' qualities rather than giving a free good as a promotion. However, a firm marketing a product very similar to that of its competitors may wish to emphasise a lower price or use some method of promotion.

■ The market they are selling to. Firms selling consumer goods aimed at the mass market are likely to emphasise the promotional and price aspects of their marketing mix. Firms selling machinery or industrial goods are likely to stress the product itself.

■ The degree of competition it faces. A firm operating in

a competitive market, with many close rivals, is likely to stress the importance of price in its marketing mix. In less competitive markets price might not be seen as being so important.

■ The marketing mix of competitors. Firms cannot afford to ignore the mix chosen by competitors. For example, confectionery manufacturers lay particular emphasis upon the availability of their products in a wide range of retail outlets. These include petrol stations, newsagents, off-licences and DIY stores. The emphasis here is on place. Any firm wishing to compete in this market would, therefore, be unable to overlook the importance of place in this marketing mix.

An advertisement stressing product quality.

QUESTION 2 $50 million (£34.4 million) was spent on the launch of Gio, the women's perfume developed for Giorgio Armani, the Italian fashion designer, by L'Oreal, the French cosmetics group. Gio is pitched in the middle of the fragrance market with prices starting at $40.

The process of launching this product began with the search for a new fragrance. 1,100 tests were conducted over a 15 month period to choose a scent which would appeal in both Europe and the US, where consumers tend to prefer stronger, less subtle smells.

The aim is for Gio to make annual sales of more than $120 million. Past experience of firms operating in this market indicates that profits are negligible initially. This is because advertising typically absorbs 75 per cent of sales in the first year and 50 per cent in the second. But from the third year the advertising budget falls to 30 per cent of sales. Given small production costs, a strong selling perfume can then produce annual profits of around $80 million.

However, the risk of failure is high. The fragrance market is intensely competitive thanks to the combination of recession and the expansion of the large perfume producers. The competition is especially intense with regard to distributing such products. Manufacturers have to be very careful not to jeopardise relations with retailers.

Source: adapted from the *Financial Times*, 11.3.1993.

(a) From the information above identify two factors which may influence the marketing mix for Gio.
(b) Advise L'Oreal on the aspects of their marketing mix which they could emphasise.

The marketing plan

To help make marketing decisions a business must plan effectively. This usually means devising a MARKETING PLAN. The marketing plan is concerned with a number of questions.

- Where is the business at present? A business can only plan where it is going if it knows where it is starting from. Finding out where a company is involves a MARKETING AUDIT. This analyses the **external** and **internal** factors which affect a company's performance. Most businesses analyse their current position by using a SWOT ANALYSIS. Table 21.1 shows the information that might be found from a SWOT analysis.

Table 21.1

Internal
- STRENGTHS (the strong points of the business)
- WEAKNESSES (the problems it has at present)

External
- OPPORTUNITIES (that may arise in the future)
- THREATS (that may arise and should be avoided)

- Where does the company wish to be in the future? This involves the business setting objectives to be achieved. The objectives provide goals and targets for a business to aim at. They may include such goals as a growth in sales or gaining a certain market share in future.
- How will the business achieve its objectives? A business must decide how to get where it wants to go. It will have **marketing strategies** which it will use to achieve its objectives. Often marketing strategies are expressed in terms of the 4 'Ps'. So, for example, a company wishing to gain a '10 per cent increase in its market share' must make sure that it has the right product at the right price with an effective promotion and distribution policy.

There will be a number of factors, both internal and external to a business, which will influence its marketing plan.

Internal factors

- People. A huge range of people will be involved in devising and implementing marketing plans. The objectives of these people will determine the targets set in the plan. Also the skills and abilities of those people working for a firm will determine whether targets can be met.
- Finance. Firms can set themselves ambitious marketing goals. However, unless finance is available to fund plans, such goals are unlikely to be achieved.
- Production processes. Any marketing plan must take into account whether the firm can produce the product. There is little point in planning to increase market share unless enough of the product can be produced to achieve this. Similarly, a firm cannot plan to launch a new product if it cannot manufacture it.
- The product portfolio. Any marketing plan should

consider the existing mix of products (☞ unit 20). Firms must be careful to develop a mix of products which will allow them to meet marketing objectives.

External factors

- Competition. Marketing plans should take into account the pricing, promotion, distribution and product policies of rival firms.
- Technological change. This can affect marketing plans in a variety of ways. It can make it possible for firms to

QUESTION 3 Chairman Dennis Henderson believes that in past years marketing has not had enough attention in ICI. ICI has not, in his judgement, concentrated sufficiently on looking ahead at customers' needs, at how the markets are changing and how to present products in the optimum way to solve customers' problems.

He recognises that in some of its businesses there is a lot of market expertise. These businesses tend to be of more recent origin, international and nearer to the ultimate consumer. On the other hand some areas of ICI have been less market orientated.

He has an answer to this problem. 'Improve the flow of information about marketing across business boundaries and urge people in the various businesses that there is much valuable information within the group', Mr Henderson says. 'We have a collection of very independent businesses, each convinced that its problems and markets are unique so they can appear unwilling to learn from each other's experiences.'

'Another barrier can be the technical/commercial interface. For as long as I can remember it has been a running joke that the production people think marketing people can't move the product and the marketing people think that production can't produce in the right quantities when it is needed. A company like ICI will continue to succeed if it produces first class technology and incorporates it into the best products. There is still a bit of an attitude which says, "This commercial hype is not quite nice - why can't we stick to inventing new molecules, making the resultant products and distributing them to our customers?" One difficulty is that the market often requires fairly minimal change in the product to excite consumers, whereas the scientists, not unnaturally, want a major breakthrough.'

'One example of minimal change was the natural whites campaign in paints. Brilliant white paint had, for a long time, been a loss leader which was heavily discounted in all supermarkets. Somebody said, "How can we add value?", "How can we differentiate?" and the answer was special shades, such as apple white and rose white.'

Over the next few years Mr Henderson states that he would like to see marketing given a higher priority and suggests that ICI should be more proactive in looking at customers' needs and problems and in using science expertise to solve them.

Source: adapted from a newspaper article, source unknown.

(a) Analyse the strengths and weaknesses of ICI from the article.
(b) Identify two objectives that ICI may like to achieve in the future.
(c) Explain how one internal and one external factor may influence whether the business achieves these marketing objectives.

produce products that were previously thought to be too costly. It can also result in the obsolescence of existing products and shorter product life cycles.

- The state of the economy. A business must try to predict the likely future economic climate. If unemployment is expected to rise, for example, this may affect future levels of demand.
- Social change. Changes in society can have consequences for firms. For example, the decline of the so-called nuclear family and the changing role of women may influence how firms promote their products. Advertisements showing women at home doing the ironing are unlikely to have wide appeal today.
- Legislation. There is an increasing amount of legislation that can affect the marketing of a business (☞ units 24 and 73). Much of this is now coming from the European Community.
- Consumers' needs. The needs of consumers who buy a firm's products may change. An effective plan should anticipate these changes, as well as any other issues affecting consumers' needs.

The benefits of marketing planning

- The main benefit of marketing planning is that it ensures a firm takes the time to reflect upon its marketing activities. In today's competitive environment it is not enough for firms to carry on doing what they have done successfully in the past. They must constantly evaluate their marketing policies. The marketing plan allows them to do this and can be seen as a means of ensuring the survival of the business.
- The marketing plan makes sure that human and financial resources are used where they are most needed. It will also make sure resources will not be wasted on unprofitable activities. The plan forms the basis of a firm's marketing budget from which all other budgets are derived.
- Businesses will set marketing objectives and targets in their marketing plan. Management, as a result, will have a clear set of criteria against which they can evaluate the success of products.
- Marketing plans may encourage greater employee motivation. Employees are likely to be more prepared for changes in company policy and in the climate of trading. They should therefore be able to act in a more confident and informed manner. They are also likely to feel more secure in the knowledge that the business has planned for the future.
- A marketing plan should make banks feel more confident about offering loans to a firm. Shareholders may also be more confident about buying shares in a business.

Problems with marketing planning

For many the main problem with marketing plans lies in their confusion as to what marketing actually is.

Marketing plans often concentrate upon issues such as product development or increasing sales, but ignore customers' needs. Satisfying consumers' needs should be at the forefront of any marketing plan. A plan which centres around the expected success of a new advertising campaign, for example, is unlikely to be successful unless consumers' needs are satisfied. British Airways, Dunlop, and Woolworths are all companies which have won awards for advertising campaigns and it is arguable whether these directly led to any improvement in sales.

Many firms in the UK are organised into personnel, finance, production, and marketing departments. The success of the marketing plan will depend upon each of these areas being prepared to put aside their own goals to satisfy consumers' needs. This can be difficult, especially in a large business, where loyalty to the department can override more important goals. One suggested way of solving this problem is for firms to be organised around customer groups rather than 'functions' (☞ unit 3).

Marketing plans often include too much information for them to be useful to managers. In order to overcome this problem, plans should be brief and concentrate upon key factors.

Marketing plans often fail to **prioritise** objectives. Plans may include as many as 100 objectives. This means that it becomes difficult to decide whether objectives are being met.

QUESTION 4 Paul Rossington had just been appointed Marketing Manager of SBC PLC, a firm which had forty years experience of supplying a range of flight instrumentation and navigational aids to the aircraft industry.

Paul had decided that his first act would be to involve a range of managers in drawing up a marketing plan. To this end, he called a meeting requesting the presence of all senior managers within the firm.

At the meeting, he began with a short presentation outlining the advantages to SBC PLC of marketing planning. He then invited comments from all those assembled. The sales manager chipped in with the first comment; 'It's about time we started advertising more heavily in trade journals and stopped turning out products with the wrong specifications'. The production manager came next; ' I don't know why you dragged me up here to this meeting. You concentrate on the marketing and I'll get on with the production side. So long as you keep me informed of developments we'll be happy down in production.'

Paul was beginning to feel uncomfortable, but it wasn't until the senior accountant's remark that he really felt worried about having accepted this new post. 'I suggest you go away and write this plan and then call another meeting when you're in a position to discuss it with us', she had said.

(a) What advantages of marketing planning would you have advised Paul to mention in his brief presentation?
(b) From the comments made at the meeting, explain any problems which you think SBC PLC will have with marketing planning.

Key terms

Marketing audit - an analysis of the internal and external factors which may affect a company's performance.

Marketing mix - the elements of a firm's marketing strategy designed to meet the needs of its customers. The four main elements are price, product, promotion and place.

Marketing plan - a written document concerned with where a company is at present with regard to its marketing, where it wishes to be in the future and how it intends to get there.

SWOT analysis - an analysis of the internal strengths and weaknesses and the external opportunities and threats facing a particular business.

Summary

1. Identify the 4 elements of the marketing mix.
2. State 3 factors that influence a firm's choice of marketing mix.
3. Briefly describe how to carry out a SWOT analysis.
4. What is the difference between a firm's marketing objectives and its marketing strategy?
5. How can a marketing plan help a business?
6. Name 4 external factors that can influence a firm's marketing plan.
7. List the benefits of marketing planning.
8. What are the potential pitfalls of marketing planning?

Question

Top of the pops

In November 1989, the President of Coca-Cola's German Division was at a convention in New York when he saw the television news flash. With Germany possibly soon to be unified, Coca-Cola reacted quickly and effectively.

Supplies from its new 2,000 cans a minute plant in Dunkirk, France, were moved to East Germany within a matter of hours. Between 1990 and 1991 Coca-Cola sold more than 20 million cases of 'Coke' and in 1992 announced plans for a $450 million investment in bottling plants. 'It wasn't accidental', said Coca-Cola president Don Keough. 'It was having Dunkirk and being in the right place with the right product.'

In the early 1990s, Pepsi, the world's number two cola producer, also stormed Europe, from bases in Eastern Europe as well as the West. From 1992 onward Pepsi planned to pour $1 billion into building up their overseas market share, largely in Europe. They hoped to boost sales volume by 150 per cent by 1995. Coca-Cola, whose sales to the EC are six times higher than Pepsi's, wanted to double their already huge European stake. Both snapped up bottlers, cemented partnerships and otherwise shook up Europe's increasingly powerful retailers with brash American-style promotional methods. In the UK, the cola giants sponsored sports events, such as Wimbledon, and pushed product tie-ins with celebrities such as Tom Cruise.

In the US, each consumer gulps down, on average, 189 cans of cola a year. In the UK the figure is 61 cans, in France 26, and in Germany 111 cans a year. But while US growth has stalled, European cola consumption continues to increase by 10 per cent a year. Almost a third of Coca-Cola's $1.8 billion operating profit last year came from Europe and there's still plenty of room for expansion.

One highly successful part of Pepsi's strategy has been more widespread use of vending machines. According to company data, the US has 11 times more vending machines than Europe, relative to population. Hence the company is planning to distribute thousands, from Berlin to Brighton. The handful of machines already in place have contributed greatly to Pepsi's 15-20 per cent annual growth in Europe.

Both firms decided upon Continent-wide marketing strategies in Europe rather than relying on local bottlers with whom they had worked in partnership in the past. Pepsi, for example, discarded the services of Source Perrier, the French mineral water company which had previously distributed their products. European marketing 'mega-events', such as the opening of Euro Disney near Paris and the Barcelona Olympic games, have provided a huge range of promotional opportunities.

Source: adapted from *Business*, April 1991.

(a) Carry out a SWOT analysis of the European cola drinks market for either Pepsi or Coca-Cola.
(b) What might be Pepsi's and Coca-Cola's marketing objectives?
(c) Outline the factors that might prevent these objectives from being realised.
(d) What do you consider to be the most important elements of Pepsi's and Coca-Cola's marketing mixes? How would you explain this?

Markets and prices

A **market** is any situation where buyers come into contact with sellers to exchange goods and services. Buyers or consumers demand goods from sellers who supply them. It is the interaction of demand and supply that determines the price of a good or service in a free market or mixed economy (☞ unit 6).

Demand

DEMAND is the amount of a product that consumers are willing and able to purchase at any given price. Demand is concerned with what consumers are actually able to buy (what they can afford to and would buy), rather than what they would like to buy. So, for example, we could say that the demand for cars at an average price of £9,000 might be 130,000 a year.

Table 22.1 shows a **demand schedule** for mushrooms. These figures can be used to draw a **demand curve** as in Figure 22.1. In practice, demand curves are not a straight line, but are usually drawn in this way for simplicity.

Table 22.1 *The demand schedule for mushrooms*

Price per kilo (£)	Quantity demanded (000 kilos)
0.50	100
1.00	80
1.50	60
2.00	40
2.50	20

The curve shows the quantity of the product that will be demanded at any given price. As with nearly all such curves, it slopes downwards from left to right. This is because the quantity demanded of a product is likely to be higher at lower prices and lower at higher prices - **ceteris paribus** (assuming no other things change). We will see in the next section that they might. In Table 22.1 more mushrooms are bought at a price of £0.50 than at a price of £2.50.

A change in the price of a product will lead to a change in the quantity demanded. This is shown on the demand curve as a movement along (up or down) the curve. In Figure 22.1, a fall in price from £1.50 to £1, for example, will result in a movement along the curve from point X to point Y.

This will result in a rise in the quantity demanded from 60,000 to 80,000 kilos. The demand curve itself has not moved from its original position. Price changes only lead to an **extension** (rise) or **contraction** (fall) in the quantity demanded.

Changes in demand

As well as price, there are a number of other factors which might affect the demand for a product. Unlike price, a change in any of these factors might cause the whole demand curve to **shift**. This might result in an increase in the demand for a product. The result is that more of a product will be demanded at any given price. Alternatively, it may result in a fall in demand, so less is demanded at any given price.

Income It is reasonable to assume that the higher the incomes of consumers, the more they will be able to buy.

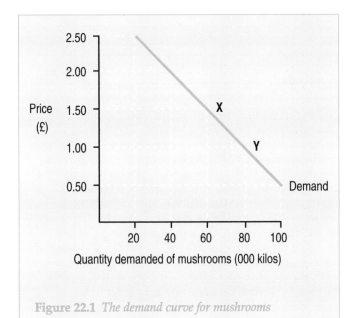

Figure 22.1 *The demand curve for mushrooms*

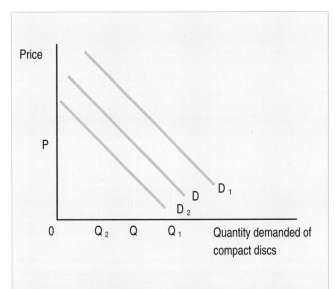

Figure 22.2 *The effect of changes in income on the demand curve for compact discs*

When incomes in the country as a whole increase, the demand for products will increase. However, the rise in income is unlikely to be the same for everyone. Some consumers will have large increases in income. Others will find that their incomes do not increase at all. Thus, demand for a product will only increase if the incomes of those consumers buying the product increase.

Assume that consumers of compact discs have had a rise in their income. The demand for compact discs increases as a result. This is shown in Figure 22.2 as a shift to the right of the demand curve from D to D_1. The demand for compact discs has increased at any given price level. In Figure 22.2, demand has risen from OQ to OQ_1. On the other hand, if consumers' incomes were to fall, this would cause the demand for compact discs to fall at any given price. The result of this would be a shift of the demand curve to the left from D to D_2 in Figure 22.2 . Demand will have fallen from OQ to OQ_2.

The price of other goods The demand for one product often depends on the price of another. For example, the demand for one brand of tea bags can be influenced by the price of other brands. A rise in the price of one brand is likely to cause an increase in the demand for others. This is often true of products which have close **substitutes**, such as canned drinks. An increase in the price of cassette tapes may result in a shift in demand from D to D_1, in Figure 22.2. Fewer tapes would be bought if prices rose, leading perhaps to increased demand for compact discs.

Complementary goods are those which are used together. Examples include cars and petrol, and video players and video cassettes. An increase in the price of one will affect the demand for the other. A fall in the price of compact disc players may lead to a shift in demand from D to D_1 in Figure 22.2. More players would be bought and so the quantity demanded of discs would also rise.

Changes in tastes and fashions Some products are subject to changes in tastes and fashions. Skateboards, for example, were bought in huge quantities in the early 1970s. They then went out of fashion for a number of years only to come back into favour again in the late 1980s. It is more usual for a company to stop producing products which have gone out of fashion altogether. Other products have shown more gradual changes in demand. In recent years, the demand for red meat has gradually declined as tastes have changed. This has caused the demand curve for red meat to shift to the left. This means that at any given price, less red meat is now demanded than in previous years. It could be argued that the demand curve for compact discs has shifted to the right as it has become 'fashionable' to buy them rather than albums.

Changes in population As well as changes in population levels, changes in the structure of population can affect demand. The increase in the proportion of over 65s in the population of Western industrialised countries will have an effect upon the demand for a number of products. They include winter-sun holidays, sheltered housing and leisure facilities. This means that, other things staying the same, the demand curve for products associated with the old will shift to the right, with more being demanded at any given price.

Advertising Successful advertising and promotion will shift the demand curve to the right, with more being demanded at any given price. A successful advertising campaign for CDs would do this.

Legislation Government legislation can affect the demand for a product. For example, a law requiring all cyclists to wear helmets would lead to an increase in the demand for cycling helmets at any given price.

QUESTION 1

Table 22.2 *The demand schedule for ice cream at a local theme park*

Price (£)	Quantity demanded
0.50	2,000
0.60	1,600
0.70	1,200
0.80	800
0.90	400

Table 22.2 shows the demand schedule for ice cream at a local theme park each month. In the next few months it has been predicted that:
- incomes will rise so that there will be 500 more bought at each level;
- the prices of substitute goods are likely to rise so that there would be another 500 bought at each price level.

(a) Draw the original demand curve from the figures in the table.
(b) Show the combined effect on the demand curve of the changes in the market.

Individual and market demand curves

So far, this unit has examined the market demand for a product or service. It is also possible to construct a demand curve for an individual business. The influences on the demand for an individual firm's product are no different from those of the market. So, for example, if a business raises the price of its product, it is likely to find that the quantity demanded will fall. If the income of consumers buying a particular firm's product increases, so will the demand for that product. If the price of a brand of tea bags such as Typhoo went up, the demand for PG Tips would increase. We will use this later to examine the effect of a change in price on the revenue of a business. The market demand curve is actually a **summing** or **totalling** of the demand curves for individual firms' products.

Supply

SUPPLY is the amount of a product which suppliers will offer to the market at a given price. The higher the price of a particular good or service, the more that will be offered to the market. For example, the amount of mushrooms supplied to a market in any given week may be as shown in Table 22.3.

Table 22.3 *The supply schedule for mushrooms*

Price per kilo (£)	Quantity supplied (000 kilos)
0.50	20
1.00	40
1.50	60
2.00	80
2.50	100

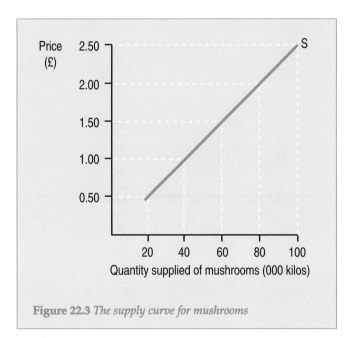

Figure 22.3 *The supply curve for mushrooms*

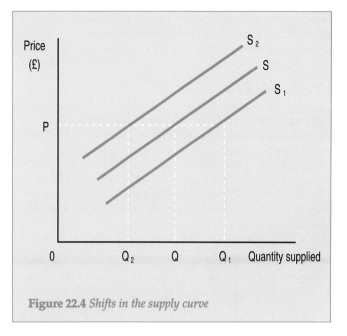

Figure 22.4 *Shifts in the supply curve*

These figures have been plotted onto a graph in Figure 22.3, which shows the supply curve for mushrooms. The supply curve slopes up from left to right. This is because at higher prices a greater quantity will be supplied to the market and at lower prices less will be supplied.

A change in price will cause a movement either up or down the supply curve. The curve will not change its position assuming that all other factors remain the same. There are a number of other factors that may affect supply other than price. Changes in these factors will cause the whole supply curve to shift.

Costs of production A fall in the costs of production due, for example, to new technology will mean that more can be offered at the same price. This will cause the supply curve to shift to the right as shown in Figure 22.4, from S to S_1. A rise in the costs of production would cause the supply curve to shift to the left, from S to S_2. A rise in raw material costs or wage costs could lead to such a shift.

Changes in production Where it is possible to shift production from one area to another, the price of other products can influence the quantity supplied. For example, many farmers are able to produce a wide range of crops on their land. A rise in the price of broccoli, might encourage farmers not only to produce more broccoli, but less of other crops such as turnips. The broccoli price change has affected the quantity of turnips supplied to the market. So a rise in the price of broccoli would shift the supply curve for turnips to the left, in Figure 22.4 from S to S_2.

Legislation A new anti-pollution law might increase production costs causing the supply curve to shift to the left. Similarly, a tax on a product would shift the supply curve to the left.

The objectives of firms Firms might seek to increase their profit levels and their market share. This might reduce the overall level of supply as other firms are forced out of business. The result of this would be a shift of the supply curve in Figure 22.4 from S to S_2.

Expectations If businesses expect future prices to rise they may restrict current supplies. This would be shown as a shift to the left of the supply curve in Figure 22.4, from S to S_2. Similarly, if businesses expect worsening trading conditions they might reduce current supply levels in anticipation of this.

The weather The weather can influence agricultural markets. For example, in the UK a late spring frost can reduce the supply of strawberries, from say S to S_2 in Figure 22.4.

It was shown earlier in this unit that the market demand curve is a summing of individual firms' demand curves. Similarly, the market supply curve is an adding up of the supply curves of individual firms.

Price determination

How does the interaction of demand and supply determine the market price? Market prices are set where the plans of consumers are matched with those of suppliers. The point at which the demand and supply curves intersect is known as the EQUILIBRIUM PRICE. This is shown in Figure 22.5. The equilibrium price of mushrooms is £1.50. The figure is drawn from Tables 22.1 and 22.2.

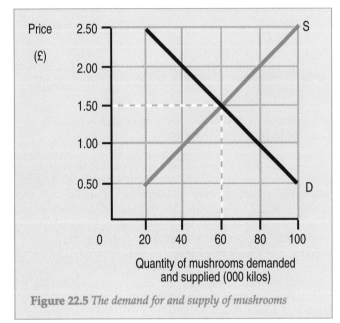

Figure 22.5 *The demand for and supply of mushrooms*

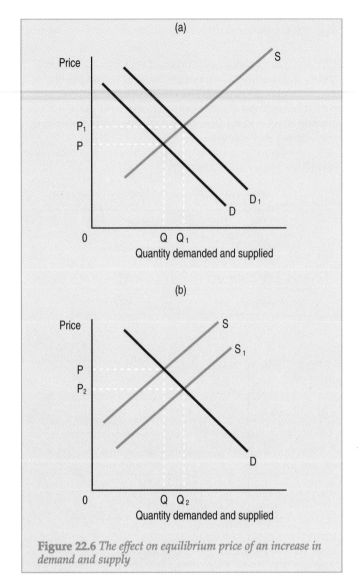

Figure 22.6 *The effect on equilibrium price of an increase in demand and supply*

What if demand does not equal supply?
■ At a price of £2.50 producers want to supply 100,000 kilos, but consumers will only demand 20,000. This is known as **excess supply**.
■ At a price of £1.00 producers want to supply 40,000 kilos, but demand would be 80,000. This is **excess demand**.

Any shifts in the demand or supply curves will cause a change in the market price. Assume that there has been a rise in income which has resulted in an increase in demand. The effect of this, as shown in Figure 22.6a, is a shift in the demand curve to the right, all things remaining the same, leading to an increase in quantity demanded from OQ to OQ₁.

This increase in demand raises the equilibrium price from OP to OP₁ in Figure 22.6a. As a result, the quantity supplied extends as well, as producers will supply more at the higher price.

Figure 22.6b shows the effect on the equilibrium price of an increase in supply. This increase may have been as a result of lower labour costs. The equilibrium price falls from OP to OP₂ as the supply curve shifts from S to S₁.

Consumers are more willing and able to buy goods at the lower price and so the quantity demanded rises as well from OQ to OQ₂ .

QUESTION 2 J Tufnell PLC is a large firm operating in the highly competitive steel market. Like all firms operating in this market, it has experienced a double blow in recent months. Not only has it seen the price of iron ore (used in the production of steel) increase by over 30 per cent, but there has been a downturn in the car industry.

Using demand and supply diagrams, illustrate the effect of:
(i)   an increase in raw material prices;
(ii) a downturn in the car industry;
on the price of J Tufnell's steel.

Price sensitivity

All firms are likely to be concerned about the sensitivity of the demand for their products to price changes. In other words, they will want to predict what will happen to the quantity demanded of their product if there is a change in price. The sensitivity of quantity demanded to changes in price is known as the PRICE ELASTICITY OF DEMAND (PED). It can be calculated using the following formula:

$$PED = \frac{\text{Percentage change in quantity demanded}}{\text{Percentage change in price}}$$

or

$$\frac{\text{Change in quantity demanded}}{\text{Original quantity demanded}} \div \frac{\text{change in price}}{\text{original price}}$$

Businesses are also concerned about how price changes affect revenue they earn. Revenue can be calculated using the formula:

$$\text{Total revenue} = \text{quantity sold} \times \text{price}$$

A price change is likely to lead to a change in revenue for the firm. Whether there is an increase or a decrease in revenue will depend upon the price elasticity of demand for that product.

Inelastic demand A firm selling its product in a particular market may face the demand schedule and demand curve in Table 22.4 and Figure 22.7. If the price is raised from £5 to £6 (a 20 per cent change), the quantity demanded falls from 10,000 to 9,000 units (a 10 per cent change). This is shown in Figure 22.7. The price elasticity of demand is:

$$PED = \frac{-10\%}{20\%} = (-)0.5$$

$$\text{or} \quad PED = \frac{-1,000}{10,000} \div \frac{1}{5} = \frac{-1}{10} \times \frac{5}{1} = \frac{-1}{2} \quad \text{or } -0.5$$

It is usual to ignore the minus sign, so that a figure that is less than 1 but greater than 0 tells the firm that demand for the product is **price inelastic**. This means that the percentage change in quantity demanded is less than the percentage change in price. In other words, consumers do not change the quantity of a good they demand proportionally more than any change in price.

What effect will a change in price have on a firm's total revenue? Table 22.4 and Figure 22.7 show that a rise in price from £5 to £6 will increase revenue from £50,000 to £54,000. This is because the rise in price is proportionally greater than the fall in the quantity demanded. A business which raises its price will hope that demand for the product is price inelastic.

A reduction in price from £5 to £4 will result in a fall in revenue from £50,000 to £44,000, even though the quantity demanded has increased from 9,000 to 11,000 units.

Table 22.4 *A demand schedule*

Price £	Quantity demanded (units)	Total revenue £
4	11,000	44,000
5	10,000	50,000
6	9,000	54,000

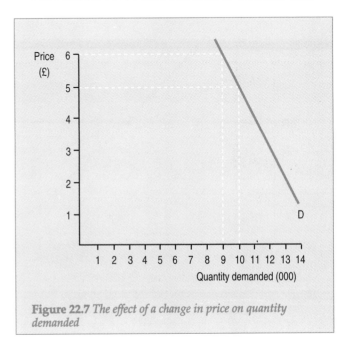

Figure 22.7 *The effect of a change in price on quantity demanded*

Elastic demand A firm operating in a different market may face the demand schedule in Table 22.5. An increase in price from £20 to £24 (a 20 per cent change) results in a fall in quantity demanded from 10,000 units to 6,000 units (a 40 per cent change). Price elasticity of demand is therefore:

$$PED = \frac{-40\%}{20\%} = (-)2$$

$$\text{or} \quad PED = \frac{-4,000}{10,000} \div \frac{4}{20} = \frac{-4}{10} \times \frac{20}{4} = \frac{-20}{10} \quad \text{or } -2$$

As this figure is greater than 1, the firm can conclude that demand for its product is relatively **price elastic**. This means that the percentage change in quantity demanded is greater than the percentage change in price. When demand is price elastic, consumers react to changes in price by changing the quantity they demand by a greater proportion.

Table 22.5 and Figure 22.8 show that if the firm reduces its price from £20 to £16, quantity demanded will increase from 10,000 to 14,000 and total revenue will increase from

£200,000 to £224,000. This is because the increase in quantity demanded is proportionally greater than the fall in price. If a business is aiming to cut its price, it will hope demand for the product will be price elastic. An increase in price from £20 to £24 will lead to a fall in revenue from £200,000 to £144,000.

Table 22.5 *A demand schedule*

Price £	Quantity demanded (units)	Total revenue £
16	14,000	224,000
20	10,000	200,000
24	6,000	144,000

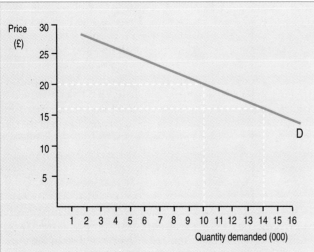

Figure 22.8 *The effect of a change in price on quantity demanded*

QUESTION 3 Ratcliffe and Sons, manufacturers of top of the range turntables for hi-fi systems, were analysing the effects of recent price changes. They had increased the price of their turntables from £200 to £240. Sales fell from 800 per month to 600 per month as a result. Questions were now being asked about the effectiveness of these price changes.

(a) Calculate the price elasticity of demand for Ratcliffe turntables.
(b) Is the price elasticity of demand relatively elastic or inelastic?
Explain why you think this is so.
(c) In terms of sales revenue, was the decision to raise prices wise?
Explain your answer showing all calculations.

Factors affecting price elasticity of demand

There are two main factors which are thought to affect the price elasticity of demand.

■ The number of substitutes for a product. A product with a wide range of substitutes is likely to be highly sensitive to price changes and relatively price elastic. This is because the more substitutes there are for a particular product, the more easy it is for consumers to purchase another product when price changes occur. For example, most types of fish are likely to be relatively price elastic. This is because if the price of one type of fish goes up, consumers can easily swap to another type of fish.

■ Time. The longer the period of time, the more price elastic the demand for a product is likely to be. The more time consumers are given, the more able and willing they are to adjust their buying habits. Take, for example, a rise in the price of gas. Over a short period of time, it would be difficult for consumers to buy less gas. Ownership of a gas cooker and gas central heating systems means in the short term that it is difficult to use other types of power. However, over a longer period of time it may be possible for consumers to switch to oil or electricity.

Income elasticity of demand

INCOME ELASTICITY OF DEMAND is a measure of the sensitivity of demand to changes in income. It can be calculated using the formula:

$$\frac{\text{Percentage change in quantity demanded}}{\text{Percentage change in income}}$$

Firms will want to know the income elasticity of demand for their products. This will help them to judge the effect of a change in their consumers' income on the demand for their products.

Price elasticity of supply

Another measure of price sensitivity is PRICE ELASTICITY OF SUPPLY. This is a measure of the responsiveness of supply to changes in price. It can be calculated using the following formula:

$$\frac{\text{Percentage change in quantity supplied}}{\text{Percentage change in price}}$$

or $\dfrac{\text{Change in quantity supplied}}{\text{Original quantity supplied}} \div \dfrac{\text{change in price}}{\text{original price}}$

Price elasticity of supply can be either relatively elastic or relatively inelastic.

■ If the quantity supplied to a market changes proportionally more than a price change, then supply is said to be relatively **elastic**.

■ If the quantity supplied to a market changes proportionally less than a price change, then supply is said to be relatively **inelastic**.

Usually, firms are more able to respond to price changes over time. Over a short period of time, the price elasticity of supply for most firms and industries will be relatively inelastic. Over longer periods it is possible for firms to adjust their supply in response to a change in price. Thus, the elasticity of supply in the long term is likely to be relatively elastic.

Prices and competition

We have seen how the price of a product can be determined by demand and supply. In free market economies, prices will be set in a wide range of different markets. These include:

■ international markets, such as foreign exchange markets;
■ national markets, such as the market for personal computers;
■ local markets, such as the market for houses in South Manchester;
■ highly specialised markets, such as the market for polo playing equipment.

Can an individual business influence the price of its product? The competition in a market will affect a firm's ability to set prices. Assessing the level of competition is not as easy as it seems. Two businesses operating a local bus route may seem to have no competition. In fact, they face competition from trains, mini-buses and taxis. A new chocolate bar will face **direct** competition from other bars, as well as competition from other firms of confectionery.

As a rule, if a business faces competition from a great number of very similar products it will have less scope to set its prices. In this case the price it charges is likely to be influenced by those of other businesses. When a business is able to make its product appear different from others, if it is different, or if there are few other businesses selling the same product, it will have more flexibility.

QUESTION 4

LOWER HALL FARM

(a) Do you think the above businesses are competing in local, international, national or specialised markets?
(b) What other businesses might:
(i) British Rail; (ii) Barclays Bank; (iii) Fred's Garage; compete against?

Degrees of competition

There are a number of widely recognised MODELS of competition or MARKET STRUCTURES. They vary according to:

■ the amount of knowledge consumers have about different products;
■ the ease with which firms can set up and compete within the market;
■ the number of firms operating within the market;
■ the extent to which rival products are different.

Perfect competition The model of PERFECT COMPETITION assumes businesses produce products which are exactly the same. Consumers have 'perfect knowledge' of the market. They are aware of what is being offered by all businesses. There are no barriers to prevent firms from setting up and there are a large number of firms in competition with one another.

Businesses in such markets are known as PRICE TAKERS. Each individual firm has no influence over the price which it charges for its products. If a firm were to charge a higher price than others then no consumers would buy its products, since every product is exactly the same and they would know exactly where to go to buy an alternative. A firm that charged a price below that of others would be forced out of business.

In reality, it is not easy to identify markets which conform to the model of perfect competition. However, there are some which have many of the characteristics of a perfectly competitive market. One example in the UK could be agriculture. There are a large number of farmers providing farm produce for the market. Farming businesses tend, generally, to be small scale and are unable to influence market price. Furthermore, it is likely that one vegetable will be much the same as another on a different farm. Information about this market is also available in trade journals.

Monopolistic competition Other market models describe situations where there is **imperfect** competition. These are markets where there is some restriction on competition. The majority of firms in the UK operate in these markets.

MONOPOLISTIC COMPETITION exists where a large number of relatively small firms compete in an industry. There are few barriers to entry. This means that it is fairly easy for firms to set up and to leave these markets. Firms will also have perfect knowledge of the market.

Each firm has a product that is **differentiated** from the others. This is achieved through **branding**, when a product is given an identity of its own (☞ unit 25). A business will face competition from a wide range of other firms competing in the same market with similar, but differentiated, products.

Firms operating under these conditions are not price takers, but they will only have a limited degree of control over the prices they charge. There are few markets of this kind in the UK. Two examples include legal services and the manufacture of certain types of clothing.

Oligopoly When only a few firms dominate a market, OLIGOPOLY is said to exist. Examples include the markets for petrol, beer, detergents, paint and sweets.

Under oligopoly, each firm will have a differentiated product, often with a strong brand identity. Several brands may be competing in the same market. Brand loyalty amongst customers is encouraged by advertising and promotion. Indeed, firms in such markets are often said to compete in the form of non-price competition. Prices are often stable for long periods, disturbed only by short price wars.

Although brand loyalty does allow some price control, businesses often 'follow' the price of a leader. In extreme cases firms might even **collude** to 'fix' a price. Sometimes this is illegal and may be called a **restrictive trade practices** (☞ unit 73).

Barriers to entry exist. If it was easy for new firms to enter the industry, they would set up and take the market share of the few large producers. Firms operate independently of each other and so information is imperfect. If a firm attempts to increase sales independently of its rivals' actions, it will gain market share only at their expense.

Monopoly MONOPOLY occurs when one business has total control over a market and is the only seller of the product. (This **pure monopoly** should not be confused with a **legal monopoly**, which occurs in the UK when a firm controls 25 per cent or more of a market.)

Monopolists are likely to erect barriers to prevent others from entering their market. They will also exert a strong influence on the price which they charge for their product. However, because monopolists are the only supplier of a product, it does not mean that they can charge whatever they want. If they raise price a great deal demand will fall to some extent. Because of the influence monopolists have on their price, they are often called **price makers**.

There are some firms operating in the UK which could be described as monopolies. One possible example has been British Gas. However, as explained earlier in the unit, such a description hinges upon the view that British Gas is operating in the market for gas. British Gas could equally be said to be operating in the energy market, in which case it faces competition from electricity and oil companies. Therefore care must be taken when describing firms as monopolies.

Table 22.6 *A summary of the characteristics of models of competition*

	Perfect competition	Monopolistic competition	Oligopoly	Monopoly
Barriers to entry	None	Few	Many	Almost impossible for new firms to enter the market
Number of of firms	Many	Many	A few	One
Influence over price	None	Some	Strong	Very strong
Differentiated product	No	Yes	Strong brands	No competition; not necessary

QUESTION 5 The market for high quality sports footwear has come to be increasingly dominated by three main operators - Nike, Reebok and Adidas. The products marketed by these companies have strong brand identities with many consumers having a very high degree of loyalty to a particular firm's shoes. Each firm has a huge advertising budget with strong campaigns designed to bolster brand identities. Indeed, some observers believe that the rising advertising costs in this market are preventing new firms from setting up.

Although most of their product ranges have been designed for use in sporting activities, they have also been taken up by the youth market, as fashion accessories. The firms competing in this market have responded by producing more and more sophisticated sports shoes and increasing the range and variety of styles available. Increasingly companies are using well known sports personalities to promote their products and are advertising in magazines and on prime time television.

(a) Which of the models of competition do you think best describes the market for sports footwear? Give reasons for your answer.
(b) Advise a competitor to Nike, Reebok and Adidas on the degree of influence they are likely to have on the price of their products. Explain your suggestions.

Summary

1. What are the factors affecting the demand for a product?
2. What are the factors affecting the supply of a product?
3. How is the equilibrium price determined?
4. How is price elasticity of demand calculated?
5. What is the difference between inelastic and elastic demand?
6. What effect will a change in price have on the revenue of a firm facing inelastic demand for its product?
7. State 2 factors affecting the price elasticity of demand for a product.
8. What determines the amount of discretion firms have in making their pricing decisions?
9. What is the difference between a price taker and a price maker?
10. What are the 4 models of market competition?
11. Under what conditions might a firm be unable to influence the price it sets for its product?

Key terms

Demand - the quantity of a product purchased at a given price.

Equilibrium price - the price at which the quantity demanded is equal to the quantity supplied.

Income elasticity of demand - the responsiveness of demand to a change in income.

Market structure - the characteristics of a market which determine the behaviour of firms operating within it.

Monopolistic competition - a market structure with freedom of entry and exit, differentiated products and a large number of small firms competing.

Monopoly - a market structure in which only one firm supplies the entire output, there is no competition and barriers to entry exist.

Oligopoly - a market structure with a small number of dominant firms, producing heavily branded products with some barriers to entry.

Perfect competition - a market structure with perfect knowledge, many buyers and sellers, freedom of entry and exit and a homogeneous product.

Price elasticity of demand - the responsiveness of demand to a change in price.

Price elasticity of supply - the responsiveness of supply to a change in price.

Price taker - a firm that is unable to influence the price at which it sells its products.

Supply - the quantity of products which suppliers make available to the market at a given price.

Question

Bodyline

Bodyline is a small firm based in the West Midlands which manufactures womens' swimwear. Their products are distributed through four main types of outlet - mail-order catalogues, department stores, womens' clothing chains and independent retailers.

The firm was set up in early 1991. The two women, Elaine and Penny, who started up the firm had originally been friends at University. One had studied for a degree in Art and Design, the other in Business Studies.

Their main product was to be a swimsuit, the Californian, which had been designed in a wide range of dazzling colours. Their marketing strategy had been to aim for the bottom end of the market, offering a cheap, but fashionable garment which would be within the reach of a wide number of consumers' pockets. Market research into the demand for the Californian showed that sales at different prices were likely to be as in Table 22.7.

Elaine and Penny found that they were able to sell all of their production at a price of £9. They sold Californians at this price for 6 months and made a fair profit. The market was fairly stable at this time and few sudden changes were expected in the near future. Penny felt that by reducing the price a little they would be able to capture more of the market. Elaine was not so sure and the two debated the decision over the next six months without taking any action.

By early 1992 a number of rival firms developed similar product lines using bright colours, having seen the initial success of Bodyline in the market.

Table 22.7

Price	Quantity of Californians
£7	18,000
£8	14,000
£9	10,000
£10	6,000

As Elaine had commented, one of the worst things about the new products was that 'the Californian designs no longer stood out in the shops and are the same as other products now available'. In what had seemed like a short period of time to these two entrepreneurs, their niche in the market had all but disappeared.

(a) Draw the demand curve for Californians from the figures in Table 22.7.

(b) Calculate the elasticity of demand for Californians for a reduction in price from
   (i)   £10 to £9;
   (ii) £9 to £8;
   (iii) £8 to £7.

(c) Given your answer to question (b) do you think Penny was right to suggest cutting the price of Californians at the time she did?
   Explain your answer using figures or a diagram.

(d) Using demand and supply diagrams, illustrate the effect on the price and quantity bought and sold of Californians as firms produce rival products.

Pricing strategies

Unit 22 showed that the extent to which a business can influence its price will depend on the degree of competition it faces. When a business does have scope to set its price there are a number of PRICING STRATEGIES or policies it might choose.

- Penetrating the market. A firm may set its price in order to gain a footing in a market. This could be a new product being launched or an existing product being launched into a new market.
- Destroying competition/capturing the market. Some firms may seek to 'capture' a market by trying to force other firms out of business.
- Being competitive. Firms may be concerned about their ability to compete with others. This may mean following another firm's price increase or cut. An example may be the pricing of petrol companies.
- Skimming or creaming. A firm may be in a position to skim or cream a market as a result of having a unique product. This usually involves charging a high price for a limited period of time in order to take advantage of the unique nature of the product. For example, video cameras were highly priced when first launched.
- Discriminating between different groups of consumers. A firm may be in a position to charge different prices to different groups of consumers for the same product. For example, British Telecom charge higher rates for telephone calls at certain times of the day.

Factors affecting pricing decisions

What factors influence the price a business sets for its product?

Objectives The pricing strategy chosen by a firm is likely to reflect the extent to which it wants to maximise profits or sales. A firm seeking to maximise short term profits may use more aggressive and perhaps risky pricing strategies.

The marketing mix The price chosen by a firm must complement the other aspects of the marketing mix (☞ unit 21). This means that the price must fit in with the nature of the product itself and the way in which it is being promoted and distributed to consumers. For example, a low quality product being sold in retail outlets at the bottom end of the market is likely to be sold at a fairly low price.

Costs A firm which cannot generate enough revenue over time to cover its costs will not survive. In the long run, a firm must charge a price which earns enough revenue to cover its total cost of production (fixed and variable) at any level of output. In the short run,

however, it is unlikely that a firm would expect to cover the fixed costs of its factory or machinery (☞ unit 10). Providing its price is high enough to generate revenue that covers its variable costs, the firm will stay in business. Revenue below this will cause the firm to cease production. As a result firms may have greater flexibility in the short term when making pricing decisions.

Competition Unit 22 explained how competition can affect pricing decisions. For a market trader, the price of her goods is largely determined by prices on nearby stalls selling similar goods. Such a trader will have very little room for manoeuvre compared to a business such as British Telecom.

Consumer perceptions and expectations Firms must pay attention to what consumers think a product is worth. A product priced above what consumers consider its value to be may generate low sales because of doubts about its **value for money**. A product priced too low may also generate low sales. This is because consumers often suspect that such products have something wrong with them or that they are of inferior quality. For example, a firm marketing high fashion clothing would be careful to ensure that its products were priced higher than those offered to the mass market.

Firms have the opportunity to influence consumer perceptions through aspects of the marketing mix, such as advertising. By improving the view consumers have of the product, firms can give themselves more scope when setting prices. In some cases firms actually encourage consumers to think of their products as expensive. For example, After Eight Mints have been marketed as a high quality luxury item which is not cheap.

Market segment Firms which produce a range of products are likely to have some aimed at particular market segments (☞ unit 19). This is true, for example, of all major car manufacturers. They are, therefore, likely to charge different prices for each segment. However, the price which they charge to one segment of the market will affect the prices charged to other segments. A product competing in the top end of the market will need to have a different price from one aimed at the middle or bottom end of the market.

Legal constraints The price of a number of products is affected by **taxation**. This raises the price above the level that might have been set by manufacturers. Products affected by taxation include cigarettes, alcoholic drinks and petrol. There are also a number of products which are offered to consumers below the price that producers would normally charge. Such products are **subsidised** by the government. An example might be low priced travel on public transport for young people and pensioners.

The price of each product in a market will have been influenced by a variety of factors. For some products the forces of demand and supply will have exerted a strong influence. For others, firms will have gone to great lengths to ensure that they have chosen just the right price.

What factors do you think have influenced the price of the products in the photographs above?

Cost based pricing

COST BASED PRICING is an example of a **marketing strategy** that a firm might use. There are a number of methods that firms use to set their prices which are based upon particular costs.

Cost plus pricing This involves setting a price by calculating the average cost (☞ unit 10) of producing goods and adding a MARK-UP for profit. If a business produces 10,000 goods costing £50,000, the average cost would be £5.00. A mark up of 20 per cent would mean goods would cost an extra £1.00 and the price would be £6.00 per product. Retailers often use this method of pricing. Say that a department store buys a colour TV from wholesalers for £200 and their mark-up to allow for

a profit is 100 per cent. The retail price to consumers will be £400.

The attractiveness of cost plus pricing is that it is a quick and simple way of setting a selling price. It also ensures that sales revenue will cover total costs and generate profit. A criticism, however, is that a fixed mark-up does not allow a firm to take market needs into account when setting prices. In addition, no attempt is made to allocate indirect costs to particular products. This means they do not reflect the resources being allocated by the business to that particular product or product range.

Contribution pricing This method takes into account that different products within a company might need to be priced using different criteria. For each product, a price is set in relation to the **direct costs** of producing that product and any **contribution** (☞ unit 12) that the firm wants that product to make towards covering its **indirect cost** and towards profit. Thus for a manufacturer of electrical goods, some prices might be as set out as in Figure 23.1.

No one product will be **expected** to account for all the indirect costs of the business. Each product's selling price would make some contribution to meeting indirect costs. If the producer expected to sell 100 items of each product

Figure 23.1 *Contribution pricing*

and had to cover indirect costs of £6,500 and generate profit of £2,000 (£8,500) then:

Product A	£45x100	=	£4,500	contribution
Product B	£30x100	=	£3,000	contribution
Product C	£10x100	=	£1,000	contribution
			£8,500	

This allows businesses more flexibility than the cost plus approach. Successful products can be priced to make a large contribution. Less successful products or new products can be priced more competitively, as they need only to make a lower contribution to overheads and profits. Indeed, new products might even be making a negative contribution, ie their price does not even cover the **marginal cost** of production. Demand factors as well as cost factors are now being taken into account.

Absorption cost/full cost pricing A business may attempt to take into account the indirect costs that can be attributable to a particular product in deciding on a price. In its simplest form (known as **full cost pricing** ☞ unit 12) a 'blanket' formula is used to allocate indirect

cost to each product, for example, a percentage of total sales of each product. The electrical goods manufacturer might charge the prices in Figure 23.2. A mark-up is then added for profit.

A more sophisticated method of allocation can also be used. This is known as **absorption cost pricing** (☞ unit 12). Instead of a 'blanket' formula being used to allocate indirect costs, each element of the cost will be treated separately. This means the selling price of a product will absorb elements of each overhead cost.

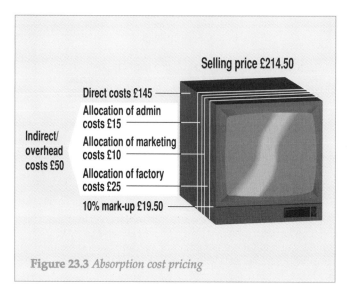

Figure 23.3 *Absorption cost pricing*

As we can see from Figures 23.2 and 23.3 the price of the TV is different according to the method used. A different costing formula will lead to a different final price. Under the full cost method a larger allocation of indirect/overhead costs was made to the television's final price than in the absorption cost approach.

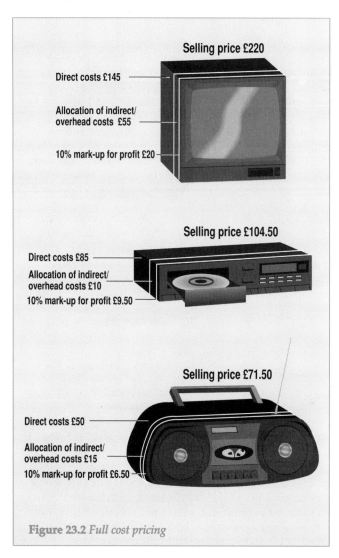

Figure 23.2 *Full cost pricing*

Problems of cost based pricing

Cost based pricing does have a number of problems. It is a product and cost orientated approach with little reference to consumers' wishes or flexibility. Contribution pricing does, however, allow more flexibility than cost plus pricing for a particular marketing strategy. Full or absorption cost pricing will result in prices being set too high or too low in relation to consumers' wishes or competitors' prices. They are also inflexible in response to market changes, as these would not necessarily be reflected in the costs of a company. The more sophisticated the costing method used when pricing, the more accurate is the allocation of costs to a product, but the further the price might be from what the market will bear.

QUESTION 2 Patel and Co have been manufacturing aluminium ladders since the business was set up in 1978. Their sales up to now have been based upon two products, a 10 metre and a 15 metre folding ladder. The firm has adopted a cost plus method of pricing for each ladder, as illustrated in Table 23.1.

Table 23.1

10 metre ladder	Average cost per unit £92	20% mark-up to cover profit £18.40	Selling price to trade £110.40
15 metre ladder	Average cost per unit £125	20% mark-up to cover profit £25.00	Selling price to trade £150.00

Because of the success of these two products and pressure from competition, the company has developed a new product, a ladder which would allow people to gain constant access to their lofts, but which will be permanently attached to the loft entrance. With a third product, the company's accountant felt that a contribution pricing approach should now be used to price each of their products. He set out some initial calculations of their likely prices, as in Table 23.2.

Table 23.2

	Direct costs per unit	Contribution to indirect cost and profit	Price
10 metre ladder	£80	£35	£115
15 metre ladder	£105	£40	£145
Loft ladder	£185	£5	£190

The pricing for the loft ladder was set at a level which was in line with the price of competitors, which was £190.00.

(a) Identify the benefits to the company of using a contribution pricing approach compared to a cost plus approach for their ladders.
(b) Is the loft ladder a viable product for the company to produce given the figures produced by the accountant? Explain your answer.

Market orientated pricing

MARKET ORIENTATED PRICING methods are those which are based upon an analysis of the conditions in the market at which a product is aimed. As such, they are much better suited to market orientated firms.

Penetration pricing This is used by firms seeking to gain a foothold in a market, either with new products or with established products being placed in new markets. It involves pricing a product at a low level so that retailers and consumers are encouraged to purchase the product in large quantities.

There are two main reasons why firms use penetration pricing.
- Consumers are encouraged to develop the habit of buying the product, so that when prices eventually begin to rise they will continue to purchase it.
- Retailers and wholesalers are likely to purchase large quantities of the product. This should mean that they will not buy from other suppliers until they have sold most of their stock. Firms can thus gain a significant slice of the market.

Penetration pricing, because of its high cost, is mainly used by large firms operating in mass markets, such as those selling biscuits, sweets, washing powder and canned drinks. A classical music monthly magazine (*Music Magazine*) launched in September 1992 was initially sold for 99p, but later for £3.50. It is not a policy that is suitable for products with short life cycles. There is usually not enough time to recover the cost of lost revenue from the initially low price.

Market skimming Market skimming involves charging a high price for a new product for a limited period. The aim is to gain as much profit as possible for a new product while it remains unique in the market. It usually means selling a product to the most profitable segment of the market before it is sold to a wider market at a lower price.

There are two reasons why firms adopt market skimming. They may try to maximise revenue before competitors come into the market with a similar product. Often new techniques or designs mean that entirely new, or new versions of a product can be offered. Examples include new fashions in clothes, new childrens' toys and new inventions. When first launched, a basic digital watch could cost as much as £50 or £60. Now they often sell for as little as a few pounds. Market skimming can also be used to generate revenue in a short period of time so that further investment in the product can be made. Companies in the electronics and pharmaceutical industries often use skimming for this reason.

Customer value pricing This involves charging the price that consumers are prepared to pay. Products which have prestige names attached to them, such as Cartier, may be able to command a higher price because of the status of these names. Products for one-off events, such as music festivals or sports finals, may be given a high price because they are unique.

Price discrimination Price discrimination occurs when a firm offers the same product at different prices when consumers can be kept separate. One example is British Telecom's policy of charging prices for phone calls made at different times of the day. It means that business users, who make the majority of their calls between 8 a.m. and 6 p.m. have to pay more for their calls than domestic users who do most of their telephoning in the evening.

British Telecom's price discrimination is **time based**. The price you pay for a phone call is based upon the time of day or the day of the week when you use the service. Other firms which use this policy are British Rail,(cheaper off peak travel), and holiday firms which charge higher prices for their product during school holidays.

Price discrimination can also be **market based**. This involves offering different market segments the same product at different prices. An example of this is students being given discounts on rail and coach travel.

Discounts and sales These tend to support the pricing strategies used by firms. They often mean a reduction in the standard price for particular groups of consumers. A very common form of discount is the seasonal 'sales' of retailers. The aim is to encourage purchasers at times when sales might otherwise be low and to clear out of date and out of fashion stock. Discounts may also be given to those customers who buy in bulk or in large quantities.

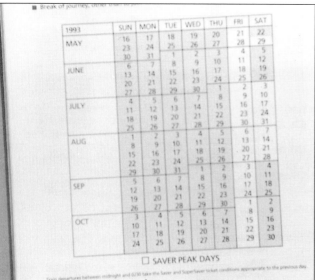

Examples of market orientated pricing.

QUESTION 3 Since the deregulation of the market for TV 'listings' magazines, a most extraordinary publishing battle has taken place.

Before deregulation only the *TV Times* and the *Radio Times* were licensed to publish. After April 1991, the market opened up. Four titles were available - the *TV Times*, *What's on TV*, *TV Quick*, and the *Radio Times*.

Bauer, the publishers of *TV Quick*, launched their magazine with a cover price of 10p, which lasted for 10 weeks. The price was then raised to 40p with the full cover price being given to newsagents for an initial period. IPC, the publishers of *TV Times* and *What's on TV*, fought back by halving the price of the *TV Times* to 25p for three weeks and cutting the price of *What's on TV* to 10p.

The BBC, publishers of the *Radio Times*, held firm at 50p, arguing that price cuts run the danger of devaluing the brand in the eyes of consumers. It has been argued that *Radio Times* has been cushioned from the 'battle' because of the up-market niche established in the market. In 1993, *TV Times* sold for 55p, *What's on TV* for 35p, *TV Quick* for 46p and *Radio Times* for 60p.

Source: adapted from *The Sunday Times*, 16.6.1991.

(a) How would you describe the pricing policy used for *TV Quick*?
(b) Why would market skimming not have been a suitable policy for *TV Quick* in this market?
(c) What might have been the pricing strategy that lay behind the *Radio Times'* decision to keep prices at 50p?

Competition based pricing

With COMPETITION BASED PRICING it is the prices charged by competitors which are the major influence on a producer's price. It is used mostly by firms which face fierce and direct competition. As a rule, the more competitive the market and the more homogeneous the products competing in that market, the greater the pressure for competition based pricing. Markets similar to the model of oligopoly (☞ unit 22) will often use this form of pricing. For example, soap powder producers tend to be influenced by the price of competitors' products.

Going rate pricing This occurs in markets where firms are reluctant to set off a price war by lowering their prices and are concerned about a fall off in revenue if prices are raised. They examine competitors' prices and choose a price broadly in line with them. It also occurs when one dominant firm establishes a position of **price leadership** within a market. Other firms will follow suit when the price leader changes its prices. This type of policy can be seen when a petrol company changes the price of a gallon of petrol.

Firms which operate in markets where going rate pricing occurs will often be frustrated by their inability to control their prices more closely. A strategy often used in such circumstances is to establish a strong **brand** identity for your product and to differentiate it from others on the market. This would be through unique design features or quality of service. BP's decision to upgrade all of their service stations is an example of an attempt to achieve this. A strong brand identity and unique product features allow firms much greater scope for choosing their own price levels.

Destroyer pricing The aim of destroyer pricing is to eliminate opposition. It involves cutting prices, sometimes greatly, for a period of time, long enough for your rivals to go out of business. An alleged example of destroyer pricing was when Laker Airways were forced out of the transatlantic airline business by the combined price cutting of the major airlines in the business.

Close bid pricing This method of pricing occurs when firms have to TENDER a bid for work which they are going to carry out. This is common practice for firms dealing with the government or local authorities. For example, if a new road is to be built then the relevant local authority will invite firms to put in a bid to win a contract for the work. Firms will clearly need to pay very close attention to the price at which they expect their competitors to bid. Usually, when a number of firms bid

for a contract those with the highest prices are likely to be rejected. Another example of this type of pricing was the bids to operate Independent Television stations. A round of bids saw TV-AM replaced by Good Morning Television for the breakfast news slot.

QUESTION 4 The Nordic Pottery company based in Stoke on Trent is a manufacturer of cheap coffee mugs aimed at the lower end of the market. Competition in the industry is sharp. Not only are there several other Potteries based firms operating in this market, but there has been a recent influx of cheap imports from the Far East. The major part of the company's sales go to high street shops and street market traders, but they also supply the Civil Service with bulk orders. Due to falling sales, the company has been forced to re-evaluate its pricing strategy.

(a) What pricing strategy do you think Nordic use? Give reasons for your answer.
(b) Given the above evidence, suggest an alternative pricing strategy for Nordic to use. Explain your answer.

Key terms

Competition based pricing - methods of pricing based upon the prices charged by competitors.
Cost based pricing - methods of pricing products which are based upon costs.
Market orientated pricing - methods of pricing based upon the pricing conditions in the market at which a product is aimed.

Mark-up - that part of a price which seeks to provide a business with profit as opposed to covering its costs. It is used in cost plus pricing.
Pricing strategy - the pricing policy or method of pricing adopted by a business.
Tender - a bid to secure a contract for work.

Summary

1. State 5 pricing strategies a business might use.
2. What are the main factors affecting a firm's pricing decisions?
3. Explain the difference between cost plus pricing and contribution pricing.
4. State one advantage and one disadvantage of cost plus and contribution pricing for a firm.
5. What is meant by absorption cost pricing?
6. Why might a firm use penetration pricing?
7. What is market skimming?
8. What types of firm might use market skimming as a pricing strategy?
9. What is meant by price discrimination?
10. Under what circumstances might a firm use competition based pricing?
11. Explain the terms:
    (a) going rate pricing;
    (b) destroyer pricing;
    (c) close bid pricing.
12. Give 2 examples of tendering.

Question

Nosing out a model profit

The World perfume business is worth £5.5 billion a year - more than the Gross Domestic Product of Kenya. Yves Saint Laurent makes £244 million from perfume and scent provides Christian Dior with £326 million.

'French designers can afford to produce a tiny collection of extortionately expensive clothes because they don't have to sell any of them', explains Anthony Price, a top London fashion designer. 'All their profit comes from perfume and cosmetics deals. And as long as their high class image promotes their perfume, the money will roll in.'

'Scent is a high risk business', says Stephen Gilbert Marketing Director of Chanel perfume. 'With a new product it is unlikely that anyone will make any money in the first year. It may take three years before a product is secure.' When Christian Lacroix launched C'est la Vie (It's Life), US based analysts dubbed it C'est la Guerre (It's War) because of the stiff competition it faced. It floundered for a few months, as American women sniffed, considered and walked away. By the end of the year its nickname was C'est la Mort (It's Death).

'C'est la Vie didn't sell as well as expected because the image was too exclusive', explains cosmetics analyst Diana Temple. 'Lacroix's image didn't mean anything to the general public.'

Advertising is essential. An aggressive launch can cost £10 million. According to *Media Register*, £37,634,000 will be spent by the fragrance industry on advertising in Britain this year. 'All the consumer is paying for is the enormous amount of advertising it takes to make the products a commercial success', says Anthony Price.

The perfume in the bottle can cost as little as five per cent of the retail price.

Source: adapted from the *Mail on Sunday*, 20.10.1991.

(a) Calculate the percentage retail mark-up on the trade price of a bottle of Chanel No.5 from Figure 23.4.
(b) Which pricing strategies are mentioned in the data? Explain your answer.
(c) Explain why the cost of the ingredients in the perfume only accounts for five per cent of the retail price.
(d) What factors do you think have influenced the pricing decisions of the perfume manufacturers?
(e) Why are the perfume companies prepared to spend so much on advertising?

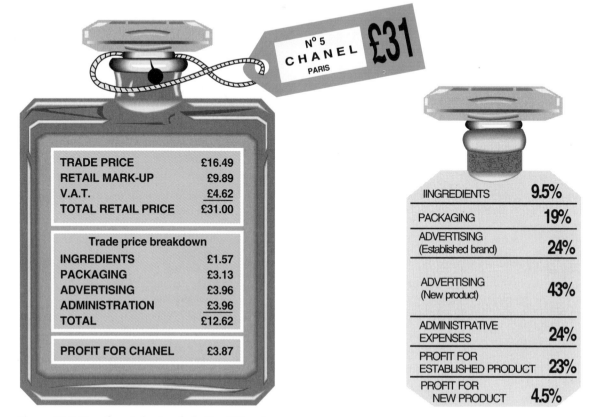

N° 5 CHANEL PARIS £31

TRADE PRICE	£16.49
RETAIL MARK-UP	£9.89
V.A.T.	£4.62
TOTAL RETAIL PRICE	£31.00

Trade price breakdown	
INGREDIENTS	£1.57
PACKAGING	£3.13
ADVERTISING	£3.96
ADMINISTRATION	£3.96
TOTAL	£12.62

PROFIT FOR CHANEL	£3.87

IINGREDIENTS	9.5%
PACKAGING	19%
ADVERTISING (Established brand)	24%
ADVERTISING (New product)	43%
ADMINISTRATIVE EXPENSES	24%
PROFIT FOR ESTABLISHED PRODUCT	23%
PROFIT FOR NEW PRODUCT	4.5%

Figure 23.4 *How the retail price of a bottle of Chanel No.5 is made up*

Figure 23.5 *Where the money goes*

What is promotion?

PROMOTION is the attempt to draw attention to a product or business to gain new customers or retain existing ones. Different methods of promotion are shown in Figure 24.1.

Firms often refer to promotion **above the line** and **below the line.** Above the line promotion is through independent media, such as television or newspapers. These allow firms to reach a wide audience easily. Most advertising is carried out 'above the line'. Some advertising, however, is carried out by methods over which a firm has direct control, such as direct mailing. These and other direct methods of promotion (known as below the line promotion) are dealt with in unit 25. This unit looks at how firms advertise their products through different media.

The objectives of promotion

A business must be clear about exactly what it is trying to achieve through its promotion. The main aim of any promotion is to obtain and retain customers. However, there are a number of other objectives, some or all of which any successful campaign must fulfil.

- To make consumers aware or increase awareness of a product.
- To reach a target audience which might be geographically dispersed.
- To remind consumers about the product. This can encourage existing consumers to re-purchase the product and may attract new consumers.
- To show a product is better than that of a competitor.

This may encourage consumers to switch purchases from another product.

- To develop or improve the image of a firm rather than a product. Much **corporate advertising** is carried out with this in mind, and is dealt with later in this unit.
- To reassure consumers after the product has been purchased. This builds up confidence in the product and may encourage more to be bought at a later date.
- To support an existing product. Such promotions may be used to remind consumers that a reliable and well thought of product is still available.

QUESTION 1 The use of 'vouchers' is a growing form of promotion. Some businesses give away free vouchers with an amount of products or services purchased. Vouchers can then be exchanged for other goods and services.

Identify the objectives businesses may have had when using the vouchers in the photograph.

The growth of advertising

Faced with competition, firms have come to realise the importance of advertising. Advertising expenditure in 1992 stood at nearly £7.9 billion, compared to less than half a billion pounds in 1948, and just over £2 billion in 1980.

The extent of advertising in the UK can be seen in numerous poster, TV and newspaper campaigns of companies as diverse as pet food manufacturers and merchant bankers. It has been estimated that the drinks industry spends over £200 million on advertising and that between 1 and 2 per cent of national income is spent on advertising in the United Kingdom.

Advertising is often placed into different categories. INFORMATIVE ADVERTISING is designed to increase consumer awareness of a product. Examples include the classified advertisements in local newspapers, new share offers, grants available to small firms and entries in the *Yellow Pages*. New products may be launched with informative advertising campaigns to make consumers

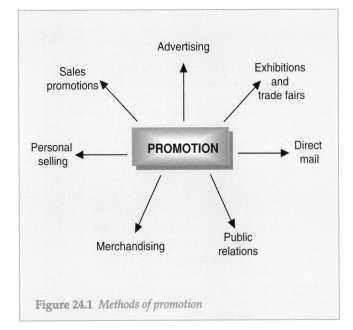

Figure 24.1 *Methods of promotion*

aware of their presence. It is usually argued that this type of advertising helps consumers to make a rational choice as to what to buy.

PERSUASIVE ADVERTISING tries to convince consumers to purchase a product, often by stressing that it is more desirable than others. It is argued that this type of advertising distorts consumer buying, pushing them to buy products which they would otherwise not have bought. In reality, almost all advertising is persuasive to some extent. Very few major campaigns aim to be entirely informative.

QUESTION 2

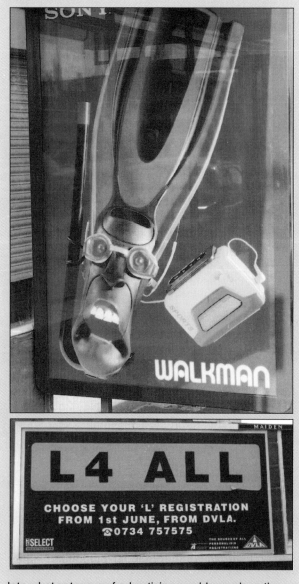

Into what category of advertising would you place the advertisements above? Explain your choices.

Choice of advertising media

There are a wide range of ADVERTISING MEDIA that firms can choose from in order to make consumers aware of their products.

Television Because of its many advantages, television advertising is often used by businesses marketing consumer goods to a mass market. As Table 24.1 shows, people of all social classes spend large chunks of their spare time watching television. Viewers are a 'captive audience' for advertisers.

One problem for the television advertisers is that commercial television tends to be watched less by social classes A and B. Another is that people are now watching less television than they were, despite breakfast and all night television. Ownership of VCRs has also reduced the effectiveness of television as an advertising medium. In 1990, 14.8 million households were estimated to have at least one video recorder. VCR owners tend to be less likely to watch television advertisements because they are able to hire and buy pre-recorded tapes. Even when programmes are recorded from television stations, owners of VCRs can 'fast-forward' through advertisements.

Table 24.1 *Television viewing by social class*

UK	Hours and minutes and percentages	
	1985	1990
Social class (hours: mins per week)		
ABC1	20:47	19:31
C2	25:18	24:13
DE	33:11	30:13
All persons	25:54	23:51

Source: adapted from *Social Trends*, CSO.

Newspapers and magazines Newspapers are a very important medium for the advertising of mass market consumer goods, because of the numbers of readers. In the UK, the figures are especially high. In 1990, for example, over 60 per cent of the adult population regularly read a daily newspaper. In the same year one quarter of all men read *The Sun*.

Newspapers can be important in reaching a **target** audience. Unlike the four main television channels, which tend to be watched by a wide range of viewers, newspapers and magazines are often read by people sharing similar characteristics. The readership of the *Financial Times* and the *Independent* is mainly from social classes A and B. Newspaper advertising is important to small firms. The only promotion they can afford may be in a local paper.

Cinema Cinema attendances have fallen greatly in the last forty years. However, during the 1980s there was an upsurge in cinema attendances, so that by 1990 64 per cent of the population visited a cinema. Advertisers, as a result, began to pay more attention to this medium. Firms such as Wrangler have even produced advertisements principally designed for use on large cinema screens. Of all the advertising media available to a business, the cinema has the greatest potential for having a strong impact on its audience.

Table 24.2 *Advertising media*

Medium	Advantages	Disadvantages
Television	• Creative advertisements can attract attention and have a great impact. • Advertisements can demonstrate the product in use. • Can reach a vast audience. • Increased scope for targeting the audience, eg Channel 4, Sky. • The message can be reinforced by continuous advertisements.	• Relatively expensive initial cost. • The message is short lived. • Consumers may not watch commercials. • Technical information is difficult to explain. • There may be a delay between seeing the advert and visiting the shops.
National newspaper	• National coverage. • Reader can refer back. • Relatively cheap. • Detail of the product can be provided.	• No movement or sound. • Usually limited to black and white. • Individual adverts may be lost amongst large quantities of other advertisements.
Regional newspaper	• Good for regional campaigns and test marketing. • Can be linked to local conditions.	• Cost per reader higher than national newspapers. • Reproduction, layout etc. may be poor.
Magazines	• Colour advertisements possible. • Targeting possible with specialist magazines. • Advertising can be linked to features. • Magazines may be referred to at a later date.	• A long time exists between advertisements being placed and magazine being printed. • Competitors' products are also being advertised. • No movement or sound.
Cinema	• Colour, sound and movement can be used. • Advertisements can be highly localised. • A 'captive' audience for advertisements. • Great impact on the consumer. • Age groups can be targeted.	• Limited audience. • Message is short lived. • Message may only be seen once.
Radio	• Enables use of sound. • Most consumer groups covered. • Minority programmes can target audiences. • Produced cheaply. • Younger audience targeted.	• Not visual. • No copy of material. • Interruptions to music may prove irritating. • May not capture the audience's attention.
Posters	• National campaigns possible. • Most groups covered. • May encourage impulse buying through location close to shops. • Seen repeatedly. • Excellent for short, sharp messages, eg, election 'promises'.	• Limited amount of information. • Difficult to measure effectiveness. • Weather and graffiti can ruin the poster.

Radio In recent years there has been a growth in the number of independent radio stations in the UK. These range from local stations, such as Capital in London and Piccadilly in Manchester, to national stations including Virgin AM and Classic FM. For advertisers this has meant an increase in both the number and type of radio stations on which they can advertise.

There has also been an increase in the amount of radio listening in recent years. The growth in the number of local commercial radio stations has been of particular benefit to small and medium sized firms.

Posters Posters appear in a variety of locations and tend to carry short messages. This is because motorists and pedestrians usually only have a few seconds to consider them. An effective poster is likely to be large, attention grabbing and placed in a site where it is highly visible to large numbers of people .

The advantages and disadvantages of different advertising media are shown in Table 24.2.

QUESTION 3 Conrack Ltd is a business that specialises in products made from 'managed' wood - wood which when cut down for timber is replaced by planting a new tree. It has produced, marketed and sold kitchen tables in the London area with great success. The Marketing Director, Neil Barnett, argued that small scale but thought provoking advertisements in the region have been particularly influential.

The company now feels it is time to market the products nationally and has decided an advertisement stressing the features of the product would be the best alternative. At the moment, funds are scarce and, although the company is convinced of its success in future, the market for the products is still likely to be limited in size.

(a) What media may Conrack have used for its 'small scale but thought provoking' advertisements?
(b) Advise Conrack on the most likely choice of media for its national campaign, given its circumstances and its product.

Choice of advertising media

How do firms decide which medium will be most suitable for their product? There are a number of factors that advertisers may take into account.

Cost Small firms will be mainly concerned with what media they can afford. Larger firms will need to consider the cost effectiveness of each of the different media. For example, although television is the most expensive medium, it reaches huge numbers of consumers. This means the cost per sale from a television advertisement may be relatively low.

The audience reached Given that many products are aimed at certain segments, it makes sense for firms to place their advertisement in a medium which the target audience is likely to see or hear. Firms must aim to reduce **wastage** in their advertising. 'Wastage' means advertising to those other than the target audience. Clearly a certain amount of wastage will occur with most TV advertising, whilst very little will occur when advertising in, say, specialist magazines.

The advertising of competitors A major TV advertising campaign by one firm may, for example, be followed by a counter campaign from its competitors.

The impact Firms will aim to make the greatest impact when advertising. Different products will require different media to do this. For example, some products such as sports equipment will benefit from being shown in action to have the most impact on an audience. Television and cinema are the obvious choice of media in such cases.

The law There are legal restrictions in the UK which mean that some products cannot be advertised in particular media. This is discussed in detail later in this unit. One example of this is the ban on advertising tobacco on TV in the UK.

The marketing mix The advertising campaign should be integrated with other types of below the line promotion (☞ unit 25). For example, sponsorship of a sports event and an advertisement for the product on the sports pages of a newspaper may be effective.

QUESTION 4 Much advertising in recent years has come from public sector organisations, financed by the government, seeking to influence public opinion over a range of issues. Twenty years ago this was largely limited to basic public information films. They were often shown on late night television, aimed at preventing people from dropping litter or persuading children to cross the road carefully. The Health Education Authority Aids awareness advertising campaign, however, was something of a breakthrough. Millions of pounds were spent advertising in a variety of media including magazines, cinemas, posters and televisions. The advertisements were also professionally made and hard-hitting.

You are preparing an advertising campaign to make consumers aware of the need for recycling paper and cans using the experience of the Health Education Authority.
(a) Decide upon your objectives.
(b) State which media you will use and explain why.
(c) Name any constraints on your campaign and how they influenced your choice of media.

The advertising budget

Advertising can be expensive. Not only must the cost of placing the advertisement in the media be met, but in most cases a company will be hired to 'create' the advert. Such organisations are known as ADVERTISING AGENCIES. These agencies, working with their clients, create and produce advertisements. Whilst some firms produce their own advertisements for newspapers, most use the services of these agencies when advertising in other media.

Setting the advertising budget can be a difficult task. This is because it is impossible to predict just how effective a particular advertising campaign is going to be and therefore how much money should be spent. However, there are a number of methods which firms might use to decide upon their advertising budget.

■ As a percentage of anticipated sales revenue. This is a simple and easy method to use. It has the advantage that resources are allocated according to their effect on sales. However, the firm is assuming that the level of advertising has a direct effect on the level of sales. This might not always be the case. For example, some products sell well no matter how much is spent on advertising them. There is also the problem that anticipated figures for sales revenue can be estimates and may, therefore, be inaccurate.

■ As a percentage of past sales. Unlike the method

described above, in this method finance allocated to the advertising budget has already been earned. However, it does not take into account market changes. A fall in sales would not result in a cut in the advertising budget. Similarly, an increase in sales would not result in a larger advertising budget.

- By comparing spending with competitors. Whilst this should help to prevent competitors from gaining market share, it can also lead to an upward spiral in the amount spent on advertising. This may result as one firm tries to match the spending of others. The major problem with this method is that it assumes competitors are spending a sensible amount on advertising.

- As a fixed amount, based upon advertising needs. For example, when introducing a new product a firm may decide upon the amount needed for advertising to successfully launch it. Advertising budgets are likely to be higher for new products than mature products.

Controls on advertising

Consumers sometimes complain that advertisements either mislead or exploit. For this reason, there are legislation and codes of practice to protect the consumer.

Legislation The **Trades Descriptions Act 1968** is the most important piece of legislation in the control of advertising. The law states that products must correspond to the claims made for them in advertisements. It is, therefore, illegal to include ingredients on a label which are not present or make unproven claims about the effects of, say, weight loss products. Descriptions of services provided by firms must also be accurate. The Act prevents firms from misleading the consumer about 'sales'. A sale can only be advertised if products were sold at higher prices for 28 days in the previous 6 months.

Under the **Monopolies and Restrictive Practices Act 1948**, the Office of Fair Trading and the Monopolies and Mergers Commission have been given powers to investigate anti-competitive behaviour by firms (☞ unit 73). Such anti-competitive behaviour may be in the form of high levels of spending on advertising. This raises costs within an industry and acts as a barrier to prevent other firms from entering the market.

Independent bodies The **Advertising Standards Authority (ASA)** is a voluntary body set up to monitor advertising in the UK. It is responsible for making sure that advertisers conform to the **British codes of advertising and sales promotion practice.** They state that advertisements must be legal, decent, honest and truthful and must not cause grave or widespread offence. Advertisements which are referred to the ASA, often by members of the public, will not be handled by the media. The ASA, therefore, has the power to ensure that the code is upheld by the advertisers. One example of an advertisement outlawed by the ASA was a poster for *Today* newspaper before the 1992 General Election. This asked 'Would Britain be better off with a hung

Parliament' above pictures of the leaders of the three main political parties, with nooses around their necks.

The Independent Television Commission (ITC) controls advertising on television and radio. There are a variety of rules which are used to judge such advertising. Examples are that current newsreaders cannot appear in adverts to endorse products, and actors cannot be used in commercial breaks during programmes in which they appear.

Pressure groups Certain pressure groups (☞ unit 71) seek to influence advertising. FOREST, for example, is a pressure group which aims to defend the rights of tobacco firms to advertise. The British Medical Association (BMA) and Action on Smoking and Health (ASH) take the opposite view. Women's groups have sought to influence firms to produce advertisements which are not sexist. Pressure groups campaigning for better safety on roads have sought to persuade car and tyre manufacturers to produce advertisements showing less aggressive driving.

How much power these bodies have is debatable. On the one hand, there is so much disagreement about what is 'decent' about an advertisement that there will always be room for dispute. However, in 1991 there were 10,610 complaints made to the ASA - a 17 per cent increase on 1990. Of these, 2,416 were upheld. Perhaps this shows a growing trend towards restricting undesirable advertisements.

Advertising and society

Advertising has the potential to affect the lives of many people. This is because, for most, regular exposure to advertising is almost unavoidable. How might advertising affect individuals?

- It adds to the cost of marketing products. This money could have been spent on improving products or price reductions. It is likely that consumers will pay more of any advertising costs than firms.

- It is argued that advertising encourages people to buy products which they might not otherwise have purchased. This may, perhaps, lead to a society where people are judged according to how much they consume rather than their value as human beings.

- Environmentalists are concerned about high levels of consumption and the role of advertising in encouraging this. They doubt whether the earth's resources can sustain current levels. There is a growing trend amongst consumers to look at the type of goods they buy and also how much they consume, as they become more aware of long term problems.

- Advertising can encourage people to buy products which are regarded as being damaging to society.

- Advertisements often encourage behaviour which might be to the detriment of society as a whole. An example is the fast 'macho' driving often seen in advertisements for cars and related products.

In its defence, the advertising industry would point to a number of arguments to justify its role.

- Advertisements offer a choice to consumers which allows them to make more informed consumption decisions.
- Advertisements give valuable information to consumers which might otherwise be difficult to come by.
- Advertisers respond to and reflect the needs, wishes and attitudes of consumers; they do not 'create' them.
- Advertising earns revenue for television and radio and allows newspapers and magazines to be sold at lower prices.
- The advertising industry employs large numbers of people. They are employed directly, through advertising agencies, and indirectly through jobs that may result from a successfully advertised product.

QUESTION 5

Discuss the possible effects of the advertisements above on consumers.

Corporate advertising

CORPORATE ADVERTISING is concerned with promoting a company as a whole, rather than individual products. An example of corporate advertising can be seen in the detergent market. Companies such as Unilever, a subsidiary of Lever Bros, now have their name on all branded packets, ie Persil. The amount spent on corporate advertising has doubled in recent years and this trend is expected to continue. Companies ranging from ICI to Benetton to BP have jumped on this bandwagon.

There are two reasons why companies need to sell themselves now more than ever. First, companies must now be seen to be responsible good 'citizens'. This means communicating. Second, there is growing pressure for the company to become a **brand** (☞ unit 25). Companies need to ensure that their corporate image is positive.

Corporate advertising often makes use of **slogans** or **catchlines.** Hanson Trust plugged their success in the USA with the catchline 'The company from over here that's doing rather well over there'. Shell has tried to build up its reputation as a much trusted institution with the slogan 'You can be sure of Shell'. British Airways advertised as the 'World's Airline', using a blinking eye made up of hundreds of people from different countries.

Corporate advertising allows a company to advertise its whole philosophy. Corporate messages are aimed at a variety of different, yet connected, audiences. These include employees, local groups, the trade, government, the media, financial institutions and the 'general public', as well as consumers themselves. There are problems, however. The corporate values of one company may not be different to those of another, so that target audiences may not be able to distinguish between the messages of different firms. Also, less may be spent on advertising individual brands, as a business uses resources to promote the whole company.

QUESTION 6 Texaco were one of the first UK companies to create a corporate advertising campaign around a social project. The oil company launched a road safety campaign with the slogan 'Children should be seen and not hurt'. As well as press, poster and TV advertisements Texaco handed out 4.3 million sets of reflective safety stickers, via its service stations, and leaflets and education packs for schools.

(a) Why might Texaco have chosen to advertise as a company rather than place an emphasis on a particular brand?
(b) What factors might have influenced the success of the way in which Texaco advertised itself?

Key terms

Advertising agencies - organisations specialising in the creation of advertisements.
Advertising media - the various means by which advertisements can be communicated to the public.
Corporate advertising - advertising which is meant to promote a whole company rather than a particular product or product line.
Informative advertising - advertising which primarily seeks to provide consumers with information about a product
Persuasive advertising - advertising which seeks to influence and persuade consumers to buy a product.
Promotion - an attempt to retain and obtain customers by drawing attention to a firm or its products.

Summary

1. What is above the line promotion?
2. Why might advertising be both above and below the line promotion?
3. What are the objectives of promotion?
4. What choices of advertising media do firms have?
5. What criteria might firms use in order to decide upon their choice of advertising media?
6. What is the role of an advertising agency?
7. What is the role of the ASA?
8. Why might an advertisement be banned under the Trade Description Act 1968?
9. State 3 arguments for and three arguments against advertising.
10. What is the objective of corporate advertising?

Question

Benetton

The last few years have been exciting for Luciano Benetton and his company. A bid to expand the profile and the market share of the company through an unusual and attention grabbing advertising campaign has not been without its problems. Benetton is an Italian manufacturer of casual clothing. It has worldwide retail outlets for its products. At its peak in the 1980s there were 700 stores in the USA alone. There are now over 6,500 shops in 100 countries. Previously, the company had produced advertisements showing children of many different races with catchlines such as 'United Colours of Benetton'.

In 1991, an advertising campaign containing a photograph of a newly born baby resulted in over 800 complaints being received by the Advertising Standards Authority. The weight of public disapproval led the Authority to ban the advertisement stating that, 'A large number of people were saying that they didn't object to the picture itself, but they did object to the exploitation of a newly born baby at its most vulnerable and frail'. It could be argued that the publicity resulting from the ban may have been more effective than the advertisement itself. Benetton argued that its advertising worked. In 1991 they raised group net profits by 23.6 per cent to £77.48 million, and turnover rose by 12 per cent. A US trade magazine, however, countered that market share was being lost and the number of stores in the US was likely to fall in the next few years.

1992 saw the launch of other disturbing, yet thought provoking, advertisements. These included a photograph of KGB officers arresting a man, a bird covered in oil in the Gulf and an empty electric chair

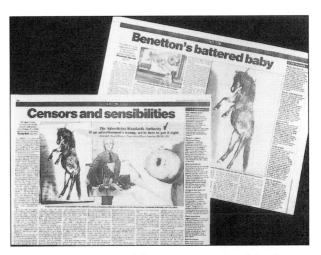

in New York. Some of these were approved by the ASA and were shown from Tokyo to Johannesburg.

Source: adapted from *The Observer*, 8.9.1991 and the *Financial Times*, 17.9.1992.

(a) To what extent might the campaign be described as corporate advertising?
(b) What might have been Benetton's objectives when launching its advertising campaign?
(c) What might have been the most suitable media for Benetton's campaign? Explain your answer.
(d) How might legal and other constraints have played a part in affecting the campaign?
(e) Argue the case for and against the use of such campaigns from the public's point of view.
(f) Evaluate the success of the campaign. State the criteria you have used for assessment.

Promoting below the line

Promotion below the line refers to those promotional methods which do not depend upon media such as newspapers and TV. Instead, it takes place by methods over which firms have some degree of control. These include direct mail advertising, exhibitions and trade fairs, sales promotions, merchandising, packaging, personal selling and public relations. A business, such as Forte, might promote its hotels by using a combination of promotions, for example public relations and sales promotions.

Below the line promotion allows a firm to aim its marketing at consumers it knows are interested in the product. Above the line advertising in newspapers means that the promotion is seen by most of the readers, even though some will not be interested. With below the line promotions, firms are usually aiming their message at consumers who are either known to them or who have been chosen in advance. For example, direct mail advertisers will pick exactly which consumers they wish to send their mail to, rather than going for blanket coverage. Firms promoting through exhibitions, such as the Boat Show, can be certain that the majority of those attending will be interested in the products on show.

There may be problems that result from below the line promotions.

- As with advertising, they are expensive and their outcome is difficult to predict.
- They are often 'one off' events, which have an impact for a limited period.
- Some types of promotion, such as direct mail and personal selling, are disliked by consumers.

Direct mailing

Direct mailing involves sending information about a product or product range through the post. The consumer can usually buy the product by placing an order by post or telephone. Although sometimes unpopular with the public, direct mail is at present the fastest growing area of promotion. It has proved very effective for firms trying to reach a target audience.

Direct mail is one means of **direct marketing** (☞ unit 26), which is often seen as part of a firm's distribution network.

Exhibitions and trade fairs

Exhibitions and trade fairs are used by firms to promote their products. They are visited by both industrial and ordinary consumers. Examples of better known fairs and exhibitions include the Motor Show, the Boat show and the Ideal Homes Exhibition. Why do businesses find them useful?

- They give the chance to show how a product actually works. This is important in the case of bulky or complex technical products. The marketing of industrial and agricultural machinery is often done through trade fairs.
- Consumer reaction to a product can be tested before it is released onto the market.
- Some trade fairs and exhibitions are held overseas. They can form a part of a firm's international marketing strategy (☞ unit 27).
- A fair or exhibition may attract press coverage. New products may be launched to take advantage of this. The Motor Show is widely used for this purpose.
- They allow customers to discuss a product with members of the management team. It is not unusual for the managing directors of a business to attend a trade fair. For industrial consumers, in particular, this can be a valuable point of contact.
- Technical and sales staff are available to answer questions and discuss the product.

QUESTION 1 One of the USA's major trade exhibitions is the PC Expo which is held at New York's Javitz Centre, the city's main exhibition venue. It draws in over 50,000 people during its three day existence, and receives a tremendous amount of press and TV coverage. The principal players in the personal computer market, such as Apple, IBM and Lucas all have stands there and it is used as a platform to make major new business announcements.

(a) Why is it important for a firm such as IBM to use a trade exhibition as part of its promotional mix?
(b) Why might trade fairs be more effective in promoting personal computers than direct mail advertising?

Sales promotions

Sales promotions are the incentives offered to consumers to encourage them to buy goods and services. They are used to give a short term 'boost' to the sales of a product. This is different to building up brand recognition and loyalty, which may be a longer term aim.

There are a variety of sales promotions that a business can use.

- Coupons and refunds. This involves refunding money or providing coupons which allow savings to be made on repeat purchases. One example was a venture between British Rail and Boots the Chemist. Consumers could obtain discounts on rail travel through the purchase of products at Boots.
- Competitions. Prizes are sometimes offered for competitions. To enter, consumers must first buy the product. Tabloid newspapers often use this type of promotion. They try to attract customers through large

cash prizes in their 'bingo' competitions.

■ Product endorsements. These are widely used by sports goods manufacturers. Sports personalities and teams are paid to wear or use particular products. They might also involve a particular personality's name actually appearing on a product. Nike 'Air Jordan' trainers are an example of this. Other uses include television and film stars opening retail outlets.

■ Product placing. This is a recent innovation. It involves a firm paying for product brands to be placed on the sets of films and TV programmes.

■ Free offers. A free 'gift' may be given with the product. An example of this was the Hoover offer in 1992 which provided two free flights to the US with the purchase of products worth over £100.

■ Special credit terms. This has been increasingly used by firms. It includes offers such as interest free credit and 'buy now pay later' schemes.

Why are these methods becoming popular?

■ Sales promotions can be used as a method to break into a new market or introduce a new product into an existing market. They can also be used as a means of extending the **product life cycle** of an existing product (☞ unit 20).

■ They are a means of encouraging consumers to sample a good or service which they might not have bought otherwise. Once the initial good has been purchased it is likely that further goods will be bought. Many magazines offer free gifts ranging from compact discs to make-up in their first issues hoping that their consumers will continue to buy.

■ Businesses use coupons to reward established customers by 'refunding' some of their spending.

■ Sales promotions provide businesses with feedback on the impact of their marketing expenditure, for example, through the number of coupons returned.

QUESTION 2 In an attempt to capture the student market, a number of firms have joined in a venture which aims to provide each higher education student with a free 'Student Welcome Pack' containing a number of different goods. The pack was launched at the beginning of the 1990-91 academic year and contained an average of 12 items worth around £12. Products placed in the pack included snack foods, toiletries, shampoo and soft drinks. In total over 350,000 packs were issued. There was also a 20 page colour booklet with advertisements and money off coupons to be used against a range of products. The total value of these coupons was approximately £100. Research before the issuing of these packs indicated that 23 per cent of recipients were likely to purchase brands contained in the pack again.

Source: adapted from *Sales Promotion*, March 1991.

(a) For what reasons might this particular sales promotion be successful?

(b) What other types of sales promotions might be used to capture the student market? Explain your answer.

Sales promotions are not without problems. The free flight offer of Hoover in 1992 is one example. The company misjudged the number of people taking advantage of the offer. This meant extreme pressure on the company to produce the goods consumers were demanding. Also many consumers did not receive the holidays on dates or at times they wished. By 1993 there were so many complaints that Maytag, Hoover's US parent company, had to intervene to make sure flights or compensation were provided. It was estimated that the cost of dealing with these problems was £21.1 million.

Branding

A BRAND is a name given by a producer to one or more of its products. The main aims of this are to differentiate the product from others and to make it distinctive to consumers. Choosing a brand name is an important part of a firm's **marketing strategy**. An effective brand name is likely to be short and easy to identify and remember. It must also project the required image and, if possible, the positive characteristics of the product. Examples of strong brands include Del Monte, Coca-Cola, Kodak, Porsche, Jaguar, Persil, Mars and Fairy Liquid.

Popular brands have often been supported and developed by CATCHLINES. These are phrases which seek to strengthen the identity of a brand. Famous examples include 'A Mars a day helps you work, rest and play' and 'Gillette, the best a man can get'.

There are three main types of branding which a firm can use.

■ Multiple branding. This involves a firm using a range of brand names for its products. Rank Hovis McDougall, for example, have a number of brands including Mr Kipling, Bisto, Mother's Pride and Hovis. Multiple brands allow the firm to develop brands for particular market segments. The travel firm Owners Abroad, for example, sells its holidays under several different brands, each targeting a different market segment. It also has the advantage that failure of one brand should not have a knock on effect on others.

■ Multiple product branding. This is the opposite to multiple branding. Only one brand name is used for a range of products. Firms which use this method of branding include Kellogg's, Cadbury's, Hitachi and Sony. The main advantage of this form of branding is that the brand can be built up over a range of products. This should allow the strengths of one product to bolster the reputation of another and allow new products to be more easily introduced to the market.

■ Retailers 'own brands'. These are products which are branded with the name of the retailer responsible for selling them. Examples include Sainsbury's, Tesco and Boots. Manufacturers of own brands can supply products to be sold under another firm's name. This allows responsibility for the marketing of a product to be passed onto the retailer. Many manufacturers, though, might see this as a mixed blessing. For retailers, own brands can help them to increase customer loyalty and increase their bargaining power when dealing with manufacturers.

There are a number of reasons why firms use branding.

- To create brand loyalty. Consumers often have a high degree of loyalty to popular, well established, brands. In many markets it can be very difficult for firms to compete unless they have a strong brand identity.
- To differentiate the product. Especially in markets where products are fairly similar, it is important for a firm that its own products can be clearly distinguished from others. A clear brand identity can help to achieve this.
- To gain flexibility when making pricing decisions. The greater the loyalty of consumers to a particular brand, the more room for manoeuvre a firm will have in its pricing decisions. A survey in 1992 by Business Marketing Services found that consumers were reluctant to switch from well known brands in the hotel, car hire, computer and transatlantic flights markets. For example, in the car hire market pricing discounts of over 20 per cent were required to persuade consumers to switch from Hertz or Avis to one of the lesser known companies.
- To help recognition. A product with a strong brand identity is likely to be instantly recognised by most consumers. This may mean consumers trust the product and are therefore more willing to buy it. Some brand names have become used to describe the product, such as Sellotape.

QUESTION 3 The age of innocence in television branding is dead. Stuart Butterfield, Channel 4's head of marketing believes that the branding of TV channels, 'seems to be one of the key developments in the nineties'.

In many ways Channel 4 set the pace for television branding when its colourful logo first appeared on our screens over ten years ago. In the words of Mr Butterfield, 'Channel 4 already projects a brand image which goes beyond its individual programmes'.

The reason why branding is likely to be of such importance for television stations in the future is the growth in the number of channels. Ten years ago there were only four channels, but today 3 million homes with satellite TV already have the choice of up to 15 extra channels. According to Paul Simons, who is now responsible for Good Morning Television's advertising, establishing a strong brand identity for a small specialist station like GMTV is likely to be far easier than doing the same for ITV. 'ITV's problem is that it has broad programming produced by 15 different companies which has to be all things to all people. BSkyB is a much smaller operation, but it could be argued that it has a much stronger identity and personality in the public's mind than ITV.'

Source: adapted from *The Observer*, 10.1.1993.

(a) Why are television companies seeking to brand their stations?
(b) What branding policy would you advise ITV to use in order to overcome the identity problem identified in the article?

Merchandising

Merchandising is an attempt to influencing consumers at the POINT OF SALE. The point of sale is anywhere that a consumer buys a product. It may be, for example, a supermarket, a department store, a bank or a petrol station. Consumers are intended to buy based on 'what they see' rather than from a sales assistant. The aim of merchandising is to encourage sales of a product and therefore to speed up the rate at which stocks are turned over (☞ unit 33).

There are a number of different features of merchandising.

- Display material. A good display should attract attention, enhance certain aspects of a product and encourage the 'right frame of mind' to make a purchase. Department stores lay great stress on window displays. Banks make sure that the services which they offer, such as insurance and loan facilities, are well displayed in their branches.
- The layout of products at the point of sale. Many retail outlets, such as supermarkets, design the layout of their stores very carefully. Their aim is to encourage consumers to follow particular routes around a store. Retail outlets often place popular items at the back or sides of a store. Consumers, on their way to these, are encouraged to walk past other items which they might buy. Another tactic is to place related products next to each other, so consumers buy both.
- Stocks. A firm must make sure that stock levels are maintained and shelves are quickly restocked. Shelf space is usually allocated according to the amount of a product which a business expects to sell. For example, a supermarket will give more space to products on special offer.
- Appropriate lighting and the creation of desirable 'smells'. Generally lighting is kept soft where browsing is encouraged and bright where there is a need to suggest cleanliness as, for example, at a cosmetics counter. Smells are used to encourage the right atmosphere. Bread smells are often wafted into supermarkets and food retailers.

Packaging

A product's packaging is important in its overall marketing. This is because consumers often link the quality and design of a product's packaging with the quality of the product itself. Unsuitable packaging may affect sales.

What factors should firms consider when deciding upon how to package their product?

- Weight and shape. These can affect the cost of distributing a product. For example, bulky packaging may mean high distribution costs.
- Protection. Products must not be damaged in transit or in storage. They must also be protected against light, dust and heat.
- Convenience. The packaging must be easy to handle by the consumer and distributors.

- Design. The design of the packaging should be eye catching and help the consumer to distinguish it from others. It should also fit in with the overall marketing of the product and project the brand image. Colour is likely to be important here.
- Information. It is likely that the package will contain information required by the consumer. For technical products, the packaging will need to include information about how the product should be used. For food products, there are legal requirements about the information that must be on the package, such as details of the ingredients contained.
- Environmental factors. Manufacturers are facing increasing pressure to cut down on the amount and type of packaging placed around products. Consumers and pressure groups (☞ unit 72) stress the wastefulness of this and its impact upon the environment. The response of some manufacturers to this pressure has been to use recyclable materials.

QUESTION 4 Caribbean Ltd is a manufacturer of soft drinks. It has recently produced a new additive-free kiwi fruit drink, which it initially aims to target at business people who are looking for something a little different for a lunchtime drink. It has arranged for retailers to stock the new drink and keep a display on view for an initial trial period.

(a) Advise the marketing department of Caribbean Ltd on the:
   (i) features of its merchandising;
   (ii) packaging;
   that it should use in attempting a successful launch for its product.
(b) What are the likely constraints on the packaging of this product and how are they likely to affect its success?

Personal selling

Personal selling occurs when a company's sales team promotes a product through personal contact. This can be done over the telephone, by setting up meetings, in retail outlets, or by 'knocking on doors'. In general, the more highly priced, technically complex or individual the product, the greater the need for personal selling. Most firms supplying industrial markets rely upon personal selling in the form of **sales representatives**.

The main advantage of personal selling over other methods is that individuals can be given personal attention. Most forms of promotion tend to deliver a 'standard message' to a 'typical' consumer. With personal selling the individual consumer's needs can be dealt with and the product shaped to meet these needs.

There are a number of purposes which personal selling can serve.
- Creating awareness of and interest in a product.
- Explaining the functions and technical aspects of a product.
- Obtaining orders and, in some cases, making deliveries.

- Encouraging product trials and test marketing.
- Providing rapid and detailed feedback from the consumer to the producer via the sales representative.

One disadvantage with personal selling is that it can be expensive. The cost of maintaining a team of sales representatives can be very high. Another problem is the dislike of 'callers' by consumers.

QUESTION 5 In recent years the so-called High Street banks, such as Lloyds, National Westminster and Midland, have been placing increasing emphasis upon the marketing of financial services, such as household insurance, holiday insurance and life assurance. Until recently they were largely seen as sidelines to the main business of banking. Merchandising, personal selling and packaging have all played key roles in a promotional mix with a high emphasis placed upon below the line promotions.

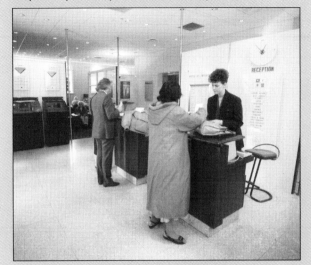

(a) What would be the likely point of sale for these services?
(b) Which aspects of their merchandising would you advise the banks to pay particular attention to?
(c) What might be the particular benefits of personal selling in marketing these 'products'?

Public relations

PUBLIC RELATIONS is an organisation's attempt to communicate with groups that form its 'public'. Such groups may include the government, shareholders, employees and customers. The aim of such communications is to increase sales by improving the image of the firm and its products. This can be done directly by the business itself through a public relations activity. On the other hand a television programme or a newspaper could be used.

Consumers appear to attach great importance to messages conveyed through public relations. Take the example of a new restaurant which has just opened. It would expect to promote a positive image of itself through its own promotional materials. Such communications may, therefore, be taken 'with a pinch of salt' by consumers. However, a good write-up in a newspaper or restaurant guide is likely to be taken much more seriously by consumers.

Businesses often use **press conferences** to attract publicity. These might involve inviting journalists to a company presentation, where they are given information. The firm may take the opportunity to launch a new or updated product. Sometimes, firms provide free products for conference members to try out. Conferences may also be used for presentations to trade customers.

Firms also make use of **press releases**. These are written accounts of events or activities which may be considered newsworthy. For example, new multi-million pound contracts gained by firms such as British Aerospace are announced on TV news bulletins. Such news stories usually originate from press releases issued by firms themselves.

Because of the importance of maintaining good relations with the media, a business may appoint a **publicity manager**. As well as promoting favourable press stories, publicity managers must respond to criticisms and try to ensure that there are no unfavourable press notices.

Other than conferences what other public relations activities may firms use?

■ Donations to charities etc. These can range from a small contribution to a college mini bus appeal to a large donation to the ITV Telethon. Whilst some make payments anonymously, others take advantage of the opportunity for a good public relations event. The approach of a firm to such an event is likely to be determined by its particular ethical stance (☞ unit 71).

■ Sponsorship. This is popular in the sporting world. Examples include the links between Coca-Cola and the Olympic Games, Sharp electronics and Manchester United, and Nike and Andre Agassi. Other types of sponsorship take place in the arts world with ballet, opera and theatre being sponsored by businesses. Firms such as ICI and BP choose to sponsor educational programmes.

■ Company visits. Jaguar Cars and Warburtons Bakeries allow members of the public to visit their manufacturing and research plants as part of their public relations activities.

Key terms

Brand - a name given by a business to one or more of its products.
Catchline - a memorable phrase which seeks to strengthen a product's brand identity.
Point of sale promotion - a promotion at any point where a consumer buys a product.
Public relations - an organisation's attempts to communicate with interested parties.

Summary

1. What is below the line promotion?
2. What is direct mailing?
3. Why do businesses promote their products at trade fairs and exhibitions?
4. Identify four different types of sales promotions.
5. What is branding?
6. What are the 3 main methods of branding?
7. Where is merchandising likely to take place?
8. Which aspects of their merchandising should firms pay attention to?
9. What factors do firms need to consider when packaging their products?
10. What is the main advantage of personal selling?
11. What is public relations?
12. Under what circumstances might public relations activities be most effective?

Question

Thomson Holidays

The crisis in the travel market of the early 1990s was something of a case of deja vu for many travel firms. The last catastrophe to hit the business was the oil crisis of the 70s, which removed market leader Clarkson's from the scene. 'Once they had gone, everyone else could survive', commented Rosemary Astles, Thomson Holiday's Marketing Director in 1991.

Following Clarkson's departure, Thomson assumed first place. After that, the company grew rapidly into a business which turned over £1 billion a year and sold three million holidays. In the midst of a world recession, the travel industry was, once again, under pressure. Rosemary Astles was only too aware of the problems. 'It won't be easy for us. We are in a position which means we won't sell as many holidays. This means there'll be pressure on our overheads', she commented at the time.

So, how did Thomson respond to the situation in terms of their promotional activities? One response was to halt all advertising, taking the view that it is pointless to hit people when they are not receptive. 'If people have strong reasons for not wanting to book at all, advertising won't make any difference', commented Astles.

Below the line, the company spent £2-3 million annually, a figure which excluded the £15-20 million a year it spent on holiday brochures. This £2-3 million was spent on a variety of promotions.

Newspaper competitions were widely used, with free holidays being awarded to the eventual winners. 'Newspaper competitions are particularly cost effective for us. We give away a small number of holidays and these often generate upwards of 100,000 entries', Astles stated.

For a number of months in 1991 Thomson's hooked up with the Air Miles scheme, allowing Air Miles collectors to redeem their vouchers against holidays as part or full payment. This involvement was particularly beneficial, according to Astles, and at very little outlay. In the period over 60,000 people booked holidays using Air Miles.

To encourage agents to sell holidays and to promote product familiarity, Thomson also targeted promotions at the travel trade - the travel agents themselves. Not surprisingly travel was a great motivator. Promotions which dangle the carrot of a holiday or a significant discount on a holiday usually attracted a great response.

Finally, to put across the right message via its retail outlets (the travel agencies) Thomson made use of

extensive point of sale materials and the showcase for its product - a glossy brochure. In all thirty titles, a total of 30 million brochures, were printed across the company's range of products which included Horizon, Skytours, HCI and Wings.

Source: adapted from *Sales Promotion*, March 1991.

(a) Identify from the passage the sales promotions techniques employed by Thomson.
(b) Why did Thomson decide that below the line promotion would be more appropriate than above the line advertising?
(c) What factors might have influenced the success of Thomson's promotions?
(d) Evaluate the likely success of the promotion in the light of the information.
(e) What role might public relations have played in Thomson's attempts to promote its products?
(f) What might have been the problems of using personal selling and direct mail for Thomson in promoting their holidays?

Channels of distribution

Distribution is about one of the 4 'Ps' of the **marketing mix** (☞ unit 21) - place. A business must get the product to the right place, at the right time. A product which is effectively priced and promoted may not be a success unless the consumer is able to purchase it easily.

A CHANNEL OF DISTRIBUTION is the route taken by a product as it passes from the producer to the consumer. Figure 26.1 shows some of the most popular channels of distribution that are open to a business. A producer can sell its products:

- directly to the consumer (channel 1);
- through a retail outlet (channels 2, 4, 6, 7);
- through a wholesaler (channels 3, 4, 7);
- using an agent (channels 5, 6, 7).

Sometimes the channel of distribution can be straightforward. Take the example of a village bakery. The bread and cakes are baked in the same place as they are sold. Consumers buy direct from the producer (channel 1 in Figure 26.1). Other examples include the sale of 'home' produced local computer software, hand made guitars or the sale of farm products 'on site'.

Many firms manufacture their goods and provide their services from large, central units in order to benefit from **economies of scale** (☞ unit 31). Their consumers, however, may be located over a wide geographical area. Having a distribution channel similar to that of the village baker could spell disaster. It is likely, in this case, that more complex methods of distributing the product are needed. This usually involves the use of INTERMEDIARIES - wholesalers, retailers or agents.

Intermediaries

What intermediaries are involved in the distribution of products?

Wholesalers These often act as links between producers and retailers. Their main task is to buy in bulk from manufacturers and to break this down into smaller quantities which can then be handled by retailers. Channel 4 in Figure 26.1 has traditionally been the most common method of distribution because of the benefits for the businesses involved. Wholesalers can benefit **manufacturers** in a number of ways.

- They have well established distribution networks and are likely to have strong links with retailers.
- By breaking the manufacturers' products down into smaller batches and taking care of distribution problems, they free the manufacturer to concentrate upon production.
- For multi-product firms, they can help to solve distribution problems, especially when wide geographical areas are involved. Figure 26.2 shows how

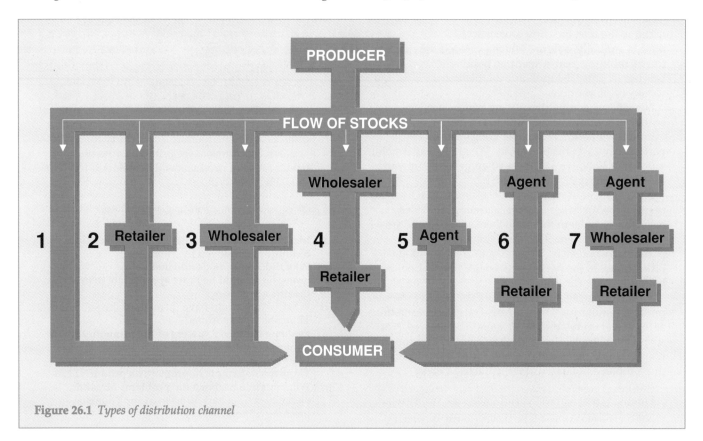

Figure 26.1 *Types of distribution channel*

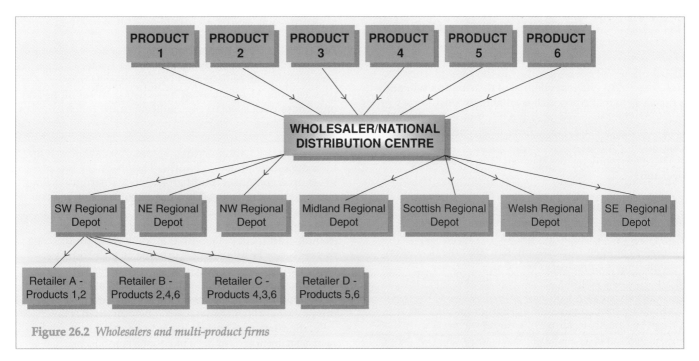

Figure 26.2 *Wholesalers and multi-product firms*

wholesalers are able to help a firm producing six products distributed over a wide area. By using a wholesaler, the manufacturer is able to deliver all six products to one site. Imagine the difficulties if the manufacturer had to deliver every one of the products to each of the retailers.

- They can bear the cost of storage or warehousing.
- They provide a source of market research information, for example, by asking retailers how their stock is selling in different areas.

Wholesalers also help **retailers**. They offer a choice of products from a variety of manufacturers and provide a 'local' service, often delivering products. Wholesalers sometimes sell direct to the public (channel 3). An example might be a kitchenware wholesaler holding a one week sale for members of the public in order to clear out old stock.

Despite the benefits wholesalers offer, they are not without their problems. Some wholesalers may not promote the products as a business might want, which might harm the firm's marketing efforts. By using a wholesaler the business is passing on the responsibility for marketing - possibly a risky venture. The wholesaler is also likely to take some of the profit.

Retailers Because of the problems of wholesalers, a number of manufacturers now prefer to deal with retailers directly, by setting up their own distribution networks. Many of the larger retail outlets, such as Sainsbury's and Marks and Spencer, deal directly with the manufacturer. This is shown as channel 2 in Figure 26.1. Retailers are an important part of distribution, particularly to manufacturers selling to consumer markets. Retailing is dealt with in more detail later in this unit.

Agents and brokers The usual role of agents is to negotiate sales on behalf of a seller. A ticket agency, for example, will sell tickets to consumers for a range of events, such as concerts and plays. The ticket agency does not usually take ownership of the tickets it offers. Instead it takes a **commission** (☞ unit 49) on those which it does sell and returns the rest.

Most travel agencies operate in this way. They earn commission on those holidays which they sell, but never actually buy 'blocks' of holidays. The agents are the link between those providing a good or service and those wishing to buy them (channel 5 in Figure 26.1).

Agents are often used by firms wishing to break into a foreign market (☞ unit 27). They are helpful to businesses which are unsure about the trading practices and legal requirements in foreign countries. They help to take the risk out of trading abroad. People and organisations which are involved in the buying and selling of commodities, such as copper, tin, coffee or sugar, in international markets are known as **brokers**. After being bought these commodities are broken down and sold on to firms for processing or to be used in manufacturing.

QUESTION 1 Six years ago, Mark Paton hit on the idea of getting a valve sound combined with the reliability of solid state electronics in a new electric guitar amplifier design. With limited funds he developed the amp in his garden shed and with £50,000 from British Telecom's Future Start fund, began Carlton Amplification.

Carlton now has the cash to diversify the range, take on staff and invest in marketing. The firm is looking to sell in 30 top UK retail outlets, targeting musicians willing to spend around £400 -£900. The aim is to sell 100 units a month, rising to more than 300 eventually.

Source: adapted from *Business News*, Autumn 1992.

(a) What channel of distribution does the article suggest Carlton Amplification is likely to use?
(b) What are the benefits to Carlton of using this method?
(c) Why might Carlton not sell directly to the consumer?

The choice of distribution channel

How does a producer decide which channel of distribution will get the product to the right place at the right time? An efficient channel of distribution will allow a business to make products available to consumers quickly, when required, and at a minimum distribution cost to the firm itself. Large firms often choose different channels for different products.

There are many factors that can influence a business' decision.

The product The nature of the product itself will influence the type of distribution channel chosen.
- Perishable or fragile goods, such as fresh fruit, require direct channels of distribution, so that the time spent handling the product is reduced.
- Technically complex goods also need a direct link between the producer and the consumer. This is so that any problems which arise from installation or use can be quickly dealt with, without the need to go through an intermediary. Firms installing computers operate in this way to maintain close links with consumers.
- Goods or services which are tailor made tend to have more direct channels, so that the consumer's needs can be passed to the producer.
- Goods which are heavy or are packaged in non-standard shapes are likely to require a direct channel of distribution. If handling is difficult, the cost of distribution is likely to be high. A producer will want to minimise the charges for the handling of such products.
- Convenience goods, such as canned drinks and food, need to be widely available through retailers. Firms that are unwilling to sell to a wide range of retailers are likely to find rival brands on shop shelves.
- Producers wishing to sell large quantities of low valued goods are likely to use a wholesaler. They will not want to keep stocks of low valued goods if they are receiving orders for more highly priced goods. Selling through wholesalers will mean they can sell low valued products in bulk, as quickly as possible.

The market
- Large and dispersed markets usually require intermediaries. Smaller, local markets can often use a system where consumers buy directly. This is also true of the size of an order, where smaller orders can be sent by a more direct channel of distribution.
- The market segment (☞ unit 19) at which the product is aimed may influence the retail outlet at which the product is made available. For example, products aimed at travelling business people may be sold near to railway stations. Consumer goods are often sold via a retailer or directly to the consumer, whereas industrial products may pass through an agent or wholesaler. International sales may also need to be made through an agent.
- The time period within which consumers expect a response to orders is sometimes an influence. A business may be forced to find the most direct means

of distribution, or lose an urgent order to a rival.

Legal restrictions Legislation may influence the channel that can be used for particular products. Certain drugs, for example, can only be sold by pharmacists through a prescription. Alcohol cannot be sold at petrol stations and only those with special gaming licences are able to operate casinos.

The company Larger companies are often able to set up their own distribution networks. They have the resources to set up warehouses, build and operate distribution sites and purchase transport. They are also often able to take advantage of **economies of scale**. For example, a large firm may be able to purchase a fleet of lorries. Manufacturers may open up their own retail outlets, but this will only be effective if the value of the product is high, a wide range of goods or services are sold or large quantities are sold. An alternative is for a producer to develop links with retailers. Raleigh bicycles, for example, provide financial and managerial help to small retailers.

Smaller firms are far less likely to be able to set up their own distribution system. They would tend to use intermediaries, such as wholesalers.

QUESTION 2 Oakham Dairies, a small Leicestershire based firm, specialise in the production of Stilton cheeses. The cheese 'rounds' which they manufacture vary in size from 10lbs to 30lbs and are proving to be very popular. Traditionally, the firm has serviced mainly the Leicestershire and South Lincolnshire markets, but a series of prizes in cheese fairs and a few flattering write-ups in national newspapers meant that their demand had spread. Requests were being received from customers in London and areas surrounding the capital. Since their cheeses had been mentioned on a television food programme, they had been besieged with requests for their product from restaurants, hotels, market stallholders, cheese shops and individual consumers, not to mention some world famous retailers. Oakham Dairies had a significant amount of excess capacity and were sure that they could go a long way to meeting this surge in demand. However, they were less sure about their ability to distribute their cheeses. They had always relied upon their 'fleet' of two vans, but one of them had broken down.
(a) Advise Oakham Dairies on which channel of distribution would best suit their purpose.
(b) Identify the main factors that influenced your choice in (a). Explain how each of these factors affected your decision.

Physical distribution

Physical distribution is the movement of products from one place to another. It is an important part of the marketing process for two main reasons.
- Failure to deliver a product in the right quantities, at the right place and at the right time can damage an effective marketing effort.
- The cost of physical distribution can be high - in some

cases higher than the cost of actually producing the product.

Two aspects of physical distribution are important to a business-holding stocks and transporting products.

Holding stocks Ideally a business would be able to guarantee every customer the product they wanted, whenever they wanted it. To do this a firm would have to hold huge amounts of stock. Holding excessive amounts of stock is very costly. Holding very low stock levels, however, could mean turning down orders.

The solution is for a business to assess the level of stocks needed to maintain an agreed level of customer service. This often means holding enough stock to satisfy regular orders, but not enough to deal with sudden changes in demand. This will depend on the market in which the product is selling.

Transporting products This is concerned with how goods can be physically delivered to markets. Firms need to consider the relative costs and speed of transporting their goods by road, rail, sea or air. For example, aeroplanes are faster than ships when transporting exports from the UK. However, firms must decide whether this advantage outweighs the costs which result from using this mode of transport. There are times when the nature of a product dictates the transport. For example, an Orkney Islands based firm which sells freshly caught lobsters to Paris restaurants has little choice but to fly this product to France.

When transporting goods, firms must also consider possible damage to or deterioration of goods. Packaging may help to reduce damage and deterioration, for example, if vacuum packs are used.

Retailing

Retailers are responsible for the sale of products to the final consumer. It is unlikely that products bought by a consumer from a retailer will be sold again, in the way that wholesalers distribute to many different retailers. Second hand exchanges are perhaps the only exception to this.

Retailers have a major role to play in the distribution of most products. This is because they have the ability to reach huge numbers of consumers, in different markets, over a wide area. Retailers, therefore, can influence manufacturers, insisting on high standards of product quality and delivery times.

Marks and Spencer, for example, are particularly concerned about the quality of products supplied to them. They have an advantage over other retailers because the products which they stock are OWN BRANDS and because of their size and influence in the retail sector. Smaller retailers may have little influence over manufacturers. This is because the success of such retailers in attracting customers is often dependent upon whether or not they stock brands which are currently in demand.

Retailers can be grouped according to their characteristics.

Multiple shop organisations These are businesses with ten or more establishments, or a group of specialist shops dealing in a particular group of products. Examples include Oddbins, the wine merchants, and B & Q, the DIY specialists. For consumers, multiple shops have two benefits. They usually offer a wide choice of products in their specialist area. Also, they have often developed an established image, so consumers will be familiar with the level of service, value for money and quality which they can expect.

Supermarkets These sell mainly foodstuffs in premises with a minimum of 400 square metres of floor space. Many buy direct from manufacturers rather than through wholesalers and sell products which are fast moving, ie with a short SHELF LIFE, in large volumes. The majority of supermarkets are part of chains belonging to Sainsbury's, Tesco, Argyll (Safeway, Lo-Cost, Presto) and Asda. There is an growing trend for supermarkets to provide 'own-brand' goods. There has also been a growth of supermarkets stressing lower prices and selling less well known brands. Examples include Aldi and Netto.

Superstores or hypermarkets These are huge stores which divide their stock nearly equally between food and other goods, such as electricals. They occupy 2,500 square metres of selling space or more and tend to be found on the outskirts of towns and cities. Their advantage is the ability to offer a wide range of goods and services under one roof. Examples include the French supermarket chain Mammouth and some Sainsbury's stores in the UK.

Department stores These sell five or more different lines of products and occupy at least 2,500 square metres of selling space. They tend to sell more highly priced goods and increasingly parts of these stores are run as **franchises** (☞ unit 8). Examples include Selfridges and Harrods.

Consumer co-operatives These differ from other types of retail organisations in terms of their ownership and the way in which their profits are distributed. They are not unlike **producer co-operatives** (☞ unit 3). They are owned by 'members' rather than shareholders and profits are distributed to customers in the form of a 'dividend', rather than being given to shareholders. After a period of decline in recent decades, they have seen something of a revival in recent years. They now account for nearly 10 per cent of the UK grocery market. Examples of stores operated by a 'co-operative' include Normid and Open Later Savers.

Independent retailers The smaller local shop, often owned by a sole trader, is still important for selling many types of products, eg newspapers and tobacco. These rely heavily on the supply of nationally known or branded goods through a wholesaler or a manufacturer's agent. Groups of independent retailers might also join together in order to benefit from the bulk purchasing of stock or joint advertising. These are sometimes known as **voluntary chains**, eg SPAR. They are an attempt by independent retailers to match the strengths of large chains.

QUESTION 3 The US fashion retailers, Gap, are riding on the crest of a wave. The Gap label, which accounts for 98 per cent of the clothes which they stock in their store, is now only second to Levis in the US. Their advertising, which has been particularly successful, includes photographs of stars such as Kim Basinger, Neneh Cherry and Spike Lee wearing Gap clothing.

Gap now have over 30 stores open throughout the UK and more than 1,000 worldwide. Their success is beginning to match that of the Italian Benetton empire which has a remarkable 6,000+ stores in 100 countries. The two companies, however, operate very differently. Benetton is not a retailer. Rather it is a manufacturer and supplier of Benetton goods to a network of independent shopkeepers who have franchises to supply Benetton clothes. All Gap's stores, on the other hand, are company owned and run.

Source: adapted from *The Observer*, 28.7.1991.

(a) What type of retail organisation is Gap? Explain your answer.
(b) Why do you think Gap have chosen to retail their clothing as well as to manufacture it?
(c) Compare the benefits of this type of retailer to those of an independent outlet from the consumer's point of view.

Trends in retailing

Retailing is a fast changing sector of the economy. Today's retail scene is very different from that which existed twenty years ago. There have been a number of important changes in retailing in recent years.

- The development of out-of-town shopping centres along the lines of American 'shopping malls'. Examples include Fosse Park on the outskirts of Leicester, or the MetroCentre in Gateshead. Such developments have often meant retailers moving from city centres in order to set up in out-of-town areas.
- The use of technology. For example, bar codes on products (read by laser beams at checkout desks) are a common feature of many retail outlets. They can be used to record sales or update stock levels. Also, many retailers now use in-store cameras to measure when and where consumers are tempted to pause and consider whether to buy a product, and for security reasons.
- Longer opening hours to fit in with patterns of work and leisure. Many larger retailers now open their doors to consumers late into the evening and on Sundays, despite the Sunday Trading Act, which attempts to regulate such activity. Flexible opening hours were previously an advantage of small retailers.
- The rise in importance of the supermarket. In the last 30 years the number of independent grocers in the UK has been cut by two-thirds. There were only 100,000 stores in 1992. During the same period the share of the grocery market held by supermarket and hypermarket chains rose from 25 per cent to over 60 per cent.

- An increasing demand by consumers for a variety of products to be sold under one roof. This has meant the continued survival of department stores, as well as the growth of shopping centres.
- The need by firms to reduce distribution costs. This has led to businesses wishing to supply in larger quantities to retailers.
- New entrants wanting to set up national chains perhaps need to be large, established firms. For example, Aldi already had many stores in Germany before setting up in the UK.

These developments affect both consumers and businesses. It could be argued that the retailing trade is monopolistically competitive (☞ unit 22). There are certainly a large number of buyers and sellers and ease of entry to the market. However, a smaller number of firms are taking a larger market share. This leaves smaller firms to compete only in local markets. Unit 31 showed that there will always be room for the small business, although sales and profit margins may be lower if current trends continue. Also, the cost of retailing is likely to increase as technology becomes necessary and businesses need to stay open for longer periods.

The extent to which the growth of 'shopping centres' and out of town supermarkets will benefit the consumer will depend on many factors. Those without transport are likely to face increased prices in local shops as retailers attempt to cover their costs. Those able to travel to larger retail outlets will benefit from buying many products from a single outlet. However, they will be unable to compare prices of similar products in different retail outlets. Shopping malls with many different outlets may offset this to some extent.

QUESTION 4

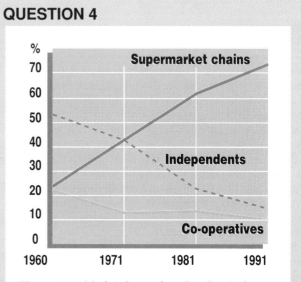

Figure 26.3 *Market shares of retail outlets in the grocery market*

(a) Using Figure 26.3, identify the changes that have taken place in the retail grocery market.
(b) What are the likely implications of these changes for:
(i) manufacturers of consumer goods;
(ii) consumers?

Direct marketing

DIRECT MARKETING is sometimes thought to be the same as direct mailing (☞ unit 25). In fact, it is just one type of direct marketing. Direct marketing occurs when sales are made without intermediaries being involved. For consumers, this means being able to make purchases from their own homes.

Direct marketing is perhaps the fastest growing means of distribution and is expected to continue into the future. There are a number of reasons for this. Changing work patterns mean that many now find it easier to shop from home. The increased range of products available, and their specialised nature, mean that certain products cannot be purchased from 'usual' outlets such as shops. Also, the increased use of credit cards makes buying in this way easy and direct.

Direct marketing also has advantages for firms. There are no intermediaries to take part of the profits. The producer is able to control its own marketing and also has a chance to reach consumers, who might not otherwise have bought from shops.

Direct marketing can be achieved through a variety of methods.

Direct mail This involves posting promotional materials to homes and workplaces. Consumers then place an order and products are sent to the buyer's address. At present, the average British adult receives five items of direct mail each month. This is just half the average in Europe, and one-tenth of what floods through the average US letterbox.

There are a number of benefits of direct mail for businesses and consumers.
- Personalised communications with the potential purchaser's name on a letter can improve sales.
- Groups of consumers or **market segments** can be targeted.
- Detailed information can be provided.
- Groups of consumers who are widely dispersed can easily be reached.

Despite its benefits, it is unpopular in some quarters and also suffers from a number of disadvantages.
- Consumers do not like the personalised nature of direct mail and the amount sent to their home address.
- The databases with potential consumers' names and addresses on them quickly go out of date, so that a large amount of mail goes to the wrong people.
- It is felt to be a 'waste of paper' which uses up a valuable resource - wood.

For many businesses direct mailing has been very successful. Readers Digest magazine sells over one million copies monthly. In addition, many charities such as Oxfam and Greenpeace are able to raise large sums.

Direct response advertisements These are advertisements placed in newspapers and magazines, and on the TV and radio. Consumers are encouraged to fill in a coupon or make a telephone call in order to purchase a product. There should be enough information in the advertisement to allow people to make a decision.

Direct response broadcasting is relatively new. It is the selling of products through TV commercials, often in late night slots. Records, CDs and car telephones have been sold in this way. There are now TV channels available which are devoted to direct response advertising.

Personal selling This can be a useful form of direct marketing. It is dealt with in unit 25.

Telephone selling This involves ringing people up at their home or workplace and trying to sell a good or service. The advantage is that the seller can deal personally with a consumer. However, it is felt to be intrusive by many consumers. It has often been used as a means of marketing financial services, such as insurance.

Catalogues This involves a range of products being included in a catalogue which people can read through at home. Orders can usually be placed by telephone or in writing. It has been seen recently as an outdated means of marketing, but innovations such as the Next Directory with 24 hour delivery have breathed new life into it. Market leaders in this area are Littlewoods and Great Universal Stores.

QUESTION 5 Despite all the criticism which direct mail has come in for, its practitioners are generally agreed that there is plenty of scope for creativity. Unlike television and press advertising, direct mail is not restricted by considerations of time and space, and does not even have to take the form of the printed word.

Some extravagant mailers have resorted to holograms, video tapes and even personal stereos to make their mail stand out. One business set out to persuade 150 car showrooms at the upper end of the market to act as cellular telephone retailers. In order to achieve this, a briefcase sized box was sent out to all of these showrooms. When opened, the briefcase revealed a replica of a car dashboard with a cardboard telephone handset. When the phone was picked up by the recipient it played a personally addressed tape recorded message.

However, such creativity is not exactly normal in the direct mailing business. Observers have noticed the tendency for firms to spend millions making TV commercials and then write to their target audience with a low quality piece of paper thrown in an envelope.

(a) What advantages of direct mailing are illustrated in the article?
(b) To what extent do you agree that there is 'plenty of scope for creativity in direct mailing' compared to advertising?
(c) How might other methods of direct marketing be used to boost the sales of cellular telephones?

Key terms

Channel of distribution - the route taken by a product as it passes from producer to consumer.
Direct marketing - a method of distributing products directly to consumers, without the use of intermediaries such as wholesalers and retailers.
Intermediaries - firms which act as a link between producers and consumers in a channel of distribution.
Own brands - products which have the brand name of their retailer on them.
Shelf life - the average length of time it takes for a product to be sold, once it has been displayed by a retailer.

Summary

1. Why is distribution so important to a firm's marketing mix?
2. What is a channel of distribution?
3. List the 5 types of organisation which can be involved in a channel of distribution.
4. What is the main role of an intermediary?
5. Explain the difference between a wholesaler and a retailer.
6. Why do manufacturers use wholesalers?
7. What is the difference between an agent and a broker?
8. What factors might influence the choice of distribution channel?
9. Explain 2 recent trends in retailing and their effect on business.
10. What is the difference between direct mailing and direct marketing?
11. Why might a business be reluctant to use direct mailing?

Question

The effects of direct selling

Booksellers are becoming increasingly concerned about the growing trend of publishers selling directly to schools. Booksellers organisations are urging publishers to consider their actions carefully. They argue, '... there are real benefits for schools in dealing with booksellers rather than direct with publishers', and that '... publishers should be persuaded that supplying through booksellers makes commercial sense, both in the short and long run'.

Previously schools had ordered bulk quantities of books through a recognised bookseller (an intermediary) that passed on orders to a variety of publishers, received the books and distributed them to the schools. The bookseller would often pass on a discount to the school for books ordered through their organisation.

Publishers argue that direct selling has increased as a result of:
- vigorous competition amongst publishers, both in terms of price and quality;
- the fact that schools can now manage their own funds and have greater choice about how much they can spend and on what;
- the need to produce highly illustrated and costly books for the national curriculum and to get them into teachers' hands quickly;
- the recession.

They have been forced, as a result, to adopt a more aggressive means of distribution. This has meant selling directly to schools, whereas in the past publishers have relied mainly on booksellers.

Why have schools started to order direct from publishers? Publishers may offer higher discounts and quicker delivery times to schools than bookshops. However, schools must weigh up the costs involved in purchasing direct. There may be greater administration involved in buying from many different publishers. Booksellers also argue that direct purchases will force bookshops to reduce stocks and choice available to schools. They also argue that bookshops can provide a wide range of books, whereas publishers can only offer their own books.

Direct mailing is increasing and sales through bookfairs and representatives are being pushed as never before. Many mail shots now have order forms attached to them, with discounts offered for quantity purchases. Some, however, do stress that orders should be made through local booksellers.

A recent survey shows that 24 per cent of all books sold to schools are now purchased directly from the publisher.

Source: adapted from *The Bookseller*, 18 September, 1992.

(a) Explain how the two channels of distribution described in the article operate.
(b) What factors might have influenced publishers to distribute through booksellers originally?
(c) Argue the case that:
  (i) 'there are real benefits in dealing with booksellers rather than dealing direct with publishers' for schools;
  (ii) 'publishers should be persuaded that supplying through booksellers makes commercial sense'.
(d) What are the implications of the trends in the article for booksellers?
(e) Advise a publisher on the effectiveness of:
  (i) direct mail;
  (ii) personal selling through sales representatives;
  in distributing their products to schools and colleges.

The importance of international marketing

At one time firms may have thought that marketing products overseas was an adventurous act. It was generally undertaken by large businesses which had grown too big for domestic markets. Today, however, the world has 'shrunk' due to, amongst other things, rapid changes in international transport and telecommunications. One effect of this is that a business now needs to consider the threat from foreign competition and the opportunities which might be gained from marketing internationally. For many firms international marketing is no longer an option. It is necessary if a firm is to survive in a competitive business environment. For British firms this is very much the case, as trade barriers between European Community nations were lifted on the last day of 1992 (☞ unit 70). The increase in the size and number of multinationals has contributed to the increase in international trading.

Why might firms market their products internationally?

■ Profits. By selling in overseas markets, a business might have the potential to increase its profits through an increase in sales. Overseas markets may be more lucrative than domestic ones. Manufacturing and distribution costs may be lower abroad. The product might also sell at a higher price on foreign markets than in the home market.
■ Spreading the risk. If a firm only produces in one country then it may face problems caused by downturns in demand due to recession (☞ unit 67). The more countries a firm operates in, the less vulnerable it is to changes in the business climate of any single country.
■ Unfavourable trading conditions in the domestic market. Businesses often find that the market for a product is saturated or in decline. One option for a firm is to try and breathe new life into the product by introducing it onto an overseas market. This is an example of an **extension strategy** (☞ unit 20). British American Tobacco industries, for example, have started to sell in developing countries as domestic market sales have declined.
■ Legal differences. Legal restrictions on the sale of products vary from one country to another. For example, developing countries have fewer restrictions on which drugs can be offered for sale. Some pharmaceutical companies (in what many regard as unethical practice) have sold drugs banned on health grounds in the UK to these nations.

Why the overseas market is different

There can be many rewards for a business entering an overseas market.

One problem that it will face, however, is that market conditions will be different to those in the domestic market. This makes selling abroad very risky. What are the differences that are likely to affect the success of foreign sales?

Political differences A firm must take into account the political stability of the country in which it plans to sell. Political instability, such as existed in Lebanon over a number of years, can make trading almost impossible. Also, a change of government can bring about a change in attitude towards foreign companies. A firm thinking of investing a large sum in its operations abroad will need to weigh up the political situation carefully. A number of firms, for example, are waiting to see how the change of government in Hong Kong in 1997 will affect trading conditions before they will invest.

Another difference between the UK and some other nations is the extent to which bribery takes place, often amongst government officials. In some countries getting things done, from electricity connection to securing an order, might require payments to corrupt officials.

Cultural differences One difference which often causes problems for British businesses is that English is not the main or even the second language in many countries. In Eastern Europe for example, German and Russian are more widely spoken than English.

QUESTION 1 When Logica, the computer systems company, began trading in 1969, they set themselves two main aims:
■ to become a top player in commercial software systems;
■ to expand as quickly as possible onto the international scene.
In order to achieve its second aim, the company began making inroads into the European market very early on by exporting its products. By 1973 it had opened an office in Holland. From there it expanded, both by internal growth and by acquisition and merger in other parts of Europe. With hindsight, now that Europe is undergoing such change with the lifting of trade barriers, Logica could not have chosen to position itself better. Not surprisingly, the achievement of its second aim gave Logica an enormous lift in its efforts to achieve the first aim.

Source: adapted from *Management Today*.

(a) Why do you think Logica was so keen to enter overseas markets?
(b) What would the threats have been for Logica if they had chosen only to trade in the UK?
(c) Why are Logica in such a good position to meet current changes in European trading?

Other cultural differences may influence the way a product is marketed. For example, a product name suitable in one country may have a totally different meaning in another - the French lemonade Pssschit would require a new name were it to be sold in the UK! Colours have different meanings throughout the world. In the Far East, white rather than black is associated with mourning. In India fashion models of the sort used to promote products in the West are considered too thin.

Differences in legislation Such differences can affect the way in which a firm produces and markets its products.
- Product labelling. US laws are far more stringent than UK laws about the amount of information which should be included on food labels.
- Product safety. Some countries have very strict legislation governing safety standards on childrens' toys. Others are less strict.
- Environmental impact. All cars now sold in California must be fitted with a catalytic convertor. This is not the case in Europe, but may be in future.
- Advertising. Cigarette advertising on television is now outlawed within EC countries.

Economic and social differences Some of the economic factors which firms must consider include levels of income, levels of sales and corporation tax, how income is distributed, the use of tariffs or other import barriers and the level and growth of population.

Social factors which firms may need to consider include literacy levels, the role of women, religious attitudes, readiness to accept new ideas, and the habits and attitudes of social groups.

Differences in business practice The usual amount of time it take to receive payment may vary in different countries. Other differences include accounting techniques, company ownership (most British companies are independent and quoted on the Stock Exchange, whereas those in other EC nations are often controlled by families or banks) and distribution (in many EC countries greater use is made of rail transport than in the UK).

What problems might businesses selling or investing in Hong Kong face after it becomes part of China in 1997?

Adapting products to fit in with local, national and regional needs can be costly. It is cheaper to have one product with one brand name and a promotional package which fits all markets. Firms must attempt to cater for national consumer tastes, whilst trying to gain economies of scale (☞ unit 31) from operating in international markets.

QUESTION 2 China has the potential to be one of the world's leading economies. It is the third largest country in the world and has a population which is by far the largest. The birth rate, though, has been falling for a number of years. The average annual income per head of population was $330 in 1988.

Since 1957 China has experienced an annual average rate of economic growth of over 5 per cent per year. This figure has been even higher since the economic reform process began in 1980. This reform programme sought to introduce market forces into the running of China's economy. It was a great success in that incomes increased significantly, consumer goods became widely available and industries boomed.

However, the reforms also brought with them rising unemployment, increased corruption, inflation and a widening of the income differences between the richest and the poorest in Chinese society. In addition, the Tiananmen Square massacre severely dented China's image abroad and reduced confidence in the political leadership.

Source: adapted from *Economics for a Developing World*, Michael P Todaro, Longman, Harlow.

What difficulties might a business seeking to enter the Chinese market face?

Methods of entering overseas markets

Once a firm has made the decision to enter an overseas market, it must decide the best way to do this.

Exporting This is often the first step for a business wishing to enter an overseas market. It involves manufacturing products at home but selling them abroad. The great advantage of exporting is that it minimises the risk of operating abroad. It can also be used as a means of testing out the ground.

Unfortunately, the business has little or no control over how the product is actually marketed in the countries to which it is sent. For this reason many firms exporting abroad make use of overseas agents (☞ unit 26). These agents are able to play an active role in the marketing of the product.

Franchising (☞ unit 8) This involves one business selling a licence to others. The licence allows one firm to use another's name, product or service in return for an initial payment and further commission or royalties.

This is a quick and relatively easy way into foreign markets and it allows the franchiser a high degree of control over the marketing of its product. However, a share of the profit does go to the franchisee. Firms such as Pizza Express, Budget Rent-a-Car, and Kentucky Fried Chicken have used this as a way of entering overseas markets.

Licensing This is similar to franchising. Franchising is used in service industries, such as fast foods and car hire. Licensing, however, involves one firm producing another's product and using its brand name, designs, patents and expertise under licence. This means that goods do not have to be physically moved abroad. Instead they are produced abroad by the foreign licensee. Also, it means that firms can avoid operating overseas. The main disadvantage is that the success or failure of the venture is largely in the hands of the licensee.

Joint ventures (☞ unit 32) This involves two companies from separate countries combining their resources. One new enlarged company is formed to launch a product onto one market. An example of this is the Royal Bank of Scotland's alliance with Banco Santander of Spain to provide banking and financial services throughout Europe. Joint ventures are increasingly being used by firms wishing to enter Eastern European markets.

One advantage of this form of venture is that the risks are shared between two firms. Also, each firm can draw on the strengths of the other. One firm may have Research and Development strength, for example, while others may have strengths in manufacturing. However, many joint ventures have broken down due to conflicts which occur.

Direct investment Direct investment requires the setting up of production facilities abroad. They can be obtained by merger or takeover, or they may be built for this specific purpose. It is an increasingly common way for firms to reach overseas markets. Mergers were widely used by European firms in the run up to 1992. This method of entering overseas markets is most often used by **multinationals** (☞ unit 70).

QUESTION 3 Stavlon, a Stourbridge firm with 200 employees producing luxury glass crystal products, had begun to investigate the possibility of selling their products within European markets. It was a process into which they had been forced. Since the removal of trade barriers in 1992 they had found themselves trading under increasing pressure from other European firms in the home market. Their 26 per cent market share was being fast eroded. The managing director was reluctant to become involved in overseas markets. 'We're better off sticking to the market we understand best, here in Britain, and fighting them on our own turf. Besides none of our staff can even speak a foreign language competently', she had said at a recent meeting. The marketing director was convinced that she was wrong and had started to prepare a paper on international marketing which she was going to issue at the next board meeting.

(a) What options for entering the European market are open to Stavlon?
(b) Which of these options do you think the marketing director should recommend to the board?
(c) Provide three arguments which could be used to persuade the managing director to reconsider her position.

Summary

1. Give 5 reasons why international marketing can be so important to firms.
2. How does entering an overseas market allow a firm to spread its risks?
3. State 3 differences between overseas and domestic markets.
4. How can an agent help a business to export its products?
5. In what ways can a business enter an overseas market?
6. What is meant by licensing?
7. What is the difference between direct investment and joint ventures?

Question

Kirin Brewery

Kirin Brewery, the world's fourth biggest and Japan's largest brewer is seeking to expand into foreign markets. Stagnation in domestic sales, due to market saturation, is forcing Kirin to turn to international expansion. Higher overseas demand for Japanese beer, due to the increasing popularity of Japanese cuisine and rising numbers of Japanese people working abroad, has also motivated Kirin to look abroad for markets. Table 27.1 shows beer exports of the major Japanese breweries in 1991.

Kirin recently signed a licensing agreement with Charles Wells Brewery of Bedford. Wells will start producing Kirin's lager in 1993. Kirin also has a licensing deal with Molson, the Canadian brewer, as well as a contract with the Hong Kong arm of Philippino brewer San Miguel.

Kirin has opted for overseas production rather than exports because it believes that freshness is the most important factor for beers. Tariff barriers can also be avoided through overseas production.

Sapporo Breweries was the first Japanese brewer to sell its beer overseas - in the 1940s. However, it does not think overseas production is warranted because of the small volume of sales abroad.

For the big four Japanese brewers, Kirin, Asahi, Sapporo and Suntory, the US is the largest market with over 70 per cent of sales. They believe, though, that the Asian markets have the greatest potential, since beer is a relatively new drink and Japanese brands are popular.

Kirin admit they are cautious about rapid foreign expansion, but they do believe that the taste of Japanese beer is gaining international acceptance. Mr Tetsuya Fujiwara of Kirin says, 'There is a high overseas demand for products which have become popular in Japan'.

Table 27.1 *Japanese beer exports in 1991 (000 litres)*

Sapporo	14,432
Kirin	13,632
Asahi	7,596
Suntory	1,704

The question is, will the Japanese brewers follow their counterparts in the electronic and automobile industries and become the Toyotas and Matsushitas of the global beer market?

'That's probably unlikely', says Mr. Fujiwara. 'The taste of beer is very cultural and personal, not like electronic goods or cars'.

Source: adapted from the *Financial Times*, 7.10.1992.

(a) For what reasons have Kirin sought to expand into foreign markets?

(b) Comment on Kirin's decision to enter the UK market through a licensing agreement.

(c) Do you think Kirin are likely to follow the success of their counterparts in the electronics and automobile industries? Explain your answer.

(d) Explain the factors which you think will determine Kirin's success in the UK market.

Dalesmoor

Dalesmoor are a Taunton based firm specialising in the manufacture of hard wearing boots. Their boots are famous for their tough, but lightweight soles, which make walking easy and comfortable.

The soles for Dalesmoor boots were initially developed in 1958 by a retired train driver, Bill Gregson, with the help of an engineer friend, while he was recovering from a knee injury which happened on Dartmoor. They were designed to enable Bill to go walking in the hills surrounding his rest home without placing undue stress upon his knees.

Bill, encouraged by the success of his boots, persuaded his son, Graham, to set up in business producing on an initially modest scale. The boots were soon selling all over the South West of England, mainly to farmers, workmen and a growing breed of ramblers who left the industrial cities at the weekends to go walking in the countryside.

By 1992, Dalesmoor had grown to become a successful medium sized business in the British footwear industry. Turnover was approaching £2.5 million per annum with 1,000 boots being produced every week. The company had four products - the lightweight fabric boot, one style for men, one for women and the leather boot, again with one for men and one for women. The sales figures for these boots are shown in Table 1.

Table 1 *Sales of Dalesmoor products*

Sales per annum

	Mens Leather	Ladies Leather	Mens Lightweight	Ladies Lightweight
1980	20,000	-	-	-
1981	29,000	-	-	-
1982	29,500	-	-	-
1983	30,200	-	-	-
1984	31,000	-	-	-
1985	31,500	4,000	-	-
1986	31,300	5,500	-	-
1987	31,800	6,100	-	-
1988	30,600	7,200	-	-
1989	30,500	8,600	-	-
1990	30,900	9,100	-	-
1991	31,000	10,800	3,000	2,300
1992	31,100	11,300	5,200	3,100

Sales were now spread throughout the UK, though the boot continued to be equally popular in its traditional base in the South West. Despite the undoubted success of its products, and the successful extension of their product range to include lightweight boots, Dalesmoor were faced with a problem.

The firm believed that it had weathered the recession of the late 1980s and early 1990s well, maintaining sales at a time of falling consumer incomes, but it was beginning to lose market share to competitors (see Table 2). The market for outdoor boots is dominated by five firms. The two leading firms have a 60 per cent market share, the other three, including Dalesmoor, have the remaining 40 per cent.

Table 2

Dalesmoor's percentage share of the outdoor boots market	
1988	15.5
1989	14.7
1990	14.7
1991	14.2
1992	13.8

The reason Dalesmoor's market share was falling during a period in which they had introduced new products and maintained sales of existing products was simple. The market had grown, and their competitors were gaining a larger share of this growing market. Outdoor boots were increasingly being worn by the young as fashion accessories.

Although sales to ramblers and other existing groups of customers had held up, Dalesmoor were failing to capitalise upon this growing youth market, especially with regard to their leather boots. Virtually all of their promotional budget went on advertisements, with photographs of men and women wearing their boots in walking and farming magazines. Dalesmoor's prices were based upon a calculation of direct production costs plus an allocation for a proportion of indirect costs (allocated according to the success of the product). This resulted in prices lower than their competitors' (see Table 3) which had always been a matter of some pride for Dalesmoor employees. They were reluctant to raise their prices for fear of alienating their traditional customers. However, feedback from retailers indicated that the lower price was actually putting off some younger customers. Indeed, as time went by, Dalesmoor were increasingly grateful for the strong links which they had built up with retailers over the years.

Table 3

Mens outdoor leather boots	prices
Dalesmoor	£65
Woodland	£87
Bergren	£91
Wolfshoe	£86
Nordshoe	£102

One of the marketing managers had been regularly saying at meetings that the company needed to pay more attention to the needs of its customers - whether they be new, potential or existing. In short, she kept saying 'we need a market based approach to our business'.

Graham Gregson was convinced that she was right and was now determined to change the company's approach to business.

(a) **What factors have caused Dalesmoor to consider becoming more market orientated?**

(b) **From the evidence in the case, describe the marketing strategy which Dalesmoor have relied upon.**

(c) **Sketch the product life cycles of each of Dalesmoor's four products.**

(d) **Identify the pricing strategy employed by Dalesmoor and comment upon any possible problems with it.**

(e) **Comment upon the income elasticity of demand for Dalesmoor's products.**

(f) **How would you describe the structure of the outdoor boots market? Explain your answer briefly.**

(g) **What are the marketing implications for the company if it adopted a market orientated approach?**

Invent and invest is the key

For Unilever, the consumer goods group whose products range from Oxo gravy cubes to Persil washing powder, brands are everything. Without investing in brands the group's business will wither. But the group's dependence on high profile premium products has recently led Unilever into trouble. In the three months to the start of June shares in the company fell by 20 per cent as doubts about brands passed around the stock market.

Unilever was caught in the aftermath as Philip Morris, the US consumer group, cut the price of its Marlboro cigarettes in an effort to beat off competition from cheaper, own label rivals. The Morris move put the skids under Unilever, along with several other companies which are reliant on brands. But it will take more than a steep short term fall in Unilever's share price to force a radical change of strategy.

Mike Perry, Unilever's chairman, reiterated his belief in brands last month. He said: 'The major assets of a consumer business, overwhelmingly, are its brands. They are of incalculable value. To succeed as a consumer products business, there is no alternative but to invent, nurture and invest in brands'.

So Unilever remains committed to its household names - names such as Wall's ice cream. About £16 million a year is spent researching and developing Wall's, or about 1 per cent of its annual turnover. Wall's R & D occupies 150 people in the UK. The programme splits into two broad categories - developing new products and revamping established products.

Peter Whittall, the manager in charge of R & D at Wall's, is as unequivocal as his chairman: 'Research and development has got to be absolutely essential. If we are to meet market challenges and keep consumers happy, we have to invest in the business. If we stand still our competitors will overtake us.'

Good marketing positioning in ice cream is worth striving for. Last year £784 million was spent on ice cream in Britain. It is particularly important to stay ahead in ice lollies. Lollies are impulse purchases, mainly by children. That market demands a new and exciting range of products. R & D feeds these needs. Dr.Whittall likens the process to a fluid passing through a funnel. At the start all ideas are considered. As the ideas are converted into reality, some are found to be impractical to make, others are thought to be unattractive to consumers. Others may make it to the shops but fail marketing trials. Dr.Whittall estimates that for every 10 ideas taken on, only one will make it through to become part of Wall's portfolio of brands.

Many advances are made possible by breakthroughs in production techniques. Twenty years ago lollies were little more than tapered blocks of ice on a stick. The technology - pouring juice into a straightforward metal mould - restricted Wall's to simplicity. Then the lolly embraced rubber technology. By casting ice in a rubber mould the lollies could be shaped more intricately.

More recently the Tangle Twister hit the high street freezer, using an ingenious invention from Wall's design engineers. They came up with a nozzle that could make a lolly from twisting three separate flavours of water ice together. The innovation represented a quantum leap in lolly technology.

Vienetta, the layered chocolate and ice cream dessert, is another good example of how advancing production techniques generates new brands. The initial idea was to spray chocolate on flat strips of ice cream. Research into production of Vienetta, however, found that by altering the shape of the nozzle waves of ice cream could be laid down. The finished product, now on sale, is a combination of flat and wavy layers of ice cream separated by wafer thin chocolate.

R & D at Wall's goes beyond dreaming up ways of making different shaped lollies and ice cream. Food scientists are continually trying to improve the taste, texture and make up of water ice and ice cream. A newish addition to the range is 'Too Good To Be True', which has very little fat content. Wall's cannot call it ice cream because it is not, but the target consumer is the weight watching ice cream lover.

In developing 'Too Good To Be True', food scientists redesigned the molecular structure of fat. Fat was changed so that a vastly smaller quantity could perform the same purpose as the much greater amounts of fat present in conventional ice cream.

The second main arena for Wall's R & D specialists is taking established products and revamping them. This may be a change of packaging, introducing new colours and flavours, altering the content or shape of the lolly or ice cream. To Dr.Whittall there is a third important area; changing operations on the factory floor to improve performance. This side of Unilever's R & D programme is a long way from the kind of work embarked on by boffins in the laboratory. It is no less vital for that.

Walking around the Wall's Plant in Gloucester, the largest ice cream factory in Britain, Dr.Whittall pointed to two examples. They had a problem with Callippo, the fruit flavoured water ice product. The tubes of Callippo were leaking. At first they thought it was because the tops were not fastened properly. But closer inspection showed that the packaging split on freezing because water expands when it turns into ice.

The answer? Carefully measure the amount of liquid put into the tubes so that the packaging will stay intact when the water turns into ice. A similarly small modification made all the difference to Cornetto production. It was noticed that in the finished product the bottom of the biscuit cone was broken. The first thoughts were that there were faults in the making of the biscuit, or in the way that it was wrapped.

However, by filming the stage where the cones are filled with ice cream, and then slowing the pictures down the problem was isolated. The bottom of the cone was hitting a component of the machinery. By moving the troublesome component a couple of millimetres, the Cornettos kept their intended shape.

While it is possible to define three broad areas of R & D in Wall's, Dr.Whittall says the system is a fluid one, where all employees can play a part. 'Constant improvement is the key', he says. 'That gives us the competitive edge'.'

Source: Robert Cole *The Independent*, 9.6.1993

(a) **What evidence is there of a market orientated approach at Unilever?**
(b) **Explain why Unilever believe 'brands are everything'.**
(c) **Describe the stages of development through which the Tangle Twister is likely to have passed.**
(d) **Explain the purpose of 'taking established products and revamping them'.**
(e) **Using evidence from the case, describe what constraints exist for Unilever in developing new products.**
(f) **Why is quality of production on the shop floor an important element for Unilever?**

Men in white coats present a caring image

Boots chemist shops yesterday stocked their shelves with a home cholesterol testing kit which the company hopes will help reduce the alarmingly high incidence of heart disease in the UK - as well as making money for shareholders. The simple kit, which requires shoppers to prick their thumbs and test their blood using a simple meter, delivers accurate results in 20 minutes. It costs £7.99.

The launch at the Ritz Hotel in London is part of a Caring for Your Heart campaign aimed at helping to meet the government's target of reducing deaths from coronary heart disease by 40 per cent by the end of the decade. Boots is also issuing leaflets on diet and lifestyle changes and has set up a free telephone enquiry line for those needing further information.

Peter Shotter, general manager of Boots' healthcare business, says: 'Awareness of cholesterol levels is about 9 to 13 per cent in the UK, compared with 70 per cent in the US. But about 150,000 people are killed by coronary heart disease each year. Cholesterol is a key factor'.

Although Boots hopes that the kit will record strong sales in its own right, the product's launch symbolises a shift of marketing emphasis that has taken place within Boots in recent years.

The company, long famed for its pharmaceutical services, has rediscovered that there are significant market opportunities in its own backyard - especially at a time when the government is trying to shift the burden of healthcare provision towards individual responsibility and preventative medicine.

'The company's strategy in the 1970s and 1980s was to expand substantially its merchandise offering. But I would say there is now a greater focus again on the core healthcare business', Shotter says. 'It is partly a recognition that this is what we are best at doing but also that there is enormous market potential.'

Extensive market research suggested that the public had great trust in Boots' 'men in white coats'. The company believes it can do more to exploit that commercial strength by moving into related healthcare areas.

Boots recruits just under one-third of all pharmacy graduates in the UK and almost all the company's 1,078 store managers are qualified pharmacists. The company is currently experimenting with offering a wide range of health screening services, such as cholesterol, blood, pregnancy and urine testing, together with full medicals at two stores at Bromley and Lincoln. 'It is early days and we are just scratching the surface at the moment', Shotter says.

But a graphic example of the lucrative business opportunities lying at the periphery of the NHS is provided by Boots' move into the nursing homes' drug supply market in recent years. The company now supplies the pharmaceutical needs of 80,000 patients at 3,600 homes.

It is a sign of the evolution of business attitudes at Boots that Shotter was recruited from outside the company following a marketing career with such fast moving consumer goods giants as Proctor & Gamble and PepsiCo. 'There has been an injection of new ideas by deliberately going out into the marketplace and bringing people with different experiences', he says.

The concept of turning Boots' stores into a chain of mini-healthcare centres is clearly attractive for potential patients and hard pressed health service managers, but as yet it remains an unproven prospect.

But Gordon Hourston, managing director of Boots the Chemist, stresses that while there are great potential opportunities in developing its primary healthcare business, he first has to be convinced that it would be in the best interests of shareholders.

Boots is a commercial enterprise; profits generated from the provision of healthcare services will have to be every bit as productive as the returns from selling soaps or photographic film.

Source: the *Financial Times*, 24.9.1992.

(a) **Explain the phrase 'Extensive market research suggested that the public had great trust in Boots' men in white coats'.**

(b) **In what ways does the article suggest Boots have changed their marketing objectives?**

(c) **How have external factors influenced the changes to Boots' marketing objectives?**

(d) **Identify the market segments in the healthcare market that Boots might be targeting.**

(e) **What are the reasons for Boots moving into the healthcare business?**

(f) **Advise Boots of possible methods of promotion they may use in future for their healthcare products.**

investigations

Aims

- To build up a profile of the type(s) of consumers purchasing a product.
- To evaluate the extent to which the marketing of a product is geared to the consumers purchasing it.

Research

Choose four entirely different and contrasting products. One may be a product which is only marketed locally, another may be a product which is available widely in a number of different countries and so on.

Once you have chosen your four products, you will need to research each of them to discover the following information.

- Which group or groups of consumers it is aimed at.
- What sort of people actually buy it. Are they young, old, male, female etc.?

The next step is to find out how each one of the products is marketed. You may examine some of the following.

- How is it packaged?
- How is it promoted?
- In which media is it advertised?
- At what stage is it in its product life cycle?
- What is its price?
- How was the price chosen?
- Where can it be purchased?

Useful sources to find out information about purchasers and marketing will include newspapers and magazines, retail outlets, company reports and visits, interviews with company representatives and purchasers. Remember that you are not able to ask all people about their views. You must therefore make sure that a representative sample is taken and use appropriate market research methods.

Presentation

Once you have collected the information you can write a report which could include the following areas.

- The typical profile of the person most likely to purchase the product. This could include age, sex, geographical area, income group, occupation etc.
- The characteristics of the products you have chosen, eg price, quality, style etc.
- The marketing techniques used by businesses.

You can then decide whether the marketing for a particular product is suitable for the type of consumer it is aimed at. Make sure you explain clearly the reasons for your conclusions.

An alternative to this investigation is to look at the profiles of consumers buying different brands or types of a single product. Newspaper readership is the obvious example, but others might be buyers of cars, shoes, trainers or clothing.

Aims

- To write a marketing plan for a business which you are intending to set up.

Research

Team up with two or three other members of your Business Studies group. Agree upon a business which you would like to, and would be able to, set up with starting capital of £1,500 each.

Research how your business should be marketed. You will need to carry out a SWOT analysis. This will involve you in doing the following in relation to your proposed business.

- Identify its potential strengths.
- Identify its potential weaknesses.
- Identify opportunities which may arise in the future.
- Identify any threats that may arise.
- Investigate any internal constraints on marketing decisions, such as finance or the skills and abilities of potential employees.
- Investigate any external constraints on your business marketing decisions, such as the state of the economy and legislation which will need to be observed.

Once this research has been carried out, you will need to decide upon:

- your marketing goals and objectives;
- the marketing strategies which you will employ.

Presentation

Once you have completed your research, write a report on your marketing plan to the manager of the small business centre of a High Street bank. The report could act as the basis for a request of a loan of up to £3,000. Point out exactly why you feel your business will be able to achieve the goals you have set. If possible use market research results and present any data in a way which shows the information you want to convey clearly.

Alternatively, you could give an oral presentation to your local Chamber of Commerce, or take a group of local business people you have invited to your school or college. After the presentation has been given, adapt and alter your marketing plan in the light of comments and suggestion made at the presentation. Once the marketing plan has been completed you could write an evaluation. This could deal with issues such as:

- how effectively you work as a team;
- the likely success of your business;
- the mistakes that your group made and how you would try to avoid them in future.

1. Explain why it has become increasingly necessary for firms to become market orientated. Is there any role today for a product orientated approach to business?

2. Outline the factors which might influence a firm's pricing decision. Why might some firms have more room for manoeuvre when making pricing decisions than others?

3. A British manufacturer of briefcases and handbags is seeking to enter the French market. Advise it on the most suitable means of achieving this.

4. Describe the possible circumstances in which businesses might prefer to use below the line promotions. Explain why direct mailing has become an increasingly popular method of promoting products.

5. What is meant by the product life cycle? How might a business alter its marketing strategy as a product passes through its life cycle?

6. What might be the impact on manufacturers of the growing importance of large retail outlets in the distribution of consumer goods?

7. What aspects of its market might a business want to research? How might market research help the business to develop its marketing plan?

8. What constraints exist on businesses wishing to promote their products?

9. What advice would you give to a firm wishing to develop a successful product mix?

What is production?

PRODUCTION takes place when resources, such as raw materials or components, are changed into goods or 'products'. Land, labour, capital and enterprise - the factors of production (☞ unit 1) - are used in the production process. The use of land and a tractor to grow cabbages is an example of production in the **primary** sector. An example in the **secondary** sector would be the use of wood, plastic, glue, screws, labour, drilling and cutting equipment to manufacture furniture.

Today production is often referred to more generally as those activities that bring the product 'into being'. Activities in the **tertiary** sector, such as services, would be included in this definition. A bank might talk about providing a 'product' in the same way as a carpet manufacturer. The financial services offered by the bank would be an example. Direct services from the producer to the consumer, such as car repairs or decorating, can also be regarded as production in this sense.

QUESTION 1

Look at the photographs. Explain why the activities are examples of production.

Production decisions

Businesses make a number of important production decisions. Some of the choices facing a business include:
■ what to produce;
■ how production is to take place, eg what materials and machinery should be used;
■ where production is to be located;
■ the scale of production, eg how big should the factory be;
■ how production can be improved and controlled.

A clothing manufacturer might decide to produce a new range of casual trousers. This could involve using a new type of cloth, changing the layout of the factory, increasing the size of its warehouse, employing more labour or introducing a new quality control system. One production decision will lead to other decisions having to be made.

This unit is concerned with the decision of what to produce and how the product is to be designed. Businesses will have carried out some market research to evaluate the likely success of a product before production takes place. The design and production of the product can then proceed. Once a business is established it is likely to redesign existing products, introduce products which are similar or even develop completely new products. This recognises that products have distinctive life cycles and that sales of products eventually decline, although at different rates (☞ unit 20).

What influences the products a firm chooses to produce?

Whether the firm is product or market orientated
Businesses in the past, and some today, have been product orientated. The nature of the product itself (what it could do and its quality) would be enough to make sure the product sold. For example, when cars were first produced they were unique and a novelty and so the product sold itself. Increasingly firms recognise the need to design products that meet consumers' wishes. These are market orientated firms. A market orientated approach means that a business must design products which meet users' needs (☞ unit 18).

Competitors' behaviour In order to survive in a competitive market, businesses must supply products which customers prefer at the expense of those supplied by competitors. This may mean developing products which are not available, or copying rivals' ideas and improving them.

Technology New inventions and innovations often result in new products. For example, telecommunications research has resulted in a range of personal telephones in the market place.

Management The choice of product is often made by

senior management. It is a crucial decision because it may decide the fate of a company. The decision by the Rover Company in 1991 not to drop the 'Mini' was deemed a success as it subsequently enjoyed strong sales growth abroad.

Financial viability Do the benefits of new or adapted goods or services outweigh the costs? The benefit to the firm might be the revenue it gains from selling the product. Accountants often act as a **constraint** on production decisions. They are unlikely to approve funds for products which will make long term losses.

QUESTION 2 For a long time the BBC had seen ITV's successful 'soap opera', Coronation Street, gain high audience ratings. In 1984 the BBC launched their own 'soap opera', Eastenders.
(a) Briefly explain 3 production decisions the BBC would have made when producing Eastenders.
(b) What factors do you think influenced the BBC's choice of product when it decided to make Eastenders?

Product design

Once the firm has found a need for a product, a **design brief** can be written. This will contain specifications or features about the product which the designers can use. For example, a firm aiming to produce a new type of ice lolly may write a design brief such as 'a new brightly coloured ice lolly is required for the age range 3 to 6; it should be shaped differently to current brands'. Designers can work from this design brief. When designing the product they may take into account:
■ the shape and the appearance of the product;
■ whether it fits the intended need;
■ how easily and cost effectively it can be produced from the design;
■ the image it gives when it is displayed;
■ whether the design should create a 'corporate identity', saying something about the image of the company.
  Well designed products are crucial for firms. They will be produced at minimum cost without sacrificing quality. Consumers are more likely to pay the price they are sold for as a result. Both of these factors determine whether the firm makes a profit from the sale of the product. Examples of well designed products may be Volvo cars, which are recognised for safety, or IKEA furniture, which is well known for its durability, simplicity and usefulness.

The design process

The design process has a number of stages which take the design from an initial idea to a final product. These stages are shown in Figure 28.1.

The design process usually begins when a need is found for:
■ a new product;
■ an adaptation;
■ a redesign of an existing product.
  These are usually identified by the marketing department in a **design brief** for the design team, like the one described for the ice lolly above.
  The next stage is to produce a **design specification** and **analysis**. One way of achieving this is for the design team, market researchers and the client to meet and discuss their ideas. The design specification and analysis will give a clear description of the purpose of the product, state any functions the product must have and mention constraints, such as cost, size or quality.
  Several techniques can be used to produce specifications. One way is to note down all the essential features of a product and be less interested in those which are only desirable. A pair of walking boots might have essential features such as durability, being waterproof, made of leather and comfortable, and desirable features such as attractiveness, lightness and economy in manufacture. Another technique is to 'brainstorm'. This involves listing all possible alternatives or solutions, even those which initially might be considered unlikely.
  Next it is necessary to find some practical **solutions** to the design brief. Solutions which the design team have

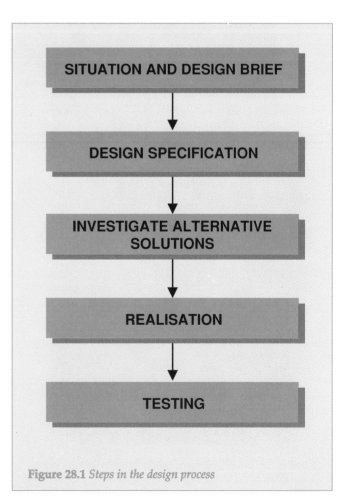

Figure 28.1 *Steps in the design process*

suggested should be assessed. Sketches and working examples will help the evaluation. Finally, the team must decide which model or prototype is the most suitable solution to the problem.

The firm can then **realise** the design solution by making the product. The first production run is likely to be very small because the total design process is not yet complete.

The final stage in the design process is **testing**. Most designs are tested to check that they satisfy the customer. It is often necessary to refine or modify the product. Sometimes new ideas might be generated once the design solution is in a working situation.

Design features

When designing any product a number of features have to be considered by the designer or design team.

Commercial viability Businesses must be able to produce and sell a product at a profit. Thought must be given to the choice of materials and the production techniques that are used so that production costs can be kept down. If the costs are likely to be too high, the design may well be dropped.

Reliability Designers must ensure their designs satisfy customers' expectations about the reliability of the product. Unreliable products may harm the company's image in the eyes of the consumer. The business will also incur costs if products are frequently returned.

Safety Designers must make sure their solutions are safe. The product itself should be technically safe. Designs may be subject to the various EC health and safety regulations, for example. Also, the user of the product should be protected. This means providing clear instructions for operation, as producers of electrical products have to by law.

Maintenance Technical and mechanical products often need maintenance. Products should be designed so that this can be easily carried out. It is particularly important in the design of machinery. The design of the Mini car has been criticised by motor mechanics. They complain that access to parts of the engine is made very difficult by the design. As a result, routine maintenance tasks take much longer and are more expensive for the owner.

Environment In recent years consumers have begun to question the effect certain products have on the environment. Designers now have to take this into account. One example is the use of 'roll on' deodorants instead of sprays which cause CFCs to be emitted.

Convenience and efficiency Products should be designed so that they are convenient and practical to use. For example, some tin openers are 'hand held' whilst others are electrically operated. Consumers are increasingly prepared to pay for products which are easier to use. Businesses also look for machinery and equipment that will lead to a more efficient workforce. Products which are well designed ERGONOMICALLY should increase efficiency and operator safety and also involve less effort for the user.

Manufacture Designers must ensure that their designs are not expensive or technically difficult to make. For

---

QUESTION 3 Many farmers have complained in the past that tractor seats are uncomfortable. Tractor drivers may have to spend up to 12 hours a day in the seat and some farmers have injured their backs as a result of poorly designed seats. Below is a description of the stages in the design process for a new type of tractor seat.

SITUATION Large agricultural producers have become increasingly concerned about the low productivity of their tractor drivers. Absenteeism caused by back complaints and an unduly high frequency of work breaks prompted by discomfort in the driving seat appear to be two of the main causes.

NEED A tractor seat which is more comfortable and supportive for the driver.

DESIGN BRIEF Design a comfortable tractor seat which is orthopaedically shaped so that back injuries are either eliminated or reduced significantly. The seat should be highly durable, able to withstand extreme weather conditions and rough treatment.

SPECIFICATION AND ANALYSIS

(SPECIFICATION) DESIGN FEATURE		(ANALYSIS) DESCRIPTION OF FUNCTION
Seat shape	-	Orthopaedically designed to protect back from injury and discomfort.
Mountings	-	Sprung or hydraulic suspension to protect spine from constant vertical shocks.
Padding	-	Strong, waterproof and soft to enhance driver comfort.
Covering	-	Very strong, waterproof and durable to protect padding.
Adjustable height	-	An efficient adjustment mechanism to accommodate different size drivers.
Swivel action	-	Swivel action to allow driver ease of movement inside the cab when operating implements.
Durable materials	-	All materials must be very strong and durable, able to withstand extreme weather conditions and possible abuse.
Minimum cost	-	The cost should not be prohibitive.

(a) Arrange the design features listed in the above specification in order of priority given the design brief. State which are essential and which are desirable.
(b) Describe any conflicts between cost and use that may arise given the order of priority which you have selected.
(c) How might the design be tested after the realisation stage?

example, they may suggest a cheaper material for lining the inside of a suitcase.

Market The designer must consider the marketing mix (☞ unit 21) when designing products. Products are very difficult to market if they are unattractive, clumsy to store and display, expensive to distribute and overpriced.

Aesthetics Designers must consider the colour, size, appearance, shape, smell and taste of products. Many consumers would not wish to be seen wearing poorly designed clothes, for example.

Legal The product should be designed so that it is legally 'fit for purpose'. For example, if a manufacturer claims that a new type of paint is designed to dry within two hours after application, then legally it must.

QUESTION 4 Look at the drawings. For each product, explain which design features you think were the most important when they were being designed?

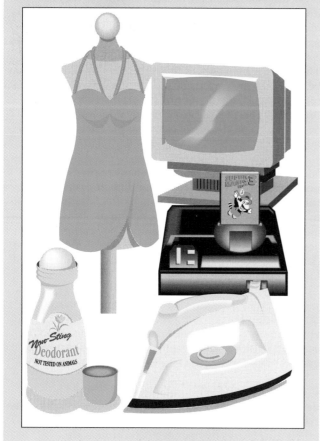

Computer aided design

COMPUTER AIDED DESIGN (CAD) is an interactive computer system which is capable of generating, storing and using geometric and computer graphics. It helps design engineers to solve design problems. CAD is used in many industries today. What benefits does CAD offer to a designer?

■ CAD has meant huge cuts in **lead time** (☞ unit 33), ie the length of time between the initial design and actual production. Long lead times result in lower profits as firms lose out to competitors in the race to launch new products.

■ A wide range of designs can be shown on the computer screen. Two and three dimensional engineering drawings, wire-framed models, electronic circuit board designs and architectural drawings are examples.

■ CAD systems handle repetitive work, allowing the designer more time to concentrate on 'creating' the design. The need for specialists is also reduced, which helps keep down costs.

■ Modifications and changes are easily made. The size or shape of a design can be changed in seconds, for example.

■ Problems are often more quickly identified. This sometimes prevents the need for expensive reworking later on. Also, the final design, once manufactured, is more likely to be right.

Value analysis

VALUE ANALYSIS is an attempt by businesses to ensure that the consumer receives value for money from the product. This technique, along with value engineering (☞ unit 29), is used by nearly every manufacturer in Japan. Designers may want to produce high quality products. This, however, may result in high prices, due to the cost of design, materials and production. Consumers may feel that products are not value for money. Value analysis attempts to produce designs for products and components which allow them to perform their function at a lower cost. For the customer, value analysis should ensure that the product is at the least cost, but not at the expense of quality and reliability.

The success of value analysis will often depend on how departments in a firm work together. Value analysis cannot be carried out by an individual and costs can only be reduced if departments take into account each other's needs. For example, in an effort to cut costs, the quality of the product may suffer to such an extent that the marketing department may find it impossible to sell the product.

Research and development

There is a constant need for invention and innovation in business. New products are required not only for a business to grow, but also to survive. Today, the pace of technological change, coupled with the rising wants and spending power of consumers, has forced firms to respond by investing in research and development (R & D).

■ RESEARCH is the inquiry and discovery of new ideas. Methods used to generate new ideas include laboratory research, product evaluation of a business' own and its competitors' products and brainstorming.

■ DEVELOPMENT involves changing ideas into commercial products. First, the idea which is expected to be the most successful must be selected. One problem in development is the time scale involved. Some projects take many years to complete and success cannot be guaranteed. The Concorde project took thirty years to develop and was eventually declared a commercial failure.

R & D is undertaken by a variety of organisations, not all of which are businesses. Universities carry out scientific research. There are also research centres, some funded by the government, which specialise in scientific research. Rothampstead experimental work station in Hertfordshire is one. This specialises in biological research, which gives information that could be used in fertiliser production.

R & D is often expensive, so it is usually large businesses which undertake it. In particular, pharmaceutical, electronic and aircraft industries devote vast funds to R & D. Small companies tend to rely on copying other firm's products. Other businesses carry out research and development without long term projects. They make use of other people's ideas which have been published.

Patents

A PATENT aims to protect the inventor of a new product or manufacturing process. It allows a business to design, produce and sell a new invention and prevents competitors from copying it. New inventions are protected for fifteen years. The developer must make details of the invention available to the Patent Office.

Obtaining a patent can be a lengthy process. To qualify for a patent the invention must be brand new. Checks are then made to ensure it is authentic. The patent is published eighteen months after its application and signed and sealed some time after this. The developer must pay annual fees to the Patent Office which become more expensive after the first four years. This is to encourage production of the new idea. Both the inventor and the consumer can benefit from patents. Some benefits to businesses of patents are:
- a higher level of sales;
- reduced competition;
- legal protection that encourages continued research;
- higher profits which can be ploughed back into further research and development;
- the industry benefits from the technical information as a result of the patent;
- high risk research and development is encouraged.

Consumers also benefit. New products mean more variety and perhaps a better standard of living. New, more efficient, productive techniques mean lower costs and lower prices.

There are a number of criticisms of the patent system. The granting of sole production and distribution rights to one firm creates a legal monopoly (☞ unit 73). If this monopoly power is abused then consumers may be exploited. Figure 28.2 illustrates some examples of ideas which have been patented in the past and the extent of their financial success.

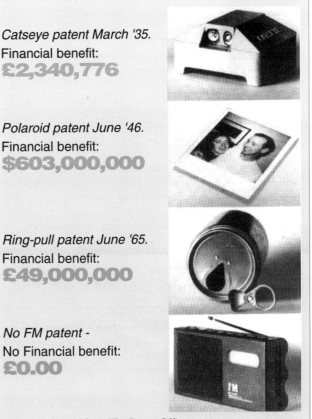

Catseye patent March '35.
Financial benefit:
£2,340,776

Polaroid patent June '46.
Financial benefit:
$603,000,000

Ring-pull patent June '65.
Financial benefit:
£49,000,000

No FM patent -
No Financial benefit:
£0.00

Source: adapted from The Patent Office.
Figure 28.2 *Examples of patented ideas*

QUESTION 5 Complex legal battles over patents are common worldwide. In the pharmaceuticals industry it is argued that the owners of patents hold the key to success. It is the patent, not the manufacture, which brings the benefits. The problem with drug patents is that they are often unclear. For example, they are taken out at different stages of development and on different presentations of the compound (injections, tablets or a slow release form). Also, they can be taken out in different countries which often have different patent periods.

An industry spokesman said, 'Patent protection is one area the industry must have, because you can spend fortunes on product development with no guarantee of success... If you come up with something, it clearly is essential that you have a reasonable period in which to market the product and get back the return not only on that, but also on the research and development of products that did not make it.'

Glaxo, a company which spent more than £500 million on R&D in 1991, holds a patent on the ulcer drug Zantac. Since its launch, Zantac has captured 40 per cent of the ulcer drug market and enjoys annual sales of £1.6 billion. The patent is due to expire in the year 2001.

Source : adapted from *The Times*, 27.1.1992.

(a) Why are patents especially important to the drugs industry?
(b) Explain the benefits of patents in the drug industry to; (i) businesses; (ii) consumers.

Key terms

Computer Aided Design - an interactive computer system developed to assist in design.

Development - the changing of new ideas into commercial propositions.

Ergonomics - the study of people in their working environment and the adaptation of machines and conditions to improve efficiency.

Patent - a licence which prevents the copying of an idea.

Production - the transformation of resources into goods and services.

Research - an investigation involving the process of enquiry and discovery used to generate new business ideas.

Value analysis - a procedure designed to evaluate the way in which products are made, in order to improve efficiency.

Summary

1. How can the behaviour of competitors and the state of technology affect the product a firm chooses to produce?
2. How might a business find out if there is a need for a product?
3. What is meant by a design brief?
4. Describe the stages in the design process.
5. What is meant by a design feature?
6. State 6 design features that a firm might consider important when designing a product.
7. How does CAD improve business efficiency?
8. How will value analysis benefit consumers?
9. What are the benefits of patents to a business?

Question

Guinness canned draught bitter

Britain is the only country in the world which produces cask conditioned (draught) beer on a large scale. Cask conditioning is the practice of delivering barrels to a pub in a state which is not quite ready to serve to customers. The brewing process continues for a short period in the pub's cellar. A secondary fermentation takes place at the natural cellar temperature, resulting in a light, naturally carbonated cask conditioned ale. Beer enthusiasts argue that the product is vastly superior to its keg, canned and bottled substitutes, which tend to be colder, gassier and much less soothing. Draught beer is fresh, the malt taste is sweet and the aroma of the hops is refreshing.

Another advantage of draught beer is that it has not been pasteurised, a process which adds stability to beer but again diminishes the quality of the drinking experience. Most kegs and all canned and bottled beers are pasteurised.

Brewers have recognised the market potential if the characteristics of draught beer could be captured in a can or a bottle. In 1961 Guinness launched a draught stout. The dispensing system released nitrogen into the beer giving it a creamy texture. This was successful, but the technique could not be applied to cans and bottles. However, after some lengthy research, Guinness discovered another technique which could be used in cans. In 1988 they launched Draught Guinness in a can which contains a capsule of a nitrogen and stout blend. This capsule is filled on the canning line and the contents are released automatically when the can is opened. This device was very successful and won Guinness the Queen's Award for Technological Achievement.

Using the same technique they launched Guinness Draught Bitter in 1991. The nitrogen not only makes the beer creamy, but produces a better head and protects against oxidation. The 'draught canned' products have levels of carbonation similar to cask-conditioned ales, and less than half those in some bottled beers. Other brewers have rapidly launched their own versions of 'draught canned' products using similar devices, eg Whitbreads, Theakstons and Courage. Guinness' design was well protected by patents so other brewers were forced to invest money in their own research and development. Whitbread spent between £5 million to £10 million in developing their own 'Draughtflow system' which has the same effect.

Source: adapted from *The Independent*, 4.5.1991.

(a) What factors might have influenced Guinness in developing their draught canned bitter?
(b) Suggest 5 features of design which might have appealed to consumers.
(c) How might the Queen's award for the brewing device benefit Guinness?
(d) What costs and benefits of research and development to Guinness are suggested in the article?
(e) Why do you think other brewers invested millions of pounds in the development of their own similar devices?

Deciding how to produce

Once a firm has decided what to produce (☞ unit 28), it must choose how to manufacture its goods or how to provide services. It is likely that products which are different will be produced differently. For example, a plastic drinks bottle may be produced using automated machinery, but a wrist watch may be assembled by hand. Products that are similar can also be produced in different ways. The Ford Motor Company and Morgan Cars both produce cars, but different processes are used. Ford builds cars using a production line and semi-skilled labour, but Morgan cars are hand built by skilled workers. There are three important decisions that businesses must make when choosing how to produce. These are shown in Figure 29.1, along with the factors which influence these decisions. In the diagram it is assumed that the firm has already decided 'what' to produce. When deciding how to produce, the objective of the firm will be to minimise the cost per unit of output, ie PRODUCTIVE EFFICIENCY.

What production method will be used? There are three alternatives for a business.
- ■ JOB PRODUCTION. One job is completed at a time before moving on to another. An example might be a costume made for a television play set in the nineteenth century.
- ■ BATCH PRODUCTION involves dividing the work into a number of different operations. Each operation is completed on the whole batch before moving on to the next. An example would be bread production, where each batch goes through several different baking stages before it is completed.
- ■ FLOW PRODUCTION involves mass production techniques. Once work has been completed on one operation, the job moves on to the next without stopping. The production of cars on a production line might be one example.

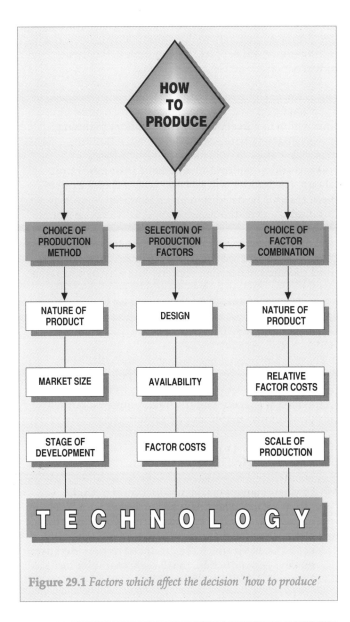

Figure 29.1 *Factors which affect the decision 'how to produce'*

QUESTION 1 Table 29.1 illustrates the amounts of capital and labour required by three alternative production methods, A, B and C, which might be used to achieve the same level of production. The weekly cost of labour and capital is also included.

Table 29.1 *The quantities and cost of labour and capital required by three production techniques*

Method	No. of machines	No. of employees	Machine rental (£/wk)	Wage rate (£/wk)	Capital cost (£/wk)	Labour cost (£/wk)	Total cost (£/wk)
A	4	20	500	100			
B	6	12	500	100			
C	10	5	500	100			

(a) Copy and complete the table. Calculate the most cost effective production technique.
(b) If the wage rate rises to £150 per week, how might the choice of production technique be affected?

The methods over the page are examined in detail later in this unit. Some industries may combine different methods of production. For example, a large brewery may produce 'batches' of beer, but then send them to a bottling line for packaging, where flow production is used. Such combinations are particularly common in the food industry.

What factors of production will be used? Businesses are often faced with a wide choice between alternative production factors. For example, a builder planning to construct a new house must decide what building materials to buy, which tools to use, which sub-contractors to employ and whether to hire any extra labour. The builder will be faced with a choice in all of these cases. If he decides to hire a labourer, there may be hundreds or even thousands of people to choose from in the area.

How will the factors of production be combined? A third production decision concerns the way in which the available production factors should be combined. For example, should an assembly plant invest in a highly automated assembly operation, or employ a large semi-skilled labour force to undertake the work?

There is a relationship between the three decisions concerning how to produce. For example, if a large UK firm produced sheet glass using flow production techniques, it is likely that it would require labour with certain skills and that it may be capital intensive.

Job production

Job production involves the production of a single product at a time. It is used when orders for products are small, such as 'one-offs'. Production is organised so that one 'job' is completed at a time. There is a wide variety of goods and services which are produced or provided using this method of production. Small scale examples include the baking of a child's birthday cake, a dentist's treatment session or the construction of an extension to a house. On a large scale, examples could include the building of a ship, the construction of the Channel Tunnel or the manufacture of specialised machinery. Job production is found both in manufacturing and the service industries. Because the numbers of units produced are small, the production process tends to be labour intensive. The workforce is usually skilled craftsmen or specialists and the possibility of using labour saving machinery is limited. Many businesses adopt this method of production when they are 'starting up'.

Advantages of job production What are the benefits to businesses?
- Firms can produce unique or 'one-off' orders according to customer needs. For example, a wedding dress may be designed and produced for the individual taste of a client. It is also possible to change the specifications of a job at the last minute even if the work has actually begun.

- Workers are more likely to be motivated. The tasks employees carry out often require a variety of skills, knowledge and expertise. Their work will be more demanding and interesting. They will also see the end result of their efforts and be able to take pride in their work. Jobs may be carried out by a team of workers aiming to achieve the same objectives. This should help raise the level of job satisfaction.
- The organisation of job production is fairly simple. Because only one job is done at a time, co-ordination, communication, supervision and inspection can be regularly carried out. Also, it is easier to identify and deal with problems, such as a defective damp proof course in a house or a poorly cooked meal in a restaurant.

Disadvantages of job production There are, however, some disadvantages with job production.
- Labour costs will be high because production tends to be labour intensive. The workforce is likely to be skilled and more versatile. Such employees will be more expensive. The amount of time each employee spends on a particular job will also be long.
- Because there is a variety of work, to many specifications, the business would need a wide range of tools, machines and equipment. This can prove expensive. Also, it may not be possible to achieve economies of scale (☞ unit 31) because only one 'job' is produced at a time.
- Lead times can be lengthy. When building a house the business has to incur costs which cannot be recovered until the house is sold. Sometimes the sale of a house can take a long time.
- Selling costs may also be high. This is likely if the product is highly complex and technical. The sales team will need to be well qualified, able to cope with

QUESTION 2 Matrix is a business that produces display stands for clients who want to promote their products at exhibitions.

(a) Explain why the activity is an example of job production.
(b) Why would it be difficult for Matrix to standardise production?

questions and deal with problems concerning sales and installation. Some firms employ agencies to help reduce their selling costs.

Once the demand for a firm's product rises, job production may become costly. Firms may prefer to use a method more suited to producing larger quantities. This is not always the case. Even if demand is high, each customer may require a unique order. In addition, many firms believe that the 'personal touch' they can offer in job production is important. As a result they may choose not to change to other production methods. Other production methods require some degree of product standardisation. This may result in more efficient production, but a loss of 'individuality'.

Batch production

Batch production may be used when demand for a firm's product or service is **continuous** rather than a 'one off'. An example might be furniture where a batch of armchairs is made to a particular design. Production is divided into a number of operations. A particular operation is carried out on all products in a batch. The batch then moves to the next operation.

A baker uses batch production when baking bread. The operations in the baking process are broken down in Table 29.2.

Table 29.2 *Operations involved in the production of a batch of bread*

1. Blend ingredients in a mixing container until a dough is formed.
2. Knead the dough for a period of time.
3. Leave the dough to rise for a period of time.
4. Divide the dough into suitable units (loaves) for baking.
5. Bake the loaves.
6. Allow loaves to cool.

These operations would be performed on every batch of bread. There is some standardisation because each loaf in the batch will be the same. However, it may be possible to vary each batch. The ingredients could be changed to produce brown bread or the style of baking tin could be changed for different shaped loaves.

A great number of products are produced using this method, particularly in manufacturing and food processing. For example, in a canning plant, a firm may can several different batches of soup, each batch being a different recipe. Products can be produced in very large or very small batches depending on the level of demand. Larger production runs tend to lower the **unit** or **average cost** (unit 10) of production.

Advantages of batch production. What benefits will this method have for a business?
- Even though larger quantities are produced than in job production, there is still flexibility. Each batch can be changed to meet customers' wishes. It is particularly suitable for a wide range of similar products. The settings on machines can be changed according to specifications, such as different clothes sizes.
- Employees can concentrate on one operation rather

than the whole task. This reduces the need for costly, skilled employees.
- Less variety of machinery would be needed than in job production because the products are standardised. Also, it is possible to use more standardised machinery.
- It often results in stocks of partly finished goods which have to be stored. This means firms can respond more quickly to an urgent order by processing a batch quickly through the final stages of production.

Disadvantages of batch production. There are also disadvantages with batch production.
- Careful planning and co-ordination are needed, or machines and workers may be idle, waiting for a whole batch to finish its previous operation. There is often a need to clean and adjust machinery before the next batch can be produced. This can mean delays. In brewing, one day of the week is used to clean equipment before the next batch begins.
- Some machinery may have to be more complex to compensate for the lower skill levels required from the labour force. This may lead to higher costs.
- The workforce may be less motivated, since they have to repeat operations on every single unit in the batch. In addition, they are unlikely to be involved with production from start to finish.
- If batches are small then unit costs will remain relatively high.
- Money will be tied up in work-in-progress (unit 33) since an order cannot be dispatched until the whole batch has been finished.

QUESTION 3

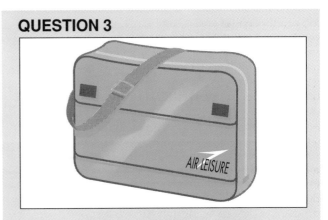

A manufacturer produces bags for a variety of businesses, such as travel firms, which use the bags as a means of promotion. Production is organised in batches.

(a) List the possible operations involved in the production of these bags.
(b) Describe the changes which might be necessary when switching production from one batch of bags to another.
(c) Explain why unit costs might fall when production is switched to a larger batch of a particular bag, eg from 100 to 1,000.

Flow production

Most people will have some idea of flow production from pictures of motor car factories. Production is organised so that different operations can be carried out, one after the other, in a continuous sequence. Vehicles move from one operation to the next, often on a conveyer belt. This type of production is often called mass or continuous production. It is also used in the manufacture of newspapers, cement and food products with very high demand, like cornflakes. The main features of flow production are:

- large quantities are produced;
- a simplified or standardised product;
- a semi-skilled workforce, specialising in one operation only;
- large amounts of machinery and equipment;
- large stocks of raw materials and components;

In recent years the traditional view of the factory has changed. New production methods have been imported from Japan, in particular,which have helped to improve efficiency. One such method is **just-in-time** (☞ unit 33) manufacturing which has helped to reduce the cost of holding stocks.

Advantages of flow production Why might a business use flow production?

Examples of flow production - valve production and the Heinz factory at Wigan.

- Unit costs are reduced as firms gain from economies of scale (☞ unit 31).
- In many industries the process is highly automated. Production is controlled by computers. Many of the operations are performed by robots and other types of machinery. Once the production line is set up and running, products can flow off the end non stop for lengthy periods of time. This can reduce the need for labour, as only machine supervisors are needed.
- The need to stockpile finished goods is reduced. The production line can respond to short term changes in demand. For example, if demand falls the line can be shut down for a period of time. If it rises then the line can be opened.

Disadvantages of flow production What are the disadvantages of flow production?

- The set up costs are very high. An enormous investment in plant and equipment is needed. Firms must therefore be confident that demand for the product is sufficient over a period of time to make the investment pay.
- The product will be standardised. It is not possible to offer a wide product range and meet different customers' needs.
- For a number of reasons, worker motivation can be a serious problem. Most of the manual operations required on the production line will be repetitive and boring. Factories with production lines tend to be very noisy. Each worker will only be involved in a very small part of the job cycle. As a result of these problems worker morale may be low and labour turnover (☞ unit 51) and absenteeism high.
- Breakdowns can prove costly. The whole production system is interdependent. If one part of the supply or production line fails the whole system may break down.

QUESTION 4 In the 1980s, Kellogg's, the giant breakfast cereal manufacturer, automated the warehousing function at its Manchester plant. Cartons of breakfast cereals roll off production lines from the main production process at an astonishing rate. The cardboard cartons are loaded automatically onto pallets and transported by computerised transport vehicles to a loading platform. The loaded pallets are placed onto the platform and moved into position automatically. When the platform is full, the entire load is automatically shifted into the back of the container ready for immediate distribution by articulated lorry. The whole warehousing and loading function is controlled by a handful of computer operators overlooking the entire operation. The number of personnel employed in the process has been reduced by several hundred due to the automation.

Source: independent research by the author.

(a) What features suggest that Kellogg's are using a flow production system?
(b) Explain three advantages to Kellogg's of using this system of production.
(c) How might the Kellogg's workforce have reacted to the introduction of the automated warehouse?

Computer aided manufacturing (CAM)

The use of computers in production is widespread. They can be used in a number of ways, but mainly to control machinery, for example robotic welders used in vehicle production. The production process is far more flexible as a result. Changing the instructions given to the computer can, for example, change the direction of a robot arm. In some plants the whole process is computer controlled. Flow production techniques make the most of computers in manufacturing. The size of investment in CAM would not be justified in job production.

Choice of production method

The method of production chosen might depend on a number of factors.

■ The nature of the product. Many products require a specific method of production. For example, in the construction industry, projects such as bridges, roads, office blocks and sewers must be produced using job production. Cereal farming involves batch production. A plot of land undergoes several processes before it 'produces' a crop.

■ The size of the market. Fast moving consumer goods like soap, confectionery and canned drinks are normally produced using flow production because the market is so big. When the market is small, flow production techniques are not cost effective.

■ The stage of development a business has reached. When firms are first set up, they often produce small levels of output and employ job or batch production methods. As they grow and enjoy higher sales levels they may switch to flow production.

■ Technology. The current state of technology will affect all decisions concerning how to produce. As technology advances, new materials and machinery become available. Changes in technology often result in firms adopting new methods of production. For example, the development of computers and robotic welders has radically changed the way in which cars are manufactured. Also, car manufacturers are now able to produce different models on the same production line at the same time.

Choosing factors of production

A firm has to choose materials, tools, equipment, machinery and labour before production can begin. The more complex the product, the more difficult this will be. There is often a variety of materials and equipment to choose from. For example, a small manufacturer of jeans has to consider which type of cloth, cotton, stud, zip, sewing machine and labour to use. What influences the factors of production a business chooses?

■ The actual design itself may specify which materials to use. For example, a new savoury snack will be made to a strict list of ingredients.

■ There may be limited amounts of labour, capital or materials. A company recruiting people with a specialist skill may find that supply 'runs out'. It may then have to recruit unskilled workers and train them.

■ Businesses will aim to use the cheapest factors, assuming that there is no difference in quality. If there is a difference in quality then the firm must decide which factor most suits its needs and budget. For example, when a company buys a new computer there is a wide range of models to choose from, at a range of different prices. They will have to select a model which suits their needs, and also one which they can afford.

Value engineering may be used to help choose materials and components. It involves studying the materials that are bought and examining whether their quality and reliability are right for a particular product's design and use.

Combining factors of production

Businesses must also decide what combination of factors of production they will use. The firm can adopt one of two approaches. LABOUR INTENSIVE techniques involve using a larger proportion of labour than capital. CAPITAL INTENSIVE techniques involve employing more machinery relative to labour. For example, chemical production is capital intensive with only a relatively small workforce to oversee the process. The postal service is labour intensive with a considerable amount of sorting and delivery done by hand.

The approach that is chosen depends on a number of factors.

■ The nature of the product. Everyday products with high demand, like newspapers, are mass produced in huge plants using large quantities of machinery.

■ The relative prices of the two factors. If labour costs are rising then it may be worth the company employing more capital instead.

■ The size of the firm. As a firm grows and the scale of production increases, it tends to employ more capital relative to labour.

Table 29.3 *The effect on output as more workers are employed, given a fixed amount of capital*

(Units)

Capital	40	40	40	40	40	40	40	40
No. of workers	1	2	3	4	5	6	7	8
Total output	4	10	18	30	45	52	55	56

Combining different amounts of labour and capital can affect the **productivity** of these factors in the short run (☞ unit 10). As more units of labour are added to a fixed amount of capital, the output of the extra workers will rise at first and then fall. This is shown in Table 29.3, where the amount of capital is fixed at 40 units. For example, when the second worker is hired the total amount produced (**total output**) rises by 6 units (10-4). When the third worker is employed, output rises by 8 units (18-10), ie a higher amount.

The amount added by each extra worker (the **marginal output**) continues to rise until the sixth worker is employed. Then output rises by a smaller amount (7 units = 52-45). This is called the law of **diminishing returns** (☞ unit 11). Output rises at first because workers are able to specialise in particular tasks, which improves the productivity of extra workers. However, there reaches a point where workers are not able to specialise any more and the productivity of the extra worker begins to fall.

QUESTION 5 Vimco Ltd are a small company which makes electrical engines. In the short run, the amount of capital is fixed at 10 units, but the size of the workforce can be varied. Table 29.4 shows the total output of Vimco Ltd in relation to the number of workers employed.

Table 29.4 *The total output for Vimco Ltd resulting from different combinations of labour and capital*

		(Units)
Capital	Labour	Total output
10	1	20
10	2	54
10	3	100
10	4	151
10	5	197
10	6	230
10	7	251
10	8	234

(a) Calculate the marginal output for each worker employed.
(b) Explain what is happening when
 (i) the fifth worker is employed;
 (ii) the eighth worker is employed.
(c) How might Vimco Ltd make use of the information contained in the table?

Key terms

Batch production - a method which involves completing one operation at a time on all units before performing the next.
Capital intensive - production methods which employ a large amount of machinery relative to labour.
Flow production - very large scale production of a standardised product, where each operation on a unit is performed continuously one after the other, usually on a production line.

Job production - a method of production which involves employing all factors to complete one unit of output at a time.
Labour intensive - production methods which rely on a large workforce relative to the amount of machinery.
Productive efficiency - production methods which minimise unit costs.

Summary

1. What are the 3 main decisions which have to be made regarding the method of production?
2. Under what circumstances might a business become more capital intensive?
3. State 3 types of products which may be manufactured using job production.
4. Describe the advantages and disadvantages of job production.
5. State 3 products that are generally manufactured using batch production.
6. Describe the advantages and disadvantages of batch production.
7. Describe 4 features of flow production.
8. What is computer aided manufacturing?
9. What is meant by value engineering?
10 What factors might affect the way a business chooses to combine factors of production?

Question

Kilburn Brackets Ltd

In March 1993, Andrew Roden decided to set up a manufacturing business. He had been employed for four years in a North London factory as a machine operator, but was made redundant when the company went into liquidation. The company made a selection of metal products, including brackets. Following the collapse of the business, Andrew felt that there was a gap in the market for metal brackets, the area of production in which he was involved. He undertook some market research to determine the potential size of the market and identified a need for a variety of steel brackets. The market research suggested that four specific designs would be popular. These designs are illustrated below.

To make the brackets required five specific operations.
- Cutting
- Bending and shaping
- Drilling
- Finishing
- Painting

Andrew purchased a cutting machine, some bending and shaping equipment, a high powered drill and a multi-use grinding machine. Initially, he employed two skilled metalworkers and a labourer and operated in a small factory. As the business became more successful, Andrew spent less time in the workshop and concentrated on the financial and marketing side of the business. During an average week the small workforce produced about 20,000 brackets. To keep up with demand it was necessary to produce a lot more, so he recruited three more workers. As a result, total weekly output rose to 50,000 brackets.

(a) What method of production would be most appropriate for the brackets? Explain your reasons.
(b) Why do you think that output more than doubled when three more workers were employed?

Andrew's business began to grow very rapidly. A Danish engineering company had placed a large order for one of the designs. The size of the order required more workers so a further 5 more employees were recruited. Andrew was disappointed to find that weekly output only rose by 10,000 units. He could see that conditions in the workshop were a little cramped and it seemed that the drilling operation was causing delays. When the Danish company trebled the size of their order Andrew visited an engineering consultant. He wanted advice on the implementation of new technology in his business. The consultant said that it would be possible to automate the entire production process, but would require an investment of £1.2 million. The product would also have to be standardised. This did not matter too much since 85 per cent of his orders were now for the one design. Andrew now had to decide whether to change the method of production.

(c) What other method of producing brackets is suggested by the advice of the consultant?
(d) Explain why you think output only increased by 10,000 units when 5 more workers were employed.
(e) Discuss the factors which Andrew should take into account when deciding whether to invest in new technology and change his method of production.
(f) What other long term action could Andrew take to cope with the rising demand?

Location decisions

The decision about where to locate is crucial to many businesses. It can affect their sales, costs, profitability and perhaps even their survival. For example, a firm which is located too far away from its market may incur extra transport costs which reduce profits.

Why might a company need to make a decision about where to locate?

- New businesses will need to carefully consider where to locate their initial premises.
- Existing businesses may need to expand, but may be unable to do so on their present sites.
- The modernisation of a business may involve moving to more up-to-date premises.
- A business aiming to cut its costs might achieve this by re-locating.
- A multinational company aiming to set up a new plant in another country for the first time may evaluate a variety of possible locations worldwide.

There are many factors which will influence a business's decision about where to locate. It is likely that any location decision will be influenced by a few or many of these factors. When deciding where to locate its premises, a business usually weighs up all potential costs and benefits of setting up in a particular area. This may be carried out with the use of **cost-benefit analysis** (☞ unit 17).

Power and raw materials

Primary industry (☞ unit 1) needs to be located near to raw materials. In the UK, agricultural production has been, and still is, found in areas such as the South, East Anglia, Wales and Scotland. The location of mining and extraction is determined by deposits of raw materials like coal, oil and iron ore. In the UK such deposits in the past have been found in the North. This is also true of offshore oil findings in recent years.

After the Industrial Revolution, secondary manufacturing industry largely located close to raw materials. This is true of most Western industrialised countries. In the UK industry moved to the North and Midlands, in Germany to the Ruhr region and in the USA to areas such as the Mid-West. One of the reasons for this was that coal was the main source of power for these industries. Also, transport systems were poor by today's standards and raw materials were costly to carry.

It could be argued that these 'traditional factors' are no longer as important as they were. Gas and electricity systems mean that being close to a power source is no longer a constraint for most firms. Also, transport systems now carry goods relatively cheaply and efficiently to manufacturers. Businesses which are still located close to raw materials tend to be ones which have extremely bulky raw materials, which are then reduced to easier-to-transport final products. For example, timber yards and saw mills are located close to forests and food canning plants are located close to agricultural areas.

QUESTION 1

Table 30.1 *Workers employed in different industries and services by region in England*

Industry or service	North		South East	
	males	females	males	females
All industries and services (000s = 100 per cent)	566	513	3,772	3,491
Agriculture, forestry & fishing	1.6	0.4	0.9	0.6
Energy & water supply	5.4	1.0	1.9	0.7
Materials, minerals & chemicals	7.5	1.6	2.5	1.3
Metal goods, eng. & vehicle inds.	16.5	4.3	11.4	3.9
Other manufacturing	9.8	7.7	7.6	5.0
Construction	9.9	1.2	6.2	1.4
Dist., hotels & catering, repairs	14.6	26.0	19.7	22.2
Transport and communication	8.3	2.3	10.6	4.0
Banking, finance, business services and leasing	7.3	9.0	16.7	17.7
Public admin. & other services	19.1	46.6	22.5	43.2
	100%	100%	100%	100%

Source: adapted from *Regional Trends*, CSO, 1992.

Compare the data for the two regions - the North and the South East. Does the comparison show that the distribution of employment is influenced by the source of raw materials? Give reasons for your answer.

Markets and transport costs

For many firms, being close to their market is often the single most important factor in choosing a location. A variety of businesses may be influenced by this factor.

- Businesses that produce products which are more bulky than the raw materials that go into them, such as North Sea Oil platforms, are likely to locate close to their market. The components and materials used to assemble North Sea Oil platforms are far less bulky than the end product - the platform itself. Therefore, the production of such platforms takes place in locations close to where they will eventually be used - the North Sea coast - in cities such as Aberdeen. If production was located elsewhere transport costs may be very high. There may also be problems transporting the product to its final destination.
- Suppliers of components and intermediate goods may set up close to their main customers. For example, a number of firms emerged in the Liverpool area supplying shipping companies with packing cases for transportation. Although the dock industry has declined in Liverpool, some of these companies still exist.

- Small retailers supply the needs of local communities. The 'corner shop', for example, relies mainly on customers from a very small local catchment area.
- Many financial service businesses locate their premises in London. Some would argue that London is the 'financial centre' of the world.
- The growth of the tertiary sector and the decline in 'heavy' industry has resulted in many FOOTLOOSE secondary and tertiary industries. These are businesses that are able to locate premises where they wish. Given this freedom many have chosen to locate by their markets. The South East of the UK developed a service economy as a result, made up of retailing, financial services, leisure industries and a small amount of 'light' manufacturing. Although there has been some movement away from the South East in the 1990s there is still evidence of a' North-South Divide' in the UK.
- Most service industries tend to be located near to markets. Businesses providing the general public with services like dentistry, dry cleaning and car maintenance must locate their premises in areas which

are accessible to people. W.H. Smith originally located their outlets in railway stations because their main market was railway passengers buying newspapers and magazines. When they moved out of railway stations they located their outlets in the nearest available premises. More recently they have returned to some stations.

Communications

The ease of communications can be important in a firm's location decision. Access to motorways, rail networks, ports and airports may all be important. By reducing travel time, motorways may encourage firms to locate premises in areas which might have been regarded as remote from markets or costly in terms of transport. The building of the M4 between London and South Wales has encouraged location along the 'M4 corridor'.

The accessibility of ports and airports might also be important. This is often true of firms which export their goods. For firms which produce light, low bulk, but high value products, air transport might be the best means of reaching both overseas and domestic markets. More bulky and heavy goods might be transported by sea. Businesses which use a great deal of imported raw materials might also locate close to a port.

The building of the Channel Tunnel will improve trade links to the Continent when it is opened in 1994. It will allow UK businesses to distribute goods easily and effectively to Europe. It is also likely to encourage firms to locate in the South East if they have markets in Europe. The Channel Tunnel became even more important when trading restrictions with Europe were lifted in 1992. Other

QUESTION 2

Look at the photographs.
(a) State whether each of these businesses is likely to locate near to the market or near to raw materials.
(b) Give reasons for your answers.

QUESTION 3 In 1991, a new Japanese-built cruiseliner, Crystal Harmony, entered service. It was built in Milton Keynes - arguably the most inland city in Britain. This shows geography is much less important than it used to be when it comes to relocating a business. One of Japan's oldest shipping lines, NYK Line, part of the Mitsubishi group, decided to set up in Milton Keynes for a number of reasons. The Japanese industrial community in the city is large, with a total of 37 companies. But NYK also found communication links good enough to site its new European operations centre there. NYK, though now one of the largest shipping companies in the world, has diversified into land and air transport, so proximity to port facilities has become less important than having the right communications links. The decision to go to Milton Keynes first is, as much as anything, down to the fact that the Japanese feel more comfortable dealing in English than in any other European language.

Source: adapted from *The Observer*.

(a) What is meant by the phrase 'geography is much less important than it used to be when... re-locating a business'?
(b) Choose one locational factor which influenced NYK and say why you think it was important.

regions in the UK may well benefit from increased trade with Europe via rail links. However, with increasing congestion on all motorways, firms with European interests are likely to favour the South East.

Land

When choosing where to locate or re-locate premises, firms need to select the 'right' piece of land. This might be a newly completed factory unit, a derelict inner city site, an old factory in need of modernisation or a piece of land never previously used for a business development. When choosing an appropriate piece of land firms are likely to take into account some combination of the following factors.

- ■ The cost relative to other potential sites. A firm must compare purchase prices of alternative sites, consider whether or not renting would be more cost effective and compare the level of business rates in each location. Some firms have re-located away from London and the South East in recent years due to the high cost of land in these areas.
- ■ The amount of space available for current needs. Some businesses require large areas of land. For example, car manufacturers need sites of several hundred acres.
- ■ Potential for expansion. It is important that firms look into the future when locating premises. When Kellogg's acquired a new cornflake manufacturing plant in Northern Italy, one of the reasons why it favoured Brescia was because of the large amount of adjacent land which they hoped to use in the future for expansion.
- ■ The availability of planning permission. This is particularly important if a firm is going to change the use of some land or premises, or construct new buildings. Local authorities will not always grant planning permission allowing land development, for example in the GREEN BELT around Greater London.
- ■ Geological suitability. Some businesses require particular geological features. A nuclear power station must be sited on a geologically stable site.
- ■ Good infrastructure. Facilities such as good road links, appropriate waste disposal facilities and other public utilities are often an important influence.
- ■ Environmental considerations. Today, firms may face pressure from public opinion when locating premises. There can be opposition from pressure groups if they attempt to locate in environmentally sensitive areas.

Some firms in recent years have opted to move their premises out of traditional industrial areas to GREEN FIELD sites. These are, literally, rural locations generally found on the outskirts of towns and cities. Here the land tends to be cheaper and more plentiful. However, there may be opposition from environmentalists and green field sites can only be developed if there is adequate access. These sites are becoming more popular and are particularly suitable for hi-tech industries. A good example is the new location which the *Lancashire Evening Post* secured. They moved from the centre of Preston to a greenfield site adjacent to junction 32 on the M6 on the outskirts of the town. Brand new premises costing

£28 million were built on a plot of land which was previously used for non-commercial purposes.

QUESTION 4

Explain why land may be an important factor in determining the location of the businesses in the photographs.

Labour

Firms re-locating from one part of the country to another will aim to take most of their staff with them. This should cut down on disruption and avoid the need to recruit and train large numbers of new staff. Sometimes, businesses try not to move very far so that staff can travel from their existing homes. For example, the Woolwich Building Society, when re-locating from North London, chose Bexley Heath in North Kent - already the home of a large number of their employees.

However, if re-location is a long way from the original position, persuading existing staff to move can be difficult. Selling existing homes, buying new homes, disrupting childrens' education and removal costs can be real obstacles. When choosing a site, firms need to find out whether existing employees can be persuaded to move and whether other sources of labour with the right skills can be recruited locally. Factors that existing staff may feel are important may be the cost of housing, the quality of the local environment, the quality of local schools and perhaps the number of traffic jams in the area. The high price of houses and the amount of traffic in the London area has contributed to a drift of employees away from the region in the late 1980s and early 1990s.

Labour skills are not evenly distributed throughout the country. If a firm needs a particular type of skilled labour there may be regions which are especially suitable. For example, a firm which is contemplating a new venture in carpet manufacturing might choose Kidderminster as a possible location. Kidderminster is famous for carpet manufacturing and could offer a firm new to the industry a ready supply of appropriately skilled and semi-skilled workers. Other examples of these regional advantages include car workers in the West Midlands, pottery workers in Stoke-on-Trent and steel workers in Sheffield. Where an industry is concentrated in a particular region advantages, such as expertise in local schools and colleges, research facilities in nearby universities and sympathetic and supportive local government agencies often exist. These are known as external economies of scale (☞ unit 31).

Telecommunications and information technology

An increasingly important factor is likely to be access to telecommunications links. Telecommunications networks, such as British Telecom's integrated services data network (ISDN), have the capacity to send and receive voices, data and pictures at great speed. Parts of the country which can provide such facilities are becoming increasingly attractive to firms. The information technology revolution has meant that firms can link separate branches or sections of their operations by computer screen. Large firms with a Head Office in London, for example, are able to place personnel in locations hundreds of miles from the Capital. Businesses no longer need to concentrate their office staff or production in one location because of communication problems. They can also employ people working at home and contact them via the computer or fax machine.

QUESTION 5 In 1991, the shortage of suitably qualified graduates in both Germany and Switzerland prompted Schindler Lifts to expand its research and development operations to Livingston, in Scotland.

This international manufacturer of lifts and escalators is spending £500,000 on its new R&D facility. The Livingston centre will take on about 20 specialist software engineers. They will be experienced in the use of advanced computer software and artificial intelligence techniques to develop new applications.

Initially the centre will work on projects originating in Switzerland, but before long it is expected to be producing its own new generation of products for the company.

'Schindler has found a ready source of graduates in Scotland', says Gordon Aitken of the Scottish Development Agency. He believes that the demographic pressures throughout Continental Europe will make it increasingly difficult for high-tech companies such as Schindler to find and retain the right calibre of staff. 'We expect other Swiss and German firms to take advantage of Scottish skills. We now have eight universities producing computer graduates of the highest quality.'

Source : adapted from *The Observer*.

(a) What was the key factor in Schindler Lifts' decision to move to Livingston? Explain your answer.
(b) How might Schindler's decision be affected by the availability of suitable information technology allowing staff to work at home?

Government influence

Since the 1920s the government has played a role in business location. Business activity is rarely geographically balanced. There have always been regions which suffer from a lack of business and employment. Also, regions which were once prosperous have suffered when the main local industry declined. For example, the North East was hit as the shipbuilding industry declined. The North West region declined when the textile industry collapsed. In the past these have been called 'assisted areas'. The government has attempted to help with the use of REGIONAL POLICY (☞ unit 65).

During the 1960s and the 1970s 'traditional' regional policy was quite successful. It was argued that around 750,000 jobs were created during this period. The government attempted to attract businesses to these areas and restrict development in the prosperous areas. A range of incentives were offered, particularly to manufacturers. Investment grants, tax breaks, employment subsidies and rent free factory space were some examples.

The Conservative Party, elected in 1979, criticised many features of regional policy. They objected to the automatic use of investment grants and felt that the chosen 'assisted areas' were too broad. They were also committed to lower levels of government spending. In 1984, the government defined areas eligible for assistance as DEVELOPMENT AREAS and INTERMEDIATE AREAS. Development areas are regions which are the most severe in terms of decline.

These have included regions such as Merseyside and the Wirral, Wales, Tyneside, Cornwall and parts of Scotland. Intermediate areas still qualify for assistance, but do not enjoy the same benefits as development areas. Over the last decade some regions have lost their status, while others have been classed as in need of assistance. New regions, in the Midlands and the South East, have been and may be, in future, designated as assisted areas.

Further reforms have included the extension of aid to smaller businesses and to service industries. The government also helped overseas investment. For example, in 1984 Fujitsu were given a grant of £30 million to locate in Durham in the UK. In the early 1990s, examples of aid to business from central government were limited to the following.

■ Selective Regional Assistance to firms which both create jobs and protect jobs.

■ Regional Enterprise Grants for firms with fewer than 25 employees in development areas. Either an investment grant (up to £15,000) or a grant towards a new product or process innovation (at 50 per cent of costs up to a maximum of £25,000).

■ Consultancy Initiative. Firms in all assisted areas, with fewer than 500 employees, could claim two-thirds of the costs of hiring consultants.

■ ENTERPRISE ZONES have been created. This is a measure designed to revitalise inner city areas. An enterprise zone is a small geographical area, usually a few hundred acres, with the offer of financial incentives for the location of business within it. Tax incentives, reduced government 'red tape' and subsidised premises are some examples.

Many policies used by the Conservative government since 1979 have been aimed at giving incentives to business, removing market restrictions and allowing businesses freedom to make decisions. It argues that these supply side policies (☞ unit 65) are most effective in creating employment and business activity. Financial help, however, has still been given by the EC and local authorities over the period.

EC influence EC funds have been available for regional development since 1973 when the European Regional Development Fund (ERDF) was set up. In 1989, EC reforms created two extra funds.

■ European Regional Development Fund. This provides financial and other help for businesses and for infrastructure projects such as roads and telecommunications.

■ European Social Fund (ESF). This provides money for training and other schemes designed to solve labour market problems.

■ European Agricultural Guidance and Guarantee Fund (EAGGF). This fund concentrates on providing job opportunities in farming areas.

In addition, the European Investment Bank offers loans at attractive rates to firms in depressed areas. The UK has benefited from these Structural Funds in recent years. For example, between 1989 and 1993 ECU 629 million was allocated for the North West and ECU 575 million for Eastern England. Many areas that have gained are those designated assisted areas in the UK.

Local authority influence During the 1980s and 1990s local authorities spent money to help promote business. Many firms benefited as a result. Local authorities channel central government funds to businesses that need them. Sometimes this involves financial aid, but it also includes providing business services such as advice. Business can benefit from:

■ grants for business start up;
■ innovation grants;
■ job creation grants;
■ re-location grants;
■ a local business directory;
■ rent and rates free periods;
■ business advice;
■ guide to sources of finance;
■ loans to businesses.

Local government has played an important role in location in recent years. There has been a change in focus, from large firms mainly in the manufacturing sector to small and medium sized firms including the service sector. Local authorities are, perhaps, more in touch with the specific needs of the area and can judge more effectively which firms should benefit from the help available.

Industrial inertia

When businesses in the same industry locate in an area with similar firms, this is called INDUSTRIAL INERTIA. Even when the original advantages cease to exist, new firms might be attracted to the area. The textile industry, although much smaller, persists in the North West. The original attractions, coal and water, have been replaced by other power sources and the natural humidity of the area can be imitated by mechanical means. In addition, natural fibres have been replaced by synthetic materials. Firms continue to locate because of other advantages. These include a supply of skilled labour, specialist marketing and support services and a range of amenities aimed at the textile industry.

Industrial inertia does have disadvantages. When a region relies heavily on one industry it will suffer if that industry declines. One example is the demise of steel producing plants in the 1970s and 1980s, which devastated areas like Consett in Durham and many parts of South Wales. In 1993 a number of coal mines were closed down in areas where the local pit was the main employer.

QUESTION 6

Wirral Welcomes Industry . . . .

Wirral is not only an attractive setting in which to live but has distinct advantages for developing businesses.
Companies are supported with a comprehensive range of sites, premises, financial assistance, training, research and communications geared for the needs of industry.

Five good reasons for choosing Wirral
1. **Wide choice of property.**
2. **Grants to help your business.**
3. **Training and education facilities geared to the needs of your business.**
4. **Easy access to U.K. and World markets.**
5. **A desirable place to live.**

For a warm welcome
Contact
David Hunt or Graham Maddrell on
051-630 6060
Department of Economic Development
Wirral Business Centre, Dock Road, Birkenhead, Wirral L41 1JW.

 **WIRRAL**
Centre for Excellence

(a) What is the purpose of this advertisement?

(b) What assistance is likely to be available to businesses locating on the Wirral?

(c) Write a brief report to the managing director of your company explaining the advantages and disadvantages of locating an importing business on the Wirral.

Source: Department of Economic Development.

Key terms

Development areas - regions with high unemployment which qualify for government help aimed at attracting business.

Enterprise zones - small inner city areas designated by the government which qualify for financial assistance.

Footloose industries - those industries which are neither influenced by their market or the source of raw materials when deciding where to locate.

Green belt - areas designated by government, usually in agricultural areas, where the development of business is prohibited.

Green field sites - areas of land, usually on the outskirts of towns and cities, where businesses develop for the first time.

Industrial inertia - the tendency for firms in the same industry to locate in the same region even when the original locational advantages have disappeared.

Intermediate areas - similar to development areas, but not as 'economically deprived'.

Regional policy - measures used by central and local government to attract businesses to 'depressed' areas.

Summary

1. What factors influenced business location during the Industrial Revolution?

2. Under what circumstances will transport costs be particularly influential in business location?

3. State 3 types of business that will benefit from locating close to the market.

4. Give 4 methods of communication that may influence a location decision.

5. For what type of business activity is land an important factor in influencing location ?

6. Why might it be important to transfer existing employees when re-locating?

7. Give 3 problems that a business might have in transferring its existing labour force to a new location.

8. How might the geographical distribution of labour affect location?

9. Describe the help which the EC gives to businesses when locating in assisted areas in the UK.

10. What is the main disadvantage of industrial inertia?

Question

Barking Steel Fabrications

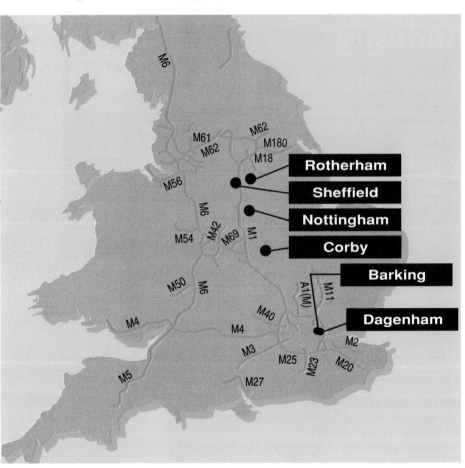

Barking Steel Fabrications is currently located in a workshop in Barking, East London. They employ 90 staff which includes 70 skilled welders. They undertake a variety of work, but in the past twelve months have enjoyed a growth in the sale of fire escapes. A lot of the new business has resulted from the appointment of a new salesperson who arrived with some useful contacts in the Nottingham area. The fire escapes are partly made up in the workshop and then transported to the site for erection. When the company was first set up in the 1960s they bought in steel from Corby steelworks near Northampton. However, following the closure of Corby they entered a contract with a Sheffield supplier. The quality of the steel was equally good but the transport costs were obviously higher. Also, with the increasing congestion on and around the M25, some deliveries had been delayed causing minor hold-ups in production. The owners of the company, Geena and Dave Parsons, had been contemplating re-location for several months. With the new orders from the Nottingham area, the workshop had become desperately overcrowded and unless some larger premises were found efficiency and quality would suffer. Geena and Dave were keen to stay in the locality because of family and social ties, but one of the two new locations under consideration was in Rotherham, just a few miles from Sheffield. Details of the two possible locations are given below.

Rotherham The premises at Rotherham were ideal in terms of size, adequate for current output and had plenty of room for expansion. Another attraction was its proximity to the Sheffield steel suppliers (8 miles) and the M1 motorway (2 miles). The area also qualified for financial assistance if a company was creating new jobs. Unemployment in the area was very high and wage rates were 20 per cent lower than in the South East. The cost of the premises was £2.1 million.

Dagenham Dagenham was less than 10 miles away from the existing base. The attraction of this new site was its proximity to the old one. There would be less disruption with a local move and the current workforce could all travel to the new premises. Indeed, 27 of them already lived in Dagenham. From a personal point of view both Geena and Dave preferred a local move. However, the cost for a slightly smaller factory unit than the one in Rotherham was £3 million.

(a) What factors led to the original site being unsuitable?
(b) Write a report describing the advantages and the disadvantages of both new sites.
(c) Under what circumstances might the Dagenham premises be favoured?
(d) If the business aims to minimise costs, which location would be the most suitable? Give reasons for your answer.

Defining size

In the UK economy there are hundreds of thousands of businesses. Their sizes vary greatly. A company like ICI has plants all over the world, employs thousands of people and has a turnover of several billion pounds. A self-employed joiner may operate in small premises, employ no other people and have a turnover no greater than a few thousand pounds. Most businesses begin on a small scale and then grow. There are strong motives for growth, but at the same time many firms remain small. What is the difference between a large firm and a small firm? When does a small firm become a large firm? Size can be measured in terms of capital employed, level of turnover, number of employees or the level of profit the firm makes. However, there is no agreement on how to measure the size of a firm.

According to the 1985 Companies Act, a firm with a turnover of less than £1.4 million is 'small'. If turnover lies between £1.4 million and £5.75 million then a firm is 'medium sized'. Firms with a turnover over £5.75 million are considered to be large. According to the same Act, firms which employ less than 50 are small and those which employ more than 250 are large.

These measures are not without problems. A highly automated chemical plant may only employ 45 staff, but enjoy a turnover of £10 million. According to the number of employees, it would be considered small. However, according to the level of turnover, it would be large, with a turnover well over £5.75 million. Using the level of profit made can also be misleading. It is possible for a very large company to make a small profit, suggesting that it is a small firm.

It is the size of the business relative to its particular sector in an industry that is important. Is it large enough to enjoy the benefits of size in the market? Is it too large or small in relation to other organisational needs of the business?

Reasons for growth

In many industries it is rare for a firm to remain exactly the same size for any length of time. Most businesses start small and then grow in size. They may aim to grow for a number of reasons.

- Survival. In some industries firms will not survive if they remain small. Staying small might mean that costs are too high because the firm is too small to exploit economies of scale. In addition, small firms, even if they are profitable, may face a takeover bid from a larger firm.
- Gaining economies of scale. As firms grow in size they will begin to enjoy the benefits of ECONOMIES OF SCALE. This means that unit production costs will fall and efficiency and profits will improve. This is dealt with later in the unit.

- To increase future profitability. By growing and selling larger volumes, a firm will hope to raise profits in the future.
- Gaining market share. This can have a number of benefits. If a firm can develop a degree of monopoly power (☞ unit 22) through growth, it might be able to raise price or control part of the market. Some personnel also enjoy the status and power associated with a high market share. For example, it could be argued that Richard Branson enjoys the publicity which goes with leading a large company like Virgin.
- To reduce risk. Risk can be reduced through diversification. Branching into new markets and new products means that if one project fails success in others can keep the company going. For example, tobacco companies have diversified into breweries to guard against a fall in demand for cigarettes.

QUESTION 1 Golden Africa Ltd is a private limited company which employs 24 staff and enjoys a turnover of £900,000. It currently specialises in long haul holidays to West Africa, Gambia and Senegal in particular. It enjoys a 7 per cent share in the long haul holiday market. In recent years it has enjoyed a 30 per cent mark-up on costs and very healthy annual profits. This year though, a number of the larger travel companies in the industry have decided to enter this market and to undercut Golden Africa's rates. The company directors have decided that diversification may be desirable and plan to organise package holidays to a number of other African destinations. The suitability of Cameroon, Ivory Coast and Mauritania is under investigation. Also, if they sell more holidays, the marketing and the administration costs are not expected to rise in proportion with the increase in sales.

(a) What evidence is there to suggest that Golden Africa Ltd is a small firm?
(b) Explain why you think that the directors have decided to grow.
(c) What risks might there be for the company in following this strategy?

Methods of growth

There are a number of ways in which a company might grow. They are shown in Figure 31.1.

Internal growth is when a firm expands without involving other businesses. ORGANIC GROWTH means that the firm expands by selling more of its existing products. This could be achieved by selling to a wider market, either at home or abroad. It is likely that internal growth will take a long time for many businesses, but will provide a sound base for development.

A quicker alternative is **external growth**. This can be by ACQUISITION or TAKEOVER of other businesses or by MERGING with them. A takeover is when one company buys control of another. A merger usually means that two companies have agreed to join together and create a new third company. In practice these terms are often used interchangeably. In recent decades merger activity has increased greatly leading to a concentration of ownership in many industries. Mergers and takeovers are discussed in unit 32.

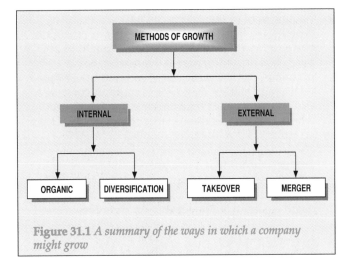

Figure 31.1 *A summary of the ways in which a company might grow*

Benefits of growth

Earlier in this unit it was argued that firms grow to achieve economies of scale. Economies of scale are the reductions in costs gained by businesses as they increase in size. Unit 10 showed that, in the long run, a firm can build another factory or purchase more machinery. This can cause the average cost of production to fall. In Figure 31.2 a firm is currently producing in a small plant and its short run costs are $SRAC_1$. When it produces an output equal to Q_1 its average cost will be AC_1. If it raises production to Q_2 average costs rise to AC_2. The rise in average costs is a result of **diminishing returns** (☞ unit 11).

If the firm expands the scale of its operations (which it

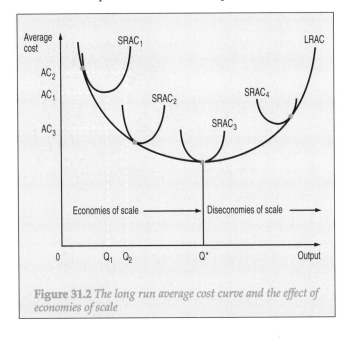

Figure 31.2 *The long run average cost curve and the effect of economies of scale*

can do in the long run) the same level of output can be produced more efficiently. With a bigger plant, represented by $SRAC_2$, Q_2 can be produced at an average cost of just AC_3. Long run average costs fall due to economies of scale and will continue to do so until the firm has built a plant which minimises long run average costs. In the diagram this occurs when a plant shown by $SRAC_3$ is built. This is sometimes called the MINIMUM EFFICIENT SCALE of plant. When output reaches Q^* in this plant, long run average costs cannot be reduced any further through expansion. Indeed, if the firm continues to grow it will experience rising average costs due to DISECONOMIES OF SCALE, as in $SRAC_4$ in Figure 31.2. This is dealt with later in the unit.

QUESTION 2 Bristol Boat Builders currently build 30 small cruisers per annum. The accountants have investigated the effect on long run costs of locating their production in bigger boat yards. The results are shown in Table 31.1.

Table 31.1 *Long run average costs for Bristol Boat Builders*

Output (cruisers)	10	20	30	40	50	60	70	80
Long run average cost (£000)	40	30	20	15	10	15	25	45

(a) Plot the long run average cost curve for Bristol Boat Builders on graph paper.
(b) How many cruisers should be built by the company? Give reasons for your answer.
(c) Over what range of output can the firm exploit economies of scale?

Internal economies of scale

What are the different economies of scale a firm can gain? INTERNAL ECONOMIES OF SCALE are the benefits of growth that arise within the firm. They occur for a number of reasons.

Technical economies Technical economies arise because larger plants are often more efficient. The capital costs and the running costs of plants do not rise in proportion to their size. For example, the capital cost of a double decker bus will not be twice that of a single decker bus. This is because the main cost (engine and chassis) does not double when the capacity of the bus doubles. Increased size may mean a doubling of output but not cost. The average cost will therefore fall. This is sometimes called the principle of **increased dimensions**. In addition, the cost of the crew and fuel will not increase in proportion to its size.

Another technical economy is that of **indivisibility**. Many firms need a particular item of equipment or machinery, but fail to make full use of it. A small business may pay £400 for a word processor. The cost will be the same whether it is used twice a week by a part time clerical worker or every day. As the business expands, more use will be made of it and so the **average cost** of the machine will fall.

As the scale of operations expands the firm may switch to mass production techniques. Flow production (☞ unit 29), which involves breaking down the production process into a very large number of small operations, allows greater use of highly specialised machinery. This results in large improvements in efficiency as labour is replaced by capital.

Firms often employ a variety of machines which have different capacities. A slow machine may increase production time. As the firm expands and produces more output, it can employ more of the slower machines in order to match the capacity of the faster machines. This is called the **law of multiples**. It involves firms finding a balanced team of machines so that when they operate together they are all running at full capacity.

Managerial economies As the firm grows it can afford to employ specialist managers. In a small business one general manager may be responsible for finance, marketing, production and personnel. The manager may find her role demanding. If a business employs specialists in these fields, efficiency may improve and average costs fall. If specialists were employed in a small firm they would be an indivisibility.

Financial economies Large firms have advantages when they try to raise finance. They will have a wider variety of sources from which to choose. For example, sole traders cannot sell more shares to raise extra funds but large public limited companies can. Very large firms will often find it easier to persuade institutions to lend them money since they will have large assets to offer as security. Finally, large firms borrowing very large amounts of money can often gain better interest rates.

In the past the government has recognised the problems facing small firms. A number of schemes have been designed to help small firms raise funds (☞ unit 8).

Purchasing and marketing economies Large firms are likely to get better rates when buying raw materials and components in bulk. In addition, the administration costs involved do not rise in proportion to the size of the order. The cost of processing an order for 10,000 tonnes of coal does not treble when 30,000 tonnes are ordered.

A number of marketing economies exist. A large company may find it cost effective to acquire its own fleet of vans and lorries, for example. The cost to the sales force of selling 30 product lines is not double that of selling 15 lines. Again, the administration costs of selling do not rise in proportion to the size of the sale. The 1990 merger of Thomson and Horizon, the package tour operators, gained them 40 per cent of the market. This allowed them to get more catalogues printed cheaper and to buy holidays in bulk from overseas.

Risk bearing economies As a firm grows it may well diversify to reduce risk. For example, many sixth form colleges have begun to offer a range of vocational courses in addition to their 'A' level courses. Also, breweries have diversified into the provision of food and other forms of

entertainment in their public houses. Large businesses can also reduce risk by carrying out research and development. The development of new products can help firms gain a competitive edge over smaller rivals.

QUESTION 3 Billy Coppock and Alex Santos are both motor mechanics operating in the same street in Oxford. Most of their customers are drawn from the same residential area. After four years of fierce competition they get together and discuss the possible advantages of forming one larger organisation in a new unit which has just become available in the next street. Billy is particularly fed up with the increasing amount of paper work while Alex admits to being intolerant of some of his customers. They approach a business consultant to help clarify the possible cost advantages.

Identify any possible
(a) marketing;
(b) risk bearing;
(c) managerial;
(d) technical;
economies of scale that could be obtained if the two firms merged.

External economies of scale

EXTERNAL ECONOMIES OF SCALE are the reductions in cost which any business in an industry might enjoy as the industry grows. External economies are more likely to arise if the industry is concentrated in a particular region.

Labour The concentration of firms may lead to the build up of a labour force equipped with the skills required by the industry. Training costs may be reduced if workers have gained skills at another firm in the same industry. Local schools and colleges, or even local government, may offer training courses which are aimed at the needs of the local industry.

Ancillary and commercial services An established industry, particularly if it is growing, tends to attract smaller firms trying to serve its needs. A wide range of commercial and support services can be offered. Specialist banking, insurance, marketing, waste disposal, maintenance, cleaning, components and distribution services are just some examples.

Co-operation Firms in the same industry are more likely to cooperate if they are concentrated in the same region. They might join forces to fund a research and development centre for the industry. An industry journal might be published, so that information can be shared.

Disintegration Disintegration occurs when production is broken up so that more specialisation can take place. When an industry is concentrated in an area firms might specialise in the production of one component and then transport it to a main assembly car plant. In the West Midlands a few large car assembly plants exist whilst there are many supporting firms, such as Lucas, manufacturing components ready for assembly.

The limits to growth

There are a number of factors which might limit the growth of business. If a firm expands the scale of its operations beyond the minimum efficient scale DISECONOMIES OF SCALE may result, leading to rising long run average costs.

Most **internal diseconomies** are caused by the problem of managing large businesses. Communication becomes more complicated and co-ordination more difficult because a large firm is divided into departments. The control of large businesses is also demanding. Thousands of employees, billions of pounds and dozens of plants all mean added responsibility and more supervision. Morale may suffer as individual workers become a minor part of the total workforce. This can cause poor relations between management and the workforce. As shown in Figure 31.2, long run average costs start to rise once a business reaches a certain size. Technical diseconomies also arise. In the chemical industry, construction problems often mean that two smaller plants are more cost effective than one very large one. Also, if a firm employs one huge plant

and a breakdown occurs, production will stop. With two smaller plants, production can continue even if one breaks down.

External diseconomies might also arise. These may occur from overcrowding in industrial areas. The price of land, labour, services and materials might rise as firms compete for a limited amount. Congestion might lead to inefficiency, as travelling workers and deliveries are delayed.

There are other constraints on the growth of firms.

- Market limitations. The market for high performance power boats is limited due to their high market price, for example. Also, unless a firm is a monopoly, growth will tend to be restricted due to the existence of competitors in the market.
- Lack of funds. Many small firms would like to grow, but are not able to attract enough investors or lenders.
- Geographical limitations. Some products are low value and bulky. High transport costs may discourage the firm from distributing to customers far away. This means it cannot grow. Bread, beer and crisps may fall into this category. However, with improved communication networks, national distributors of these products have entered the market. Also, the provision of services is often limited to local markets. For example, people are not likely to travel very far to have their hair cut.

Reasons for the survival of small firms

Despite the advantages of large scale production, many firms choose to remain small. Also, small firms sometimes have advantages over larger ones.

Personal service As a firm expands it becomes increasingly difficult to deal with individuals. Many people prefer to do business with the owner of the company directly and are prepared to pay higher prices for the privilege. For example, people may prefer to deal directly with one of the partners in an accountancy practice.

Owner's preference Some entrepreneurs may be content with the current level of profits. Some will want to avoid the added responsibilities that growth brings. Others will want to remain below the VAT threshold or will not want to risk losing control of their business.

Flexibility and efficiency Small firms are more flexible and innovative. They may be able to react more quickly to changes in market conditions or technology. Management can make decisions quickly, without following lengthy procedures.

Lower costs In some cases small firms might have lower costs than larger producers in the same market. For example, large firms often have to pay their employees nationally agreed wage rates. A small firm may be able to pay lower wages to non-union workers.

Low barriers to entry In some types of business activity like grocery, painting and decorating, gardening services and window cleaning, the set up costs are relatively low. There is little to stop competitors setting up in business.

Small firms can be monopolists Many small firms survive because they supply a service to members of the local community which no other business does. People often use their local shop because it provides a convenient, nearby service, saving them the trouble of travelling. The local shop is often open at times when its larger competitors are shut, late in the evening and on Sundays for example.

The popularity of small firms in the economy

During the 1980s there has been a significant growth in the number of small firms in the economy. At the start of 1990 there were 2.9 million small firms - firms with less than 20 employees. Self-employment has grown from less than 2 million in 1979 to over 3 million in 1992. What factors have led to this trend?

- Rising unemployment has had an important impact. People with redundancy payments have had the capital to set up in business. In some cases unemployed workers saw self-employment as the only means of support.
- The government and local authorities have introduced a number of measures to encourage the development of small businesses. For example, the **Enterprise Allowance Scheme** (☞ unit 8) was specifically designed to give financial help to unemployed people who set up in business. The rate of corporation tax on small companies was reduced. Local authorities provided special advisory services for small businesses. The government deliberately attempted to foster an 'enterprise culture' during the 1980s.
- There have been changes in the structure of the economy in recent years. The expansion of the tertiary sector has contributed to the growth in small businesses. Many services can be undertaken more effectively on a small scale.

The growth in the number of small firms has had several effects on the economy.

- Increased flexibility. Smaller firms can adapt to change more quickly because the owners, who tend to be the key decision makers, are close at hand to react to change. For example, a customer may insist that the extension to her house is finished one week before the agreed time. The business owner can put in the extra hours required and perhaps encourage employees to help out. Business owners may also react quickly when some new technology becomes available. This increased flexibility might help the UK economy win more orders from abroad.
- It could be argued that wage levels might fall as a result of more smaller firms. Employees in small businesses often negotiate their own wage rates with the owner. Since they are not in a powerful position on a one to one basis, there may be a tendency for initial wage rates and future wage increases to be relatively lower. This will help to keep business costs down.
- More casual and part time work may have been created. Small firms are often reluctant to employ full time staff because it is more expensive. For example, part time workers may not be entitled to the same level of holiday pay as full time workers. Casual and part time staff also help to improve flexibility. When a business is quiet it can lay off casual staff to reduce costs.
- Staff loyalty may have been improved. In small businesses, relationships between the owners and other staff may be quite good because they are dealing with each other at a personal level. This might improve motivation and productivity as well as staff loyalty.
- Trade union membership may have declined. In small businesses where relatively fewer workers are employed, trade union membership tends to be lower. This might have implications for the rights of workers in small businesses. It might lead to claims that in some cases, staff are being exploited by small business owners.
- Consumers might benefit from the growth in the number of small firms. More small firms often results in more competition and a wider choice in the market. For example, there has been a growth in the number of computer software producers in recent years. This has led to a variety of 'games' and programs for business and personal use.

QUESTION 4 Gerald and Pamela Watson own the only fish and chip shop in Woodstock, a small town in Oxfordshire. They have run the business for 21 years and have always enjoyed their life. The business generates a profit of about £16,000 a year, although this is not a large amount of money the couple find it acceptable. Most of their custom is from locals who over the years have grown to enjoy the service supplied by Gerald and Pamela. Ten years ago they did consider expanding. They looked into the possibility of running a mobile fish and chip shop, supplying the numerous local villages in the area with an evening service. In the end they decided not to. The local bank would only lend them money if they put up their own home as security. They also thought that the likelihood of any competition in the future was remote. Consequently, they decided to continue as they were.

(a) Why do you think that this small business has survived for so long?
(b) What is likely to have prevented Gerald and Pamela from expanding their business?

Key terms

Diseconomies of scale - rising long run average costs as a firm expands beyond its minimum efficient scale.
Economies of scale - the reductions in cost gained by firms as they grow.
External economies of scale - the cost reductions available to all firms as the industry grows.
Internal economies of scale - the cost reductions enjoyed by a single firm as it grows.

Merger - the joining together of two businesses, usually to create a third new company.
Minimum efficient scale (MES) - the output which minimises long run average costs.
Organic growth - growth achieved through the expansion of current business activities.
Takeover/acquisition - the purchase of one business by another.

Summary

1. How can the size of a firm be measured?
2. State 5 reasons for growth.
3. What is the difference between internal and external growth?
4. A business aiming to expand quickly would prefer external growth. Explain this statement.
5. What are the main sources of: (i) internal economies; (ii) external economies; (iii) diseconomies; of scale?
6. Explain 5 reasons why small firms survive.
7. Describe 5 limitations to growth.
8. Why has there been a growth in the number of small firms in recent years?
9. What effect will the growth in the small firms sector have on the flexibility of employers?

Question

Gloria's Health Centre

Gloria Peterson invested her life savings into a small business venture seven years ago. She opened a small health and fitness centre offering a range of facilities to members who joined. The centre was located in Chelmsford in Essex. It was equipped with a small swimming pool, a solarium, a sauna, a multi-gym, a steam room, a dance room and a bar with lounge facilities.

Gloria currently employs three part time staff who are responsible for the reception area and the bar. She also pays a local PE teacher to supervise aerobics and step aerobics sessions three times a week. Gloria runs dance sessions two evenings per week and supervises activities in the multi-gym. She also employs a part-time maintenance worker and a cleaner who works two hours a day. The centre is particularly busy during the school holidays, so Gloria employs two young students to help out whenever they are needed.

Revenue is generated through membership fees which are £250 per annum. In the last four years, membership has been constant at around 1,000, the majority being females within a five mile radius of Chelmsford, although male membership was starting to increase. Once the annual fee has been paid, members have access to all of the centre's facilities free of charge. Gloria generates a modest amount of turnover from bar sales. Recently, some members

asked Gloria if she would organise a special social evening offering a buffet and some entertainment. The evening was very popular and became a regular feature at the centre. Gloria was always responsive to members' suggestions and requests.

In the last financial year Gloria made a profit of £79,000. Driven by her success she was very keen to expand. Her current location was perfect. The centre was very accessible with ample public parking facilities. However, she felt that a membership of around 1,000 was as many as the centre could comfortably accommodate without becoming too crowded. Gloria believed that in order to grow she would have to open another centre in a nearby town. As she lived just outside Chelmsford, in Broomfield, she was looking for somewhere that was within travelling distance. Three possibilities were Braintree, Witham and Brentwood.

(a) Why do you think that this small business has been successful?
(b) What examples of flexibility are there in the case?
(c) What are Gloria's motives for growth?
(d) What problems might Gloria encounter when trying to expand?
(e) What economies of scale might Gloria be able to exploit if she opens another centre?

Reasons for mergers and takeovers

Mergers and takeovers (☞ unit 31) take place when firms join together and operate as one organisation. Why do some businesses act in this way?

■ It is a quick and easy way to expand the business. For example, if a supermarket chain wanted to open another twenty stores in the UK, it could find sites and build new premises. A quicker way would be to buy a company that already owns some stores and convert them.

■ Buying a business is often cheaper than growing internally. A firm may calculate that the cost of internal growth is £80 million. However, it might be possible to buy another company for £55 million on the stock market. The process of buying the company might inflate its price, but it could still work out much cheaper.

■ Some firms have cash available which they want to use. Buying another business is one way of doing this.

■ Mergers have taken place for defensive reasons. A firm might buy another to consolidate its position in the market. Also, if a firm can increase its size through merging, it may avoid being the victim of a takeover itself.

■ In recent years some mergers have taken place to prepare for the Single European Market (☞ unit 70). For example, a merger took place between the publishers Reed of the UK and Elsevier of the

Netherlands in 1992. This was mainly to develop an international business.

■ A business may want to gain economies of scale (☞ unit 31). Firms can often lower their costs by joining with another firm. This is dealt with later in this unit.

■ Some firms are **asset strippers**. They buy a company, sell off profitable parts, close down unprofitable sections and perhaps integrate other activities into the existing business.

■ Management may want to increase the size of the company. This is because the growth of the business is their main objective (☞ unit 5).

Merger activity

During the 1980s many mergers took place. Indeed, some say that there was a 'takeover binge' during the decade. Why did merger and takeover activity rise so dramatically?

■ The financial sector became more competitive. There was a large supply of funds ready to back merger activity. For example, the Unlisted Securities Market (USM) was introduced to help supply stock market funds to smaller businesses which did not want to become full stock market members. Also, institutions were perhaps more prepared to take risks than they were in the early 1990s recession.

■ The government's attitude. During the decade there was a wider acceptance of takeovers and a growth in support for them. The government aimed for an 'enterprise culture', for example, by encouraging share ownership. This may have helped firms fund takeover activity through share issues. There was also a 'hands off' approach to mergers, to encourage international competitiveness.

■ Before the 1980s takeovers had a poor image. They were thought of as aggressive and possibly unethical. This may have been due to the fact that some firms were taken over against their will. Also, merger activity often resulted in larger business organisations and consumers might be exploited. During the 1980s these fears did not seem to be as important.

Types of merger or integration

As Figure 32.1 shows, mergers can be classed in a number of ways. Not all mergers fit neatly into these categories, however. HORIZONTAL INTEGRATION occurs when two firms which are in exactly the same line of business and the same stage of production join together. An example of a horizontal merger was the joining together of BSB (owned by a consortium of firms) and Sky TV, (owned by Rupert Murdoch). They joined to form BSkyB, the satellite TV broadcasting company. This type of merger allowed greater economies of scale and market share.

QUESTION 1 In 1992, United Biscuits (UB), the biscuits and snacks group acquired Bake-Line, a private company making own-label cookies, for £47 million.

Sir Robert Clarke, UB chairman, said the purchase would 'not dilute UB's earnings in the short term and there would be merger benefits further out'.

Bake-Line should strengthen the position of Keebler, UB's branded cookie, cracker and snack subsidiary in the US. Keebler suffered a sharp drop in profits in 1992 as consumers switched to cheaper, often own-label, cookies.

Keebler had not moved into the own-label sector, although this area has been growing rapidly in the US in recent years, following a similar trend in the UK. In Britain, UB, which has the McVitie's own brand, is the leading own-label biscuit producer. Bake-Line has 25 per cent share of the own label sector in the US.

Bake-Line, based in Chicago, has a modern factory with 40 per cent spare capacity. Benefits should come from joint purchasing, distribution, technology and the use Keebler can make of Bake-Line's spare capacity.

Source: adapted from the *Financial Times*, 1992.

(a) What might have been the motives for the merger described above?
(b) What is meant by the phrase 'there would be merger benefits further out'?

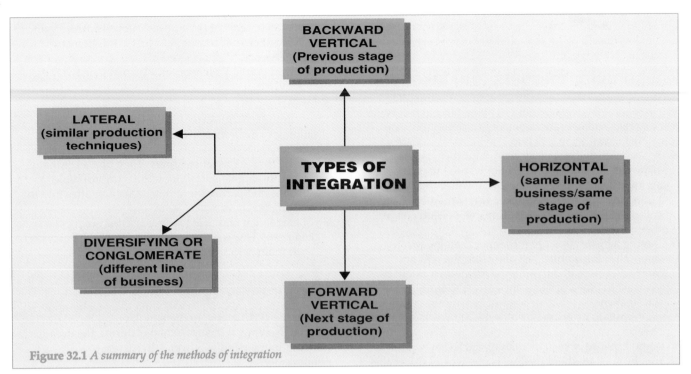

Figure 32.1 *A summary of the methods of integration*

VERTICAL INTEGRATION can be FORWARD VERTICAL INTEGRATION and BACKWARD VERTICAL INTEGRATION. Consider a firm which manufactures and assembles mountain bikes. If it were to acquire a firm which was a supplier of tyres for the bikes, this would be an example of backward vertical integration. The two firms are at different stages of production. The main motives for such a merger are to guarantee and control the supply of components and raw materials and to remove the profit margin the supplier would demand. Forward vertical integration involves merging with a firm which is in the next stage of production rather than the previous stage. For example, the mountain bike manufacturer may merge with a retail outlet selling bikes. Again this eliminates the profit margin expected by the firm in the next stage of production. It also gives the manufacturer confidence when planning production, knowing that there are retail outlets in which to sell. Vertical mergers are rare. In 1990 they accounted for only 5 per cent of all mergers in the UK.

LATERAL INTEGRATION involves the merging of two firms with related goods which do not compete directly with each other. Production technique or perhaps the distribution channels may be similar. Cadbury-Schweppes is an example. The two companies used similar raw materials and had similar markets.

There are strong motives for firms in completely different lines of business to join together. This type of merger is called a CONGLOMERATE or DIVERSIFYING MERGER. A firm might fear a loss of market share due to greater competition. As a result they may try to explore new and different opportunities. One very large conglomerate is Hanson Trust.

Takeovers

Takeovers amongst **public limited companies** (☞ unit 3) are common in today's business world. In the UK at its peak in 1988, expenditure by companies on acquisitions and mergers was almost £23 billion. One business can acquire another by purchasing its shares on the stock market. Once 51 per cent of the shares have been bought, the company is then under the control of the purchaser. For example, in March 1993 EFM Dragon, the UK investment group, claimed control of Drayton Asia by purchasing 51 per cent of its share holding. When a takeover takes place, the company that has been 'bought' loses its identity and becomes part of the **predator** company.

In practice, a firm can take control of another company by buying much less than 51 per cent of the shares. This may happen when share ownership is widely spread and little communication takes place between shareholders. In some cases a predator can take control of a company by purchasing as little as 15 per cent of the total share issue. For example, in February 1993, the advertising group Saatchi and Saatchi backed their chief executive Robert

---

QUESTION 2 A potato crisp manufacturer has recently experienced problems in receiving supplies. It has been suggested that one solution to this problem is for the business to acquire a potato farm and control production, so that supplies can be delivered when required.

(a) Explain what type of merger would take place if the businesses joined together.
(b) Describe the problems the merged business might encounter once the acquisition is made.

Louis-Dreyfus in his takeover of Adidas, the sports goods giant. Dreyfus allegedly took a 15 per cent stake in Adidas which gave him control.

Once a company has bought 3 per cent of another it must make a declaration to the stock market. This is a legal requirement designed to ensure that the existing shareholders are aware of the situation. Often a takeover bid leads to a sharp rise in the victim's share price. This is due to the volume of buying by the predator and also speculation by investors. Once it is known that a takeover is likely, investors scramble to buy shares, anticipating a quick, sharp price rise.

Sometimes more than one firm might attempt to take over a company. This can result in very sharp increases in the share price as the two buyers bid up the price. An example was the takeover of the York based confectioner Rowntree in 1988. Nestlé and Suchard, two other confectioners, bid for the company. Rowntree's share price increased from 477p to 1075p during the' battle'. Nestlé eventually won control of Rowntree.

Sometimes takeovers or mergers result in situations which may be against consumers' interests. As a result, the Department of Trade and Industry might instruct the Monopolies and Mergers Commission to investigate the merger (☞ unit 73). Mergers may be investigated if the combined value of the company's assets exceeds £30 million. This may result, in extreme cases, in the government preventing the merger from taking place. For example, in September 1992, the commission prevented an attempt by Bond Helicopters to take over British International Helicopters, part of Robert Maxwell's private empire which went into receivership in December 1991.

Hostile and friendly takeovers

Takeovers can be **hostile** or **friendly**. A hostile takeover means that the victim tries to resist the bid. Resistance is usually by the board of directors. They attempt to persuade the shareholders that their interests would be best protected if the company remains under the control of the existing board of directors. Shareholders then have to weigh up the advantages and disadvantages of a new 'owner'.

A takeover may be invited. A firm might be struggling because it has cash flow problems (☞ unit 44), for example. It might want the current business activity to continue, but under the control of another, stronger company. The new company would inject some cash in exchange for control. Such a company is sometimes referred to as a 'white knight'.

The mergers and takeovers described above all refer to public limited companies. It is possible for private limited companies to be taken over. However, an unwanted takeover cannot take place since the shares in private limited companies are not widely available.

QUESTION 3 At the beginning of 1993, Owners Abroad, a package tour operator, was the subject of a takeover bid by Airtours. Airtours were the third largest package holiday company in the UK at the time. They believed that a takeover would have left the combined company with 26 per cent of the UK holiday market and would have made it 'a significant force in the UK travel industry' according to Airtour's chairman.

In January, a £221 million bid was put in for all shares, but this was rejected as being too low. In March 1993 the Owners Abroad shareholders finally voted to reject any takeover bid for the company.

Source: adapted from the *Financial Times*, 7.1.1993

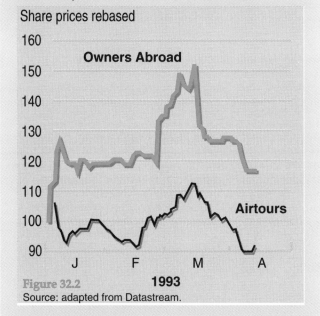

Figure 32.2   **1993**
Source: adapted from Datastream.

(a) Explain why the Owners Abroad share price might have behaved as shown in the graph.
(b) What possible motive might have existed for an investigation by the Monopolies and Mergers Commission into the above takeover bid?

QUESTION 4 In January 1992, Steetley, the aggregates and bricks group, was fighting a bid from Redland, a construction company. Steetley insisted that it was not looking for a 'white knight' to help fend off the bid and that the company was fighting only for its independence.

In its defence document, Steetley accused Redland of spoiling tactics in launching a bid to pre-empt Steetley's planned joint venture with Tarmac in brick manufacturing. The document emphasised its own strong financial record and claimed that its profit prospects were better than Redland's, once the industry recovered from the recession.

Despite this the takeover finally went through in mid-1992 for an estimated £613 million.

Source: adapted from *The Independent on Sunday*, 5.1.1992.

(a) To what extent is Redland's bid for Steetley friendly or unfriendly?
(b) What is meant by the phrase 'it was not looking for a white knight'?
(c) What evidence is there to suggest that Steetley's shareholders should be happy for the company to retain its independence?

Asset stripping

Some takeovers in recent years have resulted in ASSET STRIPPING. The asset stripper aims to buy another company at a market price which is lower than the value of the firm's total assets. It then sells off the profitable parts of the business and closes down those which are unprofitable. Such activity has often been criticised since it leads to unemployment in those sections which are closed down and generates a degree of uncertainty. Hanson Trust were allegedly criticised for their activity following the £3.3 billion purchase of Consolidated Gold in 1989. Within one year of the acquisition Hanson had sold off £1.03 billion worth of profitable assets.

Mergers and economies of scale

One of the motives for merging suggested that costs would be lower if two firms joined together. This is because when firms increase their size they can gain **economies of scale**. The effect on unit costs of increasing the scale of the business is dealt with in unit 31. It is likely that horizontal mergers will benefit most from economies of scale. For example, if two banks whose operations are similar merge together in one high street, costs can be reduced by closing down one of the branches.

A study by Professor Dennis Mueller (1980) investigated the effects on efficiency of over 800 mergers in seven countries. He found that mergers were unlikely to be undertaken to gain economies of scale. The researchers argued that small firms would gain most from mergers. However, in nearly every single case the firm initiating the merger was larger than the average for the industry. Research by Professor Keith Cowling (1980) tends to support this view. He investigated horizontal mergers and traced a range of performance indicators of the merged companies for 7 years. The study concluded that in no case were gains in efficiency greater than gains by similar firms which did not merge. Some evidence suggested that efficiency actually worsened. This may have been caused by a number of factors.

- The profits of the combined company declining from what they might have been in the absence of merger.
- A fall in turnover due to reduced capacity. Mergers often result in the 'rationalisation' of plant and other facilities and thus a loss in capacity.
- In the economy, unemployment may rise as a result of rationalisation.

Joint ventures

An alternative to a formal merger is a JOINT VENTURE. This is where two or more companies share the cost, responsibility and profits of a business venture. The financial arrangements between the companies involved will tend to differ, although many joint ventures between two firms involve a 50:50 share of costs and profits. There are many examples of joint ventures. In 1992, Forte formed a joint venture with part of Italy's state-owned

Agip. The venture, called Agip Forte International (AFI), planned to operate 18 hotels in Italy. In 1993, Richard Branson's Virgin group announced a joint venture with Blockbuster Entertainment, the Florida based video rental company. The venture involved plans to build music mega-stores in every large US city and throughout most of Europe. There are a number of advantages of joint ventures.

- They allow companies to enjoy some of the advantages of mergers, such as growth of turnover, without having to lose their identity.
- Businesses can specialise in a particular aspect of the venture in which they have experience. For example, in 1993 Unilever entered a joint venture with BSN of France, to make and market certain products worldwide. The venture enabled Unilever to specialise in ice cream and BSN in yoghurt. Both companies are world leaders in the two products.
- Takeovers are expensive. Heavy legal and administrative costs are often incurred. Also, the amount of money required to take over another company is sometimes unknown.
- Mergers and takeovers are often unfriendly. Most joint ventures are friendly. The companies commit their funds and share responsibility. Such an attitude may help to improve the success of the venture.
- Competition may be eliminated. If companies co-operate in a joint venture they are less likely to

---

QUESTION 5 During the early 1990s the aero-engine industry suffered a spiralling decline in demand. Companies in the industry had been faced with a triple problem:

- post-cold war cuts in military spending;
- the collapse of passenger travelling following the Gulf war;
- the escalating cost of developing new products.

The three big aero-engine companies - Rolls Royce, General Electric (GE), and Pratt and Whitney - responded to the recession with massive job cuts and restructuring. They had all invested in joint ventures with smaller companies. GE was working with Snecma in France, Pratt with the aero-engine arm of Germany's Motoren-und-Turbinen Union and Rolls with BMW. These partnerships helped spread the cost of research and development into larger engines.

It was suggested that the 'Big Three' should work more closely together to help 'ride out' the recession. Previously they had only worked together on minor projects. Rolls Royce were against co-operation with the other two, arguing that alone they could grab 30 per cent of the market by the end of the decade. Paul Ruddle, a sector analyst, believed that demand was not big enough for all three, although it was difficult to decide who was the most vulnerable. Rolls were the smallest but had the technical edge in the market.

Source : adapted from *The Guardian*, 4.9.1992.

(a) How might Rolls Royce have benefited from a joint venture with the other two large aero-engine companies?
(b) Explain why Rolls Royce were reluctant to invest in such a venture.

compete with each other. However, the venture must not restrict competition to such an extent that consumers' interests are harmed. For example, in 1993 Allied-Lyons the food and drinks giant, set up a joint venture with Carlsberg, the Danish brewer. The Monopolies and Mergers Commission laid down a number of conditions which the two companies had to satisfy in order for the venture to be approved.

There are some disadvantages to joint ventures:

■ Some joint ventures fail to achieve the desired results. They are often compromises when an all-out takeover would be better. There may be control struggles. For example, who should have the final say in a 50:50 joint venture?

■ It is possible for disagreements to occur about the management of the joint venture. As with any partnership, sometimes there are different views on which course of action to take.

■ The profit from the venture is obviously split between the investors. A company might regret this if it became evident at a later date that a particular venture could have been set up by itself.

Demerging

The early 1990s saw DEMERGERS taking place. This is where a company sells off a significant part of its existing operations. A company might choose to break up to:

■ raise cash to invest in remaining sections;
■ concentrate its efforts on a narrower range of activities;
■ avoid rising costs and inefficiency through being too large:
■ take advantage of the fact that the company has a higher share valuation when split into two components than it does when operating as one.

In 1993, ICI, the UKs largest manufacturer, demerged. A new company called Zeneca was 'spun-off'. ICI retained the paints, industrial chemicals, explosives, materials and regional businesses, whilst Zeneca took the pharmaceuticals, specialities and the agrochemical branches. Both Sir Denys Henderson, ICI chairman, and Ronnie Hampel, chief executive, had become very concerned that if ICI might become a 'corporate dinosaur'.

They argued that a demerger would result in two powerful companies, able to strengthen their leading positions in world markets.

In the early 1990s, Racal Electronics demerged two parts of its operations. In 1991, Racal 'spun-off' Vodaphone and in 1992 it demerged Chubb, a lock and security business. The cash raised by Racal from the demerger helped to improve its financial performance. Following the demerger of Vodaphone the City had predicted that Racal shares would eventually trade at 30p. In July 1992 they were trading for 69p - perhaps an indication of the demerger's success.

Key terms

> **Asset stripping** - the selling off of profitable sections and closing down of loss making sections of a business following an acquisition.
> **Backward vertical integration** - merging with a firm involved with the previous stage of production.
> **Conglomerate or diversifying merger** - the merging of firms involved in completely different business activities.
> **Demerger** - where a business splits into two separate organisations.
> **Forward vertical integration** - merging with a firm involved with the next stage of production.
> **Horizontal integration** - the merging of firms which are in exactly the same line of business.
> **Joint venture** - two firms sharing the cost, responsibility and profits of a business venture.
> **Lateral integration** - the merging of firms involved in the production of similar goods, but not in competition with each other.

Summary

1. Why might firms choose to join together?
2. What factors gave rise to the significant increase in takeovers and mergers in the 1980s?
3. Why might external growth be quicker than internal growth?
4. Give 2 examples of:
   (a) horizontal integration;
   (b) vertical integration;
   (c) lateral integration.
5. Why might a firm diversify?
6. Briefly explain how an acquisition is carried out.
7. Why is asset stripping often criticised?
8. Explain why mergers might not result in an improvement in efficiency.
9. What is the difference between a joint venture and a merger?
10. What might be the advantages of demergers?

Question

Grattan Mail Order Subsidiary

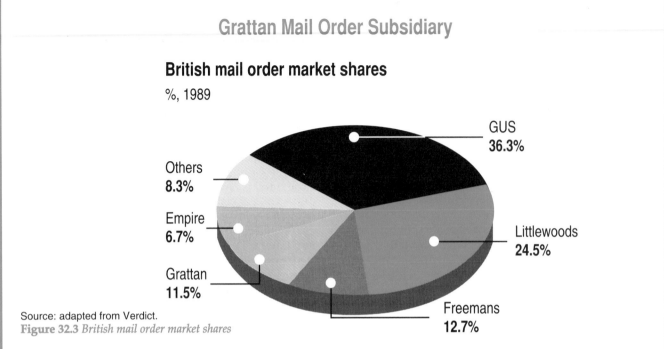

British mail order market shares

%, 1989

Source: adapted from Verdict.

Figure 32.3 *British mail order market shares*

In 1991, a battle broke out between Otto-Versand, the German based mail-order group, and Sears, best known for the Selfridges retail chain. Both companies wanted to buy Next's mail-order subsidiary, Grattan. Sears offered Next £150 million cash which was £10 million more than Otto-Versand had offered in an earlier deal.

Senior executives from Next met in Hamburg to negotiate a price with Otto-Versand. There was even speculation that Otto-Versand might bid for the whole of Next, rather than just Grattan, especially if an auction drove the Grattan asking price up further. Indeed, Otto-Versand revealed earlier that they had taken a 3 per cent stake in Next which could be upped to 10 per cent. However, it was stated that the stake in Next and the bid for Grattan were not linked.

It was also believed that Sears had a 2.9 per cent stake in Next, but had no intention of bidding for the group and inheriting its problems. Next had an estimated loss of around £222 million for the year.

Sears claimed that their offer to Next was on the same terms and conditions as Otto-Versand's. These included offering warehousing facilities for the Next Directory, Next's upmarket mail order business, which would continue to be managed by Next. Sears' chairman explained that Grattan would help Sears on the direct mail side and offer economies of scale when joined to Freemans, their existing mail-order catalogue. The chairman also pointed out that apart from the higher price the Sears bid avoided the need for clearance from the European Commission, which the Otto-Versand deal would need.

If Sears won Grattan, they would have owned around 25 per cent of the UK mail order market.

However, it was thought that the Monopolies and Mergers Commission would not investigate, since larger market shares were held by Littlewoods and GUS.

City analysts expected the battle for Grattan to be a keen one with the price rising further. They suggested that Grattan is of considerable industrial importance to both bidders. Sears wants the economies of scale and the very modern warehousing facilities while Otto-Versand wanted an entry into the UK market which they had been watching for a long time. Grattan was eventually sold to Otto-Versand for £165 million.

Source: adapted from *The Independent*, January 1991 and updated.

(a) Why might:
(i) Sears;
(ii) Otto-Versand;
have wanted to acquire Grattan?
(b) How might economies of scale have helped Sears' direct mailing?
(c) What might have been the effect on Next's share price of the battle for Grattan between Otto-Versand and Sears?
(d) Explain why the Monopolies and Mergers Commission might not have investigated the merger if Sears had won Grattan?
(e) Identify the possible arguments against a merger from Grattan's point of view.

Managing materials

Businesses purchase raw materials, semi-finished goods and components. A washing machine manufacturer, for example, may buy electric motors, circuit boards, rubber drive belts, nuts, bolts, sheet metal and a variety of metal and plastic components. These stocks of materials and components are used to produce products which are then sold to consumers and other businesses. Managing the materials is an important part of any business. Materials management involves:

■ the purchasing of stocks and their delivery;
■ the storing and control of stocks;
■ the issue and handling of stocks;
■ the disposal of surpluses;
■ providing information about stocks.

Purchasing

Purchasing involves the buying of materials, components, fuel, tools, machinery, equipment, stationery and services by the business. It also includes any method that allows the firm to obtain the goods and services it needs, such as hiring.

The various stages in the purchasing process are shown in Figure 33.1. Purchasing usually begins when the purchasing department is notified of a particular need. For example, a firm's stores or a particular department may send a **requisition form** asking for more stationery. The purchasing department will then act on this. Most purchases are repeat purchases from regular suppliers. Orders are placed with the supplier at previously agreed prices and delivery accepted under previously arranged terms. New products may need different materials and new suppliers. This will involve a period of search and negotiation, as the buyer trys to find the best deal. If there is a delay in delivery, it is the purchasing department's responsibility to find out why and speed up delivery. Once the goods have arrived the invoice is checked and then payment can be made.

In manufacturing the purchasing department works closely with the production and finance departments. Most purchasing is carried out on behalf of the production department. The finance department needs information about purchases to make payments and record the transactions.

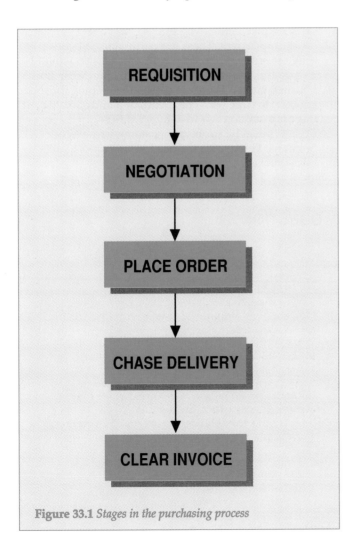

Figure 33.1 *Stages in the purchasing process*

The importance of purchasing

The importance of purchasing is likely to vary according to the nature and size of the business. In many service industries purchasing is not very important. This is because materials are only a small fraction of the total cost of the final product. For example, hairdressing involves very little purchasing, as production involves a skill and uses few materials. However, a large manufacturer requires a large amount of materials, components etc. and so the firm will employ a purchasing department made up of specialists. In order for the firm to remain competitive the department must obtain the best quality materials, at least cost, and the quickest delivery. Failure to do so may lead to increased cost. The objectives of the purchasing department are:

■ to obtain the quality and quantity of goods and materials that the firm requires;
■ to purchase goods and materials at the most competitive prices;
■ to ensure speedy delivery;
■ to arrange delivery at the appropriate site, gate or location;
■ to choose reliable suppliers and maintain good relations with them.

QUESTION 1
The Croydon Furniture Centre manufactures a variety of household furniture and supplies small retailers in the South East. It has established a reputation for speedy delivery and favourable prices. The company is about to begin manufacturing a new line of sofa and requires some fabric for covering. The purchasing manager has identified three possible suppliers. Details of their terms are shown in Table 33.1.

Table 33.1 *Prices and terms of delivery from three fabric suppliers*

Supplier	Delivery time	Cost per metre	Delivery charge per 200 metres
Crawfords (Bradford)	2wks	£2	£100
Batemans (Oldham)	3wks	£1.80	£80
Jones (London)	3days	£2.10	£30

(a) Calculate the total cost of purchasing 200 metres per month, for one year, from each supplier.
(b) Using your answers in (a), which supplier would you choose if your aim was to minimise cost?
(c) How might your answer in (b) be different if you take into account non-financial factors?

Centralised and decentralised purchasing

In some businesses, **centralised purchasing** is used. This is where the purchasing for the whole business is carried out by one department. The advantage of this method is that **economies of scale** can be gained as large scale buyers enjoy lower rates and market power. Also, the same quality and standard of materials can be set throughout the business. The distribution and warehousing of supplies can also be better planned.

Decentralised purchasing may reduce the cost and burden of administration. Purchasing officers in each department may be more in touch with the needs of that department. In retailing, if purchasing is undertaken by each store manager, the needs of each store can be better catered for. The added responsibility might also motivate store managers.

The nature of stocks

Businesses prefer to minimise stock holding because it is costly. In practice a variety of stocks are held, for different reasons.

- Raw materials and components. These are purchased from suppliers before production. They are stored by firms to cope with changes in production levels. Delays in production can be avoided if materials and components can be supplied from stores rather than waiting for a new delivery to arrive. Also, if a company is let down by suppliers it can use stocks to carry on production.
- Work-in-progress. These are partly finished goods. In a TV assembly plant, WORK IN PROGRESS would be TVs on the assembly line, which are only partly built.
- Finished goods. The main reason for keeping finished goods is to cope with changes in demand and stock. If there is a sudden rise in demand, a firm can meet urgent orders by supplying customers from stock holdings. This avoids the need to step up production rates quickly.

Stocks are listed as current assets (☞ unit 39) in the

QUESTION 2
McPhersons Ltd is a chain of twenty butchers operating in Scotland and the North of England. Its head office is attached to the shop located in Leeds. All the purchasing is currently undertaken at head office and the meat is delivered in bulk to a warehouse in Leeds. The firm employs a driver to distribute orders to the various shops twice a week. The board of directors is considering the decentralisation of the purchasing function, since the discounts from bulk buying are not particularly significant.

If decentralisation takes place each shop manager will receive a £2,000 p.a. salary increase. The discounts lost from bulk buying are expected to total £20,000 p.a. Cold storage, handling and distribution costs are expected to fall by £50,000 in total and administration costs will be £5,000 lower in total. It is expected that the quality of the meat will improve when purchasing is the responsibility of the shop managers.

(a) Advise the company whether or not decentralisation is a worthwhile change in operational policy, in purely financial terms.
(b) Explain the non-financial advantages and disadvantages to McPhersons of decentralising purchasing.

QUESTION 3

(a) From the above photograph identify examples of
    (i) stocks of raw materials;
    (ii) work-in-progress;
    (iii) stocks of finished goods.
(b) Explain the need for each type of stock.

firm's balance sheet. Stocks are fairly liquid business resources and the firm would normally expect to convert them into cash within one year. They are also part of working capital (☞ unit 44) .

Normally, at least once every year, a business will perform a **stock take**. This involves recording the amount and value of stocks which the firm is holding. The stock take is necessary to help determine the value of total purchases during the year for a firm's accounts. A physical stock take can be done manually by identifying every item of stock on the premises. Many firms have details of stock levels recorded on computer. **Stock valuation** is discussed in unit 43.

The cost of holding stocks

In recent years stock management has become more important for many firms. Careful control of stock levels can improve business performance. Having too much stock may mean that money is tied up unproductively, but inadequate stock can lead to delays in production and late deliveries. Efficient stock control involves finding the right balance. One of the reasons why control is so important is because the costs of holding stocks can be very high.

- There may be an opportunity cost (☞ unit 6) in holding stocks. Capital tied up in stocks earns no rewards. The money used to purchase stocks could have been put to other uses, such as new machinery. This might have earned the business money.
- Storage can also prove costly. Stocks of raw materials, components and finished goods occupy space in buildings. A firm may also have to pay heating, lighting and labour costs if, for example, a night watchman is employed to safeguard stores when the business is closed. Some products require very special storage conditions. Food items, may need expensive refrigerated storage facilities. A firm may have to insure against fire, theft and other damages.
- Spoilage costs. The quality of some stock may deteriorate over time, for example, perishable goods. In addition, if some finished goods are held too long they may become outdated and difficult to sell.
- Administrative and financial costs. These include the cost of placing and processing orders, handling costs and the costs of failing to anticipate price increases.
- Out-of-stock costs. These are the costs of lost revenue, when sales are lost because customers cannot be supplied from stocks. There may also be a loss of goodwill if customers are let down.

Stock levels

One of the most important tasks in stock control is to maintain the right level of stocks. This involves keeping stock levels as low as possible, so that the costs of holding stocks are minimised. At the same time stocks must not be allowed to run out, so that production is halted and customers are let down. A number of factors influence stock levels.

- Demand. Sufficient stocks need to be kept to satisfy normal demand. Firms must also carry enough stock to cover growth in sales and unexpected demand. The term BUFFER STOCK is used to describe stock held for unforeseen rises in demand or breaks in supply.
- Some firms **stockpile** goods. For example, toy manufacturers build up stocks in the few months up to December ready for the Christmas period. Electricity generating stations build up stocks of coal in the summer. During the summer, demand for electricity is low so less coal is needed. At the same time, prices of coal during the summer months are lower, so savings can be made.
- The costs of stock holding. The costs of holding stock were described earlier. If stock is expensive to hold then only a small quantity will be held. Furniture retailers may keep low stock levels because the cost of stock is high and sales levels are uncertain.
- The amount of working capital available. A business that is short of working capital will not be able to purchase more stock, even if it is needed.
- The type of stock. Businesses can only hold small stocks of perishable products. The stock levels of cakes or bread will be very small. Almost the entire stock of finished goods will be sold in one day. The 'life' of stock, however, does not solely depend on its 'perishability'. Stocks can become out of date when they are replaced by new models, for example.
- LEAD TIME. This is the amount of time it takes for a stock purchase to be placed, received, inspected and made ready for use. The longer the lead time, the higher the minimum level of stock needed.
- External factors. Fear of future shortages may prompt firms to hold higher levels of raw materials in stock as a precaution.

Stock control

It is necessary to control the flow of stocks in the business. This ensures that firms hold the right amount. Several methods of stock control exist. They focus on the RE-ORDER QUANTITY (how much stock is ordered when a new order is placed) and the RE-ORDER LEVEL (the level of stock when an order is placed).

- Economic order quantity (EOQ). It is possible to calculate the level of stocks which minimises costs. This is called the ECONOMIC ORDER QUANTITY. It takes into account the costs of holding stock, which rises with the amount of stock held, and the average costs of ordering stock, which fall as the size of the order is increased. A business must calculate the EOQ to balance these costs.
- Fixed re-order interval. Orders of various sizes are placed at fixed time intervals. This method ignores the economic order quantity, but ensures that stocks are 'topped up' on a regular basis. This method may result in fluctuating stock levels.
- Fixed re-order level. This method involves setting a

fixed order level, perhaps using the EOQ. The order is then repeated at varying time intervals.

■ **Two bin system.** This simple method involves dividing stock into two bins. When one bin is empty a new order is placed. When the order arrives it is placed into the first bin and stocks are used from the second bin. When the second bin is empty stocks are re-ordered again.

A stock control system is shown in Figure 33.2. It is assumed that:

■ 50,000 units are used every two months(25,000 each month);
■ the maximum stock level, above which stocks never rise, is 70,000 units;
■ the minimum stock level, below which stocks never fall, is 20,000 units, so there is a buffer against delays in delivery;
■ stock is re-ordered when it reaches a level of 40,000 units (the re-order level);
■ the re-order quantity is 50,000 units - the same quantity as is used up every two months;
■ the lead time is just under one month. This is the time between the order being placed and the date it arrives in stock.

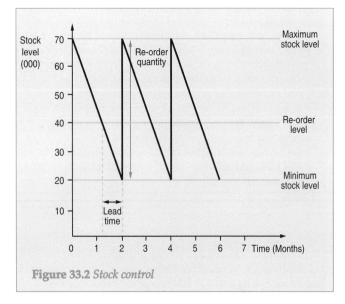

Figure 33.2 *Stock control*

This is a hypothetical model which would be the ideal for a business. In practice deliveries are sometimes late, so there is a delay in stocks arriving. Firms may also need to use their buffer stocks in this case. It is likely that re-order quantities will need to be reviewed from time to time. Suppliers might offer discounts for ordering larger quantities. The quantities of stocks used in each time period are unlikely to be constant. This might be because production levels fluctuate according to demand.

The effects of too much or too little stock

Why might having too much or too little stock be bad business practice?

Too much stock

■ Storage, insurance, lighting and handling costs will all be high if too much stock is held.
■ Large stock levels will occupy space in the premises. There may be more productive ways of using this space, such as improving the layout of the factory.
■ The opportunity cost will be high. Money tied up in stocks could be used to buy fixed assets, for example.
■ Large stock levels might result in unsold stock. If there is an unexpected change in demand, the firm may be left with stocks that it cannot sell.
■ Very large stocks might result in an increase in theft by employees. They may feel the business would not miss a small amount of stock relative to the total stock.

Too little stock

■ The business may not be able to cope with unexpected increases in demand if its stocks are too low. This might result in lost customers if they are let down too often.
■ If deliveries are delayed the firm may run out of stock and have to halt production. This might lead to idle labour and machinery while the firm waits for delivery.
■ The firm is less able to cope with unexpected shortages of materials. Again, this could result in lost production.
■ A firm which holds very low stocks may have to place more orders. This will raise total ordering costs. Also, it may be unable to take advantage of discounts for bulk buying.

QUESTION 4 Figure 33.3 shows the usage of a component, 5000XTD, for Bromley Ltd, over a seven month period. Bromley Ltd assemble electric lawn mowers using five main components. They found a new and cheaper supplier for the 5000XTD just two months ago.

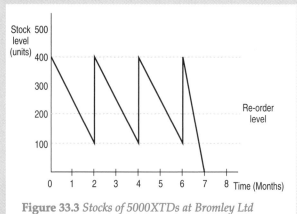

Figure 33.3 *Stocks of 5000XTDs at Bromley Ltd*

(a) Identify the; (i) lead time; (ii) minimum stock level; (iii) re-order level; (iv) re-order quantity; for the 5000XTD.
(b) Explain the reason for the change in the stock level after the sixth month.
(c) What might be the consequences of this change for the business?

Computerised stock control

Stock control has been improved by the use of computers. Many businesses hold details of their entire stock on computer databases (☞ unit 13). All additions to and issues from stocks are recorded and up to date stock levels can be found instantly. Actual levels of stock should be the same as shown in the computer printout. A prudent firm will carry out regular **stock checks** to identify differences.

Some systems are programmed to automatically order stock when the re-order level is reached. In some supermarkets, computerised checkout systems record every item of stock purchased by customers and automatically subtract items from total stock levels. The packaging on each item contains a **bar code.** When this is passed over a laser at the checkout, the sale is recorded by the system. This allows a store manager to check stock levels, total stock values and the store's takings at any time of the day. Again, the system can indicate when the re-order level is reached for any particular item of stock.

Access to stock levels is useful when manufacturers are dealing with large orders. The firm might need to find out whether there are enough materials in stock to complete the order. If this information is available, then the firm can give a more accurate delivery date.

Just-in-time manufacturing

A fairly recent innovation in manufacturing techniques in Europe and America is JUST-IN-TIME manufacturing. This system was developed in Japan in the 1950s and 1960s in the shipbuilding industry. It is a production system which is sensitive to customer demand and involves keeping stock to a minimum. Japanese shipbuilders recognised that a great deal of working capital was tied up in stocks of steel. Traditionally, one month's supply of steel was held by the shipyard. However, as the industry became more competitive, shipbuilders insisted that steel was delivered to the yards 'just-in-time'. Deliveries of steel were then put to immediate use. This reduced the need for high levels of working capital and improved the financial performance of the business.

This practice was introduced in other industries in Japan, such as the car industry. It has been used by Japanese car producers locating in the UK, such as Toyota, in the 1980s. Other industries are now adopting these methods. One example is Stoves, a small cooker manufacturer in Liverpool. The system aims to 'produce instantaneously with perfect quality and minimum waste'. In some cases the production begins only when an order is placed. Supplies of raw materials and components are delivered as they are needed on the production line. The system requires high levels of managerial and organisational skills and reliable suppliers. Figure 33.4 provides a summary of the advantages and disadvantages of Just-in-Time manufacturing.

ADVANTAGES

- It improves cash flow since money is not tied up in stocks.
- The system reduces waste, obsolete and damaged stock.
- More factory space is made available for productive use.
- The costs of stock holding are reduced significantly.
- Links with and the control of suppliers are improved.
- More scope for integration within the factory's computer system.
- The motivation of workers is improved. They are given more responsibility and encouraged to work in teams.

DISADVANTAGES

- A lot of faith is placed in the reliability and flexibility of suppliers.
- Increased ordering and administration costs.
- Advantages of bulk buying lost.
- Vulnerable to a break in supply and machinery breakdowns.
- Difficult to cope with sharp increases in demand.
- Possible loss of reputation if customers are let down by late deliveries.

Figure 33.4 *The advantages and disadvantages of just-in-time manufacturing*

QUESTION 5 Many UK companies have implemented just-in-time manufacturing very successfully. One example is JCB. JCB is said to have a manufacturing strategy. It knows what it wants manufacturing to deliver and manufacturing has a pretty good idea how to do it. The whole factory is driven by the customer's demands. Its excellence in the market place is derived from the principles of responsiveness and quality. Just-in-time manufacturing has played a key role in achieving some impressive improvements in a number of performance indicators. Between 1980 and 1987 direct labour productivity increased by 125 per cent, JCB's main product prices rose by just 4 per cent compared to general price increases of 52 per cent, the number of suppliers was reduced from 730 to 400 (future aim 100) and JCB has the highest per employee figures in the industry for turnover, profit and investment. JCB's success is also a result of internally funded investment in technology. It has islands of automation, it employs CAM and CAD to cut product development lead time, uses robots and computerised numerically controlled machine tools on production lines.

(a) Explain how the principles of 'responsiveness and quality' can be achieved through the use of just-in-time manufacturing.

(b) Compare JCB's stock control to a traditional approach using lead times.

(c) Why is a reduction in the number of suppliers (730 to 400) crucial if just-in-time manufacturing techniques are being employed?

Key terms

Buffer stocks - stocks held as a precaution to cope with unforeseen demand.
Economic order quantity - the level of stock order which minimises ordering and stock holding costs.
Just-in-time manufacturing - a manufacturing technique which is highly responsive to customer orders and uses very small stock holdings.
Lead time - the time between the order and the delivery of goods.
Re-order level - the level of stock when new orders are placed.
Re-order quantity - the amount of stock ordered when an order is placed.
Work-in-progress - partly finished goods.

Summary

1. What are the activities involved in materials management?
2. What is meant by purchasing in business?
3. Describe the various stages in the purchasing process.
4. What are the objectives of the purchasing department?
5. What effect can poor purchasing have on a business?
6. What are the advantages of centralised purchasing?
7. What is meant by
   (a) components;
   (b) finished goods?
8. What are the costs of holding stocks?
9. Why are buffer stocks held by firms?
10. Why do some firms stockpile?
11. Describe the advantages of computerised stock control.
12. Describe:
    (a) the advantages;
    (b) the disadvantages;
    of just-in-time manufacturing.

Question

Computerised stock control at Boots

At the end of 1992, Boots the Chemist completed the installation in all of its 1,100 stores of electronic point of sale scanning equipment, known as Epos. The gains from the system helped to improve the financial performance of the business. Andrew Street, director of information systems at Boots, said that Epos had contributed significantly to an increase in net profit margins. Over the last five years, margins had increased from 5 to 10 per cent and were still widening. There were a number of advantages which helped to reduce costs and raise sales.

- No need for staff to label items when stocking shelves.
- The need for counting stock was eliminated because the system allowed automatic stock replenishment techniques to be used.
- Shop shelves could be filled directly from lorries bypassing the storeroom.
- Working capital was expected to fall by between £50 million and £60 million due to a reduction in stock holding.
- A 1 per cent increase in sales had resulted from the elimination of mistakes at the till.

Other advantages were gained from the information which Epos generated about the stock levels of individual items in the stores. The information helped Boots make decisions about merchandising. For example, Boots withdrew petfood from the shelves very soon after the introduction of Epos. It discovered after taking into account shelf space, high transport costs and low gross margins that it had a negative net profit margin. More recently, product lines like dietary foods, baby products and medicines enjoyed more shelf space at the expense of others such as snacks, confectionery, and some cosmetics. The system also gave information on the effect of price changes. Boots has varied its pricing policy following the discovery that customers have different tolerance levels to price increases in the various lines. During the Christmas period Boots were able to monitor the effect of price changes on stock levels. The information provided by the system helped Boots to set prices which avoided unsold stock on December 25th. In addition, acting on more information provided by the system, Boots re-ordered a rapidly selling line of car shaped lunch boxes.

Source : adapted from *The Independent*, 12.11.1992.

(a) Explain how Epos improved stock control at Boots.
(b) How might the purchasing procedure have been assisted by Epos?
(c) In what way did Boots employ just-in-time techniques?
(d) Explain why the financial performance of Boots improved following the installation of Epos.

What is quality?

In 1986, a cargo of biscuits produced by Marks and Spencer was refused entry into Japan because it was heavier than the weight stated on the package. Also, the Japanese retailer argued that the uneven thickness of the biscuit would not be to consumers' tastes in the country. This helps to show how important quality can be to a business and that perceptions about quality can be different.

Consumers, faced with many goods at similar prices, now think about quality when making choices. Quality could be described as those features of a product or service that allow it to satisfy customers. Take an example of a family buying a television. They may consider some of the following features:

- physical appearance - they may want a certain style;
- reliability and durability - will it last for 10 years?
- special features - does it have stereo sound?
- suitability - they may want a portable television;
- parts - are spare parts available?
- repairs - does the shop carry out maintenance?
- after sales service - how prompt is delivery?

They may also consider features which they **perceive** as important, such as:

- image - is the manufacturer's name widely recognised?
- reputation - what do other consumers think of the business or product?

The importance of quality has grown in recent years. Consumers are more aware. They get information through magazines such as *Which?* that contain reports on the quality of certain products. They also have more disposable income and higher expectations than ever before. Legislation and competition have also forced firms to improve the quality of their products.

QUESTION 1

What actual and perceived features might a consumer consider important when selecting the products in the photograph?

Quality control in production

Traditionally, in manufacturing, production departments have been responsible for quality control. The objectives of quality control might be to ensure that products:

- satisfy consumers' needs;
- work under conditions they will face;
- operate in the way they should;
- can be produced cost effectively;
- can be repaired easily;
- conform to safety standards set down by legislation and independent bodies.

An example of a quality control system was one used by Kellogg's. Samples of breakfast cereal are taken from the production line every half hour and tested. The testing takes place in a food review room twice a day and is undertaken by a small group of staff. Each sample, about 50 in total, is compared with a 'perfect' Kellogg's sample and given a grade between 1 and 10. 10 is perfect but 9.8 and 7, although noticeable to the trained eye, is acceptable to the customer. Below 7 the consumer would notice the reduction in quality. The cereals are tested for appearance, texture, colour, taste etc. More sophisticated tests are carried out in a laboratory where the nutritional value of a sample, for example, is measured.

Quality control in UK organisations, in the past, often meant inspecting other people's work and the product itself **after** production had taken place. By today's standards this is not quality control, but a method of finding a poor quality product (or a problem) before it is sold to the consumer. Today we are less concerned about 'Has the job been done properly?' than 'Are we able to do the job properly?' In other words inspection is carried out during the production process. This means that problems and poor quality products can be prevented **before** final production. Such a preventative approach has been used by Japanese businesses and is known as TOTAL QUALITY MANAGEMENT (TQM). It is now being adopted by many companies in the UK.

Total quality management

Errors are costly for business. It is estimated that about one-third of all the effort of British business is wasted in correcting errors. There are benefits if something is done right the first time. Total quality management (TQM) is a method designed to prevent errors, such as poor quality products, from happening. The business is organised so that the manufacturing process is investigated at every stage. It is argued that the success of Japanese companies is based on their superior organisation. Every department, activity and individual is organised to take into account quality at all times. What are the features of TQM?

Quality chains Great stress is placed on the operation of QUALITY CHAINS. In any business a series of suppliers and customers exists. For example, a secretary is a supplier to a manager, who is the customer. The secretarial duties must be carried out to the satisfaction of the manager. The chain also includes customers and suppliers outside the business. The chain remains intact if the supplier satisfies the customer. It is broken if a person or item of equipment does not satisfy the needs of the customer. Failure to meet the requirements in any part of the quality chain creates problems, such as delays in the next stage of production.

Company policy and accountability There will only be improvements in quality if there is a company-wide quality policy. TQM must start from the top with the most senior executive and spread throughout the business to every employee. People must be totally committed and take a 'pride in the job'. This might be considered as an example of job enrichment (☞ unit 50). Lack of commitment, particularly at the top, causes problems. For example, if the managing director lacks commitment, employees lower down are unlikely to commit themselves. TQM stresses the role of the individual and aims to make everyone accountable for their own performance. For example, a machine operator may be accountable to a workshop supervisor for his work.

Control Consumers' needs will only be satisfied if the business has control of the factors that affect a product's quality. These may be human, administrative or technical factors. This is shown in Figure 34.1. The process is only under control if materials, equipment and tasks are used in the same way every time. Take an example of a firm making biscuits. Only by cooking in the same way can the quality be consistent every time. These methods can be **documented** and used to assess operations. Regular audits must be carried out by the firm to check quality. Information is then fed back from the customer to the

'operator' or producer, and from the operator to the supplier of inputs, such as raw materials. For example, a retailer may return a batch of vehicles to the manufacturer because the gears were faulty. The manufacturer might then identify the person responsible for fitting the gears. An investigation might reveal that the faulty gears were the responsibility of a component supplier. The supplier can then be contacted and the problem resolved. Quality audits and reviews may lead to suggestions for improvements - a different material, perhaps, or a new piece of equipment.

Monitoring the process TQM relies on monitoring the business process to find possible improvements. Methods have been developed to help achieve this. STATISTICAL PROCESS CONTROL (SPC) involves collecting data relating to the performance of a process. Data is presented in diagrams, charts and graphs (☞ unit 13). The information is then passed to all those concerned.

SPC can be used to reduce variability, which is the cause of most quality problems. Variations in products, delivery times, methods, materials, people's attitudes and staff performance often occur. For example, statistical data may show that worker attitudes may have led to variations in output late on Friday afternoon. Discussion might result in a change in the 'clocking on' and 'clocking off' times to solve the problem.

Teamwork TQM stresses that teamwork is the most effective way of solving problems. The main advantages are:
- a greater range of skills, knowledge and experience can be used to solve the problem;
- employee morale is often improved;
- problems across departments are better dealt with;
- a greater variety of problems can be tackled;
- team 'ideas' are more likely to be used than individual ones.

TQM strongly favours teamwork throughout the business. It builds trust and morale, improves communications and cooperation and develops interdependence. Many UK firms in the past have suffered due to lack of sharing of information and ideas. Such approaches have often led to division between sections of the workforce.

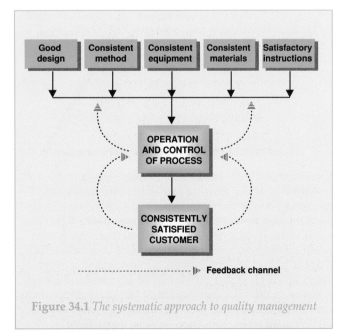

Figure 34.1 *The systematic approach to quality management*

Using TQM

TQM helps companies to:
- focus clearly on the needs of customers and relationships between suppliers and customers;
- achieve quality in all aspects of business, not just product or service quality;
- critically analyse all processes to remove waste and inefficiencies:
- find improvements and develop measures of performance;
- develop a team approach to problem solving;

- develop effective procedures for communication and acknowledgement of work (☞ unit 62);
- continually review the processes to develop a strategy of constant improvement.

There are however, some problems.

- There will be training and development costs of the new system.
- TQM will only work if there is commitment from the entire business.
- There will be a great deal of bureaucracy and documents and regular audits are needed. This may be a problem for small firms.
- Stress is placed on the process and not the product.

QUESTION 2 Baggio Ltd is a small manufacturer of sports bags and similar plastic holdalls. They operate a batch production system which allows the size of the order and the design to vary according to customer needs. Their marketing approach emphasises the company's ability to fullfil any customer order with regard to design and size. They take pride in their flexibility.

The production of the bags involves a number of straightforward processes. The first stage is design which is the responsibility of one employee who consults the individual customer. The next stage involves cutting plastic sheets into appropriate sizes so that design patterns can be copied onto them. A second cutting process provides sections ready for sewing. Before being passed onto the sewing function, one or two of the sections need to be printed with a logo according to customer design. Three sewing processes follow: one to join the sections which form the bag shape; the second to sew in piping to give the bag strength; a third to sew in a zip. A final operation involves inserting a hard base inside the bag and punching in four studs. Each completed bag is then checked for errors.

The managing director has become very concerned about the number of bags returned by customers due to faulty sewing.

(a) Describe Baggio's current quality control system.
(b) Identify problems with the system.
(c) Explain how the problems could be solved using the TQM approach.

Costs of quality control

Firms will want to monitor the costs of quality control carefully. All businesses are likely to face costs when trying to **maintain or improve** the quality of their products and services.

- The cost of designing and setting up a quality control system. This might include the time used to 'think through' a system and the training of staff to use it.
- The cost of monitoring the system. This could be the salary of a supervisor or the cost of an electronic sensor.
- There will be costs if products do not come up to

standard. Faulty goods may have to be scrapped or reworked. Product failures might also result in claims against a company, bad publicity and a possible loss of goodwill.

- The cost of improving the actual quality. This may be the cost of new machinery or training staff in new working practices.
- If the whole quality system fails, there may be costs in setting it up again. Time may be needed to 'rethink' or adjust the system. Retraining might also be necessary.

QUESTION 3 National Westminster Bank began a quality improvement service in 1983. Its aim was to differentiate the business from its competitors by developing a reputation for excellence in the delivery of financial services. All of the 100,000 staff were involved in a communications exercise, aimed at getting everyone 'to face the same way'. In 1988, internal processes were critically analysed and it was estimated that 25 per cent of NatWest's operating costs were absorbed in the difference between the cost of actually accomplishing a task and the cost which would have been incurred if the job had been done right the first time.

Figure 34.2 shows the 'iceberg effects of failure costs'. Above the waterline are the costs of failure; rework, rechecking, handling queries, handling complaints, and lost fees. Below the line, and representing a larger problem, includes the cost of lost repeat business, lost customers, staff overtime, machine downtime, and bad employee morale. NatWest researched how much time was spent dealing with customer complaints. It was significantly higher than expected.

Figure 34.2 *The total cost of failure, split between the failure costs above the water line and the more far reaching failure costs below the waterline*

Source: adapted from *The Case for Costing Quality*, DTI.

(a) Why might the failure costs below the line be more difficult to measure?
(b) Discuss any possible implications of your answer to (a) for NatWest.
(c) Describe the costs which might be incurred by NatWest if a customer telephones to complain about an incorrect debit entry on a statement.

In 1985 a survey on quality and standards undertaken by the National Economic Development Organisation claimed that between 10 and 20 per cent of a firm's revenue was accounted for by quality related costs. This meant that up to £6 billion a year could be saved by British manufacturers by cutting such costs. The vast majority of these costs is spent on appraisal and failure, which add very little to the quality of the product. Eliminating failure will also help to reduce appraisal and failure costs.

Although quality control systems are costly, it is argued that their benefits outweigh the costs. The actual quality of the product should be improved, so customers are more likely to purchase the product. Business costs may be cut if faults in products are identified before the product reaches the market. The costs of failure once the product has reached the market are likely to be much higher than those during manufacture.

Best practice benchmarking

BEST PRACTICE BENCHMARKING (BPB) is a technique used by some businesses to help them discover the 'best' methods of production available and then adopt them. BPB involves:

- finding out what makes the difference, in the customer's eyes, between an ordinary supplier and an excellent supplier;
- setting standards for business operations based on the best practice that can be found;
- finding out how these best companies meet those standards;

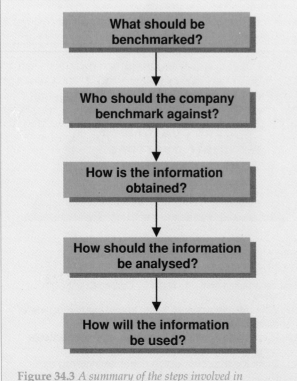

Figure 34.3 *A summary of the steps involved in benchmarking*

- applying both competitors' standards and their own to meet the new standards and, if possible, exceed them.

Figure 34.3 illustrates the five main steps in BPB. The first step is to **identify** exactly what the company intends to benchmark. For example, benchmarks that are important for customer satisfaction might include consistency of product, correct invoices, shorter delivery times, shorter lead times and improved after sales service. A few years ago, Rank Xerox chose to benchmark the way its photocopiers were built, the costs of each stage of production, selling costs, quality of services and many other aspects of its operations.

The second step involves **choosing a company** to set the benchmark against. This may be done by asking customers who they feel is the best in the field. Business analysts, journalists, stockbrokers or industrialists may also be used. Rank Xerox and Centreparc, the leisure group, have used other parts of their own organisations which have developed a reputation for excellence.

In the third step, information can be **gathered** from a number of sources, such as magazines, newspapers, trade association reports, specialist databases, customers and suppliers. Companies in the same industry often share information. An example may be businesses supplying local markets, such as garden centres. The benefits of this are that the worst performers can get advice from the best and perhaps visit their premises.

The **analysis** of information is best done with quantitative techniques (☞ units 16 and 17). For example, a firm might compare numerical data relating to delivery times.

The final stage involves **using** the information. Once standards have been found and set, they must be communicated throughout the business. Improvements must be funded, introduced and monitored. Once a

QUESTION 4 ICL, the computer company, have been involved in benchmarking for a number of years. They benchmark more than 20 of their competitors on company performance and product technology. The information obtained through their benchmarking process is distributed throughout the organisation and includes:

- average debtors/creditors as a percentage of turnover;
- research and development as a percentage of turnover;
- return on capital employed;
- revenue per head;
- a comparison of components with regard to quality;
- the speed of assimilating new technology;
- reliability of components;
- speed and reliability of delivery and payment arrangement.

Source: adapted from *The Case for Costing Quality*, DTI.

(a) How might the above information about their competitors on: (i) company performance; (ii) product technology; be beneficial to ICL in benchmarking?
(b) How might the information shown be collected?
(c) How might managers make use of the information?

company becomes the best in the field others will begin to benchmark against them. This means the company must continue to benchmark their own process.

Independent bodies and trade associations

There are a number of important pieces of legislation, independent bodies and trade associations that can affect a firm's quality or service.

Independent bodies These include the following examples.
- The British Standards Institution attempts to set standards throughout industry. It has clear quality and safety specifications for design, production, installation and servicing. Any business can apply to the BSI for an inspection of its product. If the firm can achieve and maintain the standard, it has the right to carry a **kitemark**, which shows that a certain quality has been attained. The kitemark, A in Figure 34.4, means that the BSI is able to verify any claims made by the company about the standards of their products. A firm can also apply to the BSI for a BS EN ISO 9000 certificate. This guarantees that a business' processes, procedures and systems achieve a certain quality standard. The BSI carries out regular inspections to check these standards.
- The British Electrotechnical Approvals Board (BEAB) is a body which inspects domestic electrical equipment. Manufacturers of domestic electrical appliances will be keen for the BEAB to approve their products. Approval can serve as a recognition of quality that customers will recognise.
- The Consumers Association is a body which follows up complaints by people about faulty products or services. They also make recommendations about products and services to customers. This takes into account such things as quality, reliability and value for money. Often survey results appear in their *Which?* magazines.

Trade associations
- The Association of British Travel Agents (ABTA) has drawn up a code of practice for its members. The code aims to improve the trading standards of activities related to the sale of holidays. Travel agents are allowed to register with ABTA if they agree to follow their code of practice. Their logo is shown as C in Figure 34.4.
- The Wool Marketing Board allows manufacturers to carry the label shown as B in Figure 34.4 if their garments are made entirely of pure new wool. Obtaining these trademarks is a way for a firm to give QUALITY ASSURANCE to customers. If customers know that the quality of a product is guaranteed, they are more likely to buy the product. Also, there is less need to inspect the product, and returns and re-ordering are reduced.

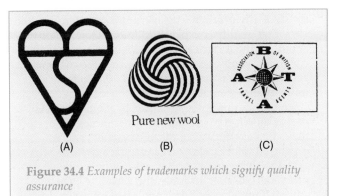

Pure new wool

(A)   (B)   (C)

Figure 34.4 *Examples of trademarks which signify quality assurance*

Legislation A number of laws exist which protect consumers from bad trading practices, but not many of them address directly the question of product quality. They tend to focus on safety aspects and consumer exploitation. The laws are enforced by local inspectors, called **Trading Standards Officers.**

An example would be the **Sale of Goods Act (1979)**. This states that goods must be of a quality fit for their normal purpose. This is called MERCHANTABLE QUALITY. It means that goods and services must perform the function for which they were intended. The **Consumer Protection Act 1987** deals with product safety and outlines certain safety regulations. Consumers that suffer injury if these regulations are broken can sue the business. Consumer legislation is dealt with in detail in unit 73.

Key terms

Best practice benchmarking - imitating the standards of an established leader in quality and attempting to better them.
Merchantable quality - the idea that a product is able to perform the function for which it was intended.
Quality assurance - the guarantee of quality by a business.
Quality chains - when employees form a series of links between customers and suppliers in business, both internally and externally.
Statistical process control - the collection of data about the performance of a particular process in a business.
Total quality management - a managerial approach which focusses on quality and aims to improve the effectiveness, flexibility, and competitiveness of the business.

Question

Plugged into the quality circuit

In 1990, Southern Electricity was privatised. It supplies electricity to more than 2.5 million customers. It has about 8,200 employees and an annual turnover of around £1.6b million. As a means of improving the performance of the business, Southern has introduced a quality control system.

Southern Electricity's managing director, Henry Casley, has been pursuing the 'Quest for Quality', as he calls it, with a great deal of commitment and enthusiasm. He says, 'Satisfied customers mean a satisfactorily profitable business.' He firmly rejects the view that quality is expensive. 'In our view, quality is about getting it right first time, identifying what the customer wants and then making sure the customer gets it. Quality is productivity and efficiency by a much more acceptable name.'

Southern's quality programme began in 1985. As part of an effort to become the most successful of the then, area electricity boards, the business was re-organised into six new divisions. Each division was asked to come up with proposals for overcoming problems like staff attitudes and image. A plan emerged for team building and team briefing which started in February 1987.

By the autumn of 1990 Casley was convinced that improving the service to customers, both internal and external, was the next challenge. He invited the briefing teams in the six divisions to name the two or three things 'that drive our customers crazy'. In reaction to the response, which was overwhelming, he appointed a 'quality manager', adopted a quality improvement programme and sought registration with Marketing Quality Assurance (MQA). MQA are an independent UK body which assess and designate compliance with BS 5750-type quality standards for marketing, sales and customer service activities. He believed that the staff should 'own the quality improvement programme' rather than have it imposed upon them. In addition, Casley exploited a friendship with Southern California Edison, a USA electricity company, to provide a benchmark and a role model.

MQA conducted an initial assessment of Southern's systems and procedures. A 48 page quality manual was written, explaining the master plan. It aimed to ensure that all Southern's employees worked together to provide a quality service which was profitable and satisfied customers. Employees were encouraged to join or set up committees called Quigs - Quality Improvement Groups - to tackle problems affecting quality. The plan was communicated to all staff through wall posters, presentations, training videos, and articles in the staff newspaper which was sent to all staff homes.

Customers benefited in a number of ways. Staff dealing with customers on the telephone gave their names. A sample of customers had their calls returned to check that a satisfactory service had been received. Engineers used mobile telephones to call customers if they were going to be late. In addition, Southern bettered the nine service guarantees imposed by 'OFFER', the industry regulator.

The company now monitors and strictly records its compliance with all externally imposed standards and has its own 39 service standards. 'Unless the company keeps a score it will not know whether it is succeeding', says Casley. Southern also draws up a comparative league table for the six divisions in the organisation to encourage competitiveness in quality. Each month a performance report is given at the management meeting, where quality is always on the agenda.

Casley has no doubt that the quality programme has already produced gain, but emphasises that it is an ongoing process. MQA awarded Southern only the second ever registration certificate and were highly complimentary about their progress regarding quality.

Source : adapted from the *Financial Times*, 21.1.1992.

(a) What features might consumers feel are important about the quality of electricity supply?
(b) Explain why Henry Casley may reject the view that 'quality is expensive'.
(c) Identify elements of TQM that are found in Casley's approach to quality control.
(d) What are the advantages of TQM for Southern?
(e) How might Southern evaluate the success of its quality programme?

Summary

1. What is meant by the quality of a product?
2. Explain the difference between actual and perceived quality.
3. Identify the objectives of quality control.
4. State 5 implications of TQM for a business.
5. Why is teamwork so important in TQM?
6. What are the costs of quality control?
7. Describe the steps in best practice benchmarking.
8. What is the role of the British Standards Institution?
9. Explain the advantage of manufacturing trademarks to a business.

Measuring efficiency

The objective of a business might be to be profitable (☞ unit 5). One way of doing this is to increase efficiency. EFFICIENCY is to do with how well resources, such as raw materials, labour and capital can be used to produce a product or service. Businesses often use costs as an indicator of efficiency. A manufacturer, for example, that finds its **average costs** (☞ unit 10) falling may well be improving efficiency as long as the quality of goods or services does not fall. Generally, as efficiency improves firms become more profitable. However firms may still be profitable without being efficient. This may perhaps be the case with firms that have a great deal of market power. British Telecom, for example, operated profitably in a market free from competition for many years. This does not necessarily mean that increased profits came from being more efficient. Why might businesses want to measure efficiency?

■ To improve control of the business. Information about the efficiency of different parts of a business will allow managers to find strengths and weaknesses.

■ To make comparisons. The efficiency of different plants can be compared, for example. The efficiency of the business compared to one of its competitors may also be useful.

■ To help negotiations. Efficiency indicators can help a business when discussing wage rates, levels of staff and working practices with trade unions, for example.

How might efficiency be measured? Lower average costs or rising profitability are only **indicators** of efficiency. It is difficult to measure efficient business practice as many factors influence it. It is possible, however, to measure the efficiency of a process or an input such as labour or capital.

QUESTION 1 Majid Khan owns a small business in Sparkhill, Birmingham, where he produces standard undercovers for a local furniture manufacturer. Over the last three years the unit cost has fallen from £6 to £4 per cover. The number of staff employed has also fallen, from 23 to 16 employees. His annual profit has risen from £90,000 to £140,000. Majid Khan believes that the improvements have resulted from a drive to become more efficient.

(a) What evidence is there to suggest that efficiency has improved?

(b) How might employees use the above information to press for higher wages?

Measuring labour productivity

Labour PRODUCTIVITY can be found by dividing the output over a certain period by the number of workers employed:

$$\text{Labour productivity} = \frac{\text{Output (per period)}}{\text{Number of employees (per period)}}$$

If a small market garden employs 20 pickers who pick 40,000 lettuces a day, their productivity is 2,000 lettuces per worker each day.

This ratio measures the output per employee and is a useful indication of the efficiency of the labour force. There are, however, problems when calculating the ratio. For example, which workers should be counted? Should the maintenance crew, management, and clerical staff be counted, or should the ratio concentrate on direct labour only, ie shopfloor workers ? How should part time workers and the long term sick be treated? How can the ratio accommodate a multi-product plant, where an employee's efforts might contribute to the production of more than one product?

Considerable improvements have been made in the productivity of labour in recent years based upon broad calculations. For example, the productivity of coal face workers doubled between 1983 and 1989. This does not mean that coal face workers worked twice as hard. In fact, it may have been as a result of a number of other things.

■ There may have been a change in the amount or

QUESTION 2 Quest Aircraft Ltd are a small company that manufactures light aircraft for the UK market. They are an established company and operate from a Coventry factory where up until 1988 the planes were entirely hand built. In 1990 the management reviewed the company's production system. They were concerned that costs were growing too rapidly and decided to introduce some new machinery into the factory. Table 35.1 shows the output, the number of hours worked and the number of employees of the business.

Table 35.1 *Production data for Quest Aircraft Ltd*

Year	Output (planes)	Employees	Average hours worked	Labour productivity per employee	Labour productivity per total time worked
1987	100	40	38		
1988	102	40	39		
1989	103	41	40		
1990	120	40	40		
1991	127	39	41		
1992	132	38	41		

(a) Complete the above table by calculating labour productivity per employee and the labour productivity per total time worked.

(b) Explain the differences between the two measures in (a).

(c) What might be responsible for the productivity pattern in the time period shown?

quality of another input. For example, the tools and equipment used by miners may have been replaced by more up to date and effective ones.
- ■ The way in which labour and shifts were organised could have been improved.
- ■ During that time period, many of the inefficient coal mines with very low labour productivity were closed. This would obviously help improve the industry's average.

It is likely that some of the improvement will have resulted from increased effort from the workforce.

Measuring capital productivity

A business may be interested in the productivity of its capital.

This is becoming increasingly likely as more and more firms become capital intensive (☞ unit 29). A capital productivity ratio can be calculated by dividing output by the amount of capital employed in a given time period.

$$\text{Capital productivity} = \frac{\text{Output}}{\text{Capital employed}}$$

If a factory employed 10 sewing machinists and the total number of garments sewn in a day was 900, the productivity of capital would be 90 garments per machine each day.

Again, improvements in the productivity of capital may not be the result of more efficient capital alone. For example, the performance of an engine can be improved if it is serviced regularly and used carefully.

The labour and capital productivity ratios above are 'partial factor' productivity ratios. They measure the efficiency of just one input. A firm might want to measure the efficiency of the combined inputs it uses.

$$\text{Multi-factor productivity} = \frac{\text{Output}}{\text{Labour + materials + capital + etc.}}$$

This ratio takes into account that efficiency can be influenced by the quality and effectiveness of all inputs.

Other measures

There are other measures which can also be used to measure the efficiency of parts of a business.

Utilisation Managers may wish to measure the efficiency of certain activities. The **utilisation** of particular machines, or even the whole production process could be measured. This can be done by comparing the actual rate of utilisation with what is physically possible. For example, a food processing plant may be capable of 20 hours per day with two 8 hour shifts. In one working day, the processing line was in operation for 14 hours. So:

$$\text{Actual utilisation} = \frac{\text{Number of hours actually worked}}{\text{Total possible hours per day}} \times 100$$

$$= \frac{14}{20} \times 100$$

$$= 70\%$$

This 70 per cent rate needs to be compared with the rate which would be possible under standard operation. This can be calculated (assuming that two 8 hour shifts are worked) as:

$$\text{Possible utilisation} = \frac{16}{20} \times 100$$

$$= 80\%$$

The results show that the production line is being under-utilised. This could be due to a machine breakdown caused by poorly trained staff or poor maintenance.

Value added measures In recent years some firms have calculated the value added by the business where:

$$\text{Value added} = \text{Sales revenue} - \text{external expenditure}$$

This is a measure of overall company performance and shows the money available for reinvestment in the business and distribution to shareholders.

Assessing business efficiency is a complicated task. A whole variety of measures are required and there is no

---

QUESTION 3 Focart Ltd assemble mountain bikes. The total possible number of hours on an assembly line is 7,000 hours per annum. The standard rate of usage is 6,000 hours in both years.

Table 35.2 *Production data for Focart Ltd*

	Output (bikes)	Labour force	Capital (£)	Line utilisation per annum (no. of hours actually worked)
Year 1	20,000	100	400,000	5,000
Year 2	30,000	70	800,000	5,500

(a) Calculate: (i) labour productivity; (ii) capital productivity; (iii) actual line utilisation; (iv) possible line utilisation; for years 1 and 2.
(b) Given your answers in (a), which are favourable and which suggest problems for the business?
(c) What reasons might you suggest for the changes between year 1 and year 2 in each measure of productivity?

single indicator which reflects accurately the overall efficiency of a business. A range of financial ratios (☞ unit 45) may also be used to help assess the performance of a business.

Work study

WORK STUDY is an attempt to find the 'best' or most 'efficient' way of using labour, machines and materials. The work of F W Taylor (☞ unit 48) is said to have formed the basis of work study methods.

Work study uses two techniques - **method study** and **work measurement.** Method study involves identifying all the specific activities in a job, analysing them, and finding the best way to do the job. This could be an existing job or a new one. Method study will allow a firm to:
- identify an optimum way to carry out a task;
- improve the layout of the factory or the workplace;
- minimise effort and reduce fatigue;
- improve the effectiveness of processes;
- improve the use of labour, machines and materials;
- establish the costs of particular activities to help with accounting;
- achieve results in the least time.

Once the best work method has been found, work measurement can be used to find the effort needed to carry out a task to an acceptable standard. The results can be used to design incentive schemes and determine staffing levels.

How is work measurement carried out? One example might be a worker being observed by a work-study assessor. The assessor might watch a worker set up a cutting machine, cut 10 patterns, reset the machine for a different pattern, and cut 10 more patterns, and record the findings. The performance might be rated against a scale of, say, 0 - 100, such as the British Standard Rating Scale (where 100 is the standard performance of an average, experienced, motivated worker). It is possible for an efficient and motivated worker to exceed 100 on this scale. Work-study assessors are often disliked by employees. Some regard these time and motion officers with suspicion and feel threatened. Workers are sometimes

expected to work harder in the future as a result of their observations.

Ergonomics is also an important feature in work study. Machines and the environment should be adapted so that the individual can achieve the best performance. A study of the working area might concentrate on such things as air temperature, humidity, radiation, noise levels and lighting. A study of the positioning of dials might be used when studying machines. EC legislation has laid down a set of rules relating to the use of VDUs by employees, for example.

The role of the labour force

Although industry has become more capital intensive in recent years the role of the labour force is still very important. Improvements in efficiency can be achieved by making labour more productive. In the last decade labour has been used more efficiently as a result of a number of factors.

Labour flexibility Labour is being used more flexibly by businesses.
- More use has been made of part-time and temporary employees, such as in retailing.
- Flexible working practices are becoming more widespread. In manufacturing, employees have been involved in job rotation, job enrichment and job enlargement (☞ unit 50).
- Disputes that arise if one worker is thought to be doing another's job (known as **demarcation disputes**) have been eased. For example, in some factories production workers have been allowed to carry out routine maintenance work.
- Employees have been asked to work new shifts which make more use of capital equipment. Also, flexitime systems have been introduced. These allow staff to choose their own working hours in each day, within limits.
- Flexible payment systems have been introduced. For example, Aldi, the German supermarket chain, pays relatively high wage rates to its employees, but can send them home at any time if there is not enough work.

Although more flexible working practices may help improve efficiency, there are some disadvantages. It is argued that they lead to higher levels of labour turnover (☞ unit 51) and absenteeism. To prevent this, employers must make sure that new practices are explained to the staff and care should be taken with recruitment, selection, and induction. Increased flexibility also requires more resources for training.

During the 1980s, the government attempted to make labour more flexible. Policies introduced by the government were aimed to reduce the influence of trade unions, reduce the cost of employing labour and improve labour mobility. Some examples of measures which arguably lead to more labour flexibility are:
- legislation has been passed to reduce the power of trade unions - the need for a secret ballot before a strike, for example;

QUESTION 4 Sheena Styles runs a manufacturing business which produces a range of neon signs. The business operates in two small factories on an industrial park. The second factory was acquired when one of their customers offered it as a payment for a debt. Both factories employ about 30 workers and similar machinery. When the second factory was equipped and opened it very quickly became a success. Indeed, its productivity rate was about 40 per cent better than the existing factory. The second factory is perhaps cleaner, brighter and more spacious. However, the production manager, who has worked in both factories, does not believe that this is the sole reason why productivity is better.

(a) How might a work study help Sheena Styles?
(b) In what way is the second factory better ergonomically?

- government training schemes to improve the chances of changing jobs;
- financial assistance to individuals to improve geographical mobility;
- abolition of Wages Councils (☞ unit 56) to allow firms to set their own wage rates;
- the 'tightening up' of the benefit system to encourage people to take lower paid jobs, the exclusion of school leavers and undergraduates, for example.

Quality circles Management and production techniques developed in Japan have been imported into the UK. The use of quality circles (☞ unit 50) is a management approach which allows people to become more involved in decision making. The approach was originally developed in America and was based on the work of Douglas McGregor (☞ unit 48).

It was during the 1950s and 1960s that Japanese companies first used this approach. A quality circle is a group of between 4 and 10 workers who work for the same supervisor. They meet regularly to identify, analyse, and attempt to solve work related problems. Meetings are usually one hour, weekly meetings in paid time. At the meetings workers use problem solving techniques to analyse and solve problems, and then pass on their findings to the management. Quality circles place faith in the capabilities of workers and emphasis teamwork. For example, in the Honda car plant at Swindon, workers are placed in teams on the assembly line and are responsible for organising their own work and developing their own jobs. The three main goals of quality circles are staff

involvement, people development and the generation of benefits. If quality circles are successful they will motivate the workforce, improve efficiency and raise profitability.

Incentive schemes One way to improve labour productivity is to provide the workforce with some sort of incentive. The incentive might be in the form of a reward for being more productive or the threat of punishment for not being productive. One of the reasons for carrying out a work study is to see whether it is possible to introduce such incentive schemes.

Standardisation

STANDARDISATION involves using uniform resources and activities or producing a uniform product. It can be applied to tools, components, equipment, procedures and business documents.

Changing systems can be very expensive, although there are benefits. A construction firm that builds a range of flats, for example, would benefit if all were fitted with standard cupboards. Savings are made in a number of ways. Bulk purchases can be made, the same tools and procedures could be used for fitting and training time could be reduced. This is an example of **internal** standardisation. Standardisation can also be more general. For example, efficiency will improve if there are standard components like nuts, bolts, pipe, screws and wire or standard measurements terminology, procedures and equipment, such as containers for ships and lorries.

The creation of the Single European Market in 1992 aimed to standardise regulations, procedures and specifications about quality, health and safety. This should benefit all businesses in member countries (☞ unit 70).

The main disadvantage is that the designers are constrained. They can not change production easily to suit the individual consumer. Designers may also face a more demanding job if they have to design products which must contain certain standard components and dimensions. Standardisation may also lead to inflexibility, which could result in a slower reaction to change.

Factory layout

The way in which a factory or workshop is set out can affect efficiency. The machinery and work stations should be set out so that effort and cost are minimised and output is maximised. This will be achieved if:

- the factory is safe and secure;
- handling and movement are minimised;
- good visibility and accessibility is maintained;
- flexibility is maximised;
- managers are co-ordinated.

Quantitative techniques (☞ units 16 and 17) might be used to find the most effective way of organising the production area. Work studies might also help to design the best layout. There is no standard method of factory layout because different products need different techniques. Also, different companies producing the same

---

QUESTION 5 Worldtours Ltd are an established travel agent located in Ipswich. They employ five workers, who have all been with the firm for nine years, and a manager. Lorraine, Darrias, Dwight and Tracey specialise in sales to Spain, Greece, the rest of Europe, and USA respectively, while Tricia handles all the administration. Stanley, the long serving manager, retired three weeks ago. Julia was appointed as the new manager after a very impressive interview with the owner. She drew attention to some modern management techniques which she had picked up on a training course last year.

One or two problems had developed in recent years which Stanley had failed to address. When one of the sales staff was absent, all enquiries to their specialist destination were delayed until their return. This frequently lost the firm business because customers simply enquired elsewhere and thus a potential booking was lost. When Tricia was absent the administration got into a serious mess because nobody could understand her filing system or operate the word processor. Julia checked the attendance records of all staff for a two year period. They were unacceptable, due, it seems, to staff boredom with the job.

(a) In what ways are the staff inflexible?
(b) What might help to improve staff flexibility?
(c) Explain how quality circles might improve efficiency in the business.
(d) What problems might Julia encounter when introducing quality circles?

product might choose different methods. For example, both Bass Charrington and Brakspears produce beer, but the layouts of their breweries are very different. Brakspears use very traditional brewing techniques compared with Bass, who use more up to date methods. What are the common types of factory layout?

Process layout This system involves performing similar operations on all products in one area or at one work station. For example, the manufacturing of wellington boots involves:

- a mixing process where P.V.C. resin and stabiliser are mixed;
- a moulding process which takes place on a moulding machine;
- a trimming operation where the boots have unwanted material cut off;
- packaging ready for distribution.

Each of these processes is undertaken on all boots at each work station, and work stations are located in different parts of the factory.

This type of layout is often used with batch production (☞ unit 29) because of its flexibility. Planning is needed to avoid machines being overloaded or remaining idle.

Product layout With this method, machinery and tasks are set out in the order required to make the product. The products 'flow' from one machine or task to another. Flow production techniques (☞ unit 29) use this method. It is popular because handling time is reduced and there is greater control. However, it can only be used if there is large demand for the product.

Fixed position layout This involves performing operations on the work-in-progress and then returning it to a fixed location after each process. Alternatively, resources are taken to a site at which production occurs. An example would be the construction of a bridge.

Other methods of promoting efficiency

Total quality management (TQM) Inefficiency may come from correcting errors. If a job is done properly the first time savings can be made. Total quality management (TQM) is an approach aimed at improving the effectiveness of the business as a whole. It emphasises teamwork, puts customer needs at the centre of the whole business operation and is a constant process of improvement. TQM is dealt with in unit 34.

Automation and technological change Advances in technology have led to major improvements in efficiency. One of the most recent changes has been the use of micro-computers in business. Computers are used in production, finance, administration, design and many other areas. Enormous savings have been made. The introduction of robots is another fairly new innovation in production. The need for unskilled and semi-skilled workers has been reduced as a result. Automation also improves the quality of the product, reduces errors, helps control and improves decision making. This is discussed in unit 36.

The size of the firm As a business increases in size it can reduce costs by gaining economies of scale (☞ unit 31).

Key terms

Efficiency - how well inputs, such as raw materials, labour or capital can be changed into outputs, such as goods or services.
Productivity - the ratio of outputs to inputs in a production process, such as the output of a given amount of labour or capital.
Standardisation - the use of uniform resources and activities.
Work study - a process which investigates the best possible way to use business resources.

Summary

1. Why might businesses wish to measure efficiency?
2. How might; (a) labour productivity; (b) capital productivity; be measured?
3. What is meant by multi-factor productivity?
4. What does 'value added' measure?
5. What are the benefits of work study for a business?
6. Explain what is meant by method study and work measurement.
7. What role can ergonomics play in improving efficiency?
8. Describe 4 examples of labour flexibility.
9. How might quality circles improve efficiency?
10. What are the advantages and disadvantages of standardisation?

Question

Morgan Cars

Morgan Cars Ltd are small sports car manufacturers located in Malvern. They are a family business and were founded in 1909. The company has done very well to survive in a such a highly competitive industry for so long. Similar business enterprises have disappeared from the scene. Morgan Cars have survived because they have an enthusiastic market, according to one of their directors, so enthusiastic that buyers are prepared to wait around 6 or 7 years for the delivery of a new car.

In 1989 production was 9 cars per week. The directors wanted to raise production in order to match some of the excess demand. The cars are entirely hand built from a range of selective, high quality raw materials. For example, the wood used is 100 year old Ash imported from Belgium. This makes a significant contribution to the tremendous appeal the cars have. The car is 'coach built' using the same method as the luxury cars of the 1930s. The appeal of this method is durability and strength combined with light weight.

In the workshops there is little evidence of automation. It is limited to some handling equipment, air tools and overhead conveyors. The cars themselves are pushed manually from one work station to the next. In 1989 the company did not use any computers. Morgan also manufacture and store spare parts for cars which were made in the 1950s. In 1989, they operated a visual stock control system and reordered when it appeared that stocks were low.

There are about 130 employees, many of whom have been working for the company between 30 and 40 years. Most of them have completed a 4 or 5 year training programme and have been working in the same workshop ever since they were recruited. Production is organised into four main departments:
- wood shop;
- sheet metal shop;
- upholstery shop;
- machine shop.

Staff are trained in a variety of jobs in a particular workshop, but do not normally switch between workshops. For example, carpenters do not turn their hand to upholstery. On the financial side, one disadvantage is the amount of capital tied up in work-in-progress. Around 100 partly finished cars were present in the workshops on any typical working day in 1989. However, Morgan receive a 10 per cent deposit on all cars before manufacture and payment is made as soon as the car is completed. This means stocks of finished cars are not accumulated.

A sales director is responsible for the unique approach of the company to its consumers. For example, there is a vast choice of colours, running into thousands, cars can be customised to customers' needs and buyers can even watch the cars being built. A

product development officer is employed to ensure changes in specifications to meet safety and emission standards and to make the up to 50 modifications to the design each year. In 1993 Morgan, for example, were developing safety 'air bags' for the American market. However, the company is still keen to keep the traditional 1930s 'look' of the car.

Since 1989, Morgan cars have enjoyed some significant improvements in terms of efficiency.
- The time taken to complete a car has been reduced from more than 10 weeks to between 7 and 9 weeks, depending on its specification.
- Production has been increased from 420 to 480 cars per annum.
- Work-in-progress has been reduced from over 100 cars to 85.
- An integrated computer system for stock control, accounts and production planning has been introduced.

There is a factory held belief that the company must continually make changes, but that they must not harm the core reasons for their customers buying its products.

Source: approved by Charles Morgan, Morgan Motor Company Ltd.

(a) **Why might Morgan wish to become more efficient even though they are a profitable business?**
(b) **Calculate the labour productivity assuming that 130 workers are employed and that 480 cars are produced in a year.**
(c) **Explain: (i) two advantages; (ii) two disadvantages; of workers being trained for employment in one work shop only.**
(d) **Explain why product standardisation might not benefit Morgan.**
(e) **How have Morgan been able to deal with the problem of a high level of work-in-progress?**
(f) **Write a short report outlining how Morgan have improved efficiency since 1989.**
(g) **Choose 2 other methods which might be used to improve efficiency and explain the possible advantages and disadvantages if they were introduced by the company.**

The nature and impact of technology

One of the most significant factors affecting how businesses have operated in the twentieth century has been the impact of new TECHNOLOGY. It is easy to see its impact when we consider some of the changes that have taken place in business.

■ New products and services, such as camcorders, compact discs, laptop computers and direct purchasing from television.

■ New production processes, such as robotic welding, and computer controlled cutting machines.

■ New materials such as silicon chips for computer circuit boards and polystyrene for packaging.

■ Changes in business operations and new skills. For example, as a result of automatic cash tills in banking, many staff have been retrained to sell financial services.

There are many ways in which technology can be defined. One approach is to say that it is 'a creative process which uses human, scientific and material resources to solve problems and generate better efficiency'. Some examples make this clear. A business that uses video conferencing to communicate with branches spread all over the country is using technology. So is a plant which uses lasers to detect faults in products as they move along the production line.

How does technological progress take place? It is usually by means of **invention** and **innovation**. Invention is the discovery of something new. Some recent examples include the Laser beam in 1960 by Dr. Charles Townes, the micro-processor in 1971 by Marcian Hoff in the USA and the Rubik Cube in 1975 by Professor Erno Rubik in Hungary. Inventions are then developed into products. The laser beam has been used for cutting in industry, micro-surgery in hospitals and spectacular lighting shows in displays.

Inventions are sometimes made by creative people 'outside' business. For example, the ball point pen was invented by a sculptor, and the pneumatic tyre by a veterinary surgeon! Today, most research is carried out by teams of people working for a business, university or the government. The rewards to inventors can be very high indeed, if their inventions can be used commercially and patented (☞ unit 28).

In business innovation is the commercial exploitation of an invention. An invention is not usually in a form that consumers will buy. The product must be developed to meet consumers' needs, so that it can be sold profitably by business. UK firms have, perhaps, been reluctant to do this in the past. For example, in the UK, Babbage developed the first working computers about 150 years ago. Since then Japan and America have led the world in hardware production and computer research. Enormous investment is often required to innovate once a technical breakthrough has been achieved.

QUESTION 1 In 1993 new technology was used to make line decisions in the Australian Open tennis championships at Flinders Park in Melbourne. The new system was developed by a company called Tel (for Tennis electronic lines). It took five years to develop and used technology associated with weapons detection and radio. The computerised system cost £130,000 to install on three courts at Flinders Park. The courts had to be relaid with a special surface of rubberised concrete. Underneath the surface is a network of flat wires following the path of the court markings. The equipment picks up signals from the tennis ball, which contains iron particles, when it hits the court. It relays the exact position within 30cm of the line to a monitor at the umpire's chair. Tel say that it is accurate to within three millimetres, compared with the naked eye which is accurate to one centimetre. Tel was awaiting approval of the system for international play from the Association of Tennis Professionals, which runs the men's professional game. If it was approved the financial benefits would be considerable. Tel are also developing similar systems for clay, grass and indoor courts. They have already spent £4.5 million on development.

Source : adapted from the *Financial Times*, 15.1.1993.

(a) Explain why the above case is an example of innovation.
(b) What will be the benefits of the system to the business if it is successful?
(c) What problems might Tel encounter in the initial stages of implementation?

Applications

There are few, if any, areas of business which have not been influenced by technology.

Production has been one of the main areas. Increasingly products are being mass produced using flow production methods (☞ unit 29). This gives a business more scope to use developments in machinery.

In the **primary** sector, the agriculture and mining industries have seen great changes in production methods. Advances in mechanical engineering and electronics have led to huge increases in productivity, cuts in the labour force and better working conditions.

In the **manufacturing** sector technology has had a similar impact. A great deal of specialist machinery is used on production lines, for example, computer driven robots and lasers. Welding and spraying can be performed by robots, which have been installed in most car manufacturing plants all over the world. Lasers have many uses. On production lines they can be made into sensors to find faults.

The development of technology has also helped to

Old and new farming techniques.

improve efficiency in the **tertiary** sector. For example, businesses which supply dental and health care, financial services and marketing services, have all introduced new technology into their operations. Distribution has seen great benefits. The introduction of containers has made the handling of freight quick and easy. Containers are easily hauled on trailers and locked into position. There is far less danger of damage and stealing, so insurance rates are lower. At container terminals containers are transferred between road and rail transport by gantry cranes in minutes.

The packaging of products has changed greatly in recent years. New materials such as polystyrene and strong plastic wrap have improved the way in which goods are packaged. The materials have been lighter and stronger, have provided better protection, and have been easier to handle. Many marketing departments have redesigned the packaging of products to increase sales. In some cases new technology has helped. For example, Lucozade and other soft drinks have been packaged in flexible bags instead of cans and bottles.

Advertising has also used new technology. Television adverts have become more sophisticated, both in filming and special effects. There is also a wider selection of advertising media. For example, advertisers have used rotating messages on the 'touchlines' of sporting events.

QUESTION 2 Congestion on Britain's roads, particularly in London, prompted the Department of Transport to commission the University of Newcastle to research into electronic road charging. Several devices have been developed. The most up to date one involves fitting vehicles with meters. These would be activated by microwave signals emitted by roadside beacons once they entered a charging zone. The meter would deduct payments from a rechargeable 'smart card' inserted into the device by the driver at the beginning of a journey. Any vehicle entering the zone without a meter would be automatically photographed. The driver would then be traced via the vehicle number plate and fined. There are a number of advantages to this particular system.

- It can operate at high vehicle speeds.
- It can operate in multi-lane traffic.
- It assures anonymity providing drivers obey the rules.
- The roadside beacons can transmit traffic information to the meters.
- The smart card could be used to pay for travel on public transport.

Source : adapted from the *Financial Times*, 2.4.1993.

How might the installation of the above technology affect the following businesses if they were located inside the charging zones?
(a) A supermarket.
(b) A manufacturer.
(c) A taxi service.

Information technology

INFORMATION TECHNOLOGY (IT) is the recording and use of information by electronic means. It is not just about the use of computers in business. For example, machines can be used to transmit documents overseas. IT has a variety of applications.

Administration There have been large savings in staffing due to computerisation. Many routine tasks can be done quickly with new machines, such as customer orders, invoicing and billing. IT allows business managers to manipulate information, use it to help design new products, create models and run simulations.

Communications Communications technology can store messages and documents electronically, then send them over telephone lines in a fraction of a second. This saves money and ensures information is passed on accurately. Mobile telephones allow business people to work from a variety of locations. Facsimile machines can transmit copies of documents over any distance. Satellite communications help scientists, engineers and managers to use specialised databases.

Personnel Most firms keep staff records on databases and use computerised payroll systems. Even the training of staff has used new technology, such as training videos.

People working from home can be linked by computer to their company and to other colleagues in a variety of locations.

Finance Many firms record all financial transactions on databases and spreadsheets (☞ unit 13). Some systems are able to produce immediate profit and loss accounts, balance sheets, cash flow statements, and up to date budgets at the end of the trading day. The value and movement of stocks in a business can be monitored by computers. Credit control can also be tighter with the use of up to date information.

Production One example of information technology in production is the checking of product quality. This is vital in high speed manufacturing, mining and in chemical processing. IT has been developed to control self-regulating systems. A good example would be a factory with two production lines. A computer controlled system would run the lines, switching materials between them so that the system runs efficiently.

Research and development Computer Aided Design (CAD) (☞ unit 28) is one obvious use of IT. Recording, monitoring, regulating, forecasting and analysing data are all tasks in R & D which can be carried out more easily.

Security Data about potential customers, suppliers and employees can be obtained easily with the use of IT. An example could be a retailer checking a customer's credit rating.

Data protection

The rapid development of IT has prompted the government to pass legislation about the collection, storage, processing and distribution of personal data. The **1984 UK Data Protection Act** only applies to information which is processed by a computer. However, European legislation may make some paper records subject to this law in the near future.

The Act makes people or businesses who use personal data register with the Data Protection Registrar. The reasons for which they hold the data must be stated. For example, it may be information about a person's credit rating or loans they have taken out.

The Act gives rights to individuals about whom information is recorded on a computer. They may find information about themselves, challenge it and claim compensation. The Act sets down 8 conditions with which users must comply.
■ Personal data should be obtained and processed fairly and lawfully.
■ Personal data can only be held for specified and lawful purposes.
■ Personal data cannot be used or disclosed in any manner which is incompatible with the purpose for which it is held.
■ The amount of data held should be adequate, relevant and not excessive.
■ Personal data should be accurate and kept up to date.
■ Personal data should not be kept for longer than is necessary.
■ An individual shall be entitled to:
(a) be informed by any data user if he or she is the subject of personal data and also have access to that data;
(b) where appropriate, have data corrected or erased.
■ Security measures must be taken by data users to prevent unlawful access, alteration, disclosure, destruction, or loss of personal data.

QUESTION 3

Table 36.1 *Information technology budget increases by sector, 1990 over 1989 (UK av. = 30%)*

Above average		Below average	
Utilities	147%	Finance	26%
Education	83%	Retail/dist.	10%
Process	63%	Other industry	0%
Engineering	48%	Public admin.	12%
		Computer services	24%

Source : Price Waterhouse Computer Opinion Surveys.

Since privatisation many UK utilities, such as water, gas and electricity, have enjoyed a monopoly position in their markets. They have also invested heavily in information technology. During the 1990s the water industry plans to spend £25 billion on capital projects, of which 10 per cent will go on support systems. Thames Water have recently bought a very expensive customer information system. National Power, which inherited a fragmented information technology system after privatisation, planned a three year information technology strategy. They planned to implement a company-wide communications network and install new hardware systems and software in data centres. They also aimed to design and build a variety of applications: office and purchasing systems, work management, financial reporting, and an innovative operational information system which gives the business access to a reservoir of operational power plant data.

Source : adapted from the *Financial Times*, July 1992.

(a) What scope might there be for the use of information technology in the water industry?
(b) Why might investment in information technology be below average in the sectors described in Table 36.1?
(c) Given their monopoly status, why do you think the utilities have invested heavily in customer information services?

Benefits of new technology

There are a number of benefits to business of using new technology.

Increased productivity More can be produced with less and, as a result, businesses may gain higher profits. In addition, fewer of the environment's resources may be used up.

Reducing waste Introducing new technology often results in time being saved and fewer materials being used. For example, technology has created printing machines which waste less paper when printing books or magazines. How resources are used has attracted a great deal of attention in recent years. As the world's population continues to grow it will be necessary to improve resource use even further.

Improving the working environment Statistics on accidents at work show that the working environment is safer as result of new technology. Mining and manufacturing in particular have benefited. Modern equipment has made work easier and more tolerable. For example, fork lift trucks mean workers no longer need to load goods by hand. These improvements also help to remove workers' dissatisfaction.

Benefits to society Many new products have come onto the market in recent years. Personal stereo systems, video recorders, satellite TV, high performance cars and microwave ovens are some examples. New products mean wider consumer choice and possibly higher living standards. Other developments have helped to make our lives easier, such as automatic cash dispensers and mobile telephones.

Improvements in communications Faster means of transport (such as the jet aircraft), answerphones, computer network links and fax machines are all examples of inventions which have helped to improve the speed of communications.

Higher incomes If firms enjoy greater profits they can afford to pay higher dividends to shareholders and higher wages to employees. Also, if efficiency is improved then products may be sold at lower prices. As the country's income increases the government collects more tax revenue. This could be used to improve the quality of public services or alternatively to reduce the overall level of taxation or public sector borrowing (☞ unit 65).

Problems with new technology

The introduction of new technology can also cause problems for both business and society.

Cost Development, installation and maintenance can often prove costly. Also, businesses may have to lay off and retrain staff, leading to redundancy payments and retraining costs. If firms borrow to meet these costs, they will have to pay interest. Reorganisation may also be needed. Production may be changed from batch to flow

Figure 36.1 *An advertisement for Innovations, a mail order company in Swindon*

production (☞ unit 29), job descriptions may be changed (☞ unit 52) and in some cases a larger or smaller plant may be needed.

Labour relations In the past, trade unions have resisted the introduction of some new technology because of the threat to their members' jobs. There have been several cases of bitter disputes between employees and management. Changes in the newspaper industry caused such problems at News International.

Job skills New technology creates jobs which require new, technical skills, but replaces manual jobs. These new jobs cannot be done by the existing workforce unless they can be retrained. Often, this is not possible.

Breakdowns Automated production lines are interdependent. If one part of the line breaks down the whole process may stop. There may also be teething problems. Breakdowns occur when technology is first installed. For example, it is argued that the Stock Exchange Automatic Quotation (SEAQ) share dealing system was partially to blame for the 1987 Stock Exchange crash. The system automatically triggered selling instructions, causing big falls in some share prices.

Motivation Some staff may dislike working only with machines. This may affect their motivation (☞ unit 48).

Management The management of technological change is considered very difficult. One reason is due to the rapid pace of the change. When new technology becomes available business managers have to decide whether or not to purchase it, or wait for the next important breakthrough. Deciding when to invest in new technology is very difficult. The management of the human resources leading up to the change, and during the change, requires great skill. People are often unhappy about to change in their lives.

Unemployment In the last 14 years unemployment has more than trebled. Some unemployment will be as a result of new technology (☞ unit 68).

Leisure time People have gained more leisure time as a result of new technology. They need to learn how to use this extra time in a constructive way. Businesses are taking advantage of this. For example, it is argued that there is enough demand in the UK for many more golf courses.

An ageing population Medicine has benefited greatly from new technology. One effect of this is that the population of many countries is now 'ageing'. As a result the pressure has increased on those in work to support the aged. Demands on public funds will also increase and the government will have to find money for facilities which are needed for the elderly.

Key terms

Information technology - the recording and use of information by electronic means.
Technology - a creative process which uses human, scientific and material resources to solve problems and improve efficiency.

Summary

1. What is meant by technology?
2. What is the difference between invention and innovation?
3. State 4 areas of a business that might benefit from new technology.
4. How has new technology been used in marketing?
5. How might a business exporting products abroad make use of new technology?
6. How has information technology been incorporated in production?
7. How has business security used information technology?
8. Why was the Data Protection Act (1984) introduced?
9. In what ways has new technology benefited
   (a) business owners;
   (b) management?
10. Briefly explain problems that:
    (a) workers;
    (b) management;
    may face with the introduction of new technology.

Question

Wapping

In the mid-1980s Rupert Murdoch introduced new computer technology to the newspaper industry. Its introduction caused a major industrial dispute which lasted for more than a year. The new technology was expected to result in significant cost savings which would be achieved in five ways.

- Journalists and advertising staff could 'key in' copy to computers, linked to page make-up and plate-making, thereby dispensing with 'hot metal' type and making redundant most composing, lithographic, and paste-up staff.
- Powerful new web-offset machines would be used, reducing the number of printers needed.
- Facsimile transmission, enabling simultaneous production at satellite printing plants, could also reduce distribution costs and enable more intensive use of printing presses.
- The social organisation of production would be changed. The bargaining power of the print unions would be reduced, and production workers would be employed at lower wage levels or be replaced by more unskilled labour.
- Production would be on a continuous basis.

The introduction began with the location of a new plant in Wapping, East London. Rupert Murdoch told the print unions that he was just extending his plant to accommodate the printing of a new, local daily newspaper. In fact, the new factory, which cost £66 million, was sufficiently large to print all of his newspapers. He recruited a whole new workforce, with the help of the Electricians' union and trained them in the new technology. In addition, he negotiated an alternative distribution contract with an Australian firm, Thomas Nationwide Company. This was to prevent sympathy action by a group of organised labour. Finally, as a precaution, the Wapping plant was established as an independent company so that any picketing outside by the Fleet Street staff would be technically illegal. The unions were then asked to sign a legally binding contract which involved no strike action, acceptance of the new technology and resultant staffing levels, and an agreement to instant dismissal without appeal if any member was involved in industrial action. It was the latter part of the contract which proved to be the crucial stumbling block for the unions.

They could not sign and decided to call a strike. The Fleet Street production workers organised picket lines outside Murdoch's Wapping plant. There were frequent battles as the pickets tried to prevent workers from entering the plant and newspapers from leaving it. During the strike violence erupted between the police and the pickets. Many print workers were jailed, unions heavily fined and people seriously injured. After more than a year the strike was called off and the unions had lost. Murdoch had taught them a lesson in multinational business management.

Source: adapted from *Power without Responsibility* by James Curran and Jean Seaton, Routledge, 1988.

(a) **Explain why the introduction of new technology was an innovation.**

(b) **Identify the areas of the newspaper business that would have benefited from the introduction of the new technology.**

(c) **Describe the financial and non-financial benefits of the new technology to Murdoch's newspaper business.**

(d) **How might the consumer ultimately benefit from the new technology?**

(e) **Do you think that the print unions were justified in not signing the agreement? Give reasons for your answer.**

The nature of investment

Investment refers to the purchase of **capital goods**
(☞ unit 1). Capital goods are used in the production of
other goods, directly or indirectly. For example, a
building contractor who buys a cement mixer, some
scaffolding, a lorry and five shovels has invested. These
goods will be used directly in production. If the
contractor buys a typewriter, a filing cabinet and a
photocopier for the firm's office, this is indirect
investment. Although these items will not be used in
production the business would not run as efficiently
without them.

Investment can be **autonomous** or **induced**.
Autonomous investment is when a firm buys capital
goods to replace ones which have worn out. Any new

QUESTION 1

(a) State which of the above examples are categories
      of construction, plant and machinery, stocks or
      public sector investment.
(b) Why might the crane be an example of
      autonomous investment?

investment by the firm resulting from rising sales or
expansion is induced investment.

Types of investment

Investment can be placed into various categories.
■ Plant and machinery. This includes the purchase of a
    whole variety of mechanical and technical equipment.
    Vans, lathes, computers, robots, tools and information
    technology are examples.
■ Construction. This includes spending on new
    buildings that are bought or constructed by the firm.
    Factories, shops, warehouses, workshops and offices
    are examples.
■ Stocks. This is a less obvious item of investment, since
    it does not fit neatly into the earlier definition.
    However, because stocks of finished goods and work-
    in-progress (☞ unit 33) will earn income in the future
    when they are sold, they are classed as investment.
■ Public sector investment. Central and local
    government fund about twenty five per cent of all
    investment in the economy. Examples of public sector
    investment include the building of schools,
    motorways, hospitals and expenditure on goods like
    buses, dustcarts and equipment for the civil service.
    The factors which influence the level of public sector
    investment are often very different from those which
    affect private sector investment. This is dealt with later
    in this unit.

Risk in investment

The decision to invest by business is the most difficult it
has to make because of the risk involved. There is often a
number of alternative choices. A firm buying a new fleet
of cars for its sales staff has to decide which model of car
will suit the company best of all. There may also be a
considerable choice of projects. For example, a firm may
need to choose whether investment in a new packaging
machine which increases efficiency would be more
profitable than a new computer system.

If all cost and revenue data upon which a decision
would be based was accurate, there would not be a
problem. However, revenue information in particular
comes from predictions. It may be based on forecasts of
future demand and conditions in the economy. Even
costs, which are perhaps easier to predict, can vary. For
example, few would have predicted the oil price increases
in 1974, 1979 and 1990.

Most investment decisions are uncertain because they
are long term decisions, where resources are committed
for a period of time. Investment projects have failed both
in the private sector and the public sector. Examples in
the private sector include the Sinclair C5 and London's
Canary Wharf, where buildings were constructed but
much of the floor space was unoccupied. In the public

sector, the government spent a lot of money on equipment which was used in the development of the Concorde aircraft. This also proved to be commercially unsuccessful.

QUESTION 2 In 1991, Crosswell Brothers, a motor service centre, invested in a new breakdown vehicle costing £48,000. The company had to borrow heavily to buy the vehicle. However, provided the number of breakdowns continued to increase as they had done over the previous 18 months, the expected returns would provide them with a good profit.

Unfortunately, in 1992 a specialist breakdown service was set up in the area. This led to a dramatic drop in callers to Crosswell Brothers and by the end of the year the new breakdown vehicle was hardly ever used. The company were forced to sell the vehicle for £32,000 at a loss.

(a) Explain how the above case illustrates risk when making an investment.
(b) How might the business be affected by this investment failure?

The factors affecting private sector investment

Figure 37.1 shows the factors which might affect private sector investment decisions.

Motives To begin with, firms must have a reason to invest.

■ All firms have to replace worn out equipment.
■ To be competitive on costs, price and quality, firms may have to invest or risk losing customers to their rivals. For example, most building societies invested in the refurbishment of their branches in the late 1980s and early 1990s. Once one society improved its branch most others copied.
■ The availability of new technology (☞ unit 36) may persuade firms to invest. When technology becomes available, firms are often keen to use it if they can afford to.
■ Firms may wish to grow, to be more profitable or to increase their market influence. Growth involves investment in more plant, equipment and other productive assets.

Return If firms have a reason to invest, they must then decide whether it is worthwhile. One influence on this is the return on the investment. The return on an investment project can be found by subtracting the cost of the project from the expected revenue. There are three major costs. Capital costs might be the cost of a new factory. Opportunity costs (☞ unit 6) are the foregone alternatives the investment funds might have been used for, eg higher dividends to shareholders. Direct variable costs include the running costs of the project, eg labour or fuel costs.

Calculating the expected revenue is not easy. Expected

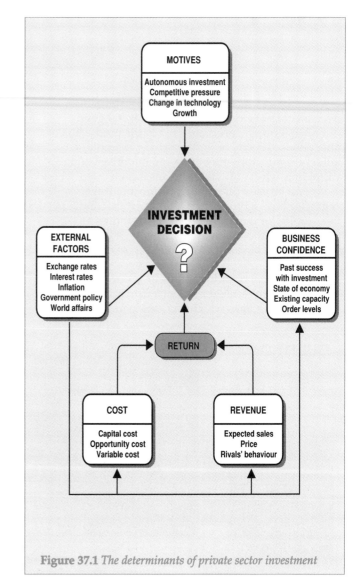

Figure 37.1 *The determinants of private sector investment*

sales are hard to predict with accuracy because many factors affect them. Market research (☞ unit 19) can only predict sales to some extent. Sales can also be influenced by the price set by the business in the future and by rivals' behaviour. Both of these factors are unpredictable.

Confidence Entrepreneurs and managers will be either optimistic or pessimistic about the future. Confidence may be influenced by a range of factors. These include whether or not previous investment has been a success, the state of the economy, the existing level of capacity and future order levels. A pessimistic business person may be less likely to invest than an optimistic one.

External factors External influences can be direct or indirect. For example, high interest rates may directly affect the cost of investment. If money is borrowed the business will pay back more. This can indirectly affect confidence. Inflation could affect costs, revenue and confidence. World affairs, like the Gulf crisis in 1990, or rising exchange rates (☞ unit 69), may make investment abroad seem less attractive.

The factors affecting public sector investment

What factors influence investment by central government and local authorities?

■ Investment in new schools, roads, and hospitals, for example, will be influenced by national and local needs. As the size of the population grows, more of these facilities will be needed.

■ Political factors may also influence the quantity and type of investment. In the recent past, the government has aimed to reduce public investment in order to reduce the size of the public sector in general. It has also reduced it in specific areas, such as on defence.

■ The availability of government funds and the opportunity cost of investment spending. If revenue from taxes is falling, there may be fewer investment funds. If the opportunity costs of investment projects are high, then they may be cancelled. The state of the economy will be important. For example, the UK has faced periods of high unemployment in recent years. This forced the government to spend on unemployment benefits, leaving fewer funds for investment or for local authority investment grants.

Investment appraisal - payback method

INVESTMENT APPRAISAL describes how a private sector firm might objectively evaluate an investment project, to determine whether or not it is likely to be profitable. It also allows firms to compare projects.

PAYBACK PERIOD refers to the amount of time it takes for a project to recover or pay back the initial outlay. For example, a farmer may invest £500,000 in new milking machinery and estimate that it will lead to income over the next five years, as in Table 37.1.

Table 37.1 *Expected income from some new milking machinery*

Year 1	Year 2	Year 3	Year 4	Year 5
£100,000	£125,000	£125,000	£150,000	£180,000

Here the payback period is four years. If we add together the income from the project in the first four years it amounts to £500,000.

When using this method to choose between projects, the project with the shortest payback will be chosen. Assume a farmer is appraising three investment projects, all of which cost £70,000. The flow of income expected from each project is shown in Table 37.2.

Table 37.2 *Expected income from three investment projects*

(000)

	Year 1	Year 2	Year 3	Year 4	Year 5	Year 6	Total
A	£10	£10	£20	£20	£30	£40	£130
B	£20	£20	£20	£20	£20	£20	£120
C	£30	£30	£20	£10	£10	£10	£110

In this example project C would be chosen because it has the shortest payback time, ie slightly less than three years. Project A's payback stretches into the fifth year and project B's into the fourth. Note that total income is not taken into account in this method. In fact project C has the lowest total return over the six years!

Advantages

■ This method is useful when technology changes rapidly, such as in the agriculture industry. New farm machinery is designed and introduced into the market regularly. It is important to recover the cost of investment before a new machine is designed.

■ It is simple to use.

■ Firms might adopt this method if they have cash flow problems. This is because the project chosen will 'payback' the investment more quickly than others.

Disadvantages

■ Cash earned after the 'payback' is not taken into account in the decision to invest.

■ The method ignores the profitability of the project, since the criterion used is the speed of repayment.

QUESTION 3 Denwood Ltd manufacture a range of camping equipment. The company has three investment projects under consideration:
■ the purchase of some new computer equipment - cost £20,000;
■ the purchase of a new delivery vehicle - cost £40,000;
■ installing a new security system - cost £15,000.
The expected stream of income from each project is shown in Table 37.3.

Table 37.3 *Expected income from three investment projects for Denwood Ltd*

(£000s)

Year	1	2	3	4	5	6	7	8	9	10	Total
Computer	4	4	4	4	4	4	4	4	4	4	40
Vehicle	10	10	10	6	6	6	4	4	2	2	60
Security	1	1	1	2	2	2	2	3	3	3	20

(a) Calculate, to the nearest month, the payback period for each project.
Which project would the business select?
(b) In what ways might the payback method of investment appraisal be inadequate in this case?

Investment appraisal - average rate of return

The AVERAGE RATE OF RETURN (ARR) method measures the net return each year as a percentage of the initial cost of the investment.

$$\text{Average rate of return (\%)} = \frac{\text{Net return (profit) per annum}}{\text{Capital outlay (cost)}} \times 100$$

For example, the costs and expected income from three investment projects are shown in Table 37.4.

Table 37.4 *The costs and expected income from three investment projects*

	Project X	Project Y	Project Z
Cost	£50,000	£40,000	£90,000
Return Yr 1	£10,000	£10,000	£20,000
Yr 2	£10,000	£10,000	£20,000
Yr 3	£15,000	£10,000	£30,000
Yr 4	£15,000	£15,000	£30,000
Yr 5	£20,000	£15,000	£30,000
Total	£70,000	£60,000	£130,000

A business would first calculate the total net profit from each project by subtracting the total return of the project from its cost, ie £70,000 - £50,000 = £20,000 for project X. The next step is to calculate the net profit per annum by dividing the total net profit by the number of years the project runs for, ie £20,000 ÷ 5 = £4,000 for X. Finally, the ARR is calculated by using the above formula, ie

$$\text{ARR (Project X)} = \frac{£4,000}{£50,000} \times 100$$

$$= 8\%$$

The results for all three projects are shown in Table 37.5. Project Y would be chosen because it gives a higher ARR (10 per cent) than the other two.

Table 37.5 *The average rate of return calculated for three investment projects*

	Project X	Project Y	Project Z
Cost	£50,000	£40,000	£90,000
Total net profit (return - cost)	£20,000	£20,000	£40,000
Net profit p.a. (profit ÷ 5)	£4,000	£4,000	£8,000
ARR	8%	10%	8.9%

The advantage of this method is that it shows clearly the profitability of an investment project. Not only does it allow a range of projects to be compared, the overall rate of return can be compared to other uses for investment funds. In the example in Table 37.5, if a company can gain 12 per cent by placing its funds in a bank account, it might choose to postpone the investment project until interest rates fall. It is also easier to identify the **opportunity cost** of investment.

However, the method does not take into account the effects of time on the value of money. The above example assumes that, for project X, £10,000 of income for the firm in two years time is the same as £10,000 in one years time. Some allowance must be made for the time span over which the income from an investment project is received for it to be most useful.

QUESTION 4 Worldwarm PLC is a multinational company which manufactures electrical heating equipment. The company has three investment projects under consideration:
■ the building of a new research centre;
■ the location of a new plant in the USA;
■ the opening of a training centre.
 The cost of the three projects are £30 million, £40 million and £25 million respectively. The income from the projects is shown in Table 37.6.

Table 37.6 *Expected income from three investment projects for Worldwarm PLC*

(£m)

Year	1	2	3	4	5	6	7	8	9	10	Total
Research centre	0	0	5	5	5	8	8	8	12	12	63
New plant	4	5	6	6	8	8	9	9	12	12	79
Training centre	5	5	5	5	5	5	5	5	5	5	50

(a) Calculate the average rate of return for each project.
(b) Calculate the payback period for each project.
(c) Which project should the business select? Give reasons for your answer.

Investment appraisal - discounted cash flow

This method of appraisal has certain advantages. It deals with the problems of **interest rates** and **time**. The return on an investment project is always in the future, usually over a period of several years. Money earned or paid in the future is worth less today. Why?

What if £100 is placed in a bank account when the rate of interest is 10 per cent? At the end of the year it will be worth £110 (£100 + £100 x 10 per cent) or (£100 x 1.1). At the end of two years it will be worth £121 (£110 + £110 x 10 per cent) or (£110 x 1.1). This shows that money grows over time if it is deposited or lent with interest. Table 37.7 shows how the value of £100 grows over a 10 year period if left in a bank account when the rate of compound interest is 10 per cent.

Table 37.7 *The value of £100 over a 10 year period if left in a bank account when the compound rate of interest is 10 per cent (rounded to the nearest pound).*

Year	Value of £100 at compound rate of interest of 10 per cent
0	£100
1	£110
2	£121
3	£133
4	£146
5	£161
6	£177
7	£195
8	£214
9	£236
10	£259

Put another way, a **fixed** sum paid in the future is worth less than a fixed sum paid today. Why? The £100 could have been placed in a bank account for 3 years and could have grown to £133. So a fixed sum of £100 received in 3 years time will be far less than £100 today. The value today of a sum of money available in future is called the PRESENT VALUE. What is the present value of £100 in 3 years? This can be found by the formula:

$$\text{Present value} = \frac{A}{\frac{(1+r)^n}{100}}$$

where A = amount of money, r = rate of interest and n = number of years. The present value of £100 received in three years time is (assuming a 10 per cent interest rate):

$$\text{Present value} = \frac{£100}{\frac{(1+10)^3}{100}} = \frac{£100}{(1.1)^3} = \frac{£100}{1.331} = £75.13$$

This shows the £100 received in 3 years time is worth less than £100 today. How much less depends on two things.
- Interest rates. If interest rates rise to 20 per cent then present value would be:

$$\frac{£100}{\frac{(1+20)^3}{100}} = £27.78$$

- The length of time. If £100 was received in 25 years

time the present value would be:

$$\frac{£100}{\frac{(1+10)^{25}}{100}} = £9.23$$

DISCOUNTED CASH FLOW takes into account that interest rates affect the present value of future income. It shows that the future cash flow is **discounted** by the rate of interest.

How can this be used to decide whether investment should take place? Assume an investment project costs £100,000 and yields an expected stream of income over a 3 year period - year 1, £30,000; year 2, £40,000; year 3, £50,000. The rate of interest remains at 10 per cent over the time period. The present value of the future income stream using the technique described above is shown over the page.

QUESTION 5 Brightwell Plastics Ltd are considering the purchase of a new plastic moulding machine which is to cost £10 million. The investment is expected to earn a return for the company over a four year period as follows: year 1, £3 million; year 2, £3 million; year 3, £4 million; year 4, £4.5 million. It is anticipated that the rate of interest will remain at 10 per cent.

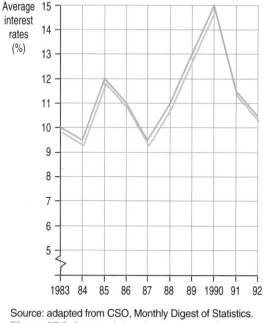

Source: adapted from CSO, Monthly Digest of Statistics.
Figure 37.2 *Average interest rate movements (1983-1992)*

(a) Assuming that the rate of interest remains at 10 per cent calculate the present value of future income from the investment.
(b) Calculate the net present value and state whether the business should invest in this project.
(c) How might the information contained in Figure 37.2 affect the accuracy of investment appraisal using the DCF approach?

$$\text{Present value} = \frac{£30,000}{(1+0.1)^1} + \frac{£40,000}{(1+0.1)^2} + \frac{£50,000}{(1+0.1)^3}$$

$$\text{Present value} = \frac{£30,000}{(1.1)^1} + \frac{£40,000}{(1.1)^2} + \frac{£50,000}{(1.1)^3}$$

$$\text{Present value} = \frac{£30,000}{1.1} + \frac{£40,000}{1.21} + \frac{£50,000}{1.331}$$

$$\text{Present value} = £27,272 + £33,057 + £37,565 = £97,894$$

The above investment project is not viable since the present value of the return (£97,894) is less than the cost (£100,000). The NET PRESENT VALUE (NPV) of the project which shows the return on the investment less the cost is:

$$\text{NPV} = \text{Present value of return - cost}$$
$$= £97,894 - £100,000 = -£2,106$$

Before the DCF procedure was applied, the total income would have been £120,000 (£30,000 + £40,000 + £50,000). A decision maker may have thought the project profitable without the use of DCF. It is sometimes thought that DCF is used to take the effects of inflation into account. In fact it is used to take into account the effect of **interest rates.**

Investment appraisal - internal rate of return

This technique also makes use of discounted cash flow. To decide on the INTERNAL RATE OF RETURN (IRR) a firm must find the rate of return (x) where the net present value is zero. This internal rate of return is then compared with the market rate of interest to determine whether the investment should take place. Assume an investment project costs £10,000 and yields a one year return only of £13,000. The market rate of interest is 14 per cent. To calculate the IRR (x):

$$\text{Cost} = \frac{A}{(1+x)^1}$$

$$10,000 = \frac{13,000}{(1+x)^1}$$

$$(1+x) = \frac{13,000}{10,000}$$

$$1 + x = 1.3$$

$$x = 1.3 - 1$$

$$= 0.3 \text{ or } 30\%$$

Since the IRR (x) of 30 per cent is greater than the market rate of interest (14 per cent) the firm should invest in the project. When this is applied to projects over a longer period the calculation becomes more complex. However, the method remains the same.

An alternative approach is to use trial and error. This means choosing a discount rate, calculating the net present value (NPV) and seeing whether it equals zero. If it does not then another rate must be chosen. This process is continued until the correct rate is found. For example, assume that an investment project costs £50,000 and earns a five year return.

Table 37.8 *The NPV of an investment project at three different discount rates*

(£)

Year	Income	Present value of income at:		
		10%	7.5%	5%
1	5,000	4,545	4,651	4,762
2	5,000	4,132	4,325	4,555
3	10,000	7,513	8,045	8,643
4	20,000	13,661	14,970	16,447
5	20,000	12,442	13,828	15,661
Total	60,000	42,273	45,919	50,048
NPV		-7,727	-4,081	48

Table 37.8 shows the actual return and the present value of the return over the five year period at different discount rates. If a 10 per cent discount rate is used the NPV is less than zero, ie -£7,727. Also, if a 7.5 per cent discount rate is used the NPV is less than zero, ie -£4,081. If a 5 per cent rate is used the NPV is as near to zero as is needed, ie just £48. Thus, 5 per cent is the internal rate of return. Figure 37.3 shows the relationship between the discount rate and the NPV. As the discount rate increases the NPV falls. The IRR is shown on the discount rate axis where NPV is zero.

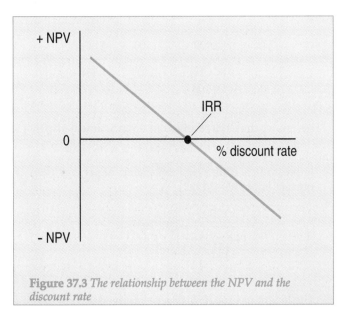

Figure 37.3 *The relationship between the NPV and the discount rate*

Summary

1. What is meant by the term investment?
2. Explain the difference between autonomous and induced investment.
3. State the 4 types of investment.
4. Why is the investment decision risky?
5. State the factors that might influence: (a) private sector; (b) public investment?
6. What is the function of investment appraisal in business?
7. Explain briefly how a business would appraise investment using the payback period.
8. What are the advantages and disadvantages of the payback method?
9. What does the average rate of return method of investment appraisal aim to measure?
10. Why is the discounted cash flow method of appraisal used in business?

Key terms

Average rate of return (ARR) - a method of investment appraisal which measures the net return per annum as a percentage of the initial spending.
Discounted cash flow (DCF) - a method of investment appraisal which takes interest rates into account by calculating the present value of future income.
Internal rate of return (IRR) - the rate of return (x) at which the net present value is zero.
Investment appraisal - the evaluation of an investment project to determine whether or not it is likely to be worthwhile.
Net present value - the present value of future income from an investment project, less the cost.
Present value - the value today of a sum of money available in the future.
Payback period - the amount of time it takes to recover the cost of an investment project.

Question

Grant Engineering

Grant Engineering are a medium sized company with a workforce of 140 and an annual turnover of around £5 million. Their main factory is located on a small industrial site on the edge of Norwich. They produce mainly sheet metal components and claim to be one of the UK's leading sub-contractors in sheet metal and powder painting.

Their commitment to capital investment is impressive. They have recently purchased a new robotic welder and a new computer system for the office. They have also opened a new plant in Harwich, concentrating on the coating of metal sheets. The directors openly emphasise the importance of capital expenditure in their business. They feel that customer confidence will increase if new technology is continually introduced.

In the past, the company has never used any investment appraisal techniques. Instead, they have stressed the relevance of capacity, order levels and in particular, 'intuition'. A particular machine would be bought if it was needed to fulfil orders and improve the security of the company in the eyes of the customers. In addition, the effect of interest rates on investment expenditure was said to be unimportant. The business would not delay buying a machine if it was needed just because the interest rate happened to be high. Similarly, they would not purchase a machine because interest rates were low. Only if high interest rates adversely affected customer demand would Grant Engineering change its investment plans.

The directors of the company are considering more investment in the future. They have identified two alternatives - a new fleet of company cars costing £160,000 and a computerised cutting machine costing £200,000.

Table 37.9 *Return on two investment projects for Grant Engineering*

(£000)

Year	1	2	3	4	5	6
Return: Car fleet	30	30	40	40	50	50
Cutting machine	50	50	50	60	60	60

Table 37.9 shows the expected income from the projects over a six year period. Grant's accountants have suggested that a quantitative approach to investment appraisal should be tried.

(a) Explain how factors like capacity, order levels and intuition could affect the investment decision.
(b) Calculate the ARR for each project.
(c) Calculate the NPV for each project (assume that r = 10 per cent).
(d) Based on your answers in (b) and (c), which project do you think Grant Engineering should select?
(e) Under what circumstances will interest rates: (i) influence the investment decision; (ii) not influence the investment decision?
(f) Why do you think Grant's accountants suggested using a quantitative approach to investment appraisal?

Woodlands PLC

Woodlands PLC were formed in 1976 when Wooden Products Ltd, a cabinet maker, and Greenlands Ltd, a timber yard, merged on a friendly basis. They went public in 1980 and enjoyed a 10 year period of profit growth. The company:

* employs 2,800 people;
* produces a range of wooden products, mainly for the furniture industry;
* owns three timber yards in Scotland;
* operates 5 factories, one in Fort William, 2 in Inverness and 3 in Glasgow.

Recently, the board of directors has been criticised for the poor financial performance of the company. Details of the performance, which compares 1990 and 1993, are shown in Table 1.

Table 1 *Financial information for Woodlands PLC*

	1990	1993
Turnover	£146m	£142m
Profit	£34m	£1.2m
Share price	92p	31p

In August 1993, a board meeting was held to discuss the poor trading position and the company's future. The production manager was also invited to give his views. The company's turnover in the last three years had not fallen too sharply, given that the recession had hit the furniture industry quite severely. The problem appeared to be rising production costs and inefficiency. The production manager was vague when questioned. He identified machinery breakdowns at two of the timber yards and generous wage increases at the production plants as possible reasons. The board meeting was a short one. The directors decided a work study should be undertaken by an independent specialist to see how efficiency in the business could be improved.

The key results of the work study were received at the end of September. Four key recommendations were made to Woodlands PLC.

* Reduce the product range from 45 to 30 by standardising some products.
* Close the Fort William factory.
* Close one of the timber yards.
* Introduce new technology in the remaining factories.
* Rationalise the workforce and introduce new working practices.

On the whole the directors agreed that all of the recommendations would benefit the firm. However, there were going to be problems following these changes. Some of the firm's customers would not be happy at the reduction in the product range. Although the workforce could be redeployed when one of the timber yards closed, it would mean a 15 mile journey for most workers. The other two recommendations were going to be expensive and could not be undertaken at the same time due to a lack of funds. The installation of new technology was expected to cost £24 million. Rationalising the workforce and introducing new work practices which involved making 600 staff redundant (as a result of the closures) and retraining a further 500 would cost £48 million. The company accountant suggested that the choice with the shortest payback should be undertaken first. Table 2 shows the cost and expected revenue from the two recommendations over a ten year period.

Table 2 *The cost and expected returns from two of the recommendations made by the work study team at Woodlands PLC*

(£m)

	Cost	Expected returns									
		Yr1	Yr2	Yr3	Yr4	Yr5	Yr6	Yr7	Yr8	Yr9	Yr10
New technology	24	8	8	8	8	8	6	6	6	6	4
Rationalisation and new working practices	48	10	10	10	20	20	25	25	30	30	30

(a) State the type of integration used when Wooden Products Ltd merged with Greenlands Ltd. Explain 2 possible advantages of this type of merger.

(b) Explain how the business may use work study and identify 3 advantages to Woodlands PLC.

(c) What might be the impact on the business of reducing the product range?

(d) Calculate the payback for the two recommendations described in Table 2. Which of the recommendations should be undertaken first according to the suggestion made by the accountant?

(e) Calculate the average rate of return for the two recommendations and state which of them is the most profitable for Woodlands PLC.

(f) Write a report to the board of directors explaining the problems Woodlands might encounter when implementing the final recommendations.

Bensons Crisps

Mr Sidney Benson set up Bensons Crisps in the 1940s during the war. At the time, Smiths, virtually the only UK volume crisp maker, drastically reduced production due to the shortage of vegetable oil for frying. Mr Benson was a fish and chip shop proprietor and decided to produce crisps using lard for frying. Today Bensons Crisps is the fourth largest quoted savoury snack maker in a UK market worth about £1.4 billion.

The company has just launched an ambitious investment programme in an attempt to secure its future. It is centralising its production operation. This involves moving most of its production from three factories and a warehouse in Kirkham, Lancashire, to a purpose built plant nearby. The main reason for this move is to match the efficiency of its larger competitors. Indeed, once the relocation is complete, Bensons believe that they will be one of the most efficient producers of snack foods in the country.

The investment will cost £9.7 million. The new plant will overcome Bensons' main problem - lack of capacity. Without the efficiency gains from volume production available to its larger rivals, the company's capacity to remain competitive is questionable. With operations split between two factories and a warehouse in Kirkham and one factory in Newport, Gwent, the ability of Bensons to survive has been in doubt. Also, in the late 1980s, Bensons failed to take changes in the market into account. Consumers switched from purchasing single packets of crisps from independent retailers, to the lower margin multipacks, sold at supermarkets. The big multiples now account for about 50 per cent of retail sales.

In the last five years five independent crisp producers have been absorbed by larger competitors. Mr Malcolm Jones, managing director, considered selling up but then decided against it. Instead, the company chose to invest in a greenfield site. This option was considered more difficult, but potentially far more rewarding for shareholders and employees.

In the last six years Bensons has spent £5 million on new equipment, most of which will be transferred to the new site. The total investment, however, is less than the sum invested by Snack Factory, a private company 40 miles away in Skelmersdale, which claims they are Europe's most efficient snack producer. Bensons' new 9.8 acre site will allow for improved materials flow and greater capacity. It will replace, for example, an existing 700kg per hour fryer with one that can handle 2,000kg per hour. The new fryer will feed an automated packaging machine which is capable of responding to orders. Bensons reckon that cost savings of around 10 - 13 per cent will be made. This represents about £1 million a year.

On the marketing side the new facility should mean a change in the sales mix. It currently sells 40 per cent of turnover to supermarkets, 10 per cent through van rounds and 50 per cent to wholesale cash and carry business. It is negotiating with multiples for shelf space and expects to sell over 60 per cent of its turnover to supermarkets after the move, with the remainder going to the independent sector.

It is a bold strategy which, although based on sound assumptions about how technology can improve efficiency, depends on other factors beyond the control of Bensons and everyone else in the market. It is argued that Bensons will remain vulnerable in the market, particularly to the price pressures exerted by the 'big' competitors. Bensons believe though that they can stand up to price competition through improvements in efficiency. Mr John Hase, a snack specialist in the City, said, 'It is a very competitive business and the big players are very serious, particularly PepsiCo and United Biscuits, about dominating the market. With competition like that it will not be easy to carve out and maintain an adequate and profitable market share.'

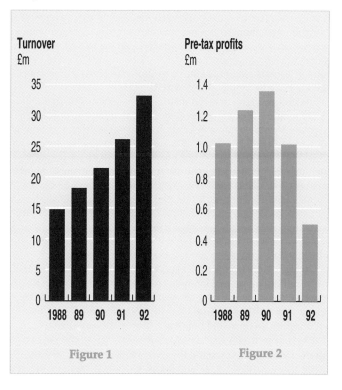

Figure 1

Figure 2

Source: adapted from the *Financial Times*, 14.7.1993.

(a) Look at the Figure 1 and Figure 2 and comment on the financial performance of Bensons over the five year period.
(b) Explain the possible method/s of production that maybe used to manufacture potato crisps.
(c) Explain Bensons' motives for investment.
(d) Explain 3 advantages to Bensons of centralising production.
(e) What is meant by a greenfield site and what are the advantages of moving to one?
(f) Why is the decision by Bensons 'not to sell up' potentially rewarding to: (i) shareholders; (ii) employees?
(g) Explain two technical economies of scale which Bensons will gain when it begins production at the new site.
(h) Explain the marketing implications of the move to the new site.

Lotus eater

Frazer Nash, Austin Healey, Triumph and MG may have pulled into the pits long ago, but a clutch of small firms still carries the chequered flag of Britain's sports-car makers. Lotus and TVR have led the way. Of the two firms, Lotus looked as if it had the best chance of surviving. Surely its giant parent, General Motors, had the money and expertise to succeed in the sports-car business. But then Lotus startled the motor industry by killing the Elan, its most popular model, barely two years after it went into production because the car was making heavy losses. Perhaps Lotus's managers should have taken a look at their much smaller, independent rival. TVR continues to make profit selling a smaller number of cars to the same kind of customers that Lotus was trying to woo with the Elan.

Both firms have steered their cars towards enthusiasts seeking more speed than is offered by the most popular sports car, the Mazda Miata, or MX-5 as it is known in Britain, where it costs £15,000 ($27,800). TVR's new £25,000 Griffith, for instance, hits 60 mph (96 kph) from standstill in 4.5 seconds flat, half the time it takes the Miata. This market is small. Mazda sells 80,000 Miatas each year. TVR, which makes three basic models, sells fewer than 1,000. But sales to such enthusiasts can nevertheless be lucrative, and for companies bigger than TVR a snazzy sports car can boost the prestige of other models. That is why Britain's Rover (partly owned by Japan's Honda) is reviving the MG badge on a powerful, limited-edition sports car.

Lotus planned to produce 3,000 of its £22,000 Elans each year, but ended up making only half that number. But the firm's mistake was to apply GM's mass production techniques to the Elan's tiny production runs. It spent six years and £30 million developing the Elan and building a new, partly automated factory. After losing around £13 million in each of the past two years, it stopped producing the Elan, reducing its 500-strong car-making workforce by 300, because it saw no chance of ever recovering its investment. Lotus will concentrate on its profitable R&D consultancy and on making its £48,000 Esprit supercar.

Compare the debacle at Lotus with the success of TVR, whose Griffith model took just 18 months and £500,000 to develop. Based in Blackpool, a faded seaside resort, TVR employs only 280 people but made an after-tax profit of £750,000 on sales of £15 million last year. Most of that profit, says Peter Wheeler, TVR's chairman and owner, will be ploughed into R&D. That investment may look small, but it will enable TVR to renew its entire model range during the coming year, he claims.

Car makers worldwide are trying to slim their manufacturing operations and make them more flexible. TVR's factory looks old fashioned, but it is a showcase for the sort of 'lean manufacturing' that will probably dominate the car industry within a decade. TVR has made a virtue of necessity. While Lotus had access to GM's huge parts catalogue to build the Elan, TVR has found it hard to excite components suppliers with its low volumes. Obliged to manufacture inhouse, the firm now makes 70 per cent of the parts that go into its cars. By doing this, TVR can also tighten its grip on quality.

TVR has not, however, splashed out on sophisticated machine tools to make its components. Such machinery can produce cheaper parts, but only at far higher volumes than TVR needs, as Lotus discovered to its cost. Instead, TVR's approach is to design parts with its own assembly techniques in mind. 'Tooling a machine would take too long and cost too much', explains Mr Wheeler. That is why TVR builds its car bodies from composites which, although ten times more costly than

steel, have exceptionally low tooling costs.

All this makes TVR highly labour-intensive. But for companies trying to become lean manufacturers, the crucial investment is in a flexible, innovative workforce. 'We have clever people here, but they all have to use their hands. We wouldn't employ an engineer who couldn't weld', says Mr Wheeler.

TVR is close to the ultimate goal of lean manufacturing - to build products to order, at lower prices than much bigger rivals, and still make a profit. Every TVR is built to the customer's specification, which means a choice, for example, of a bewildering 12,000 colours. And lean-manufacturing techniques mean that TVR can quickly change its product mix to suit the whims of the market.

Poor quality contributed to the Elan's downfall; the Griffith's quality, say industry insiders, is among the best in the business. But then TVR does have a secret weapon - Ned, Mr Wheeler's pointer puppy. Each day Ned selects a component from the factory and attempts to chew it to destruction. If a part can survive that, reckons Mr Wheeler, it can survive anything.

Source: The *Economist*, June 1992.

(a) Describe the market needs that the Lotus Elan and the TVR Griffiths attempt to fulfil.

(b) Describe the mistake made by Lotus in its selection of production technique for the Elan.

(c) How can car manufacturers achieve flexibility by trimming down their operations?

(d) Why has TVR not invested in sophisticated machine tools?

(e) What are the advantages and disadvantages of TVR employing a labour intensive production operation?

(f) What are the advantages and disadvantages of TVR's ultimate goal 'to build products to order'?

Aims

- To produce a business register and a map of your local area showing the location of different types of business activity.
- To determine the reasons why these firms are established in these locations.
- To compare the actual reasons for business location with the theoretical ones.

Research

Depending on the size of your local area, the best way to conduct your research is to split up into groups and concentrate on specific areas. This will allow the work load to be shared and avoid duplication. You start by obtaining a street map of your locality and dividing the area amongst your groups. It might also be useful to elect group leaders and an overall co-ordinator.

Once the areas have been agreed, you can plan your research. You need to identify businesses in your particular area and then collect some very basic information from them. All groups should collect the same information from the businesses they visit. The information needed will include the following.

- Exact location of the business (name and address).
- Type of business organisation (eg sole trader, partnership, private limited company, public limited company etc.).
- Business sector (primary, secondary or tertiary).
- Brief description of its activities.
- Reason for location.

Presentation

When this information has been collected it needs to be transferred to a central register and a large copy of your local map. The names and addresses and description of activities should be entered in a business register or database. This will prove useful in the future. On the map you could show the locations of the different businesses by sector and/or according to their legal status. Use a colour code.

The reasons for business location should be collated. It might be useful to produce a graph or chart which shows the reasons for business location in your area.

You can now look at the reasons for business location and discuss whether they conform with business theory. You need to discuss whether the reasons given by business owners are the reasons which business theory would predict. Present your discussion in a report using the following headings.

- An analysis of the graph, ie explain any trends or observations.
- A brief explanation of the theoretical locational factors.
- A comparison of your findings and business theory.
- Conclusion.

Aims

- To investigate and compare the methods of production used by two different manufacturing companies.
- Identify any changes in production methods which have occurred in the last 10 years or so.

Research

You need to organise two visits to very different manufacturers. Many manufacturing companies are pleased to accommodate small parties of visitors for tours of their factories. Indeed, some of the larger companies encourage such visits and are experienced in guided tours and answering questions. Even small companies are often proud to show visitors around their plants. Start by telephoning a number of companies and enquiring whether such a visit can be organised. It is important to book dates well in advance, several months in some cases. Companies may send you details of their tours and guidelines regarding conduct, health and safety factors and suitable dress.

You need to plan in advance so that you can make the most of your visit. It will be useful to make notes as you tour the factory and have a list of questions ready to ask the guide. Notes and questions could be made under the following headings.

- What method of production is used?
- What material and components are used and where do they come from?
- How is the factory laid out - why?
- Is production labour or capital intensive - ask for numerical information on the number of people employed, the categories of workers employed, the wage bill and how these have changed in the last 10 years.
- How is productivity measured?
- What is the system of remuneration?
- What is the breakdown of costs?
- How much stock is held?
- What use is made of computers?
- What new technology has been introduced in the last 10 years - why?
- How is the quality of the product maintained?
- How long is spent training employees?
- What are the future plans regarding production?

You should try to add to this list and obtain as much information as possible. Ask for any diagrams

or production documents which might be available. Ask permission to take photographs (firms often refuse permission in order to retain secrecy).

Presentation

You could write a report on your investigation including the following headings.

Introduction Outline the aims of your investigation.

Description of production in factory 1 Write a description of the production methods used in the first factory. You could use some of the headings suggested above to help your report structure. Remember to write about the changes that have taken place.

Description of production in factory 2 As above.

A comparison of production techniques Suggest reasons for any similarities or differences which you notice in the methods of production in the two factories. Produce some graphs or charts showing comparisons of numerical information if possible. For example, you could draw pie charts showing a breakdown of production costs for each factory or the category of workers employed.

Changes in production methods This is an important part of the report. You need to explain and account for any changes that have taken place. Again make comparisons between the two factories.

Conclusion Write a short summary of the main points in your report.

1. Explain the role of research and development in business organisations. Discuss the factors which must be considered when designing products in business.

2. Discuss the advantages and disadvantages of flow production. In what ways has the development of new technology affected production techniques in recent years?

3. Discuss the factors which have led to:
   (a) a movement of business towards the South East;
   (b) a movement of business away from the South East;
   in the last decade.

4. Outline the motives for business growth. Assuming that growth is a desirable business objective, why do so many firms tend to remain quite small?

5. Discuss the advantages and disadvantages of Just-in-time manufacturing.

6. Due to the increased competition in the business environment more and more firms have concentrated on improving the quality of their products. Explain the main features of Total Quality Management and outline the advantages of quality assurance.

7. What is meant by efficiency in business? Discuss ways in which the efficiency of the labour force might be improved in business organisations.

8. Outline some applications of Information Technology which you are aware of in business. What are the disadvantages of technological development in business organisations?

9. What factors affect the level of investment a business organisation undertakes? What policies might the government use to encourage more business investment?

Recording business transactions

All businesses, whatever their size and nature, must keep records and accounts of their FINANCIAL TRANSACTIONS. At the very least, they must provide financial information for the Inland Revenue. For example, a sole trader might use the document below to declare income for tax purposes. Larger companies need to provide financial information for their shareholders and for internal use, eg to show their performance.

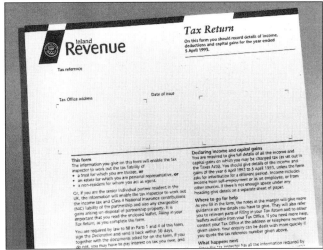

An Inland Revenue tax return. A document used by sole traders to declare annual income or profit.

A wide range of financial information needs to be collected if records are to be accurate. Figure 38.1 illustrates how financial information can be used and who might need it. The information may be useful to people both within and outside the company.

Who uses the records? - internal needs

The main users of financial information are likely to be **management**. Up to date and accurate financial data will help to improve the running of the business. It can also be used for a number of other activities.

■ Recording. The values of all of a company's resources and lists of its transactions can be recorded by hand or on computer. The records can then be used to show company **assets**, **liabilities** and **capital**, for example. These are dealt with in units 39-41. Here it is enough to say that assets are the resources of the business, such as equipment, liabilities are amounts of money owed by the business, such as a bank loan, and capital is the money introduced into the business by the owners.

■ Analysis and evaluation. It is possible to evaluate the performance of the company, make comparisons with competitors and keep a record of the firm's progress over a period of time.

■ Control. Financial information helps the control of

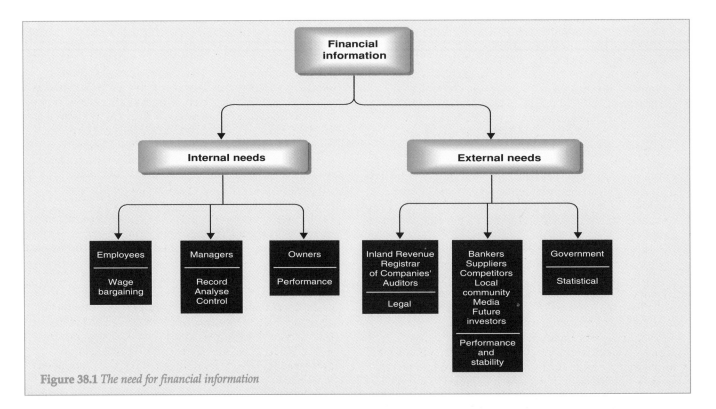

Figure 38.1 *The need for financial information*

money flowing in and out of the business. This becomes more important as the firm grows and the amounts of money used increase.

Employees are another group of people who might need financial information. During wage bargaining, information about the profitability, liquidity and financial prospects of the business could be used to decide if management can meet a particular wage demand.

The **owners** (internal or external, or both) will have a vested interest in the company's financial position. They will naturally assess its performance. For example, shareholders will decide whether any dividend is satisfactory or not. On the other hand, a sole trader might look at the annual profit and decide whether or not they could earn more from another activity.

Who uses the records? - external needs

Certain external parties, from time to time, need financial information about the company.

There are **legal needs** which businesses must satisfy. Every year the accounts of limited companies have to be checked by independent auditors. In addition, companies must send a copy of their final accounts to the Registrar of Companies. All businesses must declare their annual income to the Inland Revenue at the end of a trading year, so that their tax position can be assessed.

Some groups might be interested in the **performance** and **stability** of the business.

- Bankers. If a firm is trying to obtain a loan, or has already received a loan, bank managers will insist on access to records. This will allow them to assess whether the company can repay the loan.
- Suppliers. If a business intends to order large quantities of materials or components on credit, the supplier might wish to assess its creditworthiness.
- Competitors. It is usual for businesses to make comparisons with their rivals using financial information. Also, if a company is thinking about an aggressive takeover it can use the information to help make a decision.
- Local community. From time to time the local community might show an interest in the stability of a company, to assess employment prospects perhaps.
- Media. Newspapers and television companies, for example, often make use of financial information when reporting.
- Future investors. Companies, financial institutions and private investors may require information when deciding where to invest their funds. Venture capitalists provide sources of funds (☞ unit 40) for a business. They invest in up-and-coming businesses which they feel will do well in future.

Finally, the **government** may have an interest in a company's financial information. It employs personnel to compile statistics on output, income and employment in the economy. Much of this data is published in journals and is available to the public in libraries.

Who produces the accounts?

Accountants are responsible for supplying and using financial information. They are employed by businesses specialising in accountancy, or by large firms which have their own financial departments. Accountancy specialists sell their services to small and medium sized firms as well as self-employed individuals. They use the transactions recorded by these groups to produce final accounts. They may also advise clients on various financial matters such as taxation and investment. Another function of these specialists is AUDITING. Businesses which produce their own final accounts must by law have them checked for authenticity by an independent firm of accountants. This audit is performed annually.

There are two branches of accounting - FINANCIAL ACCOUNTING and MANAGEMENT ACCOUNTING. The role of financial accountants is to make sure that a company's accounts are a 'true and fair' record of its transactions. They supervise the book-keeping process, which involves recording the value of every single business transaction. From time to time they summarise these records and convert them into statements which may be used by those parties described earlier in the unit.

Financial accountants are concerned with the past. They need to know about accounting techniques, company law, auditing requirements and taxation law. The ability to work under quite severe time pressure with a variety of personnel, at all levels in the business, is also important.

Management accountants are more concerned with the future. They do need knowledge of accounting concepts and methods, but they also require training in economics and management science. Such accountants are involved in decision making and problem solving in the business. They are responsible for producing cost and financial data, interpreting financial statements and preparing forecasts and budgets. They act as 'information servants' to the management team, but also help in planning and control.

A subsidiary of management accounting is cost accounting. Cost accountants carry out detailed costing projects. This involves working out the cost of particular business activities, such as calculating the cost of opening a new store, launching a new product or changing working practices.

QUESTION 2 The role of accountants has changed in recent years. At the beginning of the century accountants were mainly concerned with financial accounting. They were professionally qualified and worked on the accounts of businesses. However, as society developed so did the world of business and commerce. Today the accountancy profession is more diverse, involved and complex. The contributions which accountants make to the running of businesses are clearly reflected in the size of their salaries.

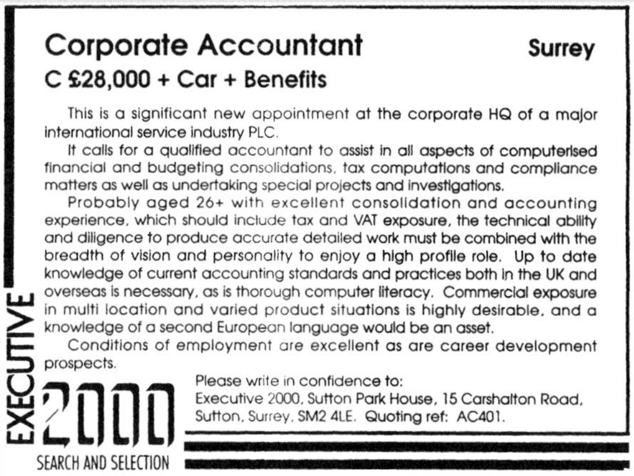

Corporate Accountant   Surrey
C £28,000 + Car + Benefits

This is a significant new appointment at the corporate HQ of a major international service industry PLC.

It calls for a qualified accountant to assist in all aspects of computerised financial and budgeting consolidations, tax computations and compliance matters as well as undertaking special projects and investigations.

Probably aged 26+ with excellent consolidation and accounting experience, which should include tax and VAT exposure, the technical ability and diligence to produce accurate detailed work must be combined with the breadth of vision and personality to enjoy a high profile role. Up to date knowledge of current accounting standards and practices both in the UK and overseas is necessary, as is thorough computer literacy. Commercial exposure in multi location and varied product situations is highly desirable, and a knowledge of a second European language would be an asset.

Conditions of employment are excellent as are career development prospects.

Please write in confidence to:
Executive 2000, Sutton Park House, 15 Carshalton Road, Sutton, Surrey, SM2 4LE. Quoting ref: AC401.

EXECUTIVE 2000
SEARCH AND SELECTION

Figure 38.2 *A newspaper advert for an accountant*

(a) What type of accountant is the firm seeking to employ?
(b) What does the advert tell you about the expected role of an accountant within a business?
(c) What are the possible advantages and disadvantages to a business employing its own accountant?

How are accounts constructed?

The accounting process must produce accurate business statements which reflect a 'true and fair view' of a company's financial position. To achieve this a series of accounting conventions and concepts are used. These allow accountants to communicate in a common language. However, the interpretation of business statements relies on the judgement of accountants. Therefore, even using these concepts and conventions it is possible for different individuals to draw different conclusions from the same information. What are the main concepts used in accounting calculations?

Going concern Accountants assume that the business will continue for an indefinite period of time. Assets are valued as if they will continue in their present use, rather than at NET REALISABLE VALUE - the value the asset would raise if it were sold. Assets are therefore valued at the cost when they are bought, known as HISTORICAL COST (☞ unit 43). This holds even if the asset is bought at a bargain, eg half the manufacturer's recommended price. If things change, and it is necessary for the business to cease trading, assets may be valued according to what they 'might realise'. In some cases this might be less than their cost. Special accounting techniques will then be used to deal with the situation.

Accruals or matching This means that costs and revenue should be matched with the period in which they occur. For example, at the end of the trading year a company may have an outstanding electricity bill for power used in that trading period. According to this principle, the cost should be included even though the bill is unpaid. Related to this is the **realisation** concept. This states that profit occurs when goods or services change hands and not when payment is made.

Consistency Once a decision has been made about the allocation of costs or the valuation of assets it should not be changed. This will make comparisons more meaningful and reduce the chance of figures being distorted.

Prudence and caution If an asset is bought at a bargain price, rather than the recommended price, the lower value is always recorded. This conforms with the concept of **prudence** and **caution**. Accountants undervalue future revenue or profit until it is realised. In contrast, they make provision for costs or losses immediately they occur, even if they are only forecast.

There are also a number of common conventions which are accepted by all accountants.

Separate entity A business is a 'legal' person in its own right and has a separate identity from that of the owners. Where a sole trader, for example, uses a van for personal reasons and business, it is important to divide the running costs between the owner and the business.

Double entry Double entry accounting is a system of recording transactions. It uses the fact that there are always two sides to a transaction, ie a 'source' of funds and a 'use' of funds. This will be explored later in this unit.

Money terms When recording business transactions, it has long been common practice to record them in **money terms**. Money acts as a unit of account (☞ unit 1). This allows the values of goods and services to be expressed accurately and makes comparison easier. Financial statements only include those matters which can be easily expressed in money terms. For example, the skills of the workforce would not be included.

Historical cost All assets are valued according to their original cost rather than what they are currently worth. Accountants prefer to deal with values which have, in the past, been confirmed with evidence. They do not like to rely on estimates, even if the historical entries are dated. This convention has been subject to change, particularly when, due to inflation, the historical cost values become inaccurate and do not provide a true and fair view of the company's financial position.

becomes cost effective to take on a book-keeper, part time perhaps. In large businesses, with their own finance departments, book-keepers will work under the supervision of accountants.

Figure 38.3 illustrates the stages in book-keeping. When a transaction takes place, it should be verified by a **document** - an invoice, receipt or cheque stub perhaps. From these documents entries are made in the company's books. The first entries are likely to be made in the **subsidiary** books, where details of all transactions may be recorded almost as they happen. The **day books** will contain records of purchases and sales, while the **cash book** lists the flows of money into and out of the business. At the end of the month, entries in these books will be totalled and recorded in **ledgers**. The main purpose of these subsidiary books is to avoid overloading the ledgers.

Ledgers form the basis of any book-keeping system. A ledger contains details of individual business accounts. The **sales ledger** records transactions with customers and the **purchase ledger** records those with suppliers. The accounts of customers and suppliers are called personal accounts. All others are impersonal and are recorded in

QUESTION 3 Sunnil owns a small restaurant and is updating his business records before visiting the accountant. Three transactions are giving him some concern.

■ During the year Sunnil employed a new chef, Sandhu. Sandhu came from a neighbouring restaurant and news of his appointment resulted in a very welcome drift of custom in Sunnil's favour. By the end of the year Sandhu's reputation had doubled turnover. Sunnil is not sure how to record this valuable acquisition.

■ Two days before the end of the trading year Sunnil received a quarterly bill for the leasing of some kitchen equipment. The bill for £600 has not been paid and relates to a period which includes two months before the end of the trading year and one month after. Sunnil decides not to record it at all because it is still unpaid.

■ At the beginning of the year Sunnil purchased some dining furniture at a second hand shop for £300. Six months later, a regular customer who is in the antiques trade kindly advised him that the furniture was Edwardian, and possibly worth £2,000. Sunnil now wonders whether the assets should be revalued.

Explain how Sunnil should treat the above transactions according to the appropriate accounting concepts and conventions.

Recording business transactions in practice

Book-keepers are responsible for recording transactions. Many sole traders keep their own records because they cannot afford to employ book-keepers. As a firm grows, it

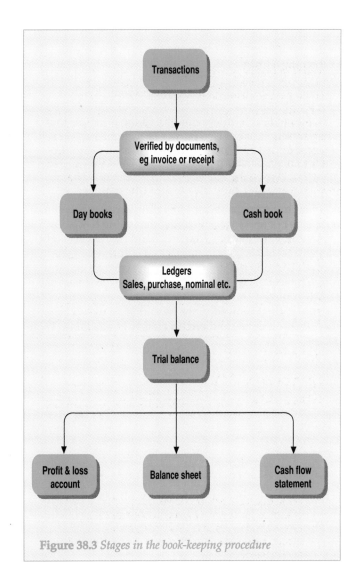

Figure 38.3 *Stages in the book-keeping procedure*

the nominal ledger. The headings in the nominal ledger might include:

■ the wages account, which records the wages paid to employees;
■ the purchase account, which records all business purchases from suppliers;
■ the sales account, which records all business sales.

From time to time a company may wish to check that all previous entries were made correctly. This can be done by producing a TRIAL BALANCE. Finally, various accounts can be produced using the information gathered from book-keeping. The trial balance and the different accounts are discussed in the next sections.

In recent years, computers have been increasingly used in business. A variety of software is available to help with book-keeping, accounting, stock control, financial control, costing and payroll. Considerable savings can be made, both in the time taken and the cost involved in using the data.

Double entry

All businesses keep a record of their transactions. During the trading year, this could involve hundreds, thousands, or even millions of entries being made in the records. The system used today was probably developed by Luca Pacioli in the fifteenth century. It was called the 'Italian method' and forms the basis of the present DOUBLE ENTRY SYSTEM.

The term double entry comes from the principle that every transaction has two parts. For example, if you sell something you give away that item, but gain cash. In order to explain how the system works it is necessary to define two terms - **debit** and **credit.**

A debit involves an entry on the left hand side of an account, indicating a **receipt of value**. A credit is entered on the right hand side, indicating that **value has been given out**. For example, a second hand car dealer might put £20,000 of his own money into the business. Two entries are made in the records (which contain many different accounts). The cash account is debited because cash is received and the capital account is credited because capital is owed to the owner. Here we will show the effects on debits and credits simply in one table (Table 38.2).

Table 38.2 *The effect of the introduction of new capital*

Receipt/debit		Payment/credit	
Cash received from owner	£20,000	Capital owed to owner	£20,000

Similarly, what if a car was sold for £10,000? The cash account would be debited because cash was received. The sales account would be credited because the car was 'given out'. Again, we can show this more simply using one table (Table 38.3).

Table 38.3 *The effect of a car sale on the business accounts*

Receipts/debit		Payments/credit	
Cash received from owner	£20,000	Capital owed to owner	£20,000
Cash received from sale of car	£10,000	Car sold	£10,000

We can see that every transaction has two equivalent entries in the records. Debits and credits affect a business' assets, liabilities and capital.

We can write:

Debits - increase assets
          - decrease capital and liabilities
Credits - decrease assets
          - increase capital and liabilities

In the above example the debit entry for the car sale increased the firm's cash balance. The credit entry has reduced the company's stock of cars. In other words, the debit entry has increased one of the assets and the credit entry has reduced another.

You will notice that the debit and credit side of the accounts are both equal (£30,000). This must be the case if equal and opposite entries are made. The advantage of this process is that it provides a self-checking facility. This is the **trial balance** mentioned in the last section. Since every transaction appears twice, when all different account balances are added (such as from the sales account, cash account, purchase account etc.). The debit total must equal the credit total. If it doesn't there must have been a mistake when recording took place.

Bank accounts treat the terms debit and credit differently. If you are overdrawn at the bank then you are said to be in debit. If there is money to withdraw, then you are in credit.

QUESTION 4 In a four day trading period T W Norman, a second hand car dealer, recorded the following transactions:
3.7.93 Introduced £1,000 capital to fund the business venture.
3.7.93 Bought a car for resale for £600 and paid cash.
3.7.93 Bought some spare parts for £50 cash.
5.7.93 Sold the car for £850 cash.
6.7.93 Paid £100 wages to a mechanic in cash.
7.7.93 Bought a car on credit from Fast Motors Ltd for £500

(a) Produce a simple receipts and payments table to illustrate these transactions.
(b) Why must the totals on both sides be equal?
(c) Explain the effect that each transaction would have on:
  (i) assets;
  (ii) liabilities.

An introduction to business statements

At the end of a trading year all businesses produce final accounts. These are the result of the process shown in Figure 38.3. A balance sheet and a profit and loss account generally form the basis of these accounts, although public limited companies publish a full annual report which contains a wider range of financial statements and reports.

Balance sheet A balance sheet provides information about the company's funds and how they are used in the business (☞ unit 39). It lists the assets, liabilities and capital of the business and, to some extent, shows the wealth of the company. A balance sheet describes the financial position of a business at a particular point in time.

Profit and loss account The profit and loss account provides a summary of the year's trading activities, stating the revenue from sales (the turnover), business costs, profit/loss and how the profit is used (☞ unit 42).

Cash flow statement From 1992 onwards companies were required to produce cash flow statements in their accounts. A cash flow statement shows the flows of cash into and out of a business in a trading year (☞ unit 44).

Notes to the accounts The balance sheet and profit and loss account show summarised information. 'Notes to the accounts' are a more detailed analysis of some entries in these statements.

Directors' report This statement, written by the directors, is required by law. It contains information which might not be shown in other financial statements, such as the number of employees, changes of personnel on the board of directors and any special circumstances arising.

Chairperson's statement One of the chairperson's roles is to communicate with the shareholders. She can do this by making a statement in the annual report. The chairperson discusses the company's general performance and comments on events during the trading year which might be of interest to the shareholders. Future prospects are also discussed and shareholders are encouraged to remain loyal to the company.

Auditor's report Auditors must make a brief report to confirm that the accounts give a 'true and fair view' of the firm's financial position, assuming, of course, that they do!

Statistics Companies often include tables and graphs in their annual report. They can be used to illustrate trends and comparisons. They might show turnover, profit, dividends or earnings per share, for example.

Key terms

Auditing - an accounting procedure which checks thoroughly the authenticity of a company's accounts.
Double entry system - a recording system which enters every business transaction twice in the books, once as a debit and once as a credit.
Financial transactions - payments made when buying goods and services and money received from selling them.
Financial accounting - the preparation of company accounts from business records.
Historical cost - the value of an asset when purchased, ie the amount paid.
Management accounting - the preparation of financial statements, reports and data for use by managers.
Net realisable value - the value of an asset when sold, ie the amount received.
Trial balance - a statement which lists all the balances on all the accounts in the double entry system.

Summary

1. Why is it so important for management to have access to financial information?
2. List all potential users of accounts and state whether they are internal or external.
3. What might be the role of a management accountant in a business?
4. What are the fundamental concepts and conventions which aim to make the accounts a 'true and fair view' of the firm's financial position?
5. Why are concepts and conventions needed in accounting?
6. Explain how a double entry system of book-keeping 'balances'.
7. Define the terms 'debit' and 'credit' in double entry accounting.
8. What is the difference between day books and ledgers?
9. What is the function of the trial balance?
10. List the financial statements which might appear in the annual report of a public limited company.

Question

Castings PLC

Castings PLC is a medium sized company based in the West Midlands. It supplies blackheart, pearlitic, free cutting and weldable malleable iron castings to a variety of manufacturing industries from its fully mechanised foundries at Brownhills.

CHAIRPERSON'S STATEMENT

Despite indifferent trading conditions for a substantial part of the year it is satisfactory to report that profits are only slightly reduced from £4.460 million to £4.369 million. The results are after taking into consideration a bad debt in excess of £200,000 due to the collapse of Leyland Daf.

The board are recommending a final dividend of 3.05p per share making a total of 4.35p compared with 4.07p last year.

This is the third year in succession we have had difficult trading conditions. Demand has been variable and unpredictable, requiring our employees to react at short notice. I wish to thank them for their continuing support and understanding of the markets we supply.

The Brownhills foundries have felt the major reduction in demand and profits because of the problems in the commercial vehicle and building industries. W.H. Booth and William Lee have enjoyed a reasonable year's trading and slightly improved profits.

Prospects
The prospects for this coming year so far look reasonable, as demand has improved and our order book and schedules are at the highest levels for over a year. However, we have seen these improvements before only to be disappointed after a short while.

Major plant modifications, involving capital expenditure of over £600,000 will be implemented during July/August to update moulding and melting plant at one of the Brownhills foundries. All three companies are involved in continual improvements to maintain their position in the market place. The company has adequate reserves to conform to health, safety and environmental requirements.

The concern for the immediate future is first of all energy charges for major users. These have risen rapidly and it does not seem to concern the electricity industry or government to increase costs to industry and jeopardise future employment. Secondly, with devaluation, the costs of raw materials, including steel scrap, are increasing at an unacceptable rate. These cost increases have to be recovered in the market as the industry cannot continue to absorb increases outside its control.

The Board
On January 28th, 1993, Brian Grice, Managing Director of W. H. Booth and Terry Woodhouse, Managing Director of William Lee, were appointed to the board. I fully believe that the appointments will strengthen the board as both have many years experience in manufacturing and the foundry industry.

The board does not feel a need to appoint further non-executive directors and in this respect I hope our shareholders will support us in our efforts to run the company in a responsible way with integrity and competence.

BRIAN J. COOKE
Chairperson

28 May 1993

PROFIT AND LOSS ACCOUNT
for the year ended 31st March 1993

	1993 £000	1992 £000
Turnover	33,751	35,075
Cost of sales	24,767	25,507
Gross profit	8,984	9,568
Operating costs	5,296	5,683
Operating profit	3,688	3,885
Other income	681	575
Profit on ordinary activities before taxation	4,369	4,460
Taxation on ordinary activities	1,354	1,405
Profit on ordinary activities after taxation	3,015	3,055
Dividends	918	859
Retained profit for the year	2,097	2,196
Earnings per share	14.30p	14.66p

Figure 38.4 *An example of a chairperson's statement and a profit and loss account (Castings PLC)*

(a) **Given that the chairperson's statement is not a legal requirement, why is it included?**
(b) **Using the information in Figure 38.4 as evidence, describe in your own words the general outlook which the chairperson is trying to convey.**
(c) **If you were:**
   (i) a shareholder;
   (ii) an employee;
   how might the information be useful?
(d) **In what way is the chairperson's report 'prudent and cautious?**
(e) **What might account for the fall in turnover?**

Introduction to the balance sheet

What does a BALANCE SHEET show? It is like a photograph of a company's financial position at a particular point in time. The balance sheet contains two sections - a list of a company's assets and a summary of its liabilities and capital.

- ASSETS are the resources that a company **owns** and which have value for the company. They are resources that can be **used** in production. Assets are usually divided into current assets (those that are used up in production, such as stocks of raw materials) and fixed assets (such as machinery which can be used over and over again for a period of time).
- LIABILITIES are the debts of the company, ie what the company **owes** to other companies, individuals and institutions. Liabilities are a **source** of funds for a company. They might be short term, such as dividends paid to shareholders, or long term, such as a mortgage.
- CAPITAL is the money introduced by the owners of the business, for example when they buy shares. It is another source of funds and can be used to purchase assets.

This is the benefit of producing a balance sheet. It shows exactly the funds a business has and how they are being used. Sources and uses of funds are discussed in more detail in units 40 and 41.

In all balance sheets the value of assets will equal the value of liabilities and capital. Why? Any increase in assets must be funded by an increase in capital or liabilities. A firm wanting to buy machinery (an asset) may need to obtain a bank loan (a liability), for example. Also, a reduction in capital or liabilities will mean a reduction in the value of assets. So we can say:

$$Assets = capital + liabilities$$

This is shown in the balance sheet of AJ Crisp Ltd in Table 39.1.

It is often argued that the balance sheet reflects the value of the company. Certainly, the balance sheet does give an indication of a company's wealth. However, there are certain assets which are very difficult to value accurately. Some intangible assets (☞ unit 41) may not be included for this reason.

A disadvantage of the balance sheet is that it fails to show that businesses are dynamic. The balance sheet only shows transactions that have taken place up until the time it is produced, and not those that are actually taking place at the time. It is a static statement.

Table 39.1 shows the types of asset and liability that might appear on the balance sheet of a limited company. You will see later in this unit that there are differences in the assets and liabilities shown in the balance sheets of sole traders and limited companies.

QUESTION 1 Look at Table 39.1.
(a) Explain why the total value under sources of funds is equal to the total value under uses of funds.
(b) What is the value of AJ Crisp Ltd's long term liabilities if the value of its:
- fixed assets is £1.2 million;
- current assets is £0.9 million;
- capital and reserves is £1.1 million;
- current liabilities is £0.4 million?

Table 39.1 *A balance sheet illustrating assets and liabilities of a limited company as at 31.7.93*

AJ CRISP LTD
Balance sheet as at 31.7.93

Liabilities (sources of funds)	£000	Assets (uses of funds)	£000
Capital and reserves		**Fixed assets**	
Shareholders' capital	400	Premises	200
Retained profit	170	Plant and equipment	100
		Financial investments	120
Long term liabilities			
Mortgage	150		
Current liabilities		**Current assets**	
Trade creditors	120	Stocks of goods	180
Taxation	70	Debtors	200
Dividend	80	Cash at bank	190
	990		**990**

Transactions and the balance sheet

How might a business record its transactions on a balance sheet? We know that there are two sides to every transaction (☞ unit 38) and that a transaction can affect both assets and liabilities. For example, when a company makes a sale it will receive cash (an increase in assets) but reduce its stocks of finished goods (a decrease in assets). Let us examine the effect of four transactions on the balance sheet of Kingstreet Ltd, a business owning a chain of night clubs, shown in Table 39.2.

- Transaction 1. Kingstreet buys some new lighting equipment for £200,000 on credit. This will increase fixed assets (equipment) by £200,000 and increase current liabilities (trade creditors) by £200,000. The balance sheet totals will also rise by £200,000.
- Transaction 2. A consignment of drinks is bought for £100,000 on credit. This will increase current assets (stocks) by £100,000 and increase current liabilities (trade creditors). The balance sheet totals will also rise by £100,000.
- Transaction 3. Kingstreet pays £150,000 tax to the Inland Revenue. This will decrease current assets (cash at bank) by £150,000 and decrease current liabilities (taxation) by £150,000. The balance sheet totals fall by £150,000.
- Transaction 4. A debtor repays £300,000 to the company. This will only affect the asset side of the balance sheet. Debtors will fall by £300,000 and cash at the bank will increase by £300,000. This transaction will leave the totals unchanged.

It is assumed here that all these transactions are carried out on 1.8.93. The collective effect of these four transactions is shown in the balance sheet in Table 39.3.

Table 39.2 *A balance sheet for Kingstreet Ltd as at 31.7.93*

KINGSTREET LTD
Balance sheet as at 31.7.93

	£000		£000
Shareholders' funds		**Fixed assets**	
Ordinary share capital			
(2,000,000 shares at £1)	2,000	Premises	1,200
Retained profit	700	Fixtures & fittings	1,100
		Equipment	700
Long term liabilities			
Mortgage	1,100		
Bank loan	200		
Current liabilities		**Current assets**	
Trade creditors	200	Stocks	800
Taxation	300	Debtors	500
Dividends	200	Cash at bank	400
	4,700		**4,700**

Table 39.3 *The balance sheet for Kingstreet Ltd illustrating the collective effect of the four transactions*

KINGSTREET LTD
Balance sheet as at 1.8.93

	£000		£000
Shareholders' funds		**Fixed assets**	
Ordinary share capital			
(2,000,000 shares at £1)	2,000	Premises	1,200
Retained profit	700	Fixtures & fittings	1,100
		Equipment	900
Long term liabilities			
Mortgage	1,100		
Bank loan	200		
Current liabilities		**Current assets**	
Trade creditors	500	Stocks	900
Taxation	150	Debtors	200
Dividends	200	Cash at bank	550
	4,850		**4,850**

The balance sheet for Kingstreet Ltd may also be shown in a vertical format as shown in Table 39.4. The advantage of this format is that there is no need to work out the **working capital** (current assets - current liabilities) and **net assets** (total assets - current liabilities) of the firm. These are very important. For example, the working capital a firm has indicates whether or not it can afford to pay its bills (☞ unit 44). Businesses now use this method when presenting their accounts and in their published accounts.

Table 39.4 *The balance sheet of Kingstreet Ltd as at 1.8.93 in a vertical format*

KINGSTREET LTD
Balance sheet as at 1.8.93

	£000	£000	£000
Fixed assets			
Premises			1,200
Fixtures and fittings			1,100
Equipment			900
			3,200
Current assets			
Stocks		900	
Debtors		200	
Cash at bank		550	
		1,650	
Less current liabilities			
Trade creditors	500		
Taxation	150		
Dividends	200	850	
Working capital			800
NET ASSETS			**4,000**
FINANCED BY			
Shareholders' funds			
Ordinary share capital (2,000,000 shares at £1)		2,000	
Retained profit		700	2,700
Long term liabilities			
Mortgage		1,100	
Bank loan		200	1,300
CAPITAL EMPLOYED			**4,000**

> **QUESTION 2** Look at Table 39.3. During the next day three other transactions took place.
> - Dividends (£200,000) are paid to the shareholders from cash.
> - A trade creditor is repaid (£250,000) from the bank account.
> - The company secures another bank loan (£300,000).
> (a) Produce a balance sheet for Kingstreet Ltd as at 2.8.93 which takes the above transactions into account. Use the horizontal format.
> (b) Repeat the above exercise, but use the vertical format.

The balance sheets of public limited companies

Table 39.5 shows the balance sheet of a public limited company, Adamowicz Welders PLC. Company law requires a business to show both this year's and last year's figures in published accounts which are available to the public.

Table 39.5 *A balance sheet for Adamowicz Welders PLC as at 31.7.93*

ADAMOWICZ WELDERS PLC
Balance sheet as at 31.7.93

	1993 (£m)	1992 (£m)
Fixed assets		
Tangible assets	220	200
Intangible assets	100	100
Investments	170	150
	490	450
Current assets		
Raw materials	70	60
Work-in-progress	100	120
Debtors	300	100
Cash at bank	100	210
	570	490
Current liabilities (amounts falling due in one year)	(450)	(300)
Net current assets (working capital)	120	190
Total assets less current liabilities	610	640
Creditors - amounts falling due in more than one year	(60)	
	550	640
Capital and reserves		
Called up share capital	300	300
Revaluation	100	100
Retained profit	150	240
	550	640

This allows a comparison to be made. A number of new balance sheet terms are included compared to that of a private limited company. They reflect the type of transactions of a public limited company. This balance sheet in Figure 39.5 is typical of most PLCs. The figures in brackets are negative.

Depreciation and the balance sheet

The value of an asset falls over time. A machine bought in one year will be worth less the next. This is **depreciation**. Accountants must make an allowance for this when showing the value of assets. They estimate the amount by which asset values depreciate, and then deduct the depreciation from the value of assets before placing the value in the balance sheet. Details about depreciation are shown in the **notes to the accounts**. Unit 43 shows how depreciation can be calculated.

Sole trader balance sheets

Earlier it was mentioned that sole trader balance sheets will be different to those of limited companies.

Table 39.6 *Balance sheet for Joanna Cullen as at 31.5.93*

JOANNA CULLEN
Balance sheet as at 31.5.93

1992 £		1993 £	£
	Fixed assets		
10,000	Car		8,000
7,900	Fixtures and fittings		7,000
17,900			15,000
	Current assets		
30,000	Stocks	35,000	
4,000	Debtors and prepayments	5,000	
3,000	Bank account	4,000	
1,000	Cash in hand	1,000	
38,000		45,000	
	less **Current liabilities**		
20,000	Creditors and accrued charges	25,000	
18,000	Working capital		20,000
35,900	**NET ASSETS**		35,000
	FINANCED BY		
30,000	**Opening capital**		35,900
-	Capital introduced		4,500
48,100	*add* Net profit		59,600
78,100			100,000
42,200	*less* Drawings		65,000
35,900			35,000

Take the example of Joanna Cullen, a sole trader running a retail outlet that sells computer software. Her balance sheet is shown in Table 39.6. The main differences between a sole trader and a limited company balance sheet occur on the liabilities 'side'.

■ The sole trader has a capital account rather than a 'capital and reserves' section. Sole traders are set up with the personal capital introduced into the business by the owner. Joanna Cullen introduced a further £4,500 into the business during 1993, according to the balance sheet in Table 39.6.

■ It is likely that a sole trader will need to withdraw money from the business for personal reasons during the year. This is subtracted from the capital account and is shown as DRAWINGS in the balance sheet. The balance on the capital account is the amount owed to the owner. This is equal to the assets of the company.

■ A limited company has many sources of capital and reserves. However, all companies will show shareholders' funds (often listed as capital and reserves), which will not be in a sole trader's balance sheet.

■ The shareholders of a limited company are paid a dividend. This appears in the figure for current liabilities. As sole traders do not have shareholders no such figure will be included in their accounts.

QUESTION 3 Look at Table 39.6 showing the balance sheet for the year ending 31.5.93 for Joanna Cullen.
(a) In next year's balance sheet, what will be the value of opening capital?
(b) Give two reasons why the value of fixed assets might have fallen from £17,900 to £15,000.
(c) According to the capital account, Joanna introduced £4,500 into the business during the year. Explain why an owner might do this.

Key terms

Assets - resources owned by the business used in production.
Balance sheet - a summary at a point in time of business assets, liabilities and capital.
Capital - a source of funds provided by the owners of the business used to buy assets.
Drawings - money withdrawn by a sole trader from the business for personal use.
Liabilities - the debts of the business which provide a source of funds.

Question

Helen and Philip Hardwick Ltd

Helen and Philip Hardwick Ltd is a family limited company which manufactures a variety of catering equipment. Their products include large food mixers, slicing machines, pans and cutlery.

Table 39.7 *The balance sheet for Helen and Philip Hardwick Ltd as at 30.6.93*

HELEN AND PHILIP HARDWICK LTD
Balance sheet as at 30.6.93

	1993 £000	1993 £000	1992 £000	1992 £000
Fixed assets		2,900		3,500
Current assets				
Stocks	500		400	
Debtors	1,200		300	
Cash at bank	100		900	
	1,800		1,600	
Creditors				
Amounts falling due in one year	1,300		1,000	
Working capital		500		600
NET ASSETS		3,400		4,100
FINANCED BY				
Shareholders' funds				
Ordinary share capital (3,000,000 £1 shares)		3,000		3,000
Retained profit		400		1,100
CAPITAL EMPLOYED		3,400		4,100

(a) Reproduce the balance sheet in a horizontal format as at 30.6.93, and calculate the value of total assets.
(b) If £400,000 worth of fixed assets were sold during the year, why has the total value of fixed assets fallen from £3,500,000 to £2,900,000, ie by £600,000?
(c) State three examples of the likely fixed assets this company might have.
(d) What might account for the changes in the firm's:
(i) debtors;
(ii) cash at the bank;
between 1992 and 1993?
(e) How has the position of the company changed over the year? Use your answers to question (d) in your explanation.

Summary

1. Explain what is meant by a balance sheet and why it is a static business document.
2. Why must the 2 sides of the balance sheet be the same value?
3. What is the difference between fixed and current assets?
4. Why might a vertical balance sheet be preferable to a horizontal one?
5. How will a balance sheet be affected if a business buys a new computer with cash?
6. State 3 items which might appear on the balance sheet of a public limited company but not a sole trader.

Unit 40 Sources of Funds

The need for funds

Firms need money to get started, ie to buy equipment, raw materials and obtain premises. Once this initial expenditure has been met, the business can get under way. If successful, it will earn money from sales. However, business is a continuous activity and money flowing in will be used to buy more raw materials and settle other trading debts.

QUESTION 1

Equipment

Building materials

Petrol

Look at the photographs, which show items bought by a business through various transactions.
(a) Which transactions to buy these items are capital expenditure and which are revenue expenditure?
(b) Under what circumstances might the expenditure on the item in the first photograph be repeated?

If the owner wants to expand, extra money will be needed over and above that from sales. Expansion may mean larger premises, more equipment and extra workers. Throughout the life of a business there will almost certainly be times when money has to be raised from outside.

The items of expenditure above fall into two categories - REVENUE EXPENDITURE or CAPITAL EXPENDITURE. Capital expenditure is spending on items which may be used over and over again. A company vehicle, a cutting machine and a new factory all fall into this category. Revenue expenditure refers to payments for goods and services which have either already been consumed or will be very soon. Wages, raw materials and fuel are all examples.

Internal sources of funds

Figure 40.1 is a summary of all sources of funds, both internal and external. This unit is concerned mainly with external sources, but there are three internal sources for a company.
- Profit. A firm's profit, after tax, is an important and inexpensive source of finance. A large proportion of finance is funded from profit.
- Depreciation. This is a financial provision for the replacement of worn out machinery and equipment. All businesses use depreciation as a source of funds (☞ unit 43).
- Sale of assets. Sometimes businesses sell off assets to raise money. Occasionally a company may be forced to sell assets because it is not able to raise finance from other sources.

External long term sources of funds

External long term capital can be in the form of share capital or loan capital.

Share capital For a limited company this is likely to be the most important source of funds. The sale of shares can raise very large amounts of money. Share capital is often referred to as PERMANENT CAPITAL. This is because it is not normally **redeemed**, ie it is not repaid by the business. Once the share has been sold, the buyer is entitled to a share in the profit of the company, ie a **dividend** (☞ unit 2). Dividends are not always declared. Sometimes a business makes a loss or needs to retain profit to help fund future business activities. A shareholder can make a CAPITAL GAIN by selling the share at a higher price than it was originally bought for. Shares are not sold back to the business. The shares of public limited companies are sold in a special share market called the STOCK MARKET or STOCK EXCHANGE, dealt with later in this unit. Shares in private limited companies are transferred privately (☞ unit 3).

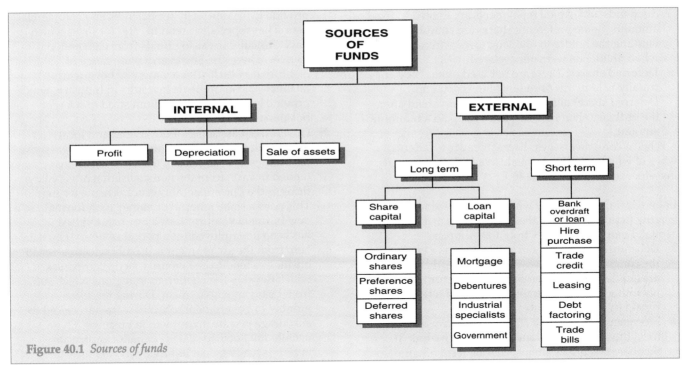

Figure 40.1 *Sources of funds*

Shareholders, because they are part owners of the business, are entitled to a vote. One vote is allowed for each share owned. Voting takes place annually and shareholders vote either to re-elect the existing board of directors or replace them. Different types of shares can be issued:

■ **Ordinary shares**. These are also called EQUITIES and are the most common type of share issued. They are also the riskiest type of share since there is no guaranteed dividend. The size of the dividend depends on how much profit is made and how much

the directors decide to retain in the business. All ordinary shareholders have voting rights. When a share is first sold it has a nominal value shown on it - its original value. Share prices will change as they are bought and sold again and again.

■ **Preference shares**. The owners of these shares receive a fixed rate of return when a dividend is declared. They carry less risk because shareholders are entitled to their dividend before the holders of ordinary shares. Preference shareholders are not strictly owners of the company. If the company is sold, their rights to

Table 40.1 *Summary and explanation of the ways in which new shares can be made available to investors*

BY PROSPECTUS

Public issue	Potential investors might apply to an ISSUING HOUSE, such as a merchant bank, after reading the company prospectus. This is an expensive method, but suits big issues.
Offer for sale	Shares are issued to an issuing house, which then sells them at a fixed price. This is also expensive but suits small issues.
Sale by tender	The company states a minimum price which it will accept from investors and then allocates shares to the highest bidders.

PLACING

Private placing	Unquoted companies (who do not sell on the Stock Exchange) or those with small share sales approach issuing houses to place the shares privately with investors.
Stock exchange placing	Less popular issues can be placed by the stock exchange with institutional investors, for example. This is relatively inexpensive.

AN INTRODUCTION	Existing shareholders get permission from the Stock Exchange to sell shares by attracting new shareholders to the firm. No new capital is raised.
RIGHTS ISSUE	Existing shareholders are given the 'right' to buy new shares at a discounted price. This is a cheap and simple method and creates free publicity.
BONUS ISSUE	New shares are issued to existing shareholders to capitalise on reserves which have built up over the years. No new capital is raised and shareholders end up with more shares, but at lower prices.

dividends and capital repayments are limited to fixed amounts. Some preference shares are **cumulative,** entitling the holder to dividend arrears from years when dividends were not declared.

■ **Deferred shares**. These are not used often. They are usually held by the founders of the company. Deferred shareholders only receive a dividend after the ordinary shareholders have been paid a minimum amount.

When a company issues shares there are a variety of ways in which they can be made available to potential investors as shown in Table 40.1.

Loan capital Any money which is borrowed for a lengthy period of time by the business is called loan capital. Loan capital comes from four sources.

■ Debentures. The holder of a debenture is a creditor of the company, not an owner. This means that holders are entitled to an agreed fixed rate of return, but have no voting rights. The amount borrowed must be repaid by the expiry date.

■ Mortgage. Only limited companies can raise money from the sale of shares and debentures (☞ unit 3). Smaller enterprises often need long term funding, to buy premises for example. They may choose to take out a mortgage. A mortgage is a long term loan, from, say, a bank or other financial institution. The lender must use land or property as security on the loan.

■ Industrial loan specialists. A number of organisations

provide loans especially for business and commercial uses. These specialists tend to cater for firms which have difficulty in raising funds from conventional sources. There are, however, a wide range of institutions which offer a variety of borrowing facilities. One example is Investors in Industry, which provide loan capital for medium sized and larger businesses.

■ Government assistance. Both central and local government have been involved in providing finance for businesses. The scale of the involvement has tended to vary, from the nationalisation of very large firms to the Enterprise Allowance Scheme (☞ unit 8). This pays a small amount of money each fortnight to a new business venture started by an individual who has been unemployed for a period of time. Financial help from the government is usually selective. Small businesses tend to be favoured, as do companies which develop their activities in regions which suffer from heavy unemployment. During the 1980s, a number of government schemes were introduced to encourage private investment in business. These usually involved special tax benefits for private investors, eg Personal Equity Plans (PEPs), a 'tax friendly' scheme to encourage the purchase of shares.

External short term sources of funds

Bank overdraft This is probably the most important source of funds for a very large number of businesses. Bank overdrafts are flexible. The amount by which a business goes overdrawn depends on its needs at the time. Interest is only paid by the business when its account is overdrawn, and is usually slightly lower than interest on a bank loan.

Bank loan A loan requires a rigid agreement between the borrower and the bank. The amount borrowed must be repaid over a clearly stated time period, in regular instalments. Compared with a bank overdraft the interest charged is slightly higher. Most bank loans are short or medium term. Banks dislike long term lending because of their need for security and liquidity. Sometimes, banks change persistent overdrafts into loans, so that firms are forced to repay at regular intervals.

Hire purchase This is often used by small businesses to buy plant and machinery. Sometimes, a hire purchase agreement requires a down payment by the borrower, who agrees to repay the remainder in instalments over a period of time. FINANCE HOUSES specialise in providing funds for such agreements. Figure 40.3 illustrates the working of an agreement and the parties involved. The buyer places a down payment on a machine with the supplier and receives delivery. The finance house pays the supplier the amount outstanding and collects instalments (including interest) from the buyer. The goods bought do not legally belong to the buyer until the very last instalment has been paid to the

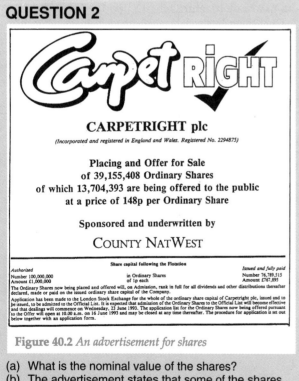

QUESTION 2

CARPETRIGHT plc

(Incorporated and registered in England and Wales. Registered No. 2294875)

**Placing and Offer for Sale
of 39,155,408 Ordinary Shares
of which 13,704,393 are being offered to the public
at a price of 148p per Ordinary Share**

Sponsored and underwritten by

COUNTY NATWEST

Figure 40.2 *An advertisement for shares*

(a) What is the nominal value of the shares?
(b) The advertisement states that some of the shares are being placed and some are being offered publicly (by prospectus). What is the difference?
(c) What might be the implications for the business of selling ordinary shares to the public?

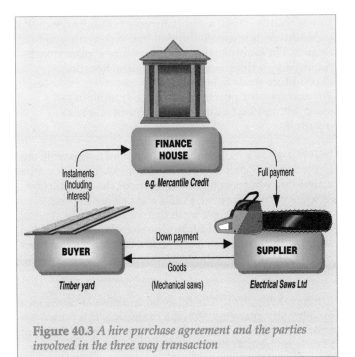

Figure 40.3 *A hire purchase agreement and the parties involved in the three way transaction*

finance house.

If the buyer falls behind with the repayments the finance house can legally repossess the item. Finance houses are less selective than banks when granting loans. Hence their interest rates are higher. They add a servicing charge for paying in instalments which also leads to higher rates.

Trade credit It is common for businesses to buy raw materials, components and fuel and pay for them at a later date, usually between 30 - 90 days. Paying for goods and services using trade credit seems to be an interest free way of raising finance. It is particularly profitable during periods of inflation. However, many companies encourage early payment by offering discounts. The cost of goods is higher if the firm does not pay early. Delaying the payment of bills can also result in poor business relations with suppliers.

Leasing Leasing is becoming increasingly popular. It allows businesses to buy plant, machinery and equipment without having to pay out large amounts of money. When equipment is leased the transaction is recorded as revenue expenditure rather than capital expenditure. An **operating lease** means that the leasing company simply hires out equipment for an agreed period of time. The user never owns the equipment, but it is given the option to purchase the equipment outright if it is leased with a **finance lease**. There are some advantages of leasing.
■ No large sums of money are needed to buy the use of equipment.
■ Maintenance and repair costs are not the responsibility of the user.
■ Hire companies can offer the most up to date equipment.
■ Leasing is useful when equipment is only required occasionally.
■ Leasing payments can be offset against tax.

However:
■ over a long period of time leasing is more expensive than the outright purchase of plant and machinery;
■ loans cannot be secured on assets which are leased.

Debt factoring When companies sell their products they send invoices stating the amount due. The invoice provides evidence of the sale and the money owed to the company. Debt factoring involves a specialist company (the factor) providing finance against these unpaid invoices. A common arrangement is for a factor to pay 80 per cent of the value of invoices when they are issued. The balance of 20 per cent is paid by the factor when the customer settles the bill. An administrative and service fee will be charged.

Trade bills This is not a common source of funds, but can play an important role, particularly in overseas trade and commodity markets. The purchaser of traded goods may sign a **bill of exchange** agreeing to pay for the goods at a specified later date. Ninety days is a common period. The seller of the goods will hold the bill until payment is due. However, the holder can sell it at a discount before the maturity date to a specialist financial institution. There is a well developed market for these bills and all holders will receive payment at the end of the period from the debtor.

QUESTION 3 Neil Jones is a self-employed musician. He needs a new electronic keyboard. His business account is overdrawn by £1,500 and he decides that a hire purchase agreement is the only way he can raise the finance to pay for the keyboard. The keyboard costs £2,000 and the supplier requires a 10 per cent down payment. Neil takes out a two year agreement and the finance company involved charges 20 per cent per annum.
(a) Calculate the monthly repayments to the finance company.
(b) Why did Neil choose to use hire purchase rather than a bank in this situation?
(c) What are the advantages to the supplier of hire purchase compared with leasing?

Capital and money markets

As we have seen, businesses have to look to external sources for their funds. **Financial intermediaries** are the institutions responsible for matching the needs of **savers**, who want to loan funds, with those of **investors**, who need funds. These groups do not naturally communicate with each other. Intermediaries provide the link between them.

A number of financial institutions hold funds for savers, paying them interest. In addition, they make funds available to investors who, in turn, are charged interest. Some deal in capital, ie long and medium term finance; others in money, ie short term loans and bills of exchange. They offer a variety of commercial and financially related services.

The stock market The capital market is dominated by the London Stock Exchange, which deals in second hand shares. The main function of a stock exchange is to provide a market where the owners of shares can sell them. If this market did not exist, selling shares would be difficult because buyers and sellers could not easily communicate with each other. Savers would be less inclined to buy shares and so companies would find it more difficult to raise finance by the issue of shares.

A stock exchange enables mergers and takeovers to take place smoothly (☞ unit 32). If the price of a company's shares begins to fall due to poor profitability, a predator may enter the market and begin to build up a stake in that company. Once the stake is large enough a predator can exert control over the company.

A stock exchange also provides a means of protection for savers. Companies which have a stock exchange listing have to obey a number of Stock Exchange rules and regulations, which are designed to safeguard savers from fraud.

Finally, it is also argued that the general movement in share prices reflects the health of the economy. However, there are times when share price movements could be very misleading, eg if they rise when the economy is in a recession as they did in the second half of 1992.

Insurance companies, pension funds, investment trusts, unit trusts and issuing houses (merchant banks) are some of the institutions which trade in shares.

Banks and other financial institutions The money market is dominated by the major commercial banks, such as the National Westminster Bank or the Midland Bank. They allow payments to be made through the cheque system and deal in short term loans. Savings banks and finance corporations also deal in short term funds. Discount houses and acceptance houses deal in bills of exchange and have very close links with the commercial banks. Building societies also provide a source of finance. They tend to specialise in long term loans for the purchase of land and property.

At the heart of this highly complex market system is the **Bank of England**. This is the government's bank and tends to play a role in controlling the amount of money loaned, and to some extent, interest rates (☞ unit 65).

In recent years many of the above institutions have changed in nature. Due to competition and a change in legislation there has been a great deal of diversification. In particular, there is now little real difference between the role of a building society and that of a bank.

The choice of the source of funds

A number of factors are important when choosing between alternative sources of funds.

Cost Businesses obviously prefer sources which are less expensive, both in terms of interest payments and administration costs. For example, share issues can carry high administration costs while the interest payments on bank overdrafts tend to be relatively low.

Use of funds When a company undertakes heavy capital expenditure, it is usually funded by a long term source of finance. For example, the building of a new plant may be financed by a share issue or a mortgage. Revenue expenditure tends to be financed by short term sources. For example, the purchase of a large amount of raw materials may be funded by trade credit or a bank overdraft.

Status and size Sole traders, which tend to be small, are limited in their choices of finance. For example, long term sources may be mortgages and perhaps the introduction of some personal capital. Public and private limited companies can usually obtain finance from many different sources. In addition, due to their size and added security, they can often demand lower interest rates from lenders. There are significant economies of scale (☞ unit 31) in raising finance.

Financial situation The financial situation of businesses is constantly changing. When a business is in a poor financial situation, it finds that lenders are more reluctant to offer finance. At the same time, the cost of borrowing rises. Financial institutions are more willing to lend to secure businesses which have **collateral** (assets which provide security for loans). Third World Countries which are desperate to borrow money to fund development, are forced to pay very high rates indeed.

QUESTION 4 Look at the photographs below which illustrate examples of agricultural expenditure.

(a) How might each item of spending be funded if the farm was a partnership? Describe the advantages and disadvantages of each method of funding.
(b) When, during the year, do you think a farmer is in a strong position to secure finance?

Finally, the ratio of share capital to loan capital, ie the **gearing ratio**, may also affect the choice of capital source (☞ unit 44).

Sources of funds and the balance sheet

Unit 39 showed how a balance sheet is produced. The liabilities 'side' shows the debts of the company, ie the money owed to others. It is made up of:
- capital - money introduced by the owners of the company;
- other liabilities - money owed to people and institutions other than the owners, such as a bank.

It was also stated that these are the **sources** of funds used by the business, for example to buy assets. We can now show how the different sources discussed so far in this unit appear on the balance sheet, under liabilities.

The liabilities side is divided into three sections - capital and reserves, long term liabilities and current liabilities.

Capital and reserves Capital is the amount of money owed by the business to the owners. If all the company's assets were sold and the liabilities paid off, any money remaining would belong to the owners. Initially, capital represents the amount of money used to start a business.

During the life of a business the amount of capital changes. It will increase if the owners introduce money or if profits are retained. If the owners withdraw money from the firm or a loss is made then the capital of the business will fall. Because of this, capital is known as an **accumulated fund**. Capital is not physical in nature, and the term is used differently by business personnel and economists. To the accountant, capital is the difference between assets and liabilities.

Capital = total assets - total liabilities

If there is negative capital, where liabilities are greater than assets, then the firm is said to be INSOLVENT. In this situation it is illegal for the firm to continue trading.

WORKING CAPITAL, or circulating capital, is the amount of money a business needs to fund day to day trading. This could be payment of wages and energy costs or the purchase of components. Unit 44 shows how a business calculates its working capital. Here we can say:

Working capital = current assets - current liabilities

In the case of a sole trader or a partnership, capital might be introduced from personal savings or a loan. For a public limited company, the main source of capital is from the sale of **ordinary shares**, ie SHARE CAPITAL. The total value of ISSUED SHARE CAPITAL is shown in the **shareholders' funds**. This is the money raised from the sale of shares. It is calculated by multiplying the number of shares sold by the price at which they were originally sold, ie the nominal value. In the notes to the accounts the AUTHORISED SHARE CAPITAL will be stated. This is the maximum amount of share capital that shareholders want the company to raise. The authorised share capital is often larger than the issued share capital, but never smaller, as companies keep their options open to issue more shares later. For tax reasons preference shares are much less popular in today's business.

Reserves are shareholders' funds which have been built up over the life of the company. Three kinds are shown in the balance sheet.
- Share premiums. If a company issues shares, and the price they charge is higher than the nominal value, the share premium will be the difference. For example, if a 25p share is issued at 40p, the share premium is 15p. Dividends cannot be declared by the business as a result of such premiums.
- Revaluations. At times, particularly during periods of high inflation, some of the company's assets increase in value. If the values are updated on the asset side of the balance sheet then it is necessary to make an equal adjustment on the liabilities side. The entry is recorded under the heading of revaluation. It is a reserve because the benefit of any increase in asset values will be enjoyed by the owners of the company.
- Retained profits. The directors always retain a part of the company's profits as a precaution or to finance new business activities. When profits are not paid as dividends they are retained in reserve.

Long term liabilities Long term loans over a year must be repaid by the company and are called LONG TERM LIABILITIES. The most common listed in company balance sheets are debentures and mortgages.

Current liabilities CURRENT LIABILITIES are those short term financial debts which must be repaid within one year.
- Trade creditors. This is when goods are purchased from suppliers and paid for at a later date. Another current liability which is very similar is an accrued charge. Certain expenses occur from day to day, but are only invoiced periodically. For example, most firms use electricity every day but are billed only four times a year. If at the end of a trading year a bill has not been received, accountants will estimate the charge for the electricity used and record it in the balance sheet as an accrued charge.
- Bank loans and overdrafts. Loans which are repayable within twelve months are classed as current liabilities. In addition, even if bank overdrafts last for more than a year, because they are repayable 'on demand' they are shown as current liabilities.
- Taxation. Most firms pay tax at the latest possible date. When a company has been notified by the Inland Revenue, the amount owed to them is shown in the balance sheet as a current liability.
- Dividends payable. Once a dividend has been declared it has to be approved at the Annual General Meeting by the shareholders. It is assumed that the proposed dividend will be approved and because it will be paid shortly after it is listed as a current liability.

Key terms

Authorised share capital - the maximum amount which can be legally raised.
Capital expenditure - spending on business resources which can be used repeatedly over a period of time.
Capital gain - the profit made by selling a share for more than it was bought for.
Current liabilities - amounts owing which are expected to be repaid within one year.
Equities - another name for an ordinary share.
Finance house - a specialist institution which provides funds for hire purchase agreements.
Insolvency - where a company does not have enough assets to meet its liabilities; an inability to meet debts.
Issuing house - any institution which deals with the sale of new shares.

Issued share capital - amount of current share capital arising from the sale of shares.
Long term liabilities - amounts owing which are not repayable for at least one year.
Permanent capital - share capital which is never repaid by the company.
Revenue expenditure - spending on business resources which have already been consumed or will be very shortly.
Share capital - money introduced into the business through the sale of shares.
Stock market - a special share market, usually where second hand shares can be traded.
Working capital - current assets less current liabilities. Funds available to meet immediate business expenditure.

Question

Manchester United FC

In January 1991 Manchester United FC became a public limited company. The directors believed that a Stock Exchange flotation would be in the best interests of the club. It would enable them to:
- raise £6.7 million towards the development of a new all-seater stand;
- widen the ownership of the club by giving employees and supporters an opportunity to invest;
- provide increased liquidity to all shareholders by creating a wider market for their shares.

At the beginning of 1991 Manchester United's major sources of funds were as in Table 40.2 (figures for July 1990 are shown in brackets).

Table 40.2

	£000	
Share capital	1,009	(1,009)
Retained profit	4,879	(1,992)
Long-term creditors	1,142	(752)
Short-term creditors	3,478	(6,014)

The directors offered 4.6 million ordinary shares of 10p for sale at 385p per share, of which 2 million were placed with institutional investors and 2.6

million were offered for sale to the public. However, the flotation came at a time when recession was just beginning to affect the economy. The public share offer was 40 per cent undersubscribed, with the underwriters having to buy the unsold shares. Following the first day's trading the share price fell from 385p to 314p.

The flotation was considered to be a flop by some at the time.

Source: adapted from *The Independent on Sunday*, 2.6.1991 and *The Guardian*, 31.5.1991.

(a) What comments would you make about the financial position of the club at the time of the flotation?
(b) Why do you think the share price fell so dramatically from 385p to 314p on the first day of trading?
(c) What are the implications for the club of the relative failure of the share issue to the public?
(d) Without a flotation, how else might the club have funded the development of the new all-seater stadium?
(e) What was the value of Manchester United's total assets at the beginning of 1991?

Summary

1. Why do businesses need to raise funds?
2. State the internal sources of funds.
3. What is the difference between ordinary, preference and deferred shares?
4. State the advantages to a business of a bank overdraft compared with a bank loan.
5. What is the difference between a finance lease and an operating lease?
6. What is the function of financial intermediaries?
7. Describe the functions of a stock exchange.
8. What factors affect the choice of source of finance?
9. Why is share capital described as permanent capital?

Uses of funds and the balance sheet

Table 39.1 in unit 39 showed the main headings we might expect to find in a balance sheet. This unit is concerned with the asset side of the balance sheet. Assets are the **resources** used by business. A company will **use** the funds it earns to purchase assets which add value to a company. Most assets are physical in nature and are used in production. However, there are some, such as goodwill, which do not fall into this category, although they still add value. They are called intangible assets because they are non-physical. One of the functions of a balance sheet is to provide a summary of all business assets and their values. Assets are usually valued at their original cost, less a deduction for depreciation (☞ unit 43).

Fixed assets

Resources with a life span of more than one year are called FIXED ASSETS. Fixed assets, such as machinery, can be used again and again until they wear out. Some fixed assets like land and property do not depreciate, although they have to be repaired. In the balance sheet, fixed assets are divided into **tangible**, **intangible** and **financial** assets. Each of these are dealt with in detail in the following sections.

Tangible assets

TANGIBLE ASSETS are physical assets that can be touched. The most long term or the least **liquid** of these assets (the most difficult to turn into cash) appear at the top of the list of fixed assets on the balance sheet. For a farmer or a small manufacturing company these are likely to be the most important and largest fixed assets, if owned.

Land and property can either be **freehold** or **leasehold**. Freehold property is owned outright by the business. It is valued on the balance sheet at its original cost, less depreciation. In the past, inflation has resulted in soaring property prices. Accountants have advised many companies to revalue their land and property so that the accounts reflect more accurately a 'true and fair view' of the company. When assets are revalued in this way on the assets side of the balance sheet, an equivalent entry must be made on the liabilities side in reserves to balance the accounts.

Leasehold land and property is rented from an owner and is a company asset. Any capital amount paid for the lease appears separately as 'leasehold property'. This amount is **written off** (☞ unit 43) over the period of the lease. This means the value of the lease is reduced by an amount each year as it depreciates.

Fixed assets which are not land or property are referred to as plant, machinery and equipment. Again, they are valued at cost less depreciation. Large companies often have vast amounts of these assets. The balance sheet will, in this case, not list separate assets, but give only a total.

QUESTION 1

Assets of a car manufacturing business.

(a) Which of the assets above can be classified as fixed assets?
(b) Which of these assets is/are not directly involved in production?
(c) What are the advantages to a business of:
  (i) leasing rather than owning assets such as a delivery van;
  (ii) a freehold rather than a leasehold factory?

Intangible assets

Some fixed assets are not tangible, but are still valuable, income-generating resources. These are INTANGIBLE ASSETS.

Goodwill Over many years of trading companies build up goodwill. They may have gained a good reputation, which means that customers will use their services or purchase their products. If the company is to be sold in the future, some value needs to be placed on this goodwill and included in the purchase price. From an accountant's point of view, goodwill is equal to the amount by which the purchase price of a business exceeds the NET ASSETS (total assets - current liabilities).

Take the example of Amanda Storey, a young, newly qualified accountant, who decides to set up in business. She considers renting an office, advertising her services in the local press and distributing business cards. However, she is approached by Geoff Horrocks, an accountant who is considering retirement. Clearly it would pay Amanda to buy Geoff's list of established clients. The agreed price would represent goodwill.

Patents, copyrights and trademarks If a company or an individual invents and develops a unique product, a patent (☞ unit 28) can be obtained from the patent office. This is a licence which prevents other firms from copying the product. Patents have been granted in the past for products as diverse as cats eyes in 1935 to Polaroid cameras in 1946.

Copyright prevents the re-use of published works, such as books, plays, films and music without the author's consent. Michael Jackson allegedly paid £48 million in 1985 for a back catalogue of 250 Beatles' songs, out-bidding former Beatle Paul McCartney. Substantial fees are paid to copyright owners of music used in TV advertisements. Occasionally, certain magazines will allow a part of their publication to be used free of charge eg *Employment Gazette*. Trademarks generally signify a manufacturer's name. The right to sell another company's products may have to be registered if they carry a trademark and a fee may be charged.

Research and development Normally research and development (R & D) costs are classified as revenue expenditure (☞ unit 40). However, if a project is expected to earn a substantial income in the future, its costs may be recorded as capital expenditure and included as an intangible asset in the balance sheet. The costs are written off over the period when income is generated.

Brand names Many companies enjoy successful brand names. Recently, some of these companies have debated the inclusion of these intangible assets in the balance sheet because they generate income for a lengthy period of time in some cases. This means that the amount a successful brand name is estimated to be worth should be included as an intangible asset on the balance sheet, so that the true value of a company's assets is made clear.

When an intangible asset is written off it is described as **amortisation** rather than depreciation.

Financial assets

These are often called **investments** in the balance sheet. They usually refer to shares held by one company in other companies. If the shareholding in a particular company is more than 50 per cent then that company is classified as a **subsidiary**. If the holding is between 20 per cent and 50 per cent then the company is described as an **associated company**. Finally, any holdings of less than 20 per cent are called **trade investments**.

There are a number of motives for holding shares in other companies. These are shown in Figure 41.1. Some companies hold shares to earn income. **Holding companies** (☞ unit 3) such as Hanson, for example, specialise in buying and controlling other companies. In some cases, businesses are bought, broken up, and parts

> **QUESTION 2** In 1988 the value of brand names was a focus of attention following the acquisition of the York based chocolate manufacturer, Rowntree, by the Swiss company, Nestlé. The true value of Rowntree's attractive brand names, Polo, Kit Kat and Aero, became apparent when the share price of Rowntree increased rapidly from 447p to 1075p. The share price soared as Nestlé and another confectioner, Suchard, engaged in a bidding war. It was believed that £1.9 billion of the £2.3 billion paid by Nestlé for Rowntree was for the value of their brand names. The chairman of Grand Metropolitan, the hotels and drinks giant, whose main brand names include Ski, Ruddles and Smirnoff, has since argued that the true worth of a company should be shown to the shareholders by including these brand names in the balance sheet. According to standard accountancy convention, if a particular business asset can be 'stripped', identified, and sold separately then it may be valued as such. Some accountants believe that, on acquisition, brand names can be listed on the balance sheet. However, it must be remembered that brand names do not have an infinite life.
>
> (a) What are the advantages and disadvantages of including brand names on a company balance sheet?
>
> (b) What difficulties would be encountered if a company decided to write off a brand name?

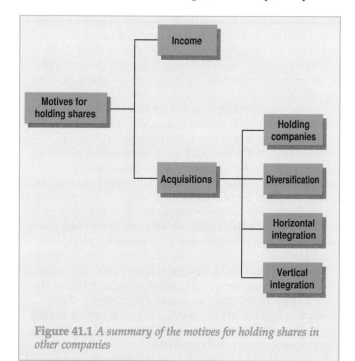

Figure 41.1 *A summary of the motives for holding shares in other companies*

sold at a profit. This activity has been described as **asset stripping**.

Another motive for holding shares is to diversify in order to reduce risk. Companies also buy firms in the same line of business to exploit economies of scale, ie horizontal integration (☞ unit 31). They may also seek to buy out their suppliers or distribution network, ie vertical integration.

Finally, other financial investments might include government bonds or deposits of foreign currency. All financial assets are listed at cost in the balance sheet.

QUESTION 3

Table 41.1 *An extract from the notes on the accounts (Castings PLC)*

11 Investments

	1993 Group £000	1993 Company £000	1992 Group £000	1992 Company £000
Subsidiary companies				
At cost		4,441		4,441
Other investments other than loans				
At cost	111	111	116	116
Other loans	-	-	5	5
	--------	--------	--------	--------
	111	4,552	121	4,562
	--------	--------	--------	--------

The company owns 100% of the issued share capital of W.H. Booth & Co. Limited and William Lee limited, companies which are incorporated and operate mainly in the United Kingdom.

The other investments are listed on a recognised stock exchange and their market value at 31st March 1993 was £209,000 (1992 - £173,000).

(a) What evidence is there in the above information to suggest that W.H.Booth & Co.Limited and William Lee Limited are subsidiaries of Castings PLC?
(b) Why is the market value of 'other investments' different to the value listed in the accounts?

Current assets

Short term assets which can be changed into cash within one year are called CURRENT ASSETS. There are four common current assets.

Stocks Most businesses hold stocks of finished goods. Stocks are classed as current assets because the business would hope to sell them within twelve months. The quantity of stocks held by a company will depend on the nature of the company.

Work-in-progress is also classified as stock. It represents partly finished goods, eg half built properties.

We also include stocks of raw materials and components in current assets. The business would expect to change them into finished goods which would then be sold, hopefully within a year.

Debtors In some lines of business, when a sale is made, it is common to receive payment at a later date. Any amounts owing by these customers at the end of the financial year are listed as **debtors** in the balance sheet. In order to speed up the payment of bills some firms offer cash discounts. In addition, debt factors offer a debt collecting service.

Related to debtors is another current asset - **prepayments**. A prepayment is a sum, such as, insurance, rent or uniform business rate, which is paid in advance. At the end of the financial year any service which has been paid for but not fully consumed is listed in the balance sheet as a prepayment.

Cash at bank Most businesses deposit their takings in a bank. From the bank account various business expenses are paid for. If the bank balance is positive at the end of the trading year the amount will be shown as a current asset in the balance sheet.

Cash in hand Many businesses have cash on their premises. This is often called **petty cash**. Cash is used to pay for small or unexpected transactions, eg the purchase of toilet paper.

Together, cash at bank and cash in hand represent the firm's most **liquid resources**. Businesses need to hold just the right amount of cash. Too much cash means business opportunities are being wasted as the money could be invested in other assets. Too little cash may prevent the business from making urgent purchases. Cash management is dealt with in more detail in unit 44.

Liquidity

LIQUIDITY refers to the speed or ease with which assets can be converted into cash without suffering any capital loss. For example, a house is an illiquid asset. It could be sold for cash for, say, £100, but the owner would be likely to lose money. In the balance sheet the least liquid assets (fixed assets) are listed at the top and the most liquid (current assets) are placed at the bottom.

Fixed assets like land and buildings tend to be very illiquid. It can sometimes take a long time to sell such assets. Possibly the most illiquid of all assets is a highly specialised item of machinery, ie a machine which has been especially made for a company. This type of capital good will prove very difficult to sell since demand will be limited.

Some fixed assets may be much easier to sell and are therefore more liquid. Vehicles, non-specialised machinery like a cement mixer or a JCB, and standard tools and equipment, which have a variety of uses, are all examples.

The least liquid of the current assets is stock. Stocks of finished goods are expected to be sold, but business fortunes change and sales can never be guaranteed. The liquidity of raw material stocks can vary. Non-specialised materials like coal will be more liquid than specialised components since they are easier to sell. Debtors are more liquid than stocks because goods have been sold and the business is legally entitled to payment. However, money has not been received so it cannot be spent. In addition, there are times when firms cannot pay and so the debt has to be written off (known as bad debts).

Cash at the bank and cash in hand are obviously the most liquid assets of all.

Asset structure

The ASSET STRUCTURE of a business refers to the amount of capital employed in each category of asset. Asset structures will vary according to the nature of the industry in which a business is competing. Manufacturing companies will tend to have a large amount of capital tied up in plant, machinery and equipment. Construction firms will have a significant amount of work-in-progress. Businesses which face seasonal demand may hold large stocks of finished goods

QUESTION 4

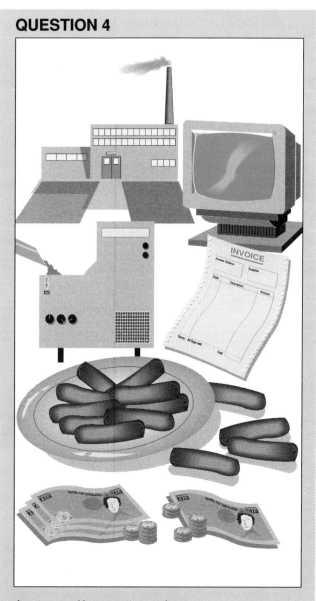

Assets owned by a sausage producer.

(a) Place the assets illustrated above in ascending order of liquidity.
(b) Where would you expect to find these assets in the balance sheet?

QUESTION 5

Figure 41.2 contains two pie charts which represent the asset structures of two different businesses. The value of each company's total assets is the same.

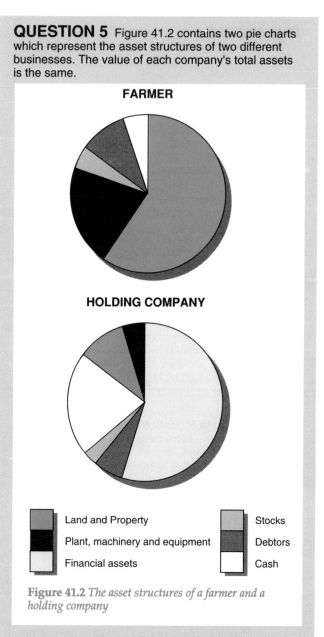

Figure 41.2 *The asset structures of a farmer and a holding company*

(a) Account for the different asset structures in Figure 41.2.
(b) In each case what might cause the asset structures to radically change?
(c) Which is the most liquid of the two companies? Explain why.

at particular times of the year. In the retail trade, public houses and restaurants will have very few debtors, or even none.

A profit maximising company will want to purchase those assets which yield the greatest return. Fixed assets are the productive assets of a business, so firms will want to invest as much of their capital as possible in these. However, some capital must be kept in current assets to fund day to day expenditure. It is not possible to conduct business activity without current assets. Some firms may exist with very little capital employed in fixed assets. Retailers often have a large proportion of current assets if they rent premises (stock in particular).

Company law and the balance sheet

According to the **1948** and the **1967 Companies Acts** the following information should be included in the balance sheet.

- The authorised and issued share capital.
- The amount of share premium.
- The amount of reserves.
- Details of debentures, mortgages, long term loans, short term loans, overdrafts, trade creditors, proposed dividends, taxation due and amounts due to subsidiaries.
- The separation of fixed and current assets.
- The method of valuation of fixed assets.
- The aggregate amounts provided for depreciation of fixed assets.
- Values of trade investments and shares in subsidiaries and any amounts due from subsidiaries.
- Details of current assets.
- The corresponding figures for the end of the previous year should be given.

These legal requirements are attempts to make company accounts standard and help protect the interests of shareholders. Much of the legislation is designed to clarify certain financial information so that the readers of accounts are not misled. The legislation does not place any unnecessary financial or administrative burden on the company and does not affect its decision making.

Key terms

Asset structure - the proportion of capital employed in each type of asset.
Current assets - short term assets which are expected to be converted into cash within one year.
Fixed assets - the long term resources of a business.
Intangible assets - non-physical business assets.
Liquidity - the ease with which assets can be converted into cash without suffering any capital loss.
Net assets - total assets less current liabilities.
Tangible assets - assets which are physical in nature.

Summary

1. What is the difference between tangible and intangible assets?
2. How is it possible to calculate the value of goodwill?
3. Distinguish between a subsidiary, an associated company and a trade investment.
4. What is meant by asset stripping?
5. What is the difference between debtors and prepayments?
6. What is the difference between a liquid and an illiquid asset?
7. Why is a specialised machine an illiquid asset?
8. What is the main determinant of a firm's asset structure?

Question

Castings PLC

Table 41.2 shows the balance sheet of Castings PLC, a company based in the West Midlands supplying a range of metal castings.

Table 41.2 *The balance sheet for Castings PLC (two entries have been removed - debtors and net current assets)*

CASTINGS PLC
Balance sheet as at 31st March 1993

	1993 £000	1992 £000
Fixed assets		
Tangible assets	8,804	8,892
Investments	111	121
Current assets		
Stocks	2,502	2,669
Debtors	?	7,412
Short term deposits	8,564	6,497
Cash at bank and in hand	50	86
	18,333	16,664
Creditors - amounts falling due within one year	10,318	10,670
Net current assets	?	5,994
Total assets less current liabilities	16,930	15,007
Provisions for liabilities and charges	245	453
	16,685	14,554
Capital and reserves		
Called up share capital	2,113	2,108
Share premium	201	172
Profit and loss account	14,371	12,274
Shareholders' funds	16,685	14,554

(a) What was the value of debtors and net current assets in 1993?

(b) What is the main reason for the increase in shareholders' funds?

(c) What major changes took place in the asset structure of the business between 1992 and 1993? Comment on these changes from the company's point of view.

(d) If the company was sold for £20,000,000 what would be the value of goodwill?

The nature of profit

Profit is the driving force in most businesses. There are few, if any, which attach no importance to making profit, the exceptions perhaps being charities. Even state run industries, whose major objective has been to provide a comprehensive service (☞ unit 5), have pursued profits in recent years.

Profit has a number of functions. The prospect of making profit motivates people to set up in business. Without profit there would be little incentive for individuals to commit their time and personal resources to business activity. Economists often refer to **normal profit**. This is the minimum reward an entrepreneur must receive in order to maintain interest in the business. If the business does not earn this amount of profit the owner will pull out and pursue other opportunities.

Profit also helps resource allocation in market economies (☞ unit 6). Businesses that make profits are able to purchase more raw materials and labour in order to expand production. Investors are attracted to those businesses that are likely to give the greatest financial reward. Economists call this abnormal profit - the amount by which total profit is greater than normal profit.

The amount of profit that a business makes is a measure of how well it is performing. Those firms that supply quality products which are efficiently produced and sold at prices which are attractive to consumers will tend to be more profitable. However, there are other factors which affect the performance of a business, such as the amount of market power a firm enjoys (☞ unit 22). From an accountant's point of view, profit is the amount of money left over in a particular trading period when all business expenses have been met. Profit can then be:
- retained;
- distributed to the owners of the company;
- used to pay tax.

If expenses exceed sales revenue in a trading period then there will be a loss. It is the accountant's definition of profit which we will be referring to in this unit.

QUESTION 1 Gabrielle Fisher terminated her contract with a large fabric manufacturer and set off on a tour of Malaysia and the Phillipines. On return, and inspired by her trip to the Far East, Gabrielle set up in business designing fabrics based on Oriental patterns. She had given the venture a great deal of thought. Gabrielle was highly regarded in the industry and could command a £30,000+ salary as a fabric designer. She felt that unless she could clear £25,000 after all business expenses had been met, the venture would not be worth her while.
(a) What is the value of normal profit for Gabrielle?
(b) Why might she accept a lower return than her previous salary?
(c) If Gabrielle cleared £40,000 in her first trading year what would be the value of abnormal profit?

Measuring profit

At the end of the trading year most owners like to see how well their company has performed. One initial indication of performance is the amount of profit (or loss) that the business has made during that year. Figure 42.1 illustrates how profit (and loss) is measured. It is the

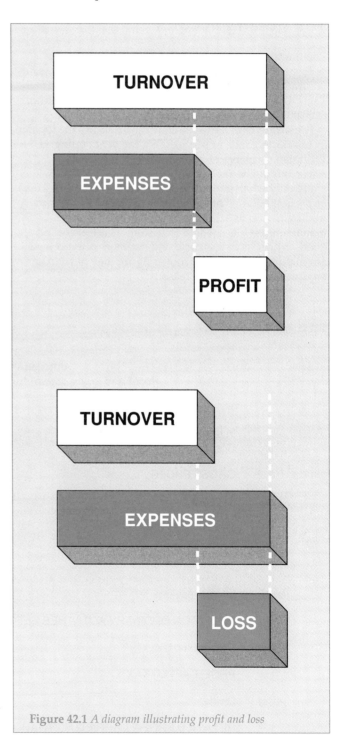

Figure 42.1 *A diagram illustrating profit and loss*

difference between turnover and business expenses. Businesses measure their profit by compiling a **profit and loss account**. This is a summary of all business transactions and shows the flow of expenditure and income in a trading period. A profit and loss account for the year ending 31 January 1993 is shown in Table 42.1. It shows the business transactions for Virginian Carpets Ltd, a carpet wholesaler which specialises in Moroccan carpets. It is divided into three sections: the TRADING ACCOUNT; the PROFIT AND LOSS ACCOUNT; the PROFIT AND LOSS APPROPRIATION ACCOUNT.

The trading account

The trading account shows the revenue earned from selling products (the turnover) and the cost of those sales. Subtracting one from the other gives GROSS PROFIT. In Table 42.1, Virginian Carpets Ltd made a gross profit of £400,000 in the year ending 31.1.93.

The **turnover** or **sales revenue** figure shows the income from selling goods or services. For the year ending 31.1.93, Virginian Carpets Ltd had a turnover of £900,000. According to the **realisation concept** (☞ unit 38) a sale is made only when goods are delivered to customers. This is important because profit must be **included** in the same trading period as sales. Goods which have been manufactured but not sold to customers are **excluded** and goods which have been sold and payment not received are **included**. The final turnover figure may have to be adjusted for a number of reasons.

- Businesses must exclude indirect taxes such as VAT from the turnover figure. VAT is added to the sale price of goods. It is paid by consumers to businesses, which then hand it over to the government. Including VAT would overstate a firm's turnover.
- Sales of goods which are returned because they are faulty or unwanted must be removed from the turnover figure. Turnover will be overstated if their value were included.
- Errors often occur on invoices - documents which tell the purchaser how much is owed for the goods that are purchased. If there is an error which overstates the value of a sale, an adjustment must be made to turnover. Businesses usually send a credit note to cover the exact amount that the purchaser has been 'overcharged'.
- Sometimes a customer who has bought goods on credit is unable to pay for them. The turnover figure is usually left unchanged. However, businesses do record the value of an unpaid sale as a business expense in the profit and loss account as a bad debt.

The second figure listed in the trading account is the **cost of sales**. This refers to all costs of production. It will include direct costs such as raw materials, the wages of labour and other indirect costs or OVERHEADS associated with production (known as production overheads) such as fuel and rent.

It is often necessary to adjust the cost of raw materials for changes in stock. The cost of sales for Virginian Carpets Ltd in Table 42.1 is £500,000. This is mainly the cost of buying carpets for resale from Morocco. However,

Table 42.1 *The profit and loss account for Virginian Carpets Ltd for the period ending 31.1.93*

VIRGINIAN CARPETS LTD
Profit and loss account for the year ended 31 January 1993

		£
	TURNOVER	900,000
(less)	Cost of sales	500,000
	GROSS PROFIT	400,000
(less)	Expenses	300,000
	OPERATING PROFIT	100,000
(plus)	Non-operating income	20,000
		120,000
(less)	Interest payable	10,000
	PROFIT ON ORDINARY ACTIVITIES BEFORE TAXATION	110,000
(less)	Corporation tax	27,500
	PROFIT AFTER TAX	82,500
(less)	Dividends	40,000
	RETAINED PROFIT CARRIED FORWARD	42,500

it is likely that during the trading year some of the carpets sold were bought in previous trading years and held in stock. Also, some of the carpets bought during the trading year will remain unsold and so the cost of sales must be adjusted.

Table 42.2 *Cost of sales adjusted for stock*

	£
Opening stock 1.2.92	80,000
Purchases during the year	600,000
	680,000
less Closing stock 31.1.93	180,000
Cost of sales	500,000

In Table 42.2, at the beginning of the trading year, Virginian Carpets had £80,000 worth of carpets in stock. During the trading year £600,000 worth of new carpets were imported from Morocco. At the very end of the trading year the stock of carpets unsold was valued at £180,000. Therefore the cost of sales was £500,000. Only purchases of goods for resale are included in 'cost of sales' figures. Expenditure, such as stationery, that is not for resale is not included.

The gross profit of £400,000 in Table 42.1 is found by subtracting the cost of sales from the turnover.

QUESTION 2 Medicon Ltd manufacture equipment for hospitals, selling to both the UK and Europe. During the year ended June 30 1993, the company earned revenue of £370,000 from sales in the UK and £220,000 from sales overseas. The sales had involved direct costs of production of £285,000 for wages and £165,000 for raw materials. Over the trading period Medicon's stocks of raw materials had fallen from £75,000 to £48,000.
(a) Based on the figures given above , draw up Medicon's trading account for the year ending June 30 1993, and calculate the gross profit.
(b) How would gross profit change if:
  (i) all the sales to Europe had been on three months credit;
  (ii) a large hospital had returned £12,000 of equipment due to faulty manufacture;
  (iii) the level of stocks on June 30 1993 was valued at £55,000?
Explain your answers.

The profit and loss account

The profit and loss account is an extension of the trading account. In practice, there is no indication where the trading account ends and the profit and loss account begins. However, once a business has calculated its **gross profit** it can then calculate how much profit (or loss) it has made by adding any extra income it has earned and subtracting its expenses and tax. In Table 42.1 the **profit**

after tax earned by Virginian Carpets Ltd for the year ended 31 January 1993 was £82,500.

The first item to be subtracted from the gross profit figure is expenses. This gives a figure for **operating profit**. Expenses are those overheads or indirect costs that are not involved in production of goods and services. They include expenses, such as advertising and promotion, wages of the administration staff and depreciation. Table 42.3 gives a breakdown of the expenses incurred by Virginian Carpets Ltd during the trading year. They reflect the type of costs associated with companies. The breakdown of these figures is normally shown in the notes to the accounts or a separate Trading and Profit and Loss Account.

Table 42.3 *Operating (administrative) expenses of Virginian Carpets Ltd*

Expenses	£	£
Wages and salaries (admin.)	110,000	
Rent and rates	40,000	
Heating and lighting	30,000	
Advertising	15,000	
Motor expenses	24,000	
Telephone	8,000	
Printing and stationery	13,000	
Insurance	9,000	
Accountancy fees	4,000	
Provision for bad debts	12,000	
Depreciation	35,000	
		300,000

The company will then add any **non-operating income** to their operating profit. Non-operating income is income which is not earned from the direct trading of the company. This could include dividends from shares held in other companies, interest from deposits in financial institutions such as banks, or rent from property that is let out.

At this stage it is usual to subtract any interest which has been paid out by the firm. Interest is usually shown separately in the accounts. When this final adjustment has been made the resulting figure is the **profit on ordinary activities before tax** (sometimes known as NET PROFIT) - £110,000. In the notes to the accounts there are often further details of expenses incurred during the year. For example, by law, the notes must show the directors' rewards, ie salaries, the auditor's fee, depreciation of fixed assets, donations and the number of employees receiving payments.

The final entry in the profit and loss account is the profit after taxation £82,500. All limited companies have to pay corporation tax on profits over a certain amount to the government. The amount paid by Virginian Carpets Ltd is £27,500.

QUESTION 3 Oldfields Ltd are a grocery wholesaler based in Shrewsbury. They supply grocery products to local retailers, public houses and hotels. Their trading account and profit and loss account for the last trading year are shown in Table 42.4.

Table 42.4 *Trading account and profit and loss account for Oldfield Ltd for the year ending 31.8.93*

OLDFIELDS LTD
Profit and loss account
for the year ended 31.8.93

	£000
TURNOVER	1,500
(less) Cost of sales	???
GROSS PROFIT	450
(less) Expenses	210
OPERATING PROFIT	???
(plus) Non operating income	10
	250
(less) Interest payable	80
PROFIT ON ORDINARY ACTIVITIES BEFORE TAXATION	???

(a) What is the value of:
   (i) cost of sales;
   (ii) operating profit;
   (iii) profit on ordinary activities before tax?
(b) Describe Oldfield Ltd's 'ordinary activities'.
(c) List 4 examples of Oldfield's likely expenses.

QUESTION 4 Table 42.5 shows a summary of financial information for Renovation Enterprises Ltd. The company specialises in renovating old machinery and industrial equipment which they then sell to collectors. The company also owns some farm buildings which they converted into two luxury flats and let out.

Table 42.5 *Financial information for Renovation Enterprises Ltd, year ending 31.7.93*

	£
Turnover	500,000
Interest received	5,000
Cost of sales	100,000
Interest paid	2,000
Distribution costs	50,000
Taxation	120,000
Administration costs	40,000
Dividends paid	100,000
Rental income	20,000

Produce a complete profit and loss account for Renovation Enterprises Ltd, year ending 31.7.93. Include the trading account, the profit and loss account and the profit and loss appropriation account.

The profit and loss appropriation account

The final section in the profit and loss account is the **appropriation account.** This shows how the company profit or loss is distributed. The profit after tax is distributed in two ways. In Table 42.1 the profit after tax for Virginian Carpets Ltd is:

- distributed to shareholders in the form of dividends - £40,000;
- retained within the company and carried forward for internal use in the following year - £42,500.

Most companies retain a proportion of profit for investment or as a precaution. The amount paid out in dividends is determined by the board of directors and approved by the shareholders at the Annual General Meeting. Although the business is not legally obliged to pay dividends, shareholders may be dissatisfied if they are not paid.

The relationship between the balance sheet and the profit and loss account

Some of the information contained in the profit and loss account is transferred to the balance sheet.

- The **retained profit in the business** is placed in **reserves** on the liabilities side of the balance sheet. Retained profit belongs to the shareholders until it is used to fund some venture in the future. If a loss is made, the retained profit figure in the balance sheet will be reduced.
- The **taxation** payable and the **proposed** dividend are shown in the **current liabilities**. Tax is owed to the Inland Revenue and dividends are paid to the shareholders.
- The **depreciation** figure from operating expenses has an effect on the **fixed assets** section of the balance sheet. The value of fixed assets is written down each year by the amount shown as depreciation in the profit and loss account.

Public limited company accounts

Public limited companies have similar accounts to those of private limited companies, such as Virginian Carpets. They must also publish their accounts by law. This allows the public to see the financial position and performance of the company and decide if buying its shares is worthwhile. Existing shareholders can also gauge the company's performance.

It is likely that the published profit and loss account of a large public limited company will be slightly different from that of a private company. Accounts often show the **earnings per share** in the appropriation account. This is calculated by dividing the profit after tax by the total number of issued shares. For example, if a company's net profit after tax is £1.6 million and 5 million shares have been issued:

$$\text{Earnings per share} = \frac{\text{Net profit after tax}}{\text{No. of shares issued}}$$

$$= \frac{£1.6m}{5m}$$

$$= 32p$$

The earnings per share gives an indication of a company's performance and is discussed in more detail in unit 45.

■ PLCs usually pay dividends twice a year. About half way through the financial year a company might pay an **interim dividend**, usually less than half the total dividend. At the end of the financial year the **final dividend** is paid.

■ From time to time business may make a 'one-off' transaction. An example of an **exceptional item** might be a very large bad debt which is deducted as normal in the profit and loss account, but disclosed separately in the notes. In recent years some of the commercial banks have had to make such entries after incurring bad debts from Third World countries. An example of an **extraordinary item** might be the cost of

management restructuring. Such an item was disclosed in the published accounts of British Telecom in 1990. Generally they arise from events outside the normal business activities and are not expected to occur again. The expenditure would normally be listed in the profit and loss account, below the line showing profit after tax.

■ Finally, in the profit and loss appropriation account of a public limited company, the retained profit figure is sometimes called **transfer to reserves**.

Sole trader accounts

Table 42.6 shows the trading and profit and loss account for Joanna Cullen, a retailer selling computer software. The differences and similarities between the profit and loss account of a sole trader and a limited company can be illustrated from Table 42.6. The profit and loss account of a sole trader normally shows how the year's purchases are adjusted for stock by including opening and closing stocks. In addition, a more detailed list of expenses is included. This allows a comparison with the previous year. A profit and loss appropriation account is not included since there is only one owner and all profit is transferred to the capital account in the balance sheet.

QUESTION 5 Compare the two accounts in Table 42.1 and Table 42.6.
(a) Why do you think that more detail is shown in a sole trader's profit and loss account compared with a limited company?
(b) Explain why a £20,000 increase in turnover for Joanna Cullen between 1992 and 1993 only led to a £11,500 increase in net profit.

Key terms

Gross profit - turnover less cost of sales.
Net profit - profit on ordinary activities before taxation.
Overheads - indirect business expenses which are not chargeable to a particular part of work or production, eg heating, lighting or wages.
Profit and loss account - shows net profit after tax by subtracting business expenses and taxation from operating profit.

Profit and loss appropriation account - shows how the profit after tax is distributed between shareholders and the business.
Trading account - shows operating profit by subtracting the cost of sales from turnover.

Table 42.6 *The profit and loss account of Joanna Cullen, a sole trader*

JOANNA CULLEN
Trading and profit and loss account for the year ended 31.5.93

1992 £		1993 £	£
130,000	Turnover		150,000
25,000	Opening stock	30,000	
65,000	Purchases	70,000	
90,000			100,000
30,000	*less* Closing stock at selling price	35,000	
60,000			65,000
70,000	Gross profit		85,000
	less:		
1,000	Casual labour	2,000	
2,500	Motor expenses	3,000	
800	Telephone	1,000	
2,500	Printing, stationery and advertising	3,000	
1,300	Electricity	1,500	
8,000	Rent and rates	9,000	
400	Insurance	500	
2,500	Bank interest and charges	2,500	
2,000	Depreciation - car	2,000	
900	Depreciation - fixtures and fittings	900	
21,900			25,400
48,100	Net profit		59,600

Summary

1. What is meant by profit from an accountant's point of view?
2. What is likely to happen to a business if normal profit is not made?
3. Distinguish between gross and operating profit.
4. What adjustments might need to be made to turnover during the year?
5. Why is it necessary to adjust purchases for changes in stock levels?
6. What is meant by non-operating income?
7. How might a limited company appropriate its profits?
8. How are earnings per share calculated?
9. What is the difference between the interim and the final dividend?
10. What is the difference between an extraordinary item and an exceptional item?
11. How might the profit and loss account of a sole trader be different from that of a limited company?

Question

Aston Cross Fittings PLC

Aston Cross Fittings PLC are established manufacturers of metal fittings which they supply to machine tool makers. They operate from a factory and office in Walsall which employs 370 workers. They have been trading for thirty years and have enjoyed a steady growth in profitability. However, during the last trading year a substantial part of the factory was damaged by fire. Unfortunately the company was underinsured and had to bear part of the cost of rebuilding themselves. In addition, production had to be halted for six weeks so that reconstruction could take place. This led to some late deliveries of orders and the loss of one very important customer. However, benefits of the reconstruction were the improvement of the factory layout and the installation of two new, more efficient, machines. The factory fire and the heavy costs of rebuilding resulted in a loss for the year and undermined shareholder confidence. Table 42.7 shows the profit and loss account for Aston Cross Fittings PLC.

Table 42.7 *The profit and loss account and an extract from the notes to the accounts for Aston Cross Fittings PLC*

ASTON CROSS FITTINGS PLC
Profit and loss account for the year ended 31.3.93

	Note	1993 £m	1992 £m
Turnover	1	124.1	146.2
Cost of sales		(100.4)	(104.1)
Gross profit		23.7	42.1
Selling and distribution expenses		(12.0)	(15.9)
Administrative expenses		(9.8)	(12.1)
Operating profit		1.9	14.1
Investment income	2	1.4	4.7
		3.3	18.8
Interest payable		(3.4)	(3.8)
Profit on ordinary activities before tax		(0.1)	15.0
Taxation	3	0.0	4.8
Profit on ordinary activities after tax		(0.1)	10.2
Extraordinary item	4	(13.9)	-
Profit (loss) for the financial year		(14.0)	10.2
Dividends	5	2.5	5.2
Transferred to reserves	6	(16.5)	5.0
Earnings (loss) per share	7	(34.31p)	25p

4 Extraordinary item

Factory reconstruction	(13.9)	-

(a) Explain and give an example of the terms:
   (i)   administrative expenses;
   (ii) investment income;
   (iii) extraordinary item.
(b) What effect might the extraordinary item have on
   (i)   the profits for the year;
   (ii) future profitability?

(c) How is it possible to pay a dividend in a year when the company has made a substantial loss?
(d) Calculate the number of shares the company has issued.
(e) Write a statement from the chairperson to the shareholders explaining significant changes in the profit and loss account.

How are assets valued?

One of the problems in financial accounting is how to place a value on assets. Unit 38 stated that accountants value assets at **historical cost**, ie the cost of the asset when it is first purchased.

There are reasons why assets should be valued in this way. Business transactions are entered into records as they occur. For example, if a firm buys a vehicle for £15,000 and pays cash, two entries will be made in the records. Also, accountants would argue that historical cost can be checked. It is based on actual costs and is better than methods which involve estimates. Other methods of valuation, such as those which take into account inflation, are also used. As yet, though, a suitable replacement has not been found.

One problem with historical cost accounting is how to put a value on fixed assets like property. In recent years there have been times when the values of land and buildings have risen sharply - as much as 30 or 40 per cent in one year. Unless the accounts are amended, they will not reflect the true value of the business. It is common now to revalue assets such as property every few years. Inflation distorts the value of assets and any other value which is measured in money terms.

This unit considers the valuation of two sets of assets - fixed assets, such as machinery, and current assets, such as stock. The valuation of these assets causes particular problems for accountants.

Valuing fixed assets - the use of depreciation

Fixed assets are used again and again over a long period of time. During this time the value of many assets falls. This is called DEPRECIATION. Figure 43.1 shows the

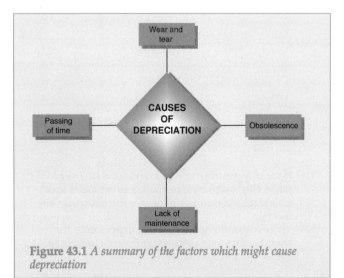

Figure 43.1 *A summary of the factors which might cause depreciation*

reasons why the value of assets might fall.
- Some assets fall in value because they wear out. Vehicles, machinery, tools and most equipment all deteriorate when used, and have to be replaced.
- Changing technology can often make assets OBSOLETE. Although a machine may still work, it may not be used because a new machine is more efficient.
- Capital goods which are hardly used or poorly maintained may loose value quickly. The life of machinery can be prolonged if it is 'looked after'.
- The passing of time can also reduce the value of assets. For example, if an asset is leased, the 'buyer' can use the asset for a period of time. As the expiry date gets close, the lease becomes worth less and less.

Depreciation and the accounts

Each year accountants must work out how much depreciation to allow for each fixed asset. This can then be used in the balance sheet and the profit and loss account.

The balance sheet (☞ unit 39) will show the BOOK VALUE of assets. This is their original value minus depreciation. So if a piece of machinery is bought for £10,000 and depreciates by £3,000 in the first year, its book value would be £7,000. The book value falls each year as more depreciation is deducted.

Depreciation is shown in the profit and loss account under expenses (☞ unit 42). This indicates that part of the original value is 'used up' each year (known as revenue expenditure (☞ unit 40). Eventually the entire value of the asset will appear as expenses, when the asset depreciates fully. This process of reducing the original value by the amount of depreciation is known as **writing off**.

There are good reasons why a firm should allow for depreciation each year in its accounts.
- If it does not, the accounts will be inaccurate. If the original value of assets was placed on the balance sheet this would overstate the value. The value of assets falls each year as they depreciate.
- Fixed assets generate profit for many years. It seems logical to write off the value of the asset over this whole period, rather than when it is first bought. This **matches** the benefit from the asset more closely with its cost.
- A sensible firm will know that assets must be replaced in future and allow for this. Even though depreciation appears as an expense on the profit and loss account, it is actually a PROVISION. Expenses involve paying out money. In the case of depreciation, no money is paid out. A business simply recognises that assets have to be replaced and provides for this by placing a value in the accounts. In practice, it is unlikely that the firm would actually put money aside each year to replace the worn out asset.

QUESTION 1

Table 43.1 *Extract from the Homecare Charity Accounts 1993*

	1993	1992
Fixed assets - equipment at cost	30,259	22,083
(less) depreciation	2,767	2,026
Net value	27,492	20,057

(a) What type of fixed asset is the Homecare Charity likely to own?
(b) Why might the value of these assets have depreciated?
(c) Why might the Homecare Charity see depreciation as a provision rather than an expense?

Calculating depreciation - the straight line method

The STRAIGHT LINE METHOD is the most common method used by business to work out depreciation. It assumes that the net cost of an asset should be written off in equal amounts over its life. The accountant needs to know the cost of the asset, its estimated **residual value**, ie its 'scrap' value after the business has finished with it, and its expected life in years. The formula used is:

$$\text{Depreciation allowance (each time period)} = \frac{\text{Original cost - residual value}}{\text{Expected life (years)}}$$

Assume, a delivery van costs £28 000 to buy and has an expected life of 4 years. The residual value is estimated at £4 000.

$$\text{Depreciation allowance} = \frac{£28,000 - £4,000}{4 \text{ years}}$$

$$= \frac{£24,000}{4}$$

$$= £6,000$$

When calculating depreciation it is helpful to draw up a table to show how an asset is written off over its lifetime. Table 43.2 shows the depreciation allowance charged to the profit and loss account each year, and the net book value which is listed in the balance sheet. We can illustrate this on a graph (Figure 43.2). These are some advantages to using this method.

■ It is simple. Little calculation is needed and the same amount is subtracted from the book value each year.
■ It is useful for assets like a lease, where the life of the asset and the residual value is known precisely.

Table 43.2 *A summary of the annual depreciation allowance and book value of the van using the straight line method*

Year	Depreciation allowance (each year) £	Net book value £
	£	£
1	6,000	22,000
2	6,000	16,000
3	6,000	10,000
4	6,000	4,000

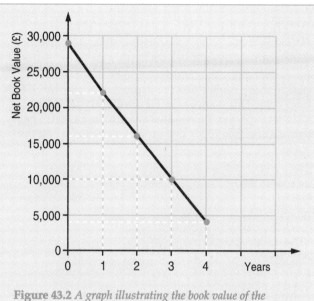

Figure 43.2 *A graph illustrating the book value of the delivery van over its lifetime (straight line method)*

QUESTION 2

A company purchases a new furnace for £200,000 and expects it to remain in use for 10 years. At the end of its useful life it is estimated that the furnace will have a scrap (residual) value of £10,000.
(a) Calculate the annual depreciation allowance using the straight line method.
(b) Draw up a table showing how the furnace is written off over its life.
(c) What is the book value at the end of year 6?
(d) Draw a line graph showing the annual book value over the life of the furnace.

Calculating depreciation - the reducing balance method

The REDUCING BALANCE METHOD assumes that the depreciation charge in the early years of an asset's life should be higher than in the later years. To do this, the asset must be written off by the same percentage rate each year. This means the annual charge falls.

Assume a vehicle is bought for £28,000 and has a life of four years. Table 43.3 shows how the vehicle can be written off using the reducing balance method. A 40 per cent charge will be made each year and the firm expects a residual value of £3,629.

Table 43.3 *A summary of the depreciation allowance and book value of the vehicle using the reducing balance method*

Year	Depreciation allowance (each year)	Book value
	£	£
1	11,200 (28,000 x 40%)	16,800
2	6,720 (16,800 x 40%)	10,080
3	4,032 (10,080 x 40%)	6,048
4	2,419 (6,048 x 40%)	3,629

Table 43.3 shows the depreciation allowance in the profit and loss account in each of the four years. It also shows the book value which would be listed in the balance sheet. Notice that the depreciation allowance falls every year. This is shown in Figure 43.3. What if the business expected the residual value to be £4,000? The depreciation charge for this can be calculated using the formula:

$$\text{Depreciation rate} = \left[1 - \sqrt[n]{\frac{\text{Residual value}}{\text{Cost}}} \right] \times 100$$

Where n = estimated life of the asset, ie 4 years, so:

$$\text{Depreciation rate} = \left[1 - \sqrt[4]{\frac{4,000}{28,000}} \right] \times 100 = 38.52\%$$

There are some advantages to using the reducing balance method.

■ It takes into account that some assets, machinery for example, lose far more value in the first year than they do in the fifth year, say. So the book value reflects more accurately the real value of the asset in the balance sheet.

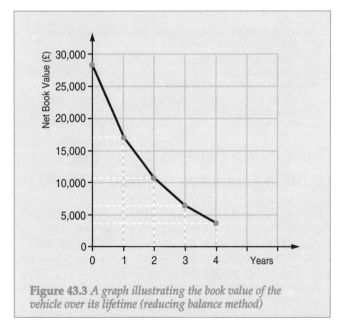

Figure 43.3 *A graph illustrating the book value of the vehicle over its lifetime (reducing balance method)*

■ For many assets, maintenance and repair costs grow as the asset ages. Using the declining balance method results in a more equal total expense each year for fixed assets related costs. For example, at the end of year 1 the depreciation charge for a machine might be £4,500 with only a £500 maintenance charge. In year 5 the depreciation charge might have been £1,500 and repairs and maintenance may have been £3,000. Although the two totals are not the same (£5,000 and £4,500), as the depreciation charges fall the maintenance and repair costs rise. American companies use this method.

QUESTION 3 A large building contractor buys a new mechanical digger costing £150,000. The firm has a policy of replacing expensive machinery after 5 years while it is possible to obtain a reasonable second hand sale price. The contractor expects the residual value to be £49,152.
(a) Using a spreadsheet, draw up a table showing the annual depreciation allowance and the book value at the end of each year. Use the reducing balance method and write off 20 per cent per annum.
(b) Draw a graph to show the annual book value over the period the digger is used by the firm.
(c) Why might the contractor choose a discount rate of 20 per cent?

Other methods of calculating depreciation

The **sum-of-the-years' digits method** assumes that fixed assets depreciate quicker in the early years. The calculation is based on the sum-of-the-years' digits, given the expected life of an asset, less the residual value. For an asset which has an expected life of 4 years the sum-of-the-years' is 10, ie 4+3+2+1 = 10. The depreciation charge for the first year will be 4/10 of the original cost, the second year it will be 3/10 of the original cost and so on.

Assuming a cost of £28,000, a life span of 4 years and a residual value of £4,000, the **net value** of the asset is £24,000 (£28,000 - £4,000). We can draw up a table to show the annual depreciation charge and the book value each year (Table 43.4).

Table 43.4 *A summary of the annual depreciation allowance and book value for the asset above, using the sum-of-the-years' digits method*

Year	Depreciation allowance (each year)	Book value
	£	£
1	9,600 (24,000 x 4/10)	18,400
2	7,200 (24,000 x 3/10)	11,200
3	4,800 (24,000 x 2/10)	6,400
4	2,400 (24,000 x 1/10)	4,000

From Table 43.4 we can see that the depreciation allowance falls in a similar way to the reducing balance method.

The **usage method** (or **machine hour method**) takes into account that some assets wear out more rapidly the more they are used. Thus, depreciation is based on the number of hours a machine, for example, is used during the accounting period. It is not a method that is often used by firms.

The disposal of assets

The book value of assets very rarely reflects their true value. So if an asset is sold, a business usually makes a profit or a loss. This is likely if the asset is sold before the end of its expected life. For example, if a machine is bought for £100,000 with an expected life of 10 years and residual value of £15,000, the depreciation allowance each year will be £8,500 (using the straight line method). If the firm decides to sell the machine at the end of year 7 and receives £44,000, it earns a profit of £3,500 because the book value at the end of year 7 is £40,500. A firm must show this in the accounts. It is common practice to deal with profit or loss on disposal by adjusting that year's depreciation charge. If a profit is made, the depreciation charge will be reduced by the amount of the profit. If a loss is made, the depreciation charge will be increased by the amount of the loss. If the profit or loss is very large then it will be treated as an exceptional item in the accounts (☞ unit 42).

> **QUESTION 4** A small retailer buys a delivery van for £3 000 with an estimated scrap value of £200 and an expected life of 7 years. Assuming that the straight line method of depreciation is used, calculate the profit/loss on disposal if the van is sold for £1200 after 3 years.

Valuing current assets - stock valuation

When accounts are produced, a firm must calculate the quantity and value of the stocks which it is holding. The value of **stocks** at the beginning and the end of the trading year, ie the **opening stock** and the **closing stock**, will affect the gross profit for the year. This is because the cost of sales in the trading account is adjusted for changes in stock. If, for example, the closing stock is overvalued, then the cost of sales will be lower and the gross profit higher. This is shown in Tables 43.5 and 43.6. In Table 43.5 the closing stock is £11,300, the cost of sales (adjusted for stock) is £57,400 and gross profit is £40,500.

In Table 43.6 the closing stock is now valued at £14,100 instead of £11,300, so the cost of sales (adjusted for stock) is lower at £54,600 and the gross profit higher at £43,300.

A **stock take** can be used to find out how much stock is held. This involves making a list of all raw materials, finished goods and work-in-progress. Stock valuation is more difficult. The 'prudence' concept in accounting

Table 43.5

	£	£
Turnover		97,900
Opening stock	12,300	
Cost of sales	56,400	
	68,700	
Less closing stock	11,300	
		57,400
Gross profit		40,500

Table 43.6

	£	£
Turnover		97,900
Opening stock	12,300	
Cost of sales	56 400	
	68,700	
Less closing stock	14,100	
		54,600
Gross profit		43,300

(☞ unit 38) does not allow selling prices to be used because profit is only recognised when a sale has been made. So stocks are valued at historic cost or net realisable value, whichever is the lowest. Normally stocks would be valued at cost. But there are circumstances when net realisable value is lower. If goods are damaged in stock, they may sell for a lot less than they cost to produce. Also, some products face severe changes in market conditions. Clothes tend to fall in value when fashions change, and may need discounts to sell them.

What happens to stock valuation when the cost of stock changes over time? Say a business buys some goods at the start of the year, but finds that half way through their cost of replacement has gone up. How are they valued? Three methods can be used.
- FIFO (first in first out).
- LIFO (last in first out).
- Average cost.

First in first out

The FIRST IN FIRST OUT method assumes that stock for production is issued in the order in which it was delivered. Thus, stocks that are bought first are used up first. Any unused stocks at the end of the trading year will be those most recently bought. This ensures that stocks issued for production are priced at the cost of earlier stocks, while any remaining stock is valued much closer to the replacement cost. Assuming that the opening stock is zero, consider the following stock transactions in Table 43.7.

On 1.6.93 a business receives 100 units of stock at £5, which means it has £500 of goods in stock. On 4.6.93, an

Table 43.7 *A record of stock transactions showing how a closing stock figure is calculated using the FIFO method of stock valuation*

Date	Stock received and price	Stock issued and price	Stock valuation	
			Goods in stock	Total £
01.6.93	100 @ £5		(100 @ £5 = £500)	500
04.6.93	200 @ £6		(100 @ £5 = £500) (200 @ £6 = £1,200)	1,700
25.6.93		100 @ £5	(200 @ £6 = £1,200)	1,200
02.7.93		100 @ £6	(100 @ £6 = £600)	600
12.7.93	200 @ £6.50		(100 @ £6 = £600) (200 @ £6.50 = £1,300)	1,900
23.7.93		100 @ £6	(200 @ £6.50 = £1,300)	1,300
24.7.93		100 @ £6.50	(100 @ £6.50 = £650)	650

extra 200 units at £6 (£1,200) are added, making a total of £1,700. On 25.6.93, 100 units are issued from stock for production. As it is first in first out, the goods are taken from the 1.6.93 stock, priced at £5 - the first stock to be received. This means £500 is removed from stock leaving 200 units valued at £6 (£1,200) left in stock.

By using the FIFO method, the value of stocks after all the transactions is £650.

Last in first out

The LAST IN FIRST OUT method assumes that the most recent deliveries are issued before existing stock. In this case, any unused stocks are valued at the older and probably lower purchase price. Table 43.8 shows how the previous transactions are adjusted for a LIFO stock valuation. On 1.6.93, 100 units of stock are received at £5, meaning £500 of goods are in stock. On 4.6.93 an extra 200 units of stock valued at £6 are added (£1,200) - a total of £1,700. When 100 units of stock are issued on 25.6.93 they are taken from the most recent (last) stock received, priced at £6. So £600 of stock is removed. This leaves 100

units at £5 and 100 units at £6 in stock - a total of £1,100.

This time the value of stocks remaining after the transactions is £500. If the value of stocks is rising, the LIFO method gives a lower finishing stock than the FIFO method.

Average cost

This method involves recalculating the average cost of stock every time a new delivery arrives. Each unit is assumed to have been purchased at the **average price** of all components. In practice the average cost of each unit is a weighted average and is calculated using the following formula:

$$\frac{\text{Existing stock value} + \text{value of latest purchase}}{\text{Number of units then in stock}}$$

Using the same stock transactions as before we can find the closing stock by drawing up Table 43.9 This time the weighted average cost method is used.

Table 43.8 *A record of stock transactions showing how the closing stock figure is calculated using the LIFO method of stock valuation*

Date	Stock received	Stock issued	Stock valuation	
			Goods in stock	Total
				£
01.6.93	100 @ £5		(100 @ £5 = £500)	500
04.6.93	200 @ £6		(100 @ £5 = £500) (200 @ £6 = £1,200)	1,700
25.6.93		100 @ £6	(100 @ £5 = £500) (100 @ £6 = £600)	1,100
02.7.93		100 @ £6	(100 @ £5 = £500)	500
12.7.93	200 @ £6.50		(100 @ £5 = £500) (200 @ £6.50 = £1,300)	1,800
23.7.93		100 @ £6.50	(100 @ £5 = £500) (100 @ £6.50 = £650)	1,150
24.7.93		100 @ £6.50	(100 @ £5 = £500)	500

Table 43.9 *A record of stock transactions showing how the closing stock is calculated using the weighted average cost method of stock valuation*

Date	Receipts	Issues	Weighted average cost £	Stock valuation	Total £
01.6.93	100 @ £5		5.00	(100 @ £5 = £500)	500
04.6.93	200 @ £6		5.67	(300 @ £5.67 = £1,701)	1,701
25.6.93		100	5.67	(200 @ £5.67 = £1,134)	1,134
02.7.93		100	5.67	(100 @ £5.67 = £567)	567
12.7.93	200 @ £6.50		6.22	(300 @ £6.22 = £1,866)	1,866
23.7.93		100	6.22	(200 @ £6.22 = £1,244)	1,244
24.7.93		100	6.22	(100 @ £6.22 = £622	622

When the weighted average cost method is used the value of stock following the transactions is £622. This stock figure lies closer to the FIFO method of stock valuation. It is often used when stock prices do not change a great deal. In practice it is the FIFO and average cost methods which are most commonly used by firms. Once a method has been chosen it should conform with the 'consistency' convention and not change. This is also true for calculating depreciation.

QUESTION 5 During a trading period the following stock transactions were recorded for a company:

01.7.93 50 units were bought @ £2 per unit.
03.8.93 100 units were bought @ £2.20 per unit.
19.8.93 100 units were issued.
23.9.93 200 units were bought @ £2.30 per unit.
25.9.93 150 units were issued.

(a) Assuming that the opening stock was zero, calculate the value of closing stock using the:
(i) FIFO method; (ii) LIFO method; (iii) average cost method. Present your answers in tables using a spreadsheet.
(b) If the stock listed in the transactions above was perishable, which of the three methods is most suitable for the physical issuing of stock? Explain why.
(c) Why do you think that the LIFO method is the least favoured by firms?

Inflation accounting

Inflation could cause quite serious problems when valuing assets. Inflation causes the value of assets to rise, whilst a balance sheet would show them at historical cost. During periods of very high inflation the effects can be quite serious. Profit may be overstated. This may lead to dividend payments and wage settlements which are too high, and inadequate funds to replace worn out assets. Any value which is measured in money terms will be distorted. During the 1970s, when inflation was over 20 per cent for a time, the problem was given a great deal of thought by accountants. Two possible solutions were suggested - constant purchasing power accounting and current cost accounting.

Constant purchasing power accounting (CPP) During periods of high inflation, measuring values in terms of money becomes unreliable. CONSTANT PURCHASING POWER ACCOUNTING replaces money values with an index of general purchasing power, ie the Retail Price Index (☞ unit 15). All transactions measured in money terms are translated into 'units of constant purchasing power', depending on the date when they took place. There are two main advantages of this method.
■ It reflects the general increase in the price of goods and services.
■ Since shareholders spend dividends from profit, the amount that they can buy depends on inflation and hence the Retail Price Index.
There are two main disadvantages.
■ The Retail Price Index is a measure of the general price level. Some items in the Index may be moving far more quickly or slowly than others. Thus a general index can be misleading.
■ The Retail Price Index is based on consumer goods and may not reflect business assets and expenditure.

Current cost accounting CURRENT COST ACCOUNTING involves changing all historic cost entries in the profit and loss account and the balance sheet into current values. A variety of indices are used to value stocks and fixed assets. Any adjustments made to fixed asset values are shown on the liabilities side of the balance sheet under revaluation (☞ unit 39). In the profit and loss account, adjustments are made for depreciation and cost of sales (similar to the LIFO method).

Concern about accounting for inflation has declined in the 1980s and the 1990s as inflation rates have remained relatively low. Accountants have returned to traditional conventions of 'money terms' and 'historical cost' as a result.

Key terms

Book value - the historical cost of an asset less depreciation accumulated each year.

Constant purchasing power accounting - a complete accounting system which replaces money with an index of general purchasing power.

Current cost accounting - a method of accounting which replaces all historic cost values with current valuations.

Depreciation - the falling in value of an asset.

First in first out (FIFO) - a method of stock valuation which involves issuing stock in the order in which it is delivered, so that the remaining stock is valued closer to its replacement cost.

Last in first out (LIFO) - a method of stock valuation which involves issuing more recent deliveries first, so

that closing stock is valued at the older and possibly lower purchase price.

Obsolete - an asset that is no longer any use to a company.

Provision - an allowance made in the accounts for depreciation.

Reducing balance method - a method used to calculate the annual depreciation allowance which involves writing off the same percentage rate each year.

Straight line method - a method used to calculate the annual depreciation allowance by subtracting the estimated scrap value from the cost and dividing the result by the expected life of the asset.

Writing off - the process of reducing the value of an asset by the amount of depreciation.

Question

Alexander Black Ltd

Alexander Black began trading as a paint wholesaler at the beginning of 1993. He would take in delivery from a number of manufacturers and supply local hardware stores. Trade in the first 6 months was poor so that by June he was finding that stocks were building up. At the same time, the average price he was paying for the paint went up from £2 to £2.20 per litre at the end of March. His stock movements

Table 43.10

Date	Purchases (litres)	Stock issued (litres)
01.1.93	5,000 @ £2	
04.1.93		3,000
02.2.93	5,000 @ £2	
15.2.93		4,000
01.3.93	5,000 @ £2	
24.3.93		4,000
10.4.93	4,000 @ £2.20	
27.4.93		3,500
04.5.93	4,000 @ £2.20	
06.5.93		3,000
10.6.93	2,000 @ £2.20	
24.6.93		3,000

for the first 6 months are shown in Table 43.10.

(a) Calculate the value of the closing stock at the end of each month using the FIFO method.

(b) Assuming the turnover for Jan - June 1993 was £82,000, calculate Black's gross profit for that 6 month period.

(c) How would the gross profit be different if closing stock was calculated using the LIFO method?

Alexander had bought a delivery van in January for £12,000. When he visited the accountant at the end of June, one of the decisions made was to use the straight line method of depreciation. It was felt that the van would last for five years, with a residual value of £2,000.

(d) Calculate Alexander Black's depreciation allowance over the five years using the straight line method of depreciation and hence show the net book value of the van at the end of each year.

(e) Would it be appropriate for Alexander Black to use a different method of depreciation? Explain your answer.

Summary

1. Why are assets valued at historical cost in the accounts?
2. Explain why assets fall in value.
3. Why is it necessary to provide for depreciation?
4. What are the main differences between the straight line and reducing balance methods of calculating depreciation?
5. What is meant by opening stock and closing stock?
6. Explain the difference between the LIFO and FIFO methods of stock valuation.
7. Why is stock not valued at its selling price?
8. What effects might inflation have on the valuation of assets?
9. Distinguish between current cost accounting and constant purchasing power accounting.

The importance of cash

Cash is the most liquid of all business assets. It is the notes and coins that are kept on the premises and the amount of money the firm has in the bank. Cash is part of, but not the same as, **working capital**. Working capital contains other assets, such as money owed by debtors, which are not available immediately if a firm needs to, say, pay bills.

Why is cash so important to a business? Without cash it would cease to exist. There are a number of reasons why firms fail. The most common tend to be:

■ lack of sales;
■ inadequate profit margins;
■ poor choice of location;
■ reliance on a small customer bank;
■ poor cash flow.

In 1992 around 62,000 business failures were reported by the media, the highest for many years. It has been argued that very high interest rates during the late 1980s and at the beginning of the 1990s were one of the reasons for these failures. High interest rates force up business costs and squeeze profit margins. Many of these businesses offered good products for which there was demand. They have the potential to be profitable and yet still went into RECEIVERSHIP (☞ unit 67). Probably the most likely cause of this is that they ran out of cash. The role of cash in a business is shown in Figure 44.1 which shows a simple CASH FLOW CYCLE. This is the continuous movement of cash in and out of a business. Initially, cash is used to buy or hire resources. These resources are converted into goods or services which are then sold to customers in exchange for cash. Some of the money from sales will be used to finance further production. In a successful firm, this flow of cash is endless. If this flow of cash ceases at some stage then the business will be unlikely to continue. The problem often stems from a lack of understanding and control of the working capital cycle.

Working capital

Unit 40 defined working capital or circulating capital as the amount of money needed to pay for the day to day trading of a business. Cash and other liquid assets are needed to pay wages and energy costs, and to buy components to make products. They also allow firms to give trade credit, enabling customers to pay for products at a later date. Working capital is the amount left when all current debts have been paid. It can be calculated by subtracting current liabilities from current assets:

Working capital = current assets - current liabilities

Provided that current assets are twice the size of current liabilities, working capital is usually large enough for most businesses to avoid problems. If the value of current assets is less than one and a half the size of current liabilities, the firm may well be short of working capital and have problems meeting its immediate debts.

> **QUESTION 1** Given the financial information contained in Table 44.1, calculate the value of the firm's working capital and state whether you consider it to be sufficient.
>
> **Table 44.1** *A summary of financial information relating to current assets and current liabilities*
>
> | | £000 |
> | --- | --- |
> | Bank overdraft | 21 |
> | Stocks of finished goods | 11 |
> | Cash in hand | 2 |
> | Trade creditors | 15 |
> | Trade debtors | 19 |
> | Work in progress | 5 |
> | Bank loan (less than 1 year) | 5 |

Managing working capital

Managing working capital in a business is crucial. In many types of business, manufacturing in particular, delays or **time lags** exist between buying the materials, components or goods to sell and the receipt of cash from the sale of finished goods. Only a small number of businesses receive cash immediately after a sale. The

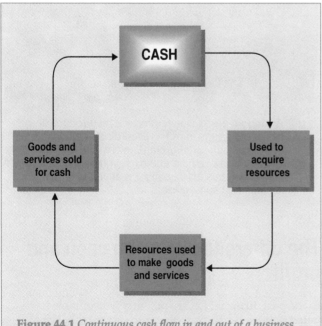

Figure 44.1 *Continuous cash flow in and out of a business organisation.*

length of these time lags will vary. How cash flows into and out of business is often called the WORKING CAPITAL CYCLE and is shown in Figure 44.2. This is a more complete picture of Figure 44.1. The cycle particularly illustrates the intervals between the payment and the receipt of cash.

- Part A. Initially, a firm will buy materials and components from suppliers on credit. Does this mean a business could start without any cash? This is unlikely. Creditors will require some proof of ability to pay or, indeed, may even demand some cash. These resources are then combined with the fixed assets and production begins. As a result of production, work-in-progress is created and costs are incurred, eg wages and power. Production is over when finished goods have been made ready to sell.

- Part B. There is often a lag between the time finished goods are completed in the factory and the time they are sent to customers. Storing finished goods can be expensive, both in terms of warehousing costs and also the opportunity cost of holding stocks. When finished goods are distributed other costs, such as transport costs, must be paid. Even when customers receive orders, a further time lag exists as the firm awaits payment. When debts are settled the cash is then used to carry on business activity.

- Part C. Figure 44.2 also shows that a business may have injections of extra cash from time to time. Loans, profit and the sale of assets can all increase the firm's cash. At the same time, though, there may be drains on a firm's cash resources. Dividends, taxation, new fixed assets, loan repayments and business losses are all examples.

Each stage of this working capital cycle needs careful management. Cash flow will be improved if a firm can reduce the intervals described above.

In order to do this a firm may:

- offer cash discounts to encourage customers to pay more quickly;
- eliminate the need to store finished goods;
- speed up the production process.

A business manager will aim to have enough cash to meet up and coming debts, but also employ all resources as productively as possible.

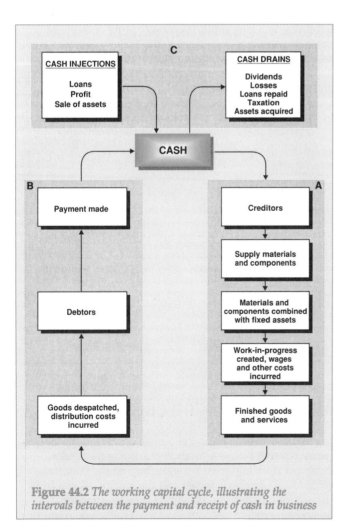

Figure 44.2 *The working capital cycle, illustrating the intervals between the payment and receipt of cash in business*

QUESTION 2

(a) Arrange the activities to produce the products in the photographs in order, according to the length of their working capital cycle. Explain your answer.

(b) Choose one example and explain how a business involved in this activity might reduce the length of its working capital cycle.

The difference between cash and profit

In the past, firms which are potentially profitable have failed in business because they run out of cash. For example, if a company sells some goods for £60,000 more than they cost to manufacture, this represents a profit.

QUESTION 3 Jeremy Munday, a building contractor, purchased land in a desirable residential area, drew up plans for an attractive detached house and found a buyer who agreed a price of £150,000. A £10,000 down payment was made and contracts were signed for a completion date in twelve months.

Jeremy estimated that construction would take ten months but extra time was allowed for unforeseen circumstances. He also costed the project. Details are shown in Table 44.2.

Table 44.2 *Costs of building the detached house*

Land	£15,000
Materials	£35,000
Labour	£25,000
Interest	£10,000
Legal fees	£ 2,000
Contingency	£ 3,000
Total	£90,000

A profit of £60,000 would be made. His bank manager agreed to lend £60,000 provided he contributed £30,000 from his own savings. His cash position on day one was sound. He had £100,000 less the cost of the land and legal fees. Materials could be purchased on 30 days credit. After six weeks the project was a week ahead of schedule. Jeremy decided that this would be an opportunity to take a family holiday (cost £5,000).

Whilst he was away, two employees discussed their financial rewards, and felt they could be improved. They put forward a sound case and Jeremy agreed to pay another 20 per cent. Jeremy had tried to persuade the men to accept a completion bonus of £4,000 each, but they insisted on a weekly pay rise. The productivity of the two workers improved. However, Jeremy was concerned. Interest rates had risen, forcing the interest charge up to £13,000. Also, material costs had risen to £50,000.

Profit would now be reduced to £32,000 (including the £5,000 spent on the holiday). This was adequate, but there was not enough cash to buy materials and pay the wages. Jeremy decided a further loan would be necessary. He approached the bank, but they refused a further advance. They argued that he was dangerously overdrawn, the extra interest charges would reduce profitability, interest rates were likely to rise again and a £2,500 tax bill had been overlooked. Jeremy contacted the buyer, explained that the house would be completed in one months time and asked for a further £15,000 to fund the final stages of construction. The buyer was sympathetic but could not raise the money. Jeremy ceased trading. His business venture guaranteed a profit of around £25,000, but since he could not raise the cash to pay for materials and wages, his business failed.

(a) Show Jeremy's cash position at the time he asked for the second loan.
(b) Why do you think Jeremy tried to persuade his employees to accept a completion bonus of £4,000, an amount which was higher than the 20 per cent he actually paid?
(c) What does the example show about the relationship between cash and profit?

However, if the customer fails to pay for these goods then the business may run short of cash. There are times when cash shortages are so severe that the business cannot continue to pay immediate bills like wages and fuel. In these circumstances the firm cannot trade and will be forced into receivership.

Sources of cash flow problems

When a business runs short of cash it is not normally due to one single reason. Liquidity crises often result from a number of errors in the control of working capital.

Overtrading Young and rapidly growing businesses are particularly prone to OVERTRADING. Overtrading occurs when a business is attempting to fund a large volume of production with inadequate working capital. Established companies trying to expand can also face this problem. This was arguably one of the factors leading to the demise of Sock Shop in 1990, after expansion plans in the USA failed, and the problems of Next, the clothes retailer in the 1980s.

Investing too much in fixed assets In the initial stages of a business, funds are limited. Spending large amounts quickly on equipment vehicles and other capital items drains resources. It may be better to lease some of these fixed assets, leaving sufficient cash funds.

Stockpiling Holding stocks of raw materials and finished goods is expensive. Money tied up in stocks is unproductive. Stocks may become obsolete. In addition, stocks of raw materials in particular cannot be easily changed into cash without making a loss. Stock control is an important feature of cash management. Firms should not buy in bulk if discounts are not enough to compensate for the extra cost of holding stocks.

Allowing too much credit A great deal of business is done on credit. One of the dangers is that firms allow their customers too long for payment. This means that the firm is waiting for money and may actually be forced to borrow during this period. Failure to control debtors may also lead to bad debts. Taking early action is the key to the effective control of debtors. At the same time businesses must maintain good relations. Small firms are particularly vulnerable if they are owed money by much larger companies. Powerful businesses are often accused of endangering smaller companies by delaying payments to them.

Taking too much credit Taking more credit might appear to help a firm's cash position since payments are delayed. However there are some drawbacks. Taking too much credit might result in higher prices, lost discounts, difficulties in obtaining future supplies and a bad name in the trade. At worst, credit might be withdrawn.

Overborrowing Businesses may borrow to finance growth. As more loans are taken out interest costs rise. Overborrowing not only threatens a firm's cash position, but also the overall control of the business. It is important to fund growth in a balanced way, by raising some capital from share issues. A well publicised example was the overborrowing by Robert Maxwell from the employees' pension fund of Maxwell Communications.

Underestimating inflation Businesses often fail to take inflation into account. Inflation raises costs, which can cause cash shortages. This is often the case if higher costs, such as wages or raw materials, cannot be passed on in higher prices. Inflationary periods are often accompanied by higher interest rates which place further pressure on liquid resources. Inflation is also a problem because it is difficult to predict future rates. Although it can be built into plans, firms often underestimate it.

Unforeseen expenditure Businesses are subject to unpredictable external forces. They must make a financial provision for any unforeseen expenditure. Equipment breakdowns, tax demands, strikes and bad debts are common examples of this type of emergency expense.

Unexpected changes in demand Although most businesses try to sustain demand for their products, there may be times when it falls unexpectedly. Unpredicted changes in fashion could lead to a fall in demand. This could lead to a lack of sales and cash flowing into a company. Travel companies in the UK arguably faced this problem in 1991 and 1992. Companies have to 'buy' holidays before they are sold. External factors, including the recession, led to many of these holidays remaining unsold as consumers changed their holiday buying patterns. Firms also lost revenue as holidays were discounted in an attempt to sell them.

Seasonal factors Sometimes trade fluctuates for seasonal reasons. In the agriculture industry, cereal farmers have a large cash inflow when their harvest is sold. For much of the year, though, they have to pay expenses without any cash flowing in. This situation requires careful management indeed, although it is possible to predict these changes.

Resolving a liquidity crisis

Liquidity problems can be prevented by keeping a tight control on working capital. Inevitably though, there will be occasions when firms run short of liquid resources. When this does happen the firm's main aim will be survival rather than profit. The following measures might be used to obtain liquid resources.
- Stimulate sales for cash, offering large discounts if necessary.
- Sell off stocks of raw materials - below cost if necessary.
- Sell off any fixed assets which may not be vital for operations.
- Sell off fixed assets and lease them back.
- Mount a rigorous drive on overdue accounts.
- Sell debts to a factoring company.
- Only make essential purchases.

- Extend credit with selected suppliers.
- Reduce personal drawings from the business.
- Negotiate additional short term loans.

In all cases, action must be taken quickly. If the firm survives the liquidity crisis, it is important to identify the causes and make sure it does not happen again.

QUESTION 4 Since its takeover of Leyland vehicles in 1987, Leyland Daf had been the largest truck maker in the UK. It had 25 per cent of the UK truck market and 8 per cent of the Western European market. In the late 1980s and early 1990s sales declined by over 50 per cent - from 69,234 in 1989 to 31,398 in 1992. In February 1993 the company was taken into receivership with cumulative losses of £300 million over the period. It was argued that Leyland Daf had faced a number of major problems.
- Opposition by banks to granting it emergency short term funding.
- Too much dependence on the UK market, where profit margins were slimmest and which had been hardest hit by the recession.
- Production of too wide a product range. This along with limited sales meant a slow stock turnover.
- As a result of a wide product range, too much investment was needed given its limited resources.
- A high interest burden - 120 million Dutch guilders a year.

Source: adapted from the *Financial Times*, 3.2.1993 and 5.2.1993.

(a) From the information above, give reasons for the likely cash flow problems Leyland Daf may have faced.
(b) Why might:
   (i) negotiating extra funds;
   (ii) selling off stocks of raw materials;
   not have been options for solving the crisis?

Credit control

Most businesses have some sort of CREDIT CONTROL system, so that money owing can be collected quickly and easily. A 'tight' or 'easy' credit policy may be adopted. Tight credit terms may be used to improve liquidity, reduce the risk of bad debts, exploit a sellers market, or maintain slender profit margins. Easy credit terms may be designed to clear old stocks, enter a new market or perhaps help a regular customer with financial difficulties.

The company accountant and the sales manager often work closely with the credit controller, since credit policy will affect the financial position of the firm and sales. Between them they set targets for the credit control department such as the value of bad debts or the length of time it takes to collect debts.

Firms have procedures to help credit control. Figure 44.3 shows an example. Many firms will not do business with a new customer until their creditworthiness has been checked. This can be done by asking for references from a supplier, a banker's reference, or a credit rating agency's report. From this information the credit controller can set

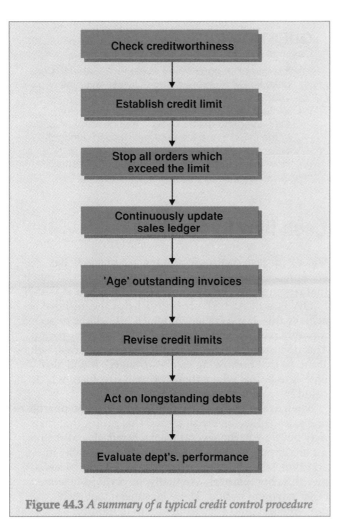

Figure 44.3 *A summary of a typical credit control procedure*

a credit limit based on the risk involved.

When an order exceeds the credit limit, the credit controller should investigate. The result may be a stop being placed on the order, a request to the customer to pay any outstanding debt, or simply allowing the order to go ahead.

Credit control records, which show customer orders and payments, must be upto date. Every month outstanding invoices must be 'aged', to identify customers who owe money over 30, 60 and 90 days.

If there are persistent debts, the credit controller must take action. A statement of the account should be sent, followed by a second one with a letter. Next a telephone call to the debtor followed by a personal visit. Finally, as a last resort, it may be necessary to take legal action to recover the debt. Some firms use an independent debt factor to assist in credit control. There has been quite a growth in this type of business in recent years.

QUESTION 5

(a) Given the information in Question 3, what measures could Jeremy Munday have taken to avoid his cash crisis?

(b) What might be the disadvantages of the measures you have suggested?

Funds and cash flow statements

The management of funds is easier if there is documented data on liquidity. The balance sheet shows the assets and liabilities of a firm at a particular point in time. The profit and loss account partly explains the changes in assets and liabilities, showing how the year's profit is distributed. Since 1975 companies were required to publish a **funds flow statement** (also known as the Source and Application of funds statement). This statement showed where a business obtained its funds from during the trading year and how they were used. For example, it could have shown that a firm's sources of funds were profits, depreciation, the sale of assets and some new loans. During the year these funds may have been used to acquire new assets, pay dividends, pay taxation or repay some loans. The statement also showed changes in the level of working capital over the year.

In 1991, the Accounting Standards Board (ASB) published its first Financial Reporting Standard, FRS 1 'Cash Flow Statements'. The new standard required companies to publish a CASH FLOW STATEMENT instead of a funds flow statement in the annual audited accounts. It was argued that a funds flow statement contained a reorganisation of existing figures in the profit and loss account and changes in the financial position between the opening and closing balance sheet dates. A funds flow statement offered little in the way of new information. In contrast, cash flow statements may include receipts and payments not disclosed elsewhere in the published financial statements. Another advantage of a cash flow statements is the standardisation of the document. The format of funds flow statements were decided by managers. This made comparisons between different companies difficult since different managers could choose different formats.

FRS 1 requires cash flows to be disclosed under standard headings, These are:
- operating activities;
- returns on investments and servicing of finance;
- taxation;
- investing activities;
- financing;

and in that order. Table 44.3 shows a cash flow statement for Castings PLC. In 1993 the net cash inflow from operating activities was £5,104,000, a breakdown of which is in note (a). Added to this was £681,000 interest received and subtracted was the £858,000 paid in dividends to shareholders. During the year taxation paid to the Inland Revenue was £1,738,000 and new tangible assets worth £943,000 were purchased. After taking into account two other smaller inflows of cash, investments (£10,000) and the disposal of assets (£14,000), the net cash inflow before financing was £2,270,000. Most of this (£2,304,000) was used to increase the company's cash (or cash equivalent) balance, a breakdown of which is shown in note (b).

Most agree that the replacement of funds flow statements with cash flow statements is an improvement in financial reporting. However, there are some criticisms.
- In practice, little new information is shown in the statements. The new law encourages disclosure but

Table 44.3 *Cash flow statement for Castings PLC 1993*

CASH FLOW STATEMENT
FOR THE YEAR ENDED 31ST MARCH 1993

	Notes	1993		1992	
		£000	£000	£000	£000
Net cash inflow from operating activities	(a)		5,104		4,731
Returns on investments and servicing of finance:					
Interest received		681		575	
Dividends paid		(858)		(796)	
Net cash outflow from returns on investments and servicing of finance			(177)		(221)
Taxation - corporation tax paid			(1,738)		(1,386)
Investing activities:					
Purchase of tangible fixed assets		(943)		(852)	
Investments made		10		24	
Disposal of tangible fixed assets		14		112	
Net cash outflow from investing activities			(919)		(716)
Net cash inflow before financing			2,270		2,408
Financing:					
Issue of ordinary share capital			(34)		(200)
Increase in cash and cash equivalents	(b)		2,304		2,608
Net financing			2,270		2,408

Notes to the consolidated cash flow statement
(a) Reconciliation of operating profit to net cash flow from operating activities

	1993	1992
	£000	£000
Operating profit	3,688	3,885
Depreciation and adjustments on disposals	1,017	960
Decrease/(increase) in stocks	167	(190)
Decrease/(increase) in debtors	195	(2,549)
Increase in creditors	37	2,625
Net cash inflow from operating activities	5,104	4,731

(b) Analysis of the balances of cash and cash equivalents as shown in the balance sheet

	1993	1992	Change in year
	£000	£000	£000
Short-term deposits	8,564	6,497	2,067
Cash at bank and in hand	50	86	(36)
Bank overdraft	(146)	(419)	273
	8,468	6,164	2,304

does not enforce it.

- Small limited companies are not bound to publish a cash flow statement because they are owner managed. However, medium sized firms are. This seems to lack a little logic since most medium sized firms are also owner managed.
- Cash flow statements, like funds flow statements, are based on historic information. It is argued that cash flow statements based on future predictions are more useful. Cash flow forecasting is dealt with in the next section.

QUESTION 6 Look at the cash flow statement for Castings PLC in Table 44.3.
(a) Explain what contributed to the increase in the net cash inflow from operating activities over the two years.
(b) Write a brief report for the managing director explaining the main changes that have taken place in the inflows and the outflows of cash during the year.
(c) How might this document be useful to Castings?

Cash flow forecasting

Successful cash control would mean a business has enough cash to meet immediate needs, but not so much that resources are held in unproductive assets. A CASH FLOW FORECAST STATEMENT helps the business to achieve this. It is a statement which lists all the expected monthly receipts and payments for a particular period. This document will help identify times when cash will be short, so that borrowing can be arranged. It will also highlight points where there are cash surpluses which could be used for investment.

When drawing up a cash flow forecast, some purchases and sales will be on credit terms. This means that cash may not flow in for several weeks. Similarly, payments for credit purchases will not be made for a while. In addition, some business expenses do not take place monthly, but quarterly, annually, or perhaps in some other payment period. These **lags** mean that cash movements could vary from month to month.

Most of the entries will be estimates. For example, it is not possible to predict precisely what the level of sales revenue will be in six months time. In addition, many costs are unpredictable. Businesses keep a record of the monthly cash flows so that a comparison can be made with predictions. Managers will be able to improve the accuracy of their estimates with experience.

Table 44.4 *A cash flow forecast statement for Dillip Sanjay Ltd*

£000s

	MAR	APR	MAY	JUN	JUL	AUG
Opening balance	344	355	49	84	- 1	17
Add Receipts from cash sales	611	634	680	650	690	684
Total cash	955	989	729	734	689	701
Less expenses						
wages	20	20	20	22	22	22
purchases	450	470	480	480	500	520
overheads	130	450	145	233	150	368
Total outflow	600	940	645	735	672	910
Closing balance	355	49	84	- 1	17	- 209

Table 44.4 illustrates a cash flow forecast statement for Dillip Sanjay Ltd, a large high street supermarket. The statement is drawn up for a six month period in 1993 and shows the estimated opening and closing cash balance, ie the money at the start and end of each month. The statement shows that the cash position of the firm will get worse over the time period. The business will need to borrow money at the end of June, and more significantly, at the end of August.

In Dillip Sanjay's business all payments are made in cash. In other types of business goods and services are sold and payment is not received until a later date. The receipts from these **credit sales** will appear in a cash flow statement in later months. Take an example of a small grocery wholesaler who sells £4,000 of goods to retailers on 30 days credit terms in April. Payment would not be received until May. If the wholesaler had an opening balance of £20,000 and cash sales of £8,000, the cash flow forecast in May would be as in Table 44.5.

Table 44.5 *Cash flow forecast statement for a wholesaler in May*

	£
	May
Opening balance	20,000
Receipts from cash sales	8,000
Receipts from credit sales	4,000
Total cash	32,000
Less Total expenses	10,000
Closing balance	22,000

Key terms

Cash flow cycle - the continuous movement of cash in and out of a business.

Cash flow forecast statement - a prediction of all expected receipts and expenses of a business over a future time period which shows the expected cash balance at the end of each month.

Cash flow statement - a financial statement which shows sources and uses of cash in a trading period.

Credit control - the process of monitoring and collecting the money owed to a business.

Overtrading - a situation where a firm attempts to raise production without increasing the size of its working capital.

Receivership - the liquidation (selling) of a firm's assets by an independent body following its collapse.

Working capital cycle - the flow in and out of a business of liquid resources.

Summary

1. Explain the operation of the cash flow cycle.
2. How is the value of working capital calculated?
3. Why do time lags exist in the working capital cycle?
4. How is it possible for a profitable business to collapse?
5. Describe the factors which may result in cash flow problems.
6. List the measures which can be employed to help prevent a liquidity crisis.
7. What is the objective of the credit control department?
8. Explain, briefly, how a business might manage its credit control.
9. Why are many of the entries in a cash flow forecast statement estimated?

Question

Leroy Simmons - meat wholesaler

Leroy Simmons runs a meat wholesale unit in Reading. He employs two butchers and pays them £1,000 per month each. He also employs a van driver and an office clerk who both earn £700 per month. Leroy buys carcass meat and cuts and prepares it for retail outlets in the area. Most of his sales are made on 30 day credit terms, although some small customers pay immediately in cash. All of his purchases are made with cash to take advantage of discounts offered in the trade by local dealers. Table 44.6 shows a summary of anticipated sales and purchases for the next six months.

In December Leroy doubles the wages of his staff for a Christmas bonus. Electricity bills are settled in September and December and are estimated at £900 and £2,500 respectively. Estimated telephone charges of £200 and £250 will be paid in August and November. Annual insurance and rent are due to be paid in November. He expects these to total £12,000.

Each month Leroy withdraws £1,500 from the business for his own personal use. He also provides a £500 allowance for motor expenses and spending on other miscellaneous items.

(a) Leroy's cash balance at the end of June is £1,700 and the value of credit sales from June is £8,000. Produce a cash flow forecast statement for the six month period showing clearly the expected cash balance at the end of each month. Assume that all outstanding customer debts are settled at the end of the 30 day credit period.

(b) What advice would you give to Leroy in preparation for the financial situation in November and December?

(c) Why might the cash position improve in January?

(d) Leroy's cash balance is held in a current account. How might this affect the performance of the business?

Table 44.6 *A summary of Leroy Simmons' expected sales and purchases for a six month trading period*

						(£)
	Jul	Aug	Sep	Oct	Nov	Dec
Cash sales	2,000	2,000	2,000	2,000	4,000	10,000
Credit sales	8,000	9,000	9,000	10,000	16,000	30,000
Purchases	3,000	3,500	3,500	4,000	8,000	16,000

The investigation process

Unit 38 showed people who may be interested in a company's accounts. Different users are interested for different reasons. For example, shareholders may want information to assess the rewards for holding shares. Managers may try to gauge performance. This unit explains how the information in the final accounts can be interpreted. It is possible to base investigation on some of these figures alone. Also, information can be obtained by combining some of these figures and carrying out a RATIO ANALYSIS. The chairperson's report, the directors' report and the notes to the accounts provide extra material as well.

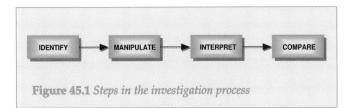

Figure 45.1 *Steps in the investigation process*

The investigation process is shown in Figure 45.1. The first step is to **identify** the figures that are relevant from the final accounts. Suitable data must be used. For example, an accountant might need information on current assets and current liabilities, rather than total assets and liabilities, in order to assess the solvency (☞ unit 40) of the business.

Once the correct figures have been chosen they can be **manipulated** into a useful form, such as percentages.

To **interpret** ratios an understanding of their significance is needed. Ratios can be used to find out the firm's financial position, assess performance, analyse capital structure and help shareholders when deciding whether to invest.

Finally, ratios may be used to make a variety of **comparisons**. For example, it is common to compare this year's figures with those of last year.

What are ratios?

Financial ratios can be calculated by comparing two figures in the accounts which are related in some way. It may be one number expressed as a percentage of another or simply one number divided by another. For an accounting ratio to be useful the two figures must be connected, eg profit is arguably related to the amount of capital a firm uses.

Ratios on their own are not particularly useful. They need to be compared with other ratios. For example, knowing that a firm has a net profit to sales ratio of 11 per cent may not be helpful. However, if it was 9 per cent the year before, this can be compared with the present figure.

There are a number of ways in which ratios can be compared.

Over time The same ratio can be compared in two time periods, eg the current financial year and the previous one. Comparisons over time also show trends. This allows a business to decide whether or not certain aspects are improving.

Interfirm comparisons It is possible for a business to compare its results with others in the same industry. This could highlight particular strengths or weaknesses. For example, a handbag manufacturer with a turnover of

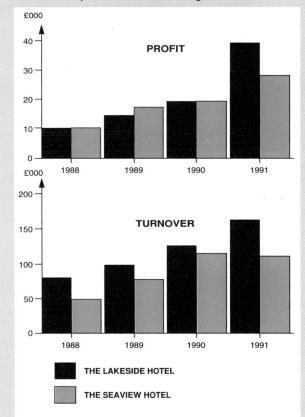

QUESTION 1 The Lakeside and The Seaview are two hotels of a very similar size situated in Scarborough. Some information regarding their turnover and profit is illustrated in Figure 45.2.

Figure 45.2 *Turnover and profit of The Lakeside and The Seaview hotels over four years*

(a) Study the data in Figure 45.2 and make an interfirm comparison over time. Write a brief report showing your findings. (The use of mathematical ratios is not required.)

(b) Explain why it is important to compare 'like with like' when making statistical comparisons.

£120,000 might think its £30,000 profit satisfactory. Another manufacturer may have a profit of £50,000 on a turnover of £130,000. Assuming that the two firms are very similar, the relative profit of the first business is not as good. It is important that firms compare 'like with like'.

Interfirm comparisons over time Using the two standards above we can make interfirm comparisons over time. This shows trends that may exist. Such comparisons are quite popular and could help analyse the behaviour of a whole industry, over a lengthy time period.

Results and forecasts Management, for example, may want to compare actual results with predicted results. Management prepare budgets and make forecasts about

the future. Decision makers will also try to account for differences which exist between the actual results and their estimates. This is called **variance analysis** (☞ unit 46).

Ratio analysis

Table 45.1 and 45.2 show the profit and loss account and balance sheet for Crowmarsh PLC and some additional information from the notes to the accounts. The company produces a wide range of clothes and sportswear and sells to a worldwide market. These figures can be used to calculate ratios and show what they mean for a business.

Table 45.1 *Crowmarsh PLC profit and loss account and additional information extracted from the notes to the accounts*

CROWMARSH PLC PROFIT AND LOSS ACCOUNT
Year ended 31st July 1993

	1993 £000	1992 £000
Turnover	69,618	63,718
Cost of sales	45,272	39,945
Gross profit	24,346	23,773
Operating expenses	19,476	18,160
	4,870	5,613
Income from investments		35
Interest receivable	351	218
Net profit before tax and interest	5,221	5,866
Interest payable	1,058	568
Profit on ordinary activities before taxation	4,163	5,298
Tax on profit on ordinary activities	1,494	1,987
Profit on ordinary activities after taxation	2,669	3,311
Extraordinary items	1,224	-
Profit for the financial year	1,445	3,311
Dividends	761	712
Retained profit	684	2,599
Earnings per share	41.42p	51.41p

ADDITIONAL INFORMATION

		1993	1992
(i)	Loan capital	£2.454m	£2.589m
(ii)	Preference share capital	£0.250m	£0.250m
(iii)	Preference shareholders' dividend	£0.009m	£0.009m
(iv)	Number of ordinary shares	6.423m	6.423m
(v)	Share price 31st July	1950p	1845p

Table 45.2 Balance sheet of Crowmarsh PLC

CROWMARSH PLC BALANCE SHEET
31st July 1993

	1993 £000	1993 £000	1992 £000	1992 £000
Fixed assets				
Tangible assets		10,092		9,811
Investments		59		44
		10,151		9,855
Current assets				
Stocks	18,162		16,981	
Debtors	11,488		10,674	
Cash at bank and in hand	7,219		3,516	
	36,869		31,171	
Creditors (current liabilities)				
Amounts falling due within one year	20,203		14,148	
Net current assets		16,666		17,023
Total assets less current liabilities		26,817		26,878
Creditors				
Amounts falling due after more than one year	2,514		2,834	
Provisions for liabilities and charges	997		1,010	
Minority interests	-		75	
Deferred income	279		485	
		3,790		4,404
		23,027		22,474
Capital and reserves				
Called up share capital		1,856		1,856
Share premium account		169		169
Revaluation reserve		893		893
Other reserves		147		278
Profit and loss account		19,962		19,278
		23,027		22,474

Types of ratios

Ratios fall into one of four categories.

Performance ratios These help to show how well the business is doing. Performance ratios focus on profit, capital employed and turnover. When measuring efficiency the firm must take into account its objectives. A performance ratio using profit would be unsuitable if the firm's main objective is not profit related.

Activity ratios can also be used. They are still related to performance, but concentrate on how well a business uses its resources.

Liquidity ratios These investigate the solvency of a business. They involve short term assets and liabilities and assess whether firms are able to pay their debts. Short-term lenders, eg banks and trade creditors are often interested in a firm's liquidity ratios.

Gearing ratios Such ratios are more concerned with the long term financial position. Gearing ratios identify the amount of capital which comes from shareholders compared with the amount raised from outside. Companies are highly geared if the proportion of loan capital (from outside) is high in relation to its share capital (from shareholders).

Creditors and shareholders have conflicting interests. Creditors prefer shareholders to have a large stake in a company for security reasons. Shareholders prefer to control the business through a small share capital, raising extra capital from outside. Thus if a company can earn 25 per cent on its capital and interest rates are 10 per cent, it pays the shareholders to borrow at 10 per cent and enjoy 15 per cent profit. Highly geared companies are said to be 'riskier' than those which are low geared.

Shareholders' ratios Shareholders' ratios are of obvious interest to the owners of the business (also known as investment ratios or stock market ratios). They help investors and their advisers when deciding where to invest savings. Shareholders ratios combine dividends, profits, share prices and the number of shares issued.

QUESTION 2

(a) If growth was a company's main objective, how might its performance be measured?

(b) How might it be possible to measure the efficiency of a school?

(c) Which of the above ratios would be of particular interest to:
   (i) the Inland Revenue;
   (ii) a debenture holder;
   (iii) a pension fund manager?

Performance ratios

Assuming that a firm's main aim is to make profit, performance ratios will focus on the trading year's profit. The profit figure alone is not a performance indicator. In 1993 Crowmarsh PLC made a pre-tax profit of £4.163 million and in 1992 it made a profit of £5.298 million. Does this mean that in 1993 Crowmarsh performed less effectively? To answer this question it is necessary to find out how the profit was generated.

Return on capital employed (ROCE) This ratio expresses the profit of the business as a percentage of the capital invested in it. Taxes are ignored because they are set by outside factors, eg the government. Interest paid is also ignored because we want to measure the total return, ie profit plus interest payments, resulting from the use of all sources of finance. This is an important ratio because it relates profit to the size of the business.

$$\text{RETURN ON CAPITAL EMPLOYED} = \frac{\text{Net profit before tax and interest}}{\text{Total capital employed (Total assets)}} \times 100$$

For Crowmarsh PLC the net profit before tax and interest in 1993 was £5.221 million. The total capital employed can be found by adding fixed assets and current assets together. For Crowmarsh PLC this would be £10.151 million + £36.869 million = £47.02 million. Using the formula above:

$$\text{ROCE} = \frac{£5.221m}{£47.02m} \times 100$$

$$= 11.1\%$$

The return on capital employed will vary according to the industry in which a business competes. The higher it is the better. Crowmarsh's figure should ideally be higher than the return from interest earning accounts.

Return on net assets This ratio is very similar to ROCE, but measures the return on long term business funds. Short term liabilities, such as creditors, are excluded. However, if a business often uses short term sources such as trade creditors and a bank overdraft, they should be dealt with as long term and included.

$$\text{RETURN ON NET ASSETS} = \frac{\text{Net profit before tax and interest}}{\text{Net capital employed (net assets)}} \times 100$$

For Crowmarsh the net profit before tax and interest in 1993 was £5.221 million. The net capital employed or the net assets figure in the balance sheet was £23.027 million.

$$\text{Return on net assets} = \frac{£5.221m}{£23.027m} \times 100$$

$$= 22.7\%$$

The return on net assets will be higher than the return on total capital employed since the denominator is lower in the former ratio. Whether the figure for Crowmarsh is high enough can only be found by comparing it with similar firms and over time.

Gross profit margin This shows the gross profit made on sales.

$$\text{GROSS PROFIT MARGIN} = \frac{\text{Gross profit}}{\text{Turnover (sales)}} \times 100$$

For Crowmarsh in 1993 gross profit was £24.346m and turnover was £69.618m. So:

$$\text{Gross profit margin} = \frac{£24.346m}{£69.618m} \times 100$$

$$= 35\%$$

Obviously higher profit margins are better than lower ones. As a rule, the quicker the turnover, the lower the gross profit margin. For example, a car retailer with a low rate of turnover would enjoy a higher margin than a clothes retailer with a higher rate of turnover. Car distributors have high stock values with slow turnover. Higher profit margins help compensate for this. For a clothing manufacturer a return of 35 per cent is perhaps low. Interfirm comparisons would help to confirm whether this was the case.

Net profit margin This ratio is the net profit expressed as a percentage of turnover. It is an indicator of management's ability to control indirect costs, such as overheads, as net profit equals gross profit minus overheads. For example, if gross profit remains the same percentage and the net profit falls then this must mean that overheads have risen.

$$\text{NET PROFIT MARGIN} = \frac{\text{Net profit}}{\text{Turnover}} \times 100$$

Crowmarsh's turnover for 1993 was £69.618 million and net profit before tax was £4.163 million (note that the net profit figure is inclusive of interest payments). So:

$$\text{Net profit margin} = \frac{£4.163\text{m}}{£69.618\text{m}} \times 100$$

$$= 6\%$$

Again higher margins are better than lower ones. Whether 6 per cent is good or not would depend on the figure in previous years. If it was low, this suggests that the indirect costs are higher than the business might want. The net profit margin is only suitable for comparisons over time. Interfirm comparisons could be misleading because different businesses have different patterns of spending, which affect this ratio.

Activity ratios

Activity ratios or asset usage ratios allow a business to measure how effectively it uses its resources. Several activity ratios exist, although only two tend to be used by firms.

Stock turnover This ratio measures the number of times in a trading year that a business sells the value of its stocks.

$$\text{STOCK TURNOVER} = \frac{\text{Cost of sales}}{\text{Stocks}}$$

The cost of sales for Crowmarsh PLC in 1993 was £45.272 million. Crowmarsh's closing stock figure on the balance sheet was £18.162 million. So:

$$\text{Stock turnover} = \frac{£45.272\text{m}}{£18.162\text{m}}$$

$$= 2.5 \text{ times}$$

It is also possible to show stock turnover in terms of the number of days money is tied up in stocks. This is found by:

$$\text{Stock turnover} = \frac{\text{Stocks}}{\text{Cost of sales}} \times 365$$

$$= \frac{£18.162\text{m}}{£45.272\text{m}} \times 365$$

$$= 146 \text{ days}$$

Crowmarsh's stock turnover for 1993 may give cause for concern. A turnover of 2.5 a year means that, on average, money is tied up in stock for 146 days. Again though, the nature of the business has to be taken into consideration.

A high stock turnover is better. The higher the stock turnover rate, the quicker the profit is earned on the stock sold, and thus a business with a high stock turnover can operate with a lower profit margin.

A declining stock turnover might indicate higher stock levels, a large amount of slow-moving or obsolete stock, a wider range of products being stocked or a lack of control over purchasing.

Debt collection period Businesses can calculate the number of days it takes to collect debts on average. The following equation can be used:

$$\text{DEBT COLLECTION PERIOD} = \frac{\text{Debtors}}{\text{Sales revenue}} \times 365$$

$$= \frac{£11.488\text{m}}{£69.618\text{m}} \times 365$$

$$= 60 \text{ days}$$

Businesses in different industries have different periods over which outstanding debts are paid. Some businesses have payment terms over 30, 60 and 90 days. Small firms may struggle to survive if many of their outstanding debts are not paid within 30 days. Crowmarsh's figure may be satisfactory for a firm of its size.

Businesses draw up lists of the 'ages' of all the firm's debts. These 'age debtors' will be the names of customers who have owed money to the business for the longest period of time. They can then concentrate on the collection of the longest outstanding debts.

QUESTION 3
(a) Using the information contained in Table 45.1 and Table 45.2 calculate all the performance and activity ratios for Crowmarsh PLC for 1992.
(b) Write a brief report for the managing director drawing attention to any changes that have occurred between 1992 and 1993.

Liquidity ratios

Unit 44 showed that making a profit was not the only criterion for survival. A firm must also have liquid assets - assets that can be turned easily into cash - to meet day to day payments. Liquidity ratios are concerned with the firm's ability to convert its assets into cash. Two of the ratios already considered, the stock turnover and the debtors turnover, throw some light on to the firm's liquidity. If these ratios are low then it means that money is tied up in stocks and debtors. Thus money is not available to make payments. Two other ratios which show liquidity can be used.

Current ratio The current ratio shows the relationship between the current assets and the current liabilities.

$$\text{CURRENT RATIO} = \frac{\text{Current assets}}{\text{Current liabilities}}$$

For Crowmarsh PLC in 1993 these were £36.869 million and £20.203 million respectively. The current ratio was:

$$\text{Current ratio} = \frac{£36.869m}{£20.203m}$$

$$= 1.82$$

It is argued that a business should aim for a current ratio of between 1.5 and 2. Below this there is a danger of running out of cash and above this shows that the business has too much cash tied up in unproductive assets. Crowmarsh PLC is in a comfortable position, with a current ratio of 1.82.

Acid test ratio The acid test or quick ratio is similar to the current ratio, but excludes stocks from current assets in the calculation. Stocks are the least liquid of the current assets, since they have not yet been sold.

$$\text{ACID TEST RATIO} = \frac{\text{Current assets - stock}}{\text{Current liabilities}}$$

All the figures required in this ratio are listed in the balance sheet. The acid test ratio for Crowmarsh in 1993 was:

$$\text{Acid test ratio} = \frac{£36.869m - £18.162}{£20.203m}$$

$$= 0.93$$

A quick ratio of 1 : 1 is desirable. Many firms operate on much lower ratios. Crowmarsh's ratio of 0.93 : 1 is very close to 1 : 1, and so could be satisfactory.

Gearing ratios

The capital structure of a business can be considered by looking at the proportions of capital raised by debt and equity, such as loans or share capital. In the USA, gearing is called **leverage** and this term is often used in the UK today. The following two ratios can be used to explore the gearing of a company.

Gearing ratio The gearing ratio shows the relationship between equity capital (from shareholders) and fixed interest/dividend bearing capital (from sources such as banks):

$$\text{GEARING RATIO} = \frac{\text{Loan capital + preference share capital}}{\text{Total capital (loan + preference + equity)}} \times 100$$

The information needed to calculate this ratio is found in the notes to the accounts or the balance sheet. For Crowmarsh in 1993 loan capital was £2.454 million, preference share capital was £0.250 million and equity (including reserves) was £23.027 million. The gearing ratio was:

$$\text{Gearing ratio} = \frac{£2.454m + £0.250m}{£2.454m + £0.250m + £22.777m} \times 100$$

$$= \frac{£2.704m}{£25.481m} \times 100$$

$$= 10.61\%$$

The gearing ratio can also be expressed as:

$$\frac{\text{Loans}}{\text{equity}} \times 100 = \frac{£2.454m}{£23.027m} \times 100 = 10.65\%$$

If the ratio is less than 100 per cent then the company is said to be low geared. If it is over 100 per cent then it is highly geared.

Crowmarsh's gearing ratio of 10.65 per cent is very low. This shows that the majority of long term funding comes from the owners of the company, ie the shareholders. This company is not a risk-taker, and the potential for growth is higher.

Interest cover The gearing ratio is a balance sheet measure of financial risk. Interest cover is a profit and loss account measure. This ratio assesses the firm's ability to pay interest by comparing profit and interest payments.

$$\text{INTEREST COVER} = \frac{\text{Profit before tax and interest}}{\text{Interest paid}}$$

For Crowmarsh PLC in 1993 profit was £5.221 million

and interest was £1.058 million.

$$\text{Interest cover} = \frac{£5.221m}{£1.058m}$$

$$= 4.9 \text{ times}$$

A figure of 1 means that the firm would need to use all its profit to pay interest. This is not a good position to be in! A figure of 1–2 may also cause problems. Crowmarsh's figure of nearly 5 would be satisfactory.

QUESTION 4

(a) Using Table 45.1 and Table 45.2, calculate the gearing and liquidity ratios for Crowmarsh PLC in 1992.

(b) Write a brief report for a bank. Describe any changes that have taken place between 1992 and 1993 and explain those you feel are most important.

Shareholders' ratios

Investors are interested in the return they might get from buying ordinary shares. A number of ratios can be used to do this. Returns only vary on ordinary shares. Returns on other shares are fixed (☞ unit 40).

Return on equity This ratio measures the 'return on investment'. It shows the profit to the shareholder as a percentage of the shareholders' equity.

$$\text{RETURN ON EQUITY} = \frac{\text{Profit accruing to ordinary shareholders (or profit after tax, interest and preference dividends)}}{\text{Ordinary share capital + reserves}}$$

The profit after tax and interest less any payment to preference shareholders for Crowmarsh in 1993 was £2.669 million - £0.009 million = £2.660 million. The total value of share capital and reserves was £23.027 million as stated in the balance sheet. From this we must subtract the value of preference share capital which was £0.250 million. This gives a new total of £22.777 million. So:

$$\text{Return on equity} = \frac{£2.660m}{£22.777m} \times 100$$

$$= 11.7\ \%$$

The higher this return is, the better. Whether 11.7 per cent is high or not depends on how much could be earned from other interest bearing accounts. This ratio does not measure the amount which ordinary shareholders actually receive. Other ratios are designed for this purpose.

Earnings per share This ratio measures the amount each share is earning for the investor.

$$\text{EARNINGS PER SHARE} = \frac{\text{Profit accruing to ordinary shareholders}}{\text{Number of ordinary shares}}$$

For Crowmarsh PLC in 1993 the earnings per share were:

$$\text{Earnings per share} = \frac{£2.660m}{6.423m}$$

$$= 41.42p$$

To determine whether this is a satisfactory return we need to take the share price into account.

Price/earnings ratio The earnings per share is a more useful ratio when compared with the current market price of the share. Market prices are not listed in the annual reports since they are liable to change every day. However, they are published daily in some of the 'quality' newspapers.

$$\text{PRICE/EARNINGS RATIO} = \frac{\text{Market price}}{\text{Earnings per share}}$$

The share price for Crowmarsh on 31.7.93 was 1950p. Thus, the price earnings ratio was:

$$\text{Price/earnings ratio} = \frac{1950p}{41.42p}$$

$$= 47.08$$

The price/earnings ratio may reflect the confidence in the future of the company. So high ratios are better. Ratios vary from company to company and industry to industry. For Crowmarsh, 47.08 might appear on the high side compared with what we might expect (a price/earnings ratio of around 10 is very common for most industries). This might be due to:
- the high status of the company;
- the share price being overvalued;
- investors expecting future profits to grow.

Dividends per share This ratio shows the amount of money ordinary shareholders actually receive. It is not the same as earnings per share. This is only the dividend paid to shareholders. The earnings of the company are also made up of retained profits.

$$\text{DIVIDENDS PER SHARE} = \frac{\text{Dividends}}{\text{Number of shares}}$$

According to the profit and loss account the dividend for Crowmarsh in 1993 was £0.761 million. We then subtract the £0.009 million paid to the preference shareholders. So:

$$\text{Dividends per share} = \frac{£0.752m}{6.423m}$$

$$= 11.7p$$

This ratio is often contained in the notes to the published accounts and is possibly the most important one to the investor. Higher returns are better, but the investor must take into account what was paid for the share and what would be earned elsewhere.

Dividend yield This ratio shows the amount the investor receives as a percentage of the market price of the shares:

$$\text{DIVIDEND YIELD} = \frac{\text{Dividend per share}}{\text{Market price}} \times 100$$

The market price for Crowmarsh was 1950p in July 1993, and the dividends per share were 11.7p. So:

$$\text{Dividend yield} = \frac{11.7p}{1950p} \times 100$$

$$= 0.6\%$$

Comparison with other firms could tell whether this is satisfactory. If low, this may be because investors expect the rate of dividend per share to grow.

Dividend cover This ratio takes into account the chance of capital growth. There are two financial motives for buying shares - to earn dividends and to make capital gains. If a company's share price rises over time an investor can make a capital gain when the shares are sold. Dividend cover links profit after tax and dividends.

$$\text{DIVIDEND COVER} = \frac{\text{Profit accruing to ordinary shareholders}}{\text{Dividends}}$$

For Crowmarsh PLC in 1993 this was:

$$\text{Dividend cover} = \frac{£2.660m}{£0.752m}$$

$$= 3.5$$

This measure shows how many more times the dividend could have been paid out of the current earnings. For Crowmarsh the cover is good because the dividend could be paid $3^1/_2$ times over. It suggests there may be growth in future. Investors looking for higher annual payouts might feel the cover was too high, and that a higher dividend could have been paid.

Limitations to ratio analysis

Ratio analysis does not provide a complete means of assessing a company's financial position. There are also problems when using ratios.

When making comparisons over time, it is necessary to take into account the following:
- inflation;
- any changes in accounting procedures;
- changes in the business activities of a firm;
- changes in general business conditions and the economic environment.

It is also important that firms compare 'like with like' when using ratios, especially when making comparisons between businesses. Even firms in the same industry may be different. Their size, product mix or objectives might differ. Different accounting techniques might be used, eg different stock valuation and depreciation methods. The financial year endings may not be the same. We also need to account for differences in human judgement. Some information is estimated, eg provision for bad debts. Firms may window dress their final accounts to show they are in a better position. One way of doing this is by chasing debts just before the end of the financial year.

Ratio analysis is based on historic information and does not include other useful information, such as the chairperson's and directors' reports. It does not include some of the positive factors within a business such as the quality of the staff or the location, both of which affect performance.

Providing these problems are recognised, ratios can be a useful tool for evaluating the accounts.

Key terms

Acid test ratio - similar to the current ratio but excludes stocks from current assets. Sometimes called the quick ratio.
Current ratio - assesses the firm's liquidity by dividing current liabilities into current assets.
Debt collection period - the number of days it takes to collect the average debt.
Dividend cover - how many times the dividend could have been paid from the year's earnings.
Dividends per share - the amount of money a shareholder will actually receive for each share owned.
Dividend yield - the amount received by the shareholder as a percentage of the share price.

Earnings per share - the amount each ordinary share earns.

Gearing ratios - explore the capital structure of a business by comparing the proportions of capital raised by debt and equity.

Gross profit margin - expresses operating profit before tax and interest, ie gross profit, as a percentage of turnover.

Interest cover - assesses a firm's ability to meet interest payments by comparing profit and interest payable.

Net profit margin - shows the firm's ability to control overheads and expresses net profit before tax as a percentage of turnover.

Price/earnings ratio - relates the earnings per share to its market price and reflects the return from buying shares.

Ratio analysis - a numerical approach to investigating accounts by comparing two related figures.

Return on equity - measures the return on shareholders investment by expressing the profit earned by ordinary shareholders as a percentage of total equity.

Return on net assets - expresses profit as a percentage of long term assets only.

Return on capital employed - the profit of a business as a percentage of the total amount of money used to generate it.

Stock turnover - the number of times in a trading year a firm sells the value of its stocks.

Question

Northern Textiles

Table 45.3 contains financial information for three companies, Rochdale Textiles PLC, Bolton Textiles PLC and Liverpool Textiles PLC. As an employee working for a firm of stockbrokers in Greater Manchester you have been asked to answer the questions below for a client.

Table 45.3 *A summary of financial information from three textile companies*

	Rochdale	Bolton	Liverpool
Turnover	£10m	£20m	£100m
Gross profit	£3m	£5.5m	£40m
Net profit before tax	£1.5m	£2.5m	£22m
Earnings per share	12.1p	9.9p	31.9p
Dividend per share	7.2p	7.1p	10.8p
Current share price	130p	198p	240p

(a) Calculate the gross profit margin and the net profit margin for each of the three companies and comment on each firm's overheads.

(b) Discuss the factors which might account for the differences in the above ratios for each of the companies.

(c) Calculate the price/earnings ratio and the dividend yield in the case of each company.

(d) On the basis of your answers to (c) which company would you advise a client to invest in if:
   (i) they wanted fast financial returns;
   (ii) they wanted capital growth?
   Explain your answers.

(e) What other information might be helpful to you when providing the advice in (d) above?

Summary

1. Briefly describe the steps involved in the investigation process when analysing a set of accounts.
2. Why might interfirm comparisons be useful?
3. What is the difference between performance and activity ratios?
4. What is the difference between liquidity ratios and gearing ratios?
5. How do gross and net profit margins differ?
6. What do stock turnover and debtors turnover measure?
7. Describe the difference between the current ratio and the acid test ratio.
8. What is meant by a highly geared company?
9. Why is interest cover a profit and loss account measure of financial risk?
10. Which of the shareholders' ratios measures the actual financial return shareholders receive?
11. Which ratio reflects the prospect of capital growth?
12. Describe the limitations of ratio analysis.

Unit 46 Budgeting

What is budgeting?

As businesses expand the need for control grows and becomes more difficult. A small business can be run informally. The owner is the manager, who will know everyone, be aware of what is going on and will make all decisions. In larger firms work and responsibility are delegated, which makes informal control impractical. To improve control budgeting has been developed. This forces managers to be accountable for their decisions.

A BUDGET is a plan which is agreed in advance. It must be a plan and not a forecast - a forecast is a prediction of what might happen in the future, whereas a budget is a planned outcome which the firm hopes to achieve. A budget will show the money needed for spending and how this might be financed. Budgets are based on the objectives of businesses. They force managers to think ahead and improve co-ordination. Most budgets are set for twelve months to coincide with the accounting period, but there are exceptions. Research and Development budgets, for example, may cover several years.

Information contained in a budget may include revenue, sales, expenses, profit, personnel, cash and capital expenditure. In fact, budgets can include any business variable (known as a budget factor) which can be given a value.

One well known budget is 'The Budget'. It is a statement made by the Chancellor of the Exchequer every year. The Budget gives details on government expenditure plans in the coming financial year, and how this will be financed by taxes and other sources.

Approaches to budgeting

Budgets can be divided into different categories. Objectives budgets and flexible budgets take different approaches to planning.

- **Objectives budgets** are based on finding the best way on achieving particular objectives (☞ unit 5). They contain information on how a business will achieve these objectives. For example, a sales budget might show how a sales target will be met.
- **Flexible budgets** are designed to change as business changes. Changes in business conditions may result in very different outcomes than those budgeted for. A flexible budget takes these into account. For example, the sales budget may be altered if there is sudden increase in demand resulting in much higher sales levels.

A business will also set budgets over the long term and short term.

- **Capital budgets** plan the capital structure and the liquidity of a business over a long period of time. They are concerned with equity, liabilities, fixed and current assets and year-end cash balances.
- **Operating budgets** plan the day to day use of resources. They are concerned with materials, labour, overheads, sales and cash. There are three important operating budgets. The **profit budget** estimates the annual business costs, the year's turnover and the expected profit for the year. The **cash budget** simply plans the receipts and payments. It shows a firm its cash balance at specified times in the budget period. The **budgeted balance sheet** incorporates the budgeted profit and loss account and the closing balance in the cash budget. It also takes into account planned changes in assets and liabilities.

The preparation of budgets

The way in which a budget might be prepared is shown in Figure 46.1. It is a step by step process. The first step is to decide upon a budget period and state the objectives which are to be achieved. The budget period may vary according to the type of budget, but one month or one year is usual. Often the objectives will be set at board level. Targets for performance, market share, quality (provided it can be quantified) and productivity are all examples.

The next stage involves obtaining information upon which the budget can be based. Some information can be obtained from previous results. Historic information can be useful, although some budgetary techniques ignore the past and make a fresh start. This is called **zero-based budgeting**. Forecasts are another source of information. These are estimates of likely future outcomes. Some

---

QUESTION 1 Michael Herriot is a student who works part time for a local hotel. He hopes to tour Europe in the summer holidays and is wondering whether or not he can afford the £500 cost. He draws up a budget showing his planned income and expenditure for the next ten months before the date of the proposed holiday in August.

Table 46.1 *A budget showing Michael Herriot's planned income and expenditure for a ten month period*

(£)

	Oct	Nov	Dec	Jan	Feb	Mar	Apr	May	Jun	Jul
Income	80	80	120	80	80	80	120	80	80	200
Expenditure	40	40	100	40	40	40	40	100	40	100

(a) Given the information in Table 46.1 calculate whether or not Michael can afford the proposed holiday based on his current plans.
(b) Explain how the preparation of this budget can help Michael.

business variables are easier to forecast than others. It is fairly easy to predict future costs, but difficult to estimate future sales. This is because sales levels are subject to so many external factors.

It is now possible to prepare two important budgets - the sales budget and the production budget. These budgets are related and affect all other budgets. For example, sales targets can only be met if there is productive capacity. Also, a firm would be unlikely to continue production if it could not sell its products. The sales budget will contain monthly sales estimates, expressed in terms of quantities per product, perhaps, and the price charged. From the sales budget, and with knowledge of stock levels, the production budget can be determined. This will show the required raw materials, labour hours and machine hours. At this stage the business should know whether or not it has the capacity to meet the sales targets. If it is not possible, then it may be necessary to adjust the sales budget.

Subsidiary operating budgets can be drawn up next. These will be detailed budgets prepared by various departments. Budgets are often broken down, so that each person in the hierarchy (☞ unit 63) can be given some responsibility for a section of the budget.

The master budget is a summary statement. It shows the estimated income, anticipated expenditure, and, thus, the budgeted profit for the period. The cash budget can also be prepared when all other budgets are complete. This budget is particularly useful since it shows the monthly flows of cash into and out of the business. It will help to show whether future cash flow problems might occur.

The final step is to prepare the projected balance sheet. This shows the financial position that will result from the firm's budgets.

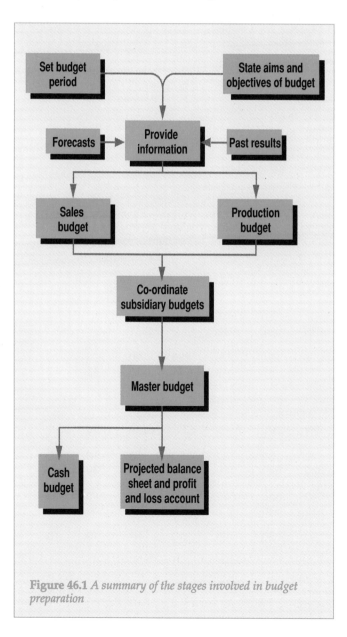

Figure 46.1 *A summary of the stages involved in budget preparation*

Preparing a sales revenue budget

A sales revenue budget will show the planned revenue for a period of time. Emerald Artwork produce four products, AD23, AD24, AE12 and AE13. They sell for £12, £20, £25 and £30 respectively. The planned sales levels for a four month period in 1994 are shown in Table 46.2.

Table 46.2 *Planned sales figures for Emerald Artwork*

	FEB	MAR	APR	MAY
AD23	100	100	100	100
AD24	50	80	80	100
AE12	40	50	40	50
AE13	30	30	50	50

The sales revenue budget is prepared by showing the planned revenue in each month. This is calculated by multiplying the predicted sales levels by the prices. The sales revenue budget is shown in Table 46.3

Table 46.3 *A sales revenue budget for Emerald Artwork*

	FEB	MAR	APR	MAY
AD23	£1,200 (£12x100)	£1,200 (£12x100)	£1,200 (£12x100)	£1,200 (£12x100)
AD24	£1,000 (£20x50)	£1,600 (£20x80)	£1,600 (£20x80)	£2,000 (£20x100)
AD12	£1,000 (£25x40)	£1,250 (£25x50)	£1,000 (£25x40)	£1,250 (£25x50)
AD13	£900 (£30x30)	£900 (£30x30)	£1,500 (£30x50)	£1,500 (£30x50)
Total	£4,100	£4,950	£5,300	£5,950

A production budget

Once Emerald Artwork has produced a sales budget, it is possible to calculate its production budget. The example in Table 46.4 assumes stock levels stay the same throughout the 4 month period. The figures are based on expected sales in Table 46.2.

Table 46.4 *A production budget for Emerald Artwork covering production of all 4 products*

	FEB	MAR	APR	MAY
Cost of materials (£3 per unit)	£660 (£3x220)	£780 (£3x260)	£810 (£3x270)	£900 (£3x300)
Direct labour costs (£4 per unit)	£880 (£4x220)	£1,040 (£4x260)	£1,080 (£4x270)	£1,200 (£4x300)
Indirect labour costs (£2 per unit)	£440 (£2x220)	£520 (£2x260)	£540 (£2x270)	£600 (£2x300)
Overheads (10% of direct & indirect costs)	£1,320x10% = £132	£1,560x10% = £156	£1,620x10% = £162	£1,800 = £180
Total	£2,112	£2,496	£2,592	£2,880

Budgetary control

BUDGETARY CONTROL involves a business looking into the future, stating what it wants to happen, and then deciding how to achieve these aims. The control process is shown in Figure 46.2.

■ Preparation of plans. All businesses have objectives (☞ unit 5). If the sales department increases sales by ten per cent, how does it know whether or not this is

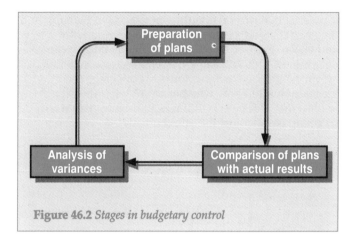

Figure 46.2 *Stages in budgetary control*

QUESTION 2   Seaforth Cornmills process maize for a breakfast cereal manufacturer. The production manager has prepared a twelve month budget for labour and raw materials based on the sales budget. The cost of direct and indirect labour is £3 and £4 per hour respectively. Factory overheads per month are estimated at 10 per cent of total variable cost (labour and materials).

Table 46.5 *The labour and raw materials budgets for Seaforth Cornmills*

Labour budget hours 000

	JAN	FEB	MAR	APR	MAY	JUN	JUL	AUG	SEP	OCT	NOV	DEC
Direct labour	200	200	200	200	200	220	220	220	220	220	220	220
Indirect labour	10	10	10	10	10	11	11	11	11	11	13	13

Raw materials budget £ 000

	JAN	FEB	MAR	APR	MAY	JUN	JUL	AUG	SEP	OCT	NOV	DEC
Opening stock	10	20	20	20	10	20	30	30	20	10	10	10
Purchases	500	500	500	500	520	520	520	510	510	520	530	540
	510	520	520	520	530	540	550	540	530	530	540	550
less production	490	500	500	510	510	510	520	520	520	520	530	540
Closing stock	20	20	20	10	20	30	30	20	10	10	10	10

(a) Prepare a twelve month production cost budget for Seaforth Cornmills.
(b) How might the raw materials budget help the production manager?
(c) What is the danger of basing production budgets on sales budgets?

satisfactory? Targets are usually set which allow a business to determine if its objectives have been met. The results it achieves can then be compared with the targets it sets.

■ Comparison of plans with actual results. Control will be effective if information is available as quickly as possible. Managers need budgetary data as soon as it is available. Recent developments in information technology have helped to speed up the supply of data. For budgeting purposes the financial year has been divided into smaller control periods - usually four weeks or one calendar month. It is common to prepare a budget for each control period. At the end of the period the actual results can then be compared with the targets set in the budget.

■ Analysis of variances. This is the most important stage of control process. Analysing the VARIANCES involves trying to find reasons for the differences between actual and expected results. An unfavourable variance, when planned sales are 1,000 units and actual sales are 800 units, for example, might be due to inefficiency. It is then up to the management to take some action. A variance may be the result of some external factor influencing the business (☞ unit 1). In this case a firm may need to change its business plans and adjust the next budget.

The benefits of budgetary control

■ Budgets provide a means of controlling income and expenditure. They regulate the spending of money and draw attention to losses, waste and inefficiency.

■ They act as a 'review' for a business, allowing time for corrective action.

■ Budgets can emphasise and clarify the responsibilities of executives.

■ They enable management to delegate responsibility without losing control, because subordinates are expected to meet budget targets which are known in advance by senior management.

■ Budgets help ensure that capital is usefully employed by checking that the capital employed is consistent with the planned level of activity.

■ They help the co-ordination of the business and improve communication between departments.

■ Budgets provide clear targets which can be understood by personnel lower down in the organisational structure (☞ unit 63). They should also help to focus on costs.

The drawbacks of budgetary control

■ Budgets might lead to resentment from some of the firm's personnel, particularly if they are not involved in the preparation. This could result in poor motivation and targets being missed.

■ If budgets are too inflexible then it is possible that the business could suffer. For example, a member of the sales team may be prevented from finalising an overseas contract because the overseas travel budget is spent.

■ If the actual business results are very different from the budgeted ones then the budget can lose its importance as a means of control.

QUESTION 3 The sales budget for Derby Drains is shown in Table 46.6. It was prepared by the managing director for a six month period and passed to the sales manager for distribution in the department. The company had experienced some selling difficulties in recent months due to a recession and a decline in the building industry. A great deal of dissatisfaction was expressed by many of the sales team since the targets (to which bonuses were related) were, in their opinion, very optimistic.

Table 46.6 *Sales budget for Derby Drains*

Sales budget						units
	JAN	FEB	MAR	APR	MAY	JUN
North	3,000	3,000	3,500	3,500	4,000	5,000
South	6,000	6,000	7,000	7,000	8,000	10,000
East	2,000	3,000	3,000	3,000	3,500	3,500
West	3,000	3,000	4,000	4,000	5,000	6,000
Total	14,000	15,000	17,500	17,500	20,500	24,500

(a) What might the forecasts in the sales budget be based on?
(b) Describe the disadvantages of preparing the sales budget without the assistance of the sales manager.
(c) What are the dangers of setting over-optimistic targets in budgets?

Variance analysis

VARIANCE ANALYSIS involves investigating and giving reasons for the differences in the actual results and the budgeted figures. It is the most important part of budgetary control. The first step is to calculate the appropriate variances and determine whether they are **favourable (F)** or **adverse (A)**. Favourable variances could occur because sales revenue is higher than expected or costs are lower. Adverse variances are when sales revenue is lower or costs are higher than expected.

There are a number of important variances which are used. The **profit variance** is probably the most important. It shows the extent to which the actual profit differs from the planned profit. Other examples include the sales variance, materials variance, wages variance, overheads variance and the production variance. Variances may be shown in terms of money, but can also be written as quantities. For example, the production budget in a particular month may be 100,000 units. If the actual level of production was 115,000 units the production variance will be 15,000F. If the actual level was 90,000, the variance would be 10,000 A. The profit variance will be influenced by all other variances. For example, if the overheads variance is favourable, then the profit variance will also be favourable as long as nothing else changes.

It is arguably easier to calculate variances than to find their causes. The possible causes of just two types of variance are summarised below.

Sales margin variances

Selling prices	● Sales discounts **A**.
	● Quantity discounts **A**.
Quantities	● Adverse economic conditions **A**.
	● Ineffective marketing **A**.
	● Competitors cease trading **F**.
	● Favourable change in consumer tastes **F**.
	● Deterioration in reputation **A**.

Direct materials variance

Direct wage rate	● General rise in wage rates **A**.
	● Fall in specific wage rates **F**.
	● Employing non-standard grade workers **A**.
Direct labour efficiency	● Slow employee **A**.
	● Improved working conditions **F**.
	● Poor supervision **A**.
	● Incorrect recording of hours worked **A**.
	● Fall in absenteeism **F**.
	● Employee restricts output **A**.

The above examples are not exhaustive. It may be possible to identify other causes for the two variances. Once the causes have been identified, management must take action to correct the variances.

QUESTION 4 Market Data is a market research agency with an office in Bristol. Clarissa Dortman, one of the business partners, has produced some information concerning overhead variances. The information is shown in Table 46.7.

Table 46.7 *Overhead expenditure variances for Market Data*

(£)

Overhead	Total budget overhead allowance	Actual overhead	Overhead expenditure variance
Power	3,000	2,900	100F
Rent	14,000	14,000	-
Indirect labour	20,000	22,000	2,000A
Telephone	800	1,200	400A
Insurance	900	900	-
Heat and light	1,500	1,100	400F
Total	40,200	42,100	1,900A

(a) What is likely to have happened to profit given the information in Table 46.7? Give reasons for your answer.
(b) Explain what might have caused the large variance in indirect labour.
(c) What would the management do with this information when forming the next budget?

Key terms

Budget - a quantitative economic plan prepared and agreed in advance.
Budgetary control - a business system which involves making future plans, comparing the actual results with the planned objectives and then investigating causes of any differences.

Variances - differences between actual results and planned expectations.
Variance analysis - the process of calculating variances and attempting to identify their causes.

Summary

1. How might a budget improve managerial accountability?
2. What is meant by budgetary control?
3. Describe the benefits of budgetary control.
4. Describe the drawbacks of budgetary control.
5. What is the difference between objectives budgets and flexible budgets?
6. What is meant by zero-based budgeting?
7. What is a master budget?
8. What might cause a sales variance?

Question

Cockleberry Aircraft Components PLC

Cockleberry Aircraft Components PLC are a firm of electronic engineers supplying aircraft manufacturers with a range of hi-tech electronic equipment worldwide. Table 46.8 shows the master budget and actual results for the last financial year (1993).

During the last couple of years the company has lost orders due to the recession. Many of its customers are cutting back on aircraft manufacturing and, unfortunately, Cockleberry are almost entirely reliant on the aircraft industry. It hopes to win some new orders in Australia, where the sales team is currently operating an expensive sales drive. There has been some discussion at the board level regarding the control of business costs. Some departments have consistently overspent their budgets in the past. The directors have experienced some conflict with the heads of department when agreeing budgets. The overheads budget and actual overheads are shown in Table 46.9.

Table 46.8 *The master budget and the actual results for Cockleberry Aircraft Components PLC*

£m

	Master budget		Actual results	
Sales		459		420
less Cost of sales				
Opening stock of finished goods	12		12	
Add cost of goods supplied	231		250	
	243		262	
less Closing stocks	13	230	14	248
Gross profit		229		172
less Overheads		108		127
Net profit		121		45

Table 46.9 *Overheads budget and actual results for Cockleberry Aircraft Components PLC*

£m

Department	Budget	Actual
Marketing	30	40
Administration	11	17
Personnel	16	18
Production	30	30
R & D	21	22
Total	108	127

(a) Calculate the:
   (i) overheads variance;
   (ii) sales variance;
   (iii) gross profit variance;
   (iv) net profit variance;
   from the information in Table 46.8.
   In each case state whether the variance is favourable or adverse.

(b) In a report account for the sales variance, the overheads variance and the net profit variance using the information in Tables 46.8 and 46.9

(c) How could the business make use of its sales budget?

(d) Explain how budgetary control might help this business.

(e) Discuss the likely impact of the company's activities in Australia on the budgets it prepares.

Dan-Air

In September 1992 Davies & Newman, the owner of Dan-Air, approached Virgin Atlantic about a possible merger to save the company. Dan-Air had suffered in recent years due to poor financial performance, continual restructuring and serious liquidity problems. Richard Branson, Virgin's boss, expressed an interest in the company with his eye on some of Dan-Air's routes to Spain, Germany and France. Branson had announced earlier in the month that he would like to establish a regional airline based at Gatwick to serve Europe. Dan-Air's routes would provide a bedrock for the new airline.

The new airline, whose suggested name might be Virgin Elite, would use Dan-Air's new fleet of Boeing 737-400s. This would allow Virgin to transfer many of its Japanese and transatlantic passengers on to other routes in Europe. Virgin was losing this traffic to British Airways and its American competitors which all had intra-European routes. A merger would also threaten BA and British Midland on its European routes where profit margins are tight.

Davies & Newman and Virgin had already planned some business links. In October Dan-Air joined Virgin's boosted frequent-flyer programme. Also Gatwick Handling, which is 50 per cent owned by Davies & Newman, bid for Virgin's ground handling contract at its Sussex headquarters. Lord Caithness, the air minister, was keen for the merger to go ahead in order to save Britain's oldest private sector airline. He was also enthusiastic about the possible competition which would materialise, forcing BA to offer quality services at competitive prices.

The financial crisis at Davies & Newman was such that £50million was owed to a consortium of banks. A key question in the negotiations was how much of the debt would be guaranteed by Virgin? City analysts were not in agreement as to whether the merger would work. On one hand 'a sprinkle of Branson's business magic' may well have been sufficient to turn the company around and finally bury the old 'Dan Dare' image. However, others were more doubtful, pointing out that in the previous month BA had scrutinised Dan-Air's books and walked away. Although Dan-Air's market capitalisation was less than £2million at 11p per share (compared with 550p three years ago), BA knew that they could 'raid the grave' should Dan-Air die, and pick up the best routes.

Branson was in a position to strike a hard bargain with Davies and Newman since he was widely perceived to be Dan-Air's only hope for survival. Given that they were under pressure to repay very heavy loans and that projected losses were around £30 million for the year, they were 'clutching at straws'. In addition, none of the American carriers had expressed an interest in buying the company.

Dan-Air was eventually bought by British Airways for £1 at the end of the year. Even though they had originally walked away from the company they were obviously attracted by the prospect of controlling 80-90 per cent of all Heathrow slots held by British carriers. A significant reorganisation was planned by BA involving the lay off of around 2,000 of Dan-Airs 2,500 workforce.

Source: adapted from *The Sunday Times*, 20.9.92 and updated.

Table 1 *Financial information for Davies & Newman*

	1991 £000	1990 £000
Fixed assets		
Intangible assets	1,142	1,308
Tangible assets	69,960	100,367
Investments	2,635	2,357
	73,737	104,032
Current assets		
Stocks	994	10,880
Debtors	31,915	37,457
Pension scheme prepayment	11,512	13,364
Short term deposits	1,352	1,854
Cash at bank and in hand	6,122	7,502
	51,895	71,057
Current liabilities	(57,483)	(115,607)

(a) What might have been the financial and non-financial advantages to Virgin of the possible merger?

(b) Calculate the current ratio and the acid test ratio for 1990 and 1991 and comment on the liquidity of Davies & Newman in 1991.

(c) Why do you think that the share price of Davies and Newman fell from 550p to 11p in three years?

(d) Explain 3 possible reasons why Dan-Air suffered in their market in the three years leading up to 1991.

(e) What type of assets do you think contributed to the £69.96 million total for tangible assets in 1991?

(f) What was the value of long term liabilities if capital and reserves were £42,757,000 in 1991.

(g) Why did British Airways pay such a low price (£1) for Dan-Air?

Simon Carruthers PLC

Simon Carruthers PLC are a large national supplier of building materials. They have 340 builders yards in the British Isles. They employ 51,000 people and have expanded steadily in the last 20 years. An important part of their business operation is the buying and selling of land. Unfortunately, in the last trading year, the company has suffered its first ever heavy loss. The recession which resulted in a sharp decline in building activity and a fall in land values is largely responsible. The balance sheet and profit and loss account are shown in Table 1.

Table 1 *Balance sheet and profit and loss account for Simon Carruthers PLC*

SIMON CARRUTHERS PLC
BALANCE SHEET
AS AT 27.2.1993

	1993 £m	1992 £m
Fixed assets		
Tangible assets	3,550	3,700
Investments	120	390
	3,670	4,090
Current assets		
Stocks (goods for resale)	750	660
Debtors	950	200
Cash at bank and in hand	50	140
	1,750	1,000
Creditors		
Amounts falling due within one year	970	650
Net assets	4,450	4,440
Creditors		
Amounts falling due after more than one year	890	560
Provisions for liabilities and charges	120	40
	3,440	3,840
Capital and reserves		
Called up share capital	100	90
Share premium	730	700
Profit and loss account	2,610	3,050
	3,440	3,840

SIMON CARRUTHERS PLC
PROFIT AND LOSS ACCOUNT
FOR THE YEAR ENDING 27.2 1993

	1993 £m	1992 £m
Turnover (excluding VAT)	7,900	8,400
Cost of sales	6,430	6,900
Gross Profit	1,470	1,500
Administration expenses	550	420
Operating profit	920	1,080
Net profit/loss on the sale of land	(960)	(410)
Less interest payable	(120)	(40)
Profit on ordinary activities before tax	(160)	630
Tax on ordinary activities	-	180
Profit for the year	(160)	450
Dividends	280	290
Transferred to reserves	(440)	160

(a) Calculate the:
   (i) gross profit margin;
   (ii) return on capital employed;
   (iii) stock turnover in days;
   (iv) debt collection period;
   for1992 and 1993.
(b) Calculate the:
   (i) current ratio;
   (ii) acid test ratio;
   (iii) interest cover;
   for 1992 and 1993.
(c) Present your results from (a) and (b) in a table.
(d) Draw two pie charts showing the asset structure for 1992 and 1993. Comment on, and try to account for, any significant changes in the asset structure which have taken place over the two years.
(e) Write a chairperson's report explaining the 1993 results to the shareholders and account for any changes that have taken place.

Tony Freehan and Keith Areety are partners in a Manchester management agency. They manage a number of rock bands working in and around the area. Tony and Keith were members of a group called 'The Clout' in the 1970s, but retired in 1979, after which they decided to set up in business. They had accumulated many contacts, particularly in the Manchester area where they used to play regularly.

For ten years the business flourished. They managed two quite popular local bands. Most of their income came from a 25 per cent commission charged on bookings which they secured for bands. They also handled promotions for bands and occasionally staged concerts. Most of the concerts organised by Tony and Keith did not make any money, but did provide an opportunity to publicise the bands which they managed.

In 1993, Tony took more of an interest in the staging of concerts and decided that money could be made if they invested more into their organisation. Tony convinced Keith that a concert should be arranged at an appropriate venue somewhere in the North West. Tony had plans to sign up four bands for an evening in October. The date would coincide with the return of students to universities in the area.

One of the problems of staging concerts is that some money has to be laid out in advance. This is not included in the calculations of net concert revenue. The income from concerts was received on the night of the concert. Tony and Keith knew they would need a bank loan in order to stage the concert. They also knew that before visiting the bank manager it would be necessary to draw up a cash flow forecast statement. Tony and Keith are currently overdrawn at the bank by £1,800 (31.1.93). Their current overdraft limit is £3,000. Details of expected cash inflows are shown in Table 1.

The following financial details are also available.
- Tony and Keith draw £2,500 each every month for personal use.
- They employ a secretary who costs £600 per month.
- Rent for their office is £6,000 each year paid in equal amounts each month.
- They lease two cars for business use which cost £600 per month.
- Telephone bills are estimated to be £600 each in January and April and £400 each in July and October.
- Concert staging costs are expected to be £4,500, £4,000 and £10,000 in March, June and September respectively.
- Advertising costs are £200 every other month, payable in February to start with.
- Insurance is £1,200 payable in August.
- £400 per month is provided for miscellaneous expenses.

(a) **Draw up a twelve month cash flow forecast statement for Tony and Keith's business starting in February. Show clearly the balance at the end of each month.**

(b) **When might they need to extend their overdraft and by how much?**

(c) **What other information might the bank require before extending Tony and Keith's overdraft?**

(d) **Explain how they might improve their cash flow position without having to borrow from the bank.**

(e) **How might variance analysis be used at the end of the twelve month period to help Tony and Keith in running their business?**

(f) **Assuming that the above cash inflows and cash outflows actually occur during the year, calculate the profit the business makes.**

Table 1 *Expected cash inflows for Tony and Keith's business*

(£)

	FEB	MAR	APR	MAY	JUN	JUL	AUG	SEP	OCT	NOV	DEC	JAN
Commission	4,000	3,000	6,000	7,000	6,000	6,000	7,000	7,000	6,000	5,000	8,000	2,000
Net concert revenue			5,000			4,000			25,000			
Promotion fees	3,000	2,000	2,000	4,000	2,000	1,000	2,000	0	3,000	0	3,000	4,000

Aims

- To examine the current financial performance of a business (public limited company).
- To compare the performance, liquidity and returns to the shareholders of two companies operating in the same industry.

Research

The first step is to obtain sets of published accounts from two businesses operating in the same industry. Probably the quickest way to obtain accounts is to telephone the company directly explaining the reason why you want copies. Usually the accounts are sent out immediately. If you know the name of the company their telephone number can usually be obtained from directory enquiries.

Make sure that the companies are in the same industry so that comparisons are meaningful. You could choose from the examples given below:

- Supermarkets - Sainsbury's, Tescos, Kwik Save, Asda, Aldi or Safeway.
- Banks - Nat West, Barclays, Midland or Lloyds.
- Electricity - Manweb, Norweb, Southern, Eastern or Seeboard.
- Confectionery - Cadbury's, Nestlé or Mars.
- Petrol - Shell, Esso, BP, Jet or Q8.
- Brewing - Bass, Courage, Scottish & Newcastle or Whitbread.
- Pharmaceuticals - Zeneca and Glaxo.

There are hundreds to choose from. If you want to find the names of more companies look at the listings of companies and their share prices in one of the broadsheet newspapers.

Use ratio analysis to examine the financial performance, liquidity and return to shareholders of each company. For both companies and over the two trading years calculate the ratios listed below.

(a) Performance:
    (i)   gross profit margin;
    (ii) return on capital employed;
    (iii) net profit margin;
    (iv) stock turnover in days;
    (v) debt collection period.

(b) Liquidity:
    (i)   current ratio;
    (ii) acid test ratio.

(c) Return to shareholders:
    (i)   earnings per share;
    (ii) price/earnings ratio;
    (iii) dividends per share;
    (iv) dividend yield.

(**nb** you will need to obtain the current share price and last year's share price for some of these ratios. These can be obtained from past copies of newspapers, CD ROM or by contacting your local stockbroker.)

Presentation

Probably the best way to present your results is in tables. For example, the performance results could be shown in a table like the one illustrated in Table 1. Notice that there is a column to show the percentage change over the two years.

Table 1 *A suitable table for presenting results*

	Company 1			Company 2		
	Yr 1	Yr 2	% change	Yr 1	Yr 2	% change
Gross profit margin						
ROCE						
Net profit margin						
Stock turnover						
Debt collection period						

You could also draw some pie charts to show the asset structure of the two companies in each trading year.

You then need to produce a report which explains your findings. It could be presented in four sections.

Introduction Give a brief history of each company explaining their location, scope of activities and any other introductory material you consider appropriate.

Interpretation of ratios Write a brief comment on the value of each ratio and the percentage change over the two years. State whether the value of each ratio is satisfactory or not. You might also try to account for any changes that have taken place over the two years.

Interfirm comparison Write some comments based on direct comparisons between the two companies. You should discuss both similarities and differences. Again, if possible, try to account for any notable observations. Do not forget to comment on the asset structures if you have drawn them.

Conclusion You need to write a general comment on the overall performance of each company. You might argue that one company has performed better than the other. You might also advise a potential investor which company to buy shares in.

investigations

Aims

- To compare the role of financial accountants with that of management accountants.

Research

You need to arrange appointments with two accountants. One should be with a financial accountant at a local firm of chartered accountants. The other should be with a management accountant at a large company in your area. Arrange appointments by telephoning the companies directly. Explain who you are and the purpose of your visit. Also explain that you will not take up too much of their time (half an hour at the most). An alternative to these interviews is for you or your college to arrange a work experience period at a firm of chartered accountants or a large firm in the accounts department.

You need to be well prepared for your visit so that you can obtain as much information as possible. You could produce a questionnaire based on the areas below.

- What qualifications are needed to become a financial/management accountant?
- How long does it take to become qualified?
- What particular skills and knowledge are required in the job?
- What is your job description?
- What specific tasks might be undertaken in a typical day at work?
- How much responsibility do you have?
- How much time do you spend out of the office?
- How much use do you make of information technology?
- How much time is spent working with other people?
- What stress levels are involved in the job?

You may have to ask slightly different questions to each type of accountant. For financial accountants in a chartered accountancy practice focus on the running of the business, eg the organisation, advertising, charges etc. in addition to the above questions. For management accountants in industry focus on their decision making contribution in the business. Remember that you are making a comparison, so ensure that your questions investigate any differences.

You are representing your school or college and are building a link with the local business community. Business people are often very busy but they are generally very happy to talk to students. This is provided that students are prepared for the visit and do not take up an unnecessary amount of their time. It is better not to go alone, but in pairs or very small groups. You can take it in turns to ask questions and share the workload.

Ask permission to tape record or video the interview. Ask for copies of any documents which you think might be useful. If you cannot record the interview you may need to take notes.

Presentation

You need to present your investigations in a report. It could be divided into five sections.

Introduction Write a brief note about your aims.

Financial accountants Write about the role of financial accountants based on the discussion you had on your visit. Use the questions above as a means of structuring your report.

Management accountants As above, but for management accountants.

Comparison Write a section which explains clearly the differences between the two different types of accountant. Are there any similarities?

Conclusion Write a brief summary of the main points discussed above. You might like to add some comments of your own. For example, which type of job is more demanding and stressful? Which of the above jobs is the most interesting?

Essays

1. Explain why it is necessary for a business organisation to keep a record of all its financial transactions and outline any principles upon which the recording of financial information is based.

2. Distinguish between capital expenditure and revenue expenditure. Compare the ways in which a sole trader and a public limited company might raise £50,000 to purchase some computer equipment.

3. Distinguish between long term and short term sources of finance. What factors might have given rise to the current popularity of debt factoring as a means of raising finance?

4. What does a balance sheet show? How might the asset structure of a retailer differ from that of a manufacturer?

5. Distinguish between tangible and intangible assets. What are the arguments for and against the inclusion of brand names as assets in a firm's balance sheet?

6. Discuss the relationship between the profit and loss account and the balance sheet. What effect might an extraordinary or exceptional item have on net profit in the profit and loss account?

7. Why is it necessary for a business organisation to provide for depreciation? Discuss the advantages and disadvantages of two different methods of calculating the annual depreciation allowance.

8. Explain what is meant by a 'liquidity crisis' and the possible outcomes of such a situation. What measures might a firm take to resolve a liquidity crisis?

9. How far is it possible to assess accurately the performance of a business organisation using ratio analysis?

10. What is meant by a budget in business? Explain the role that variance analysis plays in budgetary control.

Individuals, groups and organisations

A business is made up of **individuals**. Individual production workers, office workers or managers etc. belong to **groups** within the firm. Many tasks in modern business are technically complex, such as the production of a vehicle, and can only be carried out in groups using the combined skills of individuals. Other tasks, such as market research, may require people to work together as a co-ordinated 'team'. As well as these formal groups, individuals will also belong to informal groups, for example a group of workers who become friends after joining a company at the same time.

Individuals and the groups they belong to make up the business **organisation**. Units 57-64 examine how groups and organisations function. Units 47-56 concentrate on how individuals operate at work.

No two individuals are the same. They have different characteristics, attitudes, needs and personalities. Why does a business need to know something about these differences? It will help a business to:
- make sure it has chosen the most suitable person for a job from a number of applicants;
- make certain employees' skills are used effectively;
- ensure workers are satisfied and motivated;
- tell how individuals in the workforce will react when faced with a decision or a situation at work.

QUESTION 1 Jackson PLC are a large retail organisation. They place great emphasis on both the customer and the employee. The company believes that if it can recruit individuals because they are interested both in retailing and putting the customer first then there is more chance that they will be motivated. They recognise that different individuals have differing abilities and that the organisation needs both good till operators and good managers. Jackson PLC also believe in team work and good communications. Individuals are encouraged to work as part of groups and these groups are given responsibility for the tasks allocated to them. The effective harmonisation of individual, group and the business is how the company would like to be known.

(a) What are Jackson PLC looking for in the individuals they employ?
(b) Why might individuals need to work together in groups in the business?

Physical differences

It is very rare indeed for two individuals physically to be the same in all respects. It is possible, however, to group people based on their shape, size, hair colour etc.

Sometimes certain groups are more suitable for a job than others and this may be part of the **job description** (☞ unit 52). For example, people wanting to join the police force must be over a minimum height and an applicant to the fire service must have a certain chest expansion. A business, however, must be careful not to restrict physically demanding jobs to men as this type of **discrimination** is unlawful (☞ unit 55).

Personality differences

An individual could be described by the way they behave, such as 'happy-go-lucky' or 'quiet'. These give an indication of that person's personality. Psychologists call these words TRAITS. They form the basis of important theories of personality, some of which are used by businesses to make decisions about individuals at work.

In 1965 **Raymond Cattell** suggested that people have 16 main traits. To measure these traits he developed a test known as 16 Personality Factor (16PF). Figure 47.1 shows the 16 traits or factors that are measured in the test. Each one has a scale of 1-10. For example, factor 'A' could be reserved (1), outgoing (10) or somewhere in between. People taking the test choose a point on each scale which reflects their personality. Linking together the 'scores' will give a **personality profile.**

The 16PF is widely used in the selection of business managers. Kellogg's the cereal manufacturer, has used it successfully in the past. By looking at the profiles of successful managers a firm is able to build up a 'suitable' personality profile. When interviewing candidates in future, the business could ask them to fill in a 16PF test and compare their results with the 'ideal profile' to see if the candidate is suitable. Figure 47.1 shows the results of a study by Makin, Cooper and Cox. The line linking the scores shows the average personality profile of managing directors.

In 1975 **Hans Eysenck** reduced the number of scales upon which personality traits could be measured to two:
- stable-unstable;
- extroverted-introverted.

The stable-unstable scale showed emotional stability. Stable people tended to be calm and reliable, whilst those with low stability tended to be anxious or reserved. The extroverted-introverted scale described people who were either passive, quiet and withdrawn (introverted) or changeable, outgoing and impulsive (extroverted). Using these traits, Eysenck built a matrix of an individual's personality. This is shown in Figure 47.2. Individuals can be placed in one of the four quarters. A stable-introverted person may be calm and reliable, and perhaps suited to a job such as librarian. However, if the library needed an injection of new ideas a 'stable-extrovert' may be more suitable.

The matrix can have a number of uses for a business.

	LOW SCORE DESCRIPTION		HIGH SCORE DESCRIPTION
A	Reserved, detached, critical, aloof	1 2 3 4 5 6 7 8 9 10	Outgoing, warm-hearted, easygoing
B	Less intelligent, concrete thinking	1 2 3 4 5 6 7 8 9 10	More intelligent, abstract thinking
C	Affected by feelings, easily upset	1 2 3 4 5 6 7 8 9 10	Emotionally stable, calm, mature
E	Humble, mild, conforming	1 2 3 4 5 6 7 8 9 10	Assertive, competitive
F	Sober, prudent, taciturn	1 2 3 4 5 6 7 8 9 10	Happy-go-lucky, enthusiastic
G	Expedient, disregards rules	1 2 3 4 5 6 7 8 9 10	Conscientious, moralistic
H	Shy, timid	1 2 3 4 5 6 7 8 9 10	Socially bold
I	Tough-minded, realistic	1 2 3 4 5 6 7 8 9 10	Tender-minded, sensitive
L	Trusting, adaptable	1 2 3 4 5 6 7 8 9 10	Suspicious, hard to fool
M	Practical, careful	1 2 3 4 5 6 7 8 9 10	Imaginative, careless
N	Forthright, natural	1 2 3 4 5 6 7 8 9 10	Shrewd, calculating
O	Self-assured, confident	1 2 3 4 5 6 7 8 9 10	Apprehensive, troubled
Q1	Conservative, respects established ideas	1 2 3 4 5 6 7 8 9 10	Experimenting, radical
Q2	Group dependent, good 'follower'	1 2 3 4 5 6 7 8 9 10	Self-sufficient, resourceful
Q3	Undisciplined, self-conflict	1 2 3 4 5 6 7 8 9 10	Controlled, socially precise
Q4	Relaxed, tranquil	1 2 3 4 5 6 7 8 9 10	Tense, frustrated

Figure 47.1 *Cattell's 16 Personality Factor questionnaire showing managing directors' average personality profile*

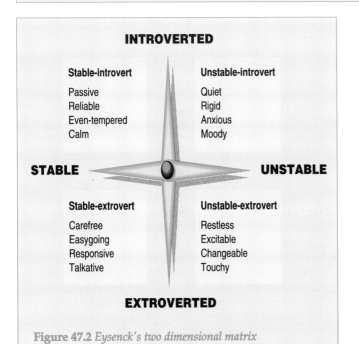

Figure 47.2 *Eysenck's two dimensional matrix*

For example, it could help judge how an employee might deal with a new situation or indicate how well a candidate might suit a particular job. A business may also use the information to build up a team of workers whose personalities complement each other to carry out a task.

There are, however, limits to how useful these theories can be. They do not precisely predict what a person will do in any situation, only indicate what a person is likely to do given their personality. Behaviour might, for example, change when faced with stress. Also, people with different personalities may still be able to do a 'good' job when faced with the same situation. Another problem is that they assume an individual will give an honest response. But often it is easy to pick out the acceptable answer or the one that is best in terms of the job. For these reasons, the theories are usually used only for selection and internal promotion (☞ unit 53).

QUESTION 2 **John Hardman** is an unlikely pop star. The chairman of Asda, Britain's third largest supermarket group, is a small, round man with glasses and a bluff Liverpudlian style.

On his own admission, he is not a man for detail, preferring the broader picture. 'I like to do things at my pace in my time ... I don't like to be disciplined or organised.' He can be stubborn.

He has none of the seriousness which goes with his job. He likes having a good time outside work, playing golf and supporting Liverpool FC. He has the type of mind that grasps issues quickly. 'I'm the sort of person who enjoys life', he says. 'I see these career guys working in business today - working and worrying. You have to have a life outside and a sense of humour.' His critics, however, argue he is a 'lightweight'.

Hardman is convinced he will regain the ground Asda lost to Sainsbury's, Tesco and Safeway in the 1980s. Derek Hunt, who worked closely with Hardman at Asda, believes that the current superstore formula is right.' He has had a lot of adversity, but he's a sticker and a survivor', he says about Hardman.

There are few insipid, tedious people in the world of advertising but, by his own admission, **Martin Sorrell** is one. He is the Chief Executive of WPP, the world's largest advertising and communications group, yet he describes himself as a 'dull, boring, little clerk'.

A graduate of Cambridge University and Harvard Business School, he is falling over himself to tell you he is not a clever person. But stupid people do not end up running an international advertising business with a £629,000 a year salary.

One colleague of Sorrell's says, 'He is petrified of being portrayed as a high flyer about to crash land. He knows that, to keep the city sweet, he has to project the image of the dull stable statesman. In reality he is a single-minded ruthless guy.'

'He's not the most affable man I've ever come across', says another ex-colleague. 'He has a stick and carrot approach to his employees. If you perform well you are rewarded. If not, then you are out. He doesn't suffer fools gladly. Everything has to be done immediately. He can be ruthless at times. I like working with him; he is pretty unflappable.' Sorrell commands a strong degree of loyalty and respect from his colleagues.

Source: adapted from *The Times*, 17.11.1990 and 8.12.1990.

(a) Using the evidence from these two descriptions, categorise the two men using Eysenck's personality traits matrix.
(b) How could Asda make use of the personality profile of John Hardman in the future?

Assessing personality in practice

The work of Cattell and Eysenck tried to 'measure' personality. In business, however, people judge the personality of others in less formal ways, and often fairly quickly. The decision may be based on what they themselves think is important. It could also be influenced by a 'stereotype' (☞ unit 55), where personality is linked to race, sex or age. For example, it may be claimed that female managers are more emotional than male.

It is argued that people get an impression of someone from the first piece of information they receive about that person's characteristics. In an interview, for example, recruiters often make up their minds in the first four minutes and rarely change them. A candidate that did not seem prepared, looked untidy or was abrupt may well have lost the job straight away. People make these decisions because they do not like being uncertain about others. A decision based on first impressions may make the interviewer feel more secure, even if it is wrong. It may take time and further contact before people are seen 'as they really are'. Employers and employees must be prepared to change their minds about people they meet and work with. Only then will they be able to make an 'accurate' assessment of someone's personality.

Differences in intelligence

As well as differing in personality, people differ in intelligence or IQ. There is considerable debate about what intelligence is. One definition, by American psychologist Arthur Jensen, is that it is the ability to discover rules, patterns and principles, and apply these to problems.

Intelligence is usually measured by using **IQ tests**. They test an individual's ability to reason. A simple IQ test question may ask for the next number in the sequence 1,3,6,10. This tests the ability to find a sequence and to apply it. An IQ 'score' is usually given at the end of the test. A high score is supposed to indicate a higher level of intelligence. Such tests are often criticised, particularly when comparing the intelligence of people in different social groups.

There are a number of factors which are thought to influence an individual's IQ although there is little agreement on exactly how they affect the IQ.

■ Culture and class. Many researchers argue that IQ tests are biased in favour of the middle classes, since tests are largely constructed by members of this group. Working class people tend to do less well on tests, so comparisons of intelligence between people in these groups are not really valid. It has also been shown that 'Western' IQ tests are not suitable for non-Western people. Cultural differences can mean they often approach and carry out the tests in an inappropriate way.

■ Genes. There is general agreement that intelligence can be inherited. Some psychologists, such as Hans Eysenck in Britain, suggest that some 80 per cent of intelligence is inherited from parents. The rest is influenced by environmental factors such as the environment where we live and grow up, diet, quality of housing and family size.

■ Environment. Some argue that differences in IQ are largely due to environmental factors. Research has shown that IQ test results can be affected by the education, motivation and physical health of the person taking the test. They can also be influenced by the person's rapport with whoever is carrying out the test and the language the test is set in.

Businesses today are now less likely to use IQ tests as a means of assessing an individual. Evidence suggests there is little connection between a person's IQ and how well he might do a job. It may be more important for a business to find out about an individual's knowledge and skills (which may include elements of IQ) as this could give a greater understanding of how a person might contribute to the organisation.

Differences in knowledge and skills

A business needs to know what knowledge and skills an employee has so that she can be given a position in the business where she will be of most use.

Knowledge can be technical, job specific, vocational or general. To be a plumber, a worker would need the technical knowledge of the trade, eg what types of materials and techniques are used for certain jobs. Also, the plumber would need to have knowledge about the way tasks should be carried out and a thorough knowledge of what is involved in the trade - the vocational aspects of being a plumber. In addition, the plumber may need to have more general knowledge, such as the ability to do simple mathematics.

As well as having knowledge, an employee will also need skills. These are the abilities needed to complete a task. The skills required at work can be job specific, communication skills, IT skills, numeracy and literacy skills or problem solving skills. A plumber would not only need to know how to complete a task, but have the appropriate skills to carry it out. The ability to communicate with customers may also be a useful skill.

Businesses in the 1990s want a more qualified and more skilled workforce. They expect workers to update their skills through training, and to develop new and different skills. This makes employees more adaptable and flexible.

Problem solving and decision making

Businesses are not only interested in the abilities of their employees, but in the way they use them to solve problems. The way in which an employee prefers to work

---

QUESTION 3

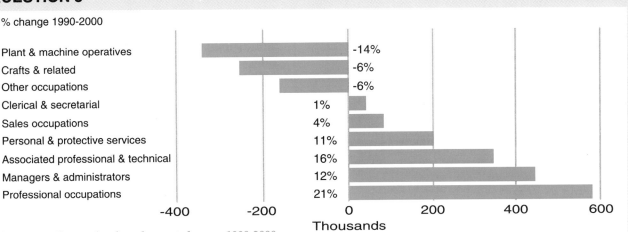

Figure 47.3 *Occupational employment changes, 1990-2000*

A report by the Institute of Careers Guidance entitled *1990s: Where Will the New Jobs Be?* suggests that highly skilled 'knowledge' workers will be well-placed to win the small number of new jobs with prospects in the UK during the rest of this decade. They will be the survivors as people struggle to avoid slipping into the group of temporary and less-skilled workers in the labour market of the 1990s. The scale of new job creation after the recession will be small. About 1.9 million new jobs will be created in service occupations, at a time when 1.2m blue-collar jobs will go. The report further indicates that business will continue the trend of retaining a small core workforce, with a temporary 'periphery' of staff with limited prospects. Skilled knowledge workers at all levels in the organisation and in whatever occupation will benefit from this shift at the expense of the less well-trained.

The report does, however, also indicate that skilled knowledge workers are not always ideal for employers. Their typically attractive higher-level qualifications and impressive work experience will be frequently offset by a high sense of self-worth, individualism, autonomy and enterprise which make them difficult to manage. Worse still for employers, these people are unlikely to consider loyalty to an organisation as important as loyalty to their 'craft' and will move jobs in search of greater job satisfaction and more money.

Even the most skilled worker is, however, unlikely to survive in the workplace of the 1990s without a talent for juggling 'multiple' careers and a commitment to continuous training.

Source: adapted from the *Financial Times*, 13.11. 1992.

(a) What are the trends for employment within business indicated in the article?
(b) Why might skilled knowledge workers be able to take advantage of these trends?
(c) What are the disadvantages of skilled knowledge workers to employers?

may cause problems if it differs from the way colleagues work or from what the business expects.

In 1984, Michael Kirton studied the way management initiatives in a business might succeed or fail. He suggested that success may depend on how **problem solving** was tackled and identified two approaches. ADAPTORS tend to solve problems by using existing or slightly modified approaches. They do not make rapid changes in the way problems are solved. INNOVATORS, however, try to find exciting and possibly unexpected ways of solving problems. Take the example of a small business having problems finding information quickly and easily when it is stored in files. The adaptor might suggest a better method of organising the files. An innovator, however, may feel that replacing the paper filing system with a computer system will be a better solution. These are two extremes. It is likely in business that people will have a combination of the two appproaches.

Both these approaches have their strengths and weaknesses. The adaptor can effectively work within the present system, but does not find it easy to seek new solutions. For example, an 'adaptor' working in marketing might look for new product developments using existing products. The innovator, on the other hand, may produce ideas for new products.

This approach often means that the innovator finds it difficult to get ideas accepted. Innovators may be seen as extroverts, generating lists of new ideas, but ignoring the needs of the business. Their attitude can often mean that an adaptor feels uncomfortable working with them. The adaptor, however, may appear conservative and always willing to agree with a superior.

What can managers do to minimise clashes? A study in 1991 by Makin, Cooper and Cox argued that the solution lies in understanding, together with an acceptance of the other person's position. Knowing someone else's style allows a manager to predict what they are likely to do in any situation.

Key terms

Adaptors - individuals who tend to solve problems by using existing or slightly modified approaches already used by the business.
Innovators - individuals who tend to solve problems by finding new, exciting and unexpected solutions to problems in a business.
Traits - words used in identifying an individual's personality.

Summary

1. State 3 reasons why businesses need to know about the different characteristics of individuals.
2. What is meant by the 16 Personality Factor?
3. Explain the terms:
   (a) stable;
   (b) unstable;
   (c) extrovert;
   (d) introvert;
   in relation to the work of Eysenck.
4. What characteristics might an unstable-extrovert have?
5. How might Eysenck's analysis of personality traits be used by business?
6. State 3 factors which are thought to influence an individual's intelligence.
7. What are the problems a business might face in using IQ tests?
8. State 5 differences in skills and knowledge that one employee might have from another.
9. Explain the difference between an innovator's and adaptor's approach to problem solving.
10. What might cause a clash between an innovator and an adaptor in the work setting?

QUESTION 4 The 1980s saw major problems emerging for British Home Stores (BHS), the UK high street retailer. The 1986 merger with Habitat-Mothercare resulted in the Storehouse Group. An attempt to improve the dowdy image of the stores over the next two years failed to improve sales and profits. Profits slumped from 71.1 million in 1987 to 27.5 million in 1990 and as recession gripped the company appeared to be heading for a crisis.

At the leading edge of BHS's revival has been David Dworkin, who was appointed in 1989 as chief executive of BHS and then later in 1992 assumed the same role at Storehouse. He studied BHS and found an overstaffed static company with little strategic vision. He did, however, believe that BHS had a great deal of potential - it was simply a question of unlocking it.

There followed a period of reorganisation under his guidance, where a number of simple and yet fundamental changes were made. Before his appointment the policy of BHS had been to keep products on the shelves at full price until they were sold. Unsold products were returned to stock and 'brought- out' at reduced prices for sales at Christmas and other times of the year. Against the advice of his colleagues, Dworkin implemented a system where slow selling stock was reduced in price immediately to clear. This allowed new ranges to be put on sale immediately, so that winter clothes, for example, would be available immediately at the end of summer - the summer stock being cleared at reduced prices.

With the help of outside consultants, Dworkin studied every link in the company's supply chain, speeding up the time it took to bring goods from the factories to the shop floor and reducing the number of suppliers from 850 to 500. By doing this BHS increased the volume of goods it bought from any one supplier, thereby improving buying terms. By July 1992 sales were up and profits rose to £37 million.

Source: adapted from the *Financial Times*, 28.10. 1992.

(a) How would you describe the approach of David Dworkin to decision-making?
(b) What potential advantages and disadvantages are there for BHS with his approach?

Question

A woman with ideas

Jane is a personnel officer in a large advertising agency. She has achieved rapid promotion in the company from her role as a secretary in the sales department to personnel officer with responsibility for recruitment. She did this by completing the Institute of Personnel Management qualifications through evening and weekend courses over a four year period. She was determined to do it and had the intelligence and perseverance finally to achieve her goal.

She has been in personnel for 2 years and has developed skills and knowledge in many different areas of the profession - in employee legislation, industrial relations issues and in her main interest of recruitment. Jane is outgoing (she had been tested and categorised as stable and extrovert using Eysenck's typology of personality) and popular with her peers. She has always believed in finding new ways to solve particular problems.

The latest problem she faced was the shortage of well qualified administrative staff who were competent in using the newly-installed computer system. The training given by the company was extremely comprehensive and it was difficult to replace lost employees with the same level of expertise.

Jane recognised that the problem consisted of two main elements. Firstly, not enough men were attracted to this area of work and, secondly, some of the women who had been trained were leaving to start a family. Due to poor local nursery provision, these women tended to stay at home rather than return to work after having children.

Her plan of action encompassed both aspects of the problem. She devised an educational campaign for the company aimed at men, in order that they might review their own ideas about the suitability of administrative work for males. In it she wanted to emphasise the promotion opportunities in administration work and how it was possible to achieve management status through the administrative route. She showed how administrative work had changed from traditionally repetitive office tasks to ones where high technology and problem solving skills were vital. She targeted the male sector by demonstrating that administrative work required types of skills that were often associated with men. At the same time, she planned to introduce creche facilities for the female employees of the company that would cost them far less than a private nursery and would also be cost effective for the organisation.

She drew up her plans and costed them out. The campaign materials and accompanying workshop sessions would be £5,000 for the year. The creche facilities would need capital expenditure of approximately £15,000. The ongoing costs would be met by the employees willing to make use of the service. At present it was costing them £35,000 to recruit and train the staff required for the administration vacancies in the company. She presented her findings to the executive board in a confident and assertive way.

The plan was rejected by senior management as too expensive in the short term and too far fetched. She was told to improve her selection procedures so that she recruited people that would stay. She was also told not to involve herself in other aspects of personnel work that were not her reponsibility.

Jane felt saddened and disillusioned by this experience.

(a) **How would you describe Jane's personality from the information?**
(b) **Identify the characteristics that have gained Jane rapid promotion in the business.**
(c) **What would be her approach to problem solving? Explain your answer using examples from the passage.**
(d) **What potential problems might her decision making approach cause for the business?**
(e) **Why do you think Jane's ideas were rejected by senior management?**
(f) **Suggest an alternative approach that Jane might have used when putting forward her plan.**

The satisfaction of needs

If asked, most people who work would probably say they do so to earn money to buy goods and services. However, this is not the only **need** that is satisfied by working.

A list of people's needs that may be satisfied from work might be very long indeed. It could include, for example, the need for variety in the workplace, which may be satisfied by an interesting job. Employees may also need to feel appreciated for the work they do, which could be reflected in the prestige attached to their job.

Unit 47 showed that individuals are not the same. Therefore, it is likely that lists made by any two people of their needs and how they can be satisfied will be very different. There are some reasons for working that could apply to everyone, such as the need to earn money. However, some reasons have more importance for particular individuals than others. One employee may need to work with friendly colleagues, whereas another might by happy working on his own.

Why is it important for a business to find out what satisfies the needs of its employees? It is argued that if an individual's needs are not satisfied, then that worker will not be MOTIVATED to work. This can affect the efficiency of the business as a whole. Businesses have found that even if employees are satisfied with pay and conditions at work, they also complain that their employer does not do a good job in motivating them. This applies to all levels, from the shopfloor to the boardroom. It appears in many companies that employers are not getting the full potential from their employees because they are not satisfying all of their employees' needs.

Figure 48.1 shows one example of how a business might make decisions, having first identified an employee's needs.

QUESTION 1 Rapid change and large scale redundancies have resulted in worsening morale among British Telecom's employees, a company survey has shown. Staff reported dissatisfaction with top management, with retraining, with input into decisions and, most of all, with the changes in the organisation. 59 per cent of the 126,000 respondents to BT's questionnaire - a 75 per cent response rate - said the changes introduced were bad for them, and 45 per cent believed they were bad for BT.

Follow-up discussion groups found most employees were concerned about the pace and unpredictability of the changes and how these would affect their future prospects.

The survey revealed that 92 per cent of staff liked their jobs, but only 49 per cent said they had job satisfaction, and 33 per cent reported they were satisfied with the recognition they received. It also found a low level of confidence in the reliability and performance of senior management. Only 32 per cent were confident that senior managers would do what they said, with 28 per cent expressing confidence in divisional managers. A mere 12 per cent had confidence in those running the company as a whole.

BT said that overall the results showed an increase in staff satisfaction in 20 areas but a deterioration in satisfaction in 41 areas. The company admitted to being disappointed at the results, but argued they were expected given the large wave of redundancies over the past few years.

Source: adapted from *Personnel Management*, March 1993.

(a) Identify the needs of the employees mentioned in the passage.
(b) How might the dissatisfaction shown in the survey affect the operation of British Telecom?
(c) Suggest how management may attempt to satisfy one of these needs.

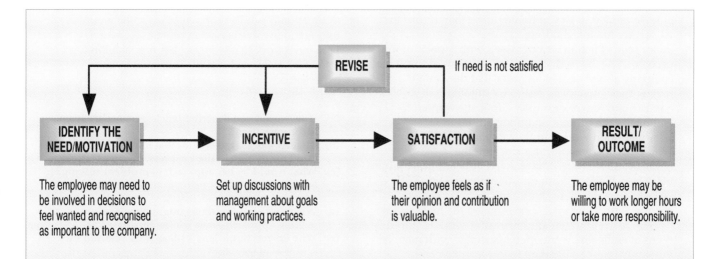

Figure 48.1 *Satisfying an individual's needs*

Maslow's hierarchy of needs

The first comprehensive attempt to classify needs was by **Abraham Maslow** in 1954. Maslow's theory consisted of two parts. The first concerned classification of needs. The second concerned how these classes are related to each other.

Maslow suggested that 'classes' of needs could be placed into a **hierarchy**. The hierarchy is normally presented as a 'pyramid', with each level consisting of a certain class of needs. This is shown in Figure 48.2.

The classes of needs were:

- physiological needs, eg wages high enough to meet weekly bills;
- safety needs, eg job security;
- love and belonging, eg working with colleagues that support you at work;
- esteem needs, eg being given recognition for doing a job well;
- self-actualisation, eg being promoted and given more responsibility.

Figure 48.2 can also be used to show the relationship between the different classes. Maslow argued that needs at the bottom of the pyramid are basic needs. They are concerned with survival. These needs must be satisfied before a person can move to the next level. For example, people are likely to be more concerned with basic needs, such as food, than anything else. At work an employee is unlikely to be concerned about acceptance from colleagues if he has not eaten for six hours.

Once each level is satisfied, the needs at this level become less important. The exception is the top level of SELF-ACTUALISATION. This is the need to fulfil your potential. Maslow argued that although everyone is capable of this, in practice very few reach this level.

Each level of needs is dependent on the levels below. Say an employee has been motivated at work by the opportunity to take responsibility, but finds he may lose his job. The whole system collapses, as the need to feed and provide for himself and his dependents again becomes the most important need.

Maslow's ideas have great appeal for business. The

SELF-ACTUALISATION
- Realising your full potential

ESTEEM NEEDS
- Gaining the esteem and respect of others
- Gaining self-esteem and self-respect
- Feeling competent

LOVE AND BELONGING
- Receiving and giving love, affection, trust and acceptance
- Affiliating with or being part of a group

SAFETY NEEDS
- Protection from dangerous objects or situations
- Protection from physical and psychological threats
- The importance of routine and familiarity

PHYSIOLOGICAL NEEDS
- Obtaining food, drink, air, rest and activity

Figure 48.2 *Maslow's hierarchy of needs*

message is clear - find out which level each individual is at and decide on suitable rewards.

Unfortunately the theory has problems when used in practice. Some levels do not appear to exist for certain individuals, while some rewards appear to fit into more than one class. Money, for example, needs to be used to purchase 'essentials' such as food, but it can also be seen as a status symbol or an indicator of personal worth.

There is also a problem in deciding when a level has actually been 'satisfied'. There will always be exceptions to the rules Maslow outlined. A well motivated designer may spend many hours on a creative design despite lack of sleep or food.

QUESTION 2 Sarah Geddes has recently been appointed as production controller in a printing works. She was chosen for the job because of her experience in operating the machines and her knowledge of the use of computer generated film, which was increasingly being employed. When Sarah arrived she found that mistakes were being made because the printing works was not yet used to working with this type of film. The other employees in the production department were a little sceptical about how Sarah wanted to reorganise the department. Whilst realising the need to change with the new technology, they were not yet prepared to accept the changing work methods.

Sarah felt that a great deal of work was necessary in the reorganisation. She was often found at eleven at night working on plans. She had even been known to work over weekends to make sure that the new equipment was being installed correctly.

(a)   What might you conclude about the 'level' on Maslow's hierarchy that Sarah has achieved at the moment?

(b)   What need do you think the printing workers are being motivated by at present? Explain your answer.

(c)   What might be the problem in using Maslow's ideas in describing Sarah's motivation?

Taylor's Scientific Management

Research into the factors that motivate individuals had been carried out long before Maslow's 'hierarchy' of needs. **Frederick W. Taylor** set out a theory of SCIENTIFIC MANAGEMENT in his book **The Principles of Scientific Management** in 1911. Many of the ideas of today's 'scientific management school' come from the work of Taylor.

The turn of the century in the USA was a time of rapid expansion. Compared to today, the organisation of work on the shop floor was left much more in the hands of workers and foremen. Workers often brought their own tools and decisions about the speed of machines were left to operators. There were few training programmes to teach workers their jobs and skills were gained simply by watching more experienced colleagues. Decisions about selection, rest periods and layoffs were frequently made by foremen.

Taylor suggested that such arrangements were haphazard and inefficient. Management did not understand the shop floor and allowed wasteful work practices to continue. Workers, on the other hand, left to their own devices, would do as little as possible. 'Soldiering' would also take place (working more slowly together so that management did not realise workers' potential) and workers would carry out tasks in ways they were used to rather than the most efficient way.

Taylor's scientific principles were designed to reduce inefficiency of workers and managers. This was to be achieved by 'objective laws' that management and workers could agree on, reducing conflict between them. Neither party could argue against a system of work that was based on 'science'. Taylor believed his principles would create a partnership between manager and worker, based on an understanding of how jobs should be done and how workers are motivated.

Taylor's approach How did Taylor discover what the 'best way' was of carrying out a task? Table 48.1 shows an illustration of Taylor's method.

Table 48.1 Taylor's method, designed to find the 'best way' to carry out a task at work

- Pick a dozen skilled workers.
- Observe them at work and note down the elements and sequences adopted in their tasks.
- Time each element with a stop watch.
- Eliminate any factors which appear to add nothing to the completion of the task.
- Choose the quickest method discovered and fit them in their sequence.
- Teach the worker this sequence; do not allow any change from the set procedure.
- Include time for rest and the result will be the 'quickest and best' method for the task. Because it is the best way, all workers selected to perform the task must adopt it and meet the time allowed.
- Supervise workers to ensure that these methods are carried out during the working day.

Taylor had a very simple view of what motivated people at work - money. He felt that workers should receive a 'fair day's pay for a fair day's work', and pay should be linked to output through piece rates (☞ unit 49). A worker who did not produce a 'fair day's work' would face a loss of earnings; exceeding the target would lead to a bonus.

In 1899 Taylor's methods were used at the Bethlehem Steel Works in the USA, where they were responsible for raising pig-iron production almost 400 per cent per man per day. Taylor found the 'best way to do each job' and designed incentives to motivate workers.

Taylor's message for business is simple - allow workers to work and managers to manage based on scientific principles of work study. Many firms today still attempt to use Taylor's principles. In early 1993 the Bishop of Salford, when shown around a Littlewoods store was told by the store manager that what he was looking for from potential Littlewoods workers was 'strong backs and nimble fingers'. This may not have been the official approach from Littlewoods, but it was seen locally as the use of Taylor's ideas.

Problems with Taylor There are a number of problems with Taylor's ideas. The notion of a 'quickest and best way' for all workers does not take into account individual differences (☞ unit 47). There is no guarantee that the 'best way' will suit everyone.

Taylor also viewed people at work more as machines, with financial needs, than as humans in a social setting. There is no doubt that money is an important motivator. Taylor overlooked that people also work for reasons other than money. A survey in the early 1980s (Warr, 1982) asked a large sample of British people if they would continue to work if it were not financially necessary to do so. Nearly 70 per cent of men and 65 per cent of women said they would. This suggests there may be other needs that must be met at work, which Taylor ignored, but were recognised in Maslow's ideas which came later.

QUESTION 3 Anmac Ltd are a small expanding high-tech company. They employ approximately 25 workers in two factories, one at Chester and one at Stafford. The employers organise work on a fairly informal basis. Workers work at their own pace, which often results in a variable level of output. Recently orders for their advanced micro-electronic circuit boards have increased rapidly. The firm has decided that, to cope with the orders, increased production is needed. Two suggestions have been put forward.
- Encourage the workers to work overtime at the Chester plant.
- Redeploy some of the workers from Chester to Stafford where there is a shortfall of workers.
The workers at the Chester plant are mainly married women in their twenties, many with young, school aged children and husbands who also work.

(a) How can Taylor's scientific management principles be used to solve the problems faced by Anmac Ltd?
(b) What problems might Anmac Ltd find in using such principles?

Human relations

Taylor's scientific management ideas may have seemed appealing at first glance to business. Some tried to introduce his ideas in the 1920s and 1930s which led to industrial unrest. Others found that financial incentives did motivate workers, and still do today. However, what was becoming clear was that there were other factors which may affect workers' motivation.

The Hawthorne studies Many of the ideas which are today known as the 'human relations school' grew out of experiments between 1927 and 1932 at the Hawthorne Plant of the Western Electric company in Chicago. Initially these were based on 'scientific management' - the belief that workers' productivity was affected by work conditions, the skills of workers and financial incentives.

Over the five year period, changes were made in incentive schemes, rest periods, hours of work, lighting and heating and the effect on workers' productivity was measured. One example was a group of six women assembling telephone relays. It was found that whatever changes were made, including a return to the original conditions, output rose. This came to be known as the HAWTHORNE EFFECT.

The study concluded that changes in conditions and financial rewards had little or no effect on productivity. Increases in output were mainly due to the greater cohesion and communication which workers in groups developed as they interacted and were motivated to work together. Workers were also motivated by the interest shown in their work by the researchers. This result was confirmed by further investigations in the Bank Wiring Observation where fourteen men with different tasks were studied.

The work of **Elton Mayo** (and Roethlisberger and Dickson) in the 1930s, who reported on the Hawthorne Studies, has led to what is known today as the human relations school. A business aiming to maximise productivity must make sure that the 'personal satisfactions' of workers are met for workers to be motivated. Management must also work and communicate with informal work groups, making sure that their goals fit in with the goals of the business. One way to do this is to allow such groups to be part of decision making. Workers are likely to be more committed to tasks that they have had some say in.

There are examples of these ideas being used in business today. The Volvo plant in Uddevalla, opened in 1989, was designed to allow workers to work in teams of 8-10. Each team built a complete car and made decisions about production. Volvo found that absenteeism rates at Uddevalla averaged 8 per cent, compared to 25 per cent in their Gothenburg plant which used a production line system. Other examples might be:
- Honda's plant in Swindon where 'teamwork' is emphasised - there are no workers or directors, only 'associates';
- McDonald's picnics, parties and McBingo for their employees where they are made to feel part of the company;
- Mary Kay's seminars in the USA, which are presented like the American Academy awards for company employees;
- Tupperware sales rallies, where everyone gets a 'badge' and has their achievements recognised.

Problems There are a number of criticisms of the human relations school.
- It assumes workers and management share the same goals. This idea of workplace 'consensus' may not always exist. For example, in 1983 Austin Rover tried to introduce a programme called 'Working with Pride'. It was an attempt to raise quality by gaining employee commitment. This would be achieved by greater communication with employees. The programme was not accepted throughout the company. As one manager stated, 'Since 1983 we've tried the face-to-face

communications approach. It works to a degree, but we are not too good at the supervisory level ... enthusiasm for the Working with Pride programme is proportionate to the level in the hierarchy. For supervisors it's often just seen as a gimmick ...'.

■ It is assumed that communication between workers and management will break down 'barriers'. It could be argued, however, that the knowledge of directors' salaries or redundancies may lead to even more 'barriers' and unrest.

■ It is biased towards management. Workers are manipulated into being productive by managers. It may also be seen as a way of reducing trade union power.

QUESTION 4

Table 48.2 *The effect of introducing a piece rate system into clothes manufacture*

Group	Number in group	Action taken to introduce system	Resignations within within 40 days of introduction	Change in output
A	100	Group told the changes will take place next week	17%	-2%
B	150	Management introduces changes with the help of group to suit their needs	0%	+10%
C	200	Group told the changes will take place next week	7%	0%
D	50	Management explains the need for change to group	2%	+2%
E	100	Management explains the need for change and discusses this with the group	0%	+5%

Table 48.2 shows the results of a survey carried out in Bryant and Gillie, a manufacturer of children's clothing. The company introduced a piece rate system of work - a system where employees are paid according to the number or quantity of items they produce. Five groups were involved in the new system. Different actions were taken to introduce the system to each group. The table shows the effect on labour turnover and output of these actions.

(a) To what extent do the results support the human relations explanation of workers' motivation?

(b) Using the results of the survey in Table 48.2, advise the management on the likely action needed to motivate workers when changing work practices.

Theory X and Theory Y

In 1960 **Douglas McGregor** published *The Human Side of Enterprise*. It was an attempt to apply the implications of Maslow and the work of Taylor and Mayo to business. In it, he gives different reasons why people work. He coined the terms Theory X and Theory Y to describe these differences. Table 48.3 shows the main ideas of the two theories.

Table 48.3 *Theory X and Theory Y*

Theory X	Theory Y
• Workers are motivated by money	• Workers have many different needs which motivate them
• Workers are lazy and dislike work	• Workers can enjoy work
• Workers are selfish, ignore the needs of organisations, avoid responsibility and lack ambition	• If motivated, workers can organise themselves and take responsibility
• Workers need to be controlled and directed by management	• Management should create a situation where workers can show creativity and apply their job knowledge

Theory X assumes that people are lazy. If this is accepted, then the only way to get people to work is by using strict control. This control can take one of two forms. One method is to use coercion - the threat of punishment if rules are broken or targets not achieved. This is often known as the 'stick' approach. The problem with threats is that they are only effective if the person being threatened believes that they will be carried out. Modern employment laws (☞ unit 56), and company wide agreements, have made this difficult for managers. For this reason, a 'carrot' approach may be more suitable. People have to be persuaded to carry out tasks by promises or rewards. In many ways this theory is similar to Taylor's view of people at work as shown earlier in this unit.

Theory Y, on the other hand, assumes that most people are motivated by those things at the top of Maslow's hierarchy. In other words, people are responsible, committed and enjoy having control over work. Most people, given the opportunity, will get involved in work, and contribute towards the solution of a problem that may arise. This theory is similar in some ways to the **human relations school.**

Business managers tend to say that their own assumptions are closer to Theory Y than to Theory X. But tests on management training courses tend to show that their attitudes are closer to Theory X than they might like to admit. In addition, many managers suggest that, while they themselves are like Theory Y, workers are closer to Theory X.

In practice, it could be argued that most firms behave according to Theory X, especially where shopfloor workers are concerned. The emphasis is on the use of money and control to encourage workers to behave in the 'correct way'. The same organisations might behave according to the assumptions of Theory Y when dealing

Barton Air Conditioner Ltd produce air conditioner equipment for the construction industry. Over the last 5 years they have had 3 redundancy programmes because of a downturn in sales caused by the recession. The workers were naturally very defensive about their jobs and morale was very low. This was reflected in the poor delivery and quality of performance. 65 per cent of deliveries were over 14 days late, and poor quality output was costing approximately £1 billion, accounting for 15 per cent of the total manufacturing bill.

Paul James, from the US, was recently appointed as the new managing director. His first statement on arrival to the company was to announce to staff a promise of no more redundancies and a four year programme for 'growth through teamwork'. The first action taken was to order the sales department to aim for steady growth. The second action was to set the factory the objective of establishing an efficient system of production control. The third action, which surprised staff, was not to dictate how this objective should be achieved as the previous management had done. Instead he encouraged managers to work in teams with engineers and shopfloor workers to decide on the correct strategy. This encouraged the workforce to participate in the decision making. The higher motivation showed through in product quality. Paul James also made sure that managerial vacancies at the company were filled by candidates who were not only technically qualified but who were also committed to a bottom-up approach to employee involvement. Authoritarian, top-down managers were rejected.

(a) Discuss the management styles of the previous management and of Paul James in terms of McGregor's Theory X and Theory Y.
(b) What implications does the approach taken by Paul James have for the company?

with management. A representative of a banker's union wrote in the *Independent on Sunday*, 'The lower down the ladder you are, the less control you have over your work environment. Managers can do as they please, stretch their legs whenever they want. Clerical workers , if they are working in a data-processing centre, for example doing entries for cheques or credit cards, are disciplined if they don't complete a given number of key strokes in an hour or a day. Half the time they don't know what they are doing. They don't see any end product. More and more work has been downgraded.'

Herzberg's two-factor theory

In 1966 **Fredrick Herzberg** attempted to find out what motivated people at work. He asked a group of professional engineers and accountants to describe incidents in their jobs which gave them strong feelings of satisfaction or dissatisfaction. He then asked them to describe the causes in each case.

Results Herzberg divided the causes into two **categories** or **factors**. These are shown in Figure 48.3.
■ MOTIVATORS. These are the factors which give workers **job satisfaction**, such as recognition for their effort. Increasing these motivators is needed to give job satisfaction. This, it could be argued, will make workers more productive. A business that rewards its workforce for, say, achieving a target is likely to motivate them to be more productive. However, this is not guaranteed, as other factors can also affect productivity.
■ HYGIENE FACTORS. These are factors that can lead to workers being **dissatisfied**, such as pay or

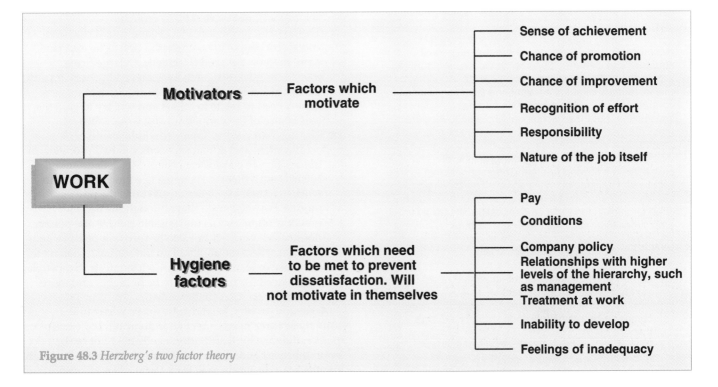

Figure 48.3 *Herzberg's two factor theory*

conditions. Improving hygiene factors should remove dissatisfaction. For example, better canteen facilities may make workers less dissatisfied about their environment. An improvement in hygiene factors alone is not likely to **motivate** an individual. But if they are not met, there could be a fall in productivity.

There is some similarity between Herzberg's and Maslow's ideas. They both point to needs that have to be satisfied for the employee to be motivated. Herzberg argues that only the higher levels of Maslow's hierarchy motivate workers.

Herzberg's ideas are often linked with **job enrichment** (☞ unit 50). This is where workers have their jobs 'expanded', so that they can experience more of the production process. This allows the workers to be more involved and motivated, and have a greater sense of achievement. Herzberg used his ideas in the development of clerical work. He selected a group of workers in a large corporation. Performance and job attitudes were low. Herzberg redesigned these jobs so that they were given more responsibility and recognition.

Problems Herzberg's theory does seem to have some merits. Improving pay or conditions, for example, may remove dissatisfaction at first. Often, however, these things became taken for granted. It is likely that better conditions will be asked for in following years. Evidence of this can be seen in wage claims which aim to be above the rate of inflation in some businesses every year. Job

enrichment may also be expensive for many firms. In addition, it is likely that any benefits from job improvements will not be seen for a long time and that businesses will not be able to continue with such a policy in periods of recession.

Surveys that have tried to reproduce Herzberg's results have often failed. This may have been because different groups of workers have been examined and different techniques used. Also, there is a problem in relying too much on what people say they find satisfying or dissatisfying at work as this is subjective. For example, if things go wrong at work individuals have a tendency to blame it on others or factors outside of their control. On the other hand if individuals feel happy and satisfied when they are at work then they tend to see it as their own doing.

McClelland's managerial needs

David McClelland suggested that what motivates people is that they learn in early childhood that certain types of behaviour lead to 'gratification'. They develop needs based on this behaviour. For example, a girl may have a great need to achieve, encouraged by parents who help her to be successful at school. When she becomes employed, she will behave in a similar way. There are, McClelland argues, three basic needs - achievement, affiliation, power.

- The need for achievement. This is one of the keys to a company's success. People who have high achievement needs often become successful entrepreneurs (☞ unit 2). Such people like to take responsibility and risks, and want quick feedback on how they have performed. They like to set their own goals and standards and achieve these on their own. However, it is also likely that people with a need to achieve will not work well in groups.
- The need for affiliation. McClelland found that some successful people in business did not, as he expected, score high on the need to achieve. In large firms, managers' goals can often by achieved by working with others, rather than their own efforts. Such managers have a need to relate to others and will try to gain the acceptance of their superiors and work colleagues.
- The need for power. Some individuals with high achievement and affiliation needs still had problems in influencing or controlling others, McClelland found. To be successful there was often a need to get people to work together. McClelland called this the power motive. He recognised that although the need for power is often seen as undesirable (where one person dominated others) it can also be seen in a positive light. It might reflect the ability of an individual to persuade, influence or lead people. Research suggests that people with a need for power tend to be in higher and more influential positions in business.

According to McClelland, a business needs to know how these three needs affect an individual. For example, a person that has high affiliation needs may not make a good marketing manager. Such a person would, based on the theory, constantly look for acceptance and support for

---

QUESTION 6 Job satisfaction and well-being among employees in the public sector falls significantly following privatisation, according to a recent research study. An analysis of over 600 employees in a water company showed that six months after privatisation, levels of job satisfaction and mental and physical well-being had dropped markedly among all levels of employees.

The research found that the causes of increased job dissatisfaction revolved around the organisational structure and climate. It was felt to be less supportive, with increased competition and less trust. Added to this were fears over job security and a feeling of loss of control. All employees experienced a drop in satisfaction, but those at manual and staff level were more affected than managers by a feeling of a lack of control.

The research showed that after one year of privatisation following re-organisation people feel secure and satisfaction rises again. The conclusions to the research were that it is more effective to implement change quickly and that communicating effectively to all employees increases their feeling of control.

Source: adapted from *Personnel Management*.

(a) Identify from this article the factors that might increase workers' dissatisfaction.
(b) How might the management of a privatised water company increase motivation using Herzberg's theory?
(c) Why might an increase in job satisfaction not necessarily lead to increased productivity?

all decisions. It is likely that this job would need someone who was far more self-motivated.

Vroom/Lawler and Porter

The theories of motivation that have been dealt with so far assume that people try to meet goals and so satisfy their needs. Vroom's and Lawler and Porter's theories state that this relationship is not so simple. First, each individual will have different goals. Secondly, people only act to achieve their goals if they feel there is a chance of success. Thirdly, the value of the goal to the individual will also affect that person's motivation.

These theories might affect the way a business designs its pay and benefit systems and also the design of tasks and jobs to enable people to satisfy their needs. They take into account that people have different needs, and that some may want autonomy and responsibility at work, whereas others may not.

Criticisms of motivation theories

At first sight it would appear that a business interested in increasing its employees' motivation at work has a fairly simple task. The theories in this unit are divided into two groups. The scientific management/Theory X group argues that workers are lazy, need controlling and are only interested in monetary rewards. The human relations school/Theory Y/Vroom group argues workers have many needs that might be achieved if they have more control and responsibility. A business, it seems, only needs to identify which view is effective and use the findings to motivate its workforce.

In practice it is difficult to conclude whether either one of these broad perspectives is 'right or wrong'. Any one view may be right or wrong depending on the circumstances. If the business is geared towards hierarchy and authority, and work is routine and monotonous, people may choose to do such work in return for cash. For example, in 1969 Goldthorpe and Lockwood in their famous study, *The Affluent Worker*, found that workers on a Vauxhall car assembly line saw work as a means to earn high wages. This would allow workers to enjoy life outside work more. Wedderburn

and Crompton's study in 1972 of a large chemical plant in North East England found much the same thing. Their results showed that the level of pay, job security and good welfare benefits were far more important to workers than job interest. In such cases, individuals regard monetary rewards as being more important than such factors as responsibility.

However, at other times, job interest and involvement may outweigh financial rewards. This may be true, for instance, in worker buyouts, when employees are prepared to accept lower financial rewards to maintain job security and have a say in the running of the business.

What conclusion can be drawn from these points?
- Employees are likely to have different priorities at different times and in different circumstances.
- Employees aiming to increase their wage or salary are not likely to show much interest in job satisfaction (at that time).
- When employees are not involved in pay bargaining then they are likely to be interested in the quality of working life and job satisfaction.
- A business cannot generalise about what motivates people. It must try to understand the views workers may have at any one time, before deciding how best to motivate them.

Key terms

Hawthorne effect - the idea that workers are motivated by recognition given to them as a group.
Hygiene factors - those things that can lead to workers being dissatisfied.
Motivated - being encouraged to do something.
Motivators - those things that can lead to workers being satisfied.
Self-actualisation - a level on Maslow's hierarchy where an employee realises his or her full potential.
Scientific management - a theory that suggests that there is a 'best' way to perform work tasks.

Summary

1. Why is it important for business to satisfy workers?
2. Name 5 needs in Maslow's hierarchy that an individual might have at work.
3. What are the aims of Taylor's scientific management theory?
4. According to Taylor, how are people motivated?
5. What is meant by the human relations school of thought?
6. What, according to the human relations school, is the main motivator at work?
7. Explain the difference between Theory X and Theory Y.
8. How is Theory X like Taylor's view of scientific management?
9. According to Herzberg's theory, what factors are likely to:
   (a) increase job satisfaction;
   (b) reduce dissatisfaction at work?
10. What conclusions can a business draw from the criticisms of motivation theory?

Question

British Telecom

British Telecom's (BT) quality programme was launched by its chairman in 1987. It was split into two phases: a 'commitment to action' programme for all 35,000 managers, to end in 1990, followed by a similar training programme for the rest of the workforce.

The training looked at what Total Quality Management (TQM) was, the impact it might have on BT, the priorities for change and a few simple problem solving and team working techniques. Quality projects were set up and quality certainly improved in many areas of the business. Training laid the groundwork for later quality initiatives. The main problem with the programme, however, was that it was too slow in being brought down BT's hierarchy. People at lower levels viewed the improvement projects as some sort of management game - not real business. In 1989 the chairman decided to rejuvenate the quality programme. The new project was to make the company more customer focused. It was named Project Sovereign.

Sovereign was a complete restructuring of BT into customer-orientated divisions in place of the old geographical divisions and a reduction in management levels from 12 to 6. This meant the loss of 5,000 managers' jobs and enormous changes for those that remained.

The announcement of Sovereign led to great uncertainty and for much of 1990 TQM lost its way at BT. Then in November the chairman made an important speech on quality, setting out priorities. The initiative on quality seemed to regain its momentum. So, having given Project Sovereign a year to get established, the company relaunched its training initiative, to cascade quality down to the 160,000 non-managerial staff. This was named the 'Involving Everyone' project.

'Involving Everyone' is seen by BT as the key to embedding quality at the grassroots. It has a number of new features. First, the initial one day course is followed up by at least four team meetings in the workplace. Secondly, quality specialists are deployed to provide back-up in the workplace.

So far, including team leaders, 30,000 have been through the programme at the rate of 1,000 a day, and another 130,000 are still to go. At the very least delegates appear to enjoy the day and are motivated by the idea of team-working. Many examples of successful projects using team work are filtering back to senior management. One particular example of effective team-working is based in BT's Guildford region where a group of 20 jointers - the engineers who join up cables - set up a quality improvement team of four. Its task was to examine why reports were coming in of failures in the underground ironwork which supports the cable joints. In previous times the jointers would have correctly identified this as a problem originating outside their group and, having apportioned the blame, washed their hands of it. Instead they carried out a survey, masterminded by the quality improvement team - to find out precisely how many joints were suffering from poor support and who supplied the supports. The team then informed the suppliers and discussed what action to take next. The team members recognise that they are more involved in why things go wrong and therefore more inclined to find solutions. They feel it has improved the job that they do.

But there are still problems. BT announced a further wave of voluntary redundancies, known as 'Release 92' in early 1992, triggered chiefly by new technology. This produced a glut of volunteers - around 40,000 compared with 20,000 planned initially. While this could be attributed to a generous redundancy package, it also indicated that morale was rock-bottom: an internal audit in spring 1993 showed only a third of those responding were happy with the company.

Arguably, a TQM approach is more urgent than ever in this climate. But some in BT believe cosy notions of working in teams - described as 'families' in the training literature - go down like a lead balloon among people who are cynical about the company and nervous about the future. Peter Burgess, an engineer and a delegate on 'Involving Everyone' had recently been informed of his second job change in months. The first one, he said, had come after only 24 hours' notice:

'There seems to be a conflict between the quality philosophy and the way staff seem to be treated as numbers on budget sheets, being moved around without any consultation. So I think low morale needs to be tackled first.'

Source: adapted from *Personnel Management Plus*, October 1992.

(a) Why did the quality initiative not succeed in the initial stages from 1987 - 1990?
(b) Using your understanding of motivation theories what would you have done to ensure the initial programme might have been more successful?
(c) Why do you think BT set up the 'Involving Everyone' campaign when they did?
(d) Using Herzberg's theory, why do you think the jointers in the quality improvement team experienced greater levels of job satisfaction?
(e) Explain why more workers than expected were interested in taking voluntary redundancy in 1992.
(f) What do you feel BT could do to enhance motivation, more generally, across the workforce?

Financial and non-financial rewards

Unit 48 outlined theories which have tried to explain the factors that motivate people at work. Some of these theories stress that money is the most important factor. The scientific/Theory X approach, in particular, argues that workers respond to **financial rewards**. It is argued that such rewards are necessary to motivate a reluctant workforce. Employees see work as a means to an end. As a result they are far more likely to be interested in monetary rewards.

In contrast, the human relations/Theory Y view argues that workers are motivated by a variety of factors. An employee working in a car assembly plant, for example, may be highly motivated by working as part of a team. Poor pay may lead to employees being dissatisfied, which can make other **non-financial rewards** less effective in motivating them.

The next two units examine how these theories can be used. This unit looks at how a business might use financial rewards and incentives.

Payment schemes

How are employees rewarded for the work they do? There are a number of methods that may be used.

Time rates TIME RATES are used when workers are rewarded for the amount of time they spend at work. Employees are paid in the form of weekly **wages** or monthly **salaries**. For most workers in the UK, pay is fixed in relation to the standard working week of 36 hours. Workers who work longer than this may be paid **overtime**, perhaps at a higher rate. In addition, holidays with pay are included for most British industries. Examples of time rates are the £19,000 a year paid to teachers with experience at the top of the standard national scale or the £3.30 per hour paid to a cleaner in, say, Newcastle.

Time rates are a simple way of calculating pay for a business. They are useful when a firm wants to employ workers to do specialist or difficult tasks that should not be rushed. Employees can ensure that work is of a high quality without worrying about the time they take.

Time rates are also useful when working out the pay of service sector employees or people working in groups. In these cases it is very difficult for a firm to work out the exact value of the employee's output. An example might be doctors, where it is virtually impossible to calculate the value of work. From an employee's point of view, time rates guarantee income.

Piece rates A system of PIECE RATES is the easiest way for a business to make sure that employees are paid for the amount of work they do. Employees are paid an agreed rate for every item produced. For this reason it is known as a PAYMENT BY RESULTS system. It is often used in the textile industry. Piece rates are arguably an INCENTIVE to workers. The more they produce, the more they earn.

From a business' point of view, this system links pay to output. However, there are a number of problems. Employees have no basic pay to fall back on if machinery fails or if the quality of the goods produced is unacceptable. Trade unions, in particular, have campaigned against this method of payment as it often results in low pay and low living standards. There have also been disputes in the past about what 'rate' should be paid. Some firms may feel that the method encourages workers to sacrifice quality in favour of higher rewards.

Because of the problems of lack of basic pay, most firms use a system where pay is made up of two elements. There is a fixed or basic pay, calculated on the time worked and a variable element, often when a **target** has been reached. It is argued that this extra element motivates workers to increase productivity, while the time element gives security. Incentive schemes are dealt with later in this unit.

Commission In some businesses COMMISSION makes up the total earnings of the workers. This is true of some insurance salespeople and some telesales employees. Commission, like piece rates, is a reward for the quantity (or value) of work. Employees are paid a percentage of the value of each good or service that is sold. It could be argued that it suffers from the same problems and gives the same incentive as a piece rate system. The benefit to the employer is that it can indicate the level of business 'won' rather than just output achieved. Earnings surveys have shown that the numbers of people receiving commission is falling. The proportion of people's total earnings made up of commission is also declining.

Fees Fees are payments made to people for 'one-off' tasks. Tasks tend to be geared towards the needs of the client, rather than a standard service or product. The amount paid will depend on a variety of factors. These might include the time taken to finish the task or the difficulty of the task. Often fees are paid to people providing services, such as solicitors, performers etc.

Fringe Benefits Fringe benefits are payments other than wages or salaries. They include things like private medical insurance, profit-related bonus schemes, a company car, subsidised meals, transport allowances, loan or mortgage facilities etc. Fringe benefits have grown in importance since the 1960s. This is especially the case in the executive, management and professional area. From an employer's view, providing benefits rather than pay may actually be cheaper. For the employee, receiving benefits rather than pay might also be preferred. For example, the AA calculated that in 1986 the cost of owning a car for a 10,000-mile-a-year driver was £3,770 each year. Despite their attraction, fringe benefits can cause status problems. Also, benefits such as a company car may be liable for tax.

QUESTION 1 The car is still the most common perk offered by British companies, although one in five is now letting employees trade cars for a higher salary. The findings, published by the CBI (Confederation of British Industry), indicate that employee benefits have not generally been cut during the recession. Fringe benefits have survived relatively unscathed despite the heavy cost they add to pay bills. Benefits typically add 10 per cent-15 per cent to the salary costs of basic level employees and 40 per cent-50 per cent for executives.

Almost all companies surveyed - 98 per cent - offer cars to at least some of their employees. Cars even outstripped pensions, which were provided by 93 per cent of companies, and life assurance, also offered by 93 per cent. Bottom of the perks league were vouchers for childcare, at 2 per cent, with on-site creches not far ahead on 4 per cent.

The CBI said the survey showed that the type of benefit paid lagged behind changes in the workforce. Companies said the main changes in their workforce were the growth of employees with partners who were also earning, an increase in employees' average ages and an increase in the number of women workers.

Companies had not adapted benefits to those changes. For example, a majority of companies continued to pay for private medical insurance cover for husbands and wives when it was possible that they now qualified for medical cover in their own right. There was also evidence that older workers valued non-monetary benefits such as being allowed to act as mentors to younger colleagues.

Many employers are reviewing their policies on cars because of increasing costs and because Inland Revenue reforms may mean that tax payments increase by up to 40 per cent for company car drivers. Companies in the financial sector and those with US parents were leading the field in substituting cash for company cars or eliminating car schemes altogether, the survey found.

Source: adapted from the *Financial Times*, 1992.

(a) Why might fringe benefits be considered a method of payment for workers?
(b) From the information in the article, suggest the types of benefit that will decrease and increase in the next 10 years.
(c) Why might older people be less interested in fringe benefits?

Employer objectives for pay

There are a number of objectives employers will have when paying their workforce.

Motivation It has been argued that workers are motivated by money (☞ unit 48). This may be a rather simple view of workers' behaviour. Yet it is clear from the way that employers use money incentives that they believe employees react to the prospect of increasing their earnings. For example, many firms are attempting to link pay with performance because they believe that employees care about pay.

Employers must give consideration to any system they use. For example, if payments are made when targets are achieved, these targets must be realistic. Payment systems are often negotiated between **groups**, such as company representatives and trade unions.

Cost Employers are interested in the profitability or cost-effectiveness of their business. Any system that is used by the business must, therefore, attempt to keep the cost of labour as low as possible in relation to the market wage in that industry. This should enable the firm to increase its profits.

Prestige Managers often argue that it is a 'good thing' to be a good payer. Whether high pay rates earn an employer the reputation of being a good employer is arguable. What seems much more likely is that the low-paying employer will have the reputation of being a poor one in the eyes of employees.

Recruitment and labour turnover Payment rates must be competitive enough to ensure the right number of qualified and experienced employees stay within the business. This will prevent a high level of **labour turnover** (☞ unit 51). This is also true of vacant posts. A business must pay rates which encourage the right quality and quantity of applicants.

Control Certain methods of payment will reduce costs and make the control of labour easier. These are examined later in this unit.

Employee objectives for pay

Employees will have their own objectives for the payment they receive.

Purchasing power A worker's standard of living is determined by the level of weekly or monthly earnings. The **purchasing power** of those earnings is affected by the rate of inflation (☞ unit 66). Obviously, in periods of high inflation workers are likely to seek higher wages as the purchasing power of their earnings falls. Those whose earnings fall behind the rate of inflation will face a decline in their purchasing power.

Fair pay Employees often have strong feelings about the level of payment that is 'fair' for a job. The employee who feels underpaid may be dissatisfied and might look for another job, be careless, or be absent a great deal. Those who feel overpaid may simply feel dishonest, or may try to justify their pay by looking busy.

Relativities Employees may be concerned about how their earnings compare with those of others. 'How much do I get relative to ... ' is an important factor for a worker. Workers with a high level of skill, or who have trained for a long period, will want to maintain high wages relative to less 'skilled' groups. **Flat rate** pay increases, such as £10 a week for the whole workforce, would erode differences. A 5 per cent increase would maintain the differences.

Recognition Most people like their contribution to be recognised. Their pay gives them reassurance that what they are doing is valued.

Composition Employees often take into account the way their earnings are made up. It is argued that younger employees tend to be more interested in high direct earnings rather than indirect benefits like pensions. Incentive payments are likely to interest employees who want to increase their pay. Married women and men are generally less interested in overtime payments, for example, and regard other factors more highly.

QUESTION 2 In late 1992 the Confederation of British Industry rejected suggestions that private sector pay should be limited to the 1.5 per cent increase which the government wanted to impose on the public sector.

Mr Howard Davies, director general of the CBI, said public sector pay rose 20 per cent in the past two years while that in the private sector increased by only 14 per cent.

'It would not be reasonable to expect the private sector slavishly to follow the public sector in the next year', he stated.

Mr Davies rejected the suggestion by some ministers that public sector pay restraint might act as an example for the private sector.

He told East Midlands business leaders in Nottingham that pay rates should be determined by the profitability and productivity of individual companies. A 1.5 per cent rise for the one in seven manufacturing companies already in a pay freeze would therefore be inappropriate, he said.

Mr Davies said the engineering industry's total pay bill last year increased by 1 per cent, although average earnings rose by 6 per cent with a 5 per cent fall in employment.

Source: adapted from the *Financial Times*, 1992.

(a) Explain why the CBI and private sector employers might want to give their workers more than a 1.5 per cent pay increase.
(b) Why might the government, as the employer of public sector workers, have wanted a 1.5 per cent limit on pay rises?

Incentive schemes

Paying money for more output can be an incentive to make workers work harder. Incentive payments have been widely used in the management of manual workers in the past. Increasingly, incentives are being paid to workers not directly involved in production. Schemes are now being used for administrative workers and in service industries. For example, a business may set sales targets for its departments. Employees in those departments can then be rewarded with bonuses once targets are reached. Sales representatives in many companies are set targets each month and are paid bonuses if they reach them.

Bonus payments come in many forms. One method is a bonus paid per extra output above a target as in the **piece rate system**. However, one-off payments are often used by businesses to motivate workers. Bonuses can be paid at certain times of the year in a lump sum (often at Christmas). They can also be built into the monthly salary

of some workers, such as staff working in certain hospitals.

Although the bonus may be paid for reaching a target, it may also be for other things. Rewards for punctuality or attendance are sometimes used. Some businesses reward their 'best' salesperson with a bonus. One unusual example of this is Richer Sounds, the hi-fi retail outlet, where workers in a retail outlet that performed best over a period was rewarded with a Rolls Royce!

The problem with regular bonuses is that they are often seen as part of the employee's basic pay. As a result, they may no longer act as a motivator.

Productivity agreements are also a form of bonus payment, where rewards are paid providing workers, achieve a certain level of 'productivity'. They are usually agreed between employees' groups and management to 'smooth over' the introduction of new machinery or new techniques that workers need to learn.

Incentive schemes fall into three categories.
- Individual schemes. Individual employees may be rewarded for exceeding a target. The benefit of this scheme is that it rewards individual effort and hence employees are more likely to be motivated by this approach.
- Group incentives. In some situations, like assembly lines, the need is to increase group output rather than individual output. Where one worker relies on the output of others, group incentives may also have benefits. They can, however, put great pressure on all group members to be productive. It can also be difficult for a new recruit to become part of the group, as existing members may feel they will have to compensate for his inexperience.
- Factory-wide schemes. Employees are given a share of a 'pool' bonus provided the plant has reached certain output targets. The benefit to management is that incentives are related to the final output rather than sections of the plant. Furthermore, in theory at least, employees are more likely to identify with the company as a whole.

The difficulty with this type of scheme is that there is no incentive to work harder, as there is no direct link between individual effort and reward. Some employees that work hard may have their rewards reduced by others who do not - the same problem as group incentives.

Types of incentive scheme

Piece rate schemes We have already seen that piece rates can be an incentive. Producing more will earn the worker more. Each unit, over and above a target, is rewarded with a BONUS or commission payment. In the past there have often been disputes about the rate that should be paid for each unit produced. Businesses have tried to solve this by using individual time-saving schemes - the incentive is paid for time saved when carrying out a task. Using Taylor's work study methods (☞ unit 48) a work study engineer calculates the **standard time** that an employee should take to complete a task. The employee then receives incentive payments if the task is completed in a shorter time. If it is not possible to work due to shortage of materials or some other reason, the time involved is not counted. Such schemes, however, mean employees still suffer from variable payments. Despite these problems this type of incentive can be used when carrying out short, manual tasks where output can vary.

Measured daywork The idea of measured daywork may provide the answer to the problems of piece rate schemes. Instead of employees receiving a variable extra amount of pay depending on their output, they are paid a fixed sum as long as an agreed level of output is maintained. This should provide stable earnings and a stable output, instead of 'as much as you can, when you can, if you can'.

The first major agreement based on the principles of measured daywork was the National Power Loading Agreement in coal mining in 1966. Chrysler followed in 1969 and in 1970 British Leyland began the transfer to measured daywork. By 1973 the system was being used by a number of manufacturing and other industries, but it was also found that in some instances productivity went down. London Docks and British Leyland both reverted to more traditional 'payment by result' methods in the late 70s. Although productivity gains may not have been great, most surveys found that measured daywork improved industrial relations and that less expenditure was spent on dealing with grievances. Furthermore, measured daywork seemed to give management a greater control over such payment schemes.

Profit sharing/share ownership Profit sharing usually involves employees being paid a cash bonus as a proportion of the annual profits of the company. This is liable for tax and National Insurance. Profit sharing is not widespread and suffers several problems. Payments are not linked to individual performance and can fluctuate from year to year, depending on the performance of the business.

An alternative is the Approved Deferred Share Trust (ADST) which was set up under the Finance Act 1978. Here the company pays a proportion of profit not in cash to employees, but to a trust fund which buys company shares on behalf of the employees. The shares are then allocated to employees on some agreed formula. One advantage is that employees only pay tax if shares are sold and neither employee or employer pays National Insurance.

In a recent survey, three out of four management teams believe that employee share ownership plans have a positive effect on employee motivation and productivity. The main obstacle was the expense of setting up and operating the plan.

Performance related pay PERFORMANCE RELATED pay (PRP) schemes link the annual salary of an employee to their performance in the job. PRP schemes have spread rapidly in recent years and now form an important part of white collar pay in the public and private sector. Nearly all the major banks, building societies and insurance companies now use performance systems. A number of large manufacturers, such as Cadbury's and Nissan, have introduced schemes (at times extending them to the shop

floor) as well as public sector industries, such as the civil service, NHS and local government.

The shift towards PRP can be seen as part of a more general movement towards 'pay flexibility' in British industry.

- Organisations have sought to tie pay increases to measures of business performance, not just through PRP schemes but through other mechanisms, such as profit sharing.
- There has been a move away from national, industry-wide pay agreements to local, plant-wide agreements. This has given managers greater discretion in the way they match rewards to particular business units.
- There is a new focus on the individual employee and rewards which reflect her performance and circumstances, which has meant that collective methods of pay determination have become less important.

PRP schemes come in many forms, but the majority have some common features.

- Individual performance is reviewed, usually over a year. This may take the form of comparing performance against agreed objectives.
- At the end of the review the worker will be placed in a 'performance category'. The 'excellent' performer, for instance, may have exceeded all his agreed targets and produced work of a high standard. The category the worker falls into will determine the size of payment or whether payment is made at all.
- The performance payment can vary. Sometimes there

QUESTION 3 PRP schemes tend to demotivate staff rather than motivate them, suggests a report from an ACAS (Advisory, Conciliation and Arbitration Service) adviser.

Ted Riley, principal adviser in the ACAS Work Research Unit, describes PRP as the 'flavour of the month' and recommends a move to team related incentives, profit-related pay and employee share ownership. 'There is something wrong with the proposition that you can measure in reliable terms the output and effort of people in a wide variety of jobs', says Riley. 'People are attempting to measure the unmeasurable.'

Riley claims that PRP is fashionable because it fits in with the current government's philosophy. He says that the system is equally disliked by those appraised and those carrying out the appraisal. 'People shouldn't fall into the trap of believing that there is one universally applicable reward system. All of them have their faults - it just seems to me that PRP has far more faults than most of the others', he says.

In some instances Riley believes that PRP can be successful. 'In a small organisation with highly dynamic whizz-kids it might work. But most organisations are not like that.'

(a) Why do you think the ACAS adviser feels that PRP is trying to 'measure the unmeasurable'?
(b) Why does he suggest moving incentive schemes from PRP to team related incentives, profit related pay and employee share ownership?
(c) Why might PRP work in an organisation that is small and dynamic?

may be a small cash bonus or the award of increments on a pay scale. In others, the entire salary and progression through scales can depend on the results of the performance review. This kind of 'merit only' scheme means a 'poor' performer will be punished, as they will not receive extra pay.

There are problems with PRP. It is based on individual achievement, so the better a person does the more that person is paid. However, there may be disputes about how performance is to be measured and whether a person has achieved enough to be rewarded. Also, the system is not likely to work if people do not react to the possibility of rewards by working harder.

The following example of two sales consultants highlights some practical problems. Jane and Ruth are sales consultants for an insurance company and both had set targets for a six month period. Ruth met her target comfortably and received the agreed bonus of £5,500 for reaching on-target earnings. Jane failed to reach her agreed target because her sales manager left the company and poached three of Jane's best customers just before they signed agreements with Jane. Jane's bonus was therefore reduced to only £2,500 for a lower level of sales. Jane had no control over this, but felt she had worked just as hard as Ruth and therefore deserved a similar bonus.

Problems with incentive schemes

There are a number of problems that financial incentives schemes have.

- Operating problems. For incentives to work, production needs to have a smooth flow of raw materials, equipment and storage space, and consumer demand must also be fairly stable. These conditions cannot be guaranteed for long. If raw materials did not arrive or ran out, for example, the worker may not achieve a target and receive no bonus for reasons beyond his control. If this happens the employee is unlikely to be motivated by the scheme, and may negotiate for a larger proportion of earnings to be paid as guaranteed 'basic' pay.

- Fluctuating earnings. A scheme that is linked to output must result in fluctuating earnings. This might be due to changes in demand, the output of the worker or machinery problems. As in the case above, the worker is likely to press for the guaranteed part of pay to be increased, or store output in the 'good times' to prevent problems in the 'bad'. Alternatively, workers may try to 'slow down' productive workers so that benefits are shared out as equally as possible.

- Quality. The need to increase output to gain rewards can affect quality. There is an incentive for workers to do things as quickly as possible and this can lead to mistakes. Workers filling jars with marmalade may break the jars if they work too quickly. This means the jar is lost and the marmalade as well, for fear of splinters. For some

businesses, such as food processing, chemicals or drug production, errors could be disastrous.

- Changes in payment. Because of the difficulties above, employers constantly modify their incentive schemes. Improved schemes should stop workers manipulating the system and may give renewed motivation to some workers. However, constant changes mean that employees do not always understand exactly how to gain rewards.

- Quality of working life. Incentive schemes which use payment by results require a certain type of job design (☞ unit 50). This often means tight control by management, routine and repetition. Theory X (☞ unit 48) argues that production will only be efficient if workers know exactly what to do in any situation and their activities are tightly controlled by management. The result of this is that boredom and staleness may set in and the worker's 'standard of life' at work may be low.

- Jealousy. Individual workers may be jealous of the

QUESTION 4 Insurance salespeople have a long tradition of part or all of their earnings being made up from commission payments. A salesperson may be paid a percentage, for example, of a customer's annual premium.

There is, therefore, an incentive for employees to increase their sales and the value of premium payments in order to maximise their income. Customers, in the past, have had no real knowledge of how much the salesperson earns from each policy sold and there has been no obligation to declare this figure.

From January 1995 onwards, new rules will force insurance salespeople to declare how much they earn on the sale of policies. These regulations have been brought in by the Securities and Investments Board (SIB) - the watchdog of the industry. Under the new system the costs of setting up and the commission earned on a life assurance policy or a pension policy, for example, must be declared to customers before they sign. Companies will be forced to revise policies and cut out the jargon often associated with the sale of insurance.

The SIB argues that these changes will encourage more informed choices for consumers, greater competition and, as a result, lower commission payments. It has been suggested that these changes could lead to a £1 million reduction in commission.

Source: adapted in part from the *Daily Express*, 29.4.1994.

(a) Outline the possible problems of the pre-1995 commission system for:
   (i) insurance salespeople;
   (ii) insurance companies;
   (iii) consumers.

(b) Discuss the likely effects of the new regulations on salespeople and businesses in the insurance industry.

rewards earned by their colleagues. This can lead to problems in relationships and a possible lack of motivation. Increasingly, businesses are using group or plant-wide incentives to solve this.

Given these problems, why are financial incentive schemes still used by many firms? Managers may find a use for a certain incentive scheme. For example, a scheme can be used to overcome resistance to change. A business introducing new technology, such as computers, may offer

an incentive for staff to retrain or spend extra time becoming familiar with the new system. Employees often see benefits in such systems of payment. They may feel that they are gaining some control over their own actions in the workplace, being able to work at their own pace if they so wish. Furthermore, many businesses believe that incentive schemes ought to work as it is logical to assume that employees work harder if they are offered financial rewards.

Summary

1. What is the difference between financial and non-financial rewards?
2. What are the problems for employees of using a piece rate system?
3. Why might a piece rate system be used as an incentive?
4. Give 3 examples of the use of commission.
5. State 4 objectives that employees may have for pay.
6. State 4 objectives a business might have for a system of payment.
7. What is the difference between an individual and a factory-wide incentive scheme?
8. Why might a group incentive scheme discourage some workers rather than encourage them?
9. Describe how a measured daywork system operates.
10. What is meant by profit sharing?
11. Briefly explain 4 problems with incentive schemes.

Key terms

Bonus - usually an extra payment made in recognition of the contribution a worker has made to the company.
Commission - a payment system where employees are paid a percentage of the value of each good or service that is sold.
Incentive - a reward given to employees to encourage them to work harder.
Payment by results - payment methods that reward workers for the quantity and quality of work they produce .
Performance related pay - management's attempts to increase worker productivity by linking pay with performance.
Piece rates - a payment system where employees are paid an agreed rate for every item produced.
Time rates - a payment system that rewards workers for the amount of time they spend at work.

Question

Cheshire Plastics

The management of a medium sized plastics company in Cheshire, which had always prided itself on good management/employee relationships within the company, were becoming concerned about the growing level of dissatisfaction that appeared to be emerging on the shop floor. Increased absence notes, poorer quality of output and recent opposition to the introduction of some new machinery were outward signs of poor motivation. Basic wage levels for shop floor workers calculated at £295.00 per week, plus time and a half for overtime, were competitive in relation to similar companies in the area. But there had been a lack of overtime opportunities over the last 6 months, due to a period of recession and a number of vacancies had been left unfilled by management as an economy measure. Thus the workforce felt that they were not being rewarded for the extra work required.

In consultation with the union representatives of the shop floor workers, the management decided to introduce an incentive payment scheme to improve motivation. Two alternative schemes were developed and a final decision would depend upon the views of both management and workforce following a period of consultation.
■ Alternative A. The basic wage would be maintained at

£295.00, but there would be an output/production bonus if output reached certain targets across the whole factory. This bonus would mean take home pay of up to £330 if output targets were achieved. No overtime pay would be available under the new scheme.
■ Alternative B. A lower basic wage would be paid at £275.00 and the bonus payments would be calculated section by section, according to targets agreed by management and section leaders. Bonuses in one section could take pay up to £350.00, with all the workers in that section benefiting.

(a) Why might this management have decided to change the basic time system of pay that they had used?
(b) Identify whether Alternative A and Alternative B apply to individuals, groups or the whole plant.
(c) As an employee on the shop floor, which alternative would you prefer, A or B? Explain your answer.
(d) As a representative of management in the company, which alternative would you prefer? Explain your answer.
(e) Explain two other methods which the business could have used as an incentive for employees.

The need for non-financial rewards

Financial rewards have been used for most of this century by firms in an attempt to motivate employees to improve productivity. However, in the last two or three decades firms have realised that:

■ the chance to earn more money may not be an effective motivator;

■ financial incentive schemes are difficult to operate;

■ individual reward schemes may no longer be effective as production has become organised into group tasks;

■ other factors may be more important in motivating employees.

If other factors are more important than pay in motivating workers, it is important for firms to identify them. Only then can a business make sure its workforce is motivated. Figure 50.1 shows some of the factors that employees might consider important in their work environment. Many of these have been identified by the theories of Mayo and McGregor (☞ unit 48). A firm may consider introducing non-financial incentives to help employees satisfy these needs.

QUESTION 1 The findings of a Mori poll (November 1992) conducted for the General Municipal Boilermakers Union (GMB) concludes that pay is low on the list of criteria by which employees judge their well-being. This is supported by research carried out by the Institute of Personnel Management, which shows that employees are far more concerned with non-pay factors such as job security, prospects for job enrichment and, most importantly, the degree to which they feel fully involved in their enterprise. According to the research, employee involvement has great benefits for both management and staff. Management will find that where employees are fully aware of the organisation's objectives and the constraints within which it operates, their expectations are realistic.

To what extent do the findings of the MORI poll and the research support the view that workers have a variety of factors which motivate them?

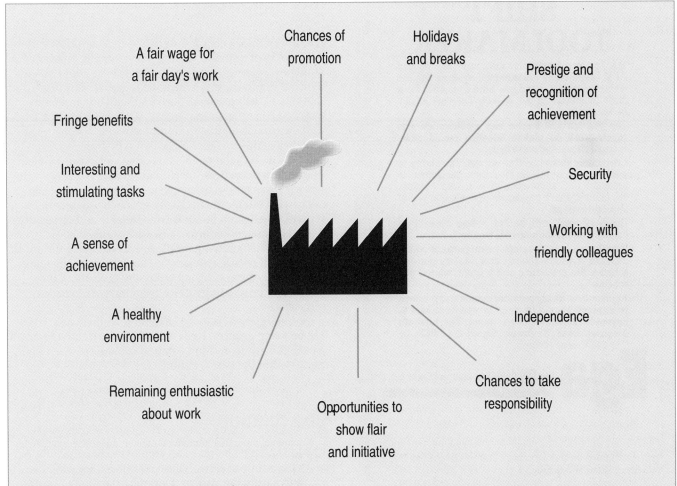

Figure 50.1 *Employees' needs from the work environment*

Job design and redesign

The dissatisfaction with financial incentive schemes reached its peak in the 1960s and 1970s. In response the 'Quality of Working Life Movement' began to develop ideas which were based around the 'human relations school', as first outlined by the Hawthorne studies (☞ unit 48). It was argued that workers were likely to be motivated by non-monetary factors and that jobs needed to be DESIGNED or REDESIGNED to take these factors into account. Five principles were put forward which any incentive scheme needed to consider.

- The principle of closure. A job must include all tasks necessary to complete a product or process. This should ensure that work is meaningful for employees and that workers feel a sense of achievement.
- Control and monitoring of tasks. Jobs should be designed so that an army of inspectors is not needed. The worker, or the team, should take responsibility for quality.

- Task variety. There should be an increase in the range of tasks that a worker carries out. This should allow job rotation to occur and keep the worker interested in their work.
- Self-regulation. Employees should have control of the speed at which they work and some choice over work methods and sequence.
- Interaction and co-operation. The job structure should allow some social interaction and the chance for an employee to work in a group.

Various methods were devised to try and put these principles into practice. They included job enrichment, job enlargement, job rotation, quality control circles and employee participation in groups. These are examined later in this unit.

One likely result of poor job design is that employees will not achieve their full potential. This means that the firm's output may suffer as a result. For example, an architect who is constantly having her work checked for accuracy is unlikely to be as productive as possible, due to constant interruptions. Another problem with jobs which do not meet workers' needs is that they are likely to lead to poor motivation, absenteeism and a lack of quality in work.

Job enlargement

JOB ENLARGEMENT involves giving an employee more work to do of a similar nature. For example, instead of an employee putting wheels onto a bicycle he could be allowed to put the entire product together. It is argued that this variety prevents boredom with one repetitive task and encourages employees' satisfaction in their work, as they are completing the entire process.

Critics of this method argue that it is simply giving a worker 'more of the same'. It is often called the problem of **horizontal loading** - instead of turning five screws the worker turns ten! In many businesses today such tasks are carried out more effectively by machines, where repetitive tasks can be completed quickly and efficiently without strain, boredom or dissatisfaction. It could even be argued that allowing employees to complete the entire process will reduce efficiency. This is because the fall in productivity from carrying out many tasks more than offsets any productivity gains from increased worker satisfaction.

Job enlargement is more efficient if workers are organised in groups. Each worker can be trained to do all jobs in the group and **job rotation** can take place. This is discussed in the next section.

Job rotation

JOB ROTATION involves an employee changing jobs or tasks from time to time. This could mean, for example, a move to a different part of the production line to carry out a different task. Alternatively, an employee may be moved from the personnel to the marketing department

Figure 50.2 A job advertisement

(a) Comment on the job above in the light of the five principles of job design.
(b) How might it be redesigned better to meet these principles?

where they have skills which are common to both. From an employee's point of view this should reduce boredom and enable a variety of skills and experience to be gained. An employer might also benefit from a more widely trained workforce.

Although job rotation may motivate a worker, it is possible that any gains in productivity may be offset by a fall in output as workers learn new jobs and take time to 'settle in'. Worker motivation is not guaranteed if the employee is simply switched from one boring job to another. In fact some workers do not like the uncertainty that job changes lead to and may become dissatisfied. Although used by firms such as Volkswagen in the 1970s, where employees carried out a variety of production tasks, job rotation has been less popular in the last decade.

Working in teams

The Swedish car firm Volvo is a well quoted example of a company that has effectively introduced 'teamwork'. In both its plants at Kalmar and Uddevalla, it set up production in teams of 8-10 highly skilled workers. The teams decided between themselves how work was to be distributed and how to solve problems that arise. It is

arguable whether these practices led to an increase in productivity, but the company firmly believed that this method of organisation was better than an assembly line system. A similar system is used at Honda UK, but with 4 person teams.

Job enrichment

The idea of JOB ENRICHMENT came out of the work of McGregor and his views about Theory Y management (☞ unit 48). Whereas job enlargement expands the job 'horizontally', job enrichment attempts to give employees greater responsibility by 'vertically' extending their role in the production process. An employee, for example, may be given responsibility for:
- planning a task;
- quality control;
- work supervision;
- ordering materials;
- maintenance.

Job enrichment gives employees a 'challenge', which will develop their 'unused' skills and encourage them to be more productive. The aim is to make workers feel they have been rewarded for their contribution to the company. Employees will also be provided with varied tasks, which may possibly lead to future promotion.

It is not, however, without problems. Workers who feel that they are unable to carry out the 'extra work', or who consider that they are forced into it, may not respond to incentives. In addition, it is unlikely that all workers will react the same to job enrichment. Trade unions sometimes argue that such practices are an attempt to reduce the labour force, and disputes about the payment for extra responsibilities may arise. In practice, job enrichment has been found to be most successful in administrative and technical positions.

Job enrichment at ICI

ICI received a good deal of publicity in its attempt to introduce job enrichment in the 1960s. Many accounts have talked about the benefits it brought to ICI. These included new working relationships, increased satisfaction and greater efficiency. Workers welcomed it despite union hostility. Other studies, however, cast doubts on these findings. In 1971 Cotgrove, Dunham and Vanplew reported that there were only marginal changes in work. At most boredom was reduced, rather than positive interest being generated. They argued there was only an **enlargement**, not an **enrichment** of tasks.

Job enrichment was only one part of a strategy to make the company appear 'participative' in its dealings with employees. However, ICI stated that schemes, such as profit sharing, could not be expected to motivate directly, but rather create a general 'ethos' of a humane employer. In the decade after the introduction of these changes it was difficult to see any real sign of job enrichment.

In the face of recession, this approach almost totally disappeared. In 1980 a cut of 4,000 jobs in the fibres division was announced, followed in 1981 by a merger of

---

QUESTION 3 Land Rover introduced total quality management ideas and 'cell manufacturing' in the mid - 80s. The Land Rover assembly line, which is non-robotic, is divided into cells of about 60 people and subdivided into zones, each run by a team. Teams are self-managed; they work out schedules and organise new assignments, keep attendance records and identify training needs.

In 1991 a new union agreement, the 'New Deal', brought in single-table bargaining, single status and a guarantee of no compulsory redundancies in return for further flexibility. It also underlined the commitment to teamwork, continuous improvement and two-way communication.

The personnel director, Jim Newell, believes these changes set the right climate for greater employee involvement. 'I see the suggestion scheme as one aspect in a package. We are seeking a new level of responsibility and commitment from the workforce compared with the old British Leyland days, where people just came to do their job and managers did everything else.'

Involvement is encouraged by regular employee meetings and the suggestion scheme itself. There are team briefings each morning. Also, on the Land Rover site, the monthly discussion groups are a big feature. These involve about six people in a cell who set their own agenda and pick their own problems to solve. Ten per cent of the workforce are involved. Finally there are quality action teams meeting occasionally to sort out specific problems.

Source: adapted from *Personnel Management Plus*, April 1993.

(a) Why do Land Rover believe that team work increases quality?
(b) Does the Land Rover approach make use of the principles of job enlargement? Explain your answer.

plastics and petrochemicals, leading to further job losses. In neither case was the consultation process used. Job enrichment faded from the scene as the recession hit hard. It could be argued that, based on ICI's experience, it seems that as money becomes tight, job enrichment schemes are first to be cut.

Quality control circles

QUALITY CONTROL CIRCLES are small groups of workers (about 5-20) in the same area of production who meet regularly to study and solve production problems. In addition, such groups are intended to motivate and involve workers on the shopfloor. Unlike job enlargement and job enrichment, they allow the workforce directly to improve the nature of the work they are doing.

Quality control circles are becoming popular in Britain. They started in America, where it was felt workers could be motivated by being involved in decision making. The idea gained in popularity in Japan in the 60s and 70s, and was taken up by Western businesses in the late 1970s. An example of their use can be found in Japanese companies setting up plant in the UK in the 1990s. Honda at Swindon have 52 teams of six people looking at improvements that can be made in areas allocated to the groups, for example, safety.

Quality control circles are only likely to work if they have the support of both management and employees. Businesses have to want worker participation and involvement in decision making, and set up a structure that supports this. Workers and their representatives also need to support the scheme. Employees must feel that their views within the circle are valued and must make a contribution to decisions.

The problems of job redesign

A business may decide to redesign jobs to increase workers' motivation. The actual process of redesigning existing jobs is often difficult to carry out in practice for a number of reasons.

- Employees' reactions. Employees may be familiar with the old approach to doing a job and may resent new changes. They might not want the extra duties that result from job redesign.
- Employers' views and costs. Job redesign may be expensive. New methods often require extra training. In addition, redesigned jobs might lead employees to claim extra pay for new responsibilities. There is no guarantee that the redesign of jobs will increase productivity in the long term.
- Technology. The introduction of new machinery can make job redesign more difficult. Certain jobs have had to be redesigned almost totally as new technology has changed production processes. In some cases employees have had to learn totally new skills, such as when newspaper page design on computer screens replaced old methods of cutting and pasting type onto pages. At other times skills may be made redundant. When Morgan cars produced their front panels in the late 1980s with machinery instead of their usual 'handmade' techniques, workers were arguably turned from skilled panel makers to non-skilled machine operators.
- Effects on output and productivity. Redesigned jobs need to be evaluated to gauge whether they have actually motivated the workforce to increase output.

Goal setting and management by objectives

Goal setting is part of a more general theory of **management by objectives** (MBO). MBO was put forward by Peter Drucker in 1954 and is covered in unit 58. It suggests that a business should define objectives or targets for an individual to achieve and revise these targets after assessing the performance of the worker.

In 1984 Ed Locke wrote *Goal Setting: A motivational technique that works*. According to Locke, the idea that in order to improve job performance you need to motivate workers by making jobs more satisfying is wrong. He argued that satisfaction comes from achieving specific **goals**. In addition, the harder these goals are, the greater the effort and satisfaction. His message was for businesses to set specific goals that people can achieve and that have been negotiated. 'Do your best', he argued, is not specific. Employees must also have feedback on the progress they are making and then they will perform. The assumption behind the theory is that people will do what they say they will do, and then will strive hard to do it.

QUESTION 4 Wedgwood has been a famous name in pottery for over two hundred years. The 1980s, though, saw high interest rates, which pushed up costs, prompted a sharp rise in the value of the pound when inflation was higher than in most western countries and a cut back in spending by consumers worried by the recession. Large scale redundancies were necessary as cost reductions meant staff cutbacks. Between 1979 and 1983, 4,000 jobs were lost and several factories were closed down.

Having survived the recession the company decided that its future would depend on the skills and flexibility of its workforce. The company's personnel and production departments were determined to introduce quality control circles as a way of involving staff in decision making. Male employees were resistant to these changes because they had borne the brunt of the redundancies and were suspicious that productivity improvements would mean more job cuts. Women workers, however, enjoyed greater say in the running of their sections; the men seemed more inclined to stick to a traditional management-worker division of responsibilities.

Source: newspaper article, source unknown.

(a) What might be the benefits to Wedgwood of introducing quality control circles?
(b) Comment on the male and female employees' reactions to the introduction of quality control circles.
(c) How might Wedgwood have evaluated the success of using quality control circles?

Organisation behaviour modification

In recent years businesses have used the theory of organisation behaviour modification (OBMod) with management by objectives when motivating employees. OBMod assumes that workers' behaviour is determined by the consequences of their actions. For example, a worker who receives a reward as a result of increasing productivity is likely to work harder. Similarly, workers try to avoid behaving in ways that produce no reward or lead to punishment.

OBMod is based on the work of psychologists such as Thorndike and Skinner, who argue that since we cannot observe people's attitudes we should observe their behaviour. Managers should therefore observe how employees' behaviour is affected by the consequences of their actions. These consequences can be broken down into four categories.
- The employee receives something he likes.
- Something the employee dislikes is taken away.
- Something the employee likes is taken away.
- Something the employee dislikes is given.

The first two categories are known as **reinforcers**, as they lead to an increase in the behaviour that precedes them. If a junior manager gives a good presentation and receives praise (something he likes), then the behaviour that resulted in praise (the good presentation) will be reinforced. This is an example of **positive reinforcement**. If something the employee dislikes is taken away, this is called **negative reinforcement**.

The other two categories are kinds of **punishment**. They tend to reduce the behaviour that precedes them. For example, if a worker is constantly late, and is fined (something he dislikes), he may try to reduce the number of times he is late.

Two examples of companies trying to put OBMod into practice are Xerox and American Airlines. At Xerox, 'X' certificates, redeemable for $25, were introduced into the personnel department. Every member of the department, can give Xs to others in the company. They may be given for many things, for example good attendance or co-operation. At American Airlines, passengers are given coupons that they may give to staff who they feel deserve recognition. These are both examples of positive reinforcement.

QUESTION 5
Greater Alchurch Hospital is having a problem with absenteeism among its nurses, porters and clerks. Employees are still paid when they are off work. In fact, as in the case of many companies, an employee benefit scheme is in operation. On the basis of the scheme, employees can be absent for 3 days, without providing a certificate. Absences of between 4 and 7 days require completion of a 'self-certificate' and afterwards a doctor's certificate is required. As a 'caring employer' the hospital makes statutory sick pay up to normal pay.

The present approach to excessive absences has involved the use of sanctions. These have included a series of formal warnings, which lead eventually to the termination of employment, and secondary sanctions, such as threats relating to the effect of excessive absence on promotion opportunities and wage increases. Trade union influence and activities are virtually non-existent, with only 15 per cent of the employees being members.

Although the actual daily cost to the hospital has not been calculated, the minimum cost has been estimated at about £80 per person in terms of wages and fringe benefits paid, loss of productivity and the cost of temporary staff where necessary.

There are some staff turnover problems although these are minor. The problem seems mainly to be one of absenteeism.

(a) What staffing problems have the Greater Alchurch Hospital experienced?
(b) Why might these problems have affected employee motivation?
(c) Explain how organisation behaviour modification could be used as a cost effective solution to motivate the workforce.

Key terms

Job design (redesign) - changing the tasks and activities of a job, perhaps in an attempt to motivate workers.
Job enlargement - giving an employee more work to do of a similar nature.
Job enrichment - an attempt to give employees greater responsibility and recognition by 'vertically' extending their role in the production process.
Job rotation - the changing of jobs or tasks from time to time.
Quality control circles - small groups of workers (about 5-20) in the same area of production which meet regularly to study and solve all types of production problems.

Summary

1. State 5 possible non-financial rewards that may be an incentive for individuals.
2. What principles would a 'good' job have according to the 'Quality of Working Life Movement'?
3. State 4 methods of job redesign.
4. 'Job enlargement is simply a method of horizontal loading.' Explain this statement.
5. Under what circumstances might job rotation not lead to an increase in productivity?
6. Why is job enrichment said to extend an employee's role in the firm vertically?
7. How does a quality control circle operate?
8. What are the advantages to an employee of quality control circles?
9. What is meant by goal setting?
10. Show, using an example, how positive reinforcement can motivate a worker.

Question

Honda

The receptionist at Honda's manufacturing complex has not yet had to leave her desk to help screw widgets together on the engine assembly line. But, if asked, she is prepared to do so. Indeed, it would be expected in the event of a sudden shop-floor crisis at the Japanese car-maker's £370 million plant at Swindon, 80 miles west of London. The receptionist would even be appropriately dressed. As a matter of daily routine she wears overalls similar to those of Shojiro Miyake, managing director of Honda manufacturing in the UK and president of Honda Motor Europe. They are the same overalls that are worn by the other 844 employees and directors currently working at the site making Honda Accords.

She could find herself swapping spanners on the assembly line with Andrew Jones, the plant manager. Jones makes clear that, if the need is sufficiently urgent, no one in the plant is too senior, or exempt for any other reason, from helping out on even the most humble of tasks.

There are other cultural aspects of Honda's Swindon operation which are similar to other Japanese companies who have sited plants in Europe. Everyone at Swindon is on the same pension scheme, sick pay conditions and holiday entitlement. There is no reserved parking. Everyone uses the same changing rooms and canteen. There are no formal job descriptions and there are no workers or directors, only 'associates'.

Currently only a handful of Accords are coming off the line each day - a result of what Jones acknowledges to be an obsession with quality, and of the small teams grouped on the assembly line learning for themselves how best to organise their work.

'Teamwork' crops up in almost every sentence Jones says. 'It's critical. So many people talk of good teamwork as if it's some kind of philosopher's stone. In our case it translates as an overriding objective to develop together. If you were to go out on the line, you would find no work study or industrial engineers timing everything - we expect our people to develop their own jobs and functions.'

Working in teams of four means that they have gained breadth and understanding from each other. Initial teams were formed by one Japanese training one 'Brit'. Both would train two more Britons. All four would train another four - and so the process continues today.

'Teamwork means we reject class differentiation and job demarcation. We don't accept anyone as being more important than anyone else. If we are recruiting at a senior level, that recruit spends at least one month on the shop floor. So if you want high status, a secretary and an expensive desk to keep everyone at a distance - don't come and work here... ' says Jones.

The majority of the current workforce has been recruited locally, many during a period when unemployment in the Swindon region was under 3 per cent. Now it is 9 per cent but the recruitment programme continues, with recommendations spreading by word of mouth. Each candidate has to pass two interviews and, more recently, an aptitude test. All staff are involved in daily start-of-shift briefings and are fully briefed from weekly management meetings. At the start of each month all staff review with Jones and his associates the company's current position and operating activities as well as welcoming new 'associates'. There are also monthly 'birthday party' get-togethers in which all staff with a birthday that month meet socially and to swap ideas with Miyake, Jones and other senior colleagues.

Regular 'Y-Gaya' meetings take place involving all groups of employees. The phrase stands for 'free, frank interchange of views'. The idea, says Jones, is continually to widen understanding and spread knowledge.

There are now 52 new 'Honda circles' - teams of six people looking for continuous improvement within defined areas that the team itself selects. They include new ideas, training, environment and safety. As an example, one 'associate' was burned while deep in the foundry area, undertaking maintenance. His circle devised a new system which now means that no one needs to enter the hazard area.

Source: adapted from the *Financial Times*, 1993.

(a) What non-financial rewards do employees benefit from at Honda's plant?
(b) Why might Honda not need to employ work study or industrial engineers?
(c) Using an example from the article, explain how Honda have made use of;
  (i) job enrichment;
  (ii) quality circles.
(d) Explain the possible:
  (i) benefits;
  (ii) problems;
  for Honda in having employees work in teams.

The work of the personnel department

Many large and medium sized businesses today have a personnel department. Its main role will be to manage the firm's HUMAN RESOURCES. These are the employees or personnel in a business that help it to achieve its objectives. They might include production workers, office staff, members of the marketing team, accountants or cleaners.

The personnel department will deal with many factors associated with employees. These include:

- human resource and manpower planning;
- recruitment and selection;
- induction and training;
- promotion and transfers;
- appraisal and termination of employment;
- discipline;
- rewards and conditions of employment;
- working conditions;
- career development and welfare;
- wage bargaining and disputes.

Many British firms have shown a renewed interest in the management of human resources in recent years. For example, there has been an increase in the use of psychological testing for managers and staff at Austin Rover, Jaguar and Peugeot. There is greater interest in performance related pay as a way of rewarding managers in major clearing banks and the NHS. Appraisal systems built around skills that managers should develop have been used by companies such as Shell, National Westminster Bank, BP and Whitbread. After a report by Coopers and Lybrand (1985) that outlined the lack of training in the UK, companies seem to be placing greater stress on this area. Examples can be found in Jaguar's open learning programme and British Airways, with its 'customer care' approach.

Human resource planning

One of the most important tasks of the personnel department will be to ensure HUMAN RESOURCE PLANNING is carried out. This, like marketing planning, is part of the overall planning of the business. A firm is only likely to achieve its business objectives if its employees are used effectively. Planning how best to use human resources will help a business to do this. Although the personnel department has expertise in planning of human resources, it is not only their responsibility. Marketing, production and finance managers will also have a responsibility to see it is carried out.

What is involved in human resource planning? It is often said that it has a 'soft' and a 'hard' side. This is shown in Figure 51.1. The soft side is mainly concerned with the way people are managed. It may include:

- planning how to motivate and satisfy workers;
- planning how to develop a certain ORGANISATIONAL CULTURE or approach in employees, for example good relations with customers, or quality at all stages of production (TQM ☞ unit 34);
- planning how to support or develop employees, for example, training.

The hard side is concerned with quantifying the number, quality and type of employees that will be needed. It is often known as the MANPOWER PLAN. It may include:

- analysing current employment needs;
- forecasting the likely future demand for employees by the business;
- forecasting the likely future supply of workers that will be available to hire;
- predicting LABOUR TURNOVER - the extent to which workers leave the business. This is dealt with later in this unit.

Planning can be **short term** or **long term**. Short term planning is aimed at the immediate needs of the business, such as filling vacancies left, say, as a result of maternity leave. Long term planning will try to plan for the future. For example, if a company was aiming to change its production techniques in the next few years, it would need to plan the number of employees, training needed

---

QUESTION 1 In 1989, ICI, the pharmaceutical company, faced major challenges, such as the expiry of a patent on a main product and fierce competition from rivals. In response, they decided the best way to improve their chances in the market was to improve workers' performance. The personnel department (along with senior management) decided that a performance management system was needed. Various comments were made about the system by ICI management:

'Improved communication, targets, personal development, visibility of line managers.'

'The whole process I am outlining is aimed at people ... it will only happen if line managers are visible and drive the process.'

'The future success of the various businesses in ICI depends on developing the talents and performance of its employees.'

ICI predicted that the system would give certain benefits.

- An emphasis on training and development to help individuals achieve these targets.
- A closer relationship between individuals and line managers, involving coaching, encouragement and motivation.
- A more objective assessment of performance against targets, leading to a better performance related reward system.

Source: adapted from *Personnel Management*, November 1992.

(a) Why did ICI introduce the system in 1989?
(b) What were likely to be the main features of ICI's performance management system?

and perhaps the incentives and motivation that workers would require.

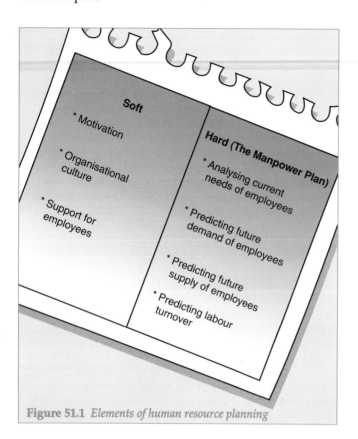

Figure 51.1 *Elements of human resource planning*

Planning methods

There are various methods that a business could use when planning for human resources. Take the example of a hotel with a variety of staff working in different jobs. How might it prepare a plan?

Changing business aims into employee goals The hotel may have decided that its main aim was to provide an excellent service to customers. To achieve this aim, goals would have to be set for the behaviour of employees of the hotel, such as always being polite to the customer. It is likely that staff training in customer care would be built into the plan to help employees.

Examining the environment There are various factors 'outside' a business that could affect human resource planning. They are dealt with in detail in the next section. The hotel would aim to gather as much information as possible to predict the effects of changes in these factors. For example, if health and safety regulations changed that affected the working of the kitchen, staff would need to be aware of these changes and may need training or support to carry them out. Information about external factors can be found from many sources, ranging from industrial journals to competitors' annual reports.

Analysing the current situation It is important for the hotel to be aware of current staff needs. It could do this by using:

- questionnaires to staff and customers;
- interviews with staff;
- discussions with managers;
- performance data;
- recruitment or promotion information.

A questionnaire given to staff and customers at a hotel, for example, might find that customer service is not as good as it could be at the checkout desk because staff are too concerned about getting the paperwork right. A solution might be to simplify the checkout system or use extra staff at busy times. This would help to motivate employees and improve the chances of meeting the goal of improved customer service.

The three methods so far are all aimed at planning how a business can motivate and manage its employees, and achieve the 'organisational culture' it wants. There are other methods, however, which attempt to measure the number of employees the business will need and whether they are available. These make up the hard side of planning - known as the **manpower plan**.

Forecasting employee demand The hotel will need to predict the number of employees it is likely to need in future. How can it do this?

- Time series data. This is a **forecasting** technique (☞ unit 15) which involves predicting the future from past figures. If the hotel had a steady increase in staff of 2 per cent a year over the last five years, it might expect this to continue. The problem with this method is that it does not take into account that changes both inside and outside the business can affect demand for employees.
- Demand linked to the business. Say that the hotel had 55 rooms and employed 60 people. This means it has a ratio of nearly 1:1.1 staff per room. If a new extension was built to include another 20 rooms then 22 extra staff would be needed (20 x 1.1). More detailed methods take into account **economies of scale** (☞ unit 31).
- Work study. This allows the business to find the numbers of staff needed to carry out a task efficiently. If the hotel was hosting a conference, then this method may help to predict the extra duties or staff that would be needed.
- The hotel may ask experienced managers or employees for their views on the employees needed in future. For example, the kitchen manager may know if demand for evening meals has fallen off, and that perhaps fewer staff are needed.

Analysing current supply Statistics can be gathered on a wide range of factors to do with employees in the business. These might include numbers of employees in certain jobs, qualifications, age, length of service, performance results etc. If the hotel wanted to plan retirements, it might look at the ages of employees in different jobs. This might perhaps indicate that the business has two gardeners and one porter over the age of sixty, but no other employees over the age of fifty five.

Forecasting internal employee supply This allows a

business to predict how the supply of employees will change over time. If an employee leaves to join another firm, or if he is promoted, a vacancy exists that may need to be filled.

It is possible to calculate the number of staff leaving a business as a percentage of those who could have left. This deals only with those leaving, not those retiring. The hotel, for example, may have found that 18 out of the 70 staff left during the previous year. So the **percentage wastage rate** or **labour turnover index** is:

$$\frac{\text{Number of staff leaving per period}}{\text{Average number of staff in post during the period}} \times 100 = \frac{18}{70} \times 100 = 25.7\%$$

This could then be used to predict the likely numbers leaving in future, and the need to recruit new employees. Similar predictions can be made about the number of employees that are likely to be promoted.

Forecasting 'external' employee supply There are a number of local factors which have to be taken into account when forecasting the likely supply of workers from outside the business.

■ Closing/opening of other businesses in the area.
■ Housing developments.
■ Transport and ease of travel to work.
■ Local unemployment levels.
■ Whether people with certain skills are difficult or easy to recruit.
■ Local education and government training schemes.
■ Population or demographic trends in the area.

Factors affecting human resource planning

There are many factors that could cause planning in a business to change.

Changing goals of a business If a chemical company, for example, decided that the most effective way to increase profits or turnover was to become more **market orientated** (☞ unit 18), this is likely to change the personnel the business needs. There would be a need perhaps for employees with market research skills or training in how to promote products. The move in recent years by British Rail to close down unprofitable lines has meant fewer workers are required as a result. This is an example of how changing goals can affect the demand for labour.

Changes in the market Changes in purchasing patterns of consumers may mean that the demand for labour or labour skills have to change. One example might be the redundancies in the coal industry as a result of demand for cheaper forms of power. Another might be the need to develop good customer relations in fast food retail outlets as competition has increased.

Changes in the economy can also affect human resource planning. In a recession, a business is likely to reduce its workforce as demand for its products falls.

Technology The introduction of new technology may lead to retraining or a need to recruit workers with specialist skills. For example, many former typists have become computer operators with the introduction of computer systems for storage, retrieval and presentation of information. The business may also have to consider the effect that new technology could have on the motivation of its employees and how to deal with this.

Competition Competition by other firms for workers may affect the supply of labour available to a business. If competitors offer high wages to workers with specialist skills then a business may have to raise its wage levels to recruit the staff it needs.

Competition for customers may also affect a human resource plan. Many firms are now aiming to meet BS 5750 quality standards, as customers refuse to use their services without this. An example might be in the electronics industry, where if one firm does not have approval it may lose business to another supplier. A business that obtains the quality standard must employ workers with specialist skills to check the standard is maintained. This can be costly for some small firms.

Population As well as the total population size, the distribution of population in a country can affect the supply of workers available. It is argued that the UK in the 1990s faces a number of changes in population distribution that are likely to affect the human resource planning of most businesses.

■ An ageing population, with a growing number of 'baby-boomers' (born just after 1945) as part of the workforce. This means that businesses will have to find more jobs for older workers and attempt to attract women 'back to work'. It is also possible that more mature workers may be motivated by factors other than money. The John Lewis partnership is one business that recruits older employees.
■ Fewer school leavers and young workers (the so-called **demographic timebomb**), so that employers are likely to have fewer to choose from and they will have to pay higher wages.

An older population is also likely to affect the demand for certain goods. Businesses are having to switch their products to appeal to older people. Examples include the revival of 1960s and 1970s music on compact disc and the growth in residential care homes.

Trade unions A business may have negotiated a wage agreement with a union based on increases in the productivity of employees which can affect how much they are paid. Increasingly, single union agreements are taking place, where a business is only prepared to discuss the conditions and rewards to workers with one union (☞ unit 59).

Government Government legislation on equal opportunities, for example, has affected the wage costs of businesses and their recruitment and selection procedures. Businesses may also operate a policy where they guarantee disabled workers or ethnic minorities a proportion of jobs. This is dealt with in unit 55.

Finance The finance available to employ or reward workers will depend on many factors, such as the overall performance of the business, cash flow (☞ unit 44) and the liquidity of the company. A small business that is building a new factory is unlikely to have funds available to hire new employees or pay large bonuses.

QUESTION 2 Like many firms in the engineering industry, Bilders Ltd have found it difficult to retain talented staff. Of the 45 graduates that started in October 1992, 16 had left after a year. Bilders have changed their recruitment patterns in recent years, using self-employed or temporary staff that can be hired or let go as conditions change.

The changes in recruitment have been brought about by uncertainty in the economy and increased competition. The business has also suffered from diversification in the industry. Traditional skills in oil and petrochemicals are no longer needed in new areas such as power plants or food processing.

The personnel manager has become increasingly concerned about the ability to find staff for the business to achieve goals it has set. She argues, 'We just don't have the resources to cope with training demands. Our clients are getting tougher - vetting our staff and quality systems as a condition of working with us. We are unlikely to keep our bright young graduates if we don't offer them enough training.'

Source: adapted from *Case Studies in Personnel*, eds. D. Winstanley and J. Woodall, Institute of Personnel Management.

(a) Calculate the labour turnover index for new graduates at Bilders Ltd and discuss how the business might use this in future.
(b) Outline the factors that have influenced the planning of human resources in the business and explain the effects they are likely to have had.

The problems of human resource planning

There are a number of problems a business will face when planning how to use its personnel.

■ Problems with predicting the behaviour of people. A business may have filled a position, but after being appointed the individual may decide he does not want the job. This could mean another costly and time consuming series of interviews for the firm.

■ Problems with predicting external events. Sometimes it is difficult to predict exactly how many employees are required. We have seen that many factors can affect human resource planning. For example, the opening up of former communist countries to trade from the West in the early 1990s would have meant changing plans for businesses aiming to break into these markets. It is likely that employees with knowledge of the business and language of these

countries would have been in demand.

■ Planning has to be constantly monitored. It is unwise for a business to plan its human resource needs and not alter them in the light of changing events. Planning has to be checked, revised and updated as other factors change.

■ Human resource planning must be well thought out or it is likely to lead to industrial relations problems. Cuts in the workforce or wage reductions that are not negotiated could affect workers' motivation and may even lead to industrial action (☞ unit 61).

Labour turnover

One of the most important tasks in the management of personnel is to make sure that labour turnover is minimised and that all vacancies that exist are filled. Labour turnover is a measure of the number of people that **leave** a business in a given period of time as a percentage of the average number of people employed during that period.

If labour turnover is high, how will this affect a business? There are likely to be costs as a result. These include:

■ the cost of advertising, interviewing and training a new employee;
■ a loss of production while the place is filled;
■ low morale amongst other employees;
■ reorganisation before the place is filled and perhaps after a new worker is hired.

The business will need to identify groups that are likely to leave and be ready to fill any vacancies that occur. Employees may leave because they are ill, retiring or having children. In some cases, they may be dismissed. These are all unavoidable.

However, some workers leave voluntarily because they are not satisfied with the job. It is these workers that a

---

QUESTION 3 The turnover in jobs among experienced nurses in the health service costs up to £24 million each year, or almost £5.50 a day for each patient. Using research commissioned from Sussex University's Institute of Manpower Studies, the cost to the National Health Service of losing a nurse, including the cost of a temporary replacement and of the eventual replacement's induction and training, varies between £1,250 and £7,760 a year.

The Institute says that a 350-bed hospital employing 700 nurses would, under present turnover rates, incur nurse turnover costs of £525,000 a year, or 6.8 per cent of its pay bill. The average turnover rate of 25 per cent is equivalent to 80,000 nurses leaving the NHS every year. At an average cost of £3,000, that is a £24 million loss.

Source: adapted from *The Times*, March 1992.

(a) What does the study suggest about the importance of reducing labour turnover in the health service?
(b) What suggestions could be made to the NHS to reduce labour turnover and what problems may be associated with each suggestion?

business should be most concerned about. Evidence suggests that those workers who leave voluntarily tend to be younger employees, who are often new recruits. They may be looking for promotion and better pay. To prevent dissatisfaction, a firm may:

- set up an internal promotion system;
- develop a staff training programme;
- make sure there is good communication between management and workers to avoid grievances and ensure that employees' views are taken into account;
- increase levels of pay.

Implications of human resource planning

Human resource planning will affect both the business and the employees that work in it. There are likely to be some benefits for workers and also some problems.

Motivation, training and support Employers will attempt to motivate workers and make sure they are satisfied in the workplace. This may be in the form of rewards such as bonuses or other incentives (☞ unit 49), or non-monetary incentives, such as job redesign (☞ unit 50).

Employees may also benefit from training and support. Marks and Spencer, for example, employ counsellors for employees, giving advice on areas such as how single parent families can cope.

Flexible work practices Employers have always wanted workers to be as flexible as possible. In the past this has meant paying overtime for extra hours worked, or higher rates for 'shift' work.

Faced with competition, today's businesses are trying to use their existing employees more effectively. Sometimes this can benefit the employee. A single woman with a child may be able to work between the hours of 9am to 3pm each day while her child is at school. Working flexible hours could mean an employee may take time off for personal reasons and still work their required number of hours a week.

Training may also be given to workers so they become **multi-skilled** - able to switch from one job to another if needed. This example of job rotation may perhaps lead to the employee being more motivated. From a firm's point of view, an employee that can change jobs may prevent the need to have temporary workers to cover for illness etc. and so reduce labour costs. An example of this is the 'workstyle' initiative at Birds Eye/Walls, where team working has been introduced so that workers can change from one process to another and do the work of others in the team if necessary.

A flexible workforce Increasingly employers are looking to make plans that allow a business to respond to changes. For example, if a large unexpected order arrives, a business will need workers that can 'get it out on time'. Using a FLEXIBLE WORKFORCE will enable a business

to react effectively to changes that take place outside the business. Examples of workers that may be used by a business include:

- part time employees, such as cleaners, who only work a few hours a day;
- temporary employees to deal with increases in demand, such as agricultural workers;
- office temporary workers to cover for illness or sickness;
- self-employed workers, such as management consultants, for specialist tasks;
- job sharing, where two workers are employed to do a full time job that may in the past have been carried out by one person.

It has been argued that there are both benefits and disadvantages for these types of employee. On the one hand, a single parent may be able to find work at a convenient time, and job sharing could mean employment for two people, instead of unemployment for one of them. However, part time workers may be paid at a lower rate and may be entitled to fewer employment rights than full time workers. The position of flexible staff is often a source of industrial relations problems for businesses and may lead to conflict with trade unions.

Recruitment, redundancy and redeployment If a business is aiming to expand production it may employ extra workers. However, when a plan calls for reductions in staff then redundancies often follow. Cuts in staff can be achieved in a number of ways.

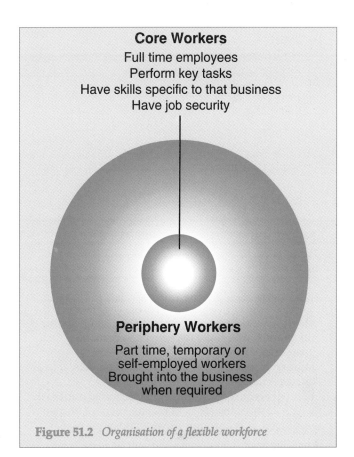

Figure 51.2 *Organisation of a flexible workforce*

- It may be possible to lose some workers through natural wastage. This simply means that employees that leave the business are not replaced.
- The business may ask for voluntary redundancies where workers agree to leave the company and are compensated by redundancy payments (☞ unit 56). The company could offer early retirement to workers close to the compulsory age (65 for men, 60 for women).
- Compulsory redundancy may take place, if there is no longer enough work for employees.

Workers may also be **redeployed** within a business. Although the worker will have to adjust to a new work environment, this should not be too difficult with induction and training. Redeployment to another part of the country, however, is more of a problem for employees.

In 1985 John Atkinson and the Institute of Manpower Studies developed the idea of the **flexible firm**. They suggested that firms have a 'core' and a 'periphery', as in Figure 51.2, and that as a result of competition in the 1980s, firms have deliberately planned to make the workforce as flexible as possible to reduce costs. The business would try to motivate core workers, and give them job security, whilst employing temporary workers on the periphery only when needed. Others have criticised this idea suggesting that firms do not plan to have a core and periphery, but that it has come about as a result of high unemployment and reduced union power (☞ unit 59).

QUESTION 4 Golden Wonder employs 3,000 people on six sites. The company has taken a co-ordinated series of initiatives on human resource planning. The workload in crisp manufacturing fluctuates depending upon seasonal peaks and special sales promotions. A temporary workers' agreement caters for employees engaged for periods of up to 26 weeks. In any one factory the number of temporaries can range from zero to as many as 500. On average, however, there would be some 200 temporaries for a few peak months. There is also 24-hour, three shift working.

In the late 1980s a proposal was put to the unions, suggesting three categories of employees: Category One was the permanent workforce; Category Two would be permanent part timers - that is those working two to three days per week with an 'agreed flexibility' to work the extra two or three days in the week (for which no overtime would be paid until 39 hours was reached); Category Three was to be composed of the temporary staff. A ballot of the workforce led, however, to rejection of this scheme.

With the help of a team of management consultants the company then turned to what was known as an 'annual hours' package. This involved the averaging out of total hours worked over a 12 month period, so that the time worked in any particular week was no longer regarded as the critical factor. It entailed a planned reduction in work hours for the first category and an increase for the other two categories. The planning of the annual hours and the mixed composition of the labour force to reach the total required was accompanied by an integrated approach. A policy document was produced which linked the issues of conditions, training, progression, rewards and the flexible use of the different categories of labour.

Source: adapted from *The Management of Human Resources*, John Storey, Basil Blackwell, 1992.

(a) Why might Golden Wonder have needed to be flexible when planning its human resource needs?
(b) Explain how Golden Wonder have aimed to use flexible work practices and a flexible workforce.
(c) What might be the implications for:
  (i) workers;
  (ii) the business;
  of these practices?

Key terms

Flexible workforce - a workforce that can respond (in quantity and type) to changes in demand a business may face.

Human resources - the employees or personnel in a business that help it to achieve its goals.

Human resource planning - an integrated approach which ensures the efficient management of human resources. It is part of the overall business plan.

Manpower plan - the suggested quantity, quality and type of employees a business will require in future.

Labour turnover - the number of people that leave a business over a period as a percentage of the average number of people employed.

Organisational culture - the shared norms and values of a business.

Question

Engindorf PLC

Engindorf PLC are a multinational engineering and manufacturing company. They have a large information technology department that employs over 1,000 people in various European locations, although most are employed in two sites in the UK and Germany. The business has grown rapidly in recent years and the demands of the department have increased.

In the mid-1980s, recruitment was accelerating each year. Mimi Tsui, the IT director, began a recruitment policy aimed at employing graduates and then developing them in the company with training. At first there were problems and the rate of new recruits leaving the business rose from 10 per cent to 21 per cent. Mimi, however, was able to reduce this fairly quickly by involving recruits in decision making and by mapping out a career development plan for each employee.

The early 1990s brought a change in the economic climate in Europe. Demand fell and, faced with overcapacity, the company changed its objectives to cutting costs and getting products to the market as quickly as possible. The IT department was to be an important part of this. It was likely in the future that more emphasis would be placed on computer aided design and computer integrated manufacturing. The department would also move from having a data processing role to providing management with up to date information quickly so that decisions could be made effectively. This was all likely to put pressure on management time, so Mimi had started to develop a number of initiatives, giving responsibility to IT managers in her department for recruitment, appraisal and promotion boards. This, she felt, would make the department more efficient.

It was clear to Mimi that what she needed was clear human resource planning which would be geared to the objectives of the company. She approached Brian McGhee, the business planning manager and together they aimed to plan the likely effects on the department's human resources over the next five years. Before writing the plan, Brian gathered some useful information.

■ The number of employees in the department had grown by between 11 and 13 per cent per annum over the last three years.

■ The UK recruitment market consists mainly of graduates aged 21 and the German recruitment market consists mainly of post-graduates aged 25-26.

■ Projections show a fall in the number of graduates in both these markets in the next 5 years.

■ At the moment, the company's initial graduate pay rates are broadly competitive with those of other companies.

■ Three years ago the department started to recruit increasing numbers of female graduates.

(a) Why might Engindorf have had problems with its new recruits initially?

(b) What problems might an increase in labour turnover of new recruits have had on the business?

(c) Using information from the passage, suggest how the IT department might plan its human resources.

(d) Discuss the likely factors that might affect the human resource planning of Engindorf PLC in the next five years.

(e) How might the business react to the changes taking place in the next five years?

Summary

1. State 6 tasks that a personnel department may carry out.
2. Explain the difference between short and long term planning.
3. How might a business forecast the:
   (a) employees;
   (b) internal employee supply;
   it may need in future?
4. Briefly describe 5 factors that may affect human resource planning by a business.
5. How might a business react to an ageing population?
6. 'A business that does not plan how to use its personnel effectively may face industrial relations problems.' Explain this statement with an example.
7. Why is a high level of labour turnover such a problem for a business?
8. Suggest 3 methods a business may use to reduce labour turnover.
9. State 3 examples of:
   (a) flexible practices;
   (b) flexible workers.
10. What are the advantages to a business of having a flexible workforce?

The need for effective recruitment

This unit concentrates on the first stage in human resource management - recruitment. From the personnel department's point of view, the objective of recruitment is to attract the 'best' candidates for the job, and then to choose the most suitable. If the wrong person is recruited, and then finds the job boring or too difficult, then the business will not get the most out of its human resources. Also, where employees need to be flexible and autonomous and where direct control over employees is difficult, recruitment is becoming more and more important. To make sure the 'best' person is chosen, personnel departments must be clear about:
■ what the job entails;
■ what qualities are required to do the job;
■ what rewards are needed to retain and motivate employees.

Job analysis

Before a business recruits new employees, the personnel department usually carries out some form of JOB ANALYSIS. Job analysis is a study of what a job entails. It contains the skills, training and tasks that are needed to carry out the job.

Job analysis can be used by firms in many ways. These include selecting employees, setting pay, disciplinary interviews, promotion and job appraisal (dealt with later in this unit). For example, if a firm was trying to choose an applicant for the post of systems analyst, it may use job analysis to find out exactly what a systems analyst does in that firm.

In order to find out about what is involved in a job, the personnel department must gather data about all the different elements in that job. It is likely that people associated with the job will have different views about what is involved.
■ The occupant of the job. She will have the most detailed knowledge of what the job requires. However, she might change the information to exaggerate her own status, or leave parts of the job out because they are taken for granted.
■ The job holder's superior. She will have her own view of what the job involves, but is unlikely to be fully aware of all job details.
■ Subordinates and others with whom the job holder is in regular contact. They are likely to have observed the behaviour of the job holder over a period of time. Once again, any bias or error which the observer may have must be taken into account.
■ Specialist observers, such as job analysts. These can provide an independent view of the work being carried out. The major problem is that the job holder, knowing she is being observed, may adjust her behaviour.

Having collected this information, it must then be analysed. This is often done by using five categories.

Task analysis This involves the study of those tasks an employee carries out when doing their job. Any job will be made up of a variety of tasks. A task is seen as a collection of activities that result in an objective being achieved. For example, an employee may have the task of reporting on stock levels in the company.

Activity analysis This is a study of the activities which make up a task. These will include physical activities and the intellectual demands of the job. So an employee whose task is to do a stock check might need to understand how to use the computerised stock control program and understand the concept of lead time (☞ unit 33).

Skills analysis This involves a study of the skills that

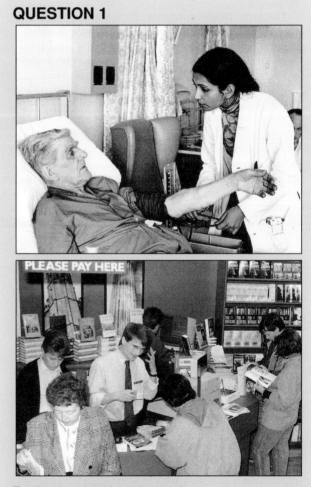

QUESTION 1

PLEASE PAY HERE

For the above two jobs discuss the:
(a) tasks that might need to be carried out;
(b) skills that the job holder may need;
(c) criteria that could be used to assess their performance.

are needed to do the job. These could be motor skills, such as the ability to use a computer program, or other skills, such as the ability to work with others.

Role analysis This is the information gathered from the job holder, superiors and colleagues. The duties, responsibilities and behaviour expected from the job holder are discussed to produce a role description which all involved agree upon.

Performance analysis This attempts to set the criteria that will be used when evaluating how well a job holder carries out the job. It involves identifying standards and expectations. For example, an employee may need to ensure that stock wastage is kept to a certain level. This will give a target to aim at while carrying out stock control.

Job description

Once a business has analysed what a job entails, it is important to draw up a description of the job. The JOB DESCRIPTION is a simple 'word picture' of the job. It will often contain some of the elements in Table 52.1.

Table 52.1 *Possible job description of a design artist*

General information	Job title, such as 'designer'. Place of job within the business. Job summary, eg main tasks.
Job content information	Tasks involved, eg details of tasks. Purpose of tasks, eg develop designs for products. Methods involved, eg drawing, CAD etc. Other duties, eg part of design team. Responsibility, eg control of other staff.
Working conditions	Physical environment, eg work area. Social environment, eg holidays. Economic conditions, eg length of working day.
Performance information	Criteria for measuring performance, eg quality of designs.

The job description has a number of uses. It allows the firm to tell candidates for a job what is expected of them. It also helps personnel officers to decide on the qualities that successful candidates must have.

When candidates are appointed, the job description can be used to gauge whether the employee is doing the job 'properly', by comparing their activities with the description. Disputes about the work an employee has to do can also be settled by looking at the job description.

A good example of 'tight' job descriptions are those for

McDonald's employees. They are given because employees are expected to be very flexible and interchangeable in their jobs (☞ unit 51) - so that when a worker comes to a job or task, they know exactly what to do. McDonalds has a 385 page operations manual which is given to each employee. It is full of details on how each task should be performed. For example, it includes instructions such as 'Cooks must turn, never flip, hamburgers... once, never two at a time ... Cashiers must make eye contact and smile at every customer'.

The job description is a means of communication (☞ unit 62). It suffers from the usual problems of misunderstanding and distortion. It is also a simplification, as it is rarely possible to include every feature of a particular job.

Person specification

Once the skills and knowledge needed to perform a particular job have been outlined in the job description, they are often reworded into a PERSON SPECIFICATION (sometimes referred to as the human specification or the job specification). This shows a profile of the type of person needed to do the job.

Such a description can then form the basis for the selection of the most suitable person to fill the job. Table 52.2 shows a possible example.

Table 52.2 *A possible personal specification of a draughtsperson*

Attainments	Essential to have evidence of application and capacity for detailed work.
	Desirable to have some knowledge of technical drawing and of engineering terms.
	Must have at least technical training and possess 4 GCSEs grade C or above, or NVQ in engineering or manufacturing at equivalent level.
	Previous experience of record keeping in technical office or library is essential.
	Experience of working with engineering drawings is desirable.
General intelligence	Brisk reactions and accurate memory are needed.
Specialised aptitudes	Neat, quick and accurate at clerical work.
Interests	Practical and social.
Disposition	Self-reliant, helpful, friendly.
Circumstances	Likely to stay for at least 3 years.

QUESTION 2

Figure 52.1 *A job advertisement*

Use the information in the advertisement above to show the difference between a job description and a person specification.

Job evaluation

A business can use JOB EVALUATION to compare the value of different jobs. Any job can be broken down into a number of factors. These are the skills, effort, responsibility, knowledge and tasks that the job entails. This allows the business to decide on the wages or salary for that job. If another job has greater skill or responsibility, then the business may award it at a higher rate of pay.

Job evaluation has become more popular over the last decade. It has been seen by businesses as a rational way of working out why some jobs are paid more than others. It has also been used in equal pay cases (☞ unit 55). For example, if there is a dispute about equal pay, the job evaluation will help to show if employees are doing work of equal value. When using job evaluation, a business must remember certain points.

- Job evaluation is about the job and not the performance of the employee in the job.
- Experienced people decide on the value of a job. Whilst this is likely to give useful results, they are not 'perfect'.
- It allows firms to set differential rewards for jobs. This

does not rule out collective bargaining (☞ unit 59) to raise these rates.
- Only pay is determined, not other earnings, such as incentives.

The most popular method of job evaluation is a points scheme. A number of factors (skill, problem solving etc.) are found which are common to all jobs. Each factor is given a weighting according to its importance. A job description is then prepared and points are allocated to each factor. The total number of points determines the value of the job, and the wages or salary to be paid.

Whilst it can be useful, job evaluation is costly for firms. Also, some jobs will still be 'underpaid' or 'overpaid', as it is a matter of human judgement.

Methods of recruitment

If vacancies do exist then the personnel department must fill them. Often firms fill vacancies by recruiting new employees - **external** recruitment. An alternative is to appoint **internally** from within the business. In the short term, particularly if funds are not available for extra workers, it may be possible to reorganise the work in

QUESTION 3

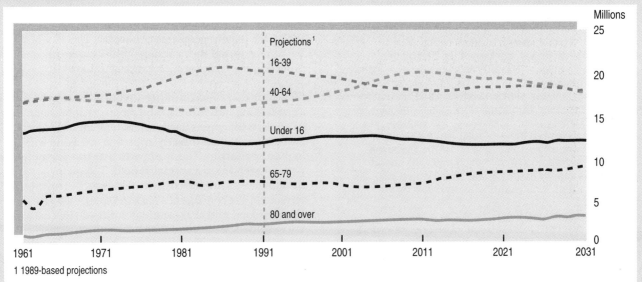

Figure 52.2 *Population projections*
Source: adapted from OPCS, Government Actuary's Department, General Register Offices (Scotland and Northern Ireland).

(a) What trends can be identified from Figure 52.2 over the next 20 years?

(b) A producer of plastics has been growing steadily and is likely to need an extra 100 workers for a new factory in Glasgow. The management has suggested that 20 per cent should be school leavers who can be trained for the future. Given the trends you have identified, advise them on the implications of such action and suggest any alternative strategies.

order to fill the 'gaps' left by vacant positions. For example, the work could be shared out between the remaining employees.

This option might be used if the workload was felt to be too light in the department before the vacancy existed, or if the section is very 'tightly knit'. A further option is to pay existing workers overtime rates to cover the output lost by the employee who has left. Internal reorganisation is not without its problems. These include how the work should be divided and what rewards employees should receive for 'extra' work.

External recruitment to fill vacancies is likely to become increasingly difficult in the 1990s given the population trends in some Western developed countries. In the UK, skills shortages and forecasts of a 'demographic timebomb' (☞ unit 51) will make recruitment from outside more difficult. Employers will either need to change their strategies to take into account the falling number of potential recruits in competitive markets, or be faced with vacant positions.

This may require the use of innovative forms of recruitment, employing previously inactive workers, flexible working (☞ unit 51) or job sharing.

Internal recruitment

It is argued that internal recruitment strengthens employees' commitment to the company. The personnel department of Kellogg's have the following courses of action in their recruitment policy handbook.

'(a) Offer the job to an existing employee, as a promotion or transfer.

(b) Advertise internally, if a suitable candidate is likely to be available internally.

(c) Advertise externally if no suitable candidate is likely to exist internally (and display notice internally to the effect that the advertisement is appearing).

Except in special cases, all vacancies should be advertised internally before external recruitment methods are used.'

There are a number of advantages to advertising jobs 'inside' the business.

■ It gives employees within the company a chance to develop their career.

■ There may be a shorter induction period as the employee is likely to be familiar with the company.

■ Employers will know more about internal candidates' abilities. This should reduce the risk of employing the 'wrong' person.

■ Internal recruitment may be quicker and less expensive than recruiting from outside the business.

However, there are also disadvantages.

■ Internal advertising limits the number of applicants.

■ External candidates might have been of better quality.

■ Another vacancy will be created which might have to be filled.

■ If, having investigated ways of filling the vacancy internally the business still does not appoint, then it must find ways to obtain candidates externally.

QUESTION 4 The Sunshine company, a cereal manufacturer that has its European headquarters in Birmingham, needed to appoint a new sales statistics controller. The post was not at a particularly high level in the clerical structure with a salary higher than a departmental secretary, but lower than that of an administrative officer. The job required individual work more than group work.

Sylvester Osei, the personnel officer, was looking for a 'number cruncher' who could work independently and whose personality fitted 'quick work'. He wanted candidates who were thirty or over, had the relevant experience and knew something about the Sunshine company, and who could do the job well. His added incentive to appoint internally was that it would help him reach his targets for advertising expenditure for the year.

Sylvester appointed Eric Giles to the job after a number of internal candidates had been interviewed. He gives a short life history and character profile of Eric.

'He is 48 years old, single and his character is quietly confident. He works very hard and is reliable. He is content doing responsible clerical jobs and doesn't see it as a necessary evil that has to be done. He has worked in the Sunshine company for 20 years in the same sort of job. He has never applied for any other job apart from this one. There seems to be no financial incentive involved as the salary of his present job is comparable to that of the sales statistics clerk. He has been a steady influence on his department for twelve years.'

(a) Give two reasons why Sylvester wanted to appoint someone internally to the Sunshine company to the post of sales statistics controller.
(b) Why do you think the appointment of Eric to the post was a good decision?

External recruitment

There are many ways of attracting candidates from outside the company. The choice of method often depends on the type of vacancy and the type of employee a business wants. Each method has its own benefits and problems, although it could be argued that the overall advantages of external advertising are the opposite of the disadvantages of internal advertising, for example, there are a wider number of applicants.

Commercial employment agencies These are companies that specialise in recruiting and selection. They usually provide a shortlist of candidates for a company to interview, but can also provide temporary workers. Examples include Alfred Marks, HMS and Kelly Accountancy Personnel.

The advantage of commercial agencies is that they are experienced in providing certain types of worker, such as secretaries and clerical staff. They also minimise the administration for the employer involved in recruiting staff. Their main drawback is that they tend to produce staff who only stay in a job for a short time. Another problem for the business is the cost of paying fees to the agency.

Job centres and professional recruitment agencies These are government run and private organisations which try to help people obtain work. Their main advantage is that they can find applicants easily and can quickly draw from local or national databases.

Headhunting 'Headhunting' involves executive agencies approaching individuals, who have a reputation in a field of work, with employment offers. The main advantage is that a business can directly approach someone with a known specialism. This is of particular use to employers not experienced in a specialist field. The main disadvantages are the cost, the fact that the recruit may remain on the consultant's list even after they have changed jobs, and that candidates outside the 'network' are excluded.

The Careers Service As well as providing careers guidance to young people and adults, the Careers Service also collects local job vacancies and distributes them to their clients in schools and in the local area. Their main advantage is that they can produce regular enquiries from young people who are likely to be looking no further than the local area for employment and who would be able to take up a post quickly. Their disadvantage is that they work on a local rather than a regional or national basis.

Youth training Youth training schemes provide training for all under 19s not in full time education or a job. They involve training for school leavers in a variety of vocational trades (☞ unit 54) in the form of.
- traineeship - where training is given, but not leading to a job;
- careership - where the trainee is given job status and trained by the business.

The advantage to a business of offering such a scheme is that costs are reduced as trainees are given an allowance by the government. The firm will also be able to have a 'free trial' of a prospective employee.

Visiting universities - 'the milkround' This involves companies visiting universities around the country with the aim of recruiting employees. Its main advantage is that it provides easy access to candidates of graduate standard. It is also fairly inexpensive and convenient through using the free services of the University Appointments Service. The main drawbacks are that often the interviewees are simply enquiring about a job and that interview schedules can be very time consuming and tiring.

Advertising agencies Apart from using the above methods, employers will often advertise their jobs to a wider audience. They may deal with advertising agencies to gain help with drafting advertisements and placing them in suitable media. The agency will usually book the space in the chosen media, prepare the layout, read and correct proofs, and check that the right advertisement has appeared in the right publication, at the right time. The agency will usually be aware of the following methods of job advertising.

- ■ Vacancy lists, outside premises. This is an economical method, but it will only be seen by a few people and little information can be included.
- ■ Advertising in the national press. This has the advantage of wider coverage, but can be costly and may reach people who are not interested.
- ■ Advertising in the local press. This will be read by local people seeking employment, but evidence suggests the local press is not read by professionals, for example.
- ■ Advertising in the technical press. This reaches the appropriate people, but may be published infrequently.
- ■ Television advertising. This reaches large numbers, but can be expensive.

A job advertisement

As important as choosing the most appropriate media through which to advertise a vacancy is the drafting of the advertisement. The decision on what to include in a recruitment advertisement is important because of the high cost of space and the need to attract attention. Both factors will encourage the use of the fewest number of words. Figure 52.3 shows some of the items that could be included.

Key terms

Job analysis - a study of what the job entails, such as the skills, tasks and performance expected.
Job description - a simple word picture of what the job entails.
Job evaluation - a method used by businesses to compare the value of different jobs and perhaps set wages or salaries.
Person specification - a profile of the type of person needed to do a job.

QUESTION 5 In November 1991, Independent Television broadcast what was thought to be the first television commercial for a single job vacancy. Its success will be only partly based on whether the company found a person to fill its own opening for an international sales manager for Europe. Independent Television hoped to convince other employers of the effectiveness of television for recruitment by showing it.

Although critics claim television recruitment advertising is expensive, the fact that it has happened at all highlights employers' problems in filling executive posts. Advertising costs have been rising in traditional recruitment media, such as national newspapers and the trade press, while typical headhunter fees are 33 per cent of the basic annual salary.

The decision to harness a mass medium for such a narrow task rested with Jonathan Shier, Independent Television's sales and marketing director. The campaign consisted of a 50 second commercial, appearing on Channel 4 and ITV a dozen times. The commercial was fairly low-budget, made up of computer-generated graphics and background music.

The commercials were broadcast in prime-time programmes such as the evening news and during French and Spanish films, which a multilingual person might watch. A similar campaign would cost an outside company up to £10,000. 'You would spend all that and more if you found somebody through a headhunter', Mr Shier said. Peter Myles, a director of Hunter-Myles, an executive search company specialising in marketing, said television cannot be sufficiently targeted for such a narrow purpose. 'It is a scattergun approach', he argued, 'The advertising wastage must be high.'

Pound for pound, the cost of television advertising compares favourably in certain situations with that of advertising in national newspapers.

Television recruitment is swimming against a trend. Recruitment consultancies continue to spring up while the use of advertising has fallen. The number of management vacancies in marketing and sales advertised in British newspapers and trade magazines for 1991 to June was 34 per cent below that for the previous 12 months, according to the human resource consultancy MSL International. For senior-level positions, non-advertising recruiting methods are prevalent. It is the search consultants or headhunters who focus on these top jobs.

Although headhunting is no longer taboo, concerns have been raised that employers are delegating an important management responsibility to an outside contractor. Although the final hiring decision remains with the client, the headhunter acts as the gatekeeper. Because search consultancies have agreements not to poach from their other clients, some qualified candidates are not considered. If television recruitment advertising proves effective, employers could regain control of the selection process.

Source: adapted from The Times, November 1991.

(a) Identify all the external methods of recruitment mentioned in the article.
(b) What factors might have encouraged the use of TV advertising as a medium?
(c) 'It is a scattergun approach.' 'The advertising wastage must be high.'
What disadvantages are implied in these statements for businesses using TV to advertise vacancies?
(d) Why might headhunting have overcome some of the limitations of TV advertising?

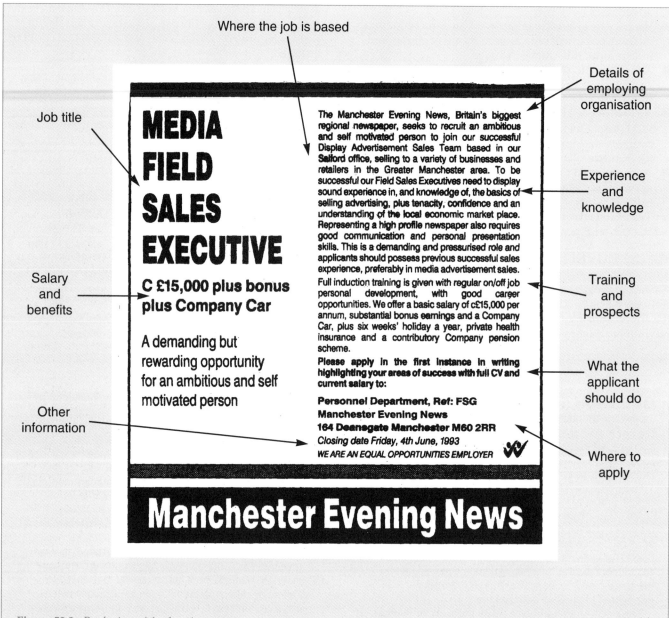

Figure 52.3 *Producing a job advertisement*

Summary

1. Why do businesses need to recruit effectively?
2. Give 2 reasons why companies carry out job analysis.
3. How is a job description useful to the personnel department?
4. What is the difference between a job description and a person specification?
5. Give 5 factors that might appear on a person specification.
6. How might job evaluation be used by a business?
7. State two ways in which a business could reorganise instead of appointing internally or externally to cover a vacancy.
8. What is meant by:
   (a) internal recruitment;
   (b) external recruitment?
9. Give 3 reasons why a business might recruit internally.
10. State 5 methods of external recruitment.
11. Why might a business recruit using an advertising agency rather than from a job centre?
12. What factors are important to show in a job recruitment advertisement?

Question

Two approaches to recruitment

The recruitment policy that a business adopts depends on a number of factors. These could include the product/service sold by the business, the type of employees required, the views of the recruiting staff and the size and organisation of the business.

Aero Industries (AI) are a long standing UK business, supplying the aerospace industry with equipment. A great deal of their production is defence related. They employ 950 staff. 200 of these employees work in the engineering department where product design takes place. This year the business estimates it will need to recruit 30 engineers. Logo Services, in contrast, are a small UK business. They offer a computer software consultancy, production and installation service. Out of 50 employees, 30 are graduates who work in the technological area. This year 6 new staff are required.

Who is responsible for recruitment?
AI sometimes experience difficulties over recruitment policy. An engineering manager, working together with the personnel department, is responsible for recruiting new engineering staff. He has worked in engineering for many years, building up contacts, and only late in his career was he made responsible for recruitment. He favours this informal use of contacts, whereas the personnel department would prefer a common, formal approach to recruitment throughout the company.

The finance director is responsible for technical staff recruitment at Logo Services. This may appear unusual, but it reflects the desire of the company to achieve greater flexibility of function. This is particularly important for a small company operating in a changing competitive environment. Engineers are also encouraged to take on managerial responsibilities.

Temporary and contract staff
AI use over 30 contract engineers. As the engineering manager puts it, 'It gives us flexibility. We've only had contract staff for the last three or four years ... lots of jobs that we do are fairly short term projects, so we really need a bit of flexibility ...'.

Logo Services, however, use no temporary or contract staff. As one manager said, 'You don't know what you are getting, and you don't know their standards of working. You have no control over them because ... they can up and go somewhere else.' The company recruits only full time permanent staff. They come in as trainees, start as junior analysts/programmers, and can then become either team leaders (doing technical work and running a team) or senior analysts/programmers who do a more technical job. The business stresses the need for staff to work flexible hours, if necessary, in order to respond to consumer requirements.

Recruitment methods
One disadvantage that AI face in recruitment is their image. They are not a 'household' name, as they do not supply products to consumers. They operate from ageing industrial buildings. From a survey of engineers, AI were seen in comparison with their main competitors as being technologically on the 'second rung of the ladder'. An advertising agency had been employed to change this image and had produced adverts based on research into potential candidates. The adverts showed a picture of a rebellious-looking young man as a typical recruit.

AI have changed their recruitment methods in an ad hoc fashion. They targeted experienced candidates through occasional national advertising campaigns and have started using hotel walk-in presentations on competitors' doorsteps, which are advertised in the local press. At these walk-ins, candidates can browse round a display of the company's activities, talk informally to AI engineers, read the recruitment literature, take refreshments and possibly be given a preliminary interview. Recently the engineering manager has been forced to use recruitment agencies as his contacts have been 'used up'. In one case, he paid for access to an agency's recruitment register, based on engineers it had placed in firms two to five years previously.

Logo Services recruit only graduates into technological positions and most of these are new graduates. All their graduate recruits are from the local university or are people who have lived in the district. This is because the managers believe it is important for a recruit to fit in with life in the surrounding countryside. The intake of computer programmers/analysts is fifty-fifty arts people and scientists. The biggest difficulty, the financial director believes, in recruiting arts graduates for such jobs is getting them to apply at all, and educating the career service that these graduates are what they want. The company tries to get over this prejudice by putting up posters on notice boards. They prefer to recruit new graduates, feeling that if people have not worked elsewhere they are easier to train. As one manager said, 'They are not starting with any preconceptions of the work and the atmosphere, so they're more amenable to our culture and way of working'.

Source: adapted from *Case Studies in Personnel*, eds. D. Winstanley and J. Woodall, Institute of Personnel Management.

(a) Summarise the main aspects of AI's and Logo Services' approaches to recruiting staff.
(b) In what ways do their different approaches reflect the differences in the way they are organised and the product/services they sell?
(c) What are the advantages and disadvantages of using contract staff in the engineering industry?
(d) How effective do you think: (i) hotel walk-ins; (ii) recruitment agencies; (iii) a national advertising campaign; are likely to be as aids to recruitment for AI?
(e) Why might Logo Services want to use internal recruitment methods for team leaders or senior analysts/programmers in the company?

Effective selection - making the right choice

Selection is growing in importance for firms. Reduced job mobility has meant that staff are likely to stay with the business for a longer period. If the candidate chosen is unsuitable, the business may be faced with the cost of poor performance by the employee. There will also be extra costs in selecting and training a replacement when that employee leaves.

Businesses have also realised the need for a fair and valid choice of candidate. The most suitable applicant will only be chosen if selection is based on ability, skills and knowledge, rather than race or sex. **Equal opportunities** legislation has helped to make impartial selection more likely, although there are still arguments about the `fairness' involved in selection (unit 55).

Effective selection should lead to the most suitable candidate being employed, in terms of their skills and motivation, as well as reducing the cost of selection. Personnel managers play an important part in this. They help to prepare the job analysis, job description, and person specification, and decide exactly how to recruit. They also advise on the nature of application forms, how to SHORT LIST from them, and how to conduct tests and interviews. Finally, they will influence how the information is evaluated and what decisions should be made about candidates.

Application forms

Growing use is being made of application forms in selection. They have many benefits for a business. All applicants give details in a standard way, rather than the different approaches of letters of application. This makes sorting applications and short listing far easier. The form is often used as the basis of the interview and can be a starting point for personnel records. The application form covers:

- personal details (name, address, nationality, etc.);
- educational qualifications;
- hobbies and interests;
- past job experience;
- reasons for wanting to join the company;
- references.

Certain forms leave out some of the above, while others include much more. Whatever the format, the form helps applicants 'present' their case. Also, by gaining biographical information, the personnel department has a simple way of matching the applicant's qualifications, interests, past experience etc. to their person specification (unit 52). This allows the firm to decide quickly which of the applicants is suitable for a job.

Table 53.1 shows a checklist of points which can be used to help a business design an application form.

Table 53.1

- Handwriting is often larger than type. Do the boxes/areas on the form give enough room for the applicant to complete the information?
- Forms that take too long to complete may be completed haphazardly or not at all. Is the time the form takes to complete appropriate to the information the employer needs?
- Some questions may be illegal, offensive, or not essential. Does the form ask only for information appropriate to the job?
- Word processors make it possible to produce separate application forms for each post advertised and to make them user friendly. One way of doing this is to use introductory paragraphs explaining why the information in each section is being sought.

QUESTION 1 Frost Frame are a small company producing double glazed windows. They have decided to expand production. In particular, they are looking for someone with skills in working with stained glass. Having placed an advertisement in the local newspaper, the company sent out application forms. The standard application form was used which had been devised for all general workshop employees. It did not ask any questions related to the applicant's specific skills. After four weeks they have received three applications and only one candidate looks worth interviewing. However, it is unclear from his answers whether he will be entirely suitable.

(a) Identify problems that Frost Frame may have had with their application form.
(b) Suggest one way in which they could improve it.
(c) What might be the implications for the company if they decide not to interview the candidate?

Testing

Businesses appear to be taking a greater interest in testing. There are strong arguments for and against the use of tests in selection. Those in favour argue that interviews (dealt with in the next section) do not really allow a business to predict performance and point to the greater accuracy and objectivity of test data. Those against dispute this objectivity. They also argue that predictions from test results can mislead. For example, does a high test score mean high job performance and a low score mean low job performance?

There are a number of tests that are used in selection. These are often associated with different levels of staff.

- Aptitude tests measure how well a candidate can cope when faced with a business situation or problem.
- Attainment tests measure an individual's ability using skills they have already acquired. For example, a candidate for an administration post may take a word processing test.

■ Intelligence tests aim to give an indication of overall 'mental' ability. A variety of questions are asked in such tests covering numeracy and literacy skills, as well as general knowledge. It is assumed that a person who scores highly will be able to retain new knowledge and to succeed at work (☞ unit 47).

■ Personality tests examine the **traits** of employees (☞ unit 47). The use of these depends on whether the business wants to use this method of selection and whether qualified personnel are available to carry out the tests. Such tests do have problems. It is dangerous to assume that there is a standard personality profile of the 'ideal employee'. Another problem is that they rely on an individual being honest. Candidates often try to pick out the answer that is wanted. Also some traits measured by the test will not be relevant in terms of job performance.

QUESTION 2 The world's top hotels have much to teach industry about the art of staff selection. The most expensive bed for the night in London's second biggest hotel will cost £2,500, and at that price guests expect service with style. An American hotel management company, Rosewood, scoured the world to recruit the best senior staff for its Lanesborough Hotel, London.

Rosewood is using the personal profile analysis from Thomas International for selection and recruitment. Interviewees assess their own qualities, such as gentleness, confidence, outspokenness and willingness.

Michael Willis, Rosewood's director of human resources, says, `I thought it would be like reading tea leaves. Three days after trying out the test on my assistant, I did his annual appraisal and found his strengths and weaknesses had come out on the form.'

The Ritz-Carlton is using a different approach, called targeted selection, to staff the Windsor Hotel. Members of staff at other hotels were asked to assess the qualities and qualifications required to perform their responsibilities. The responses by the best staff were used to prepare a list of questions to ask interviewees.

Source: adapted from *The Times*, March 1992.

(a) What type of tests are the hotels using?
(b) What reasons might the hotels in the article give for using testing in the selection of employees?
(c) Identify the problems that may be faced when using such tests.

Interviews

Most people have at least one experience of being interviewed prior to employment. Few people enjoy interviews. Often this is because the interviewer appears to be more interested in finding fault than being helpful.

The personnel department is usually involved in interviewing, both in carrying them out and helping managers to adopt good interview practice. By following certain guidelines, the business hopes to employ the 'right' person for the job. It also aims to carry out the interview in a way that is fair to all candidates. These guidelines might include the following.

■ The interview should allow information to be collected from candidates which can be used to predict whether they can perform the job. This can be done by comparing replies with the criteria that successful applicants should have.

■ The business should give candidates full details about the job and the organisation. This will help them decide whether the job would suit them.

■ The interview should be conducted so that candidates can say that they have had a fair hearing.

The interview has, however, been criticised as not always being an effective 'tool'. Some of the main criticisms are:

■ interviewers often decide to accept or reject a candidate within the first three or four minutes of the interview, and then spend the rest of the time finding evidence to confirm their decision;

QUESTION 3 A number of executives attended a conference at the Institute of Directors in 1991, titled `Changing Jobs in a Recession'. They realised that there would be changes in future and that when that time came, they would be ready.

A key subject of the conference was the interview, including the preparation and techniques. The 25:75 ratio was mentioned. This means you spend 25 per cent of your effort presenting yourself and 75 per cent on the other person, listening for clues, watching body language and picking up hidden messages in the tone of voice. Afterwards, one delegate said she was surprised that nothing had been said about the interview being as much about the candidate interviewing the employer as the other way round.

The speakers' emphasis was on how to select and present aspects of experience and skills relevant to the job and the organisation. Although this is extremely valuable, if such advice is not tempered with the view that the candidate can take some of the initiative, it can encourage interviewees to assume that they must answer to a predetermined description of the `ideal' person for the job.

There was no mention of how candidates could use the interview to select the most suitable organisation. Instead, the clues were hidden in the advice given on networking - finding out from contacts who have information about certain businesses.

At the informal meeting, the job-seeker will have prepared his set of questions and will show his real interest and enthusiasm, quite naturally, not only through his attentive listening, but also through the nature of his questions. If more candidates could behave as naturally in the interview, both they and employers would have a greater chance of making the right decisions, because they will have started to explore more openly their `degree of fit'.

Source: adapted from the *Financial Times*, 1991.

(a) What factors mentioned in the article are employers likely to be looking for from a candidate at an interview?
(b) Explain the potential problems of the interview as a method of selection using examples given at the conference to illustrate your answers.

- interviews seldom change the initial opinion formed by the interviewer seeing the application form and the appearance of the candidate;
- interviewers place more stress on evidence that is unfavourable than on the evidence that is favourable;
- when interviewers have made up their minds very early in the interview, their behaviour betrays their decision to the candidate.

The problem with these criticisms is that they do not solve the problems, only identify them. No matter what other means of selection there may be, the interview is crucial. If it is thought to be unreliable, it should not be discarded. Businesses must simply make sure they carry it out properly.

Conducting an interview

There are a number of factors which could be taken into account when carrying out interviews. The interview should be conducted around a simple plan and be based on a number of questions against which all candidates will be assessed. It is also considered good practice to prepare a suitable place for the interview, such as a warm, quiet, ventilated room. The interviewer should also ensure that the candidates have a friendly reception and are informed of what is expected of them.

The average interview takes around 30 minutes. The interview plan organises the time to cover the important areas in assessing applicants. The plan must be flexible enough to allow the interviewer to explore areas that may come up during the interview. An example is shown in Table 53.2.

Many recruitment handbooks spell out the 'dos and don'ts' of interviewing. Some of the 'dos' that the interviewer may take into account include the following.

- Introduce yourself to the candidate.
- Adopt a suitable manner, show respect and be friendly.
- Make sure the interview is not interrupted.
- Conduct the interview at an unhurried pace.
- Have a list of questions that need to be asked.
- Encourage the candidate to talk by using 'open' questions such as:
  'Tell me about your present/last job ...'
  'What is your opinion on ...?'
  'What do you find interesting in ...?'
- Concentrate on those areas not fully covered by the application form.
- Be alert for clues in the candidate's answer, probe where necessary, and be more specific in the questioning if you are not satisfied.

Table 53.2 *Organising an interview*

Organisation	Tasks	Time (minutes)
Introduction	Who are they?	2
	Who are you?	3
Body of interview	Begin questioning. Ask questions which probe what they have learnt from their experiences/qualifications /interests and how they would apply this to their new position.	10
	Let the candidate ask questions. Explain about the organisation.	5
	If any questions are left, clear them up.	5
	Tell the candidate what happens next, eg 'We will let you know in 10 days'.	3
Close of interview	Finish tidily.	
After the interview	Assess the candidate.	10/15
	Prepare for next interview.	10/15

QUESTION 4 Research into graduate recruitment has shown that personnel managers use many different approaches to interviews. Some use a standard approach. Others felt that this means graduates are too well rehearsed for the interview, which leads to a false picture of the candidate. Some comments made during research included the following.

Personnel manager from Scicon - a computer software house
'I don't ask the standard questions about why have you applied to Scicon or what in your degree has prepared you for this job, because all that's testing is one's ability to prepare for interviews. So I ask questions candidates haven't remotely prepared for. I might talk about what's going on in the teachers' dispute with testing, not because I'm interested in the subject itself ... but I'm interested in how people think quickly on a subject they haven't been expecting.'

Personnel manager from Great Universal Stores
'We are obviously anxious to get the right people for the right job. Having said that if we give the game away and say this is the sort of person we want then there are some clever people around who can manipulate their behaviour and do it in a way to show they are best. I want to make sure that they know where they stand with us as well as us finding out about them. It is very difficult to hit a happy medium between not leaving them totally confused in the questions asked but at the same time not giving so much away that some candidates can manipulate their behaviour to put on a good performance. It is very difficult.'

A comment made by a 'typical' candidate
'The interviewer asks about GCSEs, A levels, why are you doing your present degree, why this company - you know, the usual thing. You get to the situation with interviews where you know what they are going to ask and what your answers are going to be.'

Source: Independent research by the author.

(a) What might be meant by 'the standard approach to interviewing'?
(b) Why might some personnel managers be unhappy with adopting a 'standard approach'?
(c) What methods could personnel managers adopt which might avoid the pitfalls of a 'standard approach'?
(d) Based on these comments, do you think that interviewing is a reliable way of selecting individuals for jobs?

■ When the interview has ended, make sure the candidate has no further questions and let the candidate know when the decision will be made, eg within seven days.

■ Write up your assessment notes immediately.

■ Prepare for the next interview.

The interviewer will have gained a great deal of information from the interview. It will help the interviewer to have a checklist of the criteria used when assessing candidates. Table 53.3 shows two possible lists. The interviewer can make notes about candidates next to each criterion and compare the information with the person specification after the interview, to decide if the person is suitable.

Table 53.3 *Criteria used in assessing candidates*

Rodgers' 7 point plan	Munro-Fraser 5 point plan
Physical make-up	Impact on others
Attainments	Qualifications
General intelligence	Innate abilities
Specialised aptitude	Motivation
Interests	Emotional adjustment
Disposition	
Circumstances	

Evaluating selection

How can a business tell if selection has been effective? It could simply decide that if it has appointed the 'right' candidate, then its aim has been achieved. However, selection will involve costs to a business. There will be expenses in sending out application forms and perhaps travelling expenses for candidates. Staff will also have to give up time to carry out the interviews.

So, for example, if 10 people were interviewed for 3 posts, but only one applicant was suitable, selection may not have been effective. In this case the firm would have to readvertise and interview other candidates as 2 posts would be unfilled. The personnel department's role would be to check all stages of selection to find out where problems had arisen. For example, when short listing, a suitable candidate may have been 'left out'. At an interview a possible candidate may have been rushed, so he was not given the chance to do his best.

Appointment

Once a business has made a choice, the successful candidate must be **appointed**. Nearly all new employees are given a CONTRACT OF EMPLOYMENT. This is a written statement which must be given within 13 weeks of appointment. This is stated in the Employment Protection (Consolidation) Act of 1978. The contract shows the terms and conditions of employment and any additional notes on disciplinary or grievance procedures.

Some common features of a contract of employment are shown below.

■ Name of employer, name of employee.

■ Date on which employment began.

■ Job title.

■ Rate of pay, period and method of payment.

■ Normal hours of work and related conditions, such as meal breaks.

■ Arrangements for holidays and holiday pay.

■ Terms and conditions relating to sickness, injury and sick pay.

■ Terms and conditions of pension arrangements, including a note about whether or not the employment is contracted out under the provisions of the **Social Security Act 1975**.

■ Length of notice due to and from employee.

■ Disciplinary rules and procedures.

■ Arrangements for handling employee grievances.

■ Conditions of employment relating to trade union membership (where applicable).

Full and part time employees usually have different conditions. Employees who work sixteen hours a week or more have the same legal rights as full timers. Those who work between eight and sixteen hours only gain these rights when they have been in continuous service with the employer for five years. Employers are not legally obliged to pay the same rates of pay to those working part time as to those working full time, but they are bound by the **Equal Pay Act 1970** (☞ unit 55). This means that part timers could claim for equal pay if they can identify a full time worker of the opposite sex carrying out similar work.

Key terms

Contract of employment - a written document given to a successful applicant for a post stating the conditions and terms under which he or she is employed.

Short listing - reducing the original number of candidates to a manageable number to be interviewed.

Summary

1. Why has selection become increasingly important to businesses?
2. State 5 features covered in an application form.
3. What criteria might a personnel department take into account when designing an application form.
4. Name 4 types of tests that a personnel department might carry out when selecting applicants for a job.
5. What are the main problems with personality tests as a method of selection?
6. Explain the main problems with interviews.
7. State 5 'dos' when conducting an interview.
8. How might a firm evaluate its selection procedure?
9. What is the use of a contract of employment to an employee?

Question

A careful approach to caring - the London Borough of Southwark

There is increasing concern about the quality of staff selected to care for youngsters in Britain's children's homes. The Staffordshire 'Pindown' affair, where children were locked in their rooms for long periods, is just one example. The Warner Committee, examining various cases of mistreatment of children, reported that employers must tighten up their selection and appointment procedures, as well as their training and staff supervision. The London Borough of Southwark responded to the Warner Report's recommendations, with procedures aimed to prevent unsuitable candidates finding work in children's homes.

Their recruitment process starts with production of detailed job descriptions and person specifications. Vacancies are then advertised internally and externally. The Warner Report pointed to the fact that homes where problems had occurred had tended to prefer mainly internal applicants. Although the report points to problems of using agencies in recruitment, Southwark does use them. However, it ensures that agencies carry out detailed checks on staff background.

How do Southwark carry out selection? Before their interview, shortlisted candidates carry out written exercises to test if they can do the particular job they are applying for. So an applicant for a care plan officer's post might be asked to show an understanding of budgeting. As well as testing a candidate's practical abilities, these exercises test communication and literacy on the grounds that, as the Warner report puts it, 'the staff who cannot express themselves clearly are likely to make young people in their care confused and possibly angry'. The report suggests that personality tests might be used to determine how far a candidate fits a personnel specification, though it warns of the limitations of these tests.

Southwark is, in fact, currently looking at tests that can assess personality without disbarring certain groups of candidates, including those who speak English as a second language. With members of ethnic minorities making up a large proportion of the borough's population, this is a vital consideration if staff in the authority's four children's homes are to mirror the wider community and understand the backgrounds of the young people in their care. For the same reason, interviewing panels have to reflect a mixture of gender and race. These panels consist of three managers, all trained in interviewing techniques. 'Even if you have been interviewing for years, as I have done, you have to go through this training to identify how Southwark's procedures are different from those of the other authorities', says Esther McLaughlin, assistant director for finance, personnel and strategy in the Social Services department.

The Warner Report claims some authorities apply equal opportunities processes 'in ways which unreasonably constrain the process of interviewing'. For example, it argues, insisting that interviewers ask only set questions, without any follow up or informal discussion, increases the risk of appointing unsuitable people. Southwark is aware of this risk. Although interviewers use questions prepared in advance, they are not constrained from probing further. 'The interview works on the basis of set questions for each recruitment exercise to start with, and then it flows more freely once the candidate has given an initial response', says Kirk Lower, personnel and industrial relations manager.

The interview, however, is more than just a question-and-answer session. For most jobs in children's homes, candidates must also make presentations to show their ability to cope with practical problems, often revolving around 'what if?' scenarios, such as 'What would you do as head of a home if you arrived to find all of your staff stricken with flu?'

Southwark's use of a range of selection techniques, including police checks into candidates' backgrounds, is along the lines recommended by the Warner Committee, which heard evidence from the Institute of Personnel Management that relying on an interview alone is no better than making decisions on the toss of a coin. But on the question of candidates' references, the authority's practice is out of step with Warner, which says references from previous employers should be taken before shortlisted candidates are formally interviewed.

Like most London authorities, Southwark takes up references only after identifying the successful applicant. If these references or the police checks raise issues of concern, the candidate is invited for a second interview. As Kirk Lowler says,'there are mixed views not only about taking up references in advance of interview but about the whole validity of references as a selection tool'.

Although staff are selected more carefully than ever before, Southwark is not complacent, according to McLaughlin. 'You can get your procedures as strong and as flexible as you can make them, but if someone wants to find a way around them, it is very difficult to stop them. That is why this department strongly supports Warner's recommendation for a central register for approved staff.' A central register would make it easier for employers to vet job applicants and help raise standards in children's homes throughout the country to the level already found in a few authorities.

Source: adapted from *Personnel Management Plus*, April 1993.

(a) Why is effective selection especially important for the choice of staff for children's homes?

(b) What types of test are used by Southwark before the interview takes place?

(c) How useful are the results of these type of tests likely to be?

(d) Using examples from the article, illustrate the:
(i) advantages; (ii) disadvantages;
of using interviews as a means of recruiting staff for children's homes.

(e) Discuss the value of other methods used to help selection mentioned in the article.

Induction

Newly appointed employees are most likely to leave the business in the early weeks of employment. This is called the **induction crisis**. How can employers prevent this? One approach is to help the new employee settle in quickly and feel comfortable in the new job by using an INDUCTION programme. Induction programmes are not usually about a specific job the employee will be doing, but the way in which the business works. They may contain information about some or all of the following.

- The organisation - history, development, management and activity.
- Personnel policies.
- Terms of employment - including disciplinary rules and union arrangements.
- Employee benefits and services.
- Physical facilities.
- General nature of the work to be done.
- The role and work of the supervisor.
- Departmental rules and safety measures.
- The relationship of new jobs to others.
  They may also contain:
- a detailed description of the employee's job;
- introduction to fellow workers;
- follow up after several weeks.

Even with these, induction is unlikely to work without careful timing and without making sure that the employee adjusts to the new social and work environment. Experiments have shown that it is possible for the time taken for induction to be halved and costs reduced by two-thirds if it is well planned. To do this, the programme must focus on the anxieties of the new employees, instead of on what it is thought they should be told.

The aims of training

Training involves employees being taught new skills or improving skills they already have. Why might a business train its employees? It is argued that a well trained workforce has certain benefits for the business.

- Well trained workers should be more productive. This will help the business to achieve its overall objectives, such as increasing profit.
- It should help to create a more flexible workforce (☞ unit 51). If a business needs to reorganise production, workers may have to be trained in new tasks.
- It will help the introduction of new technology. New machinery or production processes can be introduced more quickly if workers are trained to use them effectively.
- It should lead to increased job satisfaction for employees. Well motivated workers are more likely to

be more productive.
- It should reduce accidents and injuries if employees are trained in health and safety procedures.
- It may improve the image of the company. Customers are more likely to have confidence in personnel who are confident, competent and have knowledge of products or processes. Good applicants are also more likely to be attracted if a training programme is part of the job.
- It can improve employees' chances of promotion. The business, as a result, should have qualified people in important posts.

The cost of training

A report by the then Manpower Services Commission in 1985 on training stated:

> 'Britain's future international competitiveness and economic performance will be significantly influenced by the speed with which substantial improvements can be made in the scale and effectiveness of training by British companies.'

> 'Few employers think training sufficiently central to their business for it to be a main component in their corporate strategy; the great majority did not see it as an issue of major importance - a few openly stated as much.'

On the one hand, employers can see benefits in training the workforce. They will be better educated and more

QUESTION 1 Companies faced with declining sales and profits will become sceptical of statements by management 'gurus' about the need for training. Increasing competitive pressures will bring a return to basics, corporate slim-downs and cost-cutting exercises. The balance has to be held, though, between short term gain and long term loss.

The challenge is not just to survive the recession, but to remain in good corporate health until the year 2000 and beyond. A key ingredient in an organisation's ability to meet short term demands without sacrificing its potential will be its management of human resources.

The early signs are far from encouraging. A recent survey by *Personnel Today* of 400 personnel specialists showed that they are finding it 'difficult to win enough money for training' and that up to two-thirds expected to have 'a tougher fight to get enough training cash' this year. If the 1990s are to herald a return to basics, the essential challenge for companies will be how to get more from fewer. For that to become a reality will require companies to release the untapped talents and abilities of the workforce.

(a) Why might training be seen as an expensive luxury by so many British companies?
(b) Explain why there might be 'short term gain and long term loss' if companies cut expenditure on training in a recession.

skilled and should be more productive. In times of recession, however, spending on training may be seen as a luxury and may be cut. The recession of the late 1980s and early 1990s may have caused firms to question whether the cost, time, effort and resources needed for training were essential. In 1991 the total employees of working age receiving job-related training fell by 177,000 from the 1990 figure. This was the first time the figure had fallen since statistics were first recorded in 1984.

The response, in 1992, was the setting by the Employment Department of National Education and Training Targets for business and individuals. They were devised by the Confederation of British Industry (CBI) after consultation with employers, employees and trainers.

- By 1996, all employees should take part in training or development activities.
- By 1996, 50 per cent of the workforce aiming for NVQs or units towards them.
- By 1996, 50 per cent of medium to large organisations to be 'investing in people'.
- By 2000, 50 per cent of the workforce qualified to at least NVQ3 or equivalent.

The need for training

How does a firm know if training is required? One method might be to use the job description (☞ unit 52) to find the skills and knowledge needed to do the job. If there is a difference between the knowledge and skills of the employee and those actually required, this may indicate a need for training.

Employees can also be asked about areas where they feel their performance is inadequate, areas where they have problems, and any 'gaps' in their knowledge and skills. This should make them more committed to training. Training needs are found at different levels within a business.

- The organisational level. A business may need to train workers if there have been changes in a company's goals or objectives, or an introduction of new processes. For example, a move to 'Just-in-time' methods of stock control (☞ unit 33) may mean that workers must be able to constantly monitor stock. Training may also be needed as a result of company surveys or changes in the law.
- The departmental level. An indication of the need for training may come from personnel statistics, such as absence levels, turnover levels, production levels and customer complaints. Any differences between departments could show that training is needed.
- The individual level. At this level information from appraisal may be useful. Managers may also request that employees receive extra training. Increasingly, however, workers are identifying their own needs and designing their own personal development plans.

Once a need for training has been identified, a business must decide what skills and approaches should be achieved at the end of the training period. They may be something as simple as 'be able to replace a tyre'. There may also be some criteria to measure how

well the trainee has learnt the skill, such as 'type a letter with no more than one mistake', and details on how to perform a task, such as 'always be polite and helpful when taking telephone calls'. Table 54.1 shows one example of how this could be done if a business is trying to improve customer relations.

Table 54.1

Training need	Learning requirement
A need to establish a better rapport with customers	The employee will immediately attend to a customer unless already engaged with another customer.
	The employee will greet each customer, using the customer's name where known.
	The employee will apologise to every customer who has to wait to be attended to.

Training needs may be put together as a training or staff development plan. However, the business must take into account whether it has the financial resources to carry out the plan. This will depend on its **training budget**.

QUESTION 2 A group of regionally based managers, having the same job title and performing the same or very similar duties, had at various times, expressed difficulties in carrying out their jobs. As there was no other obvious cause of the problems they faced, it was decided to investigate their training needs. As the officers were geographically widely spread, a short questionnaire, which they could fill in at their place of work, coupled with a half-day training needs seminar for the whole group, were felt to be the appropriate methods of identifying training needs.

In the questionnaire managers were asked to write a job description of their job, in a guided format, and their performance objectives. They were asked about areas where they experienced difficulties and problems and where they felt they weren't meeting their performance objectives. They were asked their opinions of what caused these problems, and how they might be overcome.

When the managers met as a group they were asked the same issues. Their previous preparation and the benefits of working as a group produced even more ideas. The trainer then joined the group and went through the ideas to ensure full understanding of what was meant, to ensure the appropriate solutions were adopted, and to ensure commitment to the training initiative which was to follow.

(a) How does the article suggest that opportunities for training can be identified?
(b) What problems might a business have with taking this approach?

Methods of training

The 1991 *Labour Force Survey* showed that nearly 4.3 million people of working age said that they had received some form of job-related training in the four weeks before the survey. The figure in 1984 was less than 2.6 million people during the same period. It could be argued that the previous decade had seen a growth in emphasis on training by business.

Training is often divided into **on-the-job training** and **off-the-job training**. The former takes place when employees are trained while they are carrying out an activity, often at their place of work. Off-the-job training takes place away from the job, at a different location. It may involve the employee being released for periods of time to attend courses at colleges or other institutions. This is by far the most popular form of training. 72 per cent of people of working age in employment in the UK who receive training do so 'off-the-job'.

On-the-job training

On-the-job training can take a number of different forms, but all involve the worker being trained whilst carrying out their job.

- Sitting next to 'Nellie'. This is where 'Nellie', the experienced worker, shows the trainee exactly what to do. It can vary from working next to a machine operator to travelling with a salesperson.
- Coaching. This is where a coach will guide the trainee through the use of the equipment or a process in the same way that swimmers are trained. An example might be a technician being trained how to operate a heart monitor whilst working in a hospital.
- Mentoring. This involves the trainee being 'paired' with a more experienced employee. The trainee carries out the job but uses the 'tutor' to discuss problems that may occur and how best to solve them
- Job rotation. In some large companies this has been used for the training of 'high fliers'. The employee works in different departments for short periods - picking up skills from each. The aim is that when the person is promoted and reaches the 'top' of the business, she will have a range of experiences which can be used.
- Apprenticeships are a declining form of training that can take place at the workplace, sometimes with some off-the-job training. In the past, 'trainees' served an apprenticeship over a certain period, often in a skilled trade. When they qualified, they were made employees of the firm.

Many of these methods require a single 'tutor' to work with an employee. One-to-one training has complications for a business. In cases where one employee is training another, the quality of the training will depend on the ability, willingness and time available to the tutor. Such training may mean that one employee does not 'produce' themselves, while they are training the other employee. In cases where a specialist is employed to train others, this can be costly for the business.

Off-the-job training

Off-the-job training takes place where employees attend courses. Again, it can take a variety of forms.

In-house courses Businesses may put on courses for their employees and staff them from their own workers. One example discussed earlier is induction courses, which are used to introduce new recruits to a business and help them settle in. A firm might also run a course aimed at achieving a specific goal. For example, if a new computer system was introduced into a department, employees in the section may be trained in its use on a short course. Courses may also be run by the personnel department for marketing and finance managers in the business, to help them improve staff motivation. Some businesses have their own training centres. An example is Yorkhill NHS Trust in Glasgow, which has its own centre where staff can learn skills as varied as word processing to negotiating. Barclays Bank and many insurance companies have similar centres.

Another option is for a business to run its own courses away from the place of work. It could be for one day, a weekend, a week or a longer period. Courses are often for specialist reasons, such as working in teams or Total Quality Management (☞ unit 34). These courses can make use of simulations. One example is in the training of pilots, when trainee pilots can learn to fly a plane without the worry of accidents. Businesses sometimes simulate business activity during courses. Trainees are divided into teams and compete with each other, making business decisions and carrying out tasks. Other forms of simulation might include an 'in-tray exercise', where the trainee might be told they are leaving the country tomorrow and must clear an in-tray of letters and memos.

Businesses today are likely to offer courses leading to qualifications. These are dealt with in the next section.

'External' vocational courses Businesses, colleges, universities, training 'providers' (such as private or local authority agencies) and, increasingly, schools, offer vocational training in work-related skills. The type of training can take a number of forms, but trainees who complete the course successfully usually gain a qualification. These are awarded by 'external' bodies, such as the Business and Technical Education Council (BTEC). What type of training courses are available?

- Youth training. This is a guaranteed 2 year training course for under 18s (☞ unit 52). The trainee follows a course and has work experience with a business.
- Vocational training leading to National Vocational Qualifications (NVQs) and general NVQs (gNVQ). These courses offer training in 'competencies' or skills (NVQ) and knowledge and skills (gNVQ). They vary from training in business to hairdressing to engineering. Again, trainees will follow a course and have work or work simulated experience. Those who 'pass' the course are awarded a qualification from a body such as City and Guilds. It is likely that most courses in future will aim to provide these awards.
- Professional courses. Certain professional bodies such as the Institute of Personnel Management and the Royal College of Nursing offer qualifications in their own areas.

In the early 1990s, the government has tried to encourage training in the UK. Various training targets have been set by the Department of Employment, as discussed earlier in this unit. The Training, Enterprise and Education Directorate (TEED), formerly the Training Agency, works to promote training and education. In particular, they work closely with regional Training and Enterprise Councils (TECs), which help to develop training courses in local areas and may also contribute to the costs of running these courses for a business, college or agency.

Self-paced/distance learning There are a number of terms for self-paced learning. These include distance learning, open learning and flexible learning. The main feature of all these approaches is that the trainee controls the pace and the timing of their own learning. Learning is often from materials provided by a tutor. There may be a meeting at the end of a certain period. The main problem with this form of training is the lack of help when the trainee finds the materials difficult.

Evaluation of training

As businesses have demanded greater value for money, it has become important to evaluate training. Evaluation is simple when the result of the training is clear to see, such as when training workers to use new technology. Where training is designed to give a certain result, such as:

- a health and safety course;
- a word processing course;
- a design course;

evaluation can be based on observed results. This may be a reduction in accidents, increased typing speed or designs with greater impact.

It is more difficult to evaluate the success of a management training course or a programme of social skills development. It is usual to use end of course questionnaires, where course members answer a number of questions. The problem is that the course will have been a break for most employees from the normal work

---

QUESTION 4 Trainee solicitors are to get more practical experience in legal work and less theory. Understanding the commodities market and learning how to use a telephone seem unlikely preparations for a legal career. After 300 years, however, methods and titles are changing. Articled clerks have become trainee lawyers, with as much importance placed on the training as the law. A recent report by the Law Society, *Training Tomorrow's Solicitors*, suggests the establishment of a legal practice course that places greater emphasis on skills training and less on legal theory. The present syllabus includes a small proportion of skills training, but there is no formal system to ensure that students receive a grounding in non-legal techniques.

Some solicitors have anticipated the move towards more practical qualifications. One of the first leading City practices to spend considerable time on non-legal training is Frere Cholmeley. Sophie Hamilton, the partner responsible for training, says 'Trainee solicitors join us with a good working knowledge of the academic principles of law. But they have not learnt how to communicate that knowledge, verbally or in writing. To be a successful solicitor, you need far more than just technical competence. You have to communicate, whether with colleagues, clients or a group.'

Robin Palmer, a management development consultant, runs Frere Cholmeley's course on human relations and communications skills, which includes telephone manner, managing a meeting and producing reports. 'Even law graduates with a first-class degree are not always familiar with the conventions of letter writing', he says. 'Time management is another area that is often dismissed initially as merely common sense, but lawyers are usually quick to recognise that they can benefit from learning how to structure their working day. The most popular part of the training programme is oral presentation, which gives trainees the confidence to speak before a group. As solicitors progress, there is a need for training in negotiation skills, grievance handling and disciplinary procedures.'

Source: adapted from *The Times*.

(a) Why might it be necessary for solicitors to change the way new entrants are trained?
(b) Where might a small business, like a solicitor's, go to get skills training for employees?
(c) What problems might solicitors face in evaluating the training of skills mentioned in the article?

routine. This can make the participants' view of training appear of more value than it is. Also questionnaires tend to evaluate the course and not the learning. This often means that the person attending the course is assessing the quality of the tutors and visual aids, instead of what has been learnt.

To overcome these problems a business might:
■ ask participants and managers to complete a short questionnaire at the start of the course to focus their minds on what they hope to get from it;
■ give out another questionnaire at the end of the course focusing on learning and what could be applied back at the job;
■ give further questionnaires to review the effects of the course on performance when the employee is back at work.

This helps employees to concentrate on what has been learnt. This process may, however, be costly for the business.

Appraisal

After a period of time working in a job (and regularly after), a firm may APPRAISE the employee. This is an attempt by the business to find out the qualities, usefulness or worth of its employees.

Appraisal can be used by a business to:
■ improve performance;
■ provide feedback;
■ increase motivation;
■ identify training needs;
■ identify potential for promotion;
■ award salary increases;
■ set out job objectives;
■ provide information for human resource planning;
■ assess the effectiveness of the selection process.

The problem with having all of these aims is that the person carrying out the appraisal may have conflicting roles. If appraisal is designed to help performance and to act as a basis for salary awards, the appraiser would have to be both judge and helper at the same time. This makes if difficult to be impartial. It is also difficult for the person being appraised. A worker may want to discuss problems, but is likely to be cautious about what they say in case they jeopardise any possible pay rise. One way around this is for the appraisal system to review the performance of the worker only.

Carrying out appraisal

Appraisal has, in the past, been seen as most suitable for employees in management and supervisory positions. Increasingly clerical, secretarial and manual staff, with skilled or technical jobs, are also being appraised.

How does appraisal take place?
■ Superiors. Most appraisals are carried out by the employee's superior. The advantage of this is that the supervisor usually has intimate knowledge of the tasks that a worker has been carrying out and how well they have been done.
■ People 'above' the immediate superior can be involved

in appraisal in two different ways. They may 'approve' the superior's appraisal of the employee. A manager further up the hierarchy may also directly carry out the appraisal. This is more likely to happen when individuals decide if a worker has the potential for promotion, for example.
■ Self appraisal. This is a relatively new idea and not greatly used. Individuals do carry out self appraisal in traditional appraisal schemes, although the superior's decision officially 'counts'. The ratings that the employer has given may be changed, however, in the light of the employee's comments.
■ Peer appraisal. It is sometimes argued that appraisal by peers is reliable and valid as they have a more comprehensive view of the employee's job performance. The main problem, though, is that peers may be unwilling to appraise each other. This can be seen as 'grassing'.
■ Subordinates. Appraisal by subordinates is another less well used method. It is limited, as subordinates will only know certain aspects of the work of other employees.

Many firms have used appraisal systems only to find that they have to change or abandon them after a short time. Others 'battle' on with the system, but recognise that it is inadequate or disliked. What factors influence the success of an appraisal system?
■ Purpose of the system. Effectiveness will be greater if all involved are clear about what the system is for.
■ Control. It is vital that the system is controlled by senior and line management and isn't something done simply 'for the personnel department'.
■ Openness and participation. The more feedback that appraisees are given about their ratings, the more likely they are to accept the process. Similarly, the more the employee is allowed to take part in the system, the greater the chance of gaining their commitment.
■ Appraisal criteria. The criteria must be related to the job, be easy to use and appear fair to the worker.
■ Training. Training may be needed in how to appraise and how to conduct interviews.
■ Administrative efficiency. Appraisal must be carried out so that it causes as few problems as possible for both parties. It also needs to be confidential.
■ Action. Appraisal needs to be supported by follow-up action. Plans that are agreed by appraiser and workers must be checked, to make sure they take place.

Key terms

Appraisal - evaluating the usefulness of the employee to the business.
Induction - the introduction of a new employee to the business.

Summary

1. Briefly explain the purpose of induction.
2. Why is training important to a business?
3. Give 5 aims of training.
4. State 4 methods which could be used to identify training needs.
5. What is the difference between on-the-job and off-the-job training?
6. Briefly explain 3 methods of off-the-job training.
7. How can training be evaluated?
8. What is meant by performance appraisal?
9. How can appraisal help a business?
10. Who might carry out appraisal in a business?

Question

Yorkhill NHS Trust Open Learning Centre

Catherine Campbell works part time as a cleaner at Glasgow's Yorkhill NHS Trust. But she does not intend to sweep floors all her life. One day she hopes to do office work or become a mid-wife. In preparation she has learnt computer skills and is currently in the middle of a typing course at the hospital's open learning centre.

The centre was set up in 1992. Its aim is to make training accessible to roughly 2,000 employees at the maternity hospital and nearby children's hospital which make up the Trust, along with community child health staff. One of the features of the centre is its wide range of trainees. Consultants sit shoulder to shoulder with nurses, childminders, porters, therapists and secretaries.

The idea for the centre came from the Trust's current chief executive, Gerry Marr. Lynda Hamilton, who shares the personnel manager's job with Irene Shields, took the project forward at the start. She began a 2 year plan to make the Trust a 'learning organisation'. At the time, training was focused on off-the-job classroom courses, mainly for professional staff. Nurses could specialise, but cleaners had nothing and managers very little.

Changes in the NHS were geared at getting employees to take more responsibility, and at improving personnel work. Hamilton commissioned management consultants KPMG to produce a report on the training needs of senior and middle managers. This recommended taking on a training manager. Margaret Hunter was appointed in April 1992, having worked previously at Woolworths.

The report also suggested a series of courses to be run by hospital staff. Often managers from one area would teach others. For example, the finance director ran courses on managing a budget and personnel specialists taught skills in recruitment, selection and negotiating.

The centre developed courses to help secretaries, nurses and speech therapists with presentation skills. 'We have got some junior people and it has really boosted their self confidence', said Hamilton. By far the most innovative move was to negotiate a contract with the specialist open learning company, Applied Learning.

Yorkhill was to 'pilot' the concept of learning centres for the Greater Glasgow Health Service. This meant it received a grant for the first year's hardware and training materials.

Margaret Hunter's first task was to convince staff to use the centre. There was a tremendous response from the portering manager, although some of the nursing staff were not totally convinced. One aim of the centre was to take away the fear of learning. 'We had quite a few technophobes, whom we pressed into trying it out and once they are in they are ours!', Margaret said.

The main criticism of the centre is that people would use it more if they had more time. Few trainees were there in work time. Another difficulty was the isolating effect of open learning. Few trainees really found this a major problem although trainee Jeanette McIntyre, a play group leader, would like a learner's group, where discussions about courses could take place.

Margaret Hunter would like to open the centre for longer hours, although a cash shortage holds her back. Whatever the problems, out of 2,500 employees more than 300 have used the site, many for multiple courses.

Source: adapted from *Personnel Management Plus*, June 1993.

(a) **Explain the term 'off-the-job training' and give three examples mentioned in the article.**
(b) **Discuss the benefits of the centre for:**
    (i) **employees;**
    (ii) **the hospital.**
(c) **What possible problems of running the training centre are outlined in the article?**
(d) **Discuss the effectiveness of open learning packages in the training centre from the information in the article.**
(e) **How might the Trust evaluate the success of the courses on offer?**

What are equal opportunities?

Unit 53 explained the methods used to select candidates. Choosing one candidate rather than another is known as DISCRIMINATION. If a man is chosen rather than a woman, the business has discriminated in favour of the man, and against the woman.

Some discrimination is legal and may be considered reasonable. For example, a firm may choose a candidate for the post of quality controller in a meat factory because he has 10 years experience, rather than a school leaver. However, if the school leaver did not get the job because she was a woman, or from an ethnic minority, this is illegal in the UK. It could also be said to be unreasonable. The rest of the unit will use the term discrimination in this way. Discrimination occurs not only in selection, but areas such as training, promotion and wages.

EQUAL OPPORTUNITIES mean that everyone has the same chance. In other words, a candidate or employee is not discriminated against because of their sex or race. UK legislation helps to promote this. So do EC laws. The Treaty of Rome, article 119 states men and women should receive 'equal pay for equal work'.

Why are businesses concerned about equal opportunities? We will see that giving everyone the same chance can affect the productivity, costs and organisation of a business.

Reasons for discrimination

There are certain groups of individuals in society and in business that are arguably discriminated against. Such groups may be:
- women;
- people from ethnic minorities;
- disabled people;
- older people.

By far the most attention has been paid to the first two groups. There are, however, laws relating to disabled people and age discrimination laws. In the USA, for example, compulsory retirement is illegal in most industries.

Discrimination often occurs because of **unproven** ideas or stereotypes about certain groups, such as the following examples.
- Women should not work because their place is in the home or with children; women don't want to take too much responsibility at work because of home commitments; women who are married are less likely to want to be relocated; women with children will be less reliable than men because their main responsibility is to their children.
- Sikhs or Muslims are difficult to employ because of problems with religious holidays; Indians or Pakistanis overstate their qualifications; Black Afro-Caribbeans are 'culturally lazy'.
- A person in a wheelchair will be an embarrassment to other workers or is somehow 'mentally' disadvantaged; someone who has suffered from mental illness will crack up under the pressure.
- Older people are less adaptable, are not interested in coping with new technology and work much more slowly.

All these and many other unproven ideas can affect the way people view these groups during recruitment and selection, and when they are employed.

QUESTION 1 Women working in information technology (IT) tend to remain with their employers for much longer than their male counterparts and are being recommended as a 'better investment', according to a report published in 1990 by the British Computer Society (BCS). The survey of 750 women members of the BCS shows that 44 per cent remained with their employers for at least nine years, compared with the industry average of two years.

Many companies are desperate to reduce the turnover of IT staff because of the high cost and difficulty of recruiting replacements. The BCS findings may encourage companies to introduce policies that attract more women.

The Institute of Manpower Studies has examined various companies which have encouraged the employment of women. It argues that 'this has more to do with the growing recognition that women are a vital skills resource than the so-called demographic crisis'. It also says that women have more 'holistic attributes'. For example, they have higher educational attainment, a greater ability to work in teams and are more supportive towards colleagues.

Source: adapted from The Times, 1992.

(a) To what extent does the article disprove the myth that women are a liability to a business?
(b) What potential advantages does the article suggest a firm will gain by employing women?

Women at work

Women form a large and increasing proportion of the working population. In 1979 women accounted for around 38 per cent of all people of working age in employment. By 1991, this had risen to nearly 43 per cent and should be near to 44 per cent by 1995.

There is evidence to suggest that women are discriminated against at work.
- In 1992, women's average gross weekly earnings were 71 per cent of men's in all occupations.
- Certain occupations, such as construction work, are almost exclusively male. This is shown in Figure 55.1.
- Those occupations that employ mainly women tend to involve low paid, often part time work. Personal services, such as hairdressing, might be an example, as

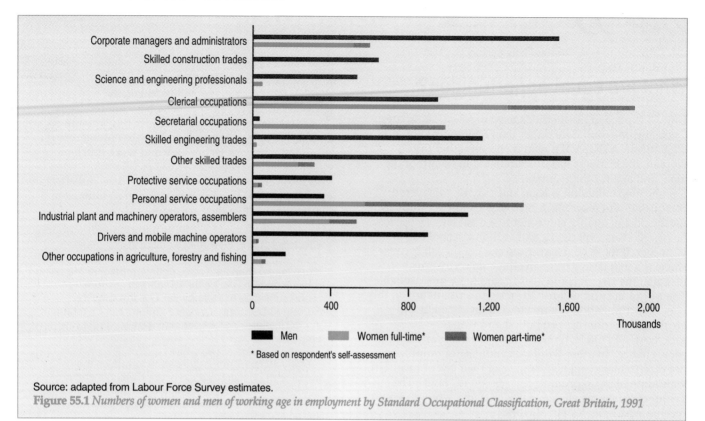

Men Women full-time* Women part-time*

* Based on respondent's self-assessment

Source: adapted from Labour Force Survey estimates.

Figure 55.1 *Numbers of women and men of working age in employment by Standard Occupational Classification, Great Britain, 1991*

shown in Figure 55.1.

In 1992, a survey of 500 employers in the UK, *Best Companies for Women*, gave details of the top 50 companies for women, stating their number of female staff, provision for female employees and their record of training. The study argued that discrimination still existed. Relatively few women were found in management posts, although women expected equal treatment and did not want to choose between children and their career. Top of the list was the Civil Service. In 1993 141 private and public sector businesses took part in 'Opportunity 2000'. This was a business-led initiative to improve the position of women in work.

It is likely that the 1990s will see a growth in women's employment opportunities, as more women gain qualifications and take advantage of changes in work practice and demographic trends (☞ unit 67). Attempts by firms to offer facilities, such as creches, will also help.

Legislation

There are two main laws that deal with the promotion of sexual equality at work.

The **Equal Pay Act 1970** stated that an employee doing the same or 'broadly similar' work as a member of staff of the opposite sex is entitled to equal rates of pay and conditions. The Act aimed to eliminate discrimination (mainly against women) in wages and other conditions of work, such as holidays, overtime, hours and duties. The Equal Pay Act was amended in 1983 to allow female employees to claim equal pay for work of 'equal value' to that done by a man. The 1970 Act ruled that women

should be paid equal pay for work which is 'like work' or 'work rated as equivalent' to that of a man. But the 1983 amendment made it possible for equal pay to be claimed for work of equal value in 'terms of the demands made on her'. Such demands could include the effort, skills and decisions made by a woman. Whether the work was of equal value or not would be determined by job evaluation (☞ unit 52).

The **Sex Discrimination Act 1975** made it illegal to discriminate against someone on the grounds of sex or whether they are married. This may be in areas such as job advertisements, interviews, selection, promotion and training, dismissal and terms of employment. In 1986 this was updated so that restrictions on women's hours of work were removed. This meant that women were more able to take jobs with flexible hours or shift work.

These two Acts have implications for recruitment and selection.

■ Advertisements must not discriminate on the basis of sex or marital status. This means that job titles should be sexless, as in 'cashier' or 'salesperson.'

■ There is a greater need for job analysis, job descriptions and person specifications (☞ unit 52). In particular, a person specification must not restrict the job to men or women.

■ Interviews carried out in a structured way can help to limit any prejudice that an interviewer may have.

The effects on the whole business are dealt with later in this unit. If employees feel that they have been discriminated against, they can take their cases to an **industrial tribunal**. They can also request help from the **Equal Opportunities Commission**, a government body which:

- works toward eliminating discrimination;
- tries to promote equal opportunities;
- helps employees making complaints;
- investigates complaints of discrimination;
- issues notices preventing a business from discriminating;
- reviews the Equal Pay Act.

An example of the work of the tribunal was the case of Hilary Williams, reported in *The Guardian* in March 1992. She lost her £45,000 a year job to a male colleague at British Gas following privatisation. The tribunal ruled that she should be reinstated and awarded £8,000.

Table 55.1 *Ethnic groups in the labour force (Great Britain, summer 1992, not seasonally adjusted)*

All persons aged 16+ (Thousands)	White	All minority groups	Black	Indian	Pakistani & Bangladeshi
All	41,980	2,090	570	690	390
Males	20,220	1,040	280	350	200
Females	21,760	1,050	290	350	200

Source: *Employment Gazette*, January 1993.

QUESTION 2 Britain's employers faced huge and potentially inflationary wage increases from women demanding equal pay for work of equal value, from the day when Miss Julie Hayward joined a Merseyside shipyard as a cook. In a landmark legal decision in 1988, the Law Lords ruled that Miss Hayward's job was as important as that of males who were painters, joiners and thermal insulation engineers at Cammell Laird, Birkenhead. She was backed by the Equal Opportunities Commission and her union, the union of General Municipal Boilermakers (GMB), which warned other employers to expect similar legal challenges.

The legal precedent she set, of equal pay for work of equal value, meant employers were confronted with the dilemma of having to treat women equally, while facing the wrath of men whose differentials and status as 'bread winners' are under threat.

In 1990 Marks & Spencer gave its 44,000 sales assistants, mainly women, a 26 per cent pay rise over three years, but froze the wages of 3,000 warehouse staff, mainly men. M&S warehousemen at Derby who had been given only a one-off £500 payment, staged a one-day protest strike, although the company denied knowledge of their action.

Marks & Spencer denied its award was influenced by equal pay legislation. Its move came only a day after Sainsbury gave rises of between 8.5 per cent and 21 per cent to 60,000 retail staff after a job evaluation exercise designed to comply with the concept of equal pay for work of equal value.

Source: adapted from *The Times*, 1990.

(a) Why was Miss Julie Hayward able to claim equal pay from her employers?
(b) What potential problems does the case highlight which Equal Pay legislation might present to employers?
(c) Advise employers in other sectors on how they might use job evaluation to help comply with Equal Pay legislation.

Legislation and guidance

An awareness of the position of ethnic groups has led to anti-discrimination legislation. **The Race Relations Act 1976**, when dealing with recruitment, states that it is unlawful for an employer to discriminate on grounds of race:

- in making arrangements for deciding who should be offered the job;
- in the terms offered;
- in refusing or deliberately omitting to offer employment.

The implications for the employer or personnel manager of these laws are similar to those of the Sex Discrimination Act. Advertisements should be worded so that there is no indication that some ethnic groups are preferred to others. Writing a job description and person specification will also be useful.

The use of selection tests should be monitored. Many tests discriminate against people from minority backgrounds in the way they are designed. Also, people from some ethnic backgrounds may be at a disadvantage because the method of testing is alien to their culture.

The **Race Relations Code of Practice** helps employers and personnel managers when recruiting. It states that:

- employers should not confine advertisements to those areas or publications which could exclude or reduce the number of applicants of a particular ethnic group;
- employers should avoid stating requirements, such as length of residence or experience, and should make clear that overseas qualifications are acceptable;
- any literature sent to applicants should include a statement that the business is an equal opportunity employer.

Guidance is also given when using employment agencies and about selection testing and applications.

A guidance pack for employers was published in 1992 by the Department of Employment titled *Ten Point Plan for Equal Opportunities*. It dealt with ethnic monitoring - the collection, presentation and analysis of data about employment procedures. The pack outlined 'best practice' used by businesses in the selection of candidates. This included, for example, monitoring to find out what proportion of minority group applicants were short listed, interviewed and appointed. This might indicate whether the recruitment and selection procedure was fair.

Ethnic minorities

There is evidence that certain ethnic groups are discriminated against, often in recruitment and selection. Table 55.1 shows the number of workers in these groups compared to white workers.

QUESTION 3 Computer Ltd is an American based business that has Federal contracts. It is required by American law to submit evidence to the Equal Opportunities Commission about its ethnic record keeping.

Computer (UK) Ltd is also committed to equal opportunities. In its handbook, it states:

'Each community has its particular set of social problems. Our company must help to solve these problems. As a major step in this direction, we must strive to provide worthwhile employment opportunities for people of widely different backgrounds. Among other things, this requires positive action to seek out and employ members of disadvantaged groups and to encourage and guide their progress towards full participation at all positions and levels.'

Computer (UK) Ltd does not stop there, however, for the references in the handbook are simply statements of intent. It also has an action plan designed to promote its policy. In a management evaluation form, one of the questions asked is:

'What leadership has been evidenced in planning and implementing an on-going, positive affirmative action programme of employment and development for minorities, women and other people subject to discrimination? What have been the results?'

In practice there is less evidence of the company's commitment being carried out. Managers in the UK ignored the section on affirmative action for minorities in the handbook, putting a line through it and writing 'not applicable in the UK'. Suggestions by researchers that an active recruitment policy was an obligation on the part of Computer Ltd management invoked the reaction, 'we're not a welfare organisation'.

Source: adapted from *Management and the Multi-racial Labour Force*, P. Torrington, D. Knight and T. Hitner, Gower, 1982.

(a) What is meant by the term 'affirmative action' in this passage?
(b) What indication is there that Computer (UK) Ltd is an equal opportunities employer in relation to ethnic minorities?
(c) What problems does the article indicate there may be in operating such a policy?

Other types of discrimination

Disabled people The disabled have tended to experience higher levels of unemployment than the workforce as a whole. Once unemployed they also have greater difficulty in finding work and so remain unemployed for longer periods. They have less choice and when they do find work it is likely to be in low paid, less attractive jobs. Employers often have concerns about employing disabled people. These include worries about attendance and health, safety at work, eligibility for pension schemes and changes to premises and equipment.

Legislation to help the disabled includes the **1944 Disabled Persons (Employment) Act**, the 1958 Act of the same name and some extra regulations in 1980. The Acts set up a 'quota' scheme and a system of reserved places for the disabled. The quota scheme is a method of **positive discrimination**, where every employer of more than twenty people has to employ sufficient disabled people to make up

3 per cent of their total workforce. In addition, certain jobs are reserved for disabled people, such as car park and lift attendants. Disabled people employed in reserved occupations cannot be counted towards the 3 per cent quota.

In 1992 a study by Incomes Data Services found that companies including the TSB and Hewlett Packard were making efforts to improve the job prospects of the disabled. These included guaranteed interviews and training.

Older people The main protection for the older employee is against redundancy. In this case they must be compensated (☞ unit 56). But there is no protection for older people seeking employment, training or promotion. Older people are far more likely to be made redundant in a recession and may accept voluntary redundancy as a form of 'early retirement'. Some argue that there are actually advantages to a business in employing workers 'over 40'.

- The over 40s have greater experience and better judgement in decision-making.
- The over 40s have already satisfied many of their needs for salary and status and are able to concentrate more on job responsibilities.
- The over 40s have a greater 'social intelligence' and the ability to understand and influence others.

B & Q, the chain of DIY stores, have recognised the benefits of employing older people, and have adopted a policy of hiring over 50s in their stores.

QUESTION 4 'Disability does not mean inability' is the message of a nationwide media campaign being run by the Employment Service. The aim is to publicise the revamped disability symbol and five new commitments all companies using the symbol will be asked to implement from next year. A new catchline, 'Positive about disabled people', added to the familiar 'two ticks' logo makes it easier for jobseekers looking through advertisements to recognise those companies which are committed to employing disabled people. Moreover, from 1 June 1993, companies using the symbol agreed to:

- interview all disabled applicants who meet the minimum criteria for a job vacancy and consider them on their abilities;
- ask disabled employees at least once a year how their organisation can enable them to develop and use their abilities at work;
- take action to ensure that key employees develop the awareness of disability;
- make every effort when employees become disabled to make sure that they stay in employment;
- each year review these commitments and what has been achieved, plan ways to improve them and inform all employees about progress and future plans.

'If you exclude disabled people when looking for ability', said Viscount Ullswater launching the campaign, 'you could be missing the best person for the job.'

Source: *Employment Gazette*, December 1992.

(a) How might the use of the logo benefit:
   (i) disabled people;
   (ii) businesses; using the logo?
(b) Explain 3 effects that following the commitments in the article are likely to have on a business' selection procedure.

Equal opportunities policies

Certain businesses operate an **equal opportunities policy**. This means that the firm is committed to giving all applicants an equal chance of, say, selection, no matter what their sex, sexuality, race, age, marital status, religion or disability. The aim of such a policy is to remove discrimination in all areas of the business, including promotion, training and financial rewards. Examples of employers that operate such a policy are some local authorities, for example Tower Hamlets Education Department, and Lucas.

How will such a policy affect business?

- A business is far more likely to employ the 'best' person for the job if everyone is given an equal opportunity. The quality of applicants may also improve.
- Equal opportunities for training are likely to lead to a better qualified workforce in key positions, altough the cost of training could increase.
- Workers may become better motivated if, for example, the chances of promotion are more equal.
- Production may need to be reorganised. This might include more flexible hours, job rotation or even job sharing. For example, an office job could be carried out by a mother in the morning (when children are at school) and by a male in the afternoon. A more flexible workforce may be better able to respond to change (☞ unit 51).
- There may be extra wage costs. Paying women equal wages to men will raise the total wage bill.
- Extra facilities may be needed. This can vary from ramps for wheelchairs to children's creches.
- The selection procedure may have to change. In some cases there may even be POSITIVE DISCRIMINATION. This is where employers discriminate in favour of minority groups or women during selection.
- The image of the business or jobs in it may have to change. This could improve the image to the customer. Rank Xerox, for example, found that jobs in the firm were often seen as 'men's' jobs or 'women's' jobs and tried to change this.

An example of how a policy that promotes equality can affect a business is the ICL career break scheme. This allows all employees a 'break' of up to two years in their career for training to improve their skills.

QUESTION 5

QUESTION 5 Cathy Powell, general manager of organisational change at Manchester Airport argues quality products or services must go hand-in-hand with equality for all employees. And this means women, people from ethnic minorities and people with disabilities as well as white males. She urged a breakdown of the old barriers; ' It's time we did away with stereotypical assumptions - both men's and women's - about each other's roles'. She put forward several reasons for equal opportunities at work guaranteed to appeal to even the most reactionary employer.

First, she pointed out, successful organisations need talent but, 'we are not awash with superb managers. Talent is equally distributed between the sexes; opportunities are not. It's not enough for companies to attract women; they've got to do much more to develop and utilise their skills. A crucial factor in any total quality/total equality strategy is a radical change in leadership style. Out should go the mass production 'sheep dip' approach to training managers; in should come a more flexible system, to bring out people's individual strengths, be they male or female, black or white.'

Companies, she stressed, need to appreciate that people have a life outside work. They should create flexible working - and training - arrangements to accommodate this. Moreover, companies with a family-friendly image in the recruitment market place will attract the best people.

Finally, in an increasingly competitive business world, everybody needs to be 'switched on' and performing well. Inequality simply breeds discontent, and short-changing employees on fairness issues only serves to lower service and efficiency levels. In contrast, equality of opportunity improves people's attitude to their work and their productivity.

Source: *Employment Gazette*, May 1992.

(a) Discuss the advantages to the Airport of Cathy Powell's suggestions.
(b) What effects are the suggestions made by Cathy Powell likely to have on the business if they are introduced?

Key terms

Discrimination - to make a selection or choice from alternatives, such as an applicant for a job. The term is often used to mean an illegal or unreasonable selection in the context of equal opportunities.
Equal opportunities - where everyone has the same chance. In business this can mean the same chance of selection, promotion etc.
Positive discrimination - actively favouring women or minority groups when selecting candidates for a job, training, promotion etc.

Summary

1. Name 4 groups that are often discriminated against by businesses.
2. Why might there be an improvement in employment opportunities for women in the next decade?
3. What are the main points of:
   (a) The Equal Pay Act 1970 and the 1983 amendments;
   (b) The Sex Discrimination Act of 1986;
   (c) The Race Relations Act of 1976?
4. What effect will equal pay legislation be likely to have on wages and opportunities for women in the UK?
5. State 3 ways in which an employer might avoid discriminating against minority groups when recruiting for jobs.
6. What advantages might candidates over 40 have for a business when compared to younger applicants?

Question

The Women in Lucas Project

The 'Women in Lucas Project' shows how a well-structured approach can lead to a positive, all-round equal opportunities strategy that's good for women and good for business.

'We recognise that women are a vital part of the workforce. The perspective and style they bring to managerial work contributes significantly to improved performance. Therefore, it makes good business sense to attract and retain our share of all available talent and remove barriers which prevent women realising their full potential.' So says Sir Anthony Gill, chairman of multinational engineering firm Lucas Industries, explaining why he initiated the 'Women in Lucas Project'.

Of Lucas' 25,000 workforce in the UK, just under a third are women. The majority work in light assembly work, with a much smaller number in professional and managerial positions - a situation which is typical of the engineering industry as a whole.

But far from neglecting its female staff, Lucas has recognised the need to adapt to changing patterns in the labour force. It is essential, it believes, to move away from one standard set of employment policies to reflect a broader diversity in the workforce. And this belief has the full commitment and support of senior management.

In 1990 the company launched the 'Women in Lucas Project' based on the findings of a thorough investigation of the situation inside and outside the company. The project was designed to answer the questions, 'Why does Lucas have such a poor record in developing women with professional and managerial potential - and what can we do about it?'

Data was collected on national trends and statistics relating to demographic changes, employment patterns, education and skills acquisition. Other organisations in a range of sectors were contacted to find out what action they were taking. Information was also collected inside the company from a target group of women already in professional/managerial roles and those likely to reach these levels in the future.

This produced interesting insights into women's experience of working for Lucas. For example, only half of the sample expected to stay long term within Lucas - giving lack of prospects as the main reason for leaving. What would encourage them to stay? Flexible working

'When I joined Lucas, I felt I had to prove myself as a woman in a predominately male world, but the intensive training and the opportunity to assume responsibility soon helped me build up my confidence.'

Swati Shah, manufacturing systems engineer.

arrangements, childcare support, and planned career development. Gathering all the information together, Lucas then drew up proposals for action.

These are now being developed through the 'Women in Lucas Project', which includes moves to:
- introduce career development programmes for women;
- examine recruitment and selection criteria;
- develop flexible working, maternity and childcare support;
- promote networking;
- liaise with schools to promote engineering as a career for girls.

As well as encouraging women's career development through networking, conferences and training opportunities, the project puts equal emphasis on the 'demand side'.

Line managers are urged to set and work towards measurable targets in promoting women up the line. A key goal is to increase the representation of women in the top three bands by 1996, a target which will in turn stimulate a long-term structural change throughout the company. Lucas reports that steady progress is being made, backed up by regular monitoring and evaluation.

As Kate Corfield, director of the project, explains, 'Our aim is to put in place processes which, over time, generate and sustain continuous improvement rather than an ad hoc set of quick fix solutions. In this way, Lucas can make sure it continually attracts and retains enough talented people. It is not about favours for women but ensuring the company has competitive capability. It is about creating the conditions which enable all employees to give of their best.'

Source: *Employment Gazette*, February 1993.

(a) **Why might women have been unfairly discriminated against in the engineering industry?**
(b) **State 3 ways in which unfair discrimination may have taken place.**
(c) **Why might Lucas think 'Women are a vital part of the workforce'?**
(d) **Explain the methods used by Lucas to promote equality.**
(e) **Discuss the possible benefits to Lucas of the 'Women in Lucas Project'.**

Why is protection needed?

Why might a business protect its employees? There are certain laws protecting people in the workplace. Legislation has laid down rules about:

- health and safety;
- employment protection (dismissal and redundancy);
- wage protection;
- recruitment, selection and training (☞ unit 52-54).

This legislation provides guidelines and acts as a constraint on how a business makes decisions (☞ unit 70). In addition, from a purely practical point of view, it makes sense for a firm to protect its workers. Satisfied employees are far more likely to help a firm achieve its goals. A business may also feel it has a moral obligation to protect employees. As their employer, it should look after their interests in the workplace.

Health and safety at work

Providing a healthy and safe environment can mean many things. It could include some of the following.

- Providing and maintaining safety equipment and clothing.
- Maintaining workplace temperatures.
- Ensuring adequate work space.
- Ensuring adequate washing and toilet facilities.
- Guaranteeing hygienic conditions.
- Providing breaks in the work timetable.
- Providing protection for the use of hazardous substances.

It is likely that the conditions for a healthy and safe environment will vary depending on the nature of the task carried out. Ensuring the health and safety of a mine worker will require different decisions by a business to protecting an office worker. Although both must be protected from adverse effects of equipment, for example, protection is likely to be different.

Businesses must protect people outside the workplace who might be affected by activities within it, eg those living near a chemical or industrial plant. They must also protect visitors or customers to shops or premises.

It is in the interest of a business to protect its workforce. A healthy and safe work environment should prevent accidents, injury and illness amongst workers. Any one of these may result in staff absence and lost production for the firm. The percentage of working days lost due to sickness or injury per week in different occupations is shown in Figure 56.1. In extreme cases, the business may even be taken to court for failing to provide protection. The court may order the business to pay compensation to the employee and perhaps a fine. Also, loss of employees may require costly recruitment of full or part time workers. Furthermore, it has been argued that high or low temperatures and lack of workspace may lead to a fall in production by employees.

In 1990 it was estimated that 1.43 million people suffered a workplace injury in England and Wales that required a doctor or absence from work. It was also estimated that 21.1 million days work were lost due to workplace injury.

QUESTION 1

In 1993 new controls were introduced to protect workers using Visual Display Unit (VDU) equipment. From January 1993 onwards, employers must assess display screen workstations and reduce any risks found, ensure that VDUs meet minimum design requirements, plan work so that users get breaks or changes of activity, and provide information and training to users. Screen users would also be entitled to eye tests paid for by the employers, and special glasses if needed.

The regulations would apply where employees 'habitually use the equipment as a significant part of their normal work'. For office tasks the risk could be based on an 'ergonomic checklist', covering how much time is spent at the screen, or whether the VDU can be used in comfort with correctly adjusted seating.

Action should be taken by employers to solve 'posture' problems, (which can lead to upper limb disorders affecting muscles, joints and tendons), visual problems (like eyestrain), fatigue and stress. Employers would also have to ensure that VDU equipment conforms to minimum standards of screen flicker, brightness and contrast, adjustability, keyboard design, glare and reflection.

Source: adapted from *Employment Gazette*.

(a) Explain the possible health and safety dangers faced by workers using VDU equipment.
(b) How might a business solve these problems?
(c) Discuss the costs and benefits of the controls on the use of VDU equipment from the point of view of:
   (i) the business;
   (ii) the workforce.

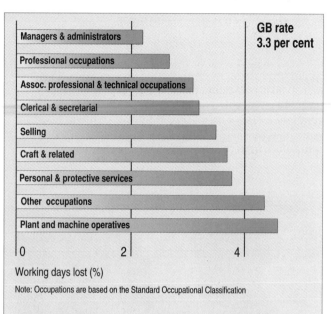

Figure 56.1 *Percentage of working days lost in the reference week due to sickness or injury by occupation (Great Britain, Spring 1992).*

Health and safety legislation

In the areas of health and safety at work, laws have been passed to protect employees for well over 100 years. Increasingly, regulations have been based on EC directives, covering such factors as noise control and the manual handling of heavy loads. There are also a number of **codes of practice** which act as 'guides' for a business.

·There are thousands of regulations concerning health and safety at work. They are updated from time to time as work conditions change. What are the main laws protecting the health and safety of employees?

The Factories Act, 1961 This Act applies to all premises where two or more people are employed in manual labour. This includes garages to engineering works. The act sets out to ensure that minimum standards of cleanliness, space for people to work, temperature and ventilation, lighting, conveniences, clothing, accommodation and first-aid facilities are maintained.

The Offices, Shops and Railway Premises Act, 1963 This was introduced to extend protection for factories to other buildings. The provisions are similar to those of the Factories Act, and deal with cleanliness, lighting, ventilation etc.

The Fire Precautions Act, 1971 This Act lists premises for which a fire certificate is required. The list includes premises being used as a place of work. When issuing a certificate a fire authority can impose requirements on the holder. These may concern such things as the means of escape from the building, instruction and training for employees on what to do in the event of fire and limits to the number of people on the premises.

The Health and Safety at Work Act, 1974 The aim of this Act is to raise the standard of safety and health for all individuals at work, and to protect the public whose safety may be put at risk by the activities of people at work.

Every employer is required to prepare a written statement of their general policy on health and safety. Employees must be advised of what the policy is. Management have the main responsibility for carrying out the policy. In the case of negligence, proceedings can be taken against an individual manager as well as against the business. The Act also places a duty on employees while they are at work to take reasonable care for the safety of themselves and others. The employee is legally obliged to comply with the safety rules drawn up by management. Employers or employees who fail to comply can be taken to court and fined. Part of the Act requires a business to give training, information, instruction and supervision to ensure the health and safety at work of employees.

The Act is backed up by the Health and Safety Executive, which has the responsibility of seeing that the Act is carried out. Health and Safety inspectors are appointed by the Commission to make sure the law is being carried out. They have the power to enter employers' premises, carry out examinations and investigations, take measurements, photographs and recordings, take equipment and materials and examine books and documents. The Commission also has the power to issue codes of practice to protect people in various situations, for example:

■ the protection of individuals against ionising radiation;
■ the control of lead pollution at work;
■ time off for training of safety representatives;
■ control of substances hazardous to health (various).

A major concern recently has been the lack of inspectors to police the Act, as highlighted by such 'disasters' as the Zeebrugge ferry.

QUESTION 2 In the summer of 1992, the Health and Safety Executive's (HSE) 'Roofwork Safety Campaign' singled out an 'unscrupulous get-rich-quick brigade' as damaging to the trade. Between May and August inspectors made 2,500 visits, issued over 600 prohibition notices and received over 600 complaints. Such roofers, it was argued, were attempting to under - cut competitors by skimping on safety. Examples of bad practice included workers with no guard rails, unsecured ladders and working over uncovered holes. Some roofers were found working over a glass conservatory without scaffolding, and without protection for the workers or the person inside the conservatory. In cases of bad practice, businesses were fined by the courts. The HSE also distributed 32,000 information packs to firms on good practice.

Source: adapted from *Employment Gazette*, November 1992.

(a) Identify the health and safety dangers to:
     (i) workers;
     (ii) the public;
     from the roofing trade.
(b) How might legislation on health and safety operate to influence businesses in the roofing industry?

Control of Substances Hazardous to Health Regulations, 1988 These regulations, which came into force on 1 October 1989, were made under the Health and Safety at Work Act, 1974. They comprise nineteen regulations, plus four approved codes of practice. The legislation protects all employees who work with any substance hazardous to their health. Employers must take into account the way and extent that such substances are handled, used and controlled. This is particularly important for workers in the nuclear fuel, chemical and asbestos industries.

Employment protection

Unit 53 showed that employees are entitled to a contract of employment when they are first appointed to a job. As well as protection that an employee receives by having an employment contract, there is further security provided by the **Employment Protection (Consolidation) Act, 1978**. The Act ensures that every employee who has been with an employer for two years has the right not to be unfairly dismissed. Certain people cannot claim unfair dismissal. These include those on fixed term contracts and freelance agents, for example.

There are a number of reasons why employees might have their contract ended which may be **unfair** dismissal under the conditions of the Act (and its amendments).

■ Because they were trying to become or were a member of a trade union. Alternatively, because they refused to join or make payments to a union.
■ On the grounds of pregnancy, even though she was able to do the job.
■ Making workers redundant without following the correct procedure. This is dealt with later.
■ As a result of a transfer of a business, such as when one business is bought by another. However, if the business can prove it was for economic, technical or organisational reasons, it may be considered fair.

There are reasons why dismissal may be **fair**. The employer must have a valid reason and must act 'reasonably' when dealing with this reason.

■ The employee is incapable of doing the job or unqualified.
■ 'Misconduct' of the employee, such as persistent lateness (minor) or theft (major).
■ The employer is unable to employ the worker. For example, a lorry driver may no longer be employed if he has lost his driving licence.
■ Any other substantial reason. For example, false details may have been given on the application form.
■ Redundancy can take place if the employer needs to reduce the workforce. This could be because a factory has closed or there is not enough work to do. The job must have **disappeared**. In other words, it is not redundancy if another worker is hired as a replacement. Certain procedures must be followed by employers. They must consult with trade unions over any proposed redundancy. If the union feels the employer has not met requirements, it can complain to a tribunal. Employees are entitled to a period of notice, as well as payment based on how long they have been in continuous employment.

If a worker feels that he has been unfairly dismissed, he can take his case to an **industrial tribunal**. This is dealt with in the next section. For example, a tribunal may decide that an employee who resigns as a result of the employer's actions has been **constructively** dismissed. To do this the employer must have acted in a way that is a substantial breach of the employment contract. An example might be where the employer demoted a worker to a lower rank or lower paid position for no reason.

Unfair dismissal - what to do

If an employee feels that he has been unfairly dismissed, what can he do about it? If may be possible for a worker and a business to settle the dispute voluntarily. If not, the employee may decide to complain to an industrial tribunal. Figure 56.2 shows the stages involved in this.

The complaint must be made within 3 months of the end of contract. A notice of application is sent to the employer asking if they wish to contest the case. Details of the case are then sent to the **Advisory, Conciliation and Arbitration Service** (ACAS) (☞ unit 60). Their role is to help settle the dispute before it reaches the tribunal through conciliation.

Before the complaint does reach the tribunal, there may be a pre-hearing assessment. If either party has a case that is not likely to succeed, they can be told and also informed that they may be liable for costs. The aim of this stage is to 'weed out' hopeless cases.

Once a complaint goes to a hearing at a tribunal, the employee is entitled to legal advice. After the hearing the tribunal will make a decision. If this is in favour of the employee then the tribunal can order:

■ the employee to be reinstated in the same job;
■ the employee to be re-engaged in another job;
■ compensation to be paid.

It is possible to appeal against a tribunal's decision. This will be heard by the Employment Appeal Tribunal.

QUESTION 3 John Smart was employed by Jones and Harcourt, a paper merchant in Oxford. The company buys paper in bulk from foreign mills and distributes it to users in the UK. In the early 1990s, trade and paper prices began to fall. The company was looking for ways of cutting costs. John had been employed as warehouse manager to control the arrival and delivery of paper. With no prior consultation, one Monday in early 1993, a director informed John that his services were no longer required. John was told that he was to be made redundant at the end of the week. The following week the company employed a younger man to do John's job, at a far lower salary.

(a) Comment on the fairness of John's dismissal.
(b) What advice would you give John about his next course of action?

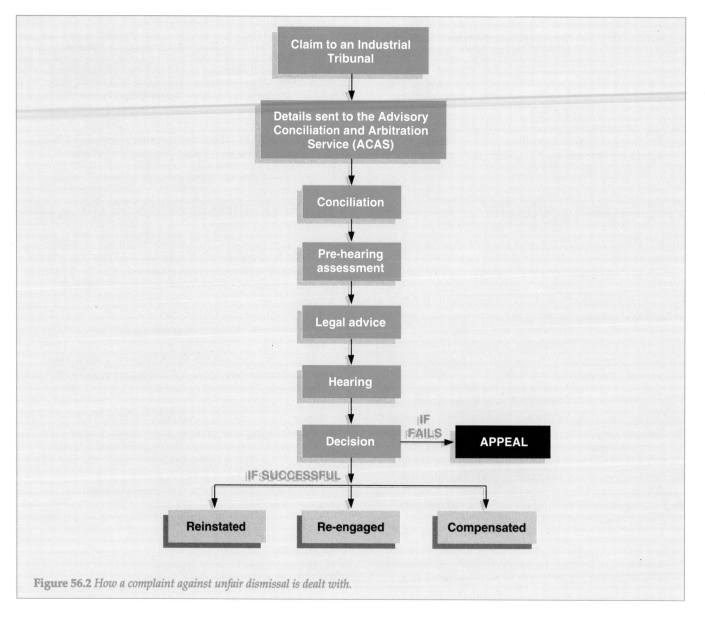

Figure 56.2 *How a complaint against unfair dismissal is dealt with.*

Wage protection

The main legislation relating to pay in the UK is the **Wages Act, 1986**. This sets out conditions for payments to workers and deductions from wages. Wages are defined as any sum paid to the worker by the employer in connection with the job. This includes fees, bonuses, commission, sick pay, gift tokens or vouchers. Certain payments, such as redundancy payments, expenses or loans are not included.

Deductions made from wages that are covered by the Act include:

■ those that must be taken or are agreed upon, such as income tax or National Insurance;
■ those shown in the contract of employment;
■ those agreed by the worker in writing, such as trade union payments;

providing that these are the agreed amounts. If the employer deliberately decides not to pay part of a worker's wages, then employees can complain to a tribunal. This is a similar process to complaints about dismissal. Wage protection is also covered by the **Equal Pay Act, 1970** (☞ unit 55).

Before 1993, some workers had minimum wages set by Wages Councils. Their role was set out in the Wages Act, 1986. Councils had the power to fix a basic minimum hourly rate of pay, fix overtime rates and decide the number of hours a week worked before overtime was paid. It was illegal to pay adults less than these rates. Wages Councils were found in industries with traditionally low paid workers. These included:

■ retailing (sale of books, clothing, stationery, toys, groceries, magazines etc.);
■ licensed establishments (public houses, inns, clubs, restaurants, hotels, holiday camps etc.);

- clothing manufacture;
- unlicensed refreshment (restaurants, cafes, snack bars etc.);
- hairdressing;
- laundry.

In 1993 Wage Councils were dismantled by the government.

The Social Chapter

The European Community's Social Chapter is an attempt to encourage minimum wages and conditions of work in member countries. It was argued that a business may attempt to respond to falling profits or greater competition by cutting costs. This could lead to poor pay and work conditions for employees. To prevent this, member countries outlined an agreement which covered such areas as:

- a limit on hours of work;
- 'fair and reasonable' rewards;
- minimum social security;
- free collective bargaining;
- access to training;
- workers' involvement in company decision making;
- health and safety;
- equal opportunities.

All member countries signed at Maastricht in December 1991 except for Britain. This meant that British workers remained outside the protection of the agreement. The Conservative government argued that signing would have prevented businesses from operating freely. It would also have worked against attempts to make wages and labour more flexible by trade union reforms. By 1993 Britain had still not signed.

QUESTION 4 In 1992 the Trade Union Reform and Employment Rights Bill was proposed by the Conservative government. The Employment Secretary at the time, Gillian Shephard argued, '... it is designed to increase the competitiveness of the economy and remove obstacles to the creation of new jobs..'.

Mrs Shephard explained why the government believed the time had come to abolish the Wages Councils. 'One of the most important developments of the last ten years has been the decisive move away from traditional, industry-wide collective bargaining which fixes pay without any regard to the skills and performance of individual employees or the need to contain costs in order to create jobs. The Wages Councils are an example of those damaging, outdated practices. They have no role to play in the 1990s. Where the Wages Councils force companies to pay more than they can afford, they destroy jobs.'

The Act was debated in Parliament in 1993. It was given the Royal seal of approval in July 1993.

Source: adapted from *Employment Gazette*, December 1992 and updated.

(a) Discuss the possible advantages to businesses of the removal of Wages Councils.
(b) How might the removal of Wages Councils:
  (i) harm;
  (ii) be of benefit to;
  employees in those industries where Wage Councils operated?

Summary

1. Why might it be in a business' interest to protect its workers?
2. State 5 types of health and safety dangers that may exist in business.
3. Briefly explain 3 pieces of legislation regarding health and safety at work.
4. Under what circumstances might dismissal be:
   (a) fair;
   (b) unfair?
5. What is the role of an industrial tribunal in protecting the employee at work?
6. 'An employee without a strong case for unfair dismissal may face problems if a tribunal finds against them.' Explain this statement.
7. Briefly explain the wage protection stated in the Wages Act, 1986.
8. What has been the role of Wages Councils in the UK?
9. Discuss 2 effects that signing the Social Chapter may have on the business of a country that signed the agreement.

Question

British Aerospace, Humberside

The British Aerospace factory in Brough near Hull makes the Hawk military aircraft and components for several others. It has an old-fashioned feel about it - brown and mustard paintwork in the corridors, deafening machines and men who call each other 'lads'.

But appearances can be deceptive. The site is rapidly modernising. Along with a smart, 'single status' restaurant and cheerful medical centre, there is 'cell' manufacturing, delayered management and an approach to health and safety which has just won the company an award. The winning formula was to integrate health, safety and environmental issues through the formation of a single department.

Brian Rylance, the health and safety manager over the past 10 years, and the new site personnel director, Tony McCarthy, have worked to increase the status of health and safety in the plant. Rylance believes the secret of good health and safety lies not in gimmicks, but by ensuring people are always alert. That is not to say that he lacks fancy schemes. The snazziest have been a traffic light symbol in the dining room where food has been marked for cholesterol content (red for chips, green for tomatoes etc) and a programme of health checks which was kicked off by sports celebrities.

Underlying the glitz was a philosophy which stated that what was good for executives, who had long had access to medicals, was good for everyone. There is also a belief, although no proof as yet, that a healthier workforce will lead to greater productivity.

All 4,200 staff have been invited to an on-site health check by the 'Look after your heart' campaign, at which nurses from the site's own health centre provide full medical screening on top of a basic check-up. Both the check-ups and the traffic lights are part of a long term 'Well being at work' campaign. Smoking has already been tackled and stress counselling is now being introduced. Private counselling has always been available for those in particular trouble, but McCarthy says the department is trying to 'roll that out' to cover anyone who wants it. The attempt, evident in the site's health policy, to break workplace class barriers and involve all employees, also underlies the changes in safety procedure.

Under the Health and Safety at Work Act, shop stewards have a right to make their own checks every three months. But Rylance says that, in the past, the regularity and thoroughness of these varied.

Meanwhile, if there was a problem, one of the 11 shopfloor representatives on the 18 strong safety committee would bring it up at the monthly committee meeting. He believes this reinforced a confrontational approach and created undesirable, even dangerous, delays.

So Rylance and his team worked with the trade unions to restructure their statutory audit, redesign the form and raise the profile to ensure it happened at least every six months. Rylance says the steward agrees a date for the audit with the team leader and they usually 'walk the four walls together'. If not, they talk about the audit before the form is circulated to relevant managers and union officials.

Similarly, the auditing of health and safety on new machines and processes and drafting of guidelines is now carried out by the engineers, managers and operators most closely involved.

Much of the literature accumulating through this process is being compiled by Rylance's team into a 300 page health and safety manual, which is constantly updated.

However, shopfloor relationships possibly pose the stickiest issue for personnel professionals who are trying to modernise health and safety management. Training supervisors to work with safety representatives is one problem which Rylance does not believe he has entirely overcome. The other side of the coin is the attitude of shop stewards. The stewards were highly critical of the attempt, as they saw it, to bypass the unions. This is because Rylance is trying to involve the whole workforce in health and safety. 'I'm not bypassing them. I would have them in on any meeting about safety. But I'm not necessarily directly asking their opinion. I'm not smart enough to know every nuance of everyone else's job, and I think the safety representative has to accept that he's not either.'

Source: adapted from *Personnel Management Plus*, November 1992.

(a) Identify health and safety problems that the article suggests might exist at the British Aerospace plant.
(b) What solutions to these problems have the company introduced?
(c) How might the suggested health and safety policy affect the business?
(d) What problems of introducing new health and safety procedures are the company likely to face?

Pasta Italiana

John and Betty Cotrozzi set up Pasta Italiana in June 1982. The business was a partnership, located in a small factory in North London. At that time it produced a range of fresh pasta dishes, including some traditional Genovese recipes that Betty Cotrozzi had had passed down to her by her grandmother. A home delivery service was provided for customers in the area. The business employed two part time staff in 1982. The turnover of the business was £35,000.

After 1982 the business expanded enormously. Turnover had reached £975,000 a year by 1988. The company had become a limited company with the Cotrozzis as major shareholders. The factory had expanded to enable it to cope with a large increase in demand. Ten retail outlets had opened in the area and the home delivery service had expanded. In addition Pasta Italiana sold many of its products to local restaurants. The major development though had been to supply the catering departments of universities and colleges in the South with a budget version of their products. These developments had been the ideas of John. Betty was more cautious suggesting that expansion should occur using the same format that had always been successful, ie more home deliveries.

The product mix of the business had changed over time. Some lines, such as the meat Cannelloni with tomato sauce, had come to the end of their life cycle. The Cotrozzis decided to replace these pasta dishes with traditional pizzas cooked in old fashioned wood burning ovens. The pizzas were an immediate success.

By 1988, the business had become too big to handle by the Cotrozzis themselves. They appointed a finance manager, a personnel manager, a marketing manager and a production and distribution manager to take over the responsibility of running the day to day aspects of the business. Each manager was paid £20,000 per annum. All, apart from the personnel manager, were male. Other employees were also recruited to the business. There were 10 female clerical staff, 5 of whom were part time. The hourly rate for the full time staff was £3.50 an hour and for the part time staff £2.80. Each retail outlet had a full time manager and a full time shop worker. Three of the bigger outlets also had two part time workers in each. All employees in the retail outlets were women. The managers were paid £11,000 per annum and the full time assistants were paid £6,800. The part time shop assistants were generally still at school and were paid £2.00 an hour.

The expanded factory had 20 workers. This included 3 male chefs each earning £12,000, with the rest catering assistants, 8 of whom were men and 9 female. Only 8 of the catering assistants were full time. The rest were part time. The catering assistants all earned £8,000 per annum. Overtime was available for these workers. In addition the company employed 10 drivers to deliver products to the company's shops and its customers. These were all male drivers and they earned £10,000 per annum. Again there were opportunities for overtime.

A cleaning staff of 5 part-timers was employed to keep the premises clean and up to health and safety standards.

Business tended to be seasonal. The summer months were the least busy. This was because the university and college catering departments didn't have students to cater for. Winter months seemed most popular, particularly around Christmas time when families order more for the festivities and restaurants were at their busiest.

By 1991 the recession started to have an effect on Pasta Italiana. Demand for the products had fallen, particularly in the restaurant and university trade and turnover was down to £500,000. The finance manager, Jim, recognised that the company needed to cut costs. He suggested that the production manager examined ways of improving productivity. Ben, the production manager, had just come back from a fact finding mission in Italy and had been impressed with the new technological developments in fresh pasta production. These included computer controlled ovens and boilers and semi-automated packaging techniques. He recognised that he could improve productivity by 50 per cent. In order to invest in this new capital equipment he worked out that he would have to make 10 (including at least 2 chefs) of his staff redundant but also employ a specialist production assistant who was computer literate. He acknowledged that it would be difficult to carry out either one of these initiatives. The staff had always been loyal and some had been with the company before he had started. In addition, specialist production assistants would be hard to come by.

The personnel manager had also been asked to examine ways of increasing the productivity of the staff. She examined ways of increasing motivation amongst all employees. She recognised there were both monetary and non-monetary ways of doing this. She examined job enrichment programmes and performance related pay. In addition she suggested an appraisal system. These schemes, she felt, would increase individual motivation to the business because it recognised the individual efforts of employees. In addition, she felt that certain jobs might be contracted out. In particular, the distribution might be contracted out to a distribution specialist and cleaning might be more effectively done by professional cleaning agencies. Her aim was to try and create a core full time workforce that had job security and were fundamentally committed to the business with a periphery that included part-timers and contract workers. By early 1993 things had worsened and turnover had reduced further to £350,000. The Cotrozzis wanted to see action and they expected to see their managers make the appropriate changes.

All of this talk of change had caused some anxiety amongst the staff. They felt that they were never communicated with on any major initiatives. They started to feel undervalued. Some of the staff, in particular the clerical staff, felt underpaid in comparison with other staff. They also felt that some of the proposed initiatives that had been heard on the grapevine were about to be introduced more because of crisis management than due to forward planning. Absenteeism started to increase and productivity had fallen. In addition 5 employees, during the 1992-93 period, decided to leave because of what they viewed as potentially worsening conditions at the company. As one of the young chefs commented, 'I've had very little formal training since I've been here and I'm unlikely to remain much longer. I've got to get a job where my skills will be developed and where my future might be assured.'

(a) Using any theories on motivation, explain why the workforce in 1993 is demotivated.

(b) What evidence is there in the case for suggesting that Pasta Italiana have not carried out any human resource planning?

(c) What type of payment systems are presently being used by Pasta Italiana to pay their employees?

(d) Why has the personnel manager suggested examining different payment systems?

(e) What could the personnel manager do to address the problem of employees feeling that they are not paid fairly?

(f) In what ways could Pasta Italiana redesign jobs in order to motivate their employees?

(g) What methods could the personnel manager and production manager use to recruit a new production assistant?

German workers go back to school and get ahead

German manufacturers never cease to complain that their labour costs are the world's highest, especially when non-wage benefits are included.

But press them a bit harder and they will admit that their highly-trained German workers are a key to the country's manufacturing success.

The cost of employing skilled workers is causing German industry to shift lower-value production abroad.

Klaus Krone, chairman of Krone in Berlin, a medium-size producer of telecommunications components, says German manufacturers are switching to higher technology products.

This had been the experience of his own company, even though labour represents less than 5 per cent of total costs. Germany is famous for its training system. This provides for three year apprenticeships during which most trainees from the age of 16 work on three days a week and attend vocational school for the other two.

Management at Krone, which has 4,100 employees in 17 countries, say this training gives the company's German labour force a significant advantage in both theoretical and practical knowledge over its workers in Britain and Australia which favour on-the-job training.

Thomas Mickeleit, a spokesman for Krone, says, 'A worker in the UK has a more narrow training than here and lacks the theoretical background which would make him more flexible.' Krone workers in Berlin said they found it difficult to imagine how foreign workers could cope without having been apprenticed or having attended a vocational school.

Jurgen Rinner, a 38 year old, did his three and a half year apprenticeship at Krone when the company was desperate for skilled workers in isolated west Berlin. At that time he earned only DM145 (£57) a month compared with the DM800 which a 16 year old apprentice starts off with today. He attended vocational school once a week, doing practical work and studying technical drawing, maths and materials science.

Today, young German apprentices go to vocational school twice a week - to the dismay of many small companies which rely heavily on them - and the range of subjects is far greater and more specialised. One language is required, usually English, and a social science.

'You can't know enough today', says Rinner. In fact, a growing number of the 100 young people who are apprenticed at Krone each year have Abitur school leaving certificates, qualifying them for university studies but instead choose to learn a trade through fear of unemployment.

Rinner is one of a handful of maintenance and control workers in an automated hall producing quick connection components for copper and optical fibre networks. He doubts that on-the-job training could give a worker the skills he gained during his apprenticeship and vocational school.

'The foundation would be missing', he says.

A colleague, Karsten Vogel, is one of Krone's nearly 200 east German employees hired since the Berlin Wall came down in 1989. They proved to be as well-qualified as their west German counterparts, according to the company.

Vogel, a 28 year old electronics worker did his apprenticeship at an east Berlin television plant equipped with modern Japanese equipment.

At the same time, he studied to gain the coveted Abitur. 'You learned more than you need but you never know where you will end up', he says.

Vogel attended a number of training courses offered by Krone and was soon able to cope with its different control system for the automated equipment.

At first, western workmates kept their distance but finally accepted him when he proved his competence.

Vogel would like to become a technician but says the two years of evening classes he would need to attend are not possible while he continues to work in a three-shifts-a-day pattern.

Source: the *Financial Times*, August 1992.

(a) Why does the German training system, according to management at Krone, give German companies a significant advantage over British or Australian firms?

(b) Discuss why there might be greater flexibility from German workers than British workers.

(c) Outline any disadvantages with the German training system.

(d) What lessons can the British government and industry learn from this article?

Aims

- To identify what makes a good equal opportunity employer.

Research

You might research the recruitment practices and equal opportunities policies of two companies - one that has positively stated that it is an equal opportunity employer and one that has not. You might have a hypothesis, for example, that an equal opportunity employer is more likely to recruit women into traditionally male jobs than employers that do not have an equal opportunity policy. Alternatively, you may include ethnic minorities, disabled or older workers in your hypothesis. The data that might enable you to see the difference between the companies could include the way the two companies recruit and select candidates for middle/senior management jobs, the proportion of women in management positions, the training given to women to allow progression in the company, and the physical and contractual allowances made for women, eg creche facilities or 5 year breaks to start a family with a guarantee that they can return to their job at the same level in the organisation.

From comparing and contrasting the approaches of two companies and reading literature on equal opportunities you might at the end of your report make recommendations as to what makes a good equal opportunity employer in practice. You must stress that the work carried out will at all times be confidential and that it is being used solely for project work. You might also say that you are happy to show them the final project.

Preparation for this type of research activity is vital. You will need to gain the co-operation of two companies. Try and obtain the contact names and addresses of at least 4 companies so that if one or two companies refuse to help you will have a number in reserve.

It would be very useful if you had contact names, particularly in the personnel department, who might help you with this research. Write to them explaining the nature of the project. You need to be precise about what you want from them and how much of their time will be needed. Make sure you have the letter checked by your teacher. Send the letter as soon as possible so that time isn't wasted.

You will be able to gather your own information.

- Information about equal opportunity employers and general information about equal opportunities can be obtained from the Equal Opportunities Commission.
- Does your college/school or local library have a CD-ROM? You might find they have *Guardian/Financial Times/Independent/Economist* CD titles. These are very good for researching a project.

You may also be able to get information from the companies themselves.

- An organisational chart with a breakdown of male/female job holders.

- A percentage male/female split for categories of jobs. The categories of jobs will depend on the type of company you investigate, eg:
  (i) shop floor workers or sales assistants;
  (ii) clerical and administration staff;
  (iii) supervisory staff;
  (vi) junior/middle/senior management.
- A policy document on recruitment.
- An equal opportunity policy document (if they have one).
- Examples of application forms.

Presentation

Before presenting your data, consider the following questions.

- Does the company promote training and internal promotion for women in the company?
- How does the company recognise when it has a vacancy and does the company then do a job analysis, person specification, and job description? Does anyone check the descriptions?
- What types of general criteria are used in pre-selection and in the interview for middle/senior management jobs?
- Does the company use a recruitment agency and for what jobs?
- Does the recruitment agency positively encourage the placement of women in non-traditional jobs?
- Do the companies feel there are problems in recruiting women to middle and senior management positions?
- How does the company positively encourage women to apply for jobs at the company?

These are some questions you might use, but talk with other students and your teacher about other issues that might be examined. The final report might then be structured in the following way.

- Introduction. What was the aim of the project and how did you go about investigating it?
- Description of the results for the two companies.
  (i) Physical provisions made for women at work, eg creche etc.
  (ii) Training and promotion paths for women in middle/senior management.
  (iii) Job analysis/person specification/job descriptions. Do they exclude women?
  (iv) Criteria used in pre-selection through application form and interview. Do they seem to exclude women?
  (v) How are certain categories of jobs segregated between men and women, eg are all shop floor workers women and all distribution workers men etc.?
  (vi) Views about women in senior management.
- Compare and contrast the results for the two companies. If they are the same why are they the same? If they are different why are they different?
- Recommendations. From your study what do you think is good practice for encouraging equal opportunities in recruitment.

Aims

- To examine how a business attempts to motivate its workers using monetary and non-monetary rewards.
- To evaluate if motivation is seen as important by the business.

Research

You might want to investigate the idea that a company is unlikely to motivate its employees by just using monetary rewards. Try to interview the personnel manager about any new schemes they have recently adopted in the organisation, such as performance related pay, appraisal schemes, job redesign schemes. Ask the personnel manager why they have adopted such schemes. Do they relate to any motivation theories that you know of? In addition you might attempt to construct a questionnaire to be given to a cross section of employees, asking them about what factors motivate or demotivate them at work.

You must stress that information received will at all times be confidential and that it is being used solely for project work. You might also say that you are more than happy to show them the final project when it is completed.

Preparation for this type of research activity is vital. You will need to gain the co-operation, in principle, of two companies. Choose one company that will give you greatest access to people you might need to talk to or give questionnaires to. It would be very useful if you had contact names, particularly in the personnel department, who might help you with this research. Write to them explaining the nature of the project. You need to be precise about what you want from them and how much time will be needed. You must obviously keep this down to a minimum.

Make sure you have letters/questionnaires checked by your teacher. Send the appropriate details to the company as soon as possible so that time isn't wasted.

Presentation

Factors to be included in your report might include the following.

- What types of payment systems are used at present? Do they vary depending on the category of job? Why is this the case? In the eyes of the organisation is pay the primary motivating factor?
- Does the company use any other incentive schemes to motivate its workers? What are these?
- What is the general view concerning employees in the organisation? Do personnel managers (or any other managers) adopt a theory X position or theory Y? Why? Do the ways the jobs are organised/designed indicate theory X or theory Y, ie:
  - (i) theory X - close supervision, narrow number of activities, little responsibility;
  - (ii) theory Y - autonomous, job enrichment, quality circles.
- Do the views of employees coincide with those of management concerning motivation? If not, why not?
- How closely do your results match the results of other theorists concerned with motivation?

Your report should make recommendations as to what appears to motivate/demotivate employees in the organisation.

Essays

1. 'The motivation of employees is only a priority for a firm when the firm faces increased competition and a reduction in supply of labour. The view that companies are genuinely concerned about the welfare of employees is a gross misrepresentation of reality.'
Discuss this statement.

2. 'Recruitment practices should be objective and fair.' How might a business ensure that this is the case?

3. What methods of training might be used by a business? Discuss why training is vital to health of the economy and the performance of individual companies.

4. To what extent are the health and safety procedures in a business the responsibility of all employees?

5. Why is it important for the management of businesses to develop and implement equal opportunities in the workplace?

6. 'A fair day's pay for a fair day's work.' How far is this quote relevant to today's workforce in the UK?

7. How might the management in a large local authority introduce a system of performance related pay for its council workers? What other methods might it use to motivate the workforce?

8. What factors might influence the success of an interview? Discuss the implications of an unsuccessful interview from a business's point of view.

9. What trends in the structure of the workforce may be of interest to a business? Discuss the effect of changes in the structure of the population over the next 10 years on a business of your choice.

Individuals in groups at work

Working with other people in groups is something that many employees do in business. An employee in a marketing consultancy business may be part of a team developing TV adverts for a client, part of a group set up to think of ideas to improve working methods and may meet with friends for lunch. Only in a small number of cases will individual employees work on their own, as in the case of a freelance journalist. Even an employee delivering goods on his own from a van will interact with staff and management when he returns to the office or factory.

Individuals may behave differently when working in a group than if they were working on their own. For example, an employee on a building site might want to work at a leisurely pace or find ways to avoid carrying out a task immediately. Group pressure could persuade or embarrass the employee into working harder than he would have wished. The group may want to finish the job early or earn any bonus that is available. In this case the employee's behaviour has changed as a result of being a group member. He is behaving in a way that conforms to the GROUP NORM. In other words, he is behaving in a way that is 'normal' for that group.

There is a certain amount of evidence to support the idea that individual behaviour is influenced by the group. The Hawthorne Studies (☞ unit 48) showed that group behaviour can influence workers' motivation. It is possible to identify certain common features of groups that exist in businesses.

■ The behaviour of the group influences all members, eg if a decision is made to take industrial action (☞ unit 61).
■ Members of the group have some common interests and objectives, eg a production team may want to increase its level of overtime payments.
■ Members meet and discuss common interests, eg assembly line workers might discuss the latest changes to working conditions.
■ There are rules or norms influencing members' behaviour, eg members of the finance committee of a business are expected to report back to the managing director after each meeting.

It could be argued that, given the emphasis on team work in many modern organisations, it is essential for businesses to understand how people work in groups. If employees in a group do not work 'well' together, this may reduce productivity and make decision making more difficult.

Types of group

It is possible to distinguish different groups that exist in business. One common method is to divide them into FORMAL and INFORMAL groups.

Formal groups These are groups which are set up by a business specifically to carry out tasks. Formal groups are an actual part of the organisation, with arranged meetings and rules determining their behaviour and actions. Examples of formal groups might be management teams that control one aspect of a business, such as the finance department.

Other examples of formal groups might be groups which are set up to deal with certain problems. For example, a unit might be set up by a business to monitor

---

QUESTION 1 Allied Corporation is a multinational. Part of the company is an engine manufacturing division, which became the focus of an investigation. A researcher spent time working in this factory as a participant observer. She observed the following about how groups, made up of operators, schedule co-ordinators and crib attendants, worked on the shop floor.

At the beginning of the shift, operators assembled outside the time office on the shop floor to collect their production cards, punch in and set up for the first task. Usually operators know from talking to their counterparts, before the beginning of the shift, which task they are likely to receive. Knowing what is available on the shop floor for their machine, operators are sometimes able to bargain with the scheduling man, who is distributing the tasks.

After receiving their first tasks, operators have to find the blueprint and tooling for the operation. These are usually in the crib, although they may be already out on the floor. The crib attendant is therefore a strategic person whose co-operation an operator must secure. If the crib attendant chooses to be unco-operative in dispensing tools, blueprints, fixtures etc. and particularly, in the grinding of tools, operators can be held up for considerable lengths of time. Occasionally, operators who have managed to gain the confidence of the crib attendant will enter the crib themselves to speed up the process. Since, unlike the scheduling man, the crib attendant has no real interest in whether operators achieve output targets his co-operation has to be gained by other means. An employee commented, 'For the first five months of my employment my relations with the crib attendant on second shift were very poor, but at Christmas things changed dramatically. Every year the local union distributes a Christmas ham to all its members. I told Harry, the crib attendant, that I couldn't be bothered picking up mine from the union hall and that he could have it for himself. He was delighted and after that, I received good service.'

Source: adapted from *Manufacturing Consent*, M.Burawoy, University of Chicago Press.

(a) Explain how being a member of a group in the above example has affected the workers' behaviour.
(b) Why might this be important for the business?
(c) What common interests might the groups of workers in the factory have?

the introduction of new machinery. The group may include the production manager, an engineer, a supervisor and a number of operators. Its task may be to make sure the changeover is as efficient as possible and it would meet to discuss ways in which this could be achieved.

Formal groups can be **temporary** or **permanent**. A temporary group might be a working party to investigate a computerised information system. Permanent groups include standing committees, such as health and safety committees or a trade union, which is a formal group, but not one created by management. The type of group depends on whether the task involved is recurrent or a 'one-off'.

Informal groups Informal groups are made up of employees with similar interests. They are not a formal part of the business itself. They do not have any formal 'rules', although there are often unofficial norms which influence members' behaviour. An example of an informal group might be a casual meeting over lunch between managers in the production, marketing and finance departments to discuss a new product launch. It could also be a group of hospital workers discussing possible job cuts in their rest room.

There are a number of reasons why informal groups exist. It is argued that these groups meet the psychological needs (☞ unit 47) of employees. These might be some of the following.

- The need to be with other people.
- Status is determined by membership of various groups. This will also influence the view people have of their personal value and self-esteem.
- Groups offer a feeling of security and mutual support. By doing so, they reduce uncertainty and anxiety.
- The group may act as a problem solver for its members.

The informal groups that develop will be determined, to a large extent, by the physical layout required for work. Distance has a powerful influence on who will interact with whom. In general, the more frequent the interactions, the more likely informal groups are to be formed. Informal groups can have considerable influence on group members and the norms and values that a group develops may or may not support those of the organisation.

It may appear that formal and informal groups are separate. This is not the case. Groups that start off as formal often develop powerful informal relations. 'Part' of a company, as well as being a department, may be a department of friends. Japanese organisations, such as Sony, deliberately encourage this. Informal groupings, such as friendships outside work, can provide useful channels of communication for the organisation. The **grapevine** is a term used for such channels (☞ unit 62).

It is also possible to divide groups into primary and secondary groups.

- Primary groups are small groups where people can have regular contact, eg a small department or office, or a youth club.
- Secondary groups are large groups where people have less regular contact, eg a large open-plan office or a large meeting.

Group decision making

The aims of businesses are to try and create groups that are effective and efficient. If the business can motivate the group to work harder in order to achieve goals, the sense

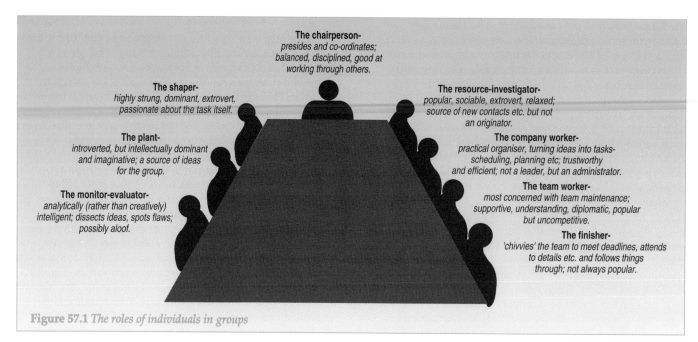

Figure 57.1 *The roles of individuals in groups*

of pride in the group's own competence might create job satisfaction.

There are a number of factors that can help group organisation and decision making.

Group members The characteristics and goals of the individual members of the group will help to determine the group's characteristics and goals. An individual is likely to be influenced more strongly by a small group than by a large group. In a large group the person may feel overwhelmed and, therefore, unable to participate effectively in team decisions.

It has been suggested that the effectiveness of a group depends on the blend of the individual skills and abilities of its members. A group might be most effective if it contains:

- a person of originality and ideas;
- a 'get-up-and-go' person with considerable energy, enthusiasm and drive;
- a quiet, logical thinker, who ponders carefully and criticises the ideas of others.

This is why groups set up to consider new products often draw members from a number of different departments in the business. This means the group will have a wide range of skills and abilities.

Group roles The most comprehensive study of group roles within a work setting is most probably that of **Meredith Belbin** (1981). He found that successful teams consisted of a mix of individuals, each of whom performed a different role. A summary of these roles is shown in Figure 57.1.

According to Belbin each person has a preferred role and for a group to be effective all the roles need to be filled. So a business might select people to ensure that they fill one or more of the roles which a group lacks. This is not always possible. Most formal groups within business are predetermined by who has the technical expertise to carry out the task.

How then can a knowledge of these roles help?

- For a group to work efficiently the business must be aware of the roles people prefer. These may become apparent through observation. People should be given tasks which allow them to operate in their preferred roles, whether in a sporting team or in a team of medical staff in a casualty department.
- There should be an understanding of which roles are missing that may cause inefficiency. For example, some researchers conducted a study into why some quality circles (☞ unit 34) continued to meet, while others ceased to. They found that all the groups that failed lacked someone who preferred the 'finisher' role. Apparently these groups were good at problem solving and finding solutions but never carried their ideas through.

The group's task The nature of the task may affect how a group is managed. If a job must be done urgently, it is often necessary to dictate how things should be done, rather than to encourage participation in decision making. Jobs which are routine and undemanding are unlikely to motivate individuals or the group as a whole. If individuals want authoritarian leadership, they are also likely to want clearly defined targets.

The characteristics of an effective work group

If a business is to try and improve the effectiveness of groups it must be able to identify the characteristics of an effective work group. These may include some of the following.

- There is a high commitment to the achievement of targets and organisational goals.
- There is a clear understanding of the group's work.

■ There is a clear understanding of the role of each person within the group.

■ There is a free and open communication between members of the group and trust between members.

■ There is idea sharing.

■ The group is good at generating new ideas.

■ Group members try to help each other out by offering constructive criticisms and suggestions.

■ There is group problem solving which gets to the root causes of the work problem.

■ Group members seek a united consensus of opinion.

■ The group is motivated to be able to carry on working in the absence of its leader.

Factors influencing group decision making

There are a number of factors which determine how effective groups are when making decisions.

Size of the group Research has been carried out into the effects of group size on decision making. It has been argued that groups become ineffective once they have 21 members. Other researchers have tried to measure an optimum size for groups. It is felt, in many cases, that the best size is between 3-7 members, with 5 often being quoted as an ideal number.

Why might groups containing these numbers be effective? Larger groups often have communication problems, as more and more people wish to contribute to group discussions. In a small group, the chairperson's role may be fairly informal. When groups get large, however, more formal management may be needed. To address all remarks through the chair in a meeting of 4 people is perhaps being over-formal. To do so in a meeting of 20 may be a necessity.

The size of the task can determine group size. A group designing and building a motor racing car may require many people, with a variety of skills. Each member is likely to make some contribution to the task of the group. But a group which decides who is to drive the car in a Grand Prix may be small in order to reach a clear decision.

Communication Communication in groups can influence how group decisions are made. A distinction is often made between two types of group.

■ Centralised groups are groups where individuals can only communicate with other group members via a central member.

■ Decentralised groups are groups where every member can communicate directly with every other member.

Communication in groups can take place in a number of ways.

■ The wheel. This is where a person at the centre of the group can communicate with all the other members. They, on the other hand, can only communicate with him or her. If they wish to communicate to other members they can only do so through the same central person. This might be the case in a formal meeting.

■ The chain. Information is passed from one individual to the next before it reaches the last person in the group. Any individual only ever communicates with one other person. This might be the case in a police operation, for example.

■ The circle. Communication is circular, in other words, messages pass between certain people, who pass it on to others, such as in a large office.

■ The all-channel. Every member of the group can communicate directly with every other member, as in an open discussion on where an 'awards' evening should be held.

The degree of centrality is highest in the wheel and is less in the chain and circle. The all-channel has no centre; decisions are made by reaching an agreement. The degree of centralisation can affect the group's efficiency, but this also depends on the complexity of the task. When the task is simple, eg deciding on the recruitment policy for a particular job, centralised groups like the wheel are faster and make fewer errors. When the task is more complicated, eg organising and putting into practice a recruitment policy for a particular job, decentralised groups maybe more suitable.

Unit 62 explains the methods and problems of communication for the business in more detail.

Leadership It is likely that a group will have a 'leader' to control or guide it. Leadership may be informal, in the sense that one person 'dominates' a group because of their personality, position or access to information. Leaders can also be elected or nominated by the group, such as chairperson.

Leadership styles and their effects on the business are discussed in detail in the next unit. It is enough to say here that types of leaders can be classified as follows.

■ Autocratic. This involves one-way communication between the leader of others in the group. The leader makes all the decisions and gives out instructions, expecting them to be obeyed by other group members without question. An example might be a powerful head of a large business like Rupert Murdoch.

■ Persuasive. The leader makes all the decisions, but believes that other group members need to be motivated to accept them before they will do what she wants them to. She therefore tries to explain her decisions in order to convince them of her point of view, as a teacher or lecturer in a class might.

■ Consultative . This involves discussion between the leader and the other group members involved in making a decision, but the leader retains the right to make the decision herself. By consulting with her group members before making any decision, the leader will take into account their advice and feelings. A council leader might have to operate in this way.

■ Democratic. This is an approach where the leader makes a decision based on consensus and agreement within the group. Group members with the greatest knowledge of a problem will have greater influence over the decision. A trade union representative is likely to adopt this style.

Skills used in groups For individuals to work well in groups, they need to have a variety of skills. These skills can be categorised into three general areas.
- Contribution. Individuals need to communicate their ideas effectively, informing group members of their thoughts, views and motives. They also need to be able to initiate ideas and evaluate both their own contribution and those of others.
- Co-operation. Individuals need to support other group members so that everyone is involved. This is more likely if individuals share their ideas and listen to others. They should also be able to negotiate and consult, so that everyone feels part of the group's activities.
- Production. Group members need to gather information, materials and ideas, and share them with other group members. They need to show the skills of perseverance and reliability especially if the group is struggling with a problem.

Advantages and problems of group decisions

To what extent are groups more effective in making decisions than individuals? There are a number of advantages in groups making decisions for a business and for the members themselves.
- Groups can pool ideas and draw on a variety of expertise. This makes them particularly good at finding errors. For example, in the design and construction of nuclear reactors, a whole variety of groups working on safety aspects are more likely to ensure that all safety measures are thought of and solutions found to safety problems.
- Groups can handle a great deal of information and involved tasks in a shorter period of time than an individual would take. An example might be the design and writing of a computerised information program.
- Group members may support, motivate and help other members when making decisions.
- Groups provide a basis for accountability within a firm. They can also be used as the basis for a bonus system to increase productivity.

Despite these advantages, there are sometimes problems in group decision making.
- Group decisions may take time. When a decision needs to be made quickly, such as an investment decision on the Stock Exchange, an individual may be more effective from a business point of view. There will be no debate, which will delay any decision that is made.
- Where one person is an obvious expert in the field, that person may make a more accurate and effective decision, for example, a personnel manager in deciding how best to train certain employees.
- There could be conflicting views and personalities within groups. This can lead to a lack of cohesion,

with no shared aims or objectives. The result is that the group becomes inefficient in carrying out a task.
- There may be a possibility of 'risky-shift' decisions. Groups may make riskier decisions than individuals would, due to too much group cohesion. For example, a board of directors might decide as a group to take over a potentially profitable, but inefficient, firm. An individual entrepreneur might have considered this decision too risky to take.

Inter-group conflict

One problem that may result for the business from group activity is a conflict between groups. Many managers would agree that some inter-group competition is inevitable and perhaps useful. If there was no competition the business may become stagnant, with few pressures to make changes. This could lead to inefficiency. The other extreme, of very high levels of competition and conflict, may also cause problems. It could lead to anxiety and tension in the workforce which are counter-productive.

Why might conflict result between groups?
- Groups are often in competition with each other over resources. One example might be where the sports and leisure department in a local council needs funds for a swimming pool, but this may result in another group such as the social services department having less. Another example would be where an employee who is an integral part of a production team may have to leave the team at a vital time to attend a health and safety meeting. Conflict results from the groups' competition for the employee's time.
- There may be conflict between groups at different levels in the business organisation. For example, non-graduate entrants to a bank may be restricted because of the promotion or higher pay of graduate entrants.
- Conflict can result when groups have different goals. Unit 2 showed that when there is a divorce of **ownership and control** managers may attempt to satisfy their own aims, such as market leadership by a series of price cuts. At the same time they would attempt to make a satisfactory profit for shareholders, who may have wanted the business to maximise profits.
- There are certain psychological factors which can often lead to conflict between groups. When groups are in competition, each will tend to underplay its weaknesses, overestimate its strengths and degrade the other group. The other group may also be seen as hostile or aggressive. As a result it becomes the enemy - 'them' against 'us'. Because of these two factors, interactions between the two groups become strained and decline.

How can conflict either be avoided or, if it already exists, defused? One method that involves low levels of risk is by getting members of one group to work with the other group. This can be achieved by organising joint projects or by some form of exchange. The leaders of the group could initially either work together or exchange roles for this approach to be effective. It can be further developed by communication and swapping of group members. This technique is often used when one organisation takes over another (☞ unit 32) and there is a need to avoid conflict at all levels within the 'new' business. Another possibility is for a business to rotate membership of groups to prevent divisions taking place.

QUESTION 3 IceCool, a major ice cream manufacturer, are concerned with two major business problems - reduced profitability due to rising costs and lack of corporate appeal among the youth market. They have asked the production and marketing departments for their diagnosis of the problem. Both departments are keen to impress, as it could mean greater resources being dedicated to them if they won the argument.

The marketing department managed to have funds allocated to them so that they could carry out market research on the development of a new ice-cream snack. The results of their work suggest that a market segment of 16-19 year olds would particularly like a dynamic, sports and fitness orientated ice-cream snack - a 'Lucozade Sports' ice cream. The price for this product would have to be in the 80p-90p bracket and the packaging would have to be bright, young and dynamic. The advertising approach would be a nationwide television campaign backed up by national billboard displays. They forecast that the payback period will be 2 years, but that high profit margins will then be generated for a further 2 years before going into decline. They have presented their plans to the board of directors.

The production department were far more concerned with the lack of productivity caused by poor capital investment over the last two years. Without any extra allocation of funds, they presented a paper to the board of directors that suggested attacking the problem of poor productivity first so that it might compete more effectively using the product range that was already tried, tested and successful. They were particularly scathing about introducing a new product without solving the underlying problems. Likewise marketing were amazed at the lack of vision from the production department.

(a) Why did conflict arise between the production and marketing departments at IceCool?
(b) What benefits might there be for the company in this conflict?
(c) How can IceCool ensure that the two departments work together when a final decision is made?

Key terms

Formal groups - groups specifically set up by a business to carry out tasks. They have certain formal rules of behaviour.
Group norm - the usual characteristics of behaviour of a group.
Informal groups - groups made up of individuals in business with similar interests. They are not part of the formal business organisation.

Summary

1. 'Group behaviour is different from individual behaviour.' To what extent is this statement likely to be true in business?
2. State 4 common features that groups in business organisations have.
3. Why might a business set up a temporary formal group rather than making it permanent?
4. Give 4 advantages for employees of informal group membership.
5. Give 6 characteristics of effective groups.
6. Briefly explain why optimal group size may be between 3-7 members.
7. What is likely to influence the size of a group?
8. Explain the difference between centralised and decentralised group decision making.
9. What are the advantages to the business of group decision making?
10. In what circumstances might individual decision making be more beneficial to a business?
11. What factors within a business might lead to inter-group conflict?

Question

High Lane VI Form College

High Lane VI Form College acquired designated status on 1st April 1993. This meant that control for the funding of the college moved from the local authority to central government. In addition, the complete management of the budget would be carried out by the principal of the college rather than the local education authority. Finances for the college would be allocated by the Further Education Funding Council and could depend, in the main, on the number of students it could attract and on whether the college had achieved its mission statement. This is a document that sets out the college's future goals and objectives in terms of curriculum development and delivery and the pastoral programme for student guidance and support.

The principal and governors of the college decided to restructure in order to meet the challenge of the future. In the past the structure had four levels - the senior management team (the principal and two vice-principals), senior tutors (responsible for the pastoral programme), heads of departments and main scale teachers. It was recognised that the senior management team needed to be expanded. Senior tutors were given extra responsibilities and made part of the senior management team. In addition a new team of curriculum leaders (CLs) was created. The team was made up from heads of departments in the different curriculum areas, such as the social sciences and sciences etc. and was responsible for curriculum development and delivery. Much of the success of the college would depend on how well this group worked together.

The group certainly had a variety of personalities in it - from those with new, innovative ideas to those that more concerned with administration and day to day problems. The group met formally once a fortnight to discuss issues concerning a quality curriculum. It became apparent, however, that the meetings rarely achieved concrete suggestions for future action. The meetings seemed to be used as 'talking shops' for curriculum leaders to air grievances about the happenings of the week.

Some of the curriculum leaders were also part of an informal group of friends who would socialise at lunchtimes and after college. It was often at these informal gatherings/meetings that the real issues were raised and ideas discussed. Other curriculum leaders who were not at such gatherings would usually have any important issues raised communicated to them through the 'grapevine'.

The informal meetings became a focal point for CLs to attack the lack of focus in the official meetings and also the fact that their ideas were very rarely accepted by senior management. They felt that senior management was made up of individuals who had caused a decline in the number of students by their inaction over the last five years. Their main complaint, however, was that although they had been assured by the principal that they would be the ones who would make decisions on curriculum matters, the senior management team would often intervene and veto their proposals. For example, CLs suggested that gNVQs (general national vocational qualifications) should be more fully developed in the college to attract students that had normally gone to the local FE colleges.

This idea was rejected by the senior management team as not fitting into the academic tradition of the college. Joan, the CL for Economics and Business, felt exasperated by this decision. She said: 'CLs were meant to be part of the management of the college with responsibilities for curriculum development and delivery. We meet formally and informally, communicating in a variety of ways to each other, trying to advance a common view on curriculum development. But at times we just don't seem to have the authority to make things happen. I just don't know what we can do.'

(a) What new formal groups did the Principal and Governors set up in April 1993?
(b) How did communication take place in formal and informal groups at High Lane?
(c) Comment on the likely effectiveness of :
  (i) formal groups;
  (ii) informal groups;
  at High Lane.
(d) What problems might High Lane face as a result of the way group decision making is organised?
(e) Suggest 2 methods High Lane management could have used to solve the problems suggested in your answer to question (d).

What is management?

Unit 2 explained that managers are an important group involved in business activity. It is difficult to define exactly what is meant by 'management'. However, many agree that managers are responsible for 'getting things done' - usually through other people. The term manager may refer to a number of different people within a business. Some job titles include the word manager, such as personnel manager or managing director. Other job holders may also be managers, even though their titles do not say it.

It could be argued that managers:
■ act on behalf of the owners - in a company, senior management are accountable to the shareholders;
■ set objectives for the organisation, for example, they may decide that a long term objective is to have a greater market share than all of the company's competitors;
■ make sure that a business achieves its objectives, by managing others;
■ ensure that corporate values (the values of the organisation) are maintained in dealings with other businesses, customers, employees and general public.

The functions of management

Henri Fayol, the French management theorist working in the early part of this century, listed a number of functions or 'elements' of management.

Planning This involves setting objectives and also the strategies, policies, programmes and procedures for achieving them. Planning might be done by line managers (☞ unit 63) who will be responsible for performance. However, advice on planning may also come from staff management who might have expertise in that area, even if they have no line authority. For example, a production manager may carry out human resource planning (☞ unit 51) in the production department, but use the skills of the personnel manager in planning recruitment for vacancies that may arise.

Organising Managers set tasks which need to be performed if the business is to achieve its objectives. Jobs need to be organised within sections or departments and authority needs to be **delegated** so that jobs are carried out. For example, the goal of a manufacturing company may be to produce quality goods that will be delivered to customers on time. The tasks, such as manufacturing, packaging, administration, etc. that are part of producing and distributing the goods, need to be organised to achieve this goal.

Commanding This involves giving instructions to subordinates to carry out tasks. The manager has the authority to make decisions and the responsibility to see tasks are carried out.

Co-ordinating This is the bringing together of the activities of people within the business. Individuals and groups will have their own goals, which may be different to those of the business and each other. Management must make sure that there is a common approach, so that the company's goals are achieved.

Controlling Managers measure and correct the activities of individuals and groups, to make sure that their performance fits in with plans.

QUESTION 1 The large crane that can hoist 50,000 tonnes of steel is a reminder to Otto Söberg of the management challenge faced at the Warnow Shipyard in East Germany. Söberg is the new chief executive installed by Kvaerner, the Norwegian shipbuilder that is aiming to turn the shipyard around. Shipbuilding is the sole industry in the region, which offers the chance to take advantage of cheap labour and a favourable location on the Baltic.

Söberg argues, 'the old management wasn't close enough to the workforce'. One of the first tasks he faces is to cut the workforce by 70 per cent - what he calls the 'dirty work.' The plan for the shipyard, agreed with the Treuhand (the German investment agency) and the unions, aims to eliminate uncertainty. Management has to establish better contacts with the existing workforce, but Söberg knows that it is no good pouring in money for nothing. Investment only stands a chance of success if the workers are trained properly and take pride in their jobs.

No easy challenge faces Kvaerner. Inefficiency is rife. The administrative to worker ratio is 3:1, compared to the Western equivalent of 1:1. Financial aid from the Treuhand will be useful, but the business faces the task of removing enormous overcapacity. The large crane will have to go. Ships will be built by fitting them together in steel chunks in docks, rather than as one large ship manufactured in a berth.

Source: adapted from the *Financial Times*, 2.4.1993.

Discuss the likely functions of management involved in revitalising the East German shipyard.

The management process

Peter Drucker worked in the 1940s and 1950s as a business adviser to a number of US firms. He is credited with the idea of MANAGEMENT BY OBJECTIVES (☞ unit 50), used by some businesses today. Drucker grouped the operations of management into five categories.
■ Setting objectives for the organisation. Managers

decide what the objectives of the business should be. These objectives are then organised into targets. Managers inform others of these targets.

■ Organising the work. The work to be done in the organisation must be divided into manageable activities and jobs. The jobs must be integrated into the formal organisational structure (☞ unit 63) and people must be selected to do the jobs (☞ unit 53).

■ Motivating employees (☞ unit 48) and communicating information (☞ unit 62) to enable employees to carry out their tasks.

■ Job measurement. It is the task of management to establish objectives or yardsticks of performance for every person in the organisation. They must also analyse actual performance and compare it with the yardstick that has been set. Finally, they should communicate the findings and explain their significance to others in the business.

■ Developing people. The manager should bring out the talent in people.

Every manager performs all five functions listed above, no matter how good or bad a manager, Drucker suggests. A bad manager performs these functions badly, whereas a good manager performs them well. He also argued that the manager of a business has a basic function - economic performance. In this respect the business manager is different from the manager of other types of organisation. Business managers can only justify their existence and authority by the economic results they produce.

Being a manager

In contrast with Fayol or Drucker, **Charles Handy** argued that any definition of a manager is likely to be so broad it will have little or no meaning. Instead he outlined what is likely to be involved in 'being a manager'.

The manager as a general practitioner Handy made an analogy between managing and staying 'healthy'. If there are 'health problems' in business, the manager needs to identify the symptoms. These could include low productivity, high labour turnover or industrial relations problems. Once the symptoms have been identified, the manager needs to find the cause of trouble and develop a strategy for 'better health'. Strategies for health might include changing people, through hiring and firing, reassignments, training, pay increases or counselling. A manager might also restructure work through job redesign, job enrichment (☞ unit 50) and a redefinition of roles. Systems can also be improved. These can include communication systems, reward systems, information and reporting systems budgets and other decision making systems, eg stock control.

Managerial dilemmas Handy argued that managers face dilemmas. One of the reasons sometimes given for why managers are paid more than workers is because of the dilemmas they face.

■ The dilemma of cultures. When managers are promoted or move to other parts of the business, they have to behave in ways which are suitable for the new

position. For example, at the senior management level, managers may deal more with long term strategy and delegate lower level tasks to middle management more often. If a promoted manager maintains a

---

QUESTION 2 Alex Krauer knows the gap between rhetoric and reality is nowhere greater than in the area of management. While chairmen pronounce their latest vision for their company, more often than not, in the bowels of the organisation, their instructions are interpreted, subverted or ignored.

Ciba, the Swiss chemicals and drugs group where he is chairman, is a perfect example. For two years, senior management at the company have been struggling to implement a cultural revolution. Their aim is to make the organisation more flexible by giving its shop floor employees greater responsibility. The scheme, called Vision 2000, is, in current management jargon, all about 'empowerment'.

The implementation of Ciba's vision has not run smoothly. Heini Lippuner, chief operating officer, admits 'We do not have a uniform adoption of the leadership style we would like. There's a difference between the various divisions. Some are far advanced. In some others, I'm sorry to say, there is not much difference. The causes for the different degrees of implementation are multiple', says Lippuner. Partly they depend on the attitudes of the individuals at the top of Ciba's 14 divisions. Partly they are a result of the cultural difference between countries.

Krauer identifies a further key component for successful implementation. 'The critical area is middle management. If it stops there, then the whole exercise is wasted. Some fully support the changes, while others are afraid. Others refuse to delegate because they believe that by doing so, they lose power', says Krauer. Lippuner explains, 'I meet young people on the shop floor who tell me they like the vision, they believe we are sincere about empowerment. But they complain there has been no real change. To put it pointedly, it looks as though we have a layer of clay that prevents anything going either way - up or down. That layer is middle management.'

Senior management plans to crack the layer of clay by creating pressure from both above and below and through education. Questionnaires were sent to the 20,000 employees in Switzerland about their superiors' leadership behaviour. The aim, says Krauer, was to set up a level of expectation from employees and use that expectation to force middle managers into dialogue.

Krauer believes 90 per cent of managers are capable of adopting the vision. 'A few, and I hope only a few, will not want to co-operate and they had better look for a job outside Ciba', says Krauer. 'There's too much at stake for people in key positions not to be part of the process'.

Source: adapted from the *Financial Times*, December 1992.

(a) Using Drucker's ideas, how would you describe Ciba's attempt at 'implementing a cultural revolution'?

(b) Using the ideas of Charles Handy, explain what 'managerial dilemmas' exist for senior management at Ciba.

(c) At what aspects of management are middle managers of Ciba failing?

'culture' that she is used to, which may mean taking responsibility for all tasks, she may not be effective in her new position.

- The trust-control dilemma. Managers may want to control the work for which they are responsible. However, they may have to delegate work to subordinates, trusting them to do the work properly. The greater the trust a manager has in subordinates, the less control she retains for herself. Retaining control could mean a lack of trust.
- The commando leader's dilemma. In many firms, junior managers often want to work in project teams, with a clear task or objective. This can mean working 'outside' the normal bureaucratic structure of a larger organisation. Unfortunately, there can be too many project groups (or 'commando groups') for the good of the business. The manager must decide how many project groups she should create to satisfy the needs of her subordinates and how much bureaucratic structure to retain.

The manager as a person Management has developed into a profession and managers expect to be rewarded for their professional skills. Managers must, therefore, continue to develop these skills and sell them to the highest bidder.

Managerial roles

Henry Mintzberg suggested that, as well as carrying out certain functions, the manager also fulfils certain **roles** in a firm. He identified three types of role which a manager must play.

- Interpersonal roles. These arise from the manager's formal authority. Managers have a **figurehead** role. For example, a large part of a chief executive's time is spent representing the company at dinners, conferences etc. They also have a **leader** role. This involves hiring, firing and training staff, motivating employees etc. Thirdly, they have a **liaison** role. Some managers spend up to half their time meeting with other managers. They do this because they need to know what is happening in other departments. Senior managers spend a great deal of time with people outside the business. Mintzberg says that these contacts build up an informal information system, and are a means of extending influence both within and outside the business.
- Information roles. Managers act as channels of information from one department to another. They are in a position to do this because of their contacts.
- Decision making roles. The manager's formal authority and access to information means that no one else is in a better position to take decisions about a department's work.

Through extensive research and observation of what managers actually do, Mintzberg drew certain conclusions about the work of managers.

- The idea that a manager is a 'systematic' planner is a myth. Planning is often carried out on a day-to-day

basis, in between more urgent tasks.
- Another myth is that a manager has no regular or routine duties, as these have been delegated to others. Mintzberg found that managers perform a number of routine duties, particularly 'ceremonial' tasks.
- Mintzberg's research showed that managers prefer verbal communication rather than a formal system of communication (☞ unit 62). Information passed by word of mouth in an informal way is likely to be more up to date and easier to grasp.

Leadership

The ability to lead within organisations is of growing interest to businesses. This interest has resulted from the need to lead companies through change, brought about by an increase in competition and a recessionary climate in the late 1980s and early 1990s.

Earlier in this unit it was shown that a manager might have a leadership **role.** To be a good leader in business it has been suggested that a manager must know what direction needs to be taken by the business and plan how to achieve this. Leaders will also be able to persuade others that the decisions that they have taken are the correct ones.

Leaders are often thought to be charismatic people who have 'something about them' that makes them stand out from others. It has been argued that there are certain personality traits (☞ unit 47) that are common to leaders. However, studies have failed to prove this is the case.

In order to identify 'leadership', studies have shifted to examine what leaders, and in particular managers, do - that is, what behaviour is associated with leadership. This is dealt with in the next sections.

The qualities of leadership

One approach to find out what makes good leaders is to identify the qualities that they should have. A number of **characteristics** have been suggested.

- Effective leaders have a positive self image, backed up with a genuine ability and realistic aspirations. This is shown in the confidence they have. An example in UK industry might be Richard Branson, in his various pioneering business activities. Leaders also appreciate their own strengths and weaknesses. It is argued that many managers fail to lead because they often get bogged down in short term activity.
- Leaders need to be able to get to the 'core' of a problem and have the vision and commitment to suggest radical solutions. Sir John Harvey-Jones took ICI to £1 billion profit by stirring up what had become a 'sleeping giant'. Many awkward questions were raised about the validity of the way things were done, and the changes led to new and more profitable businesses on a worldwide scale for the firm.
- Studies of leaders in business suggest that they are expert in a particular field and well read in everything else. They tend to be 'out of the ordinary', intelligent, and articulate.

QUESTION 3 In 1989 Rupert Murdoch delivered a speech at the Edinburgh International Television Festival which saw a shocking future for British Television. He warned that regulation was protecting a monopoly and championed a multi-channel environment. At the time top brass at the BBC and ITV laughed.

In August 1993 Murdoch was preparing another speech for the celebrity launch of multi-channels, BSkyB's package of new TV channels. His predictions about the future of TV had been disquietingly accurate and, despite a shaky start, his satellite channel was now flourishing. Not only had Murdoch revolutionised British TV, he was now making people pay for it. At the launch it was expected there would be an announcement about future policy of the company, stressing the importance of technology and its future potential. There was even talk of a flotation of the business at a later date.

In early 1993 Murdoch had clinched a $525 million deal for a 63 per cent stake in the South-East Asian satellite operator Star TV, a company well placed to carry advertising to Asia's growing middle class audience. This further expanded the possible business opportunities for the Murdoch empire.

Whilst still sprightly at 64, some were questioning who might take control of the company as Murdoch became older. Guy Lamming, a media analyst suggested that, 'while his son is working for the organisation ... he (Murdoch) .... will choose the best management for the company'.

Source; adapted from *The Observer*, 29.8.1993.

Explain the leadership characteristics shown by Rupert Murdoch which are mentioned in the article.

■ Leaders are often creative thinking and innovative. They tend to seek new ideas to problems, make sure that important things are done and try to improve standards. One example might have been the restructuring of BHS by David Dworkin so that unsold stock did not remain on the shelves.

■ Leaders often have the ability to sense change and can respond to it. A leader, for example, may be able to predict a decline of sales in an important product or the likelihood of a new production technique being available in the future.

Leadership styles

Another approach is to examine different styles of leadership. There are a number of styles that managers might adopt in the work setting. Table 58.1 shows the different ways in which leaders can involve others in the decision making process.

Autocratic An AUTOCRATIC leadership style is one where the manager sets objectives, allocates tasks, and insists on obedience. Therefore the group become dependent on him or her. The result of this style is that members of the group are often dissatisfied with the leader. This results in little cohesion, the need for high levels of supervision, and poor levels of motivation amongst employees.

Autocratic leadership may be needed in certain circumstances. For example, in the armed forces there may be a need to move troops quickly and for orders to be obeyed instantly.

Democratic A DEMOCRATIC leadership style encourages participation in decision making. Managers may consult employees or could attempt to 'sell' final decisions to them. It is argued that, through participation and consultation, employees know and believe the objectives of management because they have had some involvement with it. This will result in employees being more motivated and willing to work harder.

Democratic leadership styles need good communication skills. The leaders must be able to explain ideas clearly to employees and understand feedback they receive (☞ unit 62). It may mean, however, that decisions take a long time to be reached as lengthy consultation can take place.

Laissez- faire A LAISSEZ-FAIRE type of leadership style allows employees to carry out activities freely within broad limits. The result is a relaxed atmosphere, but one where there are few guidelines and directions. This can sometimes result in poor productivity and lack of motivation as employees have little incentive to work hard.

Table 58.1 *Leadership styles*

	Autocratic		Democratic	Laissez-faire
Type of leadership	Autocratic	Persuasive	Consultative	Laissez-faire
Method	Leader makes decisions alone. Others are informed and carry out decisions.	Leader makes decisions alone. Others are persuaded by the leader that the decision is the right one, ie leader 'sells' the decision to the group.	Leader consults with others before decision is made. There will be group influence in the final decision, even though it is made by the leader.	There is no formal structure to decision making. The leader does not force his or her views on others.

Factors affecting leadership styles

The type of leadership style adopted by managers will depend on various factors.

- **The task.** A certain task may be the result of an emergency, which might need immediate response from a person in authority. The speed of decision needed and action taken may require an authoritarian or autocratic style of leadership.
- **The tradition of the organisation.** A business may develop its own culture which is the result of the interactions of all employees at different levels. This can result in one type of leadership style, because of a pattern of behaviour that has developed in the organisation. For example, in the public sector (☞ unit 4) leadership is often democratic because of the need to consult with politicians etc.
- **The type of labour force.** A more highly skilled workforce might be most productive when their opinions are sought. Democratic leadership styles may be more appropriate in this case.
- **The group size.** Democratic leadership styles can lead to confusion the greater the size of the group.
- **The leader's personality.** The personality of one manager may be different to another manager and certain leadership styles might suit one but not the other. For example, an aggressive, competitive personality may be more suited to an authoritarian

leadership style.
- **Group personality.** Some people prefer to be directed rather than contribute, either because of lack of interest, previous experience, or because they believe that the manager is paid to take decisions and shoulder responsibility. If this is the case, then an autocratic leadership style is more likely to lead to effective decision making.
- **Time.** The time available to complete a task might influence the leadership style adopted. For example, if a project has to be finished quickly, there may be no time for discussion and an autocratic style may be adopted.

Why do leaders adopt different styles?

A number of theories have been put forward to explain the most appropriate leadership style when dealing with certain situations or groups at work.

Fiedler In 1976, F. Fiedler argued that 'it is easier to change someone's role or power, or to modify the job he has to do, than to change his leadership style'. From his 800 studies he found that it is difficult for people to change leadership styles - an 'autocrat' will always lead in autocratic style whereas a leader that encourages involvement will tend to be 'democratic'. Different leadership styles may also be effective depending on the situation. He concluded that, as leaders are unable to adapt their style to a situation, effectiveness can only be achieved by changing the manager to 'fit' the situation or by altering the situation to fit the manager.

In business it is often difficult to change the situation. Fiedler suggested that a business should attempt what he called **leadership match** - to choose a leader to fit the situation. Leaders can be either **task orientated** or **relationship orientated**. So, for example, a business that faced declining sales might need a very task orientated manager to pull the business around, even if the tradition of the firm might be for a more democratic style of leadership.

Hersey and Blanchard P. Hersey and K.H. Blanchard argued that a leader's strategy should not only take account of the situation, but also the maturity of those who are led. They defined maturity as the ability of people to set targets which can be achieved and yet are demanding.

A leader will have **task behaviour or relationship behaviour**. Task behaviour is the extent to which the leader has to organise what a subordinate should do. Relationship behaviour describes how much support is needed and how close personal contact is. Together these will decide which of the following leadership styles will be used.

- **Delegating** leadership is where a leader allows subordinates to solve a problem. For this type of leadership style to work, subordinates need to be mature and require little support at work.

QUESTION 4 On 11 March 1993, Dr Ernest Mario, chief executive of Glaxo, the pharmaceutical company, departed abruptly. Dr Mario, it is said, had an excessively hands-on style in dealing with Glaxo's overseas territories. The older Glaxo tradition was to allow regional directors considerable freedom, subject to stringent financial targets. Dr Mario, a manager with an impressive grasp of detail, seems to have practiced a more interventionist style with his fellow directors. He was also occasionally given to ill-judged public statements. In February 1993, he caused a stir by advocating a means test for prescriptions in the UK.

It was argued that he had lost the confidence of directors and the chairman, Sir Paul Girolami. It was also believed that Dr Mario wanted to focus the company on over-the-counter (non-prescription) medicines, whereas in the past it had concentrated on 'prescription' drugs.

Some also felt that he did not fit in with changes in the company. A new structure was being developed to cope with change. Glaxo had become very big and the board structure was to be changed so that those at the top were free to deal with strategic issues around the world. This meant, perhaps, being less involved in hands-on running of the company.

Source: adapted from the *Financial Times*, 12.3.1993.

(a) What type of leadership style did Dr Mario use at Glaxo? Explain your answer.
(b) How did the style of Dr Mario differ from the traditional style of the company?
(c) Explain why Dr Mario's leadership style may not be suitable for Glaxo in future.

- **Participating** leadership is where a leader and subordinates work on a problem together, supporting each other. In this situation subordinates are slightly less mature than when a leader delegates and so need more support.
- **Selling** leadership is where a leader persuades others of the benefits of an idea. Workers are likely to be only moderately mature and require a great deal of support.
- **Telling** leadership is where a leader tells others what to do. Workers are fairly immature. They are told exactly what to do and little contact or support is needed.

Wright and Taylor In 1984, P. Wright and D. Taylor argued that theories which concentrate on the situation or maturity of those led ignore how skillfully leadership is carried out.

They produced a checklist designed to help leaders improve the performance of subordinates. It included the following.

- What is the problem? An employee may, for example, be carrying out a task inefficiently.
- Is it serious enough to spend time on? This could depend on the cost to the business.
- What reasons may there be for the problem? How can it be solved? These are shown in Table 58.2.
- Choosing a solution and evaluating if it is the most effective one.
- Evaluation of the leader's performance.

This can be used to identify the most suitable leadership style in a particular situation. For example, if the problem above is caused because the employee has been left to make his own decisions and is not able to, a more autocratic leadership style may be needed. On the other hand, if the employee lacks motivation or does not have the authority to make decisions, greater discussion or delegation may be needed.

Table 58.2

Possible reasons for performance problem	Possible solutions
Goal clarity. Is the person fully aware of the job requirements?	Give guidance concerning expected goals and standards. Set targets.
Ability. Does the person have the capacity to do the job well?	Provide formal training, on the job coaching, practice, etc.
Intrinsic motivation. Does the person find the task rewarding in itself?	Simplify task, reduce work load, reduce time pressures etc.
'External' motivation. Is good performance rewarded by others?	Arrange rewards for good performance and penalties for poor performance.
Feedback. Does the person receive adequate feedback about his or her performance?	Provide or arrange feedback.
Resources. Does the person have adequate resources and delegated authority to carry out the task?	Provide staff, equipment, raw materials; delegate if necessary.
Working conditions. Do working conditions interfere with performance?	Improve lighting, noise, heat, layout; remove distractions etc.

Key terms

Autocratic leadership - a leadership style where the leader makes all decisions independently.
Democratic leadership - a leadership style where the leader encourages others to participate in decision making.

Laissez-faire leadership - a leadership style where employees are encouraged to make their own decisions, within limits.
Management by Objectives (MBO) - a management theory which suggests that managers set goals and communicate them to subordinates.

Summary

1. State 5 functions of management.
2. Briefly explain the process of management by objectives.
3. Give 3 examples of a managerial dilemma.
4. Why might a good manager not always be a good leader?
5. Briefly explain 5 qualities of leadership.
6. Under what circumstances might an autocratic leadership style be useful?
7. State 6 factors which might affect the choice of leadership style.
8. According to Fiedler's theory, why should a business attempt a leadership match?

Question

Ford at Dagenham

One of the plant managers, working with his area managers at Ford's Dagenham plant, had devised a plan for reducing costs by reorganising the work in the area of machine operation. The problem was that if the plan was to work it required two important changes from the workforce - first their co-operation in moving from the production of one set of parts to the production of another set half-way through each week. Second, it required the introduction of a new twilight shift. No extra money was on offer nor were any other inducements held out. The 'case' had to be sold direct to the workforce (some 80 people) by the relevant area manager. This was to be attempted at a special meeting in the old canteen at the start of the morning shift.

At the appointed hour, the workers were assembled and seated in a rather cold and uncomfortable setting, unconducive to extended debate. The shop stewards for the area were seated out at the front. The area manager arrived 'chauffeur-driven' in one of the plant's electric vehicles. Flanked by section heads he strode to the front and commenced his delivery. The style was relaxed, down-to-earth, occasionally jovial, but very direct. In essence, 'the problem' was explained as uncompetitive costs in the production of two power-train assemblies. The danger of at least one of these ceasing production altogether, unless the 'uneconomic' low volume levels could be compensated for by more flexible switching each week between one job and another was explained.

The 'solution' was then described. This involved the introduction of a 'swing shift' and the necessity for the shift, on certain days of the week, to be ready to finish the scheduled run in 'Power Train I' and relocate themselves to a different area of the factory to commence work on 'Power Train II'. Questions were then invited and the area manager fielded these himself. One issue of concern was the extra time that would be needed reporting to work and in lost break time because of the distance between the two work locations. The area manager dealt with this by promising to keep it under review during the first few weeks of the new work scheme.

After about 40 minutes the area manager and the rest of the management team departed and the shop stewards were left to address the meeting. The tone was essentially a realistic one of the economics of competition and the poor state of 'Power Train I' because of its age and its low volumes. While some minor problems were noted with the management plan, the overall message was that reorganisation was necessary. There was very little opposition from the floor. A vote was taken and the plan was accepted almost unanimously.

Source: adapted from *Management of Human Resources*, John Storey, Blackwell, 1993.

(a) **Identify the aspects of management that are taking place in this situation.**
(b) **What leadership qualities did the plant manager and the area manager demonstrate?**
(c) **What type of leadership style is the area manager adopting?**
(d) **What factors may have influenced this choice of leadership style?**
(e) **Use the leadership theory of Fiedler to explain why the strategy adopted by the area manager was successful.**

How are groups represented?

There are many different organisations which represent employees and employers in business. Although they are not part of actual businesses themselves, they influence how firms operate.

Trade unions These are perhaps the best known of the representative bodies. A TRADE UNION is an organisation of workers who join together to further their own interests. Trade unions have existed in the UK for over 200 years. Early unions were made up of workers with similar skills and interests, for example the General Union of Operative Spinners set up in 1829. Today's unions vary from the Transport and General Workers Union (TGWU), with over one million members in different industries, to the National Union of Journalists.

What features are trade unions likely to have? It is likely that a trade union would:
- register itself as a union;
- become affiliated to the Trades Union Congress;
- become affiliated to the Labour Party;
- be independent of employers in negotiations;
- regard collective bargaining (☞ unit 60) and the protection of its members' interests as its main function;
- be prepared to use industrial action (☞ unit 61) to further its members' interests;

although the make-up and role of unions has changed over the last decade. This is dealt with later in this unit.

The National Union of Mineworkers (NUM), Rail, Maritime and Transport Union (RMT) and the Union of Construction Allied Trades (UCAT) are well established unions with many or all of these features. There are other representative bodies which are not unions, but which still have some of these characteristics.

Staff associations Staff associations represent workers, but perform only some of those functions carried out by trade unions. These might include consultation and bargaining with management. Bodies like the Balfour Beatty Group Association, the Britannic Field Staff Association and the Sun Life Staff Association are examples of staff associations.

In some cases, staff associations develop into trade unions. A number of organisations, such as the National Union of Teachers, the National and Local Government Officers Association, the Banking Insurance and Finance Union and the Engineers and Managers Association, started as staff associations.

Professional associations Professional associations perform similar functions to trade unions, but are not registered as unions. Examples include the Police Federation, the National Association of Fire Officers (NAFO) and the National Association of Head Teachers (NAHT). Professional associations, such as the British Medical Association (BMA), represent their members in collective bargaining with employers. They are also responsible for the setting and maintaining of standards. For example, the BMA insists on certain qualifications before admitting employees to its membership. For this reason professional associations tend to be associated with 'white collar' workers and higher paid groups of employees.

Employers' organisations Just as certain bodies represent workers, there are organisations which help and support employers. They are often useful for small firms that may be negotiating with a large union. These organisations give advice to employers about collective bargaining and help with technical problems and overseas trade. They may also provide research and training facilities and act as a pressure group (☞ unit 71) for industries. Examples include the Newspaper Society and the Engineering Employers' Federation.

All of the groups mentioned above will aim to protect or further their members' interests. The rest of this unit will concentrate on the role of trade unions, although many of the points dealt with apply to other representative bodies.

The functions of trade unions

What is the role of a union in a business situation? We have already seen that unions are an example of a representative body that aims to further its members' interests. It could be argued that this includes some of the following.
- Obtaining satisfactory rates of pay.
- Securing adequate work facilities.
- Ensuring satisfactory work conditions, such as the number of hours worked or the number of breaks in any period of work.
- Negotiating bonuses for achieving targets.
- Obtaining job security for members.
- Negotiating employment conditions, such as contracts of employment or rights relating to redundancy and dismissal.
- Negotiating grievance procedures.
- Negotiating job descriptions and job specifications (☞ unit 52).

Trade unions are responsible for **collective bargaining** in the workplace. They bargain on behalf of their total membership with employers and attempt to obtain the best possible conditions. It is argued that unions are in a far better position to negotiate with management than an individual employee, who will have little bargaining 'power'.

Trade unions are also responsible, along with management, for **industrial relations**. They communicate their members' wishes to employers and try to negotiate the most favourable conditions. However, successful industrial relations means that each party must take into account the wishes of the other when bargaining. It may not be in members' interests for a union to push for a longer work break if this reduces the efficiency of the business, perhaps resulting in job losses in future. However, it may not be in employers' interests to reduce breaks, even if this cuts costs, if it results in worker dissatisfaction.

The ability of a trade union to carry out these functions may depend on the union membership and UNION DENSITY. A small union, with few members, is unlikely to have as much influence as the Union of Shop Distributive and Allied Workers (USDAW) with its 350,000 plus membership. Union density is expressed as:

$$\frac{\text{actual union membership}}{\text{potential union membership}} \times 100$$

So, for example, if a union only represented a small percentage of all workers in an industry, it would be less likely to have influence. The union density of the National Union of Mineworkers (NUM) was reduced when the Union of Democratic Mineworkers (UDM) split it in 1987.

QUESTION 1 'I start with a basic premise; people who work in organisations have a right to a say in their destiny. If you believe this, then it logically and intellectually follows that trade unions can be a positive force in organisations. Collective bargaining should not be within the gift of the employer. Rather it should be viewed as a basic right.

Organisations are only as good as the people they employ, and management neglects this principle at its peril. People in organisations, particularly when organised collectively, can be a force for good. Certainly in these difficult times for local government we will only survive by working in partnership with the unions.

Some trade union reforms have been necessary and needed to be externally imposed. However, contrary to what some people think, influential unions and successful organisations are compatible.

As Disraeli said, 'No government can be long secure without a formidable opposition.'

Fred Smith
Director of Personnel
Oldham Metropolitan Borough Council
and Secretary, Society of Chief Personnel
Officers in Local Government

Source: *Personnel Management*, July 1993.

Using examples from the quote above, argue the case for trade unions representing employees in business.

Types of union

There are a number of ways in which unions can be classified. The most common method is to place unions into one of three categories.

- Craft unions are the oldest type of union, developed directly from traditional crafts. Workers with common skills often joined together to form unions. An example today might be the Musicians Union or the National Union of Journalists.
- Industrial unions. In the past a number of unions have been formed by employees of particular industries, such as coalminers, railway or gas workers. An often quoted example of an industrial union has been the National Union of Mineworkers (NUM). It is made up of employees with different skills in the mining industry.
- General unions. These unions are made up of workers with a wide range of skills in many different industries. Examples today might be the General Municipal Boilermakers and Allied Trade Union (GMB) or the Manufacturing Science and Finance Union (MSF).

Although this division appears straightforward, it does have problems.

- It forces unions into one category, whereas many unions often have features common to all classes. The Amalgamated Electrical Engineering Union (AEEU), for example, has a large number of engineering craftworkers as members, but also recruits foundry workers and unskilled employees.
- Very few unions actually fall into the 'craft' category.
- Mergers of unions in recent years have blurred many of these distinctions. This is dealt with later in this unit.

A more useful way of dividing unions today might be into those with **open** and **closed** recruitment policies. Although there are few traditional craft unions left, they usually restrict their membership to employees with certain skills. Other unions, such as those representing mineworkers, also follow closed membership policies. They do not recruit members from outside their immediate 'areas'. This means their membership expands or contracts according to the changing levels of manpower needs in their industries.

Open membership policies are usually associated with the big general unions, such as the TGWU. They seek membership growth almost regardless of their members' jobs or the industry in which they work. Such unions organise themselves to cope with the different membership needs. This can sometimes lead to conflict, as unions are accused of 'stealing' members from other areas, which may be represented by craft or industrial unions.

Unions and pay

One criticism often made of unions is that if they negotiate very high wage increases, a business can only pay for these and maintain profits by making workers redundant. This is shown in Figure 59.1. We can use the demand and supply curves from unit 22 to show how the labour market (☞ unit 1) works. D is the demand curve for labour by an industry at any wage rate. S is the amount of labour that workers will supply at any wage rate. At a wage rate OP, OQ workers are employed. If a union now negotiates a higher wage, OP_1, the number of workers demanded at the higher wage rate will be only OQ1. This leads to a fall in employment of $OQ-OQ_1$. For the unions it represents a 'trade-off' between higher pay for its members and fewer employed. This view also suggests that union action to raise wages, or stop them falling, prevents firms from operating as efficiently as possible. For example, faced with competition from abroad, a business may need to reduce costs. Reduced costs should allow the firm to charge a more competitive price, expand sales and output, and employ more workers.

Against this it could be argued that:
■ if there is an increase in productivity by employees, this should pay for higher wages, without the need for job losses;
■ other countries, such as the former West Germany, have similar unit costs of production to the UK, and pay skilled workers relatively high wages, and yet have not had such high unemployment rates;
■ there is evidence in the UK that unemployment still exists even if wages are held down or cut (☞ unit 65).

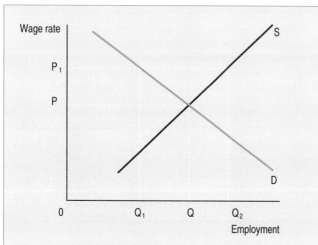

Figure 59.1 *The effect of a higher wage settlement by trade unions on employment*

QUESTION 2 In March 1993 nearly 20,000 Sheffield council workers voted to take a 3.25 per cent pay cut in exchange for short time working to stop the city council making 1,400 redundant. The deal, believed to be the first of its kind in the UK, would have kept the council budget below the £366 million ceiling imposed by the government.

In exchange for the pay cut, workers were allowed to work one hour less a week or take 7 days extra holiday. 2,000 works staff refused the deal. Works department shop stewards campaigned against the deal, which may have led to its refusal by these workers. The only exceptions to the pay cut were low paid workers earning less than £90 a week, who were mainly part time.

Source: adapted from the *Financial Times*, 3.3.1993.

(a) What are the possible benefits to:
  (i) employees;
  (ii) the employers;
  of agreeing such a deal?
(b) Discuss why shop stewards may have campaigned against this deal.

Trade unions and legislation

The election of a Conservative government in 1979 proved to be a turning point in union regulation. Its election manifesto contained the statement:

> 'Between 1974 and 1976 Labour enacted a militants' charter of trade union legislation. It tilted the balance of power in bargaining throughout the industry away from responsible management and towards trade unions.'

The government argued that:
■ trade union power was becoming excessive, particularly in wage negotiations;
■ unions were often disruptive in preventing changing work practices or the introduction of new machinery;
■ unions were increasingly creating industrial stoppages;
■ unofficial picketing was disrupting business;
■ SHOP STEWARDS were disrupting industry by calling **unofficial** strikes - strikes not supported by the unions (sometimes called 'wildcat strikes');
■ there was undemocratic decision making within unions, especially about industrial action;
■ closed shops restricted the rights of employees not to belong to a union;
and that these factors were harming the efficiency of British industry and its ability to compete.

Others have argued that it is not trade union power that has made British business uncompetitive, but a lack of good management (☞ unit 64) over a number of decades and poor levels of education and training within the workforce. They suggest that union legislation does not address the long standing causes of UK businesses - the lack of capital investment and the 'laissez-faire' approach of management.

The effects of legislation

Throughout the 1980s and 1990s the Conservative government passed many Employment and Trade Union Acts which attempted to regulate trade union action. Legislation focused on a number of areas.

Legal immunity Certain Acts have dealt with whether unions can be sued by a business or individuals as a result of damages caused by their actions. The **1974 Trade Union and Labour Relations Ac**t prevented employers from taking civil action in court for damages resulting from industrial action by unions. The Act covered disputes as a result of terms and conditions of employment, suspension or termination of employment, allocation of work duties between workers or groups of employees, matters of discipline, membership or non-membership of a trade union, trade union recognition, and disputes arising from negotiation and consultation. **The 1982 Employment Act**, however, made unions liable for any action which was not in 'furtherance' of an industrial dispute. In other words, unions taking action that was not covered by conditions in the 1974 Act were liable to pay civil damages to businesses.

One result was that courts became willing to grant injunctions, preventing unions taking action not covered in the Acts. Injunctions are court orders instructing unions to refrain from action while a court hearing over a dispute is taking place. Judges might grant the injunction if they feel a business would suffer if the action continued.

Since the **1990 Employment Act**, unions have also been liable for damages to customers or suppliers as a result of action which is not covered in the conditions of legislation.

Picketing PICKETING involves the rights of workers on strike to assemble and persuade others to help or join them. **Official pickets** (those nominated by unions) can stand outside a workplace to inform the public, employees, suppliers and managers that a strike is taking place. A code of practice is set out governing their conduct when dealing with such people.

Picketing has changed greatly since the 1970s. During that period, mass picketing of employers' premises and flying pickets (members of one union or factory picketing another's premises) were common features of strike action.

The two national coalmining strikes in the early 1970s saw the picketing of power stations and coal and coke depots to prevent the generation of electricity and the delivery of fuel to consumers. At the same time, the use of mass picketing by thousands of people, the majority of whom were sympathisers not directly involved in the dispute, led to problems for the police. The 1974 Act above made SECONDARY PICKETING unlawful, but it was difficult to enforce. The police could only act under criminal law if picketing ceased to be peaceful.

The **1980 Employment Act**, however, made it possible for civil action to be taken against secondary picketing. It also limited peaceful picketing for employees to at or near their place of work, and the number of pickets at any one time.

The closed shop A CLOSED SHOP (or union membership agreement) is an agreement between an employer and a trade union that makes it a condition of employment for each employee to be a member of that trade union. It could be argued that such a union membership agreement is sensible as it allows a union to represent all employees. This removes the possibility of conflict or bad feeling between members of the union and non-members. However, a closed shop may make employees join a union against their will. The **1980** and **1982 Employment Acts** changed the regulations in relation to closed shops. Previously employees were obliged to be a member of the union if a closed shop agreement existed. Anyone refusing to join had no defence against unfair dismissal by the employer for that reason.

Any union membership agreement coming into existence after August 1980 had to be approved by an 80 per cent vote in a secret ballot. Dismissal for non-membership of a union was made unfair if this 80 per cent vote was not achieved.

Members', business' and consumers' rights Certain legislation has been passed to make the unions more democratic and to protect the rights of workers belonging to unions. The **1984 Trade Union Act** forced unions to conduct secret ballots before industrial action took place if action was to be legal. The **1988 Employment Act** gave union members the right not to strike if they wished. In 1993, the **Trade Union Reform and Employment Rights Act** further attempted to support employees' and consumers' rights and protect business from union action with the following measures.

- The right for workers to have a postal ballot on union action and the right not to have union subscriptions deducted without consent.
- The right for workers not to be expelled or excluded from a union other than for certain reasons, such as not belonging to a certain trade as stated in union rules.
- The right for employers to have 7 days' notice of industrial action.
- The right for people deprived of goods or services by industrial action to take action to prevent it happening.

QUESTION 3 In September 1993 staff at the Asda supermarket were voting on strike action, following a rejection of a pay offer and a breakdown of talks with ACAS.

Around 40,000 GMB union members were eligible to vote - about two-thirds of Asda's total staff. If strike action was agreed the union was planning sporadic strikes of up to four hours and a ban on staff working in excess of contracts.

The pay offer had been a 2 per cent pay rise, backdated to May, a regrading from December 1993 to boost the earnings of low paid staff, and extended pension rights. The company argued 'We have put to the GMB a good deal.' Asda had had a few difficult years with operating losses of £365 million in 1991-92 but they were back in profit at the time.

Source: adapted from *Personnel Management*, September 1993.

(a) Why might the company have argued that they had offered a good deal?
(b) Advise the union on how legislation may affect:
  (i) the decision whether or not to take industrial action;
  (ii) the activities of members if they carry out industrial action.

The changing face of trade unions

Over the last 10-15 years a number of important changes which have taken place have affected trade unions.

Membership We have already seen that the numbers of members a union has (and union density) can influence its ability to perform its functions. Figure 59.2 shows that between 1950 and the late 1970s, there was a steady increase in membership, but since then there has been a sharp decline. In early 1992, there were estimated to be 9.6 million members, the lowest total since 1954. It has also been estimated that trade union density was 32 per cent in autumn 1992, a 2 per cent fall from Spring 1989.

Although the overall trend was for membership to fall, the number of female union members rose between 1991 and 1992 by 20,000. The union with the highest proportion of female members is the Royal College of Nursing (90 per cent).

What factors are likely to influence union membership?

- The economy. It is argued that in a period of recession union membership falls as people become unemployed and allow their membership to lapse. In a period of growth the opposite is likely to happen. In periods of inflation, people may join unions in order to protect their standard of living. They hope that unions can negotiate wage settlements that will keep pace with inflation. The low inflation rates and recession of 1990-1992 are both likely to have contributed to falling membership over the period.

- Economic, technological and labour market change. The decline in the steel and shipbuilding industries are examples of how change can affect employment and membership in unions related to these industries. Some unions may well have seen a growth in their numbers as a result of increased employment. Examples could be workers in service sector industries of the South East in the 1980s.

- It could also be argued that the growth of the smaller independent business in the 1980s has led to a fall in membership. Many of these businesses employ less than 10 people, some part time. Such employees are less likely to belong to unions. The use of a flexible workforce, with part time or temporary staff (who tend not to be union members) may also have led to a fall in membership.

- Government. Since 1979 the government has introduced Acts which make it far easier for employees to 'opt out' of union membership.

- Leadership. Dynamic leaders that are seen by potential members as furthering their interests may encourage them to join a union.

- Demographic trends. The UK faces a 'demographic timebomb' in the near future with falling numbers of school leavers and an ageing population. This is likely to mean that fewer new recruits will be available as union members, although this might be offset to some extent by women returning to work in greater numbers.

Trade union power Has trade union influence diminished? Some suggest that falling union membership has led to a reduction in the power of unions. Other factors are also quoted.

- Government legislation, dealt with earlier in this unit, has limited the ability of unions to carry out industrial action. The Trades Union Congress (TUC), once an important contributor to future government policy was, after 1979, removed from the consultation process by the Conservative government.

- Public opinion. Union action is likely to be more effective if there is support from the public. In recent years unions have been portrayed by the media as being disruptive to UK business and unwilling to change in the face of competition, and have lost support as a result.

- Managers' and employees' views. Some have suggested that new human resource management techniques (☞ unit 51) require managers to deal more directly with employees, who need to be flexible. This marginalises the role of unions in business. It is also suggested that managers have developed an aggressive attitude towards unions as a result of government legislation and uncertainty.

It could be argued, however, that unions still remain powerful when they are well organised. In 1993, manual and white collar workers resisted Ford UK's attempt to impose compulsory redundancies in UK plants. The GPMU print union forced the British Printing Industrial Federation to abandon a national 1.7 per cent offer. In company negotiations, however, a settlement of 3.9 per cent was agreed with the Lawson Mardon Group.

Amalgamation Figure 59.2 shows that the number of trade unions in the UK has fallen constantly since 1950. In early 1992 there were 275 unions, compared to 600 in the mid-1960s. This fall in number is partly as a result of a growth in mergers between unions. In 1992 the Amalgamated Engineering Union (AEU) and the Electrical Electronic Telecommunication and Plumbing Union (EETPU) joined to form the AEEU. In 1993 the public services unions NALGO, NUPE and COHSE joined to form Unison - potentially the largest union in the UK.

The fall in membership in some unions may have led to mergers. However, unions may have joined to become

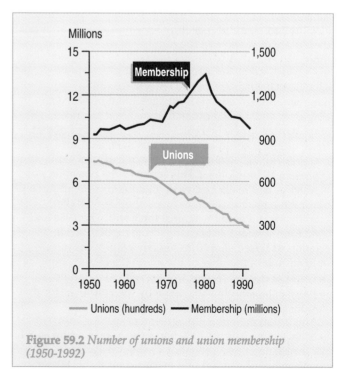

Figure 59.2 *Number of unions and union membership (1950-1992)*

larger bodies which represent more workers in an industry. This would place them in a far stronger bargaining position with employers. These larger unions will also have more finance to offer the range of services that today's members demand. This is dealt with in the next section.

Non-union businesses and derecognition In the UK non-union firms have tended to be small businesses in the private sector. The exceptions are companies such as Marks and Spencer and IBM (UK). There has been a trend in recent years to 'derecognise' certain unions by some businesses. This avoids the problem of dealing with many different unions when negotiating pay, for example. It also means that the restrictions placed on a business by the rules of different unions are reduced, which should improve the flexibility of workers. In 1992, for example, Shell derecognised the AEEU and GMB at its oil refinery in Cheshire. This left only the TGWU to represent workers.

QUESTION 4 A growing relationship was developing in 1992-93 between the Transport and General Workers Union (TGWU) and the General Municipal Boilermakers Union (GMB). Both unions have large numbers of members in similar industries - plastics, chemicals, glass, food, clothing, textiles - and in local government. In many of these industries union officials attend similar meetings and argue the same points with employers. It was suggested that a possible merger in future would save thousands of working hours by sending one rather than two officials to meetings. There could also be rationalisation of office space.

There were, however, political, cultural and organisational differences which could prevent a merger. For example, in the TGWU shop stewards had considerable power; in the GMB it lay mainly with officials.

The idea of a merger developed because of:
- financial difficulties;
- the mergers of other unions which could weaken the TGWU's position as the largest UK union;
- recruitment problems.

Source: adapted from the *Financial Times*, 1993

(a) Why might a merger between the TGWU and GMB have been suggested?
(b) What effects might such a merger have on:
  (i) the unions involved;
  (ii) the industries in which they operate?

The changing role of trade unions

In the last decade the 'traditional' role of unions has perhaps changed. A number of new practices have become part of the activities of many unions.

Single union/no strike agreements In the 1980s, some unions began to sign single union/no strike agreements with employers. The first such agreement was between

Toshiba and the then, EETPU in April 1981. Although not common (only 26 were listed in 1988), they are important as they have 'broken the mould' of traditional negotiation. Most agreements have been in smaller companies in high-tech industries on greenfield sites (☞ unit 30), although large companies such as Nissan (with the AUEW) and Thorn EMI (with the EETPU) have also agreed deals.

There are certain features of these agreements which benefit employers.
- Single union recognition, so that employers recognise only one union when negotiating over pay, conditions etc. This reduces time, complexity, conflict and administrative costs.
- Single job status for 'white' and 'blue' collar workers so that differentials in salaries, conditions, uniforms, car parking etc. are removed.
- Job flexibility in the business. The benefits of this are dealt with in unit 51.
- Union acceptance of training and re-training of employees. This gives greater flexibility and improves the quality of the workforce.
- The use of arbitration rather than industrial action. This prevents potentially damaging strikes etc. taking place.

Unions such as the EETPU believed that they had to become more aware of the needs of business, the workforce and economic changes. Such agreements took these into account.

The TUC, however, argued that such agreements hinder the bargaining rights of other unions. Where one union only is recognised by employers, other unions do not have the opportunity to negotiate on behalf of their members. When the EETPU refused to withdraw from deals with Orion Electric and Christian Salvesen it was expelled from the TUC in 1988.

Negotiations The nature of negotiated agreements between unions and employers has changed in recent years. Unions are far more likely to negotiate on aspects other than pay. These may include facilities for women members or for older or disabled workers, reflecting the changing nature of the workforce.

The 1990s saw the beginning of a number of agreements:
- at plant or local level rather than national level to take into account the needs of a particular business activity (mainly in the private manufacturing sector);
- over a larger fixed period, so that a business has knowledge of its future costs and can build these into its budgets.

Services Unions increasingly offer a wide range of services to employees. These may include:
- insurance schemes;
- pension schemes;
- financial and legal advice;
- discounts on travel and goods;
- education courses;
- mortgage discounts;
- welfare and sickness benefits.

QUESTION 5 A report by the CBI in 1993 said that more companies should consider withdrawing from collective bargaining. Mr Robbie Gilbert, CBI director of employment affairs, recommended in a paper on pay setting that companies should consider increasing the proportion of employees on short term and fixed contracts and locking labour costs into pay deals of more than one year.

He also stated that companies should consider withdrawing recognition from trade unions. After a discussion of single union deals, which he said might soon be on the increase, Mr Gilbert argued, 'But for many (companies), no union at all may now make more sense.'

Source: adapted from the *Financial Times*, 1993.

(a) Explain the statements:
  (i) 'locking labour costs into pay deals of more than one year';
  (ii) 'single union deals';
  and their benefits for business.
(b) Briefly explain why the CBI might suggest that 'no union at all now' would make sense for businesses.

The TUC

The Trades Union Congress (TUC) is an organisation which represents all major trade unions in the UK. In 1993 affiliated unions had a total of over 9 million members.

In September each year a conference is held and TUC policy is decided. Member unions send delegates to the conference, the number sent depending on the size of the union. The conference also elects the General Council of the TUC. This is responsible for carrying out policy and running TUC affairs in between conferences. A General Secretary is elected, who is often seen as the mouthpiece of the TUC and is directly involved in TUC negotiations with member unions and government. The TUC has a permanent staff which deals with the day to day issues in between the annual Congress.

The main activities of the TUC are to:
■ act as a pressure group to influence government policy on labour and union issues;
■ decide on the rules and regulations for member unions, but not to interfere with their everyday running.

Although the TUC's political role has diminished over the last decade, it continues to be represented on a number of public bodies such as the Advisory, Conciliation and Arbitration Service (ACAS), the Commission for Racial Equality (CRE) and the Equal Opportunities Commission (EOC).

The CBI

The Confederation of British Industry (CBI) was formed in 1965. It has a similar role to the TUC, but voices the opinions of employers rather than union members. CBI membership is drawn from private sector industry, service and commercial enterprises, major public sector employers, and some employers' associations, trade associations and Chambers of Commerce.

The internal organisation of the CBI is complex, but it has a ruling council which decides on policy. It also employs permanent staff, headed by the Director General. Detailed policy proposals are examined by standing committees. The CBI is organised to deal with local and area issues through its 13 regional councils. These aim to keep in touch with the needs of small firms and local employers and help them solve their day to day business problems. The membership services of the CBI are wide ranging, both nationally and locally, and are backed up by skilled professional advice from lawyers, accountants and tax specialists.

What role does the CBI have? It attempts to represent its members' interests in a number of ways.
■ Government policy. Just like the TUC, it attempts to influence government policy.
■ Services. It provides legal, financial and economic advice to its members.
■ Local businesses. It provides support and advice to local businesses through its 13 regional offices.
■ EC. Through its office in Brussels, the CBI acts in the interests of British industry.
■ Trade unions. The CBI works with the TUC on consultative bodies such as ACAS (☞ unit 60).
■ Other groups. The CBI provides information for a variety of other organisations and the public in general.

Summary

1. Explain the difference between a trade union and an employers' organisation.
2. State 6 functions of trade unions.
3. Why are good industrial relations important to a business?
4. What is meant by:
  (a) a craft union;
  (b) an industrial union;
  (c) a general union?
5. Explain 3 reasons why union legislation has taken place.
6. Briefly discuss 3 effects that legislation has had on union activity in business.
7. State 4 factors that have contributed to changes in the organisation and role of trade unions in the UK business.
8. What is meant by:
  (a) single union agreements;
  (b) no strike deals;
  (c) union derecognition?
9. What are the main functions of:
  (a) the TUC;
  (b) The CBI?

Key terms

Closed shop - a practice which prevents workers from being employed in a business unless they belong to a trade union.
Picketing - involves the rights of workers on strike to assemble and persuade others to help or join them.
Secondary picketing - where union members from one place of work picket an unrelated place of work.

Shop steward - an elected union official who represents workers' interests in the place in which the shop steward works.
Trade union - an organisation of workers that join together to further their own interests.
Union density - the actual membership of a trade union as a percentage of the total possible membership.

Question

Unison

On July 1, 1993 the 3 main public service unions merged to form one large union - Unison. The merger was supported four to one by the 550,000 voters from:

- the National Association of Local Government Officers (NALGO), a large proportion of which are local government employees;
- the National Union of Public Employees (NUPE);
- the Confederation of Health Service Employees (COHSE), with members largely based in the health service.

Combined, these three unions had a membership of 1.4 million, which would make Unison potentially the largest trade union in the UK (the TGWU having just over 1.1 million members). Mr Alan Jinkinson, the former NALGO general secretary who would lead Unison stated, 'This is a historic day for ... Britain's cash-starved public services.'

Supporters of the merger argued that changes were needed to the unions involved in response to changes in the health service and local government. In hospitals and local authorities bargaining over pay and conditions was increasingly becoming decentralised. This meant that individuals or groups of members faced the prospect of wages etc. being determined not at a national level, where unions would bargain for all employees with employers, but at local, area or even organisation level.

One feature of the new larger union was the merging of COHSE and NUPE political funds, although the NALGO fund remained separate. Another was that Unison would have 44 out of its 67 executive seats reserved for women (13 for women on low pay). This reflected the make-up of its membership - about two-thirds women and one-third men. This compares with an 82-18 per cent male-female split in the TGWU and a 61-39 per cent split in the GMB.

Unison placed great stress on the support and services that the new, larger, union could offer to its members. Alan Jinkinson stated in the September 1993 Unison magazine that, 'A third of low paid workers are now in the public sector and it's getting worse', and that, 'Unison will not allow this to continue'. New improved membership benefits, welfare and legal services were offered to all members. These include advice and representation at work, welfare and sickness benefits, mortgage and financial services and competitive holidays and travel. The union linked up with companies such as Frizzell to offer insurance and the Britannia Building Society to offer discounts, savings and high lending levels on mortgages. Another development was Unison Education and Training - a distance learning package for public service qualifications.

Table 59.1

Facts on the merger
Membership 1.4 million: 900,000 in local government and 500,000 in the following sectors: healthcare, higher education, police authorities, water, transport, electricity, gas. Unison is divided into seven service groups - one for each of the sectors except police - each with its own annual conference and executive. The union is made up of: NALGO (National and Local Government Officers' Association) with 764,000 members; NUPE (National Union of Public Employees) with 551,165 members and Cohse (Confederation of Health Service Employees) with 201,993 members. An interim 127-member executive, consisting of the three unions' executives, will manage Unison from 1 July. Within two years, a 67-strong executive will be elected, including 13 seats reserved for low-paid women members. Unison will set targets for proportional representation of women at every level of the union to be reached by the year 2000.

Source: adapted from the *Financial Times*, 17.12.1992 and *Unison* magazine, September 1993, and *Personnel Management*, July 1993.

(a) **What category of union is Unison likely to be? Explain your answer.**
(b) **Explain why the amalgamation of the three public service unions may have taken place.**
(c) **Using examples from the article, explain the potential benefits of the new, larger, union to members.**
(d) **How do the activities of Unison reflect the make-up of its membership?**
(e) **Why might the merger be;**
   (i) a benefit;
   (ii) a difficulty;
   for local government and health service employers?

Employer and employee conflict

Unit 57 showed that conflict can exist between different groups working in business. One type of conflict which may lead to major problems is between the objectives of employers and employees. Conflict between these two groups may result from a number of factors.

- Rates of pay. Employers could attempt to keep wage costs down to remain competitive, whereas unions could try to maximise employees' rewards.
- The introduction of machinery. For example, a business may want to introduce machinery which requires workers to learn new production techniques. Employees, however, may feel that this extra responsibility is an unwanted burden.
- Flexible working (☞ unit 51). Businesses often require a more flexible workforce. A printing works might decide to operate a 24 hour shift, for example, to cope with extra work. Employees may be unwilling to work at night.
- Work conditions. Workers may feel that better canteen facilities are needed, but employers could see this as an unnecessary increase in costs.

QUESTION 1 In 1992, Dillons the Booksellers indicated that they were introducing a 'group-wide' wage freeze as a means of reducing costs. In a letter to employees, Mr Terry Maher, the chairperson, explained that the recession in the UK 'has proved longer and deeper than anyone had expected. Wages and salaries are normally reviewed in December each year, with any increases taking effect on 1st January. This year, that review will be deferred until June 1993. Pay increases, which will be assessed in the light of trading conditions at that time, will then be effective from 1st July 1993.'

Frank Brazier, chief executive, said that although the book business was doing well, some of Dillons' other businesses were operating in very difficult markets and that a very generous pay award, above the rate of inflation, had already been paid in January 1992.

Other bookshops had made similar attempts to control wage bills. Waterstones resolved a threatened dispute with staff after proposals to scrap an incentive scheme, which enabled staff to earn bonuses for beating sales targets, were put on hold.

Hammicks Bookshop announced that it was switching from set salary scales to a new incentive-based pay structure. The group said salaries would be reviewed annually and staff would be judged according to performance.

Source: adapted from *The Bookseller*, 6.11.1992.

(a) Identify possible sources of conflict between bookshop employers and employees.
(b) Explain why:
   (i) Dillons' management may have felt that a wage freeze was justified;
   (ii) employees may have disagreed with such a policy.

The aim of **industrial relations** procedures (☞ unit 59) is to make sure that each party finds an acceptable solution to any conflict that may exist. Successful industrial relations should prevent the need for industrial action (☞ unit 61) by employers' or employees' groups.

Collective bargaining

COLLECTIVE BARGAINING is one way of minimising conflict in the workplace. It involves determining conditions of work and terms of employment through **negotiations** between employers and employee representatives, such as trade unions. These bodies represent the views of all their members and try to negotiate in their interests. One individual employee working for a large company would have little or no influence in setting their wages or conditions. The representative body has more strength and influence and can negotiate for its membership. Without such a bargaining process, employers and managers would be able to set wages and conditions without taking into account employees' interests.

For collective bargaining to take place:
- employees must be free to join representative bodies, such as trade unions;
- employers must recognise such bodies as representative of workers and agree to negotiate with them;
- such bodies must be independent of employers and the state;
- bodies should negotiate in good faith, in their members' interests;
- employers and employees should agree to be bound by agreements without having to use the law to enforce them.

The result of collective bargaining is a COLLECTIVE AGREEMENT. These agreements are usually written and are signed by the parties and will be binding. Collective agreements can either be **substantive agreements** or **procedural agreements**. Substantive agreements are concerned with terms and conditions of employment. They include pay, work conditions and fringe benefits. Procedural agreements set out how the parties in the bargaining should relate to each other on certain issues. They include negotiating, redundancy, dismissal, recruitment and promotion procedures.

Levels of negotiation

Collective bargaining can take place at a number of different levels.

National level Employers and employees may agree a deal which applies to all employees. Negotiations may take place to set wage or salary scales, or to discuss national conditions of work. For example, an agreement could be reached on the number of hours that teachers or lecturers should work a year, or their length of holidays, between teachers' unions and the government. A private sector example might be negotiations over a pay increase between GEC and AEEU, the engineers' union.

Local level Discussions may take place at a local level, so that any settlement can reflect local conditions. An example of local negotiations might be wages or salaries based on the area of operation. From time to time the weightings given to local authority workers for working in the London or surrounding areas are revised. These weightings are added to workers' salaries to take into account the higher cost of living in the area. A locally based engineering company may negotiate with regional union representatives about the need to reduce the workforce because of falling sales. Again, this is likely to take place at local level.

Factory or plant-wide level Negotiations at factory or plant-wide level can take place over a variety of aspects of work. They may involve the personnel department, departmental managers, shop stewards and employee representatives.

Examples of matters that might be agreed upon could be:
■ productivity targets;
■ the introduction of new machinery;
■ hours of work and flexibility within the plant;
■ health and safety conditions.

Increasingly businesses are arguing that negotiations should take place at factory or local level. National negotiations over pay do not take the 'local' situation into account. A business that wants flexibility to react to changes in the market is better able to do this if each plant can negotiate based on the individual conditions it faces. Such an argument has been strongly put forward by former public sector operations which have now 'opted out', such as NHS trusts.

The negotiation process

For negotiation to be successful in collective bargaining, an agreement must be reached which satisfies all parties. This is far more likely to be achieved if a pattern is followed during negotiation.

The agenda A meeting between all parties involved in negotiation needs an agenda. This will outline what is to be discussed and all parties must agree to it. The order of items on the agenda may influence the outcome of negotiations. If, for instance, all the employees' claims come first and all the management's points come later, then anything that is agreed at the beginning of the meeting cannot be accepted until the management side is given. An agenda that places management and employee items in alternate and logical order can make negotiations easier.

Information Both parties need 'facts' to support their arguments. Negotiators have to collect the information they need, analyse it and make sure that each member of the negotiating team has a say in its interpretation. Often managers make information about a company's financial position available to representatives before meetings. This ensures that both parties have the correct information on which to base discussions.

Strategy It is important for each side in the negotiations to prepare a strategy. This will help them to achieve their objectives. Developing a strategy could include the following stages.
■ Agreeing objectives. What do negotiators seek to achieve? The objectives set by employers or unions should, if achieved, lead to improvements. For example, a change in employment rules might improve efficiency or motivation. Negative objectives that emphasise not 'losing ground' are not usually helpful.
■ Allocating roles. Who will do what in the negotiations? Negotiators need specific roles. For example, there may be a chairperson to lead the discussion, someone to put the case and a specialist to provide advice. The roles of group members are discussed in unit 57.
■ Predict what the other side might do. Strategies are unlikely to remain the same during negotiations. Their chances of success are improved if the negotiators have tried to predict what they will hear from the opposition. Negotiators must be prepared not only to put forward their own arguments, but also to respond to arguments put to them.

Unity Because negotiation involves different sets of interests, each team must work out a united position before negotiations begin. If the group's position changes, all members must agree. It is important that a group shows unity at all times during negotiations or its position may become weaker.

Size of the group The number of people representing each side will influence the negotiations. The larger the group the greater the problem of managing communications between group members (☞ unit 62). When asked to suggest a number, most experienced negotiators opt for three or four in each group. Meetings of fewer people may be accused of 'fixing' an outcome.

Stages of the negotiation Negotiators begin by making it clear that they are representing the interests of others. They often emphasise the strength of their case and start by saying they are unwilling to move from that position. The displays of strength are necessary to convince themselves and the 'opposition' that they are willing to fight for their position. By the time this part of the negotiations starts, both sides should be very clear on the matters that divide them. After the differences have been explored, the next stage is for negotiators to look for solutions that might be more acceptable to each party. Each party will sound out possibilities, float ideas, ask questions and make suggestions. No firm commitments are made at this stage. Negotiations are likely to be more successful if each group is willing to change its position.

Decision making The next stage is to come to some agreement. The management may make an offer. The decision about what to offer is the most difficult and important task in the whole process. The offer may be revised, but eventually it will be accepted or rejected. Agreement is usual in all but a small minority of situations. Employees do not really wish to disrupt an organisation. Even if they take strike action, they will eventually return to the firm. The management need the employees to work for them. They have to reach an agreement no matter how long it takes.

Written statement Producing a brief written statement before the negotiation has ended will make it clear what both parties have decided, if agreement has been reached.

Commitment of the parties So far, agreement has been reached between negotiators only. This is of no value unless the groups represented by the negotiators accept it and make it work.

Employee representatives have to report back to their members and persuade them to accept the agreement. Management representatives may also have to do the same thing. Once the terms have been agreed by both employees and employers, the negotiating process is complete. It is the joint responsibility of both parties to carry out and monitor the agreement.

QUESTION 2 Korvac and James are manufacturers of industrial valves. They operate from a factory in Newcastle. Despite a number of years of falling sales in the late 1980s and early 1990s, they have recently had 2 good years of orders.

This year's pay negotiations are due to take place, and the management have offered a 2 per cent pay increase, which they feel is a good offer given the need to grow in future and the current rate of inflation. The local shop steward thinks this is poor given the work by employees to pull the business around. He has suggested to two local union officials who will be involved in negotiations that a 6 per cent increase should be bargained for or strike action should be considered. He feels certain that the company can afford this, although no figures are yet available on this year's profits. The local officials are not so sure. They suggest that other options are available before calling for a vote on strike action. In particular, they are concerned that higher wages will result in redundancies, although they feel in a strong position to argue that increased productivity by workers will pay for any wage increases.

Another unknown factor is the likely installation of new machinery for the next year, which could lead to new grades for certain workers, but also redundancies in some areas.

Write a letter from one of the union officials to the shop steward outlining the steps that should be taken and the strategy that should be adopted before they enter negotiations with management.

Consultation

Negotiation, as we have seen, is an activity by which the two parties make agreements which may cover pay and conditions at work and relations between management and employees. JOINT CONSULTATION, by contrast, is the process where management representatives discuss matters of common interest with employee representatives before negotiating or making a decision. There are three types of consultation.

Pseudo-consultation Pseudo-consultation is where management makes a decision and informs employees of that decision through their representatives. Employees have no power to influence these decisions. Although this is less common today than it was in the past, there are certain parts of the private sector, where unions are weak, that use this type of consultation. Some have suggested that it would be more accurately described as information-giving. An example might be a small, non-unionised plant, where the owner decides to move premises and informs the workforce when this will take place. In a large company it may be where the board of directors and shareholders discuss a possible merger and 'consult' with workers after they have reached a decision.

Classical consultation Classical consultation is a way of involving employees, through their representatives, in discussions on matters which affect them. This allows employees to have an influence on management decisions. For example, for many years train drivers and guards have been consulted on training, health and safety and work rosters at regional level by British Rail.

Integrative consultation Pseudo and classical consultation do not directly involve employees in decisions which affect them. Integrative consultation is a more democratic method of decision making. Arguably it is neither consultation nor negotiation. Management and unions discuss and explore matters which are of common concern, such as ways of increasing productivity or methods of changing work practices. The two groups come to a joint decision having used, in many cases, problem solving techniques (☞ units 16-17). An example of an integrative approach to consultation might be the use of quality circles (☞ unit 50) in a number of UK businesses and in foreign firms setting up in the UK.

The advantages of consultation

Consultation with employees and representative groups is likely to have a number of advantages for a business.
- It may avoid damaging industrial action.
- It may motivate employees more as they feel part of the decision making process (☞ unit 7).
- It may lead to an input of new or different ideas which could, for example, make any changes easier to carry out.
- It may help to develop a more open organisational culture in the business (☞ unit 51) and allow a firm to

achieve its objectives. Workers in the business might feel their opinions are valued and be prepared to put forward ideas, for example in suggestion boxes.

- It may encourage worker representatives to take a long term view and adopt similar strategies to management, by making them better informed about the reasons behind decisions.
- It might make management more sympathetic to workers' needs. This might put them in a better position to decide if changes in work organisation will be accepted or not by employees.

QUESTION 3 In the late 1980s the Kingston local authority management team wanted to review the formal and informal arrangements for consultation and negotiation. The team commissioned an outside employee relations consultant to carry out a survey of employee relations, with particular reference to consultation.

The main findings of the survey were about the 'departmental consultative groups'. These were designed to bring together management and staff in consultation, with the objective of maintaining an effective service. However, their record was described by both managers and unions as very patchy. This verdict was confirmed by the survey, which revealed the system having little effect. Some changes that affected employer/employee relations had taken place. The most frequently mentioned were new equipment and new methods of working. When employees were asked to indicate the way the changes were made, half reported the decision as 'managerially determined', with no consultation. By contrast, half the managers reported some form of discussion prior to decision making.

When asked to indicate the communication and consultation methods by which the changes were handled, half the employees could not say. Only 5 per cent mentioned their departmental consultative group. A quarter mentioned some other face-to-face arrangement, eg a departmental or sectional meeting. Managers, likewise, reported consultative groups as playing a limited role in this process of change.

The problems of the system were reflected in two other ways.

- Limited knowledge about communication arrangements. So, for example, only 17 per cent of employees and 36 per cent of managers said that they had the consultation arrangements explained to them.
- Limited feedback from departmental consultative group meetings. Eighty per cent of employees and 51 per cent of managers never attended briefings concerning feedback from the consultative groups. Few read the group minutes.

Source: adapted from *Case Studies in Personnel*, eds.D. Winstanley and J. Woodall, The Institute of Personnel Management, 1992.

(a) From the employee survey how would you classify the type of consultation strategies adopted by Kingston local authority?

(b) How could consultation be improved in the borough and what might be the positive effects of these improvements?

The Advisory, Conciliation and Arbitration Service (ACAS)

Sometimes parties fail to reach agreements after consultation and negotiation. In these situations the Advisory, Conciliation and Arbitration Service (ACAS) can be of great value to both sides.

During the period of industrial action in the 1970s, groups of employers and employees called for the setting up of a conciliation and arbitration service, independent of government control and of civil service influence. The result was ACAS, which took up its formal duties in September 1974. ACAS has a chairperson, appointed by the Secretary of State for Employment, and a council of nine members. One-third of these members are nominated by the TUC, one-third by the CBI and the remaining third are independents - mainly academics with special knowledge of industrial relations. ACAS was given the role of improving industrial relations and encouraging reform of collective bargaining procedures.

ACAS provides a wide range of services to employers and employees in business.

Industrial disputes ACAS has conciliation duties. It can intervene in industrial disputes (☞ unit 61) at the request of either management or unions. Its role is to try and encourage a settlement that all parties may agree to, using procedures that both parties accept.

Arbitration and mediation Arbitration is where both parties in a dispute put forward their case to ACAS. ACAS then independently assesses each case and recommends a final decision. Mediation is where ACAS makes recommendations about a possible solution and leaves the parties to find a settlement.

Advisory work ACAS carries out advisory work with employers, trade unions and employers' associations. This can be short visits to answer specific questions or long term, in-depth, projects and surveys. The questions ACAS deal with are wide ranging and can include issues such as contracts of employment, industrial relations legislation, payment systems and personnel policies.

Codes of practice ACAS issues codes of practice. These contain practical guidance on how to improve industrial relations between employers and employees.

Enquiries During the 1980s, ACAS carried out enquiries into the flexible use of labour, appraisal systems, labour turnover, employee involvement, handling redundancy and the use of quality circles (☞ unit 50). Much of this research is published by ACAS as advisory booklets. Employers use them to help improve industrial relations and personnel management practices.

Individual cases ACAS investigates individual cases of unfair discrimination (☞ unit 55) and unfair dismissal (☞ unit 56). The number of cases dealt with has increased from around 4,100 in 1987 to over 72,000 in 1992.

During the 1980s and into the 1990s, ACAS has developed its services to meet the needs of a changing industrial relations climate. While the bulk of its work continues to be conciliation, mediation and arbitration, it has steadily developed advisory and training services. ACAS has become less involved in collective bargaining and more involved in helping business to improve personnel and management practices. These include:

- effective recruitment and selection of employees;
- setting up and operating equal opportunities policies;
- improving communications and joint consultation;
- developing the skills of managers to help them introduce changes in work organisation.

Key terms

ACAS - a body which mediates where conflict exists in business.

Collective agreements - the agreements reached through the process of collective bargaining.

Collective bargaining - a method of determining conditions of work and terms of employment through negotiations between employers and employee representatives.

Joint consultation - discussion between management and employee representatives before a decision is taken.

Summary

1. What factors may lead to conflict between employers and employees?
2. Why is collective bargaining important to a business?
3. What are likely to be the results of collective bargaining?
4. Explain the difference between collective bargaining at national and plant level.
5. Briefly explain the stages in negotiation that may help to lead to a satisfactory outcome.
6. Explain the different types of consultation.
7. What are the advantages of consultation for a business?
8. Briefly explain the main areas of activity that ACAS are involved in.

QUESTION 4

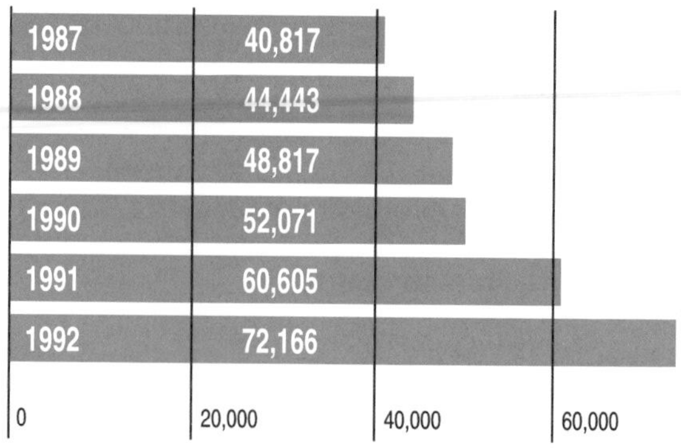

Year	Cases
1987	40,817
1988	44,443
1989	48,817
1990	52,071
1991	60,605
1992	72,166

(scale: 0, 20,000, 40,000, 60,000)

Figure 60.1 *'Individual' cases received by ACAS*

1992 ACAS figures showed that requests for conciliation in collective bargaining disputes fell by 13 per cent after several years of increase, while the number of strikes in Britain fell by a third. In nearly 85 per cent of the cases ACAS was involved in a settlement was reached.

However, requests for ACAS involvement in individual cases of unfair dismissal or sex discrimination rose by one-fifth from 1991 to 1992. Many of the 5,780 sex discrimination cases were accounted for by some 2000 complaints against the Ministry of Defence for its refusal to allow workers to return to work following pregnancy. Most of the involvement in requests for unfair dismissal were due to disagreements over termination of contract by employers. In all, 67 per cent of individual cases produced a conciliated settlement or a withdrawal, with the remaining third going to industrial tribunal.

Source: adapted from *Employment Gazette*, May 1993.

(a) Identify the types of dispute that ACAS investigated over the period 1991-1992.
(b) Give reasons for the changing trends in the disputes investigated by ACAS.
(c) How successful do you think ACAS were over the period? Explain your answer.

Question

A move to local bargaining

An increasing number of organisations are moving away from national bargaining to negotiate pay and conditions locally. These include NHS trusts, local authorities, locally managed schools, HMSO and the Passport Office. What opportunities are associated with these changes, how can they be realised and what are the pitfalls?

Such a change can affect all aspects of employment, not just terms and conditions. A move to locally negotiated conditions could suggest changes in organisation structure, considerations about who will carry out the local negotiations and what the relationship will be between the 'negotiator' and the line manager.

Management should be cautious and plan prudently. It is unwise to rush into derecognising or sidelining trade unions. Employees may well be apprehensive at an apparently hostile time for them and will look for protection.

Senior management should not retire into isolated planning but should seek out and take into account the attitudes of staff and of trade unions. Above all, they should be aware of the attitudes of middle and junior management, on whom they will depend to implement company proposals. The Transfer of Undertakings (Protection of Employment) Regulations should be examined carefully. There may be legal problems about reducing rates of pay and offering less favourable conditions, and the advice of an employment lawyer could be invaluable.

Two aspects of local bargaining that must be examined carefully are pay and negotiations.

Pay Job descriptions should be examined to ensure they are up to date. Then a decision needs to be made on a system of job evaluation, ensuring that it does not run counter to the 'equal pay for work of equal value' regulations. The Northern Ireland Electricity Service endured lengthy legal action after comparing a 'male' manual worker job and a 'female' office worker job.

A decision also has to be made on how much staff participation to encourage in, for example, preparing job descriptions, committee membership and so on, and how many job grades are appropriate. A sound objective is to have as few grades as possible, to encourage work flexibility and to avoid pay differentials which could bring the system into disrepute.

The salary bands attached to the grades should be broad enough to allow progression. These scales may well overlap to allow pay increases on promotion to a higher grade.

It may be advisable to link pay awards to an appraisal of individual performance, but there should be an appeals system. A 'harmonised' structure, covering both white-collar and blue-collar jobs, may help to avoid running foul of the equal pay regulations. Individual incentives are held to be more motivating, whereas group and organisation-wide systems often encourage teamwork. The system should be based on individual annual appraisal; this requires setting objectives and monitoring progress, but the danger is that all staff are given the highest assessment.

Negotiation A new structure may well be required at local level to accommodate pay determination. The trade unions may feel under threat, and it is usually better to encourage co-operation rather than impose change. If relationships have been good, build on them.

The final stages of the procedure at national level will probably need to be replaced by local arrangements. This could involve ACAS or arbitration by another independent person. To be effective, the arrangements should be agreed with the trade unions as soon as possible.

Some organisations have taken management grades out of collective bargaining and constructed personal salary contracts. It is claimed that this facilitates appraisal and, in some cases, performance-related pay. An example is British Rail, where all the managerial jobs were removed from the collective bargaining structure; this was painstakingly carried out and was eventually successful, despite considerable apprehension on the part of the unions and the managers.

In 1990 the *Daily Mail* announced that it was derecognising trade unions and offered a pay rise to those staff who signed personal contracts. Derecognition has its pitfalls; a test case ended at the Court of Appeal, which found on behalf of the union. However, the government has since introduced a new section into the Trade Union Reform and Employment Rights Act allowing employers to give more favourable terms, including pay, to those who accept personal contracts.

It may be appropriate to introduce 'single-table bargaining'. This can help to ensure that negotiated outcomes with different unions are compatible and can save a lot of managerial time. A recent Labour Research Department study found that such agreements have been introduced in 43 of the 65 NHS trusts and nine of the 10 privatised water companies.

Source: adapted from *Personnel Management*, September 1993.

(a) Identify possible areas of conflict that might exist between employers and employees suggested in the article.
(b) What types of consultation might there be before the switch to local negotiation takes place?
(c) How might local negotiations be different to national negotiations?
(d) Discuss the possible advantages and disadvantages to:
(i) management;
(ii) employees;
of local negotiation.
(e) What role might ACAS have in local negotiations?

Industrial action in the UK

Conflict between employees and employers can lead to **industrial action**. Industrial action can be taken by both employers against employees (such as close supervision of work, or a lock out) and by employees against employers (ranging from an overtime ban to strike action). It is in the interests of both groups to reconcile differences through negotiation and consultation (☞ unit 60) before taking action, although this is not always possible.

The number of stoppages and the working days lost through stoppages in the UK have fallen greatly over the last decade. This is shown in Figure 61.1. In part this is due to legislation which has made union action more difficult to take (☞ unit 60). It is also, perhaps, due to a movement away from the 'hostile' attitudes taken by employers and trade unions towards industrial relations. In the 1980s and 1990s, unions have appeared more willing to discuss and solve disputes. Management might also have become more interested in the area of human resource management, with its emphasis on employee involvement and direct communication.

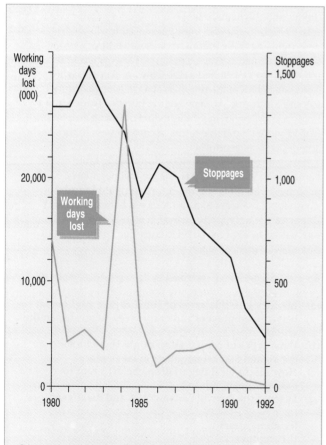

Source: adapted from *Employment Gazette*.
Figure 61.1 *Working days lost (000) and number of stoppages in the UK 1980-1992*

Employers' industrial action

Action by management against employees can take a number of forms. Sometimes sanctions can be imposed by individual managers. Some may include, for example, close supervision of employees' work, tight work discipline, discrimination against certain groups, lay offs, demoting workers or speeding up work practices. These actions are usually taken by one member of the management team and will not be repeated in other departments in the company. They might lead to individuals or groups of workers starting grievance proceedings against the manager concerned.

Sanctions can also be organised and carried out throughout the business. Management may use some of the following actions when dealing with trade unions.

Withdrawal of overtime and suspension Withdrawing overtime (☞ unit 49) or mass suspension are sometimes used by management to impress upon unions that they will be standing firm during negotiations over pay and conditions.

Lock-outs A LOCK-OUT by employers involves closing the factory for a period of time. Employees' wages are not paid during this period. Businesses tend to use this action very rarely today. It often adversely affects the image that the public have of the company. Also, the business is able to achieve the same ends by other, less drastic means. Perhaps one of the most well known was the lock out of News International employees at Wapping in a dispute over the introduction of new printing machinery (☞ unit 36).

Changing standards and piecework rates Management may change work standards or alter piecework rates when in dispute with employees. This can have the effect of making the employees' task more difficult or reducing the earnings of employees unless they work a lot harder.

Sometimes a management tactic may be to use a strategy of increasing work standards so that unions will call a strike. This might happen when order books are low and stocks are high. By causing a strike, management do not need to lay anyone off or pay redundancy money. At the same time further stockpiling is reduced. This type of action is only used in extreme cases.

Closure The closing down of factories and offices, or the threat by management to remove plant and machinery from their premises, is a much more likely managerial tactic in modern business. Some people would not even view such activities as industrial action. They would see them as the normal rights of management to shut down uneconomic enterprises or force uncooperative workers to comply with employers' needs in the workplace. Managerial action of this sort can lead to SIT-INS or WORK-INS by employees in an attempt to prevent closure. These are discussed in the next section.

Employees' industrial action

Industrial action used by employees can be wide ranging. It is possible to distinguish between **unorganised** action and **organised** action. R Hyman in his book *Strikes*, wrote that: '... in unorganised conflict the worker typically responds to the oppressive situation in the only way open to him as an individual ... Such reaction rarely derives from any calculative strategy ... Organised conflict, on the other hand, is far more likely to form part of a conscious strategy to change the situation which is identified as the source of discontent.'

Unorganised (or unofficial) action by employees can come in a number of forms.

■ High labour turnover (☞ unit 51).
■ Poor time keeping.
■ High levels of absenteeism.
■ Low levels of effort.
■ Inefficient work.
■ Deliberate time wasting.
■ Unofficial strikes not backed by the employees' union. These are often taken when workers 'down tools'

immediately in reaction to employers actions.

Such action can be disruptive for a business if it continues for a long period of time. The business, however, can use disciplinary procedures against employees and may even be able to terminate contracts in some cases (☞ unit 56). However, unofficial action may lead to organised action backed by the union. Organised action can take a number of different forms.

Work to rule or go slow Organised and group industrial action by trade unions against management can take the form of WORKING TO RULE or GOING SLOW. A work to rule means employees do not carry out duties which are not in their employment contract. They may also carry out management orders to the letter. This can result in workers strictly observing the safety and work rules which are normally disregarded. Working to rule does not mean that employees are in breach of contract, simply that they carry out tasks exactly according to their contract. This means that tasks are not carried out efficiently. The impact of train drivers working to rule, for example, could mean that trains are late arriving or are cancelled. Drivers may delay taking trains out until rigorous checks are carried out. A go slow is where employees deliberately attempt to slow down production, whilst still working within the terms of their contract.

Overtime ban An overtime ban limits workers' hours to the agreed contract of employment for normal hours. Overtime bans are usually used by trade unions to demonstrate to management that the workforce is determined to take further collective action if their demands are not met. An overtime ban does have a disadvantage for workers as it results in lost earnings. It can lead to a reduction in costs for the business, but may also lead to lost production. It can be especially effective where production takes place overnight, eg coal mines, large production lines.

Sit-ins and work-ins Sit-ins and work-ins are mass occupations of premises by workers. A work-in is where employees continue production with the aim of demonstrating that the factory is a viable concern. It is sometimes used when there is a threat of closure. In a sit-in, production does not continue. The aim is to protest against management decisions and, in the case of factory closure, prevent the transfer of machinery to other factories. A **redundancy sit-in** or work-in is a protest against the closure of a plant or company. A **collective bargaining sit-in** may be used instead of other forms of industrial action such as working to rule, overtime bans, and all out strikes, to give employees a position of strength in negotiations.

Sit-ins and work-ins mean the illegal occupation of premises by workers. They also allow workers to gain control over the factory. Why are these tactics used? Firstly, they offer some degree of control over the factory or plant being occupied, which is obviously important in redundancy situations where the removal of plant and machinery to other locations is being threatened. Also by working-in or sitting-in, employees are better able to maintain their group solidarity.

Strikes The ultimate sanction used by trade unions against employers is the strike or industrial stoppage. Stoppages at work are normally connected with terms and conditions of employment. Strikes can be **official** or **unofficial.** Official strikes are where a union officially supports its members in accordance with union rules during a dispute. Unofficial strikes have no union backing or support. They have, in the past, been called by shop stewards in particular factories, often in response to a particular incident. Such strikes are likely to be short term, local, unpredictable and disruptive for a business.

There is no single reason that explains the trend in stoppages in Britain. A study of strikes in Britain over an extensive time period was carried out by researchers for the Department of Employment. They discovered that:

- strikes appear to be over major issues;
- strikes are concentrated in a very small proportion of plants - often the larger ones in certain industries and in certain areas of the country;
- industries and regions that have large factories, on average, tend to experience relatively high numbers of strikes. These strikes occur fairly often.

QUESTION 2 It was reported in December 1992 that *Daily Mirror* journalists were to hold talks with Mr David Banks, their new editor, on a range of issues, including the sacking of 100 part time employees.

The agreement to negotiate followed a consultative ballot, in which 101 *Daily Mirror* journalists voted in favour of industrial action. Although there was a clear majority in favour of action, 69 voted against.

A further ballot needed to be held before industrial action was taken. If the National Union of Journalists called for industrial action it appeared it would be for a work to contract instead of a strike.

NUJ representatives would meet Mr Banks to negotiate three issues;

- The reinstatement of part time employees who have been dismissed.
- The terms of a new contract drawn up for those who work on the *Sunday Mirror* and *The People*.
- People being moved to different departments without consultation.

Mr Trevor Davis, an NUJ official at the *Daily Mirror*, said 'We hope that something positive will come out of these negotiations.'

Apart from re-hiring the sacked workers, *Daily Mirror* journalists were concerned about new personal contracts for the Sunday editions.

Source: adapted from the *Financial Times*, 12.12.1992.

(a) Identify the possible forms of industrial action which were open to the NUJ from the article.
(b) Discuss the possible effects on the business if employees took the preferred action.

Factors influencing the success of employees' industrial action

Whether industrial action by workers and unions is successful in helping them achieve their aims depends on a number of factors.

Nature and strength of the union A large union negotiating with a small business is more likely to be able to influence the employer. Where large unions are negotiating with large multinational companies or with the government, action may not always be successful. In the 1980s and 1990s strikes by the mine workers, railway workers and parts of the health service arguably failed to make any real impact on the government.

It has also been argued that unions are less influential if representation in the industry is split. This was perhaps the case when some mine workers left the NUM to form the Union of Democratic Mineworkers in the 1980s. It may also have been a reason for the merger of NALGO, NUPE and COHSE in 1993 to form Unison.

Smaller unions tend to have less influence. The Musicians Union, for example, whilst having rates per hour for performers is unlikely to be able to force club owners to pay the 'going rate' for performances.

Location and organisation of the workforce It has been suggested that unions are in a stronger bargaining position if a number of their members are employed in the same 'place'. Farm workers, for example, have traditionally been in a weak bargaining position with employers, as few are employed on any one farm. Also, their places of employment are geographically dispersed. This makes meetings and support difficult.

Public support and union views Public support for a dispute may strengthen a union's position. This may be particularly true of public sector workers, where the public often 'feel' workers deserve higher wages or not to be made redundant. However, public opinion may change once industrial action begins. The prolonged miners' strike of 1984-85 arguably caused public opinion to change to a view of mine workers being disruptive. This may also be the case in industrial action by railway workers, for example, especially in commuter belts around London.

Health unions have traditionally refused to strike because of the damaging effects on patients. The Royal College of Nursing (with its near 300,000 members), is one example. In recent years, however, members of other unions have been prepared to take industrial action within hospitals.

Management tactics Union action is likely to be less effective if management action can reduce the problems for business. In the car industry, a strike by employees may not affect a producer if there are stocks of cars and orders can still be met.

Management may encourage non-union workers or even union members to cross the picket line (as in the dispute at the Timex factory in 1993), or even be prepared to 'bus in' workers from other areas. The government has, in the past, been prepared to use army vehicles and members of the armed forces when fire service workers have taken industrial action.

Legislation and economic climate

The **1984 Trade Union Act** (☞ unit 59) forced unions to conduct secret ballots before strike action took place. It could be argued that this reduces the strength of unions. It has the effect of delaying any action, giving members a chance to consider whether they want to take action, and allows businesses to prepare for the outcome. Legislation that has restricted picketing has also reduced union power.

The economic climate is also likely to influence union membership and strength. In a period of growth or boom (☞ unit 67), more people are employed, have an income, and are more likely to belong to a union.

QUESTION 3 On December 1, 1992, more than 600 dock workers at the Port of Sheerness on the Thames (the country's largest car and fruit port) voted to strike. Action was taken because of the possible cut in earnings of up to 10 per cent. Employers argued that cuts would prevent redundancies and allow the business to remain competitive. They also stressed that many other companies were doing the same in the current climate.

The new contracts would give a more flexible system. Instead of 2 shifts (with extra shift payments), employees would have to work 39 hours a week and be available for work at any time between 6am and 10pm. Many workers were skilled former dock workers with salaries of over £20,000 a year. Cuts in pay had previously been rare, even during the recent recession.

The employer, Medway Ports, was created by a management buy-out, with two-thirds of the workforce being shareholders. Medway management had certain undisclosed plans to keep the docks open even if strike action took place.

Source: adapted from the *Financial Times*, 2.12.1992.

What factors mentioned in the article were likely to influence the success of the industrial action by dock workers?

Problems of industrial action

There are certain problems which result from industrial action, both for employers and employees.

Employers' problems

- Industrial action can lead to lost production for the business. A go slow or work to rule may reduce output. Strike action could mean that orders are unfulfilled and revenue and profits could fall.
- If industrial action results in production being stopped, then machinery and other resources will be lying idle. A business will have many fixed costs (☞ unit 10) which have to be covered, even if production is not taking place. If output ceases,

revenue will not be earned to pay for these costs.
- Industrial action may lead to poor future relationships in a business. Sometimes grievances can carry on after a dispute. This could result in poor motivation and communication.
- Industrial disputes divert managers' attention away from planning. If a business is concerned with solving a dispute that exists now, it may neglect plans for the future.
- Loss of output and delays in production or deliveries caused by action can harm the firm's reputation. This may lead to lost business in future.

Employees' problems

- A work to rule, go slow or strike can lead to a reduction or a loss of earnings.
- Prolonged industrial action may, in some cases, lead to the closure of the business. Employees would then be made redundant.
- Action is likely to place stress on the workforce. It can also cause friction between levels of the hierarchy (☞ unit 63). For example, managers on the other 'side' in a dispute are unlikely to find their employees motivated.
- If action is unsuccessful, the employees' position may be weaker in future. Members may also leave a union if they feel that it is unable to support their interests.

Benefits of industrial action

Industrial action is often used as a 'final' measure by unions and employers because of the disruption it causes. There are, however, some benefits for both groups.

- It 'clears the air'. Employers and employees may have grievances. Industrial action can bring these out into the open and, once the dispute is solved, this could improve the 'atmosphere' in the business.
- Introducing new rules. How groups operate in businesses is influenced by rules, such as rates of pay or what is meant by unfair dismissal. Conflict is often about disagreement over these rules. When industrial action has been resolved, this often leads to new rules which each group agrees upon.
- Changing management goals. Management often change their goals and the ways they are achieved after industrial action. For example, a business may have attempted to introduce new working practices without consulting unions, which led to industrial action. In future it may consult with unions before changing work practices.
- Understanding the position of each group. Industrial action often makes the position of employers and employees very clear. It allows each group to hear the grievances of the other, consider them and decide to what extent they agree.

QUESTION 4 On March 3, 1993, Ford workers walked out of the Dagenham plant after leaked news that the company was to close most of its general services business. It was revealed that Ford was intending to contract out services, affecting 3,000 jobs in the UK and Germany. Services workers staged an unofficial 24 hour strike. Ford argued that it needed to cut its costs and could not afford to retain in-house services of maintenance engineers or drivers of parts from Europe to the UK.

Ford assessed the costs of strike action if restructuring went ahead.

■ It believed 'the most serious risks' lay with the truck drivers who supply key components to its production plants. 'A British truck fleet dispute would probably result in the progressive closure of all Ford European manufacturing plants within three days'.

The company calculated that if it decided to reassign or re-source the truck fleet business this would 'result in a dispute of at least two weeks duration' because of the threatened loss in earnings and jobs.

■ Another danger area for disruption would be boiler operations, where a strike could halt production quickly, although Ford believed the personnel concerned 'would be willing to explore re-sourcing and reassignment terms before reacting'. Ford calculated that it would not be possible to stockpile to protect continental manufacturing plants because of the limited time available. It also believed there would be 'major difficulties' for management in maintaining boiler operations.

■ Ford also believed there would be a disruption of 'general services'.

Source: adapted from the *Financial Times*, 4.3.1993.

Discuss the potential problems of further strike action over restructuring for:
(a) Ford workers;
(b) The Ford Motor Company.

Key terms

Go slow - the reduction of output by workers whilst still carrying on tasks in their contract of employment.
Lock-out - action by employers which prevents employees entering the factory to work.
Sit-in/Work-in - the illegal occupation of premises by workers, which allows workers to gain control of the factory.
Work to rule - when employees do not carry out duties which are not in their employment contract.

Summary

1. Why might the number of days lost through stoppages in the UK have fallen over the last decade?
2. Explain 4 types of industrial action that employers can take.
3. State 6 types of unorganised employee action.
4. Why might employees be reluctant to use strike action?
5. Explain the difference between a sit-in and a go slow.
6. What factors might influence the success of employees' industrial action?
7. State 3 problems of industrial action for:
   (a) employees;
   (b) employers.
8. How might industrial action benefit a business?

Question

The rail dispute, 1993

The latter part of 1992 saw growing unrest amongst workers and unions in a number of UK industries. November's published figures showed strikes at a 100 year low, but public sector workers, in particular, were gathering to take action over their position. In 1989 there had been 17 day-long Tube strikes on the London Underground - mostly wildcat action. Rail unions were now prepared to support their members in official strike action.

April 2, 1993, witnessed the first of the one day strikes call by the RMT, the main rail union. Its members voted 26,097 to 10,314 to take action. Jimmy Knapp, RMTs general secretary, said that the vote to strike had been 'about jobs'. Workers feared that 20,000 jobs were at risk as a result of privatisation, in addition to 7,000 redundancies planned for 1993. The union wanted British Rail to guarantee no compulsory redundancies and no use of contract labour. Other rail unions such as ASLEF (the foot platemans' and drivers' union) and TSSA, the staff union, were not involved in the strike. If the RMT did strike, the railway system could not operate, as many of its members were signal workers.

Some disputed the effectiveness of the strike. They argued that action was low key and had failed to win the public support that was achieved in 1989. It was also suggested that not even the majority of the union's own members wanted action (the RMT got 70 per cent support from a 55 per cent turnout). In fact, it was even felt that disruption to passengers and bedlam on the roads could turn public opinion against the railway workers.

A second one day strike was called by the RMT for 16 April 1993. British Rail estimated this would cost a further £10 million in lost gross revenue and might even threaten long term business contracts. The strike followed a breakdown in talks between RMT and BR. On the same day strike action was also being taken by ASLEF members. Although talks between BR and ASLEF were taking place and were described as 'constructive', ASLEF stated that it was 'too late to call off its 24 hour strike'. In response to the strike by members of both unions, Royal Mail said it was hiring four extra flights capable of carrying 400,000 letters to take mail around Britain.

In May 1993, against the advice of union leaders,

RMT members voted to support a 'peace' formula put forward by British Rail, who had settled with ASLEF. BR made a number of important concessions to RMT. BR said they saw no reason for redundancies over the next couple of years or contract work over the same period. They also promised no compulsory redundancies in work-shops for the next 12 months. However, BR did say that it had not changed its decision to end the check-off system under which BR paid members' union subscriptions direct to unions from their wage packets.

Source: adapted from the *Financial Times*, 23.3.1993, 2.4.1993, 16.4.1993, 18.5.1993.

(a) **What were the reasons for conflict between railway workers' representatives and the employers, British Rail?**

(b) **Discuss the possible effects of strike action on:**
 (i) **railway workers;**
 (ii) **British Rail;**
 (iii) **customers of British Rail;**
 (iv) **other businesses.**

(c) **What factors suggested in the article might have affected the strength of the two sides in the strike.**

(d) **What possible benefits might there have been from the strike action for British Rail and railway workers?**

(e) **How might the ending of the check-off system by British Rail affect the rail unions?**

What is communication?

Communication is about sending and receiving information. Employees, managers and departments communicate with each other every day in business. For example, in a sole trader organisation, the owner may inform the workers verbally that an order for goods has to be sent out in the next two days. In a company, the personnel manager might send a 'memo' to all departments informing them about training courses that are available.

Good communication is vital for the efficient running of a business. A company exporting goods abroad is likely to have major problems if it fails to give the exact time of departure to its despatch department. Similarly, problems will also arise if instructions are not clear and goods are delivered to the wrong address.

Effective communication will only happen if information is sent, received and then understood. Some examples of information and methods of communicating in business might be:

- information on how to fill out expenses claims forms in a memo sent from the accounts department;
- verbal comments made by a manager to an employee informing them that continued lateness is likely to result in disciplinary action by the company;
- employment details given to a new employee on a written contract of employment (☞ unit 53);
- information on sales figures sent from the sales manager to the chief executive on computer disk to be called up on screen;
- face-to-face negotiations between management and employee representatives over possible rewards for agreeing to changes in work practice;
- a group meeting taking place to discuss how quality could be improved in a work section.

The communication process

Communication within business can take many forms. There are, however, some common features of all communications that take place in the workplace. Figure 62.1 shows an example.

Who sends and receives information? Information must be received and understood by the person or group to whom it was sent. Communication can take place between managers and employees, as well as between representative bodies, such as trade unions. Information is also passed to people and organisations outside the company. For example, company newspapers such as *Ford News* not only inform employees about the firm, but presents a picture to the outside world of its operations.

What message is being communicated? For communication to be effective the correct **message** must be sent and received. Messages can be sent for a number of reasons.

- To provide information about the company. Management might inform the workforce about production levels achieved during the previous year. Some information is required by law, for example, the business has to tell employees about their conditions of employment.
- To give instructions, for example, to instruct market research to be carried out.
- To persuade people to change attitudes or behaviour, for example, to warn an employee who is consistently late of the likely action.

What channel is being used? Communication can be along different routes or CHANNELS in the organisation. Sometimes this can be between a manager and a subordinate (**vertical**) or between two departments (**horizontal**). As well as this **formal** type of communication, information is often passed **informally** between departments and employees.

What medium is being used? Information can be communicated in a variety of ways or through different COMMUNICATION MEDIA. These vary from written methods, such as annual reports, to oral methods such as discussions, to the use of information technology, such as a modem or a 'fax' machine.

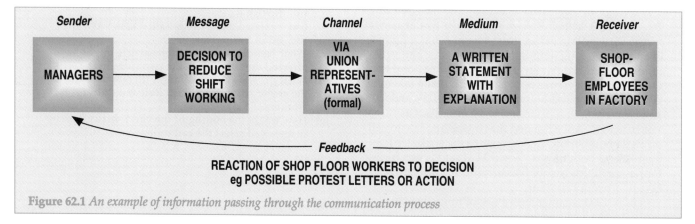

Figure 62.1 *An example of information passing through the communication process*

Feedback Communication is not complete until the message is received and the receiver confirms that it is understood through feedback of some sort, for example, written or verbal confirmation.

Formal/informal communication

Within a business there are both formal and informal channels of communication. Formal channels are recognised and approved by employers and employee representatives. An example of a formal channel would be a personnel department giving 'notice' to an employee about redundancy.

Informal communication channels can both help and hinder formal communications. Information that is communicated through the **grapevine** (☞ unit 57) may become distorted. This might, in extreme situations, cause industrial relations disputes. However, the grapevine can be acknowledged by management and actively approved of. Some firms issue a 'leak' along the grapevine to see what reaction it might provoke, making changes based on the reaction of employees to proposals, before issuing final instructions. Rumours, such as of a launch of a new product by a competitor, can be useful to a business.

Research has shown that effective communication requires both formal and informal channels. Formal statements can then be supported by informal explanations. A business might inform employees that it is introducing new machinery and then management may discuss this with employees and their representatives to find the best way to do it.

It is also possible to make the distinction between **line** and **staff** communication (☞ unit 63). Line communication has authority behind it. Staff communication does not. An example of staff communication may be where a manager attempts to persuade a worker that it is a 'good idea' to do something.

QUESTION 1 The personnel manager of an electrical components company has to communicate two pieces of information to employees. The first is the good news that the company has won a new contract to supply electrical components to a local manufacturer. However, the personnel manager also has to communicate some bad news to 20 operators on the shop floor. Due to increased levels of automation, their employment will no longer be required next month. They are to leave their work at the end of the week, will be paid in full until the end of the month and receive statutory redundancy payments.

For each message:
(a) identify who is sending and receiving the message;
(b) state what message is being communicated;
(c) suggest whether a formal or informal channel would be most suitable and explain your answer.

Vertical and lateral communication

Information can be communicated downwards, upwards and laterally. These different channels of communication are shown in Figure 62.2. **Downwards** communication has, in the past, been used to tell employees about decisions that have already been made. It may be important as it:
■ allows decisions by managers to be carried out by employees;
■ ensures that action is consistent and co-ordinated;
■ reduces costs because fewer mistakes should be made;
■ should lead to greater effectiveness and profitability as

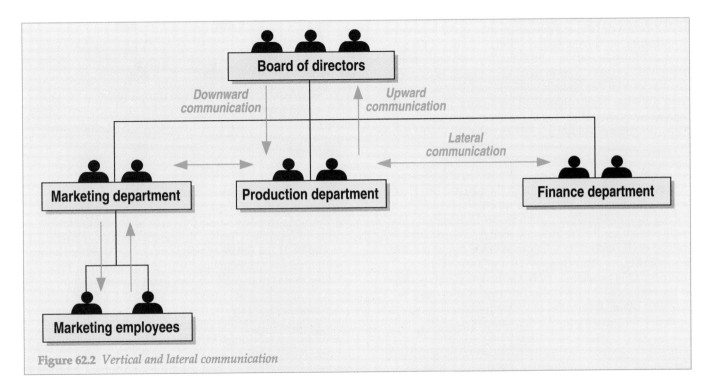

Figure 62.2 *Vertical and lateral communication*

a result of the above.

There is evidence, however, that the flow of information **upwards** can also help in decision making.

- It helps managers to understand employees' views and concerns.
- It helps managers to keep more in touch with employees' attitudes and values.
- It can alert managers to potential problems.
- It can provide managers with the information that they need for decision making and gives feedback on the effects of previous decisions.
- It helps employees to feel that they are participating and can encourage motivation.
- It provides feedback on the effectiveness of downwards communication and how it can be improved.

Lateral communication takes place when people at the same level within an organisation pass information. An example might be a member of the finance department telling the marketing department about funds available for a sales promotion. One problem that firms sometimes face is that departments may become hostile towards each other if they don't understand the problems that each face. The marketing department may want these funds, but this might adversely affect the firm's cash flow.

Communication networks

Communication between group members was discussed in unit 57. We can also show how these ideas can be applied to communication within parts of a business and between a business and outside bodies. There are advantages and disadvantages to a business of using each of these types of NETWORK.

The circle In a circle, sections, departments etc. can communicate with only two others, as shown Figure 62.3a. This type of communication may occur between middle managers from different departments at the same level of the organisation. The main problem with this type of network is that decision making can be slow or poor because of a lack of co-ordination. If middle managers from different departments had been given the task of increasing sales and profits in the short term, they may have difficulty developing a strategy that all would agree on.

The chain The chain (Figure 62.3b) is where one person passes information to others, who then pass it on. This approach tends to be the formal approach adopted by hierarchical organisations, such as the Civil Service. The main advantage is that there is a leader/co-ordinator at the top of the hierarchy who can oversee communications downwards and upwards to different areas of the business. One problem may be the isolation felt by those at the bottom of the network. Their motivation may be less than others if they feel at the periphery. This network does not encourage lateral communication.

The wheel In the wheel pattern (Figure 63.3c) there is a person, group or department that occupies a central

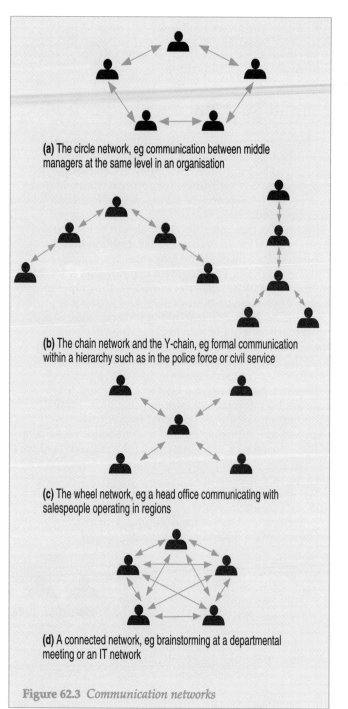

(a) The circle network, eg communication between middle managers at the same level in an organisation

(b) The chain network and the Y-chain, eg formal communication within a hierarchy such as in the police force or civil service

(c) The wheel network, eg a head office communicating with salespeople operating in regions

(d) A connected network, eg brainstorming at a departmental meeting or an IT network

Figure 62.3 *Communication networks*

position. This network is particularly good at solving problems. If, for example, the North West region of an insurance company had been asked to increase sales by central office, then the North West regional manager would be at the centre of policy initiative communicating with local managers about the best way forward. The leader in this network is the regional manager.

A connected or 'all channel' network The 'all channel' communication system (Figure 62.3d) might be used in small group workings. With its participatory style, and more open communication system, the connected network provides the best solutions to complex problems.

This type of network might be used, for example, when a department needs to 'brainstorm'. Its disadvantages are that it is slow and that it tends to disintegrate under time pressure to get results when operated in a group.

One solution to the problem of passing complex communications has been solved by the use of information technology (IT) (☞ unit 36). A complex connected network can be set up where instructions and information are passed between many people or departments, or even parts of a business overseas.

QUESTION 2 Which communication network may be most suitable for the following types of message?
(a) An instruction to despatch an order by a certain date.
(b) Discussions about possible extension strategies for a mature product.
(c) A message from head office to local building societies to change mortgage interest rates.
(d) Reacting to a bomb alert in an office block.
(e) Imposing budget cuts in a local authority.
(f) Organising a retirement party.
(g) Developing a brand identity for a consumer product.
Explain your answer in each case.

Communication media

There are a number of methods or media that can be used to communicate information in businesses. Methods are either written or oral. Sometimes a distinction is also made between oral and face-to-face methods.

Written communication The **letter** is a flexible method which provides a written record. It is often used for communications with others outside the organisation. It can also be used internally where a confidential written record is needed, eg to urge employees against strike action, to announce a redundancy etc.

A **memorandum** is the same as a letter, but is only used for internal communications. It is sent via the internal mail system. Memoranda are useful for many sorts of message, particularly for confirming telephone conversations. Sometimes they are used instead of a telephone. One criticism often made of firms is that they have too many 'memos', when short written notes would do the same job. Some businesses send 'memos' via electronic mail. This allows a person to send a message to another person's computer, which stores it in an electronic mailbox. The memo can then be called up and read by the person receiving it.

Reports allow a large number of people to see complex facts and arguments about issues on which they have to make a decision. A written report does not allow discussion or immediate feedback, as does a meeting, and it can be time-consuming and expensive to produce. However, it does have advantages for passing messages to groups. Firstly, people can study the material in their own time, rather than attending a meeting. Secondly, time that is often wasted at meetings can be better used.

Thirdly, the report is presented in an impartial way, so conflict can be avoided.

Routine information can be communicated through the use of **forms**. A well designed form can be filled in quickly and easily. They are simple to file and information is quickly retrieved and confirmed. Examples of forms used in business include expense forms, timesheets, insurance forms, and stock request forms.

The **noticeboard** is a method which cheaply passes information to a large number of people. The drawbacks to noticeboards are that they can become untidy or irrelevant. In addition, they rely on people reading them, which does not always happen.

Larger companies often print an internal **magazine** or **newspaper** to inform employees about a variety of things. These may include staff appointments and retirements, meetings, sports and social events, results and successes, customer feedback, new products or machinery and motivating competitions, eg safety suggestions. The journal usually avoids being controversial. It may not deal with sensitive issues such as industrial relations (☞ unit 59) or pollution of the environment (☞ unit 72), and may stop short of criticising management policy or products. It is designed to improve communication and morale, and it may be seen by outsiders (especially customers) who might get a favourable impression of the business.

Face-to-face communication Face-to-face communication involves an oral message being passed between people talking to each other. Examples might be:
- a message passed between two workers about how long is left before lunch;
- an instruction given to an employee to change jobs in a job rotation scheme (☞ unit 50);
- a warning given by a health and safety officer to a worker.

Unit 57 dealt with how groups operate. Group meetings involve face-to-face communication. Meetings can take a number of forms. They may be formal meetings which are legally required, such as the Annual General Meeting of a limited company. They might also be meetings of groups within the business to discuss problems, such as collective bargaining negotiations (☞ unit 60) or meetings of quality circles (☞ unit 50). Team briefings are also a common method of face-to-face communication in business. Many meetings, however, are simply informal discussions taking place to pass information between employees or managers, such as a 'chat' over lunch.

Face-to-face communication has several advantages. It:
- allows new ideas to be generated;
- allows 'on the spot' feedback, constructive criticism and an exchange of views;
- encourages co-operation;
- allows information to be spread quickly among a group of people.

However, face-to-face communication, such as meetings, can have problems, especially if:
- the terms of reference (defining the purpose and power of the meeting) are not clear;
- the people attending are unskilled or unwilling to

QUESTION 3 Team briefing is a method of face-to-face communication in groups of about 10-20 employees. The leader of the group provides up-to-date organisational information, with explanation and rational, and the group members are given an opportunity to ask questions.

The team briefing system works from the top downwards in gradual stages. The system starts with the board meeting, followed by briefing groups being held at the next level down, using as their base briefing notes issued by the first meeting, but adding any other information that may be relevant at this level. The last level of briefing group is the level of supervisor briefing the shopfloor. Briefing notes from the next level of briefing group are used here, together with local information. It is usually suggested that those who are briefers and lead the briefing group should, between meetings, make notes of any items of importance that should be included in the next meeting. Meetings are held at intervals, from fortnightly to quarterly, depending on the circumstances, but it is important that meetings are arranged well in advance so that they are clearly seen as part of the structure.

Briefing groups are not intended to replace other channels of communication, but to operate at the same time. Urgent matters should of course be dealt with immediately and not saved for the next team briefing session. However, the importance of team briefings can be shown by a comment from Mike Judge of Talbot Motors. 'Team briefing is the cornerstone of our communications policy'.

A survey of Britain's largest companies and public sector organisations, 222 organisations in all, undertaken in 1987 by the employee consultants, Vista, found that 86 per cent had installed a system of team briefing and 59 per cent claimed that it reached beyond the supervisory grades to all levels of staff.

Research by John Storey in the late 1980s revealed, however, that the real issue was not whether an organisation 'had team briefing' but how it was used in practice, and with what coverage across the organisations. His research suggests that there were difficulties on each of these fronts. For example, it was hard to find a case where the system was being uniformly applied in practice. There were usually whole departments where briefings had not taken place. In companies with trade unions, shop stewards were in some instances rather better informed than the first line supervisors who were supposed to be giving the briefings. These supervisors said they felt exposed in transmitting a brief about topics where they might be challenged and be made to look foolish. This was particularly a complaint made by supervisors in British Rail, for example.

(a) How does the team briefing work as a communication method?
(b) Why are team briefings not used solely as a communication method within the organisation?
(c) What are the benefits of team briefing to the business?
(d) What, according to the John Storey, are the main problems with team briefings as a communication method?

communicate;
- there is insufficient guidance or leadership to control the meeting;
- body language creates a barrier.

Oral communication Oral communication can take place other than in face-to-face situations in a business. The **telephone** is a common method of oral communication between individuals in remote locations or even within an organisation's premises. It provides some of the interactive advantages of face-to-face communication, while saving the time involved in travelling from one place to another. It is, however, more 'distant' and impersonal than an interview for the discussion of sensitive matters and does not provide written 'evidence'. This disadvantage can be overcome by written confirmation.

Sometimes messages can be communicated to groups of employees through a **public address system**. This might operate through loudspeakers placed at strategic points, eg in workshops or yards, where staff cannot be located or reached by telephone. The more recent, electronic method of paging individuals who move around and cannot be located is the 'bleeper'. This alerts the user to a message waiting for him at a pre-arranged telephone number. Finally, many businesses now subscribe to **mobile communications** services, such as Cellnet or Vodaphone.

Communications and information technology

A communication network in a business is concerned with the movement of data between one part of the organisation and another. We have seen the different networks that can be used. The communication networks above tend to use the more traditional communication media, such as telephones, memos, face-to-face, etc.

Information technology (IT) has revolutionised our ability to store, retrieve and send data to any user. Videoconferencing, for example, allows individuals all over the world to interact as if they were sitting in the same meeting room in the same location. 'Faxes', electronic mail and telexes let a business transmit information in both text and image form anywhere and at any time.

Answerphones can record telephone messages if an individual is not at her desk. So, for example, if a company has a subsidiary on the other side of the world, it can still communicate with it during or outside normal office hours. Information is sent and will be received when individuals start work at the subsidiary. Cellnet phones, notebook computers and modems mean that individual managers can deal with clients while they are on the move.

IT can be effective for 'sending' written information, eg printed memos stored on floppy disks. It can also be very useful when sending information in a less tangible form, eg the tone of voice, facial expression or the general atmosphere in which the communication takes place.

Teleconferencing systems, for example, incorporate live TV links, to allow visual as well as verbal communication.

Factors affecting choice of medium

There are a number of factors that affect which medium a business will use in any situation.

- Direction of communication. Some methods may only be suitable for downward communication, such as films and posters. Other methods are useful for upwards communication only, such as suggestion schemes. Many methods are useful for both.

QUESTION 4

Identify 2 types of message that would be suitable to send by each of the media above and 2 types that would be unsuitable. Explain your answers.

- Nature of the communication. The choice of communication method may depend on the nature of the message being sent. For example, a comment from a manager to a subordinate about unsatisfactory work may need to be confidential. It is important for the manager to choose a method which does this.
- Many messages are best sent by the use of more than one communication medium. Company rules, for example, might most effectively be communicated verbally on an induction course and as a written summary for employees to take away as a reminder.
- Costs. Films, videos and some tapeslides can be expensive. A business must decide whether the message could be sent just as well by other media.
- Variety. If, for example, a company tries to communicate too many messages by means of a noticeboard, then employees may stop reading it. To make sure messages are sent effectively, a variety of media should be used.
- Speed. If something needs communicating immediately then verbal or electronic communications tend to be quickest.
- Is a record needed? If it is, there is no point in verbally passing on the information. If it is communicated verbally, it may need written confirmation.
- Length of message. If the message is long, verbal communication may mean the receiver does not remember everything that has been said. If a simple yes or no answer is needed, written communication might not be suitable.

Barriers to communication

We have seen that effective communication will take place if the message is received and understood by the receiver. There are a number of factors that might prevent this from happening.

The skills of the sender and receiver The ability of the sender to explain a message and the receiver to understand it are important in communication. If an order must be sent out by a certain date, but the sender simply asks for it to be sent as early as possible, communication would not have been effective. If the receiver does not understand what stocks to take the order from, incorrect goods may be sent.

Jargon A word or phrase which has a technical or specialised meaning is known as jargon. The terms understood by a certain group of people may be meaningless to those who don't have this knowledge. One example of this was in Schools of Motoring, where for many years drivers were given the instruction 'clutch in' or 'clutch out', which nearly always confused the trainee. Later the instruction was changed to 'clutch down' and 'clutch up'. Technical information about a product which is not understood by the marketing department may result in misleading advertising and poor sales.

Choice of communication channel or medium

Sometimes the channel or medium chosen to send the message may not communicate the information effectively. An example of this might be where a manager attempts to pass a message to an employee, but would have been more successful if the message had gone through a representative. Another example is that safety campaigns are sometimes unsuccessful because slogans and posters are used to persuade individual employees about the importance of safe working practices rather than changes being discussed.

Perceptions and attitudes How employees perceive other people can affect how they interpret the message that is sent. Employees are more likely to have confidence in people they trust, because of past experience of their reliability. On the other hand, if an employee has learned to distrust someone, then what she says will be either ignored or treated with caution. Unit 57 also showed that the way employees view things can be affected by being part of a group.

Form of the message If the message is unclear or unexpected the receiver is unlikely to understand it or remember it. The rate at which we forget is considerable. We have probably forgotten half of what we hear within a few hours of hearing it, and no more than 10 per cent will remain after two or three days.
The sender of the message must make sure it:
■ does not contain too much information;
■ is not poorly written;
■ is not presented too quickly;
■ is not presented in a way that the receiver does not expect;
■ conveys the information that he actually wants to communicate;
■ is written in a way that the receiver will understand it.

Stereotypes People can often have beliefs about others. This may result in a **stereotype** (☞ unit 55) of some people. It is possible that, if one person has a stereotype of another, this may affect how they interpret a message. So, for example, if a male manager has a certain stereotype of women being less rational and able than men, his first reaction might be to ignore a female manager's communication because he believes she does not understand the information.

Length of chain of command or distance If information is passed down by word of mouth through a number of receivers, it is possible for the message to be distorted. This may result in the wrong emphasis or wrong information being received by the individual or group at the end of the communication chain. Industrial relations problems in business have sometimes been a result of a long chain of command (☞ unit 63).

Wrong target for the message Businesses sometimes send the wrong information to the wrong person. This can result in costly delays and errors and perhaps a poor image in the eyes of the public.

Breakdown of the channel This could be due to technical problems. For example, a business may rely on its management information system on the computerised network. If this breaks down, businesses might have problems dealing with enquiries. Banks, for example, are unable to tell customers what their balances are if computer terminals are not working.

QUESTION 5 Dave Almond of Repro Ltd has just installed two Apple Macintosh computers which make use of design software. Computers had not been previously used by the business for design. Part of the package when he bought them was an intensive three day training period where he would be shown the basic operations of the machine and how to use the software. This is only designed to get him started. He has been told that any other problems should be solved by consulting Operations Manual or by trial and error. If all else fails, there is a number to ring where an experienced operator can answer his problems, although the operator is unlikely to be there all the time.
   Dave now has to train his staff. They are used to designing page layouts, but have only a limited knowledge of computer operation. Dave will spend the next week showing them how to use the equipment, with hands on experience and worksheets to follow. Some of the staff are a little nervous and also wonder whether Dave's own training period was long enough.

What problems are there likely to be in:
(a) Dave interpreting the information about the computer he gets from the training;
(b) Dave passing the information to his staff?

Key terms

Channel of communication - the route by which a message is communicated from sender to receiver.
Communication media - the written, oral or technological methods used to communicate a message.
Network - the links that allow a message to be communicated between a number of people.

Summary

1. Why is good communication important for a business?
2. Why might a business want feedback in the communication process?
3. Explain the difference between:
   (a) formal and informal communication;
   (b) lateral and vertical communication.
4. How might upward communication be useful to a business?
5. Give an example of a message that might be sent using the following communication networks.
   (a) The circle.
   (b) The chain.
   (c) The wheel.
   (d) A connected network.
6. State 5 methods of written communication that a business might use.
7. When might face-to-face communication be more useful than written communication?
8. Explain 3 benefits to a business of using IT to communicate information.
9. State 5 factors that might affect the choice of communication.
10. State 5 barriers to communication.

Question

Pearson's Brewery Distribution Depot

'If there's something wrong, I was usually the last person to know about it; messages from the pubs never seemed to be getting through to the right people.' This was one of the first comments Bob Englefield heard when he took over as distribution manager of Pearson's Brewery, a medium sized business located in Essex, which served the East Anglia region.

The comment was made by one of the local planners in the large distribution depot of the brewery. Bob was carrying out a series of interviews with his staff to find out both his own workforce's and the publicans' views about how the depot was operating.

The depot's organisation was divided into 3 sections.

■ In the office were 4 clerical assistants who took incoming calls from the publicans whom the brewery supplied. The publicans were usually phoning in their weekly orders, but would also phone if deliveries were late or incomplete.

■ Also in the office, but in a sectioned off area, were 4 load planners who worked at computer terminals, sorting and organising the delivery loads between pubs.

■ In the rest of the depot there were 65 delivery employees who carried out the deliveries to the pubs. They communicated with the office via their supervisor, who collected the delivery plans at the start of the day and gave them to the employees making the deliveries.

The present system was that when the telephone rang in the office with an order any one of the 4 assistants would answer it. The load planners would then try to group orders together, but there were no regular delivery rounds. The supervisor prided himself on getting orders out quickly - he would give them out on a random basis to the delivery workers who, therefore, rarely made regular visits to one set of pubs.

Through his interviews, Bob detected a number of problems with the system.

■ Deliveries were often late. The delivery workers were not very motivated by the work and would 'spin out' a delivery in order to earn overtime.

■ Communication between the office and the delivery workers was poor, resulting in poor relations between the two groups.

■ Within the office the 2 groups appeared to work in isolation. Each did not know what the other group was doing.

■ Publicans felt that there was a lack of interest in their problems. If publicans phoned in on Friday with a rush order, or to find out why a delivery had not been made, they got the impression that no one wanted to help them.

Bob had previously worked in a small brewery where everyone was on first name terms and where good communications with customers was a major objective. He was surprised with the contrast between Pearson's and his old company.

(a) Identify and explain an example of
   (i) poor vertical;
   (ii) poor lateral;
   communication within Pearson's brewery distribution depot.

(b) Why do problems exist in the way Pearsons communicate with their customers, the publicans?

(c) Why might communication within a large brewery be more difficult than within a smaller brewery?

(d) Devise a new way of organising the office workers and delivery workers to improve the communication within the business and with the publicans.

(e) If Bob was to introduce your new plan, suggest and explain how he might be able to communicate the changes he proposes to:
   (i) the workforce;
   (ii) the publicans.

The structure of a business organisation

Unit 3 explained that a business is an example of an **organisation**. There are certain types of business organisation, including sole traders, partnerships and limited companies which may have similar financial and legal structures. However, each business organisation will have a different internal STRUCTURE - the way in which it is organised. The internal structure will take into account such things as:

- the relationships between individuals;
- who is in charge;
- who has authority to make decisions;
- who carries out decisions;
- how information is communicated.

This is often known as the **formal** organisation of the business. Although organisations will vary from one business to another, there are some similarities. For example, many large companies are controlled by a few directors, are divided into departments with managers, section heads and have many workers in each department.

One method of organising a business is where managers put people together to work effectively based on their skills and abilities. The structure is 'built up' or it 'develops' as a result of the employees of the business. In contrast a structure could be **created** first, with all appropriate job positions outlined, and then people employed to fill them. The entrepreneur Richard Branson allegedly worked out a complete organisation structure for his Virgin Atlantic airline before setting up the company and then recruited the 102 people needed to fill all the positions.

Organisation charts

Many firms produce ORGANISATION CHARTS. These illustrate the structure of the business. Figure 63.1 shows a 'traditional' type of chart. It is a chart for an engineering firm, Able Engineering. Different types of businesses are likely to have different charts. The chart in Figure 63.1 may be simpler than one drawn for BP or ICI, although the style will be similar. It may be more involved, however, than a chart for a partnership.

Why do businesses draw such charts?

- To spot communication problems. An organisation chart indicates how employees are linked to other employees in the business. If information is not received, the business can find where the communication breakdown has occurred by tracing the communication chain along the chart.
- Organisation charts help individuals see their position in a firm. This can help them appreciate their responsibilities, who has authority over them and who they are accountable to.
- Organisation charts allow firms to pinpoint areas where specialists are needed. For example, in Figure 63.1, Able Engineering recognises it needs designers and draughtspeople as part of the production 'team'.

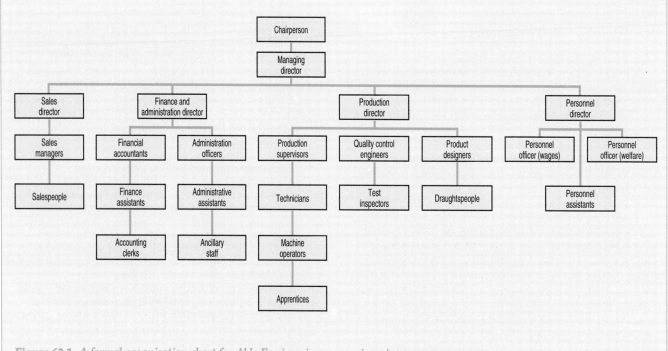

Figure 63.1 *A formal organisation chart for Able Engineering, an engineering company*

■ Organisation charts show how different sections of the firm relate to each other. For example, the chart for Able Engineering shows the relationship between salespeople and technicians. They are both at the same level in the hierarchy, but work in different departments and are responsible to different managers.

Simply producing an organisation chart is of limited use to a business. The firm will only achieve its objectives if it understands the relationships between employees and other parts of the business.

QUESTION 1 Ainscough Ltd produce ground support equipment for the aviation industry. The company has a traditional organisational structure. The managing director is responsible to the chairperson and has a sales director, finance director, personnel director and production director accountable to her. On the production side of the business, there are a works manager, technicians, test engineers and machine operators. In addition, the company employs a number of personnel assistants, financial and administrative staff, and salespeople.

(a) Draw an organisation chart from the information about Ainscough Engineering Ltd.
(b) Briefly explain two ways in which the business might use the chart.

Chain of command and span of control

When deciding on its organisation structure, a business must take into account two important factors - the management **hierarchy** and the **span of control**.

The HIERARCHY in a business is the order or levels of management in a firm, from the lowest to the highest rank. It shows the CHAIN OF COMMAND within the organisation - the way authority is organised. Orders pass down the levels and information passes up (☞ unit 62). Businesses must also consider the number of links or levels in the chain of command. R. Townsend in his book *Up the Organisation* , estimated that each extra level of management in the hierarchy reduced the effectiveness of communication by about 25 per cent. No rules are laid down on the most effective number of links in the chain. However, businesses generally try to keep chains as short as possible.

Another factor to be taken into account is the SPAN OF CONTROL. This refers to the number of subordinates working under a superior or manager. In other words, if one production manager has ten subordinates his span of control is ten. Henri Fayol (☞ unit 58) argued that the span of control should be between three and six because:

■ there should be tight managerial control from the top of the business;
■ there are physical and mental limitations to any single manager's ability to control people and activities.

A narrow span of control, has the advantage for a firm of tight control and close supervision. It also allows better

co-ordination of subordinates' activities. In addition, it gives managers time to think and plan without having to be burdened with too many day to day problems. A narrow span also ensures better communication with subordinates, who are sufficiently small in number to allow this to occur.

A wide span of control, however, offers greater decision making authority for subordinates and may improve job satisfaction (☞ unit 48). In addition, there are likely to be lower costs involved in supervision. Figure 63.2 shows two organisation charts. In the first (a), there is a long chain of command, but a narrow span of control. The second (b) shows a wide span, but a short chain.

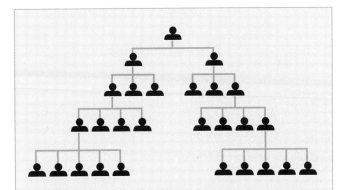

(a) A long chain of command and a narrow span of control. A production department may look like this. One manager is helped by a few assistant managers, each responsible for supervisors. These supervisors are responsible for skilled workers, who are in charge of a group of semi-skilled workers. Close supervision is needed to make sure quality is maintained.

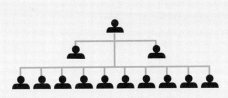

(b) A short chain of command and a wide span of control. A higher or further education department may look like this, with a 'head' of department, a few senior staff and many lecturing staff. Staff will want a degree of independence.

Figure 63.2

Authority and responsibility

Employees in the hierarchy will have responsibility and authority. Employees at lower levels have less responsibility and less authority. However, these terms do not mean the same thing. Although a task may be **delegated** (or passed down) from a superior to a subordinate, eg a manager to an office worker, the manager still has the **responsibility** for making sure the job is done.

Authority, on the other hand, is the ability to carry out the task. For example, it would make no sense asking the office worker to pay company debts if she did not have the authority to sign cheques. It is, therefore, possible to delegate authority, but not responsibility.

QUESTION 2 Developments at Austin Rover, Ford, Peugeot, Massey Ferguson and other manufacturers have resulted in a new type of production line manager. At one time production managers would concentrate on responding to instructions and on meeting schedules. In the companies mentioned, there would be a number of production managers in a variety of departments, such as process engineering, production engineering, quality control and so on. Each area would have its own separate and independent hierarchy. Over the last few years things have changed. The production manager's role has changed into a new one - that of manufacturing manager. Manufacturing managers have greater responsibilities and undertake a wider range of tasks. They are more aware of budgets and costs. The management accounting practice of allocation of costs (both variable costs and a proportion of fixed costs) to zones of production has become widespread. Manufacturing managers heading 'cost centres' are expected not merely to ensure a regular smooth operation but, additionally, to find imaginative ways of reducing costs.

But the expanded role of manufacturing managers has extended beyond budgets and accounting. They now also need to be aware of customer needs by searching for continuous improvements. The days of just being responsible for planned schedules have now gone. When asked whether their roles have changed at all, the typical response is to emphasise the drastic nature of the change and to mention the additional responsibilities they now have for quality, efficiency, costs, people, and for managing change. The separate hierarchies have gone. The span of control of manufacturing managers has increased as they have taken responsibility for a wider mix of employees.

A senior manufacturing manager at Austin Rover, Longbridge explained: 'Yes, there has been a massive shift! Fundamentally, we have moved from how a production person would run it to how a businessperson would ... that is, it is no longer just a question of meeting schedules, we do that now with monotonous regularity ...'

Source: adapted from *Management of Human Resources*, J.Storey, 1992, Blackwell.

(a) Explain the changes in the hierarchy and span of control of businesses in the article.
(b) What are likely to be the effects of the changes on:
  (i) the businesses mentioned;
  (ii) employees lower down the chain of command?

Line and staff authority

Line and staff are terms used to describe the type of relationship that managers may have with others in the hierarchy.

Line authority Line authority is usual in a hierarchy. It shows the authority that a manager has over a subordinate. In Figure 63.1, the production director would have line authority over the designers. Communication will flow down from the superior to the subordinate in the chain of command. The advantage of this is that a manager can allocate work and control subordinates, who have a clear understanding of who is giving them instructions. The manager can also delegate authority to others if they feel this will make decision making more effective.

In large organisations, the chain of command can be very long. This means that instructions given by those at the top of the chain of command may take time before they are carried out at a lower level.

Staff authority Many organisations now have within them both line and staff (or functional) authority. Staff authority might be when a manager or department in a business has a function within another department, for example, giving specialist advice. A marketing manager may give advice to the production department based on market research into a new product. Personnel managers have responsibilities for personnel matters in all departments. Although the specialist can give advice, they have no authority to make decisions in the other department.

Problems may occur in a business if people do not understand where authority and responsibility rest. This means that managers must know whether their authority is line or staff. Unfortunately, this can lead to friction. Line managers are sometimes thought of as 'first class citizens' and staff managers are thought of as costly 'overheads' who are not contributing anything of worth to the organisation.

Centralisation and decentralisation

Centralisation and decentralisation refer to the extent to which authority is DELEGATED in a business. If there was complete centralisation, then subordinates would have no authority at all. Complete decentralisation would mean subordinates would have all the authority to take decisions. It is unlikely that any business operates in either of these ways. Even if authority is delegated to a subordinate, it is usual for the manager to retain responsibility.

Certain functions within a business will always be centralised, because of their importance. For example, decisions about budget allocation are likely to be centralised as they affect the whole company. The decision to distribute profits is also taken only by a few.

Advantages of centralisation Why might a business centralise authority?
■ Senior management have more control of the business, eg budgets.
■ Procedures, such as ordering and purchasing, can be standardised throughout the organisation, leading to

economies of scale.

■ Senior managers can make decisions from the point of view of the business as a whole. Subordinates would tend to make decisions from the point of view of their department or section. This allows senior managers to maintain a balance between departments or sections. For example, if a company has only a limited amount of funds available to spend over the next few years, centralised management would be able to share the funds out between production, marketing, research and development, and fixed asset purchases in different departments etc.

■ Senior managers should be more experienced and skilful in making decisions. In theory, centralised decisions by senior people should be of better quality than decentralised decisions made by others less experienced.

■ In times of crisis, the firm may need strong leadership by a central group of senior managers.

Advantages of decentralisation or delegation Some delegation is necessary in all firms because of the limits to the amount of work senior managers can carry out. Tasks that might be delegated include staff selection, quality control, customer relations and purchasing and stock control. A greater degree of decentralisation - over and above the minimum which is essential - has a number of advantages.

■ It reduces the stress and burdens of senior management.

■ It provides subordinates with greater job satisfaction by giving them more say in decision-making, which affects their work (☞ unit 48 on McGregor's Theory Y).

■ Subordinates may have a better knowledge of 'local' conditions affecting their area of work. This should allow them to make more informed, well-judged choices. For example, salespeople may have more detailed knowledge of their customers and be able to advise them on purchases.

■ Delegation should allow greater flexibility and a quicker response to changes. If problems do not have to be referred to senior managers, decision-making will be quicker. Since decisions are quicker, they are easier to change in the light of unforeseen circumstances which may arise.

■ By allowing delegated authority, management at middle and junior levels are groomed to take over higher positions. They are given the experience of decision making when carrying out delegated tasks. Delegation is therefore important for management development.

Alternative forms of business structure

Despite the variety of business organisation that exists, there are four main types of structure most often found.

The entrepreneurial structure In this type of business structure, all decisions are made centrally. There are few collective decisions and a great reliance on 'key' workers. It is often found in businesses where decisions have to be made quickly, such as newspaper editing.

Most small businesses also have this type of structure, as illustrated in Figure 63.3 (a). These businesses rely on the expertise of one or two people to make decisions. However, as the firm grows, this structure can cause inefficiency as too much of a load is placed on those making decisions.

The bureaucratic or pyramid structure This is the traditional structure for most medium sized and large businesses and perhaps the most well known. It is illustrated in Figure 63.3 (b). Decision making is shared throughout the business. Employees are each given a role and procedures are laid down which determine their behaviour at work.

Specialisation of tasks (☞ unit 1) is possible. This means

QUESTION 3 Federalism is a growing trend in business. Countless companies, from Benetton to BP, and from Coca-Cola to IBM, have adopted a variety of new structures which have been dubbed 'federal'. The principle of federalism is that power resides with

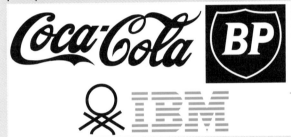

'constituent parts'. These 'parts' do, however, give some of that power to the centre for the benefit of all. Federalism is distinct from decentralisation, which implies a delegation of power from an all-powerful centre. The ideal federation is non-centralised rather than decentralised; power is withheld from the centre by constituent units, not handed down from it. It allows the parts to maintain their own strategies and vision while unifying for common purposes. They can reap the advantages of smallness and independence on some issues, such as sales and service, with the benefits of economies of scale and integration on others, such as finance and purchasing.

An example of a new, supposedly 'federal' organisation is Benetton, the Italian clothing combine. This consists partly of subcontracted production by suppliers and retailing by franchises, plus centralised finance, design, development, purchasing and planning. But can it really be called a federation when the main task of the suppliers is to serve the centre? Most franchises are also controlled with iron authority by the central organisation.

Source: adapted from the *Financial Times*, December 1992.

(a) How does federalism differ from decentralisation?
(b) How has Benetton applied federalism to its business?
(c) What benefits might there be of federalism over centralisation for a business?

that a departmental structure, with finance, personnel, production and marketing employees, can be set up (☞ unit 3). Specialisation may allow the business to enjoy economies of scale. Recently, this type of structure has been criticised for its inability to change and meet new demands.

The matrix structure This emphasises getting people with particular specialist skills together into project teams, as illustrated in Figure 63.3(c). Individuals within the team have their own responsibility. The matrix structure was developed to overcome some of the problems with the entrepreneurial and bureaucratic structures.

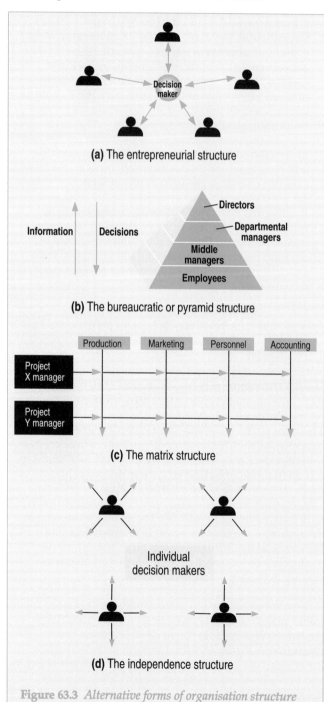

(a) The entrepreneurial structure

(b) The bureaucratic or pyramid structure

(c) The matrix structure

(d) The independence structure

Figure 63.3 *Alternative forms of organisation structure*

Managers often argue that this is the best way of organising people, because it is based on the expertise and skills of employees and gives scope for people lower down the organisation to use their talents effectively. For example, a project manager looking into the possibility of developing a new product may draw on the expertise of employees with skills in design, research and development, marketing, costing etc. A college running a course for unemployed people may draw on the skills of a number of lecturers in different departments. In this way, a matrix structure can also operate within a business that has a bureaucratic structure. The matrix model fits in with managers who have a Theory Y view of employees (☞ unit 48). It has recently lost favour because it often needs expensive support systems, such as extra secretarial and office staff. There are also problems with co-ordinating a team drawn from different departments.

The independence structure This emphasises the individual and is almost a 'non-organisation'. The other three methods put together the contributions of a number of people so that the sum of their efforts is greater than the parts. All efforts are co-ordinated so that the business benefits. The independence structure is a method of providing a support system. Barristers' chambers and doctor's clinics have worked in this way. It is attractive to independent people who are confident of their ability to be successful. This form of organisation tends to be unsuitable for most types of business because of the lack of control and co-ordination.

Factors influencing organisational structures

There are a number of factors which might influence the organisation and the structure of a business.

■ Size. As a business grows, it is likely to move away from an entrepreneurial structure towards one where authority is passed to other employees. A large firm will also tend to have a longer chain of command, with more levels in the hierarchy.

■ Views of the owners or leadership styles. If owners wish to retain control in the business, they will want a narrow span of control. Owners or managers who wish to motivate or encourage employees may delegate decision making.

■ Business objectives. If the business decides to expand rapidly, perhaps by merger, it is likely to find that its span of control gets wider. An example might be a business setting up an operation in a foreign country or deciding to sell into a foreign market.

■ External factors. Changes in external factors can often influence business organisation. In periods of recession or rising costs, a business may be forced to reduce its chain of command to cut costs. Similarly, in a period of growth (☞ unit 67), a firm may employ extra managers as specialists to gain economies of scale.

■ Changes in technology. The introduction of new technology can change the structure of a business. For example, a new system of production may remove the need for quality controllers, or an information technology system could reduce the role of administration.

QUESTION 4 J. McCague and Sons Ltd have grown quickly as an insurance broker, benefiting from the increase in commissions from household and car insurance as a result of increased premiums in recent years. They have a family business, with McCague and his 2 sons acting as managing director and managers of the household and car sections. No one else in the organisation (which employs 30 people) has any major decision making role.

McCague wants to move into the travel insurance business as he has seen other brokers making good rates of commission in this area, especially with the growing number of independent travellers. But he does not have the time or expertise to develop customers in this area. Within his company, however, he knows that there are several employees who have shown flair for marketing or who have had some experience in the travel trade. He also wants to bring his daughter into the business, who has just graduated from the Warwick Business School.

(a) What type of organisation structure do McCague and Sons Ltd have at present? Explain your answer.
(b) What reorganisation would you suggest McCague would need if he is going to cater to the travel insurance business?
(c) What problems will he face in trying to create a new structure?

Key terms

Authority - the right to command a situation, a task or an activity.
Business structure - the way in which a business is organised.
Chain of command - the way authority and power are passed down in a business.
Delegation - authority passed down from superior to subordinate.
Hierarchy - the order or levels of management of a business, from the lowest to the highest.
Organisation chart - a diagram which illustrates the structure of an organisation.
Responsibility - the duty to complete a task.
Span of control - the number of subordinates working under a superior.

Summary

1. What are the features of the internal structure of a business?
2. How might an organisation chart be used in a firm's induction programme?
3. Draw a simple organisation chart showing:
   (a) a partnership with two partners and 6 employees;
   (b) a large company with a board of directors, six departments, and two more levels in the hierarchy.
4. What is meant by a 'wide span of control'?
5. What problems might a 'wide span of control' have for a business?
6. Explain the difference between line and staff authority.
7. Why might businesses have both line and staff authority?
8. Give three situations where centralised decision making may be useful for a business.
9. State 4 advantages of delegation.
10. What problems might a matrix structure cause for a business?
11. What type of business might be organised with:
    (a) an entrepreneurial structure;
    (b) an independence structure?

Question

General Accident and the insurance industry

It's 16.32 on a Friday afternoon. The electronic indicator board high on the wall of General Accident's new Glasgow offices shows that 1,365 calls have been handled by the claims staff. Five staff are on the phone dealing with customers' enquiries.

No calls are waiting to be answered, a pleasing statistic for Alistair Waters, at 32, one of a new generation of insurance managers at the UK's second biggest insurance company. He says that 98 per cent of calls are handled within three seconds and most claims are handled within two days.

It is a far cry from the recent past when it could take General Accident weeks to respond to its policy holders. But, in common with other insurers, GA is changing its ways, over-hauling its traditional bureaucratic organisation to transform relationships with its customers.

Stung by losses of more than £2 billion in 1990 and 1991 and spurred by competitors who have been quick to take advantage of new technologies, the UK's biggest insurers have cut jobs, reducing numbers by up to a third in some cases. But there is more to the industry's reorganisation than a simple reduction in staff. In many companies whole layers of middle management have been removed, while new responsibilities are being given to lower-grade staff. Status-conscious hierarchies are giving way to flatter, more responsive and more goal-oriented businesses.

The changes are all the more striking at General Accident because the company has long been one of the industry's most conservative, dominated by generations of Scottish actuaries. Yet two years of losses have underlined the need for change. One of the main aims of the reorganisation - orchestrated by the head of UK operations, Bob Scott - has been to improve the speed with which claims are paid, as well as the quality of back-up services and complaints procedures.

Such changes have had an important influence on the organisation's culture, with the company shifting from what Scott calls an 'administrative-centred' approach to one based on 'long-term customer service', heavily influenced by the experience of companies such as Toyota. GA has been turned 'inside out', says Ray Andrews, a former Saatchi and Saatchi executive, recruited in 1990 to head an overhaul of GA's internal communications.

Scott explains how management and organisational changes have paved the way for much more rapid handling of claims. 'The goal is to handle all claims within five days', says Scott. Five years ago 'a claim would have been processed by the clerk, sent to the under manager, then the manager to be checked and finally back to the clerk. The whole process could take weeks', says Scott. 'You could justify the old system on the grounds that it guaranteed accuracy. But it destroyed people's initiative.' Under the new system GA's lower-grade claims staff have been given more responsibility to carry out basic tasks. 'They have to get it right. They are responsible'.

Computers have helped. Over the past three years, GA has abolished its typing pool and has weaned staff away from the use of paper files. Staff at GA's 'new-model' office in Dundee - where the new systems were first introduced - make extensive use of computer training techniques, as part of a programme which equips them to handle all aspects of insurance transactions - underwriting, claims and accounts, and the like - instead of the much narrower focus of the past.

While lower-grade staff are being asked to be more responsible, managers are under pressure to take a more active interest in the development of the company's business. For a start there are fewer of them. Scott has pushed through a radical overhaul of GA's branch structure, replacing over two-thirds of the company's 60 or so branch managers. A middle management position, responsible purely for office administration, has been scrapped.

Relieved of many of their control and checking functions, managers are being encouraged to develop areas of new business. John Munro and his management team in Dundee, for example, are examining ways of persuading motor policy holders to take out home or creditor insurance.

'There is much more emphasis on accountability', says Munro, who runs the group's Dundee office. 'We have much more room to take initiatives.' There are now six management layers, against eight previously, improving the company's responsiveness and increasing the opportunities for younger managers such as Waters and Munro to rise within the organisation, where promotion is no longer tied to seniority and time serving.

Performance-related pay is becoming common and information about the company more widely disseminated. In the past, middle management has seen its control over information as a source of power, says Scott. By contrast GA senior management now report details of the company's performance.

All this is good news for younger managers such as Waters, who began working with GA 13 years ago at the group's offices in Ayr and began building up GA's direct motor subsidiary at the age of 29, a position of prominence unimaginable for a young manager even 10 years ago.

'Everyone is on first-name terms', says Waters. 'We are trying to develop an operation that downplays concern for status. It's much more open - more frank and more goal-orientated than in the past. All the layers have been taken away.

Source: the *Financial Times*, 1.3.1993.

(a) **What does the study indicate about the likely structure of General Accident before reorganisation took place?**

(b) **What factors may have influenced GA's decision to reorganise?**

(c) **What changes in the organisational structure took place during reorganisation?**

(d) **Discuss the likely effects of the move to greater authority and responsibility by subordinates on the operation of GA.**

(e) **What potential advantages will the reorganisation have for:**
    (i) GA;
    (ii) GA's customers;
    (iii) GA's junior managers;
    (iv) GA's senior managers?

What causes change in business?

Businesses today have to operate in rapidly changing markets and conditions. They can no longer rely on a constant stream of customers, the same production process or the same product over a long period of time. They must constantly be aware of, and be prepared to respond to, changes in a number of areas.

Developments in technology Unit 36 showed that the introduction of new technology can affect a business in many ways. There have, for example, been rapid changes in communications technology, production techniques and electronic components, in recent years.

Market changes Businesses must respond to changes in the markets in which they sell. This could mean a sudden increase in competition from new businesses, as was the case with computer software producers. It could also be competition for previously nationalised industries, such as when Mercury was allowed to compete with British Telecom or when private firms were allowed to bid for local government cleaning services. The Single European Market (☞ unit 70) and the opening up of markets in former communist countries are also likely to affect business activity.

Consumer tastes Businesses must also be prepared for changes in the tastes of consumers. Examples might be the purchase of environmentally friendly products, the desire for greater knowledge about products or the need for more efficient methods of shopping, such as purchasing based on information on Teletext.

Legislation Government legislation can force changes in business activity. Taxation of pollution (☞ unit 72) would affect the production methods of many firms. Safety standards, such as EC regulations for VDU users, are also likely to affect how employees operate. Government aid or subsidies may affect the possible location of a business (☞ unit 30).

Changes in the workforce Population changes will affect the age and make-up of the workforce. The 'demographic timebomb' (☞ unit 51) in the UK in the 1990s will result in changing recruitment policies for businesses. A falling population is also likely to change how a business plans its human resources.

The effects of rapid change

The rapid changes illustrated in the last section can have a number of effects on business.
- Product life cycles (☞ unit 20) could become shorter. This means that businesses must constantly be looking to develop new and profitable products or services.
- The role of market research is likely to increase. A firm must not be 'surprised' by sudden changes in the market. Research and forecasting techniques should help a firm to predict more accurately the situation in future. Even product-led firms are starting to become aware of the need to become more market-orientated.
- Research and development will be essential in industries where rapid change is taking place. As well as anticipating market changes, a business must be prepared to respond to the needs of the market with new products, which can compete with those of competitors.
- Retraining of managers and 'shop floor' workers might be necessary. This may be to learn skills associated with new technology or to develop skills to meet changing consumer tastes. Examples might be the training of many typists in word processing or the learning of foreign languages by UK business people wishing to enter developing markets.
- Businesses must take account of changes in their human resource planning (☞ unit 51). This could mean employing a more flexible workforce that could be changed quickly to meet the needs of the business, for example part time workers or the use of job sharing.
- A business must develop a culture and organisation which is prepared to respond to change.

QUESTION 1 In 1993, a Luxembourg based company, Société Européanne des Satellites (SES), decided to launch two new satellites with digital TV capacity, which would enable a far greater number of channels to be transmitted.

The Astra satellite system which currently operates carries everything from Sky TV to Cable News Network and Eurosport on 2 satellites. A third is being completed and the two new 'digital' systems will allow 180 channels to be available by 1995.

Apart from the extra channels available to existing users, the main business opportunity was seen as charging for individual films. 50 or 60 channels can be devoted, for example, to the top 10 films, with staggered times.

Talks had begun with microchip manufacturers and SES believes the new satellite channel decoders could be available by 1994. SES argued that to be successful, it was vital that there was a single transmission standard which can be unscrambled and unlocked with a 'smart card'.

Source: adapted from the *Financial Times*, 23.2.,1993.

(a) Describe the changes which are likely to take place in this industry in the future.
(b) Discuss the effects on:
   (i) existing TV companies;
   (ii) new businesses wishing to enter the market;
   (iii) satellite decoder manufacturers.

■ Quality is likely to become more important as consumer awareness develops and competition increases. Firms must consider the quality of their products and also their after sales service and customer relations. An example in the early 1990s has been the aim of many producers to achieve a BS5750 quality standard.

Why manage change?

The management of change in business has grown in importance in recent years. Under pressure from competitors, higher costs and the early 1990s recession, many firms in the UK have developed company-wide change programmes. Companies such as BT, British Airways and ICI have 'turned around' their organisations through managed change.

There are some examples of firms that have made only minor changes to their business operations and remained successful. The Morgan Car Company (☞ unit 35) still retain many of the original production methods and design features that have been part of their operation since the 1930s. They argue that it is exactly these 'original' features that attract consumers. However, many firms have refused to change or did not respond and went out of business, such as the British motorcycle industry and certain holiday firms. In the face of rapid change and competition, it is likely that firms must respond or go out of business.

Criticisms of management

Some (eg T. Nichols, 1986) have argued that, historically, the problems of British business in managing change and increasing productivity have resulted from the ineffectiveness of management. It has been suggested that British managers in the past have not:
■ scored highly in their ability to plan and organise production compared to management in Germany and Japan;
■ been as market orientated as those in America and Japan, often producing goods which were uncompetitive;
■ been as highly qualified as managers in other countries - in the 1970s a Department of Industry enquiry found it 'Disquieting that there is evidence that industrial managers in Britain tend to be less qualified in academic and vocational terms than Continental counterparts';
■ invested in skilled workers - in 1980 German management were making six times more apprenticeships available than those in Britain;
■ been concerned with long term growth generated by major investment, but only in short term profits.

Today it could be argued that British management are far more aware of what is required for businesses to achieve success in markets. The ways in which they manage change are dealt with in the sections that follow.

The role of the personnel department

Unit 51 explained the role of the personnel department. It has been suggested that a new approach to human resources is needed if a business is to manage change effectively. Traditionally, personnel managers enforced rules and procedures, and were less concerned with change. It has been suggested that if they became human resources managers, and more concerned with the following, then change would take place more effectively in business.
■ A move away from job evaluation and fixed grades towards performance related pay.
■ Pay and conditions negotiated with individuals rather than collectively.
■ An emphasis on team work rather than individual job design.
■ A flexible workforce trained in a variety of skills.
■ Encouraging people to be self-motivating rather than 'controlled'.

Some have argued that these aims would be achieved better if a business developed a company wide **culture** for change. This is dealt with in the next section.

Businesses are likely to face some resistance to change from parts of the workforce. Workers and certain levels of management sometimes fear the unknown. They feel safe with work practices, conditions and relationships that they have been used to for a period of time. Employees and managers may fear that they will be unable to carry out new tasks, may become unemployed or may face a fall in earnings. Individual workers might be concerned that they will no longer work with 'friends', or may be moved to a job which they dislike. If change is to be carried out effectively, the business must make certain that these fears are taken into account. Only if employees feel they can cope with change, will the business be operating to its potential.

QUESTION 2 In 1993, a new code of practice on managing change was introduced by Royal Mail. The code ensured that employees were informed of changes in working practices, such as the function of an office or its location, well before they took place. It also provided training and other assistance to help staff moving to new locations, changing from full to part time work or taking sabbaticals.

Employees who left would be offered workshops on getting a job, including interview skills training, and advice on setting up small businesses would also be made available.

The code was endorsed by both the Communication Managers' Association and the Union of Communication Workers. A spokesperson for the UCW said that the union's sole concern was over the interpretation of 'major changes'; something which seemed a minor change to a manager could represent a major change to the person affected.

Source: adapted from *Personnel Management*, July 1993.

(a) What methods suggested in the new Royal Mail code can help employees deal with change?
(b) Why might employees working for Royal Mail be resistant to change?

Developing an organisational culture for change

An **organisational culture** (☞ unit 51) includes the beliefs, norms and values of a business. It is a generally held view about how people should behave, the nature of working relationships and attitudes. Many companies, especially Japanese firms such as Honda, Toyota and Sony, place great emphasis on all employees understanding the company's 'culture'.

It has been suggested that a business which creates a culture of change is likely to manage it far more effectively. Management at the top must have a clear idea of how they expect the business to change. Structures, methods of training, management styles etc. must then alter to reflect this. Finally a culture must be established where all employed are aware of the new relationship and methods of working.

One model that has been used to implement change is total quality management (TQM). Unit 34 discussed how this can change the production techniques of a business and its operation. One feature of TQM is that everyone in the business is responsible for maintaining

and improving quality, including the quality of the product, production methods and the supply to the customer. TQM's motto is 'getting it right the first time' and this is applied to external customers and what are known as 'internal customers' - the people employees work with.

This approach helps develop a culture where all employees, managers etc. are trying to achieve the same goal, which should motivate, develop teamwork and improve communication, accountability and rewards.

Different approaches to managing change

Research by John Storey has suggested that the way businesses manage change can be classified into four different approaches, as shown in Table 64.1. Four studies of different companies can be used to illustrate these approaches.

Austin Rover One approach to managing change is for people at the 'top' of the business to plan out major restructuring programmes, without consultation. The 'Working with Pride' package at Austin Rover was designed by management without the involvement of unions. The main advantage of this method is that a company has a 'vision' of where it is going. It can compare where it is 'now' with where it was 'then'. It is possible, using this approach, to prepare departmental and personal action plans, set timetables and measure how far change has been achieved.

The main disadvantage of planning change from the top is that middle managers, supervisors and employees may not feel involved.

Massey Ferguson A different approach is to have unplanned or piecemeal initiatives designed to bring about change. Examples might be team briefings, quality circles (☞ unit 50) and performance appraisal (☞ unit 54).

At Massey Ferguson, the managing director held 'meetings with the chief' with unions and members of the workforce. A human resource director was also appointed. A number of initiatives took place at various times. These included:
■ small group meetings;
■ open communications;
■ a re-examination of incentive payments;
■ greater flexibility;
■ subcontracting.

A disadvantage of piecemeal initiatives is that they sometimes have different objectives. One might be trying to improve managerial leadership; another might be trying to encourage greater participation. They also tend to be short lived. In the face of cutbacks in the late 1980s, many Massey Ferguson initiatives were dropped.

British Rail Productivity agreements (☞ unit 49) are often used to help change take place. Unions agree to changes in work practices in exchange for extra payments based on achieving a certain output. These negotiated

---

QUESTION 3 Bosch is a German multinational with business activities in automotive components, electronics, telecommunications, consumer products and capital goods. It has recently set up its first manufacturing operation in the United Kingdom on a 200 acre site just west of Cardiff to make compact alternators for car-makers. Bosch Cardiff have adopted a total quality approach. The corporate values of the company include:
■ total quality to achieve a world market leadership position;
■ training and development to achieve continuous improvement in quality, productivity and individual skills;
■ meeting its responsibilities to customers, employees, suppliers and the local community;
■ being a single-status company;
■ having an organisational climate which encourages open communication, minimises hierarchy, and invites involvement and partnership;
■ being a responsive organisation, which not only encourages flexibility, teamworking and team development but which focuses on the individual in terms of accountability, recognition and reward.

A lot of effort was put into designing a statement of corporate values with the aim of motivating new employees, guiding everyone's actions in putting in place policies and procedures and developing a unique Bosch Cardiff culture. The corporate culture that is being developed there is a mixture of German, Welsh and Japanese influences.

Source: adapted from *Personnel Management*, July 1993.

(a) Why would Bosch need to take into account 'German, Welsh and Japanese influences' in developing a new company culture in Cardiff?
(b) How might the corporate values that have been introduced help the management of change?

Summary

1. State 5 factors that may cause change in a business.
2. How might change affect:
    (a) market research;
    (b) research and development;
    in a business?
3. Why is it important for businesses to manage change?
4. Explain 4 ways in which the personnel department can plan human resources to deal with change.
5. What is meant by 'developing an organisational culture for change'?
6. Briefly explain 4 approaches to change.

changes tend to be ad-hoc, without any co-ordinated policy by the business. British Rail is an example of an employer that has used this method, but others include Rolls Royce and Plessey.

Ford Motor Company A fourth method of change is where a 'total package' for change is put together. This is negotiated by both employers and unions together - a practice rarely found in British industry. Ford, however, is one example. In 1985, it informed the workforce about what it saw as a 'performance gap' between its British and overseas plants - and between British and Japanese producers. It also involved line managers in designing a negotiated national package. The negotiated package of new working practices in exchange for a 4 per cent productivity allowance was then passed to plant-by-plant negotiating teams.

Table 64.1 *Four different approaches to managing change*

	Imposed by management	Negotiated
Total package	AUSTIN ROVER'S WORKING WITH PRIDE	FORD MOTOR COMPANY
Ad-hoc initiatives	MASSEY FERGUSON	PRODUCTIVITY AGREEMENTS, EG BR, ROLLS ROYCE, PLESSEY

Question

Xerox

Xerox is a US document processing company, famous for its photocopying machines. In 1992 the chairman, Paul Allaire, revealed a radical plan to redesign the company's management structure in an attempt to solve a problem for many large companies - how to retain the flair and flexibility of a small business, without losing the advantages of being big.

The company became one of the fastest growing firms in the US after inventing the plain paper copier in 1959. It then faced anti-monopoly problems and competition from Japanese firms. In the 1980s, it fought back and was one of the few US firms to reclaim market share from the Japanese. This was largely due to its policy of total quality management (TQM) and benchmarking.

Allaire, who took over in 1990, decided a restructuring was needed whilst retaining the strengths of TQM and benchmarking. He looked at other companies that had introduced 'Act Small' policies. The shake up stemmed mainly from sweeping changes in the office equipment business. The photocopier was becoming part of a larger information technology business, including fax, full colour printing and scanning facilities. These new developments were also likely to lead to new competition. Allaire believed that Xerox must be more responsive to consumers' needs.

Under the new system at Xerox, there would be 9 'stand alone' businesses, each with responsibility for their own profits. The research and development department would feed ideas into all 9 'businesses', instead of operating as a traditional department.

Sceptics wondered whether Xerox would be able to speed up their notoriously slow ability to bring products to the market. However, the company was recently able to quicken this process by involving fewer levels of the hierarchy in decisions.

Allaire was anxious to develop a culture where each business would keep in mind the needs of the group as a whole. He argued that Xerox's strength came from its combined technological and global marketing abilities. One method used to establish a culture was to change the pay system. Middle management bonuses were based on the performance of the group rather than the individual.

Allaire was pleased with the changes in the company, but argued there was no room for complacency. Xerox, he says, will 'have to change more in the next five years than we have in the last ten'.

Source: adapted from the *Financial Times*, 1993.

(a) **Explain the factors which may have influenced the need to restructure the company in 1990.**
(b) **Discuss the effects that these changes had on the business.**
(c) **Why might total quality management and benchmarking have helped Xerox to regain market share in the 1980s?**
(d) **Explain one method Xerox used to develop an organisational culture and any problems that this might have led to.**
(e) **What approach to the management of change by Xerox is indicated in the article? Discuss the possible advantages and disadvantages of this approach.**

National Power

The staff who lived through the privatisation of the electricity supply industry may have thought they had had enough change to last them a lifetime. National Power staff, however, had been warned that change was to become a way of life. The company's chief executive, John Baker, made the point early in the life of the company that 'Change is the price of success in a tough and competitive world'.

The last two years have seen staff numbers fall by almost a half, reorganisation of the non-operational functions, increased flexibility and changed working practices throughout the company. During the same period productivity increased by 18 per cent. What effects did these changes have on industrial relations?

National Power inherited from the public sector a system of wage bargaining split into three tiers: one across the whole industry; one at company level; one at local committee level. There were also separate agreements for each of the three different groups of staff - manual employees, engineers and administrative staff. All the electricity boards negotiated with the trade unions on an industry-wide basis.

While this type of negotiation was appropriate to a public utility, to continue with this approach would have meant National Power, as a private company, sitting down with other generators, who are their competitors in the market, and with the distribution companies, who are their clients. They would also be fixing wage rates with the unions which bore no relationship to local market rates or the profitability of the company. They decided, therefore, that they must negotiate on their own.

In addition, because of the number of negotiating tiers involved, the system tended to be inefficient and slow to solve disputes. A grading appeal could take up to three years to be resolved and could involve ACAS. Also, the three groups of staff had a number of demarcation areas which prevented the flexibility in working practices that National Power wanted.

Within each of the three agreements, terms and conditions of employment and, to a large extent, the basis for grading, were standardised. This meant that individuals doing the same work would be paid within the same salary range, wherever they worked. Local markets and company profitability tended to be ignored.

Finally, National Power was changing its organisation and management style by reducing the number of staff dramatically and giving line managers greater responsibility and authority. Any revised negotiating arrangements would have to be consistent with this philosophy.

National Power first had to stop the existing negotiation arrangements. Trade unions had not been receptive to informal approaches to change, despite recognising the need for change. In order to comply with the terms of the existing agreements, National Power gave notice at the end of 1991 that they intended to leave the bargaining system on 1 January 1993. This gave about 12 months in which to put new arrangements in place.

Secondly, National Power felt it was important to overhaul the existing terms and conditions of employment, wherever possible to improve flexibility.

The unions and National Power jointly decided that the best chance of making progress was to reach as much agreement as possible about the proposed negotiating machinery and terms and conditions. This approach seemed to work well and by the beginning of September many of the loose ends were tied up,

with only a few issues of principle and negotiations about the cost of the new agreement to be agreed. At this point both sides in each of the three separate negotiations - manual, administrative and engineers - decided that the best solution was to hold a two-day negotiating session, on neutral ground, to reach a final settlement. These meetings took place during October and November, and final agreements were hammered out which the unions could put to their members.

Each of the three agreements has a two-tier negotiating structure. A company-level committee discusses issues which it has jointly agreed should be consistent across the whole company, for example, basic pay increases, length of the working week, sick pay, holidays, and overtime rates. Local committees will discuss issues which can vary between locations, such as shift rotas.

The terms and conditions have also been simplified by removing much of the complex guidance which limited managers' freedom to reach agreements appropriate to site circumstances. Apart from the issues which it has been agreed will be dealt with at company level, local managers will be free to negotiate local terms and conditions, such as certain shift payments, annual hours, etc.

This structure clearly reflects the company's desire to devolve decision making to the level of the individual power station or department. In line with the policy of devolution, National Power have also introduced revised disputes and grievance procedures which keep issues firmly in the control of the line manager, with discussion of issues which arise on site always taking place on site.

The trade unions have achieved a number of their objectives. They have seen their members properly compensated for the changes. They have a commitment from the company that training and staff development will have the highest priority, as well as ensuring that staff use their full range of skills. They also have a commitment to greater consultation on changes to working practices.

Overall, the unions regarded the package as attractive and recommended acceptance to their members. In 1993 the manual staff and the engineers voted overwhelmingly to accept the package. The clerical and administrative staff were still balloting.

Source: adapted from *Personnel Management*, February 1993.

(a) Explain the phrase 'Change is the price of success in a tough and competitive world' mentioned in the article.
(b) How would you describe the system of collective bargaining that National Power inherited from the public sector?
(c) Why does this system not seem appropriate now that National Power is a private company?
(d) From your understanding of the negotiating process, why did both sides think it was a good idea to hold a two day negotiating session?
(e) What factors may have influenced the new structure for collective bargaining?
(f) What benefits might the new system of collective bargaining have for both sides?

Unions and industrial peace

As Britain crawls out of recession, industrial relations present a picture of almost unprecedented passivity. But some employers are warning that beneath the surface lies a spirit of sullen acquiescence rather than co-operation, which does not bode well for pay bargaining come the upturn.

In spite of recent one-day strikes, a small spate of high-profile disputes in Scotland and the threat of action by fire-fighters, the Department of Employment recorded only 22 strikes in progress in January, less than the year before, itself a record low.

The number of pay freezes continues to grow and average settlements are still falling to around 3 per cent. Behind the huffing and puffing from public sector unions, the government's 1.5 per cent public-sector pay limit looks like being accepted with little resistance.

The once militant Civil Service unions NUCPS and CPSA have even recommended acceptance of a 1 per cent increase and there is little evidence of the return of the 'fringe benefit' to by-pass the pay limit.

Nalgo, the local government union which yesterday had its 5 per cent claim firmly rejected by the employers, may still be capable of some disruption and the Fire Brigades Union might successfully flex industrial muscle over its pay formula.

There may even be a slight upturn in industrial action, as there was right at the end of the early 1980s recession, as companies finally take the tough decisions on redundancies or benefit cuts they have been trying to avoid. But a return to significant labour militancy is not expected.

Yet, in spite of passive unions, earnings have been rising - last year average earnings rose 6.1 per cent, well above the inflation rate of 3.7 per cent. And even three years into recession some companies have been paying very generous bonuses for changes in working practices - 14.5 per cent rises at ICI and several deals of 5 per cent plus at the privatised utilities.

There are signs that employers have made little use of the recession to change bargaining arrangements. A senior official at one employer's organisation said 'Employers have missed a golden opportunity. Things like annualised hours and individual contracts are still the exception.' A recent report found that less than 100,000 employees had been affected by union derecognition over the last five years.

Mr Robbie Gilbert, director of employment affairs at the Confederation of British Industry, also points to employer passivity. He says that a recent survey found managers in less than one-in-four private-sector workplaces believed there were significant restrictions on their freedom to organise work.

He adds, 'But the willingness to take advantage of this new freedom turns out to be much more patchy. Over 60 per cent of private sector managers reported no actual increase in job flexibility or reductions in job demarcation over the previous three years.'

There are other signs that the power of unions remains considerable where they are still well organised. Manual and white collar workers at Ford UK recently resisted the company's attempt to impose compulsory redundancies.

The continuing decline of industry-wide pay agreements may increase upward pressures on pay in unionised companies as recovery begins. After the GPMU print union refused a 1.7 per cent offer from the British Printing Industry Federation the employers abandoned national negotiations for this year.

The GPMU is now pressing its claim company by company and, according to pay analysts Incomes Data Services, had agreed a 3.9 per cent deal at the Lawson Mardon Group. There have been similar developments at the National Bed Federation and in the lock, latch and key industry.

IDS concludes, 'Decisions made in recession may have awkward consequences in the future, for employers and unions alike.'

Source: *The Financial Times*, 7.4.1993.

(a) Why do you think 'the government's 1.5 per cent public sector pay limit looks like being accepted with little resistance'?
(b) Why might businesses still be paying high wage increases despite the existence of 'passive unions' to negotiate with?
(c) What evidence is there in the article that unions have not lost all their power?
(d) According to the article, what are the effects of a continuing decline in industry-wide agreements?
(e) What evidence is there to suggest that employers have not used three years of recession to win greater employee flexibility?

investigations

Aims

- To investigate how union representation and collective bargaining have changed over a period of time in an industry, focusing on a particular business.
- To explain why changes in union activity may have taken place.

Research

Choose an industry where there have been changes in industrial relations in recent years. You will need to select a business which is representative of the industry. For example, you could choose the Ford Motor Company, Nissan, Toyota etc. to reflect the motor car industry or a newspaper or magazine group to represent the printing or publishing industry. If you are looking at the public sector (or businesses that were previously part of the public sector) you may choose British Rail to reflect the rail industry or an NHS trust to reflect the 'health' industry.

Over the last four or five years, find out the trends taking place in industrial relations in the business you have chosen. You may be able to find information in newspapers such as *The Times*, the *Financial Times*, *The Guardian* and *The Independent*. You could also look under appropriate headings using CD Rom. If a dispute is ongoing during your research, follow it on television, radio or in newspapers and take notes. You may also be able to find details of changes in industrial relations in company bulletins or magazines published by trade unions.

When gathering information you might consider the following questions.

- What areas of pay and conditions were negotiated at national level?
- Were there any negotiations at local level?
- How has the focus of collective bargaining changed?
- Have there been any single union, no-strike or long term agreements?
- How have unions been consulted about change, for example?
- What have been the trends in union density or membership for unions represented in the business?
- Has industrial action taken place?
- What type of employee/employer action was used?

Presentation

Try to identify any trends that have taken place in industrial relations in the business you have chosen. You could give reasons why these trends have taken place. For example, if successful union action resulted in a better deal for employees, what influenced its success? You may also be able to give reasons for, say, a move to local rather than national bargaining.

Also consider the effects on the business of the trends you have found. Is there more or less consultation and what is likely to be the impact of this? How will it affect employees? You could present your findings in a report or write a newspaper or magazine article.

You could also comment on whether the business you have chosen is representative of the industry. Is it the only business in the industry where union representation and collective bargaining have changed?

investigations

Aims

- To study the formal organisation of a company.
- To examine how and why the company may have changed its formal structure.

Research

Choose a company that has undergone change in recent years. You may be able to get ideas from newpapers such as the *Financial Times*, *The Guardian*, *The Independent* or *The Times*, or magazines such as *Personnel Management*. Alternatively, you may know someone who works for a business where change has taken place. Information about organisational change could also be found in articles on CD Rom. You might consider investigating a business which is now part of the private sector, but was previously part of the public sector or a private sector business.

Write to the company and ask for an organisation chart. If possible try to obtain a chart before and after the company was restructured. Try to find out as much information about the changes that have taken place at the company as you can. Newspapers etc. will contain some information. However, you may also be able to arrange an interview with a manager or someone in the personnel department. The manager may be able to give you reasons for changes which have taken place and the possible effects on the business. Try to find out if any major initiatives have been undertaken, such as an attempt to gain BS5750 certification or the introduction of Total Quality Management. Remember to arrange your interview in plenty of time, prepare a questionnaire and follow the guidelines for interviews explained in earlier investigations in this book.

Consider the following questions when you have obtained your information.
- What type of structure is it - pyramid, matrix?
- What is the length of the chain of command?
- What avenues are there for lateral or vertical communication?
- How have the above changed with restructuring?

Presentation

You will need to show clearly how the organisational structure of the company has changed. Present the charts before and after the changes. Highlight the main areas of change, commenting on any reduction or increase in tiers, or any change in the span of control etc.

Try to account for the changes that have taken place, mentioning both internal and external factors. Discuss the effects on the business of these changes.

Have they improved communication? How has authority changed, if at all? What possible benefits could the changes have for the business?. What lessons have been learned from the restructuring that could be used by other businesses?

Essays

1. What is meant by a no strike agreement between unions and employers? Why might some unions agree to such deals and why might the TUC be against them in principle?

2. What is meant by leadership style in business? How might the leadership style adopted by management affect how employees operate at work?

3. Examine the implications for management and the workforce of the possible emergence of 'superunions' in the 1990s as a result of union amalgamation and mergers.

4. 'Survival in a competitive environment depends on the management of change.' To what extent do you agree?

5. How has the role of trade unions in business changed in the last 10 years? Discuss the extent to which these changes have been forced upon unions.

6. What is the difference between consultation and negotiation? To what extent is consultation necessary before changing work practices?

7. Why have some businesses in recent years decided to decentralise and delegate decision making to the lowest possible level?

8. 'Changes in the formal organisation of a business may be necessary if a business is to be efficient.' Suggest why such changes may be needed and explain possible ways in which a business could alter its structure to achieve its objectives.

9. What communication problems might be faced by a multinational company developing a new product in different sites throughout the world?

10. Why have 'flexibility' and 'quality' become such important phrases in the business organisation of the 1990s?

What external factors affect a business?

Business decisions will be influenced by many factors within the business itself. For example, what if a firm was considering whether or not to produce a new product? This may depend on several factors.

- Marketing - are consumers likely to buy this new product?
- Finance - are there enough funds within the firm to produce the product?
- Production - does the firm have the necessary technology to produce it?
- Labour - do workers have the right skills or is training needed?

Firms do not operate in a vacuum. Unit 1 showed that they must take into account what is happening in the external environment when making decisions. There are factors outside the business that could affect any decision, such as the one above about a new product. We have seen some of these in earlier units. The rest are dealt with in the units that follow.

- Legislation. There might be laws that affect the product, eg controls on the ingredients that can be used in food.
- Technology. The rate of change of technology may influence the type of good produced, eg the development of the microchip has made possible a whole new range of products.
- Political factors. A firm may delay a decision until after a General Election because it is concerned about the effects of a new government's policies.

- Social factors, eg an increase in the amount of crime directed against businesses will affect firms differently. Some, such as security firms, may benefit; others may find that their costs increase due to, for example, higher insurance premiums.
- Population. The size, age and sex distribution of the population can affect demand for a product, eg an increase in the birth rate would affect firms marketing baby products.
- The state of competition. A new competitor entering a market could lead to a reduction in the sales of existing firms.
- Environmental factors. Increased consumer awareness has led many firms to re-evaluate their impact upon the environment.
- Economic factors and the economic system. Unit 6 showed there are different types of economic system. The aim of each is to **allocate resources**. We are mainly concerned in the sections which follow with the free market system and the problems that result from it. These have a major effect on businesses. Government policy to solve problems that result from the operation of markets also affects firms.

How a simple economy operates

A useful tool for analysing how an economy works is the CIRCULAR FLOW OF INCOME. It is often used in **macroeconomics** - the study of the whole economy. The circular flow shows how money flows around the economy. In Figure 65.1, businesses (or producers) buy land, labour and capital from households - the users of goods and services (point 1). Households receive rent,

QUESTION 1 Gurrinder Niijer owns a small business that manufactures carpet slippers. She is considering expanding her production in the near future by taking on 5 extra workers. The existing workers are concerned about how much the new employees will be paid. They feel that there need to be pay differentials between themselves and the new workers.

Although Gurrinder has £5,000 of her own money to invest she is likely to require a loan. Her bank has indicated that now is a good time to borrow as interest rates are low. However, it has also warned her that the government could force up rates in future if they needed to control the exchange rate or if inflation started to increase.

Gurrinder feels happy that she can pay back the loan quickly, because although the economy is still in recession, there is a strong local demand for her goods.

(a) Identify the:
   (i) internal;
   (ii) external;
   factors that may affect Gurrinder's decision to expand.
(b) How might the business be affected if the 'strong local demand' for its products decreases?

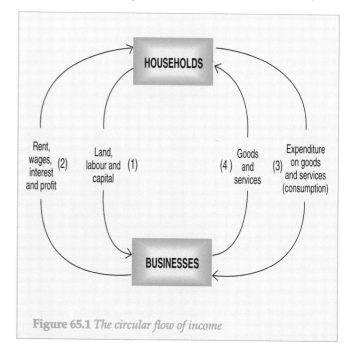

Figure 65.1 *The circular flow of income*

wages, interest and profit (income) in return. This is shown as point 2. The money they earn is spent (point 3) on goods and services produced by businesses (point 4). So, money (or **income**) flows from businesses to households and back again - a circular flow of income around the economy.

How much money is flowing around the economy? The money earned by households, their income (Y), is spent on goods and services (E), which are produced by businesses - their output (O). In the national accounts of economies these are all defined so that they are equal. We can say that the value of:

$$Y \equiv E \equiv O$$

(where ≡ represents **must equal**)

In practice, the way that economies work is more complex, as we will see in the next section.

A more complex economy

In Figure 65.1 households spend all of their money on goods and services. Is this likely? In practice they will spend some money (known as consumption) and save some as well. Saving takes money out of the circular flow - a WITHDRAWAL.

What about businesses? They are not likely to spend all their revenue on rent and wages. They will also invest some in machinery and equipment. These are used to produce goods and services which increase money in the economy - an INJECTION.

There are a number of injections and withdrawals in a more complex economy. Injections into the UK economy include:

■ investment (I) - spending on fixed capital, such as machinery and factories, and circulating capital, such as stocks and work-in-progress (☞ unit 41) which enter the circular flow;

■ government spending (G) - spending by government on new schools and motorways, for example, or subsidies to firms;

■ exports (X) - goods and services sold abroad, earning money for the UK which enters the circular flow of income.

Withdrawals can be:

■ savings (S) - money saved by households, for example in bank accounts, which is not then available to spend;

■ taxation (T) - money taken out of the economy from businesses and households by government through taxation, such as income tax;

■ imports (M) - goods and services coming into the country paid for by money leaving the circular flow to be paid to overseas producers.

Injections and withdrawals are shown in Figure 65.2.

How can we measure how much money is flowing around the circular flow? The value of a country's **economic activity** is known as its GROSS NATIONAL PRODUCT (GNP). Figures 65.1 and 65.2 can be used to show how GNP can be measured.

■ Income method - adding up all the income earned by households (rent, wages, interest and profit).

■ Output method - adding up the value of all goods and services produced by businesses.

■ Expenditure method - adding up the spending of consumers (C), the investment of business (I), the expenditure of government (G) and the spending of people overseas on exports minus the spending of a country on imports from abroad (X - M). These are often known as items which make up AGGREGATE DEMAND. The relationship is often expressed as:

$$Y = C + I + G + (X - M)$$

where Y equals GNP.

Whichever method is used, it will give the same figure for GNP because by definition income = output = expenditure. This is true of all circular flows of income. Another measure of economic activity is GROSS DOMESTIC PRODUCT (GDP). This is GNP less net earnings from property overseas.

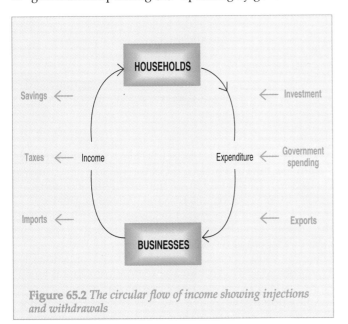

Figure 65.2 *The circular flow of income showing injections and withdrawals*

QUESTION 2 Using Figure 65.2, describe the possible impact on the UK leisure and entertainment industry of the following events. Explain your answers and, for each event, say whether it will be an injection into or a withdrawal from the circular flow of income.
(a) Greater availability of grants for setting up new businesses.
(b) An increase in the number of British groups in the US album charts.
(c) A developing trend for consumers to devote more of their income to savings.
(d) An increase in the number of British tourists taking holidays in Europe and the US.
(e) A 2 per cent reduction in income tax.

Equilibrium

Look at Figure 65.2. If injections in any year are the same as withdrawals, the money flowing around the circular flow would remain the **same**. This is known as

EQUILIBRIUM. If injections and withdrawals are not the same, the money flowing around the circular flow will change. We can say that:

■ if injections = withdrawals - income remains the same;
■ if injections > withdrawals - income will rise because more money is entering the economy than is leaving it;
■ if injections < withdrawals - income will fall because more money is leaving the economy than is entering it.

Even if the economy is in equilibrium, does this mean that everyone is employed? Say an economy is in equilibrium, with £6,000 billion flowing around it, but £8,000 billion was needed for **full employment**. This 'gap' of £2,000 billion (known as a DEFLATIONARY GAP) would mean that there was unemployment in the economy. These ideas were first put forward by John Maynard Keynes in his book *The General Theory of Employment, Interest and Money* (1936). Supporters of this view (sometimes known as KEYNESIANS) argue it is the role of government to fill any gap that exists by spending more than it receives in taxes. This is known as a **budget deficit.**

Other economists suggest that the economy will be in equilibrium at full employment only if markets are allowed to operate freely. They argue that government spending will only lead to inflation and government policy should be aimed at making markets more efficient.

We will look at this debate in the sections that follow.

Government objectives

We have seen that problems can result from the operation of an economy. These can affect businesses and households. There is an expectation that the government will try to solve these problems. The success of government policy will affect a firm's external environment. For example, if a business is thinking of expanding, its decision will be affected by future inflation, which may raise the price of components needed to produce goods. Government policy which controls inflation will result in a more stable climate and will allow the firm to expand with confidence. So if the government is able to meet its objectives, it is likely to create an environment where businesses are also successful. It is argued that governments have some common economic objectives.

Control of inflation Inflation is a rise in the general level of prices. Some are rising and some may be falling, but overall prices are increasing. Governments usually set **target rates** at which they want to keep inflation. In practice, the targets which governments set themselves often depend upon the inflation rate from previous years. So, for example, in the late 1980s when inflation was relatively high in the UK, the British government set itself an inflationary target of below 5 per cent. Once this had been met in the early 1990s, a new target of 0 per cent inflation was set. In other countries, such as Poland and Russia, where more severe inflationary problems existed, much higher rates such as 20 or 30 per cent may have been acceptable.

Governments aim to achieve an inflation rate at or below the level of those of their competitors. An inflation rate which is higher than those of competitors can mean higher prices for exports and a loss of sales by UK businesses to those of other countries. Inflation can also restrict a government's ability to achieve its other economic objectives. The problems that inflation can cause for business are dealt with in unit 66.

Full employment Full employment occurs when all who want a job have one at a given wage rate. It is argued that the UK came closest to achieving this in the 1960s. For example, between 1950 and 1970 the rate of unemployment never reached above 4 per cent (about one million unemployed). Since then unemployment levels have risen considerably. Levels of over 3 million have been recorded in the 1980s and 1990s. UK governments over this period arguably abandoned the objective of full employment. The aim now is to reduce unemployment to an acceptable level.

The level of unemployment in an economy can be seen as an indicator of its success. A falling rate may show an economy doing well. Firms employ extra workers to produce more goods and services and new businesses set up in order to take advantage of opportunities which may occur. A rising unemployment rate, on the other hand, could indicate an economy which is in recession (☞ unit 67). Firms will be making some of their employees redundant. Others may be closing down and new ventures will be put their ideas on ice until conditions improve. Unemployed people will have less to spend and this will affect firms' revenue and profits. The effects of unemployment on business are dealt with in unit 68.

Economic growth Economic growth (☞ unit 67) is said to exist if there is a rise in economic activity or gross national product (GNP). Most governments judge the performance of an economy by the figures for growth. Economic growth is good for most businesses. A growing economy should mean that trading conditions are favourable and that there are new business opportunities. However, there is another view that growth harms the environment and that sustaining growth in the long term may be impossible as the world's resources begin to run out.

A growth rate of 3-4 per cent per year may be considered good in Western economies. But some developing countries (☞ unit 70), such as Singapore and Thailand, have in recent years recorded rates of around 10 per cent per year.

The balance of payments and exchange rates
Governments usually attempt to achieve equilibrium or a surplus on the current account of the balance of payments (☞ unit 69). This would mean that the value of exports going out of a country is either the same as or greater than the value of imports coming into a country. At worst they would aim to prevent a long term deficit on the current account of the balance of payments. This occurs when the value of imports exceeds the value of exports. The problem with a current account deficit is that it must be financed either by borrowing from abroad or by running down savings. For one or two years this may not be a problem, but if the deficit persists then the country's

debts will increase. The UK's balance of payments deficit in the early 1990s was of particular concern. The economy was in recession. In other recessions, with less money to spend, people bought fewer imports leading to a surplus on the balance of payments. In the early 1990s, however, the UK balance of payments remained in deficit.

Government policy to prevent a balance of payments deficit can have a major effect on business and is dealt with in unit 69.

It is unlikely that a government will achieve all of its objectives at the same time. For example, say that the government was concerned about the level of unemployment and decided to spend to create jobs. This may lead to a rise in GNP and economic growth.

However, with more money being spent, prices may rise. Also some of the spending may be on imports, which may lead to a current account deficit. The government could try to stop the inflation and deficit happening. In practice achieving all objectives has proved very difficult for governments.

Government policy

Governments have a range of policies which they can use to achieve their objectives. They will use those policies they believe are most effective in controlling the economy. The effects of those policies on business and how they aim to achieve government objectives are dealt with in units 66-70.

Monetary policy MONETARY POLICY is designed to control the amount of money flowing around the economy - the **money supply**. It is mainly used to tackle inflation and balance of payments problems. There are a number of methods the government can employ which affect the supply of money.

■ Interest rates. Raising interest rates may reduce the amount of borrowing in the economy. This is because it makes borrowing more expensive. The amount of money flowing around the system (the quantity of money) will be reduced. Interest rates can also affect the value of the pound. Higher interest rates will attract overseas investors to put money in UK banks etc. They will buy pounds to do this, forcing up the value of sterling (☞ unit 69).

■ The government can control the amount of credit financial institutions are allowed to give. For example, it may set limits on the amount and type of lending banks can make.

■ The central bank (the **Bank of England** in the UK) can control the assets of banks and the amount of lending they can make by a variety of means (☞ unit 66).

Fiscal policy FISCAL POLICY aims to manage the level of total spending (or aggregate demand) in the economy. There are a variety of methods the government can use.

■ Changes in government spending. If the economy needs a boost, government expenditure can be raised. For example, spending on building new hospitals can create jobs, income and increased spending by the people in those jobs. On the other hand, if the economy needs to be slowed down, government expenditure can be lowered.

■ Changes in direct taxation. **Direct taxes** are those which are levied directly on individuals or businesses. Income tax rates, as part of a fiscal policy, can be lowered in order to encourage consumers to buy more goods and services. This should raise the level of aggregate demand. Raising income tax is likely to have the opposite effect, ie to lower the level of aggregate demand.

■ Changes in indirect taxation. **Indirect taxes** are taxes on goods or services. The main indirect tax in the UK is VAT. Governments raise indirect taxes as part of fiscal policy in order to raise the price of goods and

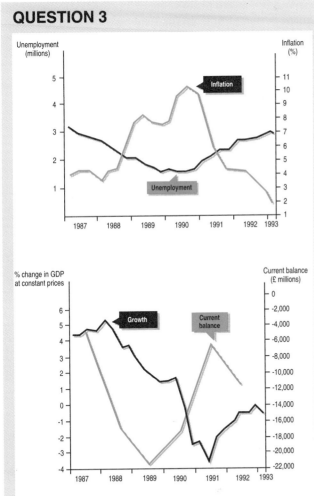

QUESTION 3

Source: adapted from CSO, *Economic Trends Annual Supplement*; CSO; *Monthly Digest of Statistics*.

Figure 65.3 *UK economic growth, balance of payments, inflation and unemployment*

(a) Describe the likely trading conditions for UK businesses in (i) 1987 and (ii) 1990.

(b) What does the data tell you about the chances of the government achieving all of its economic objectives at the same time? How will this affect UK businesses?

services and discourage spending. Indirect taxes are also used by governments as a means of raising revenue in order to finance spending plans. There is much debate as to whether it is individual businesses or consumers who have to pay for indirect taxes. Take the example of a 2 per cent increase in VAT. If this was passed on to consumers in the form of a 2 per cent price rise, then consumers would be paying for it. However, firms might be reluctant to pass on the price rise to consumers because of fears of falling demand for their product. In this case, they might only raise the price by 1 per cent and pay the other 1 per cent VAT increase themselves. This would lead to a 1 per cent increase in their costs.

If a government spends more than it receives in revenue from taxation and other sources, then it is said to have a budget deficit. This will mean it has to borrow money from a variety of sources, such as individual members of the public or banks. This will increase in the PUBLIC SECTOR BORROWING REQUIREMENT (PSBR). This is the amount of money borrowed by the government over a given time period. In the late 1980s, the UK had a public sector debt repayment (PSDR). This meant the government had a budget surplus, ie higher revenue than spending, and was able to pay off some of its past debts.

Supply side policies These policies allow the SUPPLY SIDE of the economy, ie producers, to operate more effectively. They aim to increase the amount of competition in markets and give incentives to work and innovate. Examples of supply side policies would be:

- reducing income or corporation tax to encourage entrepreneurs and employees to be more efficient by allowing them to keep more of their income or company profits;
- cutting state benefits to encourage the unemployed to return to work;
- privatising nationalised industries to open them up to competition from other businesses;
- supporting firms that provide training in order to create a more efficient and productive workforce;
- control of trade unions that may prevent wages from being flexible;
- removal of restrictions to employment, such as a maximum number of working hours in a week;
- reduction of the amount of 'red tape', such as form filling and returns required of businesses;
- reducing the National Insurance contributions (☞ unit 8) of employers in order to reduce the cost of taking on new employees.

Exchange rate policy The exchange rate is the price of one currency in relation to another. The value of the pound can be shown against other currencies, such as the dollar, yen and the deutschmark. Changes in exchange rates can affect the economy and businesses within it. Take, for example, a fall in the value of the pound from £1 = $2 to £1 = $1. UK exports become cheaper and imports more expensive. UK firms that export goods should gain increased sales and possibly hire more workers. However, at the same time, the prices of imported goods will be higher. Businesses that import

raw materials or components will have to pay higher costs. The overall effect will therefore be uncertain.

Whether or not the government should control the value of the exchange rate has been a major issue in the 1990s. The exchange rate not only affects exports and imports, it can also affect inflation. One of the arguments for the UK joining the Exchange Rate Mechanism in the early 1990s was that it could lead to lower inflation. This is discussed in unit 69.

Regional and urban policy Regional policy aims to provide aid to businesses in different parts of the country. It has been used to support regions that have suffered from a decline in important industries (☞ unit 30). It has included a range of measures to attract business to these areas, from government spending on grants and loans to the offering of 'tax breaks' for a limited period of time. In the 1980s and 1990s in the UK, regional policy involving government spending has been limited, although funds have been provided by the EC.

Urban policy has been designed to stimulate business mainly in inner-city areas. It has involved the creation of enterprise zones throughout the country, such as in Salford and Gateshead, where firms are encouraged to locate through incentives. These include no rates in the first year and a reduction in 'red tape' through a relaxation of planning permission. Urban Development

---

QUESTION 4 The 1993 Budget aimed at boosting industry and exports, whilst at the same time trying to prevent any consumer recovery escalating into a boom. The government finances for the financial year 1993-94 were:

Total expenditure - £280 billion
Total revenue - £230 billion

The following measures were announced by the Chancellor of the Exchequer during his speech.

- VAT to be imposed on domestic fuel and power bills.
- Fuel duty on petrol and diesel increased by 10 per cent.
- £125 million package of measures to help the unemployed including a package allowing 30,000 long term unemployed to be funded for full time vocational courses and 10,000 places to be available under the Business Start-up scheme to help people setting up their own business.
- The building of a £300 million high speed rail link to Heathrow.
- National Insurance contributions raised by 1 per cent.

(a) Calculate the size of the Public Sector Borrowing Requirement required in 1993.
(b) Identify the policies which the government has used in this Budget.
(c) How do you think:
   (i) the imposition of VAT on domestic fuel and power bills;
   (ii) the £125 million package of measures for the unemployed;
   (iii) the building of the rail link;
   will affect businesses?

Corporations have also been set up in a number of towns and cities to encourage private sector investment in previously run down sites. By far the biggest of these is the London Docklands Development Board.

Industrial policy Industrial policy is aimed at supporting specific industries and firms. An example is the government help given to a number of micro-electronics firms during the 1970s. Industrial policy was used far less during the 1980s. In the 1990s an example of its use is the Enterprise Initiative, which provides aid to firms with less than 500 employees.

Incomes policy This is a means of controlling inflation by imposing limits upon pay or price increases. During the 1960s and 1970s it was widely used in the battle against inflation. It was not used at all in the 1980s. Although not an official incomes policy, there have been attempts in the 1990s to restrict pay rises. An example might have been the pay freeze for public sector workers in 1993.

Policy disagreements

Earlier in this unit it was stated that economists have different approaches to solving economic problems. One approach favours the free operation of markets. Supporters of this believe that the role of government should be limited to providing the right environment for businesses to flourish. Another approach to policy favours using government intervention in the economy.

The operation of markets The free market approach suggests that markets will achieve equilibrium providing they are free to operate. Take the market for labour. Say that in a depressed area there are more workers wanting jobs than are available. This would put pressure on wages to fall. Employers would offer lower wages to workers and some workers would, as a result, not offer their labour to employers at this wage rate. This would occur until the labour market returned to equilibrium, ie to the point where the demand for labour was equal to the supply of labour at a given wage. This approach would argue for the removal of all restrictions to markets and the free movement of wages and prices.

Interventionists argue that the operation of a market economy results in a variety of problems, such as:
- high levels of unemployment;
- inadequate merit goods, such as housing, health care and education (☞ unit 4);
- a lack of provision of some public goods, such as defence;
- inequalities in income.

Wages and unemployment Market supporters suggest that if **real** wage rates (that take into account inflation) are free to move up and down, the economy would always achieve full employment. Workers must be flexible in their demands and prepared to react to changes in the market. If there is any unemployment, it is likely to be voluntary. Some people may not want to work by choice at a given wage rate. This is known as the **natural rate of unemployment**.

Interventionists believe that in the 1930s depression (and arguably the 1980s and 1990s recession) wage rates fell, or were held down, but unemployment was still high. They dispute whether real wage rates will actually operate to allow markets to achieve equilibrium at full employment. In modern economies this is because:
- labour may be reluctant to move from one area to another;
- trade unions protect the real wage rates of their members;
- businesses may not reduce wages because of the dissatisfaction it may lead to.

Instead they argue that unemployment is caused by a lack of aggregate demand in the economy - a deflationary gap. It is the government's role to fill this gap by using policies which will lead to an increase in consumption, investment, government spending and exports.

Inflation Providing markets operate freely, the economy will achieve full employment, according to market economists. At this point an increase in output would only be possible if the state of technology changed. Increases in aggregate demand by government would simply lead to inflation. Businesses could not take on more workers or produce more output even if they wished. Price increases would be the only result of government spending. One group which is often considered part of a market approach is MONETARISTS. They argue that increases in the money supply over and above increases in output lead to inflation.

Interventionists argue that money supply increases merely reflect the state of the economy and do not cause inflation. Instead, they believe that inflation is caused by an excess of consumer demand in the economy as a whole or a rise in firms' costs.

Government policy Market economists argue that obstacles to the operation of markets should be removed by government. These occur on the **supply side** of the economy. For example, workers may not be able to move to other jobs because they do not have the skills needed. This will prevent the labour market from working. Incentives to businesses to retrain workers may help solve this. The aim of supply side policies is to increase the level of output in the economy as a whole. This is known as AGGREGATE SUPPLY. Supply side economists believe that this can be increased by using the supply side policies mentioned in the last section.

Interventionists argue that government should attempt to solve problems of the market. They argue that government policy should include:
- fiscal and regional policy to increase employment, generate economic growth, help ailing industry and encourage firms to invest in new plant and machinery;
- protection for UK firms against foreign competition;
- the use of prices and incomes policy to prevent wage costs rising as a result of increases in aggregate demand;
- government ownership or close involvement in particular sectors of the economy.

QUESTION 5 A new importance was attached to supply side policies in the 1980s. Fiscal, monetary and exchange rate policies could not, it was argued, remedy fundamental problems in the economy. The introduction of supply side policies resulted in a range of measures. These included reducing government expenditure as a proportion of GDP; introducing market forces into education, health and local government, and intensifying competition in a number of markets by allowing firms to enter them more freely. In addition, government-owned nationalised industries were transferred to the private sector through privatisation and more stress was placed on the individual rather than the collective. For example, managers were encouraged to bargain with individual workers rather than unions.

(a) What is meant by the phrase 'Fiscal, monetary and exchange rate policies could not ... remedy fundamental problems in the economy'?
(b) What evidence is there in the above passage to suggest that supply side policies stress the operation of a free market?
(c) Explain briefly how one of the supply side policies in the article might affect business.

Key terms

Aggregate demand - a measure of the level of demand in the economy as a whole.
Aggregate supply - the level of output in the economy as a whole.
Circular flow of income - the flow of money around the economy.
Deflationary gap - when planned expenditure is less than the level of income needed for full employment.
Equilibrium - a balanced state, for example, when withdrawals equal injections in an economy.
Fiscal policy - a policy designed to manage the level of aggregate demand in the economy by changing government spending or taxation.
Gross Domestic Product (GDP) - like GNP, a measure of economic activity, but it does not include net property income from abroad.
Gross National Product (GNP) - a measure of the amount of income generated as a result of a country's economic activity.
Injection - any factor causing income to enter the circular flow.
Keynesians - economists who favour the use of government intervention in the economy.
Monetarists - economists who believe that inflation is caused by excessive increases in the money supply.
Monetary policy - a policy designed to control the supply of money in the economy.
Public Sector Borrowing Requirement (PSBR) - the amount of money borrowed by a government over a given period of time.
Supply side policies - policies designed to make markets operate more efficiently.
Withdrawal - any factor causing income to leave the circular flow.

Summary

1. What is meant by a firm's external environment?
2. Give examples of 3 injections and 3 withdrawals in the circular flow of income.
3. Explain the terms:
    (a) income;
    (b) output;
    (c) expenditure;
    in a complex economy.
4. 'Income must equal output, which must equal expenditure.' Explain this statement in relation to the circular flow of income.
5. What will be the effect on the circular flow if injections are greater than withdrawals?
6. Why might an economy be in equilibrium but not have full employment?
7. State 4 government objectives.
8. Give 3 examples of:
    (a) fiscal policy;
    (b) monetary policy;
    (c) supply side policy.
9. Explain the difference between direct and indirect taxation.
10. What effect would cutting income tax have on:
    (a) businesses;
    (b) consumers?
11. Briefly explain the free market approach to:
    (a) the operation of markets;
    (b) reducing unemployment .
12. Briefly explain the interventionist approach to:
    (a) the operation of markets;
    (b) reducing unemployment.

Question

Sky Travel 2000

Sky Travel 2000, a travel firm based in Bristol, were considering expanding the range of holidays which they would offer to the public in the next summer season. They already offered packages to traditional destinations such as the Greek Islands, the Costa del Sol and the Balearic Islands. They wished to expand into the long haul market, offering holidays to destinations previously out of the reach of mass tourism. Such destinations were likely to include India, Thailand and Bali.

Due to the sensitivity of the travel business to changes in the economic climate, a firm of economic consultants had been employed to provide them with a report on possible government policy in response to economic conditions.

Before the consultants had presented the report, there had been concern expressed about the expansion plan by the firm's chief accountant, Errol Lee. He was worried about the building up of debt. He believed that economic conditions were such that it was unlikely sufficient revenue could be generated in the current year to finance expansionary plans.

Anne Doyle, the marketing director, who had been carefully researching the market for long haul flights, felt that consumer demand for long haul flights to some of these exotic locations might dry up just as quickly as it had initially grown. There was growing evidence of fickle behaviour amongst consumers of such holidays. In addition, concern about the link between sunbathing and skin cancer was leading to a trend towards taking holidays in countries with more moderate climates. The firm's personnel director, John Bryden, also expressed doubts about the extent to which staff currently employed in comfortable Mediterranean locations would cope if transferred to potentially much more difficult long haul destinations.

At the next board meeting a number of these concerns were discussed, but the managing director, Chris Boughie, insisted that no decision could be made until the presentation by the economic consultants which was to take place the next day.

That evening, all directors watched the evening news in the comfort of their homes. The main stories were the redundancies to be made by several leading firms, rising unemployment and a large current account deficit on the balance of payments.

They arrived at work the next day in a gloomy mood. Erica Harper, a young economist working for the firm of consultants, gave the presentation. 'It could be argued that the UK faces a deflationary gap at the moment. Industrial output is down, unemployment is rising and there has been an upsurge in business failures. It has been suggested that in future the government might consider adopting more direct measures designed to expand the economy. Such measures would probably involve a number of new investment projects, such as the building of new public transport systems in major cities and the funding of a variety of new housing projects. There could also be more widespread availability of investment grants to new firms wishing to expand their plant and machinery. The net result of these measures could be an increase in GNP and an improvement in trading conditions, although costs may rise.

It was more likely, however, that the government would continue with policies to make markets more efficient. This would involve maintaining low tax rates or possible future cuts in tax, control of trade unions and incentives to encourage free trade, training by business and new firms to start up.

(a) **Identify 3 external factors which might have influenced Sky Travel 2000's decision to expand their business.**

(b) **What internal factors might act as a constraint on Sky Travel 2000's expansion plans?**

(c) **From the evidence given, what do you think might have been the government's two main objectives?**

(d) **What is meant by the term deflationary gap mentioned in the article?**

(e) **If the government used direct measures, and the consultant's predictions were correct, how might this affect Sky Travel 2000?**

(f) **Suggest 2 effects on Sky Travel 2000 of government policy to encourage the operation of markets.**

What is inflation?

INFLATION can be defined as a persistent tendency for prices to rise. It occurs when there is a general increase in the price level, not if just one firm raises its prices.

In the UK, inflation is measured by the Retail Price Index (☞ unit 15). If the index rises from, say, 100 to 105 over a year, then there is an inflation rate of 5 per cent. Although governments, consumers and businesses may prefer a lower rate, 5 per cent is usually considered acceptable. Rates of 10 per cent or more may lead to problems. HYPER-INFLATION, such as the Brazilian inflation rate of nearly 1,200 per cent in 1992, can cause serious difficulties.

Governments may try to reduce a rate of inflation from perhaps 10 per cent to 5 per cent. This does not mean prices are falling, just that the rate of increase is slowing down. DEFLATION is a situation where prices actually fall. Figure 66.1 shows inflation rates in the UK between 1979 and 1992-93.

The causes of inflation

What causes inflation? Three arguments are usually put forward.

The money supply This view is often associated with **monetarists**. They argue that inflation is caused by increases in the MONEY SUPPLY - the total amount of money circulating in the economy (☞ unit 1).

Monetarists believe that any increase in the money supply which is not in line with growth in the output of the economy will lead to inflation. If, for example, the money supply was to increase by 10 per cent, in the short period, consumer spending would increase, but the output of producers would not be able to expand as quickly. Instead, there would be an increase in prices. So monetarists argue strongly that it is important for governments to ensure that the rate of growth of the money supply is kept in line with the rate of growth of output or there will be inflation.

Demand Unit 65 showed that too much spending or demand can lead to inflation. This is known as DEMAND-PULL INFLATION. **Keynesians** in particular, argue that this is the major cause of inflation.

The result is similar to that described under changes in the money supply, but the cause is different. Demand-pull inflation comes about when there is excessive spending in the economy. This expenditure leads to an increase in demand which cannot be matched by the level of supply. Because demand is greater than supply, prices rise. The increase in demand can be due to:
- a rise in consumer spending;
- firms investing in more machinery;
- government expenditure increasing;
- more exports being bought abroad.

These economists argue that inflation in the UK at the end of the 1980s and early 1990s was caused by earlier tax cuts, leading to increases in consumer expenditure.

Increasing costs Another argument is that rising costs lead to inflation. This is known as COST-PUSH INFLATION, as rising costs force firms to push up their prices. What causes costs to increase?

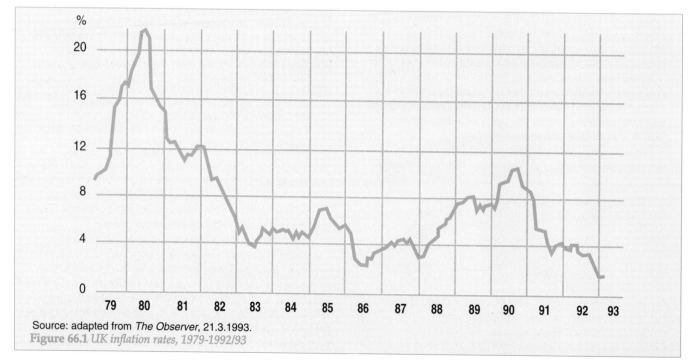

Source: adapted from *The Observer*, 21.3.1993.

Figure 66.1 *UK inflation rates, 1979-1992/93*

- Rises in wages and salaries. There may be an increase in labour costs as workers and unions push for and receive an increase in their wages. Unions have been blamed by some, particularly in the 1970s, for creating inflation.
- Tax increases. Increases in indirect taxes, such as VAT, can increase the costs of production and cause firms to raise their prices.
- Profits. A push by firms to raise profit levels, due to pressure from shareholders, can increase production costs.
- Imports. An increase in costs can be 'imported' from abroad. The prices of imported raw materials or semi-finished products, such as components, may rise. This could increase the price of home produced goods which use these in production. A rise in the price of imported finished goods can more directly lead to inflation, as it adds to the general level of prices.

Many economists believe that the inflation experienced in the UK during the mid-1970s was a result of the huge oil price rises which preceded it. In addition, inflation in the late 1970s and early 1980s was put down by some to excessive wage increases.

QUESTION 1 A number of UK manufacturers are pushing up their prices in the wake of sterling's devaluation on 'Black Wednesday'. Some believe this is putting pressure on the government's anti-inflationary strategy and its plans to keep inflation between 1 and 4 per cent. Price rises in the past few weeks include:
- more than 7 per cent on electrical goods from Siemens UK;
- 8 per cent on float glass from Pilkingtons;
- up to 13 per cent on steel from British Steel;
- up to 7.5 per cent on Ford cars;
- up to 12.5 per cent on personal computers.

Importers of goods from the continent have pointed out that devaluation has meant cost increases of 15 per cent. However, it is not yet clear that all the suggested price rises will take place. Pilkington and British Steel have tried to raise prices without success in the past few years. In glass, steel and personal computers prices have actually fallen sharply. In cars, it is not yet clear whether the latest price rises will be whittled away by discounts.

If the price rises do fail to stick, it will be principally because the UK economy is not recovering as fast as companies hoped.

Source: adapted from the *Financial Times*, 20.1.1993.

(a) What causes of inflation are indicated in the article? Explain your answer.
(b) Explain why businesses that have to increase their prices might eventually have to reduce them.

Effects of inflation on business

Reducing inflation has been the main economic objective of the UK governments in the 1980s and 1990s. The government has had strong support from the Confederation of British Industry (CBI) and other business groups in following this approach. Why is inflation seen as such a problem? There are a number of effects that relatively high rates of inflation might have on business, and on consumer demand and confidence.

Increasing costs Inflation leads to an increase in business costs. Examples might be:
- increases in the cost of components or raw materials;
- increase in wages and salaries of employees to keep pace with inflation;
- increasing energy costs;
- rising 'service' costs, such as the cost of calling out technicians.

If a business cannot pass on these costs to consumers in higher prices or 'absorb' the costs in greater productivity, profits can fall. Higher prices are likely to mean fewer sales. Whether this results in a fall in turnover depends on the response of consumers to a rise in price (☞ unit 22). Businesses may be able to raise the prices of essential products a great deal with little fall-off in sales.

Shoe leather costs During periods of price stability firms are likely to have good knowledge of the price that they will pay for various goods and services. Such purchases might include delivery vehicles, premises insurance, computer equipment and stationery. However, during periods of rising prices firms may be less able to recognise a 'reasonable' price. They may need to spend more time shopping around for the best price (hence the term shoe leather costs). The extra time spent on this can be extremely expensive for some small firms.

Menu costs This refers to the time and money which firms have to spend on changing their price lists. It is a problem for firms displaying their price either on the actual product or on its packaging. Some firms, such as those distributing their goods via vending machines, are particularly affected.

Wage negotiating When inflation is high, firms will be under strong pressure to upgrade wages and salaries in line with expected levels of inflation. As well as the increased wage costs there will be some administrative costs in these changes. Conflict between employees and employers can result from disagreements about the extent to which wages need to be raised to compensate for inflation.

Reduced purchasing power When prices are rising the REAL VALUE of money will fall. This is the value taking into account inflation. A consumer with £200 to spend will buy far less if prices are increasing. So will a business aiming to purchase £20,000 worth of raw materials. There is said to be a fall in their **purchasing power**.

In periods of inflation, sales of certain goods are particularly affected. Businesses that produce 'luxury' goods, such as designer footwear, are likely to suffer as consumers switch to more essential products. Producers of goods and services sold to groups that are badly hit by inflation may also lose sales. It is argued that **fixed income groups**, such as pensioners, are affected most because their earnings do not always keep pace with inflation.

Businesses unable to increase their turnover in line with their costs will suffer similar effects. This may be the case, for example, with a local retailer with a geographically 'fixed' market, who is unable to raise prices for fear of losing customers to a local superstore. Profits will decline as costs, which are not covered by increased turnover, rise.

Borrowing and lending Inflation redistributes money from lenders to borrowers. A business that has borrowed £20,000 is likely to pay back far less in **real** terms over a ten year period if inflation is high. Businesses that have saved will lose out. Interest rates may fail to keep up with inflation, especially when inflation reaches levels of 10 per cent or more. So, if interest rates are 10 per cent and inflation is 20 per cent, the saver will lose 10 per cent of the real value of savings, but the borrower will find the value to be paid back falls 10 per cent a year.

Investment Views are divided as to the effects of inflation upon investment decisions. Some argue that, in the short term at least, it might increase the amount of investment undertaken by firms. This is because the real rate of interest (taking into account the rate of inflation) is often low during inflationary periods as inflation figures get close to, or exceed, the rate of interest. This makes investment using borrowed money relatively cheap.

Others believe that businesses are less likely to go ahead with investment projects. This is because inflation makes entrepreneurs less certain about the future and less willing to take risks.

Uncertainty Uncertainty may affect decisions other than investment that a business makes. Firms are often unwilling to enter into long term transactions in inflationary periods. Take, for example, a business ordering stocks of sheet metal in March to be delivered in June and paid for in August. Inflation of 24 per cent a year may mean that the price of the good increases by 12 per cent during this period. The firm supplying the sheet metal will receive the amount quoted in March when the payment is made in August. However, by August the value of this money will have declined as a result of the inflation.

Unemployment, growth and trade It is sometimes argued that inflation can actually cause unemployment and lower economic growth. The uncertainty that inflation creates in the minds of business people means they are less willing to take risks, invest in new ventures, expand production or hire workers. Also, if UK inflation rates are higher than those of our competitors, UK products would be relatively more expensive in markets abroad, whilst foreign products would be relatively cheaper in the UK. An inability to compete on price in both domestic and foreign markets could mean the loss of many jobs. It could also result in a deterioration in the balance of payments (☞ unit 69) as the number of exports sold abroad falls and the number of imports coming into the country increases.

Control of inflation

There are a number of policies that can be used to control inflation. To some extent, the policies a government chooses will depend on its view of the causes of inflation.

Control of the money supply The solution to inflation, according to monetarists, is to control the rate of growth of the money supply. Government must make sure that increases in the money supply are matched only by increases in output.

The money supply can be controlled with the use of monetary policy, carried out through the Bank of England (☞ unit 65).

■ Changing interest rates. An increase in interest rates can reduce the money supply. If interest rates increase, the cost of borrowing can influence businesses and consumers to borrow less money from banks and building societies. Raising interest rates may also add to inflation. This is because higher interest rates increase firms' costs and these may be passed on to consumers in the form of higher prices.

■ Restricting bank loans. By restricting the ability of banks to give out loans, the size of the money supply can be regulated. The Bank of England can instruct banks to keep a higher proportion of their assets in reserve. This means that they are able to lend less. The government can also sell financial securities, such as **Treasury Bills**, to the public. This will cause the public to withdraw money from their bank accounts, reduce the size of the bank's assets and leave banks with less to lend out.

QUESTION 2

Table 66.1 *Inflation in selected countries*

Percentages

	June 1992	1987	1980		June 1992	1987	1980
Japan	2.3	0.0	7.7	Sweden	2.1	4.2	13.7
Belgium	2.6	1.6	6.6	USA	3.1	3.7	13.5
Germany	4.3	0.3	5.4	India	14.7	8.8	11.4
France	3.0	3.3	13.3	UK	4.3	4.2	18.0
Yugoslavia	577.9	120.0	30.9	Brazil	909.2	229.7	82.8

Source: adapted from *International Financial Statistics*, September 1992 and the 1987 Yearbook.

(a) Describe the UK's inflation rate relative to that of its international competitors during the period.
(b) Explain how inflation in 1992 may have affected:
   (i) a small firm that considered investing in a new machine which had to borrow £20,000;
   (ii) a manufacturer of drinks machines for sports centres etc. which had to buy parts from a variety of sources overseas;
   (iii) an exporter of men's suits to the USA.

■ Credit or hire purchase restrictions. The government can place controls on the amount of credit and hire purchase agreements which banks and other financial institutions are allowed to give to businesses and consumers. In the 1980s the UK government encouraged competition in financial markets. This led to an explosion in the amount of credit available and made restricting credit much more difficult.

■ Control of the Public Sector Borrowing Requirement (PSBR). A high PSBR (☞ unit 65) can lead to an increase in the money supply as the government seeks to find ways of financing it. Thus, one way of controlling the money supply is to restrict the growth of the PSBR.

Control of the level of demand The solution to demand-pull inflation is to reduce the level of demand in the economy as a whole. This can most effectively be achieved, Keynesians argue, by using **fiscal** policy. There are two main options open to a government.

■ Changes in taxation. An increase in income tax will remove a certain proportion of consumers' income. We have seen in unit 65 that taxation is a withdrawal from the economy. If consumers have less income, they are likely to spend less. Government will be reluctant to use increases in indirect taxes, such as VAT, for the purpose of controlling inflation. If goods are highly priced, people may buy less. However, VAT might actually lead to inflation, as it is included in the price of the good!

■ Reducing government spending. Government spending is an injection into the economy. If it is restricted, then the level of demand in the economy as a whole should fall.

Cost controls The policies a government uses to control cost-push inflation depend on which costs it feels are the most important factor.

■ If wage increases are causing cost-push inflation, the government may use an incomes policy to restrict pay increases. Alternatively, if unions are believed to be pushing for excessive pay increases, then direct attempts can be made to curb their powers. For example, legislation which limits their ability to take industrial action may reduce the amount of pressure for higher wages which unions can place on employers.

■ If increased profits or taxes are believed to be behind the cost-push inflation, then governments can reduce corporation tax or indirect taxes, such as VAT.

■ If a government decides imported inflation is the main problem it must support its exchange rate. To do this the government must prevent a **depreciation** or **devaluation** of the currency (☞ unit 69). This is because a devaluation of the exchange rate increases import prices. One of the main reasons, many economists believe, for the rise in inflation in the latter part of 1992 was the devaluation of pound sterling during the so-called 'Black Wednesday'.

QUESTION 3 Inflation fell rapidly in the early 1980s. From over 20 per cent in 1980, it remained below 6 per cent from early 1983 to late 1988. There then followed inflationary increases in 1989 and 1990. Will Hutton in *The Guardian* wrote, 'So 11 years of public privation in the name of fighting inflation has come to this, an inflation rate of 10.6 per cent.

This is an inflation that will keep interest rates and the exchange rate unnecessarily high for too long as the government sticks to the policy it most favours for bringing inflation down - squeezing the consumer and the economy. So what has caused this inflation level? Not wage inflation or a growth in public expenditure, but a growth in the money supply as the credit boom has led to a huge increase in lending by financial institutions.'

(a) What might the government have seen as the main cause of inflation given the policies it used?

(b) Explain how high interest rates might have affected inflation during this period.

(c) Why might banks have been keen to lend money during periods of high inflation?

Effects of anti-inflationary policy on business

The effects of anti-inflationary monetary policy There are two main effects depending upon the type of monetary policy used. Firstly, if interest rates are raised this will make borrowing by businesses more expensive and might lead to the cancellation of investment projects. Higher interest rates will also hit the pockets of many consumers. They will find it more expensive to borrow money on credit and their mortgage repayments will increase. This is likely to lead to fewer sales, particularly for those firms manufacturing and selling consumer goods. Secondly, if bank lending is restricted, loan capital will be harder to come by, particularly for small firms. Again this may result in less investment and a lower level of demand from consumers as they find credit harder to come by.

The effects of anti-inflationary fiscal policy This can be in the form of tax (usually direct) increases or public expenditure cuts. Tax increases will mean that consumers have less money in their pockets and they are therefore likely to spend less. This will affect the sales of many firms. Public expenditure cuts will mean less money spent on, for example, schools, colleges, hospitals, road building, and local leisure services. This will hit a wide range of firms, especially those who work for local authorities and central government. The construction industry, for example, is always adversely affected by cutbacks in public expenditure.

The effects of anti-inflationary exchange rate policy Such a policy will try to ensure that the exchange rate does not fall too greatly. This was the policy pursued by the British government from the moment it joined the ERM (☞ unit 69) until its departure in September 1992. What effects does such a policy have on firms? It causes the price of UK products in export markets to be relatively high, which makes it difficult to sell products in foreign markets. It also causes the price of imported goods to be relatively cheap, making it difficult for UK firms to compete 'at home'.

Maintaining exchange rates at a particular level often requires a high interest rate. This will lead to major problems for businesses.

QUESTION 4 With inflation rising to over 10 per cent at the beginning of the 1990s, a firm anti-inflationary policy became top priority for the government. A policy of maintaining the exchange rate value of the pound sterling relative to that of the Deutschmark was favoured rather than tax increases. This was accompanied by interest rates of 15 per cent. In October 1990, the government joined the European Exchange Rate Mechanism and thus became even more committed to its policy of holding the exchange rate within targeted levels (although the UK actually left in September 1992).

What effects would such policies during 1990-1992 have had on:
(a) A firm specialising in large scale construction projects;
(b) A Scottish salmon farming business exporting over 50 per cent of its output to Western Europe?

Key terms

Cost-push inflation - inflation which occurs as a result of businesses facing increased costs, which are then passed on to consumers in the form of higher prices.
Demand-pull inflation - inflation which occurs as a result of excessive spending in the economy.
Deflation - a situation where prices are falling.
Hyper-inflation - a situation where inflation levels are very high.
Inflation - a continuing or persistent tendency for prices to rise.
Money supply - the total amount of money circulating in the economy.
Real terms - any value which takes into account the rate of inflation.

Summary

1. How is inflation measured in the UK?
2. Describe the 3 main causes of inflation.
3. What is imported inflation?
4. List 5 ways in which a business might be affected by inflation.
5. How might inflation lead to unemployment?
6. What are the 4 main methods of controlling the money supply?
7. How can the government control the level of demand in the economy?
8. In what ways might businesses be affected by anti-inflationary policies?

Question

Doing business in Brazil

The managing director of Cook and Jeffries, a leading manufacturer of foodstuffs, was concerned about the rising level of inflation in the UK and its possible effects upon the business. To this end, he had asked Andy Hulme, one of his high-flying young executives, to write a report for Cook and Jeffries' senior managers about the potential pitfalls of inflation and possible strategies to overcome them. Andy had spent the last two years in Brazil overseeing Cook and Jeffries' interests in that country. His experiences in Brazil were felt to be especially relevant to this issue because of the particular problems caused by inflation in that country. Below are a selection of extracts from his report.

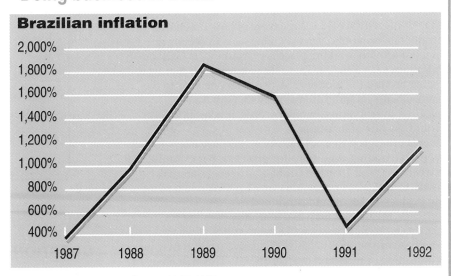

Figure 66.2 *Brazilian inflation, 1987-1992*

- So persistently high is Brazilian inflation, that the Central Bank has run out of famous Brazilians to put on its banknotes and has resorted to Amazonian fish, of which there are more than 2,000 varieties. A good lunch costs more than £39 and calculators can only be used by dropping three zeros. All this is despite two changes of currency in the last five years. Figure 66.2 shows Brazilian inflation rates over the last six years.
- Investment decisions are very hard to make. No capital intensive business likes the Brazilian climate. Many firms need to plan investment decisions over five years, but in Brazil you can't even forecast six months ahead.
- Terms of payment are especially important. Firms aim to have a long lead time in paying suppliers, but fast collection of debts. For retailers, turning over stock as quickly as possible takes on great significance. If retailers can sell within 15 days, but have 30 days to pay, the cash can be invested in money markets for 15 days.
- Investing cash in money markets in this way is highly profitable because of the level of interest rates. The Brazilian government tends to maintain interest rates at 5 per cent above inflation rates as part of its anti-inflationary strategy. Many firms generate a substantial proportion of their profit through taking advantage of these interest rates. However, profits have been hit by a 10 per cent erosion of consumer spending power over the last 3 years.
- Pricing is dominated by inflationary expectations. Firms tend to ignore production costs and the value which consumers place on their products when making pricing decisions. Full-scale price negotiations with unions and suppliers occur at least monthly - most activities which would only happen annually in other countries. For retailers which may stock up to 80,000 different items, this can involve monthly negotiations with 6,000 suppliers on a case-by-case basis.
- Many firms must walk a tightrope in their pricing decisions. Rapid turnover is essential, but prices must also be kept up to keep pace with inflation. Low prices can mean high turnover, but being overtaken by inflation. High prices can allow a firm to keep up with inflation, but can lead to loss of turnover and loss of customers to competitors. Added to this is the total impossibility of planning more than three months ahead.

Source: adapted from the *Financial Times*, 1993.

(a) How would you describe the inflation being experienced in Brazil?
(b) What problems has inflation caused for Brazilian firms?
(c) Explain one measure, other than interest rates, that the government of Brazil could use to control its inflation.
(d) Explain why, during a period of high inflation, it is particularly important for a business 'to have a long lead time in paying suppliers, but fast collection of debts'.
(e) Explain why investment decisions are so difficult for businesses during periods of high inflation.
(f) How do you think Brazilian businesses have been affected by high interest rates?

What is economic growth?

ECONOMIC GROWTH is a measure of how much the output of an economy increases. One way an economy can tell if growth is taking place is to examine its GDP or GNP figures (☞ unit 65). These show how much money is flowing around the economy. A rise from one year to the next is usually an indication of growth. Growth is measured in **real** terms, in other words, it takes into account the rate of inflation.

If economic growth is taking place, there are likely to be favourable trading conditions for business. For example, between 1980 and 1988 the UK had an average annual growth rate of 2.2 per cent. This was a period when many new businesses set up and continued to grow. In periods of growth, businesses may find a healthy demand for their products. Businesses will tend to suffer when growth is zero or even negative. Negative growth may be an indication of recession in an economy. This will have the opposite effect to a period of growth, with declining sales and many firms going out of business.

The growth rate of one country compared to others is also important. It has been argued that Britain has had poor relative growth rates in the post-war period. In the early 1990s growth rates in the UK have been very low. However, so have those of many other countries as they have experienced the effects of a world recession.

The business cycle

The BUSINESS CYCLE (also known as the TRADE CYCLE) is a useful way of showing a country's growth record. It shows the 'ups' and 'downs' which most economies go through over a period of years. At the bottom of the cycle the rate of economic growth will be low or even negative. At the top of the cycle the growth rate will be relatively high. It is argued that all economies go through these cycles, which illustrate fluctuations in economic activity.

For example, in the UK there was a boom in the mid-1980s, but a slump at the beginning of the 1990s. Figure 67.1 shows a typical business cycle. There are four parts to the cycle.

■ Peak or boom. A BOOM occurs when an economy is at a peak. GNP will be high, as will consumption and investment. Many firms will be experiencing high levels of demand from consumers with increasing disposable income. Profits should be high for most firms, but wages are likely to be rising.

■ Recession. A RECESSION occurs when incomes and output begin to fall. Businesses will face a fall in demand for their products and some may begin to lay off workers.

■ Trough or slump. A SLUMP occurs when the economy is at the bottom of the business cycle. Many

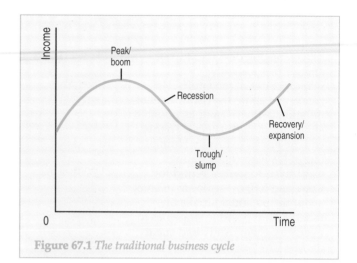

Figure 67.1 *The traditional business cycle*

QUESTION 1

Table 67.1 *New company formations*

	Total	Percentage change
1983	96,190	10.3
1984	97,937	1.8
1985	104,655	6.9
1986	117,378	12.2
1987	128,138	9.2
1988	129,182	0.8
1989	130,478	1.0
1990	121,194	-7.1
1991	110,108	-9.1
1992	107,375	-2.5

Evidence that the worst of the recession may have been over was contained in figures on new company registrations in 1992. In addition, businesses were more optimistic that sales and profits would improve the following year, according to a survey by Dun & Bradstreet, the business-information group. It suggested that confidence increased significantly after the first quarter of 1992, with light industry and the service sector expected to lead a revival in sales over the three months from January 1993.

In a separate report, Jordans, another business-information company, said that the number of companies formed in 1993 fell for the third year running, but the rate of decline was lower than in either 1990 or 1991. In particular, the decline in company formations slowed in the second half of 1992, underlining expectations that the recession may have been ending.

Source: adapted from the *Financial Times*, 11.1.1993.

(a) From the data provided, identify:
(i) a boom year;
(ii) a slump year.
(b) What evidence was there that the British economy was moving out of recession in 1992-1993?
(c) What effect might the end of a recession have had on new businesses?

firms will be going out of business and unemployment levels will be very high.

- Recovery or expansion. During this stage of the business cycle, income and business output will begin to increase. Firms will be investing more and consumers will be spending more. Many firms will be taking on more employees.

Factors affecting growth

There are a number of factors that can lead to economic growth.

Land Land includes all natural resources such as forests, lakes and oil and coal deposits, as well as land itself. It is possible for countries to experience economic growth through more effective exploitation of their natural resources. Saudi Arabia, for example, has generated the vast majority of its wealth from its oil reserves and the UK has benefited from North Sea oil.

Labour force/population Increasing the quantity of the labour force can contribute to economic growth.
- One relatively easy way of increasing the labour force is to encourage immigration. The success of the US economy has been partly attributed to the effects of immigration.
- Changes in the demography (unit 51) of a country can be important. More young people will swell the size of the workforce, but an increase in the birth rate will create more dependents for a number of years. The UK is at present experiencing an ageing of its population, resulting in a relative decline in the number of people of working age.
- One of the biggest increases in the UK's workforce over the last thirty years has come about through the increasing participation of women in work. At any given time, there are usually large numbers of women willing to enter the workforce should suitable employment become available.

Whilst the quantity of labour in a country can be important, the quality of it tends to be especially significant in influencing growth rates. A well trained, well educated workforce, which is flexible and able to respond to change is particularly useful for business and can lead to growth.

Investment and technology Economic growth requires an increase in the capital stock of the economy. This means the development of and investment in new technology (unit 36) and the updating of capital equipment. Technological development also allows new products to be created. It is not just the quantity of investment in an economy which is important. Investment needs to be directed into growth industries whose products are likely to be in high demand in the future.

Government policy Governments can use a combination of fiscal, monetary, exchange rate and supply side policies to stimulate growth. The policies a government chooses

will reflect its views about the operation of the economy (unit 65). The choice of policy is important. Even if an economy has great natural resources, a well trained workforce and high levels of investment it may be held back by inappropriate government policy.

Demographic change and business

Changes in the structure of a country's population can have important implications for firms.

Recruitment A decline in the size of the working population may cause firms to turn to sections of the population often overlooked in less difficult times. These include the young, the elderly and women with young families. An ageing population, with relatively fewer young workers might result in firms seeking to recruit retired people. B & Q, for example, have a policy of specifically hiring more elderly workers. A decline in the numbers of people of working age may also prompt firms to provide creche facilities in order to encourage more women back into the workforce. They might also employ more part time workers on flexible hours, hoping to attract students and others unable to commit themselves to full time work.

Marketing Changes in the structure of the population may result in a decline in the age group primarily purchasing a particular product. Baby products, for example, would be likely to experience a fall off in demand if there was a decline in the birth rate. Manufacturers could either seek to reduce their production of these products or attempt to find new

---

QUESTION 2 Britain's population is ageing. The number of people of pensionable age rose 16 per cent between 1971 and 1991 and will increase a further 38 per cent - to 14.6 million - by 2031. There will be twice as many people over 65 in the Britain of 2021 as there were in 1951. Within this ageing process there will be a particularly sharp rise in the very elderly, who demand the most extensive - and expensive - medical and social care. People in their late 80s consume about ten times the health expenditure of 40 year-olds.

During the 1980s the increase in the numbers of elderly coupled with a decline in long-stay hospital provision led to rapid growth in the numbers accommodated in private homes. It was good news for the private residential care sector, but social security benefits paid the bills. Social security payments for people in private and charitable residential and nursing homes made an astonishing leap from £10 million in 1979 to £2.5 billion this year.

Source: adapted from the *Financial Times*, 1993.

(a) What effect do you think these trends will have on economic growth in the UK?
(b) Discuss how demographic trends might affect:
   (i) a business aiming to find a niche market for a new magazine;
   (ii) a supermarket chain;
   (iii) the pharmaceutical industry;
   (iv) the NHS.

markets for them. Producers of talcum powder for babies have been successful in marketing it to adults. Firms may also seek to diversify into areas where demand is likely to be higher. Boddingtons the brewers, for example, now own residential homes for the elderly.

Business location Changes in the geographical distribution of the population may cause firms to consider their location decisions. One of the most significant population movements in the UK today is the shift of people from urban to suburban and semi-rural locations. Retailers, such as supermarkets, must respond rapidly to such population shifts. Businesses providing a wide range of goods and services may well wish to locate or re-locate close to their consumers.

Business and economic growth

The majority of firms benefit from a growing economy. There are some, such as pawnbrokers and scrap-metal dealers who perhaps do better in recessions, but these tend to be exceptions. If a business is operating in a growing economy, experiencing economic growth rates of 3 per cent per annum or more, this is likely to have a number of effects upon it. Not all of them, however, are positive.

Sales revenue Consumer spending should be high during a period of economic growth. This will increase the demand for many firms' products and should lead to an increase in sales revenue. If a firm is able to keep its costs under control, this should also mean an increase in profits.

Expansion An increase in the demand for a firm's products generated by a sustained period of economic growth may lead to expansion. Some businesses are forced into expanding where they find that they cannot meet demand. Others plan their expansion well in advance. Expansion may involve some or all of the following:
- recruiting new staff;
- raising finance;
- increasing the size of premises;
- moving to new premises;
- purchasing more assets, for example, production facilities, machinery or office equipment;
- taking over competitors.

Security In a healthy business climate, a firm is likely to feel more secure in its decisions. It will be able to order from suppliers with greater confidence. This may lead to a better and more effective relationship. Firms should also be able to hire employees without concern about being forced to lay them off within a short period of time. This may result in a firm committing itself more to the workforce, for example, by investing in training programmes.

Planning for the future Economic growth should provide businesses with more confidence in planning for

the future. Higher profit levels, for example, should help to provide investment funds for new projects. Year to year or even day to day survival is likely to become less of an issue as a firm seeks to consolidate its future position. However, confidence in planning for the future will hinge upon how long the business expects the growth to last. Due to the UK's past record of rapidly moving from boom to slump, there is evidence that many British firms do not regard a period of economic growth as sufficient reason to undertake investment projects.

Increasing costs As mentioned earlier in this unit, it is not unusual for high economic growth rates to be accompanied by rising costs. Land costs often rise during such periods. This was especially evident in the South East of England during the mid-1980s, when property prices spiralled. Labour costs may also increase as employees and trade unions seek to benefit from the success of their business.

The effects of lack of growth on business

A lack of growth or negative growth in the economy can have a number of effects on business.

Changes in consumer demand Many firms will face a fall in the demand for their products. This is because the incomes of consumers tend to fall during such periods, forcing them into cutting back on spending. The effect of this is not spread evenly amongst firms. For some the impact can be dramatic, leading to redundancies and even closure. The construction industry is notoriously vulnerable to recessions. The Costain Group, for example, which is involved in the construction of the Channel Tunnel, experienced a £979 million fall in sales in the year to April 1993. Producers of consumer goods tend to suffer less in a recession than producers of goods for industrial markets.

Confidence There tends to be a general lack of confidence amongst businesses during a recession. This can lead to investment projects being cancelled and orders being lost. Some firms will be affected not only for the period of the recession itself, but also in the longer term. It may also lead to a loss of profitability and competitiveness.

Effect on small firms Small firms tend to be especially vulnerable to recession. They often do not have the finance to withstand periods of negative cash flow (☞ unit 44) which occur during such times. Also, small firms tend to rely upon banks. This means that they may suffer as banks are reluctant to lend during recessions. Banks also tend to call in loans at short notice.

Possible benefits Those firms which survive during a recession may benefit from a reduction in competition, as their rivals go out of business. This should put them in a position to gain a greater share of the market, especially when the economy picks up again. The recession may also force businesses to become leaner and fitter operations. Government policies designed to bring an economy out of recession can be an advantage to many firms. For example, interest rates are often reduced to help bring a recession to an end.

Business failure

Recession often leads to the failure of businesses. Figure 67.2 shows the extent of the problem. Over 60,000 firms, more than 1,000 a week, went out of business in 1992. These failures range from the collapse of small businesses which have barely managed to get off the ground, to huge multinational corporations such as the Bank of Credit and Commerce International (BCCI). When BCCI collapsed it had liabilities of $10.6 billion and assets of only $1.1 billion.

However, the vast majority of business failures are accounted for by small firms. Only 40 per cent of small businesses started up after 1989 were still trading after three years. This is shown in Figure 67.3. A number of terms are used to explain business failure. Businesses ultimately fail because they are **insolvent**. This means that they are unable to pay their debts. The **Insolvency Act 1986** sets out certain regulations for terminating businesses that become insolvent.

Sole traders and partnerships can be declared BANKRUPT. The process of a person being declared bankrupt begins when one or more creditors of a business present a petition to a court. Petitions can only be presented by creditors who are owed £750 or more by a business. If this is successful, then a receiving order will be made out against the debtor. An OFFICIAL RECEIVER is then appointed who has legal rights over all of the owner's property. Nothing can happen to this property without the permission of the Official Receiver. If the Official Receiver believes that the business is still a going concern, a manager will be appointed to run the business on the Receiver's behalf. Within fourteen days of the bankruptcy being declared, a meeting of creditors will be called. At this meeting the debtor has the opportunity to present proposals to meet debts. If this is unsuccessful, the debtor will return to court and, if the court is satisfied, the debtor will be declared bankrupt.

Private or public limited companies face LIQUIDATION. Liquidation can be either compulsory or voluntary, depending upon the circumstances. It involves the appointment of an Official Receiver as a **Liquidator**. This person is responsible for the winding-up of a company, taking control of a company's affairs and gathering assets with a view to finding a buyer. The liquidator is also responsible for paying off any debts the company may have. The law states the order of priority in the payment of debts. For example, payment of taxes comes before payments to firms. Some creditors may receive nothing if the company was heavily in debt.

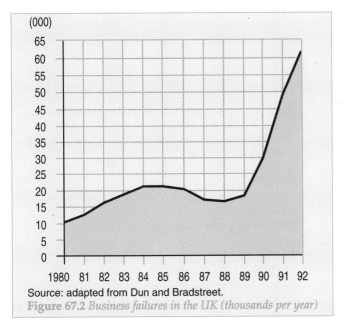

(000)
Source: adapted from Dun and Bradstreet.
Figure 67.2 Business failures in the UK (thousands per year)

QUESTION 3 Within a few hours of the liquidator arriving at Ms Jennifer Bond's Leicestershire leather-processing business a £65,000 order arrived. The order, for the tanning and dyeing of about 50,000 feet of leather, would have kept the factory busy for more than a month. But underfunding had already brought about the demise of the five year old business, and a meeting of creditors is expected to put it into voluntary liquidation. Ms Bond said, 'The recession has passed but we can't finance the orders we are getting.'

Ironically the Leicestershire company's fate was sealed by its efforts to expand the business. It increased turnover from £300,000 in 1991 to £500,000 in 1992 by switching from the cheaper leathers and varied colours used in women's shoes to better quality leather for men's shoes, most of which are dyed black. The improvement in business increased the company's need for working capital and put further pressure on its already overstretched finances. 'We were very successful in opening up new markets but we didn't have the money to go on', said Ms Bond. 'We couldn't afford to buy in the chemicals or the other raw materials.'

The problem of how to finance growth is one which faces many businesses in a recession. Ms Bond's company had barely established itself when the recession began to bite and it lost money in 1991 and 1992. The company was unable to return to profit and finally Ms Bond decided to call in the liquidator.

If the creditors approve, the liquidator will sell off the plant and equipment, the remains of the lease on the factory and any other assets he can find. Ms Bond, in spite of her disappointment at the loss of the business and concern at the personal liability she may still face when the business is liquidated, is relieved that it is all over. 'I feel better', she said, after her first meeting with the liquidator. 'It has been two years of ifs and buts.'

Source: adapted from the Financial Times, 1993.

(a) What factors contributed to the collapse of Ms Bond's business?
(b) Why was Ms Bond not declared bankrupt?
(c) How would an increase in economic growth have affected Ms Bond's business?
(d) Why are small firms likely to suffer from a recession more than larger firms?

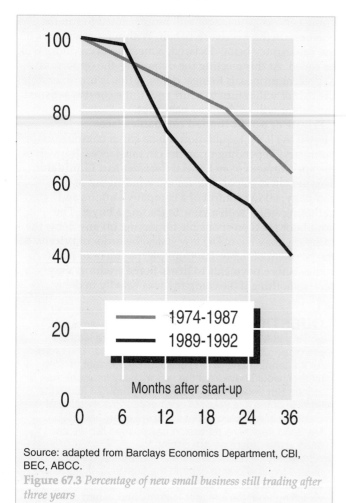

Source: adapted from Barclays Economics Department, CBI, BEC, ABCC.

Figure 67.3 *Percentage of new small business still trading after three years*

Survival in a recession

It is useful for businesses to find strategies which they can use to weather a recession or increase their chances of doing so. Possible strategies may include some of the following.

■ Focusing upon parts of the market where a firm has an advantage. A firm, for example, may produce a number of product lines.
■ Accurate and up to date financial information. Firms need to identify quickly where losses are being made and act decisively with the use of this information.
■ Credit control. Small firms, in particular, are often forced to close down due to the failure of a major customer to pay their bills. A tight credit control policy which involves promptly chasing up slow payers and taking out credit insurance can be useful.
■ Realistic planning. Too many firms set their business plans (unit 8) on the assumption that nothing will go wrong. In a recession it is vital that firms build room into their plans for setbacks.
■ Diversification into other markets. Businesses may move into new markets. They could include more 'secure' home markets or those in such countries as Germany or Japan, which are less prone to recession.

QUESTION 4 Lucas, one of the UK's leading manufacturers and suppliers of parts to the motor industry, is one example of a firm affected by the recession. The company was not 'overweighted', but it was investing heavily in itself to keep up with international competitors. The financial strain imposed by three years of recession finally made this expenditure unaffordable. After slashing its workforce and selling off businesses to stay alive, however, Lucas will find it increasingly hard to compete with foreign rivals.

Source: adapted from *The Independent on Sunday*, 18.10.1992.

(a) What strategy have Lucas employed in order to survive the recession?
(b) What positive effects might the recession have had on Lucas?

Key terms

Bankruptcy - declared by a court when a sole trader or partnership cannot meet its debts.
Boom - the stage when an economy is at the peak of its activity.
Business or trade cycle - a measure of the regular fluctuations in the level of economic activity.
Economic growth - a measure of how much the output of an economy rises over time.
Liquidation - declared by a court when a company is unable to meet its debts.
Official Receiver - the person called in to handle the affairs of a business facing bankruptcy or liquidation.
Recession - when income and output begins to fall in an economy.
Slump - the bottom stage or lowest point of the trade cycle.

Summary

1. What are the 4 main parts of the business cycle?
2. How might land contribute to economic growth?
3. In what ways might a firm be affected by demographic change?
4. How might a business benefit from economic growth?
5. What problems might economic growth cause for a firm?
6. Why are small firms especially vulnerable to recession?
7. What is the difference between bankruptcy and liquidation?
8. What strategies might a business pursue in order to survive a recession?

Question

Daf

On February 2 1993 Daf, the Anglo-Dutch commercial vehicle maker, was forced to file for protection against its creditors in the Netherlands. The number of truck makers in Europe had already dropped from 25 in 1975 to 10 by the end of 1991, and the group was still shrinking.

Financially, Daf has been the weakest of the leading European truck makers, but it has tried hard to compete in the industry's premier league. Daf is the biggest truck maker in the UK - since its takeover of Leyland vehicles in 1987 - and it is the UK truck market leader, with a market share of 25 per cent. It has just over 7 per cent of the west European truck market.

Daf's single biggest shareholder is British Aerospace, with a 10.9 per cent stake. As Daf's problems have grown it has, however, been Dutch companies, who between them own over 40 per cent of shares, that have answered the distress call. Daf insisted yesterday that its attempt to engineer a financial rescue had failed because of the opposition of a minority of its banks, mainly in the UK, to its proposals for securing emergency short-term funding.

As news of the financial collapse spread, some suppliers immediately began to stop deliveries of components. With just-in-time delivery of parts to plants spread from Lancashire to Eindhoven in the Netherlands, the impact of such actions on the assembly process can be almost immediate.

'Where possible we are producing, but in some areas supplies of components have stopped. What happens tomorrow, I don't know', said one Daf executive in the UK. As Daf fortunes have waned, it has proved unable to find a rescuer within the industry, despite desperate overtures in recent months to Mercedes-Benz, the world's biggest truck maker. It has also searched in vain in recent months for a Japanese partner. Daf's competitors have enough troubles of their own. Volvo, Renault and Iveco are all losing money on their truck and bus operations. In the US the heavy truck industry has been deep in loss for five of the past 11 years. In Japan the truck market has been falling for more than two years.

The fortunes of the truck makers fluctuate widely as the industry suffers from exaggerated trading cycles. In west Europe the last year of strong growth was 1989, the year that Daf went public. European truck sales have been falling for the past three years, and there is little prospect of relief during 1993 with demand forecast to fall particularly sharply in Germany and Italy.

Each lurch downwards in the trading cycle claims new victims, and Daf has long looked most exposed. Its financial demise has abruptly ended its brave dream of becoming one of the leading players in the European truck industry, able to challenge the likes of Mercedes-Benz, Iveco and the Franco-Swedish alliance of Renault and Volvo. Its strategy for climbing into the top flight started with the takeover in 1987 of the then British Leyland truck and van operations. The move transformed it from being essentially a heavy truck and bus maker into a commercial vehicle producer with a full product range from vans to

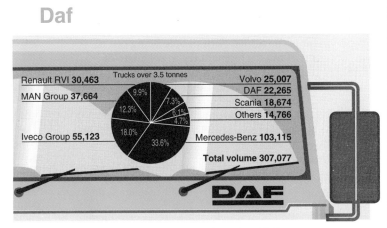

Figure 67.4 *The Western European truck market, 1991*

light, medium and heavy trucks and buses.

The UK became its biggest single market after the merger with Leyland and by 1991 the UK still accounted for 29.4 per cent of group sales. In 1991 it ousted Iveco from the leadership of the UK truck market.

But market leadership has been small consolation when overall UK truck sales have fallen to their lowest level since the early 1950s. In the past three years, the number of trucks sold in the UK market has declined by more than 50 per cent, from 69,234 in 1989 to only 31,398 in 1992. Daf has tried hard to reduce its dependence on the UK by expanding its dealer network and sales overseas - in particular in Germany and in France. But other markets have weakened too.

Excluding the German market, the impact of recession has been savage. According to Mr Peter Schmidt, an analyst at the UK-based Automotive Industry Data, the west European truck market excluding Germany, has plunged from 255,000 in 1989 to 160,000 in 1992, the lowest level for at least two decades. Including Germany, truck sales in western Europe have fallen from 321,000 in 1989 to an estimated 281,000 last year.

Daf has had its own problems. It has been exposed by having the breadth of product range of the biggest manufacturers without their production and sales volumes. As a result, it has been unable to achieve economies of scale. But if Daf's problems have been exaggerated by its relatively small size, its rivals are unlikely to feel reassured. The problems of the European truck industry are likely to get worse before they get better. Some of Daf's larger competitors may also find themselves forced onto the hard shoulder before the end of the decade.

Source: adapted from the *Financial Times*, 3.2.1993.

(a) To what extent was recession to blame for Daf's problems?

(b) What are 'exaggerated trading cycles'? Why should the truck industry suffer from them?

(c) In what ways have Daf attempted to avoid calling in the receivers?

(d) Why do you think Daf's problems were 'exaggerated by its relatively small size'?

(e) Describe the likely role of the Receiver in this matter.

What is unemployment?

Unemployment is concerned with people being out of work. Measures of unemployment try to calculate or estimate the number of people out of work at a given point in time. In the UK, unemployment is measured by counting those claiming benefit for being unemployed. Figure 68.1 shows unemployment rates from 1972 to 1992 in the UK. It illustrates the unemployed as a percentage of the labour force (ie those either in work or officially counted as unemployed).

Source: adapted from *The Observer*, 21.3.1993.

Figure 68.1 *UK unemployment rates, 1972-1992*

Types of unemployment

There are a number of different types of unemployment.

Seasonal unemployment Some workers are employed on a seasonal basis. In the UK construction, holiday and agricultural industries, workers are less in demand in winter because of the climate. Seasonal unemployment is therefore high. In summer it falls, as these workers are hired. It is difficult in practice for governments to 'solve' this type of unemployment, which may always occur. In producing unemployment statistics, governments often adjust the figures to allow for seasonal factors.

Search and frictional unemployment These two types of unemployment are very similar. FRICTIONAL unemployment occurs when people are moving between jobs. Usually it only lasts for a short amount of time. For example, an electrician who had been working in the North East may have a few weeks 'off' before starting a new job in London. It is not seen as a serious problem by government. SEARCH unemployment, however, can last

longer. People often spend time looking for a new job. The greater the information on job opportunities, the lower search unemployment is likely to be.

Structural unemployment STRUCTURAL unemployment is caused by changes in the structure of a country's economy. Examples include the decline of the coal and steel industries during the last twenty years. Between 1963 and 1993 almost half a million jobs were lost in the coal mining industry. This indicates the size of the problem in the UK. Because certain industries have traditionally been located in particular parts of the country, their decline can have a dramatic effect upon those regions. As a result, structural unemployment is closely linked with regional unemployment.

Technological unemployment This occurs when new technology replaces workers with machines. For example, new technology introduced to the newspaper industry has meant the loss of many print workers' jobs.

Cyclical unemployment CYCLICAL unemployment results from the cycles which occur in most economies. These ups and downs in economic activity over a number of years are known as the **business cycle** (☞ unit 67). In a recession, at the 'bottom' of a business cycle, unemployment results from a lack of demand. It is argued that demand is not high enough to employ all labour, machines, land, offices etc. in the economy. This **Keynesian** view was explained in unit 65.

Real wage unemployment We saw in unit 65 that those who argue for a free market approach believe an economy will achieve full employment if wage rates are flexible. They suggest that the number of workers a business employs depends on its wage costs. Relatively high real wages mean that businesses will employ fewer workers. The real wage rate is the wage rate that determines the supply of labour. Unemployment occurs when the REAL WAGE RATE is above that needed to employ all workers. In other words, it is argued that workers 'price themselves' out of jobs. There are vacancies, but businesses will only be willing to pay wages which are lower than workers are prepared to accept.

Voluntary and involuntary unemployment Some suggest that unemployment can be voluntary or involuntary. Voluntary unemployment occurs when workers refuse to accept jobs at existing wage rates. Involuntary unemployment occurs when there are not enough jobs in the economy at existing wage rates. The natural rate of unemployment (☞ unit 65) is the percentage of voluntarily unemployed workers.

QUESTION 1 Guinness, the brewing and spirits group, is to cut 700 jobs in its United Distillers' Scotch whisky production operations. The group, which employs 5,000 people in Scotland, will close five distilleries and three bottling plants as part of a cost-cutting and modernisation programme. The move has come to help restore the balance between the industry's output and estimated demand during the 1990s.

Mr Tony Greener, Guinness chairman and chief executive, said £100 million would be invested over the next three years in modernising production facilities. 'The investment in new technology requires significant reorganisation to achieve improved productivity, efficiency and profitability', he said. Trade union officials described the decision as 'devastating'.
Source: adapted from the *Financial Times*, 13.1.1993.

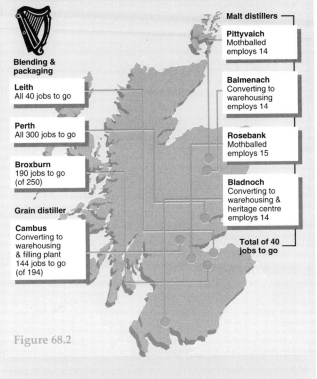

Blending & packaging

Leith
All 40 jobs to go

Perth
All 300 jobs to go

Broxburn
190 jobs to go
(of 250)

Grain distiller

Cambus
Converting to warehousing & filling plant 144 jobs to go (of 194)

Malt distillers

Pittyvaich
Mothballed employs 14

Balmenach
Converting to warehousing employs 14

Rosebank
Mothballed employs 15

Bladnoch
Converting to warehousing & heritage centre employs 14

Total of 40 jobs to go

Figure 68.2

(a) What types of unemployment might the loss of these jobs create?
(b) Explain why moves to 'restore the balance between the industry's output and estimated demand' should lead to unemployment.
(c) How might these job cuts lead to increased efficiency and profitability for the business?

Effects of unemployment on business

High levels of unemployment have a number of effects on businesses. Not all of them are harmful.

Demand The obvious effect of unemployment is that people are not earning income and are likely to have less to spend. Businesses will suffer a loss of demand for their products and reduced profits as a result. Producers of goods, such as clothing and footwear, and providers of services, such as insurance and holidays, are all likely to suffer.

There are, perhaps, a number of 'side-effects' to unemployment. Research has indicated a link between unemployment and illnesses related to poverty and stress. There is also evidence that it can lead to 'social' problems, such as vandalism and crime, resulting in higher insurance premiums for firms.

Organisation Unemployment can have a number of effects on the internal organisation of a business. It may mean that a firm can no longer afford to recruit new members of staff because of low demand for its products. New, often young, recruits to a firm will no longer be coming through. In addition, new posts which arise may be filled through retraining of existing staff rather than recruitment.

Redundancies are also a common feature of a period of high unemployment. Whilst the work of some who are made redundant will not be replaced, the responsibilities and roles of others may be added to the job descriptions of those who remain with the firm.

During periods of high unemployment, some firms reorganise their internal structure. This may mean the loss of a whole tier in the hierarchy or the changing of individual job descriptions. Part of IBM's reorganisation, for example, has been to remove many of their middle managers.

Output During periods of unemployment, many firms reduce their level of output to compensate for falling demand. This can lead to excess capacity and under-utilisation of capital equipment. In addition, falling levels of demand can interrupt the flow of production, causing production and stock control problems (☞ unit 33).

Payments Businesses may be faced with making redundancy payments to workers. These tend to vary between firms depending upon the average length of service of the employee.

The cost of any reorganisation caused by redundancies will also have to be borne by firms. Such costs may include lost productivity after a reorganisation, as employees struggle to cope with new responsibilities.

It may be easier for firms to recruit new employees during a period of high unemployment. This is because there is a larger pool of people to choose from, with more applicants for each available post. In addition, because of the increased competition for new jobs, people may be prepared to work for less money. In this way firms can lower their labour costs.

Government spending High levels of unemployment mean that government spending on social security will be high. Also, the government will lose revenue from tax and National Insurance contributions which people would have paid had they been in employment. It was estimated in 1989 that the cost of this was £5,700 million in lost revenue for every one million people unemployed.

To make up for this the government is likely to either borrow, increase taxation or reduce other items of spending.

Increased trade and reduced costs The services offered by some firms depend upon other firms going out of business. Firms specialising in receiverships and pawnbrokers may see an increase in the demand for their services. Firms also benefit from 'trading down', ie buying cheaper alternatives. Retailers and manufacturers selling goods aimed at lower income segments of the market tend to do well during periods of unemployment. Supermarkets, in particular, have benefited. It has been argued that this is because consumers spend more on home entertainment and less on going out during periods of high unemployment.

QUESTION 2 In 1990, English China Clay employed 4,500 people in their china clay works close to the Cornish town of St Austell. They very much formed the backbone of the local economy. There was great concern in the town of 20,000 people when they announced that 14.5 per cent of the workforce would lose their jobs in across-the-board redundancies. In company towns such as St Austell, it is common for a family's links with the company to go back for generations, and several members of the same family may work there at any one time. When redundancies occur, almost everyone has a relation or friend who is affected.

ECC's job cutting continued in 1991 when more than 1,000 jobs in the British part of ECC disappeared. In 1992, the company had to set aside £14.3 million. Most of this was to cover a write-down in the value of land for ECC's house building business. £5.5 million was for redundancies and other cutbacks.

However, despite these cutbacks, things are still not looking rosy for ECC's European operations. One of their biggest groups of customers, paper manufacturers, are, according to ECC's chief executive Andrew Teare, 'having a hard time, and they are trying to pass some of the pain on to their suppliers'.

Source: adapted from *Management Today*, December 1990 and *The Guardian*, 16.3.1993.

Explain the potential impact of these redundancies on:
(a) English China Clay itself;
(b) the local business community in St Austell;
(c) the government's revenue and spending.

Employment policies

As with other problems, such as inflation, there is great debate about the policies which should be used to solve unemployment. Such policies are similar to those used to generate economic growth (☞ unit 67).

Policies to increase demand If the government believes that unemployment is caused by a lack of aggregate demand there are a number of policies it can use.

- Government can increase its spending. An increase in spending on sporting facilities would mean more work for construction firms and those businesses supplying the construction industry. Grants to industry, spending on roads, or employing workers in government departments or nationalised industries, would also create employment. Increased child benefit or other benefits could lead to increased consumer spending, which may create jobs.
- Cuts in direct taxation will increase the disposable income of consumers and may lead to more spending and jobs.
- Reducing interest rates may encourage both businesses and consumers to borrow. This should lead to an increase in the amount of consumption and investment.
- Increasing the money supply (the amount of money in the economy), some economists believe, will increase the overall level of demand.
- Governments could provide grants and/or loans to firms attempting to sell in foreign markets.

Supply side policies These are policies that:
- encourage the workings of the free market;
- encourage competition;
- attempt to change the aggregate or total supply in the economy;
- give incentives to business and individuals.

Such an approach is advocated by those who feel full employment will be achieved if the labour market works freely. Unemployment can result, as we saw earlier, from real wages being too high. Policies to deal with this may include the following.

- The power of trade unions can be reduced. This would result in them being less able to force wage levels up.
- Social security benefits could be reduced. This would allow firms to reduce their wage levels and still be able to attract workers.
- Cuts in taxation will leave businesses with more profit and give them an incentive to employ more workers and expand production. Cuts in taxation will also give workers an incentive to take low paid jobs, as they will be left with more of their income.
- Retraining incentives for workers and businesses will allow people to develop skills to help them gain employment. For example, in the 1993 Budget £67 million was allocated to the 'learning for work' scheme. This gives the chance for 30,000 unemployed people to follow vocational full time courses of education.

This approach also argues that search unemployment can be important. To overcome this, a number of measures may be used, such as:
- greater availability of information about jobs;
- improving the mobility of labour, for example, by making the buying or selling of houses more straightforward;
- 'job clubs', where people seeking work can find advice and facilities to help them apply for jobs, eg telephones and word processors.

QUESTION 3 More and more people are using Career Development Loans (CDLs) to help them pay for vocational training, says the first annual report on the scheme.

In 1991-92 over ten thousand people took out a Career Development Loan - a 30 per cent increase on the year before. Almost 60,000 more loans will be available over the period 1992-1995.

Just over half of all CDL trainees are aged 25-39, and the average loan is for about £2,600. The type of courses undertaken are extremely varied, for example, secretarial, windsurfing, managing people, HGV driving, law, computer programming, oceanography, and dental hygienist courses. Seven out of ten people using CDLs are in or go into jobs straight after their training.

Career Development Loans enable individuals, who may not otherwise have been able to afford it, to take up a training course. Courses can be full, part time or distance learning and CDLs can support up to one year of training. The Co-operative, Barclays and Clydesdale Banks make the loans which range from £300 to £5,000 to cover up to 80 per cent of course fees, the full cost of books and materials and, where appropriate, a contribution towards living expenses for full-time courses. The other 20 per cent of course fees is paid for by the trainee.

Source: *Employment Gazette*, December 1992.

(a) Explain why loan schemes may be considered a supply side solution to unemployment.
(b) How might such a scheme help to solve 'search' unemployment problems?
(c) What are the advantages of the scheme for:
 (i) the government;
 (ii) the business sector?

Effects of policy on business

Policies to increase demand Firms can both benefit and suffer from government policy to increase demand in the economy. Fiscal policy involving increases in the amount of government spending on new capital projects, such as hospitals and colleges, can lead to an increase in the demand for many firms' products. Cuts in income tax may also increase demand. Similarly, monetary policy that reduces interest rates can make the cost of borrowing cheaper for firms, allowing them to invest in new plant and machinery. Lower interest rates also make it cheaper for consumers to borrow. This can increase the demand for a variety of goods, particularly those, such as consumer durables bought on credit.

However, the government may have to finance its spending by borrowing or taxation. The former may involve a rise in interest rates, which makes loans to firms more expensive. Increased corporation tax or income tax will take away a firm's profits or income. Increasing the money supply or government spending may lead to inflation, which can also be harmful to businesses.

Supply side policies Supply side policies can also affect firms.

■ Policies which aim to cut wages reduce the cost of employing labour for firms.
■ A more mobile workforce would make recruitment easier for businesses.
■ A better trained workforce would mean less training would be needed within firms.
■ A problem with supply side policies is that they can lead to the creation of significant numbers of low paid jobs. Not only may this reduce the morale and motivation of low paid workers, but it may also lead to a lower level of demand in the economy.
■ There is also concern that supply side policies, giving greater freedom to businesses, could result in damage to the environment. This is because businesses, left to themselves, often fail to take account of the true social costs (☞ unit 72) of their activities.

QUESTION 4 As the economic depression worsened in 1992, the award for the most inappropriate economic contribution of the year became intense. Amongst the leaders were the Organisation for Economic Co-operation and Development (OECD) with their calls for a reduction in public spending and the government for their repeated assertion that beating inflation remained the number one policy.

What we needed were policies to expand demand, not policies which depressed it even further. The most powerful ways of achieving this are by reducing taxes or stepping up public expenditure. Public expenditure increases would have directly helped the hard pressed construction industry and would have stimulated consumption and then industrial investment across the economy as a whole.

Source: adapted from *The Observer*, 18.8.1992.

(a) How would you describe the author's approach to solving unemployment?
(b) Explain what methods the government might use to increase demand and how this might have directly helped the 'hard pressed construction industry'.

Key terms

Cyclical unemployment - unemployment resulting from the ups and downs (cycles) which occur in most economies.
Frictional/search unemployment - unemployment caused by people moving from one job to another.
Real wage rate - wage rates that take into account the effects of inflation.
Structural unemployment - unemployment caused by changes in the structure of the economy.

Summary

1. How is unemployment defined?
2. What are the different types of unemployment?
3. Why is frictional unemployment not regarded as a problem by government?
4. What are the possible negative effects of unemployment on firms?
5. What are the possible positive effects of unemployment on firms?
6. State 3 policies to:
   (a) increase demand;
   (b) increase supply.
7. How might government policy to solve unemployment benefit a firm?
8. Give 2 reasons why government spending to solve unemployment may be a problem.
9. Briefly explain the benefits of supply side policies to firms.

Question

IBM to cut 25,000 more jobs

International Business Machines (IBM), reeling from a global economic slowdown and a rapidly changing computer market, yesterday announced plans to cut its worldwide workforce by 25,000, or 8 per cent, next year and sharply reduce its manufacturing capacity. It will take a $6 billion (£3.9 billion) fourth-quarter charge to cover the costs.

In a sign of the severity of the crisis facing the world's largest computer company, IBM made clear that a policy of no forced redundancies was no longer safe. Mr John Akers, the chairman, said that while IBM would try to achieve job cuts voluntarily, if current business conditions did not improve significantly 'it is likely that some business units will be unable to maintain full employment in 1993'.

IBM declined to spell out precisely where job cuts would fall. Since 1986, IBM has already cut its workforce by about 100,000 to some 300,000. The extent to which the restructuring will affect IBM Europe was unclear as each country's managers and personnel directors held urgent meetings. Individual countries are being left to make their own provisions. Many divisions have yet to learn details of the cuts.

IBM Germany, however, said that next year it would cut rather more than the 2,000 jobs that it shed in 1993. It would not rule out further redundancies as a way of reducing the workforce. IBM UK said it expected to cut up to 1,000 jobs in 1993, the same as this year. By the end of 1993, IBM's workforce could be down to 13,000 in the UK, about 5,000 less than in 1990.

Worldwide, the company is to cut its development spending by about $1 billion, reduce capital spending, and cut sales, general and administrative expenses by $1 billion. IBM added that its fourth-quarter operating results were only likely to be around break-even (well below Wall Street forecasts) because the unexpected depth of the business downturn, particularly in Europe, prolonged worldwide economic weakness, and market pressures had cut hardware prices. It warned that it expected unfavourable conditions to continue into 1993.

This is latest in a long series of restructuring by IBM since the late 1980s as it has struggled with the global economic slowdown, which began in the US, and the extremely rapid pace of change in the computer industry. IBM, which has dominated the market for large, mainframe computers, has suffered from the shift of demand to smaller, desk-top models because its bureaucratic structure has not responded sufficiently quickly.

Source: adapted from the *Financial Times*, 12.11.1992.

(a) Identify the possible causes of unemployment mentioned in the article.
(b) What is meant by the statement 'it is likely that some business units will be unable to maintain full employment in 1993'?
(c) Explain the likely effects that job cuts at IBM are likely to have on:
(i) IBM itself;
(ii) other firms in the same industry.
(d) Outline 2 policies to increase demand and 2 policies to improve the supply side of the economy that the UK government might use in dealing with unemployment.
(e) What are the possible implications for IBM UK of your answer to question (d)?

The balance of payments

Business transactions often take place across country borders. A UK manufacturer may buy components from the USA. Japanese businesses may use British insurance companies. A UK business may invest in a land reclamation project in a developing country.

All these transactions would be shown in a country's BALANCE OF PAYMENTS. It is a record of transactions between one country and the rest of the world. The balance of payments is usually divided into two sections - the current account and the capital account.

The current account The current account of the balance of payments is also divided into two sections.
- Visible trade. This is the trade in **goods**. Examples might be computer hardware, machine tools and chemicals. It includes visible IMPORTS, goods which come from abroad but are bought in this country, and visible EXPORTS, goods which are made in this country and bought abroad. A visible export, where goods are sold abroad, earns money for UK businesses, which flows into the UK. The difference between visible imports and visible exports is known as THE BALANCE OF TRADE.
- Invisible trade. This is trade in **services**, such as banking, shipping, insurance and tourism. It includes invisible imports and invisible exports. Services sold abroad are invisible exports. If a UK insurance firm insures goods for a Japanese firm, money flows into the UK. The difference between invisible imports and exports is known as the INVISIBLE BALANCE. As well as services, the invisible balance also includes transfers of money earned in one country to another. For example, the profits of a Japanese car firm being sent back to Japan would be an invisible import to the UK as money is leaving the country. The earnings sent home by a British computer programmer working in Libya would be an invisible export because money is flowing into the UK.

The difference between total exports and total imports (both visible and invisible) is known as the CURRENT BALANCE.

The capital account This deals with the flow of capital into and out of a country. It usually involves transactions for investment, saving and borrowing. An example of a transaction on the capital account might be a British company investing abroad by setting up a new factory in South East Asia. This would be a minus figure (or an outflow) on the capital account.

Investment abroad is called a transaction in assets on the capital account, as it is creating assets abroad which earn money for UK businesses. Note that any interest or profit earned from the investment would be an invisible export (shown as a plus figure) on the current account.

Other examples of transactions shown on the capital

account might be a Spanish business buying shares in a UK company or a UK firm borrowing from a Swiss Bank. In each case, a plus figure would be shown on the UK's capital account as there is an inflow of money. These would be known as transactions in liabilities, as they are borrowing by UK firms abroad.

QUESTION 1 Jobson PLC is a British based multinational business. They have plants in Singapore, the USA, the UK and Australia. They specialise in the manufacture and distribution of a wide variety of food and drink products. Below are some of their transactions over the past 12 months.
- Profits from their plants in Singapore, Malaysia and Ireland taken back to the UK.
- Buying shares in a French drinks producing firm.
- Exporting £30 million of soft drinks to EC nations from its UK plant.
- Holding a conference for senior managers from all of their plants in Bermuda.
- Paying for a team of Japanese management consultants to help with the restructuring of their London headquarters.
- Buying new production machinery from Germany for their UK plant.
- Investing £50 million on upgrading production facilities in their USA, Singapore and Australian factories.

Explain which of the above would be shown as:
(a) invisible exports;
(b) invisible imports;
(c) visible exports;
(d) visible imports;
(e) capital inflows;
(f) capital outflows;
in the UK's balance of payments account.

Balance of payments problems

The balance of payments must always 'balance'. Take a situation where a country has a **current account deficit** - in other words, visible and invisible imports are greater than exports. (This also means that outflows of money are greater than inflows to that country.)

Where does the money come from to finance this deficit? The UK may, for example, borrow from foreign banks or sell its assets abroad to bring money back in. The Bank of England (☞ unit 65) could sell some of the country's gold or foreign currency reserves. Whatever happens, the deficit on the current account would be made up by a surplus on the capital account. In practice, if the values do not actually balance a **balancing item** is added. This is a figure for errors and omissions in the figures, large or small enough so that the accounts always balance.

Although the accounts always balance, individual parts of the balance of payments may not. What if the current account deficit carried on for a long period? This could lead to a number of problems for the UK government and for UK business.

■ The country as a whole will get more and more into debt. Other countries may refuse to lend more money, and may insist upon repayment of any debt. Third World and Eastern European countries have faced such problems over the past few decades.

■ Loss of jobs. If consumers buy imports, they will not buy home produced goods or services. Thus opportunities for job creation are lost. Similarly, low levels of exports mean the demand by businesses for employees will be lower.

■ UK businesses may become dependent on imports of components and raw materials. This may mean that costs are dependent upon the exchange rate value of the pound sterling. This is dealt with later in this unit. It may also make the UK economy more vulnerable to imported inflation (☞ unit 66).

Figure 69.1 shows the UK's current account over the period 1970 to 1992. The most striking feature is the large deficits of the late 1980s and early 1990s.

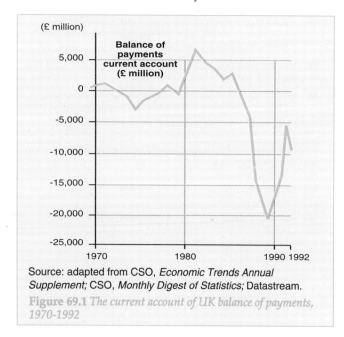

Source: adapted from CSO, *Economic Trends Annual Supplement*; CSO, *Monthly Digest of Statistics*; Datastream.

Figure 69.1 *The current account of UK balance of payments, 1970-1992*

Government policy and business

We have seen that current account deficits cause problems. One government objective is a balance of payments equilibrium, or a small surplus if possible. There are a number of policies it can use to achieve this.

Protectionism This involves the use of controls to restrict the amount of imports coming into a country. TARIFFS are a tax on imports. They raise the price of imports and, hopefully, discourage consumers from buying them. For example, there is a Common External Tariff (☞ unit 70) on goods entering the EC. QUOTAS are a limit on the number of goods that are allowed to enter a country. For

example, a government may specify that only 1,000 Japanese television sets are allowed to enter the country each month.

A more subtle approach is to impose technical restrictions or 'waiting' periods on goods entering a country. For example, Japan has been known in the past to reject imports because they do not meet standards they have set for products being sold in domestic markets.

Why might a government impose tariffs?

■ To protect INFANT INDUSTRIES or newly emerging industries which have yet to find their feet. This is often used by Third World countries to protect their manufacturing industries.

■ To protect strategic or declining industries which governments feel are important to the future of the country. Also industries whose decline may lead to a loss of jobs are sometimes protected. Many believe that the UK coal industry should have been protected for this reason.

■ Anti-dumping. Dumping occurs when goods are sold in foreign markets at prices below their cost of production. This may occur because of excess capacity in an industry or as a deliberate attempt to quickly gain market share at the expense of domestic businesses. Because dumping is seen as unfair, many governments act to protect their own businesses from its effects.

There are some difficulties with protectionist policies.

■ They may lead to retaliation by the exporting country. This may 'cancel out' the effect of protection. It will also harm the imposing country's exports to other countries.

■ They can lead to inflation in the country imposing the tariff. This may be the case if, despite the tariff, the country still has to buy the goods. They might be essential raw materials, for example.

■ International agreements such as GATT, the General Agreement on Trade and Tariffs (☞ unit 70), prevent the use of tariffs by individual countries except for those agreed by the countries involved.

Supply side policies These policies are aimed at increasing the efficiency of firms and their ability to compete (☞ unit 65). Their impact in the short term on the balance of payments would hardly be noticeable. However, in the long term, they could help to solve a balance of payments deficit by improving the performance of firms in both domestic and export markets.

Fiscal and monetary policy These two policies could be used to tackle a balance of payments deficit by reducing the spending power of consumers. A reduction would reduce the amount of money available to spend on imports. This could be achieved by, for example, raising taxes and interest rates. The problem, however, is that such policies can also affect domestic firms by reducing the demand for their products, possibly leading to redundancies and even bankruptcies.

Note that these policies are similar to the use of anti-inflationary policies discussed in unit 66 and have similar effects on business.

Exchange rate changes A government, faced with a balance of payments deficit, can allow its exchange rate to fall or DEPRECIATE under a **floating** rate system. This is where the value of a currency is allowed to rise or fall without restriction against the value of other currencies. The result should be higher import prices and lower export prices, which in the longer term arguably lead to an increase in exports and a reduction in imports.

Under a **fixed** rate system, such as the Exchange Rate Mechanism, a DEVALUATION of a currency (a fall in its value) can only be achieved with the agreement of other countries. The factors which cause exchange rates to rise or fall are dealt with in the next section.

Government restraint If there is a large and persistent current account surplus a country may restrict the amount of exporting its businesses undertake. Due to its large current account surplus, there has been international pressure on Japan to exercise export restraint in recent years.

QUESTION 2 On 27 January 1993, the US government imposed tariffs on the import of carbon steel products from 19 countries. The highest, 109.22 per cent, was placed on steel plate exported by British Steel. The US argued the tariffs were necessary to prevent dumping taking place in the US. The EC attacked the decision as heavy handed, commenting that they would 'defend the community steel industry' and seek talks with the US over GATT procedures. They did not comment at the time about possible retaliation.

Mr Phil Wolfinden, for British Steel, said that the company's sales to the US in 1991 of 35,000 tonnes was less than 0.7 per cent of the US market. He also believed that such action would not help the US steel industry. EC producers particularly resented the tariffs as they came at a time when they operated under a voluntary restraint agreement with the US. The EC Trade Commissioner, Sir Leon Brittan, argued that EC producers had respected this agreement and had not even used up their quotas.

Source: adapted from the *Financial Times*, 28.1.1993.

(a) What reasons might the US have for imposing these restrictions?
(b) What effects might the restrictions have on:
  (i) US steel producers;
  (ii) the British steel industry and other UK businesses;
  (iii) the policy of countries within the EC?
(c) Briefly explain one other policy which the US could have used.

Exchange rates

An EXCHANGE RATE is the price of one country's currency in relation to that of another. So, for example, an exchange rate of £1 = 2DM means that one pound is worth two deutschmarks or that one deutschmark is worth 50p.

Exchange rates are determined on foreign exchange markets throughout the world. If an exchange rate is freely floating, then changes in the demand for or supply of a currency will result in a change in that country's exchange rate. For example, a fall in the demand for sterling will cause its value to fall. This is the same type of analysis that was used to show the effect of changes in the demand for and supply of goods on prices in unit 22.

There are a number of factors that can affect the exchange rate of a currency.

The volume of exports An increase in exports by UK firms will mean that more pounds are required to buy these exports. This will result in an increase in the demand for sterling and cause the value of sterling to rise. A decrease in UK exports will have the opposite effect, resulting in a fall in the demand for sterling and a fall in its value.

The volume of imports An increase in imports coming into the UK will mean that more sterling has to be sold in order to purchase the foreign currencies needed to buy imports. This will cause an increase in the supply of sterling, leading to a fall in sterling's exchange rate. A decrease in imports will have the opposite effect, resulting in a fall in the supply of sterling and a rise in its value.

The level of interest rates A rise in interest rates in the UK will attract savings from abroad. This will raise the demand for sterling and thus its price. A fall in interest rates will have the opposite effect.

Speculation The short term price of a country's currency is mainly influenced by speculation. If dealers on foreign exchange markets expect the value of a currency to fall in the future, they may sell their reserves of that currency. This will cause the supply of that currency to increase and its price to fall. It has been argued that speculation led to the collapse in the price of the pound on the so-called 'Black Wednesday' in September 1992. If, however, speculators expect the value of a currency to rise in the future, then they will begin purchasing that currency leading to an increase in its value.

Government intervention Governments may intervene on foreign exchange markets. They may try to influence the price of either their own currency or that of another country. For example, the UK government may attempt to raise the value of the pound by purchasing it on foreign exchange markets. Governments may also raise interest rates in order to increase the value of the pound.

Investment and capital flows An inflow of funds for long-term investment in the UK will cause the demand, and therefore the price, of sterling to rise. Similarly an outflow of investment funds will cause the supply of sterling to rise and its price to fall, other factors remaining the same. Thus, French investment in a UK water bottling plant would cause a rise in the exchange rate.

Capital flows are largely determined by the rate of interest. Thus an increase in UK interest rates would lead to an inflow of funds into the UK and a rise in the value of sterling. Such inflows of funds following interest rate changes tend to be short term money moving from one of the world's financial centres to another in search of the highest rate of return.

QUESTION 3 Discuss the likely effects on the value of the pound against the franc of the following:
(a)   increases in UK residents taking holidays in France;
(b)   the French franc coming under speculative selling pressure as an election comes nearer;
(c)   an increase in UK aircraft sales to France;
(d)   UK interest rates increased to 6 per cent whilst French interest rates remain at 4 per cent.

Exchange rates and business

The main reason why exchange rates are so important to businesses is because of their influence on the price of imports and exports. All but a very few small firms use at least some goods and services imported from abroad. Increasingly, large numbers of businesses are finding that they have to export their products in order to grow or survive. Thus the majority of firms are affected in some way by exchange rates.

The effect of falling exchange rates A fall in the exchange rate (a **depreciation** or **devaluation**) will affect the price of a business's exports and the price it pays for imports. Look at Table 69.1 which shows the effects of a fall in the value of the pound.

Table 69.1 *The effects of a fall in the value of the pound on the price of exports and imports*

	Exchange rate	UK price	German price
Exported goods	£1 = 2.75DM	£10	27.5DM
	£1 = 2.25DM	£10	22.5DM
Imported goods	£1 = 2.75DM	£10	27.5DM
	£1 = 2.25DM	£12.23	27.5DM

At an exchange rate of £1 = 2.75DM, a book priced at £10 that is exported to Germany would cost Germans 27.5DM. If the value of the pound fell to £1 = 2.25DM, Germans would now be able to buy the same book for 22.5DM. So a fall in the exchange rate can make UK exports cheaper. What about imports to the UK? A picture frame priced at 27.5DM imported to the UK would cost £10 before the depreciation of the exchange rate. If the exchange rate fell to £1 = 2.25DM, the picture frame would now cost £12.23. So a fall in the exchange rate can cause the price of imports to rise.

The overall effect should be beneficial for UK businesses. The price paid for UK exports should fall, allowing businesses to sell more in export markets. The price paid by UK businesses and consumers for imports should rise. This might encourage them to switch their purchases from foreign goods to UK products.

There are problems, however, for firms if exchange rates are falling.
■ Rising import prices mean that the amount paid for any inputs, such as raw materials or components bought in from abroad, will rise.
■ Rising import prices can lead to inflation and the problems for firms of this.
■ Uncertainty over future prices of raw materials and components can result.
■ Constant price changes may affect foreign demand for products as they are unsettling for customers.

The effect of rising exchange rates This has the opposite effect to devaluation. A rise in the exchange rate can cause the price of exports to rise and the price of imports to fall. For example, in Table 69.1 an increase in the exchange rate from £1=2.25 DM to £1=2.75 DM will cause the price of a £10 export to rise from 22.5DM to 27.5DM and the price of a 27.5 DM import to fall from £12.23 to £10.

The overall effect is likely to be negative. Not only will it became more difficult for UK firms to compete on price in export markets, but it will put pressure on them in UK markets, as they struggle to compete with lower priced imported goods. However, a rise in the exchange rate could allow UK businesses to buy cheaper imports from abroad.

The stability of exchange rates Unstable exchange rates can make it very difficult for firms to plan for the future. A rise in the exchange rate, for example, could turn a previously profitable export order into a loss maker. A devaluation, on the other hand, could mean that exports which looked unprofitable could now earn a profit for the firm.

How much are businesses affected?

Not all businesses are affected to the same extent by changes in exchange rates.

The response of consumers Some products have a strong brand identity. Even if their prices increase, consumers do not reduce the amount purchased by a great deal. Unit 22 referred to these products as having an **inelastic** demand. What effect will a fall in the value of the pound from £1=2.75 DM to £1=2.25 DM have on UK businesses exporting such goods?

A firm selling 1,000 pre-recorded cassette tapes to Germany each month for 27.5DM at an exchange rate of £1 = 2.75DM, would receive 27,500DM (£10,000) in revenue. If the exchange rate fell to £1 = 2.25DM, and the demand for cassette tapes were price inelastic, then the business may be able to keep the price at 27.5DM. At this new exchange rate the 27,000DM would be worth £12,222 (27,500 ÷ 2.25). Thus, revenue would increase by £2,222.

Firms with products which are sensitive to price changes are likely to feel the impact of even minor exchange rate changes. If export prices rise the volume of sales will fall by a greater degree, and the overall revenue for exports will fall. If export prices fall, revenue should be greater because the increase in quantity sold is relatively greater than the fall in price.

The degree of control over prices Not all businesses have the same degree of control over the price at which their products are sold. Those with a high degree of control over their prices can adopt market based methods of pricing, such as customer value pricing (☞ unit 23) . They might decide not to allow exchange rate changes to alter the price of their exports, although their sales revenue may change. For example, a business selling sportswear with a strong degree of brand loyalty amongst its customers might be unwilling to alter its price as a result of relatively small exchange rate fluctuations. This is because prices will have been carefully chosen to suit particular markets. In this case, only a large rise in the exchange rate, which threatened profits, would cause a pricing re-think.

Importing components and raw materials The effect of a change in the exchange rate on firms that imported components or raw materials would depend on a number of factors. Firstly, whether or not the firms from which they are importing decide to alter their prices. Secondly, whether or not any long term agreements on prices had been reached. Thirdly, whether the firm had already bought foreign currency to pay for future imported components etc. A firm importing fabric from Hong Kong might want to buy a year's supply of Hong Kong dollars to make sure it was unaffected by changes in the exchange rate.

QUESTION 4 Business Systems PLC imported 1,000 personal computers from the USA each month at a price of $1,500 each. With an addition of 20 per cent to their imported price they sold them in the UK for £900 at an exchange rate of £1 = $2. Because of the strong brand identity which these computers had and their reputation for quality, Business Systems were never left with any unsold at the end of the month.

(a) Show how Business Systems arrived at a price of £900 for their American computers.
(b) Assuming price changed in line with the exchange rate change, how would a change in the exchange rate to £1 = $1.60 affect:
  (i) the US personal computer manufacturer;
  (ii) Business Systems?
(c) What would be the effect on business revenue if sales fell by 10 per cent in the UK ?

The Exchange Rate Mechanism

The Exchange Rate Mechanism (ERM) is the means by which European Community (EC) (☞ unit 70) currencies are linked together to form the European Monetary System (EMS). It is very similar to the system of fixed exchange rates described earlier in this unit. However, under the ERM, currencies are fixed within agreed limits. They are allowed to float against other ERM currencies so long as they remain within these limits.

The aim is to create exchange rate stability within the EC. The ERM tries to achieve this by making sure that the exchange rates of member currencies remain within a limited band of a weighted average of all currencies. The weighted average is known as the European Currency Unit (or ECU).

Governments maintain their currencies within the ERM limits by intervening on foreign exchange markets and adjusting interest rates. So for example, if the French government thought the franc was in danger of rising above its agreed maximum level, the French government might lower its interest rates or sell francs on foreign exchange markets.

On the other hand, if the currency looked like falling below the minimum of its band, the government of that country must raise interest rates or buy home currency. This is what happened to many countries in late 1992. The UK, having joined the ERM in October 1990, found the pound falling to below its minimum of £1 = 2.78 deutschmarks. In this extreme case, even government action was not enough to keep the pound within its band and the UK was forced to leave on September 16, 1992.

Membership of the ERM has other effects on member countries and their businesses.

Competitiveness When not in the ERM, governments can allow the value of their currency to fall. This should make exports cheaper and imports more expensive. However, under the ERM this is less of an option, so the main way in which businesses can become more competitive on foreign markets in terms of price is to keep their costs down. In order to achieve this wage costs must be kept down and productivity (output per worker) must be raised. Thus the ERM is seen by some as a means of imposing discipline upon an economy and the businesses within it. It also means that there is less chance for inflation, via increased wages, to build up in an economy.

Stable exchange rates Because the ERM results in more stable exchange rates between those involved, many businesses view it in a positive light. This is because exchange rate stability allows firms to plan ahead. Under the ERM, firms are better able to predict the price of materials bought in from other ERM countries and the revenue which they will gain by selling their products abroad. Outside the ERM, neither can be predicted with any certainty.

Interest rates Governments can use interest rates as a means of influencing exchange rates. Under the ERM the use of interest rates becomes especially important because of the need to meet exchange rate targets. Interest rates may, therefore, be set with the needs of the exchange rate rather than with the needs of businesses in mind. Thus, businesses may be punished by high interest rates during a recession, when this is exactly the opposite of what they need. This may cause some businesses to fail and result in unemployment.

The widening of ERM bands to 15 per cent in 1993 lessened the restrictions placed on governments and the effects on business. Currencies were able to fluctuate more widely than they did previously.

Monetary Union

Some believe that EC countries and their businesses would benefit from European monetary union (EMU). In the case of Europe, this would mean:
- the establishment of a single currency (the ECU) which would replace the pound, the lira, the peseta and all other member currencies;
- the free movement of capital between countries;
- the establishment of a European Central Bank;
- member countries giving up control of their budgets and monetary policy to the Central Bank.

There are considerable advantages for businesses arising out of European Monetary Union (EMU).
- One currency would be used throughout the EC, so firms would no longer incur charges when buying foreign exchange to do business in other EC countries.
- Businesses would no longer need to worry about exchange rate fluctuations when making plans for trading in other EC countries.
- It would encourage firms to trade in other EC nations because, other than language barriers, there would be no difference to trading in a firm's home country.
- It is also argued that an independent central bank will

make decisions for the long term benefit of EC nations. This is as opposed to the current system where national central banks have been accused of making decisions for short term political gain, such as before a General Election.

As well as these, there are the benefits that would have already been gained from the ERM. However, many remain sceptical about the benefits of monetary union. They are concerned that the common fiscal and monetary policies required, although suited to the majority of EC nations, may not be suitable for individual countries. It would no longer be possible for individual governments to pursue economic policies designed for the needs of their businesses. This may result in some countries having economic prosperity with others getting left behind. For example, one country may want to reduce interest rates to encourage investment, spending and employment. This would not be possible under EMU unless such a policy was considered suitable for the rest of the EC.

Because of those problems it has been suggested that EMU should take place only when EC economies converge, ie when interest rates, inflation rates, budget deficits as well as exchange rates are all in line with each other. The **Maastricht Treaty**, signed by all EC member countries in December 1991 at Maastricht in the Netherlands, committed the EC to such convergence by 1 January 1999. It is unlikely by then that members will have achieved the targets that have been set.

Key terms

Balance of payments - a record of the transactions between one country and the rest of the world over a given period of time.
Balance of trade - the difference between visible imports and visible exports.
Current balance - the difference between total imports and total exports.
Devaluation/depreciation - a decline in the value of an exchange rate.
ECU - the European Currency Unit.
Exchange rate - the price of one currency in relation to another.
Exports - goods and services which leave the country and are sold to foreigners.
Imports - goods and services which enter the country and are bought from foreigners.
Infant industries - newly set up industries that are unable to compete with established foreign competition.
Invisible balance - the difference between the import and export of services.
Quota - a limit placed upon the number of particular categories of goods allowed to enter the country.
Tariff - a tax upon imports.

QUESTION 6 The main benefit of EMU is not the savings in transactions costs, which would amount to almost 1.5 per cent of GDP, but the removal of long term exchange rate uncertainty. Under a system of floating rates, this increases the risk of doing business in EC countries.

For the UK economy as a whole, there is the prospect of escaping from the inflationary cycles which have characterised economic policy in the past. The larger credibility of an independent European central bank makes it likely that this can be reached at lower cost than is possible under present arrangements. There is also no reason why EMU should result in an increase in unemployment as a result of the loss of national monetary policy. In the past, temporary gains in competitiveness from devaluation have been quickly eroded through higher inflation. Britain has never been able to price itself back into world markets simply by devaluing.

Source: adapted from a letter to the *Financial Times*, 14.12.1992.

(a) Identify the benefits pointed out by the author for UK business in being part of EMU.
(b) Why might 'the loss of national monetary policy' lead to unemployment?

Summary

1. What is meant by:
   (a) the current account;
   (b) the capital account;
   of the balance of payments?
2. What is the difference between visible and invisible trade?
3. Give 3 examples of invisible trade.
4. Give 3 examples of capital transactions.
5. Why must the balance of payments always balance?
6. Briefly explain 2 policies used to tackle a balance of payments deficit and how they can affect business.
7. State 5 factors that determine exchange rates.
8. What is the difference between a fixed and a floating exchange rate system?
9. State 3 ways fluctuating exchange rates can affect firms.
10. What is the ERM?
11. What are the possible consequences of ERM membership for UK businesses?
12. What are the likely advantages for firms of EMU?

Question

Black Wednesday

When the UK joined the ERM in October 1990, the minimum value below which the pound sterling was not allowed to fall was £1 = 2.78 Deutschmarks (DM). If there were signs that the pound was in danger of falling below this level, then the Bank of England would intervene on foreign exchange markets. This was done by increasing the demand for, and therefore the value of, sterling

by buying appropriate quantities of it. Similarly if the pound sterling was in danger of rising above its agreed limit, then it would sell sterling on the foreign exchange, therefore increasing its supply and lowering its price.

However, there were signs that this approach was going wrong in the week beginning 14 September 1992. On the Tuesday, the moment London foreign exchange dealers began work they started selling sterling. Its value slid. The Bank of England dug into its reserves to buy pounds. Sterling survived the day - bolstered by the Bank of England's support.

Overnight, foreign exchange dealers in New York and Tokyo were frantically selling sterling. London dealers joined in on the Wednesday morning. At 11 am, the Government increased interest rates from 10 per cent to 12 per cent. The government's message was clear: we mean business. Norman Lamont the Chancellor of the Exchequer, repeated that he would 'do whatever was necessary' to maintain the value of sterling. However,

pressure on sterling continued. At 2.15 pm a further interest rate rise, to 15 per cent, was announced by the government. Again it made no difference. This time, the government threw in the towel and it was announced that the pound had been suspended from the ERM.

It has been estimated that the government spent over £10 billion on intervention to support the pound. Despite this, in just one day the value of the pound sterling fell from £1 = 2.78 DM to £1 = 2.70 DM.

Source: adapted from *The Times*, 17.9.1992 and *The Guardian*, 9.9.1992.

(a) Explain why the government raised interest rates in order to support the value of the pound sterling.
(b) Using calculations, show the possible effect of the fall in the value of sterling on Black Wednesday to a UK firm selling ten £5,000 computer systems to Germany each week.
(c) Many economists had predicted a fall in the value of sterling before the events of Black Wednesday. Explain how a firm importing components from France, Germany and Holland might have cushioned itself against the effects of such a devaluation.
(d) Describe the possible impact of Black Wednesday on the UK's current account.
(e) How might UK firms have been affected by the UK leaving the ERM at that time?

The European Community

The European Community was set up (then as the European Economic Community) in 1958. The six member countries (West Germany, France, Italy, Belgium, the Netherlands and Luxembourg) committed themselves, in the Treaty of Rome, to establishing a **Common Market**.

By 1993 the UK, Spain, Portugal, Greece, Denmark and Eire had also joined. In future, countries such as Sweden and Finland, and former communist countries such as Hungary and Czechoslovakia, may also apply to join. Austria, Malta, Turkey and Cyprus have applied to join in the near future.

A COMMON MARKET exists when a group of countries form a CUSTOMS UNION, with free trade between member countries, and establish a common external tariff on imports of goods and services from outside. Free trade should take place in goods and services, as well as factors of production such as land, labour and capital. For example, it should be possible for a worker from Denmark to work in Newcastle on the same terms as in her home country. Also, a German company should be able to buy land in London to develop offices. In practice, the free movement of factors of production has proved a lot more difficult than mobility of goods and services.

A common external tariff is placed on all imports into a customs union. If tariffs were different for different EC countries, this might lead to problems. Say Germany had a 10 per cent tariff and France a 20 per cent tariff. An American firm exporting to France could bring products in through Germany, paying the lower tariff, and then import them into France paying no extra tax. To avoid this, a common external tariff **harmonises** all tariffs on imports. This means the tariff is the same for imported products into all member countries.

There are some advantages to businesses operating in countries belonging to a customs union or common market.

■ Firms operating within customs unions have free access to markets which would otherwise be protected by tariffs or quotas (☞ unit 69). In this way British firms, for example, have access to all other EC markets. For many firms this provides them with the opportunity to operate in EC markets in much the same way that they would at home. A Blackburn based firm would operate in Berlin or Bilbao in much the same way as they would in Brighton or Birmingham.

■ Firms will have access to the most appropriate factors of production. A British firm might purchase cheap land in Southern Portugal for a new factory location, skilled designers from Italy or capital equipment from France.

■ Customs unions provide firms with large markets to sell to. The bigger the market a firm is selling to, the greater the economies of scale it is able to benefit from. The EC provides firms with access to 360 million consumers.

■ Businesses operating within a common market will be protected from competition from outside this area by an external business. Such protection allows

Table 70.1 *How Euro-brand prices vary*

Lowest price = 100	BELGIUM	GERMANY	SPAIN	IRELAND	FRANCE	UK	ITALY
Biggest differences:							
Kellogg's Cornflakes (500gm)	165	190	208	126	227	100	243
Pedigree Pal dog food (100gm)	175	175	223	127	172	100	182
Twix (standard, two fingers)	104	149	138	130	204	100	138
Nescafé (100gm)	213	229	132	114	182	100	214
Coca Cola (330ml can)	127	113	117	200	100	117	120
Palmolive hand wash liquid (500ml)	210	218	192	163	210	100	253
Whiskas cat food (400gm)	178	179	210	133	174	100	209
Schweppes tonic (500ml bottle)	147	203	140	149	100	115	110
Evian (3 litre bottle)	153	183	124	203	100	150	110
L'Oreal Freestyle hair mousse (150ml aerosol)	148	171	175	120	203	100	126
Smallest differences:							
Tampax regular (Pack of 32)	128	103	130	107	105	100	110
Nutella chocolate spread (400gm)	117	100	116	136	117	127	126
Bailey's Irish Cream (70cl/75cl)	123	111	100	133	115	135	101
Duracell batteries (AA size)	143	123	105	126	129	100	114
Colgate toothpaste (regular 100ml)	124	120	129	120	112	100	137

Source: adapted from A C Neilson.

businesses to be sheltered from the potentially damaging effects of competition such as price wars.

- Increased competition from European firms may act as an incentive for British firms to increase efficiency and standards.

There are, however, disadvantages for businesses operating within a customs union or common market.

- Before Britain joined the EC, British firms could buy goods and services from the lowest cost producers around the world. Foodstuffs were imported in huge quantities from New Zealand and the USA in this way. Since joining the EC, however, British firms have had to pay far more for foodstuffs from New Zealand and Australia because of the common external tariff.
- Whilst a British based firm will have free access to other EC markets, businesses based in these markets will also have access to the UK market. Such competition may reduce the market share which domestic businesses have established.
- Protection from external tariffs is not always beneficial to firms operating from within a common market. This is because being sheltered from external competition may result in less incentive for a firm to become more efficient. In the long run, this may lead to a deterioration in the firm's performance.
- Firms may have to adapt their marketing strategies to suit the needs of consumers in each country within the customs union. For example, a *Financial Times* survey in January 1993 found that of the thousands of products commonly sold in European supermarkets, only 45 'Euro-brands' were widely on sale in identical format in at least the four largest countries. As shown in Table 70.1, prices of products within EC nations vary widely.

QUESTION 1 P Clark Ltd, a Stafford based firm specialising in the manufacture of hi-tech exercise machines, had enjoyed enormous success in the US market with their rowing machines and running tracks. However, they could not have failed to notice a fall in their share of the UK market as a result of competition from Italian and French firms.

They had been poised to enter the European market for over a year, but had been held up by recurrent production difficulties which meant that they could barely satisfy the demand for their products in the UK and US markets. With free access to EC markets and unlike in the US no tariff barriers to overcome, they had begun planning for the launch of their products in Europe. Their initial plan was to increase production by 50 per cent. If successful, their long term plan was to open a new manufacturing and distribution plant in a suitable EC location.

(a) In what ways will P Clark be able to benefit from operating within a common market?

(b) What problems has operating from within a common market brought them?

EC policies and business

The European community has economic policies which are designed to help businesses within member countries.

These policies vary from employee protection (☞ unit 56) and consumer protection (☞ unit 73) to transport and energy policies. Here we will concentrate on three policies and their effects on business.

The Common Agricultural Policy (CAP) This policy operates in all EC countries. Article 39 of the Treaty of Rome states 5 objectives of agricultural policy:

- to increase the productivity of agriculture;
- to ensure a fair standard of living for farmers;
- to stabilise markets;
- to guarantee supplies;
- to ensure fair prices.

The CAP aims to achieve this. Farmers are guaranteed a fixed minimum price by the EC for their produce. The EC will buy up any amount that farmers produce at this price. Farmers could, of course, always sell on world markets if the market price was higher. If the market price drops below the minimum, however, CAP maintains the price to farmers, thus guaranteeing their income.

For farmers the CAP guarantees them a price for their produce so that they are not at the mercy of fluctuations in price. This means that fewer farmers will go out of business during difficult years and, to some extent, their incomes will be guaranteed.

The CAP has a number of problems associated with it.

- Overproduction. The setting of high, guaranteed prices has often caused excess supplies (☞ unit 22) of a variety of agricultural products. Any excess supply is purchased by EC authorities. They prevent it from being sold on markets by storing it, resulting in butter mountains, wine lakes etc.
- High prices. The minimum price set by the EC for agricultural products as part of CAP is very often higher than the price which would have resulted without their intervention. It is consumers and businesses such as food retailers who suffer as a result of these high prices.
- Purchasing excess supplies of agricultural products is expensive for the EC. It is possible that the money spent on this could be better diverted to projects such as providing grants to firms engaged in producing new high technology products.
- It prevents non-EC countries from competing in EC markets. It therefore represents an obstacle to the signing of international trading treaties, such as GATT, dealt with later in this unit.

The Regional Fund This provides funds to member states to help reduce unemployment in depressed parts of the EC. It also aims to encourage development in areas on the edge of the EC, such as Southern Italy and Northern Ireland. For example, construction firms may win contracts to build new roads or industrial units could be financed through the Regional Fund. Similarly, firms may receive investment grants if they locate in particular parts of the EC. This is dealt with in more detail in unit 30.

The Social Chapter The **Maastricht Treaty** was signed by all EC member states in December 1992 (☞ unit 69). One section of this treaty is the Social Chapter. The aim of the Social Chapter is to standardise working conditions throughout the EC so that all workers within the community are guaranteed basic rights. These include the following.

- A minimum wage to be paid to all workers.
- A maximum working week of 48 hours.
- A minimum of four weeks paid holiday per year.
- The freedom to join a union.
- Access to appropriate training.
- The right to be consulted and informed about company plans.
- The protection of young workers.

The UK has opted out of the Social Chapter, but all other EC nations have signed it. What might be the implications of the Social Chapter for businesses?

- Workers may be better motivated. This should make them more effective and productive employees, able to raise the efficiency of the firm for which they work.
- Industrial relations may improve as employees are involved in making company decisions and consulted about the work which they carry out.
- It may raise the labour costs of those firms currently employing workers at wages below the minimum level set out in the Chapter. Those firms expecting their employees to work longer than 48 hours per week, or to take less than 4 weeks holidays, may also find their costs rise as they are required to employ more people.
- Higher labour costs may make it more difficult for EC based firms to compete with businesses in low wage countries, such as China or South Korea.

The Single European Market

A major event in the EC's move towards free trade was the signing of the Single European Act in 1986, which established a SINGLE EUROPEAN MARKET to come into being on 31 December 1992. Despite the existence of a customs union for over 30 years, there were still many non-tariff barriers to trade in the EC. This Act aimed to remove those barriers between EC member countries. The effects of this should be to encourage the freer movement of people, goods, services and capital. Three categories of barriers were removed.

- Barriers which prevented entry into markets. For example, differing technical standards were required of products by different member states. This made it difficult for firms to enter certain markets. Also, the practice of public sector contracts being given only to domestic firms prevented free trade.
- Barriers which caused firms' costs to rise. Often complex documents were needed in order to move goods from one country to another. Also, there were long delays waiting to get exports through customs posts.
- Barriers which lead to the market being distorted. Such barriers are said to prevent firms from competing on equal terms. They included differing rates of VAT in EC countries and subsidies given by EC governments to domestic industries.

Not all firms have been affected to the same degree by the Single Market. In some industries, very few barriers to trade existed between EC countries before December 1992. Firms operating in such industries have seen little or no changes to their situation. However, in other industries, where trade barriers were high, the Single Market has resulted in major changes for those firms operating within them. What effects will the Single Market have on firms in member countries?

- Product standards. Firms may have to alter their products so that they meet new product standards. Many firms have had to improve the safety aspects of their products in order to meet new EC regulations.
- Harmonisation of tariffs and taxes. There have been attempts to harmonise VAT rates throughout the EC. For businesses this may mean that the selling prices of their products rise or fall in line with VAT rate changes. In the UK, a number of products such as childrens' clothes and books, which have previously not attracted any VAT, may now have to face this tax as the UK seeks to fall into line with other EC countries. The rates of VAT in the EC in 1992 are shown in Figure 70.1.

  Attempts will also be made to harmonise EXCISE DUTIES on products such as petrol, tobacco and spirits. This will affect the price at which these products are sold and, therefore, the companies marketing them.
- Ease of trading. The reduction in the number of customs posts, and the amount of paperwork which is required for goods traded between EC countries, should save businesses time and reduce costs.

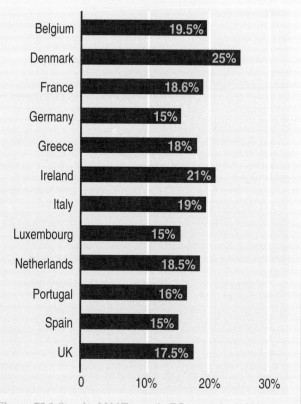

Figure 70.1 *Standard VAT rates in EC countries (1992)*

QUESTION 2 Europe's two largest trailer and truck rental companies have a double vision of the single market. Central Trailer Rentco, a subsidiary of Tiphook, the British transport group, has visions of a unitary Europe, where its trailers can be picked up or dropped off in any country to suit customer needs.

TIP Europe, another British company, sees Europe as a collection of separate markets which must be addressed individually. The difference in outlook stems mainly from each company's customer base. CTR serves a few large transport groups, such as Frans Maas, while TIP works with smaller, local customers in 10 separate countries.

Despite their alternative strategies, both companies agree that the Single European Act has removed some important barriers. Equally, they say, problems remain which could take years to solve.

Road haulage permits, which were needed to cross some national boundaries, were abolished on January 1. Vehicles no longer require customs documentation for their loads, which in turn no longer need to be bonded. This should save time and paperwork for trailers making cross border journeys.

However, the benefits will only be fully felt if vehicles are making return journeys to their place of origin.

Because of a number of structural problems, the free movement of vehicles remains difficult. Once a border has been crossed, it will still be difficult, or sometimes impossible, for vehicles to make onward journeys after unloading. French hauliers, for instance, find it very hard to transport goods between two points in Germany.

Price differentials also exist between markets. Germany's preference for heavy loads to be carried by rail rather than road has led to average road taxes for articulated lorries being almost twice levels in the UK. UK rental rates are 30 per cent below continental rates, partly because of competition and partly because UK fleets tend to be older.

These remaining barriers within the EC could take years to erase. In the US, similar problems have only recently been ironed out - 10 years after deregulation.

Source: adapted from the *Financial Times*, 4.1.1993.

(a) In what ways will TIP Europe and Central Trailer Rentco benefit from the Single European Market?
(b) What evidence is there to suggest that trade barriers between EC nations have continued to exist since the establishment of the Single European Market?

'Western' developed economies

Western Europe and, in particular, the EC is now the single most important market for British firms. However, there are many other parts of the world which are significant trading partners for the UK, such as the US, Japan and Canada. They provide large export markets and have rival firms operating in the UK market. The way these countries trade with the UK and the EC is largely determined by two organisations - the group of seven (G7) and the General Agreement on Tariffs and Trade (GATT).

The Group of Seven (G7) The G7 nations are the seven leading industrial countries - Germany, Japan, US, UK, France, Italy and Canada. Between them they are responsible for over two-thirds of the world's total output, and a similar proportion of its expenditure. The main aim of G7 is to promote growth in the world economy.

The success of G7 nations in reaching agreements has implications for firms trading in all parts of the world. For example, the break-up of G7 nations into rival trading groups centred around Europe, North America and the Pacific Rim could lead to a reduction in the quantity of goods and services traded. This may result in a reduction in business opportunities for firms. The failure of G7 nations to reach agreement on promoting economic growth could have similar effects.

Trading agreements between non-EC G7 nations can also affect EC-based firms. For example, the US and Canada along with Mexico have recently formed the North American Free Trade Area (NAFTA). This is a regional trading bloc similar to the EC. Such regional trade blocs place barriers in the way of external firms seeking to export into them. Trade barriers of this kind can be damaging to firms wishing to enter such markets. However, there is an organisation to which all G7 nations belong, and which seeks to prevent trade barriers and encourage free trade between countries - GATT.

The General Agreement on Tariffs and Trade (GATT) GATT is a binding agreement between 105 countries that together account for 90 per cent of world trade. It aims to encourage trade by bringing about reductions in trade barriers agreed by all its members. Such barriers include tariffs and quotas (☞ unit 69). There are three main ways in which GATT seeks to achieve this.
- It can act as a forum for negotiations on trade.
- It can provide a set of rules governing trade behaviour.
- It can act as a court in which governments can settle their differences.

The most recent round of GATT talks, known as the Uruguay Round, began in 1986. This has involved years of negotiation about levels of subsidies given to European farmers through the Common Agricultural Policy (CAP). These subsidies were seen as giving an unfair advantage to EC farmers, resulting in strong objections from America in particular.

The reason GATT is important is because of its potential for increasing the amount of trade in the world. Such an increase in trade, many believe, can lead to greater prosperity. Indeed, the increase in the wealth of many nations since the Second World War has, perhaps, been due to the success of GATT in lowering trade barriers. There are concerns that, without GATT, the world could divide up into trading blocs resulting in a reduction in trade and possibly a worldwide depression. For individual firms, GATT makes it more likely that they can operate in export markets on equal terms with locally based companies. As such, GATT acts as a 'door opener' to overseas markets.

GATT talks are often dominated by the advanced industrial countries. They have been criticised for ignoring the needs of less wealthy countries in Eastern Europe and the South of the world. For example, it is argued that attention has not been paid to protectionist policies which seek to exclude these countries from Western markets. An example is the Multi-Fibre Trade Agreement, which continues to exist despite GATT. Many believe that this agreement protects Western textile manufacturers from equal and fair competition from poor countries like Bangladesh. The agreement is only allowed to continue because poorer countries are unable to wield enough power at GATT talks.

A European Economic Area (EEA) has also been proposed. This would include all EC nations and those countries which are members of the European Free Trade Area (EFTA) - Austria, Finland, Iceland, Norway, Switzerland and Sweden. The EEA would be the world's largest single market, with 19 countries and a population of over 375 million. It would be likely to account for 46 per cent of world trade.

The aim of the EEA is to extend the benefits of the Single Market to EFTA countries by removing the trade barriers which exist between EC and EFTA countries. For EC businesses this means increased trading opportunities within EFTA countries. However, it also means that EFTA-based firms may pose a threat within EC markets.

Eastern Europe

The fall of the communist governments of Eastern Europe and the countries' attempts to move to market economies in the early 1990s present many opportunities for UK and EC businesses.

Countries such as the former Soviet Union, Poland and Hungary are, with varying degrees of success, introducing the operation of markets into their economies (☞ unit 6). In 1992, East Germany united with West Germany to form one country. This meant that businesses in the former East Germany were faced with the prospect of competing in a market economy with domestic and foreign businesses.

Before the change took place, most products in this part of the world were provided by state-owned monopolies. These were protected from overseas competition by trade barriers. Today, most of these state-owned monopolies have been privatised and investment from foreign firms is positively encouraged.

For British firms, the changes in Eastern Europe present a number of opportunities. UK firms see these economies as untapped export markets for their products.

- The opening up of these markets has provided Western-based firms with access to a huge number of consumers. They can be used as a manufacturing base for Western firms, taking advantage of workforces and land prices which are relatively cheaper than those in Western Europe.
- There are opportunities for joint ventures (☞ unit 32) with former state-owned firms. This allows British and other Western firms to combine their international business skills with local knowledge of markets and trading conditions.
- Firms and individual entrepreneurs have the

opportunity to sell their expertise and skills to Eastern European businesses.

There are however, a number of problems with trading in Eastern Europe and the former Soviet Union states.

Bureaucracy Many of the institutions and regulations under the old planned system are still in existence. These can present a number of obstacles. For example, there are huge delays in receiving permits and licences for Western businesses wishing to set up and trade in these countries.

Political instability Since their transition to market economies, there has been political instability in a number of these countries. This ranges from full scale war, as in Bosnia and Croatia, to weak and fragile governments, as found in many of the CIS. Such instability may be off-putting for potential business investors. They may argue that their businesses are unlikely to flourish in the 'turmoil' which results from such instability.

Low incomes Although Eastern Europe and the CIS represents a huge potential market for Western-based businesses, opportunities are likely to be limited whilst average incomes remain low. The bulk of the population

---

QUESTION 3 The revolution which swept communism out of eastern Europe helped make Jan Kulczyk rich. This 42-year-old Polish millionaire, clad soberly in grey slacks and a blue blazer, has moved with apparent ease from the old world of communist rule to the new one where capitalism holds sway - and where the whole of Europe now appears a place to make money.

Controlling 36 companies with sales approaching 3,000 billion zloty (£124 million), Mr Kulczyk's interests include banking, Volkswagen vehicle distribution in Poland and, above all, agribusiness. Mr Kulczyk made his fortune selling fruit, vegetables and meat to the EC. Now, in addition, he buys western food processing machinery to sell in the east. Prospects for increased EC commerce depend crucially on improving transport links. Mr Kulczyk and other businessmen want to build a 270km toll motorway linking Berlin to his native Poznan and beyond.

In another example of his activities, Mr Kulczyk has teamed up with Krupp to help build, near Poznan, a $100 million 150,000 tonnes per year processing plant, a venture which will increase Poland's rape seed processing capacity by a quarter. 'Workers in the European Community shouldn't feel that low wage employees in Poland are a threat to their jobs', he declares. 'Rather, this offers a chance to expand their companies' business.'

Mr Kulczyk's European horizons stretch east as well as west. Last year he helped set up Euro Agro Centrum, a company which aims to sell food processing equipment from western Europe to countries like Ukraine.

Source: adapted from the *Financial Times*, 4.1.1993.

(a)   What evidence is there in the article of EC firms taking advantage of opportunities in Poland?
(b)   What problems related to doing business in Poland are suggested by the article?

of these countries is unlikely to be able to afford many of the products manufactured by Western-based firms. This should, however, be less of a problem over time as business in these countries develops and earnings increase.

Infrastructure The INFRASTRUCTURE of a country includes roads, railways, schools, airports, hospitals and office accommodation. In many ways the infrastructure of the Eastern European and CIS nations is of a high standard. For example, the hospitals and public transport in some of these countries are better than those found in some Western countries. However, there are also problems. Poor telecommunication systems, banking services and law enforcement are all problems which may affect the prospects of Western firms.

Less developed economies

These economies are almost always found in the southern hemisphere. They are often known as 'the South', Third World Countries, developing countries or LESS DEVELOPED COUNTRIES (LDCs).

The main features of LDCs are that they have poorly developed infrastructures and low average incomes per head of population. However, it is difficult to place countries in the South into one single group. This is because some are developing a wide range of industries which can compete with those in the West. Such countries are known as the Newly Industrialised Countries (NICs). Others are hardly developing at all. They continue to struggle with a range of economic and social problems on a scale almost unimaginable in the west.

The Newly Industrialised Countries (NICs) Many of these countries are found in South East Asia and include Taiwan, Singapore, South Korea, Malaysia and Hong Kong. Others are in South and Central America, including Mexico and Brazil. Such countries have been developing home-grown industries with products which are increasingly able to compete in the domestic markets in the West. An example of this is Proton cars from Malaysia. In addition, multinational companies are locating their production facilities in NICs, often in order to take advantage of their relatively cheap wage costs. NICs, therefore, present competition to Western countries and their businesses on two fronts.
■ Undercutting the costs of Western producers of cars and other domestic goods.
■ Companies based in SE Asia are expanding via takeovers or via inward investment into Western countries where their imports have reduced the strength of the competition.
These countries have also experienced a rise in overall income levels. As a result, they now provide significant export markets for Western produced consumer goods.

Poorer countries in the South Most of these countries are to be found in Africa, Asia and Central/South America. For Western businesses, such countries can either provide a base for manufacturing products or act as potential export markets. The infrastructure of such countries however, is often poor. It can be very difficult for multinational companies to establish manufacturing facilities. For example, in Sudan, the largest African country, there is only one purpose-built road of any great distance. Income levels are also very low. Export opportunities for most Western firms are limited to providing goods to very small sections of the population who enjoy Western incomes and lifestyles.

Many of these poorer countries are crippled by debt arising from balance of payment deficits and loans which they had been given by Western banks and governments. This means that they are required to make large, regular payments to Western banks. As a result, despite the aid which is given by those in the richer North, there is a net

---

QUESTION 4 Mr Bob May, a blunt straight talking Scot, is managing director of Dunlop Zambia. Despite the environment within which he works, his approach is a blend of optimism, hard headed realism and entrepreneurial flair.

After more than 25 years of debilitating mismanagement and regional wars, Zambia is making a fresh start. Peaceful elections in October 1991 marked the collapse of one party rule. Although aid and debt relief have been substantial, Africa's newest democracy is under strain. The infrastructure is frail, social services are impoverished and industry needs re-equipping. GDP per head of population is £240 and Zambia is one of the world's most indebted nations - its 8 million people owing external creditors over £4 billion.

He has to convince his London shareholder, BTR, with its reputation for running a tight ship, that Zambia is a country worthy of a $7million investment in the modernisation of the tyre factory. In a country with three-digit inflation and a tumbling exchange rate, this is no easy task. Dunlop is able to beat the imported competition partly because it can undercut suppliers burdened with transport costs, devaluation, import duties and massive importer margins.

Dunlop plans a modest investment - $7million over four years - in modernising its plant, drawing on technology from Dunlop International Technology in Birmingham. By mid-1993, Dunlop Zambia will introduce a new generation of tyre, capable of doubling the mileage of existing products.

The Dunlop story is a familiar one for those with experience of Africa. After 15 years or more of monopoly, Dunlop is now faced with competition from half a dozen direct importers. An industry where marketing used to mean rationing supplies to desperate buyers has changed beyond all recognition. 'We have to change the marketing mindset,' says Mr May, who is sending his sales staff to work with Dunlop Nigeria to learn how to market in a competitive environment.

Source: adapted from the *Financial Times*, 17.12.1992.

(a) Explain the problems likely to be faced by Dunlop when trading in Zambia.
(b) Using evidence from the above article, explain why Dunlop are considering investing $7 million in Zambia despite these problems.

outflow of money. For example, in 1985, the year of the Ethiopian famine and 'Live Aid', the poorest countries in Africa gave twice as much money to the West as we gave to them!

Despite these problems, many Western-based businesses continue to operate in these countries. They represent an enormous market; the majority of the world's population lives in these countries and they can provide low cost facilities. Unfortunately, such business activities have often attracted bad publicity.

■ Some Western businesses have provided aid for military goods or inappropriate projects, such as enormous hydro-electric schemes, which are unlikely to meet the needs of the majority of the population.

■ Some companies have been accused of acting unethically by persuading poor consumers to purchase goods which can be harmful, such as drugs banned in the West.

■ Large multinationals are said to exploit cheap labour and raw materials and provide little in return.

Multinationals

A MULTINATIONAL company is an organisation which owns or controls production or service facilities outside the country in which it is based. This means that they do not just export their products abroad, but actually own production facilities in other countries.

These companies usually have interests in at least four countries, but there are many which operate in a huge range of countries throughout the world. Examples of multinationals include Ford, British American Tobacco, Volkswagen, Matsui (producers of electrical goods), Unilever, Mobil, Sony and Ciba-Geigy (producers of chemicals). The very largest of the multinationals such as Exxon (which trades as Esso in the UK), General Motors and Royal Dutch Shell are enormous organisations. They have turnovers that are in excess of the GNPs of all but the wealthiest countries.

There are a number of reasons why firms become multinationals.

■ To avoid protectionist policies. By actually producing within a particular country, a firm can usually avoid any tariffs or quotas which that country may impose. This is why Japanese car firms, such as Nissan, Toyota and Honda, have established themselves within EC countries in recent years.

■ The globalisation of markets. National boundaries, many believe, are becoming irrelevant for firms as instant communications and high speed travel make the world seem smaller. This is known as the 'global village'. Multinationals, which are global or international in outlook, are the ideal type of business organisation to take advantage of this situation.

The influence of multinationals

There is great debate as to the actual effects of multinationals. Whilst there are clear benefits of multinationals operating in a particular country, there are also a number of problems associated with them.

The balance of payments and employment One benefit of multinationals is their ability to create jobs. This, along with the manufacturing capacity which they create, can increase the GNP of countries and add to the standard of living. As well as this, multinationals benefit the balance of payments of a country if their products are sold abroad. The setting-up of a car manufacturing plant by Toyota in Derby helps to illustrate this. Not only has this plant created jobs, but it has raised the GNP of the UK. The balance of payments has also been helped as large proportion of the Derby plant's cars are shipped out to other EC nations.

However, whilst multinationals can create jobs, they are also capable of causing unemployment for two reasons. Firstly, they create competition for domestic firms. This may be beneficial, causing local firms to improve their efficiency, but it can also be a problem if it results in these firms cutting their labour force or closing down plants. Secondly, multinationals often shift production facilities from one country to another in order to further their own ends. The effect of this is that jobs are lost and production is either reduced or completely stopped.

In addition, multinationals can have a negative impact upon the balance of payments. This is because many of them receive huge amounts of components from their branches abroad, thus adding to the total quantity of imports.

Technology and expertise Multinationals may introduce new technology, production processes and management styles and techniques. This has been one of the benefits to Western countries of Japanese multinationals. Techniques such as just-in-time stock control (☞ unit 33) and management methods such as quality control circles (☞ unit 50) have been successfully used by Japanese firms in foreign countries. Such techniques have also been adopted by home based firms. These raise the standards of local firms who become aware of these new developments. The process by which multinationals benefit countries in this respect is known as **technology transfer**.

Technology transfer can be especially important to developing countries, which may lack technical expertise and know-how. However, this is not always the case. Managers and supervisors are often brought in from the multinationals' home country, with little training being given to locally recruited staff. As a consequence locals are likely to be employed in low skilled jobs.

Social responsibility Multinationals have often been criticised, especially in their dealings with LDCs. The Union Carbide disaster in Bhopal, India, when hundreds were killed by the release of poisonous gases into the atmosphere, raised serious doubts about the safety measures used by multinationals in LDCs.

They have also been accused of marketing harmful products. One example was the aggressive selling of milk powder to mothers with new born babies when medical research indicated that breast feeding is far more likely to benefit infant health. In addition, environmentalists are concerned about the impact of multinationals on tropical rainforests and other natural resources.

Government control Because of the size and financial power of many multinationals, there are concerns about the ability of governments to control them. For example, they may be able to avoid paying corporation tax in particular countries.

Taxation can be avoided by the use of TRANSFER PRICING. This involves declaring higher profits in those countries with lower taxation levels, thus reducing the overall tax bill. A company may charge subsidiary branches in low taxation countries low prices for components bought in from overseas branches of the same firm. This means that costs in the low tax country are kept low and high profits can be declared. Similarly, subsidiary branches in high tax countries are charged high prices for components bought in from overseas branches. This means little or no profit is recorded.

QUESTION 5 Unilever is an Anglo-Dutch business formed in 1930. It is one of the world's largest producers of consumer goods and is known for its branded food and drinks, detergents and personal products. Such brands include Birds Eye, Surf, Walls, Timotei, Mentadent, Batchelors and Brooke Bond. Unilever operates in more than 75 countries and employs around 300,000 people worldwide.

UAC International is a substantial and integrated group of companies which together form an important part of Unilever. UAC mainly operates in tropical Africa and the Middle East. The principal product areas include: African textiles, beers, foods and personal products; electrical and diesel equipment; agricultural equipment and commercial and passenger vehicles. To an increasing extent, these products are manufactured or assembled using local raw materials, skills and labour, thus stimulating the economy of the area and reducing the need for imports.

Unilever are constantly looking for further opportunities for growth and are at present focusing on the Middle East, Vietnam and China, where they recently began making skin care products.

Operating profits in Unilever's 'Rest of the World' sector (excluding Europe and the USA) have been £497 million in a year. Total sales in this sector amounted to £5.34 billion.

Source: adapted from Unilever External Affairs Department Booklet

(a) Why is Unilever described as a multinational?
(b) Why do you think Unilever became a multinational?
(c) Why might a country benefit from Unilever establishing a plant there?

Key terms

CAP - the Common Agricultural Policy of the European Community. It is designed to stabilise EC agricultural markets by fixing minimum prices for agricultural products.
Customs union/Common market - a group of countries with free trade between them and a common external tariff.
Excise duties - taxes levied on fuel, alcohol, tobacco and betting.
GATT - the General Agreement on Tariffs and Trade, an organisation which seeks to promote free trade between nations.
Infrastructure - those aspects of a country which support its economy. These include schools, roads, airports, telecommunication systems, hospitals etc .
Less developed countries - the poorer, less economically developed countries of the world.

Multinational - a company which owns or controls production or service facilities outside the country in which it is based.
NICs - Newly Industrialised Countries. These are countries such as Singapore, Malaysia and Mexico which have recently gone through the process of industrialisation.
Single European Market - an agreement by EC countries to remove all barriers to trade.
Transfer pricing - a system operated by multinationals. It is an attempt to avoid relatively high tax rates through the prices which one subsidiary charges another for components and finished products.

Summary

1. Why is the EC said to be a customs union?
2. What is the Common Agricultural Policy?
3. What changes have occurred as a result of the Single Market?
4. State 5 implications of the Single Market for British businesses.
5. What is the aim of the G7 group of countries?
6. How might GATT affect British firms?
7. What opportunities have the changes in Eastern Europe presented for British firms?
8. What problems exist in poorer LDCs which can make it difficult for Western firms to operate within them?
9. For what reasons do firms become multinationals?
10. What benefits might the expansion of Japanese businesses into world markets have had?
11. What are the potential benefits of multinationals?
12. What problems might be created by multinationals?

Question

General Motors - the lean machine

Factory openings are not usually very exciting affairs, but this one was different. Helmut Kohl, Germany's Chancellor, took time out from the political crisis engulfing Europe to attend, and Jack Smith, the GM chairman, flew in from the company's headquarters in Detroit. They were there to celebrate a $666 million investment in the former East Germany; a welcome gesture towards reviving the East's tottering economy. The new factory in Eisenach will build 150,000 cars a year for Opel, GM's German subsidiary and employ 2,000 people. It will employ production techniques pioneered by the Japanese, which are expected to drastically undercut the costs of other German car makers.

For Mr Smith, the opening was a bittersweet affair. It vindicated his stewardship of GM's European business, but it was in stark contrast to what had kept him busy for much of the year; closing factories in America.

Ironically, the opening of the Eisenach plant comes at a time when Germany is becoming a less competitive place to make cars, even for companies like BMW and Mercedes-Benz which charge premium prices. This is partly as a result of the EC market being opened up to greater competition from Japanese car manufacturers locating plants within the EC. Some German car makers are switching production abroad. Volkswagen, Europe's biggest producer, already makes cars in Spain and it has taken charge of Skoda in Czechoslovakia. BMW are building a plant in America and Mercedes may well follow.

Opel's Eisenach plant could hasten the departure of the German car industry from the western part of the country. Instead of taking 40-50 man hours to make a car, as even the most efficient German plants do, Eisenach aims to make cars in only 20 man-hours. That would match the productivity of the joint-venture car plant which GM operate with Toyota in California. Indeed, some of the managers at the new German factory come from this Californian plant, whilst others come from another joint-venture plant which GM operate with Suzuki in Canada. These managers have carefully studied the manufacturing techniques of GM's Japanese partners.

Source: adapted from *The Economist*, 19.9.1992

(a) Why do you think GM opened their new plant in Eastern Germany?
(b) How might the Single European Market affect GM's European operations?
(c) What problems do you think GM might encounter in their new Eisenach plant?
(d) Other than Eastern Europe, which parts of the world do you think GM might have considered investing in? Explain your answer.
(e) Assess the impact of the opening of the Eisenach plant upon the former East Germany.
(f) Explain how GM might use transfer pricing in order to avoid paying German corporation taxes.

What are business ethics?

Ethics are a set of values and principles which influence how individuals, groups and society behave. BUSINESS ETHICS are concerned with how such values and principles operate in business. They help firms to decide what actions are right or wrong in certain circumstances. Ethics might influence the following business decisions.

- Should products which might damage the health of consumers be withdrawn from the market?
- What efforts, if any, should be made to ensure that business activities do not damage the environment?
- Should money be spent on wheelchair access to workplaces and retail outlets?
- Should a firm reject a bribe given to secure an overseas contract?
- Should part time staff be offered the same employment rights as full time staff?
- Should a workplace creche be provided for working mothers?
- Should a contribution be made to a local charity?

A business that says 'yes' to some of these questions might be described as ETHICAL. A firm which is ethical with regard to society as a whole and the community within which it is based might also be described as 'socially responsible'.

Different individuals and groups have different viewpoints. It is these which can determine what they see as ethical business behaviour. For example, a firm polluting a river might only be able to take action against further pollution through savings made by job losses. What is ethical behaviour in this case - preventing the pollution or saving jobs?

To some extent the law attempts to ensure that businesses act ethically. However, obeying the 'letter' of the law does not necessarily mean that a firm is behaving in an ethical way. For example, some would regard water companies which pump untreated sewerage into the sea as unethical, even if the activity is legal. This is due to the possible pollution and health problems associated with such an activity.

In recent years there have been a number of businesses that could be described as acting unethically. Examples which some believe fall into this category include British Airways for the 'dirty tricks' which they allegedly used against their competitor Virgin Airlines and Exxon for the safety standards on their oil tanker Exxon Valdez which sank in Alaskan waters. Other examples may include the large salary increases given to the chief executives of newly privatised companies, insider share dealing in the City of London, the trade of some businesses with countries that have oppressive regimes, or the trade in arms. Individuals within businesses also act 'unethically'. A well publicised example is the behaviour of Robert Maxwell, former owner of Maxwell Communications Corporation. In 1992, after his death, it was found that he had been supporting his business empire with money 'borrowed' from his employees' pension fund.

QUESTION 1

YOU GET EXCELLENT COFFEE. YOU DON'T GET COCAINE.

The coffee growers of Latin America face a problem. Either they get paid a fair price for their coffee, or they face bankruptcy and may have to turn their land over to the illegal production of the coca plant for cocaine.

Cafédirect helps avoid this problem, because more of the money you pay for Cafédirect roast and ground coffee goes directly to the growers.

The result? They continue to produce high quality Arabica coffee for Cafédirect.

cafédirect
MEDIUM ROAST
FILTER AND CAFETIERE

Cafédirect.
Fair trade. Excellent coffee.

Figure 71.1

Would you describe the above as ethical behaviour? Explain your answer.

Increasingly firms are keen to be seen as acting ethically. This has led some to draw up a **code of ethics**. For example, Body Shop's Green Book contains 50 pages covering everything about the company's commercial and personal relations policy. Indeed, a study in 1993 suggested that almost a third of Britain's large firms have a code of ethics. In the US in the same year the figure was more than three-quarters of all firms.

The benefits of ethical behaviour

There are a number of possible advantages for businesses in behaving in an ethical or socially responsible way.

Consumers' views Increasing numbers of consumers are taking into account a firm's 'behaviour' when buying products. As a result, ethical behaviour can be good for sales. Body Shop is a good example of this. A feature of Body Shop's marketing is that its products are not tested on animals. The company has also lent support to groups helping firms in the world's poorest countries. This stance has perhaps helped Body Shop become one of the most successful newcomers in Britain's retail industry. There are a number of other firms which have responded in a similar way. The Co-operative Bank, for example, has conducted a wide ranging campaign. They refuse to invest money in or finance a variety of concerns. These range from countries with poor human rights records to companies using exploitative factory farming methods. This policy was introduced as a result of a survey carried out amongst the bank's customers, which found that they regarded a clear ethical policy as important for the bank.

Improvements in the recruitment and retention of staff Firms with an ethical approach believe that they will be more able to recruit well qualified and motivated staff. In addition, ethical firms argue that they are able to retain their staff better if they adopt a more caring approach to employees. Polaroid in the US, for example, subsidises child-care expenses for their lower paid workers. Marks and Spencer provide their staff with a range of benefits, over and above those usually provided in the retail sector. They have benefited by achieving one of the lowest rates of staff turnover in the UK. This has cut their recruitment and retraining costs.

Improvements in employee motivation Firms which behave in an ethical manner believe that their employees are more committed to their success as a result. They may be prepared to work harder to allow the business to achieve its aims.

Effects of ethical behaviour

What effect will acting in an ethical way have on a business?

Increasing costs Ethical behaviour can result in an increase in costs for a firm. An ethical firm may, for

---

QUESTION 2

The SKANDIA ETHICAL SELECTION FUND

What screening criteria is applied?

The screening criteria applied to ensure that all investments in the Fund are ethically/environmentally sound is obviously of paramount importance to clients. Unlike some funds however, Skandia Life felt it inappropriate to set up a formal advisory panel as this inevitably leads to extra costs to the fund.

Instead, Skandia Life utilises the services of a recognised expert in the field of ethical investment - Lee Coates of the Ethical Investors Group. Lee works closely with the fund manager to ensure that strict screening criteria is maintained and provides his expertise free of charge. Screening is based on both negative and positive selection i.e.

Negative Selection

The screening-out of companies which have a negative social or environmental effect:
- Armaments and nuclear weapons
- Animal exploitation and experimentation
- South Africa and other oppressive regimes
- Alcohol
- Tobacco
- Environmentally damaging practices
- Gambling
- Pornography

Positive Selection

The selection of companies which make a positive contribution to the environment:
- Environmental protection
- Pollution control
- Conservation and recycling
- Safety and security
- Equal opportunity provision for employees.

'The ethical and environmental investment sector is holding its own in the performance stakes. Public awareness of ethi-green policies suggests that it will continue to do so.'

Pensions Management - March '92

Figure 71.2 *The screening process used by Skandia life assurance company to decide upon investments*

(a) Why might the screening process by Skandia be an example of ethical behaviour?
(b) Explain the terms negative and positive selection.
(c) What might be the benefits to the business of such behaviour?

---

example, be forced to turn down cheaper supplies from a firm which tests its products on animals. Similarly, PowerGen's costs may have been raised by the pollution reducing filters which they have put on their coal-fired power stations.

Loss of profit Firms may be forced to turn down profitable business due to their ethical stance. A business, for example, may reject a profitable investment opportunity in a company which produces animal fur, as this is against its ethical policy. However, the ethical firm would hope that the gains it makes from its policy, by attracting increased numbers of customers, would outweigh these costs.

Conflict When a firm's overall profitability comes into conflict with its ethical policy, problems may result. In such cases the shareholders of a firm may object to the ethical policy as the return on their investment is harmed.

Business practice. A firm seeking to act more ethically may need to alter the way in which it approaches a huge range of business matters. Such a firm might, for example, need to consider the impact of its activities on the environment (☞ unit 72), whether or not its recruitment policy was providing equal opportunities for all applicants regardless of age, sex, ethnic background or disability (☞ unit 55), the extent to which its advertisements are offensive or in poor taste, and the protection given to consumers buying their products (☞ unit 73).

QUESTION 3 Pedigree Pet Foods, which employs 1,200 of its 1,500 workforce around Melton Mowbray in Leicestershire, claims to be one of the pioneers of more orthodox corporate responsibility through practice evolved gradually over the past 40 years.

This can range from support, in cash and kind, of local schools to the development of a pet-food nutrition centre, work with animal charities and a guiding principle of 'mutuality' aimed at sharing benefits with employees and suppliers. Local help varies from a cheque to a quiet word with suppliers who might be able to help a school or charity with savings on a project.

Richard Evans, external affairs director of the Third World trade and development company, Traidcraft, said the producers' perspective was vital to its commercial policies. 'Right from the beginning we have been trying to promote fair trade with the Third World, but a very strong secondary objective has been to demonstrate that this is not just a good thing to do but that it's commercially feasible'.

Traidcraft is based on an industrial estate in Gateshead, supporting 115 jobs as part of its commitment to the North-East. Its trading policies reflect its impact on overseas suppliers, its community (including its workforce, supporters, shareholders, and commercial neighbours) and the market, through continuing debate on trade issues, said Richard Evans, who recently returned from Tanzania with fresh proposals for company policy on imports.

Source: *The Guardian*, 9.1.1993.

(a) Identify the elements of ethical behaviour that can be found in the examples above.
(b) Why might Richard Evans argue 'a strong secondary objective has been to demonstrate that it is not just a good thing, but that it's commercially feasible' to behave in an ethical way?
(c) What might be the effects on:
   (i) Pedigree Pet Foods;
   (ii) Traidcraft;
   of their policies?

Should businesses be expected to act ethically?

There is considerable debate about how businesses should actually behave.

Some argue that businesses have a responsibility to act ethically. Those who hold this view stress the fact that firms do not operate in isolation. They are a part of society and have an impact upon the lives of those communities in which they operate. As such they should act in a socially responsible manner and consider the possible effects of any decisions they make. This means that profit making should not be the only criterion used when making decisions. Other factors which firms might consider include the effect of their decisions upon the environment, jobs, the local community, consumers, competitors, suppliers and employees.

Others argue that businesses should not be expected to act ethically. There are two main views in support of this argument. The first is from supporters of free market economics (☞ unit 65). They argue that the primary responsibility of businesses is to produce goods and services in the most efficient way, and make profit for shareholders. Firms should attempt to do this in any way they can, providing it is legal. Only by doing this will the general good of everyone be served. If firms are expected to act 'ethically', then consumers may suffer because the ethical behaviour could lead to inefficiency, higher costs and higher prices.

A second argument is that in most cases it is naive to expect businesses to act ethically. Whenever there is a conflict between acting ethically and making greater profits, the vast majority of firms will choose the latter. Those firms which do act in an ethical manner only do so because it is profitable. This view is often held by those who favour government intervention to regulate business. They argue that it is necessary for the government to force firms to behave responsibly through a variety of laws which it must enforce.

Are businesses becoming more ethical?

It could be said that the late 1980s and 1990s have seen a move towards a more 'caring' attitude by businesses. The growth of companies producing health care products which are not animal tested, the use of recyclable carrier bags and the sale of organically grown vegetables by many retailers could all be an indication of this. Some pension funds and a number of investment schemes are now termed 'green'. They will only invest savers' money in companies which promote the environment.

Others argue that ethical attitudes have failed to penetrate the boardrooms of the UK and that firms continue to act unethically in a variety of ways. According to an extensive survey undertaken by the University of Westminster in 1991 and 1992, many company directors still believe in the greed-driven motives of the past. The results of the survey showed that junior executives and women took the moral 'high ground', with more concern about green issues, staff relations and trade with countries that had records of abusing human rights. The majority of British business is, they found, run by people who are old and male. One respondent summed up the climate. 'In general, business ethics does not come very high in the scale of human behaviour. Professional standards and levels of caring sometimes leave a lot to be desired.'

QUESTION 4 Mr Richard Branson and his Virgin Atlantic airline won near record libel damages of £610,000 at the end of a two year 'dirty tricks' legal battle against British Airways. In charging BA with going 'beyond the limits of commercially acceptable practice', Mr Branson listed details of its rival's campaign to discredit Virgin. These included:

- the illegal use of Virgin Atlantic computer information;
- the poaching of Virgin passengers by bogus Virgin representatives;
- the shredding of documents relating to Virgin activities;
- the spreading of hostile and discreditable stories to destabilise Virgin.

BA, which also had to meet several million pounds in legal costs, apologised 'unreservedly' to Mr Branson in court for alleging that Virgin Atlantic, in claiming BA was conducting a 'dirty tricks' campaign, was only seeking publicity.

Sir Colin Marshall, BA's chief executive and deputy chairman, said his airline was taking steps to ensure 'regrettable incidents' undertaken by BA employees did nor occur again.

In a special message to BA staff intended to bolster morale, Sir Colin said the 'overwhelming majority' of the airline's workforce had no involvement whatsoever in the campaign against Virgin. He urged them not to be distracted by the publicity surrounding the affair.

Mr Branson also demanded BA directors give a full explanation of a separate covert activity targeted at Virgin which, he alleged, was carried out by private investigators.

Source: adapted from the *Financial Times*, 12.1.1993.

(a) What elements of BA's behaviour could be termed
 (i) illegal;
 (ii) unethical?
(b) What evidence is there to suggest this was the action of individuals rather than a corporate policy?
(c) Which view about the behaviour of the firms would BA's actions lend support to ? Explain your answer.

Pressure groups

PRESSURE GROUPS are groups without the direct political power to achieve their aims, but whose aims lie within the sphere of politics. They usually attempt to influence local government, central government, businesses and the media. They aim to have their views taken into account when any decisions are made. Such influence can occur directly, through contact with politicians, local representatives and business people, or indirectly by influencing public opinion.

There are many different types of pressure group and many ways of classifying them. One way is to divide groups into those which have a single cause and those which have a number of different causes.

- Single cause groups include the Campaign for Nuclear Disarmament, Survival International and the Campaign for Press and Broadcasting Freedom. Such groups mainly try to promote one cause.
- Multi-cause groups include trade unions, Greenpeace and the Confederation of British Industry. Pressure groups falling into this category tend to campaign on a number of issues. Trade unions, for example, have campaigned on a variety of issues, including the rights of the unemployed, boycotting goods from South Africa under apartheid and improving the pay and conditions of their members.

Over the last few decades there has been a huge increase in the number of pressure groups and in the scale of their activities. Inevitably this has brought them into much closer contact with businesses. As a result there are now a number of groups which focus their activities upon businesses in general or particular businesses and industries.

- Environmental groups such as Friends of the Earth campaign to prevent businesses from polluting the environment.
- Consumer groups, such as the Consumers' Association seek to protect the rights of consumers in general. Others' include The Football Supporters' Association and rail users' groups.
- Local community groups may, for example, seek to prevent particular business developments or influence the policies of individual firms which operate in their local area.
- Employee groups, such as trade unions and professional associations, try to influence firms about issues such as conditions of work and pay levels.

Pressure groups vary in size. Some, like a local group aiming to divert a by-pass, may be made up of a few local people. Others are national organisations such as the Royal Society for the Protection of Birds, or international groups such as Amnesty International.

Factors influencing the success of pressure groups

The success of any group, no matter how large or small, will depend on a number of factors.

- Finance and organisational ability. A pressure group with large funds will be able to spend on well organised campaigns. This has been a tactic employed by trade unions and professional groups. A well financed pressure group may also be able to employ full time professional campaigners. Such people are likely to organise more effective campaigns than enthusiasts devoting some of their spare time to such

an activity.
- Public sympathy. Capturing the imagination of the public will play an important role in the ability of a pressure group to succeed. The Campaign for Real Ale has been effective in this respect. Almost single handedly they caused a change in the types of beer available in public houses and in the brewing methods of the big brewing companies. As with many successful campaigns, CAMRA's ability to present a clear and simple message to the public was vital.
- Access to politicians. Pressure groups which have access to politicians are able to apply pressure for changes in the law. For example, the International League for the Protection of Horses persuaded the government to ban the export of live horses for human consumption within the EC. Their contacts with politicians were vital in this campaign. The process of applying pressure on politicians is known as lobbying. It has become dominated by skilled professional lobbyists, the fees of whom are out of the range of all but the wealthiest of groups.
- Reputation. Gaining a favourable reputation amongst politicians can be important. The British Medical Association, for example, has a good reputation amongst a variety of politicians and is therefore often consulted on a variety of health matters by the government.

> **QUESTION 5** The carefully planned retailing strategy of developing large out of town supermarkets with plenty of parking spaces has run into problems. Pressure groups, in both Sheffield and Bristol, were formed by local residents opposed to the development of green field sites for this purpose. These groups were at pains to point out the inconsistency of supermarket chains' claims to be environmentally sensitive, when at the same time they were encouraging their customers to use more petrol and building on sites of local beauty or interest.
>
> (a) Which category of pressure group is described in the above passage?
> (b) What might determine the success of the local residents?

The effects of pressure groups on business

There are a number of ways in which pressure groups can affect firms.
- Pressure groups often seek to influence the behaviour of members of the public about a particular product, business or industry. Friends of the Earth attempt to persuade the public to use cars less and public transport or bicycles more in order to reduce emissions into the atmosphere. This campaign, if successful, would have important implications for a wide range of firms involved in the transport industry.
- Political parties, through their representatives in Parliament, are able to pass laws which regulate the activities of businesses. Therefore it is not surprising

that many pressure groups devote resources to lobbying politicians. An example of this is the attempt by the anti-smoking group, ASH, to change the law so that the advertising of tobacco is made illegal.
- The actions of pressure groups can reduce the sales of firms. This is often most successfully achieved when efforts are targeted at particular firms. Consumers are then called upon to boycott these firms. For example, in the 1970s and 1980s the National Union of Students boycotted banks which invested in South Africa.
- Firms can face increased costs as a result of the activities of pressure groups. This may involve new production processes or waste disposal methods. Firms may have to counteract any negative publicity from a pressure group. For example, many believe that British Nuclear Fuel's campaign to attract visitors to its Sellafield site was a result of the negative publicity which it received from environmental groups.
- Businesses with a tarnished reputation as a result of pressure group activity may find it more difficult to recruit employees.

How might businesses react to pressure groups?
- By positively responding to the issues raised by pressure groups. For example, due to the campaign against investment in South Africa by a number of pressure groups, some of the major banks did pull out of the country. Similarly, local pressure groups have been successful in persuading some firms to change building plans and landscape nearby areas.
- Through promotions and public relations. Firms can attempt to counteract negative publicity through their own promotional and public relations work. For example, a number of oil companies which have been criticised for their impact upon the environment have sought to deal with this by promoting the 'greener' aspects of their industry, such as the availability of lead free petrol.
- A number of leading firms either lobby politicians themselves or pay for the services of professional lobbyists to represent their interests.
- Legal action. Where pressure groups make false allegations about a business, this can be dealt with by the legal system. For example, allegations by pressure groups that McDonalds were contributing to the destruction of the Amazonian rainforest were dealt with through legal action in the courts.

Key terms

> **Business ethics** - the influence of moral values and principles upon the conduct and operation of businesses.
> **Ethical** - morally correct.
> **Pressure groups** - groups of people without direct political power who seek to influence decision makers in politics, business and society.

Summary

1. Give 5 examples which might indicate a business is behaving ethically.
2. Give 5 examples which might indicate a business is behaving unethically.
3. Why might firms draw up a code of ethics?
4. Briefly explain 5 effects that ethical behaviour may have on businesses.
5. 'Businesses should not be expected to act ethically.' Explain the two sides to this argument.

6. What are the 2 main types of pressure groups?
7. Give 3 reasons why a pressure group campaign may fail.
8. How can pressure groups affect the sales of a firm's product?
9. How might a business respond to negative publicity generated by a pressure group?

Question

The Co-operative Bank

The Co-operative Bank have strict guidelines governing the conduct of their business. They believe that all commercial enterprises, whatever their size, should have a policy which controls the way their business is conducted. They also believe that such a policy must be actively implemented, otherwise it is 'no more than a collection of fine words'.

The guidelines are in the form of a thirteen point ethical policy. They will:

- not invest or provide financial services to oppressive organisations or regimes;
- not finance the manufacture or sale of weapons;
- not invest in businesses involved in animal experiments;
- not finance individuals or businesses using factory farming methods;
- not support organisations involved in blood sports;
- not finance tobacco manufacturers;
- try to make sure their services are not used for money laundering, tax evasion or the trafficking of drugs and to be constantly vigilant of their dealings in order to avoid these areas;
- encourage business to support the environment;
- promote business relations with firms that have a similar ethical stance;
- improve and strengthen their customer charter which sets standards for their dealings;
- consider their consumers' views and change its policies to suit them;
- not speculate against the pound during periods of crisis (this was added in May 1992 as a result of the international currency crisis).

This ethical stance taken by the Co-operative Bank has found support amongst their customers. Research revealed 85 per cent support for the Bank's stance among a survey of 30,000 customers. Among the

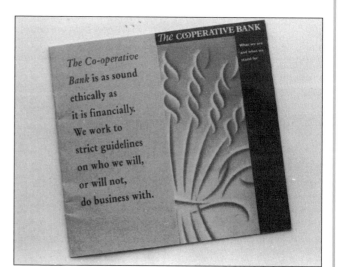

general public, however, only 15 per cent were strongly in favour, 75 per cent neutral and 10 per cent opposed. The bank aim to keep their charter under constant review. A bank spokesman has commented 'Basically what we are saying is we are trying; we are not perfect.'

Source: adapted from The Co-operative Bank booklet, *What we are and what we stand for* and *The Guardian*, 9.1.1993.

(a) Why might the Co-operative Bank be said to be operating in an ethical way?
(b) Why might the bank have adopted this stance?
(c) Discuss 3 effects that such a policy is likely to have on the bank's business.
(d) How might pressure groups have influenced the bank's decisions?
(e) Explain possible conflicts that may arise between the bank and other interested parties from this stance being taken.

The costs and benefits of business activity

When businesses produce and sell a product or a service it is relatively easy for them to see the costs involved and the benefits they will gain. These costs are known as PRIVATE COSTS. They might include such things as the wages paid to employees, the cost of an advertising campaign or the purchase of raw materials. The PRIVATE BENEFITS to the business and its owners include the total revenue earned from sales, any resulting profit and the dividends paid to shareholders.

A business may find, however, that it creates other costs. Take a factory producing cement which is located in a small 'scenic' town. The firm may dispose of some of its waste in a local river or discharge dust into the atmosphere. Lorries making deliveries to the factory may disturb the local residents. The factory may be sited close to a local beauty spot, ruining the view. These are all examples of spillover effects or EXTERNALITIES. So the costs to the whole of society, the SOCIAL COSTS, are made up of the private costs of the business plus **negative externalities** (the costs to the rest of society).

There may also be **positive externalities** which result from the business. It may create other jobs in the area for companies producing components or design a factory that complements the landscape. The firm may create skills which can be used for other jobs in the area. We can say that SOCIAL BENEFITS to society are the private benefits to business plus positive externalities (the benefits to the rest of society).

There are obvious problems that result from negative externalities. Furthermore, when firms set their prices these usually only reflect the private costs of production. Prices will not, therefore, reflect the cost of pollution, noise etc. As a result of this firms may not be concerned about negative externalities as they do not have to pay for them. For example, a chemical company may produce toxic waste from its production process. It might be faced with two choices - disposing of this waste in a nearby river without treating it, or treating it and removing any toxins. The first measure would cost next to nothing, but the second measure could be relatively expensive. The rational choice for the firm, assuming this is legal, is to dispose of the waste untreated in the river. However, for

> **QUESTION 1** In January 1993, the Braer oil tanker broke up after hitting rocks on the coastline of the Shetland Islands. Thousands of tonnes of oil leaked out of the tanker, whose engines failed as it was transporting oil from Norway to North America.
>
> Outline the possible:
> (a) private costs to the company that owned the tanker;
> (b) negative externalities to the rest of society;
> that may have resulted from the disaster.

other users of the river, such as anglers and water sports enthusiasts, this decision would have serious effects.

In order to assess the impact of business activity, cost - benefit analysis is sometimes used, particularly for large projects (☞ unit 17).

Negative externalities

There are many different types of negative externality that may result from business activity. Some are dealt with in other units, eg consumer exploitation (☞ unit 73) and employee exploitation (☞ unit 56). This section will focus on environmental costs.

Air pollution This is pollution from factories, machines or vehicles emitting poisonous gases into the atmosphere. We need only look into the sky above some factories to see evidence of this. Other forms of air pollution may be catastrophes such as at the Chernobyl nuclear plant in 1986, when massive quantities of radioactive materials were released into the atmosphere and surrounding countryside. The results have been seen in many countries in Europe. Even now the area around the Chernobyl nuclear plant is uninhabitable.

What effects do the emission of gases have?
- Acid rain. Thousands of acres of forests have been destroyed by acid rain, as a result of sulphur dioxide emissions into the atmosphere.
- Chlorofluorocarbons (CFCs). The use by some firms of CFCs in aerosols and refrigerators has contributed to the breakdown of the earth's ozone layer. The ozone layer acts as a filter for the sun's rays. Without it, exposure to sunlight can increase the risk of skin cancer.
- Carbon dioxide (CO_2) and other gases. There has been a growing awareness that the release of CO_2, and other gases such as methane and nitrous oxide, into the atmosphere is causing a 'greenhouse effect'. The build-up of these gases is associated with the rise in the use of cars and with the generation of electricity with fossil fuels such as coal.

  Scientists argue that the 'greenhouse effect' could result in the earth's atmosphere warming up (**global warming**) to such an extent that the polar ice caps melt. This could lead to significant areas of land being submerged by rising sea levels. The 'greenhouse effect', many scientists believe, has also been responsible for the climatic extremes experienced in parts of the world in the 1980s and 1990s.

The rise since 1970 in some greenhouse gases emitted into the atmosphere is shown in Figure 72.1.

Water pollution Water pollution can occur in a number of ways. Many industries, such as brewing and chemical production, use water in production. Their plants are usually located by rivers and it is fairly easy, therefore, for

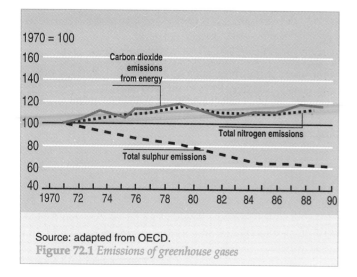

Source: adapted from OECD.

Figure 72.1 *Emissions of greenhouse gases*

them to dispose of waste into nearby water. It is also possible for our drinking water from reservoirs to be polluted by chemicals used in agricultural production. People are starting to drink bottled water or have water filters fitted to their water supply in the home as a result.

The sea has also been polluted over many years. Industries sited near to the coast have used the sea as a dump for their waste. The effluence and cargo of ships are also sometimes dropped into the sea. The North Sea, for example, is now one of the most polluted seas in the world as a result of years of discharges from a variety of industries. These have included sewage and the by-products of chemical production. A number of beaches in the UK are unsafe for bathing, according to the European Community, which grades the quality of beaches.

Congestion and noise Business activity has resulted in more roads becoming congested with traffic. For example, many firms now transport their goods by rail rather than road. Recent estimates have put the cost of this congestion on British roads as high as £15 billion. A recent study suggests that traffic in central London now moves more slowly than it did in the last century, before the days of motorised transport.

Some business activity can also result in noise pollution. For example, a decision by an airport to open a new runway would affect noise levels experienced by local residents.

Destruction of the environment One example of this is logging and associated industries, which have been responsible for the destruction of sections of the Amazonian rainforests. Another example might include the effects of new buildings in a rural area. A new housing estate in a village, for example, may deprive villagers and visitors of a previously unspoilt countryside. It may also increase noise and congestion levels in the village.

The impact on the environment of business is not always negative. In derelict urban areas, for example, businesses have converted rundown buildings into office space and have landscaped waste land around the site. Also, some of the buildings may be thought to have architectural merit.

QUESTION 2 A publication by the Department of Trade and Industry in 1992, *Energy-related carbon emissions in possible future scenarios for the United Kingdom*, argues that recession and the decline of coal fired power stations are combating global warming (as shown in Figure 72.2). According to the paper, the UK will emit around 10 per cent less carbon dioxide, one of the main greenhouse gases, than was feared two years earlier. On its most cautious projections, the UK is on course to bring carbon dioxide emissions back to 1990 levels by the year 2000, in line with international targets.

The paper suggests that the reason for the reduction in the projections for CO_2 can be explained by two main factors. Firstly, the decline in big energy using manufacturing industries and second, the slowdown in the UK economy. However, forecasts of emissions in 2005 still look disturbingly high.

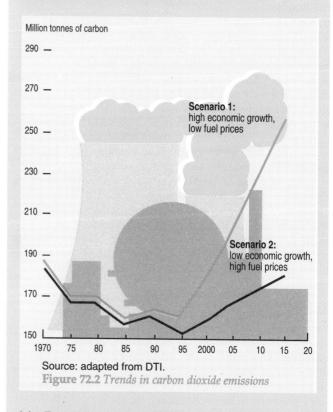

Source: adapted from DTI.

Figure 72.2 *Trends in carbon dioxide emissions*

(a) Explain why carbon dioxide emissions might be regarded as negative externalities.
(b) What externalities, other than carbon dioxide emissions, might be produced by the energy industry?
(c) Why should a slowdown in the economy reduce carbon dioxide emissions?

Controlling negative externalities

Because of concern about the impact of business on the environment, attention has been focused on how pollution, congestion etc. can be controlled. There are a number of ways this can be done.

Government regulation Laws can be passed which make it illegal for firms to pollute the environment. The **Clean Air Act** and the **Environmental Protection Act** seek to achieve this in the UK. They set limits on the maximum amount of pollution. For example, there are controls on the quantities of certain gases which firms are allowed to release into the atmosphere.

In the US a highly powerful body, the Environmental Protection Agency, attempts to ensure that US firms do not contravene legislation.

Taxation The aim of taxation in this context is to ensure that the social cost of any pollution caused by a firm is paid for. This means that the government must estimate the actual cost to society of different types of pollution. As a result prices would more accurately reflect the true cost of using environmental resources. So, for example, a firm which produced a £5 product with 'environmentally unfriendly' packaging might be taxed 50p for this packaging, raising the price to £5.50. There are two advantages to this. Firstly, the tax revenue might be used to minimise the impact of this packaging on the environment. Secondly, it might act as an incentive for the firm to produce more environmentally sensitive packaging, so that the tax is either reduced or removed.

In this example the consumer pays for the environmentally unfriendly packaging in the form of a price rise. Some would argue that the firm itself should pay for such costs. In this way, the price would remain at £5.00, but the firm would be taxed 50 pence for externalities created by its packaging. The consumer would not directly suffer as a result of the taxation.

In May 1992, the European Commission proposed a carbon tax on fuels. It was intended to reduce the demand for fuels and to go some way towards ensuring that some of the costs of fuel consumption were paid. The proposed tax would put about 1p a litre on the price of petrol at the pumps in the UK.

Compensation Firms could be forced by law to compensate those affected by externalities. For example, it is common for airports to provide grants to nearby residents. This allows them to purchase double glazing and other types of insulation, which provides protection from aircraft noise.

Government subsidisation This involves governments offering grants, tax allowances and other types of subsidy to firms in order to encourage them to reduce externalities. Such subsidies can allow environmentally desirable projects, which otherwise might not be profitable, to go ahead. For example, a firm may be given a grant so that it could build a recycling plant for plastics. This should encourage domestic and industrial users to recycle rather than dump plastic products.

Government subsidies could also be used to encourage more environmentally friendly habits amongst consumers. For example, Manchester City Council are attempting to encourage the use of bicycles through schemes such as setting up cycle lanes and giving grants to employees wishing to use bicycles for travelling to and from work.

Road pricing Charging road users could be used to reduce pollution and congestion. There is a long history of charging for motorways in European countries such as France, Spain and Italy and the first toll motorway will soon be built in Britain in the West Midlands. Similarly, vehicle users could be charged for entering cities at certain times of the day as is currently happening in a scheme in Cambridge.

Education Governments and other agencies, such as charities, could try to influence consumers and producers through educational and promotional campaigns.

Consumer pressure Consumers have forced a number of firms to consider the impact of their activities on the environment. There is evidence that a new breed of consumer is emerging, who considers factors other than price and quality when buying products. NEW CONSUMERISM involves consumers taking into account the effect on the environment and society of those products which they purchase. So, for example, such a consumer may not buy aerosols containing CFCs, furniture made from trees which have been chopped down in the Amazonian rainforest or cosmetics which have been tested on animals.

Although this new approach has influenced a wide range of firms, it does have one major problem. Consumers often do not have sufficient information with which to evaluate the impact of business activity upon the environment. Such information is often not disclosed to members of the public. Also, many firms have not been slow to realise that presenting themselves as being environmentally conscious can be very good for sales. However, the actual record of such firms with regard to the environment may well fall short of the claims which they make for themselves. For example, a battery company placed an environmentally friendly label on its products. However, this had to be removed when it was revealed that batteries use up more energy in their construction than they create in their use.

An environmental audit is one method by which consumers have a fairer chance of assessing the environmental impact of a firm. This could be much like the financial audits which all companies are at present required to have by law. In 1992, there were 339 companies in the UK which carried out an environmental audit, compared to 125 in 1989. This perhaps indicates the growing pressure put on firms to be concerned about their impact on the environment.

QUESTION 3 Time is running out for road users. With congestion becoming a worldwide problem, drivers may have to get used to the idea of paying for their journeys.

This is certainly true in Britain, where new solutions are being looked at more closely than ever. While recession may have taken some of the heat out of the traffic crisis, it will not be long before vehicle ownership and use resume their rapid rise. In barely a decade, according to UK government forecasts, traffic levels could be 50 per cent worse than they are already (as shown in Figure 72.3).

The question is: just how is this traffic growth to be accommodated? Many large towns and cities already experience intolerable levels of congestion, but few have room for more roads. Many trunk roads and motorways are also packed, but even where environmental considerations allow for widening or new construction, the government cannot afford the huge sums required.

Source: adapted from the *Financial Times*, 3.12.1992.

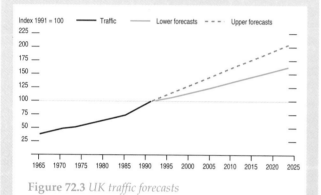

Figure 72.3 *UK traffic forecasts*

(a) How might road pricing help to deal with the problem of congestion on British roads?
(b) Explain three other ways in which attempts could be made to deal with this problem.

Business and environmental policies

With public concern increasing about the dangers of damaging the environment, pressure is building on many firms to become more environmentally friendly. Adopting such environmental policies can affect businesses in a number of ways.

■ They may need to change production techniques or the materials which they use. Such changes may range from the simple, such as the use of recycled paper in offices, to the complex, such as the installation of new recycling plants.

■ Firms may find that their costs increase. For example, a firm previously dumping waste products into the sea would find it more expensive to process this waste. Similarly, a firm which encouraged its employees to use bicycles rather than cars on company business might find that this takes employees longer and is, therefore, more expensive. Such increases in costs may well be passed on to customers in the form of higher prices.

■ Some activities which improve a firm's environmental practices may lead to lower rather than higher costs. For example, a firm which sought to improve its energy efficiency might insulate the workplace, turn down heating appliances and turn off unused lights. Such actions are likely to reduce fuel bills and thus reduce costs. Encouraging employees to re-use items, such as paper clips, envelopes and elastic bands, is likely to have a similar effect.

■ There may need to be a change in its ethical stance (☞ unit 71). This may have a knock-on effect on other aspects of a firm's activities and lead to a re-examination of a number of its business practices.

■ There is growing evidence that consumers are attracted to firms with environmentally friendly policies. Adopting such policies may lead to an increase in sales and possibly in profit levels.

■ Research and development expenditure may need to increase as a firm seeks to find new, more environmentally friendly, products and production processes. Such an increase in expenditure may go on testing and creating new packaging materials or materials to be used in production.

QUESTION 4 Hattersley, Newman and Hender, an Ormskirk based firm that produce industrial valves, have installed two new electric furnaces designed to get rid of the problem of smoke emission. Prior to their instalment, nearby houses and a local school were regularly smoked out. Mr John McBryer, the firm's industrial director, commented: 'We had either to make the change or close down because of our new obligations under the Environmental Protection Act.'

Mr James Rigby, headteacher at Ormskirk CE Primary School, said, 'We have heard that the smoke should be gone by the middle of the year and that is brilliant.'

Source: adapted from the *Ormskirk Advertiser*, 18. 2.1993.

In what ways might Hattersley, Newman and Hender be affected by the installation of the new furnaces? Explain your answer.

Conservation

All businesses depend, to a greater or lesser degree, on the use of non-renewable resources (☞ unit 1). These are resources which cannot be replaced and which might in some cases, with current usage, run out within the next 100 years. Such resources range from raw materials, like oil, iron, copper and aluminium, to living creatures like whales, elephants and dolphins.

Conservation ranges from banning the use of such resources altogether, to encouraging businesses to use them sparingly. There are a number of measures which seek to conserve non-renewable resources.

■ Recycling schemes. Bottle banks set up to help the recycling of glass are now a common sight in supermarket car parks. Not only do glass recycling schemes help to conserve natural resources, but they can be profitable for those companies involved. Recycling schemes also exist in the paper, plastics and aluminium industries.

■ Multilateral agreements. These are agreements between a number of countries which seek to limit the use of natural resources. Agreements now exist which place limits on the amount of fishing and whaling which countries are allowed to carry out. In addition, some countries now have import bans on commodities such as ivory which come from endangered species. The Earth Summit at Rio in 1992 was an attempt to get governments to agree on a range of conservation measures, from the preservation of forests to ending the destruction of rare plants and animals.

■ Government subsidies. These have been used to encourage farmers to conserve the countryside through retaining features such as dry stone walls and hedgerows, for example.

QUESTION 5 The obstacles created when waste management is left entirely to the free market can prove insurmountable and can be illustrated by the difficulties faced by the polystyrene food packaging recycling plant officially opened in July by Linpac, the UK plastics group.

Mr David Eggleston, Linpac's environmental manager, says such plants are vital if the UK is to increase its rate of recycling, but their existence is crucially dependent on the government introducing incentives. The plant, which has the capacity to recycle 2,000 to 2,500 tonnes of waste a year, is testing the technical and commercial viability of recycling plastic containers, but in the existing market conditions it is uneconomic.

The government 'must encourage the consumption of recycled materials of all kinds at prices which make recycling economically viable,' he says. The UK government has hesitated in introducing sweeping environmental initiatives, waiting for the European Commission to finalise the details of its directive on the avoidance of packaging waste.

This summer, the EC published its far-reaching proposals aimed at harmonising environmental laws across the Continent. However, it is likely that it will take another two years before its modified principles become enshrined in national laws.

Its hierarchy of preferred solutions is minimisation of the packaging used in particular products, followed by recovery and recycling, with final disposal in landfill sites remaining as a last resort.
Source: adapted from the *Financial Times*, 10.11.1992.

(a) What advantages might there be for:
(i) Linpac;
(ii) its consumers;
in recycling products?
(b) Why might Linpac argue that it is crucial that the government introduces incentives?
(c) What implications might EC proposals have for Linpac?

Key terms

Externalities - occur when private costs are different to social costs and private benefits are different to social benefits.
New consumerism - a trend for increasing numbers of consumers to take into account the costs to society of producing products when making purchasing decisions.
Private benefits - the benefit of an activity to an individual or a business.
Private costs - the cost of an activity to an individual or a business.
Social benefits - the benefit of an activity to society as well as to a business.
Social costs - the cost of an activity to society as well as to a business.

Summary

1. Give an example of:
(a) a private cost;
(b) a positive externality;
(c) a private benefit.
2. State 5 examples of negative externalities that may be created by a business.
3. Briefly explain the effect that:
(a) a tax on a business;
(b) a subsidy from government to a business;
might have on the creation of negative externalities.
4. Why might a business be concerned about the views consumers have about how it affects the environment?
5. Briefly explain 3 consequences of following an environmentally friendly policy for a business.
6. 'Conservation can be profitable for a business.' Explain this statement with an example.

Question

Getting the green light - three companies which have become more environmentally aware

Increasingly, companies are paying more attention to their environmental performance. While many do it to ensure they are meeting UK and EC legal requirements, others are interested in calculating their environmental impact and using the information to maintain good relations with their local community, customers, suppliers and investors.

Berger Aus Berg, manufacturers of metal drum closures in Peterlee, County Durham, are one such firm. They commissioned an independent environmental review to see what environmental improvements could be made. Several of the recommendations made in the review have already been implemented. For example, it advised the company to reduce its energy consumption by altering the factory's lighting. The factory had previously had to have all its lights on when only half were needed. Future electricity bills for lighting are expected to be 50 per cent less. The review also advised the company to take pallets and bags it receives from suppliers and re-use them when sending products to its consumers. This it has done with impressive results. In the past, most transport packaging costs were passed on to customers. By re-using packaging the costs have been significantly reduced. Customers have been informed about this reduction in charges.

Conservation Papers, a Reading based firm which recycles paper to the business community, joined an Environmental Business Challenge launched by Reading Borough Council. This scheme was designed to help companies develop and implement an environmental policy. A number of changes were made as a result including simple steps such as turning down thermostats and switching off heating at weekends.

Dragon International, a London based marketing consultancy, assessed the environmental impact of all they did from the first day the business was set up. They purchased second hand 'recycled' furniture, bought a photocopier for double-sided copies and decided against supplying company cars. Staff are encouraged to use bicycles or public transport.

The company buys recycled non-chlorine bleached paper, re-uses scrap paper, fits long life light bulbs, uses environmentally sensitive cleaning equipment and supplies china rather than disposable cups.

Being environmentally sensitive brings costs with it. Berger Aus Berg has spent £600 on an electrician's bill. Conservation Papers spent £70 on automatic door closures and Dragon International's main expenditure will be on better insulation and a more efficient boiler for its offices costing several hundred pounds.

All companies spent several hours discussing environmental practices with staff and have found that they are quick to change their attitudes, often suggesting further improvements.

Source: adapted from the *Financial Times*, 30. 3. 1993.

Easy steps to improving a company's environmental practices

🔍 Review energy efficiency. Reduce consumption by turning down the thermostats and turn off un-needed lights and equipment.

🔍 Encourage employees to re-use as much equipment as possible - paper clips, scrap paper, elastic bands, bull-dog clips etc.

🔍 See whether there are ways to reduce waste or generate a further income by selling your waste as scrap.

🔍 Reduce vehicle use. Encourage staff to use public transport or walk. If employees live locally, set up a company bike scheme.

🔍 Review purchasing policy. For example, save money or improve your public image by purchasing recycled paper. Only buy ozone-friendly products and cleaning materials which are free of phosphates and are readily biodegradable.

🔍 Reduce paper usage. Encourage staff to write on both sides of any paper and use double-sided photocopies when sending long memos.

🔍 Recycle paper, glass, plastics and cans.

Figure 72.4

(a) Using evidence from the article, what negative externalities might each of these firms have created before they made changes to their environmental practice?

(b) How might the pricing of these companies be affected by the changes in environmental practice?

(c) For what reasons might these companies have implemented their environmental changes?

(d) What examples of conservation are mentioned in the article?

(e) How have these companies been affected by becoming more environmentally sensitive?

The growth of protection

At the beginning of the century consumers and producers were seen as having equal responsibility. Indeed, consumers were expected to ensure that their purchases were satisfactory. This approach can be summarised by the expression *caveat emptor* - 'let the buyer beware'.

Today, the relationship between consumers and businesses is viewed differently. Many see consumers as being at the mercy of powerful and well organised producers. This has led to a rise in interest about consumer affairs and increasing pressure on governments to pass legislation to protect consumers. Consumer magazines, such as *Which?*, and consumer television and radio programmes, such as 'Watchdog' and 'Talkback', have lent pressure to this movement seeking to protect the rights of consumers. There are a number of reasons why consumers may need protecting more than they did in the past.

- The increasing complexity of many goods and services. Technological advance, in particular, have increased the gap between the knowledge of consumers and producers about products. Few consumers have the ability to properly assess the quality of the technology which goes into everyday items such as televisions, washing machines or refrigerators. Such ignorance can leave consumers at the mercy of unscrupulous producers.
- The environment within which firms operate is becoming increasingly competitive. Some believe that this degree of competition encourages firms to take advantage of consumers. This may be in the form of reductions in the level of service or the quality of goods offered, for example.
- The disposable income of many consumers has increased greatly over the last four to five decades. This means that the average consumer purchases far greater quantities of goods and services than would have been the case in the past. It is argued that more protection needs to be offered to consumers as a result.
- The increase in the number of goods and services from abroad. Now that consumers are purchasing increasing numbers of goods and services imported from abroad, they may need protection against the different standards which may operate in other countries. Safety standards on children's toys, for example, are often far lower in goods produced in the Far East.
- Scientific advances have created a variety of materials that were not previously available. For example, there are an increasing number of food additives and techniques for preserving foods which have only recently been discovered. Consumers may need to be protected against any possible harmful effects of such scientific discoveries.

Consumer protection legislation

Unit 71 showed that some businesses are aware of ethical considerations when making decisions. However, it could be argued that, in a number of areas, businesses cannot be relied upon to regulate themselves. These include their dealings with employees (☞ unit 56) and other firms, as well as consumers. Governments in the past have found it necessary to regulate businesses, by passing laws which protect consumers from their activities.

Weights and Measures Act, 1951 This act makes it possible for inspectors to test the weighing and measuring equipment used by businesses. Use of false or unfair weighing equipment is an offence. It is also an offence to give short weights or short measures. The Act states that all prepacked goods must have information about the net quantity of their contents.

Trade Descriptions Act, 1968 This prohibits false or misleading descriptions of goods or services. For example, a pair of shoes which are described as made of leather cannot be made of plastic.

Unsolicited Goods Act, 1971 This law seeks to prevent the practice of sending goods to consumers which they had not ordered, and then demanding payment. It states that unsolicited goods need not be paid for and that consumers can keep such goods after six months if the seller does not collect them.

Consumer Credit Act, 1974 This aims to protect the rights of consumers when they purchase goods on credit, such as hire purchase or credit sale agreements. For example, it states that consumers must be given a copy of any credit agreements into which they enter. It also ensures that only licensed credit brokers can provide credit. There are many other offences listed which constitute a breaking of the law. These include credit firms sending representatives to people's homes to persuade them to take credit and credit agreements which have high interest rates.

Consumer Safety Act, 1978 This law was passed in order to prevent the sale of goods which might be harmful to consumers. It concentrates, in particular, upon safety matters relating to children's toys and electrical goods.

Sale of Goods Act, 1979 This law states that goods sold to consumers should meet three main conditions. Firstly, that they are of merchantable quality which means that goods should not have any serious flaws or problems with them. Secondly, that they are fit for the purpose for which they were purchased. For example, paint which is sold to be used outdoors should not begin to peel or flake with the first outbreak of poor weather conditions. Thirdly, that they are as described. Thus, an anorak described as waterproof should not leak in the rain.

Supply of Goods and Services Act, 1982 This seeks to protect users of services, ensuring services are of 'merchantable quality' and at 'reasonable rates'. For example, a holiday firm which booked clients into a four star hotel which turned out to be of lower quality would be in breach of the conditions.

Food Act, 1984 This Act, along with the 1955 Food and Drugs Act, enforces the hygienic preparation and sale of food. It also sets guidelines for the labelling of food products.

Consumer Protection Act, 1987 This law was introduced to bring Britain in line with other European Community nations. It ensures that firms are liable for any damage which their defective goods might cause to consumers. For example, a firm supplying defective electrical equipment would be liable for any injuries caused to consumers using that equipment. It also seeks to outlaw misleading pricing, such as exaggerated claims relating to price reductions on sale items. An example might be a statement that a good is '£2 less than the manufacturer's recommended price' when it isn't.

QUESTION 1 Which of the consumer protection Acts might the following contravene?
- Winston Stanley buys a cotton tee shirt from a shop in Bath. When he takes it home, he discovers that it is made of polyester and cotton and has a small hole in its collar.
- Lena Hardman buys a 400 gramme box of chocolates, but later discovers there are only 250 grammes of chocolates in the box.
- A car dealer advertises that all of his cars have been approved by the AA. Irfan Patel, who has just bought a car from this dealer, rings up the AA and discovers that the car dealer has had no dealings with them.
- Bill Dean urgently requires £1,000 to pay a long overdue loan back to a friend. He goes to a credit agency and arranges a loan of £1,000 to be paid back over 12 months. His repayments on this loan will be £250 a month.

Effects of protection on business

The increase in the number of consumer laws and the concern about protecting consumers has a number of possible implications for firms.
- Increases in costs. Improving the safety of a good or ensuring that measuring equipment is more accurate can increase the costs of a firm. For example, an electrical firm producing table lamps may find that its product contravened the Consumer Safety Act of 1978. The firm would have to change or improve the components used to make the lamps or re-design the lamp itself. Such changes would be likely to raise the firm's costs.
- Quality control. Many firms have needed to improve their quality control procedures as a result of legislation. For example, firms involved in bagging or packaging goods must ensure that the correct

quantities are weighed out. Failure to do so could result in prosecution. In addition, businesses must be careful not to sell substandard or damaged products.
- Dealing with customer complaints. Many businesses now have a customer service or customer complaints department to deal with customers. These allow firms to deal with problems quickly and efficiently and to 'nip problems in the bud' - dealing with any problems before the customer turns to the legal system.
- Changes in business practice. Attempts to ensure that customers are treated fairly by a firm may place pressure on it to become more market orientated (☞ unit 18). The firm would attempt to ensure that it is actually meeting the needs of those people it is attempting to serve. Such a change, for example, may lead to greater use of market research.

QUESTION 2 Describe the possible effects of consumer protection legislation on the following firms.
- A firm which specialises in bagging and packaging flour for a leading food business.
- An advertising agency which specialises in campaigns for small and medium sized firms.
- A manufacturer of household plugs.
- A retailer which specialises in the sale of 'own brand' goods.

Monopolies and mergers

It is argued, by some, that competition between businesses benefits consumers. Legislation and government action have, in the past, attempted to achieve this by control of monopolies and mergers.

A LEGAL MONOPOLY in the UK is defined as any business which has over 25 per cent market share. Examples might include British Gas and British Telecom. A merger is the joining together of two or more firms (☞ unit 32). In recent years there has been a growth in mergers and takeovers. Well known examples include mergers between Nestlé and Rowntree, and Renault and Volvo.

In some cases just one firm or a small group of firms control the market for a particular good or service. Such market strength puts these firms in a position where they have the potential to exploit their consumers. They can also prevent other firms from competing against them. Some criticisms of monopolies and mergers include the following.
- They raise prices in order to make excess profits.
- They fix prices. When a small group of firms control the market for a product, it is believed that they may act in unison to fix prices at an artificially high level.
- They force competition out. It has been suggested that monopolists sometimes pursue pricing or promotional strategies designed to force competitors out of the market. In the early 1980s, it was alleged that some of the big airlines forced Laker Airways out of the transatlantic airline market through price cutting techniques.
- They prevent new firms from entering markets. It has

been alleged, for example, that British Airways attempted to prevent Virgin Airlines from entering the airline industry.

- They carry out a range of restrictive practices. Examples include putting pressure on retailers not to stock the goods of rival firms and attempting to prevent suppliers from doing business with new entrants to the market.

There are, however, a number of arguments which support the continued existence of monopolies.

- Because monopolies often operate on a large scale, they are able to benefit from economies of scale (☞ unit 31). The cost advantages from this can allow monopolies to set prices lower than would be the case if there were a number of firms competing, and still make profits.
- Monopolies can use their large profits to undertake research and development projects. Many of these projects, which result in technological and scientific breakthroughs, could not be afforded by smaller firms.
- Monopolies are much better placed to survive in international markets. It is argued that this is only possible if a firm operates on a large scale.

Legislation

In the UK there is legislation to protect consumers and other businesses from the problems created by monopolies and mergers.

Monopolies and Trade Practices Act, 1948/ Monopolies and Mergers Act, 1965 The 1948 Act established a Monopolies Commission with powers to investigate any unfair dealings. If the commission believed that a particular monopoly was against the 'public interest', then it would pass the matter on to the government for further action.

The Monopolies Commission was criticised for not undertaking sufficient investigations, but its work did reveal that some monopolies were abusing their position. The 1965 Act extended the powers of the Monopolies Commission to investigate proposed mergers. Mergers involving the takeover of assets in excess of £5 million pounds, or which would result in control of one-third of the market, could be referred to the newly created Monopolies and Mergers Commission (MMC).

1973 Fair Trading Act This act defined exactly what constitutes a monopoly or a merger.

- Monopolies are said to exist if they have a 25 per cent or greater share of a market.
- Mergers are said to exist if the combined total assets of firms that join together are greater than £5 million.

It also established the role of the **Office of Fair Trading**. This has the responsibility for referring cases to the MMC. Under the supervision of the Director General of Fair Trading, the Office of Fair Trading is responsible for overseeing all policy relating to competition and consumer protection.

The Monopolies and Mergers Commission

The role of the MMC is to reach a judgement as to whether or not a particular monopoly or proposed merger is in the public interest. On its own the MMC has no power to act, but it can recommend the break-up of a firm or propose that a particular merger should not take place to the Secretary of State for Trade and Industry. The Secretary of State for Trade and Industry then has the power to act on the recommendations of the MMC.

Since the **1980 Competition Act**, the powers of the MMC have been extended to include two new areas - the investigation of public sector businesses and authorities and the investigation of anti-competitive practices. The MMC's approach has always been on a case by case basis, refusing to condemn outright certain types of business behaviour. This has meant that each investigation tends to be fairly lengthy. With a staff of only about 100 people, the number of investigations which it can make is limited. In most years it completes less than 20 investigations and under 5 per cent of mergers are referred to the MMC.

QUESTION 3 Government attempts to reduce takeover activity and increase competition in the bus industry received support when the Monopolies and Mergers Commission won its final appeal in the Sheffield bus mergers case.

The House of Lords ruled that the Commission had the power to investigate local bus company mergers under the terms of the 1973 Fair Trading Act and restored a 1990 MMC recommendation that South Yorkshire Transport (SYT) should sell four rival bus companies it acquired in 1989. The decision was a blow to private sector bus companies hoping to build up their strength through mergers.

Mr Richard Boardman, the lawyer who handled the case for SYT, said the decision 'opened the floodgates for thousands of other investigations' into small, local mergers. The MMC report, which was accepted by Mr Peter Lilley, then Trade and Industry Secretary, recommended that SYT should sell Sheffield and District Transport, Sheafline (PSV), Michael Groves and SUT on the grounds that each merger might be expected to operate against the public interest.

As a result of the acquisitions, SYT's share of bus miles in Sheffield increased to the point at which the commission said competition to SYT in Sheffield had, in effect, ceased.

It said each acquisition could result in higher fares as well as lower standards, declining quality and frequency of service and less choice.

Source: adapted from the *Financial Times*, 1993.

(a) Why should the government wish to increase competition in the bus industry?
(b) Why did the MMC recommend that South Yorkshire Transport sell off the four companies it had taken over?
(c) What problems might result for South Yorkshire Transport from being required to sell off the four companies it had taken over?

Examples of MMC activities have included the following.

■ The tool producer Black & Decker withdrew distribution from B&Q stores in response to B&Q's discount campaign. The MMC forced Black & Decker to supply goods again.

■ In an investigation into the brewing industry, the MMC reported the practice by big brewers of producing, distributing and selling their own beer in 'tied' public houses restricted competition. It recommended that no brewer should own more than 5,000 public houses, and that guest beers should be provided in those pubs owned by breweries. As a consequence of this, around 11,000 pubs have been sold off by the big brewing companies.

■ An investigation into new housing warranty schemes by the MMC looked at the rule of the National House Building Council, which required builders to present every new house for inspection to obtain a warranty from the NHBC. The Commission found that this deterred builders from using other schemes, such as those provided by insurance companies.

The European Community now has powers to investigate monopolies and mergers. A merger which would result in a combined worldwide turnover of £5 billion ECUs (approximately £6.25 billion) can be referred to the EC Commission. This means that only so called 'mega' mergers will be referred to the EC. The rest will continue to be dealt with on a national level.

Competition policy

Competition policy is concerned with influencing the degree of competition in individual markets in the economy. Its aim is usually to control anti-competitive practices on the grounds that consumers tend to suffer from such actions. In the UK, the Office of Fair Trading under the leadership of the Director General is responsible for implementing competition policy. The role of the MMC in encouraging competition was discussed earlier. The control of RESTRICTIVE TRADE PRACTICES is another feature of competition policy. Examples of restrictive practices include the following.

■ A firm which is a dominant supplier in a particular market may set a minimum price for the re-sale of its products. Such firms may also seek to ensure that retailers stock their products alone. In return, retailers are often given exclusive rights to sell this product within a particular area.

■ Firms forming agreements to fix prices and/or limit the supply of a product. Such agreements between firms are often referred to as COLLUSION.

■ A dominant supplier requiring retailers to stock the full range of their product lines.

The **1956 Restrictive Trade Practices Act** regulated such practices. It established a Restrictive Practices Court. All firms engaged in restrictive practices have to register them with this Court, which then decides whether or not they are acceptable. Firms have to prove that their practices are in the public interest. Judgements made by the Court are backed by law. The 1956 Act laid down 8 gateways through which a restriction could be approved.

If a business could prove a restrictive practice would prevent the public from injury, for example, it may be allowed to continue. The **1976 Restrictive Practices Act** extended the powers of the Court to cover services as well as goods.

The Commission for the EC is also able to intervene on matters which affect competition between member states. It has no power, however, within individual countries. The main aim is to prevent agreements which prevent free trade between member countries.

Control of former state monopolies

During the 1980s, state owned monopolies were sold off as part of the government's privatisation (☞ unit 4) programme. The aim was to increase efficiency in these firms by removing them from the public sector. However, the creation of private monopolies led to concern that these newly privatised firms would take advantage of their market position and exploit consumers. Agencies were set up to regulate them as a result.

■ The Office of Telecommunications (OFTEL) - set up in 1984 when British Telecom was privatised.

■ The Office of Gas Supplies (OFGAS) - set up in 1986 when British Gas was privatised.

■ The Office of Water Services (OFWAT) - set up in 1989 when the water boards were transferred to the private sector.

■ The Office of Electricity Regulation (OFFER) - set up in 1990-1991 during the privatisation of the electricity industry.

Each of the regulators have different powers, but all of them are required to carry out two main functions.

■ To operate a system of price controls. All regulatory authorities operate according to a Retail Price Index (☞ unit 15) plus or minus formula. Where a firm's costs are falling due, for example, to improvements in technology, it will probably be set an RPI minus figure. As an example, British Telecom was given a figure of RPI minus 7.5 per cent for 1993. BT was also not allowed to increase the price of any single service apart from line rental by more than the RPI.

■ To help bring about the introduction of competition wherever this might be possible. In some respects, this is more difficult than implementing price controls. This is because telephone lines, gas pipelines, water pipes and the National Grid are examples of **natural monopolies**. If every house, factory and office were connected with a number of different water pipes or telephone lines from which to choose, the costs within these industries would significantly rise. It therefore makes sense for the regulated firm to operate such services.

However, there is no reason why other firms should not be allowed to transmit their power, gas, telephone calls or water down the existing National Grid, gas pipeline network, telephone lines and water pipes. Indeed, this is the way in which competition has been introduced into these industries. Mercury, for example, a right to use British Telecom lines.

QUESTION 4 In March 1992, the Office of Fair Trading signed an agreement with British Gas seeking to reduce its control on the gas industry. The agreement forced British Gas to create a new company which would own all British Gas pipelines. This meant that British Gas, along with any other company that wished to enter this market, would have to pay the new company to transmit gas down its pipelines. Charges for use of the pipelines were be set so that all suppliers of gas paid the same.

The agreement also forced British Gas to limit its share of the industrial gas market to 40 per cent from 1995. British Gas at the time had a 100 per cent share of this market.

Source: adapted from the *Financial Times*, 1992.

(a) How might this agreement have helped to increase competition in the gas industry?
(b) How else would it be possible to regulate British Gas?
(c) How might gas consumers be affected by the agreement described above?

Key terms

Collusion - agreements between businesses designed to restrict competition.
Legal monopoly - in the UK, any business with over 25 per cent of the market.
Restrictive trade practices - any attempt by businesses to prevent competition

Summary

1. What is meant by the term *caveat emptor*?
2. For what reasons might consumers need more protection today?
3. List 5 main consumer protection acts.
4. In what ways might firms be affected by consumer protection legislation?
5. What are the possible advantages and disadvantages of monopolies?
6. How is a monopoly defined by UK law?
7. What are the roles and responsibilities of the Monopolies and Mergers Commission?
8. What is the Restrictive Trade Practices Court?
9. What are the 4 main bodies set up to regulate the former state monopolies?
10. Explain 2 main functions of bodies set up to regulate former state monopolies.

Question

Europe's new cold warriors

The European cold war between Unilever, the Anglo-Dutch consumer products group, and Mars, the US food manufacturer, is hotting up. This month, a new front was opened when Britain's Monopolies and Mergers Commission launched an investigation into ice cream makers' distribution practices.

The inquiry, which will focus on the £350 million UK market for 'impulse' ice creams typically sold by small corner shops, marks an important advance for Mars' three-year assault on Unilever's grip over ice cream sales across Europe.

The ferocity of the conflict, and the boisterous public relations campaigns mounted by the two sides, show that this is no ordinary trade dispute. At its heart lies a struggle for a rapidly-expanding business worth billions of pounds a year, which is central to both companies' future.

Unilever is defending a commanding 40 per cent of European ice cream sales, valued at about £6 billion annually at retail prices. Ice cream is among the most profitable and fast-growing of all the group's £11 billion worldwide food operations - owing to a stream of product innovations which have recently injected new life into a previously unexciting business.

The catalyst was Mars' launch in 1989 of premium-priced ice cream versions of its chocolate bars. Almost overnight, it created a thriving luxury sector of the market into which many other manufacturers, including Unilever, have moved and which is now the industry's biggest source of profits growth.

The problem for Mars is to avoid becoming a victim of its own success, as rivals increasingly challenge its early lead. The company needs to secure its position quickly to achieve satisfactory returns from its heavy investments in ice cream - but also because it is under increasing competitive pressure in its other businesses worldwide.

Mars' answer has been to attack Unilever's control over distribution and, in particular, its long-standing use of a practice known as 'cabinet exclusivity'. This involves supplying freezer cabinets free of charge to small retailers who sell the bulk of impulse ice creams, on condition that the freezers do not carry competitors' products.

Mars contends that cabinet exclusivity unfairly inhibits entry into the ice cream market and penalises smaller producers, particularly in the many small retail outlets which have room for only one freezer.

Unilever counters that it is entitled to exclusive use of its own cabinets, and that its strength in ice cream stems largely from its products and marketing expertise. It also points out that six companies have entered the UK ice cream market in the past five years.

These arguments have failed to convince Sir Bryan Carlsberg, the Director General of Fair Trading. When referring the case to the MMC, he suggested that cabinet exclusivity was 'a major factor' in the growth of Unilever's share of ice cream sales and that consumers would benefit if retailers were free to stock a wider choice of products.

Source: adapted from the *Financial Times*, 19.5.1993.

(a) Why might 'cabinet exclusivity' be an example of an uncompetitive practice?
(b) For what reasons have the MMC launched an investigation into ice cream makers' distribution practices?
(c) Why might the European Commission become involved in this case?
(d) How might:
(i) consumers;
(ii) small retailers;
(iii) Unilever and Mars;
be affected if 'cabinet exclusivity' deals were outlawed?

Table 73.1 *Unilever's European ice cream sales, 1992*

	Market volume (litres m)	Market value* (£m)	Unilever market share	Share of Unilever's European sales
Germany	520	1,000	40%	25%
Italy	400	700	40%	19%
UK	420	500	40%	13%
Scandinavia	300	400	35%	11%
Spain	180	300	30%	7%
France	320	400	20%	5%
Benelux	160	300	30%	7%
Other	200	300	50%	11%
Total	2,500	3,900	40%	100%

* at manufacturers' selling price
Source: adapted from Henderson Crosthwaite.

J Chadwick Ltd

J Chadwick Ltd manufacture a range of furniture aimed at the 'top end' of the market. Their products include period style Regency and Victorian furniture, including desks, wardrobes, dining tables and drawers. The prices of their products range from £350 to £1,270.

Jean Chadwick, the managing director, was preparing to write her annual report for the company's shareholders. Although all of the shareholders were members of the close knit Chadwick family, it was an exercise which she took very seriously. The reason was that this report allowed her a rare opportunity to survey and reflect upon the performance of the company.

Overall, J Chadwick Ltd had performed well in recent years. There had been a 50 per cent increase in profits in the previous year, a remarkable feat for a company operating in a period of recession, which had seen the closure of a range of firms in the furniture industry. Perhaps most significantly, one of J Chadwick's main competitors were facing liquidation, with the Official Receiver winding up its affairs. Jean was increasingly coming to the conclusion that the success of the company was largely due to the closure of rival firms. Events had conspired to create some of the worst trading conditions she could remember. She had listed three main factors responsible for this.

- A depression in the housing market with extremely low numbers of houses being bought and sold.
- Over 2 million unemployed, with particularly large increases in the unemployment rate in the South East - the principal market for J Chadwick's products.
- A government committed to a restriction in the growth of the money supply, targeted at reducing inflation. One feature of this policy had been high interest rates, despite the recessionary climate.

However, there did seem to have been an improvement in trading conditions in the past few months. Confidence amongst business leaders in the UK was growing and two of its main trading partners, the USA and Germany, had experienced increases in economic growth rates. Jean was considering a recommendation to the shareholders that the company explore the possibility of finding new markets. This could mean exporting furniture to countries in the EC in future.

A feature of the company's performance over the past year which was bound to interest shareholders was the change in Chadwick's buying policy. Previously wood used in the manufacture of their furniture had been purchased from Brazil. It was mahogany which had been chopped down from the Amazonion rainforest. Although this type of wood had been used for centuries in the manufacture of furniture, Jean's daughter Susan had persuaded her to seek alternatives. Susan was an active member of the environmental pressure group Friends of the Earth which was campaigning to save the Amazonion rainforest. The alternative which Jean's buying manager had found was yarra, a hard wood very similar to Mahogany, which was imported from Australia. Unfortunately, however, yarra was more expensive than mahogany at 20 Australian dollars per cubic metre, and the decline in the

exchange rate from £1 = $Australian 2.2 had worsened this situation.

(a) Discuss how unemployment and high in have affected businesses in a recession

(b) Discuss possible reasons why J Chadw been able to increase profits during a r

(c) How might an improvement in trading affect J Chadwick in future?

(d) In pounds sterling, how much would 1, yarra cost J Chadwick:
(i) before the exchange rate change;
(ii) after the exchange rate change?

(e) What might be the costs and benefits changing their wood suppliers from F

Agony and excess

od 1988-1993 saw the collapse of some well known
ies (Coloroll) and the slimming down of others (Next,
nd Saatchi). For most senior business leaders the
as seen the worst recession they have ever
nced.

sis of the performance of a large number of leading
ies shows how few have been unaffected and builds up
e of the state of British business as it emerges from
n. Barely a handful of companies has escaped
d from the fall in demand and high interest rates at
lus an overvalued currency affecting dealings abroad.
150 businesses included in *The Guardian Guide to
Top Companies* only 16 managed to increase earnings
of the last five years; 14 companies ended the period
er sales than at the beginning (despite inflation which
ated to about 33 per cent over the period); in spite of
and British directors' reluctance to cut dividends, 30 of
npanies paid a lower dividend in 1992 then they did in
s suggests that while all companies faced recession,
onded more sensibly than others, and many
ded the economic difficulties with financial problems
wn making.

hat have done more than survive have done so partly
ey operate in the most promising sectors such as
ets and drugs. But that alone has not been enough, as
r Fisons, Gateway and Asda in those two sectors
ed. Even in those sectors where it has been easiest to
od management has also been necessary to achieve
performance.

rd clearly shows that performance is by no means
on the business sector a company is in. In the drinks
r example, Allied-Lyons managed to end the period
shareholders' funds than at the start, only Scottish &
and Whitbread were able to increase sales in each
ly Whitbread ended the period employing more

rience of the engineering industry illustrates also
tor has not been as disadvantaged as is sometimes
ployment grew at Siebe, TI and Trafalgar House, for
ile Rolls-Royce, Smiths Industries and TI all
aintain investment above depreciation levels.
easures of success is not easy, especially when
e been known to make their figures 'look good'.
ten a useful measure in the absence of clear
ut it can also be misleading. The list of
large negative cash flows during this period
Aerospace, Burton, Forte, Lonrho and Ratner.
businesses such as Sainsbury, Tesco, Cable &
ed Biscuits. Their cash outflows were
xpansion, rather than recession.
re is sufficient to capture business
collection of indicators does separate the
osers.
earnings, employment, investment and net
stand out. These few winners all managed
earnings per share in each of the last five
estment above depreciation levels,
fs, and ended the period employing more
t. They include three supermarket
nsbury and Tesco), Cadbury Schweppes,

the services group Rentokil, and Glaxo. Rentokil stands out
even amongst this group as the only one also to have increased
return on capital during the period. (It was one of only 27
companies which achieved that.)

All of the leading half-dozen are renowned for the strength of
their managements. Sadly the same cannot be said for many
other leading British companies in recent years.

The typical picture is of companies highly optimistic after the
boom of the mid-1980s, so that they ignored the possibility of
contraction.They attempted to become bigger rather than
better, which led to heavy borrowing. The combination of over-
optimism, over-ambition and over-borrowing was fatal for some
but also damaged a large number of Britain's biggest businesses.

The greatest losers, shown in Table 1, cross the business
spectrum from service to heavy manufacturing.

The ability of these businesses to pay their interest bills
(measured by interest cover) weakened considerably between
1988 and 1992. In aggregate, the interest cover for all these
companies fell from 11 in 1989 to 6.7 in 1993. As many as 14
companies saw interest cover fall below three, not just once
but at least twice during the five year period.

Some of the most over-borrowed companies included the
builders Barratt and Costain, Burton Group, the conglomerates
Lonrho and P&O, and probably the best examples of companies
that threw caution to the winds, the advertising group Saatchi
and Saatchi and WPP.

The effect of the recession and poor financial management
can be seen in investment. It is difficult to determine how
much a company should spend to maintain its capital base, but
the annual depreciation charge is a reasonable minimum. It is
based on historical asset costs, and therefore tends to
understate the extent to which asset values are depreciating.
Nevertheless only 44 companies exceeded this target in every
year. As many as 36 companies failed to invest as much as their
depreciation charges in at least two years.

Not all these companies were in hock to their bankers,
although several of them also appear in the list of those with
minimal interest cover and uncovered dividends. Many are
companies that simply will not invest in hard times because
they cannot see quick returns. The list includes GEC, GUS,
Hanson, Kingfisher, Thorn-EMI and Tomkins - companies
regarded as highly successful on conventional financial
measures, especially shareholders' returns. The engineering
group Siebe failed to invest as much as its depreciation charge
in every year.

At the other end of the scale, a small group of companies has
invested heavily and grown through the recession. Only nine
companies meet the growth criteria shown in the table. These
included a number of supermarket chains, Cable & Wireless
and Enterprise Oil, as well as the more predictable Body Shop
and Glaxo.

Employment, even in those companies which survived the
recession, has also suffered. Only 62 of these companies ended
the period with more employees than at the beginning.

Source: adapted from *The Guardian*, 18.9.1993.

Table 1

Winners	Losers	Growers	Shrinkers
• Cadbury Schweppes • Glaxo • Kwik Save • Sainsbury • Tesco • Rentokil Criteria: sales increased each year, earnings increased each year, employment higher at end of period, investment greater than depreciation each year, positive net profit each year.	• Costain • Royal Insurance • Saatchi & Saatchi • Storehouse • Trafalgar House Criteria: earnings fell in at least three years, investment less than depreciation in at least two years, net loss in at least three years, lower assets per share and shareholders' funds at end of period.	• Argyll • Body Shop • Cable & Wireless • Enterprise Oil • Glaxo • Kwik Save • Wm Morrison • Sainsbury • Tesco Criteria: Investment more than double depreciation each year, employment higher at end of period, positive net profit each year, assets per share, and shareholders' funds higher at end of period.	• Barratt Developments • Slough Estates • Vickers Criteria:sales, earnings, dividends, employment, assets per share and shareholders' funds all lower at end of period.

(a) What criteria does the article use to measure the success of a business?

(b) Explain, with examples, why some companies were able to expand during the recession.

(c) Why did the 'losers' do badly during the recession?

(d) To what extent does a healthy cash flow determine the ability of a business to survive a recession?

(e) How would you advise a business to approach its investment during a recession?

(f) How might government policies to end a recession affect business?

ICI rethink about Europe

It must rank as one of the most rapid corporate rethinks ever. Amid a fanfare of proclamations by its senior managers about the need to 'reshape for the Single Market challenge', the world's fourth largest chemicals multinational creates a new regional organisation based in Brussels. Then, barely 16 months later, it decides quietly - although amid internal controversy - to shut it down.

On the face of it, this about face by ICI, Britain's largest manufacturer in any industry, looks like an embarrassment of the first order. But behind the scenes the U-turn over ICI Europe reflects the company's new-found willingness to adjust to changing circumstances far more rapidly than in the past.

By reversing its decision, ICI has done two things. First, it has recognised that it had overrated the potential demand from multinational customers - ranging from BMW to several household appliance makers - for cross-border European sales co-ordination across its various businesses. Instead, it now feels that any pan-European sales can be handled within individual ICI businesses.

Second, the turnaround represents the final triumph within ICI of a movement which, as in many multinationals today, was already on the rise inside the chemical company before the Brussels decision was taken; the need to speed decision-making and cut costs by streamlining the complex 'matrix' structures through which they had managed since the 1960s.

Under these, control had been shared between international or global product divisions (ICI's 'businesses'), and geographic units. The latter were either regional, as in the case of ICI Europe, or national, as with the 15 ICI country organisations whose responsibilities it was supposed largely to subsume.

In September 1990, when ICI celebrated the opening of ICI Europe, there was a clear shift of influence towards the global businesses, away from its existing regional organisations and national companies. So although the reasons for ICI Europe seemed powerful to those involved, it was seen elsewhere as being 'out of time'. Trevor Gazard, planning manager of ICI Europe, says ICI Europe 'was really a project, not a permanent organisation'. This is because its most trumpeted purpose, the creation of 'corporate coherence' towards customers in continental Europe, proved 'a bit ahead of its time'. Car companies, for instance, still prefer not to purchase through a single point, even if four ICI businesses supply them separately with paint, polyurethane for bumpers, materials for engines, and fibres for seats. ICI seemed to be far too ready to swallow the now mainly discredited 'supermarket' theory of business-to-business purchasing.

ICI Europe's main tasks from the start actually turned out to be transitional.
- To establish an orderly transfer of sales activities and staff from the 15 national companies to ICI's global businesses, splitting sales staff into European sub-regions such as Benelux, Nordic and what ICI calls 'mid-Europe' (Germany, Austria and Switzerland).
- To support the businesses across Europe by creating half a dozen sub-regional centres for shared 'support services'. such as information technology, finance, health and safety, public affairs and personnel.
- To streamline the old way of maintaining a 'corporate presence' in each country.

By the time the chairman of ICI Europe came back to London in the Summer of 1991 to report on progress, several things had happened.
- Most of the first two tasks were well in hand or complete.

- The business climate had changed for the worse, and ICI's profits had slumped. The Hanson group had taken a threatening stake in the company, and a desperate hunt was under way within ICI to simplify structures and cut costs.
* From the beginning of 1991 the group's 14 businesses had been agglomerated into eight larger units, all with revenues of more than £1 billion. 'If regional co-ordination in Europe was needed, it could be done at that level', says Trevor Harrison, ICI's head of planning.
* The role of ICI Europe 'was causing some distress to the businesses', continues Harrison. For one thing, they claimed its upkeep was affecting their European selling costs. They also 'felt that they didn't have enough control over their entire business process, from the customer right back to the factory', explains Harrison; 'Brussels was getting in the middle'. It was decided that ICI Europe had, in effect, fulfilled much of its remit. It should be shut down, and its remaining activities split up.

The provision of shared services would be transferred to the strongest business in each country or sub-region. At the same time a senior manager in each business within a country or sub-region would be selected to act as a part time representative there. The first to take on such a role, for the whole Nordic area, was the head of ICI Pharmaceuticals.

Both these moves follow the growing tendency within other multinationals of streamlining their bureaucracies by dispersing such geographic 'head office' responsibilities among senior divisional managers on a part-time basis.

The costs saved by shutting ICI Europe are hard to estimate, since about 20 of its 60 staff have been transferred, either to the UK head office or to the businesses. More significant, Gazard says, is that its efforts cut the cost of ICI's continental support services by a fifth between 1990 and 1992. There is still at least as much again to be saved, he estimates, through streamlining within the businesses.

Paradoxically, ICI's costs in mainland Europe may soon be increased slightly by a much more striking rethink than the closure of ICI Europe - the demerger of the entire group into two companies, the Zeneca bio-pharmaceutical side and the remaining five ICI businesses.

Both companies will maintain the new principles of dispersing shared support services and national representation. But each company will need its own string of support centres and national ambassadors, so overheads will rise somewhat.

That should be a small price to pay if it helps achieve the demerger's promised benefits. But this further rethink does underline the speed with which ICI's European structure is continuing to change. It is unlikely to be the last upheaval.

Source: The *Financial Times*, 1.2.1993.

(a) What evidence is there in the article to suggest that ICI is a multinational?
(b) For what reasons was ICI Europe initially set up?
(c) Explain the:
   (i) internal;
   (ii) external;
   factors that may have influenced the company to close down ICI Europe after only 16 months.
(d) How might ICI benefit from the operation of the Single European Market?
(e) Discuss the possible impact of the creation of a new chemical plant in Belgium by ICI in the future.

investigations

Aims

- To evaluate the impact of a pressure group on business.
- To collect information on the means by which a pressure group seeks to influence business.
- To assess the response of business to pressure group activity.

Research

Identify a local, regional or national pressure group involved in a campaign designed to influence the behaviour of a particular business, group of businesses or business in general.

Establish the reasons for the pressure group activity and research the methods employed in order to alter the behaviour of the targeted firm or firms. Information can be found by monitoring the media, interviewing people involved in the campaign and by writing to the parties involved and requesting information. Get hold of copies of any campaign material issued either by business or the pressure group. Establish clearly the views of both sides by arranging interviews with representatives of the pressure group and the business. You could also arrange an interview with other interested parties, such as politicians, or talk to your local Member of Parliament or a representative on the local council.

For campaigns, monitor the campaign in magazines and newspapers, and on television and radio. For local campaigns, look in local newspapers and listen to local radio. You might also interview people in the local area that are affected.

Monitor the response of the targeted firm or firms. Identify the extent to which their behaviour has been affected. Identify the implications for the firm or firms behaving differently. Judge whether or not you believe the campaign was successful or, where appropriate, predict its likely success.

Presentation

Write a report including the following sections.
- An introduction outlining the aims of your investigation.
- The findings of your research. Include any relevant campaign material.
- Present clearly the views of both the relevant business and the pressure group about the issue which you are researching.
- Evaluate the likely success or failure of the campaign. Provide a full explanation of any judgements which you make.

Aims

- To gather data on how small businesses respond to the current economic climate.
- To identify the strategies which small firms use to adapt to the current economic climate.
- To evaluate the relative effectiveness of the various strategies used by small businesses.

Research

You will need to gather data on this topic from a range of sources. Firstly, you should construct a questionnaire which will allow you to interview members of your local business community. You might be able to make use of your family, your friends, or others that have connections with or work in small firms in your locality. Be sure to take up as little of your interviewees' time as possible. Follow the guidelines for interviews outlined in other investigations in this book.

Conduct a search of your local media for any relevant information. This might include local newspapers and radio programmes. Your local Economic Development Unit may have data on business failures or business start-ups.

In order to evaluate the relative effectiveness of the strategies which firms have employed you will need to develop criteria by which you can judge success. Such criteria might include profitability, whether or not a firm is still trading, sales turnover or the amount of investment undertaken.

If the current climate is one of recession, you could concentrate on the survival strategies of firms. Consider such things as their relationship with banks or their credit control. You might also identify those firms that are thriving in a recession and explain why they are able to do this.

If the current climate is one of growth, where business confidence is high and trading conditions are encouraging, you could focus on areas of the business such as recruitment, investment, new products, promotions etc. Identify the factors that allow small firms to take advantage of these conditions. Also try to identify possible problems that might result from a growing economy for small businesses.

Presentation

Write a report including the following sectors.

- An introduction outlining the aims of your investigation.
- The findings of your research. The use of graphs and tables may help you to present this data.
- Your evaluation of the relative success of the various strategies identified.
- Any conclusions you may have arrived at.

An additional activity would to be to present your findings in the form of an oral presentation to an invited audience including members of your local Chamber of Commerce and trade union representatives. Alternatively, send a copy of your report to one or more members of your business community and invite comments upon your findings.

Essays

1. Examine the external factors which may influence the success of the launch of a new product.

2. Discuss the ways in which the policies of a government committed to reducing inflation might affect business.

3. 'Devaluation of the pound sterling will allow UK firms to compete more effectively in overseas markets.' To what extent do you agree with this statement?

4. 'External pressures are not required to ensure that businesses act ethically. It is in their own interest to do so.' Do you agree with this statement?

5. Examine how businesses might be affected by an increase in the level of concern about the deterioration of the environment.

6. What strategies would you advise a business to employ in order to survive a recession?

7. Why are national boundaries becoming increasingly irrelevant for large businesses?

8. Discuss how UK businesses might be affected by the election of a government committed to intervening in the economy.

9. To what extent is there a conflict between profitability and ethical behaviour for businesses?

Index

C

N

Y

W

Z